The

W

Na

JOHN EVERETT-HEATH

John Everett-Heath is a former military diplomat (Belgrade) and
was a civil servant for thirteen years, during which he was
concerned with Russia, Central Asia, and the Caucasus. He is also
a Fellow of the Royal Geographical Society. HIs most recent
publication is *Place Names of the World: Europe* (Macmillan, 2000)

OXFORD
UNIVERSITY PRESS

OXFORD
UNIVERSITY PRESS

Great Clarendon Street, Oxford OX2 6DP

Oxford University Press is a department of the University of Oxford.
It furthers the University's objective of excellence in research, scholarship,
and education by publishing worldwide in

Oxford New York

Auckland Cape Town Dar es Salaam Hong Kong Karachi Kuala Lumpur
Madrid Melbourne Mexico City Nairobi New Delhi Shanghai Taipei Toronto

With offices in

Argentina Austria Brazil Chile Czech Republic France Greece
Guatemala Hungary Italy Japan Poland Portugal Singapore
South Korea Switzerland Thailand Turkey Ukraine Vietnam

Oxford is a registered trade mark of Oxford University Press
in the UK and in certain other countries

Published in the United States
by Oxford University Press Inc., New York

British Library Cataloguing in Publication Data
Data available

Library of Congress Cataloging in Publication Data
Data available

Typeset in Swift and Frutiger by SPI Publisher Services, Pondicherry, India
Printed in Great Britain by Clays Ltd, St Ives plc

ISBN 0-19-860537-4
ISBN 978-0-19-860537-9

1

For
Catharine, Alexandra and Thomas

Contents

Preface

A dictionary of place-names depends heavily on the myriad works devoted to the subject which have been published over many decades and acknowledgement is therefore due to their authors and researchers. A selection of these publications is listed in the bibliography.

No dictionary can be compiled without a great deal of assistance. I owe a deep debt of gratitude to a host of people who have given so generously of their time and knowledge, and who have taken great trouble to explain the finer points of their language and of a particular translation. Whatever errors there are are mine alone. It is a pleasure to acknowledge, in particular, my grateful thanks to Sir Mark Allen, Catherine Cheetham, David O'Connor, Derek Hird, František Krs, Bill Nicolaisen, John Shipman, and Akiko Yuba Frellesvig who always responded with alacrity and good humour to a bombardment of questions. I received sterling help and advice from Dorairajan Balaji, Chong Wei Yee, Catharine de Rienzo, Ben de Wet, Dragan Djukić, Ana Carla Duta, Tom Everett, Tom and Claudia Everett-Heath, Lotsmart Fonjong, Carolyn Ford, Paata Gaprindashvili, Lara Goodbody, Olga Grahor, Jarmo Jaakola, Hans Magnusson, Boris Malakhov, Bayram Mammedov, Bill Manktelow, Sergey Mirzoyan, Halin Ngatidjan, Henry Plater-Zyberk, Udomak Reosanguanwong, Chris Rundle, Ria Russell, Tae Kon Tim, Thelma Theodoridou-Walters, Truong Hong Vo, Linda van Huyssteen and Paul Woodman. They, too, provided specialist knowledge, found answers to specific questions, and, in some cases, read relevant entries.

My thanks are also due to my publisher, Ruth Langley, who kept me along the right lines, Jane Robson, my editor, who has performed wonders in bringing this dictionary to publication, and to Andrew Hawkey, the proof-reader of a difficult manuscript. Lastly, I must thank my wife who provided tireless encouragement throughout.

E.J.E-H.
January 2005

General Note

British Isles: from 1536 these have included the following states:

9th century–1651, 1660–1707: Kingdom of the Scots.
1536–1649, 1660–1707: Kingdom of England and Wales.
1541–1649, 1660–1800: Kingdom of Ireland.
1649–54: Commonwealth of England, Wales and Ireland.
1654–60: Commonwealth of Great Britain and Ireland.
1707–1800: (united) Kingdom of Great Britain.
1801–1922: United Kingdom of Great Britain and Ireland.
1922– : Irish Free State (later Éire (1937) and the Republic of Ireland (1949)).
1922– : United Kingdom of Great Britain and Northern Ireland.

For the sake of simplicity and where appropriate, the term Britain has been used from the Roman occupation until 1707, Great Britain between 1707–1800, and the UK thereafter. In common usage today 'Britain' is very often used rather than 'the UK'.

Calendar: the Gregorian calendar is used. This superseded the Julian calendar from 1582 when 4 October was followed by 15 October since the Julian calendar year was too long. It was not adopted in Great Britain and its colonies until 1752, in China until 1912, in Russia until 1918 and in Greece until 1923.

Dates: the dates after the name refer to birth and death.

Nobility: below royalty, in descending order, the five degrees of nobility in the UK on the male side are duke, marquess, earl, viscount, and baron; on the female side, duchess, marchioness, countess, viscountess, and baroness. The title of 'lord' may be used instead of marquess (of), earl (of), viscount, and baron; thus the Marquess of Salisbury or Lord Salisbury. Lady is the female equivalent.

Personalities: where names are marked with † the reader can find more information in the Personalities appendix.

Cross-references are marked with an *.

Introduction

Over 8,000 names from around the world appear in the following pages. They cover continents, geographical regions (such as the Maghreb and South-East Asia), countries, administrative units (cantons, counties, departments, districts, divisions, governorates, prefectures, provinces, regions, republics, states and territories), bays, capes, cities, towns, deserts, islands, lakes, mountains, rivers, ruins, oceans, and seas. The focus has been on the more important of these, although a few lesser known names have been included. Regrettably there is no space for such place-names as Compton Pauncefoot, Middle Wallop, Rolling Fork and Scratch Ankle. Names whose meaning is self-explanatory have been omitted unless there has been a good reason to include them (see Newcastle). In looking through this dictionary it is readily apparent that many places share the same name, although the spelling may not be identical: there are at least 31 places or features called Victoria in nineteen different countries. In the USA, for example, one can find twelve cities called Athens, nine Berlin, four London, four Madrid, eight Paris, and five called Rome. Many other European names recur in North and South America, often after the birthplace of the founder.

This dictionary does not claim to be definitive or comprehensive, aims that are impossible to achieve. Quite often there is no satisfactory etymology for a place-name and therefore no precise meaning can be established, at least at the moment; or its origins are clouded in the mists of time. It is almost impossible to provide a definitive derivation for some Native American and African names. Despite considerable research the meaning of London, for example, is not known. Nevertheless, this does not mean that various theories cannot be put forward; some of these depend on intriguing, and sometimes entertaining, legend. This, however, is usually a poor basis for discovering the truth, Rome being a classic example. The danger is that, popularly, the name is derived from the legend or a person, often mythical, associated with it and it is this 'folk etymology' that is remembered. Despite this, legends are included here where appropriate. To add to the confusion, toponymists differ in their interpretations of the known facts while sometimes those facts conflict. One can only offer the most plausible explanation based on the information available and if even this is unwise more than one explanation is presented.

The study of place-names, toponymy, involves language (of which there are thought to be about 6 800 spoken today), history, and therefore personalities and peoples, geography and topography, religion and cultural tradition, politics, and even local industry; superstition, too, can play a role (see Cairo). There is no populated place, however obscure, without a name. It will have been chosen, presumably, for a particular reason, although now this may not be known. The approximate date of founding, or naming in the case of a natural feature, the language, religion, and social and political attitudes of the namer, if known, may offer clues. However, the older the name, the more difficult it will be to discover these facts. A place-name is a window that can shed light on the past—from the language can be deduced who the inhabitants were at that time, where they went and who they communicated with. Scandinavian place-names in England indicate where the Norwegian and Danish population was concentrated. Birkby, from Bretarbý 'Village of the Britons', shows that this was a village inhabited by Britons rather than Anglo-Saxons. The migration of peoples has had a profound influence on the naming of places and features. When East Prussia was overrun by Soviet forces in 1945 and the German population expelled, the northern half, annexed by the Soviet Union, was renamed Kaliningrad and its German names changed to Russian ones. River names, usually adopted by immigrants and left unchanged, can indicate the presence of ancient peoples: the Ésera in Spain, the Isar in Germany, the Isère in France; and the Jizera in the Czech Republic advertise the existence of pre-Celtic tribes along these rivers.

Simple translation is often the key to the meaning of a name; for example, *Novgorod* means 'New Town' in Russian, *Los Angeles* 'The Angels' in Spanish, and *Shanghai* 'By the Sea' in Chinese. It is not always as easy as this. Some places have names whose meaning is not readily apparent from their current form, having evolved over time. To try to ascertain the present meaning it may then be necessary to go back to the original name if that is possible; this may be in a different language or use obscure or unknown words. Modification of the name may make the search more difficult. There are names whose literal translation appears to be irrelevant to their situation or even have no real meaning. The majority of place-names in the British Isles are of Old English (Anglo-Saxon) and Old Scandinavian (Old Norse and Old Danish) origin, and from the

Celtic group of languages (Brithonic, Irish and Scottish Gaelic etc.) employed earlier (and often Latinized in written sources, but not actually changed, with the arrival of the Romans). The most common Latin loan-word, *castra* 'fortified place', evolved into the Old English *ceaster* '(Roman) camp', 'station', or 'walled town' from which the present *-chester* and *-caster* are derived: thus, Chester, Winchester, Doncaster, and many others which indicate a former Roman protected establishment. Western Europe abounds with Greek and Roman names which have been modified, perhaps because newcomers could not pronounce them correctly. *Mérida* in Spain, for example, was developed as a retirement settlement for Roman veterans (*emereti*). Dedicated to the Emperor Augustus, it was at first called *Augusta Emerita*, which in due course became *Mérida*. Some modern names have resulted from misunderstandings between explorers and indigenous peoples. Without a knowledge of the local language it was inevitable that a word or words uttered by local people were misheard or misinterpreted. European explorers in Africa would sometimes ask the name of a place only to be told what it was that the locals were doing (see Abidjan and Banjul).

A state can have more than one official language, a fact which may be reflected in its place-names. Switzerland, for example, has three, French, German, and Italian together with the Rhaeto-Romance dialects. To its inhabitants it is known variously as La Suisse, Die Schweiz, and La Svizzera. The small island state of Singapore has four: Chinese, English, Malay, and Tamil. China's official language is Mandarin (*Putonghua* 'common speech'), but it is no surprise that in the most populated country on earth several other major languages are spoken: Cantonese (*Yue*) is spoken in southern China and Hong Kong, *Wu* in Shanghai and *Min* in Fujian and Taiwan (although Mandarin is the official language). Because of the Chinese diaspora, various Chinese languages are spoken throughout Asia and indeed in the UK and USA (where at least seventeen states have cities called Canton). Conversely, both Austrians and Germans speak German, and the official language of Angola, Brazil, Cape Verde, Guinea-Bissau, Mozambique, Portugal, and São Tomé and Príncipe is Portuguese. Dutch, English, French, and Spanish are also spoken around the world due to the empires they forged. The biggest was the British Empire which, in the first decade of the 20th century, covered approximately a quarter of the world's land surface. It is no surprise, therefore, that numerous names in Canada and the USA are of Dutch, English, French, and Spanish origin. From their locations information on the colonization of the USA can be gleaned. Happily, some Aboriginal names have been retained in Australia and a greater percentage of Maori ones in New Zealand. Where translation is involved the language has only been indicated when it is not clearly apparent, for example, a Chinese name in Vietnam.

Few states have borders which encompass a population with a single ethnic identity and culture to form a genuine nation state. There are states that comprise more than one nation: the UK, for example, with its English, Scottish, Welsh, Irish and immigrant nationalities, and Russia with a fifth of its population being non-Russian. On the other hand, there are nations that are spread over more than one state: 25 million Russians live outside Russia, mainly in the republics of the former Soviet Union which are now sovereign states in their own right. For Muslims the concept of nation is less important than that of religion which they see as being divided into nations. This is the House of Islam (*Dār al-Islam*), regions where Islamic government and law prevail. Language, clearly, does not define a state, but it is strongly influential in defining a nation. A state, therefore, may have place-names in different languages and place-names in the same language may be found across the globe.

It is tempting sometimes to assume the meaning of a name which appears obvious. This should be resisted. One might suppose that Cambridge means 'Bridge over the River Cam' but this is incorrect. It means 'Bridge over the River Granta'; it was Norman influence that changed *Grant* to *Cam*. The river was named Cam after the city, a back-formation. Furthermore, place-names spelt the same way may not have the same meaning or origin: the *hampton* of Northampton and Southampton has different origins, although the *North* and *South* were added to distinguish between the cities. Conversely, some places spelt differently do have the same meaning: Krasnoye Znamya in Turkmenistan and Krasnoznamensk in Russia both mean 'Red Banner'.

The coining of names often follows in the wake of historical developments. The Greeks began to settle round the Black Sea during the 7th century BC and their presence led, in the 18th century, to some new towns being given Greek-style names: Melitopol', Nikopol', and Sevastopol' and Simferopol' in the Crimea (not all towns ending in *pol'*, however, are a shortening of the Greek *polis* 'city'; some come from *pole* 'field'). The expansion of the Russian Empire southwards and eastwards resulted in new towns and settlements which were named after the Russian emperor or empress, members of the imperial family, or senior servants of the state. Ukraine derives its name from the Russian *okrainy*, meaning the border lands or marches, denoting the territory between the open steppes of Russia and Asia to the east and the populated lands of the Polish-Lithuanian Commonwealth to the west.

Many names were imposed by European explorers and colonists within the approximately 10 000 independent African kingdoms, minor states, and tribal associations which, with the exception of Abyssinia (Ethiopia) and Liberia, were merged into some 40 European colonies and protectorates between 1884 and 1913, following the footholds gained in previous centuries. Many of these have been, or are now being, superseded by locally chosen ones. Most of today's inhabitants of South-East Asia originally came from China. It grew into the most powerful and sophisticated country in the region and spread its influence far and wide, as far north as Korea. Annam and Tonkin, for example, in Vietnam are Chinese names. In Australia, New Zealand and islands of the Pacific names are either of local origin or coined by European settlers. The British Isles have experienced five major invasions by foreigners who spoke a different language: Celts, Romans, Anglo-Saxons, Vikings, and Normans. Where they displaced their predecessors they adopted existing names, modified others to suit their own language and devised new ones. The Anglo-Saxons made the greatest impact on the naming of places and features, the Romans the least, although they did give a Latin form or ending to Celtic names. Many Welsh names were Anglicized when the shire system was introduced during the reign of Henry VIII (1509–47)—one such being Cardigan for Ceredigion. The 17th-century plantation maps hastened the process of Anglicizing Irish names—at which time the Gaelic *Baíle* became *Bally*, for example—but it was not until after the Act of Union in 1707 that the same process for Scottish names began. As they were founded, the towns of New England in the north-east of what is now the USA were often given English names—Andover (Massachusetts), Cambridge (Massachusetts), Dover (New Hampshire), Norwich (Connecticut)—to provide a sense of familiarity, a link to the past.

Individual events may be reflected in a name. For new governments coming to power and wishing to make an impact, or when they acquire new territory by conquest or peace treaty, the temptation to rename can be difficult to resist. The desire to exorcize the past can be very strong and changing names can be a way of underpinning the new 'legitimacy'. Following the Bolshevik revolution in 1917 many Tsarist names disappeared to be replaced by the names of Bolshevik leaders, Civil War military commanders or other luminaries, and to commemorate events, such as the October Revolution itself, glorifying the emergence of communism. They, in their turn, were overturned following the dissolution of the Soviet Union in 1991 and many of the former names were readopted. Christmas Island received its name when it was discovered on Christmas Day 1643 and Easter Island when the Dutch saw it at Easter 1722; Regis was added to Bognor after King George V had visited it in 1929.

Wishful thinking is not unknown, with 'bad' names being changed to 'good': the Cape of Good Hope which was previously the Cape of Storms. Malventum was thought by the Romans to mean 'Ill Wind' so they changed it to Beneventum (now Benevento) 'Fair Wind'. The original name for the Black Sea was *Pontos Axenos* 'Inhospitable Sea', but this was renamed *Pontos Euxenos* 'Hospitable Sea' as the Greeks settled round it.

Changing the title of a country is a practice favoured by rulers who wish to advertise their hopes or suppress the nature of their regime. 'Democratic' features widely, quite often with states that are anything but: a good example was the group of 'People's Democracies' in Eastern Europe during the cold war. 'United' and 'Union' are less common, but most unions have failed to stand the test of time: the United Arab Republic (see Egypt and Syria) and the Union of Soviet Socialist Republics, for example. Politics also intrudes when states are in dispute over a piece of territory. The capital of Nagornyy-Karabakh, an Armenian enclave in Azerbaijan, is called Stepanakert by the Armenians; the Azeris, however, call it Xankändi (Khankendy). Indeed, the Armenians have taken to calling Nagornyy-Karabakh itself Arts'akh. It may be counter-productive politically to dispute a name, but it happens nevertheless. When Yugoslavia disintegrated in 1991 Macedonia, one of its constituent republics, became a sovereign state. Greece, however, protested over the name Macedonia and so internationally the country is known as 'The former Yugoslav Republic of Macedonia'.

People and places interact. Many places and features take their name from the person or people who founded them or began their development, owned them, or discovered them; for example, Kristiansand founded by the Danish King Christian IV, and Tasmania after the Dutch navigator, Abel Tasman. Antarctica is a good example of this with all its names in European languages usually commemorating a person's name or occasionally that of a ship. However, many are named after individuals about whom we know little or nothing. A few countries are named after the people who inhabited them (not necessarily the first), such as Croatia, England, France, Mongolia, and Slovakia. Some cities and towns take their name from local peoples, a practice quite prevalent in the USA where Native American tribes and the names of tribal chiefs provide a good source: Cheyenne, Wichita, and many others. It is common in Europe too, where Amiens comes from the Gaulish tribal name *Ambiani*, Bohemia from the *Boii*, and Cherkasy and Cherkessk in Ukraine from the Cherkess or Circassians. It is not always easy to decide whether a natural feature takes its name from the people living nearby or vice versa. In the case of Niger and Nigeria, however, it is clear that both countries' names are derived from the Niger River.

Historical events occur in space as well as in time. The naming of a place is a historical event. Where an examination of local history cannot help in discerning the meaning or origin, geography may provide a clue. In this case it is likely to be descriptive of its appearance, e.g. the Rocky Mountains and the Yellow River; or of its location, or because of its association with a physical feature, natural or man-made. The Turkish town of *Trabzon* takes its name from the Greek *trapeza* 'table', a reference to the flat-topped mountain close by. Natural features often have old names for obvious reasons. Rivers have always been important in providing fertile soil, a supply of water and fish, and as a means of communication. Thus, they frequently have the oldest names and it is common for places to be named after the river on which they lie; often, too, the river's name may simply be the local word for water or river. The Adriatic port of *Rijeka* means 'river' in Croat, as does the Mekong River in Thai. Those features that until modern times were more or less inaccessible have often been named by and after their discoverers: Lake Champlain on the American–Canadian border, the Barents Sea, and the Strait of Magellan. Descriptive names abound and these may take various forms: size (Great Bear Lake in Canada); colour (Krasnoyarsk 'Red Bank' in Russia and Belgrade 'White City' in Serbia and Montenegro); shape (Table Mountain); climate (Coldstream); location (Interlaken 'Between the Lakes' and any number of names alluding to a ford or river crossing). Fairview, Chad 'lake' in Arabic, and Pyatigorsk 'Five Peaks' in Russian are all simple descriptive names. A significant number of American names are translations from Native American languages, usually descriptive but modified over time, and therefore open to dispute. Twenty-six states have Native American names, although of the thirteen original colonies only two had: Connecticut and Massachusetts.

Descriptive names also include other elements: time, in so far as many places start with 'New' even though they may now be ancient: Naples from *Neapolis* 'New Town' in Greek. Points of the compass sometimes qualify a name: East Anglia, North and South Carolina, and the West Indies. Some places owed their development to the success of their market days and this has been reflected in their names: Dushanbe 'Monday' in Tajikistan and Szombathely 'Saturday Place' in Hungary, both a reference to market day. Some names are simply manufactured: Pakistan, Pasadena, Tanzania, and Texarkana, for example.

A local natural resource, flora or fauna, or even man-made objects can precipitate a name. *Srebrenica* in Bosnia and Herzegovina is so-named because of the silver mining in the area; similarly Tuzla in the same country because of its salt mines, and Shakhty in Russia simply means 'pits'. Some, but not all, places called Buffalo indicate the former presence of this animal. Such associative names are quite common. Leipzig in Germany takes its name from its lime trees and there is a plethora of names associated with bridges, fords (although in Ireland these often refer to inlets from the Old Scandinavian *fjǫrthr* 'fjord'), and ports since these were natural places for settlements to spring up. Names can therefore offer clues to local topography.

Conversely, places can give their names to manufactured goods. The Czech plastic explosive known as Semtex derives its name from the village of Semtín where it is made. Croatia, in Croat *Hrvatska*, has given us cravat, a scarf worn by Croat mercenaries in French service at Versailles, Bayonne the bayonet, and Kashmir cashmere. Items of food are also qualified by the name of a place: Parma ham, Budweiser beer, and champagne. Some personal names are taken from names of places or natural features: Alma, Chelsea, India, Lourdes, Paris, and Phoenix. This is also true of dogs: Dalmatian, Labrador, Pekinese, and Pomeranian.

This dictionary provides many examples of places and natural features being named in honour of a particular person, perhaps because he or she was royal, or in a position of power or influence, or who had achieved some conspicuous feat or explored new territory: Adelaide, Gagarin, Kimberley, and Mt Everest are well-known examples. The name of Christopher Columbus, in its various forms, is famous in the New World even to the extent of the Republic of Colombia being named in his honour. The names of kings and queens, and their equivalents, are widespread: Alexandria, Georgetown, Victoria, Terezin, and Yekaterinburg. Places with names such as Kingston and Kingstown, and Kraljevo in Serbia, proclaim their association with royalty. Titles, rather than names, are also evident: New York after the English Duke of York; and epithets: Virginia after Queen Elizabeth I, the Virgin Queen. The cult of personality loomed large during the Soviet period and several places and natural features, not only in the Soviet Union, were named after Lenin, Stalin, and other communist heroes, although most of these have since reverted to their pre-Soviet names. Saigon was renamed after Ho Chi Minh, the Vietnamese leader, and Krasnovodsk in Turkmenistan is now called Türkmenbashi in honour of the current president who has taken this title. During the age of colonialism, many senior administrators achieved comparative immortality by having places named or renamed after them, notably in the British Empire. Decolonization, however, usually demands the readoption of historical or traditional names, or a linguistic correction and this accounts for the disappearance of some of these names. Where several places have been named after a particular person, a dagger has been added to the name and brief details can be found in the Personalities appendix.

The names of saints and religious leaders are to be found across the world, particularly in California, Central and South America, and the Caribbean, as a result of the Spanish and Portuguese presence. Some result from having been founded or sighted on a saint's feast day: the island of St Helena; some because they were the personal saint of the founder: St Petersburg in Russia; or because the saint was thought to have been martyred there: St Albans in England. A substantial number of places has taken its name from its first church or mission dedicated to a particular saint: Zlatoust in Russia is just one.

The trend towards using indigenous names is growing. However, where Anglicized names are still in use the indigenous name follows in brackets in this dictionary; in important cases they are cross-referenced. So we have Belgrade rather than Beograd, Damascus rather than Dimashq, Moscow rather than Moskva, Munich rather than München, Naples rather than Napoli, Vienna rather than Wien, and so on. Every country is introduced in its conventional English form with its name in the official national language in roman script following in brackets.

The spelling of names is full of pitfalls, given the diversity of the world's languages and scripts used. There is usually no standard method of transliterating them into Roman script. Nevertheless, the United Kingdom Permanent Committee on Geographical Names (PCGN) and the United States Board on Geographic Names (BGN) approve romanization systems whereby names that are written in non-Roman scripts or in Roman alphabets which have special letters can be rendered in Roman script. PCGN systems have been used where appropriate.

Transliterating Arabic and Persian is more an art than a science. Systematic transliterations are really only of use to those who know Arabic and more informal methods can be misleading. Arabic consonants are not the same as in English and Arabs themselves pronounce their vowels in a variety of ways, depending on region. In this dictionary every effort has been made to be consistent; as far as possible, geographical, personal, and other names and words have been presented in their conventional English spelling, although with diacritical marks included except for the most common: for example, Ahmad, Ali, Islam, Khan, Shah, and a few others. Muhammad has been preferred to Mohammed or any other alternative. The Arabic definite article is *al-*, but it sometimes appears as *el-* when this has been adopted as the more usual English spelling, as in El Alamein, for example.

Although Pinyin was adopted as China's official romanization system in 1958, it was 1979 before it made any real impact in the West. It romanizes Chinese characters which represent Mandarin names. Even so, a few well-known place-names are still common from the previous Wade-Giles system. Peking is the traditional Anglicized spelling, although its use is becoming increasingly rare. The Chinese characters on which it is based are exactly the same as those for *Beijing* which is the correct pronunciation in Mandarin (China's official language). Only Mandarin speakers pronounce place-names according to their Pinyin spelling; in Cantonese the capital is pronounced *Bak-geng*. Pinyin was not designed principally for English speakers and so some letters do not represent the sounds they make in English; for example, *q* represents a sound similar to *ch* as in *Ch*ina. The Pinyin system has been used here except in a very few cases, such as Hong Kong, where the conventional Anglicized spelling is still common.

The ELOT 743 system, as produced by Greece and approved by the United Nations, has been used for Greek; it is based on the pronunciation of the modern language. The modified Hepburn system has been used to romanize the Sino-Japanese characters (known as *kanji*) in which Japanese place-names are usually written. Although the characters, which can have different sounds depending on context, have a meaning, where there are two characters or more, their meaning together is sometimes 'meaningless': Ashikaga is one example. For Korean (*Han'gul*), both North and South, PCGN/BGN use the McCune-Reischauer system, although South Korea officially adopted a new phonetic system (the Ministry of Culture and Tourism system) in 2000. Similarly the PCGN systems for Russian Cyrillic, and indeed for Serbian and Ukrainian Cyrillic which are very similar, have been adopted.

The entries are ordered alphabetically. After the conventional English name, with its local counterpart if only found in a single country, comes a list of the countries which have a place or feature with this name; this list does not claim to be comprehensive because other countries may have lightly populated places or sites with the same name. Names are cross-referenced where more than one is in use: Beijing and Peking, Burma and Myanmar, Ho Chi Minh City and Saigon, among a number of others. To assist in locating some places, the administrative region in 22 selected (large or heavily populated) countries in which they are located has been included; in the case of Indonesia, Japan, New Zealand, and the Philippines, this has been restricted to islands; for the UK to England, Northern Ireland, Wales and Scotland. For Russia, the unit is assumed to be a province unless otherwise stated; Primorskiy Territory has not been translated as Maritime Territory because the former is more commonly used. In countries where there is more than one place with the same name, particularly prevalent in the USA, the administrative region is given in the text for those places selected. Alongside the header in italics is a selection of former names, a selection only because of the variety of ways in which they have been spelt and lack of space. These former names often provide a clue as to the meaning of the present name.

Some places or features have more than one name in different languages or the same name may be pronounced differently in other languages: Montenegro to its inhabitants is Crna Gora and London to the French is Londres. The same river that flows through different countries may have a series of names: the Brahmaputra and the Nile among others. However, in this dictionary foreign language names for the English name, except where it is the local name, have not been given.

Although the modern pronunciation of a name sometimes gives a clue to its etymology no attempt has been made to indicate how any name is pronounced. Nevertheless, as mentioned above, diacritical marks have usually been included. Without a knowledge of their effect, however, there is little chance of getting the correct pronunciation: Orël (pronounced Oryol), Priština (Prishtina), and Wrocław (Vrotswaf). This is also true of some names with no such marks: Arkansas (Arkansaw), Gloucester (Gloster), Kirkcudbright (Kercoobry), Mobile (Mobeel), Myitkyina (Meechinar), and Rzeszow (Zheshoov). Arabic place-names very often include the written al- but this is pronounced differently depending on the following consonant: for example, the Empty Quarter is correctly written al-Rub' al-Khali in Arabic but pronounced ar-Rub' al-Khali. Where an Arabic place-name appears in an atlas in the way it is pronounced rather than with its correct written form, then the former spelling has been used. There are other names that are spelled identically but which have different pronunciations: Paris, which in French is pronounced 'Paree', in English 'Paris', and in German 'Parees'.

Personal names have generally been Anglicized: for example, Alexander for the Russian Aleksandr, Christian for the Scandinavian Kristian, and Charles for Karl. Where specific names are more widely known, such as Kaiser Wilhelm II or Tsar Ivan IV, then they have been used. This is also true of titles: imam, khan, shah, shogun; and gods: Shiva, Vishnu.

The description of a populated place as being a city, town, or village is often locally subjective: a city in one country might only be a town in another. Many quite small places in the USA, for example, are described as cities by their own authorities whereas in the UK (where there are 66 cities) the matter is carefully controlled at a national level and certain criteria have to be met before a town can achieve city status.

The glossary should be consulted for the meaning of Old English and foreign words or elements of words that occur more than once. To avoid repetition in most cases they have not been translated in the individual entries.

Names change. With the help of PCGN every effort has been made to keep pace with this. Nevertheless, between delivery of manuscript and publication, it is likely that some new names will have been coined or former names readopted. A famous Englishman had decided views on place-name changes. Sir Winston Churchill wrote to the Foreign Office in April 1945: 'You should note, by the way, the bad luck which also pursues peoples who change the names of their cities. Fortune is rightly malignant to those who break with the traditions and customs of the past.'

There are reasons why languages have their own names for places and features in other countries—the English Cologne for the German Köln, Finland for the Finnish Suomi, and a host of others. There is a good case, however, for states to standardize their geographical names and indeed the problems associated with international standardization have been under serious study for nearly 200 years. Today the United Nations Group of Experts on Geographical Names works to promote the consistent use world-wide of accurate place-names, a task which naturally entails the standardization of romanization systems. However, while the benefits of consistency and accuracy are easy to perceive, a little charm and fascination would surely be lost were idiosyncratic names to be abandoned.

Aachen, NORTH RHINE-WESTPHALIA/GERMANY
Aquis Granum, Aix-la-Chapelle
Derived from the Old High German *aha*
'water', a reference to the springs here. The
springs of Grannus were named after the
Celtic god of healing and later used as baths by
the Romans. The 'la-Chapelle' of the French
name refers to the fact that Charlemagne[†] is
buried here in the chapel built by him and is
used to differentiate it from other towns
beginning with 'Aix' which itself evolved from
the Latin *aquis*, the ablative plural of *aqua*.
Occupied by the French in 1794, the city was
annexed by France between 1801 and 1815; it
then passed to Prussia after the Congress of
Vienna that year.

Aalsmeer, THE NETHERLANDS
A municipality with a name meaning 'Eel
Lake' from *aal* 'eel', and *meer* 'lake' which was
known for its eels.

Aarau, SWITZERLAND
Located on the River Aare from which it gets
its name. *Au* is a form of *Aue* 'meadow'.
Founded in *c.*1250, it was the temporary
capital of the Helvetic Republic in 1798.
Nearby is the Habichtsburg 'Hawk's Castle',
the ancestral residence of the Habsburg
family. One of the great dynasties of Europe,
the family took its name from a contraction of
Habichtsburg.

Aargau (French: **Argovie**), SWITZERLAND
A canton which joined the Swiss
Confederation in 1803. It is drained by the
River Aare from which it takes its name with
the additional German *Gau* 'district'.

Aasiaat, GREENLAND/DENMARK *Egedesminde*
'The Spiders' in Inuktitut. The original
Inuktitut name was Asiaat. In the centre of a
populated region on the west coast of
Greenland, the name gives the idea of a
spider's web, although the spiders that live
here do not spin webs. It was named in 1759 by
Niels Egede, after his father, Hans, a
missionary and trader, who founded the first
trading company in 1721.

Ābādān, IRAN, TURKMENISTAN
1. Iran: an island and city possibly named after
'Abbad ibn al-Hussein, a holy man who
founded a garrison here in the 8th century.

However, it has also been suggested that its
Arabic form 'Abbādān is derived from *'abbād*
'worshipper'. Another possibility is that it
comes from *āb* 'water' and the root *pā* 'watch'
or 'guard' to give 'guard post'. In subsequent
years it declined, but later became the object
of a long-running dispute between the
Persians and Ottoman Turks. Finally acquired
by the Persians in 1847, it developed from a
village after the discovery of oil nearby in
1908.
2. Turkmenistan: spelt Abadan. It was
formerly Bezmein.

Abakan, KHAKASIYA REPUBLIC/RUSSIA
Ust-Abakanskoye, Khakassk
Founded in 1707 as a fortress, it was named
after the River Abakan with *usta* 'mouth (of the
river)'. The meaning of the river's name is not
known. It was renamed Khakassk (1925–31) as
the capital of the republic.

Abancay, PERU
Named after the *amankay*, the Quechua for a
flower similar to the white lily.

Abay, KAZAKHSTAN *Churubay-Nura*
Renamed in 1961 after the inventive Kazakh
poet Abay Kunanbayev (1845–1904).

Abbeville, FRANCE, USA
France (Picardy): derived from the original
Latin name, Abbatis Villa, the present 'Abbot's
Village', from *abbé* 'abbot' and *ville*, belonged to
the abbots of St Riquier during the 9th
century.

Abbotsbury, ENGLAND/UK *Abbedesburie,*
Abedesberie
'Fortified Manor of the Abbot (of Glastonbury)'
from the Old English *abbod* and *burh*.

Abbottābād, NORTH-WEST FRONTIER/
PAKISTAN
Founded as a military garrison in 1853 and
named after Major (later Major General Sir)
James Abbott, who was deputy commissioner
for Hazara and who pacified this area of the
North-West Frontier Province between 1849
and 1853. He was one of a band of young
officers who distinguished themselves on
the Punjab frontier at this time in the service
of the English East India Company. To his
name has been added *ābād* to give
'Abbott's Town'.

Åbenrå, DENMARK *Obenroe, Apenrade, Aabenraa*
Derived from Åen ved Opnør, 'Stream by
Opnør', an ancient village which has since
disappeared, from *å* 'stream'. It took the name
Apenrade, still the modern German name,
during Prussian rule (1864–1920). Å has replaced
Aa, except in non-Danish languages that do not
have *å*, and the name of the town was officially
spelt Aabenraa between 1920 and 1948.

Abeokuta, OGUN/NIGERIA
'Refuge among Rocks' or 'Refuge under the
Rocks' in Yoruba. This is a reference to the
town's situation on the rocky east bank of the
Ogun River. The town was founded in *c.*1830
by Egba refugees, a branch of the Yoruba, who
initially hid in a cave fleeing slave traffickers.
As a kingdom, in 1893 it signed an alliance
with the British, who recognized its
independence. It was incorporated into the
British Colony and Protectorate of Nigeria in
1914.

Aberdare, KENYA, UK
Kenya: a forested mountain range named in
1884 after Henry Austin Bruce, 1st Baron
Aberdare, British Home Secretary (1869–73)
and president of the Royal Geographical
Society (1880–5, 1886). He took his name from
Aberdare in Wales. The local Kikuyu name is
Nyandarua 'Drying Hide'.

Aberdeen, ANDAMAN ISLANDS, CHINA, SOUTH
AFRICA, UK, USA
UK (Scotland): formerly Aberdon '(Place at the)
Mouth of the (River) Don' from *aber* 'river
mouth'. The ancient river name was Devona,
which was also the name of a goddess.
Although Aberdeen now lies between the
mouths of the Rivers Dee and Don, it was
developed from Old Aberdeen, which lies at
the mouth of the Don and which was almost
completely destroyed by the English in 1336.
The famous breed of cattle, Aberdeen Angus,
derives its name from two adjacent counties in
which the cattle originated, Aberdeenshire
and Angus.

Abergavenny (Welsh: **Y Fenni**), WALES/UK
Gobannio
'(Place at the) Mouth of the (River) Gafenni'
from *aber* and the river name, possibly
meaning 'forge', a reference to the ironworks
here. The Roman fort was called Gobannium, a
name clearly associated with that of the river.

Aberystwyth, WALES/UK *Aberestuuth*
'(Place at the) Mouth of the (River) Ystwyth'
from *aber* and the river name which means
'Winding One'. The mouth of the Ystwyth has
been diverted into the River Rheidol and the
town now lies at the mouth of this latter river.

Abhā, SAUDI ARABIA *Manadhir/Menadir*
Garrisoned by the Ottoman Turks up to the
First World War and captured in 1920 by Abd
al-Aziz ibn Saud (*c.*1880–1953), the first King of
Saudi Arabia (1932–53), when the Turkish
name gave way to Abhā. This could mean
'More splendid' or 'More beautiful' from the
root word *bhy* 'beautiful'. Alternatively, *abaha*
means 'to be aloof' or 'to look down on' and
this may explain the name, given that Abhā is
7 500ft (2 290 m) above sea level.

Abidjan, CÔTE D'IVOIRE
According to popular tradition, when asked
where they were by a group of French settlers,
some local women replied '*T'chan m'bi djan*'
'Coming from gathering leaves' from *m'bi*
'leaves' and *djan* 'to gather' or 'to cut'. With
misunderstanding on both sides, the French
named the town Abidjan. Founded in 1903, it
replaced Bingerville as the capital of the
French Ivory Coast Colony in 1934 and
remained the capital when the country
became independent in 1960. The legislative
capital was moved to Yamoussoukro in 1983,
but Abidjan continued as the *de facto*
(administrative) capital.

Abilene, USA
1. Kansas: founded in 1860 and so named by
the pious owner of the settlement. She read of
the Tetrarch of Abilene in the Gospel
according to St Luke 3: 1, and found the name
appealing. Abilene, from the Greek meaning
'from around Abila', itself said to mean 'grassy
plain', was a region north-west of Damascus in
which the Greco-Roman city of Abila Lysaniou
was located. Abilene in Kansas was bought and
developed by Joseph McCoy, famous as 'the
real McCoy', as a railhead for cattle moving up
from southern Texas. It is now little more than
a village.
2. Texas: founded in 1881, it took its name
from the Abilene in Kansas since it was
developed for the Texan railhead for cattle
drives.

Abingdon, UK, USA
UK (England): derived from the first Anglo-
Saxon names, Æbbandun and then Abendone,
meaning 'Æbba's Hill' from an Old English
personal name and *dūn*. The town was founded
by the Saxons around a Benedictine monastery
*c.*680. When the abbey was moved from the
hill to low ground near the River Thames the
name went with it.

Abitibi, ONTARIO/CANADA
A river named after its source, Lake Abitibi,
from the Algonquian words *abitah* 'middle' and
nipi 'water', a reference to the lake's position

halfway between the Ottawa Valley and James Bay on a canoe route.

Abkhazia (Abkhaz: **Aqa**; Georgian: **Ap'khazet'i**), GEORGIA *Colchis/Kolkhis, Abasgia/ Abasgoi, Avocasia*
An autonomous republic named after the Abkhaz(ians), considered to be one of the aboriginal peoples of the Caucasus. Colonized by the Greeks in the 6th century BC, Colchis lay on the Black Sea and comprised what is now western Georgia; Abkhazia was only a part of Colchis, the other parts being Egrisi (the Old Georgian name, now Samegrelo, and also known as Mingrelia in Russian) and Lazica which extended into modern Turkey and was called Lazistan under the Ottoman Empire. In Greek mythology, it was to Colchis that Jason and the Argonauts went in search of the Golden Fleece. After Colchis and Lazica were united in the 4th century and then joined with Abasgia in the 8th century, Abkhazia became independent. It was later incorporated into Georgia, but achieved independence again in 1463. This was lost to the Ottoman Turks in 1578. Abkhazia became a protectorate of Russia in 1810 called Avocasia and was annexed by Russia in 1864. It was upgraded to a Russian republic in 1921 and at the end of that year joined with Georgia in a special treaty of alliance on the basis of equality. In 1931, however, it was reduced to an autonomous republic within Georgia. Abkhazia declared itself an independent state in November 1994 and has existed as a *de facto* independent country since then, although this independence has not been recognized by the Georgian government or internationally.

Abomey, BENIN
'Within the Fortification', corrupted from *agbo* 'fortification' and *mi* 'within'. It was the capital of the Kingdom of Abomey, later Dahomey (*Benin), in the 17th century and was known for its magnificent palace compound which was enclosed by a 33ft (10 m) high wall.

Abovyan, ARMENIA *Elar*
Founded in 1963 on the site of a settlement called Elar and named after the celebrated Armenian writer Khachatur Abovyan (1805–48).

Abruzzo, ITALY *Aprutium*
A mountainous region, originally with a Latin name, possibly after an ancient tribe, the Praetutii, or from the Latin *abruptus* 'steep', a reference to the Apennine mountain range known as the Abruzzi.

Abu Dhabi (Abū Ẓaby), UNITED ARAB EMIRATES *Abothubbee*
The largest and wealthiest of the seven emirates of the UAE; the city of Abu Dhabi is the capital of the UAE. Literally, the name means the 'Father, *abū*, of Ẓaby', a personal name derived from *ẓab* 'gazelle'. According to legend, in 1761 a Bani Yas hunting party from Liwa Oasis found a gazelle drinking at a spring around which a fort was built in 1793. Under the terms of an Exclusive Agreement in 1892, the UK took control of Abu Dhabi's foreign affairs in return for British protection until independence was achieved 1971. The British Royal Navy mapped the coastline of the Emirates in the 1830s and referred to Abu Dhabi as Abothubbee.

Abuja, ABUJA FEDERAL CAPITAL TERRITORY/ NIGERIA
A Federal Capital Territory and city named after Abu Ja, King of the Hausa Kingdom of Zazzau, who founded the original town of Abuja in 1828. It was renamed Suleja in the 1970s when work was under way on a new capital city. Present-day Abuja is nearby and has been the purpose-built capital of Nigeria since 1991. Located close to the geographical centre of Nigeria, the new capital was intended to relieve the congestion in the previous coastal capital, Lagos, besides taking advantage of the equable climate and the rough ethnic balance in the area.

Abukir (Abū Qīr), EGYPT
Named after a 4th-century Christian doctor, Abū Kyr 'Father Cyr', who was martyred in Canopus, just to the south-west.

Abu Simbel, EGYPT
Also spelt Abū Sunbul. It is the site of two temples with four huge statues of the builder, King Ramses II (1279–1213 BC). They were rediscovered in 1813 and, because of the rising waters of Lake Nasser, were moved to higher ground in 1964–8. The ancient site of Abu Simbel was then allowed to disappear beneath the waters of the lake. The name means 'Father of Sunbul' which itself means 'spikenard', a perfumed ointment highly valued in ancient times.

Acadia (French: **Acadie**), CANADA
The 17th and 18th century French possessions on the Atlantic coast of North America, principally Prince Edward Island, Nova Scotia, and New Brunswick. The name, however, is derived from an Algonquian word *akadi* 'fertile land'.

Acapulco (Acapulco de Juárez), GUERRERO/ MEXICO

'Place where the Reeds were destroyed' or 'Place of Giant Reeds' from the Nahuatl *acatl pulco*. The natural harbour was discovered in 1530 by the Spanish conquistador Hernán Cortés[†] and a settlement founded in 1550.

Accra, GHANA
Derived from the Akan word *nkran* 'ant', a reference to the black ants common in the area. Developed from several small Ga villages by the British, Danish, and Dutch who built three fortified trading posts in the 17th century; these grew into towns. The Danes (1850) and the Dutch (1872) ceded their possessions to the British and left. Accra replaced Cape Coast as the capital of the British Gold Coast Crown Colony in 1877 and became the capital of Ghana on independence in 1957.

Accrington, ENGLAND/UK *Akarinton*
'Farmstead where Acorns are found, or stored' from the Old English *æcern* 'acorn' and *tūn*.

Aceh, SUMATRA/INDONESIA
A province and once a sultanate. The name comes from the Malay *aci* 'beech', a reference to their profusion here.

Achaea (Akhaía), GREECE *Ægialus, Ionia*
A department and historic region also called Hellas (*see* GREECE). During Mycenaean times it referred to the whole of the Peloponnese, but otherwise to a region on the north coast of the Peloponnese. Its original name, Ægialus, meant 'shore' from its location. When the Ionians settled here they called the place after themselves. It received the name Achaea when the Achaei superseded the Ionians. As the Achaean League, a military alliance, it passed to the Romans in 198 BC, becoming part of the Roman province of Macedonia in 146 BC and a province in its own right in 27 BC. It was under Ottoman Turkish rule between 1460 and 1828.

Acireale, SICILY/ITALY *Aquilia, Reale*
The first syllable of the name is derived from the ancient River Acis which, according to legend, was formed from the blood of the mythological Acis, a shepherd, when he was crushed to death. Called Aquilia by the Romans, it was renamed Reale 'royal' in 1642 by Philip IV, King of Spain (1621–65) and King of Portugal (1621–40). The Spanish Houses of Aragon and Bourbon ruled Sicily from 1282 to 1860.

Aconcagua, ARGENTINA, CHILE
1. Argentina: a mountain named after the river in Chile.
2. Chile: a river, rising in the foothills of Mt Aconcagua, whose name is derived from the Araucan *konka* 'sheaf of straw' and *hue* 'place

abundant in', a reference to the fertility of the land.

Acre[′] BRAZIL, ISRAEL
1. Brazil: a state named after the River Acre, formerly the Aquiri. Disputed territory, it became part of Bolivia in 1866 before being transferred to Brazil in 1903 under the terms of the Treaty of Petrópolis.
2. Israel: the city has had several names including Accho, Ptolemais, and St Jean d'Acre. The name may be derived from a Hebrew word for 'enclosed', given its position at the northern end of the Bay of Haifa. The Old Testament name was Accho. The city was conquered in 336 BC by Alexander III the Great[†] and by Ptolemy II Philadelphus[†] who renamed it Ptolemais. Later it came under Roman, Persian, and Arab rule before falling to the Crusaders during the First Crusade in 1104. They held it until Saladin, the Muslim Sultan of Palestine, recaptured it in 1187. The Third Crusade, led by Guy of Lusignan, Richard I of England, and Philip II of France, won it back in 1191 and they gave it to the Knights of St Jean, who located their headquarters here. It was renamed St Jean d'Acre, Acre being the French version of Akko. It was captured in 1291 by the Mamlūks. From 1516 to 1917 the city was mainly under Ottoman Turkish control, before being taken over by the British, becoming part of the British mandate in 1922. Acre was captured by Israeli troops in 1948. Locally it is known as Akko.

Actópan, HIDALGO/MEXICO
Founded in 1546 and called 'In thick and fertile Soil'.

Ada, USA
1. Idaho: named after Ada Riggs, the first white child born in Boise County.
2. Minnesota: named after the deceased six-year-old daughter of William H. Fisher.
3. Oklahoma: named after Ada Reed, the daughter of the first postmaster; he built a log store for the community in 1889.

Adamawa, NIGERIA
A state, created in 1991 and based on a Fulani emirate founded in 1809 by, and named after, Modibbo Adama, from *adam* 'man'. He started a holy war against the non-Muslims in the area. The state was partitioned in 1901 between British Northern Nigeria and German Cameroon, which came under French rule at the end of the First World War. Adamaoua (the French name) is a region in Cameroon.

Adam's Peak (Samanala), SRI LANKA
The top of the mountain contains a depression resembling a human footprint. It is a place of

pilgrimage for Buddhists, Hindus, and Muslims who consider it to be the footprint of Buddha, Shiva, and Adam respectively; Adam is supposed to have descended here when ejected from Paradise.

Adana, TURKEY
A very old city believed to take its name from a Phoenician word *adan* 'delight'. Having been conquered by Alexander III the Great[†] in 335 BC, it later fell under Arab and Turkmen rule before being taken by the Ottoman Turks in 1516.

Ad Dakhla, WESTERN SAHARA *Villa Cisneros*
'The Inner', a reference to the fact that it is located on a finger of land that creates an 'inner' sea known as Bahía de Río de Oro, a bay in the former Spanish territory of Río de Oro. Its original name meant the 'Community of Cisneros', the Spanish cardinal Francisco Jiménez de Cisneros (1436–1517) who strongly supported the Spanish conquests in North Africa. The town is also known as Dakhla.

Addis Ababa (Adīs Ābeba), ETHIOPIA
'New Flower' from the Amharic *āddis* 'new' and *ābāba* 'flower'. A region in, and the capital of, Ethiopia. It was founded in 1887 by Empress Taitu, wife of Menelik II, Emperor of Ethiopia (1889–1913). Unhappy with the cold and dismal conditions in the capital, Intoto, Taitu persuaded her husband to build a new palace and military camps on the site of hot springs at the foot of the high plateau on which Intoto was situated. The city was captured and occupied by the Italians in 1935, becoming the capital of Italian East Africa before being recaptured by the Allies in 1941.

Addo, NIGERIA, SOUTH AFRICA
South Africa (Eastern Cape): a European modification of the Khoikhoin *kadouw* 'river passage', a reference to the ford over the Sundays River here.

Adelaide, AUSTRALIA, SOUTH AFRICA
1. Australia (South Australia): founded in 1836 by British Captain John Hindmarsh and named after Queen Adelaide (1792–1849), the wife of William IV[†], at her request.
2. South Africa (Eastern Cape): founded as a military outpost in 1834, it was also named after Queen Adelaide.

Adélie Coast, ANTARCTICA
Also known as Adélie Land. Discovered by the French naval explorer, Jules-Sébastian-César Dumont d'Urville, in 1840, who named it after his wife, Adélie.

Aden ('Adan), YEMEN *Adane, Athenae, Eudaemon Arabia, Arabia Emporion*
A governorate and a port city. The derivation of the name is not known. It is possible, but unlikely, that it is related to the biblical Garden of Eden; it may come from *edinnu* 'plain' or 'steppe', an Akkadian word; this language, spoken in Mesopotamia (Iraq) before the birth of Christ, is extinct. In the 1st century Aden was sometimes referred to by the Greeks as Eudaemon Arabia 'Happy Arabia', or Arabia Emporion 'Arabia the Market', the name of the entire country. The port was occupied by the Ottoman Turks in 1538. It was captured by the British in 1839 after which it was administered by the Bombay Presidency until it became a British crown colony in 1937. In 1963 it joined the Federation of South Arabia, which included the Aden Protectorate. It then became the capital of the People's Democratic Republic of Yemen (popularly known as South Yemen) in 1968 and remained so until North and South Yemen merged in 1990 to form Yemen. The capital was then transferred to Şan'a.

Adige, ITALY *Athesis*
A river in the north whose name is derived from the Indo-European *at* 'swift', a reference to its flow.

Adirondacks, NEW YORK/USA
A mountain range named after an Algonquian-speaking Native American tribe, the Adirondacks, whose name is said to mean 'eater of tree bark', although the original meaning has been lost.

Adıyaman, TURKEY *Hüsnümansur*
The previous name comes from the Arabic Ḥiṣn Manṣūr, the name of the Manṣūr Castle, from the Arabic *ḥiṣn* 'fortified place' or 'fortress', built as a defensive fort by Arabs against the Byzantines in the 7th century; Turkish *hüsnü* means 'good'. Adıyaman, which was adopted in 1926, is said to come from *Vadi-i-Leman* 'Beautiful Plain'. Locals claim that the name is derived from Yedi Yaman, seven brothers who rebelled against pagans and consequently were killed.

Admiralty Islands, PAPUA NEW GUINEA
The 21 Islands
Discovered in 1616 and originally named by the Dutch navigator, Willem Schouten[†]. They were renamed in 1767 by the British sea captain Philip Carteret in gratitude to the British Admiralty, the government department that directed the Royal Navy, which sponsored his expedition. They were part of German New Guinea from 1884 until their capture by Australian troops in 1914. Six years later they were included in an Australian League of Nations mandate. The islands came

under Japanese occupation in 1942–4, and then became part of the UN Trust Territory of New Guinea in 1946 before finally joining Papua New Guinea on its independence in 1975.

Adrano, SICILY/ITALY *Hadranon, Adranum, Adernò*
Founded in about 400 BC near a temple dedicated to the god Hadranus after whom the town is named. It was Latinized to Adranum in 260 BC by the Romans and this name evolved into Adernò. It assumed its present name in 1929.

Adrar, ALGERIA, MAURITANIA
1. Algeria: formerly named Timmi after the Timmi, a local Berber people. The present name means 'mountain' in Berber. It was taken from the Moroccans in 1900 by the French. It joined Algeria in 1962.
2. Mauritania: Adrar is an upland region.

Adria, VENETO/ITALY *Atria*
Founded by the Etruscans, the origin of the name is not certain. It may have a connection with the Illyrian *adri* 'rock', or the Latin *atrium* (plural *atria*) 'hall'. Originally a port, although now 12 miles (19 km) inland, it gave its name to the Adriatic Sea, *Mare Adriatico*.

Adrian, USA
Michigan: settled in 1826 as Logan and renamed two years later after Hadrian, Roman emperor (117–38). The 'H' was dropped in 1838.

Adriatic Sea (Italian: **Mare Adriatico**; Serbo-Croat: **Jadransko More**)
Lying between the Balkans and Italy, it takes its name from *Adria, once a Venetian port.

Adygeya, RUSSIA
A republic since 1991, having been the Adygei Autonomous District since 1922, named after the Adygei people. Their name, which may come from the Abkhaz *adzi* 'water', is also spelt Aydgey. They are descended from the Circassians (see KARACHAY-CHERKESSIA), but the Adygei, collectively, include the Abkhaz and Kabardins, the Circassians/Cherkess, and a number of other minor tribes.

Aegean (Greek: **Aigaíon**; Turkish: **Ege**)
A sea and islands named, according to legend, after Aegeus, the mythical King of Attica (Athens). When his son, Theseus, returned, having been offered up to the Minotaur in place of the yearly tribute, he forgot to change the colour of his sails from black to white to indicate his survival. When Aegeus saw the black sails he flung himself into the sea. Northern Aegean and Southern Aegean

comprise two administrative regions of Greece.

Aegina (Aíyina), GREECE *Oenome*
An island, whose chief town has the same name, which is named after Aegina. She was one of the twenty daughters of one of two river gods called Asopus. She is said either to have been abducted to the island which was then called after her or, more drastically, was actually changed by Jupiter into the island.

Aeolian Islands (Isole Lipari), ITALY
Also known as the Eolie Islands. A group of seven volcanic islands, including the semi-active Stromboli, named by the Greeks after Aeolus, king of the winds. In Homer's epic poem, the *Odyssey,* Odysseus (in English, Ulysses), King of Ithaca, was given a favourable wind by Aeolus to help him on his way back to Ithaca, and also a bag which contained unfavourable winds. Odysseus opened the bag, allowing the ill winds to escape; these swept him back to the island of Aeolia.

Afghanistan *Ariana, Albania*
The Islamic Republic of Afghanistan (Jomhūrī-ye Eslāmī-ye Afghānestān) since 2004, having been the Transitional Islamic State of Afghanistan since 2002. Previously the Islamic Emirate of Afghanistan since 1996; the Republic of Afghanistan (1987); the Democratic Republic of Afghanistan (1978); the Republic of Afghanistan (1973) when the monarchy was abolished; and the Kingdom of Afghanistan (1747). Only in 1747 did Ahmad Shah Durrānī, a Pashtun leader, create the nation of Afghanistan after centuries of rule by invaders. Some sources claim that Afghan is derived from the Sanskrit *Avagana*, which in turn may come from a Sumerian word for the mountainous region of Badakshan, *Ab-bar-Gan* meaning 'Mountainous Country'. The region was known as Ariana to the Greeks *c.*200 BC. In the 3rd century AD the Persian Sāssānians referred to the 'Abgan'. Northern Afghanistan was part of the ancient, and huge, historical region of Khorasan, 'Land of the Sun'. Modern Afghanistan comprises the ancient regions of Aria, Arachosia, Bactria, and Sogdiana, either completely or in part. Excepting subjugation by Alexander III the Great[†] in 330–327 BC, Afghanistan has been under the nominal domination only of Greeks, Kushans, White Huns, Arabs, Seljuk Turks, Mongols, the British, and the Soviet Union; it has also been subject to Persian, Mughal, and Russian influence. The Romans called the area Albania, 'mountainous country'. A popular, rather than official, name was Yaghistan meaning the 'Land of the Ungovernable' or 'Rebellious' from

the Persian *yāghī* 'rebel', so-called by Abdur Rahman Khan, the Emir (1880–1901). He was referring to the tribal fastnesses (in what has since become the North-West Frontier Province of Pakistan) used by those fighting the British in the 19th century. According to a Persian translation, *afghan* means 'wailing' or 'moaning'. Afghanistan itself means 'Land of the Afghans' and only came into use about the middle of the 18th century when the Afghans had established their superiority. The country was given the title 'Islamic Emirate' by the Taliban, a militant Islamic movement, after its fighters captured the capital Kabul in September 1996. The Taliban was overthrown in 2001. An Afghan is any person who lives in Afghanistan while the largest ethnic group is the Pashtun, or Pushtun or Pakhtun (also previously known as the Pathans by the British), who comprise many different tribes. The Pashtun got their name from the Tajik *pasht*, meaning the 'reverse side of a mountain range'; this is the Sulaiman Range (now in Pakistan) lying just west of the River Indus. In 1893–5 the Durand Line fixed the border between Afghanistan and British India (and now Pakistan); although some Pashtun tribes then found themselves outside Afghanistan, successive rulers in Kabul never gave up the idea of Pashtun unity. Amānullāh Khan, the ruler (1919–29), declared independence from the UK (which controlled the kingdom's foreign policy) on ascending the throne in 1919; this was recognized at the Treaty of Rawalpindi the same year. The country has given its name to the Afghan hound, a dog bred as a hunter.

Africa Following their destruction of Carthage at the conclusion of the Third Punic War in 146 BC, the Romans originally named their province after the Berber tribe of Afrigi, who lived in what is now Tunisia and eastern Algeria. As the Romans increased the size of the province by expanding southwards and eastwards, and then westwards, so the name came to be applied to these additional regions until in time it embraced the whole of the continent. Afrigi may have been derived from the Berber word '*afar* 'dust', to mean 'People from the Dusty Land'. 'Black Africa' refers to that part of the continent south of the Sahara where the majority of the population is black.

Afyon, TURKEY *Acroënus, Nikopolis, Karahisar-i-Sahip, Afyon Karahisar*
The first name was Byzantine and the town was later given the Greek name the 'City of Nicholas'. Having been captured by the Seljuk Turks under Sahip Ata in the 13th century, it was renamed Karahisar, 'Black Castle', after

the fortress overlooking the town, in honour of Sahip. In the chief opium-producing region of Turkey, the town's name was given the prefix *afyon* 'opium' in place of Sahip in 1923, although in 1933 the amount of opium grown was limited to that required for medicinal purposes only. This ban, except to approved pharmaceutical companies, was reinforced in 1971. By common usage the town's name has been abbreviated to Afyon.

Agadez, NIGER
Founded by the Tuaregs and the capital of a Tuareg sultanate in the 15th century, it was a centre for wandering herdsmen and appropriately means 'Meeting Place'.

Agadir, MOROCCO *Santa Cruz*
'Embankment', possibly from the Tuareg *ağādir* to describe the slope on which the town was built overlooking the harbour, or from the Phoenician *gadir* 'masonry wall enclosing a town'. The Portuguese, who occupied it in 1505–41, called it Santa Cruz 'Holy Cross'. The Agadir Crisis erupted in 1911 when a German gunboat appeared offshore to challenge the French position in Morocco by claiming to 'protect German interests' and, indeed, to enhance them. The Germans backed down and French troops occupied the town in 1913.

Aghdam, AZERBAIJAN
'White-covered Roofs'. Largely destroyed by Armenian troops in 1992 when they overran this part of Azerbaijan which they still occupy.

Āgra, UTTAR PRADESH/INDIA *Agrabana, Akbarābād*
Mentioned in the epic *Mahābhārata* as Agrabana, meaning 'Paradise'. The present city was established in 1566 by Akbar[†], the great Mughal emperor, after whom it was named for a short period. It was the capital of the Mughal Empire (1566–1658) and was annexed by the British in 1803.

Ağri, TURKEY *Karaköşe*
Named after Mount Ararat (in Turkish, Ağri Daği 'Sad, or painful, Mountain', from *ağri* 'pain' and *dağ* 'mountain'), not far to the east. It is still sometimes called Karaköse, which literally means 'Black Corner' which may be interpreted as a 'little dark, out of the way, place'. It lies in a rather bleak region.

Agrigento, SICILY/ITALY *Akragas, Agrigentum, Girgenti*
Founded by the Greeks c.580 BC on a hill overlooking the sea, the original Greek name may be connected with the word for 'summit'. Sacked by the Carthaginians and Romans during the First Punic War (264–241 BC), it was renamed Agrigentum by the Romans when

they captured the town in 210 BC during the Second Punic War (218–201 BC). It was occupied by the Saracens in 828 who gave it an Arabized version of Agrigentum, Girgenti, and this name was retained until it reverted to its classical name in 1927.

Agrínion, GREECE *Vrakhóri*
The former name was an adaptation of Evrekori, meaning the 'Town of the Jews'. The present name was adopted from that of a community in the ancient region of Aetolia in north-west Greece.

Aguascalientes, MEXICO, PERU
1. Mexico: a state and town meaning 'Hot Waters', a reference to the thermal springs in the area. Founded in 1575 by the Spanish, they called it informally La Ciudad Perforada, 'The Perforated City', a reference to the many tunnels underneath it. It was first called Villa de la Asunción and then Nuestra Señora de la Asunción de las Aguascalientes. *Asunción* means 'Assumption'.
2. Peru: spelt Aguas Calientes.

Agung, Mt (Gunung Agung), BALI/INDONESIA
'Great Mountain' from *gunung* 'mountain' and *agung* 'noble' or 'high'.

Ahaggar, ALGERIA
A mountain plateau also known as Hoggar. It takes its name from the Ihaggaren, a local Tuareg people whose name means 'Members'.

Ahmadābād, GUJARĀT/INDIA
'Ahmad's Town' from the personal name and *ābād*; the Arabic *ahmad* means 'glorious'. Also called Amdavad. The town was founded in 1411 by, and named after, Sultan Ahmad Shah, the Muslim ruler of Gujarāt. It was captured by the Mughal emperor Akbar[†] in 1572 and annexed by the British in 1818.

Ahmadnagar, MAHĀRĀSHTRA/INDIA *Bhinar*
Conquered by, and renamed in 1490 after, Malik Ahmad Nizam Shah to mean the 'City of Ahmad' from *nagar*. Bhinar was in use from the early 12th century.

Ahvaz (Ahwāz), IRAN *Hormuzd Ardashīr*
Having rebuilt the town, Ardashīr I, King of the Sāssānians (224–41), named it after himself. It was renamed Suq al-Ahwāz by the Arabs when they conquered the town during the 7th century to mean 'Market of the Hūzi'. Ahwāz is the plural of Hūzi which was a local tribe.

Aiken, SOUTH CAROLINA/USA
Named after William Aiken, governor of South Carolina (1844–6).

'Ain, al-, SAUDI ARABIA, UNITED ARAB EMIRATES
United Arab Emirates (Abu Dhabi): formerly Tu'am/Tawwan and later al-Jau. It is also spelt al-'Ayn 'The Spring' (of water) from the abundant springs (Arabic *aïn*) in the area. It is situated in the Buraimi Oasis which contained nine villages. Collectively they are known as al-Ain, although Buraimi (al-Buraymī) is in Oman; there is no formal international border in the Oasis. With the prospect of oil being discovered, Saudi Arabia made a claim to the entire Oasis in 1949, based on a Saudi presence there during the 18th century. Sovereignty was not clearly defined: the British, who exercised power in south-east Arabia at the time, considered that six of the villages belonged to Abu Dhabi and three to Oman. Saudi forces occupied part of the Oasis in 1952. The question of sovereignty was sent to international arbitration, but the talks collapsed in 1955. Meanwhile, it had been agreed in 1953 by Abu Dhabi, Oman, and the UK that the six villages should be part of Abu Dhabi and the other three part of Oman. The Saudis were forcibly driven out of the Oasis in 1955. The border between Abu Dhabi and Oman was demarcated in 1966 and the dispute with Saudi Arabia was finally settled in 1974.

'Aïn Beïda, ALGERIA *Daoud*
'White Spring' from the Arabic *aïn* and *baydā* 'white'. In an area of wells and springs, the French built two forts in 1848 and 1850 to control the local Berbers.

'Aïn Sefra, ALGERIA
Founded as a French garrison in 1881 in a *wādi* (a usually dry river bed), it means 'Yellow Spring' from *aïn* and *safra* 'yellow'.

'Ain Sukhna, EGYPT
'Hot Spring' from *aïn* and *sukhna* 'hot'.

'Aïn Temouchent, ALGERIA *Albula, Ksar ibn Senar*
A province and a town. Originally a Roman site called Albula and then an Arab settlement, it was refounded in 1851 by the Spanish, who named it after the Wadi Temouchent.

Aitutaki, COOK ISLANDS/NEW ZEALAND *Ararua Enua O Ru Ki Te Moana*
A shortened version of the original name which meant 'Ru in Search of Land over the Sea'. According to the local legend, Ru, with his wives and brothers, discovered the atoll.

Aix-en-Provence, PROVENCE-ALPES-CÔTE D'AZUR/FRANCE *Aquae Sextiae*
Founded in 123 BC by the Roman proconsul Caius Sextius Calvinus, the thermal springs, *aquae*, were named after him. *Aix* is merely an

abbreviation of *aquae*. Capital of Provence, 'en-Provence' was added to differentiate this 'Aix' from others.

Aix-les-Bains, RHÔNE-ALPES/FRANCE
A spa town with 'les-Bains' denoting the baths used by the Romans.

Aizuwakamatsu, HONSHŪ/JAPAN
Aizu appears in the *Kojiki* 'Records of Ancient Matters' compiled in 712, a father meeting his son in the area. Translation of the characters gives 'meeting port' from *ai* 'meet' and *zu* 'port', and 'young pine tree' from *waka* 'young' and *matsu* 'pine tree'. The city is well inland.

Ajaccio, CORSICA/FRANCE *Ajax*
The name may be derived from the Low Latin *adjacium*, 'resting place where shepherds stopped with their flocks'. Apart from a six-year period (1553–9), the city belonged to the Genoese until the French acquired the town in 1768.

Ajaria (Ach'ara), GEORGIA *Lazica, Achara*
An autonomous republic named after the Ajars. Populated by the Laz, it was called Lazica in ancient times. The region was incorporated into the Georgian state in the mid-11th century and annexed by the Ottoman Empire in 1578. During the succeeding centuries the population was gradually converted to Islam and this is where most Georgian Muslims live. Ajaria was annexed by Russia under the terms of the Congress of Berlin in 1878. As the Ajar Autonomous Soviet Socialist Republic, it became part of Georgia in 1921. It was renamed the Ajar Autonomous Republic in 1991, although this title is rarely used. Also spelt Adzhariya.

Ajijic (Nahuatl: **Axixique/Axixic**), JALISCO/MEXICO
'Place where the Water springs forth'. The present spelling is a Spanish corruption of the Nahuatl name.

'Ajlūn, JORDAN
Named after a Christian monk who lived in the ancient monastery here. When the monastery became a ruin, the castle and then the town from which it developed took his name.

'Ajmān, UNITED ARAB EMIRATES
The smallest of the seven UAE emirates and with two exclaves, its name may conceivably be derived from *ajam*, a word of Arabic origin which in Persian means 'non-Arab' or 'barbarian'. It was formerly a British protectorate from 1892 until it joined the UAE in 1971.

Ajmer, RĀJASTHĀN/INDIA
Founded in the early 12th century by Ajayadeva, a Rājput ruler after whom it is named.

Akademgorodok, NOVOSIBIRSK/RUSSIA
An abbreviation of *Akademicheskiy Gorodok* 'Academic Campus'. It was founded in 1957 as a purpose-built town and the headquarters of the Siberian branch of the Academy of Sciences, to which some 40 000 scientists were sent.

Akaroa, SOUTH ISLAND/NEW ZEALAND
'Long Harbour', meaning an extended sheltered place rather than an open bay, from the Maori *aka* 'long' and *roa* 'harbour'.

Akashi, HONSHŪ/JAPAN
'Shining Stone' from *aka* 'shining' and *ishi* 'stone'. A different Chinese character for *aka* means 'red'.

Akbulak, ORENBURG/RUSSIA
'White Spring' from the Turkic *ak* 'white' and *bulak* 'spring', thus one with clean water.

Akdepe, TURKMENISTAN
'White Hill' from *ak* and *depe* 'hill'.

Akhali Ap'oni, GEORGIA *Novyy Afon*
A former Greek colony, both the previous Russian and the Georgian name mean 'New Athos' after a nearby monastery which had been built by monks from Athos in Greece in 1876.

Akhalkalaki, GEORGIA
'New Town' from *akhal* 'new' and *kalaki* 'town'. It was so called by the Russians after they had captured it from the Turks in 1829.

Akhaltsikhe, GEORGIA *Akhiska*
'New Castle' from *akhal* 'new' and *tsikhe* 'castle' or 'fortress'. Fortifications were present on the site before Prince Ivan Paskevich, commander of Russian troops in the Caucasus, assaulted the Turkish defences at Akhiska in 1828 and built a new fortress.

Akhdar Mountains (al-Jabal al-Akhdar**),** LIBYA, OMAN
Oman: a mountain range, the great backbone of Oman, meaning the 'Green Mountain' from the Arabic *jabal* 'mountain' and *akhdar* 'green'. It is called 'green' only because it is green in comparison with the arid areas surrounding it. The same is true of the mountain range in Libya.

Akhisar, TURKEY *Pelopia, Thyatira*
'White Castle' from *ak* and *hisar*. It may have been founded by the Lydians during the 6th century BC. It was renamed Thyatira by the Macedonians in 290 BC.

Akhmīm, EGYPT *Khenté-Min, Panopolis, Ipu, Khemmis*
The first Old Egyptian name was possibly derived from the Coptic Khmin, the town's god being Min. This became the Arabic Akhmīm. Min was associated with the Greek Pan, hence the name Panopolis 'City of Pan'; Khemmis was also a Greek name.

Akhtopol, BULGARIA *Agathopolis*
Evolved from the former name of the Greek colony 'Noble City' on this site.

Akita, HONSHŪ/JAPAN
A prefecture and city with a name meaning 'Field of Ripe Rice' from *aki* 'autumn' and *ta* 'field of rice'. The cultivation of rice is a major preoccupation here.

Aklavik, NORTHWEST TERRITORIES/CANADA
'Where there are Bears' in Inuktitut.

Akranes, ICELAND
'Field Peninsula' in Icelandic.

Akron, OHIO/USA
Founded in 1825 over 1 000ft (305m) above sea level, it means 'At the Top' from the Greek *akros*; in other words, 'High Place'. Places in Colorado, New York and Pennsylvania have this name and meaning.

Akrotiri, CYPRUS
'(Place) at the End' from the Greek *akros*. It lies on a peninsula which gives its name to Akrotiri Bay.

Aksaray, TURKEY *Archelais*
'White Palace' from *ak* and *saray*, a very ancient town founded in Hittite times.

Akşehir, TURKEY *Philomelium*
'White City' from *ak* and *şehir*.

Aksu, CHINA, KAZAKHSTAN, TURKEY
1. 'White Water' in Uighur and Turkish from *ak* and *su* 'water'.
2. China (Sinkiang Uighur Autonomous Region): it was the Kingdom of Baluka.
3. Kazakhstan: there are three towns called Aksu (Aqsū), all named after the River Aksu. The town north-east of Shymkent was formerly Belyye Vody 'White Water' in Russian.
4. Turkey: named after the Turkish River Aksu.

Aksum, ETHIOPIA *Sabea*
According to oral Ethiopian tradition, the city was named after Aksumai, the son of Ethiopic, who was the great-grandson of Noah. Sabea was also known as the biblical Kingdom of Sheba, or Saba. Queen Makeda allegedly ruled a powerful kingdom that included modern Ethiopia, Eritrea, and Yemen during the 10th century BC from her capital at Sheba, but she is better known in the West simply as the Queen of Sheba; alternatively, she is believed to be Queen Bilqis of Sheba, now Sabea in Yemen. Also spelt Axum. Aksum was also a former name for ancient Ethiopia.

Aktau (Aqtaū), KAZAKHSTAN *Aktau, Shevchenko*
Founded in 1963, to exploit the uranium deposits which had been discovered in 1953, from a Russian settlement, Aktau, 'White Hills'; Aktau itself was named after the white hills which separated the peninsulas of Mangyshlak, 'Place of Wintering', and Bozashchy. It was then renamed in 1963–91 after Taras Shevchenko, the foremost Ukrainian poet of the 19th century, who was exiled to Kazakhstan in 1847 because of his poems satirizing Russian oppression of Ukraine.

Aktyubinsk, KAZAKHSTAN
See AQTÖBE.

Akureyri, ICELAND
A sand spit, it means 'Tongue of Land' from *akur* 'field' and *eyri* 'tongue'.

Akyaka, TURKEY *Kizílçakçak*
Situated on the Arpa River, the name means 'White Bank' from *ak* and *yaka* 'bank' or 'shore'.

Alabama, USA *Alibamo*
A state and a river with a name derived from a Choctaw word for 'Thicket clearers', that is, people who clear a way through the forest, from *alba* 'thick vegetation' and *amo* 'to clear' or 'to gather'. The area was disputed between the British, French, and Spanish during the 17th and 18th centuries, passing to the USA in 1783. Mississippi Territory having been divided in two in 1817, the eastern part became Alabama and joined the Union as the 22nd state in 1819. It seceded in 1861 during the American Civil War (1861–5) and rejoined in 1868.

Alagoas, BRAZIL
A state which is characterized by its large number of lakes, hence its name 'The Lakes' from the Portuguese *lagoão* 'large lake'.

Alamo, MEXICO, USA
Cities and rivers in both countries with a Spanish name meaning 'Cottonwood' or 'Poplar' tree.

Alamogordo, NEW MEXICO/USA
Founded in 1898, the name is derived from the Spanish meaning 'Large Poplar' or 'Large Cottonwood', both *álamo* and *gordo* 'large'.

Åland Islands (Finnish: **Ahvenanmaa**), FINLAND

'Water Land' from the Swedish *å* 'water'. The Finnish name means 'Land of Perch' from *ahven* 'perch' (the fish) and *maa* 'land'. Though belonging to Finland, these islands were long inhabited by Swedes and Swedish language and culture are still predominant. The islands were seized by Russia in 1714 and when the Grand Duchy of Finland was ceded by Sweden to Russia in 1809 they were included. The Ålanders sought reunion with Sweden in 1919–21, but the islands were allocated to Finland by the League of Nations in 1923.

Alanya, TURKEY *Coracesium, Kalonoros, al-Alāiyyah*

On a virtually impregnable site, the Greek Kalonoros means 'Beautiful Mountain' from *kalon* 'good' and *oros* 'mountain'. The Seljuk Sultan of Rûm, Alâeddin (or Ala al-Din) Keykûbad I, built a formidable new citadel in 1221 and renamed the city after himself to mean 'The Noble'. Kemal Atatürk[†] changed the name to the more mellifluous Alanya in the 1920s.

Alaşehir, TURKEY *Philadelphia*

'Spotted Town' from the Turkish *ala* and *şehir*. Originally named after Attalus II Philadelphus, King of Pergamum (159–138 BC). Philadelphus meant 'loving the brethren'.

Alaska, USA

A state with a name derived from the Aleut (a branch of the Inuit–Aleut family of languages) *alakshak* 'mainland'. It was first discovered in 1741 by Vitus Bering[†], a Dane leading an expedition for Peter I the Great[†]. The first non-local settlers in 1784 were Russians. Administered by the Russian American Company from 1799, it was known as Russian America. The region was sold by Alexander II, emperor (1855–81), to the USA in 1867 for $7.2 million when it quickly became known as Seward's Folly; William H. Seward was the American Secretary of State who arranged the purchase. It became the Territory of Alaska in 1912 and finally the 49th state when it joined the Union in 1959.

Álava, BASQUE COUNTRY/SPAIN

A province with a name from the Basque *araiiar* 'among the mountains', a reference to its location on the southern slopes of the Pyrenees.

Alba Iulia, ROMANIA *Apulon, Apulum, Bălgrad, Weissenburg, Karlsburg, Gyulafehérvár*

An ancient city, the Dacian Apulon gave way to the Latin Apulum, the name of a Roman camp where the 13th Roman Legion was based. The Slavonic Bălgrad and German Weissenburg meant 'White Town', perhaps because of the town's pale walls. It was given the German name Karlsburg after Emperor Charles VI, Holy Roman Emperor (1711–40), Archduke of Austria, and King of Hungary. The present name is derived from the Latin *albus* 'white', and Julius (Gyula), a mid-10th-century Hungarian prince; it is merely a translation of the Hungarian Gyulafehérvár, 'White Town of Julius' from *fehér* and *vár*. The city was the capital of Transylvania during the 16th and 17th centuries. Prince Michael the Brave proclaimed it the capital of the three Romanian provinces of Moldavia, Transylvania, and Wallachia, thus uniting them very briefly for the first time in 1600.

Albacete, CASTILE-LA MANCHA/SPAIN *al-Basīṭ*

This may simply mean 'The Plain' from the Arabic *al-basīṭa* or 'Someone who stretches out to Others'; al-Basīṭ is one of the 99 names of Allah.

Albania (Shqipëria) *Arbania/Arbanon, Epirus*

The Republic of Albania (Republika e Shqipërisë) since 1991. Previously the People's Socialist Republic of Albania (1976); the People's Republic of Albania (1946); the Kingdom of Albania (1928); and the Republic of Albania (1925). Although its independence was recognized in principle in 1912, it was made a protectorate of the Great Powers. Nearly half the Albanian population was left outside the country's political boundaries, mainly in Serbia (Kosovo) and Macedonia. True independence was gained in 1921. Shqipëria is generally taken to mean the 'Land of Eagles' from *shqipónjë* 'eagle', a name gradually adopted during the 16th and 17th centuries, to replace Arbania/Arbanon which took its name from the Albanoi (the Byzantine Greek name; in Latin, Arbaneses) tribe which in turn took its name from the Indo-European word *alb* 'mountain'. Some three-quarters of Albania is mountainous. It was overrun by the Ottoman Turks who established control in 1478 and retained it, despite resistance, until 1912. *Epirus was an ancient country formed from modern southern Albania and north-western Greece.

Albany, AUSTRALIA, USA

1. Australia (Western Australia): developed from a penal settlement in 1826 and renamed Frederickstown after Frederick, Duke of York and Albany (1763–1827) and the second son of King George III[†]. Within six years the name Albany was more commonly used than Frederickstown.

a

2. USA (New York): originally Fort Orange and then Beverwyck and Rensselaerswyck. Finally the city was named after the Duke of York and Albany, later James II[†]. Founded in 1624 by the Dutch as Fort Orange, the attached settlement was called Beverwyck. When it was passed to Kiliaen van Rensselaer, a merchant from Amsterdam, it was renamed after him. The city passed to the British in 1664 when it was given its present name.

Albert, AUSTRALIA, CANADA, FRANCE, USA
1. France (Picardy): named after Albert, Duc de Lynes, who acquired the area some time after 1619. The current pretender to the non-existent French throne, the Comte de Paris, also has the title Marquis d'Albert.
2. USA (South Dakota): named after J. J. Abert, a colonel in the US Army; his name was misspelt Albert.

Albert, Lake, DEMOCRATIC REPUBLIC OF THE CONGO-UGANDA *Luta N'zige, Lake Mobutu Sese Seko*
The first European to see the lake, in 1864, was the British explorer, Samuel (later Sir Samuel) Baker, who named it after Prince Albert (1819–61), the husband of Queen Victoria[†]. It was renamed in 1973 after himself by Mobutu Sese Seko, president of what was then Zaire (1965–97), but this name was never generally accepted. It is also known as Albert Nyanza, a Bantu word for 'lake'.

Alberta, CANADA
A province. From 1670 the southern half was administered as part of Rupert's Land. It joined Canada in 1869 and a year later became part of the Northwest Territories. It became a province in 1905 and was named in honour of the fourth daughter of Queen Victoria[†] and the wife of the governor-general of Canada, Princess Louise Caroline Alberta (1848–1939). She took her final name from her father, Prince Albert.

Albert Lea, MINNESOTA/USA
Named after Lieutenant, later Colonel, Albert M. Lea who explored the area.

Albertville, FRANCE, USA
France (Rhône-Alpes): named after Charles Albert (1798–1849), King of Sardinia-Piedmont (1831–49), who merged two small towns in 1835.

Albi, MIDI-PYRÉNÉES/FRANCE *Albiga*
Takes its name from a Roman personal name, Albius. It gave its name to the Albigensian Crusade of 1209, a war against Catharist heretics which only ended with the Treaty of Paris in 1229, but which did not eliminate the heresy itself.

Ålborg, DENMARK *Alabu, Alaburg(um), Aleburgh*
'Town on the River' from the Jutlandish *ål* 'channel' and *borg*. Ålborg, also spelt Aalborg, lies on the south side of the Limfjord.

Albufeira, PORTUGAL
'The Lake' from the Arabic *al-Buhairah*, a diminutive of *bahr* 'sea'.

Albuquerque, NEW MEXICO/USA
Founded in 1706 and named after Francisco Fernandez de la Cueva, the Spanish Duke of Alburquerque and Viceroy of New Spain (Mexico) (1702–11). The first *r* was dropped in the place-name. Albuquerque itself means 'white oak' from the Latin *quercus* 'oak' and *albus* 'white'.

Alcácer do Sal, PORTUGAL *Salacia, Qasr Abi Danis*
'Castle of Salt', the town being named after the salt pans of the River Sado. *Alcácer* is derived from the Arabic *al-Qasr* 'The Castle'.

Alcalá de Henares, MADRID/SPAIN *Complutum, al-Qala an-Nahr*
'Fortress on the River Henares' from the Moorish name, *al-Qala* being 'fortress' and *an-nahr* 'the river'. Henares is a corruption of the Arabic. The city was destroyed by the Moors in 1000 and rebuilt by them 38 years later. The town was wrested from them in 1088 by Alfonso VI (*c*.1040–1109), King of León (1065–70) and Castile-León (1072–1109).

Alcamo, SICILY/ITALY *Manzil Alqamah*
Founded in 1233 and named after the nearby Saracen fortress to mean 'Resort of Lotus Fruit'.

Alcántara, EXTREMADURA/SPAIN *Kantarat al-Saif*
'The Bridge' from the Arabic *al-Qanṭarah*, a reference to the old Roman bridge built in 105 over the River Tagus. It gave its name to the military Order of Alcántara, founded in 1156 to defend Christian Spain against the Moors; the Order was given to the city in 1218.

Alcázar de San Juan, CASTILE-LA MANCHA/SPAIN *Alces, al-Qasr*
'Castle of St John', the 'St John' being added after the castle, *al-Qasr*, was captured by the Knights of St John of Jerusalem in 1186.

Alchevs'k, UKRAINE *Voroshilovsk, Kommunarsk*
Founded in 1895 and named after a man named Alchevsky who founded the ironworks here. The town was renamed in 1931–61 after Marshal Kliment Voroshilov[†] and Kommunarsk in 1961–92. The latter name, from *kommunar*, acknowledges the communards, members of the Paris Commune which rebelled against the French government

in 1871 and which was much admired by the Russian Bolsheviks.

Alcobaça, PORTUGAL
Named after the Alcoa and Baça Rivers, at whose confluence the town lies.

Alconbury, ENGLAND/UK *Acumesberie, Alcmundesberia*
'Ealhmund's Stronghold' from an Old English personal name and *burh*.

Aldermaston, ENGLAND/UK *Ældremanestone*
'Farmstead of the Nobleman' from the Old English *aldormann* 'nobleman' (modern alderman) and *tūn*. An aldormann was a very senior member of the hierarchy.

Alderney (French: **Aurigny**), CHANNEL ISLANDS *Riduna, Aurene/Aureneie*
An island whose name may mean 'Gravel Island' from the Old Scandinavian *aurinn*, the adjective of *aurr* 'gravel' or 'mud' and *ey*. Riduna 'In front of the Hill' was the Roman name for the port. *See* CHANNEL ISLANDS.

Aldershot, ENGLAND/UK *Halreshet*
'A Piece of Land where Alders grow' from the Old English *alor* 'alder' and *scēat* 'piece, or corner, of land'.

Aleksandriya, UKRAINE *Usovka*
Founded in 1754, but renamed in 1784 after Alexander, grandson of Catherine II the Great[†] and later Emperor of Russia as Alexander I[†], when it became a town.

Aleksandrovac, SERBIA/SERBIA AND MONTENEGRO *Koželin*
Named after Alexander Obrenović, King of Serbia (1889–1903), the last of the Obrenović dynasty (1815–1903); he and his wife were assassinated.

Aleksandrovsk-Sakhalinskiy, SAKHALIN ISLAND/RUSSIA *Aleksandrovsky Post*
Founded in 1881 and named after Alexander III, Emperor of Russia (1881–94). To differentiate it from other towns named Aleksandrovsk (as in Perm Province), Sakhalinsky was added in 1926.

Alentejo, PORTUGAL
A historical province, the name for which is derived from *além Tejo* 'Beyond the (River) Tagus'.

Aleppo (Halab), SYRIA *Khalap, Beroea*
A very ancient city which, according to legend, derived its Arabic name, Halab, from the practice of Abraham to milk, *halîb*, his cow on what is now the citadel hill. Aleppo is the westernized form of Halab. The city was conquered by the Hittites, who called it Khalap, Assyrians, Persians, and Seleucids who

redeveloped it during the 4th century BC and renamed it Beroea. In 540 it was sacked again by the Persians and in 637 conquered by the Arabs, who restored the original name. In 1260 it fell to the Mongols under Hülegü, who did not spare the inhabitants. Aleppo remained under Mamlūk control, after they had defeated the Mongols the same year, until it was incorporated into the Ottoman Empire in 1516. Between 1831 and 1840 it was under Egyptian rule. From 1920 to 1941 the city was part of the French mandate.

Alès, LANGUEDOC-ROUSSILLON/FRANCE *Alestium, Alais*
The town was founded in the 10th century BC by the Phoenicians whose name for it was said to mean 'Industry'. It is still an industrial centre. It received its present name in 1926.

Alessandria, PIEDMONT/ITALY *Civitas Nova, Cesaria*
Founded in 1168 as 'New City'. After a period as Cesaria it was renamed after Pope Alexander III (1159–81) in recognition of his support for the Lombard League, which was established to oppose Frederick I Barbarossa, Holy Roman Emperor and King of Germany (1152–90), who challenged papal authority.

Aleutian Islands, USA
Named after the inhabitants of the islands, the Aleuts, whose name may be derived from the Russian *aleaut* 'bald rock'.

Alexander Island, ANTARCTICA
Discovered in 1821 by two Russian explorers who named it after Alexander I[†].

Alexandra, CANADA, NEW ZEALAND, SOUTH AFRICA
1. New Zealand (South Island): originally Lower Dunstan and then Manuherikia, it was named Alexandra South in 1863 to honour the Danish princess, Alexandra (1844–1925), when she married the Prince of Wales (later Edward VII of the UK) that year. The name was shortened a few years later.
2. South Africa (Gauteng): now a Johannesburg township named after the wife of the founder, S Papenfus, a rich farmer who bought several farms in the area in 1904. One, Zandfontein, became the township of Alexandra in 1912 specifically for 'natives and coloured persons only'.

Alexandria, AUSTRALIA, BRAZIL, CANADA, EGYPT, JAMAICA, ROMANIA, SOUTH AFRICA, USA
1. Egypt: the earliest site was called Rakotis or Rhecates and it was to become the greatest city of the ancient world, founded in 331 BC by, and named after, Alexander III the Great[†] after he had prised Egypt from the Persian Empire.

It was the capital of Egypt from 332 BC to AD
642. It came under Roman control in 30 BC. In
116 the Romans massacred the Jewish
population and in 215 the male population for
resisting their rule. Byzantine rule replaced
Roman and led to the city's decline. This left it
to the mercy of the Persians in 616 and the
Arabs who sacked it in 642. It was bombarded
and then occupied by the British in 1882–1922,
with a British presence remaining until 1947.
In the harbour of Alexandria stood the Pharos
lighthouse, one of the Seven Wonders of the
(ancient) World built by Ptolemy II c.280 BC; it
collapsed during an earthquake in the 14th
century. Its Arabic name is al-Iskandarīyah.
2. South Africa (Eastern Cape): previously
known as Olifantshoek, 'Elephants' Corner'
because of their numbers here, it was renamed
in 1973 after Alexander Smith, a minister in
the Dutch Reformed Church in the 1820s.
3. USA: there are at least eleven towns called
Alexandria, usually named after individuals
associated with their original development.
For example, the Alexandria in Virginia is
named after a Scotsman, John Alexander, who
bought the land from an English ship captain
in 1669; a settlement was constructed in 1731
and named Belhaven, but this was renamed
when it became a town in 1749.

Alexandrina, SOUTH AUSTRALIA/AUSTRALIA
A lake named after Princess Alexandrina, later
Queen Victoria[†]. The Prince Regent, her uncle
who later became King George IV[†], insisted
that she should be named after her godfather,
Tsar Alexander I[†], and so she was christened
Alexandrina Victoria.

Alexandroúpolis, GREECE *Dedeagaç*
Founded in 1860 by the Turks as Dedeagaç,
'Tree of the Holy Man' or 'Grandfather's Tree',
derived from a colony of dervishes. It was
ceded to Bulgaria in 1913, but given to Greece
by the Treaties of Neuilly (1919) and Sèvres
(1920). In 1919 it was renamed 'Alexander's
City' after Alexander III the Great[†] with *polis*.

Alfred, CANADA, USA
1. Canada (Ontario): named after Prince Alfred
(d. 1782), the 14th child of King George III[†].
2. USA: three towns (in Maine, North Dakota,
and New York) have this name, the first two in
honour of Alfred the Great (849–99), King of
Wessex (871–99), a Saxon kingdom in the
south of England. The Alfred in New York was
possibly named after King Alfred's seat in
Hampshire, England.

Algarve, The, PORTUGAL *Cyneticum, al-Gharb*
A historical province and at one time an
independent Moorish kingdom. The present
name is derived from the Arab name and

means 'The West', a reference to the region's
location on the western edge of the Muslim
lands until it fell in 1249 to Afonso III
(1210–79), King of Portugal (1248–79).

Algeciras, ANDALUSIA/SPAIN *Portus Albus,
al-Jazīrah al-Khadrā*
First settled by the Romans as 'White Port', but
founded as a city by the Moors in 713, its
Arabic name means 'The Green Island', a
reference to the island offshore (now called
Isla Verde), from *jazīrah* and *khadrā*, the
feminine of *akhdar* 'green'. It was captured in
1344 by Alfonso XI (1311–50), King of Castile
and León (1312–50), but retaken and destroyed
by the Moors in 1368. It was redeveloped in
1704 by the Spanish.

Algeria (al-Jazā'ir) *Numidia*
The People's Democratic Republic of Algeria
(al-Jumhūrīyah al-Jazā'irīyah ad-Dīmuqrātīyah
ash-Sha'bīyah) since independence from the
French in 1962. As part of the Roman Republic
and Empire, Numidia occupied an area north of
the Sahara roughly equivalent to modern
Algeria. After the fall of Rome in the 5th
century, the coast and certain inland areas
were at one time or another under the control
of the Vandals, the Byzantines, the Muslim
western Umayyad and 'Abbāsid dynasties, the
Berber Almoravids (Arabic: *al-Murābitūn* 'People
of the *Ribat*') and Almohads (Arabic: *al-
Muwahhidūn* 'Those who proclaim the unity of
God' or 'The Monotheists'), and the Spanish
until Algeria came under the nominal
protection of the Ottoman Sultan in 1518. The
region became an autonomous province of the
Ottoman Empire in 1536. At this time the name
Algerian was applied only to those Turks who
lived in Algiers. The French invaded in 1830
and four years later the occupied areas were
annexed as a colony. Between 1830 and 1962
the country was occupied by the French, who
drew its borders and considered it an integral
part of metropolitan France. The country
takes its name from its capital city, Algiers.
The Arabic name, al-Jazā'ir, means 'The Islands'
and Algeria is the Anglicization of this name.

Al-Gharbīyah, SAUDI ARABIA
A geographic region simply called 'The
Western'.

Alghero, SARDINIA/ITALY
Founded in 1102 by the Genoese, it became a
Catalan colony in 1354. Its name is derived
from the Latin *alga* 'seaweed', a reference to its
presence off the coast.

Algiers (al-Jazā'ir), ALGERIA *Icosium*
Also known as Alger. The city takes its
name from the presence of a few islands, *jazā'ir*

(the plural of *jazīrah*), which were once in the bay, but which have since been joined to the mainland. The conventional English name is a corruption of the Arabic. Icosium was the Carthaginian and Roman name. The city was sacked by the Vandals in the 5th century, destroyed by the Arabs in the 7th, and rebuilt and renamed in the 10th. It was later seized by the Ottoman Turks in 1516 and by the French in 1830. They made it the headquarters of their North and West African Empire. It became the capital of independent Algeria in 1962.

Algoa Bay, EASTERN CAPE/SOUTH AFRICA *Angra da Roca, Bahia da Lagoa*
First named by the Portuguese 'Bay of Rocks' from *angra* 'bay' in 1488, it was later changed to 'Lagoon Bay'. The present name may be derived from the second Portuguese name. However, *algoa* means 'needles' in Old Portuguese and this name may have been chosen because of the needle-sharp rocks off Port Elizabeth.

Alhama, SPAIN
Four towns have this name, each with an affix indicating their location: de Almería, de Aragón, de Granada, and de Murcia. The name means 'The Hot Spring' from the Arabic *al-Hammah*.

'Alīābād, AFGHANISTAN, IRAN
'Town of Ali' named after Ali ibn Abī Tālib (*c.*600–61), the fourth caliph (656–61) and cousin and son-in-law of the Prophet Muhammad[†].

Ali Bayramli, AZERBAIJAN
Named after the Bolshevik revolutionary, Ali Bayramov (1889–1920), who took his name from a festival of Islam (in Azeri, *Bayram* 'celebration'), and was killed during the Russian Civil War (1918–20).

Alibunar, SERBIA/SERBIA AND MONTENEGRO
A former Turkish frontier post built in the 16th century which developed into a fortified town meaning 'Ali's Well' from the Serbo-Croat *bunar* 'well'.

Alicante, VALENCIA/SPAIN *Akra Leuke, Lucentum, al-Lucant/al-Akant*
Founded in 325 BC by the Greeks, the original name meant 'White Peak' from *akra* 'peak' or 'headland' and *leukas* 'white' or 'chalky'. The Romans, who captured it in 201 BC, named it Lucentum, the 'Place of Light'. The Moorish name, which was used 718–1249, had the same meaning.

Alice, EASTERN CAPE/SOUTH AFRICA
Named in 1847 after Princess Alice (1843–78), the second daughter of Queen Victoria[†].

Alice Springs, NORTHERN TERRITORY/AUSTRALIA *Stuart*
While surveying a route for the Overland Telegraph Line, William Mills discovered some springs in a dried-up river bed here. He named the river in 1870 after Charles Todd (1826–1910) (later Sir Charles Heavitree Todd, Superintendent of Telegraphs for South Australia (1870–1905)) and the springs Alice after Todd's wife. Todd was known as Telegraph Todd, his great project being to cross Australia from Darwin to Adelaide and set up a telegraph service. It took fifteen years (1857–72), but was not quite completed, having a 394-mile (634 km) gap. The present town originated in 1871 as a telegraph station on the Line, known as Alice Springs. When it became recognized as a town in 1890 it was called Stuart after the Scottish explorer John McDouall Stuart (1815–66). It reverted to Alice Springs in 1933.

Alīgarh, UTTAR PRADESH/INDIA *Koil/Kol, Ramgarh*
'High Fortress', the town being named from 1776 after the nearby 12th-century fort, *garh.*

Aliquippa, PENNSYLVANIA/USA *Logstown*
Settled *c.*1750, it was renamed after a Mohawk or Delaware woman, Aliquippa, whose name was said to mean 'hat'.

Aliwal North, EASTERN CAPE/SOUTH AFRICA
Founded by Lieutenant General Sir Harry Smith (1787–1860), governor of Cape Colony (1847–52), who gave it this name to commemorate his victory over the Sikhs in 1846 at Aliwal in India before he came to the Cape as governor. 'North' was added when Aliwal South (now *Mossel Bay) was established.

Al-Janūbīyah, SAUDI ARABIA
A geographic region simply called 'The Southern'.

Alkmaar, SURINAME, THE NETHERLANDS
The Netherlands: a commune developed from a 10th-century fishing village with a name meaning 'All Sea'.

Allahābād, UTTAR PRADESH/INDIA *Prayāg, al-Ilahābād*
Renamed in 1584 al-Ilahābād, 'The City of God' from *Allah* and *ābād*, by Akbar[†], the Muslim Mughal emperor. Sometimes still called Prayāg 'Place of Sacrifice' and occasionally Teerthraj. Prayāg was a holy city of great importance. Allahābād is sited at the confluence of the Rivers Ganges and Yamuna (Jumna) and the mythical underground Saraswati River. It was

ceded to the UK in 1801 and it was here that the English East India Company handed over control of India to the British government in 1858. It is one of four locations in India for the Kumbh Mela, the Festival, *Mela*, of the Pitcher, *Kumbh*, the largest Hindu religious festival (and the largest religious pilgrimage in the world), which is held four times every twelve years.

Allahüekber Daği, TURKEY
'God is Greatest Mountain' from *Allah* 'God', *ekber* 'greatest' or 'almighty', and *dağ*.

Allanridge, FREE STATE/SOUTH AFRICA
Laid out in 1950 and named after Allan Roberts, an engineer who helped to establish gold mining on the ridge here.

Allegheny, ANTARCTICA, USA
USA (Pennsylvania): a river said to have a Delaware name meaning 'Fine Stream' or 'Fairest River'. The Allegheny Mountains stretch southwards into Virginia and West Virginia.

Allentown, PENNSYLVANIA/USA *Northampton*
The town was laid out by William Allen, the mayor of Philadelphia, in 1762. He named it Northampton. It was renamed after its founder in 1838.

Alliance, OHIO/USA
So-called because of the junction of two railway lines here. It was midway between Freedom and Mount Union, both of which were incorporated into Alliance in 1854.

Alma, CANADA, UKRAINE, USA
1. Ukraine: a river in the Crimea with the name from a Turkic word for 'apple'; the modern Turkish word is *elma*.
2. There are at least seven towns with this name in the USA and at least two in Canada. Those in Illinois and Michigan, USA, are named after the Battle of Alma (20 September 1854) in the Crimea, Ukraine, which ended in victory for British and French forces over the Russians. Others bear personal names.

Almadén, AUSTRALIA, SPAIN
Spain (Castile-La Mancha): formerly Sisapo and al-Ma'din from the Moorish name, al-Ma'din 'The Mine', a reference to the very rich mercury deposits in this area.

Almalyk, UZBEKISTAN
Founded in 1951, the city derives its name, which means 'Apple Grove', from *olma* 'apple', from the local wild apple trees.

Almaty, KAZAKHSTAN *Almatu, Zailiyskoye, Verny, Alma-Ata*
Once an oasis on the Silk Road, Almatu was sacked by the Mongols in the 13th century.

It was refounded in 1854 as a Cossack military fort called Zailiyskoye. Within a year the name was changed to Verny 'Faithful', that is, one that would not surrender to the enemy. The city was renamed Alma-Ata in 1921, a Soviet version of its Kazakh name, Almaty 'Apple Orchards'; however, it is traditionally translated as 'Father of Apples' from the Kazakh *Ata* 'father' and *alma* 'apple'. It was renamed Almaty in 1994 after Kazakhstan gained independence in December 1991. It was the national capital between 1929 and 1997 because its predecessor, Qyzylorda, was considered by the Bolsheviks to be too hot. It is still sometimes called the 'Southern Capital'. It is also the name of a province.

Almeida, CASTILE AND LEÓN/SPAIN
Possibly 'The Table' from the Arabic *al-Ma'ida*'.

Almería, ANDALUSIA/SPAIN *Campus Spartarius, Urci, Portus Magnus, al-Mariyah*
The original Roman name meant 'Land of Esparto Grass' and later Portus Magnus 'Great Port'. The Arab name, from which the present name comes, meant 'Mirror of the Sea' or 'Watchtower'. The city was held by the Moors between 1157 and 1489.

Almodóvar del Campo, CASTILE-LA MANCHA/SPAIN
Derived from the Arabic *al-Mudawar* 'the defended' with the Spanish *del Campo* 'of the plain' added to distinguish this Almódovar.

Alor Setar, MALAYSIA
Named after a setar tree in the main channel of a river, or a canal, *alor*.

Alps, FRANCE-ITALY-SWITZERLAND-LIECHTENSTEIN-GERMANY-AUSTRIA-SLOVENIA-CROATIA
A major mountain range with a name probably derived from an Indo-European root word *alb* 'mountain'.

Alsace, FRANCE *Elsass*
A region with a name meaning 'Those living on the outside', that is, west of the River Rhine. It became a Frankish duchy in 496, having been seized from the Alemanni who had previously taken it from the Romans. The region was subsumed into Lotharingia in 870 and thereafter became a much disputed territory. It was ceded to Germany in 1871 after the Franco-Prussian war, returned to France in 1919, occupied by Germany in 1940 and once more restored to France in 1945. It gave its name to the Alsatian breed of dog, also known as the German shepherd. Elsass is the German name.

Altamura, APULIA/ITALY
Takes its name from the high wall, *alta mura*,
which surrounds the town and which was
built by Frederick II[†] to keep out the Moors.

Altay, CHINA, MONGOLIA, RUSSIA
1. China (Sinkiang Uighur Autonomous
Region): situated in the southern foothills of
the Altay Mountains, it takes its name from
them.
2. Mongolia: there are two towns with this
name, one previously called Yösönbulag and
which is in the Altay mountains.
3. Russia: a republic and a separate territory
named after the Altay Mountains from the
Turkic–Mongolian *altan* 'golden'. The republic
was previously the Oirot Autonomous Region,
created in 1922 and named after the
Mongoloid Oirot people. It was renamed the
Gorno-Altay Autonomous Province in 1948
and given republican status in 1992 as the
Altay Republic.

Alto Molócuè, MOZAMBIQUE
Named after the river which takes its name
from the local word *moloki* 'river' and the
Portuguese *alto* 'upper' to indicate that the
town lies fairly near the river's source.

Alton, NEW ZEALAND, UK, USA
1. USA (Illinois): founded in 1817 by Rufus
Easton and named after his son.
2. There are at least nine other Altons in the
USA, several in the UK, and one in New
Zealand. The various English Altons are all
associated with a farmstead, *tūn*, in one way or
another.

Altoona, PENNSYLVANIA/USA
Founded in 1849 and possibly named after the
Altona in Germany; or the name may be taken
from the Latin *altus* 'high', a reference to its
elevated position in the Allegheny Mountains.

Altrincham, ENGLAND/UK *Aldringeham*
'Homestead of Aldhere's Followers' from an
Old English personal name, *-inga-*, and *hām*.

Altus, OKLAHOMA/USA *Frazier*
Liable to flooding, it was moved in 1891 to
higher ground 4 miles (6 km) to the east and
renamed 'High (Place)' from the Latin *altus*.

Alverstone, Mt, YUKON/CANADA-ALASKA/USA
A mountain named after Richard Everard
Webster (1842–1915), Viscount Alverstone,
Lord Chief Justice of England and a member of
the Alaska Boundary Commission (1903).

Älvsborg, SWEDEN
A county with a name derived from the Old
Swedish *älv* 'river' and *borg*. The area contains
many rivers; the fort is the one at Vänersborg.

Alzira, VALENCIA/SPAIN *Algezira Sucro,
Saetabicula, Jazīrat Shuvr*
Originally called by Iberian settlers the 'Island
of Sucro' because it lay between two branches
of the River Sucro (now the Júcar). The
succeeding Roman, Moorish, and present
Spanish names are similar.

Ama Dablam, Mt, NEPAL
A mountain close to Mt Everest with a name
meaning 'Mother's Charm Box', a reference to
the ornament that Sherpa women wear round
their necks.

Amadeus, Lake, NORTHERN TERRITORY/
AUSTRALIA
Named in 1872 after Amadeus (1845–90), the
Piedmontese-born King of Spain (1870–3).

Amagasaki, HONSHŪ/JAPAN
'Nun's Cape', the characters representing *ama*
'(Buddhist) nun', *ga* 'of', and *saki* 'cape'. It is an
important port and centre of the fishing
industry (*ama* can also mean 'diver').

Amalfi, CAMPANIA/ITALY
Said to have been founded in *c*.320 by, and
named after, Amalfo Romano, a captain in the
army of Constantine I the Great[†].
Alternatively, it has been suggested that it may
come from a stem *melf* with the sense of a
'curve' or 'concave gulf', a description,
perhaps, of the ravine in the Mulini Valley in
which the coastal town lies. By the 9th century
it was a city-state which developed into a
maritime republic rivalling Genoa, Pisa, and
Venice in importance and influence. Having
been sacked by the Pisans in 1135 and 1137, it
went into a rapid decline, its population falling
from about 50 000 in its heyday to little more
than 5 000.

Amanzimtoti, KWAZULU-NATAL/SOUTH AFRICA
According to legend, the Zulu chief Shaka said
'Kanti amanza mtoti' 'So, the water is sweet',
a reference to the river near which he was
camping with his army. Locally, the town is
simply called Toti.

'Amārah, al-, IRAQ
'Building' or 'Structure' from *imarah*. It could
also mean 'Place of Habitation'.

Amarapura, BURMA
'City of Immortals', 'City of Immortality', or
'City where there is No Death'. It was founded
in 1783 as the new capital (1783–1823,
1841–61) of Bodawpaya (1741?–1819), King of
Burma (1782–1819). The city is often also
called Taungmyo 'Southern City' from *myo*
'city', or Myohaung, 'Old City', to distinguish it
from Mandalay, the northern city. It is now
virtually a suburb of Mandalay.

Amarillo, TEXAS/USA *Ragtown*
Founded in 1887, the name is the same as the Spanish word for yellow, a reference to the colour of the local clay.

Amarna, Tell al-, EGYPT *Akhetaton*
Ruins. In about 1350 BC the Pharoah Amenhotep IV, having transferred his religious loyalty from Amen to Aton, changed his name to Akhenaton. He built a new capital, which he called Akhetaton, to replace Thebes 180 miles (290 km) to the south. The name means the 'Horizon of Aton', a sun god represented as a solar disc; Akhenaton means 'He who worships Aton'. Akhenaton was married to Nefertiti and his son-in-law was Tutankhamen. Tutankhamen assumed power about four years after Akhenaton's death in about 1336 BC, quickly reverted to the old religion (changing his name from Tutankhaton) and moved the capital back to Thebes. Akhetaton fell into decline and was abandoned; only ruins remain. They are named now after a nearby village, 'Mound of the Amra' from *tell* 'mound' and the name of a local tribe.

Amazon, BRAZIL-PERU
A river, *Amazanu* in Tupi-Guarani, which means 'Big Wave', a reference to the rapid flow at its mouth. It has no connection with the female warriors of Greek mythology, the Amazons, although Spanish explorers brought back tales of fearsome female warriors in the jungle (who were probably men who wore their hair long).

Amazonas, BRAZIL, COLOMBIA, PERU, VENEZUELA
1. Brazil: a state named after the River Amazon, in Portuguese 'Rio Amazonas'.
2. Colombia-Peru: departments, both connected with the Amazon River basin.
3. Venezuela: a state, although it is drained by the Orinoco River. The Negro River, which forms its western border, is a tributary of the Amazon.

Ambatolampy, MADAGASCAR
'Place where there are Flat Rocks' in Malagasy.

Āmber, RĀJASTHĀN/INDIA *Ambarikhanera, Ambiner*
Founded as a fortress-palace in 1592, it became a Rājput capital. Also known as Āmer, it was named after Ambarisha, King of Ayodhyā. The original complete name was shortened to Ambiner and again to Amber.

Ambon, MOLUCCAS/INDONESIA *Nuestra Senhora da Anunciada, Amboina*
An island and a city named by the Portuguese 'Our Lady of the Annunciation' in 1521. The present name may be derived from *ambwan* 'dew' or *nusa ombong* 'dawn'. It was occupied by the Dutch in 1605 until 1796 when the British captured it; they held it until 1814 when it was returned to the Dutch. In 1950 the Ambonese refused to join the new Republic of Indonesia and declared an independent South Moluccan Republic; this was soon extinguished.

Amelia, VIRGINIA/USA
Named after Princess Amelia (d. 1786), the second daughter of King George II[†].

America The name technically includes North and South America. They can be divided into 'Anglo-America' (Canada and the United States) and 'Latin America' (Central and South America, and the Hispanic Islands of the West Indies). The name America was first applied to South America in 1507 by Martin Waldseemüller (*c*.1470–*c*.1521), a German geographer and cartographer at the court of the Duke of Lorraine, in honour of an Italian (Florentine) explorer, Amerigo Vespucci (1451–1512) (Latinized in Waldseemüller's *Cosmographiae Introductio* to Americus Vesputius). Vespucci made a landfall in modern Guyana in 1499 and then went south. This first voyage was with Spanish support, but his subsequent voyage in 1501-2 along the coast of Brazil had the backing of the Portuguese. Vespucci came to the conclusion that during the voyages he had undertaken in 1499–1502 a 'New World' had been discovered rather than the east coast of Asia. In due course the name was extended to North America. 'America' now usually refers only to the United States of America.

Americana, SÃO PAULO/BRAZIL *Vila Americana*
Founded by immigrants from the Confederate States of America (the eleven southern states that left the Union between 1860 and 1865) in 1868 as 'American Town'. Vila was dropped in 1938.

American Samoa *Navigator Islands*
An unincorporated territory of the USA. The meaning of the name is disputed. Samoa is said to mean 'Sacred Centre' because, according to legend, this is where Tagaloalagi created the world. It may, however, mean the 'Place of the Moa', an extinct bird, in the Samoan language. The first European to sight the islands in 1722 was the Dutch Admiral Jakob Roggeveen. Germany, the UK, and the USA agreed in 1889 to Samoan neutrality and established a joint protectorate. All rights to the islands east of the line of longitude 171° West were awarded to the USA in 1899 and all to the west to Germany. As a result of a decision by the High Chiefs, all 'eastern' islands were ceded to the

USA by 1904 and collectively called American Samoa; however, they were not accepted by the US Congress until 1929. The islands of American Samoa and Samoa were given the name Les Îles des Navigateurs 'Navigator Islands' by the Frenchman Louis-Antoine de Bougainville in 1772 because of the sailing skills of the local canoeists.

Americus, GEORGIA/USA
Founded in 1830 and named after Amerigo Vespucci (*see* AMERICA); or, as some locals would have it, after the 'merry cusses' who first settled here.

Amersfoort, THE NETHERLANDS, SOUTH AFRICA
1. The Netherlands: 'Ford on the Amer'. The River Amer is now called the Eem.
2. South Africa (Mpumalanga): named after the Dutch town.

Amersham, ENGLAND/UK *Agmodesham, Elmodesham*
'Ealhmund's Village' from an Old English personal name and *hām*.

Ames, IOWA/USA
Laid out in 1865 and named after Oakes Ames (1804–73), a Congressman from Massachusetts. The scandal enveloping the Crédit Mobilier, a company established to build the Union Pacific Railway in 1865, resulted in his disgrace. Nevertheless, the town was not renamed.

Amesbury, UK, USA
1. UK (England): formerly Ambresbyrig and Ambresberie, this town is near Salisbury and has a name meaning 'Ambre's Stronghold' from *byrig*, the dative of *burh*, and an Old English personal name.
2. USA (Massachusetts): the American town was founded in 1642 as part of Salisbury and was thus given the name Amesbury.

Amfipolis, GREECE *Ennea Hodoi, Amphipolis*
As a transport hub, its original name meant 'Nine Roads'. Its present name is derived from the Greek *amphi* 'on both sides' or 'around', and *polis*, to mean 'Surrounded City'; it is situated in a loop of the River Strymon.

Amherst, CANADA, USA *La Planche (Canada)*
1. Canada (Nova Scotia): the original French name 'The Land', a reference to its location on rising ground above the Tantramar Marshes, gave way to Amherst in 1759 in honour of Jeffrey Amherst, later 1st Baron Amherst, the British commander in North America who captured Canada from the French between 1758 and 1760.

2. USA (Massachusetts): founded and named in 1759 after Jeffrey Amherst.

Amherstburg, ONTARIO/CANADA
Named after Jeffrey Amherst (see previous entry); as is Amherstview, also in Ontario.

Amiens, PICARDY/FRANCE *Samarobriva, Ambianum*
Situated in the Somme River valley, it is named after the Ambiani whose name comes from the Gaulish *ambe* 'river'. Samarobriva, the pre-Roman name, means 'Bridge over the (River) Somme' from *briva*.

Amirante Islands, SEYCHELLES
Sighted by the Portuguese navigator, Vasco da Gama, in 1502, they were named in his honour as *Ilhas do Almirante* 'Admiral's Islands'.

'Ammān, JORDAN *Rabbah, Philadelpheia*
The biblical Hebrew name Rabbah, or Rabbat Bene 'Ammon, meant 'Capital City of the Sons of Ammon'. The Ammonites were a Semitic people who settled in Palestine in the second millennium BC and gave their name to the city. In the Bible (Deuteronomy 3: 11) it is mentioned as 'Rabbah of the children of Ammon'. The city was captured from the Greeks by Ptolemy II Philadelphus, King of Egypt (285–246 BC), who renamed it after himself. It was briefly occupied by the Nabataeans before falling to Herod the Great (*c.*73–4 BC), appointed by the Romans as King of Judaea (37–4 BC), *c.*30 BC. Following its conquest by the Arabs in 635, it fell into decline, becoming no more than a village. In 1878 it was resettled by Circassian refugees from Russia. When Transjordan became a protected emirate as part of the Palestinian mandate in the aftermath of the First World War, Abdullah became the emir and made Amman his capital in 1921. When Transjordan became independent as Jordan in 1946, Amman became the capital of the new state.

'Ammārīyah, al-, SAUDI ARABIA
'Camel-borne Howdah and the Virgin riding in it into Battle'.

Amo, USA
The three towns with this name in Colorado, Indiana, and Minnesota are called after a Native American word for 'bee'.

Amoy (Xiamén), FUJIAN/CHINA *Jiahe Island*
'Great Gate' from *xià* 'great' or 'large' and *mén* 'gate'or 'door'. The island is so-named due to its location at the mouth of the Jiulung River. During the Song (960–1279), Yüan (1279–1368), and Ming (1368–1644) dynasties it was called Jiahe Island from *jiahe* 'auspicious grain', a reference to the time when the island had a

bountiful crop, three to four times the normal harvest. Sometime after 1394 it was mentioned as Xiamén when the island was fortified against the depredations of pirates. However, this name was not formally adopted until the Qing (or Manchu) dynasty (1644–1911). The city-port with the same name was occupied by the British in 1841 and a year later it was opened up to foreign trade by the Treaty of Nanking. The Fujianese call both the island and port Amoy, which is a version of Xiamén in their language; Europeans preferred this because it was easier to pronounce.

Amritsar, PUNJAB/INDIA *Gurū kā Chak, Rāmdāspur, Chak Rām Dās*
Founded in 1577 by Rām Dās, the fourth Sikh Gurū, who built a temple around a pool filled with 'sacred' water known for its healing properties. Called Amrita Saras, it means 'Pool of Nectar' from the Sanskrit *amṛta* 'nectar of immortality', and *saras* 'pool' or 'lake'. The Sikh's Golden Temple was built on an island in the centre of the pool. The city was annexed to British India in 1849.

Amsterdam, FRANCE, THE NETHERLANDS, USA
1. The Netherlands: founded in 1270 as a small fishing village in a marshy area at the mouth of the River Amstel. When a dam was built between the dykes on both sides of the river the village became known as Amsteldam, the l changing to r later. It has been the nominal capital of the Kingdom of the Netherlands since 1806, but not the seat of government.
2. USA (New York): named by a Dutch settler after the Amsterdam in The Netherlands. It originated in 1783 as Veedersburg after its founder, Albert Veeder, but was renamed in 1804.

Amu Darya, CENTRAL ASIA *Jayhun, Oxus*
A river which may derive its name from the ancient city of Āmul (now Chardzhev, Turkmenistan, which lies on the river) with the Uzbek *daryo* 'river'. It assumes its name at the confluence of the Pyandzh and Vakhsh Rivers on the border between Afghanistan and Tajikistan and then flows some 880 miles (1 416 km) to the Aral Sea in Uzbekistan.

Amundsen, ANTARCTICA
A mountain, bay, and sea, all named after Roald Amundsen (1872–1928), a Norwegian explorer, who trekked to the South Pole in 1911.

Amur (Chinese: **Hēilóng Jiāng**; Mongolian: **Kharamuren**), CHINA-RUSSIA
A river which may derive its name from the Mongolian *amar* 'peace', which may be a reference to the peaceful flow of its water. The Chinese name means 'Black Dragon River' from *hēi* 'black', *lóng* 'dragon', and *jiāng*. For most of its course it forms the border between Russia and China.

Amursk, KHABAROVSK TERRITORY/RUSSIA
Founded in 1958, it is named after the River Amur, on which it lies.

Anaconda, MONTANA/USA *Copperopolis*
The creator of Montana's copper industry, Marcus Daly, an Irish immigrant, added *polis* to copper when founding the town in 1883. It was renamed Anaconda in 1888 after Daly set up the Anaconda Company to produce copper.

Anadyr', CHUKOT AUTONOMOUS DISTRICT/RUSSIA *Anadyrsky Ostrog, Novo-Mariinsk*
Founded in 1889 as a frontier post on the estuary of the River Anadyr, it was given the additional *ostrog* 'stockade' later to indicate that it was a fortified town. In due course it was renamed 'New Mary's (Settlement)' after the Danish-born Maria Fëderovna (1847–1928), wife of Tsar Alexander III, before a shortened version of the original name was adopted in 1923.

Anaheim, CALIFORNIA/USA
Said to have been named after Anna Fischer, the first child born in the settlement in 1857, with the German suffix *heim* to mean the 'Home of Anna'. Alternatively, however, founded by German immigrants that year, it may be 'Home on the Ana', a reference to the Santa Ana River on which the city lies.

Anáhuac, MEXICO, USA
Mexico: two states, Nuevo León and Zacetecas, have towns with this name. They are less well known than the region that was the centre of Aztec Mexico. The name means 'Land by the Water' in Nahuatl, a reference to the five interlocking lakes which surrounded Tenochtitlán (now Mexico City) when the Spanish arrived in 1519. They have since been drained.

Anandpur, INDIA
Punjab: 'City of Bliss' from Punjabi *ānanda* 'bliss' and *pur*. It was founded in 1664 as a Sikh holy place.

Anantapur, ANDHRA PRADESH/INDIA
'Town of Ananda', the wife of the official who founded the town in the Kingdom of Vijayanagar (1336–1614) with *pur*.

Anatolia (Anadolu), TURKEY *Asia Minor, Rûm*
The western peninsula of Turkey lying in the Asiatic and larger part of the country, now comprising four geographical regions (West, East, Southeast and Central Anatolia).

Historically called Asia Minor, it was called '(Land of the) Rûm' (Rome or Roman) by the Greeks. Anatolia is derived from the Greek *anatole* 'east' or 'sunrise', which referred to the Byzantine province situated to the east of the original Turkoman principality in north-west Asia Minor. To the Greeks this region was the outer limit of the known world, hence the name. Rumeli, 'Roman land', a name later used to describe Ottoman Turkish conquests in Europe, was replaced by Anadolu. Only in 1923 did the Treaty of Lausanne recognize Turkish ownership of Anatolia.

Anbār, al-, IRAQ
A governorate and an oasis town meaning 'Granaries' in Arabic, a reference to the fact that the Sāssānian armies used the area as a military supply depot in the 3rd century.

Anchorage, ALASKA/USA
Founded in 1915 as the central construction camp for the Alaska Railroad going north to Fairbanks and south to Seward, linking the oilfields. Before being developd into a port, the site was initially used as an anchorage for ships plying the huge Cook Inlet (named after Captain James Cook's[†] visit in 1778). It was given the name Anchorage by the US Post Office.

Ancona, MARCHE/ITALY *Dorica Ancon*
Founded *c*.390 BC, its name is derived from the Greek *ankon* 'elbow', in this case 'bend', referring to the shape of the coastline. It became a semi-independent republic in the 9th century and was incorporated into the Papal States in 1532. In 1860 it became part of Italy.

Andalusia (Andalucia), SPAIN, USA
1. Spain: an autonomous community meaning the 'Land of the Vandals' (with the *v* dropped) and which is largely equivalent to the Roman province of Baetica. The Vandals were a Germanic people who sacked Rome and invaded Spain during the 5th century. Their name means 'wanderers'. Their behaviour has given us the word vandalism. The former Arabic name Al-Andalus referred to the whole Iberian peninsula. As the Christian reconquest of the peninsula progressed the meaning changed to cover only the territory under Muslim control. It was occupied by the Moors from 711 to 1492, when it was incorporated into the Christian Kingdom of Castile.
2. USA: there are two towns with this name in the USA. One, in Alabama, was originally called New Site, because it was relocated due to flooding, before being given the Spanish name in 1846.

Andaman and Nicobar Islands, INDIA
A Union Territory. The Andamans may derive their name from the Sanskrit *hanumant*, from Hanuman, the monkey-general in the *Rāmāyaṇa*, the Romance of Rāmā, one of the two great epic poems of India. The Nicobars may have had the name Nakkavāram 'Land of the Naked' from the Hindi *nangā* 'naked'. Under Danish sovereignty 1756–1848, the Islands were annexed by the British in 1869, occupied by the Japanese 1942–5, and passed to India on independence in 1947. The Andaman Islands gave their name to the Andaman Sea.

Anderson, USA
1. Indiana: founded in 1823 and named after a Delaware chief, Koktowhanund (or Kikthawenund), who was also known as Captain William Anderson.
2. South Carolina: founded in 1826 and named after a hero of the War of Independence (1775–83), General Robert Anderson.

Andhra Pradesh, INDIA *Telinga, Telugu*
A state since 1953 with a name meaning the 'State of the Andhras'. *Pradesh* comes from the Sanskrit *pradesa* 'province'. Telugu is the local form of Telinga which was used in Sanskrit texts. The Telugu *andhramu* means 'Telugu'. Andhra is now the official name to describe the people and their language.

Andijon, UZBEKISTAN *Andizhan*
A province and a city, probably named after the Andijon River and dating to at least the 9th century. As capital of the Ferghana state in the 15th century, it was an important trading centre on the Silk Road. It was captured by the Russians in 1876 and incorporated into the Uzbek Soviet Socialist Republic when it was established in 1924. The name adopted a revised spelling in 1991.

Andorra (French: **Andorre**)
The Principality of Andorra (Principat d'Andorra). The name is derived from the local Navarrese word *andurrial* 'shrub-covered land'. However, it has also been suggested that it might come from the Arabic *al-Gandura* 'the wanton woman', a legacy from the Moors, although it is not known why. It has been virtually independent since 803 when Charlemagne[†] drove the Muslims out of the area. Because of a long quarrel between the Spanish bishops of Urgel and the French counts of Urgel, it was agreed in 1278 that Andorra should be governed jointly. True independence is dated from 1288. French rights passed to the head of state in 1572.

Andorra-la-Vella (French: **Andorre-le-Vieille**; Spanish: **Andorra-la-Vieja**)
'Andorra the Old'. The capital of Andorra.

Andover, UK, USA
1. UK (England): formerly Afondwfr, Andeferas, and Andever/Andevore. Lying on the small River Anton, previously Ann or Anna, the town's name is Celtic in origin and means '(Place by) Ash Tree Waters' from *afon*, which was sometimes pronounced *Oun* and then *onna* or *anna* to give the river name Ann 'ash tree', and *dwfr*, a generic word for 'water' or 'stream'. In due course this evolved through *dubro* into *dever* and *dover*.
2. USA: towns in Massachusetts, originally called Cochicewick, a Native American name meaning 'Great Cascade', and Vermont, are named after the town in England.

Androscoggin, MAINE-NEW HAMPSHIRE/USA
A river and a lake with an Algonquian name meaning '(Place for) fish-curing' or '(Place for) fish-spearing'.

Anegada, BRITISH VIRGIN ISLANDS
An island whose name means 'Flooded' from the Spanish *anegadizo*.

Aného, TOGO *Petit Popo, Anécho*
Founded and named after the Ane people in the 17th century. It was the capital of German Togoland 1885–7 and of the French-occupied territory between 1914 and 1920.

Angangueo, MICHOACÁN/MEXICO
'Mouth of the Cave' in Tarascan.

Angarsk, IRKUTSK/RUSSIA
Founded in 1948, it is situated at the confluence of the Kitoi and Angara Rivers, hence its name. It is not clear what Angara means.

Angeles, LUZON/PHILIPPINES
'Angels' in Spanish.

Angel Falls, VENEZUELA
Named after Jimmy Angel, a prospector who landed a light aircraft at the top in 1936. It sank in a bog and he and his wife took eleven days to walk back to civilization.

Angels Camp, CALIFORNIA/USA
Named after Henry Angel, who discovered gold in the vicinity in 1848.

Angers, PAYS DE LA LOIRE/FRANCE *Juliomagus*
Named after the Andecavi, the Roman name for a Gallic tribe, whose capital this was. Their name came from the Gaulish *ande* 'greater' and *cavi* 'allies'. Later, under the Romans, it was called 'Julius (Caesar)'s Market'. As Angers, it became the capital of the former Duchy of Anjou. Geoffrey IV Plantagenet, Count of

Anjou, married Matilda, daughter of Henry I of England, in 1128. Their son became King Henry II of England in 1154, thus founding the English House of Plantagenet which provided fourteen kings 1154–1485. The House of Plantagenet was also called the House of Anjou and the empire ruled by Henry II (1154–89) and his successors, which extended from Scotland to the Pyrenees, was called the Angevin Empire.

Angkor, CAMBODIA *Yasodharapura*
Ruins. Capital of the Khmer Empire from the 9th century until 1431, it was originally named after King Yasovarman I (889–*c.*910) who built it. His name may be derived from the Sanskrit *yasodhara* 'possessing glory' from *yasas* 'glory' and *dhara* 'possessing'; *pura* was added to indicate a town. The present name is derived from the Sanskrit *nagara* 'city'. The city gave its name to Cambodia's medieval civilization. It was abandoned in 1431 after successive Thai attacks and was lost for over 400 years before being rediscovered in 1860.

Angle Inlet, MINNESOTA/USA
So named because it is located in the Northwest Angle of Minnesota. This is an area, on the western side of the Lake of the Woods and separated from the rest of Minnesota, which was created when the border between the USA and Canada was realigned along the 49th parallel. The previous border had been further north, drawn in 1783, when maps showing the incorrect source of the Mississippi River were used.

Anglesey (Ynys Môn), WALES/UK *Anglesege, Ongulsey*
'Ongull's Island' from an Old Scandinavian personal name and *ey*. The island was invaded by the Romans in 61 and taken fully under control in 78. The English subjugated it during the reign of Edward I (1272–1307).

Angoche, MOZAMBIQUE *Vila António Enes*
Originally named after the offshore island which takes its name from the Akoti people after Akote, their leader. The Portuguese name honoured the dramatist, António Enes (1848–1901), but the first name was restored in 1975.

Angola The Republic of Angola (República de Angola) since 1991. Previously the People's Republic of Angola (1975–91) following the achievement of independence in 1975 and an Overseas Province of Portugal (1951–75). It became a Portuguese colony in 1590, although Portuguese control was confined to an area south of the Kingdom of Kongo. The Portuguese were the first Europeans to arrive in 1483. During the next century they began to

settle and establish links with the Kingdom of
Ndongo to the east. They began to call the
whole area Angola after the first word of the
title of the ruler of the Mbundu people in
Ndongo, *Ngola a kiluanje*, although the name
Angola was not officially recognized until
1914. The interior of Angola was often called
Portuguese West Africa. Its present borders
were not finally agreed until 1926.

Angra do Heroísmo, AZORES/PORTUGAL
Founded in 1464, the name means 'Bay of
Heroism', from the Spanish *angra* 'bay' or
'cove', in honour of the islanders' stout
resistance to Spanish forces in 1580–2. It was
the capital of the Azores 1766–1832.

Angrezābād, WEST BENGAL/INDIA *English Bāzār*
The location of a trading centre here,
particularly for silks, which was developed by
the English East India Company from 1676,
gave the city its original name. Angrezābād is
simply the local version of 'English-town'.

Anguilla, LEEWARD ISLANDS/WEST INDIES
Malliouhana
An island and a self-governing UK Overseas
Territory. Although colonized by English
settlers coming from St Kitts in 1650, the name
comes from the Spanish *anguila* 'eel', probably
because of its shape. According to Anguillan
tradition, it was Christopher Columbus[†] who
discovered the island in 1493. However, this is
no longer believed to be correct, French
explorers now being given the credit. In 1871
the UK formed Anguilla, St Kitts, and Nevis
into a single colony. It became a part of the
State of St Kitts-Nevis-Anguilla within the UK
in 1967. The Anguillans objected, desiring
separation from St Kitts and Nevis.
Negotiations with the British government
failed and British troops invaded the island in
March 1969. They were warmly welcomed
since maintenance of the connection with the
UK was the Anguillans' objective. The troops
remained for six months. In 1971 Anguilla
came directly under British rule as a crown
colony. Nine years later Anguilla formally left
the State of St Kitts-Nevis-Anguilla.

Anhalt, SAXONY-ANHALT/GERMANY
A former duchy and a state until 1945. Since
1990 it has been part of the state of Saxony-
Anhalt, called after the Castle of Anhalt,
which itself takes its name from *an* 'to' and
halten 'to hold'. The meaning is 'place where
one stops'.

Anhui, CHINA
A province whose name is an amalgamation of
the first syllables of two cities, Anqing and
Huizhou. The name could mean 'Peaceful

Beauty' from *ān* and *hui* 'beautiful' or
'excellent'.

Anjou, PAYS DE LA LOIRE/FRANCE *Civitas
Andegavensis*
A former county, duchy (from 1360), and
province. *See* ANGERS.

Ankara, TURKEY *Ankuwash, Ankyra, Angora*
Situated in a winding corridor called the Halys
Gates, the city may take its name from the
Indo-European root word *ang* 'bend'. The
Hittites were the first to build a city here in the
2nd millennium BC, calling it Ankuwash.
Alexander III the Great[†] conquered it in 334 BC
and the Romans, who changed the name to
Ankyra, absorbed it into their empire in 25 BC.
Later it became part of the Byzantine Empire,
but fell to the Seljuk Turks in about 1075. After
being occupied by the Ottoman Turks in 1356,
the city became part of the Ottoman Empire in
1360. The Ottoman Sultan Bayezid I (*c.*1360–
1403) was defeated at the Battle of Angora in
1402 by Tamerlane[†], the Tatar conqueror.
Angora then declined to little more than a
village before Kemal Atatürk[†] chose it for his
headquarters in 1919 because of its central
location. On Turkish independence in 1923, it
became the capital of Turkey. In 1930 the
name was formally changed from Angora, its
Europeanized version, to Ankara. Angora gave
its name to a breed of goat and rabbit.

Annaba, ALGERIA *Hippo Regius, Bône*
The present name is taken from the Arabic
Madīnat al-'Unnāb 'Town of the Jujube Tree'
which produces edible berries. The original
name 'Royal Hippo' was coined by the
Phoenicians, possibly during the second
millennium BC, to denote the presence of royal
stables here from the Greek *hippos* 'horse'. The
port was destroyed by the Vandals in 431,
passed to the Byzantine Empire in 533, and
was captured by the Arabs in 697. It fell to the
French in 1832 when it became known as
Bône. It was renamed after independence in
1962.

Annam (Trung Bo), VIETNAM *Nam Viet, Dai Viet,
Trung Ky*
A Vietnamese version of a Chinese name
meaning 'Pacified South' from *an* 'peace' and
nam. It refers to the central part of the country,
roughly between the Red River Delta in the
north and the Mekong Delta in the south. The
original Chinese 'Nam Viet' might be
translated as the 'Viets to the South' and Dai
Viet as 'Great Viet'. One of the rulers of Funan
(a Chinese version of *pnom* 'mountain' and
now southern Vietnam), Jayavarman I
(478–514), was given the title of 'General of the
Pacified South' in 503 by the Chinese after he

a

had conquered Champa (the southern coastal region of modern Vietnam). The Chinese were driven out of Vietnam in 939 and the country remained independent for almost the next 950 years. A former kingdom of the Nguyen family in what is now central Vietnam, Annam became a French protectorate in 1883. The name, however, was not used by the Vietnamese. Until 1945 foreigners called the people of this area Annamites or Annamese.

Annapolis, MARYLAND/USA *Providence, Town of Proctor's, Town at the Severn, Anne Arundel Town*
Settled in 1649 by Puritans and called Providence, it was renamed frequently until, in 1695, a year after it became the provincial capital, it was renamed in honour of Princess Anne (1665–1714), who became Queen Anne of Great Britain (1702–14), to give the name 'City of Anne' from *polis*. The previous name honoured Anne Arundel, the daughter of the 2nd Baron Arundell and wife of the 2nd Baron Baltimore, owner of the colony of Maryland. It served as the capital of the USA for six months in 1783–4.

Annapolis Royal, NOVA SCOTIA/CANADA *Port Royal*
Founded in 1605 by the French, it was captured by the British in 1710, formally annexed under the terms of the Treaty of Utrecht in 1713, and then renamed in honour of Queen Anne (1702–14).

Annapūrna, NEPAL
A mountain range in the Himalayas whose name comes from that of a Hindu goddess; her name comes from the Sanskrit *anna* 'food' and *pūrna* 'plentiful', a reference to the fertile valleys.

Ann Arbor, MICHIGAN/USA
Founded in 1824 by John Allen and Elisha Rumsey, who named the settlement after their wives who were both called Ann. Arbor was added because of its arbour-like appearance.

Annecy, RHÔNE-ALPES/FRANCE
Taken from a Germanic personal name Anerik. Having been a part of Savoy, it joined France in 1860.

An Nhon, VIETNAM *Vijaya, Singapura, Binh Dinh*
The first name was taken from the region of India when, as a state of Champa, this area was Indianized. *Vijaya* is Sanskrit for 'Victory'. It was the capital of Champa. The name was changed later to Singapura, or Simhapura, 'Lion City'. The present name means 'Peaceful Person' or 'people living in peace' from the Chinese *ān* and *nhon* 'person' or 'people'.

Anniston, ALABAMA/USA *Woodstock*
Founded in 1872. To avoid confusion with another Woodstock in Alabama, this town in Calhoun County was renamed 'Annie's Town' after Annie, the wife of Colonel Alfred Tyler, who was the president of the Woodstock Iron Company.

Annobón, EQUATORIAL GUINEA *Pagalu*
An island first visited by the Portuguese on New Year's Day 1474 and thus given the Old Portuguese name *Anno Bom*, literally 'Good Year'. In 1778–1968 it was a Spanish possession. It was given the Creole name Pagalu in 1973–9 from the Spanish *papá* and *gallo* 'cockerel', the cockerel being the emblem of President Nguema. He was deposed and executed in 1979 and the Portuguese name was readopted.

Anqing, ANHUI/CHINA *Wan, Huaining*
'Peaceful Celebration (of a Holiday)' from *ān* and *qing* 'to keep a holiday' or 'to celebrate'. It was named Wan during the 2nd century BC. This was changed to Huaining in 1147 and it retained this name until 1949 when its present name was adopted.

Anshan, LIAONING/CHINA
'Saddle Mountain' from *ān* 'saddle' and *shān*, a reference to the two peaks a little south of the city which look like a saddle.

Ansonia, CONNECTICUT/USA
Named after Anson G. Phelps, the senior partner in the firm of Phelps, Dodge & Co., who established the copper and brass mills here rather than buy land in nearby Derby at an extortionate price.

Ansonville, CANADA, USA
USA (North Carolina): named after Admiral of the Fleet Baron Anson (1697–1762), first lord of the British Admiralty (1751–6, 1757–62), who conducted operations along the Carolina coast against pirates and the Spanish in 1723–30 and again in 1735–7. He became popular with the colonists who named a county and town after him.

Antakya, TURKEY
See ANTIOCH.

Antalya, TURKEY *Attaleia, Adalia*
Named in 158 BC after its founder, Attalus II Philadelphus, King of Pergamum (159–138 BC), who wanted a port of his own on the Mediterranean. Later a Byzantine fortress, it fell to the Seljuk Turks in 1207, but did not join the Ottoman Empire until late in the 15th century.

Antananarivo, MADAGASCAR *Analamànga, Tananarive*
Founded in the 17th century, its original name meant 'Blue Forest'. The present name means

'City of a Thousand' from the Malagasy *an*, a prefix signifying the name of a place, *tanàna* 'town', and *arìvo* 'thousand'. Tananarive is the French version of the name. It was used from 1895, when the island was colonized by the French, until 1975 when the island's name was changed back to *Madagascar.

Antarctica A continent around the South Pole whose name means 'Opposite the Arctic' from the Greek *anti* 'opposite' and *arktikos* 'Arctic'.

Antequera, ANDALUSIA/SPAIN *Anticaria, Madīnah Antakira*
'Old Town', so-named by the Romans. The name may be related to *anta*, a local word for a dolmen, an ancient stone burial chamber. It was the first Granada border town to be recaptured by the Christians during the Reconquest in 1410.

Antibes, PROVENCE-ALPES-CÔTE D'AZUR/FRANCE *Antipolis*
'Opposite the City' or 'City on the Opposite Side (of the Bay)', i.e. from Nice. The current name is derived from the Greek one from *anti* 'opposite' and *polis*; they founded a trading centre here.

Anticosti Island, QUEBEC/CANADA *Assomption*
An island in the Gulf of St Lawrence, it was discovered by Jacques Cartier[†] in 1534 and named Assomption 'Assumption'. In the 17th century it was given a name that is possibly derived from the Native American word *naticosti* 'where bears are hunted'.

Antigua and Barbuda, WEST INDIES
This small nation comprises Antigua, Barbuda (previously Dulcina), and the uninhabited island of Redonda. Antigua was first visited by Christopher Columbus[†] in 1493. He named it after the Church of Santa Maria de la Antigua, 'St Mary the Ancient', in Seville, Spain. Antigua was colonized by the English in 1632 and Barbuda in 1678, the latter becoming a dependency of Antigua in the 18th century. In 1871 Antigua and Barbuda became part of the Leeward Islands Colony. After the colony's dissolution in 1956, the entity of Antigua and Barbuda was part of the West Indies Federation from 1958 to 1962; in 1967 it joined in a free association with the UK. In 1981 Antigua and Barbuda gained its independence.

Antigua Guatemala, GUATEMALA *Santiago de los Caballeros de Guatemala, Ciudad Vieja, Santiago*
Founded in 1527 as 'St James of the Knights of Guatemala' to be the capital of the Spanish colonial government, it was quickly destroyed by a volcanic eruption. It was rebuilt as Ciudad Vieja, 'Old City', although it was no bigger than a village, and in 1542 another capital city was built nearby and called simply Santiago 'St James'. When this was flattened by an earthquake in 1773 yet another capital city, New Guatemala, was built 15 miles (24 km) away (which subsequently became the present Guatemala City) and Santiago came to be called Antigua Guatemala, 'Old, or Ancient, Guatemala'.

Anti-Lebanon Mountains (al-Jebel ash-Sharqī), LEBANON-SYRIA
Running north-east to south-west along the Lebanese–Syrian border, parallel to the Lebanon Mountains, the name means 'Opposite Lebanon' from the Greek *anti*. The Arabic name means 'The Eastern Mountain' from *jabal* and *sharqi* 'eastern'.

Antilles, WEST INDIES *Antilia, Antillas*
A term applied to the whole of the West Indies except for the Bahamas. The Antilles are divided into the Greater Antilles and the Lesser Antilles. The name was coined before Christopher Columbus[†] arrived in the area, possibly by the Florentine (Italian) cosmographer Paolo dal Pozzo Toscanelli who corresponded with Columbus before his great voyage, suggesting that the shortest route to Asia was to the west and a stop could be made en route at the island of Antilia. It is possible that the word is derived from the Latin *ante* 'before', and *illas* 'islands' to suggest islands off the mainland. In 1502 the full name of the islands was given as Las Antillas de Rey de Castella 'The Antilles of the King of Castile'.

Antioch (Antakya), TURKEY, USA
1. Turkey: also sometimes called *Hatay.
A city of ancient Syria and a part of Syria until 1939, it was founded in 301BC by Seleucus I Nicator[†] who named the city Antiochia (on the Orontes) after his 24-year-old son, Antiochus I Soter ('Saviour'), Seleucid King of Syria (281–261 BC); some sources claim, however, that it was named after the father of Seleucus, Antiochus. The name Antiochus meant 'swift runner' from the Greek *anti* 'equal to', and *okhos* 'chariot'. When the younger son of Antiochus I Soter, Antiochus II (*c.*287–246 BC), captured the city of Miletus and overthrew its dictator, he was worshipped as a god, attracting the title Theos, 'God'; thus the city was renamed Theopolis, the 'City of God'. Antioch was the capital of the Seleucid Empire between 281 and 64 BC, and then of the Roman province of Syria. The Arabs held the city from 638 until 969 when it was retaken by the Byzantines. It was captured by the Seljuk

Turks in 1084, by the Crusaders in 1098 during the First Crusade, and sacked by the Mamlūks in 1268. It fell to the Ottoman Turks in 1517 and was occupied by the French 1918–39.
2. Turkey: another ancient city called Antioch was located in Phrygia (now west-central Turkey). It became a Roman colony in 25 BC and was given the name Caesarea Antiochia.
3. USA: there are three cities of the same name in the USA (in California, Illinois, and Nebraska), all named after the city in Turkey, because of the desire to recognize the importance of Antioch in the early Christian Church.

Antipodes Islands, NEW ZEALAND
Discovered in 1800 and so-called because their longitude is 180°, directly opposite to the 0° meridian of Greenwich. The name comes from the Greek *anti*, here meaning 'opposite', and *podos* 'of the foot'.

Antofagasta, CHILE
A region and a city known for its copper mines which give it its name 'Hidden Copper' from the Quechua *anta* 'copper', and *pakakta* 'hidden', to mean underground. The city was transferred from Bolivia in 1879.

Antonin, POLAND
Named after Prince Antoni Radziwiłł, who built a wooden summer residence here between 1822 and 1824 for his family. The Radziwiłł family played an important role in Polish–Lithuanian history over several centuries and owned lands larger than the state of Belgium.

Antrim (Aontroim), UK, USA
1. UK (Northern Ireland): formerly Irish Aontreibh. One of the original six counties of Ulster and a town meaning 'One Holding' or 'One House' from the Irish *aon* 'one' and *treabh* 'house'. The name remained even though the area became populated. The name was later reinterpreted as Antroim 'One Ridge'.
2. USA: there are two Antrims, one in New Hampshire and one in Pennsylvania, both named by Irish immigrants.

Antsirabé, MADAGASCAR
Founded by Norwegian missionaries in 1869, the name means '(Place where there is) Plenty of Salt' from the prefix *an*, *sira* 'salt', and *bé* 'much'. It is known for its thermal springs.

Antsiranana, MADAGASCAR *Diégo-Suarez*
'The Port' or '(Place where there is) a Port' from the prefix *an* which denotes a place-name, and *seranana* 'port'. The original name comes from a combination of the names of the Portuguese navigator, Diego Dias (brother of the better known Bartholomew Dias), who discovered

the island in 1500, and the Spanish admiral, Hernán Suarez, who first landed here in 1506. The present name was adopted in 1977.

Antwerp (Flemish: Antwerpen; French: Anvers), BELGIUM
A province and a city-port lying in the Flemish-speaking part of Belgium. The name may be derived from *aan het werp* 'at the wharf' from the Germanic *werpum* 'wharf', a reference to the city's location on the River Scheldt, or from the Germanic prefix *anda* 'against', and some noun connected with *werpen* 'to throw', to indicate some defensive fortification. According to legend, a giant, Druon Antigonus, exacted tribute from passing boatmen; he severed the hands of those who refused to pay and threw them into the river until Silvius Brabo, a Roman soldier, cut off one of the giant's own hands and threw it into the river, thus giving the literal name 'to throw a hand' from *hand* 'hand'.

Anuradhapura, SRI LANKA
Founded in the 5th century BC, it was named 'Anuradha's Town' after Anuradha, a senior official of Prince Vijaya, with *pura*. It was a kingdom from the 3rd century BC to the 10th century AD and capital of Sri Lanka from the 4th century BC to the 11th century AD.

Anyang, CHINA, SOUTH KOREA
China (Henan): 'Peaceful Sun' from *ān* and *yáng* 'sun'. *Yáng* here refers to locations on the southern sides of mountains, that is, with exposure to the sun; thus, *yáng* here has the meaning of 'facing the sun'. *Yáng* is one of the two complementary principles of Chinese philosophy and culture. It is of heaven, male, active, and light in contrast to *yin*, which is of earth, female, passive, and dark. Anyang was the last capital of the Yin (Shang) dynasty between 1300 and 1066 BC, but it was at that time called Yinxu. It was known as Xin Zhongyi during the Warring States Period (475–255 BC) and Ning Xinzhong, where *ning* means 'peaceful' or 'pacified' and *zhōng* 'inside' or 'central', just before it was conquered by the state of Qin and renamed Anyang county.

Anzio, LAZIO/ITALY *Antium*
The Roman name, from which the present name is derived, may have been taken from a Greek myth. According to this, the town was founded by Anteias, son of Odysseus, the hero of Homer's epic poem *The Odyssey*. The Romans captured the town in 338 BC.

Aomori, HONSHŪ/JAPAN
'Green Forest' from *ao* 'green' and *mori* 'forest'.

Aosta, VALLE D'AOSTA/ITALY *Augusta Praetoria*
Founded in 24 BC by, and named after,
Augustus[†], having been a stronghold of the
Celtic Salassi tribe, who were defeated by the
Romans in 25 BC. The present name is a
shortening of the original name.

Apalachicola, FLORIDA/USA *West Point*
A city, originally known as West Point, a bay
and a river, all given a Hitchiti name thought
to mean 'People on the Other Side'; they were
the Apalachee.

Apatity, MURMANSK/RUSSIA
Settled in 1935 and named after the local
apatite ore.

Apeldoorn, THE NETHERLANDS
'Apple Tree' from the Dutch *apel* and *door*, an
old word for tree.

Apennines, The (Gli Appennini), ITALY
The mountainous backbone of peninsular
Italy, the *ap* may be associated with the Latin
apex 'point' or 'summit' while *penn* may be the
Celtic for 'hill'.

Aphrodisias, TURKEY *Ninoe, Aphrodite, Caria,
Geyre*
Ruins dedicated to the ancient Greek goddess
of love, Aphrodite. Ninoe was the Carian name
for the goddess and Caria, after the Carians,
was in vogue by the 14th century. Caria
became the Turkish Geyre which is now the
name of a nearby village.

Apolda, THURINGIA/GERMANY
Derived from *Appel* 'apple', a reference to the
local apple orchards.

Appalachians, CANADA-USA
A mountain range named after a Native
American tribe, the Apalachee, who lived in
north-western Florida. *See* APALACHICOLA.

Appenzell, SWITZERLAND *Abbatis Cella*
'Abbot's Cell' from the Latin *cella* 'cell' or
'shrine'. The name applies to two autonomous
demi-cantons, each functioning as a single
canton, which joined the Swiss Confederation
in 1513, and also the name of the capital of one
of them, Appenzell Inner-Rhoden. Appenzell
Ausser-Rhoden is the name of the other
demi-canton. The name comes from their
abbot-rulers, the prince bishops of Sankt
Gallen.

Appleton, WISCONSIN/USA *Grand Chute*
Renamed after Samuel Appleton, the father-in-
law of the town's founder, Amos Lawrence
(1814–86). He called it Grand Chute because of
the strong flow of the River Fox on which the
city lay. In 1882 the first hydroelectric power
station in the USA began operations here.

Apulia (Puglia), ITALY
A region with a long coastline on the Adriatic
Sea whose name is probably derived from the
Apuli, the Latin name for the inhabitants, who
themselves may have taken a name, possibly
Iapigi, connected with *ap* 'water'.

Apurímac, PERU
A department and a river which only keeps
this name to its confluence with the Mantaro
River. Its name is said to come from the
Quechua *apu rimak* 'speaking lord' from *apu*
'lord', a reference to its power as it follows a
course through narrow canyons, waterfalls,
and rapids, and *rima* 'to speak', from the noise
it makes.

Aqaba ('Aqabah, al-), JORDAN *Eloth, Berenice,
Aelana, Ayla*
Dominated by mountains, the name is an
abbreviated form of 'Aqabat Ayla 'Pass of Ayla'
from the Arabic *q'ab* 'lowest part'. The city is
mentioned in the Bible as 'Ezion-geber which
is beside Eloth' (1 Kings 9: 26), although this is
now more properly Eilat, which is just across
the western border in Israel. It was called
Berenice by the Ptolemies and became Aelana,
the garrison for a Roman legion *c.*100. The city
was captured by the Prophet Muhammad[†] in
630, the Arabs renaming it Ayla, and by the
Crusaders in the 12th century. In 1183 it was
regained by the Muslims, who renamed it
Aqaba in the 13th century. The city became
part of Egypt during the 19th century, but was
acquired by the Ottoman Turks when the
boundary between the Ottoman Empire and
Egypt was demarcated in 1906. It was captured
in 1917 by Arab forces under T. E. Lawrence,
a British guerrilla leader. In 1925 it was placed
by the British under the control of the
Protectorate of Transjordan. The frontier,
arbitrarily drawn by the UK and which put
Aqaba in Transjordan, was disputed by Saudi
Arabia. A treaty resolved the dispute in 1965:
in return for about 4 000 square miles
(10 360 sq. km) of Jordanian territory, Saudi
Arabia recognized Aqaba as Jordanian and
itself gave up some 10 miles (16 km) of
coastline to the south of the previous
boundary.

Aqmola, KAZAKHSTAN
A province. *See* ASTANA.

Aquileia, FRIULI-VENEZIA GIULIA/ITALY
According to popular legend, an eagle, *aquila*,
swooped overhead while the town's
boundaries were being marked by a plough.
Alternatively, the town may take its name
from the River Aquilis, possibly a Celtic name,
in Istria; the suffix *-eia* could indicate the town
on the river. It was founded in 181 BC, mainly

as a military garrison. It is possible that the root *aqu-* might be connected with the Latin *aquilus* 'dark', 'gloomy', or 'obscure', or perhaps 'watery'.

Aquitaine, FRANCE *Aquitania*
A region with a name associated with *aqua* to give 'Land of Waters' after the great rivers that flow through it. Founded by the Romans as a province of Gaul, it became an independent duchy and between 781 and 877 a kingdom before reverting to a duchy. When Eleanor, daughter of the Duke of Aquitaine, married Louis VII (*c.*1120–80), King of France (1137–80) in 1137, Aquitaine and France were united. After their divorce Eleanor married the Count of Anjou, Henry Plantagenet, in 1152; two years later he became Henry II, King of England (1154–89). Aquitaine remained an English possession until 1453.

Aqtöbe, KAZAKHSTAN *Aktyube, Aktyubinsk*
A province and a city founded in 1869 as a Russian military post. The first two names were Russian versions of the Kazakh name meaning 'White Hill' from *aq* 'white' and *töbe* 'hill'. The city was renamed in 1992 after Kazakh independence in 1991, but reverted to the original name with the Kazakh spelling in 1999. The town formerly called Aqtobe, west of Kustanay, has been renamed Maylın.

Arabia (Jazīrat al-'Arab or al-Jazīrah al-'Arabīyah**)**
1. 'Island of the Arabs': a huge peninsula in south-west Asia bounded by the Red Sea, the Gulf of Aden, the Arabian Sea, the Gulf of Oman, the Persian Gulf and, in the north, Jordan and Iraq. Its area comprises seven countries: Saudi Arabia, Yemen, Oman, the United Arab Emirates, Qatar, Bahrain, and Kuwait; and parts of Jordan, Syria, and Iraq.
2. Ptolemy[†] divided Arabia into three parts: Arabia Petraea 'Rocky Arabia' in the north-west; Arabia Felix 'Arabia the Fortunate' in the south and south-west (larger than the present state of Yemen) because of its rainfall and thus fertility; and Arabia Deserta, 'Desert Arabia', in the north and centre.
3. Arabia was a Roman province during the 2nd and 3rd centuries. It comprised what is now the Sinai Peninsula, much of Jordan and a slice of the east coast of the Red Sea as far south as Madā'in Şāliḥ. It was divided into two provinces at the end of the 3rd century.
4. Named originally after the Arabs, *al-'arab*, of the central and northern Arabian peninsula whose name derives from a Semitic root denoting a nomadic lifestyle. In Arabic *'araba* means 'to cross'. In due course, Greek and Roman writers used the term 'Arabia' and

'Arab' to cover the entire peninsula. There is no Arabic word for Arabia. An Arab now is considered to be anybody who speaks Arabic as their native language.
5. It inspired the word 'arabesque', meaning 'in the Arabic style', from a decorative style that originated in Arabic and Moorish art, and is applied to ballet and music. It also gives its name to the Arabian Sea.

Arad, ISRAEL, ROMANIA
1. Israel: although only founded in 1961, it is named after the biblical Arad whose ruins are close by. The Bible (Numbers 21: 1–3) describes how the Canaanite King of Arad was defeated by Israel and his cities 'utterly destroyed'.
2. Romania: a county and a city, formerly called Ziridava. *Ara*, of Thracian–Dacian origin, means a 'Curve made by a River'. The city is situated in a curve in the River Mureş valley. It was a small Roman garrison. Between 1552 and 1699 it was in Ottoman Turkish hands, later falling to the Austrians and Hungarians. It was ceded to Romania in 1920.

Aragón, SPAIN
An autonomous community named after the river of the same name. It uses the Indo-European root word *ar* 'water'. It was a former kingdom in north-east Spain which was conquered by the Visigoths in the 5th century and by the Moors in the 8th century. Sancho III the Great (*c.*992–1035), King of Navarre (1000–35) and King of Castile (1028–35), divided his realm into four kingdoms in his will (one for each son), creating the Kingdom of Aragón from the county of the same name. His illegitimate son Ramiro (d. 1063) had governed the county during Sancho's reign and he became the beneficiary on his father's death in 1035. Ramiro became the first King of Aragón. It joined with Catalonia in 1140. In 1479 Aragón united with the Kingdom of Castile, ten years after Isabella of Castile had married her second cousin, Ferdinand of Aragón.

Arāk, ALGERIA, IRAN
Iran: formerly Sultanābād. The present name may be a corruption of its Arabic name, 'Irāq 'Ajam 'Iranian River Bank' from *ajam*, a word of Arabic origin which in Persian means 'non-Arab' or 'Iranian' and *irāq* 'river bank'. The town lies on a small river. The previous name meant 'Sultan's Town'.

Arakan (Rakhine), BURMA *Argyre, Rachani, Raksapura*
A coastal state named after the Rakhine people. Argyre 'Land of Silver' was the name given by Ptolemy[†] while the Portuguese called it Rachani. The conventional English name is the Portuguese/Bengali version of the

Arakanese name which can also be Yakhine. The Sanskrit Raksapura meant the 'Land of the Ogres', possibly named after the original inhabitants, the Bilu, which in Burmese means 'ogre'. The early Buddhists gave this name to the unconverted tribes with whom they came in contact.

Aral, KAZAKHSTAN-UZBEKISTAN
Named after the Aral Sea (in Kazakh, Aral Tengizi, and in Uzbek, Orol Dengizi) on which it used to lie. The sea received its name from *Aral-tengizi* 'Sea of Islands' from the Kazakh *aral* 'island' and *tengiz* 'sea' because it used to contain over 1 000 islands. Due to pollution and the tapping of the rivers which fed the sea to irrigate new cotton fields, most of these have disaapeared as the sea has shrunk; indeed, because of the huge drop in the water level, it became two seas in 1987 and Aral is now some 20 miles (30 km) from it.

Arandjelovac, SERBIA/SERBIA AND MONTENEGRO *Vrbica*
Named after a church dedicated to the Holy Archangel, *Sveti Arhandjel*, built on the orders of Miloš Obrenović, Prince of Serbia (1817–39, 1859–60) in 1859. He decreed the change of name.

Aran Islands (Árainn), IRELAND
A group of three islands, Inishmore 'Big Island', Inishmaan 'Middle Island', and Inisheer 'Eastern Island', with a name which means 'Islands of the Ridge', a reference to the sheer cliffs that face the Atlantic.

Aranjuez, MADRID/SPAIN *Ara Jovis*
Derived from the former name, the Roman 'Altar of Jupiter' from the Latin *ara* 'altar'; Jupiter was the principal ancient Roman god.

Arapahoe, USA
There are three towns in Colorado, Nebraska, and Wyoming, and one spelt Arapaho in Oklahoma, that are named after the Native American tribe of the Great Plains. Their name denotes 'traders'.

Ararat, ARMENIA, AUSTRALIA, TURKEY
1. Armenia: a city named after the mountain, just over the border in Turkey, which is sacred to the Armenians, who consider themselves to be the first humans to have appeared in the world after the Flood. Ararat was the biblical name for Armenia. *See* AGRI.
2. Australia (Victoria): named in 1840 by a sheep farmer, who felt his settlement resembled the grounding of Noah's Ark on Mt Ararat in Turkey.
3. Turkey: a mountain whose Hebrew name is derived from Urartu, a Babylonian kingdom in the area that existed in the 9th to 7th centuries

BC. The Turkish name is Ağri Daği 'Mountain of Sorrow'. This name was given to it after a village and monastery built on its slopes were destroyed by an earthquake in 1840. However, it is also said to mean 'Painful Mountain' from *ağri* 'pain' and *dağ*, due to the difficulty in climbing it. It is called Masik' or Masis by the Armenians.

Araucanía, CHILE
A region named after the group of South American tribes, the Araucanians.

Arauco, CHILE
'Limestone'. The town gives its name to Araucanian, the Spanish name for the Mapudungun language spoken by the Mapuche in southern Chile.

Arāvali, RĀJASTHĀN/INDIA
A mountain range with a name from the Sanskrit *āra* 'outer edge' and *āvali* 'range'. This may be a reference to its location on the eastern side of the Great Indian Desert.

Arbatax, SARDINIA/ITALY
'Fourteen' from the Arabic *'arba' at 'ashar*.

Arbīl, IRAQ *Urbillum, Arba Elu/Arba Ilha, Arbelles*
Evolved from the Babylonian name '(The City of) Four Gods'. The Greeks called it Arbelles. It is also spelt Irbīl. The *de facto* Kurdish capital, it is largely populated by Kurds and they call it Hawlēr.

Arbroath, SCOTLAND/UK *Aberbrothok, Aberbrothwick*
The full name is Aberbrothock '(Place at the) Mouth of the (River) Brothock', a Pictish river name, from the stream on which it lies, whose name means 'Seething One'; *ar* is an abbreviation of *aber*.

Arcadia, CALIFORNIA/USA
Named after the historic region in the Peloponnese, Greece, today a department called Arkadhía. In Greek mythology, the name is said to come from Arcas, son of Zeus, who became King of Arcadia. Unknowingly, he shot at his mother, Callisto, who, when pregnant, had been turned into a bear by Zeus. She was then transformed into the constellation of the Great Bear and Arcas into the Little Bear.

Archangel (Arkhangel'sk), ARKHANGEL'SK/RUSSIA *Novokholmogory, Arkhangelsky*
A province and a city which grew up round a monastery founded in the 12th century and dedicated to the Archangel Michael. The present city was founded in 1584 as Novokholmogory, New Kholmogory, after the original village of Kholmogory. It was renamed in 1613 after the monastery.

Arcos de la Frontera, ANDALUSIA/SPAIN
Colonia Arcensium, Medina Arkosh
'Arches of the Frontier', a reference to the fact
that it was on the border between Christian
and Muslim Spain. A Roman colony, it was
captured by the Moors from the Visigoths in
711 and the name Arabized. It was briefly an
independent kingdom during the 11th
century before being taken by Alfonso X
(1221–84), King of Castile and León (1252–84),
in 1264.

Arctic A region surrounding the North Pole
which takes its name from the Greek *arktikos*
'northern', which itself comes from *arktos*
'bear'. In Greek mythology Zeus placed the
nymph Callisto in the northern hemisphere in
the shape of a bear and thus this particular star
constellation was named by the Greeks *Ursa
Major* 'Great Bear'. Close by is *Ursa Minor* 'Little
Bear', which includes Polaris, the pole star,
which marks the approximate position of the
north celestial pole.

Ardennes, BELGIUM-FRANCE-LUXEMBOURG
A high forested plateau with a probable Celtic
name 'High District' from *ardu* 'high'; however
it could relate to a word for 'forest'.

Arequipa, PERU *Nuestra Señora de la Asunción del
Valle Hermosa*
A department and a city was developed in 1540
from an earlier Inca settlement as a stronghold
with the name 'Our Lady of the Assumption of
the Beautiful Valley'. Its present name is
derived from the Aymari *ari* 'summit', and the
Quechua *qipa* 'behind', a reference to its
position at the foot of the snow-capped, but
dormant, Misti Volcano.

Argenteuil, ÎLE-DE-FRANCE/FRANCE
Argentogilum
The present and Roman names may come
from the deposits of silver *'argent'* used by the
Gauls or from a Gaulish personal name. The
suffix comes from the Gaulish *ialo* 'settlement'
or 'village'.

Argentina The Argentine Republic
(República Argentina) since 1853. Previously it
was the United Provinces of South America (or
of the Río de la Plata 'River Plate') (1816–53);
part of the Viceroyalty of the Río de la Plata
(1776–1816); and part of the Viceroyalty of
Peru (1542–1776). The Spanish *plata* also
means 'silver', thus Río de la Plata is the 'River
of Silver' or 'Silver River'. The name is said to
have been coined by Spanish explorers who
were attracted to the area by rumours of great
mineral wealth and who then noticed the
silver ornaments worn by the natives. Thus the
name Argentina from the Spanish *argentino*

'silvery' is really a Latin name meaning '(Land
of) the Silver (River)'. The first Europeans to
arrive were the Spanish in 1515 and in 1534
the Spanish king despatched Pedro de
Mondoza to take control of the government of
the lands of the Río de la Plata. Two British
invasions of Buenos Aires, the capital, in 1806
and 1807, and the entry of Napoleonic forces
into Spain in 1808, encouraged the population
of Buenos Aires, much larger than the rest of
the country, to rise against the Spaniards in
1810 and independence was declared in 1816.
Sometimes called 'The Argentine'.

Argonia, KANSAS/USA
Named after the ship *Argo* in which, in Greek
legend, Jason and the Argonauts sailed to
Colchis (now Georgia) in search of the fleece of
the golden ram.

Argyll, SCOTLAND/UK *Arregaithel, Ar-gael*
Now the unitary district of Argyle and Bute
which was created in 1975. The Gaelic version,
Earraghaidheal, means the 'Coastland of the
Gaels (Irish)' from the Gaelic *oirthir* 'coastland';
early settlers called the area Ar-gael 'the
Eastern Gaels'. The Gaels originally came from
Ireland, then known as Scotia, in the 2nd
century.

Århus, DENMARK *Arosel, Arusensis, Arus*
'At the River's Mouth' from *å* 'river' and *os*
'mouth'. The river, or rather stream, is no
longer visible.

Arilje, SERBIA/SERBIA AND MONTENEGRO
Named after the original 11th–12th-century
church of Sveti Ahilije 'St Achillius', a Roman
martyr, possibly of the 2nd century. The
present royal church, which formed the basis
of an important monastery, was founded in
1295 by Dragutin, former King of Serbia (1276–
82), who became a monk. Gradually over the
centuries a small town grew up around the
monastery.

'Arīsh, al-, EGYPT *Rhinocolura*
'The Hut', so-called because Jacob allegedly
stayed in a hut here while journeying from
Canaan into Egypt. A simple hut, *'arish*, in the
Middle East, locally called a *barasti*, can be
made of date palm fronds. The Roman name
means 'Severed Nose' from the Greek *rhis*,
genitive *rhinos* 'nose', and *koloyein* 'to sever'; it
is a reference to the fact that Roman prisoners
had their noses cut off. The town became a
part of Egypt in 1906 when the border
between Egypt and the Ottoman Empire was
drawn.

Arizona, USA
A state with a name slightly modified from the
Papago *Arizonac* 'Place of the Small Spring'.

Having been explored and settled by the Spanish in the 16th century, it became part of the newly independent Mexico in 1821. That part north of the Gila River joined the USA as part of New Mexico at the conclusion of the war between the USA and Mexico in 1848. The area south of the river was acquired by means of the Gadsden Purchase in 1853. Ten years later the whole area was established as the Arizona Territory and in 1912 it became the 48th state.

Arkadelphia, ARKANSAS/USA *Blakelytown*
After 27 years of existence the town's name was changed in 1838. It is a combination of *Arkansas* and *adelphia*, from the Greek *adelphos* 'brother'.

Arkansas, USA
A state and a river which may take their name from the Native American tribe, the Arkamsea, later called the Quapaw; or it may be a Sioux word meaning the 'South Wind People'. First claimed for France in 1682, the area was ceded to Spain in 1763; however, it was returned to France in 1801. Two years later it was acquired by the USA as part of the Louisiana Purchase. Arkansas Territory was established in 1819 and it became the 25th state in 1836. Arkansas seceded from the Union in 1861, becoming a member of the Confederate States of America during the Civil War (1861–5). It rejoined the Union in 1868. It was the French who added the final *s*, although the name is pronounced 'Arkansaw'.

Arkansas City, USA
Kansas: founded in 1870 at the confluence of the Arkansas and Walnut Rivers; it was first named after the latter. It then adopted the names Adelphi and Creswell before assuming the present name after the other river in 1872.

Arkhipo-Osipovka, KRASNODAR TERRITORY/RUSSIA
Named after Arkhip Osipov, who in 1840, as a member of the small Russian garrison defending the fortress against an attack by 12 000 locals, sacrificed himself by taking a blazing torch into the room in which the gunpowder was stored.

Arles, PROVENCE-ALPES-CÔTE D'AZUR/FRANCE *Theline, Arelate*
Located where the River Rhône delta starts, the city originally had the Greek name Theline. The present name is probably derived from the Indo-European root word *ar* 'water' or 'river', to mean 'Town in the Marshes'. Having been an important Roman city, it was captured by the Visigoths in the 6th century and by the Muslims in 730. During the 10th

century it became capital of the Kingdom of Burgundy, later renamed Arles. Annexed by the Holy Roman Empire in the 11th century, it was ceded to France in 1378 by Charles IV (1316–78), Holy Roman Emperor (1355–78).

Arlington, USA
1. There are at least nineteen towns and cities in the USA bearing this name.
2. Massachusetts: its original Native American name, Menotomy, meant 'Swift Waters'. In 1807 it was renamed West Cambridge. It was renamed again in 1867 after the Virginia estate of the playwright, George Washington Parke Custis, the grandson of George Washington, the USA's first president (1789–97). Custis named his mansion after Henry Bennet (1618–85), 1st Earl of Arlington, secretary of state (1662–74) to Charles II[†].
3. Texas: the original settlement, Bird's Fort, was later renamed Johnson's Station. In 1876 it was developed and named after the home in Virginia of General Robert E. Lee (1807–70), one of the leading Confederate generals during the Civil War (1861–5). Lee was the son-in-law of George Washington Parke Custis.
4. Arlington County, Virginia: settled as Bellehaven County and then renamed Alexandria County, it was ceded to the Federal Government in 1789 and included in the District of Columbia. It was restored to Virginia in 1846 and in 1920 renamed after the 1st Earl of Arlington. Within it are sited Arlington National Cemetery, the Pentagon, and the Ronald Reagan National Airport, all of which are federal property.

Arlon (Flemish: **Aarlen**), BELGIUM *Orolaunum*
The present name is derived from the previous Roman name which denotes a settlement lying at the crossroads of two important trade routes: Reims to Trier and Tongeren to Metz.

Armada, MICHIGAN/USA
'Fleet' from the Spanish *armada*.

Armageddon (Megiddo), ISRAEL
Ruins. The name comes from the Hebrew *har megiddon* 'Hill of Megiddo'. In ancient times it was a strategically important Palestinian fortified town guarding the route, through a pass, from Egypt into Galilee and Syria. The site of many important Old Testament battles, it is mentioned in the Bible (Revelation 16: 16) as the site of the final battle between good and evil at the Day of Judgement. The name is now used to describe a cataclysmic conflict on a vast scale.

Armagh, CANADA, UK
1. Canada (Quebec): named after the Irish town.

2. UK (Northern Ireland): locally Ard Mhacha. One of the original six counties of Ulster and a city meaning 'Height of Macha' from *ard* 'height' and Macha, the district name, from *macha* 'pasture'. Macha, who is said to have come to the throne in 377 BC, is also a land goddess in the myths of the ancient Ulstermen. The name referred to the fortress around which the city developed. The city was the seat of the kings of Ulster between *c*.400 BC and AD 333.

Armavir, ARMENIA, RUSSIA
Armenia: founded in 1839 as Argishti-khinili and named after the capital of Urartu (*see* ARMENIA); its meaning is unknown. It was later renamed Oktemberyan to commemorate the Bolshevik Revolution on 25 October (Julian calendar; now 7 November using the Gregorian calendar) 1917.

Armenia (Hayastan), AND COLOMBIA *Urartu*
The Republic of Armenia (Hayastani Hanrapetut'yun) since gaining independence from the Soviet Union in 1991. Previously the Armenian Soviet Socialist Republic (1936–91), and part of the Transcaucasus Soviet Federative Socialist Republic (March 1922) which joined the USSR nine months later; the Soviet Republic of Armenia (1920–2); and the independent Republic of Armenia (1918–20). The present republic represents a fraction of historical Greater Armenia which included extensive territory in modern eastern Turkey, and parts of modern Georgia, Azerbaijan, and Iran. The Armenian name means the 'Land of Hayk', Noah's great-great-grandson from whom the Armenians claim descent. The Armenians call themselves the Hayk. The ancient Greeks used the term 'Armenian' which, according to legend, was derived from the Armen tribe who took their name from Armenios; he was, in Greek legend, one of the Argonauts who accompanied Jason in his search for the Golden Fleece. Armenia, however, may be a modification of Aramaean, a tribe which lived in northern Syria. The biblical name for Armenia was Ararat. Armenia (Armina in old Persian), whose name was already in use by 500 BC), succeeded the Kingdom of Urartu, (Western) Ararat in the Assyrian language, in the 6th century BC. Since, it has been constantly overrun by foreign invaders, particularly Persians, Turks, and Russians, although enjoying short periods of independence. By the end of the 14th century the Kingdom of Armenia had finally expired. During the 15th–17th centuries Turkey and Persia fought over Armenia, partitioning it into western and eastern halves.

In 1828 eastern Armenia was ceded to Russia, while some two and a half million Armenians lived within the Ottoman Empire. In 1915, fearful that the Armenians might help an expansionist Russia against a weak Ottoman Empire, the Turks emptied Turkish (West) Armenia of Armenians: perhaps as many as one and a half million people were deported to northern Syria and elsewhere, many of them being slaughtered or dying from disease and starvation in what was later called by the Armenians 'The Genocide' (the Turks consistently claim that this was simply a case of relocation and that there was no intention to cause loss of life). Having captured Turkish Armenia in 1916, the Russians were compelled to surrender it and part of Russian Armenia to Turkey in 1918 in the wake of the Bolshevik Revolution. A substantial Kurdish population now inhabits the area. The First World War over, Armenia enjoyed a period of independence from May 1918 to December 1920. In June 1918, however, Armenia was forced to acknowledge the pre-1878 Russo-Turkish border as its own Armenian–Turkish border. Under pressure from a rejuvenated Turkey under Kemal Atatürk[1], the Armenians abandoned all pre-1914 territory in Turkey at the Treaty of Alexandropol (now Kumayri, Armenia) on 2 December 1920. That same day Armenia was declared a Soviet republic. It had become even smaller with the loss of Nakhichevan, Nagornyy-Karabakh, and, more particularly, Mount Ararat, a sacred symbol of the Armenian homeland.

Armentières, NORD-PAS-DE-CALAIS/FRANCE
Taken from the Gallo-Roman *armentum* 'cattle for ploughing'. It was destroyed during the First World War (1914–18) when it became famous for the song *Mademoiselle from Armentières*.

Armidale, NEW SOUTH WALES/AUSTRALIA
Founded in 1839 and named by G. J. Macdonald, commissioner for crown lands, after his father's Scottish baronial estate on the Isle of Skye.

Arnavutköy, TURKEY
'Albanian Village' from *köy* 'village'.

Arnhem, THE NETHERLANDS *Arenacum*
A combination of the Latin *arena* 'sand' and the German *Heim*, to indicate a settlement on the banks of the River Rhine.

Arnhem Land, NORTHERN TERRITORY/AUSTRALIA
Discovered in 1623 by the Dutch explorer Jan Carstensz who named the area after his ship, the *Arnhem*, itself named after the Dutch city.

Arno, TUSCANY/ITALY *Arnus*
A river with both the Latin and present names coming from the Indo-European root word *ar* 'river' or 'water'.

Arnstadt, THURINGIA/GERMANY *Arnestati*
'Arn's Settlement' from a personal name and *Stadt*.

Arochukwu, ABIA/NIGERIA
Named after the Ibo's supreme deity, Chuku, and a sub-tribe, the Aro.

Arras, NORD-PAS-DE-CALAIS/FRANCE *Nemetacum/Nemetocenna*
The original Celtic name comes from *nemeton* 'sacred grove' or 'sanctuary'. It was later renamed after the Atrebates, a tribe in north-east Gaul. Their name comes from *trebu* 'tribe'. They were one of the last tribes to acknowledge Julius Caesar's[†] authority. The Peace of Arras in 1482 fixed the northern borders of modern France. The town was finally confirmed as French at the 1659 Treaty of the Pyrenees which ended the Franco-Spanish War (1648–59).

Arsenyev, PRIMORSKIY TERRITORY/RUSSIA *Semenovka*
Named in 1952 after Vladimir Arsenyev (1872–1930), an explorer in the Far East, ethnographer, and author.

Artëm, PRIMORSKIY TERRITORY/RUSSIA
Named after Fëdor Sergeyev (1883–1921), an early Bolshevik leader in the Donetsk region who was nicknamed Artëm. He had a son who was given the name Artëm; when his father was killed his mother was ill and Stalin[†] adopted the boy.

Artemisa, CUBA
Named after the Greek goddess of fertility, Artemis.

Artëmivsk, UKRAINE *Bakhmut, Artëmovsk*
Originally a fort to defend against Crimean Tatars, it took its name from the River Bakhmut on which the town lies. It was renamed in 1924 after Fëdor Sergeyev (*see* ARTËM).

Artëmovsk, KRASNOYARSK TERRITORY/RUSSIA
See ARTËM.

Artesia, NEW MEXICO/USA *Miller, Stegman*
New Mexico: founded in 1890 as a stop, known as Miller, on a stagecoach route, it was renamed in 1894 when it became a railhead for livestock. In 1905 an artesian water basin was discovered and its new name reflected this.

Artigas, URUGUAY *San Eugenio*
Founded in 1852 and named after St Eugene. The city was renamed after José Gervasio Artigas (1764–1850), the national hero of Uruguay, because of his revolutionary leadership during the wars of independence against Spain. Driven into exile in Paraguay in 1820, he did not experience the actual achievement of independence when it came in August 1828.

Artois, NORD-PAS-DE-CALAIS/FRANCE
A historic region and former province named after a Gaulish tribe, the Atrebates. *See* ARRAS.

Aruba A territory of the Netherlands 15 miles (24 km) off the Venezuelan coast which was claimed by Spain when discovered in 1499. According to local tradition, Alonso de Ojeda, a Spanish explorer, is said to have given the island the name Oro Hubo, suggesting that gold, *oro*, was to be found. The Spanish, however, did not settle. The Dutch presence, after they took the island in 1636, was also minimal. Between 1828 and 1845 the island was part of the Dutch West Indies and then of the Netherlands Antilles until 1986. The name is believed to have come from a Caiquetios Arawak word *oíbubai* 'guide'.

Arunachal Pradesh (Arunā), INDIA *North East Frontier Agency*
A state. As part of Assam, it was given its original title in 1954. In 1972 it became a union territory with its present name, meaning 'Land of the Rising Sun' from *arunāchal* 'dawn'. *Pradesh* comes from the Sanskrit *pradesa*. Its territorial status was enhanced to that of a state in 1987.

Arundel, CANADA, UK
UK (England): formerly Harundel 'Valley where Horehound grows' from the Old English *hārhūne* and *dell* 'valley'. The town lies on the River Arun, but this is a back-formation from the town's name.

Arusha, TANZANIA *Northern Region*
A geographical region established in 1963 and a city named after the Arusha (or Warusha), a Tanzanian ethnic group. It was founded as a German garrison in 1900.

Arvayheer, MONGOLIA
'Barley Fields'.

Arzamas, NIZHNIY NOVGOROD/RUSSIA
Derived from the Russian *Erzia*, the name of a group of Mordovians, and the Mordvin *mas* 'land'. Until 1991 Arzamas-16 was a secret nuclear research centre; it is now called Sarov.

Ašaghy Agdzhakand, AZERBAIJAN *Nizhniy Agdzhakand, Shaumyanovsk*
Originally 'Lower Agdzha's Town' from the Russian *nizhniy* and the Azeri *kand* 'town'. In 1938 it was renamed after Stepan Shaumyan (1878–1918), the famous Georgian

revolutionary (*see* SHAUMYANI). The present name is the Azeri form of its historical Russian one.

Asahikawa, HOKKAIDŌ/JAPAN
Lying along the River Ishikari, the name means 'River of Sunrise' and comes from the Ainu *chiupet* 'fast-flowing river'. However, the Japanese *asahi* means 'rising sun' and *kawa* 'river'.

Asaka, JAPAN, UZBEKISTAN
1. Japan (Honshū): the original name, Hizaori, was in use from the early 17th century and meant 'Bent Knee' from *hiza* 'knee' and *ori* 'bent'. However, in 1932 the Tokyo Golf Club thought that Hizaori was inappropriate and renamed the city after their honorary president, Yasuhiko Asakanomiya. The characters in his name represent 'Morning Mist of the Imperial Palace' from *asa* 'morning', *ka* 'mist', *no* 'of', and *miya* 'imperial palace'. Thus the present name means 'Morning Mist'.
2. Uzbekistan: originally Assake, it was renamed Zelensk 'Green' in 1933 and in 1934 Leninsk in honour of Vladimir Lenin[†]. It returned to a version of its original name in 1992.

Asbest, YEKATERINBURG/RUSSIA *Kudelka*
'Asbestos'. Founded and named in 1720 as a consequence of the discovery of asbestos in the area.

Asbestos, QUEBEC/CANADA
Named after the minerals on which the town's economy depends.

Ascension Island, DEPENDENCY OF ST HELENA/UK
Discovered by the Portuguese navigator, João da Nova Castella, on Ascension Day (the 40th day after Easter) 1501. It was uninhabited until 1815 when a small garrison of British marines was deployed to deter any idea of escape from St Helena, 800 miles (1 290 km) to the south-east in the South Atlantic, by Napoleon Bonaparte[†].

Aschaffenburg, BAVARIA/GERMANY
'City on the (River) Aschaff' from *Burg* and the river's name. It was developed from a Roman camp and then a castle built on the same site.

Ascoli Piceno, MARCHE/ITALY *Asculum Picenum*
Named after the pre-Roman Picentes who took their name from the Latin *picus* 'woodpecker', a sacred bird to the tribe and one used for the interpretation of omens.

Ascot, ENGLAND/UK *Estcota* (*Berkshire*)
'Eastern Cottage' from the Old English *ēast* and *cot* 'cottage' or 'hut'.

Asenovgrad, BULGARIA *Stanimaka*
The original name meant 'Defence of the Mountain Pass', but the town was renamed in 1230 after Ivan II Asen (d. 1241), Tsar (1218–41), as the 'City of Asen' from the personal name, *ov* 'of', and *grad*, in honour of his victory over the Byzantines at Klokotnitsa.

Ashanti, GHANA
A modern region and historic kingdom dating from the late 17th century and named after its people, the Ashanti or Asante 'United in War'. By the early 19th century the Ashanti Empire controlled most of the territory of modern Ghana. It became a British crown colony in 1902

Ashby de la Zouch, ENGLAND/UK *Ascebi, Esseby la Zusche*
'Farmstead where Ash-trees grow' from the Old English *æsc* 'ash'tree' and *bý* with the additional French family name de la Zuche. The family held it at the beginning of the 13th century.

Ashdod, ISRAEL *Azotus*
Refounded in 1956 some 4.5 miles (7 km) north-west of the ruins of the ancient city. It was one of the five major cities of the Philistines, but the meaning of the name is unknown. Some sources suggest 'citadel' or 'stronghold'. The Greek Azotus was used in 312–167 BC.

Asheboro, NORTH CAROLINA/USA *Asheborough*
Founded in 1796 and named after Samuel Ashe (1725–1813), governor of North Carolina (1795–8).

Asheville, NORTH CAROLINA/USA *Morristown*
Founded in 1794 and named after Robert Morris who provided funds for the American Revolution (1775–83). Renamed later after Governor Samuel Ashe (see previous entry).

Ashford, AUSTRALIA, IRELAND, UK, USA
UK (England): the town in Kent, formerly Essetesford, has a name meaning 'Ford by some Ash Trees' from the Old English *æsc* 'ash tree' and *ford*, probably denoting a particular clump of trees. The town in Surrey, formerly Ecclesford and Exeforde, however, may mean 'Ford belonging to a man (possibly) called Eccel'.

Ashgabat, TURKMENISTAN *Askhabad, Poltoratsk, Ashkhābād*
'The City of Love' or 'Lovely City' from the Turkish *aşk* or Persian *eşk*, both 'love', and *ābād*. Founded in 1881 as a Russian military fort, it was given the name of a nearby Turkmen settlement. In 1919 it was renamed after a local Bolshevik revolutionary hero, Pavel

Poltoratsky (1888–1918), who was one of the leading organizers of the struggle for Soviet power in Turkestan. In 1927 the original name was restored, although spelt slightly differently. This was changed again in 1992 to reflect Turkmen spelling after the country achieved independence in 1991. In 1924 the city became the capital of the Turkmen Soviet Socialist Republic which, a year later, joined the Soviet Union; in 1991 it became the capital of Turkmenistan.

Ashikaga, HONSHŪ/JAPAN
Named after the Ashikaga family which gave its name to a shogunate (1338–1573). The seat of government was located in the Muromachi district of Kyōto and so this era is also known as the Muromachi period. The characters represent *ashi* 'legs' and *kaga* 'profit'.

Ashland, KENTUCKY/USA *Poage's Settlement*
Founded in 1815, but renamed in 1854 after the home of Henry Clay (1777–1852), a member of the US Senate and House of Representatives; three times he was a candidate for the presidency, but was never elected. The name comes from the large number of ash trees around his estate in Lexington, Kentucky.

Ashqelon, ISRAEL *Ascalon, al-Majdal, Migdal Gad, Migdal Ashqelon*
The meaning is unknown. Because of the onion export trade which flourished during Crusader times, the city's Roman name, Ascalon, gave its name to the scallion and the shallot, types of onion. The modern city lies 1¼ miles (2 km) north-east of the ancient site.

Ash-Shamālīyah, SAUDI ARABIA
A geographic region simply named 'The Northern'.

Ash-Sharqāṭ, IRAQ *Ashur*
Named after Ashur, the son of the biblical 'mighty hunter' Nimrod. He was the primary god of the ancient Assyrians who took their name from him. Ashur was the religious capital of Assyria.

Ash-Sharqīyah, EGYPT, OMAN, SAUDI ARABIA
A governorate in Egypt and regions in Oman and Saudi Arabia, all meaning 'The Eastern'.

Ashtabula, OHIO/USA
An Algonquian name meaning 'Fish River' indicating a bountiful supply of fish.

Asia The meaning is unknown. It may be derived from the Akkadian *asu* 'east' or 'Land of the Rising Sun'. It could possibly come from Assuva or Asuwa, first mentioned by the King of the Hittites, when reporting a victory over the 'Land of Assuva' in *c.* 1235 BC. Alternatively, it could be a local name, originating in Turkey, which gradually spread to embrace territory further east. The Asiatic part of Turkey then became Asia Minor, now Anatolia, the western part of which was a Roman province from 133 BC. Traditionally, the western border with Europe runs along the eastern side of the Ural Mountains in Russia down to the Caspian Sea, to the Black Sea, through the Bosporus and the Sea of Marmara to the Aegean Sea, the eastern end of the Mediterranean Sea, and then through the Red Sea.

Asilah, MOROCCO *Arcila/Arzila, Zilis*
Derived from the Phoenician settlement, Zilis 'Beautiful'. Then variously under the control of the Romans, Idrīsids, Marīnids, Portuguese, Spanish, and Arabs. The city was reoccupied by the Spanish in 1911, becoming part of Spanish Morocco until 1956 when Morocco gained independence.

Asir, SAUDI ARABIA
An administrative region with a name representing 'Rugged Country'.

Asmara, ERITREA
'Forest of Flowers' in Tigrinya. However, an alternative theory is that the name comes from 'Arbate Asmara' which, in the Tigrinya language, means 'The Four Villages of those (Women) who brought Harmony'. The city became the capital of the Italian colony of Eritrea in 1900, the Italians having gained control of the Eritrean highlands by treaty in 1889. After the Italian defeat by the British in 1941 Asmara remained under British control until Eritrea joined Ethiopia in 1952. It became the capital of an independent Eritrea in 1993.

Aspen, COLORADO/USA
Founded in about 1878 and named after its aspen trees.

Assam, INDIA *Kamarupa*
A state named in the 13th century by, and after, the Ahoms, originally Shans, who came from Burma to establish a kingdom. The Ahoms' own name for themselves was Tai, but Ahom was pronounced Asam, hence the name of the state. It may mean 'Undulating Land'; or it may be derived from the old Ahom word *asama* 'peerless', or possibly from the Thai *ahom* 'invincible'. The area became part of British India in 1826. It was reduced in size when a portion of it was ceded to East Pakistan in 1947 on partition, and the creation of new states within it: Nagaland in 1963 and Arunachal Pradesh, Meghalaya, and Mizoram in 1972.

Assens, DENMARK *Asnæs, Asensz*
On the island of Fyn, the town's name is derived from *ask* 'ash tree' and *næs* 'point' or 'promontory'.

Assiniboia, SASKATCHEWAN/CANADA
Named after the Assinboin tribe. The name in
Ojibwa (Chippewa) means 'Stone Boilers' or
'One who cooks with Stones' from their habit
of cooking their meat by placing it in water
and then adding heated stones. The
surrounding region had the same name and it
served as the official name for the Red River
Settlement. *See* MANITOBA.

Assiniboine, Mt, CANADA
A mountain on the border between Alberta
and British Columbia and a river flowing
through Manitoba and Saskatchewan, both
named after the Assiniboins (see previous
entry).

Assyria, IRAQ-TURKEY
An ancient kingdom which ceased to exist
*c.*610 BC. It took its name from Ashur, the
primary god of the Assyrians.

Astana, KAZAKHSTAN *Akmola, Akmolinsk,
Tselinograd, Akmola/Aqmola*
Founded as a Cossack fort in 1824, it became
known as Akmola in 1830. It was officially
renamed in 1832 as Akmolinsk, 'White Tomb',
from the Turkish *ak* and Russian *mogíla* 'tomb'
when it became a town. From 1961 to 1992,
the town was called Tselinograd, 'Virgin Lands
City' from *tselina* 'Virgin Lands' and *grad*, as the
capital of a Russian government initiative.
Begun in 1954 it aimed to increase arable land
by irrigating the steppes and deserts of
Kazakhstan and Uzbekistan. This necessitated
a huge influx of workers. In 1992 the name
Akmola (Aqmola in Kazakh) was restored. It
became the capital of Kazakhstan in December
1997 in place of Almaty. Reasons for the
transfer may have included the desire to
enhance the ethnic Kazakh presence in the
north, to integrate the strong Russian presence
in the north which is rich in metals, oil and
farmland more fully into Kazakh life, and to
place the capital nearer to the centre of this
huge country. Almaty, the former capital, is
very close to the Kyrgyz border in the south. It
may also have been that Nursultan
Nazarbayev, Kazakh president (1990–),
wished to distance himself from a previous
long-term leader of Kazakhstan, Dinmukhamed
Kunayev, who was strongly associated with
Almaty. In May 1998 the city was renamed
Astana, meaning 'Capital' in Kazakh. The
province of Aqmola has retained its name.

Astorga, CASTILE-LEÓN/SPAIN *Asturica Augusta*
The present name is derived from the first
word of its original Roman name, *Asturica*;
Augustus means 'grand', thus 'Grand Asturian
(Place)' from Asturia, the Latin name for
Asturias.

Astoria, OREGON/USA *Fort Astoria, Fort George*
Named after the New York Astor family which
established a trading post here, Fort Astoria,
for the Pacific Fur Company in 1811. It was
captured by the British in 1813 and held for
five years, during which time it was called Fort
George after King George III[†].

Astrakhan', ASTRAKHAN/RUSSIA *Itil, Khadzhi-
Tarkhan*
A province and a city, moved in 1558 some 7
miles (11 km) from its original site on the right
bank of the Volga River. The previous name is
said to come from the Turkic *haci* or *hadji*, a
Muslim who has made the pilgrimage to
Mecca, and *tarhan* 'untaxed', a reference to the
city's exemption from taxes. The Arabic name
was al-Hajj Tarkhan. Astrakhan is simply a
Russian version of the Turkish name. The city
is alleged to have been founded by a local *hadji*
who became a Muslim saint and its Islamic
fervour gained it a tax-free status. The city was
captured in 1556 by Ivan IV the Terrible, tsar
(1547–84), having been the capital of the Tatar
khanate of Astrakhan formed from the Golden
Horde in 1466. It was an important trading
post between Europe and Central Asia and
gave its name to the fur first brought to Russia
by Astrakhan traders.

Asturias, PHILIPPINES, SPAIN
Spain: a mountainous autonomous
community (and officially the Principality of
Asturias) on the Bay of Biscay. Its name derives
from the Basque *asta* 'rock' and *ur* 'water'. It
was the last Christian stronghold of the
Visigothic élite, who had been driven north by
the Moors. They established an independent
kingdom between 718 and 910. Asturias was
absorbed by Léon in the 12th century and
became a principality in 1388. The title 'Prince
of Asturias' is held by the eldest son of the
king.

Asunción, BOLIVIA, PARAGUAY *Nuestra Señora de
la Asunción (Paraguay)*
Paraguay: the Spanish gave it the full name
'Our Lady of the Assumption' when they began
to build a fort here on the Feast of the
Assumption, 15 August 1537. The city became
the capital of Paraguay when independence
was declared in 1811.

Aswān, EGYPT *Sunt, Swen, Syene*
A governorate and city, also spelt Assuan,
meaning 'The Market' or the 'Place where
Business is conducted' in Coptic. The name is a
corruption of the ancient Egyptian Swen,
Souan, or Swenet, which became the Greek
Syene. In the Bible (Ezekiel 29: 10) it is
variously given as Syene and Seveneh. In
ancient times the name for the surrounding

area was Yeb 'Land of Elephants' perhaps
because the Egyptians saw these animals here
for the first time or because the shape of the
rocks resembled elephants. This name is now
restricted to Elephantine Island.

Asyūt, EGYPT *Syut, Lycopolis, Zawty*
A governorate and very ancient city, and the
centre of worship of Upuauet (or Wepwawet),
a war god in the shape of a desert wolf. It had
the Greek name Lycopolis 'Wolf City' during
the Hellenistic period. Tradition has it that a
large number of wolves roamed the area and
even repulsed an invading Ethiopian army.

Atacama, CHILE
A region created in 1974 and a desert named
after a South American tribe, the Atacama.
Their name is said to come from the Quechua
takama 'black duck'.

Atar, MAURITANIA
The name is derived from the Berber word for
mountain, *adrar*.

At Bashi, KYRGYZSTAN
'Head of the Horse'. It lies in the At Bashinski
range of the Tien Shan mountains.

Atchison, KANSAS/USA
Named after the leader of the settlers who
founded it in 1854, David R. Atchison, a
senator from Missouri.

Athabasca, Lake, CANADA
A lake on the border between Alberta and
Saskatchewan and a river in Alberta with a
Cree name meaning '(Place) where there are
Reeds'.

Athelstan, QUEBEC/CANADA
Founded by Scots who named it after their
village, Athelstaneford.

Athenry (Baile Átha An Rí), IRELAND
'Town of the King's Ford' from *baile*, *átha*, and
rí 'king'.

Athens (Athínai), GREECE, USA
Greece: according to legend, the gods of
Olympus proclaimed that a city founded by
Cecrops, a Phoenician, should be named after
the god who could produce the most valuable
legacy for mortals. Athena (in Latin, Minerva),
goddess of war, produced an olive tree, the
symbol of peace and prosperity; Poseidon, god
of the sea, produced a horse, a symbol of
strength and endurance (although it is also
said that he caused a spring of salt water to
flow on the Acropolis having struck it with his
trident). The gods chose Athena. The actual
origin of the name is unknown, but it may be
associated with *akté* 'beach' or 'raised place
(from the sea)'. The city was destroyed by the

Persians in 480 BC, captured by the Romans in
86 BC, sacked by a Germanic tribe, the Heruli,
in 267, and captured by the Crusaders in 1204.
It fell to the Ottoman Turks after a siege in
1458; they held it until 1829 (and the Acropolis
until 1833). It then became the capital of the
newly independent Kingdom of Greece.

Athlone (Baile Átha Luain), IRELAND
'Town of the Ford of Luan' from *baíle*, *átha*, and
a personal name.

Athol, NEW ZEALAND, USA
USA (Massachusetts): founded in 1735 as
Pequoiag and renamed in 1762 after Blair
Atholl, the Scottish home of the Dukes of
Atholl. The town is said to have been named
for James Murray (*c*.1690–1764), the 2nd Duke
of Atholl.

Athos, Mt (Áthos Óros), GREECE
Also known as 'Holy Mountain'. The name
comes from *thoos* 'pointed', a reference to its
marble peak. It has also been suggested that it
comes from *athoos* 'innocent' or perhaps
'pure'.

Atkarsk, SARATOV/RUSSIA *Yetkara*
The present name has evolved from the
original name which came from the Itkara
River. This is said to have received its name
from Itkar, a Mongol commander of the
Golden Horde.

Atlanta, GEORGIA/USA *Terminus, Marthasville*
Founded in 1837 as a junction for two
railroads, its name was changed to
Marthasville in 1843 after the daughter of the
governor, Wilson Lumpkin. The name was
changed again in 1845 in recognition of the
Western & Atlantic Railroad which had a line
running to the Atlantic coast.

Atlantic City, NEW JERSEY/USA
A city lying on the Atlantic coast.

Atlantic Ocean 'Sea of Atlas', possibly
named after the Titan, Atlas. *See* ATLAS
MOUNTAINS.

Atlas Mountains (Jabal al-Atlas), MOROCCO-
ALGERIA-TUNISIA
They are said to take their name from the
Titan, Atlas, who, in Greek mythology, was
believed to hold up the sky. He was supposed
at first to support the pillars which had their
bases in the sea, the Atlantic Ocean, beyond
the western horizon and which kept the sky
and earth apart. When Atlas refused Perseus
hospitality Perseus showed him the head of
the Gorgon Medusa which turned Atlas into
stone. Subsequently his name was given to the
mountains in north-west Africa which in their
grandeur could be perceived to be keeping the

sky and the earth apart. The actual origin of the name is not known.

Attica (Attiki), GREECE, USA
Greece: an ancient, and now an administrative, region whose name means the 'Territory of Athens'; Athens is its chief city. It comprises a headland jutting into the sea and the name is derived from the Greek *akté* 'raised place (from the sea)', thus 'promontory'.

Attleboro, MASSACHUSETTS/USA
Founded in 1669 and named after the Attleborough in England whence most of the settlers had come. Attleborough means 'Ætla's Hill' from *beorg* 'hill'.

Atzcapotzalco, FEDERAL DISTRICT/MEXICO
Founded in the 12th century with an Aztec name meaning 'Anthill' because of the great number of its inhabitants. Also spelt Azcapotzalco.

Aubagne, PROVENCE-ALPES-CÔTES D'AZUR/ FRANCE *Pagus Lucreti*
Its name is derived from its health springs, *Ad Bainea*.

Auburn, AUSTRALIA, USA
1. USA (Alabama, Maine, Washington): all three cities were named after the 'sweet Auburn' in *The Deserted Village*, a poem by Oliver Goldsmith, written in 1770. The city in Washington was originally named Slaughter, after an officer killed in the Indian wars. It was renamed in 1893.
2. USA (New York): founded in 1793 by Captain John Hardenberg on the site of a Native American village called Wasco, this Auburn was first called Hardenberg's Corners.

Auch, MIDI-PYRÉNÉES/FRANCE *Elimberris, Augusta Auscorum, Novempopulani*
Named after the Celtiberian tribe, the Ausci, whose capital this was.

Auckland, NORTH ISLAND/NEW ZEALAND
Founded in 1840 as the capital of the colonial government, it was named after George Eden (1784–1849), 2nd Earl of Auckland, first lord of the British Admiralty and governor-general of India (1836–42). It gave way as the capital to Wellington in 1865.

Augher (Eochair), NORTHERN IRELAND/UK *Ogher*
'Border', denoting that it lay close to an administrative border. It is now only a few miles from the border with the Republic of Ireland.

Aughnacloy (Achadh na Cloiche), NORTHERN IRELAND/UK
'Field of the Stone' from the Gaelic *achadh* 'field' and *cloch* 'stone'.

Augsburg, BAVARIA/GERMANY *Augusta Vindelicorum*
Founded in 15 BC and named by the Roman generals Drusus and Tiberius after their stepfather, the Emperor Augustus[†], and the local Celtic tribe, the Vindelici, which the Romans had subjugated. Only the first syllable of Augusta was retained to which *Burg* was added.

Augusta, AUSTRALIA, ITALY, USA
1. Italy (Sicily): founded in 1232 by Frederick II[†] and called by him Augusta Veneranda to mean 'August (Place)', that is, a place to be venerated or revered.
2. USA (Georgia): founded as a trading post in 1735 and named after Princess Augusta (1719–72), the mother of the future George III[†].
3. USA (Maine): originally with a Native American name, Koussinoc, a fort was built here in 1754. In 1797 the town which had developed from it was called Harrington, but this was almost immediately changed to Augusta after Pamela Augusta, the daughter of General Henry Dearborn (1751–1829), army officer, congressman, and secretary for war (1801–9).

Augustów, POLAND
Named after King Sigismund II Augustus (1520–72), the last Jagiełłonian King of Poland (1548–72).

Aurangābād, MAHĀRĀSHTRA/INDIA *Fathnagar, Khadki*
Founded in 1610, the city was renamed in 1653 'Town of Aurangzeb' by Aurangzeb (1618–1707), the last of the great Mughal emperors (1658–1707), after himself. The first name meant 'City of Victory' from the Arabic *fath* 'victory' or 'conquest' and *nagar*. Khadki meant 'Big Rock'.

Aurora, CANADA, GUYANA, PHILIPPINES, USA
1. There are fourteen towns and cities of this name in the USA. Most, but not all, are named from the Latin word for 'dawn', Aurora being the Roman goddess of the dawn. Aurora is also known as Eos.
2. USA (Colorado): previously named Fletcher in 1891 after its founder, Donald Fletcher. It was renamed in 1907.

Austin, USA
1. Texas: chosen in 1839 to be the capital of the independent Republic of Texas (1836–45), the small settlement of Waterloo was renamed Austin that year after Stephen F. Austin (1793–1836). He was the first major English-speaking land developer in the area (when it was still

part of Mexico) and he established several Anglo-American colonies in the 1820s. He served as secretary of state of the Republic of Texas for a few months in 1836, having bid to become president of the new republic. Austin remains the state capital today.

2. Minnesota: first settled in 1853 and named after Horace Austin, the state governor (1870–4).

Australasia A name used to describe Australia and the islands of the south-west Pacific Ocean, including New Zealand and New Guinea. It combines the Latin *australis* 'southern' and Asia.

Australia (Eendrachtsland), NEW HOLLAND, TERRA AUSTRALIS

The Commonwealth of Australia since 1 January 1901 when the six separate colonies of New South Wales, Queensland, South Australia, Tasmania, Victoria, and Western Australia were joined in a federation and retitled as states; South Australia was partitioned in 1911, a part being hived off as the Northern Territory and joining the Commonwealth as a 'territory', not a state. Imagining the existence of such a land at the beginning of the 1st millennium, the Greeks called it *Terra Australis Incognita* 'Unknown Southern Land'. So optimistic were cartographers in the 15th century that some maps bore the name *Terra Australis Nondam Incognita* 'Southern Land Not Yet Known'. The west coast was eventually discovered by the Dutchman Dirck Hartog in 1616 and named Eendrachtsland after his ship, the *Eendracht*. After another Dutchman, Abel Tasman[†], had undertaken a second voyage to the area in 1644, the land discovered was renamed New Holland (now Western Australia). Between 1801 and 1803 Matthew Flinders[†], a British naval officer, circumnavigated the entire island, proving that it was a single landmass and calling it on his chart 'Terra Australis or Australia'. 'Australia' was approved by international consent in 1817. Great Britain's claim to Australia followed Captain James Cook's[†] voyage in 1770 when New South Wales was annexed. In a referendum on 6 November 1999, a majority of Australians voted to retain the British Queen as head of state rather than alter the constitution to establish Australia as a republic and replace the Queen with a president.

Australian Capital Territory, AUSTRALIA *Limestone Plains*
Explored by Charles Throsby in 1820 and originally named by him. In 1901, with the creation of the Commonwealth of Australia, the new constitution decreed that an area at least 100 miles (160 km) from Sydney should be carved out of New South Wales and reserved for a new capital. The area was handed over in 1909 and became the Capital Territory in 1911. *See* CANBERRA.

Austria (Österreich) *Noricum, Ostmark, Ostarrichi*
The Republic of Austria (Republik Österreich) since 1918. Noricum was a kingdom established by the Celts in about 400 BC. The present name is derived from the fact that the region became a military district on the eastern border, Ostmark, of Emperor Charlemagne's[†] Frankish kingdom as a buffer against the Avars; it was also referred to as the 'Avarian Mark'. The area had been occupied by the Romans by 15 BC and by Germanic tribes by the 6th century. In 976 Austria's identity was formulated when it became an imperial fief of the Margrave Leopold (d. 994) of Babenberg (and to some it was known as Marchio Liutpold). The name Ostarrichi 'Eastern Province' was first mentioned in 996 to describe the territory over which the Babenbergs ruled and in due course this became Österreich 'Eastern Empire'. The Margravate became a duchy in 1156, the nucleus of the Habsburg Empire from 1278, and was united with Bohemia and Hungary to form a joint kingdom in the 16th century. In 1804 the Empire of Austria was created and in 1867 a Compromise (*Ausgleich*) was reached with Hungary whereby the kingdom was split to become the 'Dual Monarchy' or the 'Austro-Hungarian Empire'. While the Hungarian part of the Dual Monarchy was simply called the Kingdom of Hungary, the non-Hungarian part was officially called 'The Lands and Kingdoms Represented in the *Reichsrat*' (Advisory Council) and unofficially as Cisleithania 'Lands on this Side of the Leitha'; the Leitha was a stream which marked the contemporary border between Hungary and Lower Austria. Only in 1917 was the clumsy official title replaced by Austria and this only lasted until the dissolution of the Austro-Hungarian Empire. Under the terms of the Treaty of Saint-Germain in 1919 the dissolution was recognized together with the independence of modern Austria (and other central European countries). For the first time it became a state in its own right, having previously been just a part of the Habsburg lands. In March 1938 Nazi forces invaded the country and Austria was annexed, becoming a province of the Greater German Reich. In 1945 the republic was restored, although it was divided into four occupation zones for American, British,

French, and Soviet forces. In 1955 these forces were withdrawn and Austria's independence and pre-1938 borders were recognized on condition that it remained neutral.

Autun, BURGUNDY/FRANCE *Augustodunum*
The present name is a shortening of the Roman 'Stronghold of Augustus', referring to the Emperor Augustus[†], and *dunum*.

Auvergne, FRANCE *Arvernia*
A region named after the Gaulish Arverni tribe, formidable opponents of Julius Caesar[†].

Auxerre, BURGUNDY/FRANCE *Autessiodurum*
Probably taken from a personal name and the Gaulish *duru* 'fort' to mean the 'Fortress of Autessio'.

Ava, BURMA *Ratnapura*
Founded in 1364 as the capital of a Burmese kingdom (1364–1527, 1636–1760, 1764–1841) in central Burma of which little now remains. The earlier Pali name meant 'City of Gems'. Ava, also known as Innwa, may be a version of the Burmese *Ing-wa* 'Entrance to the Lake' because the city was built near the entrance to a lagoon by the River Irrawaddy. It was more commonly called by the Burmese A-wa 'The Mouth'.

Avalon, PENNSYLVANIA/USA
In an area of fruit orchards, the name may mean the 'Island of Apples' from the Welsh *afal* 'apple'. This is an allusion to Avalon, the island to which the legendary 6th-century British King Arthur was taken to recover from his wounds. Geoffrey of Monmouth described it as 'the island of apples' in his *Vita Merlini* 'Life of Merlin' *c.*1150.

Avanos, TURKEY *Venasa*
Corrupted from the Latin *Venasa*, a reference to the ferrous metals which colour the silt of the River Kizilirmak.

Avellaneda, ARGENTINA *Barracas al Sur*
Directly south-east of Buenos Aires, the previous Spanish name meant 'Huts to the South' from *barraca* 'hut' or 'cabin'. It was renamed in 1914 in honour of Nicholas Avellaneda (1837–85), president of Argentina (1874–80).

Avellino, CAMPANIA/ITALY *Abellinum*
The present name comes from the earlier name of a stronghold of the Hirpini some 1¾ miles (3 km) away. Abellinum is associated with the ancient Abella, a name derived from the Indo-European *abel* 'apple'.

Avernus, Lake (Lago d'Averno), CAMPANIA/ITALY
A lake whose Greek name, Aornos, meant 'Without Birds' from *a* 'without' and *ornis*

'bird'. According to legend, its sulphurous vapours killed any bird which tried to fly over it. This, and the rather sinister atmosphere gained from its still waters, reinforced the belief that it was the source of the River Styx which flowed down to Hades; it was thus regarded as the entrance to Hell.

Avignon, PROVENCE-ALPES-CÔTES D'AZUR/FRANCE *Avennio*
Lying on the River Rhône, the city takes its name from the Indo-European root word *ab* 'water'. The present name is derived from the Roman name. Factionalism in Rome led Philip IV the Fair, King of France (1285–1314), to invite the pope, Clement V (1305–14), to set up his seat here in 1309. Clement VI (1342–52) bought the city in 1348 and it remained papal property until annexed by France in 1791. In the mean time, the Avignon papacy ended in 1377. All seven popes who presided in Avignon were French.

Ávila, CASTILE-LEÓN/SPAIN *Albicella, Abula, Avela*
The full name is Ávila de los Caballeros, 'Ávila of the Knights'. The suffix was added to the Roman name in recognition of their exploits in the recapture of Saragossa in the 12th century, and Córdoba, Jaén, and Seville in the 13th. Ávila is a shortened version of the city's Roman name, Albicella, from the Latin *alba cella* 'white cell', that is, a monk's cell. The city was captured by the Moors in 714 and was not retaken by the Christians until 1088.

Avoca, AUSTRALIA, IRELAND, USA
1. Australia (Victoria): named after the Avoca in Ireland. It was founded in 1852, following the death of Thomas Moore (1779–1852), the Irish poet..
2. USA (New York): named by a resident of New York in a reference to Thomas Moore's poem *Sweet Vale of Avoca,* an allusion to the Avoca in County Wicklow, Ireland.

Avon, UK, USA
USA: there are nine cities with this name in the USA. Most, if not all, are named after the rivers in England whose name is derived from a word of Celtic origin, *abona* 'river'.

Avontuur, WESTERN CAPE/SOUTH AFRICA
'Adventure' in Afrikaans, so-called because there was no guarantee that the fruit farm established here would be a success.

Axel Heiberg, NUNAVUT/CANADA
An island first visited by a Norwegian expedition in 1899, led by Otto Sverdrup who named it after the Norwegian consul.

Axminster, ENGLAND/UK *Ascanmynster,*
Aixeministra
The town lies on the River Axe and its name
remembers the great Cistercian abbey which
was demolished after Henry VIII (1491–1547),
King of England (1509–47) gave the order to
dissolve the monasteries in 1536. It was
famous for its carpets in the 18th and 19th
centuries; its name survives for a certain type
of carpet.

Ayacucho, PERU *Huamanga*
Founded in 1539, it was renamed in 1825 from
a Quechua word meaning 'Corner of the
Dead'. In the surrounding area Spanish forces
were defeated at the Battle of Ayacucho in
1824 and ensured Peru retained its
independence which it had gained in 1821.

Aydın, TURKEY *Tralleis, Güzelhisar*
Its previous name, meaning 'Beautiful Castle'
from *güzel* 'beautiful' and *hisar*, was changed
to Aydın in the 14th century after Aydın
Oglu Mehmed Bey, founder of the dynasty
of Aydın Ogullari (*c.*1308–1425), had
taken control. About 1390 Aydın was
annexed to the Ottoman Empire, but was
captured by Tamerlane[†] in 1402. It then
enjoyed 23 years of comparative
independence before being retaken by the
Ottoman Turks.

Ayers Rock, NORTHERN TERRITORY/AUSTRALIA
The Aboriginal name, now in common use, is
Uluru 'Howling'. Sighted in 1872, it was
named the following year after Sir Henry
Ayers (1821–97), seven times prime minister of
South Australia.

Ay Khanom, AFGHANISTAN
Ruins. The settlement may have been founded
in 327 BC by Alexander III the Great[†] as
Alexandria-on-the-Oxus (now the Amu Darya
River). Its present name means 'Lady of the
Moon' from the Uzbek *oy* 'moon' and *xonim*
'lady'.

Aylesbury, ENGLAND/UK *Ægelsburg, Eilesberia*
The Anglo-Saxon name meant 'Ægel's Fort'
from an Old English personal name and *burh*.
The town gives its name to a special breed of
duck.

Aylesford, CANADA, UK
1. Canada: the original township was named
after Heneage Finch (1751–1812), 4th Earl of
Aylesford, who served the crown in different
appointments (1777–1812).
2. UK (England): formerly Æglesforda
and Ailesford, the name means 'Ægel's
Ford' from an Old English personal name and
ford.

Ayodhyā, UTTAR PRADESH/INDIA
Also called Oudh and Awadh. It is one of the
seven sacred cities of the Hindus, a place of
pilgrimage and revered as the legendary
birthplace of the god Rāma, the hero of the
epic poem, Rāmāyana. Ayodhyā means
'invincible' or 'unconquerable' in Sanskrit.

Ayr, AUSTRALIA, UK
1. Australia (Victoria): named in 1882 after the
birthplace in Scotland of Sir Thomas
McIlwraith, the state prime minister.
2. UK (Scotland): originally Inverayr 'Mouth of
the (River) Ayr' after the river on which it lies,
from the Gaelic *inbhir* 'river mouth' and the
Indo-European root word *ar* 'water'. 'Inver'
was subsequently discarded, except in the
Gaelic form of the name.

Aytos, BULGARIA
Taken from the Fortress of Aetos which is the
Greek for 'eagle'.

Ayutthaya, THAILAND *Ayodhyā*
The full name is Phra Nakhon Si Ayutthaya,
meaning the 'Sacred City of the Good and
Invincible One'. Ayutthaya took its name from
Ayodhyā, the Sanskrit for 'invincible' or
'unconquerable', while the Thai *phra* indicates
divine status, *nakhon* 'city', and *si* 'good'.
Ramathibodi (1315–69), King of U Thong from
1347, moved his capital to an artificial island in
the Chao Phraya River in 1350 and founded
Ayutthaya as a small fortified city. The next
year he became King of the Thai Kingdom of
Ayutthaya (1351–69) as Ramathibodi I and
Ayutthaya began to grow into a kingdom,
becoming one of the strongest in South-East
Asia. It was the capital of Thailand between
1351 and 1767 until being sacked and
destroyed by the Burmese. Now a town replete
with ruins from its heyday, it is sometimes
called Krung Kao 'Ancient Capital'.

Azad Kashmir 'Free Kashmir', a disputed
territory since the partition of India in 1947
when it was seized from India by Pashtun
tribesmen, supported by Pakistani troops. A
UN ceasefire line was agreed in 1949 but, after
Pakistan's defeat in the Second Indo-Pakistan
War in 1971, the 1972 Simla Agreement set
out a new 'line of control' to separate the
Indian and Pakistani-controlled areas of
Jammu and Kashmir. The Pakistani area is
called Azad Kashmir and is claimed by
Pakistan to be independent, although it has
strong links with Pakistan. *See* KASHMIR.

Azamgarh, UTTAR PRADESH/INDIA
Founded in 1665 by Azam Khan after whom
the town is named to give the 'Fort of Azam'
from the personal name and *garh*.

Azemmour, MOROCCO
Founded by the Berbers in a region with
numerous wild olive trees, the name means
'Wild Olive Tree' from the Berber *azemmūr*.

Azerbaijan (Azäbaycan), AND IRAN
1. The Republic of Azerbaijan (Azäbaycan
Respublikası) since 1991. Previously the
Azerbaijani Soviet Socialist Republic
(1936–91), having had the same title as part of
the Transcaucasian Soviet Federative Socialist
Republic (1922–36) which joined the USSR in
1922; the Soviet Republic of Azerbaijan
(1920–2) after invasion by the Red Army; and
the independent Democratic Republic of
Azerbaijan (1918–20) after the Bolshevik
Revolution in 1917. During Soviet rule the
territory of Azerbaijan was reduced by 11 000
square miles (28 500 sq. km). Some 16 per cent
of its territory, of which roughly one-third is
the autonomous province of *Nagornyy-
Karabakh, has been under Armenian control
since 1993. Until achieving independence in
1918 Azerbaijan had never existed as a state,
having been subjected to a variety of powers
through the ages: Scythians, Seleucids,
Romans, Persians, Arabs, Seljuk Turks,
Mongols, Ottoman Turks, and Russians. The
Treaties of Gulistan (in Nagornyy-Karabakh)
in 1813 and of Turkmenchai (now in Iran) in 1828
resulted in the area called Azerbaijan being
partitioned between Russia and Persia (Iran)
along the River Aras; only the northern half
now constitutes the Republic of Azerbaijan.
Azerbaijan may take its name from one of
Alexander III the Great's[†] Persian generals,
Atropates, who established a kingdom and
dynasty after the death of Alexander in 323 BC.
Atropates took his name from the Greek
atropatan 'protected by fire'. Alternatively, it
may come from Persian words meaning 'Land
of Fire', a reference to the fire-worshippers, or
to the oil seeping from the ground which
could be burnt. Having annexed it by the 3rd
century, the Romans named the area Albania
which later became known as Caucasian
Albania. The Caucasian Albanians had no links
with the 'Illyrian' Albanians in modern

Albania and disappeared without trace in the
11th century.
2. Iran: there are two Azerbaijani provinces in
north-west Iran: Azārbāyjan-e Gharbī (West)
and Azārbāyjan-e Sharqī (East). More than
twice as many Azeris live in Iran as in
Azerbaijan. The region was occupied by the
Soviet Union during the Second World War in
an effort to reunify Iranian and Soviet
Azerbaijan; the attempt failed in the face of
Western opposition.

Azogues, ECUADOR
'Mercury' from the Spanish *azogue*, a reference
to the ore in the area.

Azores (Ilhas dos Açores), PORTUGAL
'Islands of the Hawks' from the Portuguese
açor 'goshawk', although it may have been
buzzards that the first inhabitants saw. The
group of islands in the Atlantic Ocean forms an
autonomous region of Portugal. Although
known to the Phoenicians in the 6th century
BC, the islands were forgotten and not
rediscovered until 1427 by the Portuguese.
Settlement began in 1439. Between 1580 and
1640 they were annexed by Spain.

Azov, ROSTOV/RUSSIA *Tanais, Tana, Azak*
A sea and a city with a name possibly derived
from the Turkish *az* 'small' or *azak* 'low'. The
Sea of Azov (in Russian, *Azovskoye More*) is the
world's shallowest and gives its name to the
town. However, it has been suggested that it is
named after a local prince, Azum, who was
killed here in 1067. Founded as Tanais in the
6th century BC by the Greeks, it experienced a
succession of rulers. It was renamed Tana by
the Genoese in 1316, was taken by the
Venetians who retained the name, was
overrun in 1471 by the Turks who built a
fortress here to dominate the River Don and
called it Azak and then Azov. It was captured
by the Russians in 1696 and the modern town
was founded in 1708.

Azrou, MOROCCO
'Rock' from a Berber word. The town is close to
a huge volcanic outcrop.

Baalbek (Ba'labakk), LEBANON *Heliopolis*
The area having been taken by the Egyptian
Ptolemaic dynasty during the 4th century BC,
the city was given the Greek name Heliopolis
'City of the Sun' from *hĕlios* 'sun' and *polis*. It
fell to the Romans in 64 BC and to the Arabs in
637. Thereafter it was under Syrian control
until being included in the French mandate for
Lebanon after the First World War. The name
may mean the 'City of Baal' from *bakk* 'city';
Baal was worshipped as a god of fertility with
the title 'Lord of the Earth'.

Bāb al-Mandab, RED SEA
A strait, the 'Gate of the Tears', linking the Red
Sea and the Indian Ocean between Djibouti
and Yemen. The name is derived from the
Arabic *bāb* 'gate' or 'door' and *mandab*
'lamentation' or 'tears', a reference to the
navigational difficulties that used to be
experienced here.

Babbage River, YUKON/CANADA
Named after the English mathematician,
Charles Babbage (1791–1871), one of the
founders of the Royal Astronomical Society
and the inventor of a machine to calculate
numerical tables.

Bābol, IRAN *Bārfurush, Mamter*
Named after the River Bābol on which it lies.
Its former port, no longer usable after the
Caspian Sea receded, is called Bābol Sar,
previously Meshed-e Sar.

Babruysk, BELARUS *Bobruysk*
Named after the small River Bobruyka, itself
derived from the Russian *bobr* 'beaver'.
The Belarusian spelling was adopted after
Belarus achieved independence in 1991.

Babushkin, BURYATIYA REPUBLIC/RUSSIA
Mysovsk
Situated on Lake Baykal, the original name
came from *mys* 'cape' or 'promontory'. The
town was renamed in 1941 after Ivan
Babushkin (1873–1906), a Bolshevik
revolutionary who was captured by Tsarist
forces here and executed.

Babylon, IRAQ, USA
1. Iraq: ruins called Bāb-Ilān, 'Gate of the
Gods', from the Akkadian *bābu* 'gate', and *ílu*,
God'; called Aṭlāl Bābil in Arabic, and Babel or
Bavel in Hebrew. It first became important as

the capital of the Kingdom of Babylonia
(southern Mesopotamia) in 1792 BC. It was the
site of the Tower of Babel, mentioned in the
Bible (Genesis 11: 1–9), the name of which is
used to describe a confusing medley of voices
or a hubbub. Babylon was also the site of one of
the Seven Wonders of the Ancient World, the
fabled Hanging Gardens.
2. USA (New York): founded in 1872 and
named after the ancient Babylon.

Bacău, ROMANIA
A county and a town which, according to
legend, was named after Bakó. He was a
Hungarian outlaw from Calugara who was
caught and condemned to death. At that time
the condemned could escape death by
agreeing to become executioners themselves.
The Hungarian word for executioner or
hangman is *bakó*. When he returned to
Calugara, Bako opened a bar on a junction of
trade routes on the River Bistriţa and from this
the 'Town of Bako' evolved. A less fanciful
explanation may be that the name is simply
derived from the Romanian *bac* 'ferry'.

Bacchus Marsh, VICTORIA/AUSTRALIA
Lying on the Werribee River, it was named
after its founder, Captain William Bacchus, in
1838.

Bačka Palanka, SERBIA/SERBIA AND
MONTENEGRO *Pest-Ujlak, Iločka*
Before the beginning of the 17th century it had
become known as Palanka, a fortified Turkish
settlement with the Turkish *palanka* meaning
the 'redoubt of a fortress'. Bačka is a region in
Vojvodina, Serbia, and derives from the Serbo-
Croat *bačija* 'summer mountain pasture'.

Bačka Topola, SERBIA/SERBIA AND
MONTENEGRO *Mala Bajša*
'White Poplar in the Bačka Region' from
the Serbian *topola*. Bačka is included to
distinguish this town from another Topola
further south.

Bactria, AFGHANISTAN-TAJIKISTAN-UZBEKISTAN
An ancient Greek kingdom between the Hindu
Kush and Amu Darya River which took its
name from its capital, Bactra, now *Balkh. It
gives its name to the Bactrian camel which has
two humps.

Badajoz, EXTREMADURA/SPAIN *Pax Augusta,
Batalyaws, Bax Augos, Badaljoz*
A province and a city with a name corrupted
by the Moors to Batalyaws from the original
Roman name which meant the 'Peace of
Augustus[1]'. The city, situated close to the
Portuguese border, was recaptured from the
Moors in 1229 and thereafter occupied by the
Portuguese on several different occasions.

Baden, AUSTRIA, CANADA, ERITREA, GERMANY,
SWITZERLAND, USA
'Baths' from the plural of the German *Bad*.
The towns in Austria, Germany, and
Switzerland all have hot springs and were used
as spas by the Romans. Baden was also the
name of a former state in south-west Germany
and the towns in Canada and the USA are
named after it. The name also refers to the
western part of the modern state of
Baden-Württemberg.

Baden-Baden, BADEN-WÜRTTEMBERG/
GERMANY *Aquae Aureliae*
'Baths' and to distinguish them from any other
baths in Germany the town has an added *Baden*
to show that it is in the state of Baden-
Württemberg, formerly the province of Baden
and Württemberg. The Roman baths, named
for the Emperor Marcus Aurelius (161–80),
were built some 35 years after his death for the
military garrison in Strasbourg.

Bad Harzburg, LOWER SAXONY/GERMANY
A spa town, *Bad*, built round a castle, *Burg*, in
the Upper Harz mountains.

Bad Homburg, HESSE/GERMANY
The full name is Bad Homburg vor der Höhe
which denotes a spa town (since 1834) at the
foot of the (Taunus) mountains. Homburg
means 'High Fortress', a reference to the
Hohenburg Fortress, built in the 12th century
but now in ruins. The town has given its name
to the felt hat with a lengthways furrow in the
crown which was first made here.

Bad Kreuznach, RHINELAND-PALATINATE/
GERMANY
The present name is a development of
Cruciniacum, the Latin name for a Carolingian
palace in the time of Louis I the Pious (778–
840), Holy Roman Emperor (814–40). Ceded to
Prussia in 1815, it became a popular spa town,
hence the additional *Bad*.

Badlands, SOUTH DAKOTA/USA
A national park since 1978 called Mako Sica
'Land Bad' by the Oglala Sioux. Without
vegetation and little natural life, it is a rocky,
desolate area of canyons and gullies, cliffs, and
buttes. French Canadian fur trappers called it

Les mauvaises terres à traverser 'The bad lands to
cross'.

Badplaas, MPUMALANGA/SOUTH AFRICA
'Bathing Place' as a result of its mineral spa.
Locally, it is also known as Emanzana 'Healing
Waters'.

Bafatá, GUINEA-BISSAU
A region and a town with the meaning
'Confluence of Rivers' from the Mandekan
ba 'river' and *fatá* 'confluence'. The town
lies at the confluence of two rivers,
the point where the Colufi flows into the
Gêba.

Baffin Island, NUNAVUT/CANADA
Named after the English navigator, William
Baffin (c.1584–1622), who came upon the
island in 1616 while searching for the
Northwest Passage. He also gave his
name to the bay between the island and
Greenland.

Bafing, MALI
A river simply called 'Black River' from *ba*
'river' and *fing* 'black'.

Bafoulabé, MALI
'Confluence of Two Rivers' from *ba* 'river', *foula*
'two', and *bé* 'to meet'. The town lies at the
junction of the Bakoye and Bafing rivers.

Bagamoyo, TANZANIA
Formerly a slave-trading depot and port on
Arab caravan routes, the name may be derived
from the Swahili *bwaga-moyo* 'tranquil heart'.
From this various meanings having been
deduced: for example, 'where the heart lays
down its burden' or 'forget where you have
come from'.

Bagan, BURMA, CHINA, RUSSIA, TOGO
*Arimaddanapura, Tambadipa/Tainpa Deepa,
Nyaung-U, Pagan (Burma)*
Burma: a Pyu city-state, the first Pali name
meant 'City of the Tramplers on the Enemy'
because Anawrahta, King of Bagan (1044–77/
84), besieged the Mon capital, Thaton, and left
it in ruins in 1057. The second name meant
'Copper Land'. Pagan is said to come from
Pugan, itself from Pyugam 'Village of the Pyu'.
Pagan was transformed into Bagan in the 19th
century but was later corrupted by the British
back to Pagan. On their departure Bagan was
readopted. It is now only a small town, but
surrounded by hundreds of temples and
religious sites.

Bagdadi, GEORGIA *Mayakovskiy*
'Gift of God' (*see* BAGHDAD). In 1940 it was
renamed after Vladimir Mayakovsky
(1893–1930), the famous poet who was born
here and who was a strong supporter of the

Bolshevik Revolution in 1917. The present
name was readopted in 1991.

Baghdad, IRAQ *Madīnat as-Salam*
A governorate and a city founded in 762 as the
capital of the new 'Abbāsid dynasty (750–1258)
at a junction of trade routes on the site of a
Persian town called Baghdad. It was renamed
Madīnat as-Salām 'City of Peace'. The pre-
Islamic name Baghdad is a combination of two
Persian words and means 'Gift of God' or
'Founded by God'. The move of the caliphate
from Damascus, Syria, to Baghdad in 752 and
the change of dynasty from Umayyad to
'Abbāsid refocused Muslim civilization
eastwards and initiated five centuries of
'Abbāsid rule over most of the Islamic world.
Subject to two Turkmen dynasties between
1410 and 1508, the city was ruled by the
Persians in 1508–34 before falling to the
Ottoman Turks. They retained control
until 1916, the city being the capital of
Baghdad province. On the creation of Iraq
in 1920 (when it was placed under a
British-administered League of Nations
mandate) Baghdad became its capital and
remained so when independence was gained
in 1932.

Bagheria, SICILY/ITALY
Probably derived from the Arabic *baqar* 'Night
Stable'.

Bago, BURMA, PHILIPPINES
Burma: formerly Hanthawady/Hamsavati,
Pegu and Lower Burma. A division and city
named after the river in Sri Lanka by the side
of which the monks who founded the city
were ordained. Alternatively, there is a legend
that the city was founded in 573 by two Mons
princes who saw a female goose standing on a
male goose. This was considered to be a good
omen and so a town was founded here. It was
called Hamsavati 'Kingdom of the Hinthar (a
mythical goose or duck)' in Pali-Sanskrit. As
Pegu, from which it takes its present name, it
was capital of the Mon kingdom. Bago, in the
local language, is said to mean 'Conquered by
Strategem'. It was designated a province of
India by the British in 1852 and renamed
Lower Burma.

Bagrationovsk, KALININGRAD/RUSSIA *Eylau*
Founded in 1336 in what was then East
Prussia. Eylau has a Slavonic origin with the
meaning of 'mud' or 'silt' (in modern Russian,
il). In 1946, after the Soviet Union had annexed
the region, it was renamed after Pyotr
Bagration (1765–1812), a general who
distinguished himself during the Napoleonic
Wars. He fought at the Battle of Eylau
(February 1807) between the Russians and

Prussians, and the French. It ended in
stalemate, but the Russians and Prussians
withdrew from the battlefield, leaving it in the
possession of the French.

Baguio, LUZON/PHILIPPINES
Derived from the Spanish *bahia* 'bay', although
it lies inland from the Lingayen Gulf. Between
1898 and 1976 it was the summer capital.

Bahamas, The The Commonwealth of the
Bahamas since 1973 when the islands gained
their independence from the UK. Previously its
official name had been the Commonwealth of
the Bahama Islands (1969–73). The name is
said to mean 'Shallow Sea' from the Spanish
baja mar although there is some doubt about
this; it is probably derived from a much older
Lucayan word. Inhabited originally by the
Lucayans, one of the Bahama islands (possibly
San Salvador Island, Cat Island, or Samana Cay)
was where Christopher Columbus[1] first
'discovered' the New World on 12 October
1492. The Spanish did not try to settle, English
migrants from Bermuda being the first
Europeans to establish a colony in 1649. In
1717 the islands became a British crown
colony and remained so until 1973.

Bahāwalpur, PUNJAB/PAKISTAN
Founded in 1748 and named after the Nawab
Muhammad Bahāwal Khan Abbasi I, a direct
descendant of the Prophet Muhammad's uncle
Abbas. It means the 'Town of Bahāwal' with
the additional *pur*. It was a former princely
state which claimed independence in 1802
and was only incorporated into Pakistan in
1954. The smaller town of Bahāwalnagar, in
Punjab province, is also named after Bahāwal
Khan.

Bahia, BRAZIL
A state meaning 'Bay' from the Portuguese
baía. It takes its name from its capital which
was Bahia, but which is now Salvador.
Portuguese sailors entered the bay on All
Saints' Day, 1 November 1501, naming it Baía
de Todos os Santos, 'All Saints' Bay'.

Bahía Blanca, ARGENTINA *Nueva Buenos Aires*
'White Bay'. A military post called New Buenos
Aires was established in 1828 by the Spanish to
provide protection against attack and in due
course a settlement developed around it. It was
renamed in 1895.

Bahrain *Dilmun/Telmun*
The Kingdom of Bahrain (Mamlakat al-
Baḥrayn) since 2002 when a constitutional
monarchy was instituted. Previously it was the
State of Bahrain (Dawlat al-Baḥrayn) which
consisted of a group of islands in the Persian
Gulf. The name of the biggest island, Bahrain,

means 'Two Seas' from *baḥrayn*, the plural of *baḥr*, a reference to the fact that it has 'seas' to the east and west. Dilmun/Telmun is said to mean 'Land of the Sweet Waters'. It was ruled by the Persians and Arabs until 1521 when it was taken by the Portuguese. They were superseded by the Persians in 1602. The present Āl-Khalīfah dynasty took control from the Persians in 1783, although in 1861 Bahrain became a British protectorate in all but name. In 1971 it became an independent emirate.

Baḥr al-Aḥmar, al-, EGYPT
A governorate between the Nile River Valley and the Red Sea with a name meaning 'Red Sea' from *baḥr* and *aḥmar* 'red'.

Baḥr al-Ghazāl, THE SUDAN
A state called 'The River of the Antelopes', a tributary of the River Nile, from *baḥr* and *ghazāl* 'gazelle' or 'antelope'.

Baia, ITALY, ROMANIA
Italy (Campania): '(Town on the) Bay'. However, the name may come from Baios, a companion of Ulysses.

Baia Mare, ROMANIA *Neustadt, Nagybánya*
'Big Mine' in both the present name and the previous Hungarian name when the town was located in Hungary; it was transferred to Romania in 1920 after the fall of the Austro-Hungarian Empire, retaken by the Hungarians during the Second World War and finally returned to Romania in 1947. Both the Romanian *mare* and the Hungarian *nagy* mean 'big'; however, while the Hungarian *bánya* means 'mine', the Romanian *baie* actually means 'bath'. The town was the Hungarians' chief source of gold bullion. Founded by Saxon immigrants in the 12th century, the original name meant 'New Town' in German.

Baie-Comeau, QUEBEC/CANADA
Founded in 1936 and named after a local naturalist, Napoléon-Alexandre Comeau. Lying on the St Lawrence River close to the mouth of the Manicouagan River, it is not clear whether the *baie* refers to 'bay' or, in recognition of Comeau's calling, 'berry'.

Baillie, CANADA
1. Nunavut: a river named after George Baillie, agent general of the crown colonies.
2. Northwest Territories: islands discovered in 1826 by Sir John Franklin and named after George Baillie.

Bainbridge, USA
There are four cities with this name in Georgia, Indiana, New York, and Ohio. They are named after Captain William Bainbridge (1774–1833), a naval commander who

captured a British frigate off the Brazilian coast during the 1812 war.

Baja California, MEXICO
Two states in the Californian peninsula have the names Baja California 'Lower California' from the Spanish *baja* 'drop' or 'fall'—it was Baja California Norte in 1974–9—and Baja California Sur 'Lower California South'. *See* CALIFORNIA.

Bajina Bašta, SERBIA/SERBIA AND MONTENEGRO *Plijeskovo*
Now named after Osman Baja who had a large garden (in Serbo-Croat, *bašta*) here.

Bajram Curri, ALBANIA
Named after an Albanian nationalist, anti-royalist, warlord who was killed by police in a cave just outside the town in the late 1920s. He was elevated to hero status by Enver Hoxha, the Albanian communist leader (1944–85).

Bakersfield, USA
1. California: founded in 1869 and named after Colonel Thomas Baker who reclaimed marshes along the River Kern.
2. Vermont: founded in 1789 and named after Joseph Baker who owned the land on which the town was built.

Bakhchysaray, UKRAINE *Baghče Saray*
'Garden Palace' from a combination of the Persian *bāgh* 'garden' and *saray* 'palace' or 'mansion' in Turkish. A Tatar town with a 'pleasure-garden palace', it was the capital of the Crimean khans from the 15th century to 1783.

Bakoye, MALI
A river called the 'White River' from the Mandekan *ba* 'river' and *koye* 'white'.

Baku (Baky), AZERBAIJAN
Derived from the Persian *Bad Kube* 'blustery wind' or 'blown by winds'; or from *Bad Kiu* 'town of winds' from *külēk* 'wind'. Situated on the west coast of the Caspian Sea, it is exposed to strong winds. The name may, possibly, come from a tribe, the Bakan or Baki, who lived on the Apsheron peninsula between the 5th and 2nd centuries BC. It became the capital of the Shīrvān Shahs in the 12th century, fell to the Russians in 1723, but was retaken by the Persians in 1735. The Russians retook the city in 1806. It became the capital of Azerbaijan in 1920.

Balaklava, AUSTRALIA, UKRAINE
Ukraine: it is said to have received its first name, Symbalon, from the son of the Scythian prince Skiluros in the 2nd or 1st first century BC. However, it may represent the Greek *sumbolon* 'sign' and this is the more likely name to have evolved into the Genoese Cembalo.

A popular explanation for the present Ukrainian name has it coming from the Tatar *balık* 'fish' and possibly a word associated with the Turkish *yakala* 'to catch'. Originally a Greek city in the Crimea, it was conquered by the Genoese in 1357, by the Turks in 1475, and by the Russians in 1783. It was the site of the Battle of Balaklava in October 1854 during which the British Light Brigade famously charged down a valley towards retreating Russian cavalry and was cut to pieces. The town has given its name to the balaclava, a knitted woollen covering for the head and neck worn by the British against the cold and much favoured by modern criminals.

Balaton, Lake, HUNGARY
A lake with a name probably from a Slavonic word *blatt* associated with the Russian *boloto* 'marsh' or 'swamp'. It is very shallow, no more than 37 ft (11 m) deep.

Balboa, PANAMA
Founded in 1914 and named after Vasco Núñez de Balboa (1475–1519), a Spanish conquistador and explorer, who was the first European to see the Pacific Ocean in 1513.

Balchik, BULGARIA *Krunoi, Dionysopolis*
The original Greek name was taken from the local springs, while the Roman name honoured Dionysus (also known as Bacchus), the god of wine. After the harbour had silted up during the 6th century, the Turks renamed it the '(City of) Wet Clay' from *balçík*. The town belonged to Romania between 1913 and 1940.

Baldock, ENGLAND/UK *Baldoce*
Founded in the 12th century by the Knights Templar, who called it Baldac. This was an Old French name for Baghdad and probably recalled their association with that Arab city during the Crusades.

Balearic Islands (Islas Baleares), SPAIN
An autonomous community which the Greeks and Romans originally called Gymnesiae, and which today in the form of Gimnesias, refers to Majorca, Minorca, and Cabrera; the smaller western group is called the Pitiusas Islands and consists of Ibiza and Formentera. In due course, the Romans used the name Baliarides, a modification of Balharides which meant 'slingers' or 'those who hurl stones from a sling' in Iberian. Having been occupied by the Phoenicians, Greeks, Carthaginians, Romans, Vandals, Byzantines, and Moors, James I the Conqueror (1208–76), the Spanish King of Aragón (1213–76) drove the Moors out beginning in 1229. In 1298–1349 the islands constituted an independent kingdom before rejoining Aragón. Under the Treaty of Utrecht

in 1713 Minorca was ceded to the British until 1802. The islands were established as a Spanish province in 1833. *See* IBIZA/MAJORCA/MINORCA.

Balikpapan, KALIMANTAN/INDONESIA
The name has various possible meanings from *balík* 'behind' or 'reverse side of' and *papan* 'shelter' or 'board', 'plank' or 'piece of wood'.

Balkanabat, TURKMENISTAN *Nebitdag*
Renamed in 2000 as 'City of the Balkan (Province)' of which it is the capital. Established as a settlement for oil workers in 1933, its previous name meant 'Oil Mountain' from *nebit* 'oil' and *dag* 'mountain'.

Balkan Peninsula The peninsula comprises the countries of south-eastern Europe: Albania, Bosnia and Herzegovina, Bulgaria, Croatia, Greece, Macedonia, Moldova, Romania, Serbia and Montenegro, and Slovenia. In use since the early 19th century, the name means 'mountains' from the Turkish *balkan* 'wooded mountain range'. The Turkish for 'The Balkans' is *Balkanlar*. It was coined to describe those lands that had been under the direct control of the Ottoman Empire since the Treaty of Karlowitz (now Sremski Karlovci, Serbia) in 1699. Apart from the break-up of Yugoslavia in 1991, today's national frontiers derive from the peace settlement after the First World War. The term 'balkanization' is taken to mean the disintegration of an area into a number of smaller, mutually hostile, states.

Balkh, AFGHANISTAN *Bactra-Zariaspa, Bakhtrish, Vahlíka, Wazírābād*
Named after the Balkh River, the meaning of which is unknown. A great city in about 330 BC, it became the capital of the Greek Central Asian Kingdom of Bactria; Bakhtrish is the Old Persian name. Captured by the Arabs in the 8th century, it became the capital of Khorāsān. It changed hands between invading nomads many times before being destroyed by the Mongols in 1220. Although rebuilt, it fell into decline as a result of the rise of nearby Mazār-e Sharif. It is now little more than a village.

Balkhash, Lake (Balqash Köli), KAZAKHSTAN
'Marshy Place'. The town of Balkhash is named after the lake.

Ballantrae (Baile na Tràgha), SCOTLAND/UK
'Town on the Shore' from *baile* and *traigh* 'shore'.

Ballarat, VICTORIA/AUSTRALIA
Founded in 1854, the name comes from two Aboriginal words meaning 'resting place'.

Ballina, AUSTRALIA, IRELAND
1. Australia (New South Wales): founded in 1842, the name is derived from an Aboriginal word meaning the 'Place where Oysters are in Abundance'.
2. Ireland: there are two towns with this name in Mayo and Tipperary. The Irish name is Béal an Átha 'Mouth of the Ford' from *béal* 'mouth' and *átha*.

Ballymena (An Baile Meánach), NORTHERN IRELAND/UK
'Middle Homestead' from *baíle* and *méanach* 'middle'. It was, and is, a market centre and has been a district since 1973.

Ballymoney (Baile Mónaidh), NORTHERN IRELAND/UK
'Towland on the Moor' from *baíle* and *morredh* 'moor'.

Balmoral, AUSTRALIA, CANADA, UK, ZAMBIA
All five towns with this name are believed to have been named by Scottish settlers after Balmoral Castle, a royal residence in Scotland. The name originates from Gaelic *both* 'hut' and an uncertain second element. Balmoral has given its name to a highland bonnet.

Balochistan, PAKISTAN *Gedrosia*
A province meaning the 'Land of the Balochi People'. They only arrived in the area during the 14th century, having probably come from Persia. They are sometimes referred to as the Baluch. They may have taken their name from the Urdu *baluc* 'peak', since they lived in the mountains; the word can also mean 'wanderer' or 'nomad'.

Balta, ROMANIA, UKRAINE, USA
Ukraine: 'Marsh' or 'Swamp' from the Romanian/Moldovan *baltă*. In 1795 it was renamed Yelensk after the Russian Princess Yelena Pavlovna (1784–1803), a granddaughter of Catherine II the Great[†], before returning to its original name in the 20th century.

Bălţi, MOLDOVA *Belts/Bel'tsy*
'Marsh' or 'Swamp' from the Romanian/Moldovan *baltă*.

Baltic States Comprising Estonia, Latvia, and Lithuania, the region may have taken its name from *Mare Balticum* 'Baltic Sea'. This was named by the Romans after an island (which did not exist) which they called Baltica. From the middle of the 19th century the people generically became known as Balts, although the Estonians are not Balts and speak an entirely different language, one of the Finno-Ugric group of languages. The name Balt, however, may be derived from *bælt*, a Danish word used to describe some of the narrow

passages, or belts, between the Danish islands. The Russian name for the area is Pribaltika, meaning 'adjacent to the Baltic Sea'.

Baltimore, IRELAND, USA
USA (Maryland): founded in 1729, it was named after the Lords Baltimore, who owned Maryland, and in particular after the 2nd Baron, Cecilius Calvert (1605–75). Their hereditary title came from George Calvert (1579–1632), the 1st Baron, whose family seat was at Baltimore, County Cork, Ireland. Baltimore itself means 'Grand Settlement'.

Baltistān, PAKISTAN
A disputed geographic region in the Pakistani-controlled part of Kashmir with a name meaning the 'Land of the Baltis', Muslims of Tibetan origin. It was a largely inaccessible mountain kingdom until it began to expand in the late 16th century to include Chitral and Ladakh.

Baltiysk, KALININGRAD/RUSSIA *Pillau*
Originally a German town in East Prussia, it was called Pillau between 1686 and 1946. It was ceded to the Soviet Union in 1945 under the terms of the Potsdam Agreement (July/Aug. 1945) and renamed. It is not exactly clear what either name means, but Baltiysk is probably a shortening of the adjective *baltiyskiy*, with *gorod* understood, to give 'Town on the Baltic'.

Bamako, MALI
The name may be derived from *Bamma-ko* 'beyond Bamma's', to mean 'a village beyond Bamma's (settlement)' in Bambara (a version of the Mandekan language). Originally it comprised a number of villages. It became the capital of French West Africa, then known as French Sudan, in 1908 and is now the capital of Mali.

Bamberg, BAVARIA/GERMANY
A shortening of Babenberg, the ancestral castle of the Babenberg family. In 976 Leopold I of Babenberg became Margrave of Ostmark (Austria) and his descendants ruled until the male line died out in 1246. The name Babenberg is said to come from Babe, a daughter of Otto II (955–83), German king (961–83) and Holy Roman Emperor (967–83).

Bamenda, CAMEROON
A German name for the people of Mendakwe whom they called Bamendakwe. As their settlement grew into a town it became known as Bamenda; the German fort was called Bamunda.

Banat, HUNGARY-ROMANIA-SERBIA AND MONTENEGRO
A name historically used to describe any frontier district under a *ban* 'governor'; *ban* is

derived from a Persian word meaning 'lord'. The best known is the Banat of Temesvár (now Timişoara), the historic term for what is now the western marches of Romania. Until 1920 the Banat was primarily a part of Hungary; it received this title after the Treaty of Passarowitz in 1718 without ever having been ruled by a Ban. In 1920 it was divided between Hungary, Romania, and Yugoslavia under the terms of the Treaty of Trianon.

Banbridge (Droichead Na Banna), NORTHERN IRELAND/UK
A town and a district established in 1973. It was given the name after a bridge was built over the River Bann in 1712.

Banbury, ENGLAND/UK *Banesberie*
'Banna's Stronghold' from an Old English personal name and *burh*. It is known for its cross which is mentioned in a children's nursery rhyme and gives its name to a special spiced cake.

Bandar Abbas (Bandar-e 'Abbās), IRAN
Cormosa, Djarun/Gamru/Gombroon/Gāmerūn
'Port of Abbas' from the personal name and *bandar*. It was developed by, and named after, 'Abbās I the Great (1571–1629), Shah of Persia (1588–1629), in 1632 as a substitute port for Hormuz which had been captured by the Portuguese more than a century earlier.

Bandar Bushehr (Bandar-e Būshehr), IRAN
Rishehr, Abū Shehr, Būshehr/Bushire
Rishehr is an abbreviated form of Rew Shahr. From Rishehr came Abū Shehr 'Father of the Town' which became Būshehr which was then corrupted to Bushire by English sailors. The founder of the modern city-port in 1734 was Nādir Shah (1688–1747), who seized the Persian throne in 1736. He intended the port to be the principal naval base for the Persian Navy. Consequently *Bandar* was added to its name.

Bandar Khomeyni (Bandar-e Khomeyni),
IRAN *Bandar-e Shahpūr*
'Port of Khomeyni', having been the 'Shah's Port'. Shahpūr means 'Son of a King'. It was renamed in honour of Ayatollah Khomeyni (c.1900–89), religious and political leader, who was head of state (1979–89).

Bandar Seri Begawan, BRUNEI *Brunei Town*
'Distinguished Port' from *bandar* and *seri begawan* 'distinguished' or 'honoured'. It was renamed in 1970 in honour of the sultan's father, Sir Omar Ali Saifuddin, sultan (1950–67), who had abdicated in 1967. Capital of the Sultanate of Brunei.

Bandar Sri Aman, SARAWAK/MALAYSIA
Simanggang
'Abode of Peace' from *aman* 'peace' and *bandar*. Lying on the Batang River, it is a small port.

Bandar Torkmen (Bandar-e Torkman), IRAN
'Port of the Turkomans.' It lies on the Caspian Sea close to the border with Turkmenistan.

Bandirma, TURKEY *Panormus, Panderma*
Derived from the original Greek name to mean 'Safe Harbour' from *pan* 'all' and *ormos* 'chain'; this indicates a 'chain of boats', thus an 'anchorage'. The port gave its name to pandermite, also known as priceite, a mineral.

Bandundu, DEMOCRATIC REPUBLIC OF THE CONGO *Banningville*
A province and a city. Its previous name recognized a Belgian official, Émile Banning (1836–98), who was instrumental in establishing the Congo Free State in 1885. The present Bantu name, whose meaning is unknown, was adopted in 1966.

Bandung, JAVA/INDONESIA *Kota Kembang*
The previous name meant 'City of Flowers' from the Indonesian *kota* and *kembang* 'flowers'. The city was founded by the Dutch in 1810 on a plateau over 2 000 ft (610 m) above sea level as a hill station retreat from the sultry heat of the plains. The present name comes from the Malay *bandong* 'embankment' or 'dam'.

Bangalore, KARNĀTAKA/INDIA
A city which takes its name from the fact that it was founded as a mud fort in 1537 by Kempe Gowda, a local chief in the Hoysaḷa Kingdom, in an area where the population spoke mainly Bengali. The Bengalis took their name from a chief called Banga.

Bangkok (Krung Thep), THAILAND
'District of Wild Plums' from *bang* 'district' or 'village', and *makok* 'wild plum'. This is the original site which now is only a small part of the modern city. The name Bangkok evolved from Bancok which was the name printed on 17th-century Western maps. The Thai name, Krung Thep, is the shortened version of the full name—the world's longest place-name given to the city in 1782 by Rama I, King of Siam (1782–1809). It means 'City of Angels' from *krung* 'city' and *thep* 'angel'. The full name is 'Krungthep Mahanakhon Bovorn Rattanakosin Mahintharayutthaya Mahadilokphop Noppharat Ratchathani Burirom Udomratchaniwet Mahasathan Amonphiman Avatansathit Sakkathathiya Visnukarmprasit' (although there are other versions of this). This has been translated as 'The City of Angels, the Great City, the

Residence of the Emerald Buddha, the Impregnable City of Ayutthaya of the God Indra, the Grand Capital of the World endowed with Nine Precious Gems, the Happy City Abounding in Enormous Royal Palaces which resemble the Heavenly Abode wherein dwell the Reincarnated Gods, a City given by Indra and built by Vishnukarm'. It became the capital of Siam in 1782 when Rama I (1737–1809), King of Siam (1782–1809) ascended the throne and moved the court from Thonburi (capital 1767–82) on the west bank of the River Chao Phraya to a small trading post called Bangkok on the opposite bank because he thought the new location was more easily defended. The Bangkok Metropolis is a region of Thailand.

Bangladesh *Vanga/Vangala/Banga/Bangala, East Bengal, East Pakistan*
The People's Republic of Bangladesh (Gana Prajatantri Bangladesh) since its creation in 1971. When independent India was partitioned in 1947, West Bengal became part of India while East Bengal joined Pakistan. It was previously the province of East Pakistan (also referred to as the East Wing) (1947–71), part of Bengal (officially East Bengal in 1905–12) when it was part of British India (1857–1947) and of the English East India Company (1764–1857). The name means 'Land of the Bengalis' from *deś* 'land' or 'country'; the Bengalis take their name from Banga, chief of the Dravidian-speaking Bang tribe, who settled in the region *c*.1000 BC.

Bangor, UK, USA
1. UK (Wales): formerly Benchoer from which the present name, '(Row of Poles in a) Wattle Fence', comes. This protected a church built in the 6th century.
2. UK (Northern Ireland): named after the Welsh Bangor. The local name is Beannchar meaning 'Peaked', perhaps a 'Pointed Wattle Fence' around the monastery.
3. USA: there are seven towns with this name in the USA, the most important being in Maine. It was originally called Kenduskeag Plantation in 1776 and renamed Sunbury in 1787. According to one local tradition, its present name is derived from the tune of a psalm called Bangor which the Reverend Seth Noble, the town's representative in the legislature, was whistling when the new town was being registered in 1791. There are other similar stories. The Bangor in Pennsylvania was founded in 1866 by a Welshman who named it after the Bangor in Wales.

Bangui, CENTRAL AFRICAN REPUBLIC
'The Rapids'. It was founded in 1889 as a French military outpost at the confluence of

the Oubangui and Mpoko Rivers. Two years later the French moved to a site by some rapids on the Oubangui. In 1906 it became the administrative centre of the Oubangui-Chari region of French Equatorial Africa. It is now the Republic's capital.

Bangweulu, ZAMBIA
A lake meaning 'Large Water' in Bantu.

Bāniyās, SYRIA *Paneas, Caesarea Philippi*
Situated on the Golan Heights, it has been occupied by Israel since the war of 1967; the Heights were annexed by Israel in 1981. The present name comes from the original Greek name which honoured the god Pan. The Roman name honoured Caesar Augustus[†] and Philip (20 BC–AD 34), one of the sons of Herod the Great (73–4 BC) and tetrarch over part of the Kingdom of Judaea.

Banja, SERBIA/SERBIA AND MONTENEGRO
Two towns have this name which means 'Spa' because they were built close to mineral springs.

Banja Luka, BOSNIA AND HERZEGOVINA
'Baths of Luke' (St Luke) from the Serbo-Croat *banja* 'spa'. It was a Roman watering place and military centre in an area which legend associates with St Luke. Banja Luka was the capital of the Ottoman Turkish province of Bosnia between 1583 and 1639. In 1738, at the Battle of Banja Luka, the Turks defeated the Austrians and at the subsequent Treaty of Belgrade a year later the present northern border of Bosnia was demarcated. In 1998 the town became the 'capital' of Republika Srpska, the Serbian region of Bosnia and Herzegovina.

Banjarmasin, KALIMANTAN/INDONESIA *Bandar Masih*
Named after the Banjarese. Founded in 1526, it became the most important sultanate on the whole island with the exception of Brunei. *Banjar* means a 'line', 'row', or 'series' while *masin* means 'salty' or 'briny' from *asin* 'salt'. The earlier name probably indicated a port where salt was exported.

Banjul, THE GAMBIA *Bathurst*
Established as a military post in 1816 by Captain Alexander Grant in an attempt to control the illegal slave trade. He named it after Henry Bathurst (1762–1834), 3rd Earl Bathurst, the British secretary for war and the colonies at the time (1812–27). The city became the capital of The Gambia in 1965 and its original Mandinka name of Banjul was restored in 1973. It has been suggested that this name originated with the Portuguese in the 15th century. They asked the name of the place from some locals who misunderstood

the question to be 'what are you doing?'; they answered *bangjulo* 'making rope matting'.

Banks Island(s), NORTHWEST TERRITORIES/ CANADA, VANUATU
Both are named after the eminent naturalist and explorer, Sir Joseph Banks (1743–1820), president of the Royal Society (1778–1820), who sailed with Captain Cook[†] on his first voyage round the world in 1768–71.

Bann (An Bhanna), NORTHERN IRELAND/UK
A river meaning 'The Goddess'.

Bannockburn, SCOTLAND/UK *Bannokburne*
Probably '(Place on the) Stream surrounded by Peaks' from the Scottish Gaelic *banoc*, a reference to the hill from which the river flowed; both the Scottish and English *burna* means 'stream' or 'brook', *burn* being the general Scottish equivalent of 'brook'.

Bannu, NORTH-WEST FRONTIER/PAKISTAN *Pona, Fort Dalīpgarh, Dalīpnagar, Edwardesābād*
Founded as a fort in 1848 by Lieutenant (later, Major General Sir) Herbert Edwardes (1819–68) after the young Sikh ruler of the Punjab, Maharajah Dalīp Singh, the name was changed to the 'City of Dalīp' as it grew and then 'Town of Edwardes' in 1869 after his death in 1868. A one-time Commissioner of Peshawar, he won the respect of the local tribesmen by forbidding plunder and insisting that the Sikh troops pay for everything they took from the villagers. The town was renamed Bannu after its original name, Pona, sometimes spelt Bunnoo, in 1903.

Banská Bystrica, SLOVAKIA *Neusohl, Besztercebánya*
Situated at the confluence of the Hron and Bystrica (Beszterce in Hungarian) Rivers, *bystrica* means 'fast-flowing'; *banská* and *banyá* mean 'mine' or 'pit'. Since the Middle Ages the area has been known for its silver and copper mines. The first German name meant 'New Bottom' from *neu* and *sohle* 'bottom of a mine'.

Banstead, ENGLAND/UK *Benestede*
'Place where Beans are grown' from the Old English *bēan* and *stede* 'place'.

Banteay Chhmar, CAMBODIA
'Narrow Fortress', *banteay* being the Khmer word for 'fortified temple'.

Bao'an, CHINA
Shaanxi: 'Protected Peace' from *băo* 'protect' or 'keep' and *ăn*.

Baoulé, MALI
A river called the 'Red River' from the Mandekan *ba* 'river'.

Baqubah (Ba'qūbah), IRAQ
'House of Jacob' from the Aramaic *Bāya* and *'qūbā* 'Jacob'.

Bar, MONTENEGRO/SERBIA AND MONTENEGRO *Antivaris, Antibarum*
Built as a fortification on the coast against the Avars, hence its original name from which the present name has evolved. It has also been suggested that it means 'Opposite Bari', the Italian port. Bar was under Venetian rule in 1443–1571 and Ottoman Turkish in 1571–1878.

Baraboo, WISCONSIN/USA
According to tradition named after a French trapper, Jean Baribault, or after two French brothers, also called Baribault, who owned a mill at the mouth of the River Baraboo.

Baracoa, CUBA
Founded in 1512 as the first Spanish settlement, it served as Cuba's capital between 1518 and 1522. Surrounded by mountains, the port has a name which comes from a local native word for 'elevated land'.

Baranavichy, BELARUS
'(Place where) Sheep Graze' from the Russian *baran* 'sheep' or 'ram'.

Barbados, WEST INDIES
'Bearded' or 'The Bearded Ones' from the Spanish *barbados*. Visited by Spanish explorers in 1518, it was given this name because of the trails of moss which hung from the banyan (Indian fig) trees. The island was settled by the English in 1627, becoming a British colony in 1652. Barbados gained independence in 1966 as a constitutional monarchy with the British Queen as head of state.

Barbary Coast, NORTH AFRICA
The historical name for the North African coastline stretching westwards from Egypt to the Atlantic. The name comes from the region's inhabitants, the Berbers, whose name may be attributed to the Greek *barbaros* 'barbarous', that is, people who did not speak Greek, or foreigners. Muslim pirates operated from coastal cities, preying upon Mediterranean shipping during the 17th, 18th, and 19th centuries.

Barberton, SOUTH AFRICA, USA
1. South Africa (Mpumalanga): settled in the 1880s as Barber's Reef, it was a gold-buying and mining centre named after Graham Barber, one of the early successful prospectors.
2. USA (Ohio): founded in 1891 by, and named after, Ohio C. Barber as the new location for his match factory.

Barbourville, KENTUCKY/USA
Founded in 1800 and named after James
Barbour who offered land on which the city
could be built.

Barbuda *See* ANTIGUA AND BARBUDA.

Barcelona, SPAIN, VENEZUELA Spain
(Catalonia): formerly Faventia Julia Augusta
Paterna Barcino, Barcinona, Barshaluna.
The city was originally believed to owe its
name to the family of the Carthaginian general
Hamilcar Barca (c.270–228 BC). However, this is
now considered unlikely and the name may
come from a Roman, Faventia Julia Augusta
Paterna Barcino. The city was founded by the
Romans as an *oppidum* 'fortified camp',
becoming an Augustan colony by 15 BC. By 500
it was under Visigoth rule as Barcelona (and
was the capital). It fell to the Moors in 717,
being renamed Barshaluna. Barcelona was the
seat of the Republican government during
1938–9.

Bardějov, SLOVAKIA
'Bardej's Place' from the personal name.

Barents Sea (Russian: **Barentsevo More**)
Murmean Sea
Named after Willem Barents[†] who attempted
to find a northern passage between the
Atlantic and the Pacific. He died on his third
unsuccessful attempt. The new name was first
used on a chart in 1853.

Bari, DEMOCRATIC REPUBLIC OF THE CONGO,
ITALY
Italy (Apulia): a port whose Latin name was
Barium. This name comes from the Latin and
Greek *baris*, an Egyptian 'barge' or type of raft.
From 1863 to 1931 the town was called Bari of
Apulia.

Barkly West, WESTERN CAPE;
Barkly East, EASTERN CAPE/SOUTH AFRICA
Barkly West, formerly Klipdrift meaning
'Rocky Ford' in Afrikaans and then simply
Barkly, was founded in 1869 and renamed
after Sir Henry Barkly (1815–98) the following
year. Barkly East was named after him in 1874
at which time 'West' was added to Barkly. Sir
Henry was governor of Cape Colony between
1870 and 1877.

Barlaston, UK, ZAMBIA
UK (England): formerly Beorelfestun and
Bernulvestone 'Beornwulf's Farmstead' from
an Old English personal name and *tūn*.

Bar-le-Duc, LORRAINE/FRANCE *Castrum Barrum*
Originally the 'Camp of Barrum' from the
possibly Celtic *barr* 'height', it became the
capital of a county in the 10th century
and later of a duchy. Le-Duc 'the duke' was

thus added to proclaim its new status and
to differentiate between this Bar and
others.

Bärmer, RĀJASTHĀN/INDIA *Bahadamer*
The present name is a contraction of the
original name which meant the 'Hill Fort of
Bahada'; he was a local *rāja*.

Barnard Castle, ENGLAND/UK *Castellum
Bernardi*
Named after Barnard Balliol, who rebuilt the
castle in 1112–32.

Barnaul, ALTAY TERRITORY/RUSSIA
Founded as a metal works c.1738, the city lies
on the confluence of the Rivers Ob and
Barnaulka, after which it is named. The name
might be derived from any one of a number of
words for 'wolf': *büre* in Tatar, *bo'ri* in Uzbek,
börä in Uighur, or *boru* in Ket. With the
additional Ket *ul* 'river' the name could mean a
'River along which Wolves are common'.

Barnsley, ENGLAND/UK *Berneslai*
'Beorn's (woodland) Clearing' from the Old
English *lēah* 'glade' or 'forest clearing'.

Barnstaple, ENGLAND/UK *Bardanstapol,
Barnestaple*
The original Anglo-Saxon settlement by a ford
on the Taw Estuary may be named after the
Bearda family who guarded the crossing to
which has been added 'staple', a reference to
the area's main product which was wool.
Alternatively, the name may mean 'Post of the
Battleaxe' in reference to a meeting place
here, from *stapol* 'wooden post'.

Barotseland, ZAMBIA
A historic region inhabited by the Lozi. They
and their language have also been known as
Rozi. Missionaries spelt the language Rotse and
called the people baRotse. The *ba-* is the plural
of a Bantu noun which indicates human beings.

Barquisimeto, VENEZUELA *Nueva Segovia*
Founded in 1522 by the temporary Spanish
governor, Juan de Villegas, who named it after
his home in Spain. Its present name is a
corruption of Variquecemeto, an old native
word meaning 'River of Ash-coloured Water'.
This is the third site for the city which now lies
on the Turbio River.

Barrackpore, WEST BENGAL/INDIA
Also called Chanak or Achánok, the somewhat
mongrel nature of the name recognizes the
fact that it has been a military garrison since
1775 with *pur* added.

Barrancabermeja, COLOMBIA *La Tora*
'Reddish Cliffs' from the Spanish *barranca*
'gully' or 'ravine', and *bermejo* 'reddish'.

Originally a Native American settlement, it was renamed Barrancas-Bermejas, a reference to the local cliffs, after the Spanish discovered it in the 1530s.

Barranco, BELIZE, PERU
Peru: founded as a small beach resort in 1874, its name means 'Cliff' in Spanish, a reference to its position over 200 feet (60 m) above sea level.

Barre, USA
1. Massachusetts: named after Colonel Isaac Barre, a supporter of America in the British Parliament.
2. Vermont: founded in 1793 as Wildersburgh, it was soon renamed after the Barre in Massachusetts.

Barrie, ONTARIO/CANADA
A landing stage on a supply route to the Great Lakes, it is named after Commodore Robert Barrie, who commanded a naval squadron in Kingston.

Barrington, CANADA, USA
USA (Rhode Island): originally Swansea, it was renamed in 1717 after John Shute (1678–1734), Viscount Barrington, an eminent English lawyer and champion of religious freedom. The town was transferred from Massachusetts to Rhode Island Colony in 1746, becoming part of Warren. However, in 1770, Warren was split, the western half being named Barrington.

Barron, QUEENSLAND/AUSTRALIA
A river named in 1870 after T. H. Barron, a chief clerk in the state police.

Barrow-in-Furness, ENGLAND/UK *Barrai*
'Promontory Island' from the possible Celtic *barr* 'promontory' or 'height', rather than the more usual Old English *bearu* 'small wood' or 'grove', and *ey*. Furness distinguishes it from other towns named Barrow and means 'headland by the rump-shaped island' from the Old Scandinavian *futh* and *nes* 'headland'.

Barry, UK, USA
1. UK (Wales): locally Y Barri and originally Barren 'hill brook' from the Welsh *y* 'the' and *barr* 'summit of a hill'.
2. USA (Illinois): originally named Barre, after the town in Vermont, before being changed by the US Post Office.

Barstow, CALIFORNIA/USA *Fishpond, Waterman Junction*
Founded in 1880, it was given its present name in 1886 in honour of William Barstow Strong, the president of the Santa Fé Railroad at the time.

Bartle Frere, Mt, QUEENSLAND/AUSTRALIA
A mountain named in 1873 after Sir Henry Bartle Edward Frere (1815–84), commissioner of Sind (1850–62), governor of Bombay (1862–7) and governor of the Cape Colony (1877–80).

Bartlesville, OKLAHOMA/USA
Founded in the 1870s by a trading post established by Jacob Bartles who was the leading entrepreneur.

Bartow, GERMANY, USA
USA (Florida): founded in 1851 as Fort Blount, it was renamed in 1867 after Francis S. Bartow, a Confederate general killed during the Civil War (1861–5). The town in Georgia is also named after the general.

Barysaw, BELARUS *Borisov*
The present name, adopted in 1993, is the Belarusian version of the Russian name. It may indicate the site of an ancient battle, the Slavonic *bor* meaning 'battle'; or the city may be named after a 12th-century Polotsk prince, Boris Vselavich.

Bashkortostan, RUSSIA *Bashkiriya*
A republic with the name meaning the 'Land of the Bashkirs (or Bashkorts)', a Turkic people who settled here between the 13th and 15th centuries. They may derive their name from the Turkish *baş* 'head' and *kurt* 'wolf', an animal with which the Bashkirs associated themselves. Russia acquired the region in 1552 after the Kazan khanate was conquered. It became the Bashkir Autonomous Soviet Socialist Republic in 1919 and adopted the present name in 1993.

Basildon, ENGLAND/UK *Berleduna, Bertlesdon*
'Beorhtel's Hill' from an Old English personal name and *dūn*. Basildon New Town was founded in 1949.

Basilicata, ITALY *Lucania*
A region in the south whose name is derived from *basilikós* 'imperial' or 'of the king', the title given to the local Byzantine administrator or governor. Previously Lucania had been part of the Greek region of Oenotria and took its name from the Lucanians, a Samnite people.

Basingstoke, ENGLAND/UK *Basingastoc, Basingestoches*
'The Outlying Place where the Followers of Basa live' from *-ingas-* and *stoc*.

Basle (French: **Bâle**; German: **Basel**), SWITZERLAND *Robur, Basilia*
Originally a Celtic settlement and given the Roman name Robur from the Latin *roburetum*

'oak grove'. The present name is derived from the Greek *basíleia* 'royal', when Valentinian I (321–75), Roman emperor (364–75), developed the settlement into a fort in 374. In 1501 Basle joined the Swiss Confederation and in 1833 the canton was divided into two demi-cantons, one urban, Basel-Stadt, and one rural, Basel-Landschaft, although they operate as full cantons.

Basque Country (Basque: **Euskardi**; Spanish: **País Vasco**; French: **Pays Basque**), SPAIN-FRANCE *Vasconia*
A cultural and historic region extending across the western Pyrenees into south-western France and north-eastern Spain. In Spain it comprises an autonomous community named after the Euskaldunak (Basques) whose language is Euskara. The modern 'Basque' is derived from the original Vascones, the tribal name; hence, Vasconia. The Basque terrorist group calls itself ETA (*Euzkadi Ta Azkatasuna* 'Basque Homeland and Liberty').

Basra (al-Baṣrah), IRAQ *Balsora*
Founded in 638 on the site of a Persian settlement as a military post on the western bank of the Shatt al-Arab waterway, formed by the merging of the Euphrates and Tigris Rivers. The name appears to derive from the root word *baṣara* which means 'to see' or 'have an insight to'. This may allude to the strategic location of the city as a landmark or viewpoint. The city was captured by the Ottoman Turks in 1668 and became the capital of an Ottoman province. It fell under British control in 1916 and remained so until the British mandate expired in 1932.

Basse-Normandie, FRANCE
A region meaning 'Lower Normandy'.

Basse-Terre, GUADELOUPE
An island and also capital of Guadeloupe. Its French name means 'Low Land' from *terre* 'land', a reference to its location at the foot of the Soufrière volcano.

Basseterre, ST KITTS & NEVIS
'Low Land'. Founded in 1627, it is the chief town of St Kitts and the capital of the state.

Bass Strait A strait separating the mainland of Australia and Tasmania discovered by, and named after, George Bass (1771–1803), a naval surgeon and explorer who travelled around the area in 1798. He proved that Tasmania was an island.

Bastia, CORSICA/FRANCE *Marina di Cardo*
Its name was changed after a *bastiglia* 'keep' was built by the Genoese to defend the town. It

was the capital of Corsica between 1380 and 1811.

Bastrop, USA
Louisiana, Texas: both are named after the Mexican Baron de Bastrop, who was a land commissioner in Texas in 1823.

Basutoland *See* LESOTHO.

Batak, BULGARIA *Desposhovo, Desposhovo Mahallesi*
'Marsh'. The previous Turkish names meant 'Place of the Despot'.

Batalha, PORTUGAL
'Battle'. This refers to the Battle of Aljubarrota in 1385 when John I (1357–1433), King of Portugal (1385–1433), defeated John I (1358–90), King of Castile (1379–90), thereby ensuring Portugal's independence. The town actually takes its name from the Dominican Abbey, Santa Maria da Vitória 'St Mary of the Victory' or Santa Maria da Batalha 'St Mary of the Battle'.

Batavia, USA
New York: named after the Batavian Republic, created by the French after their victory in 1795 to refer to the Netherlands. Other cities so called are generally named after the Batavia in New York. Batavia takes its name from a Germanic tribe, the Batavi. *See* JAKARTA.

Bath, CANADA, JAMAICA, ST KITTS & NEVIS, UK, USA
1. UK (England): originally called Aquae Calidae '(Place of) Warm Waters' after the complex of Roman baths and sacred hot springs. It was later renamed Aquae Sulis and dedicated to the local pagan Celtic water-goddess Sulis. The Anglo-Saxon Akemanchester, from Acemannesceastre, 'Roman Town associated with a Man called Acemann', enjoyed local popularity as 'aching man's place', a reasonable description of the place to which those suffering from rheumatism went. By the time of the Domesday Book (1086) it was known as Bade. The city gave its name to Bath (invalid) chairs, which were invented about 1750 by James Heath of Bath, Bath buns, and Bath Oliver biscuits by the eminent physician, Dr William Oliver.
2. USA: the Bath in Maine is named after the English city, the city in North Carolina is named after Sir William Pulteney (1684–1764), 1st Earl of Bath, while the Bath in New York is named after Lady Henrietta, Countess of Bath and Sir William Pulteney's daughter.

Bathsheba, BARBADOS
Named after one of the wives of the biblical King David, second King of Israel, and the mother of King Solomon.

Bathurst, NEW SOUTH WALES/AUSTRALIA, NEW BRUNSWICK/CANADA, EASTERN CAPE/SOUTH AFRICA
All these cities, and the Bathurst in the Gambia now renamed Banjul, are named after Henry Bathurst (1762–1834), 3rd Earl Bathurst, secretary of state for war and the colonies (1812–27).

Batinah (al-Bāṭinah), OMAN
An administrative region and coastal plain lying on the Gulf of Oman and meaning 'stomach' from baṭn since the Omanis liken the Jabal Akhdar 'Green Mountain' to the backbone of Oman with the Batinah as the 'stomach'; additionally, baṭin means 'inner' in the sense here perhaps of 'accessible'. On the other, western, side of the mountains is the Dhārihah 'outer' and here representing the 'back'.

Baton Rouge, LOUISIANA/USA
'Red Stick' or 'Red Pole' from the French *rouge* 'red'. Named by the French in 1719 after a red pole which, according to tradition, marked the boundary between two Native American tribes. It was ceded to Great Britain in 1763, but the Spanish captured the city at the first Battle of Baton Rouge in 1779. The city's inhabitants successfully rebelled against Spanish control at the second Battle of Baton Rouge in 1810.

Battle, ENGLAND/UK *La Bataïlge*
'(Place of) the Battle'. It is named after the Battle of Hastings between the English and Normans, which took place here, some 10 miles (16 km) north-west of Hastings, in 1066. An abbey was first built here to commemorate the battle. According to tradition, the high altar of the abbey marked the spot where Harold II (c.1020–66), the last Anglo-Saxon King of England (1066), placed his standards.

Battle Creek, MICHIGAN/USA
Given the name in 1833 after a 'battle' between two Native Americans and two surveyors on the bank of the Kalamazoo River.

Batumi, GEORGIA *Batumistsikhe, Batum*
It is said to take its name from the River Bat or Bathus, a Greek name with the meaning of 'deep'. On the left bank arose the first settlement, the Greek city of Batis with the Georgian *tsikhe* 'castle'. The name may come from the Greek *bathys limen* 'deep harbour'. It was a port in the independent principality of

Guria until seized by the Ottoman Turks in the 17th century. It was ceded to Russia in 1878.

Baturin, UKRAINE
Founded by the Poles as a military post in 1625, it was named after Stephen Báthory (1533–86), Prince of Transylvania (1571–76) who was elected the King of Poland (1575–86) by the Polish nobility.

Bat Yam, ISRAEL *Bayit ve Gan*
Founded in 1926 with a Hebrew name meaning 'House and Garden', the name was changed ten years later to 'Daughter of the Sea' from the Hebrew *bat* 'daughter' and *yam* 'sea'.

Batyevo, IVANOVO/RUSSIA
'Place of Batu', a reference to Batu Khan (d. *c.*1255), grandson of Genghis Khan and founder of the Golden Horde, who is said to have pitched his camp here in 1238 before sacking Suzdal and Vladimir.

Batys Qazaqstan, KAZAKHSTAN *Ural*
A province 'West Kazakhstan' from *batys* 'west'.

Bauchi, BAUCHI/NIGERIA *Yakubu* (town)
A state and town which, according to tradition, take their name from a local hunter called Baushe. The town of Bauchi, first called Yakubu, was founded by Yakubu and named after him in 1809. The Emirate of Bauchi was founded, probably the following year, by Yakubu, its first ruler.

Baumann Peak, TOGO
Named after the Austrian explorer, Oskar Baumann (1864–99), when Togo, then Togoland, was a German colony.

Bautzen, SAXONY/GERMANY *Budissin/Budyšin*
The present name is derived from the name of the Slav settlement, which itself is taken from a Slav personal name Budych or Budiš.

Bavaria (Bayern), GERMANY
A state named after a Germanic tribe, the Baiovarii, who settled in the region *c.*500, having defeated the Romans. A duchy since 562, Bavaria was given the status of a kingdom as a result of the Treaty of Pressburg in 1805. At the end of the First World War in 1918 it became a republic and in 1919 a state.

Bay City, MICHIGAN/USA
Takes its name from its location on Saginaw Bay in Lake Huron.

Bayeux, LOWER NORMANDY/FRANCE *Baiocasses, Augustodorum, Civitas Baiocassium*
The capital of the Gauls, it derives its name from that of the Celtic Baiocasses tribe. Taken by the Romans in the 1st century BC, it was

renamed in Latin Augustodorum 'Fort of
Augustus' after the Emperor Augustus[†] and
then the 'City of the Baiocasses'.

Baykal, Lake (Ozero Baykal), BURYATIYA
REPUBLIC-IRKUTSK/RUSSIA
A lake with a name of Tatar origin from *bay*
'rich' and *kül* 'lake'. The richness is a reference
to the many different species of fish and
plants.

Baykonur (Kazakh: Bayqongyr; Russian:
Baykonyr), KAZAKHSTAN *Tyuratam, Leninsk*
There are two cities in Kazakhstan with this
name. The larger one, in Qyzylorda Province,
was built in 1955 near the village of Tyuratam
(now Töretam) as the town for the Soviet long-
range missile test centre at the Baykonyr
Cosmodrome which later became a space
launch centre. In 1966 it was named after
Vladimir Lenin[†]. The name of the town was
changed later to recognize the space centre. In
1995 the Kazakhs agreed to lease to the
Russians an area around the Cosmodrome and
the city of Baykonyr for a period of twenty
years. Over 190 miles (300 km) to the north-
east in Qaraghandy Province lies the smaller
Baykonyr. *Bay* is the Russian for a 'bay', a rich
landowner in Central Asia and *konura* means
'kennel'. However, it is much more likely that
the *bay* here is the Kazakh for 'rich'; thus
Baykonyr might have the meaning of
'Settlement with many Dwellings'.

Bayonne, FRANCE, USA
1. France (Aquitaine): formerly the Latin
Lapurdum, the present name is taken from the
Low Latin *baia* 'bay', and the Basque *on* 'good'.
First produced here during the 17th century,
the bayonet took its name from the city.
2. USA (New Jersey): originally founded by the
Dutch in 1646 as Konstable Hoeck, it was
renamed in 1869.

Baýramaly, TURKMENISTAN *Merv*
The name was changed in 1884 when the
Russians annexed Merv and then built a new
township, which they also called Merv, some
19 miles (30 km) away. The new name for the
old Merv honoured a Persian nobleman,
Bayram Ali Khan, who had reversed the
city's decline in the 18th century. The district
of Baýramaly was previously known as
Bayram-Aliyiskiy. The name Bayram Ali
means 'Festival of Ali' from the Turkish
bayram 'religious festival' or 'holiday' and Ali,
the son-in-law of the Prophet Muhammad[†]. *See*
MARY.

Bayreuth, BAVARIA/GERMANY
'The Bavarians' Clearing' from Old German
riuti 'clearing (in a wooded area)'.

Bayt al-Faqīh, YEMEN
Founded at the beginning of the 18th century
and named for Shaikh Ahmad ibn Musa, well
known as a scholarly man. The name means
'House of the Jurisprudent' from *bayt*
'dwelling', originally simply a tent, but now
also used for permanent buildings, and *faqīh*
'jurisprudent'.

Baytīn (Hebrew: **Bethel/Beit El),** WEST BANK
A Jewish town, the Arabic name is a version of
the Hebrew name and means 'House of God'.

Beacon, AUSTRALIA, USA
USA (New York): a city that takes its name from
the fires that were lit atop Mt Beacon to warn
George Washington[†] of British military
movements during the War of Independence
(1775–83).

Beaconsfield, AUSTRALIA, CANADA, UK
1. Australia (Tasmania): originally Cabbage
Tree Hill, it was renamed Brandy Creek when
gold was found in the area in 1870, it was
renamed again in 1879 after Benjamin Disraeli
(1804–81), 1st Earl of Beaconsfield, twice
British prime minister (1868, 1874–80).
2. Canada (Quebec): also named after
Disraeli's title.
3. UK (England): formerly Bekenesfelde 'Open
Country around a Beacon' from the Old
English *feld*.

Beagle Channel, ARGENTINA-CHILE
A strait at the southern tip of South America in
the Tierra del Fuego archipelago, it is named
after the *Beagle*, a ship commanded by Captain
Robert Fitzroy (1805–65), a British naval officer
who, together with Charles Darwin, explored
the area in 1833–4.

Beaufort, FRANCE, LUXEMBOURG, MALAYSIA,
USA
1. France (Nord-Pas-de-Calais and Rhône-
Alpes): there are two towns with this name
which has the meaning of a 'fine-looking fort'
from *beau* 'beautiful'.
2. USA (North and South Carolina): both are
named after Henry Somerset (1684–1714),
2nd Duke of Beaufort, one of the eight
owners of the colony of Carolina. The southern
town was founded in 1712 and the northern
in 1715.
3. The Beaufort Sea in the Arctic Ocean is
named after a British admiral, Sir Francis
Beaufort (1774–1857), who also gave his name
to the Beaufort Scale, invented in 1805, to
classify the strength of the wind at sea.

Beaufort West, WESTERN CAPE/SOUTH AFRICA
Beaufort
Founded in 1818 and named after Charles
Henry Somerset (1768–1831), 5th Duke of

Beaufort, father of the governor of the Cape Colony at the time. 'West' was added to differentiate the town from other Beauforts.

Beaujolais, FRANCE
An ancient province and famous wine-producing area, its name is derived from the small town of Beaujeu, literally 'beautiful game'. The Roman name of Beaujeu was Bellojocum 'Beautiful Mountain'.

Beaumont, BELGIUM, CANADA, FRANCE, IRELAND, NEW ZEALAND, USA
1. 'Beautiful Hill' from the French *beau* and *mont*. There are four towns in France, three in the USA, and one in each of the other countries with this name.
2. USA (Texas): the settlement of Tevis Bluff was founded by, and named after, Noah Tevis in 1825. Ten years later he sold some of his land to Henry Millard to build a town; he allegedly named it after his brother-in-law, Jefferson Beaumont.

Beaune, BURGUNDY/FRANCE *Belina, Belnocastrum*
The present name has evolved from the Roman names which recognized the Beaunois, whose capital this was.

Beauregard, MISSISSIPPI/USA
Named after Pierre Gustave Toutant Beauregard (1818–93), a general in the Confederate Army.

Beauvais, PICARDY/FRANCE *Caesaromagus, Civitas de Bellovacis*
Named after the Gaulish Bellovaci tribe whose capital it was, although its original name is not known; after Julius Caesar[†] captured it in 52 BC it was given the Roman name 'Caesar's Market' from the Gaulish *mago* 'market' or 'place' and then later 'City of the Bellovaci'.

Béchar, ALGERIA *Colomb-Béchar*
Originally named after the French Captain de Colomb, who explored the region in 1857, and after the nearby Mount Béchar.

Bechuanaland See BOTSWANA.

Beckley, WEST VIRGINIA/USA
Founded in 1838 by, and named after, General Alfred Beckley.

Bedford, CANADA, INDIA, SOUTH AFRICA, UK, USA
1. UK (England): formerly Bedanford and Bedeford 'Beda's Ford' over the River Ouse.
2. There are nine towns with this name in the USA, some named after the English Bedford. Others in the USA, Canada, India, and South Africa are named after various Dukes of Bedford.

3. Bedfordshire is a county in England named after the town of Bedford with the additional *scīr*.

Beersheba (Hebrew: **Be'er Sheva'**), ISRAEL
The name has two possible meanings: 'Well of the Oath' or 'Well of the Seven', from *be'er* 'well', and *sheva'* meaning both 'oath' and 'seven'. It was at Beersheba that Abraham and the King of the Philistines, Abimelech, agreed a covenant. Genesis 21: 27–8 mentions a covenant with Abraham setting aside 'seven ewe lambs'. Verse 31 states: 'Wherefore he called that place Beer-sheba because there they sware both of them.' The city was captured by the Arabs in the 7th century, by the Ottoman Turks in the 16th, and by the British in 1917.

Bega, AUSTRALIA, INDONESIA
Australia (New South Wales): settled in 1839 with an Aboriginal name meaning either 'beautiful' or 'camping place'.

Begusarai, BIHĀR/INDIA
Possibly derived from the Urdu *begam* 'begum', a title given in the Indian subcontinent to a married Muslim woman, and Persian *sarai* 'a palace' or 'inn for travellers'.

Beijing, BEIJING MUNICIPALITY/CHINA
Ji, Zhongdu, Yan, Youzhou, Nanjing, Zhongdu, Dadu, Khanbalik, Beiping, Peking
Built as a frontier trading town, it became the capital of the Yan Kingdom during the Warring States period (453–221 BC) and was called Ji 'Reeds', in reference to the local marshes; and sometimes Yan after the Kingdom of Yan. During the Tang dynasty (618–907) the Han people called it Youzhou. The city was destroyed by the Khitans, who founded the Liao dynasty (907–1125). They redeveloped the site as one of their capitals and named it Nanjing 'Southern Capital' from *nán* and *jīng* 'capital' in 938. When the Juchen from Manchuria overthrew the Liao they founded the state of Jin, having conquered the city in 1123; they gave it to the Northern Song who renamed it Yanshan 'Swallow Mountain' from *yàn* 'swallow' and *shān*. In 1153 the Juchen rebuilt Yanshan as their capital and called it Zhongdu 'Central Capital' from *zhōng* 'central' and *dū* 'capital'. Destroyed by Genghis Khan[†] in 1215, it was redeveloped in 1267 by the Mongol Khan, Khubilai, who wished to move his capital from Karakorum to China. He called the city Dadu 'Great Capital' from *dà* 'great' and *dū* and it became the foremost city in China. It was also given the Mongol name Khanbalik 'City of the Khan' after Khubilai. When the Mongols were overthrown in 1368 and the Ming dynasty inaugurated, Dadu was renamed Beiping 'Peace in the North' from *běi*

'north' and *píng* 'peace'. In 1403 it was renamed Beijing 'Northern Capital' and in 1421 it became the Ming capital. The city was captured in 1928 by Chiang Kai-shek, leader of the Guomindang (Nationalist Party), who made Nanjing (in Jiangsu) his capital. He changed Beijing's name back to Beiping. When Mao Zedong and the communists took the city in 1949 the name Beijing was restored. The city, with a few interruptions, has been the Chinese capital since 1272. Until the Pinyin system of transliteration was adopted in 1958 Beiping was known as Peiping and Beijing as Peking. Peking, however, is still used to describe Peking man, of the species *homo erectus*, Peking duck, and a breed of small dog, Pekinese, kept as a sacred dog by members of the Imperial family.

Beira, MOZAMBIQUE
Named after the former principality and province in northern Portugal to mean 'Close to Water' from the Portuguese *ribeira* 'river'. Although a Portuguese explorer anchored off the coast in the vicinity in 1487, it was not until 1891 that the Portuguese Mozambique Company founded the port as its headquarters. The former province of Beira is now called Sofala.

Beirut (Bayrūt), LEBANON *Colonia Iulia Augusta Felix Berytus, Beyrouth*
'The Wells' from the Hebrew *be'erot*, the plural of *be'er* 'well', an acknowledgement of the presence of numerous wells in the area. It became a Roman province in 14 BC, but by 551 had been destroyed by a series of earthquakes and a tidal wave. It fell to the Arabs in 635 and to the crusaders of the First Crusade in 1110. It was recaptured by the Muslims under Saladin in 1187, but was lost to the crusaders again ten years later. They were expelled by the Mamlūks in 1291 and in 1516 Beirut was occupied by the Ottoman Turks. Under the French mandate the city, known as Beyrouth, became the capital of the State of Greater Lebanon in 1920, of the Lebanese Republic in 1926 and of independent Lebanon in 1941.

Bei Shan, GANSU/CHINA
A mountain range 'Northern Mountains' from *běi* and *shān*.

Beja, PORTUGAL, TUNISIA
Portugal: a district and town, its present name is a corrupted form of its first Roman name, Pax Iulia. This was followed by Pax Augusta and Colonia Pacensis. All the Roman names are connected with 'peace', that is, the town's pacification during the times of Julius Caesar[†] and Augustus[†]; in particular, Caesar's peace

treaty with the Lusitanians which ended their resistance to Roman rule.

Bejaïa, ALGERIA *Saldae, Bijaya, Bougie*
Named after the Bejaïa tribe, whose name may be derived from the Arabic *baqāyā* 'survivors', who perhaps sought refuge here. By 1833 the name had evolved into Bougie as a result of the French presence. Because of its trade in wax candles with Europe, the French word for candle became *bougie*, a shortened version of *chandelles de Bougie* 'candles from Bougie'.

Bekaa Valley (al-Biqā'), LEBANON
The Arabic name means 'The Places' from *al* and the plural of *buq'ah* 'place' or 'spot'.

Békéscsaba, HUNGARY
'Peaceful Csaba' from the Hungarian *békés* and Csaba, a personal name, probably of Turkish origin.

Bela-Bela, LIMPOPO/SOUTH AFRICA *Warmbad*
Previously Warmbad 'Warm Baths', the present name was adopted in 2002 and is a Sotho word meaning 'Hot Springs' or 'Boiling Place' ('Bubble Bubble').

Belarus' *Belaya Rus, Byelorussiya*
The Republic of Belarus (Respublika Belarus) since September 1991. Previously the Byelorussian Soviet Socialist Republic before 1919 and after 1922 on the formation of the Soviet Union of which it was a founder member; the Byelorussian National Republic (1918). In 1839 Tsar Nicholas I[†] banned use of the name Byelorussia and insisted that the region be called the Northwest Territory. The present name is a shortening of Belaya Rus 'White Russia' from *belyy*. Why 'white' is not known. It may be because one of the three major branches of the Slavs settled here and they were predominantly of fair complexion. Many Byelorussian towns were sacked by the Tatars so the theory that 'white' means 'free', that is free from the Tatars, is dubious. However, 'free' may have the sense of freedom of spirit, the people always trying to defend their language and culture whatever the odds.

Bela Crkva, SERBIA/SERBIA AND MONTENEGRO *Weisskirchen, Fehértomplon*
'White Church' from the feminine of *beo* 'white' and *crkva*. It was called Weisskirchen, with the same meaning, when the town was the headquarters of an Austrian regiment serving in the 'Military Frontier' (the strip of land dividing the Muslim Turks from the Christian West which ran through Croatia and Serbia from 1578 to 1873). The Hungarian Fehértomplon also means 'White church' from *fehér* and *templon* 'church'.

Bela Palanka, SERBIA/SERBIA AND MONTENEGRO *Remesiana, Mokro, Izvor, Bunar-Baši, Su-Hazor, Musa-paša Palanka, Ak-Palanka*
'White Town'. The origin of the first two names is not known, but Mokro gave way to the Serbian Izvor, 'spring' or 'well', in the 14th century. The next two Turkish names meant 'Great Spring' and 'Source of Water'. In the 17th century it was renamed Musa Pasha's Fortress after the local Turkish pasha; a variation of this name was Mustafa-pašina Palanka (18th century). The present Serbian name is derived from Ak-Palanka (19th century) from the Turkish *ak* and *palanka* 'fortress redoubt'; the ruins of a Turkish castle are still visible. However, the Serbian *palanka* means 'country town'.

Bela Vista, MATO GROSSO DO SUL/BRAZIL, MOZAMBIQUE
'Beautiful View' in Portuguese.

Belaya Tserkov' (Bila Tserkva), UKRAINE *Yuryev*
'White Church'.

Belcher Islands, NUNAVUT/CANADA
In Hudson Bay, they were first sighted in 1610 and later named after the British Admiral Sir Edward Belcher (1799–1877), who in 1852 was appointed to lead an ultimately unsuccessful and unhappy attempt to find Sir John Franklin, who had disappeared while searching for the Northwest Passage in 1847.

Belém, BRAZIL, MEXICO, PORTUGAL
1. Brazil (Pará): on the River Pará, the name simply means Bethlehem. Its first name was Feliz Lusitânia and its second, Nossa Senhora de Belém do Grão Pará, meant 'Our Lady of Bethlehem of the Great Para (River)'.
2. Mexico: spelt slightly differently: Belem.
3. Portugal: also called Santa Maria de Belém 'St Mary of Bethlehem'.

Belfast, CANADA, NEW ZEALAND, SOUTH AFRICA, UK, USA
1. UK (Northern Ireland): the Irish name is Béal Feirste 'Mouth of the Sandbank Ford' or 'Crossing of the River' where the River Farset flows into the River Lagan, a point where it could be crossed at low tide. Capital of Northern Ireland since 1920.
2. The other towns take their name from the Irish Belfast.

Belfort, FRANCHE-COMTÉ/FRANCE
'Splendid Fort'.

Belgium (Dutch: **België**; French: **La Belgique**; German: **Belgien**)
The Kingdom of Belgium (Koninkrijk België, Royaume de Belgique, Königreich Belgien)

since 1831 after the country was created with a declaration of independence in 1830; part of the Kingdom of the United Netherlands (1815–30), of France (1795–1815), of the Austrian Netherlands (1713–95), and of the Spanish Netherlands (1579–1713). Named after the Belgae, a confederation of tribes that lived between the Rivers Rhine and Loire in Roman times. The name Belgium came into use during the Thirty Years' War (1618–48).

Belgorod, RUSSIA
A province and city, founded in 1593, with the name 'White City' from *belyy* and *gorod*. Why it should be described as 'white' is not clear.

Belgorod-Dnestrovskiy (Bilhorod-Dnistrovskyy), UKRAINE *Tyras, Ak-Libo, Akkerman, Cetatea Albă*
'White City on the (River) Dnestr' (in English, Dniester). Ak-Libo (Tatar), Akkerman (Turkish), and Cetatea Albă (Romanian) all mean 'White Fort' from, respectively, the Turkish *ak* and *kerman* 'fort' and the Romanian *cetate* 'fortress' and *alb* 'white'. Tyras was the Greek name for the Dniester, the Greeks having settled on the site in the 6th century BC. In the 13th century it began to prosper as a Moldavian city-state. It was in Ottoman Turkish hands in 1484–1812, Russian (1812–1918), and Romanian (1918–40). Its present name was adopted in 1944.

Belgrade (Beograd), SERBIA AND MONTENEGRO, USA
Serbia and Montenegro (Serbia): 'formerly Singidunum, Beli Grad, Dar ul Jihad, and Weissenburg. White City' from *beo* and *grad*; in Turkish, 'House of the Holy Wars'. The Romans named it the 'Fort of the Singi', a Celtic fort, *dunum*, having been built in the 4th century BC. Later, according to legend, it was named after the white bluff at the confluence of the Rivers Danube and Sava. It came under Serb rule for the first time in 1284, becoming the capital of Serbia in 1404. It was seized by the Ottoman Turks in 1521 and changed hands several times between them and the Austrians during the 17th and 18th centuries. The city was liberated by the Serbs in 1806, becoming the capital again in 1839. Liberated from the Austrians in 1918, the city became the capital of the Kingdom of the Serbs, Croats, and Slovenes when that country was created in 1918, of Yugoslavia when that name was adopted in 1929, and of Serbia and Montenegro in 2003 when the name Yugoslavia was superseded.

Belize *Belice, Honduran Bay Settlement, British Honduras*
Belize since 1974 and named after the Belize River. The actual name Belize may be a

Spanish mispronunciation of the name Wallace; Peter Wallace was a Scottish adventurer who is said to have established a small settlement at the mouth of the Belize River in about 1640. Earlier, in 1502, Christopher Columbus[†] named the bay the Bay of Honduras, although he did not make a landfall here. On the other hand, the name may come from an old Mayan name for the river, *be likin*, meaning the 'Way to the East'. The Mayans flourished here until *c*.900. In 1798 the Spanish failed to eject the British from their settlement and Belice virtually became a colony known as British Honduras. In 1862 it became a formal colony subordinate to Jamaica, but in 1884 it received the status of an independent crown colony. The name was changed to Belize in 1974. Independence was achieved in 1981.

Belize City, BELIZE
Named after the Belize River (see previous entry). The city was severely damaged by Hurricane 'Hattie' in 1961 and as a result it lost its status as capital to Belmopan in 1972.

Bellefontaine, BELGIUM, MARTINIQUE, USA
'Beautiful Fountain' in French.

Belleville, CANADA, FRANCE, USA
1. Canada (Ontario): originally Meyer's Creek after John Meyers, but renamed in 1816 after Arabella Gore, wife of the lieutenant-governor of Upper Canada.
2. USA: there are eight towns with this French name, all with the meaning 'Beautiful Town'.

Bellevue, AUSTRALIA, CANADA, REPUBLIC OF THE CONGO, USA
'Beautiful View' in French.

Bellingham, UK, USA
1. UK (England): 'Homestead of the Dwellers at the Bell-shaped Hill' from the Old English *belle* 'bell', *-inga-* and *hām*.
2. USA (Washington): named in 1792 after Sir William Bellingham who superintended the exploratory voyage of the North American coast by the British Captain George Vancouver[†].

Bellingshausen Sea, ANTARCTICA
Named after the Russian explorer, Admiral Fabien Bellingshausen (1778–1852), the first man to circumnavigate and penetrate the Antarctic continent during 1819–21.

Belluno, VENETO/ITALY *Bellunum*
A pre-Roman settlement, the name may be a contraction of Belodunum with the Celtic *dunum* equivalent to the Latin *oppidum* 'town' and *bel* signifying 'brilliant' or possibly 'beautiful'. It was captured by the French in

1797, passed to the Austrians in 1813, and finally to Italy in 1866.

Bellville, SOUTH AFRICA, USA
1. South Africa (Western Cape): formerly Hardekraaltje 'Hard Ground' and then Twaalfde Mylpaal 'Twelfth Mile Stone' to indicate its distance from Cape Town along the railway. It was renamed again in 1861 after Charles Bell, surveyor general of the Cape (1848–72).
2. USA (Texas): named after Thomas Bell who donated land for the site.

Belmopan, BELIZE
Following the destruction of Belize City in 1961, a new town was built 50 miles (80 km) inland, officially becoming the capital in 1972. It takes its name from the first syllables of Belize and Mopan, the tributary of the Belize River on which it lies, and the name of an indigenous tribe that successfully resisted Spanish attempts at subjugation.

Belo Horizonte, MINAS GERAIS/BRAZIL
'Beautiful Horizon' in Portuguese, a reference to the mountainous ridge which surrounds the city.

Beloeil, BELGIUM, CANADA
'Beautiful View' in French.

Belogorsk, AMUR/RUSSIA *Aleksandrovka, Kuybyshevka-Vostochnaya*
'White Hill' from *belyy* with *gorsk* being a word associated with *gora*. Founded in 1860, it was named after Alexander II[†] until 1935 when it was renamed after Valerian Kuybyshev[†]; the suffix, *-vostochnaya* 'east', was added to differentiate it from other towns with the same name. It was given its present name in 1957.

Beloit, WISCONSIN/USA *Blodgett Settlement, The Turtle, New Albany*
The name is said to be derived from the French *bel* 'beautiful' and the last syllable of Detroit, although its connection with that city is unknown.

Belomorsk, KARELIA/RUSSIA
'White Sea (Town)' from the Beloye More 'White Sea' on which it lies from the neuter of *belyy* and *more* 'sea'.

Beloretsk, BASHKORTOSTAN REPUBLIC/RUSSIA
Named after the Belaya River on which it lies. The river's name simply means 'white' from the feminine of *belyy*.

Belozersk, VOLOGDA/RUSSIA
The name is taken from Beloye Ozero 'White Lake' on which it lies from the neuter of *belyy* and *ozero* 'lake'.

Belper, ENGLAND/UK *Beurepeir*
'Beautiful Retreat' from the Old French *beau*
and *repaire* 'retreat'.

Benares, INDIA
See VĀRĀNASI.

Benbecula (Beinn na Faoghla), SCOTLAND/UK
Beanbeacla
An island in the Outer Hebrides perhaps
meaning 'Mountain of the Ford' from the Gaelic
beinn 'mountain', although 'mountain' is rather
too grandiose for the solitary 409ft (125m) hill;
the island is largely waterlogged, but connected
to North and South Uist by causeways.

Bendigo, VICTORIA/AUSTRALIA *Sandhurst*
Founded in 1840 and renamed in 1891 after a
local boxer who compared himself to a well-
known English boxer, William Thompson,
whose nickname was Bendigo.

Benelux A collective name for Belgium, the
Netherlands, and Luxembourg. They are also
called the Low Countries because significant
amounts of land are either just below or just
above sea level. The term 'Low Countries' may
have been coined by the Austrians, in
comparison to their own mountainous
country, when the Low Countries became an
Austrian Habsburg possession in 1482. The
name 'Benelux' was coined in 1948 when a
customs union was brought into effect.

Benevento, CAMPANIA/ITALY *Malies,
Malventum, Beneventum*
In Sanniti, the language of the Samnites,
Malventum meant 'Town in the Mountains'.
Thinking that it sounded like the Latin *male
ventum*, the Romans misinterpreted it to mean
'Ill wind'. They therefore changed it to
Beneventum 'Fair Wind'.

Bengal (Banga) *Vanga/Vangala/Banga/Bangala*
A historic region in the north-east of the
Indian subcontinent and a presidency of the
English East India Company named after the
Bengalis, who themselves took their name
from a chief, Banga. The British arrived in 1642
and Bengal became the base from which
expansion took place. Between 1905 and 1911
it was partitioned and again in 1947 on Indian
independence. It gave its name to the
bungalow from the Hindi *bangla* 'belonging to
Bengal', a reference to the single-storey
buildings common in the region, thus a 'House
in the Bengali style'. *See* BANGLADESH AND
WEST BENGAL.

Benghazi (Banghāzī), LIBYA *Hesperides/
Euesperides, Berenice*
Founded by the Greeks in the 7th century BC as
Hesperides 'Daughters of the Sunset', the

three daughters of Hesperus, the evening star
in Greek mythology. To this name, after the
occupation of Cyrenaica, Ptolemy III, Egyptian
Pharaoh (c.246–221 BC), added Berenice in the
4th century BC in honour of his wife. By
marrying Ptolemy III, Berenice II (c.269–221
BC), daughter of the King of Cyrene, reunited
her country with Egypt. Her name, Berenikhe
in Greek, was the name of the queens of the
Ptolemaic rulers of Egypt and was derived
from *pherenike* 'bringer of victory'. Benghazi
may come from *banī ğāzī* 'Sons of the
Conqueror' from *banī*, the plural of *íbn* 'son';
ğāzī usually means 'Defenders of Islam' or
'Warriors for the Faith'. Alternatively, it may
be named after Sidi Ghazi, a locally buried
saint.

Beni Mellal, MOROCCO
Beni comes from the Arabic *banī* 'sons' while
Mellal appears to come from a Berber root
word *mall* 'white'. This is believed to be a
reference to the purity of the water from the
Aïn Asserdoun spring.

Benin *Dahomey*
The Republic of Benin (République du Bénin)
since 1990. Previously the People's Republic of
Benin (1975–90) and the Republic of Dahomey
(1960–75). In the 17th century the King of
Abomey, Wegbaja, defeated Dã, the king of an
adjacent state, whose body was interred in the
palace that Wegbaja was building. He called
his joint kingdom *Dã-ho-mé*, 'On the Belly of
Dã'. After two years of fighting Dahomey
became a French protectorate in 1894 and in
1904 it was incorporated into the Federation of
French West Africa. It gained its independence
in 1960. In 1975 the country was renamed
Benin after the bay in the Atlantic Ocean, the
Bight of Benin, itself named after the historic
Kingdom of Benin (and known during the 18th
century as the Slave Coast), now in Nigeria.
The name Benin may be derived from the Bini,
its original inhabitants.

Benin City, EDO/NIGERIA
Sometimes called Edo, the name of the state of
which it is the capital and named after the Edo;
they are also known as the Bini.

Benkovac, CROATIA
Named after 14th-century Croatian princes
called Benković.

Ben Nevis, SCOTLAND/UK *Gleann Nibheis*
A mountain named after the River Nevis. *Ben*
comes from the Gaelic *beinn* 'mountain', while
the river's name is derived from the Celtic *nebh*
'water'. It has been suggested, however, that
the name comes from the Gaelic *nemess*
'malicious' or 'nasty', a reference to its

malevolent reputation; this derivation is unlikely.

Bennington, VERMONT/USA
Founded in 1749 and named after Benning Wentworth, governor of New Hampshire.

Benoni, GAUTENG/SOUTH AFRICA
Founded in 1904 with a name taken from the Bible (Genesis 35: 18). Ben-Oni was the name given to Benjamin by Rachel as she was dying in childbirth. The name means 'Son of Sorrow' and may be a reference to the difficulty in landscaping the valley on both sides of which the town lies and developing the mining camp that arose here in 1887.

Benton, CANADA, USA
USA: there are thirteen cities with this name in the USA (and also a Benton City and Benton Harbour), most of them named after Thomas Benton (1782–1858), who served for 30 years as the senator for Missouri. The city in New York is named after Caleb Benton, the first settler.

Benue, NIGERIA
A state named after the Benue River whose name means 'Mother of Waters' from *be* 'mother' and *nue* 'water'.

Berat, ALBANIA *Antipatria, Albanorum, Pulcheriopolis, Beligrad*
The original Greek names were superseded when the Byzantines renamed it the 'City of Pulcheria', the sister of Theodosius II (401–50), Eastern Roman emperor (408–50). The present name is probably derived from Beligrad 'White City', the name adopted by the Serbs after the city had been rebuilt in the 13th century. However, it has been suggested that Berat is a corruption of Antipatria, itself named after Antipater (*c.*397–319 BC), a Macedonian general and Regent of Macedonia (334–323 BC).

Berazategui, ARGENTINA
A district named after José Clemente Berazategui when the land was sold to him and Juan Etcheverry in 1860.

Berbera, SOMALIA
The origin of the name is by no means certain but is probably taken from the Berber people who inhabited this region at one time. Their name may be derived from the Greek *barbaros* 'barbarian' or 'outcast', or even 'foreign', to indicate that they were not Greek. It was the capital of British Somaliland until 1941.

Berchtesgaden, BAVARIA/GERMANY
'Perhtger's House' from the personal name and the Old High German *gadum* or *gaden* 'one-roomed house'.

Berdyans′k, UKRAINE *Osipenko*
Founded in 1827 and previously named (1939–58) after Polina Osipenko (1907–39), a fighter pilot in the Soviet Air Force and a Hero(ine) of the Soviet Union who set five aviation world records for women and who was born near here. The present name is probably that of a prominent founder of the original settlement.

Berenice, EGYPT
Founded in 275 BC by Ptolemy II Philadelphus (308–246 BC), King of Egypt (285–246 BC), who named it after his mother, Berenice I, Queen of Egypt and third wife of Ptolemy I Soter.

Berezina, BELARUS
A river with a name taken from the Russian *berëza* 'birch tree'.

Bergama, TURKEY *Teuthrania, Pergamum/Pergamon*
Originally named after King Teuthras of Mysia, and then after Pergamus, in Greek legend the youngest son of Andromache. It became the capital of the Attalid kingdom in the 3rd century BC, but was bequeathed to Rome in 133 BC when Attalus III (*c.*170–133 BC), King of Pergamum (138–133 BC) died without an heir. It then became the capital of the Roman province of Asia. Most of the ruins of ancient Pergamum can be found on the acropolis overlooking the modern city. Forced to use animal hides for their manuscripts, rather than pressed papyrus reeds, the people of Pergamum gave their name to the word parchment (in Greek, *pergamene*).

Bergamo, LOMBARDY/ITALY *Bergomum*
Situated in the foothills of the Alps, it became a Roman town in 196 BC. Both names are derived from a word of probably Celtic origin, *berg*; as in modern-day German, it means 'mountain'. The city was under French control between 1797 and 1815 when it was transferred to Austria. It joined the Kingdom of Italy in 1859.

Bergen, NORWAY *Bjǫrgvin*
'Mountain Pasture' from *bjǫrg* or *berg* 'mountain', and *vin* 'pasture' or 'meadow'. Founded in 1070, it was the Norwegian capital in the 12th and 13th centuries.

Bergen op Zoom, THE NETHERLANDS
Located on the River Zoom, the name means '(The Place by) the Hills on the Border (of the Marshes)'. Zoom 'border' indicates that the river flows along the edge of marshes.

Bergerac, AQUITAINE/FRANCE
'Place of Bracarius', a Gallo-Roman personal name.

Bering Island, RUSSIA
Named after the Danish-born ship's captain
Vitus Bering[†] who died on the island. Peter I
the Great[†] appointed him in 1724 as the leader
of an expedition to see if Asia and North
America were joined by land. The Bering Sea
(in Russian, Beringovo More), the Bering Strait
(Proliv Beringa), and the town of Beringovskiy,
previously Ugol'niy from *ugol'* 'coal', are also
named after him.

Berkane, MOROCCO
Takes its name from Muhammad Aberkane, a
local holy man. His name meant 'black'.

Berkeley, UK, USA
1. UK (England): formerly Berclea and
Berchelai 'Birch-tree Wood' from the Old
English *beorc* 'birch tree' and *lēah*.
2. USA (California): originally named Ocean
View in 1853, becoming the campus for the
College of California. When it and the
University of California merged in 1868, the
new campus was named after the Anglo-Irish
philosopher, Bishop George Berkeley (1685–
1753), who had arrived in America in 1728.

Berkhamsted, ENGLAND/UK *Beorhthanstædæ,*
Berchehamstede
'Homestead on a Hill' from *beorg* and *hām-stede*
'homestead'.

Berkshire, ENGLAND/UK *Berrocscire*
The only royal county in England, with the
first syllable being derived from the Celtic
berroc or *barroc* 'hilly place', and the second
from *scīr*.

Berlin, GERMANY, USA
Germany: a state and city situated among lakes
and rivers, the name may be derived from the
Slavic *birl* or *berl* 'marsh' or 'swampland'. The
city was the capital of the Duchy of
Brandenburg from 1486, of Prussia when
Brandenburg-Prussia became a kingdom in
1701, and of Germany between 1871 and 1945,
and again when East and West Germany were
reunited in 1990. The German parliament held
its first plenary session in the refurbished
Reichstag in April 1999 having moved from
Bonn, and this marked the dawn of the so-
called 'Berlin Republic'. From 1945 until the
reunification of Germany in 1990 the city was
divided into American, British, French, and
Soviet sectors. East Berlin became the capital of
the communist German Democratic Republic
in 1949 and West Berlin, an enclave within that
Republic, a state of the Federal Republic of
Germany. A fortified wall separating the
American, British, and French sectors from the
Soviet sector was erected in 1961. The collapse

of the communist regime in 1989 was
accompanied by the dismantling of the wall.

Bermejo, ARGENTINA-BOLIVIA
A river rising in Bolivia which joins the
Paraguay River. The silt that it carries down
stream gives it its name 'reddish (colour)' from
the Spanish *bermejo*. There is also a town with
this name in Argentina, but it is over 600 miles
(965 km) from the river.

Bermuda, UK *Somers Islands*
An Overseas Territory of the UK consisting of
seven main islands and about 150 smaller
ones. The archipelago is named after the
Spaniard, Juan Bermúdez, who discovered it
sometime between 1503 and 1511. In 1609
English colonists under Sir George Somers
(1554–1610) were shipwrecked on their way to
Virginia and decided to stay; the islands were
briefly named after him. In 1612 Bermuda was
included in the Third Charter of the Virginia
Company and in 1684 it became an English
crown colony. It has given its name to the
Bermuda Triangle, a local area of the Atlantic
Ocean in which ships and aircraft have
mysteriously disappeared, and to knee-length
Bermuda shorts.

Berne, GERMANY, SWITZERLAND, USA
1. Switzerland: locally Bern. A canton since
1353 and the capital of Switzerland since 1848.
According to legend, Berthold V, Duke of
Zähringen, killed a bear (in German *Bär*), while
hunting in the local area in 1191. The city's
name is said to be taken from the German
word. However, like Berlin, the name may
actually be derived from *birl* or *berl* 'marsh',
given that the city lies on the River Aare. It has
given its name to an international copyright
agreement—the International Convention for
the Protection of Literary and Artistic Works—
popularly known as the Berne Convention.
2. USA (Indiana): named after the city in
Switzerland.

Berwick-upon-Tweed, ENGLAND/UK
Berewicum super Twedam
The first part of the name means 'Barley Farm,
outlying Part of an Estate' from the Old English
berewīc, with the River Tweed added to
differentiate it from other towns simply called
Berwick. It was a subject of dispute between
England and Scotland over a period of
centuries until being definitively included in
England in 1885.

Besançon, FRANCHE-COMTÉ/FRANCE *Vesontio*
Derived from its original name which is based
on the Indo-European root word *ves*
'mountain'. The town was developed at the

foot of a high rock on which the Romans built a fort.

Bessarabia (Basarabia), MOLDOVA-UKRAINE
A region, and former principality, lying between the Prut and Dniester Rivers in the north-eastern corner of the Balkans and named after the Romanian house of Basarab which had ruled parts of Wallachia in the 14th century. Basarab is thought to come from the Turkish *basar*, itself from *baski* 'restraint' or 'oppression'. A much disputed area, it has been subject to Moldavian, Ottoman Turkish, Russian, Romanian, Soviet, and Moldovan/ Ukrainian control since the 15th century. Russian occupation was confirmed at the Treaty of Bucharest in 1812. In 1917 Bessarabia declared independence, becoming the Bessarabian Democratic Republic of Moldova; the following year, however, it joined Romania. In 1940 Bessarabia was ceded to the Soviet Union, southern Bessarabia then becoming part of the Ukrainian Soviet Socialist Republic. *See* MOLDOVA.

Bessemer, USA
There are three towns in the USA with this name and another called Bessemer City. All are named after Sir Henry Bessemer (1813–98), a British engineer who was the first person to initiate a way to manufacture steel cheaply; it was known as the Bessemer process. The town in Alabama was originally called Fort Jonesboro and was renamed in 1887.

Bethany, CANADA, WEST BANK, USA
1. West Bank: a small village with the Arabic name al-ʿAyzarīyah which is derived from Lazarus, who lived here and was raised from the dead by Jesus. The Hebrew name Bethany means 'House of Poverty' from *bēt* 'house' and *ʿanya* 'poverty'.
2. USA (Oklahoma): founded in 1909 and named after the biblical Bethany just outside Jerusalem on the West Bank.

Bethesda, UK, USA
All are named after the Pool of Bethesda in Jerusalem, Israel, where Jesus healed a lame man as described in the Bible (John 5).

Bethlehem, SOUTH AFRICA, WEST BANK, USA, US VIRGIN ISLANDS
1. South Africa (Free State): founded in 1860, it takes its name from the Bethlehem in the Holy Land because wheat grew well in the area.
2. West Bank: in Arabic Bayt Laḥm, and in Hebrew Bēt Leḥem. An ancient town within the British Palestine mandate (1923–48); it was annexed by Jordan in 1950 and captured by the Israelis in 1967. Under the terms of the 1995 Oslo 2 interim agreement, it is now under the authority of the Palestinians. The town has changed hands many times, having been under the control of the Romans, Byzantines, Arabs, Crusaders, Mamlūks, Ottoman Turks, British, Jordanians, and Israelis. The Arabic name means 'House of Meat' while the Hebrew name represents 'House of Bread', a reference to the fertility of the area from *bēt* 'house'.
3. USA (Pennsylvania): founded in 1741 and given its name by missionaries commemorating the traditional birthplace of Jesus.
4. It gave its name to 'bedlam', a contraction of Bethlehem and meaning a scene of confusion and uproar, a madhouse. The Hospital of St Mary of Bethlehem (otherwise Bethlem Royal Hospital) was founded in Lambeth, London, as the country's main asylum for the insane in the 14th century.

Bethulie, FREE STATE/SOUTH AFRICA *Groot Moordenaarspoort, Caledon, Verhuellpolis, Bethulia, Heidelberg*
The first Afrikaans name meant 'Great Murderers' Gateway', a reference to the murder of Bushmen here. In 1833 the settlement was renamed Caledon after the river but, because a Caledon already existed in the Cape, in 1835 it became the 'City of Verhuell' after Admiral C. H.Verhuell and *polis*. As a missionary station this name was considered inappropriate and the name was changed again, this time to the biblical Bethulia (Judith 6: 7; nowhere else in the Bible does this name appear and it is believed by some to be fictitious). When the settlement was upgraded to a town in 1863 it was renamed Heidelberg, surprisingly, because there was already another town of this name. Finally in 1872 a slightly amended version of Bethulia was agreed.

Beverley, ENGLAND/UK *Beferlic, Bevreli*
Probably a Celtic name meaning 'Beaver Lodge'.

Beverly, MASSACHUSETTS/USA
Named in 1668 after Beverley in England.

Beverly Hills, CALIFORNIA/USA *Rancho Rodeo de las Aguas, Beverly*
Renamed Beverly in 1906 after the town in England. Hills was added in 1911.

Beylerbeyi, TURKEY *Chrysokeramos, Ferukh fesa*
The original Byzantine name represented a church covered with golden tiles. Under Mahmud I (1696–1754), Ottoman sultan (1730–54), it was renamed 'Increasing Joy'. At some later date, possibly during the reign of Mahmud II (1785–1839), sultan (1808–39) it

was changed to Beylerbeyi. This was the title of
the highest grade of Turkish *pasha* who could
be a military commander or provincial
governor.

Bhaktapur, NEPAL
'Town of the Faithful' from the Nepalese *bhakt*
'believer' and *pur*. It is also called Bhatgaon or
Bhādgaon to mean 'Land of Rice' from *bhāt*
'rice' and *gāun* 'land'.

Bharatpur, RĀJASTHĀN/INDIA
Founded in *c*.1733 and also known as
Bhurtpore. It was the capital of the former
princely state of the same name. 'Bharata's
Town', it is named after Bhārata, probably the
first king of an Aryan tribe which took his
name.

Bhavnagar, GUJARĀT/INDIA
Founded in 1723 by, and named after, Gohil
Rājput Bhavsinghji to mean the 'City of
Bhavsinghji' with the additional *nagar*.

Bhir, MAHĀRĀSHTRA/INDIA *Champāvatinagar*
The name may be derived from the Persian *bhir*
'water'.

Bhopāl, MADHYA PRADESH/INDIA *Bhojapāl*
Said to be named after Raja Bhoj (1010–53) to
which the Hindi *pāl* 'embankment' or 'dam'
has been added. According to legend, Bhoj was
instructed to atone for the murder of his
mother by linking together the nine rivers
which flowed through his kingdom. He did
this by constructing dams and built his capital
by the lakes which were thus formed. Another
theory is that the name is derived from the
Sanskrit *bhūpāla* 'king' or 'prince'. Part of a
princely state founded in 1723, Bhopāl joined
India in 1949, having been a separate province
since Indian independence in 1947.

Bhubaneswar, ORISSA/INDIA *Ekamrakshetra,*
Bhuvaneśvara
Derived from the local name of Shiva,
Tribuhuvaneśwara 'Lord of the World' from
the Sanskrit *bhuvana* 'world' or 'universe' and
ishvara 'supreme deity'.

Bhutan *Men Jong*
The Kingdom of Bhutan (Druk-Yul) since the
17th century. In the language of Bhutan,
Dzongkha, Druk-Yul means 'Land of the
Thunder Dragon', although it is also translated
as 'Land of the Peaceful Dragon'. The previous
name, Men Jong, meant 'Land of Medicinal
Plants' because of the fertility of its valleys and
their flora and fauna. The name Bhutan may
be derived from the Sanskrit Bhot-ant, the
'End of Tibet', from *bhoṭa* 'Tibet', or Bhu-uttan
'High End', or Bhots-than 'Land of the Bhutia'
(a Himalayan people originally from Tibet).

The kingdom came under Chinese rule in
1731. British expeditions into the country
resulted in a peace treaty in 1774, but conflict
arose again in the 19th century. This was only
settled with the Treaty of Sinchula in 1865
whereby Bhutan ceded to the UK control of
its southern frontier passes. Although it
became a hereditary monarchy in 1907 and
retained its independence, the Treaty of
Punakha in 1910 provided for British guidance
in the kingdom's external affairs. The treaty
was renewed by India in 1949 and the part of
Dewāngiri annexed by the UK in 1865 was
returned.

Biafra, NIGERIA
The former Eastern Region, it declared its
independence in 1967. War and defeat
followed and in January 1970 Biafra ceased to
exist. The name comes from the Bight of Biafra
(now the Bight of Bonny) which is a
Europeanized version of Mafra, the name of a
tribe.

Białystok, POLAND
A former province and a city with a name
meaning 'White Slope' from *biały* 'white' and
stok 'slope' or 'hillside'.

Biarritz (Basque: **Miarritze**), AQUITAINE/FRANCE
'(Place of) two Oak Trees' from the Basque *bi*
'two' and *haritz* 'oak'.

Bibi-Eybat, AZERBAIJAN *Helenendorf/Elendorf,*
Hellenfeld, Khanlar
Founded in 1819 by German immigrants from
the Duchy of Württemberg and called 'Helen's
Village' and 'Clearing in the Woods'. It was
renamed in 1938 after Khanlar Safaraliyev
(1885–1907), a Bolshevik revolutionary. It was
renamed again in 1991.

Bible Belt, USA
The informal name of an area of the central
and southern USA renowned for its Christian
religious fervour.

Bicester, ENGLAND/UK *Bernecestre*
Possibly 'Beorna's Fort' from an Old English
personal name and *ceaster*.

Biddeford, MAINE/USA *Winter Harbour*
Settled in 1630 by an English group, led by
Richard Vines who first called it Winter
Harbour, having wintered there. He renamed
it later after his birthplace, Bideford in
Devon, England. This might have the meaning
of 'Ford on the (stream called) Byd' or 'Bieda's
Ford'.

Biddulph, ENGLAND/UK *Bidolf*
'(Place) by the Quarry' from the Old English *bī*
'(place) by' and *dœlf* 'pit' or 'quarry'.

Bié, ANGOLA *Silva Porto*
A province with a name slightly modified from that of a local 15th-century chief, Vié. At the end of the 19th century it was renamed after António Francisco Ferreira da Silva Porto, a Portuguese explorer who died here in 1890. After Angolan independence in 1975 the name Bié was restored.

Bielefeld, NORTH RHINE-WESTPHALIA/GERMANY *Bilifelde*
'Steep Field' from the Old High German *bil* 'steep rock' and *Feld*.

Bielsko-Biała, POLAND
Until 1951 the city consisted of two towns on either side of the Biała River, the Silesian Bielsko and the Galician Biała. Bielsko comes from *biel* 'white', while Biała is probably derived from *białawy* 'whitish', referring to the colour of its water. Until 1999 it was also the name of a province.

Biên Hoà, VIETNAM
A name representing the words 'border' from *biên* and 'peace' from *hoà*.

Bierutów, POLAND *Brückenberg*
Renamed after Bolesław Bierut (1892–1956), president of Poland (1945–52) and prime minister (1952–4). Bierut was a pseudonym; his real name was Krasnodebski.

Biggleswade, ENGLAND/UK *Pichelesuuade?, Bicheleswada*
'Biccel's Ford' from a possible Old English personal name and *wæd* 'ford'.

Bighorn, MONTANA-WYOMING/USA
Mountains, a river, a lake, and a city all have this name from the sheep found in the Rocky Mountains, often called 'bighorn'.

Big Sioux, IOWA-SOUTH DAKOTA/USA
A river named after the Sioux.

Big Spring, TEXAS/USA
Founded in about 1881 and so-called because of a big spring at nearby Sulphur Draw.

Bihār, INDIA
A state and a city. They take their name from the Sanskrit *vihāra* 'monastic retreat'. The city is sometimes called Bihārsharīf. It was a great religious centre, particularly for Buddhists. Here *sharīf* means 'exalted' or 'noble' in the sense that it enhances the status of the religious centre, thus 'Bihār the Noble'. *Sharīf* has other meanings (*see* MAZĀR-E SHARĪF). Bihār has several mosques.

Bijāpur, KARNĀTAKA/INDIA *Vijayapura*
A medieval city-state in the Deccan, it was originally named in the 10th century as the 'City of Victory' from *vijaya* and *pur* by the Chalukyas, an ancient Indian dynasty. The present name is merely a shortened version of the original.

Bijelo Polje, MONTENEGRO/SERBIA AND MONTENEGRO *Pruška, Akova*
The origin of the first name is unknown. The present and previous Turkish names mean 'White Field'. According to legend, the town received this name because the surrounding fields were covered in white flowers.

Bīkaner, RĀJASTHĀN/INDIA
'Settlement of Bika'. Founded in 1488 and named after Rao Bīka (or Bīkaji), a Rājput chieftain and one of the fourteen sons of Rao Jodha, and a shepherd called Ner. According to legend, he boasted of the courage of one of his sheep in fighting off wolves to two surveyors sent off to find the site for a new capital. The present Bīkaner district was the former princely state of Bīkaner.

Biläsuvar, AZERBAIJAN *Pushkino*
'Place of Efficient Irrigation', an apt name given that the surrounding area is the breadbasket of Azerbaijan. The previous Russian name honours Alexander Pushkin (1799–1837), widely considered to be Russia's foremost poet.

Bilbao (Basque: **Bilbo**), BASQUE COUNTRY/SPAIN *Bellum Vadum*
An adaptation of the Roman name which means 'Beautiful Ford', a reference to its position on the Nervión estuary.

Bilibino, CHUKOT AUTONOMOUS DISTRICT/ RUSSIA
Founded in 1958 and named after Yuri Aleksandrovich Bilibin (1901–52), a geologist who first discovered gold in this northerly region of Siberia. For this discovery he was awarded the State Prize of the USSR in 1946.

Billings, RUSSIA, USA
1. Russia (Chukot Autonomous District): a small port on the Chukchi Sea named after Joseph Billings, an Englishman who became an officer in the Russian Navy. He was on Captain Cook's[†] third voyage round the world in 1776–9 and later co-led a Russian expedition to explore the coasts of Siberia between 1785 and 1794.
2. USA: there are three towns with this name. The towns in Montana and North Dakota are named after Frederick Billings (1823–90), president of the Northern Pacific Railroad.

Bilohirs'k, UKRAINE *Mavron Kastron, Karasū-Bāzār*
The Byzantine name from the Greek *kastron* 'castle' gave way to 'Blackwater Market',

named after the River Karasū 'Blackwater River' from the Turkish *kara* and *su*.

Biloxi, MISSISSIPPI/USA *Fort Louis*
The name is of Choctaw origin and has been translated as either 'worthless' or 'terrapin'. However, the city, founded in 1719, might be named after the Biloxi, a local tribe whose name is said to mean 'broken pot'.

Bima, SUMBAWA/INDONESIA
The name is thought to come from the Hindu epic, the *Mahābhārata*, one of whose heroes is named Bhīma. It was a Hindu kingdom, becoming a Muslim sultanate in 1621 before a Dutch presence was established in 1669.

Bingerville, CÔTE D'IVOIRE
Named after the French explorer, Captain Louis-Gustave Binger (1856–1936), first governor of the French Ivory Coast colony (1893–5). As a lieutenant, he made a two-year journey into the interior.

Binghamton, NEW YORK/USA *Ochenang/Chenango Point*
The Iroquois name gave way in 1855 to that of William Bingham (1752–1804), a benefactor of the town, who owned considerable land in the vicinity.

Bingöl, TURKEY *Çapakçur*
'A Thousand Lakes' from *bin* 'thousand' and *göl* 'lake', a reference to the large number of lakes in the area.

Bioko, EQUATORIAL GUINEA *Formosa, Fernando Pó, Macías Nguema Biyogo*
An island thought to have been discovered in 1472, it was first called *Formosa* 'Beautiful' before the name was changed in 1494 to honour its discoverer, the Portuguese explorer, Fernão do Pó. In 1973–9 it was named after Macías Nguema Biyogo (1922–79), the first president of Equatorial Guinea (1968–79), but when he was deposed and executed in 1979 the name was changed to Bioko. This comes from the second son, Bioko, of a paramount chief of the Bubi, the original inhabitants. The island comprises the Insular Region of Equatorial Guinea. Although ceded to Spain in 1778 in return for Spanish cessions in South America, the Spanish presence was minimal and in 1827–58 the island was administered by the UK after the Royal Navy had established a base to try to minimize the movement of slaving ships along the Slave Coast. Bioko united with Río Muni on the mainland in 1900 to form a single colony under Spanish rule.

Birkby, ENGLAND/UK *Bretebi*
'Village of the Britons' from the Old Scandinavian *bretar* 'Briton' and *bý*.

Birkenhead, ENGLAND/UK *Bircheveth, Birkheued*
'Headland covered with Birch' from the Old English *birce* and *hēafod* 'headland'.

Birmingham, UK, USA
UK (England): formerly Beormingeham 'Village of Beornmund's (or Beorma's) People' from an Old English personal name with *-inga-* and *hām*.

Birni Nkonni, NIGER
'Fortress of the Konni' from the Berber *birni* 'fortified village' and the name of the local tribe who once lived in the region.

Birobidzhan, YEVRESKAYA AUTONOMOUS PROVINCE/RUSSIA *Tikhonkaya*
Founded as Tikhonkaya railway station in 1928, it was renamed after the two rivers Bira and Bidzhan in 1937. In a remote part of the Russian Far East, the Birobidzhan autonomous province was renamed Yevreskaya 'Jewish'.

Biscay, Bay of (French: **Golfe de Gascogne**; Spanish: **Golfo de Vizcaya**), ATLANTIC OCEAN
Of Basque origin, the name comes from *biskar* 'mountain country', a reference to the Pyrenees, on both sides of which the Basques live.

Bisceglie, APULIA/ITALY *Vigiliae*
Derived from its earlier Roman name, which was a reference to the watchtowers along the coast from the Latin *vigilia* 'watch'.

Bischofswerda, SAXONY/GERMANY *Bischoffswerde*
'River Island belonging to a Bishop' from *Bischof* 'bishop' and *Werder* 'plot of land surrounded by water' from old High German *werid* 'island'.

Bishkek, KYRGYZSTAN *Peshagakh, Bishkek, Pishpek, Frunze*
The city's original Sogdian name meant 'Place below the Mountains'. The Khan of Kokand built a fortress on the site in 1825 against Russian encroachment and called it Bishkek, probably a corruption of Peshagakh. However, it has been suggested that it might mean 'Five Knights' since, according to legend, these knights fought each other to gain control of the Shu River valley in which the city lies. In 1862 the Russians captured the fortress which, by mistake, they called Pishpek. A town slowly developed round it and in 1878–1926 it was called by the same name. It was then renamed Frunze after Mikhail Frunze (1885–1925), a Bolshevik revolutionary who was born in the city in 1885 and had been sent by Lenin[†] to the region in 1919 to oppose the Basmachi fighting for independence; he was appointed

People's Commissar for the Red Army and Navy in 1925. The name reverted to Bishkek in 1991 after a popular referendum. In 1924 it became the capital of the Kyrgyz autonomous province and, since 1991, of Kyrgyzstan.

Bisho, EASTERN CAPE/SOUTH AFRICA
'Buffalo' in Xhosa after the Buffalo River on which the town lies.

Bishop's Stortford, ENGLAND/UK *Storteford, Bysshops Stortford*
'Ford by a Salient of Land' from the Old English *steort* 'salient of land' and *ford*. The 'Bishop's' is a reference to the fact that it was owned by the Bishop of London.

Bismarck, CANADA, GREENLAND, PAPUA NEW GUINEA, USA
1. Canada (Ontario): named after Prince Otto von Bismarck (1815–98), prime minister of Prussia (1862–73, 1873–90) and the first German chancellor (1871–90).
2. Papua New Guinea: the Bismarck Archipelago, the Bismarck Range, and the Bismarck Sea in the Pacific Ocean are all named after Otto von Bismarck. The Bismarck Archipelago was annexed by Germany in 1884 before being occupied by Australia in 1914. The range was visited by a German explorer in 1886.
3. USA: there are four cities with this name. The capital of North Dakota, founded in the 1830s, was originally called the 'Crossing on the Missouri'. In 1873 the name was changed to honour Otto von Bismarck in an attempt to attract German investment in the Northern Pacific Railway.

Bissau, GUINEA-BISSAU
Founded as a Portuguese post in 1687 and given the Portuguese version of the name of the Bissagos tribe. It became the capital of Portuguese Guinea in 1941 and of Guinea-Bissau when the country achieved independence in 1974.

Bitola, MACEDONIA *Heraclea Lyncestis, Pelagonia, Monastir, Bitolj*
Originally a Greek settlement, and then Roman, it became an episcopal see in the 11th century. It fell to the Turks in 1382 and was renamed Monastir after *monasterium* 'monastery'. The present name is derived from the Slavonic *obitel'* 'cloister' or 'abode'. It was the capital of Macedonia in the 19th century.

Bitterfontein, WESTERN CAPE/SOUTH AFRICA
'Sour Fountain'.

Bitter Lake, CANADA, EGYPT, USA
Egypt: there were two, the Great Bitter Lake (al- Buḥairah al-Murrah al-Kubrā) and the Little

Bitter Lake (al-Buḥairah al-Murrah aṣ-Ṣughrā), through which the Suez Canal flows; they are now one large lake. They are so-called because the area is marshy and the water bitter, hence the Arabic *murrah*, the feminine of *murr* 'bitter' and *buḥairah* 'lake'; *kubrā* actually means 'greater' and *ṣughrā* 'lesser'.

Biwa (Biwa-ko), HONSHŪ/JAPAN
A lake named after the biwa, a short-necked lute, because their shapes are similar.

Bizerta (Bizerte, Banzart), TUNISIA *Hippo Diarrhytus/Zarytus*
Also known as Banzart which comes from the Arabic *binzart*, a corruption of the Low Latin *Hippo Zarytus* which is itself a corruption of the Greek *Hippōn Diarrutos* 'Flowing through the Stables', a reference to the presence of a nearby stream which supplied water to the stables; from *hippōn* 'stable' and *diarrutos* 'flowing through'. Originally a Phoenician settlement, it was captured by the Arabs in 661 and its Roman/Greek name was Arabized. It was held by the Spanish for 37 years during the 16th century and by the French in 1881–1955.

Bjelovar, CROATIA *Bjelovac, Wellewar*
'White Fortress' from the Hungarian *vár*, and built on the orders of Maria Theresa[†] as a military town in 1756. The original name means 'White Town'.

Blackburn, CANADA, UK
UK (England): formerly Blacheburne 'Dark Stream' from the Old English *blæc* 'black' or 'dark' and *burna* 'stream'.

Black Forest (Schwarzwald), BADEN-WÜRTTEMBERG/GERMANY *Silva Nigra*
The Roman, German, and English names are linguistic variations of the same name which stems from the dark fir forests that characterize the region.

Blackpool, CANADA, UK
UK (England): 'Dark-coloured Pool' from the Old English *blæc* 'black' and *pōl*. The city is named after a stretch of dark, peaty water about a kilometre from the sea.

Black Sea (Russian: **Chernoye More**; Ukrainian: **Chorne More**; Turkish: **Karadeniz**)
Also known, occasionally, as the Euxine Sea. The Persians called it *akhshaēna* 'dark', possibly because of the apparent colour of its waters during storms. Before the Greeks came to settle round it they called it Pontos Axenos 'Dark Sea' or 'Inhospitable Sea' from *pontos* 'sea' and *axenos* 'inhospitable'. Strabo[†] in his *Geography* also referred to the Sea as inhospitable because of its 'wintry storms and the ferocity of the tribes that lived around it'.

Later, however, this was changed to *Euxenos* 'hospitable' or 'friendly to strangers' when Greek city-states began to spring up along its coastline.

Blagoevgrad, BULGARIA *Skaptopara, Dzhumaja, Gorna Dzhumaja*
The first Thracian name gave way to the following Turkish names, meaning 'Mountain Market' during the Turkish occupation which lasted from 1396 to 1878. In 1950 the town was renamed after Dimitŭr Blagoev (1856–1924), a Macedonian Marxist who founded the Bulgarian Communist Party.

Blagoveshchenka, KABARDINO-BALKARIYA REPUBLIC/RUSSIA *Pervomayskoye*
Formerly 'First of May' from *pervyy* 'first' and *may* 'May' to commemorate the Soviet workers' holiday, May Day. Renamed in 1992, the present name is associated with 'The Annunciation' from *Blagoveshcheniye*, literally 'Good Tidings' from *blago* 'good' and the Church Slavonic *veshcheniye* 'tidings'.

Blagoveshchensk, AMUR/RUSSIA *Ust-Zeysk*
First settled in 1644 at the confluence of the Amur and Zeya rivers, the original name meant the 'Mouth of the River Zeya' from *usta* 'mouth'. The town was ceded to China between 1689 and 1856. A military post was then developed on the site. Two years later the Church of the Annunciation was built and the town was renamed after the church: *Blagoveshcheniye* (see previous entry).

Blandford Forum, ENGLAND/UK *Chipping Blandford, Blaneford St Mary*
Probably 'Ford where Gudgeon are found' from the Old English *blægna* 'gudgeon' and *ford*. The Latin *forum* 'market' was added in recognition of the former name Chipping Blandford from the Old English *cēping* 'market'. The church was dedicated to St Mary.

Blantyre, MALAWI, UK
1. Malawi: founded in 1876 as a Church of Scotland mission station and named after the Scottish birthplace of David Livingstone (1813–73), missionary and explorer.
2. UK (Scotland): the meaning is not known apart from the Gaelic *tir* 'land' or 'territory'.

Blarney (An Bhlarna) IRELAND
'The Small Field'. In Blarney Castle is the Blarney Stone which, if kissed, is said to give the gift of eloquence and the ability to flatter—'blarney'. The legend is said to stem from 1602 when the Lord of Blarney was able to avoid transferring his allegiance to Queen Elizabeth I[†] with effusive rhetoric.

Blenheim, CANADA, NEW ZEALAND
New Zealand (South Island): founded in 1847 and named after the Battle of Blenheim in 1704 when the Duke of Marlborough and Prince Eugene of Savoy defeated the French during the War of the Spanish Succession (1701–14). The site of the battle, in Bavaria, Germany, is now called Blindheim, *blind* being 'dull', 'false', or 'hidden' with *Heim*.

Blida, ALGERIA, LEBANON
Algeria: a province and a town; also known as el-Boulaida. The name comes from *boleida*, a shortening of the Arabic *balad* 'town'.

Block Island, RHODE ISLAND/USA *Manisses, Rhode Island*
First sighted in 1524 by Giovanni da Verrazzano (1485–1528), an Italian navigator. He called it Rhode Island because it appeared to him to resemble the island of Rhodes in the Mediterranean. It was renamed after Adriaen Block, a Dutch explorer, who visited it in 1614. The original Narragansett name meant 'Manitou's Little Island'.

Bloemfontein, FREE STATE/SOUTH AFRICA
Founded as a fort in 1846 with the name that can be translated as 'Fountain of Flowers' from the Afrikaans *bloem* 'flower'. However, it may have been named after himself by Jan Bloem, a Griqua leader who lived on a farm here before the Voortrekkers arrived. It is also known locally as Mangaung, with the Isotho meaning of 'Place of Leopards'.

Bloemhof, NORTH WEST/SOUTH AFRICA
Founded in 1864 as 'Flower Garden' from the Afrikaans *bloem* 'flower' and *hof* 'garden'.

Bloomfield, CANADA, USA
USA (New Jersey): founded by Puritans in 1660 as Wardsesson and renamed in 1796 after Joseph Bloomfield (1753–1823), a general in the War of Independence (1775–83) who became governor of the state.

Bloomington, USA
1. Illinois: orginally called Keg Grove when settled in 1822, it was renamed Blooming Grove and then in 1831 Bloomington after its profusion of wild flowers.
2. Indiana: named after an early settler, Philip Bloom.
3. Minnesota: took its name from the city in Illinois.

Bluefields, NICARAGUA
Said to be named after a Dutch pirate, Abraham Blewfeldt (or Bleuwveldt), who operated from here in the 17th century.

Blue Mountains, AUSTRALIA, JAMAICA, USA
Australia (New South Wales): so-called because of their blue appearance as a result of rays of

light being coloured by droplets of oil given off by the local eucalyptus trees.

Blumenau, SANTA CATARINA/BRAZIL
Named after one of the first Germans to arrive in 1850, the philosopher Herman Bruno Otto Blumenau.

Boa Vista, BRAZIL, CAPE VERDE
'Good View' from the Portuguese *boa*, the feminine of *bom* 'good'.

Bobo Dioulasso, BURKINA FASO *Sya*
It originated in the 15th century as a forest clearing by a river with the name Sya 'island'. In 1897 it fell to the French who renamed it after the Bobo, one of the earliest ethnic groups to settle in south-west Burkina Faso, and the Dyula, whose name means 'itinerant trader' in Mande.

Bobruysk, BELARUS
See BABRUYSK.

Boca Raton, FLORIDA/USA
'Mouse's Mouth' from *boca de ratones*, a Spanish nautical term used to refer to the sharp rocks that wore away ships' cables; from *boca* 'mouth' and *raton* 'mouse'.

Bocholt, BELGIUM, NORTH RHINE-WESTPHALIA/GERMANY
Derived from the German *Buchenholz* 'Beech Wood'.

Bodmin, ENGLAND/UK *Bodmine/Bodminian*
'Dwelling by Church Land' from the Old Cornish *bod* 'dwelling' and *meneghy* which could mean 'land assigned for the vicar's living'.

Bodrum, TURKEY *Halicarnassus*
'Dungeon' or 'Cellar', although this is entirely inappropriate. The name may have been changed to Bodrum when the Knights of St John arrived here at the beginning of the 15th century and built the Castle of St Peter. Halicarnassus was the site of one of the Seven Wonders of the Ancient World, the Mausoleum of Halicarnassus. Mausolus, King of Caria (377–353 BC), began the planning of a huge tomb for himself; its construction was undertaken by his widow, Artemisia, after his death. Mausolus has given us the word 'mausoleum' to describe any large and imposing place of burial.

Bofors, SWEDEN
The name may mean 'Settlement', *bo*, 'by the waterfall', *fors*. Alfred Nobel (1833–96), founder of the Nobel prizes, owned an armaments factory here which gave its name to a rapid-firing anti-aircraft gun, the Bofors.

Boğazkale, TURKEY *Hattusas, Boğazköy*
'Gorge Fort', and formerly 'Gorge Village' from *boğaz* 'throat' or 'gullet', a very ancient city that was the capital of the Hatti, now known as Hittites.

Bogdanovich, SVERDLOVSK/RUSSIA
Founded as a settlement on a railway line in 1885, it was named after General Yevgeny Bogdanovich who strongly supported the construction of the Transsiberian Railway.

Bognor Regis, ENGLAND/UK *Bucganora*
'Shore of the Woman called Bucge' from an Old English personal name and *ōra* 'edge' or, here, 'shore'. *Regis* 'of the king' was added as a result of King George V's stay here in 1929.

Bogolyubovo, VLADIMIR/RUSSIA
Named after Andrew I, Andrey Bogolyubsky (*c*.1111–74), Grand Prince of Vladimir (1169–74) and the son of Grand Prince Yury Dolgoruky, the founder of Moscow in the 12th century. According to legend, Bogolyubsky was leading his troops in the area in 1164 when he saw a vision of the Virgin Mary, indicating that he should build a settlement here.

Bogong, Mt, VICTORIA/AUSTRALIA
A mountain with an Aboriginal name meaning 'High Plains'.

Bogor, JAVA/INDONESIA *Buitenzorg*
'Carpet' in Sunda, a reference to its textile industry. Founded by the Dutch in 1745, the original name meant 'Without Care' from *buiten* 'without' and *zorg* 'care'.

Bogorodsk, KOMI REPUBLIC AND NIZHNIY NOVGOROD/RUSSIA
Named after their churches which were dedicated to the Virgin Mary (in Russian, *Bogoroditsa*).

Bogotá (Santa Fé de Bogotá), COLOMBIA *Bacatá*
The Chibcha capital, Bacatá, was captured by Gonzalo Jiménez de Quesada in 1538 and he added Santa Fé 'Holy Faith' to the existing name after Santa Fé, his Spanish birthplace. Bacatá was the name of a Chibcha chief. Bacatá soon became Bogotá. When the region achieved independence from Spain in 1819 Bogotá became capital of Gran Colombia, then of Nueva Granada, which in due course became the Republic of Colombia.

Bohemia (Čechy), CZECH REPUBLIC *Boiohemum*
Named after the Celtic Boii tribe with a name meaning 'Homeland of the Czechs' from the Indo-European *haimoz* 'home'. It encompasses five regions of the Czech Republic. It became a kingdom (11th century–1620) within the Holy Roman Empire and thereafter a province in the Habsburg Empire. It was part of

Czechoslovakia in 1918–39 and 1945–92.
Čechy is taken from a chieftain called Čech.
Bohemian has come to describe a socially
unconventional person—a 'gypsy'—since
gypsies were believed at one time to come
from Bohemia.

Boise, IDAHO/USA
Named by French-Canadian trappers for the
tree-lined river (in French, *boisé* 'wooded')
which provided succour for those crossing the
Snake River Plain.

Bokèo, LAOS *Hua Khong*
A province whose name means 'Gem Mine', a
reference to the sapphire deposits in the
region. The original name meant 'Head of the
(River) Mekong'.

Boksburg, GAUTENG/SOUTH AFRICA
Named 'Bok's Town' after Willem Eduard Bok
(1846–1904), the Dutch-born secretary of state
of South Africa (1884–8).

Bolesławiec, POLAND *Bunzlau*
Probably named after Bolesław III (1085–1138),
Prince of Poland (1102–38), who is thought to
have built the castle here. When Germany had
control of Silesia it was called Bunzlau.

Bolhrad, UKRAINE *Bolgrad*
Founded in 1821 by Bulgarians fleeing
Ottoman Turkish oppression and given the
name 'Big Town' from the Bulgarian *bol* 'big'
and *grad*. The Ukrainian spelling was adopted
in 1991 when Ukraine achieved independence.

Bolívar, BOLIVIA, COLOMBIA, ECUADOR, PERU,
USA, VENEZUELA
A department in Colombia, a province in
Ecuador, a state and mountain in Venezuela,
towns in the other countries; and a mountain
in Oregon, USA. All are named after Simón
Bolívar (1783–1830), the national hero of
Bolivia, Colombia, Ecuador, Peru, and
Venezuela who led the revolutions against
Spanish rule in South America.

Bolivia *Charcas* (*Upper Peru*)
The Republic of Bolivia (República de Bolivia)
since 1825 when it gained independence from
Spain. Previously the *Audiencia* 'Court' of
Charcas (1559), also known as Upper Peru, in
the Viceroyalty of Peru; it then became part of
the Viceroyalty of Río de La Plata, whose
capital was Buenos Aires, when it was created
in 1776. The country is named after Simón
Bolívar (see previous entry), although it was
Antonio José de Sucre[†] who actually liberated
Upper Peru in 1824. Rather than join Peru or
Argentina, Bolívar and Sucre decided that
Upper Peru should become independent. As a
consequence of its defeat by Chile in the War

of the Pacific (1879–84), Bolivia lost its Pacific
coast and became landlocked.

Bologna, EMILIA-ROMAGNA/ITALY *Felsina,
Bononia*
A Villanovan settlement from before 1000 BC,
it became Etruscan in about 500 BC and was
called Felsina. It fell to the Celtic Boii tribe in
about 350 BC; they made it their capital and
renamed it Bononia after themselves. In due
course, this evolved into the present name
which is widely used to describe a type of
spaghetti, spaghetti Bolognese.

Bolsover, ENGLAND/UK *Belesovre, Bolesoura*
'Boll's Ridge' from an Old English personal
name and possibly *ofer* 'ridge' or 'slope'.

Bolton, CANADA, UK, USA
UK (England): formerly Bothilton. Derived
from the Old English *bōthl* 'special building' or
'dwelling place' and *tūn*, here with its original
meaning of 'enclosure'; thus a place where
people lived rather than worked.

Bolu, TURKEY *Claudiopolis*
A very ancient city, it was renamed after
Claudius I (10 BC–AD 54), Roman emperor (41–
54). Captured by the Ottoman Turks *c*.1325,
Bolu is the Turkish pronunciation of the Greek
polis.

Boma, DEMOCRATIC REPUBLIC OF THE CONGO
Lombi, Embomma
'Place of the King' in Babwendé, according to
Sir Henry Morton Stanley[†], the British explorer
who founded the Congo Free State in 1879. A
'boma' is a tall and impenetrable hedge of
thorn branches constructed for protection
against wild animals. Between 1886 and 1926
the town was the capital of the Congo Free
State (later the Belgian Congo).

Bombay, MAHĀRĀSHTRA/INDIA
See MUMBAI.

Bonaparte, IOWA/USA
Named after Napoleon Bonaparte[†].

Bonifacio, CORSICA/FRANCE *Giola*
Named after the Genoese Count Bonifacio who
built a castle here in 828 to defend against
pirates. It gives its name to the strait between
Corsica and Sardinia.

Bonin Islands (Ogasawara Guntō), JAPAN
Discovered by the Spanish in 1543, they were
annexed to Japan in 1876. They were not
inhabited and the Anglicized name comes
from Munin Tō 'No Man Islands' from *mu* 'no',
nin 'man', and *tō* 'islands'. The Japanese name,
adopted in 1675, comes from the name of the
first Japanese explorer to see them in 1593
with *guntō* 'islands'. They were returned to

Japan in 1968, having been under American military control since the end of the Second World War in 1945.

Bonn, NORTH RHINE-WESTPHALIA/GERMANY
Castra Bonnensia, Bonna, Bonnburg
Derived from the Gaulish *bona* 'fortress' or 'city'. It was the garrison of the Roman 1st Minerva Legion. In the 9th century the Franks renamed it Bonnburg. It was the capital of the Federal Republic of Germany (West Germany) between 1949 and 1990, but the Federal government remained in Bonn until 1999 when it moved to Berlin.

Boone, USA
1. Iowa: founded in 1865 as Montana and renamed after Captain Nathan Boone, son of Daniel Boone, in 1871.
2. North Carolina: named after Daniel Boone (1734–1820), the legendary frontiersman, who led the first group of settlers through the Cumberland Gap into the wilderness in 1767.

Boonesboro, KENTUCKY/USA *Boonsborough*
Developed from a fortified settlement built in 1775 by, and named after, Daniel Boone (see previous entry). There is also a Boonsboro in Maryland and a Boonville in five other states.

Bootle, ENGLAND/UK *Bodele* (*Cumbria*)
'The Special Building' from the Old English *bōtl*.

Bophuthatswana, NORTH WEST/SOUTH AFRICA
In the Setswana language the name means 'That which binds, *bophutha*, the Tswana People', thus 'The Place of Gathering of the Tswana'; *bo*- is a prefix for abstract nouns and *phutha* means 'to gather'. A former independent Bantu homeland (Bantustan), consisting of seven separate enclaves, and nominal republic for the Tswana within the territory of South Africa from 1977, it was reintegrated into South Africa in 1994.

Bor, RUSSIA, SERBIA AND MONTENEGRO, SUDAN, TURKEY
Russia (Nizhniy Novgorod): 'Pine Forest'. It has the same meaning in Serbo-Croat.

Bora-Bora (Pora-Pora), SOCIETY ISLANDS/ FRENCH POLYNESIA
'First Born' in Tahitian. An island annexed by the French in the 17th century.

Borås, SWEDEN *Boeråås*
Takes its name from a ridge called Buaråsen. *Buar*, or *budhar*, is the genitive of the Old Swedish *budh/bodh* 'booth' or 'stall' with *ås* 'ridge' and the definite article.

Bordj Omar Driss, ALGERIA *Fort Flatters*
Originally named after Paul Flatters, a French officer who surveyed a route for the proposed Trans-Saharan railway (which was never built) and was murdered by Tuaregs. The present name means the 'Fort of Omar Driss', a Muslim leader, with *borj* 'fort'.

Borehamwood, ENGLAND/UK *Borham, Burhamwode*
'Homestead on, or by, a Hill in a Wood' from the possible Old English *bor* 'hill', *hām* or *hamm*, and *wudu* 'wood'.

Borisoglebsk, VORONEZH/RUSSIA *Pavlovskaya Krepost*
Founded in 1646 as 'Paul's Fortress' from *krepost'* 'fortress' as a bulwark against the Tatars, although which Paul is not known. It was later renamed after a church dedicated to two brothers, the princes Boris and Gleb, two of several sons of Vladimir the Great (*c*.956–1015), grand prince of Kiev (980–1015). On Vladimir's death Svyatopolk, their elder half-brother, determined to consolidate all power in his own hands and ordered the murder of his brothers. To ensure the unity of the nation Boris and Gleb submitted without trying to defend themselves in 1015. They were later revered as the first saints of the Russian Orthodox Church. Another brother, Yaroslav (*see* YAROSLAVL'), defeated Svyatopolk in 1019.

Borispol', UKRAINE
'Boris's Town'. The Boris in question may well be Boris Godunov (*c*.1551–1605), Tsar of Muscovy (1598–1605), since the first mention of the town was in 1590.

Borneo (Indonesian: **Kalimantan**), BRUNEI-INDONESIA-MALAYSIA
The island of Borneo comprises the Sultanate of Brunei, the two Malaysian states of Sabah and Sarawak, and Indonesian Kalimantan, although the Indonesians use this name for the whole island. Kalimantan is the Malay name for the indigenous inhabitants. The name *kāliman* 'blackness' itself is taken from the Sanskrit *kāli* 'black' and the Malay *tanah* 'land'. On the other hand, it is also claimed that *kalimantan* is a species of wild mango which would give a name of 'Island of Wild Mangoes'. Because of the diamond field near Martapura, Kalimantan is sometimes translated as 'River of Diamonds'. 'Borneo' is a Portuguese mispronunciation of Brunei, the capital city on the island when it became known to Europeans in the 16th century. Some people in Sarawak (the major part of the non-Indonesian part of the island) maintain that 'Borneo' comes from the Malay *buah nyior* 'coconut'. The Dutch established

predominance in the south during the 18th century while the British moved into the north. The southern two-thirds became a Dutch colony in 1863.

Bornholm, DENMARK *Burghændeholm*
An island and county with a name meaning 'Island of the Burgundians' from *holm* 'island'. They emigrated to Poland during the 1st century and during the 5th century to central France.

Borno, NIGERIA *Bornu*
A state said to mean the 'Home of the Berbers'. Historically, as Bornu, it has been a kingdom and an emirate.

Bosanski Brod, BOSNIA AND HERZEGOVINA
'Bosnian Crossing Place' from the Serbo-Croat *brod* 'boat', but meaning here 'crossing place' (over the River Sava) from Slavonia into Bosnia. *See* SLAVONSKI BROD in Croatia.

Boshof, FREE STATE/SOUTH AFRICA
Founded in 1856 and named after Jacobus Boshof, president of the Orange Free State (1855–9).

Bosnia and Herzegovina *Bosona, Hum, Zachumlje*
Bosnia and Herzegovina (Bosna i Herzegovina) since March 1992. Previously a republic of Yugoslavia (1946–92) and part of Croatia (1941). It did not have its own independent identity when the Kingdom of the Serbs, Croats, and Slovenes was formed in 1918, being annexed to Serbia at that time, or when this was renamed Yugoslavia in 1929. In April 1992 the creation by the Serbs of a Bosnian Serb Republic was proclaimed and three months later a Bosnian Croat Republic was brought into existence. Civil war erupted. Since 1995 the country has been divided into two autonomous regions: the Muslim-Croat Federation of Bosnia and Herzegovina and Republika Srpska 'Serbian Republic'. Bosnia takes its name from the River Bosna (or, in ancient times, Bosanius) while Herzegovina (which comprises 18 per cent of the country and was previously called Hum) means the 'Property of a Duke', or 'Duchy', from the Old Serbian *Herceg* 'duke', *ov*, to make the genitive case of *herceg* to indicate possession, and *ina* 'property'. The name stems from 1448 when Stephen Vukčić Kosača, a Bosnian general, was granted the title of Duke of St Sava, probably by Pope Nicholas V. It was also known as Zachumlje in the Middle Ages, this name referring specifically to the area between the Neretva River and Dubrovnik. For four centuries Bosnia and Herzegovina were Roman provinces, first as part of Illyricum and later of Dalmatia. Bosnia fell to the Turks in 1463 and Herzegovina in 1482. Together, they were placed under the control of Austria-Hungary in 1878, although still under nominal Ottoman Turkish suzerainty, and then annexed by Austria-Hungary in 1908.

Bosporus (Karadeniz Bogazi), TURKEY
A strait linking the Black Sea and the Sea of Marmara from *boğaz* 'throat'; Karadeniz means 'Black Sea'. The English name, sometimes spelt Bosphorus, comes from the Greek and means 'Ox Ford' from *bous* 'ox' and *poros* 'ford'.

Boston, PHILIPPINES, UK, USA
1. UK (England): formerly Botulustan 'Bōtwulf's Boundary Stone' from an Old English personal name and *stān*. This Bōtwulf may have been St Botulf (d. 680) who has been associated with Boston, but he is more likely to have been a landowner.
2. USA: there are four cities with this name, the best known being the one in Massachusetts which was settled in 1630 and named by prominent Puritans who had come from the Boston in England.

Botany Bay, NEW SOUTH WALES/AUSTRALIA
Stingray Harbour
Captain James Cook[†] made his first landing here in 1770. He soon changed the name as a result of the wide variety of plants collected by Joseph (later Sir Joseph) Banks (1743–1820), the chief scientist on board Cook's ship, the *Endeavour*, and President of the Royal Society (1778–1820).

Botev, BULGARIA *Yumrukchal*
The highest peak in the Stara Planina Range renamed in 1950 after Khristo Botev (1849–76), a hero of the national revolutionary movement against Ottoman Turkish rule, and a poet. He was killed by the Turks on Mount Vol shortly after he had entered Bulgaria from Romania where he had headed the movement in exile.

Botevgrad, BULGARIA *Orkhaniye*
Renamed 'Botev's Town' in 1934 after Khristo Botev (see previous entry).

Bothaville, FREE STATE/SOUTH AFRICA
Botharnia
Founded on a farm in 1889 by Theunis Botha and named after him. Four years later, with many more inhabitants, it was renamed 'Botha's Town'.

Bothnia, Gulf of (Swedish: **Bottniska Viken**; Finnish: **Phjan Lahti**), BALTIC SEA
Derived from the Swedish *botten* 'bottom'. On the west side of the Gulf is the Swedish county

of Västerbotten and on the east the Finnish Österbotten.

Botoşani, ROMANIA
A county and city which take their names from a Romanian nobleman, Botas or Botos, who founded and owned the settlement at the end of the 15th century.

Botswana *Bechuanaland*
The Republic of Botswana since 1966 when the name was changed on the achievement of independence. Previously the British Protectorate of Bechuanaland (1885–1966) in response to a request from Khama III (*c.*1837–1923), chief of the Bamangwato tribe of the Tswana people (1875–1923), for protection from the Boers (Afrikaners) in South Africa. It is named after the indigenous people, the Tswana or baTswana. Their name is said to mean 'those who went away' or 'the separators'. Bechuana was an English corruption of Batswana.

Bouaflé, CÔTE D'IVOIRE
A department and a town with a name which is a contraction of Bouavéréfla meaning the 'Place of the Bouavéré' with *-fla* or *-flé* 'place'.

Bouaké, CÔTE D'IVOIRE
Founded in 1865, the name has been corrupted from that of Gbouéké, King of the Baule people.

Bougainville Island, PAPUA NEW GUINEA
The largest of the Solomon Islands and a province, it was discovered in 1768 by, and named after, the French navigator Louis-Antoine de Bougainville (1729–1811). It was subject to German rule between 1898 and 1914 when it was occupied by Australian forces; it was occupied by the Japanese in 1942–4. Part of the UN Trust Territory of New Guinea, it passed to Papua New Guinea in 1975.

Bouira, ALGERIA
'The Small Wells'.

Boulder, COLORADO/USA
Founded in 1858 and named after the huge boulders in the area.

Boulogne, ARGENTINA, FRANCE
France (Nord-Pas-de-Calais): derived from the Gaulish *bona* 'fort'. The full name is Boulogne-sur-Mer 'Boulogne on Sea'. Former names were possibly Potus Itus, Gesoriacum, and Bononia.

Boulogne-Billancourt, ÎLE-DE-FRANCE/FRANCE
Originally two separate towns, Boulogne-sur-Seine and Billancourt. The first was so named because it was founded by people from

Boulogne-sur-Mer. Billancourt means 'Billa's Enclosure' from a Germanic personal name and the Latin *cors*.

Bountiful, UTAH/USA *Sessions' Settlement*
Originally named after Peregrine Sessions, a Mormon pioneer, it was renamed in 1855 in recognition of good harvests.

Bounty Islands, NEW ZEALAND
Discovered in 1788 by Captain William Bligh (1754–1817), an English admiral, who named them after his ship, HMS *Bounty*.

Bourbon, INDIANA AND MISSOURI/USA
Both towns are named after the French royal House of Bourbon.

Bourges, CENTRE/FRANCE *Avaricum*
Named after the Bituriges whose capital this was. Their name meant 'Kings of the World' from the Gaulish *bitu* 'world' and *rix* 'king', an indication that they considered themselves masters of the surrounding area.

Bournemouth, ENGLAND/UK *La Bournemowthe*
'Mouth of the Bourne'. Bourne, the name of the river, simply means 'Stream' from the Old English *burna*, now 'burn'.

Bourton-on-the-Water, ENGLAND/UK
Burchtun, Bortune
'Farmstead by the Hill-Fort' from *burh* and *tūn*. The 'Water' refers to the River Windrush which flows through the town.

Bou Saâda, ALGERIA
'Place of Happiness', *Bou* being a French transliteration of *Bu*, a North African shortening of *Abū* 'father'. *Saâda* or *sa'adah* means 'happiness' or 'felicity' to give an actual translation of 'Father of Happiness'.

Bouvet Island (Norwegian: **Bouvetøya**),
SOUTH ATLANTIC OCEAN
Discovered in 1739 by a French navigator, Jean-Baptiste-Charles Bouvet de Lozier, after whom it was named. It was annexed by Norway in 1930.

Bow, AUSTRALIA, CANADA
Canada (Alberta): a river so-called because the Cree made bows from the trees.

Bowling Green, USA
There are six cities with this name, all believed to be so-called because bowls were played on the green.

Bowral, NEW SOUTH WALES/AUSTRALIA
Settled in 1825 with an Aboriginal name meaning 'large'.

Boyne, AUSTRALIA, IRELAND
Ireland: locally An Bhóinn. A river possibly named after Queen Boann or Board whose

name means 'She who has white cows' or 'White Cow (goddess)' from *bó* 'cow'. According to legend, she lifted the lid of the Well of Segais at Carbury. This was sacred to her husband Nechtain, King of Leinster, and only he and his cup-bearers were allowed to go near it. In response to this act of disobedience the water rose up, formed the River Boyne on its way to the sea, and drowned her.

Brabant (Flemish: **Braband**), BELGIUM *Brachant*
A former province possibly named after Silvius Brabo (*see* ANTWERP). However, it is also possible that the name comes from the Old High German *bracha* 'new land' or 'land prepared for tillage' and *bant* 'region' to give 'Ploughed Area'. It was divided into Flemish Brabant and Walloon Brabant on 1 January 1995. Earlier still, it comprised the southern part of the Duchy of Brabant; this was split in two during the Eighty Years' War (1568–1648), the northern part going to the Dutch. North Brabant is a province of The Netherlands.

Brač, CROATIA *Elaphos, Brattia, Brazza*
An island with an original Greek name. The following Roman name may be derived from the Illyrian *bren tos* 'stag' which became Brazza in Italian and then Brač when the island became part of Croatia.

Bracknell, ENGLAND/UK *Braccan heal*
'A Parcel of Land belonging to Bracca' from the Old English *halh* 'parcel of land' and a personal name.

Bradenton, FLORIDA/USA
Named after Joseph Braden, the first person to settle here permanently in 1854.

Bradford, UK, USA
1. UK (England): formerly Bradeford '(Place at) the Broad Ford', a reference to a wide crossing place over a tributary of the River Aire in Yorkshire. There is a Bradford-on-Avon in Wiltshire, the Anglo-Saxon name for which was Bradanforda be Afne. Avon here is a Celtic river name simply meaning 'river'.
2. USA: there are ten places with this name in the USA, some named after the English town, others after people called Bradford.

Braga, PORTUGAL *Bracara Augusta*
Named after the Celtic Bracarii tribe with the Romans adding the name of their emperor.

Braganza (**Bragança**), BRAZIL, PORTUGAL
Portugal: a district and a city formerly called Brigantia and Juliobriga. The present name was taken from the Celtic settlement on a nearby hill called Brigantia. Julius Caesar[†] developed it into a Roman garrison and the Roman Juliobriga meant 'Hill Fortress of Julius'

from *briga*. It was renamed by Sancho I (1154–1211), King of Portugal (1185–1211), and became the seat of the ruling dynasty of Portugal (1640–1910) and the emperors of Brazil (1822–89), the House of Braganza.

Brahmāpur, ORISSA/INDIA *Berhampur*
'City of Brahmā', one of the major Hindu gods.

Brahmaputra, CHINA-INDIA-BANGLADESH
A river which joins with the Ganges to empty into the Bay of Bengal. Its Hindi name means 'Son of Brahmā', one of the major Hindu gods, with *putra* 'son'. Rising in Tibet, it is known to the Tibetans as the Tsangpo 'The Purifier', to the Chinese as the Yarlung Zangbo, and to the Bengalis as the Jamuna or Yamuna. In Assam, India, it is called the Dihāng and when it is joined by the Dibāng and the Lohit, the river becomes known as the Brahmaputra. On entering Bangladesh it assumes the name Jamuna.

Braintree, UK, USA
1. UK (England): formerly Branchetreu 'Branca's Tree' from an Old English personal name and *trēow* 'tree'.
2. USA (Massachusetts): named after the English town in 1640. Its previous Native American name, Monoticut, meant 'Abundance'.

Brampton, CANADA, UK, USA
1. Canada (Ontario): named after his English birthplace by John Elliott, a founder.
2. UK (England): 'Farmstead where Broom grows' from the Old English *brōm* 'broom' and *tūn*.

Brandberg, NAMIBIA
A mountain with a Dutch name 'Fire Mountain' from *brand* and *berg* , a reference to the glow it appears to give off at times.

Brandenburg, GERMANY, USA
1. Germany: a state and city (Brandenburg an der Havel 'on the (River) Havel'). Originally a Slav fortress called Branibor and later Brennaburg, its name may mean 'Burnt Fortress' from Germanic words associated with *Brand* 'burning' or *Burg*. It was at one time a *Mark* and an electorate of the Holy Roman Empire. It was the base on which the Kingdom of Prussia was founded and with which it merged in 1701. It was a province of Prussia between 1815 and 1945 when that part west of the River Oder in East Germany became a state. It lost this status in 1952 and only regained it in 1990 when East and West Germany were united.
2. USA (Kentucky): named after the Prussian province.

Brandon, CANADA, IRELAND, UK, USA
1. Canada (Manitoba): a Hudson's Bay
Company trading post called Brandon House
was founded in 1793 and named after
Archibald Douglas, Duke of Brandon. When
the Canadian Pacific Railway was built nearby
in 1881, the city of Brandon was founded.
2. Ireland: five natural features in Kerry have
this name, probably after a person called
Bréanann.
3. UK (Suffolk/England): formerly Bromdun
and Brandona 'Hill where Broom grows' from
the Old English *bröm* and *dūn*.

Brandvlei, NORTHERN CAPE/SOUTH AFRICA
'Burned Lake', a reference to the vast salt pans
to the north.

Branford, CONNECTICUT/USA
Adapted from the English Brentford which
means 'Ford over the River Brent'.

Brantford, ONTARIO/CANADA *Brant's Ford*
Named after Joseph Brant, a Mohawk chief,
who was given the land in 1784 to settle the
Six Nations Native Americans after the
American War of Independence (1775–83).

Brasília, BRAZIL
A federal district and capital city. The idea of
having the country's capital in the interior was
first proposed in 1789. However, a site was not
selected until 1956 after Juscelino Kubitschek
(1902–76), president of Brazil (1956–61), had
come to power. He was keen to develop the
economy of Brazil's interior. Government was
transferred from Rio de Janeiro in 1960. The
name is the Latin form of the country's name.

Braşov, ROMANIA *Kronstadt, Brassó, Oraşul Stalin*
Founded in 1211 by the Teutonic Knights, it
became a Saxon colony with a name meaning
'Crown Town' in German. Between the 11th
century and 1918, when it was ceded to
Romania, it was held by the Hungarians with
the name Brassó. It was renamed Stalin City
from *oraş* 'city' between 1950 and 1960 after
the Soviet leader, Joseph Stalin†. The present
name derives from the Slav name Braš and the
possessive suffix *-ov* to give the 'Town of Braš'.

Brass, RIVERS/NIGERIA *Tuwon/Twon, Brasstown*
Lying at the mouth of the Brass River, from
which it takes its name, in the Niger delta. The
name may come from the previous name of
the river, Barasin, believed to mean 'to release'
which may be connected with its role as a
slave-trading port in the early 19th century.
Brasstown was the name coined by Europeans
who added to the name of the river the name
of the previous settlement—and then
corrupted it. An alternative theory as to how
the town gots its name concerns a young

British officer who, keen to know the name of
the place, took the arm of a woman and asked
her. Allegedly, she replied 'Barasi' 'Leave me
alone' in Nembe.

Bratislava, SLOVAKIA *Posonium, Istropolis,
Pressburg, Pozsony*
A region and capital city. Named after Bratislav
(or Braslav), a Slav ruler of the town at the
beginning of the 10th century. The Hungarian
name, Pozsony, which gave way to Bratislava
in 1918, can be traced back to the 1st-century
Roman Posonium, while the German
Pressburg has its origins in Brezlauspurg, a
battle in which the Hungarians defeated the
Moravians in 907. The city was the capital of
Hungary between 1541, when the Ottoman
Turks captured Buda (part of Budapest), and
1784. Although a predominantly German
town, it was given to Czechoslovakia in 1918
because the new country needed a river port
(on the Danube). It became the capital of
Slovakia within Czechoslovakia in 1918 and of
independent Slovakia when that country was
established in 1993.

Bratsk, IRKUTSK/RUSSIA
Founded as a fort in 1631, it is named after the
Buryat people, 'brothers', from *brat*, of the
Russians. *Brat* is derived from the Old Russian
pronunciation of *buryat*.

Braunau, AUSTRIA
A shortening of Brunnenau 'Place of Many
Springs' from the German *Brunnen* 'spring' or
'well'.

Braunschweig LOWER SAXONY/GERMANY
See BRUNSWICK.

Brava, AZORES/PORTUGAL
An island with a name meaning 'Wild' or
'Untamed', although this is not the case.

Brazil (Brasil), AND USA
The Federative Republic of Brazil (República
Federativa do Brasil) since 1889 when the
monarchy was overthrown. Previously the
Empire or Kingdom of Brazil (1822–89) when
independence was declared; part of the United
Kingdom of Portugal, Brazil and the Algarves
(1815–22); and a Portuguese colony (16th
century), the Portuguese having arrived in
1500. This followed the Treaty of Tordesillas in
1494 which demarcated the spheres of
colonial interest between Spain and Portugal:
the latter's rights extended out to 370 leagues
(1 110 miles, 1 786 km; a league varied in
distance but was usually taken to be about 3
miles or 5 kilometres) west of the Cape Verde
Islands, the Spanish beyond. Thus Brazil
became Portuguese and is Latin America's only
Portuguese-speaking nation. The country is

named after the *pau-brasil* tree from which a valuable red dye is extracted. Its original Portuguese name, Ilha de Vera Cruz, meant 'Island of the True Cross'.

Brazzaville, REPUBLIC OF THE CONGO
Nkuma/Ntamo
'City of Brazza'. Named after the French explorer, Pierre Savorgnan de Brazza (1852–1905), who penetrated the Congo River basin interior and founded the city in 1884 on the site of Nkuma which had been ceded to the French in 1880. Savorgnan was Italian-born and became a naturalized Frenchman in 1874. He adopted the suffix Brazza, an island in the Adriatic Sea then under Italian rule, but now belonging to Croatia and known as Brač. Brazzaville became the capital of French Equatorial Africa in 1903 and of the independent Republic of the Congo in 1960.

Brea, CALIFORNIA/USA *Randolph*
The centre of oilfields, the name means 'Pitch' in Spanish.

Břeclav, CZECH REPUBLIC *Bratzlav*
Named after Břetislav I (*c.*1005–55), Prince of Bohemia (1034–55), who built a castle here. The settlement by it was called at first Bratzlav and this became Břeclav.

Brecon Beacons (Bannau Brycheiniog), WALES/UK
A mountain range named after the town of Brecon which itself is named after Brychan, a 5th-century prince; he was later known as Brycheiniog. The Welsh name means 'Peaks of Brycheiniog' and these were used for signalling purposes by lighting fires on them.

Breda, THE NETHERLANDS, SPAIN, USA
The Netherlands: 'Broad River' from the Old Dutch *brede* 'broad' and *a* 'river'. It lies at the confluence of the Mark and Aa Rivers.

Bredasdorp, WESTERN CAPE/SOUTH AFRICA
Founded in 1838 as 'Breda's Village' in Afrikaans by Michiel van Breda, a member of the Cape Legislative Council, and named after him.

Bregenz, AUSTRIA *Brigantium*
'Height'. Lying at the foot of Mount Pfänder, the name is derived from *briga*.

Bremen, GERMANY, USA
Germany: a state and a city formerly called Bremon or Brenun. Lying on the River Weser, the name is derived from the Old Saxon *bremo* 'edge'.

Bremerhaven, BREMEN/GERMANY *Wesermünde*
'Port for Bremen' from *Hafen* 'port'. The former name meant 'Mouth of the (River)

Weser'. Founded in 1827, Bremerhaven was absorbed by, and called, Wesermünde in 1939; it was renamed Bremerhaven in 1947.

Bremerton, WASHINGTON/USA
Laid out in 1891 by, and named after, William Bremer who was instrumental in founding the Puget Sound Naval Shipyard.

Brentwood, UK, USA
UK (England): formerly Boscus arsus and Brendewode 'The Burnt Wood' from the Old English *berned* and *wudu*. The name Boscus arsus was the Latin form of the English name; administrative documents during the Middle Ages were usually written in Latin.

Brescia, LOMBARDY/ITALY *Brixia*
In the foothills of the Alps, the name is derived from the ancient Brixia which is usually considered to have come from the Celtic *briga*.

Bressanone, TRENTINO-ALTO ADIGE/ITALY *Brixen*
Has the same origin as Brescia (see previous entry).

Brest, BELARUS, BULGARIA, FRANCE
1. Belarus: a province and a city whose former names were Berestye, Brest-Litovsk, and Brześć which may be derived from the Slavonic *berёst* 'birch bark' or 'elm', of which there are many locally. Litovsk means 'Lithuanian', indicating that the city, in the 14th century, belonged to that country. Later it became Polish as Brześć. It passed to Russia at the third partition of Poland in 1795. The city was incorporated into Poland in 1919–39, the 'Litovsk' being dropped in 1921. When Germany and the Soviet Union divided Poland after the Nazi–Soviet non-aggression pact in 1939, it became a Soviet frontier town. It was occupied by German forces in 1941–4. When Poland's borders were shifted westwards at the end of the Second World War, Brest was included in the Byelorussian Soviet Socialist Republic which became Belarus in 1991.
2. France (Brittany): derived from the Celtic *bre* 'hill', which in turn comes from *briga*.

Briançon, PROVENCE-ALPES-CÔTES-D'AZUR/FRANCE *Brigantium*
'(The Town) on the Height' from *briga*. The city is partly built on high ground.

Bridgeport, USA
Connecticut: the port here, originally named Newfield and then Stratfield, was so-called for the opening of the first drawbridge over the River Pequonnock.

Bridgeton, NEW JERSEY/USA *Cohansey Bridge*
Founded in 1686 and named after a bridge that was built over the creek here in 1718. It was renamed Bridgetown which in due course became Bridgeton.

Bridgetown, AUSTRALIA, BARBADOS, CANADA, IRELAND, USA
Barbados: the capital of Barbados was founded in 1628 and renamed in the 19th century in recognition of the bridge built by Carlisle Bay. Its former names were Indian Bridge and St Michael's Town.

Bridgnorth, ENGLAND/UK *Brug, Brugg North*
'(Place at) the Bridge' from *brycg* with the later addition of 'north' to distinguish it from another place with the same name.

Bridgwater, CANADA, UK, USA
UK (England): formerly Bruggie, Bryggia, Brycg, Brugie, and Brigewaltier '(Place at) Walter's Bridge' from *brycg* and the personal name of Walter de Dowai, the holder of the manor. The original name was Saxon and the second Old Scandinavian; the meaning then might have been 'fording place' or 'bridge' or even 'gang plank'. Only after the Norman Conquest in 1066 was the name Walter introduced. Versions of Bridgwater have sometimes included an *e* after the *g*.

Bridlington, ENGLAND/UK *Bretlinton*
'Village, or Estate, associated with, or called after, Berhtel' from an Old English personal name, *-ing-* and *tūn*.

Bridport, UK, USA
UK (England): formerly Brideport 'Port, or Market, belonging to Bredy'.

Brigham City, UTAH/USA
Settled in 1851 by Mormons who named it in 1877 after the death of their leader, Brigham Young (1801–77).

Brighton, AUSTRALIA, UK, USA
UK (England): formerly Brighthelmstone or Bristelmestune 'Beorhthelm's Settlement, or Farmstead' from an Old English personal name, meaning 'Bright Helmet', and *tūn*.

Brindisi, APULIA/ITALY *Brentesion, Brundisium*
Named originally after the deer (in Illyrian, *brento* or *bretto*) which roamed the area. In *c.*260 BC it became a Roman town and was renamed Brundisium 'Stag's Head' because of the antler-shaped harbour.

Brisbane, AUSTRALIA, USA
Australia (Queensland): originally established in 1824 as a penal colony in what was then New South Wales called Edenglassie to relieve overcrowding in the Sydney convict

settlement. The name was changed in 1834, when it became a town, in honour of General Sir Thomas Brisbane (1773–1860), a soldier and astronomer who had been governor of New South Wales (1821–5). There is also a river with this name.

Bristol, CANADA, UK, USA
UK (England): formerly Brycgstow and Bristou 'Meeting Place by the Bridge' from *stōw* and *brycg*, a reference to a stone bridge built at the place where the Lower Avon and the Frome Rivers used to join.

Britain *Albion, Britannia*
Albion (in Latin, Albionum) was the first known name for Britain, possibly taken from the Latin *albus* 'white', a reference to the white cliffs that sailors saw as they approached Dover, the shortest route across the English Channel from the continent; or, less likely, it may be taken from the Indo-European root word *alb* 'mountain'. Britannia 'Land of the Britons' was the Roman name for modern England, Scotland and Wales. The Greeks recorded the name as Pretaniké and referred to the inhabitants of the island as Prittanoi 'The Tattooed People', that is, those who customarily decorated their bodies with woad, from a word of Celtic origin meaning 'to cut' or 'to carve'. In time this became 'Britons', after the Roman name Brittani, and they gave their name to the country. A Roman province between 43 and *c.*410, Britannia was divided into two provinces in *c.*200 and four about 100 years later as Roman control was extended northwards and westwards. Old English names included Breoton, Breten, and Bryten. The epithet 'Perfidious Albion' was first used by Augustin, Marquis de Ximénèz (1726–1817), in his poem *L'Ère des Français*. It only became popular during the Napoleonic Wars, being used by Napoleon[†] to describe Britain's self-centred determination to maintain the balance of power in Europe and, in his view, its unscrupulous behaviour towards foreigners. Albion features in the name of some English football teams, notably West Bromwich Albion. *See* GREAT BRITAIN.

British Antarctic Territory, UK
Established in 1962, as a result of the 1961 Antarctic Treaty, to separate those areas of the then Falkland Islands dependent territories which lay within the treaty area from those that did not. It includes a part of the continent of Antarctica, the South Shetland Islands, and the South Orkney Islands.

British Columbia, CANADA
A province. The Colony of British Columbia was proclaimed in 1858 and in 1871 joined

Canada with the Crown Colony of Vancouver to become the Province of British Columbia. The province was planned to be called New Caledonia after the Roman name for Scotland, but Queen Victoria† allegedly vetoed this to avoid confusion with the French island of this name. Instead, it was named after the Columbia River, itself named after an American ship whose name honoured Christopher Columbus†.

British Indian Ocean Territory Established in 1965 from the amalgamation of the Chagos Archipelago and various islands bought from the Seychelles (and returned in 1976). Now an Overseas Territory.

British Isles Until 1949 a collective title for Great Britain, Ireland, and the numerous islands surrounding the two larger islands, including the Isle of Man. In 1949 the Republic of Ireland left the British Commonwealth and so could no longer be included in the title.

British Virgin Islands *See* VIRGIN ISLANDS.

Brits, NORTH WEST/SOUTH AFRICA
Developed from a farm owned by Gert Brits in 1924 and named after him. In Northern Cape Province there is a town called Britstown, but this is named after Hans Brits who owned the farm from which it developed.

Brittany (Bretagne; Breton: **Breiz**), FRANCE *Armorica*
A region. Armorica was the Romanized version of the Celtic word for seaside from *ar* 'on' and *mor* 'sea'. The region was named after the Britons who fled here in the 5th century to escape the Anglo-Saxon invasions of Britain. Between 851 and 939 it was a kingdom before becoming a duchy. Brittany did not become a part of France until 1532. It shares a Celtic heritage with Wales, Ireland, and the county of Cornwall in England.

Brno, CZECH REPUBLIC *Brünn*
Founded in the vicinity of a bridge over the River Svratka in 1314, the name means 'Settlement in a Muddy Place' from an Old Slavonic word *brn* 'mud'. It gave its name to the famous Bren gun, developed in Brno and made in Enfield, England. It was used during and after the Second World War.

Brockton, USA
Massachusetts: renamed from North Bridgewater with a variation of the name Brockville after Sir Isaac Brock (see next entry).

Brockville, ONTARIO/CANADA *Elizabethtown, Williamstown, Charlestown*
Founded in 1790, it rejoiced in three 'royal' names until the American War of 1812 against the UK when it was renamed after Major General Sir Isaac Brock (1769–1812), commander of troops in Upper Canada and lieutenant-governor (1810–12).

Brody, UKRAINE
'Fords' from the Slavonic *brod*.

Broken Hill, NEW SOUTH WALES/AUSTRALIA
So-called after a hump-backed range of hills. Alternatively, it has been suggested that the mining of silver, lead, and zinc resulted in the hill being 'broken'. The previously named Broken Hill in Zambia is now called Kabwe.

Bromsgrove, ENGLAND/UK *Bremesgrefan, Bremesgrave*
'Grove belonging to a Man called Breme' from an Old English personal name and *græfe* 'grove'.

Bronx, The, NEW YORK/USA *Keskeskeck*
A borough of New York City. Two years after local Native Americans sold the site to the Dutch West India Company in 1639, Jonas Bronck bought land here and developed a farm. The area was named after him.

Brooklyn, NEW YORK/USA
A borough of New York City settled in 1645 and named by a Dutch farmer who named it after his home village of Breukelen in the Netherlands. It experienced many different spellings before the present version was adopted towards the end of the 18th century.

Brooks Range, ALASKA/USA
Named after the geologist, Alfred H. Brooks, who surveyed it during the first two decades of the 20th century.

Broome, WESTERN AUSTRALIA/AUSTRALIA
Settled in 1883 and named after Sir Frederick Napier Broome (1842–96), governor of Western Australia (1883–91).

Brownsville, TEXAS/USA
Developed from Fort Brown, named after Major Jacob Brown, who was killed in 1846 defending it from Mexican attack.

Bruchsal, BADEN-WÜRTTEMBERG/GERMANY
'House on the Moor' from the Old High German *bruch* 'moor' or 'marsh' and probably *sal* 'house'.

Bruck, AUSTRIA
Named after the first bridge, *Brücke*, built over the River Mur.

Bruges (Flemish: **Brugge)**, BELGIUM *Municipium Brugense*
Possibly named by the Vikings from *bruggia* 'place of disembarkation'; or from the

Flemish *brug* 'bridge', around which the city developed.

Brunei Brunei Darussalam. The State of Brunei, Abode of Peace (Negara Brunei Darussalam) since independence in 1984; previously a British protectorate (1888) and an independent sultanate (15th century). At this time it controlled most of the island of Borneo, but it is now divided into two small, unequal, enclaves on the north-western coast as a consequence of the district of Limbang between them being ceded to Sarawak, Malaysia, in 1890. The name may be derived from the Sanskrit *bhūmi* 'land'.

Brunswick (Braunschweig), GERMANY, USA
1. Germany (Lower Saxony): 'Bruno's Settlement' after the Saxon Duke Ludolf's son who founded it in 861 and the Old High German *wĩch* 'settlement'.
2. USA (Georgia): founded in 1771 and named after the German Brunswick, the seat of England's royal House of Hanover.
3. USA (Maine): founded as a trading post called Pejepscot in 1628 and renamed in 1717 after the Duchy of Brunswick in Germany.

Bruntál, CZECH REPUBLIC *Freudental*
The original German name meant 'Happy Valley' from *Freude* 'joy' or 'gladness' and *Tal* 'valley' because the Bavarian founders, brought in by the kings of Bohemia, anticipated successful mining and agriculture in the area. The present Czech name is a corruption of the German with the initial *F* changed to *B* and the first two syllables reduced to one.

Brussels (Flemish: **Brussel**; French: **Bruxelles**), BELGIUM
Derived from *bruocsella* from the Germanic *broec* 'marsh' and *sele* 'village', meaning 'Settlement in the Marshes'. The city was the capital of the Spanish Netherlands between 1531 and 1713 and of the Austrian Netherlands between 1713 and 1795. It lost this status when part of France between 1795 and 1815. It shared the status of capital of the Kingdom of the Netherlands with The Hague in 1815–30 until becoming the capital of Belgium in 1830. It gave its name to Brussels sprouts.

Bruton, ENGLAND/UK *Briwetone*
'Farmstead on the (River) Brue' from the river's Celtic name meaning 'brisk' and *tūn*.

Bryan, USA
Texas: founded in 1855 and named after William J. Bryan, who inherited the land on which the city was built.

Bryansk, RUSSIA *Debryansk*
A province and a city. The name may be derived from *debri* 'the wilds' or 'thickets', a reference to the surrounding heavily wooded and uncultivated terrain.

Bryce, Mt, BRITISH COLUMBIA/CANADA
A mountain named after the Irish-born James Bryce (1838–1922), 1st Viscount, under-secretary of state for foreign affairs (1886) and British ambassador to the USA (1907–13).

Brzeg, POLAND *Brieg*
'Bank' or 'Riverside'. The city lies on the River Oder.

Buchanan, CANADA, LIBERIA, USA
1. Liberia: founded in 1835 by black Quakers from Pennsylvania and named by them Grand Bassa after the Bassa people. As more Quakers arrived Thomas Buchanan (?–1841), who had been active in the anti-slavery movement and been governor of Bassa Cove, was appointed the first American governor of Liberia (1839–41) and the colony, as it was then, was renamed after him.
2. USA: there are four towns with this name, some after James Buchanan (1791–1868), American President (1857–61).

Bucharest (Bucureşti), ROMANIA *Cetatea Dambovitei*
The earlier name means 'Dambovita Citadel', a military fortress on a tributary of the River Danube, now called the Dîmboviţa. According to tradition, the present name comes from a shepherd called Bucur, who established a forest settlement from which the city was developed during the 15th century. It was the capital of the Principality of Wallachia from 1659 and of Romania from 1862. The suggestion that the name comes from the Romanian *bucurie* 'joy' is hard to accept.

Buckingham, AUSTRALIA, CANADA, UK, USA
1. Canada (Quebec): named after immigrants from the English Buckingham.
2. UK (England): formerly Buccingahamm and Bochingeham 'Land in a River Bend belonging to Bucca's People' from *-inga-* and *hamm*. This settlement grew into a county called Buckinghamshire with the additional *scīr*.
3. USA: both towns are either named after the English town or the 17th-century 1st or 2nd Dukes of Buckingham.

Budapest, HUNGARY *Aquincum, Ofen*
Founded as a camp for a Roman legion, it acquired its present name in 1873 when the separate towns of Buda, Pest from the Slavonic *pešt* 'furnace' or 'kiln' (in German, *Ofen*), and Óbuda (Old Buda) merged. Buda and Óbuda are on the left bank of the Danube with Pest on the

opposite bank. Óbuda is the oldest and was built on the ruins of the ancient Roman settlement of Aquincum; it was soon eclipsed by Buda. Buda may be named after Attila the Hun's brother, Buda; or it may be named after the first constable of the new fortress built in the 11th century. It developed into an important settlement later than Pest and was therefore called New Pest for a time. The city was occupied by the Ottoman Turks between 1541 and 1686 and they called it Peshte. Buda was the royal capital in 1361–1873 and Budapest the Hungarian capital from 1873.

Budënnovsk, STAVROPOL' TERRITORY/RUSSIA
Svyatoi Krest, Prikumsk
Originally 'Holy Cross'. The city was called Prikumsk in 1924–35 and 1957–73 with the meaning '(Place) by the River Kuma' from *pri*- 'by' or 'near'. In 1935–57 and since 1973 it has been Budënnovsk in honour of Marshal Semën Budënny (1883–1973), commander of the Red Army's 1st Cavalry Army in the North Caucasus during the Civil War (1918–20) and first deputy commissar of defence in 1940–1. Together with Voroshilov[†], who was in charge of political affairs in Budënny's Cavalry Army, and three others (Blyukher, Tukhachevsky, and Yegorov, all shot during Stalin's[†] purges in 1937–9), Budënny was promoted to the rank of marshal in 1935.

Buea, CAMEROON
Derived from Gbea, meaning the children of Eya and Bokwango, who were the founders of the settlement from which the town developed. It was the capital of German Kamerun in 1884–1919 and of the Southern Cameroons until 1961 when it joined Cameroon.

Buenos Aires, ARGENTINA *Nuestra Señora Santa María del Buen Aire*
A province, federal district, and capital city. The port was founded twice by the Spanish: in 1536, after which the settlement quickly succumbed to the indigenous inhabitants, and again in 1580. Spanish sailors named it after their patron saint, Our Lady St Mary of the Good Air (or, perhaps, Favourable Winds). It became the capital of the Viceroyalty of the Río de la Plata in 1776, of the United Provinces of the Río de la Plata in 1816, and of Argentina in 1880.

Buffalo, CANADA, SOUTH AFRICA, USA
1. There are fifteen towns with this name in the USA and one in Canada. Some are so-called because of the former presence of buffalo in the area. The city in New York was not known for buffalo and may have received its name from a mispronunciation of the French *beau*

fleuve 'beautiful river', a reference to the creek, now called Buffalo Creek. However, the city may take its name from that of a local Native American chief.
2. Buffalo is also a common name for bays, creeks, gaps, lakes, mountains, and rivers in Canada and the USA.

Builth Wells (Llanfair-ym-Muallt), WALES/UK
Buelt
'Cow Pasture with Springs'. The 'Wells' was added in the 19th century when the springs were found. The Welsh name means 'St Mary's Church in Buallt'; and Buallt gave Builth.

Bujumbura, BURUNDI *Usumbura*
A province and a city. Originally a small fishing village founded by German colonists in 1899, it was renamed in 1962 when it became the capital of Burundi on the country's independence. The meaning of the name is not known, although the Bantu prefix *Bu* means 'land'.

Bukavu, DEMOCRATIC REPUBLIC OF THE CONGO
Costermansville
Founded in 1901 as 'Costerman's Town'; he was a Belgian official. Renamed in 1966 with a name of unknown meaning.

Bukhara (Bukhoro/Buxoro), UZBEKISTAN
Numijent, Bukhar
A province and a city. Numijent was the Sogdian name. The present name comes from *bukhar*, a Turkish-Mongol form of the Sanskrit *vihāra* 'monastery', although the Chinese and Uighur name, Bukhar, meant 'Temple of Idols'. The city was captured by the Arabs in 709 and became the capital of the vast Sāmānid Empire in the 9th century. The Emirate of Bukhara was founded in the early 16th century. It became a Russian protectorate in 1868, although still ruled by its emir, and was annexed by Soviet Russia in 1920, becoming the Bukharan People's Soviet Republic. In 1924 the Republic's territory was divided between the Turkmen and Uzbek Soviet Socialist Republics. It may have given its name to buckram, a kind of linen or cotton fabric.

Bukittinggi, SUMATRA/INDONESIA *Fort de Kock*
A hill town, it means 'High Hill' from *bukit* 'hill' and *tinggi* 'high'. It was developed round a Dutch fort, Fort de Kock, built in 1845. It is sometimes called Kota Jam Gadang, 'Great Clock Town', after its large clock tower; it is also called Tri Agra after three mountains to the south.

Bukovina, ROMANIA-UKRAINE
'Land of the Beech Trees' from the Slavonic *buk* 'beech tree'. A principality of Moldavia in the

14th century, it only acquired its own name and identity in 1775. Two years later it was ceded by the Ottoman Turks to Austria which made it a duchy in 1849 and a crown land. It was incorporated into Romania in 1918–40 after the collapse of the Austro-Hungarian Empire and again, as the German Army invaded the Soviet Union, in 1941–4. After the Second World War the Ukrainian Soviet Socialist Republic was awarded the northern part and Romania the southern.

Bulandshahr, UTTAR PRADESH/INDIA *Baran*
'High Town' from the Persian *shahr* 'town', a reference to its position on high ground.

Bulawayo, ZIMBABWE *GuBulawayo*
'Place of the Slaughter' from the Ndebele *bulawa* 'to slaughter' with the locative suffix *yo*, a reference to the battle fought in 1868 by Lobengula (*c.*1836–94), King of the Ndebele (1870–93), against a rival chief who would not submit to him. It was razed by Lobengula in 1893 to prevent occupation by Europeans. However, a new town, Bulawayo, was established a few miles to the south by the British the following year.

Bulgaria (Bulgariya)
The Republic of Bulgaria (Republika Bulgariya) since 1990. Previously the People's Republic of Bulgaria (1947–90) after the abolition of the monarchy in 1946; the Kingdom of Bulgaria (1908–46); an autonomous principality of the Ottoman Empire (1878–1908); and an Ottoman province (1396–1878). It is named after the Bulgars, possibly from the Turkic *bulga* 'mixed', meaning a mix of Turkic and Slav tribes.

Bunbury, AUSTRALIA, CANADA, UK
1. Australia (Western Australia): founded in 1843, the town is named after Lieutenant Henry William St Pierre Bunbury who explored this part of Western Australia.
2. UK (England): formerly Boleberie and then Bonebury 'Buna's Stronghold' from an Old English personal name and *burh*.

Bundaberg, QUEENSLAND/AUSTRALIA
Named after the local Aboriginal Bunda tribe.

Būndi, RĀJASTHĀN/INDIA
A former princely state and now a city, said to be named after Būndi, a 13th-century chief.

Burbank, CALIFORNIA/USA
Named after David Burbank, a dentist who established a sheep ranch here in 1867.

Burdur, TURKEY *Polydorion*
The present name is a corruption of the previous Greek name meaning 'Many Gifts'.

Burgas, BULGARIA *Pyrgos*
Derived from the Turkic *burgaz* 'fortress', itself derived from the Greek *pýrgos* 'castle'. There is a town in Turkey called Burgaz with the same meaning.

Burgenland, AUSTRIA
A state meaning 'Land of Castles' from the German *Burgen*, the plural of *Burg*. It was part of Hungary until ceded to Austria in 1920.

Burgesdorp, EASTERN CAPE/SOUTH AFRICA *Klipdrift*
Founded in 1844 with the Afrikaans name Klipdrift 'Rocky Ford'. A year later the inhabitants agreed to change it and chose 'Citizens' Town'.

Burgos, PHILIPPINES, SPAIN
Spain (Castile-León): founded in 884 as a fortress from *Burg* to protect the eastern reaches of the Kingdom of Asturia from the Moors. It became the capital of the County of Castile and then the Kingdom of Castile in 951–1492.

Burgundy (Bourgogne), FRANCE
A region named after the Burgundians, a Scandinavian tribe, who migrated from the southern shores of the Baltic Sea between the 1st and 5th centuries. During its history parts of Burgundy have been a kingdom, a duchy, and a county. Upper Burgundy was known as Jurane Burgundy and Lower Burgundy as the Kingdom of Provence. These two were united and after passing to the German king they became known as the Kingdom of Arles from the 13th century. Cisjurane Burgundy referred to the County of Burgundy (*Franche-Comté) while the Duchy was that part of the realm west of the River Saône; it was annexed by France in 1477. The colour burgundy is probably derived from the colour of the famous red Burgundy wine produced in the region.

Burkina Faso *Upper Volta*
Burkina Faso since 1984. Its three principal rivers, the Black Volta, the White Volta, and the Red Volta gave the country its previous name. This was changed in 1984 to Burkina Faso meaning 'Land of Honest Men' from the Mandekan *burkina* 'honest' or 'upright' and *faso* 'fatherland' from *fa* 'father' and *so* 'village'. Before independence in 1960, Upper Volta (Haute Volta) had become an Overseas Territory of the French Union in 1947, having been a French colony in 1919–32. Between 1932 and 1947 it did not exist as an entity, being divided between Côte d'Ivoire, French Sudan (now Mali), and Niger. A French

protectorate from 1898, it was part of the colony of Haut-Sénégal-Niger in 1904–19.

Burlington, CANADA, USA
There are fifteen places with this name in the USA and two in Canada.
1. Canada (Ontario): named after the English Burlington (now Bridlington).
2. USA (Iowa): previously known by its Native American name Sho-quo-quon 'Flint Hills', it is named after the Burlington in Vermont.
3. USA (New Jersey): originally called New Beverly and then Bridlington after a village in England; Burlington is an alternative spelling of Bridlington.
4. USA (Vermont): founded in 1763 and named after the Burling family.

Burma (Myanmar)
The Union of Myanmar (Pyidaungzu Myanma Naingngandaw) since 1989. Previously the Socialist Republic of the Union of Burma (1974–89) and renamed in 1989 on the orders of the State Law and Order Restoration Council (SLORC) (and now the State Peace and Development Council) for international use because 'Burma' was held to be a relic of European colonialism; Union of Burma (1948–74) on independence. Between 1886 and 1937 Burma was a province of the British Indian Empire, but it was detached in 1937 to become a crown colony and given a degree of self-government. Locally, from the 13th century, the country has been known as Myanma, which is taken from *Mranma*, the local name for the Burmese people and their language. *Myan* means 'swift' and *ma* 'strong'. The English 'Burma' is derived from *Bamma* which is the Burmese pronunciation of *Mranma*. Another reason why Myanmar was considered more acceptable to the SLORC than Burma is because it is not confined to a single ethnic group. (There are over 60 such groups in the country, Burman referring to the majority ethnic group. Internationally, Burmese is accepted as referring to the indigenous inhabitants generally.) Very often the *r* of Myanmar is not printed because it is merely an English addition to lengthen the pronunciation of the preceding *a*. The Burmese domestic cat takes its name from Burma, as does the Birman, the sacred cat of Burma.

Burnaby, BRITISH COLUMBIA/CANADA
Named after Robert Burnaby (1828–78), a leading businessman.

Burnie, TASMANIA/AUSTRALIA *Emu Bay Settlement*
Originally named after the River Emu, it was renamed after a director of the Van Dieman's Land Company, William Burnie.

Burnley, ENGLAND/UK *Brunlai*
'Forest Clearing by the (River) Brun' from the Old English *lēah* 'forest clearing'.

Bursa, TURKEY *Prusa/Brusa*
Named after King Prusias I of Bithynia who founded the town in 183 BC. It was captured by the Seljuk Turks in the 11th century and then by the Crusaders; it fell to the Ottoman Turks in 1326 and was the first capital of the Ottoman Empire (1326–1402).

Burundi *Urundi*
The Republic of Burundi (Republika y'u Burundi) since 1966 when the monarchy was abolished; it had been a kingdom since the 17th century. Independence was gained in 1962 before which Ruanda-Urundi (now, separately, Rwanda and Burundi) had been administered by Belgium as a UN Trust Territory after the Second World War and before that as a League of Nations mandate from 1923; part of German East Africa (1890–1919), although occupied by Belgian troops in 1916. The name comes from the language spoken, Kirundi (a Bantu language) with Bu, a prefix indicating the country, or from the name of the Rundi people. *See* RWANDA.

Bury, CANADA, UK
1. UK (England): '(Place by) the Fort' from *burh*.
2. Canada (Quebec): named after the English town.

Buryatiya, RUSSIA *Buryat-Mongol Autonomous Soviet Socialist Republic, Buryat Autonomous Soviet Socialist Republic*
A republic named after the Buryats, a people of Mongol descent. The first title was in force in 1923–58, after which the 'Mongol' was dropped; the republic was renamed in 1992 after the Soviet Union had disintegrated.

Bury St Edmunds, ENGLAND/UK *Beodriceswyrth, St Edmundsbury*
The original name meant 'Beodric's Enclosure'. The town was then renamed after St Edmund (841–69), a martyr and King of the East Angles (c.864–9) who was captured by the Vikings and, refusing to deny his Christian faith, was killed. In c.915 his body was moved the short distance to Beodriceswyrth.

Busan, SOUTH KOREA
See PUSAN.

Butare, RWANDA *Astrid*
Founded in 1927 as the prospective capital of Ruanda-Urundi. It was previously named after the Swedish-born Queen Astrid (1905–35), wife of the Belgian King Leopold III. The town was renamed in 1962 on Rwanda's independence, but the meaning of its name is unclear.

Bute, AUSTRALIA, UK
UK (Scotland): an island whose name possibly means 'Fire', thus '(Island of) Fire' from the Gaelic *bód*. Former names were Bot and Boot. The name may be pre-Celtic.

Butte, USA
There are three towns with this name in the USA. All are named after *buttes*, a French word for 'hillock', on which they are situated or which overlook them.

Butterworth, MALAYSIA, SOUTH AFRICA
1. Malaysia: named after William Butterworth, governor of Singapore and Malacca (1843–55).
2. South Africa (Eastern Cape): a former Wesleyan mission station founded in 1827 and named after Joseph Butterworth, a treasurer of the Wesleyan Mission Society.

Buturlinovka, VORONEZH/RUSSIA
Named after the Buturlin family, and specifically Marshal Count Alexander Buturlin (1694–1767), commander-in-chief of the Russian Army during the Seven Years' War (1756–63), who was given a large estate here in the 1740s by Elizabeth (1709–61), Empress of Russia (1741–61), whose favourite he was.

Buynaksk, DAGESTAN/RUSSIA *Temir-Khan-Shur*
Until 1922 it may have taken its name from Tamerlane[†]. It is now named after Ulluby Buynaksky (1890–1919), a Bolshevik revolutionary who was executed here.

Buzi, CHINA, MOZAMBIQUE
Mozambique: a river meaning 'kid', a reference to the young antelopes that were numerous here.

Byblos (Jubayl/Jbail), LEBANON *Kubna, Gebal/ Gubla, Gibelet*

A Phoenician city from the 11th century BC, the name is derived from a Phoenician word for 'hill'. Captured by the Crusaders in 1103, they corrupted the name to Gibelet. Byblos is the source of the Greek word *byblion* 'papyrus', which was exported from the city. The English word Bible also takes its name from Byblos since it was a 'papyrus book'.

Bydgoszcz, POLAND *Bromberg*
Situated near the confluence of the Brda and Vistula rivers, the name is derived from the Indo-European root word *bredahe* 'swamp'. The name used during Prussian and German rule loosely equates to *bredahe* with *Berg* added.

Byelorussia *See* BELARUS.

Byron, USA
There are seven towns with this name in the USA. All are thought to be named after Lord Byron (1788–1824), the English Romantic poet.

Byron Bay, AUSTRALIA, CANADA
Australia (New South Wales): a town situated on Cape Byron which was discovered by Captain James Cook[†] in 1770 and named after Commodore (later Admiral) John Byron, grandfather of Lord Byron (see previous entry).

Bystřice, CZECH REPUBLIC
Eight towns have this name which means 'Swift (Stream)' from Czech *bystrý* 'swift'. They are situated on rivers.

Bystrytsya, UKRAINE
A river meaning 'Swift' from the Russian *bystryy*.

Bystrzyca, POLAND
A river meaning 'Swift' from the Polish *bystry*.

Caacupé, PARAGUAY
Derived from the Guaraní *caaguycupé* 'The
Other Side of the Mountain', the town lying in
a valley of the Cordillera de los Altos.

Caála, ANGOLA *Vila Robert Williams*
Named after a local chief. The name was
changed to Vila Robert Williams in 1930 after
Sir Robert Williams (1860–1938), a Scottish
engineer. The original name was restored soon
after Angola achieved independence in 1975.

Cabinda, ANGOLA
An exclave of Angola squeezed between the
Republic of the Congo to the north and the
Democratic Republic of the Congo to the south
and east, Cabinda is the amalgamation of three
former kingdoms: Makongo, Mangoyo, and
Maluangu. After three treaties were signed
between 1883 and 1885, Cabinda became a
Portuguese protectorate. With Portuguese
decolonization in 1974–5, Cabinda became
part of Angola, although a struggle for
independence has continued since 1975. It is
named after its people.

Cabo Delgado, MOZAMBIQUE
A province named after the small peninsula
meaning 'Thin Cape' in Portuguese.

Cabo Gracias a Dios, HONDURAS-NICARAGUA
A cape 'Thanks (be) to God' in Spanish. So
named in 1502 by Columbus[†] who, having
been becalmed here, was able to proceed with
the help of a following wind.

Cabot Strait, CANADA, USA
Canada: a lake and a strait between
Newfoundland and Cape Breton Island named
after John Cabot (c.1450–c.1499), the Italian
navigator who explored this area on behalf of
Henry VII, King of England (1485–1509), at the
end of the 15th century.

Čačak, SERBIA/SERBIA AND MONTENEGRO *Gradac*
Situated on the Western Morava River, the
Turkish name means 'Frozen Mud', the Serbo-
Croat word being *čagalj*. This word also means
jackal, for which the more usual word now is
šakal, presumably a reference to the numerous
wild dogs in the area. The town was under
Ottoman Turkish rule in 1459–1815.

Cáceres, BRAZIL, COLOMBIA, SPAIN *Castra
Caecilius, Norba Caesarina, Alkazares/Quazri (Spain)*

Spain (Extremadura): possibly founded in 74
BC by, and named after, the Roman consul
Quintus Caecilius Metellus Pius (d. c.63 BC), the
present name being derived from Caecilius.
The name was given an Arabic flavour by the
Moors during their occupation from the 9th
century until 1229 when the town was
recaptured by Alfonso IX (1171–1230), King of
León (1188–1230).

Cádiz, PHILIPPINES, SPAIN, USA *Gadir, Gades, Julia
Augusta Gaditana, Jazīrat Qādis (Spain)*
1. Spain (Andalusia): founded c.1100 BC by the
Phoenicians as Gadir 'Enclosure' which came
to mean a 'Walled Place in a State of Defence'
or 'Fortress'. The port surrendered to the
Romans at the end of the Second Punic War in
201 BC and was renamed Gades and then Julia
Augusta Gaditana. It fell to the Moors in 711,
taking on the name Jazīrat Qādis 'Fortress
Island', although it is actually on a long,
narrow, peninsula, until recaptured by
Alfonso X (1221–84), King of Castile and León
(1252–84), in 1262. It was the temporary
capital of all that part of Spain not under
French control in 1810–12.
2. The city in the Philippines, spelt Cadiz, is
named after the city in Spain, as are the towns
in Kentucky and Ohio, USA.

Caen, LOWER NORMANDY/FRANCE *Catumagos*
'Battlefield' from the Gaulish *catu* 'battle' and
magos 'field' or 'plain'. The most recent
example of it being a battlefield was just after
the Allied invasion of Normandy in June 1944
when Caen was crucial to the German defence;
consequently, it suffered severe damage.

Caerleon (Caerllion), WALES/UK *Castra Legionis,
Caerleion*
The popular name of the Roman military base
was *Castra Legionis* 'Camp of the Legion' (2nd
Augustan Legion) from which the present
name has evolved from the Welsh *caer* and
legionis, the genitive of the Latin *legio* 'legion'.
The actual Roman fort was called Isca Legionis
'Isca of the Legion', with Isca being the Roman
name of the River Usk on which the town
stands.

Caernarfon, WALES/UK *Kairarvon, Kaer yn Arvon*
'Fort in Arfon' from *caer, yn* 'in' and the district
of *Arfon* 'opposite Anglesey' from *ar* 'over' and
Fôn, a form of Môn, the Welsh name for

Anglesey. It stands on the shore of the Menai Strait.

Caerphilly (Caerffili), WALES/UK *Kaerfili, Kaerphilly*
'Ffili's Fort' from *caer* and a Celtic personal name. It gave its name to the famous cheese.

Caerwent, WALES/UK *Cair Guent*
'Fort of Gwent' from *caer* and Gwent coming from the British *venta* 'trading place'.

Caesarea (Hebrew: Ḥorbat Qesari), ISRAEL
Straton's Tower, Caesarea Palaestinae/Maritima
Ruins. The Hebrew name means the 'Ruins of Caesarea'. Originally a Phoenician settlement called Straton's Tower, it was redeveloped by Herod the Great (73–4 BC), the Roman client King of Judaea (37–4 BC), between 22 and 10 BC and renamed after his patron, the Emperor Caesar Augustus†. It was given the suffixes *Palaestinae* and *Maritima* to distinguish it from the Caesarea Philippi (*see* BĀNIYĀS) north of the Sea of Galilee on the Golan Heights. An important port, Caesarea became the capital of the Roman province of Judaea in AD 6 and after 135 of the province of Syria-Palestina. It declined after capture by the Arabs in 637 and was destroyed in 1265 by Baybars I (1223–77), the Mamlūk Sultan of Egypt and Syria (1260–77).

Cagliari, SARDINIA/ITALY *Cardlis, Caralis/Calares*
The origins of the name are uncertain, but the present name is derived from the Latin Caralis which itself was derived from the Greek Cardlis. The root of the name may be from a Phoenician word *karel* 'City of God' or 'Large City', the Phoenicians beginning to settle here in the 8th century BC. Ancient sources gave the name in the plural, that is, Calares or Caralis.

Caguas, PUERTO RICO
Founded in 1775, it is named after a Native American chief who converted to Christianity.

Cahokia, ILLINOIS/USA
Founded in 1699 and named after a Native American tribe whose name perhaps meant 'Wild Geese'.

Cahors, MIDI-PYRÉNÉES/FRANCE *Cadurcum, Divona*
The original Roman and the present names are taken from the Cadurci people. The second Roman name recognizes the ancient spring, Divona, coming from a Gaulish word for 'holy well'.

Caia, MOZAMBIQUE *Vila Fontes*
'House'. In 1954–81 it was renamed after Pereira de Melo, Marquis of Fontes, a founder of the Portuguese Mozambique Company.

Cairngorms, SCOTLAND/UK
A range of mountains which take their name from their highest peak, Cairn Gorm 'Blue Rock' from the Gaelic *carn* 'rock' and *gorm* 'blue'.

Cairns, QUEENSLAND/AUSTRALIA
Founded in 1873 as a government customs collection point, it was named after Sir William Cairns (1828–88), governor of Queensland (1875–7).

Cairo (al-Qāhirah) EGYPT, USA *Babylon-in-Egypt, al-Fusṭāṭ, al-Mansūrīyah (Egypt)*
1. Egypt: Heliopolis 'City of the Sun' may be the oldest city on a site on the east bank of the River Nile now occupied by modern Cairo (district of al-Matarīyah). By *c.*3100 BC it had become an important religious centre. About 500 BC the Persians built a fortified town from which some 500 years later the Romans developed a military stronghold at On (modern Heliopolis) which they called Babylon-in-Egypt. This may be an affectionate reference to the Babylon in Mesopotamia or come from Bāb il-On 'Gate of Heliopolis'. When the Arabs arrived in 641 to besiege what was now a city, they erected a tented camp close by. They called it al-Fusṭāṭ, to mean roughly 'The Tented City' or 'Military Camp'. It became their capital and the foundation of the modern city of Cairo. In 969 the Fāṭimids, dissident Islamists from modern Tunisia under their caliph al-Muʿizz (*c.*930–75), invaded and conquered Egypt. They built a new capital just to the north-east of al-Fusṭāṭ which they called al-Mansūrīyah 'The (Place of) Victory'. According to a convenient legend, although the city boundaries had been demarcated, construction could not begin until Moorish astrologers rang their bells attached to ropes ringing the area to indicate that the propitious moment had arrived. However, a raven landed on the rope and set off the bells. The astrologers consulted their charts to discover which planet was in the ascendant. It was Mars, *al-Qāhir*, and so it was quickly decided to begin work and in 974 the city was given this name from which the present conventional English name is derived. With Mars figuratively meaning 'warlike prowess', the feminine al-Qāhirah (cities in Arabic are feminine) represents 'The Victorious' or 'The Strong'. Al-Qāhirah and al-Fusṭāṭ coexisted until 1168 when the latter was set alight to protect al-Qāhirah from the Crusaders. Capital of the Mamlūks in the 13th century, it was downgraded to a provincial capital by the Ottoman Turks when they seized the city in 1517. The British arrived in the 1880s but allowed the dynasty of Muhammad Ali

(1769–1849), viceroy and pasha of Egypt (1805–49), to continue as puppet rulers until the Egyptian Republic was created in 1952 with Cairo as its capital.
2. USA (Illinois): lying in a delta at the confluence of the Mississippi and Ohio Rivers, the site was said to resemble that of the Egyptian city and was thus named after it.

Caister, ENGLAND/UK *Caistor*
'(Roman) Camp, or Town' from *ceaster*.

Calabar, CROSS RIVER/NIGERIA *Old Calabar*
The name may be taken from the name of the first king, Kalabari. The 'Old' was dropped in 1904, having been used to distinguish it from New Calabar to the west.

Calabria, ITALY *Ager Bruttius/Brutium, Bruzzio*
A region whose name is derived from a pre-Indo-European root word *kal* or *kalabra* 'rock'. For 1 000 years up to the end of the 7th century Calabria referred to the south-eastern 'heel' of Italy rather than, as now, to the 'toe'. The name Calabria came into fashion with the Byzantines.

Calais, FRANCE, USA
1. France (Nord-Pas-de-Calais): formerly Calesium and Callis named after the Gaulish Caleti tribe. It was under English control in 1346–1558 and was the last piece of English territory in France to fall to the French.
2. USA (Maine): named after the French town in 1809.

Calatayud, ARAGÓN/SPAIN
'Ayyub's Castle' from the Arabic *qal'at Ayyub* with *qal'at* 'fort of' and Ayyūb bin Habīb al-Lakhi, the name of a Moorish prince or *wali* 'provincial governor'.

Calcutta (Kolkata; Bengali: **Kālīkāta or Kālīghāṭa**), INDIA, USA
India (West Bengal): the conventional English name is the Anglicized version of Kālīkāta which is said to be derived from the Bengali *Kālīkshetra* 'Kālī's Dwelling Place' or in this case 'Shrine', or from *Kālī-ghat*. *Kālī*, in Sanskrit, means 'black' and *ghaṭṭa* 'place of access' or 'steps' to indicate the steps going down from Kālī's temple to the water. Kālī is the ferocious Hindu goddess of the dead. The city was founded by Job Charnock in 1690; he was the local agent of the English East India Company and he wanted to establish a trading post in Bengal. He selected the site of three villages, one of which was called Kalikātā. The settlers' defensive fortification, begun in 1697, came to be known as Fort William, after William III[i] in 1700. After the city was sacked by the Nawab (ruler) of Bengal in 1756, he placed over 100 Europeans in a small room—the so-called Black Hole of Calcutta; only a few survived. The city was recaptured the following year by Robert Clive (1725–74), later 1st Baron Clive of Plassey, who went on to defeat the Nawab at the Battle of Plassey in June, thus securing the future of the East India Company's operations in Bengal. Calcutta was one of three Presidencies of the Company (the others were Bombay and Madras) and was the capital of British India between 1772 and 1912. The city gave its name to the Calcutta Cup, the trophy given to the victor in the annual rugby union match between England and Scotland. Originally the cup belonged to the Calcutta Football Club which presented it to the Rugby Football Union in 1878. In August 1999 West Bengal MPs voted to bring the name into line with Bengali pronunciation. The Bengali name is usually spelt Kolkata in the international arena.

Caldas, BRAZIL, COLOMBIA
1. Brazil (Goiás): called Caldas Novas 'New Hot Springs'.
2. Colombia: 'Hot Springs'. A department and a city.

Caldas da Rainha, PORTUGAL
'Queen's Hot Springs' after Queen Leonor (1458–1525), wife of King John II, discovered the locals bathing in the mineral springs. She sold some of her jewels and used the money to found a hospital here in 1484.

Caledon, CANADA, SOUTH AFRICA, UK
1. South Africa (Western Cape): the original name was Zwarte Berg 'Black Mountain', the town being overlooked by a mountain. It was renamed in 1813 after the Earl of Caledon, governor of the Cape (1807–11).
2. South Africa (Free State): a tributary of the Orange River rising in the Drakensberg Mountains and discovered in 1777 by a Dutch-born Scottish explorer, Robert Gordon. He called it Prinses Wilhelminarivier after Princess Wilhelmina (1751–1820) of Prussia who had married William V, Prince of Orange, in 1767. In 1809 it was renamed after the Earl of Caledon, governor of the Cape (1807–11).

Caledonia, CANADA, USA
The Roman name for Scotland has been adopted for a number of American and Canadian towns. The name comes from a tribe called the Caledonii who lived in that part of northern Britain.

Calexico, CALIFORNIA/USA
Founded in 1900 on the border with Mexico, the name is taken from a combination of *Cali*fornia and *Mex*ico. It is opposite Mexicali.

Calgary, CANADA, UK
Canada (Alberta): founded in 1875 as Fort
Brisebois, a North West Mounted Police post, it
was renamed Fort Calgary the following year
by a Canadian police officer, some of whose
forebears had lived in Calgary on the Isle of
Mull, Scotland.

Calicut, KERALA/INDIA
See KOZHIKODE.

Caliente, USA
The towns in California and Nevada both have
the meaning 'hot' or, figuratively, 'fiery' from
the Spanish word *caliente*.

California, PERU, TRINIDAD, USA
USA: a state whose name is thought to have
literary origins: derived from the Spanish
novel *Las Sergas de Esplandián* (The Exploits of
Esplandián) which describes an imaginary
island called California. The actual mainland is
said to have been so-called by Hernán Cortés[†]
before it was actually sighted by the Spanish
navigator, Juan Cabrillo (d. *c*.1543), the
discoverer of California in 1542. Sir Francis
Drake annexed the territory he annexed in 1579
New Albion in what is now California.
California became part of Mexico after
Mexican independence from Spain in 1821. In
1846 American settlers declared independence
and, following the US–Mexican War of 1848,
the territory was ceded to the USA. In 1850 it
became the 31st state. It gave its name to
californium, discovered at the University of
California in 1950.

Caltanissetta, SICILY/ITALY
Possibly derived from the Arabic *qal'at an-nisā*
'Fortress of the Women'. More likely is it that
the name comes from a Latin name, Nisa or
Nissa, with *qal'at*.

Calumet City, ILLINOIS/USA *West Hammond*
Founded in 1868, it was renamed in 1924 after
a Native American version of the French
chlamel 'little reed', itself from the Latin *calamus*
'reed' which, in its modified form, meant a
peace pipe; in other words, the pipe used to
signify the ratification of a treaty.

Calvary, GEORGIA/USA
Named after the hill outside Jerusalem on
which Jesus was crucified. Known locally as
Golgotha, this meant 'skull' in Aramaic;
Calvary means the same from the Latin *calva*.

Calvinia, NORTHERN CAPE/SOUTH AFRICA
Founded in 1851 and named after John Calvin
(1509–64), the Protestant reformer.

Camagüey, CUBA *Santa María del Puerto Príncipe*
A province and a city. Founded in 1514 on the
site of the modern Nuevitas, the city was

moved inland in 1528 to the native village of
Camagüey. It was the capital of the Spanish
West Indies during the 19th century and was
renamed after the local chief, Camaguai, in
1903.

Camberley, ENGLAND/UK *Cambridge Town*
Originally named in 1862 after the 2nd Duke
of Cambridge (1819–1904), commander-in-
chief (1856–95), who, that year, was promoted
to field marshal and established the Army
Staff College here (since moved to
Shrivenham). The name was changed,
probably for postal reasons, to avoid confusion
with the older city of Cambridge. It seems to be
a name of pure invention with no discernible
meaning.

Cambodia (Kampuchea) *Chenla, Kambuja*
The Kingdom of Cambodia (Preah Reach Ana
Pak Kampuchea) since 1993. Previously the
State of Cambodia (1989–93), the name
'Cambodia' being taken to distance the
country internationally from the 'Kampuchea'
favoured by the Communist Khmer Rouge; the
People's Democratic Republic of Kampuchea
(1979–89); Democratic Kampuchea (1976–9),
the Khmer Rouge insisting that the country be
known internationally by the local Khmer
name after their take-over in April 1975; the
Khmer Republic (1970–5), and the Kingdom of
Cambodia since independence was gained in
1953; before that the country, known to the
French as Cambodge, had been a French
protectorate since 1863. Kampuchea is the
original Khmer pronunciation of Cambodia
which itself is the Latinized form of the
Sanskrit Kambuja. From the 9th to the mid-
15th centuries the Khmer state was known as
Kambuja, a name derived from the Sanskrit
nagara 'city'. Kambuja, the name of an early
and small kingdom in northern Pakistan
supposedly in the region of Chitral, means
'Those born to Kambu', the mythical founder
of Cambodia. With the decline of Funan (the
Chinese name for what is now southern
Cambodia) in the 6th century, the Chinese
referred to Cambodia as Land (Upper) Chenla
and Water (Lower) Chenla. When Yasovarman
I, king (*c*.889–*c*.900), built his new capital at
Angkor, the Khmer civilization, until the
mid-15th century, came to be known as
Angkorian. From 1593, when the Thais
attacked, to the arrival of the French,
Cambodia was a vassal state of the Thais and
the Vietnamese.

Camborne, ENGLAND/UK *Cameron*
'Crooked Hill' from the Cornish *camm*
'crooked' and *bronn* 'hill'.

Cambrai (Flemish: **Kambryk/Kamerijk**), NORD-PAS-DE-CALAIS/FRANCE *Camaracum*
Adapted from the Roman name which probably comes from the personal name 'Camarus'. This may be taken from the Latin *cammarus*, a type of lobster, with the suffix *-acum* signifying a place-name. However, it might mean a '(Place on a) Bend (in the River Escaut)' from the Gaulish *cambo* 'curve' or 'crooked'. Changing hands many times, the town was ceded to France in 1678 by the Treaty of Nijmegen. It has given its name to cambric, a fine white linen or cotton fabric.

Cambrian Mountains, WALES/UK
A Roman name meaning now 'Welsh Mountains' from the Roman name for Wales, Cambria, which was derived from the people's name for themselves: in modern Welsh, Cymry.

Cambridge, CANADA, JAMAICA, NEW ZEALAND, UK, USA
1. UK (England): the original name, Grantacaestir, indicated a Roman fort, *ceaster*, on the River Granta. Later it became Grontabricc 'Bridge over the Granta' from the Celtic river name, whose meaning is unknown, and *brycg*. By the time of the Domesday Book (1086) the name had become Cantebrigie. The switch from 'Granta' to 'Cam' took place during Norman rule and this applied to the city before the Granta became the River Cam; thus the river name was a back-formation from the place-name. The county of Cambridgeshire took its name from the city, the most important in the district, with the additional *scīr*.
2. The other towns with this name, eleven of which are in the USA, are generally named after the English university city or various Dukes of Cambridge.

Camden, AUSTRALIA, USA
1. Australia (New South Wales): originally Cowpastures, it was renamed Camden Park in 1805 after John Jeffreys Pratt (1759–1840), 1st Marquess and 2nd Earl of Camden, who was the British secretary of state for war and the colonies (1804–5).
2. USA (Arkansas): founded in 1783 as Écore á Fabre after a Frenchman and renamed by Thomas Woodward after his hometown in Alabama.
3. USA (New Jersey): a settlement was founded in 1681 and named Pyne Point. In 1773, now as a town, it was renamed after Charles Pratt (1714–94), 1st Earl of Camden, British lord chancellor (1766–70), in gratitude for his opposition to the taxation of American colonists.

4. USA (South Carolina): founded in 1734 as Pine Tree Hill and renamed after the 1st Earl of Camden in 1768.

Cameron Highlands, MALAYSIA
A hill resort developed by the British in the 1940s and named after William Cameron, who explored the area in 1885.

Cameroon *Kamerun, French Cameroun*
The Republic of Cameroon (République du Cameroun) since 1984. Previously the United Republic of Cameroon (1972–84); the Federal Republic of Cameroon (1961–72) when the British UN Trust Territory of the Southern Cameroons joined the Republic of Cameroon (1960–1) which gained its independence from France in 1960. From 1946 to 1959 French Cameroun was a UN Trust Territory administered by the French, having been a French League of Nations mandate since 1922. The arrangements for the British Southern and Northern Cameroons (the North joined Nigeria in 1961) mirrored those for French Cameroun. Between 1884 and 1916 the Germans ruled the larger part of Cameroon as the Protectorate of Kamerun. Sailing into the Wouri River estuary at the end of the 15th century, Portuguese explorers found plentiful supplies of prawns and thus named the area *Rio dos Camarões* 'River of Prawns', which was later Anglicized to Cameroons River. There is also a Mount Cameroon.

Camogli, LIGURIA/ITALY
May be shortened from *Casa delle Mogli* 'House of Wives' from *casa* 'house' and *moglie* 'wife' or be derived from the name Camullius.

Camp David, MARYLAND/USA *Shangri-La*
Established as a retreat for American presidents in 1942, it was renamed in 1953 by Dwight D. Eisenhower (1890–1969), President of the USA (1953–61), after his grandson.

Campania, ITALY
A region whose name is derived from the Campani, the pre-Roman name for the inhabitants of Capua, the area's most important city in ancient times, and of the Campanian plain. Campani is probably an Oscan name and it may be associated with the later Latin *campus* 'plain'. Campania was colonized by the Greeks from *c.*750 BC and by the Etruscans, and only in the late 4th century BC was it conquered by the Romans.

Campbellton, NEW BRUNSWICK/CANADA *Martin's Point*
Founded *c.*1793 by Scottish fishermen, it was renamed in 1833 after Lieutenant General Sir Archibald Campbell (1769–1843), lieutenant-governor of the province (1831–37).

Campbelltown, AUSTRALIA, USA
Australia (New South Wales): originally called
Airds in 1810 by Lachlan Macquarie
(1761–1824), governor of New South Wales
(1809–21), after his wife's home town. He
renamed it after her maiden name in 1820.

Campbeltown, SCOTLAND/UK *Dalruadhain,
Kilkerran, Kinlochkerran*
Renamed for the first time after the Irish St
Ciaran (Kieran) who is supposed to have visited
the area in the first half of the 6th century. It
received its present name when James V
(1512–42), King of Scots (1513–42), gave the
land to the Campbells of Argyll.

Campeche, MEXICO
A state and a city whose name was corrupted
from the ancient Mayan province of Ah Kim
Peche by the Spanish in 1542. The Mayan
name is said to come from the Mayan *kam*
'grass snake' and *peque* 'tick', both of which
thrive here, or to mean 'Lord Sun Sheep-Tick'.

Campina Grande, PARAÍBA/BRAZIL *Porta do
Sertão*
Originally with the Portuguese name 'Gateway
to the Hinterland', it was renamed in 1864 to
mean 'Great Prairie' from the Portuguese
campina 'prairie' or 'plains'.

Campinas, SÃO PAULO/BRAZIL *Nossa Senhora da
Conceição de Campinas de Mato Grosso, São Carlos*
An abbreviated version of the original name
'Our Lady of the Conception of the Prairies of
the Mato Grosso' which is taken from the
Portuguese *campina* 'prairie' or 'plains'.

Campobasso, MOLISE/ITALY
The previous hill town was abandoned in the
18th century and a new town built lower
down. Literally, the name means 'Low Field'
and this would be apt. However, the name
could mean the 'Field of Bassus', a personal
name.

Campo Grande, MATO GROSSO DO SUL/BRAZIL
'Great Plain' in Portuguese.

Campo Maior, BRAZIL, PORTUGAL
Portugal: according to legend, three men were
searching for a good place to build a town.
Eventually one of them said 'Aqui é o campo
maior' 'Here is the best piece of land'. The
location was in fact the site of a Roman
settlement.

Campos, RIO DE JANEIRO/BRAZIL
'Plain' in Portuguese, that is savannah, a
treeless grassy plain.

Canaan, CANADA, TOBAGO, USA
These towns are all named after the ancient
name for western Palestine, the land promised
to the children of Israel, the 'Promised Land'.
The origin of the word is unknown. However,
it may be derived from a Semitic word
signifying 'reddish purple', a reference to the
purple dye made in the area or to the wool
made with such dye. Alternatively, it has also
been suggested that it may come from *kana* 'to
be low' or 'humble', thus 'lowlands'. The
ancient region was called Retinu by the
Egyptian pharaohs. The Phoenicians' name for
themselves may have been Kena'ani
'Canaanites'; the secondary meaning of the
Hebrew *kena'ani* 'merchant' well describes the
Phoenicians. In the Bible (Genesis 9: 18) a man,
Canaan, is said to be the son of Ham and the
grandson of Noah. *See* LEBANON.

Canada *New France, Quebec, British North America*
Eastern Canada (along the St Lawrence River
and around the Great Lakes) was colonized by
the French as New France largely during the
17th century. In 1763 the region was ceded to
Great Britain at the Treaty of Paris. The British
used Quebec to describe Canada for a period
after their acquisition of the country and later
British North America. The original name
Canada was restored in 1791 when it was split
into Upper and Lower Canada. In 1841 Upper
Canada (renamed Canada West) and Lower
Canada (renamed Canada East) merged to form
the United Province of Canada. In 1867 the
Dominion of Canada, a confederation, was
established to include Nova Scotia, New
Brunswick, Ontario (formerly Canada West)
and Quebec (formerly Canada East). From 1947
the title 'Dominion' was not used. In 1982
complete national sovereignty was achieved.
The name is probably derived from the Huron-
Iroquois word *kanata* 'village' or 'settlement'.
This was mistaken by a French expedition
exploring the Gulf of St Lawrence in 1534 to be
the name of the country. An alternative, and
less likely, explanation is that the name comes
from the Portuguese who sailed up the St
Lawrence in the hope of reaching the Indian
sea; on realizing their mistake they entered *acá
nada* 'here nothing' in their log. The natives
remembered this word and told later explorers
who took the word to be the name of the
country. It has given its name to a type of
goose.

Canadian, USA
A river in the southern USA, rising in New
Mexico, and probably named by French-
Canadian trappers or explorers.

Çanakkale, TURKEY *Kale-i Sultaniye*
1. Founded in the 15th century on the south
side of the Dardanelles as 'Sultan's Fortress'
from *kale* 'fortress', it became famous for its

pottery and thus was renamed in the 18th century 'Pottery Fortress' from *çanak* 'pot'.
2. Çanakkale Boğazi is the Turkish name for the Dardanelles, formerly known as Hellespont, the narrow strait between European and Asiatic Turkey which links the Aegean Sea with the Sea of Marmara.

Canary Islands (Islas Canarias), SPAIN
Canariae Insulae
An autonomous community called Canarias and, according to the Roman scholar, Pliny the Elder (23–79), named after the many large dogs, from the Latin *canis* 'dog', on the island of Grand Canary (Gran Canaria). The name was then extended to the islands as a whole. Pliny also called them the 'Blessed' or 'Fortunate Islands' and Ptolemy[†] chose them as the zero line of longitude (now Greenwich, England) because he believed there could be no inhabited place any further west. Spanish sovereignty was recognized in 1479.

Canberra, AUSTRALIAN CAPITAL TERRITORY/
AUSTRALIA *Kamberra/Kambery, Yass-Canberra*
Originally a small settlement with a name derived from an Aboriginal word *nganbirra* 'meeting place'. A capital city was required for the Commonwealth of Australia when it was created in 1901. With Melbourne and Sydney both claiming to be Australia's pre-eminent city, it was decided to build a new capital. The site was chosen in 1909 and in 1927 Canberra was inaugurated as the capital. The British Canberra bomber and photo reconnaissance aircraft was named after the city. *See* AUSTRALIAN CAPITAL TERRITORY.

Canby, USA
Three towns in California, Minnesota, and Oregon are named after the US Army General Canby, who was treacherously murdered by Native Americans.

Cancún, QUINTANA ROO/MEXICO *Cancúne*
Selected by a government computer to be an international holiday resort in 1970 on the tip of the Yucatán Peninsula, it was originally a small Mayan settlement with a name meaning 'Vessel at the End of the Rainbow'; locals also claim that it means 'Snakes' Nest' from the Mayan *cun* 'snake' and *can* 'nest'.

Cangas de Narcea, ASTURIAS/SPAIN
Lying on the junction of the Narcea and Luiña rivers, the name means 'Town on the Narcea' with a local word for 'town'.

Caniapiscau, QUEBEC/CANADA
A river with a Native American name meaning 'Rocky Point'. It rises from Lake Caniapiscau.

Çankiri, TURKEY *Gangra, Germanicopolis, Kangri*
Renamed Germanicopolis *c.*6 BC when it was subsumed into the Roman province of Galatia to mean the 'City of Germanicus'. Gaius Germanicus Caesar (15 BC–AD 19), although never achieving much himself, was the son, father and brother of Roman emperors. Captured by the Seljuk Turks in 1071, it was incorporated into the Ottoman Empire in the 15th century.

Cannanore, KERALA/INDIA *Kannūr*
'Krishna's Town'. However, it could also mean 'Beautiful Town' from the Tamil *kannu* 'eye' and *ūr* 'town' or 'village'.

Cannes, PROVENCE-ALPES-CÔTES D'AZUR/FRANCE
Canois
'Cane Harbour', a reference to the reeds that once grew in the surrounding area.

Cannock, ENGLAND/UK *Chenet, Canoc*
'The Hillock' from the Old English *cnocc*.
Cannock Chase takes its name from Cannock with the additional Middle English *chace* 'land for hunting wild animals'.

Canon City, COLORADO/USA
'Canyon City' from the Spanish *cañon*.

Canosa di Puglia, APULIA/ITALY *Canusium*
'Reedy (Place) in Apulia' from the Latin *canna* 'reed' or 'cane'. Originally a Greek town, it was finally renamed in 1863.

Canso, CANADA
A strait between Nova Scotia and Cape Breton Island with a name derived from the Micmac word *kamsok* 'beyond the cliffs'.

Cantabria, SPAIN *Santander*
A mountainous autonomous community which takes its name from an ancient Iberian tribe called the Cantabri, who derived their name from the root word *kanto* 'rock'.

Canterbury, AUSTRALIA, CANADA, NEW ZEALAND, UK, USA
1. Canada (New Brunswick): named after Thomas Manners-Sutton (1814–77), 3rd Viscount Canterbury, lieutenant-governor of New Brunswick (1854–61).
2. UK (England): the original Roman name, Durovernum, meant 'Walled Town by the Alder Marsh' from the Old British *duro* 'fort' or 'walled town' and *verno* 'alders' and 'marsh'. This had been changed to Cantwaraburg by about 900 and by the time of the Domesday Book (1086) it had become Canterburie. The present name is a modification of these names meaning 'Town (fort) of the Men of Kent' (Cantware) from the Old English *-ware* 'dwellers' and *burh*. The word 'canter' comes from pilgrims on horseback going at a

'Canterbury pace' to visit St Thomas à Becket's shrine.

3. The towns in Australia and the USA, and the regional council in New Zealand, are probably named after the English city.

Canton, CHINA, USA *Nanwu Cheng, Wuyang Cheng, Ban-Yü, Nanhai Guangzhai (China)*
1. China (Guangdong): the local name is Guangzhou. The city is the capital of Guangdong province from which Canton gets its conventional European name; this originated with the Portuguese who called it Cantão in the 16th century. It means 'Large Region' from *guǎng* and *zhōu*. However, it has been suggested that *guǎng* meant 'yellow' in the native tongue of the original inhabitants of the region and that the Chinese *guǎng* is an attempt to approximate the sound of the original language. The city gives its name to one of the two major Chinese dialects, Cantonese, spoken in the south and Hong Kong. Wuyang Cheng means 'City of Five Goats' and refers to a myth about five immortal beings who are said either to have raised five goats of different colours or who appeared as goats. The city was then named Ban-Yü after the two hills, Ban and Yü, when the city spread to embrace both.
2. USA: seventeen states have a town or city named after the city in China, either directly because they were believed to be diametrically opposite—on the other side of the earth—to the Chinese city, or because they had some other connection, such as trade.

Cap-de-la-Madeleine, QUEBEC/CANADA *Cap-des-Trois-Rivières*
Originally 'Cape of the Three Rivers', it was renamed in 1651 after a grant to the Jesuits from Sainte-Marie-Madeleine-de-Châteaudun, France.

Cape Agulhas, WESTERN CAPE/SOUTH AFRICA
The southernmost point of Africa with the name 'Cape Needles' from the Portuguese *agulha* 'needle', probably a reference to the rocks and reefs here.

Cape Breton Island, NOVA SCOTIA/CANADA
Île Royale
'Royal Island' when it was a French colony, but renamed later, possibly by Basque fishermen from Cap Breton, near Bayonne in France. Captured by the British in 1758, it became part of Nova Scotia, but in 1784 it was hived off to become a British crown colony; it rejoined Nova Scotia in 1820.

Cape Canaveral, FLORIDA/USA *Cape Kennedy*
A complex for the launch of spacecraft, it was renamed in 1964 after the assassination of

John F. Kennedy (1917–63), President of the USA (1961–3), the previous year. In 1973 it reverted to its original Spanish name meaning 'Cane Plantation'.

Cape Coast (Gua), GHANA *Cabo Corso*
The town was founded as a trading post during the 15th century by the Portuguese as Cabo Corso 'Corsican Cape'. It was then developed into a castle by Swedes in 1655 and this was taken over by the British in 1663. The present name is a corruption of the Portuguese name.

Cape Cod, MASSACHUSETTS/USA
Named in 1602 by an English explorer, Bartholomew Gosnold (d. 1607), after he had taken on board a heavy catch of codfish which are abundant in the waters here.

Cape Dezhnev (Mys Dezhnëva), CHUKOT AUTONOMOUS DISTRICT/RUSSIA
In English also known as East Cape, it being the easternmost point on the Russian mainland. In 1879 it was named after Semyon Dezhnëv (*c.*1605–73), an explorer who rounded the cape in 1648.

Cape Elizabeth, MAINE/USA
Takes its name from the cape which honours Princess Elizabeth (1596–1662), the daughter of King James I[†].

Cape Girardeau, MISSOURI/USA
Named after a Frenchman, Jean Girardeau, who had built a trading post near here in about 1705.

Cape Horn (Spanish: **Cabo de Hornos**), CHILE *Cape of Hoorn*
The most southern point of South America, Willem Schouten[†] claimed to have discovered it in 1616; he named it after his home town, Hoorn 'Horn'. However, Sir Francis Drake (*c.*1540–96) had reached the Cape in 1578 and named it Elizabetha after Queen Elizabeth I[†]. His discovery was kept as a state secret by Elizabeth to prevent knowledge of this new passage into the Pacific becoming public.

Cape May, NEW JERSEY/USA *Cape Island*
Renamed in 1869 after Cornelius Mey, a Dutch explorer who came here in 1623.

Cape of Good Hope (Afrikaans: **Kaap die Goeie Hoop**), SOUTH AFRICA *Cabo Tormentoso*
Rounding the cape on his first voyage to the east, the Portuguese navigator, Bartholomew Dias (*c.*1450–1500), failed to see land, but did so on his return journey in 1488. Suffering a rough passage, he named it Cabo Tormentoso 'Cape of Storms'. Dias was one of the sea captains of John II (1455–95), King of Portugal (1481–95). With this voyage John realized that Ptolemy's[†] view of the world had now been

proven to be wrong and that Asia and its riches could be reached by sea. To celebrate the discovery he renamed the cape Cabo Boa Esperança 'Cape of Good Hope' a few years later.

Cape Palmas, LIBERIA *Cabo des Palmas* 'Cape of Palm Trees', so named by the Portuguese in the 15th century.

Capernaum (Kefar Nahum), ISRAEL Ruins. A biblical town which was the centre of Jesus's ministry after he left Nazareth. The name means 'Nahum's Village' from the Hebrew *kefar* 'village' and a personal name.

Cape Town (Afrikaans: **Kaapstad**), WESTERN CAPE/SOUTH AFRICA *Cabo de Goede Hoop, De Kaap* Founded in 1652 by an official of the Dutch East India Company as 'The Cape of Good Hope' and then as 'The Cape', it was intended to be a food supply depot for Dutch ships sailing between the Netherlands and the Indies. Occupied by the British in 1795, it was often thereafter referred to as Cape Town. It is the legislative capital.

Cape Verde The Republic of Cape Verde (República de Cabo Verde) since 1975. Previously an Overseas Territory of Portugal (1951–75) and before that a Portuguese colony (17th century). Until 1879 Cape Verde included Portuguese Guinea (now Guinea-Bissau). The island republic takes its name from the westernmost cape on the continent of Africa to its east. This cape was called *Cabo Verde* 'Green Cape' by the Portuguese, who admired the evergreen trees on the otherwise barren coast.

Cape Virgenes, ARGENTINA 'Cape of the Virgins', so named by Ferdinand Magellan[†] who sighted it on 21 October 1521, then the feast day of St Ursula and the legendary 11 000 virgins. Her feast day was removed from the universal calendar during its reform in 1969. *See* VIRGIN ISLANDS.

Cap-Haïtien, HAITI *Cap-Français* Also known as Le Cap. Originally settled by the Spanish in the 17th century, it became French in 1697. Its name simply means 'Haiti's Cape'.

Cappadocia (Kapadokya), TURKEY An ancient region in Asia Minor, now in east-central Turkey, it was a kingdom before becoming a Roman province in 17. It may be named from the River Cappadox or after its inhabitants who may have taken their name from the Assyrian *Katpa Tuka* 'Tuka's Side'. Its Armenian name is Gamir, indicating that the survivors of the Cimmerian people finally settled here.

Capraia Island (Isola Capraia), ITALY Derives its name from the Latin *capra* 'goat' because of their presence on the island.

Capri (Isola di Capri), CAMPANIA/ITALY *Capreae* An island whose name may be derived from the Etruscan *capra* 'land of tombs', the Latin *capra* 'goat', or the Greek *kapros* 'wild boar'. It may be none of these. The island was a Greek colony and later a resort for some Roman emperors.

Caprivi Strip, NAMIBIA A 280 mile (450 km) strip of land between Angola, Zambia, and Botswana. Part of German South West Africa between 1893 and 1919, it was ceded by the UK to give the Germans access to the Zambezi River. It is named after Leo (1831–99), Graf von (Count of) Caprivi, German chancellor (1890–4). In 1919 it became part of South West Africa (now Namibia), then a South African mandate.

Capua, CAMPANIA/ITALY *Casilinum* Ancient Capua, now called Santa Maria Capua Vetere, was founded *c.*600 BC; the modern city of Capua close by was founded in 856 on the site of the old Casilinum by the residents of ancient Capua which had been destroyed by the Saracens. The most probable explanation of the name Capua is that it is derived from Capys, its Etruscan founder.

Carabobo, VENEZUELA A state named after an extinct tribe, the Carabobos.

Caracas, VENEZUELA *Santiago de León de Caracas* Shortened from the original name given by its founder, Diego de Losada, in 1567. The name comes from the patron saint of Spain, St James (Santiago), the provincial governor, Don Pedro Ponce de León, and the local inhabitants, the Caracas. When Venezuela achieved independence in 1830, Caracas became the nation's capital.

Caransebes, ROMANIA *Tibiscum* The Hungarian *sebes*, referring to the River Sebeş, means 'fast-flowing'. The meaning of Caran is not known.

Carcassonne, LANGUEDOC-ROUSSILLON/ FRANCE *Carcaso* Perched on an isolated hill, the city derives its name from the pre-Indo-European root words *kar* 'rock' or 'stone' and *kasser* 'oak'.

Cardiff, UK, USA
1. UK (Wales): formerly Kairdif, o gaer dydd, and Caer Didd. The Welsh name now is Caerdydd 'Fort on the (River) Taff' from a *caer*, built by the Romans in about 75, and the Dydd, the

Welsh name for the Taff. The city has been the capital of Wales since 1955.
2. USA: both places, one in Alabama and the other, Cardiff-by-the-Sea, in California, are named after the Welsh city.

Cardigan, CANADA, UK
UK (Wales): formerly Ceredigion and Kerdigan. The Welsh name is Aberteifi 'Mouth of the (River) Teifi' from *aber* and the river name. Cardigan itself means 'Ceredig's Land'.

Cardston, ALBERTA/CANADA
Founded in 1887 and named after Charles Card, who led the Mormon caravan from Utah. He was the son-in-law of Brigham Young (1801–77), the Mormon leader.

Carencro, LOUISIANA/USA
'Buzzard' in Creole. So named because large flocks of buzzards roosted in the cypress trees in the area.

Careysburg, LIBERIA
Settled in 1859 by freed slaves from North America and named after the Reverend Lott Carey who had arrived with the first group in 1821.

Caria, TURKEY
An ancient district of south-west Anatolia whose name is derived from *kar*, a reference to its mountainous interior.

Caribbean, The Usually accepted as meaning the region of the Atlantic Ocean between the southern West Indian islands and Central America, the Caribbean Sea. The islands used to be called the Caribbees and these included the Lesser Antilles (Windward and Leeward Islands). The Caribbees took their name from the Caribs, a Native American people who lived in the Lesser Antilles and northern Venezuela. A Spanish version of their name was Caribales and their alleged habit of torturing and eating their male captives gave the English word 'cannibal'.

Caribou, CANADA, USA
USA (Maine): settled in 1824 and given the name Lyndon Village in 1859, it was renamed in 1877 in recognition of the many caribou in the region. There are cities with this name in Alaska and Nova Scotia, Canada, and also a number of rivers and islands with the same name.

Carinthia (Kärnten), AUSTRIA
A state named after a Celtic tribe living in Karantanija, itself from *kar*, a reference to the mountainous area in which they lived. It was the centre of the Celtic Kingdom of Noricum which became a Roman province in 16 BC. An independent duchy in the 10th–13th

centuries, it became an Austrian crownland in 1335. A small part was ceded to Slovenia after the First World War (1914–18); its Slovenian name is Koroška.

Carletonville, GAUTENG/SOUTH AFRICA
Developed without authority between 1937 and 1957 as gold mining companies established their claims. Only in 1959 was it recognized as a town and named after Guy Carleton Jones, a long-serving director of Consolidated Gold Fields.

Carlisle, CANADA, UK, USA
UK (England): originally Luguvalium 'The Fort of Luguvalos', the Celtic god of arts and crafts, Lugus. 'Lisle' is a modification of the Roman name. To it was added later the Celtic *cair* 'fortified town'. The name in the 11th century was Carleol.

Carlow (Ceatharlach), IRELAND
A county and a town with a name meaning 'Four Lakes'. They are no longer evident.

Carlsbad, USA
1. California: originally Frazier's Station but renamed in 1883 because its mineral springs were thought similar to those in Carlsbad, Bohemia (now Karlovy Vary, Czech Republic).
2. New Mexico: originally named Eddy after its founder Charles B. Eddy. It was renamed in 1899 after the Bohemian Carlsbad.

Carlyle, CANADA, USA
The three places, one in Canada and two in the USA, are all named after the British historian and essayist, Thomas Carlyle (1795–1881).

Carmarthen (Caerfyrddin), WALES/UK
Maridunum, Cair Mirdin
'Fort at Maridunum', the Roman town having a Celtic name 'Fort by the Sea'. *Caer* was somewhat unnecessarily added. It has been suggested that the name might mean 'Myrddin's (Merlin's) Fort' from *caer* and a personal name. Carmarthenshire is a unitary district of Wales.

Carmel, Mt (Har Ha-Karmel), ISRAEL
A mountain range with a name derived from the Hebrew *kerem* 'vineyard' or 'orchard', a reference to its fertility.

Carnarvon, AUSTRALIA, SOUTH AFRICA
1. Australia (Queensland and Western Australia); named after Henry Herbert (1831–90), 4th Earl of Carnarvon, who was secretary of state for the colonies (1866–7, 1874–8). The Carnarvon Range in Queensland is also named after the earl.
2. South Africa (Northern Cape): founded in 1860 as Harmsfontein 'Fountain of Sorrow' before being renamed Schietfontein. It was

renamed again after the 4th Earl of Carnarvon. In 1875 he proposed a Federation for South Africa to follow the Canadian example; this did not succeed.

Carniola (Kranjska), SLOVENIA *Krain*
A mountainous region named after the Carni who probably took their name from the pre-Indo-European *kar* 'rock'. A Habsburg possession from 1335, it became an Austrian crownland in 1849. In 1918 most of it was absorbed into the Kingdom of the Serbs, Croats, and Slovenes when that kingdom was created; all of it was incorporated into Slovenia in 1947.

Carnot, CENTRAL AFRICAN REPUBLIC, USA
Central African Republic: named after Sadi Carnot (1837–94), fourth President of the Third (French) Republic (1887–94) who had just been assassinated. At the time the town lay within Oubangui-Chari, proclaimed as a French colony that year.

Carolina, COLOMBIA, PUERTO RICO, SURINAME, USA
1. Puerto Rico: formerly Trujillo Bajo and then renamed San Fernando de la Carolina. The present name is a shortened version of the previous name which honoured the Spanish King Charles II†.
2. USA: two states, North and South Carolina. Originally a single small territory named Caroline in 1564 after the Latin form of the name, Carolus, by the French as a tribute to Charles IX (1550–74), King of France (1560–74). A small English colony was established temporarily in 1585, but it was not until 1629 that the name Carolina was accepted by the English after Charles I† had granted this territory to Robert Heath. In 1663 Charles II† granted the territory to Edward Hyde (1609–74), 1st Earl of Clarendon and lord chancellor to the king (1658–67), and seven other proprietors to establish a colony and it became known officially as Carolina after him. In 1712 Carolina was partitioned when North Carolina was established as a separate province, becoming a royal colony in 1729 as did South Carolina. However, the border between the two was not agreed until 1735. South Carolina became the 8th state to join the Union in 1788, but in 1860 it was the first state to secede; it rejoined in 1868. North Carolina joined the Union as the 12th state in 1789. It seceded in 1861 and was not readmitted until 1868.

Caroline Islands, FEDERATED STATES OF MICRONESIA *Islas de los Barbudos, Islas de los Jardinos*
Named in 1528 by Spanish visitors the 'Islands of the Bearded Ones', they were renamed in 1542 the 'Islands of the Gardens'; in 1686 they were renamed again after the Spanish King Charles II†. They were sold to Germany in 1899. In 1914 they were occupied by the Japanese who, in 1921, received a League of Nations mandate to administer them. They were invaded by US forces in 1944 and became part of the UN Trust Territory of the Pacific Islands, administered by the USA, in 1947. In 1979 the Caroline Islands, less Palau, were subsumed into the newly created Federated States of Micronesia.

Carpathians, CZECH REPUBLIC-POLAND *Karpates Oros*
A mountain range with a name derived from *kar*. *Oros* 'mountain' or 'mountain range' is of Greek origin.

Carpentaria, Gulf of, NORTHERN TERRITORY-QUEENSLAND/AUSTRALIA
An inlet of the Arafura Sea first explored by the Dutch in 1606 and named in 1623 after Pieter Carpentier (1588–1659), governor-general of the Dutch East Indies.

Carrara, TUSCANY/ITALY
Derived from the Latin *quadraria* 'quarry'. It gives its name to the famous Carrara marble, much favoured by Michelangelo (1475–1564).

Carrickfergus (Carraig Fhearghais), NORTHERN IRELAND/UK
'Rock of Fergus', so named in memory of the legendary King Fergus of Ulster who is believed to have been shipwrecked off the coast some time during the first decades of the 1st millennium AD; from *carraig* 'rock', *carrick* being the Anglicized version of the word.

Carrickmore (Carraig Mhor), NORTHERN IRELAND/UK
'Large Rock' from *carraig* 'rock' and *mor/more* 'large' or 'great'.

Carson City, USA
1. Nevada: founded in 1858 as Eagle Station and then Eagle Ranch. It was later renamed after the frontiersman, trapper and Rocky Mountain guide, Kit Carson (1809–68).
2. There is another Carson City in Michigan, eight cities called Carson and another called Fort Carson, all in the USA. Not all are named after Kit Carson.

Cartagena, COLOMBIA, SPAIN
1. Colombia: settled in 1533, the full name is Cartagena de Indias. It is named after the Cartagena in Spain with 'de Indias' added to denote its location in South America.
2. Spain (Murcia): founded by the Carthaginian general Hasdrubal (d. 221 BC) in the 3rd century BC, it was named after the Carthaginian capital. It was known by the

Romans as Carthago Nova 'New Carthage' from which the present name comes, and as Colonia Urbs Julia the 'Colonial Town of Julius'.

Carthage, TUNISIA, USA
Tunisia: ruins. A Phoenician city founded supposedly in the 8th century BC. Its Phoenician name, Qart-Hadas, means 'New Town' from *qart* 'town' and *hadas* 'new'. At the peak of its power from the 6th to the 4th centuries BC it was the dominant power in the western Mediterranean. It was called Karchedon by the Greeks. As a result of the three Punic Wars (264–241, 218–201, 149–146 BC) with the Romans, Carthage was defeated and destroyed. It was rebuilt from 122 BC as a trading centre and became known as Colonia Julia Carthago. It became the capital of the Roman province of Africa. It was captured by the Arabs in 705 and was gradually abandoned.

Cary, UK, USA
1. UK (England): a river with a Celtic or pre-Celtic name derived from *car-* 'hard'.
2. USA (North Carolina): named after Samuel F. Cary, a temperance leader from Ohio who is said to have given an impassioned sermon here in the 1850s.

Casablanca, CHILE, MOROCCO
Morocco: 'White House' from the Portuguese *Casa Branca* from *casa* 'house' and *branca* 'white'. In 1515 the Portuguese built a new town with mainly white buildings on the site of a Berber town called Anfa. The city was called Casablanca by the Spanish and Maison Blanche 'White House' by French settlers. The Arabic name Ad-Dār al-Bayḍā or Dar al-Beïda has the same meaning from *ad* 'the', *dar* '(stone) house' and *bayḍā* 'white'.

Casa Grande, ARIZONA/USA
'Big House' in Spanish and so-called because of a large 14th-century building erected by Native Americans with a watchtower atop it.

Casale Monferrato, PIEDMONT/ITALY
Bodincomagus
Founded in the 8th century on the ancient site of Bodincomagus, the first word comes from the Latin *casalis* 'cabin' or 'hovel' indicating a very modest rural dwelling. Monferrato seems to indicate an open, fertile area, ideal for growing wheat. Bodincomagus was the Celtic-Ligurian name for the River Po with the Gallic root *mago* 'place', thus 'Place on the (River) Po'.

Casamance, SENEGAL
A river flowing through what was once the land, Kasa, of a *mansa* 'king'.

Casas Grandes, CHIHUAHUA/MEXICO
'Great Houses'. Settled by the Spanish in 1661, they named it after the imposing ruins of a pre-Columbian town close by.

Cascade Range, CANADA-USA
A mountain range named after the cascades near the Columbia River Gorge on the border between Washington State and Oregon.

Casper, WYOMING/USA *Fort Caspar*
Founded as a tented town by a fort in 1888 and named after Lieutenant Caspar Collins who was killed by Native Americans while trying to bring help to a stranded wagon train. In writing his report, a clerk misspelt the name.

Caspian Sea (Azeri: **Khazar Denizi**; Persian: **Daryāye Khezer**; Russian: **Kaspiyskoye More**) *Khazarsk, Khvalynsk, Girkansk*
Named after the ancient Kaspi people who used to inhabit the area to the west. The previous names also come from local tribes, the last meaning 'Country of the Wolves'. Although called a sea it is in fact a land-locked salt lake.

Cassino, LAZIO/ITALY *Casinum, San Germano*
Originally called Casinum by its founders, the Volsci, in the 5th century BC, it was abandoned in the 9th century and a new town was built close by. It was named after its patron saint, Germanus, until 1863 when its Latin name was restored. The name may be connected with Casilinus, another name for the Volturno River a few miles to the east.

Castel Gandolfo, LAZIO/ITALY
The summer residence of the Pope. It takes its name from a castle owned by the Gandolfi ducal family. It was acquired by the Holy See in 1608.

Castellammare di Stabia, CAMPANIA/ITALY
Derived from the nearby Roman resort of Stabiae, destroyed by the eruption of Mt Vesuvius in 79, and from a castle, *castello*, built on the coast (in Italian, *mare* 'sea') by Frederick II[†].

Castelo Branco, PORTUGAL *Albi Castrum*
'White Castle', a Templar castle of great strategic importance near the Spanish frontier around which the town developed.

Castelvetrano, SICILY/ITALY
'Old Castle' from the Latin *Castellum veteranum*.

Castile-La Mancha (Castilla-La Mancha), SPAIN *al-Qila*
An autonomous community famous for its castles, from the Low Latin *castilla*, built by Alfonso III the Great (838–910), King of Asturias (866–910), to defend his frontiers against Muslim assaults. It was thus named

'Land of Castles'. The Arab name means 'The Castles'. La Mancha (in Arabic, *al-Manshah* 'The Wilderness') was added to Castile in 1982 to form the autonomous community. A former independent kingdom from 1029, although Ferdinand III (1217–52) was also King of León (1232–52), until Castile and Aragón united in 1479.

Castile-León (Castilla y León), SPAIN
Formed as an autonomous community in 1983. *See* CASTILE-LA MANCHA AND LEÓN.

Castlebar (Caisleán an Bharraigh), IRELAND
'de Barra's Castle' from *caisleán* 'castle'.

Castlemaine, AUSTRALIA, IRELAND
1. Australia (Victoria): originally Forest Creek and then Mount Alexander. A gold mining settlement, it was named by the chief commissioner for the goldfields, Captain William Wright, after his uncle, Viscount Castlemaine.
2. Ireland: locally Caisleán na Mainge 'Castle of the (River) Maine'.

Castlereagh, AUSTRALIA, UK
UK (Northern Ireland): a district with the Irish name of An Caisleán Riabhach meaning 'Striped Castle' from *caisleán* 'castle' and *ria(bhach)* 'striped', the Anglicized version of which is *reagh*. In place-names, however, *ria* can often mean 'grey'.

Castletown, ISLE OF MAN, IRELAND, UK
Isle of Man: formerly Villa Castelli 'Village of the Castle', ultimately after the 10th century Castle Rushen, and now from the Middle English *castel* and *toun*.

Castres, MIDI-PYRÉNÉES/FRANCE
The site of a Gallo-Roman camp, the name comes from *castra*.

Castries, SAINT LUCIA *Le Carénage*
The original French name meant the 'Place where Ships are careened'. This was then changed in 1758 to honour Maréchal de Castries, a Minister of the French Navy and Colonies.

Çatalca, TURKEY
Derives its name from *çatal* 'fork', allegedly because the route forked here to Istanbul or south to the Sea of Marmara.

Catalonia (Catalan: **Catalunya**; Spanish: **Cataluña**), SPAIN *Spanish March*
An autonomous community whose name means 'Land of Castellans' from *castlan* 'governor of a castle'. Occupied by the Romans, Visigoths, and Moors, it was absorbed into the empire of Charlemagne[†] at the end of the 8th century when it was known as the Spanish March. It has also been suggested that the

name comes from Gothalanda 'Goths' Land' when they occupied it in the 5th century.

Catamarca, ARGENTINA *Londres*
A province and a city founded in 1559, also known as San Fernando del Valle de Catamarca. Moved to a sheltered valley in 1694 because of the hostility of the local people, the city's name comes from the Quechua *qata* 'slope' or 'incline' and *marka* 'region'.

Catanzaro, CALABRIA/ITALY *Catasarion/ Katantzarion*
Originally founded by the Byzantines in the 10th century as Catasarion, the name may mean 'Below the Terraces' from the Greek *cata* 'on' or 'near to' and the Arabic *anzār* 'terrace', a reference to the orchards and gardens that surrounded the city which overlooks the Ionian Sea.

Cathay, AND USA
The medieval name for northern China derived from the Khitay or Khitan, the Medieval Latin name applied to a semi-nomadic Tatar people from Mongolia who conquered northern China in the 10th century. Kitai survives as the Russian word for China. It is also used as part of the name of an international airline, Cathay Pacific, based in Hong Kong.

Catherine, Mt (Jabal Katrīnah), SINAI/EGYPT
Named after St Catherine of Alexandria who, according to legend, was executed in the 4th century after torture on a wheel, later called a Catherine wheel. After her death her body was supposedly taken by angels to the mountain where her remains were said to have been discovered some 300 years later by monks from the nearby monastery of St Catherine. However, she may never have existed and her feast day was removed from the church calendar in 1969.

Catherine Strait (Proliv Yekateriny), KURIL ISLANDS/RUSSIA
A strait between Iturup and Kunashir Islands and named after the ship, the *Catherine*, on which Grigory Lovtsov, a Russian Navy commander, sailed through it in 1792.

Catskill Mountains, NEW YORK/USA *Katsberg*
Mountains called Katsberg by the Dutch after the numerous wildcats in the area and the creek, which flowed from the mountains; thus, Kaaterskill 'Wildcat Creek' from *kil* 'creek'.

Catterick, ENGLAND/UK *Katouraktónion, Catrice, Catreath*
Probably derived from the Latin *cataracta* 'waterfalls' or 'rapids', itself from a

misinterpretation of the original Celtic place-name, referred to by Ptolemy[†], which meant '(Place of) Battle Ramparts', entirely appropriate now since Catterick is the UK's biggest military base.

Catumbela, ANGOLA *Quitumbela*
Named after a local chief.

Caucasus (Russian: **Kavkaz**)
1. A mountainous region, also called Caucasia, between the Sea of Azov and the Black Sea to the west and the Caspian Sea to the east, it is characterized by the Great and Little Caucasus Mountain Ranges. The area north of the Great Caucasus (Russia) is called the North Caucasus, Ciscaucasia ('this side of the Caucasus' mountains from the Russians' point of view). The area to the south (Armenia, Azerbaijan, and Georgia) is called the Southern Caucasus or Transcaucasia ('the other side of the Caucasus'). The present Latinized name may be derived from the Greek *Kaukasos*, which itself may come from the Hittite name for the people living along the southern shores of the Black Sea, the Kazkaz. On the other hand, it is possible that the name comes from an ancient Greek (Pelasgi) word *kau* 'mountain'. The Caucasus was disputed between the Ottoman, Persian, and Russian Empires for centuries. By 1878 Russia had gained control, despite stiff local resistance, and after the 1917 Russian Revolution the Soviet Union maintained control until 1991. The term Caucasian is used to describe one of the five great racial divisions of mankind—that which is light-skinned—as defined by the German anthropologist Johann Blumenbach (1752–1840). This is not to say that all the peoples of Europe belong to a single white race that originated in the Caucasus as proposed by Blumenbach.
2. In the time of Alexander III the Great[†] the Hindu Kush in Afghanistan was known as the Indian Caucasus to the Greeks. The present town of Chārīkār, north of Kabul, was founded by Alexander in 329 BC as Alexandria-under-the-Caucasus.

Cava de' Tirreni, CAMPANIA/ITALY *Cava*
Until 1862, it was known simply as Cava 'Cave' because of the caves in the surrounding hills. De' Tirreni was added because it was built on the site of the ancient Marcina, a city of the Tirreni.

Cavalla, WEST AFRICA
A river which rises in Guinea and later forms part of the border between Liberia and Côte d'Ivoire. Portuguese navigators gave it the name Cavalla 'Horse Mackerel' in the 15th century, having found these fish at the mouth

of the river. It is also known as the Cavally or Youbou.

Cavan (An Cabhán), IRELAND
Lying in a hollow, the name means 'The Hollow Place' from *cabhán* 'hollow' or 'valley'. It was one of the three counties of the old province of Ulster.

Çavdir, TURKEY
'Barley'.

Cavite, LUZON/PHILIPPINES
The Hispanized version of the local Tagalog *kawit* ' hook', a reference to the shape of the original settlement.

Caxias, MARANHÃO/BRAZIL *São José das Aldeias Altas*
Renamed in 1837 after Luis Alves de Lima e Silva (1803–80), Duke of Caxias, when he became governor of Maranhão; in 1855 he became minister of war and in 1867 commander-in-chief of the Brazilian Army. The previous name meant 'St Joseph of the High Hamlets'.

Cayenne, FRENCH GUIANA *La Ravardière*
Founded in 1643 by the French, it was renamed in 1777 with the French form of Guyana, possibly from a Carib word meaning 'worthy'. It is an *arrondissement* (an administrative subdivision of a department) and the capital city. It gives its name to a type of pepper.

Cayman Islands, UK *Las Tortugas*
An Overseas Territory of the UK. The numerous turtles (in Spanish, *tortuga*) gave the islands their original name, but this was changed to Cayman in 1530 because of the caimans, a type of alligator. The Spanish for alligator is *caimán* (possibly taken from the Carib *acayuman* 'alligator'), but in fact the islands are noted for their iguanas; in Bolivia, *caimán* means iguana. The islands were ceded to Britain in 1670 under the terms of the Treaty of Madrid and British settlement began in 1734. Since some of the settlers came from Jamaica, the Cayman Islands became a dependency of Jamaica and remained so until 1959.

Cayos Cochinos, HONDURAS
'Pig Islands' from the Spanish *cayo* 'islet' and *cochino* 'pig' or 'hog', so-called because the Spanish conquistador Hernán Cortés[†] tried to rear pigs here during his expedition to Honduras in 1524–6.

Cebu City, CEBU/PHILIPPINES *Sugbo*
Taken from the name of the island, Cebu, which is a corruption of the earlier Visayan name meaning 'walk on water', a reference to

the very shallow beaches characterizing the island.

Cedar Falls, IOWA/USA
Settled in 1845 and named for the cedar trees along the Cedar River.

Cedar Rapids, IOWA/USA *Rapids City*
Lying astride the Cedar River, it was named after its rapids. When incorporated as a town in 1849 it took on the river's name. There is also a Cedar Rapids in Nebraska, but this is not associated with the Cedar River.

Celebes (Sulawesi), INDONESIA
An island with four provinces (which include some small neighbouring islands): Central, North, South-east, and South. The origin of the name is not known, but it may have come into existence through some Portuguese misunderstanding or corruption of a local word. Possible explanations are that Celebes might come from *selîhe* or *selîre* 'sea current' or from *si-lebîh* 'the one with more islands'. On the other hand, it is claimed that the Portuguese called the island Os Célebres 'The Celebrated Ones', referring to the treacherous waters on the north-eastern coast. The present Indonesian name means 'Spear of Iron' from *sula* 'spear' or 'stake' and *besi* 'iron', a reference to the favourite weapon of the inhabitants. The Portuguese were the first Europeans to arrive in 1512 to enhance their stake in the spice trade and they were followed by the Dutch who had gained almost complete control by 1905.

Celje, SLOVENIA *Claudia Celeia, Cilia*
First inhabited by the Illyrians and then by the Celts, who gave the town its name from *kel* 'refuge' or 'place of residence'. During the reign of Claudius (10 BC–AD 54), Roman emperor (41–54), it was taken by the Romans. They added his name which was subsequently discarded.

Celle, LOWER SAXONY/GERMANY
Lying on the River Aller, the name comes from old High German *kella* 'ladle' or 'deep place in a river'.

Central African Republic *Oubangui Chari, Central African Empire*
The Central African Republic (République Centrafricaine) since 1958 when it achieved self-government as an autonomous republic within the French Community; independence was gained in 1960. Before that it had been one of the four constituent territories of French Equatorial Africa, the French having established a military post on the Oubangui River, discovered in 1870 and also spelt Ubangi, in 1889. For a considerable distance the river now serves as the border between the Republic and the Democratic Republic of the Congo, and between the two Congos. In 1894 the French declared Oubangui-Chari a colony. The name comes from the Bantu *ou* 'land' and *bangi* 'rapid', a reference to the fast-flowing river, *chari*, and the land through which it flows; there is also a river called the Chari. In 1976 Eddine Bokassa (1921–96), president (1966–79), proclaimed himself Emperor Bokassa and the country became known as the Central African Empire. It reverted to a republic in 1979 when Bokassa was overthrown. The country takes its name from the fact that it lies at the centre of Africa. Strangely, and unusually, a local name has given way to an Europeanized one.

Central America The region, lying between Mexico and Colombia, that comprises Belize, Costa Rica, El Salvador, Guatemala, Honduras, Nicaragua, and Panama. Independence from Spain was achieved in 1821 and two years later the United Provinces of Central America, which included Costa Rica, El Salvador, Honduras, Guatemala, and Nicaragua, was established. In 1838, however, Costa Rica, Honduras, and Nicaragua left the federation, thus ensuring its effective collapse.

Central Asia The region now generally agreed to comprise Kazakhstan, Kyrgyzstan, Tajikistan, Turkmenistan, and Uzbekistan. Until 1993 Kazakhstan was regarded as a separate entity, but in that year the presidents of the five republics agreed to the term *Tsentral'naya Aziya* 'Central Asia', to embrace their whole region. In the 19th century, the heartland of Central Asia was known as Russian and Chinese Turkestan and divided into three subregions: Transoxiana 'Across the (River) Oxus', the area between the Oxus (now the Amu Darya) and the Jaxartes (now the Syr Darya); Yeti Su 'Land of the Seven Rivers' in Turkish and Semirechye in Russian, the area between the Tien Shan mountains and Lake Balkhash; and Kashgaria, an area centred on the Taklamakan Desert.

Centre, FRANCE, USA
1. France: a region whose name describes its position in the approximate centre of France.
2. USA (Alabama): spelt in the Anglo-French way (as opposed to the usual American 'center'), although it is by no means near the geographical centre of the state.

Cephalonia (Kefalinía), GREECE *Same*
The largest of the Ionian Islands, it takes its name from the Greek *kephale* 'head', here with the meaning 'mountain'. It has changed hands many times, undergoing Roman, Norman,

Neapolitan, Venetian, Turkish, French, and British rule before being ceded to Greece in 1864.

Čepin, CROATIA *Oppidum Chapa*
A Roman settlement later renamed after the Adamović-Čepinski family.

Ceres, ARGENTINA, BRAZIL, ITALY, SOUTH AFRICA, USA
1. South Africa (Western Cape): founded in 1854 to process the fruits of the Bokkeveld Valley and therefore named after the Roman goddess of fruit.
2. USA (California): also named after the Roman goddess.

Cernavodă, ROMANIA
A port at the junction of the Danube River and Black Sea Canal with a Slavonic name acquired when Bulgaria occupied this part of Romania. The name means 'Black Water' from *voda* 'water'.

Česká Lípa, CZECH REPUBLIC *Lipa/Lipý/Lyppeho*
The original settlement was founded in the 13th century. In 1787 it was given its present name to mean 'Czech (settlement near) Lime Trees'. *Česká* indicates that it is a Czech town. The lime tree is considered to be the symbol of the Czech nation.

České Budějovice, CZECH REPUBLIC *Budweis*
A settlement founded in 1265 by, and named after, Budivoj, the son of the chief judge of the Czech Kingdom during the reign of Otakar II (1230–78), King of Bohemia (1253–78); *České* indicates that it is a Czech town. Otakar II was elected Duke of Upper and Lower Austria in 1251 and the city was included in the Austrian and Austro-Hungarian Empires until 1918. The German name is reflected in Budvar or Budweiser beer.

Český Krumlov, CZECH REPUBLIC *Krumau*
The former name comes from the German *Krumme Aue* 'curved meadow', a reference to a tight S-bend in the River Vltava (former Moldau), with *česky* 'Czech'. There is also a town called Moravský Krumlov 'Moravian Krumlov'.

Český Těšín, CZECH REPUBLIC *Tescin*
Derived from a colloquial form, Těša, of the Czech personal name Těšimir with the possessive suffix *-in* to give 'Těša's Settlement'. Until 1918 part of Austria-Hungary, it was an important railway junction lying at one end of the Silesian coalfield. The Czechs and the Poles could not agree to whom it belonged. In 1920 the Powers at the Peace Conference in Paris decreed that the town be split in two, the River Olše being the dividing line. The Czech part

became known as Český Těšín 'Czech Těšín'. The name of the Polish town across the river (in Polish, Olza), is Cieszyn which comes from the Polish version of the personal name Těcha from Těchoslav.

Cetinje, MONTENEGRO/SERBIA AND MONTENEGRO *Cettigne*
Named after the small Cetina River. It was the capital of Montenegro between 1484 and 1918.

Ceuta (Arabic: *Sebta*), SPAIN *Abyla, Septem Fratres*
An autonomous community and Spanish exclave on the Moroccan coast. The Roman name meant 'Seven Brothers' from the seven hills of the Jabal Musa range on the slopes of which the town stands. The present name has evolved from *septem*. The town was occupied by the Carthaginians, Greeks, who called it Abyla, and Romans before being held by the Moors between 711 and 1415. It was captured in 1415 by John I (1357–1433), King of Portugal (1385–1433) and became Spanish as a consequence of the union of Spain and Portugal in 1580; when this was severed in 1640 Ceuta remained Spanish. Opposite Gibraltar, it was regarded in the ancient world as one of the Pillars of Hercules.

Chad The Republic of Chad (République du Tchad) since independence in 1960, having become an autonomous republic within the French Community in 1958. Previously one of the four constituent territories of French Equatorial Africa (1946), a French colony (1920), it was incorporated into French Equatorial Africa in 1910. The country takes its name from Lake Chad in the west, that name coming from the Arabic *tšād* 'large lake'.

Chaillu Massif, GABON
Named after Paul du Chaillu (1831–1903), who is believed to have discovered this mountain range during his explorations along the Ngounié River in 1855–65.

Chaiyaphum, THAILAND
'Site of Victory' from *phum* 'site' and *chai-ya* 'victory' to mark the victory of the town's first governor, Pho Khum Lae, over an invading army during the reign of Rama III (1788–1851), King of Siam (1824–51). Pho was killed during the battle.

Chaleur Bay, NEW BRUNSWICK-QUEBEC/CANADA
An inlet of the Gulf of St Lawrence discovered in 1534 by Jacques Cartier[†] who gave it the name Chaleur 'Heat' in French because of the high temperature at the time of his visit.

Chalkís (Khalkís), GREECE *Euripus*
Developed from a very ancient city on the
island of Euboea, the name comes from the
Greek *khalkos* 'copper'. The town fell to the
Venetians in 1209 who retained it until 1470
when it was captured by the Ottoman Turks. It
became a part of Greece in 1830.

Châlons-sur-Marne, CHAMPAGNE-ARDENNE/
FRANCE *Durocatalaunum*
Takes its name from a Gallic tribe, the
Catalauni, as can also be seen from the Roman
name. It is identified with the River Marne to
distinguish it from Chalon on the River Saône
(Chalon-sur-Saône); its Roman name was
Cavillonum.

Chambersburg, PENNSYLVANIA/USA
Named after a Scotsman, Benjamin Chambers
(1708–83), who founded it in 1730.

Chambéry, RHÔNE-ALPES/FRANCE *Camberacium*
Derived from the Medieval Latin name which
itself comes from the Gaulish *cambo* 'curve' or
'bend' with the Latin suffix *-acum* for a place-
name. The town lies on a bend in the River
Leysse valley.

Chambly, QUEBEC/CANADA *Fort Chambly*
Founded in 1665 by, and named after, Captain
Jacques de Chambly, a French Army officer.

Champagne-Ardenne, FRANCE
A region with a name derived from the Latin
campus (in French, *champ* 'field') and Ardenne
(see ARDENNES). It includes the Plain of
Champagne and part of the forest of Ardennes.
It is known world-wide for its wine, champagne.

Champaign, ILLINOIS/USA *West Urbana*
Adjacent to Urbana, it was renamed in 1860
after the county in Ohio which itself took the
name from the nature of the countryside
which was generally open fields; the root is the
French *champ*.

Champaner, GUJARĀT/INDIA *Muhammadābād*
Possibly named after the *champa* tree or after a
person called Champaraj. So that he could
besiege the nearby fortified hill of Pawagadh
'Quarter of a Hill', the capital of the Chauhan
Rājputs and a place of pilgrimage, the Muslim
Sultan Muhammad Begarha occupied it in
1484 and renamed it Muhammadābād. With
the departure of the Muslims the original
name was restored.

Champlain, Lake, CANADA-USA
Seen in 1609 by the Frenchman, Samuel de
Champlain[†], and named after him.

Chandernagore, WEST BENGAL/INDIA
Also called Chandannagar 'Moon Town' from
the Hindi *ĉandra* 'moon' and *nagar*. Founded by

the French in 1673, it was captured by the
English in 1757, but returned to the French in
1815. It joined India in 1949.

Chandīgarh, PUNJAB/INDIA
'Fort of Chandī' from the Hindu name of the
goddess Ĉandī and *garh*. Besides being a Union
Territory, formed in 1966, and a town, it is also
the capital of both Punjab and Haryāna states.

Chandrapur, MAHĀRĀSHTRA/INDIA *Chānda*
'Town of the Moon' from the Hindi *ĉandra*
'moon' and *pur*.

Changane, MOZAMBIQUE
A tributary of the Limpopo River with a name
meaning 'reeds', a reference to the marshy
region near its upper course.

Changbai (Chinese: **Changbai Shan**; Korean:
Changbaeksanmaek), CHINA-NORTH KOREA
A mountain range along the border with a
Chinese name meaning 'Always White
Mountains' from *cháng* 'long' (as regards time),
bái 'white', and *shān*. The Korean name means
'White-topped Mountains'.

Changchun, JILIN/CHINA *Guanzhengzi,
Changchun-fu, Xinjing*
'Eternal Spring' from *cháng* 'long' and *chūn*
'spring' (the season). During the Japanese
occupation (1932–45) it was the capital of the
puppet state of Manchukuo, being renamed
Xinjing 'New Capital' from the Chinese *xīn*
'new' and *jīng* 'capital city'. The name is said to
come from the mythical 'four seasons' flower
which has leaves like a lotus and which is
green in spring, red in summer, white in
autumn, and purple in winter.

Changde, HUNAN/CHINA *Wuling, Dingzhou*
'Eternal Virtue' from *cháng* 'constant' or
'eternal' and *dé* 'virtue'.

Changsha, HUNAN/CHINA *Jingyang*
A port on the Xiang River, the name literally
means 'Long Sand' from *cháng* 'long' and *shā*
'sand'. The original name meant 'Blue Rock'. It
received its present name as a county in 589.

Channel Islands (French: **Îles Normandes**)
AND USA
1. So named because of their location in the
English Channel. They are not part of the UK,
nor a sovereign state nor a colony; they have
been a possession of the British crown since
1066, having originally been a part of the
Duchy of Normandy. They are now self-
governing.
2. USA (California): a group of islands in the
Santa Barbara Channel. Also known as the
Santa Barbara Islands.

Chanthaburi (Meuang Chan), THAILAND
Chantaboon
'City of the Moon' from *chan* 'moon' and *buri* 'city'.

Chantilly, PICARDY/FRANCE *Chantileium*
Named after Cantilius, a Gallo-Roman who built the first villa here. It has given its name to various types of lace and porcelain.

Chanute, KANSAS/USA
Founded in about 1870, it was named after Octave Chanute (1832–1910), a civil engineer whose knowledge of aeronautics did much to help the Wright Brothers achieve the first powered heavier-than-air flight in December 1903.

Chao Phraya, THAILAND
The name recognizes the fact that this is the country's major river from *chao* 'royal' or 'king' and *phraya* 'chief'.

Chapala, JALISCO/MEXICO
The origin of the name is not clear, but it has been suggested that it comes from a local chief called Chapalac whose name comes from an onomatopoeic Aztec word *chapatal* referring to the sound of waves breaking on the shores of Lake Chapala; or that it comes from a local word *chapatla* 'Place where the Pots abound', a reference to the local practice of throwing sacrificial bowls into the lake to appease the gods.

Chapayev, KAZAKHSTAN *Lbishchensk, Chapayevo*
The original name came from a local word *lbishche* 'rocky headland'. In 1939 it was renamed after Vasily Chapayev (1887–1919), a Russian hero of the First World War (1914–18) and the Russian Civil War (1918–20), who was killed by White Guards here. The final *o* was deleted in 1971.

Chapayevsk, SAMARA/RUSSIA *Ivashchenkovo, Trotsk*
Renamed in 1919 after Leon Trotsky (1879–1940), who played a prominent role in the Bolshevik Revolution in 1917 and became commissar for war. When he fell from grace the town was renamed in 1929 after Vasily Chapayev (see previous entry). There is a Chapayeva in Turkmenistan named after the same man. The River Chapayevka takes its name from the town.

Chapel Hill, NORTH CAROLINA/USA
Founded in 1792 and named after the Church of England New Hope Chapel that was erected on the hill in the middle of the settlement.

Chaplygin, LIPETSK/RUSSIA *Slobodskoye, Oranienburg, Ranenburg*
The original name from *sloboda* indicated a settlement exempt from normal state obligations. In 1702 Peter I the Great[†] gave it to Prince Alexander Menshikov (1673–1729), a general and foremost administrator who built a fortress here and changed the name to Oranienburg after the town in Germany. When a town was officially established here in 1779 it became known as Ranenburg. In 1948 it was renamed in honour of Sergey Chaplygin (1869–1942), a pioneer in high speed aerodynamics and head of the Central Aerodynamic Institute, who was born here.

Chappaquiddick, MASSACHUSETTS/USA
An island with a name derived from a Native American word *cheppiaquidne* 'separated island' because it is separated from Martha's Vineyard by a narrow strait.

Chardzhev (Charjov), TURKMENISTAN
See TURKMENABAT.

Chārīkār, AFGHANISTAN *Alexandria-under-the Caucasus, Kapisa/Kapishi*
Founded in 328 BC by, and named after, Alexander III the Great[†]. The Hindu Kush in Afghanistan was known as the Indian Caucasus.

Charleroi, BELGIUM *Charnoy*
A village developed into a fortress in 1666 by the Spanish and renamed after Charles II[†] and the French *roi* 'king'. It changed hands between the French and Spanish before coming under Austrian rule between 1713 and 1746. The Dutch fortified the city in 1816 and it became a Belgian possession when that country achieved independence in 1830.

Charlesbourg, QUEBEC/CANADA *Bourg Royal*
Originally 'Royal Borough', it was renamed after the city's patron saint, Charles Borromeo (1538–84), cardinal and archbishop of Milan (1560–84).

Charleston, CANADA, NEW ZEALAND, USA
1. USA (Illinois): named after Charles Morton, its first postmaster.
2. USA (South Carolina): previously named Charles Towne in 1670 after the British King Charles II[†], it was shortened in 1783 after the end of the American War of Independence (1775–83). The dance, the charleston, was conceived in Charleston, South Carolina.
3. USA (West Virginia): founded in 1794 as Charles Town, it was named by its founder, George Clendenin, for his father, Charles.

Charlestown, IRELAND, ST KITTS & NEVIS, USA
1. St Kitts & Nevis: named after the British
King Charles II[†].
2. USA (New Hampshire): named by a friend
of, and after, Admiral Sir Charles Knowles
(*c.*1697–1777), governor of Jamaica (1752–6).

Charleville-Mézières, CHAMPAGNE-
ARDENNE/FRANCE
The town was formed in 1966 from the
amalgamation of Charleville, named after its
founder in 1606, Charles de Gonzague, Duke
of Nevers, and Mézières which was previously
Maceriae from the Latin *maceria* 'ramparts'.

Charlevoix, MICHIGAN/USA
A lake and a city named after a French Jesuit
missionary, Pierre-François-Xavier de
Charlevoix (1682–1761), who wrote of his
travels in North America.

Charlotte, USA
North Carolina: named in 1768 after Charlotte
Sophia of Mecklenburg-Strelitz (1744–1818)
who married King George III[†] in 1761.

Charlotte Amalie, US VIRGIN ISLANDS *Tap
Hus, St Thomas*
Founded as a Danish colony in 1672 with a
name meaning 'Rum House', it was renamed
in 1730 after Charlotte (1650–1714), wife of
King Christian V of Denmark. It was
sometimes also called Amalienborg, the name
of the royal palace in Copenhagen. The USA
bought the islands in 1917. Between 1921 and
1936 the city was called St Thomas after the
island of which it is the capital; the town is also
the capital of the US Virgin Islands.

Charlottesville, VIRGINIA/USA
Named in 1761 after the Queen of George III[†]
(*see* CHARLOTTE).

Charlottetown, PRINCE EDWARD ISLAND/
CANADA *Port La Joie*
Founded as a French settlement in the 1720s, it
was renamed after King George III's[†] Queen
(*see* CHARLOTTE) when the island was passed to
Great Britain in 1763 at the close of the Seven
Years' War (1756–63).

Chartres, CENTRE/FRANCE *Autricum*
Named after the Gaulish tribe, the Carnutes.

Châteauroux, CENTRE/FRANCE
Takes its name from a castle, *château*, built in
the 10th century by Raoul le Large, Prince of
Déols; Raoul has become *roux*.

Château-Thierry, PICARDY/FRANCE *Égalité-
sur-Marne*
'Thierry's Castle'. Named after the castle built in
718 by Charles Martel (*c.*688–741), the Frankish
ruler (715–41), for Thierry (or Theodoric) IV

(713–37), the puppet Merovingian king (720–37)
under the control of Martel. During the French
Revolution (1789), the name was changed
temporarily to Égalité-sur-Marne after Louis
Philippe Joseph (1747–93), Duke of Orléans,
who was known as Philippe Égalité 'Equality'
because he supported the Revolution; the town
lies on the River Marne.

Châtellerault, POITOU-CHARENTES/FRANCE
Named after a 10th-century castle built by the
2nd Viscount Airoud.

Chatham, CANADA, UK, USA
1. Canada (Ontario): named after the English
Chatham while that in New Brunswick is
named after William Pitt (Pitt the Elder) (1708–
78), 1st Earl of Chatham, twice the British
Prime Minister in all but name (1756–61,
1766–8).
2. UK (England): 'Village at Chet' from the
Celtic *cēd* 'wood' and *hām*.

Chatham Islands, NEW ZEALAND
An island group in the Pacific, they were
discovered in 1791 by the British Lieutenant
William Broughton, who named them after
his ship, the *Chatham*. The islands were
annexed by New Zealand in 1842.

Chattahoochee, USA
A river in the south-east, the name comes from
a Creek word meaning either 'painted stone'
or 'pounded rock'.

Chattanooga, USA
Tennessee: formerly Ross' Landing and
established as a trading post on the Tennessee
River in *c.*1815 by John Ross who became a
Cherokee chief. It was given the same Native
American name, meaning 'Rock rising to a
Point', as the nearby Lookout Mountain in 1838.

Chauk, BURMA, INDIA
Burma: 'Dry', the town being in a dry zone.

Chaumont, CHAMPAGNE-ARDENNE/FRANCE
Calvus Mons
The present name from *chauve* 'bald' and *mont*
is derived from the previous name 'Bald
Mountain' from the Latin *calvus* 'bald' or 'bare'
and *mons*.

Chaves, PORTUGAL *Aquae Flaviae*
The site of a spa, fortified by the Romans and
called the 'Baths of Flavius' after the local hot
springs.

Chaykovskiy, PERM/RUSSIA
Built as settlement for construction workers in
1955, it was renamed in 1962 after the
composer Pyotr 'Peter' Tchaikovsky (1840–93),
who was born in nearby Votkinsk on the other
side of the River Kama.

Cheadle, ENGLAND/UK *Celle*
'Wood' from the Celtic *cēd* and the Old English *lēah*, also meaning 'wood'.

Cheb, CZECH REPUBLIC *Eger*
Lying on the River Ohře, it means 'Bend (in the River)'. Historically inhabited by Germans until their ejection at the end of the Second World War in 1945, the German Eger is derived from the Celtic name of the river which in Old Latin was Egire.

Chechaouene, MOROCCO
Founded as a fortress in 1471 between a pair of mountain peaks, the name means 'Horns' and is a French adaptation of the Berber *issawen*, the plural of *iss* 'horn'. The town was occupied by the Spanish in 1920–56. It is also spelt Chaouen, Chechaouèn, Xauen (Spanish), and Shafshawan (Arabic).

Chechnya (Ichkeria), RUSSIA
A predominantly Muslim republic, called by the Chechens the Chechen Republic of Ichkeria, with *chechen* meaning 'people'. The Chechen for Ichkeria is Noxçiyçö. The name is derived from the name of a village on the River Argun where the Russians and Chechens fought their first battle in 1732. The Russians finally prevailed in 1864. In 1922 Chechnya became an autonomous province; between 1934 and 1991 it was united with Ingushetia as a single autonomous province which became a republic in 1936. The republic ceased to exist in 1944–57 when Stalin deported the Chechens and Ingush for 'unsocialist acts' to Central Asia, having accused them of collaboration with the German Army. In 1957 Checheno-Ingushetia was re-established with new territorial boundaries when the two peoples were rehabilitated. In 1991 the Chechen-dominated parliament declared the republic's independence and the following year Moscow established a separate republic for the Ingush. Russian troops invaded Chechnya in December 1994 and a brutal war lasted until August 1996. The result was *de facto* independence for Chechnya. Another Russian military invasion took place in October 1999 in response to Chechen terrorist attacks into Russia. Fighting continues.

Cheddar, ENGLAND/UK *Ceodre, Cedre*
Derived from the probable Old English *cēodor* 'ravine', a reference to the gorge nearby. It gives its name to a hard cheese which originated here.

Cheektowaga, NEW YORK/USA
Derives its name from the Native American words *juk do waah geh* 'Place of the Crab Apple Tree'.

Cheju, SOUTH KOREA *Tamra-guk, T'amlla, Quelpart*
An island (Cheju-Do), a province and a city. Situated off the south-western coast of South Korea and the country's biggest island, the name means 'Island in the Province Over There' or 'End Province' from Korean *che* 'over there' or 'end', *ju* 'province' and *do* 'island'. The island was an independent kingdom known as Tamra-guk before 938, then T'amlla. It received its present name during the reign of Kojong, King of Koryŏ (1214–60), although in 1653 a Dutch sailor, Hendrik Hemel, found it and gave it the Western name of Quelpart.

Chelmsford, UK, USA
1. UK (England): formerly Celmeresfort 'Cēolmær's Ford' from an Old English personal name and *ford*.
2. USA (Massachusetts): named after the English town from which some of the first arrivals came in 1633.

Cheltenham, UK, USA
UK (England): formerly Celtanhomme and Chinteneham. The meaning of the first part of the name is not known, but it may be an Old English personal name, Celta, to give a 'River Meadow belonging to a Man called Celta' and *hamm*. It is possible, however, that the name means a 'River Meadow, or Enclosure, by a hill known as Celte'.

Chelyabinsk, RUSSIA *Chelyabi Karagay*
A well-wooded province on the eastern side of the Ural Mountains and a city. Founded as a fortress in 1736 by a Bashkir village with a Turkic name meaning 'Ancient Pinewood (Forest)' from *chelyabi* 'ancestral' and *karagay* 'pinewood'. It was renamed in 1786. So prolific was the Kirov Plant in producing the T-34 medium tank during the Second World War that the city was known informally as 'Tankograd' from *tank* and *grad*. This was not unique: Nizhniy Tagil, which had another of the three plants building the T-34, was also called 'Tankograd'.

Chemba, MOZAMBIQUE
Takes its name from the river that joins the Zambezi here. The name means 'ditch'.

Chemnitz, SAXONY/GERMANY *Karl-Marx-Stadt*
Probably derived from a Slavonic root word akin to the Russian *kamen'* 'stone', thus 'Stone (Town)'. In 1953–90 it was called the 'City of Karl Marx' (1818–83), the German political and economic theorist who inspired the creation of communism. Chemnitz was readopted in 1990 when Germany was reunified.

Chengde, HEBEI/CHINA *Rehe*
Also sometimes called Jehol (for which the
Pinyin is Rehe), as it is situated on the Je Ho
'Warm River' from *rè* 'warm' and *hé*, so-called
because of the hot springs which flow into it.
North of the Great Wall, it only became part of
China during the Liao Dynasty (907–1125). The
present Pinyin name, adopted in 1733 when
the Yongzheng emperor renamed it in honour
of his father, means 'Inherited Virtue' from
chéng 'to inherit' and *dé* 'virtue'.

Chengdu, SICHUAN/CHINA *Yizhou, Jinguan
Cheng, Fu/Furong*
'Great Capital (City)'. The founder, in the 3rd
century BC, is said to have claimed that in one
year the site would become a city and in two
years it would become a great city from *chéng*
'to become' and *dū* 'great city' or 'capital'.
Jinguan Cheng meant 'Official Brocade City'
from *jǐn* 'brocade', *guān* 'official' because the
government silk bureau was established here
during the Eastern Han dynasty (25–220), and
chéng 'city'. It was also called Fu or Furong at
one time from *fúróng* 'hibiscus'.

Chennai, TAMIL NĀDU/INDIA *Fort St George,
Chinnepatan, Machilipatnam, Masalia,
Madraspatnam/Madraspattanam, Madras*
Founded by the English East India Company as
a trading post whose fortification was begun
on St George's Day, 23 April 1640; hence its
name Fort St George. In due course this
expanded to include surrounding villages, one
of which was the fishing village of
Madraspatnam, also called Black Town to
indicate that that was where the Indians lived.
They called it Chinnepatan. The British
adopted a shortened version of
Madraspatnam, the Sanskrit *patnam* or
pattanam simply meaning 'town'. There are
several theories as to the origin of the name
Madras. It may be derived from the Sanskrit
mandarāstra 'Kingdom of Manda' from the
name of a god of the underworld and *rāstra*
'kingdom'; or from the local Muslim religious
schools, the Arabic *madrasa*; or from the Tamil
madhu-ras 'honey'. A highly unlikely theory is
that it comes from the name of a Christian
fisherman called Madarasen. In 1652 Madras
was designated a Presidency—the first of three
centres of the Company's trade and
administration with its own governor (the
others were Bombay and Calcutta). Since 1997
the city has been officially known by its Tamil
name, Chennai, although this name is not of
Tamil origin. It comes from Chennappa
Naicker, the Telugu-speaking Raja of
Chandragiri, who granted the British the right
to trade along the coast.

Chepstow (Cas-Gwent), WALES/UK *Chepstowe,
Chapestowe*
'Market Place' from the Old English *cēap*
'market' and *stōw*. Its Welsh name means
'Castle in Gwent'.

Cherbourg, LOWER NORMANDY/FRANCE
Coriallum, Carusburc
The first Roman name is derived from the
Gaulish *corio* 'army' and the Latin *vallum*
'rampart' or 'fortification'. The present name
may come from a Germanic version of the
Roman name—from *hari* 'army' and *burg*
which was also the origin of the 11th-century
name of Carusburc.

Cherchell, ALGERIA *Iol, Caesarea, Sharshal*
Founded as a small Phoenician or Carthaginian
port, it was renamed in 25 BC after Caesar
Augustus[†] and became the capital of ancient
Mauretania. The present name is a French
corruption of the previous name, itself a form
of Caesarea.

Cherkasy, UKRAINE
A province and a city named after the
Circassian people. Also spelt Cherkassy. *See*
CHERKESSK.

Cherkessk, KARACHAI-CHERKESIYA REPUBLIC/
RUSSIA *Batalpashinskaya/Batalpashinsk, Sulimov,
Yezhovo-Cherkessk*
Capital of the republic and named after the
Circassian people, in Russian *Cherkes*. This
is said to be from an Ossetic word *charkas*
'eagle'. The city's first name commemorates a
Russian victory over a Turkish force led by
Batal Pasha in 1789; this name was amended in
1880. In 1930 it was changed to credit Daniil
Sulimov (1890–1937), a local Communist
official. When he died the new name
honoured Nikolay Yezhov (1895–1940), head
of the NKVD (1936–8). The prefix Yezhovo was
dropped after his disappearance and
presumed death.

Chërnaya Rechka, KEMEROVO/RUSSIA *Yuksa*
'Black Rivulet' from *rechka* 'rivulet'. Although
the name is still in use, the town is now also
called Qarasū, its Turkish equivalent.

Chernigov (Chernihiv), UKRAINE
A province and a city, probably named after
the rich chernozem soil, also called black
earth, from the Russian *chernozëm*.

Cherni-Vrŭkh, BULGARIA
A mountain meaning 'Black Peak' from *cheren*
'black' and *vr'kh* 'peak'.

Chernobyl, UKRAINE
Derived from the Russian *chernobyl'nik*
'wormwood', an aromatic plant of the

composite family, *Artemisia absinthium*, abundant here.

Chernogorsk, KHAKASIYA REPUBLIC/RUSSIA
'Black Mountain', so-called because it lies in the Minusinsk coal basin, from *chërno* 'black' and *gorsk*.

Chernovtsi (Chernivtsi), UKRAINE *Czernowitz, Cernăuţi, Chernovitsy*
A province and a city. Having been founded in the Polish-Lithuanian kingdom, it came under Ottoman Turkish rule in the 18th century. From 1775 to 1918 it lay within the Austro-Hungarian Empire as Czernowitz, the Bukovina having been ceded to the Empire in gratitude for the emperor's mediation in one of the many Russo-Turkish wars (1768-74). In 1918-40 it was part of Romania as Cernăuţi. It was then taken by the Soviet Union as a result of the 1939 Nazi–Soviet non-aggression pact and called Chernovitsy. The city received its present name in 1944. It is clearly linked in some way to various words for 'black', in Russian *chërniy*. This may be because of the darkish skins of the people, a legacy of Turkish rule, or it may come from a personal name.

Chernyakhovsk, KALININGRAD/RUSSIA
Insterburg
Renamed after Army General Ivan Danilovich Chernyakhovsky (1908-45), commander of the 3rd Byelorussian Front, who was killed during the fighting for Königsberg (now Kaliningrad). To be a Front commander-in-chief at the age of 37 was remarkable. Its previous name indicated its position on the Instruch River.

Cherokee, USA
Six states have cities with this name, all after the Cherokee people. Two lakes also have this name.

Chersky, CHUKOT AUTONOMOUS DISTRICT/
RUSSIA
Named after Ivan Chersky (1845-92), who explored Siberia. Two Chersky Ranges are also named after him, one in Yakutia and one south of Lake Baykal.

Chervonograd (Chervonohrad), UKRAINE
Krystinopol'
Renamed from 'Christina's Town' in 1953 as 'Red Town' from the Russian *chervonnyy* 'red' and *grad*, or *hrad* in Ukrainian.

Chesapeake, USA
There are three towns in the USA (in Ohio, Virginia, West Virginia) with this name and one Chesapeake City in Maryland. The name comes from Chesapeake Bay which itself is thought to be a contraction of the Delaware

name *kitshishwapeak* 'Great Salty Bay', but this is disputed.

Chesham, ENGLAND/UK *Cæstæleshamme, Cestreham*
'River Meadow by a Pile of Stones' from the Old English *ceastel* 'pile of stones' and *hamm*. The nearby Chesham Bois has the manorial addition of Bois, a family name from the French *bois* 'wood', possibly the location of the 13th-century manor.

Cheshire, UK, USA
UK (England): formerly Cestre Scire, a county with a name shortened from Chestershire, that is, the district of the city of Chester.

Chester, CANADA, UK, USA *Deva (Deoua)/Castra Devana, Castra Legionum, Legacaestir, Cestre (UK)*
1. UK (England): '(Roman) Town, or Camp' from *castra* or the Old English *ceaster* with no geographical distinction, although Deva (Deoua) is associated with the River Dee, itself meaning 'The Goddess', on which it lies. It was the garrison of the 20th Roman Legion, hence its Roman names which meant 'Camp of the Legions'.
2. USA (Pennsylvania): first settled by the Swedes, Dutch settlers joined them in the first half of the 17th century and called the place Upland. It was renamed after the city in England, because of its Quaker centre, by William Penn (1644-1718), the founder of Pennsylvania, when he arrived in 1682.

Chesterfield, UK, USA
1. UK (England): formerly Cesterfelda and Cestrefeld 'Open Land near a (Roman) Camp' from *ceaster* and *feld*.
2. USA: there are five towns with this name, some of which are named after Philip Dormer Stanhope (1694-1773), 4th Earl of Chesterfield, an English statesman and a secretary of state (1746-8).

Chester-le-Street, ENGLAND/UK *Ceastre, Cestria in Strata*
See CHESTER. The additional '-le-Street' indicates that it was built on, or close to, a Roman road from the Latin *stratum* 'paved road'.

Cheyenne, USA
The two towns in Wyoming and Oklahoma, and the river, are named after the Plains tribe, the Cheyenne. The name is said to be a modification of a name given to it by the Sioux which meant 'aliens'. Alternatively, the name is said to come from a local word *shaia* 'talkers', with the meaning that their speech was unintelligible to everybody else.

Chhatarpur, MADHYA PRADESH/INDIA
Founded in 1707 by a Bundelā king, Chhatrasal, after whom it is named, with the suffix *pur*.

Chiang Mai, THAILAND *Zimmé*
Its full name is Nopburi Si Nakhon Ping Chiang Mai. Although founded in 1296 on the banks of the Ping River by Mengrai, King of Lanna (1296–1317), the name means 'New City' from *chiang* 'city' and *mai* 'new'. Having conquered the Kingdom of Haripunjaya in 1281, Mengrai made it the capital of his newly founded Kingdom of Lanna, the 'Land of a Million Rice Fields' from *lan* 'million' and *na* 'rice fields', in 1296 because of its central location. Lanna's name was later changed to Chiang Mai. The city was occupied by the Burmese between 1558 and 1776.

Chiang Saen, THAILAND
Founded on an ancient site in 1328 by, and named after, Phra Chao Saen Pu, a grandson of Mengrai, King of Lanna (1296–1317), to mean the 'City of Saen'.

Chiapas, MEXICO
A state named after the Chiapa people. It was within Guatemala until annexed by Mexico in 1821.

Chiba, HONSHŪ/JAPAN
'Thousand Leaves' from *chi* 'thousand' and *ha* 'leaf'.

Chicago, ILLINOIS/USA *Chickagou*
Named after the Chicago River which itself was given an Algonquian name whose meaning is still disputed. It may come from *she-kag-ong*, denoting a place along the river where wild onions grew.

Chichén Itzá, YUCATÁN/MEXICO
Mayan ruins. 'The Mouths of the Wells of the Itzá' from the Mayan *chi* 'mouths' and *chen* 'wells', and Itzá, a tribal name of Chontal origin.

Chichester, UK, USA *Noviomagus Regnensium, Cisseceaster, Cicestre* (UK)
UK (England): '(Roman) Fort belonging to Cissa', a son of Aelle, the first King of the South Saxons in the late 5th century, from an Old English personal name and *ceaster*. It was the garrison of the 2nd Roman Legion. It was also the capital of the Breton Regnenses with *noviomagus* meaning a 'new town developed from a market'.

Chickasaw, ALABAMA/USA
Named after the Chickasaw people.

Chicopee, USA
Two towns in Massachusetts and Georgia take their name from a Native American word for 'cedar tree'.

Chicualacuala, MOZAMBIQUE *Malvérnia*
Derived from the local *xi-quadja* 'quail' because they were numerous here. Until 1981 the town was named after Sir Godfrey Huggins (1883–1971), Viscount Malvern, who was prime minister of Southern Rhodesia (now Zimbabwe) in 1933–53 and of the Central African Federation (now Malawi, Zambia, and Zimbabwe) in 1953–6.

Chidambaram, TAMIL NĀDU/INDIA
The name refers to the Hindu temple dedicated to the god Shiva and is taken from the Tamil *citt* 'wisdom' and *ampalam* 'atmosphere'.

Chieti, ABRUZZO/ITALY *Teate*
The present name has evolved from the original and ancient Teate, the first *t* mutating to *k* (or *ch*), the *a* to an *e*, while the final *i* represents the fading vowel *ĕ* spoken by the people of the Abruzzi.

Chifeng (Mongolian: **Ulanhad**), INNER MONGOLIA/CHINA
'Red Mountain' from the Chinese *chì* and the Mongolian *ulan* 'red', and Chinese *fēng* and Mongolian *had* 'mountain' or 'peak'. This refers to the rosy-coloured peak overlooking the town.

Chigwell, ENGLAND/UK *Cingheuuella, Chiggewell*
Possibly 'Cicca's Stream' from an Old English personal name and *wella* 'stream ' or 'spring'.

Chihuahua, MEXICO *Villa Real de Minas, San Francisco de Cuellar*
A state and a city founded in 1709 with a Native American name meaning 'sandy' or 'dry' or, alternatively, the 'Place where Sacks are made'. When the Spanish arrived they changed the name, first to the 'Royal Town of Mines' as settlers worked the silver mines and then to 'St Francis of Cuellar' after the arrival of Franciscan and Jesuit missionaries. The original name was restored after Mexican independence in 1821. It gives its name to the smallest breed of dog, *perritos chihuahueños*.

Chile The Republic of Chile (República de Chile) since independence in 1818. Previously a Spanish colony attached to the Viceroyalty of Peru (16th century). The origin of the country's name is not known, but it is probably derived from an Araucanian word for a type of bird. It has also been suggested that it may be a local word meaning 'Where the Land Ends'.

Chililiabomwe, ZAMBIA *Bancroft*
'Croaking Frog', a reference to the abundance of frogs here. It was founded in 1955 and

originally named after the Canadian geologist, Dr Joseph Bancroft (1882–1957), who worked here in the copper industry. The present name was adopted in the late 1960s.

Chillicothe, USA
There are four towns with this name, the principal one being in Ohio. The name is derived from a Shawnee word meaning 'Main Town'; an alternative meaning is 'Man made perfect'.

Chilliwack, BRITISH COLUMBIA/CANADA
A town founded in the 1860s, a river and a lake with a Salish name possibly meaning 'Valley of Many Streams', but there are other derivations indicating a tribal name associated with water.

Chilpancingo, GUERRERO/MEXICO
Founded in 1591 with the name 'Place of the Wasps'. The full name is Chilpancingo de los Bravos, Bravos being added in honour of Leonardo, Nicolás, and Victor Bravo, local heroes of the revolution (1910–21).

Chilumba, MALAWI *Deep Bay*
A port on Lake Malawi, its previous name recognized the depth of water here. The name was changed in 1964 to a Nyanja word meaning 'island'; the Nyanja speak a dialect of Chewa, a Bantu language.

Chimanimani, ZIMBABWE *Melsetter, Mandidzuzure*
A town and mountains with a name derived from the local *Tshimanimani* 'to be constricted', a reference to the mountain defile here. Founded in 1893, it was named after the estate in the Orkneys of its founders. When Zimbabwe gained independence in 1980 the name was changed to Mandidzuzure, an expression describing people who live here. The present name was adopted in 1982.

Chin, BURMA
A state named after the Chin people of Mongol descent.

China (Zhōngguó)
The People's Republic of China (Zhōnghuá Rénmín Gònghéguó) since 1949. Previously the Republic of China (1912) and the Chinese Empire (221 BC); this was ruled by various dynasties: the Qing (Manchu) (1644–1911), the Ming (1368–1644), the Yuan (Mongol) (1260–1368), and so on. Zhōngguó means 'Middle Kingdom' from *zhōng* 'middle' and *wángguó* 'kingdom' and refers to historical China, in particular the eighteen inner provinces—the centre of the known world; it was first used as the formal term for China at the Treaty of Nerchinsk in 1689. Zhōnghuá is the contraction of two terms which together mean the 'Huaxia

(Han or Chinese) people of the Central Plain', *Rénmín* 'People's', and *Gònghéguó* 'Republic'. The conventional English name 'China' is derived from Qin (in Pinyin pronounced 'cheen'), a state which emerged supreme at the end of the Warring States Period (475–221 BC). Although only lasting until 206 BC, China was united for the first time and a Chinese identity created. The Qin ruler assumed the new title of emperor, calling himself Qin Shihuangdi 'First Sovereign Emperor of Qin' (221–210 or 209 BC). The Chinese have been subject to Mongol and Manchu rule, as well as Japanese rule of northern and eastern China in 1937–45. The final *a* was added by the Portuguese. Porcelain was first made in China which thus gave its name to china.

Chingleput, TAMIL NĀDU/INDIA
'Town of Red Lotuses' in Tamil.

Chinguetti, MAURITANIA
Said to be 'Springs of Horses'. Founded in 1262, it became the capital of Western Sahara and one of the most sacred towns of Islam.

Chinhoyi, ZIMBABWE *Sinoia*
Renamed in 1946 after a chief, Tshinoyi, who lived in the area at the beginning of the 20th century. The current spelling was only adopted in 1980.

Chinook, CANADA, USA
All three towns in Canada and those in Montana and Washington, USA, are named after the Chinook tribe which lived along the north-west Pacific coast of North America. They have given their name to a large combat support helicopter in the US Army.

Chioggia, VENETO/ITALY *Fossa Clodia*
Adapted from the Roman name, the 'Canal of Clodius', a personal Latin name. Who this particular Clodius was is not known.

Chipata, ZAMBIA *Fort James*
Founded in 1899 and named after Sir Leander Starr Jameson (1853–1917) who led the disastrous 'Jameson' raid into the Transvaal in 1895 to overthrow the Boer government. At independence in 1964 the town was renamed 'Gateway' in reference to its location on the border with Malawi.

Chippenham, ENGLAND/UK *Cippanhamme (Wiltshire), Chipeham*
Possibly a 'River Meadow belonging to a Man (possibly) called Cippa' from an Old English personal name and *hamm*. Chipeham was the name in the Domesday Book (1086) for both towns in Cambridgeshire and Wiltshire.

Chipping Sodbury, ENGLAND/UK *Cheping Sobbyri*
'Fortified Place of a Man (possibly) called Soppa' from an Old English personal name and *burh*. Chipping comes from the Old English *cēping* 'market place'.

Chirchik, UZBEKISTAN
Named after the Chirchik River which was previously known as the Parak. It and the present name may simply mean 'swift (flowing)'.

Chiromo, MALAWI
'Corner of Land', a reference to its location in the junction of the Shire River and another river.

Chișinău, MOLDOVA *Kishinëv*
First documented in 1466, it may derive its name from the Tatar *kish* or Turkish *kiş*, both 'winter' or 'winter cold'. It came under Ottoman Turkish control after the death of Stefan III (1435–1504), Prince of Moldavia (1457–1504). An alternative possibility is that the name comes from the Old Moldovan *kishineu* 'spring' or 'well'. The city adopted the Russian equivalent of Chișinău, Kishinëv, when ceded by the Ottoman Turks to Russia in 1812 until it was included within Romania in 1918–40 when it became Chișinău once more. When taken by the Soviet Union in 1940 the name Kishinëv was restored, but when Moldova achieved independence in 1991, it reverted once more to Chișinău. The city has been the capital of the Moldavian Soviet Socialist Republic and then of Moldova since 1940.

Chistopol, TATARSTAN REPUBLIC/RUSSIA *Chistoye Pole*
'Open Field' from *chistovoy* 'clean' and thus 'unencumbered' or 'open' and *pole* 'field'. It was renamed in 1781 when the village became a town.

Chita, RUSSIA
A province and a city which originated as a winter camp in 1653; a fort was built in 1690. The city lies at the confluence of the Ingoda and Chita rivers, hence its name. In Evenki *chita* means 'clay'.

Chitipa, MALAWI *Fort Hill*
Founded in 1896 as a military post to guard the route north to Tanganyika (now Tanzania), it was named after Sir Clement Hill (1845–1913), a senior official in the British Foreign Office. It was renamed in 1966 after a local former chief.

Chittagong, BANGLADESH *Porto Grande*
Also called Chittagrām or Cattagrām. Called 'Great Port' by the Portuguese, its present name is thought to come from the Hindi *čiṭṭāgǎṅv* 'white village' from *čiṭṭā* 'white' and *gǎṅv*. It could be derived, however, from the Sanskrit *Chaturgrāma* 'Four Villages'. Another possibility is that the name comes from an Arakanese inscription, *Tsit-tse-gong* 'War shall not be waged' on a pillar erected by the Buddhist king to commemorate his victory over the Muslims. The port was ceded to the English East India Company in 1760.

Chittaurgarh, RĀJASTHĀN/INDIA *Chitrakut*
Previously named after Chitrang, a Rājput chieftain. It now means the 'Fort of Chitor' from *garh*.

Chkalovo, KAZAKHSTAN
Named after Valery Chkalov (1904–38), a test pilot and aviation hero who, with two others, flew 63 hours non-stop from Moscow to Portland, Oregon, USA, using the polar route in June 1937. *See* ORENBURG.

Chkalovskoye, PRIMORSKIY TERRITORY/RUSSIA
Renamed in 1937 after Valery Chkalov (see previous entry).

Choctawhatchee, USA
A river in the south-east named after the Choctaw with the additional *hatchee* 'stream'. Their name is believed to come from the Spanish *chato* 'flat (nose)', a reference to their practice of head deformation whereby a hinged piece of wood was used to apply pressure on the foreheads of male infants.

Chodov, CZECH REPUBLIC *Codou*
Founded in the 12th century as 'the Chods' Settlement', the local peasants who guarded the border between Bohemia and Bavaria. Their name was *Chodove* 'Chods' from *choditi* 'to walk'.

Choiseul, SOLOMON ISLANDS, ST LUCIA
1. Solomon Islands: named by Louis-Antoine de Bougainville (1729–1811), a French explorer of the South Pacific (1766–9), after his patron, the Duc de Choiseul (1719–85), French foreign minister (1758–61) and minister of war (1766–70).
2. St Lucia: also named after the Duc de Choiseul at a time when St Lucia was ruled by the French.

Chokoloskee, FLORIDA/USA
'Red Houses' from a Native American word *chokoliska*.

Cholet, PAYS DE LA LOIRE/FRANCE *Cauletum*
Because the area was known for its cabbages, the name may be derived from the Latin *caulis* 'cabbage'.

Cholula (Cholula de Rivadabia), PUEBLA/
MEXICO
'Place of Springs' in Nahuatl.

Choma, ZAMBIA
Founded c.1905, the Lala name means 'Large
Drum', probably a reference to ceremonial
rituals that took place here.

Chomutov, CZECH REPUBLIC *Komotau*
Derived from the nickname of the first owner
of the original farm. He was called *chomût*
'ham-fisted, or clumsy person'.

Chongqing, SICHUAN/CHINA *Yuzhou, Gongzhou*
Established as Yuzhou in 589, the present
name means 'Twice Blessed' or 'Repeated
Celebration' from *chóng* 'double' or 'repeat'
and *qìng* 'celebrate'. It was the custom that the
place where the heir apparent resided when
he ascended the throne would acquire the
status of a prefecture at the same time. When
the heir apparent Zhao Dun became Emperor
Guangzong of the Southern Song Dynasty in
1190 Gongzhou became Chongqing
prefecture, 'Twice Blessed', because both the
retired emperor and his empress presided at
the elevation ceremony. It has also been
suggested that the name is doubly appropriate
because of the city's dominant position
between Nanzhong and Pengshui. The city was
the wartime capital of Nationalist China
(1938–46) and at that time the name was
transliterated as Chungking.

Chonju, SOUTH KOREA
A very ancient city founded c.57 BC, the name
means 'Great Province' from *chŏn* 'great' and *ju*
'province'. Formerly a civil and military
centre, it is not a province now.

Chorley, ENGLAND/UK
'Clearing of the Free Peasants' from the Old
English *ceorl* 'peasant' or 'freeman' and *lēah*.

Choybalsan, MONGOLIA *San-Beyse, Bayan
Tumen.*
Renamed Bayan Tumen in 1921 and
Choybalsan in 1941 after Khorloghiyin
Choybalsan (1895–1952), a Communist hero of
the 1921 Mongolian Revolution, who later
became a marshal, prime minister, and the
dictator of Mongolia in 1936. Although
Choybalsan was condemned in 1962, after his
death, for his cult of personality, the city's
name was not changed.

Christchurch, NEW ZEALAND, UK
1. New Zealand (South Island): there is some
dispute about the name of the city. It is
generally accepted that it was renamed after
Christ Church College, Oxford, which is where
one of the principal founders, John Robert
Godley, of the Church of England Canterbury
Association, which founded the original
settlement of Canterbury in 1851, was
educated. On the other hand, two other
principal founders were Cambridge University
graduates and it has been suggested that they
would not have agreed to call the city after an
Oxford college. Since the name Canterbury
had become the name of the region, they
decided to rename the settlement Christ
Church from the dedication of Canterbury
Cathedral.
2. UK (Dorset/England): lying at the
confluence of the Avon and Stour Rivers, it was
known formerly as Twynam 'Place between
the Rivers'. It was subsequently renamed
Christecerce 'Church of Christ' from the Old
English *Crist* and *cirice* 'church'.
3. There is also a Christ Church in Barbados.

Christmas Island, AUSTRALIA, KIRIBATI
1. Australia: an External Territory since 1958.
Although sighted in 1615, it was so-named on
Christmas Day 1643 by Captain William
Mynors of the English East India Company. It
was annexed by the UK in 1888 and was
incorporated into the British Straits
Settlements Colony in 1900. The island was
occupied by the Japanese during the Second
World War and became a dependency of
Singapore in 1946.
2. Kiribati: *see* KIRITIMATI.

Chūbu, HONSHŪ/JAPAN
A region which takes its name from its
location in the centre, *chūbu* from *chū* 'middle'
and *bu* 'region', of Honshū Island.

Chrudim, CZECH REPUBLIC
'Chrudim's (Place)' from the personal name.
Chrudim means a 'sickly man'.

Chukchi Sea (Russian: **Chukotskoye More**)
Part of the Arctic Ocean between Russia and
North America, it is named after the north-east
Siberian Chukchi people.

Chukot, RUSSIA
An autonomous district in the extreme north-
east of Siberia named in 1728 after the
Chukchi people.

Chula Vista, CALIFORNIA/USA
Named after its 'Pretty View' from the Spanish
chula 'pretty' and *vista*.

Churchill, CANADA, USA
1. Canada (Manitoba): a port named after John
Churchill (1650–1722), 1st Duke of
Marlborough, who was a governor of the
Hudson's Bay Company between 1685 and
1691 and later a highly successful general

against the French. It was developed from Fort Churchill, originally built in 1688.

2. Canada (Saskatchewan): previously the Missinipi 'Big River' and then the English River, so-called because it served as a route into the interior for the English traders of the Hudson's Bay Company. It was subsequently renamed after Fort Churchill, itself after the 1st Duke of Marlborough.

3. Canada (Newfoundland and Labrador): a river in Labrador, previously the Hamilton River, named in 1821 after Admiral Sir Charles Hamilton (1767–1849), the first governor and commander-in-chief of Newfoundland (1818–24). In 1965 it was renamed after Sir Winston Churchill (1874–1965), British prime minister (1940–5, 1951–5), after his death that year.

4. There are also mountains, lakes, and falls in Canada and the USA, all named after a British Churchill.

Churu, RĀJASTHĀN/INDIA
Founded c.1620 by, and named after, Churru, a Jāt chieftain.

Chuvashia (Chuvashiya), RUSSIA
A republic, established in 1992 having been an Autonomous Soviet Socialist Republic, named after the Chuvash, a Turkic people.

Cicero, ILLINOIS/USA
Named in the 1830s after the small town in New York State, which itself was named after Cicero (106–43 BC), the famous Roman orator, statesman, and writer.

Ciego de Ávila, CUBA
A province and a city founded in 1840. The name is derived from a certain type of savannah, with trees, called a *ciego*, and the Ávila in Spain.

Ciénaga, COLOMBIA *Aldea Grande*
The full name is San Juan de Ciénaga. Founded in 1518, the original name meant 'Large Village', but the town was renamed after the nearby Great Marsh (in Spanish, *Ciénaga Grande*) of Santa Marta after a Spanish fleet had been destroyed there in 1820. There is also a Ciénaga de Oro, Marsh of Gold, in Colombia.

Cienfuegos, CUBA *Fernandina de Jagua*
A province and a city developed from a fortress whose construction was begun in 1738 by French colonists. This was destroyed by a hurricane in 1825, but the settlement was rebuilt in 1831 and renamed after Don José Cienfuego, the Spanish captain-general who ruled the region in 1816–19. His name meant 'A Hundred Fires'.

Cieplice Śląskie Zdrój, POLAND *Bad Warmbrunn*
Both the former German name and the present Polish one mean 'Bath of the Warm Springs' from *ciepły* 'warm' and *zdrój* 'spring'. The additional *Śląskie* means 'Silesian'.

Cieszyn, POLAND
See ČESKÝ TĚŠÍN.

Cilicia, TURKEY
An ancient district of southern Anatolia which became a Roman province in the 1st century BC. It takes its name from Cilix who, in Greek mythology, was one of the sons of Agenor, King of Phoenicia. Sent by his father to find his sister Europa, he settled here, having failed in his quest.

Cimarron, USA
A river rising in New Mexico whose name may come from the Spanish *cimarrón* 'wild'.

Cincinnati, OHIO/USA *Columbia, Losantiville*
Columbia was founded in 1788 and Losantiville, nearby, in 1789. The latter is a representation of the 'Town opposite the Mouth of Licking Creek' from L(icking Creek), the Latin *os* 'mouth', the Greek *anti* 'opposite' and the French *ville* 'town'. Two years after its initial founding General Arthur St Clair, governor of the Northwest Territory, renamed the settlement in honour of the Revolutionary War Officers' Society of the Cincinnati, itself named after Lucius Quinctius Cincinnatus (5th century BC), Roman statesman and folk hero.

Cinque Ports, ENGLAND
A medieval group of ports in south-east England (Dover, Hastings, Hythe, New Romney, and Sandwich, which were later joined by Rye and Winchelsea) which provided ships and men for royal service in defence of the English Channel in return for certain privileges. The name comes from the Old French *cink porz* 'five ports'.

Circassia, RUSSIA
See KARACHAY-CHERKESSIA.

Circeo, LAZIO/ITALY
A village, San Felice Circeo, and a promontory which appears to be an island when seen from the sea and which is called Mount Circeo. Both are named after Circe, a sorceress in Greek mythology.

Cirencester, ENGLAND/UK *Korinion, Cirenceaster, Cirecestre*
'(Roman) Camp called Corinion, or Corinium' from *ceaster* and an abbreviated form of a Celtic personal name of unknown meaning. It has been suggested that the name means

Ciskei

'Town on the (River) Churn', but Churn may be a back-formation of the town's name.

Ciskei, EASTERN CAPE/SOUTH AFRICA
A former tribal homeland and republic for the Xhosa people between 1981 and 1994, the name means 'On this Side of the (River) Kei' from the Latin *cis* 'on this side of', that is the south-west side. It was the region between the Great Kei and Great Fish Rivers. *See* TRANSKEI.

Città de Castello, UMBRIA/ITALY *Tifernum Tiberinum*
To distinguish the town from other towns called Tifernum, the Romans added Tiberinum 'on the (River) Tiber', but from the 10th century it was known as 'Castle City' from *città* 'city' or 'town' and *castello*.

Ciudad Bolívar, VENEZUELA *San Tomás de la Nueva Guayana de la Angostura*
Founded in 1764 and, despite its full name 'Saint Thomas of the New Guayana of the Narrows', it was simply called Angostura because it was situated by a narrow passage of the Orinoco River; it lies some 70 miles (112 km) upstream of *Ciudad Guayana. It was renamed in 1846 in honour of Simon Bolívar (1783–1830), the liberator of Venezuela, to give the 'City of Bolívar' from the Spanish *ciudad*. Angostura gave its name to Angostura bitters, a kind of aromatic bitters used as a tonic.

Ciudad del Este, PARAGUAY *Puerto Presidente Stroessner*
Founded only in 1957, it was named after Alfredo Stroessner (1912–), Paraguayan president and dictator (1954–89), until he was overthrown in a coup in 1989. It was then renamed 'City in the East'.

Ciudadela, ARGENTINA
'Citadel' in Spanish.

Ciudad Guayana, VENEZUELA *Santo Tomé de Guayana*
'Guayana City', the name being taken from the region in north-east South America, Guiana or Guayana. The modern city was founded in 1961. The original St Thomas of Guayana was founded by the Spanish in 1576.

Ciudad Hidalgo, MEXICO *Taximaroa, Villa Hidalgo*
Michoacán: 'Noble City' from the Spanish *hidalgo* 'noble' and *ciudad* and founded on the site of a Tarascan village called Taximaroa.

Ciudad Juárez, CHIHUAHUA/MEXICO *El Paso del Norte*
Founded in the late 17th century opposite El Paso in Texas, USA, it was first known as the 'Pass of the North' for the river crossing and mountain pass into the USA first mapped in

1581. In 1888 it was renamed in honour of Benito Juárez (1806–72), president (1861–72), to give the 'City of Juárez'. He made the city his headquarters and the provisional capital of Mexico in 1865 while fighting the French. Now it is sometimes simply called Juárez, although there are three other towns in Mexico with this name.

Ciudad Obregón, SONORA/MEXICO
Named after Álvaro Obregón (1880–1928), general and revolutionary leader, and president (1920–4, 1928) who was born here. Shortly after he was elected for the second time he was assassinated.

Ciudad Real, CASTILE-LA MANCHA/SPAIN *Villa Real*
'Royal City'. Founded in 1262 by Alfonso X the Wise (1221–84), King of Castile and León (1252–84) and elevated to the status of a city, *ciudad*, in 1420.

Ciudad Rodrigo, CASTILE-LEÓN/SPAIN
Named after Count Rodrigo González who founded it in 1150.

Ciudad Victoria, TAMAULIPAS/MEXICO *Santa Maria de Aguayo*
Founded in 1750 and in 1825 renamed after Guadalupe Victoria (1786–1843), the first president of Mexico (1824–9). His original name was Manuel Félix Fernández.

Cividale del Friuli, FRIULI-VENEZIA GIULIA/ITALY *Forum Julii*
Cividale is a local form of the Latin *civitas*, here 'city', with del Friuli being a contraction of Forum Julii, either 'Market Place of Julius (Caesar)'[†], or 'Forum of the Julian People'.

Civitavecchia, LAZIO/ITALY *Centumcellae*
Also previously known as Trajan's Port after Trajan[†], it was destroyed by the Saracens in 828 and the inhabitants fled. However, in due course they returned to the 'old city', in Medieval Latin *civitas vetus*; hence the present name.

Clackmannan, SCOTLAND/UK *Clacmanan*
'Stone of Manau' from the Gaelic *clach* 'stone', a reference to the very old stone in the middle of the town, and Manau, the name of a district.

Clanton, ALABAMA/USA
Named after James H. Clanton, a Confederate general who fought in the Civil War (1861–5).

Clanwilliam, CANADA, SOUTH AFRICA
South Africa (Western Cape): originally named Jan Disselsvlei 'Jan Dissel's Vlei' from the name of the farm owner here and *vlei* 'marshy ground'. It was renamed in 1814 by Sir John Cradock (1762–1839), governor of Cape Colony

(1811–14), to honour his father-in-law, the Earl of Clanwilliam.

Clare, AUSTRALIA, IRELAND, UK, USA
1. Australia (South Australia): founded in 1842 and named after the county in Ireland in which one of the early settlers was born.
2. Ireland: locally An Clár. A county and river whose name comes from the Gaelic *clar* 'plain' to describe a level surface.
3. USA (Michigan): thought to be named after the county in Ireland.

Claremont, AUSTRALIA, JAMAICA, SOUTH AFRICA, USA
1. South Africa (Western Cape): named after Claremont House in Surrey, England, which was the residence of Sir John Molteno (1814–86), first prime minister of Cape Colony.
2. USA: there are five towns with this name, the first one being founded in New Hampshire in 1762. There is some doubt as to whether it was named after the country seat of Baron Clive of Plassey (1725–74), who was given an Irish peerage in 1762, or a member of the Holles family, specifically the 1st Earl of Clare (*c.*1564–1637). The town in California, founded in 1887, was named after the New Hampshire town.

Claremore, OKLAHOMA/USA
Settled in 1880 and named after an Osage chief whose tribe lived in the area.

Claremorris (Clár Chlainne Muiris), IRELAND
'Plain of the Children of Muiris' from the Gaelic *clár* 'plain'.

Clarence, AUSTRALIA, NEW ZEALAND
Australia (New South Wales): a river renamed after Albert Victor (1864–92), Duke of Clarence, the eldest son of the British King Edward VII. It was at first known as the Big River after its discovery in 1831.

Clarksburg, USA
West Virginia: settled in 1765 and named after General George R. Clark (1752–1818), a charismatic military leader against the British and Native Americans during the American War of Independence (1775–83).

Clarksdale, MISSISSIPPI/USA *Clarksville*
Settled in 1849 and named after Captain John Clark, brother-in-law of the governor of Mississippi.

Clarksville, USA
1. Georgia: named after General John Clarke, governor of Georgia.
2. Indiana and Tennessee: named after George R. Clark (1752–1818) (*see* CLARKSBURG).
3. Missouri: named after Captain William Clark (1770–1838), a member of the Lewis and Clark Expedition (1804–6), the first ground expedition to the Pacific Coast and back.

Claverley, ENGLAND/UK *Claverlege*
'Clearing where Clover grows' from the Old English *clæfre* 'clover' and *lēah*.

Clearwater, CANADA, USA
USA (Florida): previously Clear Water Harbour in recognition of the clear sulfate springs offshore.

Cleethorpes, ENGLAND/UK *Thorpe, Clethorpe*
'Hamlets near Clee' from the Old Scandinavian *thorp* 'hamlet' or 'outlying farmstead' and Clee from the Old English *clæg* 'clay', thus a 'Hamlet near a Place where there is Clay'.

Clermont-Ferrand, AUVERGNE/FRANCE *Augustonemetum*
Originally named after Emperor Augustus[†] with the Gaulish *nemeton* 'sanctuary'. The present city was established in 1731 with the union of Clermont and Montferrand. Clermont means 'clear mountain' from the French *clair mont*, that is, one that is visible from afar, and Montferrand 'Ferrand's mountain'; Ferrand might have been the name of a local lord. The first syllable of Montferrand was deleted so that '*mont*' was not repeated in the name.

Cleveland, AUSTRALIA, USA
1. USA (Ohio): named after Moses Cleaveland (1754–1806) from the Connecticut Land Company who helped to survey the city in 1796. In 1832 the *a* was dropped so that the name could fit comfortably on a newspaper's masthead.
2. USA (Tennessee): named after Colonel Benjamin Cleveland, a commander during the American War of Independence (1775–83).

Clifton, BAHAMAS, UK, USA
UK (England): 'Farmstead near a Cliff' from the Old English *clif* and *tūn*. A number of towns in England have this name with more having some kind of manorial or other additions.

Clinton, CANADA, NEW ZEALAND, USA
1. USA (Iowa): originally New York, it was renamed in 1855 after DeWitt Clinton (1769–1828), governor of New York (1817–23, 1825–8).
2. USA: at least six other towns are also named after the same man; others are named after George Clinton (1739–1812), another governor of New York (1777–95, 1801–4) and vice president of the USA (1804–12).

Clitheroe, ENGLAND/UK *Cliderhou*
'Hill with loose Stones' from a possible Old English word *clider* 'loose stones' and the Old

English *hōh* 'hill', a reference to the loose limestone of the hill here.

Clogher (An Chlochar), NORTHERN IRELAND/UK
'The Stony Place'.

Clonmel (Cluain Meala), IRELAND
'Meadow of Honey' from *cluain* 'meadow' or 'pasture', a reference to the fertility of the Suir Valley.

Clovis, USA
The two towns in California and New Mexico are named after Clovis I (*c*.466–511), Merovingian King of the Franks (481–511).

Cluj-Napoca, ROMANIA *Napoca, Castrum Clus, Klausenburg, Kolozsvár*
Napoca was the Dacian name which was retained by the Romans. Clus, which became Cluj in the 14th century, is from the Latin *clusum* 'closed', a reference to the surrounding hills, and was developed from Castrum Clus, the Medieval Latin name for the small fortified settlement. The city was called Klausenburg when part of the Austro-Hungarian Empire and Kolozsvár when part of Hungary; both indicate a stronghold from the German *Burg* and the Hungarian *vár* and a relationship with Cluj, although *Klause* can mean a 'mountain pass' or a 'hermit's, or monk's, cell'; *kolosz* might come from *kolosszalis* 'colossal' or *kolostor* 'monastery' or 'convent'. The suffix -Napoca was added in 1974 by Nicolae Ceauşescu (1918–89) after he became head of state in 1967 to draw attention to the city's Daco-Roman origin.

Clutha, SOUTH ISLAND/NEW ZEALAND
A river whose name comes from the Gaelic version of the River Clyde in Scotland.

Clwyd, WALES/UK *Cloid fluvium*
Named afer the River Clwyd whose name is said to mean 'hurdle'.

Coats Land, ANTARCTICA
Discovered in 1904 by the Scottish explorer, William Speirs Bruce, during a voyage in the Weddell Sea and named after the expedition's sponsors, James and Andrew Coats.

Cobán, GUATEMALA
Founded *c*.1540, it was named after Cobaóu, a Native American chief.

Cobar, NEW SOUTH WALES/AUSTRALIA
Derived from an Aboriginal word meaning 'Red Earth'.

Cobh (An Cóbh), IRELAND *Queenstown*
An Irish version of the English *cove* referring to Cork Harbour. In 1849–1922, after a visit by Queen Victoria[†] in 1848, it was known as Queenstown.

Coblenz (Koblenz), RHINELAND PALATINATE/ GERMANY *Confluentes*
Founded in 9 BC by Drusus Germanicus (38–9 BC), commander of the Roman forces between the Rhine and Elbe Rivers (12–9 BC), who built a military camp here, Castrum apud Confluentes, and named it after its position at the confluence (in Latin, *confluens*) of the Moselle and Rhine Rivers.

Cobourg, ONTARIO/CANADA *Amherst, Hamilton*
Founded in 1798 and named after Field Marshal Jeffrey Amherst (1717–97), 1st Baron, who conquered Canada for Great Britain in 1758–60; he was then governor-general until 1763. The name was changed to Hamilton and again in 1819 to Cobourg in recognition of the marriage in 1816 of the English Princess Charlotte (1796–1817), daughter of George IV[†], to Prince Leopold of Saxe-Cobourg (1790–1865), King of the Belgians (1831–65). There are towns spelt Coburg in Australia, Germany, and the USA.

Cochabamba, BOLIVIA *Villa de Oropeza*
A department and a city founded in 1574 and named after an Oropesa in Spain. It was renamed in 1786 after the Hispanicized Quechua name, Khocha Pampa, which means a 'Plain with small Lakes'.

Cochin (Kochi), KERALA/INDIA
A former princely state and now an important port, the name may come from a Tamil word *koncam* or a Malayalam word *kochchī*, both meaning 'small' or a 'small place', a reference to the size of the original fishing village from which it developed. To the Portuguese, who first arrived in 1500 and retained possession until the Dutch drove them out in 1633, it became Cochin.

Cochinchina, VIETNAM *Champa, Cauchichina, Nam Ky*
Champa was a kingdom which stretched over the southern and central coastal region of modern Vietnam between the 2nd and 17th centuries. The Portuguese first gave the name Cauchichina to the area around the mouth of the Mekong River, but in the 17th century the name began to refer to the whole country ruled by the Nguyen family. When this southern part of modern Vietnam became a French colony in 1862, the name only referred to the colony. Cauchi may be derived from the Chinese name for Vietnam, Giao Chi. 'China' was added to distinguish it from the Portuguese colony of Cochin in India. Nam Ky 'Southern Administrative Division' was the name used by the Vietnamese before and after the arrival of the French.

Cochinchina was a French Overseas Territory between 1946 and 1949 when it merged with Vietnam.

Cockermouth, ENGLAND/UK *Cokyrmoth*
'Mouth of the (River) Cocker' from the Celtic river name meaning 'twisting' and *mūtha*.

Cocos Islands, AUSTRALIA *Keeling Islands*
An External Territory of Australia discovered in 1609 by, and originally named after, Captain William Keeling (d. 1620) of the English East India Company. They now take their name from the coconut groves on the islands. They became a British possession in 1857 and were attached to the British crown colony of Singapore in 1903. They passed to Australia in 1955.

Codrington, BARBUDA
Named after the Codrington family who developed the island as a private estate in 1674–1870.

Cody, USA
Wyoming: laid out in 1895 by, and named after, Colonel William F. Cody (1846–1917), popularly known as 'Buffalo Bill' Cody, a US Army scout who fought in the Sioux Wars and a buffalo hunter.

Coeur d'Alene, IDAHO/USA
Founded in 1879 after a Native American tribe. The French name means 'Needle Hearts'. One theory is that it was given to them by members of the Hudson's Bay Company in recognition of their commercial sharpness; another that it was an expression used by a chief of the tribe to describe his opinion of the parsimony of the Canadian trappers.

Coff's Harbour, NEW SOUTH WALES/ AUSTRALIA *Brelsford*
Founded in 1847, its name was changed in 1861 to a corruption of the name of a shipbuilder, John Korff.

Cognac, POITOU-CHARENTES/FRANCE *Comniacum*
The Medieval Latin name means the 'Land of Cominius' from *-acum* and the personal name. The town gives its name to the famous brandy produced in the region.

Cohoes, NEW YORK/USA
'Pine Tree' from an Algonquian word. However, lying on the Mohawk River, it is also said to mean 'Shipwrecked Canoe'.

Coimbra, BRAZIL, PORTUGAL
Portugal: formerly Aeminium and Conimbriga. It took the name of the nearby Conimbriga (8 miles (13 km) to the south-west and now called Condeixa), after Roman and Moorish occupation. It was named after the pre-Celtic tribe, the Conii, when the see of a bishop was transferred to Aeminium. The name means 'Fort on the Hill' from the Celtiberian *cun* 'hill' and *briga*. The city was the capital of Portugal between 1139 and 1260.

Coín, ANDALUSIA/SPAIN *Lacibis, Cohine*
The Roman name gave way to the Arabic Cohine in 713; this meant 'Pleasant Paradise' and is the basis for the present name. It was recaptured from the Moors in 1485.

Colchester, CANADA, UK, USA
1. Canada (Ontario): named after the town in England.
2. UK (England): the original name Colonia Victricensis meant the 'Colony of the Victorious' after the Romans defeated Queen Boudicca in 61. Colchester was the first Roman capital of Britain, but London became the capital after Boudicca's rebellion. The second British name, Camulodunum 'Fortress of Camulos' from *dunum*, honours the Celtic war god, Camulos. The next, Saxon, name, Colneceastre, meant 'Roman Camp on the (River) Colne'. The name in the Domesday Book (1086), Colecestra, may be a shortening of the Latin *colonia* with *ceaster*.
3. USA (Connecticutt): named after the town in England.
4. USA (Illinois): originally Chester, 'Col' was added to distinguish it from another Chester in Randolph County.
5. USA (Vermont): named after Viscount Tunbridge, Baron of Enfield and Colchester in the time of King George II[†].

Coleraine (Cúil Raithin), NORTHERN IRELAND/UK
Situated near the mouth of the River Bann, the name means 'Nook of Ferns' from *cúil* 'nook' or 'corner' and *raith* '(place of) ferns'.

Colesberg, NORTHERN CAPE/SOUTH AFRICA *Toverberg*
Founded in 1829 by the British as part of the effort to pacify the violent frontier region of Trans Orangia, it was renamed after Sir Galbraith Lowry Cole (1777–1842), governor of Cape Colony (1828–33), with the additional *berg*.

Coligny, FRANCE, SOUTH AFRICA *Treuerfontein* (*South Africa*)
South Africa (Gauteng); originally named 'Fountain of Sorrows', in 1918 the inhabitants took steps to have it renamed after Gaspard II de Coligny (1519–72), Seigneur 'Lord' de Châtillon, a French admiral and Huguenot leader during the early years of the Wars of Religion (1562–98).

Colima

Colima, MEXICO *Cajitlan*
A state and a city. The previous Aztec name
meant 'Where Pottery is made'. The present
name may honour a Nahua leader, King
Colimán, or it may be a Nahuatl word meaning
'Domain of the old God'.

College Station, TEXAS/USA
A college was situated by the Houston and
Texas Central Railroad and the college was
known as a flag station where trains were
stopped by flag signals. When the area gained
a post office, the name College Station was
adopted for the developing town.

Co Loa, VIETNAM
Capital of the Kingdom of Au Lac and now a
village and ruins. The name is said to mean
'Shell City', a reference to the shape of the
citadel.

Cologne (Köln), NORTH RHINE-WESTPHALIA/
GERMANY *Colonia Claudia Ara Agrippinensis*
The Roman name meant the 'Colony of
Agrippina the Younger (15–59)', whose
birthplace this was. She was the great-
granddaughter of Caesar Augustus[†], the
daughter of Agrippina the Elder (*c.*14 BC–AD
33), the sister of Emperor Caligula (37–41), the
wife of Emperor Claudius I (41–54), and the
mother of Emperor Nero (54–68). The city,
founded by Agrippa (*c.*63–12 BC), the deputy to
Caesar Augustus[†], in 38 BC, was so-called at her
request in AD 50 when Claudius founded a
colony here. The name was later shortened to
Colonia from which the city's present name is
derived. It was the garrison of the Roman 30th
Ulpia Victrix Legion. The city gave its name to
Eau de Cologne, its Italian inventor, Johann
Maria Farina, coming to live in the city in 1709.

Colombia The Republic of Colombia
(República de Colombia) since 1886. Previously
the United States of Colombia (1863–86); New
Granada (1830–63); part of the Republic of
Gran Colombia (1819–30) (which also included
Ecuador, Panama, and Venezuela); part of the
Viceroyalty of New Granada (1740), and the
Audiencia of Santa Fé de Bogotá (1549). The
first Spaniard set foot on what is now
Colombia in 1499. Independence from Spain
was achieved in 1819, although 20 July 1810 is
celebrated as independence day, the day of the
uprising in Bogotá. The name New Granada
was chosen by Spanish settlers after the
Granada in Spain. The present name, adopted
in 1863, honours Christopher Columbus[†].

Colombo, SRI LANKA *Kao-lan-pu, Kalan-totta,
Kolambu/Kolamba*
The first name, whose meaning is unknown, is
Chinese. The port then became known as
Kalan-totta 'Kelani's Ferry', a reference to the
nearby ferry. The Arabs then changed this to
Kolambu which locally became Kolamba. The
first Europeans to settle in the 16th century
were the Portuguese who believed that the
Sinhalese name Kolamba was derived from
kola 'leaves' and *amba* 'mango'. More credible is
that *kolamba* was an old Sinhalese word
meaning 'port', although this is by no means
certain. Nevertheless, the Portuguese are said
to have taken the opportunity to 'tweak' the
name to Colombo in honour of Christopher
Columbus[†], although he never came anywhere
near here.

Colón, ARGENTINA, COSTA RICA, CUBA, EL
SALVADOR, HONDURAS, NICARAGUA, PANAMA,
URUGUAY, VENEZUELA
Panama: founded in 1850 as Aspinwall after
William H. Aspinwall (1807–85), one of the
American sponsors of the Panama Railway.
The city was renamed in 1890 with the
Spanish version of the name Columbus[†].

Colorado, COSTA RICA, PARAGUAY, USA
USA: a state named after the Colorado
River which flows through it and which was
named from the Spanish *colorado* 'ruddy',
'red', or 'coloured' by a Spanish Jesuit priest,
Father Francisco Garcez, in 1776 because its
waters were red with mud. Claimed by Spain
in 1706, the eastern part passed to France in
1802. The next year it was included in the
Louisiana Purchase by the USA, the western
part remaining Spanish until acquired by
Mexico. In 1848 part of western Colorado
was ceded to the USA by Mexico. In 1861
the area in American hands became the
Colorado Territory and in 1876 it joined the
USA as the 38th state. It gave its name to the
infamous Colorado beetle which attacks
potato plants.

Colorado Springs, COLORADO/USA *Fountain
Colony*
Founded in 1871, it was quickly renamed for
the Manitou mineral springs in the state.

Columbia, CANADA, USA
1. USA: there are thirteen places with this
name and the District of Columbia (DC) in
which the American capital, Washington, lies.
In most cases they take their name from
Christopher Columbus[†].
2. Canada-USA: a river rising in British
Columbia and named after the *Columbia*, a ship
in which a Captain Gray sailed to its mouth in
the Pacific in 1792.

Columbus, USA
There are at least sixteen cities and towns with
this name in the USA, the best known being

the city in Ohio. They are either named after Christopher Columbus[†] or after Columbus, Ohio.

Comacchio, EMILIA-ROMAGNA/ITALY
Derived from the Latin *commeatus* with the sense of '(a place where) provisions for the military on the move (could be obtained)'.

Comiso, SICILY/ITALY
Derived from Yhomisum which is itself derived from the Arabic *hums* 'fifth part' with the meaning that this was the fifth part of the land conquered by the Muslims when they took Sicily in 965.

Commander Islands (Komandosrskiye Ostrova), KAMCHATKA/RUSSIA
Named after Commander Vitus Bering[†] who joined the Russian Navy and died here.

Communism Peak (Pik Kommunizma), TAJIKISTAN *Mount Garmo, Mount Stalin*
Following Joseph Stalin's[†] fall from grace, this mountain peak in the Pamirs, discovered in 1928, was renamed in 1960, having adopted the name of Stalin in 1933. At 24 590 ft (7 495 m), it is the highest peak in the Pamirs and in the former Soviet Union, and thus naturally was reserved for Stalin when the Pamir peaks were being given new names to honour the Communist leaders in the 1920s and 1930s.

Como, GABON, ITALY, USA
Italy (Lombardy): formerly Comum and associated with a word of Celtic origin meaning 'valley'. The town lies on Lake Como.

Comodoro Rivadavia, ARGENTINA
Founded in 1901 and named after Commodore Martin Rivadavia (1852–1901), an officer in the Argentinian Navy.

Comoros The Union of the Comoros (Udzima wa Komori) since 2002 following a referendum in 2001 on granting more autonomy to the three islands. Previously the Federal Islamic Republic of the Comoros since independence in 1975. However, in 1976 the inhabitants of one of the islands, Mayotte, voted to stay under French rule and it remains a French possession to this day. Previously a French Overseas Territory (1947–75), a French colony (1912–47), and French protectorates (1886–1912); before the arrival of the French the islands were dominated by the Arabs. The name is corrupted from the Arabic *qamr* 'moon', the islands being known as *Juzur al-Qamr* 'Islands of the Moon'. The Arabs gave the name *al-Qamr* to both Comoros and Madagascar. This was the name they gave to the Magellanic Clouds, two satellite galaxies to

the Milky Way galaxy which can only be seen in the southern hemisphere, which indicated the way to the south.

Compass Berg, EASTERN CAPE/SOUTH AFRICA
A mountain from *Berg* and so-called in 1778 because it has a wonderful view from the summit over all points of the compass.

Compiègne, PICARDY/FRANCE *Compendium*
Founded by the Romans, the name comes from the Latin *compendium* 'short way', to mean a 'short cut' between Beauvais and Soissons.

Conakry, GUINEA
Founded by the French in 1884, the name being taken from a local village whose name, *Konakri*, meant 'Beyond the Water', a reference to its original location on an island, although it is now linked by a causeway. It became the capital of Rivières du Sud in 1891, of the colony of French Guinea in 1893 and of independent Guinea in 1958.

Concepción, ARGENTINA, BOLIVIA, CHILE, COLOMBIA, COSTA RICA, HONDURAS, NAMIBIA, PARAGUAY, PERU, PHILIPPINES, USA
'Conception' in Spanish, a reference to the Immaculate Conception of Mary, mother of Jesus. The towns in the Philippines and Texas, USA, are spelt Concepcion. Some of the cities were founded on the Feast of the Immaculate Conception, 8 December. There are bays, spelt Conception, in Namibia and Newfoundland, Canada.

Concord, CANADA, GRENADA, USA
1. California: previously Rancho Monte del Diablo, but a year later in 1869 it was renamed after Concord, Massachusetts.
2. Massachusetts: previously Musketaquid. It was renamed to indicate a peace accord with the local Native Americans which allowed its purchase from them. However, together with Lexington, it was where the American Revolution began in 1775.
3. New Hampshire: settled in 1727 as Penacook Plantation and renamed Rumford in 1733. It was renamed Concord in 1765 only after a dispute as to whether it lay in New Hampshire or Massachusetts was settled in 1762. The new name marked the peaceful settlement of the dispute.
4. North Carolina: named after the peaceful settlement of a dispute.

Conegliano, VENETO/ITALY
Possibly corrupted from the Latin *cuniculus* 'road' or 'underground channel' alluding to military defensive works with the suffix *-an*; or it may come from a Latin personal name

and the place-name would have originated from *fundus Connilianus* 'the estate of Connilianus'.

Coney Island, NEW YORK/USA *Konijn Eiland*
Although no longer an island, it was called by the Dutch 'Rabbit Island' and this name appears to have been Anglicized.

Congo
1. The Democratic Republic of the Congo (République Démocratique du Congo) since 1997 when Mobutu Sésé Séko (1930–97), was overthrown after 32 years as president (1965–97). Previously the Republic of Zaïre (1971–97); the Democratic Republic of the Congo (1964–71); the Republic of the Congo (1960–4) after the country achieved independence from Belgium in 1960; the Belgian Congo (1908–60) when annexed by Belgium; Congo Free State or Independent State of the Congo (1885–1908) when, at the Berlin West Africa Conference in 1884–5, Leopold II (1835–1909), King of the Belgians (1865–1909), was recognized as the legitimate authority. He treated it almost as though it were a personal fiefdom. The name of the country comes from the most important river which flows through it. Its name comes from the Kongo (also called Bakongo) people who founded the Kongo Kingdom in the 14th century astride the Congo River. The river was given the name Zaïre by a Portuguese explorer in 1482 from a local word *nzai* from *nazdi* 'river'.
2. The Republic of the Congo (République du Congo) since 1997. Previously the People's Republic of the Congo (1970–97); Congo Brazzaville (1960–70) after independence (*see* BRAZZAVILLE); Moyen-('Middle') Congo (1905–60); French Congo (1885–1905) after the Berlin Conference, when France was given the northern bank of the River Congo after the French had occupied the area in 1882. Moyen-Congo was one of a number of colonies of French Equatorial Africa in 1910–46, then an Overseas Territory of France, and in 1958 an autonomous republic within the French Community. Between the 14th and 19th centuries the coastal region comprised the Kingdom of Loango (also known as Brama). To differentiate the Republic of the Congo from the Democratic Republic of the Congo, the former is still sometimes referred to as Congo (Brazzaville) and the latter as Congo (Kinshasa), using the names of their capitals respectively.

Connaught (Connacht), CANADA, IRELAND
Ireland: a province—and one of the five ancient kingdoms in Ireland—named after the Connachta people. They may have taken their name from Conn who, according to Irish

tradition, was the first of a line of Irish kings beginning in the 2nd century.

Conneaut, OHIO/USA
Derived from *konyiat*, a Seneca word said to mean either 'many fish', 'large-mouth fish', or 'place of snow'.

Connecticut, USA
A state named after the Connecticut River whose name itself comes from an Algonquian word *quonoktacut* or *quenihtekot* 'land on the long tidal river'. First settled by English Puritans from Massachusetts in 1634, Connecticut became one of the original thirteen states of the USA, joining the Union in 1788 as the fifth state.

Constance, Lake (German: **Bodensee**), CANADA, AUSTRIA-GERMANY-SWITZERLAND
Europe: a lake named after the German town of *Konstanz. The Roman name, Lacus Brigantinus, is the Latin version of modern Bregenz, Austria, at the eastern end of the lake. The present German name is probably associated with the Carolingian imperial palatinate of Bodman, a name which may have come from an Indo-European root word for 'water'; *See* means 'lake'.

Constanta, ROMANIA *Tomis, Constantiana, Köstence/Köstendje*
A county and a town, rebuilt in 311 and renamed Constantiana after himself by Constantine I the Great[†]. The Greek city of Tomis was founded in the 7th century BC. In the early 15th century the Ottoman Turks took control and the city became Köstence or Köstendje, the Turkish pronunciation of Constantiana. When Romania gained control in 1878 the city was renamed with the Romanian version of the name Constantine.

Constantine, ALGERIA, USA *Sarim Batim, Cirta/Kirtha, Colonia Cirta Julia/Cirta Sittianorum, Qusantinah/Qasentina (Algeria)*
Algeria: named after Constantine I the Great[†] who rebuilt it in 313 and made it the capital of Numidia. Its original name was Carthaginian, while Cirta, adopted in the 2nd century BC, came from the Phoenician *qart* 'town'. The Arabs took control in the 7th century. The Arabic name is Blad al-Hawa. Qasentina has also been in use since 1981.

Conway, CANADA, USA
1. USA (Arkansas): named after Henry W. Conway, a delegate to Congress.
2. USA (Massachusetts and New Hampshire): named after Henry Seymour Conway (1721–95), an English Member of Parliament who supported the American colonies.

3. USA (South Carolina): named after General Robert Conway, an early resident.

Conwy, WALES/UK *Conguoy, Aberconuy, Aberconway, Conway*
'(Place on the River) Conway'. The river name is Celtic and means 'reedy one'. Aberconway meant 'Mouth of the (River) Conway' from the Old Welsh *aber*.

Cook, Mt, SOUTH ISLAND/NEW ZEALAND *Aorangi/Aoraki*
The first European to sight the mountain was the Dutch navigator, Abel Tasman[†], in 1642. Its Maori name comes from *ao* 'cloud' and *rangi/raki* 'sky', giving a literal translation of 'cloud in the sky'; however, with a little poetic licence, this has become 'cloud piercer'. The mountain was renamed after Captain James Cook[†] in 1851, although he never actually saw it because of cloud cover.

Cook Islands, NEW ZEALAND *Hervey Islands*
A self-governing territory in free association with New Zealand since 1965. The islands became a British protectorate in 1888 and were annexed by New Zealand in 1901. They were explored by Captain James Cook[†] in 1773–4 and 1777 and subsequently named after him. However, he named them after Vice Admiral Augustus Hervey (1724–79), 3rd Earl of Bristol, a lord of the British Admiralty (1771–5).

Cook's Harbour, NEWFOUNDLAND/CANADA
Named after Captain James Cook[†] who surveyed the coast of Newfoundland in the mid-1760s.

Cookstown, CANADA, UK
UK (Northern Ireland): the Irish name is An Chorr Chríochach 'The Boundary Hill'. The town is named after Alan Cook, an English planter who laid out the town in 1609.

Cook Strait, NEW ZEALAND
Thought by Abel Tasman[†] to be a bay when he visited it in 1642, it was discovered by Captain James Cook[†] in 1770 to be a strait separating North and South Islands, and was thus named after him.

Cooktown, QUEENSLAND/AUSTRALIA
Founded in 1873 and named after Captain James Cook[†] who had beached his ship, the *Endeavour*, here for repairs in 1770.

Cooma, NEW SOUTH WALES/AUSTRALIA
Founded in 1849, the name comes from the Aboriginal word *coombah* which is said to mean either 'lake', 'big swamp' or 'sandbank'.

Coonabarabran, NEW SOUTH WALES/ AUSTRALIA
Takes its name from an Aboriginal word meaning 'Inquisitive Person'.

Coonamble, NEW SOUTH WALES/AUSTRALIA
Takes its name from an Aboriginal word meaning 'Bullock Dung' and 'Amazing Sight'.

Coonoor, TAMIL NĀDU/INDIA
'Village of the Coons', a hill tribe, from the Tamil *oor* 'village'

Copenhagen (København), DENMARK *Hafn, Mercatorum Portus, Køpmannæhafn*
'Merchants' Port' from the medieval Danish *køpmann* 'merchant' and *havn*. The Latin name was adopted *c.*1200 before giving way to the Danish name in 1253. It has been the capital of Denmark since 1443.

Copperbelt, ZAMBIA *Western Province*
A province whose name recognizes its mineral deposits, particularly copper.

Coppolani, MAURITANIA
Named after Xavier Coppolani, French commandant of Mauritania Civil Territory for a few months in 1904–5 before being assassinated.

Coral Gables, FLORIDA/USA
So named by George E. Merrick, who developed the area, after his house which had walls of coral and many gables.

Coral Sea, PACIFIC OCEAN
The name recognizes its many coral reefs.

Corato, APULIA/ITALY
Probably derived from the Latin *quadratum*, probably in the sense of a square fortification manned by a company of some 100 men located on the outskirts of a Roman town.

Corby, ENGLAND/UK *Corbei (Northants)*
'Farmstead of a Man called Kori' from an Old Scandinavian personal name and *bý*.

Córdoba, ARGENTINA, COLOMBIA, MEXICO, SPAIN
1. Argentina: a province and a city founded in 1573 by a Spanish conquistador who named the settlement Córdoba de la Nueva Andalucía 'Córdoba of the New Andalusia' after his wife's birthplace in Spain.
2. Colombia and Mexico: the department in Colombia and the city in Veracruz state, Mexico, originally Villa de Córdoba, are both named after the city in Spain.
3. Spain (Andalusia): formerly Corduba, Colonia Patricia, and Kurtuba. It was possibly a Carthaginian town with a name of uncertain origin. It has been suggested that it may be derived from the Phoenician *karta-tuba* 'good,

or important, town'. Alternatively, it has been suggested that it comes from the Phoenician *qorteb* 'oil press'. Occupied by the Romans in 152 BC, it was given the name Corduba and was sometimes called Colonia Patricia to indicate a town for patricians as opposed to plebeians. They shipped olive oil to Rome from here. Between the 6th and early 8th centuries it was under Visigothic control before falling to the Moors in 711. They named it Kurtuba. In 756 'Abd ar-Raḥmān I (?–788) established the independent Ummayad Emirate in Córdoba and in 929 'Abd ar-Raḥmān III (891–961) founded the Córdoba Caliphate, severing all religious connections with Baghdad. In 1031 the Ummayad Caliphate collapsed and Córdoba fell to Ferdinand III (*c.*1201–52), King of Castile and León (1230–52), in 1236. It gave its name to 'cordovan' or 'cordoban', a type of shoe originally made in Cordova, and 'cordwainer', a shoemaker.

Corfu (Kérkira), GREECE *Corcyra/Korkyra*
An island in the Ionian Sea which has changed hands many times. After Napoleon's[†] defeat at the Battle of Waterloo in 1815, Corfu became a British protectorate until 1864 when it was ceded to Greece. The island was given the name Corcyra by the Corinthians in c.730 BC and the Romans retained it. The present name is an Italian version of the Greek *coryphai* 'crests', a reference to the island's twin mountain peaks.

Corinth, GREECE, GRENADA, USA
1. Greece: formerly Ephyre. Locally Kórinthos and probably derived from a pre-Greek Pelasgian word *kar* 'point', a reference to its position on the isthmus of Corinth which connects the Peloponnese with the Greek mainland. Although Nero (37–68), Roman emperor (54–68), began to carve a canal through the isthmus in 67, the Corinth Canal was not opened until 1893. The city gave its name to 'currant' from the French *raisin de Corinthe* 'grapes of Corinth', whence they were originally exported.
2. USA (Mississippi): originally Cross City and renamed in 1857 after the Greek city.

Cork (Corcaigh), IRELAND
'Marshy Place' from *corcach*. The town was developed from a church built on an island in the River Lee.

Corleone, SICILY/ITALY *Cuor di Leone*
'Lionheart' from *cuore* 'heart' and *leone* 'lion'.

Corner Brook, NEWFOUNDLAND/CANADA
Lying at the mouth of the Hudson River, it was founded in 1955 and named after a local brook.

Cornwall, CANADA, UK, USA
1. Canada (Ontario): originally New Johnstown and renamed in 1797 after the Duke of Cornwall, the eldest son of King George III[†] and the future King George IV[†] .
2. UK (England): a county, the name for which is derived from its shape (in Latin *cornu* 'horn') which became a Celtic tribal name, Cornovii, the 'Horned People', perhaps meaning people who lived on a promontory or people who wore horns on their helmets. The Old English *Walh* 'foreigner' or 'Briton' or 'Welshman' was added by the Anglo-Saxons because the language spoken by the natives was different from their own. The meaning, therefore, is '(Territory of) the Britons (or Welsh) of the Cornovii Tribe'. To the Anglo-Saxons the name was Kern-wealhas and in modern Cornish the name is Kernow. Former names include Cornubia, Cornwalas, and Cornualia, the latter being in the Domesday Book (1086).

Coro, VENEZUELA *Santa Ana de Coriana*
Named after the local Coros people.

Coromandel, BRAZIL, NEW ZEALAND
New Zealand (North Island): named after the British supply ship HMS *Coromandel* which often put into port here in the early 1800s.

Coromandel Coast, TAMIL NĀDU/INDIA *Mabar*
The earlier Arabic name from *ma'bar* 'ferry' or 'crossing place' may refer to the place where ships crossed to Sri Lanka. The present name comes from the Sanskrit *choramandala* 'Realm of Chora', Chora, or Chola, being the name of a Tamil royal dynasty with *mandalam* 'kingdom'. The name has been spelt in a number of different ways, but it was the Italians who substituted the *ch* for *c* and this was accepted by the British in 1778.

Corona, CALIFORNIA/USA *South Riverside*
Renamed in 1896 from the Spanish *corona* 'crown' or in this case 'circle' for the circular circuit which was sometimes used for motor racing.

Coronado, CALIFORNIA/USA
Named after Los Coronados, a group of Mexican offshore islands, themselves named after the Spanish explorer, Francisco Vázquez de Coronado (1510–54).

Corozal Town, BELIZE
Originally a Mayan settlement, the modern town was founded in 1849 and named after the cohune palm (*Orbignya cohune*), a symbol of fertility, found in Central America.

Corpus Christi, TEXAS/USA
Founded in 1838 as a trading post, it was named after Corpus Christi Bay in 1846. The bay was given this name because Alonso de Pineda, a Spaniard, sailed into it on the feast day of Corpus Christi, the 'Body of Christ', in 1519.

Corregidor Island, PHILIPPINES
A Spanish post was established here to register ships entering Manila Bay. This was done by a *corregidor*, a historical word for 'chief magistrate' and here a 'registrar'.

Corrientes, ARGENTINA *San Juan de Vera de las Siete Corrientes*
A province and a city with the name 'Currents', alluding to the seven rapids upstream on the River Paraná.

Corsica, FRANCE, USA
France: an island and a region with the local name of Corse. This is of uncertain origin, but may come from the Phoenician *chorsi* 'woody place'. It was known to the Romans, who completed their conquest in 163 BC, as Kyrnos. Taken by the Moors in 754, it was colonized by Pisa in 1077–1284 before falling to Genoa. Five hundred years of Genoese rule came to an end when Corsica was ceded to France in 1768; it became a province the following year.

Cortina d'Ampezzo, VENETO/ITALY *Ampezzo*
Cortina could have the meaning of 'enclosed place', or even 'cemetery', which was added to Ampezzo, the name of the valley here in the Alps, in 1923. Ampezzo comes from *pezzo* 'piece (of land)'.

Corunna, CANADA, SPAIN, USA
1. Canada (Ontario): named by Sir John Colborne in memory of his commander Lieutenant General Sir John Moore (1761–1809), who led the retreat to Corunna in Spain (1808–9) and died of his wounds there.
2. Spain: the Roman Brigantium gave way to Ardobirum Coronium before the arrival of the Moors in the 8th century. They occupied it until the 10th century. The Portuguese held it during the 14th century and it was retaken by the Spanish in the 15th. The Spanish name, La Coruña, may come from the Latin *columna* 'column', a reference to the Hercules Tower, the Roman lighthouse built here in the 2nd century.
3. USA (Michigan): named by Andrew Mack after the Spanish city after he had gone there to buy sheep.

Corvallis, OREGON/USA *Marysville*
Two years after it was founded in 1851 as Marysville it was renamed. In the Willamette Valley, the name is taken from the amalgamation of two Spanish words, *corazón* and *valle*, meaning 'Heart of the Valley'.

Corvo, AZORES/PORTUGAL
An island meaning 'Raven' in Portuguese.

Coşbuc, ROMANIA
Named after the poet Gheorghe Coşbuc (1866–1918) who was born here.

Cosenza, CALABRIA/ITALY *Cosentia*
May be derived from an Oscan word related to the Latin *consentire* 'to agree'. However, more likely, it comes from the Latin *consentia* 'confluence', a reference to its location on the junction of the Rivers Busento and Crati.

Costa Blanca, SPAIN
The south-east coast with a name meaning 'White Coast'.

Costa Brava, CATALONIA/SPAIN
'Rugged Coast'.

Costa del Sol, SPAIN
The southern coast with a name meaning 'Coast of the Sun'.

Costa Dorada, CATALONIA/SPAIN
'Golden Coast', so-called because of its golden sands.

Costa Mesa, CALIFORNIA/USA *Fairview, Harper*
Renamed in 1921 as 'Coastal Plateau' in Spanish in recognition of its position on the coast.

Costa Rica The Republic of Costa Rica (República de Costa Rica) since 1848. It was named the 'Rich Coast' by Christopher Columbus[†] in 1502, possibly in the (erroneous) belief that gold would be found here, given that the natives were wearing gold ornaments; he did not know that the gold was imported. However, the coast may have been rich in timber, fruit, and water. The name Costa Rica was officially conferred in 1539 and the next year, although there would be no permanent Spanish settlement until 1561, it became part of the Viceroyalty of New Spain; in 1568 it was included in the newly established Kingdom of Guatemala, remaining so until it declared its independence in 1821 and joined the Mexican Empire. Two years later it was a founding member of the United Provinces of Central America. In 1824 it took the name of the Free State of Costa Rica. In 1838 it left the Federation and struck out on its own, formally becoming an independent republic ten years later.

Cotabato, MINDANAO/PHILIPPINES *Magindanao*
The original name is also the language of the people inhabiting the Pulangi River basin. This

was prone to flooding, hence the possible meaning 'liable to flood'. The present name of the town comes from the Magindanaon *kuta wato* 'stone fort'

Côte d'Azur, PROVENCE-ALPES-CÔTE D'AZUR/FRANCE
'Azure Coast', also known as the French Riviera, and so-called because of the colour of the sea and sky.

Côte d'Ivoire *See* IVORY COAST.

Cotonou, BENIN *Donukpa, Ku Tonu*
The first name meant 'Near the Hole', i.e. 'near the lagoon' from *kpa* 'near'. The second meant 'Estuary of Death' from the Fon *ku* 'dead' and *tonu* 'estuary', 'lake' or 'lagoon'. According to legend, the souls of the dead drifted down the Ouémé River through the Nokwe Lagoon, on which Cotonou lies, to the sea; as they crossed the lagoon they left trails of blood which were absorbed by the trees growing on the banks, giving their barks a reddish hue.

Cotopaxi, ECUADOR
A volcano with a Quechua name meaning 'Shining Peak' from *kotto* 'peak' or 'mountain' and *paksi* 'shining'.

Cotswolds, ENGLAND/UK *Codesuualt*
A range of hills whose name means 'Cōd's Woodland' from a possible personal name and the Old English *wald* 'woodland' or 'forest'.

Council Bluffs, IOWA/USA *Council Hill, Miller's Hollow, Council Point, Kanesville*
So-called because of a meeting between members of the Lewis and Clark Expedition (1804–6) and some Native Americans on the Missouri River. Mormons settled here by the bluffs along the river in 1846, first changing the name to Miller's Hollow and then, in recognition of the historical importance of the place, to Council Point. Two years later it was changed again to Kanesville after Colonel Thomas Kane who had helped the Mormons. When the Mormons left to settle in Utah in 1853 the city was given its present name.

Courland (Kurzeme), LATVIA *Curonia*
A region meaning the 'Land of the Kursi' (in English, the Cours) from *zeme* 'land' or 'country'. Created as a duchy in 1561, it became a Polish fief. With the third partition of Poland in 1795, Courland passed to Russia which held it until the Bolshevik Revolution in 1917, when it was returned to Latvia.

Courtenay, CANADA, FRANCE, USA
Canada (British Columbia): named after George Courtenay, a ship's captain in the British Royal Navy, who was based here in 1846–9.

Coutances, LOWER NORMANDY/FRANCE *Cosedia, Constantia*
An ancient town renamed in the 3rd century after Constantius I Chlorus (d. 306), Roman emperor in the West (305–6). The present name has evolved from Constantia.

Coventry, UK, USA
1. UK (England): formerly Couentre and Couentreu 'Cofa's Tree' from a possible Old English personal name and *trēow* 'tree'. The expression 'to send to Coventry' means to ostracize somebody and arose from the inhabitants of Coventry's distaste for soldiers to the extent that any woman seen speaking to one was immediately ostracized; consequently, any soldier sent to Coventry was also ostracized by the townsfolk.
2. USA: the towns in Connecticut and Vermont are named after the English city from which some settlers came.

Covington, USA
There are ten cities with this name, most, if not all, being named after General Leonard Covington who distinguished himself at Fort Recovery in 1794 and who died in the 1812 war.

Cowra, NEW SOUTH WALES/AUSTRALIA
Founded in 1846, its name is derived from an Aboriginal word for 'The Rocks'.

Cox's Bāzār, BANGLADESH
Named after Captain Hiram Cox of the English East India Company who helped to settle Buddhist refugees here fleeing their Arakanese homeland after a Burmese invasion in 1798.

Cozumel, QUINTANA ROO/MEXICO *Cutzmil/Cuzamil*
An island and town whose name is derived from the former Mayan name meaning 'Place of Swallows' or 'Place of Wild Turkeys'.

Cracow, AUSTRALIA, POLAND
Poland: locally Kraków and named after a Polish knight, Krak or Krakus, who built a castle on a hill overlooking the River Vistula. According to a popular legend, Cracow was afflicted by a dragon which demanded a virgin every day to appease its appetite. Other knights tried to kill it without success. Krakus killed a sheep and filled its carcass with sulphur. The dragon consumed it in a mouthful, was tormented by thirst, plunged into the river, and drank so much that it burst. The city was the capital of Poland in 1370–1609. Between 1795 and 1918 it was subject to Austrian rule. The Republic of Cracow, or Free City of Cracow, was established by the Congress of Vienna and was the only part of Poland to be independent, in 1815–46, after

the third partition of the country in 1795; it was under the joint protection of Austria, Prussia, and Russia.

Cradock, SOUTH AFRICA, USA
South Africa (Eastern Cape): named in 1814 after Sir John Cradock (1762–1839), one of the first British governors of Cape Colony (1811–14).

Craigavon, NORTHERN IRELAND/UK
A district and a town founded in 1965 and named after James Craig (1871–1940), 1st Viscount Craigavon, who was Northern Ireland's first prime minister (1921–40).

Craiova, ROMANIA
Derived from the Slavonic *krai* 'edge' or 'margin' and the suffix *-ov* to give the meaning of a 'Border Land'. This refers to the border between the Vlachs-Bulgarians and the Byzantines during the 11th and 12th centuries.

Cranborne, ENGLAND/UK *Creneburne*
'Stream frequented by Cranes' from the Old English *cran* 'crane' and *burna* 'stream'. Cranborne Chase has the additional Middle English *chace* 'land for hunting wild animals'.

Cranston, RHODE ISLAND/USA
Named in 1754 after Samuel Cranston, governor of Rhode Island colony (1698–1727).

Crawley, ENGLAND/UK
At least three towns have this name which means 'Wood favoured by Crows' from the Old English *crāwe* and *lēah*. The town in Sussex was recreated as a New Town in 1947, having been called Crauleia in its previous existence.

Crediton, ENGLAND/UK *Cridiantune, Chritetona*
'Farmstead on the (River) Creedy' from a Celtic river name meaning 'sluggish river' and *tūn*.

Cremona, LOMBARDY/ITALY
Probably named after the Cenomani tribe; however, it may be derived from the pre-Latin *carra* 'stone' which later became corrupted to *carm* and then *crem*.

Crete (Kríti), GREECE *Kaptaru, al-Iķriţish, Candia, Kirid*
A region and an island with a name which may be derived from Krus, a mythical figure from whom, according to tradition, the Cretans are descended. Crete was the birthplace of the Minoan civilization. Thereafter it was under the control of the Dorians, the Romans (67 BC–AD 395), the Byzantines (395–824), the Arabs, who called it al-Ikritish, and the Byzantines together (824–1204) until the Crusaders sold it to the Venetians (1204–1669). They gave the name Candia to the island, possibly from the

Arabic *el-khandaq* 'the entrenched', thus '(Castle in) the Moat' (*Heraklion). It was called Kirid by the Ottoman Turks while they ruled in 1669–1898. Crete was united with Greece in 1913, having been proclaimed the Independent Cretan State, still under the rule of the Ottoman Sultan, by the Great Powers in 1898.

Crewe, UK, USA *Creu (UK)*
UK (England): formerly Creu, a name of Welsh origin, from *crïu* 'fish trap'.

Crewkerne, ENGLAND/UK *Crucern, Cruche*
'House at the Hill' from the Celtic *crūg* 'hill' and the Old English *ærn* 'house' or a Celtic suffix.

Crickhowell (Crucywel), WALES/UK *Crichoel, Crukhowell*
'Hywel's Hill' from the Celtic *crūg* 'hill' and a personal name.

Crikvenica, CROATIA *Ad Turres*
Derived from the Croatian *crkvica*, a 14th-century 'church', around which the town and port developed.

Crimea (Krym), UKRAINE *Chersonesus Taurica/Taunda, Gotland*
An autonomous republic with a 15th-century name derived from the Tatar *kerim* 'fort'. When the Mongol-Tatars of the Golden Horde entered the peninsula they made their first encampment beneath the remains of a stone tower which they called *kerim*; they called the place Eski Kerim 'Old Fort'. The Crimea was one of the three most important Tatar khanates carved out of the lands of the Golden Horde in 1430. It was subdued and annexed by Russia in 1783. Unofficially, it was called Gotland during the Nazi occupation in 1942–4. It was formerly part of Russia until it was transferred to Ukraine in 1954 to commemorate the 1654 Treaty of Pereyaslav which incorporated much of Ukraine into Russia. There may be a link between *kerim*, *Krym*, and *kreml* 'Kremlin'. When first settled by the Greeks in the 6th century BC, it was known as the Tauric Peninsula from *chersonesus* 'peninsula' and the Cimmerian people called the Tauri.

Croatia (Hrvatska)
The Republic of Croatia (Republika Hrvatska) since 1991. Previously the Socialist Republic of Croatia within the former Yugoslavia (1946–91); the Independent State of Croatia (1941–5); part of the Kingdom of Yugoslavia (1929–41); part of the Kingdom of the Serbs, Croats, and Slovenes (1918–29); from 1867 Croatia-Slavonia had been a Hungarian crown land, having been absorbed into Hungary in 1091;

part of what was known as the Military Frontier (against the Ottoman Turks) in 1718–1873; although retaining links with Hungary, most of Croatia between 1527 and 1699 had been under Turkish rule. The country is named after the Croats and their name may be derived from the Persian *choroatos* 'nomads' from the Caucasus and along the River Don in Russia, or from the Serbo-Croat *hrbat* 'mountain ridge', a reference to the mountains along the Adriatic coast. Croatia gave its name to the cravat (Old Slavonic *khruvat*), a form of scarf worn by Croat mercenaries in service with the French during the 17th century.

Cromer, ENGLAND/UK *Crowemere*
'Lake frequented by Crows' from the Old English *cräwe* 'crow' and *mere* 'lake' or 'pool'.

Crowborough, ENGLAND/UK *Cranbergh*
'Hill favoured by Crows' from the Old English *cräwe* 'crow' and *beorg*.

Croydon, ENGLAND/UK *Croindene* (*Greater London*)
'Wild Saffron Valley' from the Old English *croh* 'saffron' and *denu* 'valley'.

Crux Alta, RIO GRANDE DO SUL/BRAZIL
'High Cross' from the Portuguese *crux* 'cross' and the feminine of *alto* 'high' or 'elevated'.

Csongrád, HUNGARY
Derived from the Slavonic *Czernigrad* 'Black Castle'.

Cuango, ANGOLA
A river and two towns, one in Lunda Norte 'North Lunda' Province and one in Uige Province, both lying on the river. The name is the Portuguese version of the Bantu Kwango 'Great River'.

Cuanza, ANGOLA
A river which has given its name to two provinces, Kuanza Norte 'North Kuanza' and Kuanza Sul 'South Kuanza'. Cuanza is the Portuguese version of the Bantu *kwanza* 'most important', a reference to the significance of the river. The *kwanza* is also the monetary unit in Angola.

Cuba, AND PORTUGAL, USA *Juana, Fernandina* (*Cuba*)
The Republic of Cuba (República de Cuba) since 1902 when independence was achieved. Discovered by Christopher Columbus[†] in 1492 and named by him Juana after Prince Juan (1478–97), heir to the Spanish throne. After Juan's death in 1497 the island was renamed Fernandina, but this was largely ignored and the native name of Cuba (whose meaning is unknown) continued to be used. From 1511 to 1898 Cuba was a Spanish colony. The island

was occupied by American military forces between 1898 and 1902 and in 1906–9; in 1903 the Treaty of Relations authorized the establishment of an American naval base at Guantánamo Bay which still exists to this day.

Cuddalore, TAMIL NĀDU/INDIA *Fort St David*
Settled by the English East India Company in 1682–3. The name is derived from the Tamil *kūṭṭal-ūr* 'Junction Town', so-called because it lies close to the confluence of the Ponnaiyār and Gadilam Rivers.

Cuddapah, ANDHRA PRADESH/INDIA
Derived from the Telugu word *kaḍapa* 'threshold' because it is situated at the opening of the pass from the north that leads to the sacred pagoda Śrī Venkateśvara at Tirupati.

Cuenca, ECUADOR, SPAIN
1. Ecuador: founded by the Spanish in 1557, the full name of the city is Santa Ana de Cuenca. It lies in a *cuenca* 'bowl' among mountains.
2. Spain (Castile-La Mancha): previously the Roman Conca from the Medieval Latin *concha* 'shell', which gave the Spanish *cuenca*. It was occupied by the Moors until recaptured in 1177 by Alfonso VIII (1155–1214), King of Castile (1158–1214).

Cuernavaca, MORELOS/MEXICO *Cuauhnáhuac*
'Place at the Edge of the Forest' in the language of the Tlahuican people. It was renamed by Hernán Cortés[†] in 1521 after he had razed it.

Culiacán, SINALOA/MEXICO
'Where Two Rivers Meet' from a Nahuatl word referring to the confluence of the Humaya and Tamazula Rivers.

Cullinan, GAUTENG/SOUTH AFRICA
Named after Sir Thomas Cullinan who discovered a diamond mine here in 1902 and had the Cullinan diamond also named after him. It was cut into over 100 stones which are part of the British crown jewels.

Culpeper, VIRGINIA/USA
Named after John Culpeper, governor of Virginia in 1679–80.

Culver City, CALIFORNIA/USA
In Los Angeles county, it was named after Harry H. Culver who suggested it as a site for the film industry in 1914.

Cumberland, CANADA, USA
1. USA: there are seven places with this name. Some are named after William Augustus (1721–65), the Duke of Cumberland, the third child of King George II[†], who suppressed the Jacobite Rebellion in 1745 and won the Battle of Culloden against the Scots in 1746. Others

are named after the former county in England and the one in Maryland after Fort Cumberland which itself was named after the Duke.
2. USA (Kentucky): a river named after William Augustus, Duke of Cumberland. The news of his victory at the Battle of Culloden had just reached Kentucky when the river was discovered.

Cumbernauld, SCOTLAND/UK
A New Town with an old name derived from the Gaelic *comar-an-allt* 'confluence of streams'.

Cumbria, ENGLAND/UK
A county formed in 1974 from the former counties of Cumberland, Westmorland, and parts of Lancashire. The Latinized name is derived from the Welsh *Cymry* 'the Welsh' (*see* *Wales). Cumberland means 'Land of the Welshmen' while Westmorland means 'Land of the Westmoringas'—people who lived west of the moor.

Cuneo, PIEDMONT/ITALY
Derived from the Latin *cuneus* with the meaning of a 'Point on the Ground between Two Rivers'; it lies in the *v* formed by the confluence of the Stura di Demonte and Gesso Rivers.

Ćuprija, SERBIA/SERBIA AND MONTENEGRO
Horeum, Ravno
'Bridge' in Old Turkish. It acquired its present name in the mid-17th century when the Grand Vizier Mehmed-Pasha Ćuprilić built a bridge, *ćuprija*, across the River Morava on the site of the former Roman bridge.

Curaçao, NETHERLANDS ANTILLES *Isla de los Gigantes*
First discovered by the Spanish in 1499 and later settled by them. In 1634 the Dutch West India Company claimed the island after the Spanish had abandoned it. The original name meant 'Island of the Giants' because of the height of its inhabitants. Its present name comes from the Caiquetios, a subgroup of the Arawak tribe. An unlikely, but attractive, explanation for the name is that Amerigo Vespucci, on his way to South America, left on the island a number of his sailors who were suffering from scurvy. On his return later he found them to be cured, possibly by means of vitamin C-rich fruit. Vespucci thus named the island after an archaic Portuguese word for 'cure'. It is not explained why Vespucci, an Italian, and Alonso de Ojeda, a Spaniard who was sailing with him, should use a Portuguese word; however, *curación* is the Spanish for 'healing' or 'cure' which could have been corrupted to Curaçao. It is possible that the

Spanish named the island *Corazón* 'heart', which was corrupted to Curaçao by contemporary cartographers. The island has given its name to the famous liqueur.

Custer, USA
There are four cities with this name, all named after General George Custer (1839–76), a cavalry officer who distinguished himself during the Civil War (1861–5), but who was killed by Native Americans at the Battle of the Little Bighorn (River) in 1876.

Cuttack, ORISSA/INDIA *Coteka*
Derived from the Sanskrit *kataka* 'army', 'camp', or 'royal city'.

Cuvette, REPUBLIC OF THE CONGO
Two regions, Cuvette East and Cuvette West, with the French name meaning 'basin'. They lie in the basin of the Congo River.

Cuyahoga, OHIO/USA
A river and falls with a name which may be derived from an Iroquois word *cayahaga* 'crooked water' or from *cuyahogan-uk* 'lake river'.

Cuzco, PERU
Derived from the Quechua word meaning 'navel', the city was the capital of the Inca Empire from the 11th century until the Spanish sacked it in 1534.

Cwmbrân, WALES/UK
Designated a New Town in 1949, the name means 'Valley of the (River) Brân' from the Welsh *cwm* 'valley' and the river name which means 'raven', a reference to its black waters.

Cyclades (Kikládhes), GREECE
A group of 39 islands which roughly encircle the sacred island of Delos. The name comes from *kýklos* 'circle'.

Cyprus (Greek: **Kipros**; Turkish: **Kibris**) *Kypros, Makaria, Alashiya, Aeria, Iatanana*
The Republic of Cyprus (Greek: Kypriakí Dimokratía; Turkish: Kibris Çumhuriyeti) since 1960. In 1925 Cyprus had become a British crown colony, the UK having assumed responsibility for the island's administration in 1878 as a result of the Congress of Berlin and having annexed it in 1914. The Ottoman Turks had captured the island in 1571, ending 82 years of Venetian control. The discovery of abundant deposits of copper is believed to have given the island its earliest pre-Greek name, Kypros. However, it has also been suggested that that name comes from the son or daughter of Kinyras, mentioned by Homer as King of Cyprus. Makaria means 'Blessed'. Aeria probably comes from the Latin *aes* 'copper'. Rome's supply of copper came from

Cyprus and was known as *aes Cyprium* which was shortened later to *cuprum* to give the English word 'copper'. Cyprus also gave its name to the cypress tree. The Republic of Cyprus, ethnically Greek and occupying the southern two-thirds of the island, is the internationally recognized *de jure* government of the entire island; however, the northern third is occupied by the self-styled Turkish Republic of Northern Cyprus (Kuzey Kibris Türk Çumhuriyeti), proclaimed in November 1983, after the Turkish invasion in 1974, and recognized only by Turkey.

Cyrenaica (Barqah), LIBYA *Pentopolis, Cyrene,* An ancient region in North Africa, and in 1951–63 a province of Libya. Settled as early as 640 BC by the Greeks, it was first known as Pentopolis, an allusion to the five cities they established; Cyrene was one of them. The Ptolemies of Egypt took control of the region in *c.*320 BC and in 67 BC Cyrenaica, together with Crete, became a Roman province. It fell to the Arabs in 642 and to the Ottoman Turks in the 15th century. Cyrenaica was ceded to Italy in 1912 and became part of the Kingdom of Italy in 1939. In 1951 it joined the Kingdom of Libya. The region (and the ancient city—now a village, Shahhāt) is said to be named after Cyrene, a nymph in Greek mythology, and thus meant 'of Cyrene'.

Czech Republic, The The Czech Republic (Česká Republika) since 1993 when it separated from Slovakia. Previously part of the Czech and Slovak Federative Republic (1990), of the Czechoslovak Socialist Republic (1960–90), of the People's Republic of Czechoslovakia (1948–60), and of the Republic of Czechoslovakia (1918–48). Previously part of the Austrian Empire, Czechoslavakia was created in 1918 with the unification of Bohemia, Moravia, and Slovakia. The country is named after the Czechs, *Češi,* a Slav tribe which came from the east and which may possibly have taken its name from the Slavonic *četa* 'company' or 'group of warriors', or from Čech, a legendary Slav chieftain who led his people to the region.

Częstochowa, POLAND *Tschenstochau* May be derived from *częstokoł* 'palisade' which originally provided protection for the city.

D

Dachau, BAVARIA/GERMANY
'Clayey Stream' from the Old High German *daha* 'clay' and *au* from *aha* 'water'.

Dâc Lâc, VIETNAM
A province with a name meaning 'Savannah' in the local language of the Ede.

Daegu, SOUTH KOREA
See TAEGU.

Dagenham, ENGLAND/UK *Dæccanhaam*
'Dæcca's Homestead, or Village' from an Old English personal name and *hām*.

Dagestan, RUSSIA
A republic whose name means 'Mountain Country' from the Turkish *dağ* 'mountain' and *stan*. Annexed by Russia in 1813, it became an autonomous republic in 1921.

Dahab, EGYPT
'Gold', the Arabic word used to describe the local beaches with their golden sands.

Dahlonega, GEORGIA/USA
Derived from a Cherokee word *taulonica* 'yellow', a reference to the gold formerly mined in northern Georgia.

Dahomey *See* BENIN.

Dakar, SENEGAL
Having established a trading post *c*.1750, the French built a fort here in 1857. According to legend, when they asked the natives the local name of the place, they responded as though the French were asking the local name of the tamarind tree which grew in profusion along the coast. Thus Dakar is said to be derived from a Wolof word *n'dakhar* 'Tamarind Tree'. It has also been suggested that the name may come from *Deuk Raw* 'Land of Refuge', the name given to the Cape Verde Peninsula, on which Dakar lies, by refugees fleeing the oppression exercised further inland. The city became the capital of French West Africa in 1904; it was the capital of the brief Mali Federation (1959–60) and has been the capital of Senegal since 1960.

Dakhla Oasis, EGYPT
'Inner Oasis' in the sense that it is deeper into the Egyptian desert than the *al-Khārijah group of oases further east.

Dakota, USA
Two states, North and South Dakota. A large part of the two states was acquired by means of the Louisiana Purchase from France in 1803; the remainder, the north-eastern part of North Dakota, following a treaty with the UK in 1818. In 1861 the region became the Dakota Territory. It was split in two in 1889 when both North and South Dakota joined the Union as the 39th and 40th states respectively. The name comes from a Santee word *lakota*, *nakota*, or *dakota*, depending on the dialect, meaning 'allies' to describe the confederated Sioux tribes. They gave their name to the famous Douglas DC-3 transport aircraft, the Dakota.

Dalarna, SWEDEN *Dalecarlia*
A county with a name meaning 'The Valleys' from *dalar*, the plural of *dal* 'valley' and *-na* 'the', a form of the definite article.

Dà Lat, VIETNAM
Founded in 1912 by the French as a hill station, it was named after the River Da, now called the Cam Ly, and the Lat hill tribe. *Dà* itself can mean 'river', 'water', or 'land' and thus the name means the 'Land of the Lat'.

Dalby, AUSTRALIA, DENMARK, ISLE OF MAN, SWEDEN
Australia (Queensland): located on Myall Creek, it was founded in 1841 as Myall Creek Station. The name was soon changed to Dalby, probably at the request of an immigrant from the village of that name in the Isle of Man.

Dalhousie, CANADA, INDIA
1. Canada (New Brunswick): named after James Ramsay's father, George (1770–1838), 9th Earl of Dalhousie, and governor-general of Canada (1819–28).
2. India (Himachal Pradesh): named after James Ramsay (1812–60), 1st Marquess and 10th Earl of Dalhousie, governor-general of India (1847–56).

Dalian, LIAONING/CHINA *Qing-ni-wa, Dalny, Dairen, Lüda*
With acquisition of the lease of the Liaodong Peninsula in 1898 and having secured the right to build a railway through Manchuria to the Yellow Sea, the Russians decided to develop the fishing village of Qing-ni-wa as a commercial port and rename it from the

Russian *dal'niy* 'far' or 'distant'. Following the loss of the Battle of Nanshan in 1904, the Russians ceded control of the peninsula to the Japanese at the Treaty of Portsmouth (New Hampshire, USA) in 1905. The Japanese renamed the port Dairen, their rendering of the Chinese Dalian from *dà* 'big' and *lián* 'to join' or 'unite', thus a place of commercial activity. It passed to China after the defeat of Japan and the withdrawal of the Russians, who occupied it briefly, at the end of the Second World War. Uniting with *Lüshun, between 1946 and 1981 it was known as Lüda, a combination of Lüshun and Dalian.

Dalkey (Deilginis), IRELAND
'Thorn Island' from the Old Scandinavian *dalkr* 'thorn' and *ey*. Deilginis means the same with *inis* 'island'.

Dallas, UK, USA
USA (Texas): the first settlement took place in 1841. In due course, as it grew, it was probably named after George M. Dallas (1792–1864), vice-president of the USA (1845–9).

Dalmatia (Dalmacija), CROATIA-BOSNIA AND HERZEGOVINA, USA *Illyricum Superior*
Croatia: a region on the Adriatic coast including offshore islands. It is probably named after an Illyrian tribe, the Delmatae, who may have taken their name from the Albanian *delmë* 'sheep' to denote sheep breeders. During its eventful history the region has been under the rule of the Illyrians, Greeks, Romans, Goths, Byzantines, Hungarians, Bosnians, Tatars, Croats, Serbs, Venetians, Sicilians, Normans, Ottoman Turks, Austrians, Italians, and Yugoslavs. The previous name, Upper Illyricum, probably gave way to Dalmatia during the Roman Flavian dynasty (69–96), having become a Roman province. Dalmatia includes some 12 miles (19 km) of Bosnian coastline. It has given its name to the Dalmatian breed of dog, although the dogs were probably brought in to guard the borders and did not originate here.

Dal'nerechensk, PRIMORSKIY TERRITORY/ RUSSIA *Iman*
Renamed in 1973 'Far River' from *dal'niy* 'far' and *reka* 'river'. It was previously named after the Iman River.

Dalton, SOUTH AFRICA, USA
1. South Africa (KwaZulu-Natal): named after the village of North Dalton in Yorkshire, the original home of an immigrant who organized the settlement in South Africa of people from Yorkshire.
2. USA (Georgia): founded as Cross Plains in 1837, it is thought to have been renamed

either after General Tristram Dalton, speaker of the House of Representatives of Massachusetts, or after John Dalton, the engineer who designed the town.

Daly, NORTHERN TERRITORY/AUSTRALIA
A river explored in 1865 and named after Sir Dominick Daly (1798–1868), governor of South Australia (1862–8).

Damanhūr, EGYPT *Hermopolis Parva*
The present name is derived from the ancient Egyptian Timinhor 'City of Horus'. Horus was an Egyptian god in the form of a falcon whose eyes represented the sun and the moon. The previous Greek name meant the 'Little City of Hermes', a Greek god.

Damaraland, NAMIBIA
A historic region named after the Damara people.

Damascus (Dimashq), SYRIA
The origins of the name are not known, although the city has been called Damascus since at least the 15th century BC. Colloquially, it is known as *ash-Shām* 'The Northern (Region)' (which can also refer to Syria as a whole). It fell to Muslim Arab forces in 635 and thereafter was occupied by Seljuk Turks, Egyptian Mamlūks, and others before the arrival of the Ottoman Turks in 1516. They retained control until 1918, although giving way to the Egyptians in 1831–40. The city became capital of an independent Syria in 1919, but the next year it was occupied by French forces when France assumed a League of Nations mandate until 1946. It has given its name to 'damask', patterned fabrics, often of linen, originally produced in Damascus in the Middle Ages, and to 'damson', the small dark-purple plum originally called 'damascene', meaning 'of Damascus'.

Damba, ANGOLA
Named after a local Kongo chief, Fumuachi Mandamba.

Damietta (Dumyāt), EGYPT *Tamiati*
The present name is an Italian corruption of the Arabic name, which is itself a corruption of the original Coptic (the Greek name for the Egyptian language developed from ancient Egyptian with an alphabet based on Greek) name which may have meant 'City of the Cedars'.

Dampier, ASCENSION ISLAND, AUSTRALIA
Both are named after William Dampier, although the port in Western Australia is actually named after the Dampier Archipelago; further north is Dampier Land. The Dampier Strait between Papua New

Guinea and New Britain is also named after
him. Dampier (1651–1715) was a British
buccaneer, who spent some years as a pirate,
and an expert hydrographer. In 1699 he was
commissioned by the British Admiralty for a
voyage of exploration and reached western
Australia and Indonesia. On his return voyage
he had to abandon his ship off Ascension
Island due to its non-seaworthy state.

Dan, ISRAEL *Laish*
Named after the Dan, one of the twelve tribes
of Israel named after one of the sons of Jacob.

Danané, CÔTE D'IVOIRE
Named after the Dan people.

Đà Nẵng, VIETNAM *Cua Han, Tourane, Thai Phien*
The original name meant 'Mouth of the (River)
Han'. When the port-city was ceded to France
in 1787, it was given a name, Tourane, that
was the approximate French equivalent of Cua
Han. Thai Phien was only used briefly, being
replaced by Da Nang in 1954.

Danao, CEBU ISLAND/PHILIPPINES
A port-city with good beaches, it was founded
in 1844. Its name is derived from a local word
danawan 'shallow lagoon'.

Danbury, UK, USA
1. UK (England): formerly Danengeberiam
probably meaning the 'Stronghold of the
Followers of Dene' from an Old English
personal name, *-inga-* and *burh*.
2. USA (Connecticut): named in 1687 after the
town in England from which some of the
settlers had come.

Dandara, EGYPT *Ta-ynt-netert/Tentyra*
Built on the site of Ta-ynt-netert 'Divine Pillar
of the Goddess' from *yn* 'pillar' and *netert*
'goddess'. The ancient town was dedicated to
the sky and fertility goddess Hathor. It is also
spelt Dendera.

Dandenong, VICTORIA/AUSTRALIA
Takes its name from the nearby Dandenong
Ranges whose name comes from the
Aboriginal *tanjenong* 'lofty'.

Danilovgrad, MONTENEGRO/SERBIA AND
MONTENEGRO
'Danilo's Town' and named after Danilo Nikola
Petrović, prince-bishop of Montenegro (1696–
1737) with the additional *grad*.

Danube (German: **Donau**; Czech/Slovak:
Dunaj; Hungarian: **Duna**; Serbo-Croat/Bulgarian:
Dunav; Romanian: **Dunărea**), EUROPE *Danubius*
A river whose present names are derived
from the Latin name which is said to be
derived from the Indo-European *dānu* 'water'
or 'river'.

Danvers, USA
Massachusetts: founded in 1630 as Salem
Village and renamed in 1775 after Sir Danvers
Osborne, governor of New York in 1753. In
1858 South Danvers became a separate town
and in 1868 was renamed Peabody. The two
other cities with this name in Illinois and
Montana are named after the Danvers in
Massachusetts.

Danville, CANADA, USA
1. USA (Illinois): named after Dan Beckwith
who donated a part of the town site.
2. USA (Kentucky): named after its founder,
Walker Daniel.
3. USA (Vermont): named after a French
admiral, D'Anville.
4. USA (Virginia): originally The Ford at Wyn's
Falls, it was renamed after the River Dan on
which it lies.

Danzig, POLAND
See GDAŃSK.

Dardanelles (Çanakkale Boğazi), TURKEY
Hellespont
A strait between the Sea of Marmara and the
Aegean Sea. It may have received its name
from the city of Dardanus or from Dardanus,
the son of Zeus and Electra in Greek
mythology. Hellespont comes from the Greek
Hellespontos 'Helle's Sea' from Helle, a daughter
of Athamas and Nephele in Greek mythology,
who was drowned here on her voyage to
Colchis, and *pontos* 'sea'.

Dar es Salaam, TANZANIA *Mzizima*
Developed in 1862 from a small fishing village,
Mzizima 'Entire Place', by the Sultan of
Zanzibar, Mājid ibn Said, who renamed it Dār
as-Sālam 'Haven of Peace'. With a good
harbour, the *dār* might conceivably be a
shortening of *bandar* but, more likely, simply
the Arabic for 'house' with *as-* (*al-*) 'the' and
sālam 'peace'. The Sultan intended to move his
capital here from Zanzibar, but he died before
this plan could be implemented. In 1887 the
German East Africa Company took possession
of the port. Between 1891 and 1916 it was the
capital of German East Africa; it remained the
capital when the UK administered the territory
for the League of Nations and then for the
United Nations, and of Tanganyika when it
became independent in 1961; in 1964 it
became the capital of Tanzania, although
Dodoma is planned to become the capital in
2005.

Darfur, THE SUDAN
A state, and former independent sultanate
which was annexed to the Sudan in 1916, with
the name 'Realm of the Fur' from *dār*, here

'realm' and *fur*. 'Fur' was the name given to the inhabitants of the region by the Keira dynasty who ruled over them; in due course the Keira and the Fur merged.

Darjeeling, WEST BENGAL/INDIA
Derived from the Tibetan *Dorje ling* or *Dorje-glin* 'Land of the Dorje', that is, 'of the thunderbolt', the weapon of the Hindu god Indra; according to legend, the place had been struck by a mystic thunderbolt. The British bought the town from the Rāja of Sikkim in 1835 and developed it as a hill station sanatorium for their troops. It has given its name to Darjeeling tea.

Dark Continent, The Africa. So-called because, before the continent had been fully explored by Europeans during the 19th century, it was a land of obscurity and mystery to them and they were 'in the dark' about it.

Darling, AUSTRALIA, SOUTH AFRICA,
1. Australia (New South Wales): a river discovered in 1829 and named after Sir Ralph Darling (1775–1858), governor-general of New South Wales (1825–31).
2. South Africa (Western Cape): founded in 1853 as Groene Kloof 'Green Ravine'. It was quickly renamed after Sir Charles Darling (1809–70), lieutenant-governor of Cape Colony (1851–4).

Darlington, UK, USA
1. UK (England): formerly Dearthingtun and Dearningtun 'Dēornōth's Farmstead' from an Old English personal name, *-ing-* and *tūn*. As was common under Norman influence, the *n* in Dēornōth became an *l*.
2. USA (South Carolina): named after the English Darlington.
3. USA (Wisconsin): named after Joshua Darlington, a prominent resident.

Darmstadt, HESSE/GERMANY *Darmundenstadt*
The name of the city, only a small village in the 14th century, means 'Darmund's Residence' from a personal name and the Old High German *stad*.

Dartford, ENGLAND/UK *Tarentefort*
'Ford over the (River) Darent', a Celtic river name and *ford*.

Dartmouth, CANADA, UK, USA
1. Canada (Nova Scotia): it is not clear whether the town was named after the Dartmouth in England or after William Legge (1731–1801), 2nd Earl of Dartmouth, British secretary of state for the colonies (1772–5).
2. UK (England): formerly Dertamuthan 'Mouth of the (River) Dart' from the Celtic river name and *mūtha*.

3. USA (Massachusetts): named after the English town.

Darwin, AUSTRALIA, FALKLAND ISLANDS, USA
1. Australia (Northern Territory): the harbour was founded in 1839 and named Port Darwin after the British naturalist Charles Darwin (1809–82) who had visited this part of the coast in 1836. However, settlement did not take place until 1869 when the name was changed to Palmerston after Henry Temple (1784–1865), 3rd Viscount Palmerston, British prime minister (1855–8,1859–65). In 1911 the name of the growing city was returned to Port Darwin after the harbour. The 'Port' was subsequently dropped.
2. Falkland Islands: named after Charles Darwin who visited the Islands twice in 1833 and 1834.
3. USA (California): named after Charles Darwin.

Dashoguz, TURKMENISTAN *Tashauz, Dashkhovuz/Dashhowuz*
A province and a city founded as a fort in the early 19th century, the name is said to come from *dashkhauz* 'stone reservoir' from *dash* 'stone' and *khauz* 'reservoir'. The modern form of the name was adopted in 1991.

Datia, MADHYA PRADESH/INDIA
Takes its name from a mythical evil spirit called Dantavakra which ruled the area.

Daugavpils, LATVIA *Dünaburg, Borisoglebsk, Dvinsk, Latgale*
Situated on the Western Daugava River (in English, the Dvina), the name means 'Castle on the Western Dvina' from the Lettish *pils* 'castle' or 'palace'. Founded in 1278, the original German name meant 'Fort on the Dvina', although this was some 12 miles (19 km) north of the modern city. It was captured by the Russians in 1656 and given the Russian name °Borisoglebsk since Alexey I Mihailovich (1629–76), Tsar of Russia (1645–76), heard the news of its capture on the feast day of the two saints. The Poles regained the city in 1667, but once more it passed to the Russians at the first partition of Poland in 1772. In 1893 the city was renamed Dvinsk. In 1920–41, when Latvia enjoyed independence, the city was called Latgale (*see* LATGALLIA). Dünaburg was restored while the Germans occupied Latvia between 1941 and 1944.

Daulatābād, MAHĀRĀSHTRA/INDIA *Devagiri, Deogir(i)*
Founded in 1187, the original name meant 'Hill of the Gods'. It was captured in the 14th century by Muhammad Tughluq (*c.*1290–1351), Muslim Sultan of Delhi (1325–51), who

made it his capital and gave it its present name 'City of Fortune'. In 1327 he marched the population of Delhi 680 miles (1 100 km) south to populate it to consolidate Muslim conquests, but seventeen years later abandoned it and returned to Delhi.

Dauphin, CANADA, MADAGASCAR, USA
1. Canada (Manitoba): named after Lake Dauphin which itself was named by a French trader in 1739 after Louis (1729–65), Dauphin of France; this was the title of the heir apparent to the French throne between 1350 and 1830.
2. USA (Alabama): an island originally called Massacre Island because human bones were found along the coast. Planned as a base for French colonists of Louisiana, it was renamed in 1708 after Louis (1682–1712), Duke of Burgundy and known as *Le Petit Dauphin* 'The Little Dauphin'.

Daura, KATSINA/NIGERIA
A traditional Hausa emirate, the name means 'Blacksmith' in the Tuareg language.

Davenport, IOWA/USA *Oskosh, Morgan*
Named after Colonel George Davenport (1785–1845) who ran a fur company and bought the site.

Daventry, ENGLAND/UK *Daventrei*
'Tree belonging to a Man called (possibly) Dafa' from an Old English personal name and *trēow* 'tree'.

Davis Strait, ATLANTIC OCEAN
A strait between Baffin Island, Canada, and Greenland explored in 1585 by the English navigator, John Davis (1550–1605), and named after him.

Davos, SWITZERLAND
Inhabited by Romansh-speaking people during the early Middle Ages, it takes its name from the Romansh *tavau* 'behind', a reference to the fact that the valley, in which it lies, turns away behind the town.

Dawson, CANADA, USA
Canada (Yukon): founded during the Klondyke Gold Rush in 1896 as Dawson City after George M. Dawson, a geologist and explorer.

Dax, AQUITAINE/FRANCE *Aquae Tarbellicae, Acqs, Dacqs*
Originally the 'Waters of the Tarbelli People' during Roman times, its actual name is d'Ax, with *ax* representing the Latin *acqua* 'water'. It is known for its thermal springs.

Daxue Shan, SICHUAN/CHINA
A mountain range meaning 'Great Snowy (Mountains)' from *dà* 'great' or 'large' and *xuě*

'snow'. Many peaks rise above 20 000 ft (6 000m) and are snow-covered.

Daye, HUBEI/CHINA
'Great Smelting (Place)' from *dà* 'great' and *yě* 'to smelt', a reference to the nearby iron ore deposits and the smelter put in place here in the 8th century.

Dayr az-Zawr, SYRIA
Founded by the Ottoman Turks in 1867 with a name possibly derived from the ancient nearby site of Auzara. The name means 'Monastery of the Tamarisk Grove' from the Arabic *dayr* 'monastery' and *zawr* 'tamarisk'.

Dayton, USA
There are at least thirteen cities and towns with this name. They are generally named after people called Dayton or after the city in Ohio, which was named after Jonathan Dayton (1760–1824), a veteran of the War of Independence (1775–83) and one of the original owners.

Daytona Beach, FLORIDA/USA
Founded in 1870 by Mathias Day and named after him in 1876. To his name was added *ton* 'town' and a superfluous *a*, possibly to differentiate it from Dayton.

De Aar, NORTHERN CAPE/SOUTH AFRICA
'The Blood Vessel', the name being taken from the farm from which it was developed. The Afrikaans name is that used for an underground watercourse.

Dead Sea (Arabic: **al-Baḥr al-Mayyit**; Hebrew: **Yam Ha-Melakh**), ISRAEL-JORDAN *Nekrē Thalassa, Mare Mortuum*
'Dead Sea' in Arabic from *baḥr* 'sea' and *mayyit* 'dead', although it is also known as Baḥr Lūṭ 'Sea of Lot', a reference in the Bible (Genesis 19: 26) to Lot's wife being turned into a pillar of salt here. The Hebrew name means 'Salt Sea' from *yam* 'sea', *ha* 'the', and *melakh* 'salt', because it is a land-locked salt lake below sea level whose extreme salinity precludes animal and plant life. The Greek and Roman names have the same meaning.

Deal, ENGLAND/UK *Addelam, Dela*
'(Place in) the Valley' from the Old English *dæl* 'valley' or 'hollow'. The original name (found in the Domesday Book of 1086) had the Latin *ad* 'at' as a prefix.

Dearborn, MICHIGAN/USA *Ten Eyck, Bucklin, Dearbornville*
Founded in 1795 and eventually renamed in 1833 after General Henry Dearborn (1751–1829), a hero of the War of Independence (1775–83) and secretary of war (1801–9) under President Thomas Jefferson.

Death Valley, CALIFORNIA/USA
Named in 1849 by a group of pioneer settlers,
some of whom died from the extreme heat
and lack of water while trying to cross it.

Debrecen, HUNGARY
The name's origin is not clear. It may be
derived from the Slavonic *debr* 'ravine' or
'escarpment' or from a Turkish personal name
like Tebresün; the Ottoman Turks occupied
the city during the 16th and 17th centuries.

Debre Markos, ETHIOPIA *Mankorar*
The original name meant 'Cold Gaze' in the
ecclesiastical language of Ge'ez, formerly
known in Europe as Ethiopic; it is extinct as a
vernacular language. The present name means
'Mount of Mark', that is, St Mark, from *debre*
'Mount'.

Debre Zeyit, ETHIOPIA
'Mount of Olives' fom *debre* 'mount'.

Decatur, USA
There are at least ten cities with this name, all
thought to be named in honour of Stephen
Decatur (1779–1820); another is called
Decaturville. Decatur became a naval hero
when, as a lieutenant, he led a small party into
the harbour of Tripoli (now the Libyan capital)
in 1804 to set fire to the American frigate
Philadelphia which, with its captain and crew,
had fallen into Tripolitan hands. The party
achieved its aim and escaped unscathed.

Decazeville, MIDI-PYRÉNÉES/FRANCE
Named in 1829 after Élie Decazes (1780–1860),
Duc de Decazes, premier (1819–20) and a man
who did much to promote coal and steel
production in the area.

Deccan, INDIA
The southern part of the country which takes
its name from the Sanskrit *dakshina* 'The
South'.

Děčín, CZECH REPUBLIC *Tetschen*
Derived from a Slavic personal name *Deka*
'child'. From its founding in the 12th century
until the end of the Second World War it was
German and called Tetschen.

Dedham, USA
The town in Massachusetts is named after the
village of Dedham, possibly 'Dydda's
Homestead', in England whence some of the
settlers came; the one in Maine after the town
in Massachusetts.

Dee, IRELAND, UK
Rivers in Ireland, Scotland, and Wales. In
Welsh, the river is called the Dyfrdwy from
dwfr 'water' or 'river'. The name Dee is of
Celtic origin and is a form of *deva* 'goddess',

'the holy one' or 'the holy (river)' which is
what the Romans called the river. The name is
related to the Latin *divus* 'divine'.

Deep South, The, USA
The south-eastern states of the USA,
sometimes called 'The Old South', and
comprising Alabama, Georgia, Louisiana,
Mississippi, and South Carolina. These were
the states generally associated with slavery
before the Civil War and were the first states to
secede from the Union in 1860–1. Tennessee is
also sometimes included.

Defiance, OHIO/USA
Named after Fort Defiance built in 1794 in
defiance of local Native Americans (and
possibly the British).

DeGrey, WESTERN AUSTRALIA/AUSTRALIA
A town and a river named in about 1861 after
George Robinson (1827–1909), 1st Marquess of
Ripon and 3rd Earl de Grey, governor-general
of India (1880–84) and president of the Royal
Geographical Society.

Dehra Dūn, UTTAR PRADESH/INDIA
'Camp in the Valley' from the Hindi *dehra*
'camp' and *dūn* 'valley'. It was founded in 1699
in a valley of the Siwaliks, foothills of the
Himalayas, and was ceded to the British in
1816.

De Kalb, ILLINOIS/USA *Buena Vista*
Founded as Buena Vista 'Good View' in 1838, it
was renamed in 1856 after Johann Kalb, a
general in the War of Independence (1775–83).

Delareyville, NORTH WEST/SOUTH AFRICA
Founded in 1914 and named after the Boer
guerrilla leader, General Jacobus Hercules de
la Rey (1847–1914), who was killed by police
that year, with the additional *ville*.

Delaware, USA
A state, two towns in Ohio and Oklahoma, a
river, and a bay; in the state itself is Delaware
City. Named after Sir Thomas West (1577–
1618), 12th Baron De La Warr, first governor of
Virginia (1610–11). The Dutch were the first to
arrive in Delaware in 1631, but the first
permanent settlement was made by Swedes in
1638; they called their territory New Sweden.
The Dutch from New Amsterdam took the
area in 1655 but yielded it nine years later to
the English. It then became part of New York
until 1682. Although the name Delaware had
been in use since 1610 for the bay and
gradually thereafter for the surrounding area,
the name did not become official for the
colony until the Revolution broke out in 1775.
Because Delaware was the first to ratify the
constitution in 1787 it is known as the First

State. The Delaware tribe of Algonquian-speaking Native Americans, also known as the Lenni Lenape, were given their name because they lived in the Delaware River valley.

Delft, THE NETHERLANDS
Lying on the canalized Schie River, it takes its name from the Old Dutch *delf* 'canal', modern Dutch *delven* 'to dig'. It gives its name to the tin-glazed earthenware, delftware.

Delhi, INDIA, USA *Indraprastha, Dhílli, Qíla Rai Pithora, Siri, Tughlaqābād, Jahānpanāh, Ferozābād/Fīrūzābād, Purāna Qíla/Shergarh, Shāhjahānābād (India)*
India: National Capital Territory and a city. The *Mahābhārata* mentions a city called Indraprastha built in about 1400 BC. The name Delhi first emerged during the 1st century BC when Rājā Dhilu built a city and named it after himself. However, modern Delhi is said to have been founded by a Rājput chief during the 11th century as the walled city of Qíla Rai Pithora. Thereafter seven more cities of Delhi were built, each extending its boundaries. Captured in 1192 by Qutb-ud-Dīn Aykab (d. 1210), founder of Muslim rule in India, it became the Muslim Dīhli Sultanate in 1206, remaining in existence until the mid-16th century. (Dihli was the Perso-Arabic spelling of the name; Delhi was a 19th-century mistake which somehow became the official spelling.) The second Delhi was built at Siri, a couple of miles (3 km) to the north-east, in 1303. Further expansion to the east resulted in the city being renamed Tughlaqābād in 1325 after the Muslim Tughluq dynasty and then Jahānpanāh 'Refuge of the World' when Muhammad ibn Tughluq (c.1290–1351), sultan (1325–51), extended construction in the north-east. When Feroz (Fīrūz) Shah Tughluq, sultan (1351–88), moved his capital even further north in 1354 the city was renamed Ferozābād (Fīrūzābād) after him. In 1526 the city became the capital of the Mughal Empire. Purāna Qíla was also known as Shergarh (or Sher Shah) after Emperor Sher Shah, the Afghan king, who built it as the sixth city of Delhi in 1540. The city became known as Shāhjahānābād (now Old Delhi) in 1638 after Shah Jahān (1592–1666), Mughal emperor (1628–58). Delhi came under British rule in 1803. The British Indian capital was moved from Calcutta to New Delhi in 1912 (although construction was not complete until 1929), a location adjacent to and south of Old Delhi. Old and New Delhi have since merged and the city is the capital of India. Other theories as to the origin of the name include the Hindi *dil* 'eminence' and *dehlī* 'threshold' to the Rivers Ganges and Indus.

Dellys, ALGERIA *Rusucurru, Tadellast/Tadā'ilīs/ Tedallēs*
First Roman, then Ottoman Turkish between 1517 and 1844 when it fell to the French. The present name is derived from the previous name meaning 'The Cottage'.

Delmar, DELAWARE-MARYLAND/USA
So-called because it lies astride the states' common border and thus takes its name from the first syllable of each.

Delmarva Peninsula, USA
Includes parts of Delaware, Maryland, and Virginia.

Del Norte, COLORADO/USA
A Spanish phrase meaning 'of the North'.

Delos (Dhílos), GREECE
A small island in the Cyclades meaning 'clear' or 'visible' from *dēlos*.

Delphi, GREECE, IRELAND, USA
Greece: ruins originally called Thyia from *thyo* 'to rage' being associated with the Thyiades who participated in the orgies of Dionysus. In Homer's *Iliad* the place is mentioned as an oracle called Pythó from the verb *pytho* 'to rot', a reference to the fact that the carcass of the resident dragon, Python, was left to rot after Apollo had killed him. The present name is probably derived from *delphys* 'womb', 'belly', or 'cavity'. The ancient Greeks believed Delphi to be the womb or centre of the world, the 'navel of the earth', the most important oracle of the Greek world. It has been suggested, however, that it was subsequently renamed after Apollo, the most revered of all Greek gods, who took on the form of a dolphin, *delphis*, when he established his oracle here. The village of Kastri occupied the site until 1890 when it was then moved away to allow excavation of the ruins and renamed Delfoí.

Delray Beach, FLORIDA/USA *Linton, Delray*
Laid out in 1896 with the town named Linton after Congressman William L. Linton who had bought the site. After being named Delray in 1901 after a district of Detroit, the town merged with Delray Beach, lying along the Atlantic coast, in 1927.

Del Rio, TEXAS/USA
Situated on the Rio Grande, the city developed from the Spanish mission of San Felipe del Rio 'St Philip of the River' established about 1675. It retained this name until 1833 when it was shortened to Del Rio to avoid confusion with San Felipe de Austin, also in Texas.

Delta, CANADA, NIGERIA, USA
1. Nigeria: a state established in 1991 and so-called because the delta of the River Niger acts as its eastern boundary.

2. USA: there are six cities with this name, some so-called because of their triangular shape and some because of river deltas.

Demavend, Mt (Qolleh-Ye Damāvand), IRAN
A mountain with a snow-capped summit, the name means 'Snowy Mountain' from the Sanskrit *himavant*.

Demidov, SMOLENSK/RUSSIA *Porech'ye*
On the Kasplya River, it was at first known simply as 'River Place'. In 1918 it was renamed after Ya. Demidov (1889–1918), a Communist Party secretary killed here during the Civil War (1918–20).

Demirci, TURKEY
Derives its name from *demir* 'iron' in recognition of the iron ore deposits in the area.

Denbigh, CANADA, UK, USA
UK (Wales): in Welsh Dinbych meaning 'Small Fortress' from the Welsh *din* 'fortress' and *bych* 'small'. There is a unitary district called Denbighshire; in Welsh, Sir Dinbych.

Deniliquin, NEW SOUTH WALES/AUSTRALIA *Sandhills*
Settled in 1845 and renamed in 1850 from an Aboriginal word *denilocoon* 'wrestlers' ground'.

Denizli, TURKEY *Laodicea ad Lycum, Lādhīq*
'(Town of) Flowing Waters'. Lying close to the Çürüksu River, Denizli assumed the mantle of Laodicea ad Lycum 'Laodicea-on-Lykos', whose ruins stand some 4 miles (6 km) away, when it was abandoned in the 12th century. According to Ibn Battutah (1304–68/9), the famous Arab traveller, who visited Lādhīq, its alternative name was Dun Ghuzluh 'Town of the Swine'.

Denmark, AND AUSTRALIA, CANADA, USA
The Kingdom of Denmark (Kongeriget Danmark) since 1814 when Norway was ceded to Sweden. The Kingdom includes the Faroe Islands and Greenland. Named after the Danes, possibly meaning 'warrior' and applied to 'Northmen' from Sweden who settled here. However, it has been suggested that their name may come from the Old High German *tanar* 'sandbank', appropriate given the number of islands that make up the country. The provinces of Skåne and Halland (part of Sweden since 1658) formed the Danes' border territory, march, or *mark* in Danish.

Denpasar BALI/INDONESIA *Badung*
'Next to the Market' from *pasar* 'market'. Badung was a minor kingdom which rebelled against the Dutch in 1906.

Denton, UK, USA
1. UK (England): a common name meaning 'Village, or farmstead, in a Valley' from the Old English *denu* 'valley' and *tūn*.
2. USA (Maryland): originally Eden Town, from which the present name is derived. It is a tribute to Sir Robert Eden (1741–84), governor of Maryland (1769–76).
3. USA (Texas): founded in 1857 and named after John B. Denton, a frontiersman.

D'Entrecasteaux Islands, PAPUA NEW GUINEA
Visited in 1793 by, and named after, Antoine Bruni d'Entrecasteaux (1737–93), a French navigator.

Denver, COLORADO/USA
Founded in 1859 during the 'Gold rush' as two towns, Auraria and St Charles. The latter was renamed Denver City after James W. Denver (1817–92), governor of the territory in 1858. In 1860 Auraria and Denver City merged to form Denver.

Dera Ghāzi Khan, PUNJAB/PAKISTAN
'Place of Ghāzi Khan' from *dera* 'place' or 'camp'. Ghāzi Khan founded it in the late 15th century.

Dera Ismāīl Khan, NORTH-WEST FRONTIER/ PAKISTAN
'Place of Ismāīl Khan' whose father, a Baluchi chieftain, founded it in the 15th century.

Derbent, RUSSIA, TURKMENISTAN, UZBEKISTAN
Russia (Dagestan): the first name, al-Bāb, meant 'The Gate' and the second, Bāb al-Abwāb, 'Gate of Gates'. The present name is derived from the Persian *darband* 'gate'. This alludes to the pass, only 1½ miles (2.5 km) wide, between the Caspian Sea and the Caucasus Mountains. A fortress was built in 438 to control the passage of nomads, this being the principal caravan route for trade between south-east Europe and south-west Asia.

Derby, AUSTRALIA, UK, USA
1. Australia (Western Australia): founded in 1883, it was named after Edward Stanley (1826–93), 15th Earl of Derby, British secretary of state for the colonies (1858, 1882–5).
2. UK (England): the first name, Northworthy 'Northern Enclosure' comes from the Old English *worth* 'enclosure'. When the Danes arrived in the 9th century they changed the name to Deoraby 'Village where the Deer were seen' or 'Village where the Deer were kept' and thus 'Deer Village'. The name was derived from the Old Scandinavian *djúr* 'deer' and *bý*. The county of Derbyshire takes its name from the city with the additional *scīr*.

3. USA (Connecticut): a trading post established in 1642 and called Paugasset after the Paugasset people from whom the land was bought. In 1675, now a town, it was renamed after the Derby in England, probably by emigrants from that city.

Derry, NORTHERN IRELAND
See LONDONDERRY.

DeRust, NORTHERN CAPE/SOUTH AFRICA
'The Resting (Place)' from *rust* 'rest'.

Derwent, AUSTRALIA, CANADA, UK
1. Australia (Tasmania): a river named in 1793 after one of the four English rivers with this name.
2. UK (England): there are four rivers with this name, first mentioned by the Venerable Bede[†] as *Deruuentionis Fluvii*, from *dervā* 'oak' to mean 'River where Oaks were common'.

Descanso, CALIFORNIA/USA
'Rest' or a 'Break from Work' from the Spanish *descanso*.

Descartes, CENTRE/FRANCE *La Haye-en-Touraine, La Haye-Descartes*
Named after the French philosopher, René Descartes (1596–1650), who was born here. Descartes gave his name to the place in 1802 and this was shortened in 1967.

Desio, LOMBARDY/ITALY
The name is generally accepted as coming from the Latin *decem* or *ad decimum* 'ten', a reference to the fact that Desio was 10 Roman miles (one mile was 1 000 paces) north of Milan. However, Desio is not actually 10 Roman miles from Milan and the name may simply come from a Latin name *Decius*.

Des Moines, USA
There are three towns with this name, the one in Iowa being the most important. It was founded in 1843 as a fort to protect Native American rights. The origin of the name is not clear. It may be derived from a Native American word *mikonang* 'road' which became *Moingona* as the local name for the river on which the city lies. The French may have shortened this to *moin*; conveniently, after some French monks had settled here, the river came to be called *Rivière des Moines* 'River of Monks'. The name, however, probably comes from the French *de moyen* 'middle', indicating that it was halfway between the Missouri and Mississippi Rivers.

Des Plaines, ILLINOIS/USA *Rand*
Originally named after Socrates Rand in 1835, the name was changed in 1869 after the river Des Plaines, French for 'of the Plains'. It has been suggested that the name comes from a species of maple called by the French *plaine*.

Dete, ZIMBABWE
'Narrow Passage'.

Detmold, NORTH RHINE-WESTPHALIA/GERMANY *Theotmalli*
'People's Meeting Place' from the Teutonic *thiot* 'people' and *mahel* 'meeting place'.

Detroit, USA
Michigan: founded in 1701 by a French trader, Antoine de la Mothe Cadillac (1658–1730). He built a fort on the river and called it Fort Pontchartrain-du-Détroit after his patron, Comte de Pontchartrain, minister of state to Louis XIV, King of France (1643–1715), to which he added *détroit* 'strait'; this refers to the narrow passage between Lake St Clair and Lake Erie. The British shortened the name to Detroit.

Deux-Sèvres, POITOU-CHARENTES/FRANCE
A department meaning 'Two Sèvres', a reference to two rivers, the Sèvre Niortaise 'Niort Sèvre' and the Sèvre Nantaise 'Nantes Sèvre', which flow through it. Sèvre itself is derived from the pre-Indo-European *sav* 'hollow' with the root element *ar* 'water'.

Devechi (Däväçi), AZERBAIJAN
Derived from *deve* 'camel', the place once being the site of a camel market.

Devizes, ENGLAND/UK *Castrum Divisarum, Divises*
From the Old French *devise* 'boundary'. A castle was built in *c*.1132 on an earlier Roman fortification from which a town developed on the boundary between two hundreds (territorial divisions).

Devon(shire), CANADA, UK, USA
UK (England): a county whose former names, Defnum or Defena, and Defenascir (the Germanic variant), came from the British Dumnonii, the 'Deep Ones', that is possibly, those who lived in a valley or who engaged in mining. The Old English tribal name was Defnas, from the Celtic Dumnonii, and *scīr* was added.

Dewetsdorp, FREE STATE/SOUTH AFRICA
Founded in 1880 by, and named after, Field-Cornet Jacobus de Wet, father of General Christian de Wet, commander of the Orange Free State Kommandos during the Second Anglo-Boer War (1899–1902).

Dewey, USA
Two towns in Arizona and Oklahoma are named after Admiral George Dewey (1837–1917) who defeated the Spanish fleet in Manila

Bay, the Philippines, during the American–Spanish War in 1898.

Dewsbury, ENGLAND/UK *Deusberia*
'Dewi's Stronghold' from an Old Welsh personal name and *burh*.

Dezfūl, IRAN *Coprates, Andālmishk, Kantarat al-Rūm*
'Castle Bridge' from the Persian *dez* 'castle' and *pul* 'bridge'. It refers to the castle, thought to have been built *c*.375, that protected the bridge built here by Roman prisoners; in Arabic, *Kantarat al-Rūm* 'Roman Bridge'. The river is now called the Dez.

Dezhnev (Dezhnëva Mys), CHUKOT AUTONOMOUS DISTRICT/RUSSIA
A cape named after Semën Dezhnëv (*c*.1605–73) who explored the far north of Siberia during the 1640s. A bay in the Koryak Autonomous District, Bukhta Dezhnëva, is also named after him. The cape was also named East Cape by Captain James Cook† in 1778 and some maps still show this name.

Dhākā, BANGLADESH *Jahangirnagar, Dacca*
Said to be derived from the Hindi *ḍhākā*, itself from *ḍhāk*, a small bushy tree (*Butea frondosa*), abundant in the jungle, which has deep orange flowers which produce a yellow dye. Dacca was the English spelling. According to a Hindu legend, however, the city is named after its guardian goddess, Dhākéswarī 'The Hidden Goddess', whose shrine is here. According to a Muslim legend, it was named by Islam Khan, Mughal governor of Bengal, who so enjoyed the beating of drums that welcomed him that he ordered the region within earshot of the drums to be called Dhākā from *dhak* 'drum'.

Dhaulāgiri, NEPAL
A mountain massif in the Himalayas with a Hindi name meaning 'White Mountain' from the Sanskrit *dhavala* 'white' and *giri* 'mountain'.

Dhenkānāl, ORISSA/INDIA
Named after a local medieval chief, Dhenka.

Dhofar (Ẓufār), OMAN *Zafar*
A governorate with a name connected with being 'victorious' or 'successful' from *dhafara*. The name of Zafar, once a city and now a ruined site called al-Balīd 'The Town' a few miles east of Salālah, was Anglicized to Dhofar.

Dia, MALI
Takes its name from Dia-Founé 'Founder of Dia', an ancestor of the Soninké (also known as the Diankanké) people who have lived in Mali and Mauritania for thousands of years.

Diafarabé, MALI
'Meeting Place at the Junction of the (River) Dia (and the River Niger)' from *fara* 'crack', thus 'junction', and *bé* 'to meet'.

Diamantina, AUSTRALIA, BRAZIL
1. Australia: a river named in 1866 after the wife of Sir George Brown, governor of Queensland.
2. Brazil (Minas Gerais): formerly Arrail do Tejuco and renamed when it was given the status of a city in 1838 in recognition of the diamonds discovered here in 1729.

Didcot, ENGLAND/UK *Dudecota*
'Dud(d)a's Cottage(s)' from an Old English personal name and *cot* 'cottage' or 'hut'.

Diego Garcia, BRITISH INDIAN OCEAN TERRITORY
An island discovered by the Portuguese in the early 16th century, it was a dependency of Mauritius under French rule and then under British rule when Mauritius was ceded to the UK in 1814. As part of the Chagos Archipelago it joined the British Indian Ocean Territory when that was created in 1965. The name comes either from the surnames of the captain and navigator of the Portuguese ship, or from the name of the captain or navigator of that ship, or from the captains of two separate ships who both claimed the discovery.

Dieppe, CANADA, FRANCE
France (Upper Normandy): probably derived from the Saxon word *deop* 'deep' or Old Scandinavian *duipa* 'deep water', a reference to the depth of the mouth of the River Arques here.

Dijon, BURGUNDY/FRANCE *Dĭbio, Castrum Divionense*
Derived from the Latin *divus* or *divinus* 'divine' or 'godlike', from an unknown Divius. The city is famous for its mustard.

Dimbokro, CÔTE D'IVOIRE
'Dimbo's Village' from *kro* 'village'. Dimbo was a local chief.

Dimitrovgrad, BULGARIA, RUSSIA, SERBIA AND MONTENEGRO
1. Bulgaria: built in 1947 and named after Georgi Dimitrov (1882–1949), Bulgarian secretary general of the Comintern (1935–43) and communist prime minister and dictator (1945–9).
2. Russia (Ulyanovsk): previously Melekess until 1972 when it was renamed after Georgi Dimitrov on the 90th anniversary of his birth.

3. Serbia and Montenegro (Serbia): named after Georgi Dimitrov, the Bulgarian leader.

Dimona, ISRAEL
Established in 1955 for workers at the Dead Sea Plant at Sedom to the east and named after the biblical city of Dimonah.

Dinan, BRITTANY/FRANCE
Derived from the Gaulish *divo* 'holy' and *nanto* 'valley'. It lies in the estuary of the River Rance.

Dinant, BELGIUM
Probably derived from Diana, the Roman goddess and huntress.

Dindigul, TAMIL NĀDU/INDIA
Derived from the Tamil *tinti kal* 'pillow rock', a reference to the bare hill which dominates the city.

Dingwall, CANADA, UK
UK (Scotland): formerly Dingwall 'Place of the Council' from the Old Scandinavian *thing* 'council' or 'parliament' and *voll* 'place'.

Dinkelsbühl, BAVARIA/GERMANY
'Wheat Hill' from *Dinkel*, a form of 'wheat', sometimes called 'German wheat', and *Bühl* 'hill'.

Diomede Islands (Russian: **Ostrova Gvozdeva**), RUSSIA-USA
Straddling the International Date Line, the two islands are divided between Russia and the USA and were so named because they were discovered in 1728 on St Diomede's Day (16 August) by Vitus Bering[†]. Big Diomede Island is on the Russian side and is known to them as Ostrov Ratmanova *'Ratmanov Island'; Little Diomede Island is on the American side. The two islands together are called the Gvozdev Islands after the Russian scientist and explorer, Mikhail Gvozdev (d. *c.*1759), who surveyed them in 1732.

Dīr, NORTH-WEST FRONTIER/PAKISTAN
A former independent princely state, it is named after the River Dīr. The town was incorporated into Pakistan in 1962.

Dire Dawa, ETHIOPIA
'Empty Plain' in Amharic. The local area is not susceptible to cultivation. It is possible, however, that the name comes from the Somali *Dir-dabo* 'Limit of the Dir', one of the six major clans still present in modern Somalia.

Dirk Hartog Island, WESTERN AUSTRALIA/AUSTRALIA
Named after Dirck Hartog (d. *c.*1616), a Dutch navigator who visited the island in 1616 while exploring the west coast of Australia.

Diss, ENGLAND/UK *Dice*
'(Place at) the Dyke' from the Old English *dīc*.

District of Columbia, USA
A federal district established in 1791 and named afer Christopher Columbus[†].

Diu, GUJARĀT/INDIA *Dio*
Situated on an island, the name is derived from the Sanskrit *dvīpa* 'island'. It was captured by the Portuguese in 1535 and remained in their hands until 1961.

Divnomorsk, KRASNODAR TERRITORY/RUSSIA
Fal'shivyy Ghelendzhik
'Wonderful Sea' from *divno* 'wonderful' and *more* 'sea'. It was renamed in 1964 from False Ghelendzhik, a name it attracted because its bay is so similar to that of Ghelendzhik some 4 miles (7 km) away that ships' navigators were sometimes confused as to their actual position.

Dixie, USA
A name given to the southern states of the USA (those south of the Mason-Dixon Line), in particular the eleven Confederate States of America in 1860–5. The name may have come from the title of a song that became a marching song for the Confederate Army. However, it has also been suggested that it came from the \$10 notes issued by a bank in New Orleans which had the French *dix* 'ten' printed on the back, thus the 'Land of the Dixies' or 'Dixieland'. A third theory is that it came from a benevolent Manhattan slave owner, a Mr Dixy, whose good nature spread far and wide. Dixieland is also a type of jazz music said to have originated in New Orleans.

Dixon, ILLINOIS/USA
Named after John Dixon who inaugurated a ferry service over the Rock River and established a rest place here in 1830.

Diyarbakir, TURKEY *Amida, Kara-Amid, Dikranagerd*
'District of the Bakr People' from the Arabic *diyār* 'dwellings' or 'district'. Having been annexed by the Romans in 297, it fell to the Persians in 359, and to the Arabs in about 639; it was allotted to the Beni Bakr clan. Nevertheless, it was still sometimes called Kara-Amid 'Amid the Black', a reference to its impressive basalt walls. It passed finally to the Ottoman Turks in 1516. The Armenians, nevertheless, called it Dikranagerd in the mistaken belief that it was the ancient city of Tigranokeita, founded by King Tigranes II the Great (*c.*140–55 BC), King of Armenia (95–55 BC), in the 1st century BC. The present population is largely Kurdish.

Djibouti (Jībūtī)

The Republic of Djibouti (Jumhūrīyah Jībūtī, République de Djibouti) since independence in 1977. Previously the French Territory of the Afars and Issas (1967–77), the Afars being Danakil and the Issas Somalis; French Somaliland (Côte Française des Somalis— French Somali Coast) (1888–1967). The French changed the name in 1967 after a referendum on independence at which the minority Afars endorsed continued association with France; this allowed the French to downplay Somali nationalism. The port-city of Djibouti became the capital of French Somaliland in 1896 and remains the capital today of what is virtually a city-state. The name is said to come from an Afar word *gabouri* 'plate', although it is not clear to what this refers: possibly it is because the city is on the coastal plain and is surrounded by flat, arid desert.

Dnieper (Russian: **Dnepr**; Ukrainian: **Dnipro**), BELARUS-RUSSIA-UKRAINE

A river which is said to take its name from the Sarmatian *dānu* 'river' and *apara* 'deep'.

Dniester (Ukrainian: **Dnistro**; Moldovan: **Nistru**), MOLDOVA-UKRAINE *Tyras*

A river which is said to take its name from the Sarmatian *dānu* 'river' and possibly *istros* 'current' to suggest a fast-flowing river. The former Greek name is derived from a Scythian word for 'rapid'. *See* TIRASPOL'.

Dniprodzerzhyns'k, UKRAINE *Kamyansk/ Kamenskoye, Dneprodzerzhinsk*

Founded *c.*1750 as a Cossack settlement with a name meaning roughly the '(Place of) the Stone' from the Russian *kamen'* 'stone'. It was renamed in 1936 with the Russian spelling. The first part of the present name refers to the fact that the city lies on the River Dnipro (in English, the Dnieper; in Russian, the Dnepr). The second part is named after Felix Dzerzhinky (1877–1926), a Pole who founded the Soviet secret police, the Cheka, in 1917. The Ukrainian spelling was adopted after the country became independent in 1991.

Dnipropetrovs'k, UKRAINE *Yekaterinoslav, Novorossiysk, Dnepropetrovsk*

A province and a city. Lying on the River Dnieper, the second part of the name honours Grigory Petrovsky (1878–1958), a leading figure in the Ukrainian Communist Party who played a prominent role in establishing Bolshevik control in the city and thereafter throughout the Donbass region. Founded in 1783, the city was named after Catherine II the Great[†] by its founder, Grigory Potemkin (1739–91), Catherine's right-hand man and possibly her secret husband. The name meant 'To the Glory of Catherine' from *slava* 'glory'. It was renamed Novorossiysk 'New Russia' in 1796–1802; Yekaterinoslav was then restored between 1802 and 1926 when the present name was adopted as a sop to the Ukrainians. Under Stalin, it was a rare honour to have an important city named after a living person outside Stalin's inner circle, although it did not always guarantee personal security.

Dobrich, BULGARIA *Hadzhioğlu, Bazardzhik/ Bazargic, Tolbukhin*

Originally named after the Turkish merchant who built the first house here, his name meaning the son, *oğlu*, of a man who had completed the *hajj* (the pilgrimage to Mecca). During the Ottoman Turkish occupation which lasted from the 15th century until 1878 the town was called Bazardzhik from the Turkish *bazar* 'market'. It was then renamed Dobrich after the son of a local 14th-century boyar, Dobrichev. When this region of Bulgaria became part of Romania in 1913 the town was renamed Bazargic. It returned to Bulgaria in 1940 and the town was once again renamed Dobrich. Between 1949 and 1991 it was called Tolbukhin in honour of the Soviet marshal, Fëdor Tolbukhin (1894–1949), whose 3rd Ukrainian Front liberated the region from the Germans in 1944.

Dobruja (Bulgarian: **Dobrudzha**; Romanian: **Dobrogea**), BULGARIA-ROMANIA *Moesia Inferior*

Lying south of the River Danube, the northern part is in south-east Romania and the southern part is in north-east Bulgaria. First colonized by the Greeks in the 6th century BC, the region then passed to the Scythians, Romans, and Byzantines before becoming part of the First Bulgarian Empire (681–1018). It was again subject to Byzantium until 1186 when it was included in the Second Bulgarian Empire. In 1357 it became an autonomous principality founded by the Wallachian Prince Dobrotič from whom the name Dobruja probably derives. Having been conquered by the Ottoman Turks in 1411, it remained part of the Ottoman Empire until 1878 when northern Dobruja was awarded to Romania and the south to Bulgaria. As a result of the Second Balkan War in 1913 southern Dobruja was ceded to Romania. However, in 1940, at German insistence, southern Dobruja was returned to Bulgaria. There is an alternative, somewhat inappropriate, theory that the name comes from the Bulgarian *dobriče* 'stony' or 'unfertile plain'; and another that it means the opposite, 'Good (Land)' from *dobro* 'good'.

Doctor Petru Groza, ROMANIA
Named after Petru Groza (1884–1958), leader
of the left-wing Ploughmen's Front, prime
minister (1945–52), and president (1952–8).

Dodecanese (Dhodhekánisos), GREECE
'Twelve Islands' from the Greek *dṓdeka*
'twelve' and *nḗsos* 'island' although there are
more. Although they were part of the ancient
Greek world, the name was designated in the
16th century by the Ottoman Turks, who
recognized only twelve as comprising the
group because they had voluntarily accepted
Turkish rule. This lasted until the Italians took
control in 1912. The group was finally ceded to
Greece in 1947.

Dodge City, KANSAS/USA
Named after Fort Dodge, founded in 1864, so-
called after Colonel Henry I. Dodge, governor
of Wisconsin Territory.

Dodoma, TANZANIA *Idodomya*
An administrative region and a city which is
planned to become the national capital in
2005. It was founded by the Germans in 1910
in an area called in Kigogo Idodomya said to
mean 'The Place where it Sank', a reference to
an elephant which became stuck in the mud
while drinking at a waterhole.

Doha (ad-Dawḥah), QATAR *Bid', al-Bida*
'The Big Tree', presumably a reference to a
large tree around or near which the original
village developed. The city became the capital
of Qatar when independence was gained in
1971.

Dolni Chiflik, BULGARIA *Georgi Traĭkov*
'Lower (that is, Private) Estate', reflecting its
Ottoman Turkish connection. It was renamed
after Georgi Traikov (1898–1972), appointed
titular head of state in 1964, before the
original name was readopted.

Dolomites (Alpi Dolomitiche), ITALY
A mountain range composed of dolomitic
limestone which thus gave it its name.
Dolomite was discovered here by, and named
after, a French geologist, Dieudonné Dolomieu
(1750–1801).

Dolores, USA *Rio de Nuestra Señora de los Dolores*
A river rising in Colorado meaning simply
'grief' or 'sorrow' from the Spanish *dolor*. The
original name meant 'River of Our Lady of
Sorrows', a reference to the Virgin Mary.

Dolores Hidalgo, GUANAJUATO/MEXICO
Dolores
Hidalgo was added to Dolores (see previous
entry) to honour Father Miguel Hidalgo y
Costilla (1753–1811), a Catholic priest who led
a rebellion against the Spanish in 1810 and is
called the 'father of Mexican independence'.

Dominica *Waitukubuli*
The Commonwealth of Dominica since 1978.
Discovered by Christopher Columbus[†] on
Sunday, 3 November 1493, he named it after
the 'Lord's Day', in Latin *Dies Dominica*, or
'Sunday'. The native Carib people called it
Waitukubuli 'Tall is her Body', a reference to
the mountainous range that runs from north
to south. Awarded to Great Britain in 1783,
Dominica was part of various federations:
having been under the rule of the Leeward
Islands since 1833, it joined the Federation of
the Leeward Islands (1871), the Windward
Islands (1940), and the Federation of the West
Indies (1958–62). It became an Associated State
of the UK with internal self-government in
1967 before becoming an independent
republic on 3 November 1978, the 485th
anniversary of Columbus's discovery.

Dominican Republic *Santo Domingo*
The Dominican Republic (República
Dominicana) since 1821, although
independence was not gained until 1844. It
shares the island of Hispaniola, called by
Christopher Columbus[†] La Isla Española 'The
Spanish Island' when he discovered it in 1492
and Quisqueya by the Taino people, with Haiti.
In 1697, when the western third of the island
was ceded to France (later to become Haiti), the
remainder was given the name Santo
Domingo 'Holy Sunday' to mark the fact that it
had been discovered on a Sunday. Between
1795 and 1809 the entire island belonged to
France, but in 1809 Santo Domingo was
returned to Spain. After the declaration of its
independence in 1821, it was invaded by Haiti
whose troops remained until 1844.

Domodossola, PIEDMONT/ITALY *Oscela*
Lepontiorum, Domus Oxulae
The ancient capital of the Leponzi after whom
it was originally named. It then became the
administrative centre for the province of
Ossola which was established by Emperor
Augustus[†]. Domo comes from the Latin *domus*
'house', in this case meaning the parish
church.

Don, RUSSIA, UK
1. Russia: a river, the former name of which,
Tanais, is of Scythian origin and means 'water'
or 'river'. The present name represents the
first part of that name. In contrast to the
English and Scottish rivers its descent is slight
and thus its flow is gentle. This has given rise
to the title of Mikhail Sholokhov's (1905–84)
most famous four-volume novel *Tikhy Don* 'The

Silent Don'; the title of the first two volumes have been translated as *And Quiet Flows the Don*.
2. UK (England-Scotland): rivers with a Celtic name meaning 'rapidly flowing river' from *dānā* which is linked to the *Danube, but see *Aberdeen.

Donaghmore (Domhnach Mór), NORTHERN IRELAND/UK
'Big Church' from *domhnach* 'church' and *mór* 'big' or 'great'.

Donauwörth, BAVARIA/GERMANY *Schwäbisch Wörth*
Situated at the confluence of the Danube and Wörnitz Rivers, the name probably means 'Enclosed Settlement by the Danube' from *Donau* 'Danube' and Middle Low German *Wurd*. *Schwäbisch* means Swabian, Swabia being a historic part of south-west Germany, including south-west Bavaria.

Doncaster, ENGLAND/UK *Danum, Doneceastre, Donecastre*
'(Roman) Fort on the (River) Don' from *ceaster* and the Celtic river name meaning simply 'River'.

Dondo, ANGOLA, INDONESIA, MOZAMBIQUE
Mozambique: takes its name from the dondo tree which grows here.

Donegal (Dún na nGall), IRELAND *Tyrconnell (Tír Chonaill)*
A county which takes its name from the town meaning 'Fort of the Foreigners, or Strangers' from *dún* 'fort' and *gall* 'foreigner'. Some sources suggest that the foreigners were the Vikings who are alleged to have built a fort here; others, that they were the English. The previous name, still sometimes used, means 'Land of Conaill', Conaill being one of the petty kings of Ulster.

Donetsk, RUSSIA, UKRAINE
1. Russia (Rostov): formerly Gundorovka until 1955 and then renamed after the Donets River.
2. Ukraine: locally Donets'k. A province and a city originally named Yuzovka in 1872 after John Hughes, a Welsh engineer who established what later became the largest steelworks in Imperial Russia. In 1920 it was renamed after Leon Trotsky (1879–1940), Bolshevik commissar for foreign affairs and for war during the Russian Civil War (1918–20). When Trotsky fell from favour and Stalin[†] assumed the leadership the city was renamed Stalino 'Of Steel' from *stal'* in 1924–41 and 1943–61. This name was in fact appropriate for another reason because ever since the late 19th century the city had been the centre of steel production in Russia. The name reverted to Yuzovka during the German occupation (1941–

3) before returning to Stalino. When he, too, fell from favour, the new Soviet leader, Nikita Khruschev (1894–1971), Soviet leader (1958–64), who was a Communist Party secretary in Yuzovka (1925–6), renamed the city Donetsk because of the proximity of the River Donets 'Little Don'; the suffix *-ets* signifies the diminutive, the Donets being a tributary of the Don. Donetsk is the main city in the Donbas(s), a shortening of *Donetskiy Ugol'ny Basseyn*, the Donetsk Coal Basin.

Donji Milanovac, SERBIA/SERBIA AND MONTENEGRO
Named after Prince Milan III (1819–39), the son of Prince Miloš Obrenović. Milan died within a month of becoming Prince of Serbia in 1839 when his father was forced to abdicate. The Serbo-Croat *Donji* 'lower' was added in 1859 to distinguish the town from Gornji 'Upper' Milanovac.

Donji Vakuf, BOSNIA AND HERZEGOVINA
During the Ottoman Turkish occupation *vakuf* was a piece of land, given by pious Muslims, the income from which was used for the maintenance of mosques and religious charitable institutions. Fairly close to 'Lower Vakuf' is Gornji 'Upper' Vakuf.

Dorchester, CANADA, UK, USA
1. Canada (New Brunswick): named after Guy Carleton (1724–1808), 1st Baron of Dorchester, governor-general of British North America (1786–96).
2. UK (England): formerly Durnovaria, Dornwaraceaster '(Roman) Town called Durnovaria' from a Celtic name possibly meaning a 'place of fist-sized rocks' and *ceaster*. Dorecestre was the name in the 1086 Domesday Book.
3. USA (Massachusetts); founded in 1630 and named after the English town.

Dordogne, AQUITAINE/FRANCE
A department which gets its name from the river, which itself is derived from an Indo-European root word *dor* 'stream' or 'river' and *anun* 'deep'.

Dordrecht, THE NETHERLANDS, SOUTH AFRICA
1. The Netherlands: founded in 1008 with a name, Dort and then Dordt, derived from the Old Dutch *drecht* 'channel'. The town lies at the junction of four rivers.
2. South Africa (Eastern Cape): founded in 1856 by a minister of the Dutch Reformed Church and named after the city in The Netherlands.

Dorking, ENGLAND/UK *Dorchinges*
'Settlement of a Family, or the Followers of, a Man called Deorc' from an Old English personal name and *-ingas*.

Dornod, MONGOLIA
A province meaning 'Eastern'.

Dorset, CANADA, UK, USA
1. Canada (Ontario): possibly named after
Edward Sackville (1591–1652), 4th Earl of
Dorset, privy councillor and lord chamberlain
of King Charles I's[†] household (1644–6).
2. UK (England): a county, formerly Thornsæta
and Dornsætum, meaning '(Territory of) the
People living around Dorn' from the Old
English *sæte* 'settlers' and Dorn, a shortened
version of Dornwaraceaster (*Dorchester).
Although a county it did not receive the suffix
scīr.

Dortmund, NORTH RHINE-WESTPHALIA/
GERMANY *Throtmanni*
The German name suggests 'Mouth of the
(River) Dort'; however, there is no such river
and Dortmund does not lie on a river. This
name has never been satisfactorily explained.
Manni in the old spelling may mean 'water' but
Throt is opaque.

Dörtyol, TURKEY
A port and oil terminus in the Gulf of
Iskenderun, the name means 'Four Routes'
from *dört* 'four' and *yol* 'way' or 'route'.

Dos Hermanas, ANDALUSIA/SPAIN
Founded in 1248 and called 'Two Sisters' by
Ferdinand III (*c*.1201–52), King of Castile
(1217–52), in honour of the sisters of Gonzalo
Nazareno, one of his principal commanders.

Dos Palos, CALIFORNIA/USA
A Spanish phrase meaning 'Two Timbers'.

Dosso, NIGER
Comes from Do-So, a Djerma spirit.

Dostyq, KAZAKHSTAN *Druzhba*
Like its previous Russian name, it means
'Friendship'. This name may have been chosen
since the town is situated on the border with
China.

Dothan, ALABAMA/USA *Poplar Head, Dothen*
Founded in 1858 and renamed in 1911 after
the biblical Dothan, roughly halfway between
the Dead Sea and the Sea of Galilee.

Douala, CAMEROON *Kamerun/Kamerunstadt*
First developed as a station for the
Transatlantic slave trade in the 18th century, it
came under German rule in 1884. The
following year it was given the German name
Kamerun or Kamerunstadt 'Town of Kamerun'
and became the capital of German West
Africa. It was renamed in 1907 after a people
who spoke Douala, a Bantu language, who had
come from the interior and founded this city
on the coast in about 1650. From 1901 to 1916

it was the capital of the German Kamerun
protectorate and of Cameroon in 1940–6.

Douarnenez, BRITTANY/FRANCE
'St Tutuarn's Island', after the saint founded a
priory on the island here in 1118, and the
Breton *enez* 'island'.

Doubs, FRANCHE-COMTÉ/FRANCE *Dubius*
A department and a river whose present name
has evolved from the previous Roman name,
well describing its erratic course and meaning
'wavering' or 'uncertain'. Alternatively, it may
come from the Gaulish *dubi* 'dark' to describe
its waters.

Douglas, CANADA, ISLE OF MAN, FALKLAND
ISLANDS, IRELAND, SOUTH AFRICA, UK, USA
1. Canada (Manitoba and Ontario): named
after the Scottish philanthropist, Thomas
Douglas (1771–1820), 5th Earl of Selkirk, who
became governor of Prince Edward Island and
established a large settlement there in 1803;
later he was active in Manitoba creating new
settlements. *See* SELKIRK.
2. Isle of Man: formerly Dufglas, it takes its
name from the Dhoo and Glass Rivers to mean
'Black Stream' from the Old Gaelic *dubh* 'black'
and *ghlaise* or *glais* 'water' or 'stream'. Douglas
is the capital.
3. South Africa (Northern Cape): founded in
1838 as a mission station called Backhouse
after the English quaker James Backhouse, it
was renamed in 1867 after Vice Admiral Sir
Percy Douglas (1876–1939), hydrographer of
the British Royal Navy (1924–32).
4. USA (Arizona): named after James Douglas,
president of the Phelps Corporation, a mining
concern.

Douro, PORTUGAL-SPAIN
A river with a name coming from the Indo-
European root word *dor* 'water' or 'river'.

Dover, CANADA, UK, USA
1. UK (England): formerly Dubris, Dofras, and
Dovere named after the stream here, now the
Dour. This comes from a possible word *dubrās*,
the plural of the Celtic *dubro* 'water', to give
'the waters'. Dover gives its name to the strait,
in French *Pas-de-Calais*.
2. USA (Delaware): named in 1683 after the
English city.
3. USA (New Hampshire): originally Bristol, it
may have been named after a lawyer, Robert
Dover.

Dowlatābād, AFGHANISTAN, IRAN
'City of Wealth' in Farsi.

Down (An Dún), NORTHERN IRELAND/UK
Until 1973 one of the six counties of Ulster and
now a district meaning 'The Fort' from *dún*.
This refers to the fort at Downpatrick.

Downham Market, ENGLAND/UK *Dunham*
'Homestead near a Hill' from *dūn* and *hām*. The
'Market' was added later.

Downpatrick (Dún Pádraig), NORTHERN
IRELAND/UK *Dún Lethglaise*
'St Patrick's Fort' from *dún*. Previously a
stronghold, it was renamed later after the 5th-
century St Patrick who is said to be buried
here.

Downs, The, ENGLAND/UK
Rounded hills which take their name from
dūn.

Drakensberg, LESOTHO-SOUTH AFRICA
Khalamba
'Dragon Mountain' from the Middle Dutch
drake 'dragon' and -*berg* in recognition of the
spectacular and wild nature of the terrain. The
old Nguni name meant 'Barrier of Spears', a
reference to the jagged, tooth-like, peaks,
resembling the back of a stegosaurus dinosaur.

Drake Passage, SOUTH AMERICA
A strait between the Atlantic and Pacific
Oceans named after Sir Francis Drake (1540–
96), the English navigator. Sailing from the
Atlantic into the Pacific in 1578, he traversed
the Strait of Magellan, but a furious westerly
storm blew his ship into the northern part of
the Passage in 1578.

Drenthe, THE NETHERLANDS
A province with a name derived from the
Germanic *thrija hantja* 'three lands'.

Dresden, CANADA, GERMANY, USA
Germany (Saxony): first settled by Slavs, the
present name is derived from the original
Slavonic name, Drežd'ane 'Forest Dwellers on
the Plain' or 'Dwellers in the Marshy Woods'.
Dresden china is famous, although made at
nearby Meissen since 1710.

Dreux, CENTRE/FRANCE *Drocae*
Evolved from the Roman name which came
from a Gaulish people, the Durocasses.

Drobeta-Turnu Severin, ROMANIA *Drobeta*
Originally a Dacian town later fortified by the
Romans. Turnu Severin 'Tower of Severus'
from the Romanian *turn* 'tower' was built to
commemorate a military victory by Septimius
Severus (146–211), Roman emperor (193–211).
Drobeta and Turnu Severin were merged in
the 1970s.

Drogheda (Droichead Átha), IRELAND
'Bridge of the Ford' from *drohed* 'bridge' and
átha. This referred to the bridge built in place
of the earlier ford after the Vikings had built
settlements on both sides of the River Boyne in
911.

Drohobych, UKRAINE
'Woody Place' from the Slavonic *drowo* 'wood'
or 'forest'. Polish, it was seized by the Austro-
Hungarian Empire at the first partition of
Poland in 1772 and was only returned in 1918.
At the end of the Second World War in 1945 it
was incorporated into the Ukrainian Republic
of the Soviet Union.

Droitwich, ENGLAND/UK *Salinae, Wych,
Drihtwych*
'Muddy Place of Saltworks' from the Old
English *drit* 'dirt' and *wīc*, a reference to the salt
extracted from its springs or wyches. *Wīc* can
mean a place with a specialist activity, such as
an industrial settlement or works. The Roman
Salinae also indicates the saltworks.

Dromore (Droim Mór), NORTHERN IRELAND/UK
'Big Ridge' from *droim* 'ridge' and *mór* 'big'.

Drumcliff (Droim Cliabh), IRELAND
'Ridge of the Baskets' from *droim* 'ridge' and
cliabh 'baskets'.

Drummondville, QUEBEC/CANADA
Founded in 1815 and named after General Sir
Gordon Drummond (1772–1854), then British
commander in Canada who played a
significant role in the American War
(1812–14).

Druskininkai, LITHUANIA
'A Man, or People, who work with Salt' from
druskas 'salt'.

Druzhba, RUSSIA, UKRAINE
'Friendship' in Russian. The previous German
name of the town in Kaliningrad Province was
Allenburg.

Drvar, BOSNIA AND HERZEGOVINA *Titov Drvar*
Derived from the Serbo-Croat *drva* 'firewood',
a reference to the locals chopping trees to
make logs for use in the bitter winters. After
the Second World War each of the Yugoslav
republics named a town in honour of Josip
Broz Tito[†]. Thus Drvar gained the additional
Titov 'Tito's'. It was dropped after Bosnia and
Herzegovina became independent in 1992.

Dryanovo, BULGARIA
'Place of the Dogwood'.

Dry Tortugas, FLORIDA/USA *Tortugas*
A string of islands named in 1513 by Ponce de
León (1460–1521), the Spanish explorer, after
the tortoises (in Spanish, *tortuga*) that were
common here. Sailors later added the 'Dry' to
describe the terrain.

Dublin, IRELAND, USA
Ireland: formerly Eblana, Dyflin, and Duibh-
linn, and locally Dubh Linn 'Dark Pool' from
the Gaelic *dubh* 'black' or 'dark' and *linn* 'pool'

and named by the Vikings for the dark waters of the River Liffey. The Vikings destroyed the existing settlement when they arrived in the mid-9th century. They built a new settlement at the junction with the Poddle River from which an important trading post developed. The new Viking settlement was near a hurdled ford over the Liffey and this gave the official Irish name, Baile Átha Cliath 'Town of the Hurdled Ford' from *baíle*, *átha*, and *cliath* 'hurdle'. When the Irish Free State was created in 1922 Dublin became the capital. Dublin is also the name of a county in the province of Leinster. Ptolemy, the 2nd-century Egyptian geographer, called the ancient settlement Eblana.

Dubna, BELARUS, LATVIA, RUSSIA
Russia (Moscow): only designated a city in 1956, its name, from the Russian *dub* 'oak', recognizes its wooded landscaping. The same is true for the town in Belarus. In Latvia it is the name of a river.

Dubno, UKRAINE
Derived from the Russian *dub* 'oak'.

Dubossary (Dubăsari), MOLDOVA *Dubesar*
Founded in 1792 and named after the village of Dubesar. This name may derive from *dubas*, a large fishing boat used on the Dniester River here, and the suffix *-ary* to indicate that this was a place where these boats were built.

Dubrava, CROATIA
An old castle-town and market place meaning 'Grove (of oak)'. *See* DUBROVNIK.

Dubrovnik, CROATIA *Ragusium, Ragusa*
Roman refugees fleeing from Cavtat, further south on the coast, in the 7th century settled on the then island of Lava (which became Lausa 'rock' in Greek, then the Latin Rausa/Ragusium, Rhacusa, and Ragusa). A second settlement developed on the wooded mainland which had a Slav name, Dubrava, which in Russian means 'Oak wood' from *dub* 'oak'; in Serbo-Croat *dubrava* means 'grove'. The two settlements merged in the 12th century when the channel separating them was filled in. Under Venetian sovereignty, though retaining considerable independence from 1205 to 1358, the city was thereafter called the Republic of Ragusa, only losing its independence in 1808 by Napoleonic decree. At the Congress of Vienna in 1815 it was ceded to Austria until 1918 when it joined the newly created Kingdom of the Serbs, Croats, and Slovenes and became known as Dubrovnik. Between the 12th and 15th centuries the area was known as Morlacchia, named after its inhabitants, the Morlachs, whose skins were darker than their Slav neighbours. The Morlachs were a branch of the Vlachs, their name being derived from the Byzantine Greek *mauros* 'black' and *Blaxos* 'Vlach'.

Dubuque, IOWA/USA
Named after Julien Dubuque, a French trader, who was one of the first, if not the first, Europeans to settle here in 1788.

Dufourspitze, SWITZERLAND
The highest mountain peak in Switzerland, it is named after General Guillaume-Henri Dufour (1787–1875), a military officer who surveyed several peaks in the region. The German *Spitze* means 'peak' or 'summit'.

Dugi Otok, CROATIA *Isola Longa*
'Long Island' from the Serbo-Croat *dug* 'long' and *otok* 'island'. The Italian name means the same. The island is 27 miles (43 km) long and at best 2½ miles (4 km) wide.

Duisburg, NORTH RHINE-WESTPHALIA/ GERMANY *Castrum Deutonis, Diuspargum, Diotisburg, Duisburg-Hamborn*
'Diu's Fort' from *Burg*. It may be connected with Tiu, the Anglo-Saxon name for the Norse god of war who gave his name to Tuesday. By the early years of the 8th century the original Roman name had given way to the Frankish Diuspargum. Diotisburg probably means 'Fort of the Teutons'. Duisburg-Hamborn was only current between 1929 and 1934.

Duluth, MINNESOTA/USA
Named after Daniel Greysolon (c.1639–1710), Sieur Du Luth (or Du Lhut), a French officer and explorer.

Dumbarton, CANADA, UK
1. Canada (New Brunswick): probably named after the city in Scotland by Scottish immigrants.
2. UK (Scotland): the meaning of the original Alcluith or Alclut for the Britons was 'Hill Fort by the (River) Clyde' and the second Celtic name, Dunbreatain, meant 'Fort of the Britons' from *dùn*. This was built on a large rock commanding the entrance to the Clyde which was made into a defensive stronghold. Between the 6th and 8th centuries it was the capital of the Strathclyde Britons.

Dum Dum, WEST BENGAL/INDIA
Founded in 1783 and derived from the Persian *damdama* 'mound' or 'elevated battery'. Besides being the headquarters of the Bengal Artillery, it had an ammunition factory. This produced, and gave its name to, the 'dumdum' bullet, a soft-nosed bullet that expands on entry to maximize the severity of the wound.

This type of bullet was declared illegal in 1899 by the Second Hague Conference.

Dumfries, SCOTLAND/UK *Dunfres*
Derived from *dùn* and the Gaelic *preas* 'copse' to give a 'fortified position in woodland'.

Dunaújváros, HUNGARY *Intercisa, Dunapentele, Sztálinváros*
The original Roman town fell into decline to become the village of Dunapentele, that is, on the River Danube, *Duna*. This was developed in 1950 into the town of Sztálinváros, 'Stalin's Town', after Joseph Stalin[†]. The town was renamed in 1961 to mean 'Danube New Town' from *Duna*, *új* 'new', and *város*.

Dunbar, AUSTRALIA, UK, USA
UK (Scotland): formerly Dynbaer 'Fort on the Height' from *dùn* and the Gaelic *barr* 'height'. A castle was built on a rocky promontory overlooking the harbour in *c*.865.

Duncan, CANADA, USA
USA (Oklahoma): founded in 1892, it was named after William Duncan, a leading merchant from Fort Sill, Oklahoma.

Dundalk, CANADA, IRELAND, USA
1. Canada (Ontario): named by settlers after the Irish town.
2. Ireland: the Irish name is Dún Dealgan 'Dealga(n)'s Fort' after a local chieftain.

Dundee, SOUTH AFRICA, UK, USA
1. South Africa (KwaZulu-Natal): founded in 1882 and named after the Scottish birthplace of its founder, Thomas Patterson Smith.
2. UK (Scotland): formerly Dunde, it may mean 'Daig's Fort' from *dùn* and Daig, a Celtic personal name. Traditionally, however, it is said to mean 'Fort on the (River) Tay'.

Dunedin, NEW ZEALAND, USA
1. New Zealand (South Island): founded in 1848 by Scottish settlers who wanted to call it New Edinburgh. They were dissuaded from this by the mayor of Edinburgh who suggested calling it by Edinburgh's Gaelic name, Duneideann.
2. USA (Florida): originally named Jonesboro after a local shopkeeper. It was renamed in 1882.

Dungannon, CANADA, UK
UK (Northern Ireland): the Irish name is Dún Geanainn 'Geanann's Fort' after a local chief.

Dungarpur, RĀJASTHĀN/INDIA
Founded in the 14th century and named after Dungaria, a local chief, with *pur*.

Dungarvan (Dún Garbhán), IRELAND
'Garbhan's Fort', named after St Gervan who founded a monastery here in the 7th century.

Dungeness, UK, USA
USA (Washington): originally applied to some low-lying land because of its resemblance to the headland in Kent, England; the name was given later to the town. Dungeness itself means 'Headland near Denge Marsh' from the Old English *næss* 'headland'; Denge may mean 'valley district' from the Old English *denu* 'valley' and *gē* 'district'.

Dunhuang, KANSU/CHINA *Kuazhou, Shazhou*
'Blazing Beacon' since it was located at the end of the Great Wall with a line of fortified towers, constructed for protection against the Mongols to the north, extending further westwards. Nevertheless, it fell to the Mongols in 1227, became a part of Uyguristan in the 15th century, and only returned to China in 1723. It was important as a junction for two branches of the Silk Road and a major staging post. A very ancient city, it came under Chinese rule during the Han dynasty (206 BC–AD 220); its name was changed to Kuazhou in the 5th century and to Shazhou in 633.

Dunkirk, FRANCE, USA
1. France (Nord-Pas-de-Calais): locally Dunkerque and formerly Dunkerk 'Church of the Dunes' from the Middle Dutch *dune* 'dune' and *kerke* 'church', a church having been built here on the coast in the 7th century.
2. USA (New York State): originally Chadwick's Bay and renamed because the harbour here closely resembled the one in France.

Dún Laoghaire, IRELAND *Kingstown*
Named after Laoghaire, High King of Ireland in the 5th century BC, who built a fortress, *dún*, here. Between 1821 and 1921 it was known as Kingstown in recognition of the fact that King George IV[†] passed through in 1820.

Dunmore, CANADA, IRELAND, UK, USA
1. UK (Northern Ireland): 'Big Fort' from *dún* and *mór* 'big'.
2. USA (Pennsylvania): previously Bucktown after the abundance of deer in the area. Renamed in 1840 after Charles Augustus Murray, second son of George Murray, 5th Earl of Dunmore, in the hope that he might put some of his wealth to the advantage of the town; he did not, but his name has been retained.

Dunstable, ENGLAND/UK *Dunestaple*
'Dunna's Boundary Post' from the Old English *stapol* 'post' or 'pillar' and an Old English personal name.

Duque de Caxias, Rio de Janeiro/Brazil *Meriti Station, Caxias*
Its original name was changed to Caxias in 1931 and the present name was adopted in 1943. It was named after Luis Alves de Lima e Silva (1803–80), Duke of Caxias. *See* CAXIAS.

Durango, COLOMBIA, MEXICO, SPAIN, USA
1. Mexico: a state and a city (whose full name is Durango de Victoria) originally named Guadiana in 1563 by Francisco de Ibarra after a river in Spain. The same year he changed it to the name of his home town in Spain.
2. USA (Colorado): named after the city in Mexico.

Durazno, URUGUAY
A department and a city; the city's full name is San Pedro de Durazno. Founded in 1821, it was named after Dom Pedro de Alcântara, the prince regent of Brazil, and the Spanish *durazno* 'peach' or 'peach tree' in recognition of the numerous trees in the area.

Durban, FRANCE, SOUTH AFRICA
South Africa (KwaZulu-Natal): founded by the British in 1824 as Port Natal and renamed in 1835 after Lieutenant General Sir Benjamin D'Urban (1777–1849), governor of Cape Colony (1833–7), who had ordered the annexation of some territory held by the Boers; this became the new colony of Natal. Initially D'Urban, the spelling was simplified in 1854. The metropolitan area has a local Zulu name, eThekwini, which has different interpretations: 'The Place of the Lagoon' and 'The Place of the Single Testicle', a reference to the round shape of the bay and the nearby phallic-shaped promontory which overlooks the bay when seen from the Berea Hills.

Durbanville, WESTERN CAPE/SOUTH AFRICA *Pampoenkraal*
Founded in 1824 as 'Pumpkin Kraal', a *kraal* being a community with an enclosure for livestock. In 1836 it was renamed after Sir Benjamin D'Urban but, to avoid confusion with °Durban, *ville* 'town' was added in 1886.

Durg, MADHYA PRADESH/INDIA *Drug*
Derived from the Hindi *durga* 'fort'.

Durgāpur, WEST BENGAL/INDIA
'Town of Durgā'. Durgā, 'The Inaccessible' in Sanskrit, in Hindu mythology is one of the names of a goddess and wife of Shiva.

Durham, CANADA, UK, USA
1. Canada (Ontario): originally Bentinck and renamed in 1866 after the English city.
2. UK (England): formerly Dunholm 'Island with a Hill, or Promontory' from *dūn* and the Old Scandinavian *holmr* 'island'. Durham is located on a hill overlooking the River Wear and 'island' here really means firm ground surrounded by marsh. The Normans later exchanged the *n* in the hybrid English-Scandinavian Dunholm for an *r*. The county is called County Durham, there never having been a 'Durhamshire'. The centre of a great lordship, by the end of the 13th century, it had become a palatinate, the Bishop of Durham exercising regal rights over it. The palatinate was abolished in 1646 but restored after Charles II[†] became king in 1660. It lasted until 1836 and only subsequently did it become a county. To distinguish it from the city of Durham it was called County Durham.
3. USA (New Hampshire): founded in 1635 as Oyster River and then renamed after the English city in 1732.
4. USA (North Carolina): founded in about 1750 as Prattsburg after a prominent landowner, William Pratt. When he refused to make land available for a railway station to be built, the name was changed to that of a man who would, Bartlett Durham. The town was then called Durhamville and Durham Station before becoming simply Durham.

Durrës, ALBANIA *Epidamnus, Dyrrhachium, Durazzo*
Founded by the Greeks *c.*625 BC as Epidamnus before being taken by the Romans. Possibly considering the name to have an ominous meaning, in Latin *damnum* 'damage' or 'harm', they renamed it Dyrrhachium. It was held by the Ottoman Turks in 1501–1913 when it was proclaimed to be the capital of an independent Albania. It was given the Italian name Durazzo when the Italians occupied the port during the First and Second World Wars. The name may mean 'Dangerous Cliffs'.

Dushanbe, TAJIKISTAN *Dyushambe, Stalinabad*
'Monday' from the Tajik words *du* 'two' and *sanbe* 'Saturday', that is, two days after Saturday. The small village of Dyushambe was given this name to indicate that a bazaar opened there on Mondays. Part of the Khanate of Bukhara, it became the capital of the Tajik Autonomous Soviet Socialist Republic in 1929 when a branch line of the Transcaspian railway reached the city. It was renamed Stalin's[†] Town that year to mark the fiftieth birthday of the Soviet leader, a name it retained until 1961 when a new Soviet atlas was being prepared to take account of de-Stalinization. In 1991 when independence was achieved Dushanbe became the capital of Tajikistan.

Düsseldorf, NORTH RHINE-WESTPHALIA/
GERMANY
'Village on the Düssel', a tributary of the
Rhine, from the German *Dorf* 'village'.

Duxbury, MASSACHUSETTS/USA
Founded in about 1628 by Miles Standish who
gave it the name of his family seat, Duxbury
Hall, in England.

Dvůr Králové, CZECH REPUBLIC *Königinhof an
der Elbe*
The full name is Dvůr Králové nad Labem. Both
the Czech and the previous German names
mean 'The Court of the Queen on the (River)
Elbe'. The town was founded by Wenceslas II
(1271–1305), King of Bohemia (1278–1305),
who gave it to his wife, Elizabeth.

Dwārkā, GUJARĀT/INDIA
'City of Many Gates', an abbreviated version of
the Sanskrit *Dvārakā* or *Dvārāratī*.

Dyersburg, TENNESSEE/USA
Named after Colonel Henry Dyer who was
killed at the Battle of New Orleans in 1815
when American forces defeated the British.

Dzerzhinsk, BELARUS, RUSSIA
1. Belarus: the local spelling is Dzyarzhynsk.
Originally it was named Koydanovo after
Koydan, a Tatar leader, who was defeated in
battle here in 1241. In 1932 it was renamed
after Felix Dzerzhinskiy (1877–1926), a
fanatical Polish communist who founded the
Soviet secret police, the Cheka (The All-
Russian Extraordinary Commission for
Combating Counter-Revolution and Sabotage),
in 1917. He was born on the Dzerzhinovo
Estate (in Russian, *derzhat'* 'to hold') from
which he probably took his name.
2. Russia (Nizhniy Novgorod): located on the
Oka River, it was originally named
Chernorechye 'Black River' from *chërniy*
'black'and *reka* 'river', and Rastyapino,

possibly the name of local landowners, in
1919–29. It was then renamed after Felix
Dzerzhinskiy.
3. There are other towns named after
Dzerzhinskiy: Dzerzhinskiy in Kazakhstan,
now also called Aqqargha, and Dzerzhinskoye
in both Kazakhstan and Russia.

Dzhalal-Abad, KYRGYZSTAN
See JALAL-ABAD

Dzhalil', TATARSTAN REPUBLIC/RUSSIA
Named after Musa Dzhalil' (1906–44), a Tatar
poet, who was executed by the Nazis in 1944
and posthumously awarded the title of Hero of
the Soviet Union in 1956.

Dzhalilabad, AZERBAIJAN *Astrakhan-Bazar*
Originally 'Astrakhan Market', it was renamed
in 1967 after Dzhalil Mamedkulizade (1866–
1932), a militant satirist and writer.

Dzhambul, KAZAKHSTAN
See TARAZ.

Dzhankoy, UKRAINE
'New Village' from the Turkic *dzhan* 'new' and
koy 'village'.

Dzhizak, UZBEKISTAN
It may mean a 'Small Fort' in Sogdian or 'Key'
because it controls the strategic pass through
the Nuratau Mountains to the Zerafshan
Valley, Samarkand and Bukhara.

Dzierzoniów, POLAND *Reichenbach*
Founded in the 12th century from Old German
words equivalent to modern *reich* 'rich', here
meaning 'strongly flowing' and *Bach* 'stream',
a reference to the River Piława on which it lies.
The town passed to the Habsburgs during the
14th century. In 1742 it was acquired by
Prussia and only in 1945 did it return to
Poland. It was then renamed after the Polish
priest and apiculturist, Jan Dzierzoń (1811–
1906).

Eagle Pass, TEXAS/USA *El Paso de Aguila*
The present name is merely a translation of
the original Spanish name which was acquired
because of the apparent resemblance of the
hills through which the Rio Grande flows, and
on which the town lies, to the wings of an
eagle in flight.

East Africa Generally agreed to include the
countries of Burundi, Kenya, Rwanda, Somalia,
Tanzania, and Uganda.

East Anglia, ENGLAND/UK
A region, consisting of Norfolk, Suffolk, and
parts of Cambridgeshire and Essex, and one of
the seven Anglo-Saxon kingdoms of England.
The first large-scale settlement was named
after the East Angles, a folk-name which was
then applied to the area in which they lived.
They had come from Schleswig in southern
Denmark, and settled to the east of the Middle
Angles. They were composed mainly of the
northern and southern folk (Norfolk, Suffolk).
The present name is the Latinized version of
the Old English *Êast Engle*

East Bengal *See* BANGLADESH.

Eastbourne, NEW ZEALAND, UK
UK (England): formerly Burne and then
Estburne '(Place by the) Eastern Stream' from
the Old English *burna* 'stream'. 'East' was
added later to distinguish it from Westbourne.

East Dereham, ENGLAND/UK *Estderham*
'Enclosure for Deer' from the Old English *dēor*
'deer' and *hamm*.

East Greenbush, NEW YORK/USA *Het Groen
Bosch*
A translation of the original Dutch name
'Green Bush' in recognition of the nearby pine
woods which were permanently green.

East Grinstead, ENGLAND/UK *Estgrenested*
'Green Place', that is, a place for grazing from
the Old English *grēne* and *stede* 'pasture'.

East Haven, CONNECTICUT/USA *Iron Works
Village*
Part of the harbour of New Haven, it was
renamed in 1707 and detached as a separate
town in 1785.

East Liverpool, OHIO/USA *St Clair, Fawcettown*
Founded in 1798 by Thomas Fawcett, an Irish
Quaker, and very soon named after him. As it

grew into a village it was renamed after the
English city of Liverpool with 'East' added to
indicate its location on the state's eastern
border with Pennsylvania.

East London (Afrikaans: **Oos-Londen**; Xhosa:
Monti), EASTERN CAPE/SOUTH AFRICA *Port Rex*
Used as a supply base for the Kaffir War of
1846, it was probably named after a surveyor
called John Rex; popularly, it was claimed to be
named after George Rex who was said to be an
illegitimate son of King George III[†]. John Rex
worked hard to develop the port, but the name
was changed two years later in honour of the
English capital. The 'East' may indicate that it
was east of the London in England or on the
east coast of South Africa.

East Malaysia That part of Malaysia
detached from the mainland on the island of
Borneo. It consists of the states of Sabah and
Sarawak.

East Prussia (German: **Ostpreussen**), POLAND-
RUSSIA
A former German province which was
partitioned between the Soviet Union and
Poland at the end of the Second World War
and ceased to exist. Its original inhabitants
were known as the Prusi and the name Prussia
was given to the territory controlled by the
Order of the Teutonic Knights.

East Sussex, ENGLAND/UK
A county, with 'Sussex' named after the South
Saxons.

East Timor (Timor-Leste) *Portuguese Timor*
The Democratic Republic of Timor-Leste
(Tetum: Repúblika Demokrátika Timor
Lorosa'e; Portuguese: República Democrática
de Timor-Leste) since 2002, the first new
nation of the 21st century. Independence was
gained in May 2002, East Timor having been a
UN-administered territory since October 1999
when the Security Council established
UNTAET (UN Transitional Administration in
East Timor) to prepare it for independence
after the population had voted for this rather
than special autonomy under Indonesian
sovereignty two months earlier. Indonesia had
declared it to be its 27th province in 1976 after
the Indonesian Army had invaded the year
before to suppress the Democratic Republic of

East Timor proclaimed by a revolutionary
front (FRETILIN) after the withdrawal of the
Portuguese. However, this annexation was not
accepted by the population and only
recognized by Australia; the UN continued to
recognize Portugal as the administrative
power. East Timor was not, and never had
been, legally a part of Indonesia. Previously an
Overseas Province of Portugal (1945) after the
Japanese occupation (1942–5) ended; a
Portuguese colony (1701), although formal
possession was only recognized by treaty with
the Dutch in 1859 and the border between
Dutch West Timor and Portuguese East Timor
was not settled until 1914. East Timor
comprises the eastern half of the island of
Timor with a small exclave, called Ambeno
Oekussi and awarded to Portugal in 1913, in
West Timor and the island of Atauro, formerly
Kambing. The island's former Indonesian
name comes from the Malay *timur* 'east' and
thus East Timor, for Indonesians Timor Timur,
means 'East East'. *See* TIMOR.

Easter Island (Isla de Pascua), CHILE *Pito-o-te-
Henua*
The local Polynesian names are Rapa Nui and
Mata-kite-ran 'Eyes that watch the Stars', a
reference to the giant stone figures here. The
early inhabitants gave the island the name
Pito-o-te-Henua 'Navel of the Land'. According
to legend, the wife of one of the first people to
arrive gave birth to a boy and the cutting of the
umbilical cord gave rise to the name. A remote
island in the Pacific, it was discovered at Easter
1722 by the Dutch navigator, Admiral Jakob
Roggeveen. Chile annexed the island in 1888.

Easton, SOUTH AFRICA, USA
1. USA (Maryland): having been founded by
Quakers in 1682, it assumed the name Talbot
Court House in 1710–89 before becoming
Easton, a shortening probably of East Town,
because of its location east of St Michaels on
Chesapeake Bay.
2. USA (Pennsylvania): named after the estate,
Easton-Neston, of the English Earl of Pomfret,
who was the father-in-law of Thomas Penn,
who had caused the town to be built in 1752.

Eau Claire, WISCONSIN/USA
Situated at the confluence of the Eau Claire
and Chippewa Rivers, it was founded in 1844
and named 'Clear Water' after the river which
French traders had named in the 18th century.

Ebbw Vale (Glynebwy), WALES/UK
The name refers to its position in the valley of
the River Ebbw. The river name means 'colt'
(in Welsh, *ebol*) perhaps because horses lived
near the river or because the water was
'coltish', thus 'bubbly'.

Eberswalde-Finow, BRANDENBURG/
GERMANY *Neustadt Eberswalde*
'Forest of Wild Boar by the (River) Finow' from
Eber 'boar' and *Wald* 'forest' or 'wood'. The
previous 'New Town of Eberswalde' was used
between 1400 and 1876.

Eccles, UK, USA
UK (England): 'Church' from the Celtic *eglēs* to
refer to a Christian church from the Latin
ecclēsia. At that time the Old English had no
medial *g* and so *c* was substituted.

Echmiadzin, ARMENIA *Vardkesavan,
Vagarshapat*
Founded in the 7th century BC, it was renamed
Vagarshapat after a personal name and *ābād*
when the Parthian King Vologases III made it
his capital *c.*140. According to tradition, *c.*303
St Gregory the Illuminator (*c.*240–332) had a
vision of the Lord descending from heaven; he
was told where to build a church after he had
converted his cousin, King Trdat (or Tiridates)
III, to Christianity and this had become the
official religion of Armenia. In 309 he built the
church and called it *Echmiadzin* 'Descent of the
Only-Begotten (Son of God)'. In 1945 the town
was given the name of its church. It is also
spelt Ejmiatsin.

Echo, UTAH/USA
A descriptive name taken from the name of
the canyon.

Echuca, VICTORIA/AUSTRALIA *Hopwood's Ferry*
Founded in 1847 at the confluence of the
Murray and Campaspe Rivers, the name is
derived from an Aboriginal word meaning
'Meeting of the Waters'.

Écija, ANDALUSIA/SPAIN *Astygi, Colonia Augusta
Firma, Estadja*
Founded by the Greeks with a name corrupted
from the Basque *asta* 'rock' to mean 'On the
Rock'. The Roman name meant the 'Fortified
Colonial Town of Augustus[1]' while Estadja was
the Moorish name, also a corruption of Astygi.

Ecuador The Republic of Ecuador (República
del Ecuador) since 1830. Previously the
Presidency of Quito as part of the federation of
Gran Colombia (1822), having achieved
independence from Spain in 1822; part of the
Viceroyalty of New Granada (1739–1822); part
of the Viceroyalty of Peru after becoming a
Spanish colony (*audiencia*) called Quito in 1563.
The area was conquered by the Incas in the late
15th century. The name means 'Equator' in
Spanish, the equator running through the
northern part of the country.

Edam, CANADA, THE NETHERLANDS
The Netherlands: so-called because of the dam
built on the River Ye, the name of which

comes from the Old Dutch *e* 'river'. The town is famous for its semi-hard, distinctively red-rinded cow's milk cheese.

Edendale, SOUTH ISLAND/NEW ZEALAND, KWAZULU-NATAL/SOUTH AFRICA
Named after the biblical Garden of Eden.

Edenton, NORTH CAROLINA/USA
Named after Charles Eden, governor of the then colony (1714–22).

Edessa (Édhessa), GREECE *Vodina*
According to legend, Caranus, King of Macedonia, took the settlement *c*.810 BC by following some goats which were seeking shelter from the rain. He called the place Ægeas, which evolved into Edessa, from the Greek *capras* 'goat'. The Ottoman Turks subjugated the city in 1374 and completed their capture of it in 1430, giving it the name Vodina from the Slavonic *voda* 'water' because there was plenty in the area. The Edessa in Turkey is now known as *Şanlıurfa.

Edgartown, MASSACHUSETTS/USA *Nunnepog*
Founded in 1642, its Native American name, meaning 'Fresh Pond', gave way to Edgartown in 1671 in honour of Edgar (d. 1671), Duke of Cambridge and son of King James II[†].

Edinburg, USA
1. Texas: founded on a nearby site as Old Edinburgh by its founder, John Young, who came from Edinburgh in Scotland. In 1908 it was moved to Chapin which, in 1911, was renamed Edinburg, the final *h* being discarded.
2. There are five other towns with this name in the USA and an Edinboro in Pennsylvania which is also derived from Edinburgh, the *boro* being a fairly common shortening.

Edinburgh, UK, USA
UK (Scotland): the Gaelic name is Duneideann. Former names were Eidyn, Din Eidyn, Edwinesburh, and Edenburge 'Fort at Eidyn'. As the meaning of Eidyn is not certain, the name of the city cannot be taken to mean 'Fort on a Ridge', the *-dyn* being a cognate of the Gaelic *dùn*. It and the Old English *burh* both mean 'fort' or 'stronghold', in this case a hill fort. The original fort was built on a rocky basalt ridge now known as Castle Rock. A popular misconception is that it means 'Edwin's Fort', Edwin being King of Northumbria (616–32), that is, after the original fort was built *c*.500. The city developed round Castle Rock and became the capital of Scotland in 1437.

Edirne, TURKEY *Uskudama, Hadrianopolis, Adrianople*
Hadrian (76–138), Roman emperor (117–38), rebuilt the city in 125 and renamed it after

himself. The city has changed hands a number of times, finally becoming Turkish in 1922 when it adopted its present name, the Turkish version of the Greek Adrianople 'City of Hadrian'. It was the capital of the Ottoman Empire in 1413–58.

Edison, NEW JERSEY/USA *Raritan*
Renamed in 1954 after Thomas Edison (1847–1931), best known as the inventor of the light bulb and phonograph, who set up his research laboratory here.

Edmond, OKLAHOMA/USA
Founded in 1889, it is named after Edmond Townsend, a local rancher.

Edmonton, CANADA, UK, USA
1. Canada (Alberta): named originally after Fort Edmonton, a Hudson's Bay Company trading post built in 1795 some 20 miles (32 km) downstream from the present city. It was destroyed by Native Americans in 1807 and rebuilt in the present location. Fort Edmonton is said to take its name from a London borough which had been the birthplace of a Company employee.
2. UK (England): formerly Adelmetone 'Farmstead, or Estate, belonging to a Man called Ēadhelm' from an Old English personal name and *tūn*.

Edmundston, NEW BRUNSWICK/CANADA *Petit-Sault*
Settled *c*.1785 as Little Falls, it was renamed in 1848 after Sir Edmund Head (1805–68), then lieutenant-governor of the province and governor-general of Canada (1854–61).

Edo, NIGERIA
A state created in 1991 and named after the Edo people. Also known as the Bini, Oviedo, and Benim, they ruled the powerful Kingdom of Benin between the 15th and 19th centuries. *See* TOKYO.

Edward, Lake, DEMOCRATIC REPUBLIC OF THE CONGO-UGANDA *Albert Edward, Idi Amin Dada*
A lake visited by Sir Henry Morton Stanley[†] in 1889 and named by him Albert Edward Nyanza after Albert Edward, the Prince of Wales, who later became Edward VII, King of the UK (1901–10). *Nyanza* is the Bantu for 'lake'. In 1908 the name was simplified to Lake Edward. In 1973–9 the lake was renamed Lake Idi Amin Dada after Idi Amin (1924/5–2003), Ugandan president and military dictator (1971–9); when he was overthrown the previous name was restored.

Effingham, UK, USA
1. UK (England): formerly Epingeham and Effingeham 'Effa's Homestead' from an Old English personal name, *-inga-* and *hām*.

2. USA (Illinois): founded in 1854 as Broughton and renamed in 1859 after Thomas Howard, 3rd Earl of Effingham who, when a British Army officer, resigned his commission rather than fight against the American colonies in their struggle for independence.

Eger, HUNGARY *Erlau*
'Alder Tree'.

Eggleston, ENGLAND/UK *Egleston*
Probably 'Ecgwulf's Farmstead' from an Old English personal name and *tūn*.

Egham, ENGLAND/UK *Egeham*
'Ecga's Homestead' from an Old English personal name and *hām*.

Egmont, Mt (Maori: **Taranaki**), NORTH ISLAND/ NEW ZEALAND
A mountain named in 1770 by Captain James Cook[†] after Sir John Perceval (1711–70), 2nd Earl of Egmont, first lord of the British Admiralty (1763–6). *Taranaki is gradually superseding Egmont.

Eğridir, TURKEY *Acrotiri, Akridur, Felikabad*
Derived from the Byzantine Greek *acrotiri* 'promontory'. In Turkish this became Akridur/ Eğridir which meant 'It is bent'. The inhabitants did not like this name and so in the 1980s changed it to Eğirdir meaning 'She is spinning'. This is compatible with a local legend. At a time when there was no lake, the local prince was out hunting while his mother was spinning. He shot at, but missed, a deer. His arrow struck a rock from which poured out a torrent of water which drowned him. The lake was formed. Meanwhile the king remonstrated with his wife; 'Your son is dead, but you keep on spinning.' The name is now generally spelt Eğridir.

Egypt (**Mişr**)
The Arab Republic of Egypt (Jumhūrīyat Mişr al-'Arabīyah) since 1971. In 1958 Egypt and Syria together formed the United Arab Republic; in 1961 Syria withdrew, but Egypt retained the name for another ten years. (Egypt and Syria had been united under Saladin at the end of the 12th century and again in 1260.) Previously the first Arab Republic of Egypt from 1953 after the monarchy was abolished; the Kingdom of Egypt (1922–53) when it gained nominal independence; a British protectorate (1914), having been occupied by the British in 1882, although remaining nominally an Ottoman Turkish province, when Turkey entered the First World War on Germany's side; a province of the Ottoman Empire (1517), although it was under French rule in 1798–1801. The Mamlūks, emancipated military slaves of non-

Arab origin, came to the fore in 1250 and retained control until the arrival of the Ottoman Turks. Between 969 and 1169 Egypt was ruled by the Fātimids from modern Tunisia. Before being conquered by the Arabs in 642, Egypt had been a province of the Byzantine Empire (395) and of the Roman Empire (30 BC). Between 332 BC, when Alexander III the Great[†] took Egypt, and 1922 the country was ruled by people who were not Egyptians. The ancient Greek and Roman names for the country, Aiguptos and Ægyptus respectively, come from the Egyptian *hūt-kā-ptah* 'Temple of the Soul of Ptah' from *hūt* 'temple', *kā* 'soul', and the god Ptah. The Egyptian name for the country was *Khemi* 'Black Land', more probably because of the dark skins of the ancient Egyptians, but possibly because of the colour of the earth when flooded by water from the River Nile. The name *Khemi* is believed to have given us the word 'alchemy', in Arabic *al-kīmiyā*. The Egyptian language is now extinct, the last form of the language, Coptic, only surviving in the liturgy of the Coptic Church. The modern Arabic name for Egypt, Mişr, was brought by Arab conquerors from the Hejaz in the 7th century. It is an ancient Semitic word which could be interpreted as a border region or province. Egypt, not being an Arabic word, is only used by Egyptians when speaking English. Egypt has given its name to 'gypsy' since gypsies were originally thought to have come from Egypt; in fact, they came from India.

Eilat, ISRAEL *Aīla*
Also spelt Elat and Eloth. The name is derived from the Hebrew *elōn* 'oak'. A biblical city, modern Eilat was founded in 1949 after the area had been seized by the Israeli Army.

Eindhoven, THE NETHERLANDS
Derived from the Old Dutch *eind* 'end' and *hoven* 'property' to mean the village at the end of a larger settlement.

Eire *See* IRELAND.

Eisenach, THURINGIA/GERMANY
'Iron Place' from *Eisen* 'iron', a reference to the iron deposits in the area.

Eisenerz, AUSTRIA
'Iron Ore'. Iron has been mined here since Roman times.

Eisenhüttenstadt, BRANDENBURG/GERMANY
Formed in 1961 from the amalgamation of Fürstenberg, Schönfliess, and Stalinstadt, it means 'Iron Works Town' from *Eisenhütte* 'ironworks' and *Stadt*. It was at this time that many cities in the Soviet Union which bore Stalin's name were also renamed.

Eisenstadt, AUSTRIA
'Iron Town'. It belonged to Hungary between 1648 and 1920 when Burgenland was ceded to Austria after the end of the First World War.

Eisleben, SAXONY-ANHALT/GERMANY *Islebia*
Derived from its original name, the present name may mean an 'Inherited Estate belonging to a Man called Eis' from *Leben* 'Inherited Estate'. The official name is Lutherstadt-Eisleben because Martin Luther (1483–1546), a preacher who triggered the Protestant Reformation, was born here in 1483.

Ekalaka, MONTANA/USA
Named after the Sioux wife of an early settler.

Ekibastuz, KAZAKHSTAN
Takes its name from a small nearby L-shaped lake to give 'Two-Headed Lake' from *yeki* 'two', *bas* 'head', and *tuz* 'lake'.

El Aaiún, WESTERN SAHARA-MOROCCO
Also spelt Laâyoune. The name is derived from the Arabic *aïn* to mean 'sources of water' or 'springs'. Capital of Western Sahara between 1940 and 1976, when it was an overseas province of Spain, and since 1976 of the Laâyoune province of Morocco, although the international status of *Western Sahara has not yet been agreed.

El Alamein (al-'Alamayn), EGYPT
It is difficult to get the meaning. *'Alam* means 'mark', 'sign', or 'flag' with *'alamein* being the dual form. Thus it could mean 'The Two Signs', perhaps local physical features. Well-known as the site of the battles in 1942 between the British 8th Army and German and Italian forces, it is usually referred to as *el*-Alamein.

Elâzığ, TURKEY *Mezere*
Founded as a military garrison called Mezere from *mazra'a* 'hamlet' in the mid-19th century by the autocratic Abd al-'Aziz (or Abdul Aziz) (1830–76), Ottoman Sultan (1861–76). The name was changed in 1862 to Mamurat al-'Aziz; this was shortened to al-'Aziz which subsequently evolved into Elaziz. In 1937 the name became Elâzığ.

Elba, ITALY, USA
Italy (Tuscany): the original Greek name of Aethalia meant 'Smoky Place' from the Greek *aethaleos* 'full of smoke' or 'smoky', a reference to the pollution from the furnaces here. The Etruscans mined iron ore on the island. The present name comes from its second, Roman, name Ilva which is derived from the Ilvates, a Ligurian people. Having changed hands many times, the island fell to the Kingdom of Naples in 1709 before being ceded to France in 1802–15. In 1815 Tuscany took control.

El Banco, COLOMBIA *Sompallón, Barbudo, Tamalameque*
Originally a village called Sompallón, the Spanish conquistador, Gonzalo Jiménez de Quezada, renamed it Barbudo 'Bearded One' in 1537 after its bearded chief. It was renamed Tamalameque in 1544, but this is now the name of a town a few miles away. In 1749 the town became known as Nuestra Señora de la Candelaria de El Banco, 'Our Lady of Candlemas of the (River) Bank'. It lies at the confluence of the Magdalena and César Rivers.

Elbasan, ALBANIA *Scampa/Skampis, Albanopolis*
The previous name meant 'City of the Albanoi'. However, Mehmed II (1432–81), the Ottoman Sultan (1444–6, 1451–81), built a fortress here in 1466 on the site of the ancient Skampis as a base for Turkish operations against Albanian resistance. The present name is said to mean 'The Fortress'.

Elbląg, POLAND *Elbing*
Founded by the Teutonic Knights in 1237, it is named after the River Elbląg on which it lies. This name comes from the Old Norwegian *elf* 'river'.

Elburg, THE NETHERLANDS
'Ridge Town' from *elle* 'ridge' on which the original inhabitants were forced to build a settlement due to flooding in the area and *burg*.

Elche, VALENCIA/SPAIN *Ilici, Elx*
Originally an Iberian site, the name may be derived from an Iberian root word *al* 'salt'. The Roman Ilici gave way to the Arab Elx after the invasion of the Moors in 711. The present name evolved from Elx.

El Dorado, ARKANSAS/USA
1. 'The Golden' or 'The Gilded', a Spanish name allegedly given to the settlement by its first settler.
2. There are towns spelt Eldorado in Argentina, Canada, Mexico, and the USA.
3. Eldorado (or El Dorado) is also the name of a legendary country, first believed to be near Lake Guatavita in modern Colombia. It is said to have got its name from a local king, the 'Golden One', who was believed to have his body covered in gold dust during festivals (according to Sir Walter Raleigh, every day) and then washed it off by plunging into Lake Guatavita. Spanish conquistadors found the lake in the 1530s, but not the fabulous treasure they were seeking. The search led into the Amazon and Orinoco valleys to no avail. However, Eldorado appeared on Spanish maps of the 16th and 17th centuries. Now it is used to signify a place where one can make one's fortune quickly and easily.

Eldoret, KENYA *Farm 64*
Named after the River Eldare on which it lies.
Established as a post office in 1912, its previous
name alluded to the fact that it was 64 miles
(103 km) from Londiani to a point in the south-
east.

Elektrostal, MOSCOW/RUSSIA *Zatishye*
'Electric Steel' from *elektricheskiy* and *stal'*. A
steel works was built here in the early years
after the 1917 Bolshevik Revolution. The
original name, which lasted until 1938, meant
'Quiet Place', which described the site before
the steel works was built.

El Escorial, MADRID/SPAIN
'The Dump' or 'The Slag Heap', a name for the
former village and a reference to the residue of
the granite quarrying needed in 1563–84 to
build the huge monastery-palace erected as a
tomb for his father by Philip II (1527–98), King
of Spain (1556–98).

Eleuthera Island, BAHAMAS
'Freedom' or 'Free (People)' from the Greek
eleutheria, so-called in 1648 by people arriving
here, having fled religious persecution in
England.

El Faiyûm, EGYPT
See FAYYÛM, AL-.

El Ferrol, GALICIA/SPAIN *El Ferrol del Caudillo*
Takes its name from the Spanish *faro*
'lighthouse' which used to mark the entrance
to the harbour. The birthplace of General
Francisco Franco (1892–75), Spanish leader
(*caudillo*) (1939–75), *del Caudillo* was added in
1939; it was removed in the 1980s.

Elgin, CANADA, UK, USA
1. Canada (New Brunswick and Ontario):
probably named after James Bruce (1811–63),
8th Earl of Elgin, governor-general of Canada
(1846–54).
2. UK (Scotland): said to be 'Little Ireland' but
this is unlikely. The meaning is unknown.
3. USA (Illinois): founded in 1835 and said to
derive from the Scottish hymn 'The Song of
Elgin'.

El Golea, ALGERIA
'The Fortress' from the Arabic *qal'ah*.

Elgon, Mt, KENYA-UGANDA
An extinct volcano on the border between the
two countries. The name means 'Breast' from
the Masai *ilgoon*, a reference to its shape.

Elista, KALMYKIYA REPUBLIC/RUSSIA *Stepnoy*
In 1944–57 the city was known as Stepnoy
'(Town in the) Steppe' after Stalin† had exiled
the Kalmyks to Central Asia for allegedly
collaborating with the Germans. The town was

founded in 1865 and took its present name
from the Kalmyk *elstia* 'sandy' from *ilis* 'sand'.

Elizabeth, AUSTRALIA, USA
1. Australia (South Australia): founded in
1955, it was named after Elizabeth II (1926–),
Queen of the UK (1952–).
2. USA (New Jersey): settled in 1664 as
Elizabethtown after Lady Elizabeth Carteret,
wife of Sir George Carteret. Together they
shared the royal grant of New Jersey and other
land in New England. The present shortened
name was adopted in 1740.

Elizabeth City, NORTH CAROLINA/USA *Redding*
Probably renamed after Elizabeth, wife of
Adam Tooley, who originally owned the land.

Elizabethtown, USA
1. Indiana: named after Elizabeth Branham,
wife of the founder.
2. Kentucky: named in 1797 after the wife of
Colonel Andrew Hynes who laid out the town
in 1793.
3. New York: named after the wife and
daughter of William Gilliland, an early settler
here; both were called Elizabeth.

El Jadida, MOROCCO *Mazagan, al-Brija al-Jadīda*
'The New' in Arabic. Developed around a
Portuguese fort from 1502, it was known as
Mazagan after a tribe, the Mazg'anna, that had
once lived in the area. In 1821 it was settled by
Moroccan Jews who gave it the Arabic name
al-Brija al-Jadīda 'The New Fort'. In due course,
this name was shortened.

El Khārga, EGYPT
See KHĀRIJAH, AL-.

Elkhart, INDIANA/USA
Lying at the junction of the St Joseph and
Elkhart Rivers, it derives its name from an
island here, said by the local Native Americans
to have resembled an elk's heart.

Elkhorn, CANADA, USA
USA (Wisconsin): named after the prairie
called Elkhorn, so named by Samuel F.
Phoenix in 1836 when he found an elk's horn
wedged in a tree.

Elkins, WEST VIRGINIA/USA *Leadsville*
Renamed in 1890 after Senator Stephen B.
Elkins.

Ellensburg, WASHINGTON/USA *Robber's Roost*
Renamed in 1875 after his wife, Ellen, by John
Shoudy, who redeveloped the site.

Ellesmere, CANADA, NEW ZEALAND, UK
1. Canada (Northwest Territories): the largest
island of the Queen Elizabeth Islands, it was
first seen by William Baffin (c.1584–1622), an
English navigator, in 1616. However, it was

only named after Francis Egerton (1800–57), 1st Earl of Ellesmere, British under-secretary of state for the colonies (1828), in 1852 by Sir Edward Inglefield during his expedition to the region.
2. New Zealand (South Island): a lake also named after the 1st Earl of Ellesmere.
3. UK (England): formerly Ellesmeles and Ellismera 'Elli's Pool' from an Old English personal name and *mere* 'pool' or 'lake'.

Elliot, SOUTH AFRICA, USA
South Africa (Eastern Cape): founded in 1885 and named after Sir Henry Elliot (1826–1912), chief magistrate of the Transkei (1891–1902).

Ellis Island, NEW YORK/USA
Within New York City, it was named after its owner in the 1770s, Samuel Ellis. Between 1892 and 1943 it was the main immigration centre for the USA.

Ellisville, MISSISSIPPI/USA
Named after Powhatan Ellis, member of the US Supreme Court and a senator.

Ellsworth Land, ANTARCTICA *Ellsworth Highland*
By the Bellingshausen Sea, it was discovered in 1935 by the American explorer, Lincoln Ellsworth (1880–1951), who named it after his father, James William Ellsworth.

El Maḥallah al-Kubrā, EGYPT
From the 10th century an important trading centre, the name means 'The Greater Encampment' from *maḥall* 'place', here a 'place to stop', and *al-kubrā* 'the greater'.

Elmali, TURKEY
'Apple Town' from the Turkish *elma* 'apple'.

El Mansura, EGYPT
See MANSŪRAH, AL-.

Elmhurst, ILLINOIS/USA *Cottage Hill*
Renamed in 1869 after the elm trees with the common English *hurst* from the Old English *hyrst* 'wooded hill'. German immigrants arrived in the middle of the 19th century.

Elmina, GHANA *São Jorge de Mina*
The present name evolved from the previous Portuguese name 'St George of the Mine', a reference to the belief that the gold of Guinea was mined; it was not, being panned from alluvial deposits. Nevertheless, the Portuguese appreciated the quantity of gold here and called the whole Guinea coast El Mina. The first European foothold in black Africa, a fort was built here on the orders of John II (1455–95), King of Portugal (1481–95), by Diogo de Azambuja in 1482 near an African village to ensure that only Portuguese ships could trade

along this coast. Four years later fort and village combined and a wall was built round them. Elmina was the Portuguese headquarters on the Gold Coast until the Dutch conquest in 1637.

Elmira, CANADA, USA *Newtown (USA)*
USA (New York): renamed in 1828 after Elmira Neall, the daughter of an early tavern keeper.

El Monte, CHILE, USA
'The Mountain' in Spanish.

Elne, LANGUEDOC-ROUSSILLON/FRANCE *Illiberis, Castrum Helenae*
Originally known as 'New Town' from the Aquitanian *ili* 'town' and *beri* 'new'. In the 4th century it was renamed 'Helen's Fort' after Helena, the mother of Constantine I the Great[†]. The present name is derived from Helenae.

El Oued, ALGERIA
'The Dry River Bed' from a Berber variation of the Arabic *wādī*, a reference to the river that once flowed here.

El Paso, TEXAS/USA *El Paso del Norte*
Lying below a pass between Texas and Mexico where the Rio Grande emerges from the mountains, the pass was named in 1598 'The Pass of the North' in Spanish. A mission was established from which the town grew. It passed to the USA in 1848.

El Puerto de Santa María, ANDALUSIA/SPAIN *Portus Menesthei*
Originally a Roman port, it was renamed the 'Port of Saint Mary' by the Spanish.

El Qanātir el Qahirīya, EGYPT
Located where the River Nile splits into the eastern Damietta branch and the western Rosetta branch, the name means 'The Delta Barrage'.

El Qantara, EGYPT
'The Bridge'. On the east bank of the Suez Canal, this was a crossing place into and out of western Sinai.

El Reno, OKLAHOMA/USA
'The Reindeer' in Spanish, the town being named after the original Fort Reno in 1899.

El Salvador, AND MEXICO, PHILIPPINES
The Republic of El Salvador (República de El Salvador) since 1823. Previously the area had been divided into two districts by the Spanish, San Salvador and Sonsonate, and attached to Guatemala. Independence was gained from Spain in 1821 and two years later San Salvador and Sonsonate merged to form the new state of El Salvador; it became a member of the United Provinces of Central America. This

federation was dissolved in 1840 and El Salvador proclaimed itself to be a fully independent republic in 1841. The country takes its name from a Spanish fort built in 1524 on the present site of San Salvador, the capital, with the meaning 'The Saviour', a reference to Jesus Christ. Cuscatlán was the name of the area used by the Pipil tribe, a subgroup of the nomadic Nahua.

Elsinore (Helsingør), DENMARK, USA
Denmark: possibly taken from the tribal name Hælsing with *ør* 'spit of land' added.

El Tell el-Kebir, EGYPT
'The Great Mound' from the Arabic *tell* 'mound'.

El Tigre, COLOMBIA, PANAMA, VENEZUELA
In Latin America 'The Jaguar' in Spanish; elsewhere it is the Spanish word for 'tiger'. Jaguars are only to be found in Central and South America.

Ely, UK, USA
1. UK (England): formerly Elge and Elyg 'District where Eels may be found' from the Old English *æl* 'eel' and *gē* 'district'.
2. USA (Minnesota): renamed from the original Florence after Samuel P. Ely who helped to develop the mining of iron ore.
3. USA (Nevada): probably named after John Ely who helped to develop the gold and copper mining in the area.

Elyria, USA
Ohio: named after Heman Ely who owned considerable land in the area and built a sawmill. For some unknown reason, the *ria* is believed to come from the Greek Illyria.

Emden, LOWER SAXONY/GERMANY
'Mouth of the (River) E(h)e from the Old Frisian *Emutha* 'mouth' and *e(h)e* 'river'. The river is a tributary of the River Ems.

Emerald Coast (Côte d'Émeraude), BRITTANY/FRANCE
Part of the north Brittany coast by St Malo and so-named because of its green vegetation and the greenish colour of the sea.

Emilia-Romagna, ITALY *Aemilia, Romagna*
A region whose name is derived from Via Aemilia, a Roman road which joined Rimini and Piacenza; it was built during the 2nd century BC under the direction of Marcus Aemilius Lepidus (d. 152 BC), an important statesman of the Roman Republic. When five cities (Ancona, Fano, Pesaro, Rimini, and Senigallia) were seized from the Lombard King Aistulf and given to the papacy in 756 by Pepin III (*c*.714–68), King of the Franks (751–68), they were renamed collectively Romagna to mark the change of allegiance of the area from the Lombards to the Pope in Rome. Only in 1948 was the region called Emilia-Romagna.

Eminence, KENTUCKY/USA
So-called because the town stands on the highest point of land between Louisville and Lexington.

Empangeni, KWAZULU-NATAL/SOUTH AFRICA
Named by the Norwegians, when they opened a mission station here in 1851, after a river which itself had been named after the numerous hard pear trees, *mpange*, in the valley. It has also been suggested that the name comes from the Zulu word *panga* 'to seize', 'grab', or 'rob'. It is not known for certain what this might refer to, but various theories have been put forward. They include: first, it was wise to 'grab' the fertile land here so that disputes about possession would not arise later; secondly, crocodiles used to 'grab' unwary collectors of water; thirdly, when the river floods it 'robs' the people of their crops; and fourthly, cattle thieves operated in the area.

Emporia, KANSAS/USA
Founded in 1857, the name comes from the Latin *emporium* 'Place of Trade'.

Empty Quarter, The ('ar-Rub'al-Khāli), SAUDI ARABIA
A huge, desolate desert wilderness that even the Arabs call 'The Empty Quarter' from *'ar-rub'* 'the quarter' and *al-khāli* 'empty'; it is also known to them as 'The Sands'. It used to be translated as the 'Abode of Emptiness'.

Encarnación, PARAGUAY *Itapúa*
Founded in 1614, the name means 'Incarnation' in Spanish.

Enderby Land, ANTARCTICA
The London whaling firm of Enderby Brothers first sent its ships to the Southern Ocean in 1785. The coast here was discovered in 1831 by John Biscoe, an English navigator sailing on behalf of Enderby. He named it after the firm.

Enfield, AUSTRALIA, CANADA, JAMAICA, NEW ZEALAND, UK, USA
1. UK (England): formerly Enefelde 'The Open Area belonging to a Man called Ēana' from an Old English personal name and *feld*.
2. USA (Connecticut): named after the Enfield in England in 1683.
3. USA (New Hampshire): named after the English Baron Enfield in 1761.

En Gedi, ISRAEL
'Spring of the Kid (young goat)' from *gedi* 'kid'. Mentioned in the Bible (Joshua 15: 62), it was refounded as a kibbutz in 1953.

Engel's, SARATOV/RUSSIA *Pokrovka, Pokrovsk, Kazakstadt*
Founded in 1747 as a military base which was named after its church, which was dedicated to the Protection of the Virgin from *pokrov* 'cover' or 'covering'. The German population grew during the 18th century and they caused the name to be changed to Kazakstadt 'Cossack Town'; it did not catch on. The name was slightly altered to Pokrovsk in 1914. In 1922–41 the city was the capital of the Volga German Republic. It was renamed Engel's in 1931 after Friedrich Engels (1820–95), the German socialist philosopher and colleague of Karl Marx.

England, UK *Englaland*
'Land of the Angles' from the Old English *Engle*, the genitive plural of which is *Engla*, a Germanic tribe which previously lived in Angel (thought to be in Jutland, now part of Denmark) and which crossed the sea to Britain during the 5th century. At much the same time Saxon mercenaries from Germany were invited by a British king, possibly Vortigern (*c.*425–*c.*450), to help protect his kingdom from marauding Picts and Scots. These Anglo-Saxon footholds were then expanded into settlements and, in due course, kingdoms. The name England was first mentioned by the Venerable Bede[†] *c.*730. The seven main Anglo-Saxon kingdoms during the 7th and 8th centuries, known as the Heptarchy (from the Greek *hepta* 'seven' and *-archia* 'rule') since the 16th century, were those of the East Angles (East Anglia), East Saxons (Essex), West Saxons (Wessex), South Saxons (Sussex), Kent, Mercia (the border folk), and Northumbria (the land north of the River Humber). The Kingdom of England was created as a nation in the 10th century (Æthelstan became the undisputed ruler of all England in 937) and lasted until 1536 when Wales was incorporated to become the Kingdom of England and Wales in 1707, apart from the years of the Commonwealth, 1649–60. (*See* GREAT BRITAIN AND THE UNITED KINGDOM.) First World War British troops, particularly at first those who had served in India, referred to England as 'Blighty' from the Urdu *bilāyatī* 'foreign country', itself from the Arabic *wilāyat* 'kingdom' or 'province'. British troops still use the word sometimes when abroad.

English Channel (French: *La Manche*)
A waterway separating southern England from northern France and linking the Atlantic Ocean with the North Sea. The French name 'The Sleeve' is a reference to its narrowing shape from west to east. In the 2nd century Ptolemy[†] referred to it as Oceanus Britannicus.

Enid, OKLAHOMA/USA
Originally a tented city that sprang up overnight in 1893 around a land office when the Cherokee Strip was opened to settlers. The name is believed to come from Enid, a character in Tennyson's *Idylls of the King* published in 1859.

Enna, SICILY/ITALY *Hennae, Castrogiovanni*
An ancient Siculi stronghold, its Latin name was (Castrum) Hennae. This gave way to the medieval 'Camp of John' which was derived from the Arabic *Kasr-Yanni* or *Kasr-Yannah*, both a corruption of the Latin name. The Saracens occupied the city between 859 and 1087 when it was taken by the Normans. In 1927 a modern version of the ancient name was adopted.

Enniskillen, CANADA, UK
UK (Northern Ireland): in Irish, Inis Ceithleann 'Cethlenn's Island' from *inis* 'island', a reference to the fact that the city is built on an island in the River Erne.

Enschede, THE NETHERLANDS *Aneschedhe*
'On the Border' from the Old Dutch *ane* 'on' or 'at' and *schedhe* 'border' or 'boundary'. It is near the German border.

Ensenada, ARGENTINA, MEXICO, PUERTO RICO, USA
Mexico (Baja California): originally Ensenada de Todos Santos from the Spanish *ensenada* 'Cove' or 'Inlet'. It lies on the Bay of Todos Santos.

Entebbe, UGANDA
'Chair' in the Lugandan language. According to legend, Mugula, chief of the local Mamba tribe, gave his orders while seated in a chair carved out of rock. In due course the 'chair' was submerged under the waters of Lake Victoria. In practical terms, 'chair' can be taken to mean 'headquarters'. When a military post was established here in 1893 it was given the name Entebbe. It served as the capital of Uganda until 1958.

Enterprise, CANADA, GUYANA, USA
USA: there are six cities and towns with this name, all presumably so-called to indicate the attitude of their inhabitants.

Entre Ríos, ARGENTINA, BOLIVIA, BRAZIL, GUATEMALA, HONDURAS, MOZAMBIQUE
Argentina: a province with the name 'Between Rivers'. It is between the Paraná and Uruguay Rivers.

Enugu, NIGERIA
A state and a town founded in 1917. The Ibo name is *enu Ugwu* 'At the Top of the Hill'. The name comes from the Ibo village, Enugu

Ngwo, which was situated on the Udi Plateau; the present city, however, lies at the foot of it. Enugu was the capital of the short-lived Republic of Biafra in 1967.

Épernay, CHAMPAGNE-ARDENNE/FRANCE
Sparnacum
The earlier Roman name, from which the present one is derived, is based on the Gaulish *eperno* 'thorn' with *-acum*.

Ephesus (Efes), TURKEY *Haghios Theologos, Alto Lugo, Ayasoluk/Aya Suluq, Selçuk, Akincilar*
Ruins. Founded at least as early as the 7th century BC by Ionian colonists at a strategic site on the west coast of Asia Minor, the name may be derived from the Greek *eforos* 'ruler' or 'district governor' to indicate its importance. The classical Greek city surrounded one of the Seven Wonders of the Ancient World, the Temple of Artemis (called Diana by the Romans) built in about 550 BC by Croesus (d. *c.*546 BC), King of Lydia (*c.*560–546 BC). However, Ephesus has been moved four times and what little remains of the Temple is about half a mile (1 km) from the ruins of the city. It was the capital of the Roman province of Asia.

Épinal, LORRAINE/FRANCE
Derived from the Latin *spina* 'thorn'.

Épinay-sur-Seine, ÎLE-DE-FRANCE/FRANCE
Spinogelum
The original Gallic-Roman name meant 'Place of Thorns and Gorse' from the Latin *spina* 'thorn'. The present name is derived from this with the addition of 'on (the River) Seine'.

Epirus (Greek: Ípiros), ALBANIA-GREECE
A geographic region of Greece whose name comes from *ēpeiros* 'mainland' to distinguish it from the many neighbouring islands. Between the 4th and 2nd centuries BC part of it was known as the Kingdom of Molossia, which took its name from King Molossus. The Despotate of Epirus was a Byzantine principality in north-west Greece and southern Albania, formed when the Crusaders took Constantinople (now Istanbul) in 1204; it ceased to exist in 1337 when the Byzantine Empire reasserted control. After the Balkan Wars of 1912–13 Epirus was partitioned between Albania and Greece, although neither country has recognized this division.

Epping, AUSTRALIA, SOUTH AFRICA, UK, USA
UK (England): '(Place of the) People who live on the Ridge' or possibly '(Place of the) People who used the Ridge for a Lookout' from the Old English *yppe* 'ridge' or 'lookout place' and *-ingas*.

Epsom, ENGLAND/UK *Evesham, Eofeshamm*
'Ebbe's Homestead' from an Old English personal name and *hām*.

Equateur, DEMOCRATIC REPUBLIC OF THE CONGO
A province so named because it lies on the equator.

Equatorial Guinea *Spanish Guinea*
The Republic of Equatorial Guinea (República de Guinea Ecuatorial) since independence in 1968. The country consists of the island of *Bioko, the small island of Annobón 'Good Year' because it was first seen on New Year's Day, probably 1474, and previously known as Pagalu, the mainland territory of Río Muni, also sometimes known as Mbini, and three other small islands. It was formerly a Spanish colony (1778) when the Portuguese, who had claimed the lands at the 1494 Treaty of Tordesillas, ceded them to Spain. The Republic lies just north of the equator from which it gets part of its name. *See* GUINEA.

Erebus, Mt, ANTARCTICA
A volcanic peak on Ross Island named by Sir James Ross (1800–62), a British naval officer, after one of his ships which participated in his voyage here during 1841. Erebus means 'darkness', the darkest place of the underworld in classical mythology.

Erechim, RIO GRANDE DO SUL/BRAZIL *Boa Vista do Erechim, José Bonifácio*
'Small Field' in the Tupí-Guaraní language. Founded in 1909, the Portuguese *Boa Vista* means 'Good View'. Its previous name was valid only between 1939 and 1944.

Ereğli, TURKEY
1. Cappadocia: previously Heraclea Cybistra, Ereğli being the Turkish version of Heraclea or Hercules.
2. Black Sea coast: founded *c.*560 BC as Heraclea Pontica and then renamed Bender-Ereğli and Karadenizereğlisi; thus, a port, *bandar*, in Pontus, an ancient district in north-eastern Anatolia. Karadenizereğlisi means 'Ereğli on the Black Sea' from *kara* 'black' and *deniz* 'sea'.

Eretz Yisra'el 'Land of Israel' in Hebrew, the land promised to the Jewish patriarch, Abraham. It referred to the land governed by the British during their mandate in 1922–48, the biblical land of Israel of which the heartland was the West Bank. *See* PALESTINE AND WEST BANK.

Erevan, ARMENIA
See YEREVAN.

Erfurt, THURINGIA/GERMANY *Erpesfurt*
'Ford through the (River) Erpf' from a *Furt* 'ford' which lay on the River Gera. The river was formerly known as the Erpf from the Old High German *erp* 'dark'.

Erie, CANADA, USA
USA (Pennsylvania): named after the Erie, an
Iroquoian tribe, whose name may mean
'Wildcat' or 'Long Tail'. They also gave their
name to Lake Erie, one of the five Great Lakes
of North America.

Erin, CANADA, USA
Canada (Ontario): named in 1820 after the
ancient name for Ireland.

Eritrea (Tigrinya: **Ertra**)
The State of Eritrea since 1993 when
independence from Ethiopia was gained.
Previously the Eritrea Autonomous Region in
Ethiopia (1991–3); annexed by Ethiopia as its
14th province (1962–91); federated as an
autonomous state with Ethiopia (1952–62); a
British UN Trust Territory (1941–52); an Italian
colony (1890–1941). In 1889 Menelik II (1844–
1913), Emperor of Ethiopia (1889–1913),
signed the Treaty of Wichale which
recognized Italian possessions on the Red Sea
which they had gathered since 1869. The
Italians gave these the name Eritrea, which
was the Italianized version of the Latin *Mare
Erythraeum* 'Red Sea' from the ancient Greek
erythros 'red'. Disputes over the somewhat
arbitrarily drawn border with Ethiopia, which
is based on a treaty between Ethiopia, Italy,
and the UK in 1902 and which was never
properly demarcated, continue.

Erlangen, BAVARIA/GERMANY
'Field of Alder' from the Middle High German
erle 'alder' and *wang* 'field' or 'meadow.'

Erne, Lough (Loch Éirne), NORTHERN
IRELAND/UK
'Érann's Lake', Érann being a goddess. The
River Erne takes its name from the lake.

Erode, TAMIL NĀDU/INDIA
'Wet Skull', a reference to the Cōla temple
here, built in the 10th century.

Er Rachidia, MOROCCO *Ksar es Souk*
Also spelt Errachidia. Renamed in 1979 after
Moulay al-Rachid, the founder of the Alawid
(Alaouite) dynasty that rules in Morocco to this
day, who seized the throne in 1668; he was
succeeded by his younger brother in 1672. By
the French, who built a Foreign Legion fort
here during the First World War (1914–18), it
was called Ksar es Souk 'Enclosed Market'
from *ksar* 'stronghold' and *sūq* 'market'.

Er Rif, MOROCCO
A mountain range, also known as Rif, close to
the north Moroccan coast and meaning 'The
Coastland' from the Arabic *ar-rīf*.

Erzgebirge (Czech: **Krušné Hory**), CZECH
REPUBLIC-GERMANY
'Ore Mountains' from *Erz* 'ore' and *Gebirge*
'mountain'. The Czech name means the same.
The mountains are known for their mineral
wealth.

Erzurum, TURKEY *Camacha, Theodosiopolis, Arzan
ar-Rūm*
An ancient settlement called Camacha on
which was built a Byzantine fortress in 443
named after either Theodosius I the Great (347–
95), Roman Emperor of the East (379–92) and
both of the East and the West (392–5), or, more
likely, Theodosius II (401–50), Roman Emperor
of the East (408–50). The fortress-city fell to the
Arabs in 635, to the Seljuk Turks in 1071, and in
1515 it was taken by the Ottoman Turks under
Selîm I the Grim (1470–1520), Sultan (1512–20).
The Arabs called it Arzan ar-Rūm 'The Land of
the Romans', that is, the Byzantine Christians,
and the Turks retained the name from which
the present one is derived.

Esbjerg, DENMARK *Eysburgh*
Known as Eysburgh in 1502, the present name
was first associated with an estate on the west
coast of Jutland which derived its name from
the Jutlandish for 'Bank, *bjerg*, where the Bait is
put on the Hook'. When the city-port was
founded in 1868 to facilitate Jutland's exports
after the loss of North Schleswig to Germany,
it was given the same name. It has been
suggested, however, that the name has
evolved from an older name such as Eskebjerg
'Ash Tree Bank' from the Old Scandinavian *eski*
'Place of Ash Trees'. There is, however, no
certain derivation.

Escalante, PHILIPPINES, USA
USA (Utah): a river, originally named Potato
Creek by Almon H. Thompson because it
flowed out of what the Mormons called Potato
Valley, and a town named after Silvestre Velez
de Escalante, a Spanish Franciscan missionary,
who was the first white man known to have
crossed the Utah wilderness in 1776–7 while
searching for a route between Santa Fe in New
Mexico and Monterey, California. In doing so,
he rediscovered the Grand Canyon in Arizona.

Escanaba, MICHIGAN/USA
A Chippewa word meaning 'Flat Rock'.
However, it is also claimed to mean 'Red Buck'
and 'Young Male Quadruped'.

Eschwege, HESSE/GERMANY
'Ash Tree Way' from *Esche* 'ash tree' and *Weg*
'way'.

Eschweiler, NORTH RHINE-WESTPHALIA/
GERMANY
'Ash Tree Hamlet' from *Esche* 'ash tree' and
Weiler 'hamlet'.

Escondido, CALIFORNIA/USA
'Hidden' from the Spanish word, a reference to its location in a remote valley.

Esdraelon, Plain of ('Emeq Yizre'el), ISRAEL
Also known as the Valley of Jezreel. The present name is the Greek version of the Hebrew Yizre'el 'God will sow' or 'God will make fruitful', a reference to the plain's fertility.

Eşfahān, IRAN *Anzan, Gabae/Gabian Yagi, Jay, Safahan*
A province and a city called 'Place of an Army' or 'Army Camp' because, in Sāssānian times, it contained a military garrison with horses; in modern Persian *aspahān* or *sepahān*, the plural of *sepah* 'army', and *asb* 'horse'. The ancient Persian city of Gabae, it is also known as Isfahān and Ispahān. It was captured by the Arabs in 642; they named it Jay. In 1051 it was taken by the Seljuk Turks, but when the Seljuk dynasty fell, the city went into decline. It was resurrected when 'Abbās I the Great (1571–1629), Shah of Persia (1588–1629), came to the throne and made it his capital.

Esher, ENGLAND/UK *Æscæron, Aissele*
'District where Ash Trees grow' from the Old English *æsc* 'ash tree' and *scearu* 'boundary', thus 'district'.

Eshowe, KWAZULU-NATAL/SOUTH AFRICA
A Zulu onomatopoeic name describing the sound of the wind whispering through the trees, there being a pine forest within the town. Thus the name has the sense of 'Breezy Place'. However, it has also been suggested that its name comes from *ishowe*, a cold winter wind.

Esk, UK
The name of several rivers in England and Scotland from the British *isca*, simply meaning 'the water' or 'the river'.

Eskilstuna, SWEDEN *Tuna*
Renamed to commemorate St Eskil, an English priest who became a bishop and who helped to reconvert the Swedish people after they had lapsed into paganism. He was stoned to death *c.*1080 after protesting against an idolatrous festival. He was buried here.

Eskişehir, TURKEY *Dorylaeum, Darūliyah*
The name 'Old City' from *eski* 'old' and *şehir* testifies to the fact that it replaced the nearby Phrygian city of Dorylaeum, called by the Arabs Darūliyah, now in ruins. Eskişehir was rebuilt after suffering severe damage during the Turkish War of Independence (1919–22).

Esmeraldas, ECUADOR
At the mouth of the Esmeraldas River, it probably takes its name from the river, which itself may have been given the name from the emerald colour of the water or the presence of emeralds from the Spanish *esmeralda*.

Esperanza, ARGENTINA, MEXICO, PERU, PHILIPPINES, PUERTO RICO, SOUTH AFRICA, USA
'Hope' in Spanish. There are also towns spelt Esperança in Brazil, Esperance in Australia and the USA, and Esperantina and Esperantinópolis in Brazil.

Espírito Santo, BRAZIL
A state, and one of the original captaincies created by the Portuguese, called 'Holy Spirit'.

Espiritu Santo, VANUATU *Marina*
An island with the Portuguese name 'Holy Spirit'. It was discovered in 1606 by the Portuguese navigator, Pedro Fernández de Quirós (d. 1614). As with many islands in the Pacific, different maps showed different locations for the island east of Australia and New Guinea, and even on the mainland of Australia.

Espoo, FINLAND *Esbo*
Derived from the earlier Swedish Esbo, which itself comes from the name of an ancient village called Espåby 'Espå Village' once located at the mouth of the Espoo River. Espåby is said to be derived from Äspeby from the Old Swedish *äspe* (modern Swedish *asp*) 'aspen', probably a reference to the numerous aspen trees growing at the mouth of the river.

Esquimalt, BRITISH COLUMBIA/CANADA *Puerto de Cordova*
Named by an officer of the Spanish Navy in 1790 after the Viceroy of Mexico, its local Native American name meaning 'Place of gradually shoaling Waters' was subsequently restored.

Essaouira, MOROCCO *Amougdoul, Mogador*
An ancient port, its original name may have been taken from the Phoenician *migdol* 'Lookout Tower'. Mogador was a corruption of a Berber word for 'safe anchorage', although it has been suggested that it is a corruption of the Berber Magdoul, the name of a holy man buried here. It was refounded in 1765 by the new sultan, Sīdī Muhammad, who wanted to make it a commercial port to compete with Agadir; it was given its present name at the same time. This comes from the Arabic *as-saouîra* 'Little Ramparts' or 'Little Fort' from a diminutive of *sûr* 'wall', indicating a fortification here. During the period of French rule it was called Mogador but the present name was readopted in 1956 when Morocco gained its independence.

Essen, BELGIUM, GERMANY *Astride*
'Place where Kilns stand' from the Middle Dutch *ast* 'kiln' or 'anvil', cognate with the German *Esse*, and the collective suffix *-ede*.

Essex, CANADA, UK, USA
UK (England): one of the seven Anglo-Saxon kingdoms and previously East Seaxe and Exsessa; a county named after the East Saxons from the Old English *Seaxe* 'Saxons' who may have taken their name from *seax* 'knife' or 'dagger', possibly their favourite weapon.

Essoûk, MALI *Tadmekket*
'The Market' from the Arabic *es-sūq.*

Estcourt, KWAZULU-NATAL/SOUTH AFRICA
Bushmans River Post/Bushmans Drift
Founded in 1848, its name was changed in 1863 to mark the support given by Thomas Estcourt, a British Member of Parliament for Devizes and later North Wiltshire (1835–65).

Este, VENETO/ITALY *Ateste*
The present name is derived from the original one which meant the 'City on the (River) Atesis', now called the Adige. In the 6th century, however, the river changed its course and the town no longer lies on it.

Esterhazy, SASKATCHEWAN/CANADA
Named after Count Paul Otto d'Esterházy (1830–1912), a French-Hungarian who encouraged settlement.

Estevan, SASKATCHEWAN/CANADA
Founded in 1892, the town's name is believed to come from various letters within the names of George *Ste*phen and William *van* Horne who were involved with the building of the Canadian Pacific Railway.

Estherville, IOWA/USA
Named after Esther Ridley, the wife of one of those who laid out the town in 1857.

Estonia The Republic of Estonia (Eesti Vabariik) in 1918–40 and since 1991. Previously the Estonian Soviet Socialist Republic (1940–1, 1944–91) within the Soviet Union; it was occupied by German forces in 1941–4 during which time it was part of what was called Ostland 'East Land', created by Hitler and comprising Estonia, Latvia, Lithuania, and Byelorussia; a province of Russia (1721). Before that Estonia had been under the rule of Swedes, the Teutonic Knights and Danes, becoming part of *Livonia together with Latvia, in 1346. The country is named after its inhabitants, the Eesti, people living on the eastern shores of the Baltic Sea who traditionally call themselves *Maa Rahvas* 'People of the Country'. The meaning of *eesti* is not known, but is almost certainly not related to the German *est* 'east'.

Estuaire, GABON
A province with a French name meaning 'Estuary' because it includes the estuary of the Ogooué River.

Esztergom, HUNGARY *Strigonium, Gran*
Originally a Celtic settlement and then a Roman stronghold called Strigonium, its name is derived from the Frankish *Osterringun* 'Eastern Fortress' as part of the border defence system. It was occupied by the Ottoman Turks between 1543 and 1683. When part of the Austro-Hungarian Empire after the withdrawal of the Turks, it was given the German name Gran 'grain' to signify its importance as a grain market. The town was the capital of the early Arpád kings from the 10th to the mid-13th centuries.

Ethiopia (Amharic: Ītyop'iya) *Aksum, Abyssinia*
The Federal Democratic Republic of Ethiopia (Yeltyop'iya Federalawi Demokrasiyawi Ripeblik) since 1995. Previously the Peoples' Democratic Republic of Ethiopia (1987–95). Proclaimed a socialist state in 1975, it had been a monarchy for centuries with its ruler called emperor. Modern Ethiopia dates from the reign of Téwodros II (*c.*1818–68), Emperor of Ethiopia (1855–68). The country was invaded by the Italians in 1935 and annexed the following year. In 1936–41 it formed, with Eritrea and Italian Somaliland, Italian East Africa. In 1941 joint British and Ethiopian forces drove out the Italians. The name comes from its inhabitants, called by the Greeks the '(Land of) Burnt Faces', *Aithiops*, from *aithō* 'I burn' and *opsis* 'appearance'. When the Kings of Aksum wrote in Greek they referred to their country as Aithiopia. What the Greeks called Ethiopia (or Meroe), the middle Nile valley, was known to the ancient Egyptians and Jews as the Kingdom of Kās (Cush/Kush) and this extended over what is now northern Sudan; the Cushitic group of languages is spoken in the south of the country today. In the Bible (1 Kings 9: 28 and 2 Chronicles 8: 18), it is referred to as the 'Land of Ophir'. The Egyptian Pharoahs called it the 'Land of Punt'. Abyssinia is a 16th-century Latinization of the so-called Habash people from the Arabic *habasha* 'to gather' to give *habishat* 'mixed people', a reference to the ethnic mix of the people who have always lived in this part of Africa. Since ancient times Abyssinia was more or less interchangeable with Ethiopia, although it has not been used since the end of the Second World War (1939–45). Some early rulers also used *Aksum to describe the northern part of modern Ethiopia. It is one of only two African countries never to have been colonized by European powers; Liberia is the other.

Etna, CANADA, ITALY, USA
Italy (Sicily): an active volcano, sometimes called locally Mongibello from the Latin *mons* and the Arabic *jabal*; in Arabic it was called Jabal an-Nār 'Mountain of Fire'. The present

name comes from an Indo-European root *aidh* representing 'burning' or 'fire' and the Greek Aitne from *aithō* 'I burn'.

Etobicoke, ONTARIO/CANADA
'Place where the Alders grow' from a local Native American word.

Eton, CANADA, UK
UK (England): formerly Ettone 'Farmstead by the River' from the Old English *ēa* 'river' and *tūn*.

Euboea (Évvoia), GREECE *Hellopia, Egripo, Negraponte*
An island whose name may be derived from *euboia* 'rich in cattle' from *eu* 'rich' and *bous* 'ox' or 'cow'. Alternatively, it may be named after the nymph Evia. Hellopia was named after the Hellopes. Taken by the Ottoman Turks in 1470, the island joined Greece in 1830.

Euclid, USA
Minnesota and Ohio: both towns are named after the famous Greek mathematician who lived in the 4th–3rd centuries BC and taught at Alexandria during the reign of Ptolemy I Soter (*c*.365–*c*.282 BC), ruler of Egypt (323–285 BC).

Eufaula, USA
1. Alabama: originally a Creek village spelt Yufala which had the meaning 'They divided here and went to other Places'.
2. Oklahoma: named after the Eufaula in Alabama.

Eugene, OREGON/USA *Eugene City*
Founded in 1846, it was named after Eugene Skinner, its first settler.

Euphrates (Turkish: **Firat**; Arabic: **Furāt**), TURKEY-SYRIA-IRAQ
A river whose name may be derived from its Akkadian name Purat from *ur* 'river' and *at* 'father' to give 'father of rivers' or 'great river'. Euphrates in ancient Greek, from the Hebrew Perath, is said to mean 'sweet water' from *eu* 'pleasing'. The Euphrates is mentioned in the Bible (Genesis 2: 14) and in Deuteronomy 1: 7 it is called 'the great river, the river Euphrates'. Its headwaters are the Karasu 'black, or muddy, river' from the Turkish *kara* 'black' and *su* 'river' and the Murat '(river of) desire' from the Turkish *murat* 'desire' or 'wish'.

Eurasia The combined landmass of Europe and Asia.

Eureka, CANADA, USA
There are ten towns with this name in the USA and one in Nunavut, Canada. They are generally named after the Greek exclamation *Heureka* 'I have found it' by Archimedes when he discovered by chance a way to determine the purity of a gold crown he had been asked to test: any body displaces its own volume of water when immersed. The port in California was named after the 'Eureka' placed on the state seal, a reminder of the gold discovered in the state.

Europe The second smallest continent is said to be named after Europa. According to Greek mythology, she was the daughter of Agenor, King of Phoenicia, who was carried off to Crete by Zeus, the supreme ruler of the Greek gods. Geographically, it was first mentioned in a Greek poem in the 8th century BC. It applied only to the 'mainland', that is, the vast territory to the north of ancient Greek horizons. Around the turn of the first millennium AD, the name Europe was not often used. Indeed, it was rarely used until the late 17th century; more common was Christianitas or Christendom. It has also been said to be associated with the Greek *eurys* 'broad' to mean a large region. On the other hand, it might be derived from the Phoenician '*ereb* 'West' or 'Land of the Setting Sun'. Europe can be defined in geographical, historical, political, cultural, and value terms, although these are often disputed. Geographically, its eastern boundary is generally accepted as being along the eastern Ural Mountains in Russia and the Zhem (previously Emba) River, which flows into the north-eastern corner of the Caspian Sea, in Kazakhstan. Continuing southwards, Europe may then be said to include the three states of the Caucasus (Armenia, Azerbaijan, and Georgia), Turkey, despite the signpost on the south side of the Bosporus in Istanbul proclaiming the start of Asia, and Cyprus.

Evanston, USA
Illinois: named after John Evans, one of the founders of Northwestern University in 1853 and a former governor of Colorado. The town in Wyoming was also named after him.

Evansville, CANADA, USA
USA (Indiana): named after Robert M. Evans, a colonel in the local militia, who helped to lay it out in 1812.

Eveleth, MINNESOTA/USA
Named after a lumberjack, Edwin Eveleth, who proposed the site for a settlement in 1885.

Evenk, RUSSIA *Evenkia*
An autonomous district in Siberia named after its inhabitants, the Evenk or Evenki.

Everest, Mt (Nepalese: **Sagarmāthā**; Tibetan: **Chomolungma/Qomolangma**), NEPAL
DEVIDANGA, PEAK XV
Before the British began measuring the highest peaks in the Himalayas, the local name for the

mountain was Devidanga. It was called Peak XV by the British who were wary of giving a European name to a mountain that already had a local name. However, the temptation to give the highest peak in the world a name was too great and in 1865 it was renamed after Sir George Everest (1790–1866), an English East India military engineer and the surveyor-general of India (1830–43). It had been calculated to be the highest in the world in 1852 (although this was not made public until 1856 when it was first measured) by Andrew (later Major General Sir Andrew) Waugh (1810–78), Everest's successor; it was Waugh who proposed the new name. Waugh, a lieutenant in 1843, was promoted to surveyor-general over Captain Robert Shortrede, nine years his senior, on Everest's strong recommendation. Had seniority prevailed and Shortrede become surveyor-general despite Everest's opposition, it is highly unlikely that he would have suggested Everest for the new name of Peak XV. The Nepalese name represents 'Sky Head' or 'Whose Head touches the Sky' which has roughly the same meaning as the Tibetan 'Goddess Mother of the World' from *chomo* 'goddess', *lang* 'world' (literally 'elephant' to represent the world) and *ma* 'mother'. According to legend, the goddess who lives on Everest is Miyolangsangma. The summit was reached for the first time in 1953.

Everett, CANADA, USA
1. USA (Massachusetts): previously South Malden when it was founded in 1649, it was renamed in 1870 after Edward Everett (1794–1865), governor of the state (1835–39), US minister to England (1841–5), secretary of state (1852) and a senator (1853–4).
2. USA (Pennsylvania): named after Edward Everett.
3. USA (Washington): named after Everett Colby, the son of a local landowner.

Everglades, FLORIDA/USA
A vast marshland whose present name is a rough translation of the Native American name Pa-May-Okee 'Grassy Water'.

Evesham, ENGLAND/UK *Eveshomme*
'Land in a River Bend belonging to Ēof' from an Old English personal name and *hamm*. The town lies in a bend of the River Avon.

Évians-les-Bains, RHÔNE-ALPES/FRANCE *Aygueani*
A spa whose name is ultimately derived from the Latin *aqua* 'water' with Les Bains 'The

Baths'. It gives its name to the well known Evian mineral water.

Évreux, UPPER NORMANDY/FRANCE *Civitas Eburovicum*
Named by the Romans after the Eburovices, a Gaulish tribe who inhabited the area, and from whom the present name is derived. Their name comes from the Gaulish *eburo* 'yew tree'.

Excelsior, USA
A town, mountains and another town called Excelsior Springs, after its medicinal springs, with Excelsior derived from the Latin *excelsus* 'lofty', 'sublime', or 'noble'.

Exeter, CANADA, UK, USA
1. UK (England): '(Roman) Town on the (River) Exe' from *ceaster* and a Celtic river name. It was originally named Isca Dumnoniorum by the Romans after the Dumnonii tribe, with Isca being the river name and meaning 'the water'. The Saxons changed the name to Exanceaster, the name Isca giving way to Exe with the same meaning. In the Domesday Book (1086) the name appears as Execestre.
2. USA (New Hampshire): founded in 1638 by the Revd John Wheelwright who was a member of the Exeter Combination which took its title from the English city.

Exmouth, AUSTRALIA, UK
1. Australia (Western Australia): named after Exmouth Gulf which itself was named after Admiral Edward Pellew (1757–1833), 1st Viscount Exmouth by Lieutenant Phillip King who surveyed the coast in 1818.
2. UK (England): formerly Exanmouthe 'Mouth of the (River) Exe' from the Old English *mūtha*.

Extremadura, SPAIN
An autonomous community also spelt Estremadura. During the slow Christian Reconquest the name was used to describe those areas, generally along the River Duero, not under Moorish control; actual borders varied in line with events on the battlefield. Towards the end of the 11th century it took on a slightly different meaning: the 'Land beyond the (River) Duero', a reference to newly conquered territory further south.

Eyre, AUSTRALIA, NEW ZEALAND
Australia (South Australia): Australia's largest salt lake named after Edward Eyre (1815–1901), a British explorer who first sighted it in 1840. He later held governorships in New Zealand, St Vincent in the West Indies, and Jamaica.

Faenza, EMILIA-ROMAGNA/ITALY *Faventia*
Derived from its Roman name which means
'favourable' in the sense that it is located in a
very fertile area. It has given its name to
faïence, richly coloured glazed pottery.

Faeroe Islands, DENMARK
See FAROE ISLANDS.

Faial Island (Ilha do Faial), AZORES/PORTUGAL
'Beech Wood Island' from *faial* 'beech wood'.
However, this was an inaccurate description
by those who named the island because the
beech trees were in fact wax myrtle.

Fairbanks, ALASKA/USA
Founded in 1902 and named after Senator
Charles W. Fairbanks (1852–1918), later
Vice President (1905–9). Fairbanks led
a commission in 1903 to settle a dispute
with Canada over the boundary
between British Columbia and the Alaskan
panhandle.

Fairfax, USA *Earp's Corner*
Virginia: renamed in 1859 after Thomas
Fairfax (1692–1782), 6th Baron Fairfax of
Cameron, who had inherited the Northern
Neck of Virginia (an area between the Potomac
and Rappahannock Rivers, including the
Shenandoah Valley).

Fairfield, USA
1. California: named in 1859 by Robert
Waterman after his hometown in
Connecticut.
2. Connecticut: founded in 1639, it was
named after Fairfield in Kent, England, from
where an early settler came.
3. There are at least twenty cities and towns
with this name, many simply to describe the
beauty of the site.

Fair Isle, SCOTLAND/UK *Fridarey, Fáröy*
'Island of Sheep' from the Old Scandinavian *fár*
'sheep' and *ey*.

Fairmont, WEST VIRGINIA/USA *Middletown*
Founded in 1820, Middletown merged with
Palatine in 1843 to form Fairmont; so-called
because of its location on a hill.

Fairplay, COLORADO/USA
Founded and named by gold miners as a
reproof to their aggressively acquisitive
neighbours.

Fairweather, BRITISH COLUMBIA/CANADA
Mount Fair Weather
A mountain seen by Captain James Cook[†] in
1778 who was sailing offshore in 'fair
weather'.

Faisalābād, PUNJAB/PAKISTAN *Lyallpur*
Founded in 1890 and named 'Lyall's Town'
after Sir Charles Lyall (1845–1920), lieutenant-
governor of the Punjab with the additional *pur*.
In 1979 it was renamed 'Faisal's Town' after
Faisal (*c*.1906–75), King of Saudi Arabia
(1964–75).

Fakel, KIROV/RUSSIA
'Torch' or 'Flare' to signify a 'guiding light'.

Fakenham, ENGLAND/UK *Fachenham*
'Facca's Homestead' from a possible Old
English personal name and *hām*.

Falkirk, SCOTLAND/UK *Egglesbreth, Varie Capelle,*
Faukirke
'(Place of) the Speckled Church', that is, a
church built with mottled stone from Old
English *fāg* 'multi-coloured' and *cirice* 'church'.
The three former names, Gaelic, Latin and Old
French, all have the same meaning.

Falkland Islands (Spanish: **Islas Malvinas**),
UK *Davis Land, Hawkins Maidenland*
An Overseas Territory of the UK also called
Islas Malvinas by the Spanish-speaking
Argentinians. This name, given by French seal
hunters in 1764 when the first colony was
established, is derived from Isles Malouines
after the French port of St Malo from which
the French came. The English navigator, John
Davis, may have been the first European to see
the islands in 1592 and they were briefly
named after him. Two years later Sir Richard
Hawkins (*c*.1560–1622), a naval adventurer,
sighted them and gave them the name
Hawkins Maidenland in honour of Queen
Elizabeth I[†]. Nevertheless, it was Captain John
Strong who was the first to land in 1690. He
named the Sound between the two main
islands after Anthony Cary (1656–94), 5th
Viscount Falkland, who was the British Royal
Navy's treasurer and who had given financial
approval for the expedition. The British,
French, and Spanish all made settlements on
East and West Falkland during the second half
of the 18th century, but the British retained

their claim to the islands. In 1820, by which time all the early settlements had been abandoned, Argentina declared its sovereignty over the Falklands and began to colonize them. In 1831, however, the USA precipitated the eviction of the Argentinians and in 1833 the British arrived to complete the process. Within eight years a British lieutenant-governor had been appointed. In 1892 the Falkland Islands became a British crown colony. In 1982 Argentinian forces invaded the islands, but ten weeks later surrendered to the British.

Fall River, CANADA, USA
USA (Massachusetts): a city previously called Fallriver and then Troy, it readopted its original name in 1831. This was derived from the Quequechan name which meant 'falling water'.

Falls Church, VIRGINIA/USA
Named after an Episcopal church built in the 18th century on the site of an earlier church near the Great Falls of the River Potomac.

Falmouth, ANTIGUA, CANADA, JAMAICA, UK, USA
1. UK (England): formerly Falemouth 'Mouth of the River Fal' from a river name and *mūtha*.
2. USA (Massachusetts): settled by some Quakers in 1661 who retained its Native American name of Succanessett. In 1664 it was renamed after the port in England from where some of the settlers had come.

False Bay (Afrikaans: **Valsbaai**), WESTERN CAPE/SOUTH AFRICA
So named because navigators used to confuse this bay with Table Bay to the north, beyond the Cape of Good Hope.

Falster, DENMARK *Falstriam*
An island whose name is derived from the Old Danish *fjala* 'hiding place'.

Falun, SWEDEN
Probably 'Treeless Plain' in Swedish, a reference to the nature of its terrain.

Famagusta (Greek: **Ammókhostos**; Turkish: **Mağusa/Gazimağusa**), CYPRUS *Arsinoe*
Founded during the reign of Ptolemy II Philadelphus[†] and named after his wife; it is not known which one since he had two, both called Arsinoë (the second one being his sister). The name may be a Frankish corruption of the Greek name which could mean 'Buried in the Sand', a reference to the mouth of the River Pedieos which became choked with sand, from the Greek *ammos* 'sand' and *khôstos* 'built up', or '(Town by the) Sand Dune'. Some sources claim that the present name is derived from

Fama Augusta, possibly the 'Pride of Augustus' after Emperor Augustus[†]. The town was held by the Ottoman Turks between 1571 and 1878 when the British assumed responsibility for the administration of Cyprus. The island gained its independence in 1960, but in 1974 the Turks invaded and seized the town. It is now in the region called the Turkish Republic of Northern Cyprus.

Fano, MARCHE/ITALY *Fanum Fortunae*
Takes its name from its earlier Latin name meaning the 'Temple of Fortune'.

Farāh, AFGHANISTAN *Alexandria Prophthasia, Phrada*
Named after the Farāh River, having been founded by Alexander III the Great[†].

Far East The eastern countries of the Old World, now East Asia; in particular, China, Japan, North and South Korea, the Philippines, and Indonesia.

Fareham, ENGLAND/UK *Fearnham*
'Village where Ferns grow' from the Old English *fearn* 'fern' and *hām*.

Fargo, NORTH DAKOTA/USA
Founded in 1871 and named after William G. Fargo (1818–81), a leading specialist in express delivery and a founder of Wells, Fargo & Co. in 1852.

Faribault, MINNESOTA/USA
Founded in 1826 by, and named after, Alexander Faribault, a French fur trader with the Sioux.

Farīdābād, HARYĀNA/INDIA
Founded in 1607 by, and named after, Shaikh Farīd, the emperor's treasurer, to mean 'Farīd's Town' with the additional *ābād*.

Farīdkot, PUNJAB/INDIA
'Farīd's Fort' from *kot* 'fort'. The Farīd refers to Farīd al-Dīn Gandj-Shakar (*c.*1175–1225), a distinguished Muslim mystic.

Farīdpur, BANGLADESH
'Farīd's Town' after a Muslim saint, Farīd-ud-Dīn Mas'ūd, who is buried here, with the additional *pur*.

Farmington, UK, USA
1. UK (England): a village whose former name, Tormington, may have meant 'Farmstead near the Pool where Thorn Trees Grow' from *thorn*, *mere* 'pool', and *tūn*.
2. USA (Connecticut): originally Tunxis and renamed in 1645 after the Farmington in England.
3. USA (Maine): so named because it was located in good farming country.

Farnborough, ENGLAND/UK *Ferneberga*
(*Hampshire*)
'Hill covered in Ferns' from the Old English
fearn 'fern' or 'bracken' and *beorg*.

Farnham, CANADA, UK, USA
1. Canada and USA: the towns in Quebec,
Canada, and Virginia, USA, are named after the
Farnham in Surrey, England.
2. UK (England): 'Farmstead where Ferns
grow' from *fearn* and *hām*.
3. USA (New York): named after Le Roy
Farnham, an early trader.

Faro, PORTUGAL *Ossonoba, Santa Maria de
Ossonoba, Ukhshunuba, Shantamariyyat al-Gharb,
Santa Maria de Hárune*
A district and a town. To the name of the
Roman town was added St Mary by the
Christian Visigoths when they arrived in this
part of the Iberian Peninsula. After taking the
town in 713, the Moors gave the town their
version of the Roman name before renaming it
Shantamariyyat al-Gharb 'St Mary of the West'
in the 10th century; in the 11th century they
renamed it after one of their princes,
Muhammad bin Said bin Hārūn, the town's
governor (1026–42). The town was recaptured
from the Moors in 1249 by Afonso III (1210–
79), King of Portugal (1248–79), who
completed the conquest of the Algarve. Hārūn
was corrupted by the Christians to Faaron and
in due course this became Faro.

Faroe Islands (*Føroyar*; Danish: **Faerøerne**),
DENMARK *Faereyiar*
Also spelt Faeroe. 'Sheep Islands' from the
Faroese *før* 'sheep' and *oyar*, the plural of *oy*
'island'. Colonized by the Vikings *c*.800, the
islands became a Norwegian province in 1035;
Faroese is a direct descendant of Old
Scandinavian. Together with Norway, the
islands passed to Denmark in 1380.
Independence from Denmark was declared in
1945, but the Danish king dissolved the
Faroese regional parliament.

Farrukhābād, UTTAR PRADESH/INDIA
'City of Farrukh'. Founded in 1714 and named
after Muhammad Farrukh-Siyar who had
become the Emperor of Dihlī in 1713.

Fārs, IRAN *Pārs/Persis*
A province and an ancient region with a name
Arabized from the Old Persian Parsa. This
name was derived from a tribe known as the
Parsua, the ancestors of the Persians, who
settled in this part of south-central Iran in the
7th century BC.

Fāshir, al-, THE SUDAN
'The Courtyard in front of the Palace' from
fashr 'court'. This referred to an open area
where the sultan could hold public audiences.
The town grew up around the palaces of
successive Sultans of Darfur. In the late 18th
century the Fur Sultan of Darfur established
his court here.

Fastnet (Gaelic: **Carraig Aonair**), IRELAND
A rock off the south-west coast of Ireland with
a Gaelic name meaning 'Lone Rock'. It features
in the weather forecast for shipping in the
Atlantic.

Fatehpur Sīkri, UTTAR PRADESH/INDIA
A historical site with a name meaning 'City of
Victory (at) Sikri' from the Arabic *fath* 'victory'
or 'conquest'. Anxious that he might have no
male heir, Akbar[†], the Mughal emperor,
sought help from a Sufi Muslim saint, Shaikh
Salim Chisthī, who lived in Sīkri. He reassured
Akbar that he could father a son, and forecast
that the emperor's wives would give birth to
three sons; a year later in 1569 a boy (who
became Emperor Jahāngīr) was born and then
two more. In gratitude Akbar built a palace-
fort at Sīkri that year as his new capital and
renamed the site Fatehpur Sīkri. However, due
to the brackish nature of the local water, the
city had to be abandoned in 1586.

Fátima, PORTUGAL
Named after a 12th-century Moorish princess
who married a Portuguese nobleman after she
had converted to Christianity. She is buried in
the area. She will have been named after
Fatima (*c*.605–33), the daughter of the Prophet
Muhammad[†], who founded Islam. Since 1917,
when three children saw a vision of the Virgin
Mary, Fátima has been one of the world's
greatest shrines to the Virgin Mary and a place
of pilgrimage.

Fauresmith, FREE STATE/SOUTH AFRICA
Founded as a mission station in 1849, it was
later named after the Revd Philip Faure of the
Dutch Reformed Church, and Sir Harry Smith
(1787–1860), governor of Cape Colony (1847–
52).

Favara, SICILY/ITALY
'Gushing Spring' probably derived from the
Arabic *fār* or *fawwar* 'to boil' or 'gush forth'.

Faversham, ENGLAND/UK *Fefresham*
'Village of the Smith' from a possible Old
English word *fœfer* 'smith' and *hām*.

Fayetteville, USA
1. Arkansas: originally Washington Court
House and renamed in 1829 after the
Fayetteville in Tennessee.
2. North Carolina: Campbelltown and Cross
Creek merged in 1783 and together were
renamed after the Marquis de Lafayette

(1757–1834), a French aristocrat who fought with the Americans against the British during the American War of Independence (1775–83).

Fayyūm, al-, EGYPT *Madīnat al-Fayyūm*
'The Lake' from the Coptic *Fiom*; both *al-* and the initial *F* mean 'The' and *iom* 'lake'. The ancient Egyptians modified this to *pā-yom* with the same meaning; *al-* was only added later. The city lies in Egypt's largest oasis, also called al-Fayyūm (or el-Faiyūm), which was once a lake known as Birket Qārūn; it now comprises only about a fifth of the oasis on the north-western side and is known as Lake Moeris. The Greeks called the area Krokodeilōspolis because they considered the crocodiles to be sacred, and later Arsinoë after one of the wives of Ptolemy II Philadelphus[†]. The city is located in the rough centre of the dried-up part of Birket Qārūn. The name is also that of a governorate in Upper Egypt. The previous name meant 'Town of the Lake'.

Fécamp, UPPER NORMANDY/FRANCE *Fiscamnum*
Evolved from the Roman name which is derived from an Old German form for fish, *fisk*, and *hafn* 'harbour'. At one time cod fishing was a major industry.

Feira de Santana, BAHIA/BRAZIL *Feira de Sant'Anna*
Famous for its cattle fairs, it is clear from its original name that it means 'St Ann's Fair'.

Feldberg, BADEN-WÜRTTEMBERG/GERMANY
The highest peak in the Black Forest, its name means 'Field Mountain' from *Feld* and *Berg* to signify that its slopes are not tree-covered.

Feldkirch, AUSTRIA *Veldkirchae*
'Field Church' from the German *Feld* and *Kirche* 'church'.

Felipe Carillo Puerto, QUINTANA ROO/ MEXICO
Named after Quintana Roo's first socialist governor in the 1920s.

Felixstowe, ENGLAND/UK *Filchestou*
Possibly 'Filica's Meeting Place' from an Old English personal name and *stōw*. Local tradition later associated this name with that of St Felix (d. 647) of Dunwich, first bishop of the East Angles.

Feltre, VENETO/ITALY *Feltria*
Derived from *Felth(u)ri* with the suffix *-thuri* meaning the urban tribal centre of the Fel.

Feodosiya, CRIMEA/UKRAINE *Theodosia, Kaffa/ Kefe, Caiphun*
Founded by the Greeks in the 6th century BC with a name meaning 'God-given Place' from *theos* 'god'. In the 13th century the Genoese

arrived to establish a trading post and renamed the city Kaffa whose meaning is unknown. The town was captured by the Ottoman Turks in 1475 and by the Russians in 1783. In 1802 the Russian version of the old Greek name was imposed.

Ferentino, LAZIO/ITALY *Ferentinum*
An Etruscan urban tribal centre, it has a pre-Roman root *frent* which may be a variant of the Illyrian *brent* 'deer' or 'stag' to indicate a place where deer roamed.

Ferghana (Farghona), UZBEKISTAN *Novyy Margelan, Sim, Skobolev*
A province and city. The latter was founded in 1877 as the military and administrative centre of a new province to replace the recently conquered Khanate of Kokand. Until 1910 it was called New Margelan, named after the nearby, and very much older, Margelan (also Marghinen and Marghilan). For a short time in 1910 it was known as Sim 'wire', possibly to mark the arrival of the telephone. In 1910–24 it was renamed after General Mikhail Skobolev (1843–82), who played a leading role in the Russian conquest of Turkistan (1873–5, 1880–1) and fought against the Turks in 1877–8. The city became a part of the Uzbek Soviet Socialist Republic in 1924 and was renamed after the Ferghana Valley, from *pargana* 'curved valley', at that time.

Fergus Falls, MINNESOTA/USA
A city founded in 1857 and named after James Fergus who gave financial support to an expedition to the area.

Fermanagh (Fear Manach), NORTHERN IRELAND/UK
A district with a name meaning 'District of the Manaigh' who may have been monks.

Fermoy (Mainistir Fhear Maighe), IRELAND
'Monastery of the District of Fir Mhaí'. The name of the district means 'Men of the Plain' from *magh* 'plain'.

Fernandina Beach, FLORIDA/USA
Founded in about 1680 by Spanish settlers who named it after Don Diego Fernández, a local landowner.

Fernando de Noronha Island, BRAZIL
In the Atlantic, it was discovered in 1504 by the Portuguese Fernando de Noronha and named after him.

Fernando Pó, EQUATORIAL GUINEA
See BIOKO.

Ferrara, EMILIA-ROMAGNA/ITALY *Forum Alieni*
The present name, derived from the original, may have a connection with a forge or

ironworks from the Latin *ferrarius* 'pertaining
to iron'. Alternatively, it might come from
ferraria 'land where *farro* "spelt" [a primitive
type of wheat used to prepare soups, but now
not used] is cultivated'. The earlier name
meant 'Market of the Foreigners' from the
Latin *alius* 'other' and here 'aliens'.

Ferryland, NEWFOUNDLAND/CANADA
Probably derived from the Portuguese *farelhão*
'small promontory'.

Fertile Crescent, MIDDLE EAST
A term coined by the American James
Henry Breasted (1865–1935) to describe the
crescent-shaped area stretching from the head
of the Persian Gulf along the Tigris and
Euphrates Valley to the Mediterranean coast
and then along it to Lower Egypt and the Nile
Valley. It was the most fertile part of the
Middle East and the cradle of the early
civilizations.

Fès (Fās), MOROCCO
Also spelt Fez. Accounts of the founding of the
city vary. One claims that Idrīss I, Moulay of
the first Islamic Kingdom of Morocco (789–91),
built an Arab city on the right bank of the
Wādī Fās in 789 at a junction of trade routes.
Fās is an Arabic version of the Berber *sàf* which
is an abbreviation of *isaffen*, the plural of *asif*
'river'. According to a popular legend,
however, while work was proceeding on the
excavations, a pick-axe, *fās*, of gold and silver
was found. It was used to demarcate the line of
the city's walls. Then, twenty years later, his
son, Idrīss II, Moulay (803–28), founded a
Berber city on the left bank. Another account
claims that it was Idrīss II who founded two
separate cities on either side of the river,
making them together the capital of the
kingdom. During Umayyad rule (980–1012)
Moors settled in the city on the right bank
while Tunisians settled on the left bank. In
1069 the Almoravids occupied Fès. They
dismantled part of the walls and erected a
single outer wall to merge the two cities. Fès
has given its name to the *fez*, a brimless, red
felt hat with a tassel, called a *tarbush* in Arabic.
Hearing that the Ottoman Sultan was keen to
abolish the turban with its Islamic
associations, Grand Admiral Koja Husrev
Mehmed Pasha returned from North Africa to
Constantinople (now Istanbul) in 1826 with
some samples. It was not long before Mahmud
II (1785–1839), Sultan (1808–39), issued the
order that all Ottoman Turks were henceforth
to wear the fez. It was abolished in 1925 by the
first president of the Turkish Republic, Kemal
Atatürk[†].

Fezzan, LIBYA *Phazania*
A historic desert region whose name has
evolved from the Roman Phazania, itself
named after the local Phazāni.

Fianarantsoa, MADAGASCAR
Founded in 1830, the name uses a
combination of Malagasy words, *fianàrana*
'school' or 'study' and *sòa* 'good', to give the
meaning of '(a place) where one learns what is
good'.

Ficksburg, FREE STATE/SOUTH AFRICA
Founded in 1867 as 'Fick's Town' and
named after Commandant General
Johan Fick (1816–92), leader of the Orange
Free States in their conflict with the Basuto
in 1865–8.

Fidenza, EMILIA-ROMAGNA/ITALY *Fidentia Iulia,
Borgo San Donnino*
Believed to be the site of martyrdom of St
Domninus *c.*300, it was renamed after him,
borgo meaning 'small town' or 'village'. In 1927
an Italian version of its ancient name was
adopted. The 1st century Fidentia
demonstrated good omens and comes from
the Latin *fides* 'faith' or 'trust'.

Fiji (Viti)
The Republic of the Fiji Islands since 1998.
Previously the Sovereign Democratic Republic
of Fiji (1987–98) and before that simply Fiji. It
was first discovered in 1643 by the Dutch
explorer Abel Tasman[†] and visited by Captain
James Cook[†] in 1774. Fiji was ceded to the UK
in 1874, becoming a crown colony. It achieved
independence in 1970. It takes its name from
its largest island, Viti Levu, 'Great Fiji'. The
meaning of Fiji itself is not known, but as the
Tongan version of Viti, it was used by Cook.

Filipstad, SWEDEN
Named as 'Philip's Town' after Charles Philip
(Karl Filip) (1601–22), Duke of Södermanland
and son of Charles IX, King of Sweden.

Fillmore, CANADA, USA
USA (Utah): settled in 1851 and named after
Millard Fillmore (1800–74), President of the
USA (1850–3).

Findlay, OHIO/USA
Founded in 1821 and named after Fort Findlay,
built by Colonel James Findlay.

Finistère, BRITTANY/FRANCE
A department with a name derived from the
Latin *finis terrrae* 'land's end'.

Finisterre, GALICIA/SPAIN
The westernmost point of Spain, it means
'Land's End' (*see* FINISTÈRE) or 'End of the
Earth', so-called by sailors. The Cape is called

Cabo Finisterre. In British shipping forecasts Finisterre was replaced by FitzRoy in February 2002 because Spain and the UK agreed to differ on the definition of the area. FitzRoy is named in honour of Vice Admiral Robert FitzRoy (1805–65), commander of HMS *Beagle*, governor of New Zealand (1843–45) and founder of the British Meteorological Office in 1853.

Finland (Suomi), AND USA
The Republic of Finland (Finnish: Suomen Tasavalta; Swedish: Republiken Finland) since independence in 1917. Previously an autonomous grand duchy within the Russian Empire (1809–1917), having been ceded by Sweden after a Russian invasion in 1808; an integral part of Sweden (1634–1809) although occupied by the Russians between 1713–21; a grand duchy within Sweden (1581–1634). At the Treaty of Pähkinäsaari (now Schlisselburg, Russia) in 1323 Finland was confirmed as part of the Swedish kingdom, settling the territorial competition between the Swedes and Russians. It became a Swedish province in 1362. During most of the period of Swedish rule, Swedish was the language of government, education, and culture. The Finnish name may come from *suo* 'marsh' and *maa* 'land' in reference to the country's many lakes. Alternatively, it may come from the Old Swedish *somi* 'mass', meaning that the Swedes at one time considered the Finns to be inferior, 'the masses'. The English 'Finland', the 'Land of the Finns', may be from the Germanic (or Teutonic Scandinavian) *finna* 'fish scale', which is *suomu* in Finnish. This could be a reference to the type of clothing worn by the primitive Finnish tribes. The Fenni was the original name given to the Lapps, otherwise known as the Sami, by Tacitus in his *Germania* in 98. The term 'Finlandization' describes a policy of neutrality under the umbrella of the Soviet Union; it originated from that policy practised by the Finnish government during the cold war (1945–90).

Finningley, ENGLAND/UK *Feniglei, Feningelay*
'Fen Dwellers' Woodland Clearing' from the Old English *fenn*, *-inga-*, and *lēah* 'woodland clearing'.

Finnmark, NORWAY
A county whose name means 'Borderland of the Finns' from the Norwegian *finne* and *mark* 'march' or 'borderland'.

Finschhafen, PAPUA NEW GUINEA
Named in 1894 after the German explorer Otto Finsch to mean 'Finsch's Port' from *Hafen* 'port'.

Finsteraarhorn, SWITZERLAND
The highest peak in the Bernese Alps with a name meaning 'Peak of the dark (River) Aar' from *finster* 'dark' or 'obscure' and *Horn* 'peak' or 'top'. The river is obscure because of the ice covering it.

Finsterwalde, BRANDENBURG/GERMANY
'(Place of) the Dark Wood' from *finster* 'dark' and *Wald* 'wood'.

Fīrozpur, PUNJAB/INDIA
Also spelt Ferozepore. Founded in the 14th century during the reign of Fīrūz Shah Tughluq (1351–88) after whom it was named the 'Town of Fīruz' with *pur*.

Firozpur Jhirka, HARYĀNA/INDIA
Also spelt Ferozepur. Said to be founded by, and named after, Fīrūz Shah III.

Fīrūzābād, IRAN *Gūr*
Probably founded by Ardashīr I, Sāssānian king (224–41), in celebration of his victory over the Parthians; the city's name means 'City of Victory'. The name was changed in the 10th century from the previous Persian name which meant 'tomb' because of its disagreeable associations.

Fishguard (Abergwaun), WALES/UK *Fissigart, Fissegard, Aber gwein*
'Fish Yard' from the Old Scandinavian *fiskr* and *garthr* 'yard', possibly to indicate a place where fish were stored. The Welsh name means '(Place at the) Mouth of the (River) Gwaun' from the Old Welsh *aber* and *gwaun* 'marsh'.

Fitchburg, MASSACHUSETTS/USA *Turkey Hills*
Settled in 1740 and renamed after John Fitch, a leading member of the committee that organized the incorporation of the town in 1764.

Fitzroy, AUSTRALIA, UK
1. Australia (Western Australia): a river named in 1838 by Lieutenant John Stokes of HMS *Beagle* in honour of Vice Admiral Robert Fitzroy (1805–65), a British naval officer who commanded the *Beagle* (1828–30, 1831–6) and was governor of New Zealand (1843–5).
2. Australia (Queensland): a river and an offshore island named after Sir Charles Fitzroy (1796–1858), governor of New South Wales (1846–50), which at this time included this area, and governor of Australia (1850–5).
3. UK (Falkland Islands): on East Falkland, it is named after Vice Admiral Robert Fitzroy who commanded HMS *Beagle* when it made its round-the-world voyage in 1831–6.

Flagstaff, ARIZONA/USA
So-named because a group of immigrants, celebrating the first centenary of the American

Declaration of Independence on 4 July 1776, nailed a national flag to a tall pine tree and called their settlement, which until then had no name, Flagstaff.

Flakstadøya, LOFOTEN ISLANDS/NORWAY
Vargfot
An island whose previous name meant 'Wolf's Paw'. The present name may be derived from *flag* 'cliff'.

Flamborough, CANADA, UK
UK (England): formerly Flaneburg 'Fleinn's Stronghold' from an Old Scandinavian personal name and the Old English *burh*.

Flanders (Flemish: **Vlaanderen**; French: **Flandre**), BELGIUM-FRANCE-THE NETHERLANDS
A medieval region now divided between three countries. The Belgian region of Flanders has five provinces of which two are East and West Flanders. In France it is part of the Nord department and in the Netherlands of the province of Zeeland. The name probably means 'Lowland' or 'Land subject to Flooding'. The Flemish name means much the same from *vlakte* 'plain' and *wanderen* 'to wander', thus a large flat area.

Flathead, MONTANA/USA
A lake and mountain range named after the Flathead people, originally known as the Salish. They acquired the name 'Flathead' because they did not deform the shape of their heads like some other tribes.

Fleet, ENGLAND/UK
'(Place at) the Stream, or the Pool' from the Old English *flēot*.

Fleetwood, AUSTRALIA, UK, USA
1. UK (England): founded by, and named after, Sir Peter Fleetwood (1801–66), MP for Preston (1832–47), who laid out the town on his estate of Rossall in 1836. He changed his name by royal licence in 1831.
2. USA (Pennsylvania): originally Coxtown and renamed in 1859 after Sir Peter Fleetwood (1801–66) who did much to develop the railroad.

Flensburg, SCHLESWIG-HOLSTEIN/GERMANY
Flensaaburgh
'Fortification at the Flensaa Pointed River' from the Old Danish *flen* 'fork point' and Old High German *aha* 'river' or 'water'.

Flevoland, THE NETHERLANDS
A province, the name for which is taken from the Roman Lacus Flavo which referred to the Zuider Zee, the Southern Sea.

Flinders, AUSTRALIA
Islands, off South Australia and Tasmania, and the Flinders Group off Queensland, are all named after Matthew Flinders[†] who explored the coasts of Australia in 1795 and 1801–3. Also named after him are the Flinders Ranges in South Australia, the Flinders River in Queensland, Flinders Peak in Victoria, and Flinders Bay off Western Australia.

Flin Flon, MANITOBA/CANADA
Took its name in 1915 from a fictional Professor Flintabbatey Flonatin in the novel *The Sunless City* by J. E. Preston-Muddock.

Flint, UK, USA
1. UK (Wales): there is a unitary district called Flintshire, often called Flint, a reference to the nature of the rock on which a castle was built in 1277 by Edward I (1239–1307), King of England (1272–1307).
2. USA (Michigan): founded as a trading post in 1819, it was named in 1836 after the river, called by the local Native Americans Pawanunling 'River of Flint'.

Florence, CANADA, ITALY, USA
1. Italy (Tuscany): locally Firenze 'Flowering City' or 'City of Flowers' from the Old Italian *fiorenza*, itself from the Latin *florere* 'to blossom', perhaps because the city was built on a flowery meadow. Founded in 59 BC as a Roman military garrison, its Latin name Florentia meant 'The Flourishing Town'. A republic during the 15th century, it was the capital of Italy 1865–71. The 'Flo' of Florentia evolved through 'Fio' to 'Fi'.
2. USA (Alabama): founded in 1818 and named after the Florence in Italy by its Italian planner, Ferdinand Sanona.
3. USA (Arizona): founded in 1866 and named after the sister of Governor Richard McCormick.
4. USA (South Carolina): originally founded in the 1850s as Wilds, it was renamed in about 1859 after the daughter of General William Harlee, a senior railroad official.

Florenceville, NEW BRUNSWICK/CANADA
Named after Florence Nightingale (1820–1910), the English nurse who pioneered nursing training for women and who became famous for her medical care during the Crimean War (1854–6). She was called Florence because she was born in that Italian city.

Flores, BRAZIL, ECUADOR, GUATEMALA, INDONESIA, PORTUGAL, URUGUAY
1. Indonesia: one of the Lesser Sunda Islands, it was first sighted in 1512 by the Portuguese navigator, Antonio de Abreu, who called a cape at the eastern end of the island Capo de Flores 'Cape of Flowers' from which the whole island was subsequently named. To the north is the Flores Sea, named after the island.

2. An island in the Azores archipelago, Portugal, and a river in Brazil have the same name, 'Flowers'.

Floreşti, MOLDOVA, ROMANIA
Named after Florya, a personal name with the possessive suffix -*eşti* to give 'Florya's (Place)'.

Floriano, PIAUÍ/BRAZIL
Named after Marshal Floriano Peixoto (1842–95), Brazilian president (1891–94), who brought stability to the country.

Florianópolis, SANTA CATARINA/BRAZIL
Desterro
In 1700 the Portuguese founded a convict settlement with the name Desterro 'exile'. In 1893 the city lies, was captured by opponents of the Brazilian president, Floriano Peixoto (*see* FLORIANO). The insurrection collapsed, however, and the city, 'Floriano's City', was renamed after him.

Florida, ARGENTINA, BOLIVIA, CUBA, SOLOMON ISLANDS, URUGUAY, USA
USA: a state. Because Juan Ponce de León (1460–1521), the Spanish explorer, discovered the Florida peninsula at Easter time in 1513 and because of the lush vegetation, he named the area Florida from the Spanish *Pascua Florida* 'Easter of Flowers' or 'Flowering Easter'. In 1763 Spain ceded Florida to England in exchange for Havana, Cuba, and twenty years later England returned it in exchange for the Bahamas. In 1819 a treaty was signed which ceded Florida to the USA with effect from 1821. It became a territory, and in 1845 the 27th state. In 1861 Florida seceded from the Union, not rejoining until 1868. It gives its name to an island chain known as the Florida Keys.

Florissant, MISSOURI/USA *St Ferdinand*
Founded by the French c.1785, it was renamed from the French *fleurissant* 'flowering' in 1939.

Flushing (Vlissingen), THE NETHERLANDS, USA
1. The Netherlands: the conventional English name stems from the local name which means 'flowing'. The town is situated at the mouth of the western Scheldt estuary.
2. USA: there are three cities with this name; certainly the one in New York City, founded in 1645, was called Vlissingen by early Dutch settlers.

Fly, DENMARK, PAPUA NEW GUINEA, USA
Papua New Guinea: a river named in 1842 by Captain F. P. Blackwood after his ship, HMS *Fly*, after he had charted the Gulf of Papua and explored the river's estuary.

Foča, SERBIA/SERBIA AND MONTENEGRO
May be derived from the Turkish *fiçi* 'barrel'.

Foça, TURKEY. *Phocaea*
An ancient Ionian city which may take its name from Phocus, the colony's leader. In Greek mythology, he appeared to his father in the form of a seal (in Greek, *phóke*), hence his name. It may be, however, that the place gets its name from the large number of seals that used to be found here.

Foggia, APULIA/ITALY
May come from the Latin *fovea* 'hole' or 'pit' used for the storage of grain, or a deep water reservoir. *Fogge* is a local Apulian version of *fossa* 'pit' or 'ditch'.

Fokino, BRYANSK/RUSSIA *Tsementny*
Originally 'Cement' because of its cement works, it was renamed in 1964 after Ignaty Fokin (1889–1919), a Bolshevik revolutionary and bureaucrat.

Foligno, UMBRIA/ITALY *Fulginium*
According to tradition, the town is named after Bishop Feliciano who was martyred and buried here c.251. A small church was built and later, surrounded by a wall and towers, it became the 'Castle of St Feliciani' and then the 'Town of St Feliciani'. The name evolved into Fulginae with the Roman town being called Fulginium.

Folkestone, ENGLAND/UK *Folcanstan, Fulchestan*
'Folca's Stone' from an Old English personal name and *stãn*. The 'stone' here means a meeting place within the hundred (a territorial subdivision).

Fond du Lac, CANADA, USA
1. Canada (Saskatchewan): has much the same meaning as the American town (see 2), although it is not located at the end of Lake Athabasca.
2. USA (Wisconsin): founded as a French trading post in 1785, it was given a name to indicate its position '(at the) end of the lake', this being at the southern end of Lake Winnebago.

Fondi, LAZIO/ITALY *Fundi*
Possibly from the Latin *fundus* 'estate' or 'farm'. According to legend, it was founded following the slaughter by Hercules of Cacus, a three-headed monster who stole his cows. Hercules erected a temple to Jupiter here in celebration of his success and an annual festival was held thereafter.

Fontainebleau, ÎLE-DE-FRANCE/FRANCE
Fontem Blahaud
Derived fom the Latin *fons*, genitive *fontis* 'spring' or 'fountain' and a Germanic personal name. Originally a 12th-century royal hunting lodge, it was developed into a town during the 16th century.

Fontenay-le-Comte, PAYS DE LA LOIRE/
FRANCE *Fontanetum*
Derived from the Latin *fons*, genitive *fontis*
'spring' or 'fountain'. *Le Comte* 'The Count' was
added by Louis IX (1214–70), saint and King of
France (1226–70), when he appointed a count
at Fontenay.

Forbach, LORRAINE/FRANCE
Derived from the German *Föhre*, itself from
fohra 'picea', a tree of the pine family, and *Bach*
'stream'.

Forbes, AUSTRALIA, CANADA, USA
1. Australia (New South Wales): named in
1861 after Sir Francis Forbes (1784–1841), the
chief justice of New South Wales (1823–36).
2. Canada (Alberta): a mountain named after
the Scottish scientist, Professor James Forbes
(1809–68), who was an authority on heat.

Forbidden City, BEIJING/CHINA
The Imperial Palace complex within the city of
Beijing which was barred to commoners and
foreigners without special permission.

Fordingbridge, ENGLAND/UK *Fordingebrige*
'Bridge of the People living by the Ford' from
ford, *-inga-*, and *brycg*.

Forli, EMILIA-ROMAGNA/ITALY *Forum Livii*
A market place, 'Livius's Market', was
founded in 188 BC by, and named after, the
Roman general and consul Marcus Livius
Salinator.

Formby, ENGLAND/UK *Fornebei*
'Forni's Farmstead', possibly from an Old
Scandinavian personal name and *bý*.

Formentera, BALEARIC ISLANDS/SPAIN
An island whose name is derived from the
Catalan *forment* 'wheat', itself from the Latin
frumentum 'corn' or 'grain' to give 'Wheat
Island'.

Formia, LAZIO/ITALY *Formiae, Mola di Gaeta*
Derived from the Latin *formus* 'hot'. The
previous name meant the 'Mill of Gaeta', a
town on the Gulf of Gaeta.

Formosa, ARGENTINA, BRAZIL, GUINEA-BISSAU,
SOUTH AFRICA
'Beautiful' in Portuguese. A province and a
town in Argentina, a town in Brazil, an island
off Guinea-Bissau, and a peak in Western Cape,
South Africa. *See* TAIWAN.

Forrest City, ARKANSAS/USA
Founded in 1866 by, and named after, Nathan
Bedford Forrest, a Confederate general and
arguably the best cavalry general on either side
in the Civil War (1861–5).

Forst, BRANDENBURG/GERMANY
'Forest'.

Fortaleza, CEARÁ/BRAZIL *Villa do Forte da
Assumpção*
'Fortress' in Portuguese. It takes its name from
the adjacent fort built in 1654 to provide
protection against attack by local Native
Americans.

Fort Augustus, SCOTLAND/UK *Kilcumein/Cille
Chuimein*
Originally named 'Culmein's Church' after
Culmein, one of the followers of the
charismatic St Columba (*c*.521–97), who
was buried here. Developed in the 1730s
around a military garrison established to
help quell the Jacobite rebellion, it was
renamed after William Augustus (1721–65),
Duke of Cumberland and second son of
King George II[†]. He was nicknamed
'Butcher Cumberland' as a result of his
actions after the Battle of Culloden in the final
suppression of the Jacobite rebellion in
Scotland in 1745.

Fort Beaufort, EASTERN CAPE/SOUTH AFRICA
Developed in 1837 from a fort of the same
name which was built as a defence
against the Xhosa in 1822 and named
after the Duke of Beaufort, father of Lord
Charles Somerset, governor of Cape Colony
(1814–26).

Fort Collins, COLORADO/USA
Developed in the mid-1860s from a military
post named after its commander, Lieutenant
William O. Collins (1809–80).

Fort-de-France, MARTINIQUE *Fort-Royal*
'Fort of France' to indicate its allegiance. It has
been the capital of Martinique since 1680.

Fort Dodge, IOWA/USA *Fort Clarke*
Renamed in 1851 after Henry Dodge, a US
senator from Wisconsin, who had fought
against the Native Americans.

Fort Edward, NEW YORK/USA
Named after an old fort built in 1709 and
named in honour of Edward (1739–67), Duke
of York.

Fort Frances, ONTARIO/CANADA *Fort Saint-
Pierre*
Originally a fur trading post built in 1731, it
was renamed in 1830 after the wife of Sir
George Simpson (1792–1860), general
superintendent of the Hudson's Bay Company
in Canada and governor of Rupert's Land from
1821.

Fort George, GRENADA, TOBAGO, UK
UK (Scotland): the Gaelic name is An
Gearasdan 'The Garrison'. Built after the
Jacobite rebellion in 1745, the fort was named
as a tribute to King George II[†].

Fort Kent, MAINE/USA
Developed from a fort which was named after Governor Edward Kent of Maine in 1839.

Fort Lauderdale, FLORIDA/USA
Developed in 1895 from a fort, built in 1838 and named after its commander, Major William Lauderdale, commander of a force opposing the Seminole.

Fort Macleod, ALBERTA/CANADA *Macleod*
Developed from a fort built by, and named after, Colonel James F. Macleod in 1874. The town was simply called Macleod until 1952 when 'Fort' was added.

Fort McMurray, ALBERTA/CANADA *Fort of the Forks, McMurray*
Established as a fur trading post in 1790 at the confluence of the Athabasca and Clearwater Rivers, hence its first name. It was rebuilt and renamed in 1875 after an employee of the Hudson's Bay Company, William McMurray.

Fort Madison, IOWA/USA
Named after James Madison (1751–1836), President of the USA (1809–17).

Fort Morgan, COLORADO/USA
Named after a fort built in 1864 which was named after Colonel Christopher A. Morgan who fought in the Civil War (1861–5).

Fort Munro, PUNJAB/PAKISTAN
A hill station founded by Sir Robert Sandeman and named after Colonel Thomas Munro, a district commissioner who had been one of those promoting the 'Forward' policy of the English East India Company: to extend the Company's territories deep into the Indian hinterland and towards Afghanistan.

Fort Myers, FLORIDA/USA
Named after the fort built in 1839 to provide protection against the Seminole and named after Captain, later General, Abraham C. Myers (1811–89).

Fort Payne, ALABAMA/USA
Founded in 1836 and named after Captain John Payne who was involved in the forced migration of the Cherokee to the west during 1838–9; this was known as the 'Trail of Tears'.

Fort Pierce, FLORIDA/USA
Named after the fort built in 1838–42 during the Seminole Wars and named after Major, later Lieutenant Colonel, Benjamin K. Pierce.

Fort Pierre, SOUTH DAKOTA/USA
Claimed by the French in 1743 and named after a Frenchman, Pierre Choteau.

Fort Portal, UGANDA *Fort Gerry*
Named after Sir Gerald Portal (1858–94), a British diplomat in the 1880s, who was instructed to go to Uganda to explore the advisability of the British continuing to develop their presence in this part of Africa. They did so.

Fort Scott, KANSAS/USA
Developed from a military post built in 1842 and named after General Winfield Scott (1786–1866), commander-in-chief of the US Army (1841–61).

Fort Shevchenko, KAZAKHSTAN *Fort Novo Aleksandrovskiy, Fort Petrovsk/Novopetrovskoye, Fort Aleksandrovskiy*
The first fort was built in 1834 on the order of Emperor Nicholas I[†], but it was soon abandoned and replaced by Fort Petrovsk or Novopetrovskoye in 1846. This was renamed in 1857 after one of Nicholas's elder brothers, Emperor Alexander I[†]. Finally, in 1939 on the 125th anniversary of his birth, it was renamed Fort Shevchenko after the Ukrainian poet, Taras Shevchenko (1814–61), who spent 1850–7 in exile here.

Fort Smith, CANADA, USA
1. Canada (Northwest Territories): the southwestern region of the Northwest Territories created in the 1970s and a town settled in 1874 after the Hudson's Bay Company set up a trading post here and named it after Donald A. Smith (1820–1914), 1st Baron Strathcona and Mount Royal, a Canadian fur trader who was the governor of the Company (1889–1914).
2. USA (Arkansas): developed from a fort, built in 1817 on a site previously known as Belle Point, named after General Thomas A. Smith.

Fort Walton Beach, FLORIDA/USA
Developed from a fort built on the Gulf of Mexico to provide protection against the Seminole and named after Colonel George Walton. 'Beach' was added in 1953.

Fort Wayne, INDIANA/USA
Named after a wooden stockade built in 1794 by General Anthony Wayne (1745–96), who defeated the Northwest Confederation of Native American tribes at the Battle of Fallen Timbers in 1794.

Fort William (An Gearasdan), SCOTLAND/UK *Maryburgh*
The original earthen fort, built in 1654 to restrain the Highlanders, was rebuilt in stone the following year and named after Mary II (1662–94), Queen of England (1689–94), when she married William III[†] in 1677. A year after William and Mary ascended the throne together the name

was changed to honour William. The Gaelic name means 'The Garrison' (*see* FORT GEORGE).

Fort Worth, TEXAS/USA
Founded as a military post in 1849 against the Comanche, it was named after General William J. Worth (1794–1849), the American military commander in Texas at that time; he had earlier distinguished himself during the Mexican War (1846–8).

Foshan, GUANGDONG/CHINA *Nánhǎi*
'Buddha's Mountain' or 'Hill of the Buddhas' from *Fó* 'Buddha' and *shān*. According to legend, a monk placed three statues of Buddha in a hilltop shrine. The shrine later collapsed and the statues disappeared. Centuries later the statues were discovered during the Tang dynasty (618–907) and the shrine rebuilt. The city's former name meant 'Southern Sea' from *nán* and *hǎi*, it being in the Pearl River Delta. Nánhǎi is also the name of a county, but Foshan was established as a city separate from the county in 1949.

Fossano, PIEDMONT/ITALY
In popular tradition, the name is derived from the Latin *fons sana* 'healing fountain' from *fons* 'fountain'. However, it might be derived from the Latin *fossa* 'ditch' which might have been dug in or around the ancient settlement.

Fossombrone, MARCHE/ITALY *Forum Sempronii*
The present name is a corruption of the original which is named after Gaius Sempronius Gracchus (*c.*159–121 BC), a Roman tribune who was in the area in 133 BC to supervise the application of the agrarian law.

Fougères, BRITTANY/FRANCE *Fulgerii*
'Ferns' from the French *fougère* which can be traced to the Medieval Latin *filicaria*.

Foulness, ENGLAND/UK *Fughelnesse*
An island with a name meaning 'Promontory frequented by Birds' from the Old English *fugol* 'bird' and *næss* 'promontory'. The use of the word 'promontory' indicates that Foulness was at one time joined to the mainland and was not an island.

Foxton, NORTH ISLAND/NEW ZEALAND
Founded in 1855 and named after Sir William Fox (1812–93) who emigrated to New Zealand in 1842 and served four times as New Zealand's prime minister (1856, 1861–2, 1869–72, 1873).

Foz do Iguaçu, PARANÁ/BRAZIL
'Town of Great Waters' from the Portuguese *foz* 'river mouth' and the Tupí-Guaraní *i* 'water' and *guazú* 'great'. It is the site of spectacular waterfalls.

Framingham, MASSACHUSETTS/USA
Founded in 1650 and named after Framlingham in England. This name means the 'Homestead of the Followers of Framela' from a personal name, *-inga-* and *hām*.

France *Gaul, Francia*
The French Republic (République Française) since 1792. However, the monarchy was restored in 1814, but was overthrown in 1848 and replaced by the Second Republic. This lasted only until 1852 when Napoleon III (1808–73) took the title of Emperor. He was deposed in 1870 and the Third Republic was proclaimed. This survived until 1940. The Fourth Republic was instituted in 1946 and the Fifth in 1958. The name France is derived from a coalition of Germanic tribes, the Franks, who conquered Gaul (in Latin, Gallia, which also included parts of modern Belgium, western Germany, and northern Italy) during the 5th century after the fall of the Roman Empire. The name 'Frank' might have meant 'fierce' or 'brave' from an Old German word *franka* or it may have come from a personal name. Under the first Frankish dynasty, the Merovingians (481–751), Francia was the name for the area between the Rhine and Seine Rivers (*see* ÎLE-DE-FRANCE). Over a period of some nine centuries France acquired more and more territory, and it was only during the middle of the 18th century that French borders began to resemble what they are today; they took their final shape in 1919 when Alsace-Lorraine was ceded back to France from Germany. The Franks gave their name to the former French monetary unit, the franc; more than 30 other countries around the world use the same term. It has also been suggested that it has the connotation 'free' from the time in 1360 when John II the Good (1319–64), King of France (1350–64), minted new gold coins to pay his ransom in exchange for his freedom, having been captured by the English at the Battle of Poitiers in 1356. The people of the eastern Mediterranean lands used the term Franks to describe all those participating in the Crusades. The wooden shoes worn by the Gauls were called *solea Gallica* 'Gallic sandals' by the Romans, hence the word 'galoshes', waterproof overshoes. The English language uses the word 'French' in a number of phrases: for example, French bread, French dressing, French fries, and French kiss.

Franceville, GABON
Founded in 1880, and named the 'Town of France' after his country of adoption,

by Pierre Savorgnan de Brazza (1852–1905), an Italian-born count who became a French citizen in 1874.

Franche-Comté, FRANCE *Cisjurane-Burgundy*
A region meaning 'Free County'. It was the name given to the County of Burgundy (as opposed to the Duchy of Burgundy, now the Region of Burgundy) in 1137 after the count, Raynald (Reginald) III, had refused to pay allegiance to Lothair II (*c*.835–69), the Frankish King of Lotharingia. After a victorious struggle lasting ten years Raynald became known as the Free Count and the County of Burgundy was renamed.

Francistown, BOTSWANA *Nyangabgwe*
Renamed in 1869 after an English gold prospector, Daniel Francis (1840–1920), who was given land here by the canny Lobengula (*c*.1836–94), King of the Ndebele.

Franconia, NEW HAMPSHIRE/USA
Named after the Duchy of Franconia, itself named after the Franks, which was one of the principal duchies in medieval Germany.

Frankfort, SOUTH AFRICA, USA
1. South Africa (Free State): founded in 1869 and named after Frankfurt, the German city.
2. USA (Kentucky): founded in 1786, the name comes from Frank's Ford. Frank was Stephen Frank who was killed during a skirmish with Native Americans in 1780 at a place where the River Kentucky could be forded.

Frankfurt, GERMANY
1. To distinguish the two cities with this name, the rivers on which they lie are included: Frankfurt am Main 'Frankfurt on the Main' in Hesse, and Frankfurt an der Oder 'Frankfurt on the Oder' in Brandenburg.
2. Hesse: originally Franconofurt, the name means 'Ford where the Franks crossed (the River Main)' in pursuit of the Alemanni *c*.500. It was the capital of Germany 1816–66. It has given its name to a type of sausage, the frankfurter, also known as the wiener or hot dog and which originated here.

Franklin, CANADA, USA
1. There are 25 cities and towns with this name in the USA. Most, if not all, are named after Benjamin Franklin (1706–90), who did much to assist in the drafting of the Declaration of Independence and the US Constitution.
2. USA (Pennsylvania): originally a Native American village called Venango, forts were built on the site by the French, British, and Americans. The latter fort was called Fort

Franklin in 1787 after Benjamin Franklin. In 1795 a town was laid out around it.

Franschoek, WESTERN CAPE/SOUTH AFRICA
'French Corner' in Afrikaans, having been settled by Huguenots from France in 1688.

Františkovy Lázně, CZECH REPUBLIC *Egerbrunnen, Franzenbad*
'Franz's Springs' in German, both *Brunnen* and *Bad* meaning 'spring' or 'watering place', and in Czech. Famous for its springs since medieval times, it was renamed in 1793 after Francis I (1768–1835), Emperor of Austria (1804–35), who was also Francis II, the last Holy Roman Emperor (1792–1806).

Franz Josef Land (Zemlya Frantsa-Iosifa), RUSSIA
An archipelago of nearly 200 islands in the Barents Sea discovered in 1873 by an Austro-Hungarian expedition which named it after Franz Josef (Francis Joseph) (1830–1916), Emperor of Austria (1848–1916) and King of Hungary (1867–1916). The archipelago was annexed by the Soviet Union in 1926.

Frascati, LAZIO/ITALY
Derived from *frasca* 'branch' or 'bush' because the inhabitants had been given the right to go into the forest to cut branches, or simply because of the abundance of bushes and shrubs in the area.

Fraser, AUSTRALIA, CANADA
1. Australia (Queensland): an island also called Great Sandy Island. It is characterized by sand hills rising to almost 800ft (250 m). The island is named after Captain James Fraser who was killed with several companions by Aborigines in 1836.
2. Canada (British Columbia): a river named after Simon Fraser (1776–1862), a Canadian fur trader of the Northwest Company and an explorer who followed its course down to the sea in 1808, misguidedly believing it to be the Columbia River.

Fraserburgh, SCOTLAND/UK *Faithlie*
Originally a village, Faithlie was bought by the Fraser family in 1504 and became a chartered town in 1546. It was renamed Fraserburgh in 1592 after Alexander Fraser of Philorth.

Frauenfeld, SWITZERLAND
'Field of our Lady' from the German *frau* 'lady'.

Fray Bentos, URUGUAY
Founded in 1859 to mean 'Friar Benedict', a celebrated local hermit, from the Spanish *fray* 'friar' or 'brother'. Famous as a large meat-packing plant, the Fray Bentos brand of corned

beef took its name from the city-port when a London meat firm began operations here in 1864.

Fredericia, DENMARK *Friedrichsodde, Fridericia*
Founded as a fortress to defend Jutland in 1650 and named after Frederick III (1609–70), King of Denmark-Norway (1648–70).

Frederick, MARYLAND/USA
Settled in 1733 and called Frederick Town from 1745, it is allegedly named after Frederick Calvert (1731–71), 6th Baron Baltimore. However, it is possible that it is named after the Prince of Wales, Frederick Louis (1707–51), the eldest son of George II[†] and father of George III[†].

Fredericksburg, USA
1. Iowa: may be named after Frederick II the Great (1712–86), King of Prussia (1740–86).
2. Virginia: founded in 1671 and named in 1727 after the Prince of Wales, Frederick Louis (*see* FREDERICK).

Fredericktown, MISSOURI/USA
Named after George Frederick Bollinger, a member of the state legislature.

Fredericton, NEW BRUNSWICK/CANADA *Fort Nashwaak, St Anne's Point, Frederick Town*
Originally a French fort at the end of the 17th century, it was laid out as a town in 1785 and named after the Duke of York, Frederick Augustus (1763–1827), son of King George III[†].

Frederiksberg, DENMARK
A municipality founded in 1651 by Frederick III (1609–70), King of Denmark-Norway (1648–70), and named after him.

Frederiksborg, DENMARK
A county called 'Frederick's Castle' from *borg* 'castle' after the castle in Hillerød, the county's capital, which was acquired by Frederick II (1534–88), King of Denmark-Norway (1559–88).

Frederikshavn, DENMARK *Fladstrand*
Originally called 'The Beach (in the Parish of) Flade' from *strand* and *Flade* 'flat'. It was renamed 'Frederick's Port' in 1818 after Frederick VI (1768–1839), King of Denmark (1808–39) and of Norway (1808–14).

Fredonia, COLOMBIA, USA
USA (New York): settled in 1804 with a name meaning 'Place of Freedom'. This name was also proposed as a name for the United States.

Fredrikstad, NORWAY
Founded as a fortress town in 1567 by, and named after, Frederick II (1534–88), King of Denmark-Norway (1559–88) as 'Frederick's Town'.

Freeport, THE BAHAMAS, CANADA, USA
1. The Bahamas: founded in 1955 as a 'free port', thus tax exempt.
2. USA (Illinois): founded in 1835 as Winneshiek. However, Freeport was adopted as a result of the hospitality of an early settler, William Baker, and his wife.

Free State (Vrystaat), SOUTH AFRICA *Orange Free State*
A province situated between the Orange and Vaal Rivers, hence its former name; the 'Orange' was dropped in 1995. It was established in 1854 by Boers who had trekked northwards in 1836 to escape British rule, becoming a province of the Union of South Africa in 1910.

Freetown, ANTIGUA, THE BAHAMAS, CANADA, JAMAICA, SIERRA LEONE, USA
Sierra Leone: founded as Granvillestown in 1792 by Granville Sharp (1734–1813), a prominent British activist in the movement to abolish the slave trade, as a refuge for poor black people, mainly freed African slaves from North America who had sided with the British in the American War of Independence (1775–83) and had since languished in Canada. It was called Granvillestown between 1792 and 1797. In 1808 it became the capital of the British crown colony of Sierra Leone and of Sierra Leone when it became independent in 1961.

Freiberg, SAXONY/GERMANY
'Free Mountain' from *frei* 'free' and *Berg*. Founded at the end of the 12th century by Margrave Otto with a name that recognized the silver-mining rights of the 'free miner'. He abolished the monopoly on mining, but the miners did in fact have to pay him a 10 per cent tax on whatever they could earn.

Freiburg im Breisgau, BADEN-WÜRTTEMBERG/GERMANY
Founded in 1120 by the dukes of Zähringen as a free market town, hence its name from *frei* 'free' and *Burg*. Breisgau is an historic region (in German, *Gau* 'district') between the Black Forest and the River Rhine, now in the state of Baden-Württemberg. This state also has an administrative district called Freiburg.

Fréjus, PROVENCE-ALPES- CÔTE-D'AZUR/FRANCE *Forum Julii*
'Market Place of Julius'. Founded in 49 BC by, and named after, Julius Caesar[†] as a naval base and trading post.

Fremantle, WESTERN AUSTRALIA/AUSTRALIA
Settled in 1829 and named after Captain Sir Charles Fremantle (1800–69), a British naval

officer who took control of the mouth of the
Swan River to prevent French or American
infiltration.

Fremont, USA
There are at least nine cities with this name,
mostly in honour of John C. Frémont
(1813–90), an adventurer, explorer, and a
member of the Corps of Topographical
Engineers who became military governor of
California in 1847, defeated presidential
candidate for the Republican Party in 1856,
and governor of Arizona Territory (1878–83).

French Guiana *Cayenne*
Department of French Guiana (Département
de la Guyane Française) since 1946, having
been known as Cayenne until then. Settled by
the Spanish in 1503, the territory was awarded
to France by the Treaty of Breda in 1667, the
French having first arrived in 1604. In 1852
Guiana became a French penal colony, the
prisons not being shut until 1946. Guiana is a
Native American word meaning 'Land of
Waters'.

French Indo-China (Indochine Française)
Now a region of South-East Asia that consists
of Cambodia, Laos, and Vietnam. Through the
signing of separate bilateral treaties in 1950,
whereby each country became an
independent self-governing state within the
French Union, the concept of French Indo-
China (1869–1950) was effectively brought to
an end. The term 'Indo-China' acknowledges
the presence of Indian and Chinese culture in
the region.

French Lick, INDIANA/USA
Founded in 1811, it was named after the
French presence in the area and an animal salt
lick.

French Polynesia (Te Ao Maohi) *French
Colony of Oceania*
Territory of French Polynesia (French:
Territoire de la Polynésie Française; Tahitian:
Polynesia Farani), an Overseas Territory of the
French Republic since 1958 and consisting of
five archipelagos in the south-central Pacific
Ocean. The island groups became protectorates
from 1843 which were then annexed by France
in 1880–7. Administratively, they were part of
the French Colony of Oceania, also known as
French Settlements in Oceania. The name
means 'Many Islands' from the Greek *polus*
'many' and *nēsos* 'island'. The traditional name
comes from the Maohi, a Polynesian people,
and is Te Ao Maohi.

Fresco, BRAZIL, CÔTE D'IVOIRE
Rivers in both cases with the name 'Fresh' in
Portuguese, indicating fresh water.

Fresno, CALIFORNIA/USA
Settled in 1872, it means 'Ash Tree' in Spanish.

Freudenstadt, BADEN-WÜRTTEMBERG/
GERMANY
Founded in 1599 as a haven for Protestant
refugees from Salzburg, Austria, it was named
'Town of Joy' from *Freude* 'joy' and *Stadt*.

Fribourg (German: **Freiburg**), SWITZERLAND
A canton and a city which was founded in 1157
as a fort to control a ford over the Saane River;
it means 'Free Fort'. The canton joined the
Swiss Confederation in 1481. When occupied
by the French in 1798 it became part of the
Helvetic Republic until joining the remodelled
Swiss Confederation in 1803.

Friedrichshafen, BADEN-WÜRTTEMBERG/
GERMANY
'Frederick's Harbour'. Founded in 1811 by, and
named after, Frederick I (1754–1816), King of
Württemberg (1805–16), who merged the city
of Buchhorn and the village of Hofen.

Friesland, THE NETHERLANDS
A province named after the Frisians, or Frisii, a
Germanic seafaring people.

Frisian Islands, DENMARK-GERMANY-THE
NETHERLANDS
The East Frisian Islands belong to Germany,
the West Frisian Islands to the Netherlands.
They are named after the Frisians. The North
Frisian Islands lie off the west coast of
Schleswig-Holstein and are divided between
Germany and Denmark.

Friuli-Venezia Giulia, ITALY *Forum Julii*
A region, the first part of whose name is a
contraction of the Roman name which may be
'Market Place of Julius (Casear)'†, or 'Forum of
the Julian People'. Previously known simply as
'Coastland', Venezia Giulia was adopted in
recognition of the power of Venice in the
region. *See* CIVIDALE DEL FRIULI.

Frobisher, CANADA
1. Saskatchewan: a town and a lake named
after a fur trader, Thomas Frobisher.
2. Nunavut: a bay off Baffin Island discovered in
1576 by Sir Martin Frobisher (*c*.1535–94), an
English navigator who explored the north-east
coast of Canada. Some 150 miles (240 km) long,
Frobisher believed it to be a strait and it was not
until 1860 that it was correctly designated a bay.

Frome, JAMAICA, UK
UK (England): named after the River Frome, a
Celtic name meaning 'fine' or 'brisk'.

Front Royal, VIRGINIA/USA
According to local tradition, a sergeant drilling
the local militia during colonial times gave the
command 'front the royal oak' indicating a

huge oak tree, the 'royal' tree of England, which stood in the main square. Continuing use of this order gave the town its name.

Frýdek-Místek, CZECH REPUBLIC *Místek*
Originally two separate towns with Frýdek on the Silesian bank of the River Ostravice and Místek on the Moravian bank. They merged under the name of Místek in 1942 and in 1945 the town was given its present name. Frýdek comes from its previous German name which was Friedeck 'Peaceful, or protected, (Settlement) on the Bend (in the River)' from *Friede* 'peace' and *Eck* 'corner' or 'angle'. Místek was originally Friedberg 'Peaceful, or protected, (Settlement) on the Mountain' from *Friede* and *Berg*. The Czech version of this name was Frýdburk but, to avoid confusion with Frýdek, it was renamed Neuestetil 'New Small Town' in the 15th century. The Czech version of this was Miestko 'Small Town' and this became Místek in the 16th century.

Fryeburg, MAINE/USA
Named after its founder, General Joseph Frye, a veteran of the wars against the French, who received a grant of land here in gratitude for his services.

Fuente Obejuna, ANDALUSIA/SPAIN
'Sheep Spring' from *fuente* 'fountain' or 'spring' and *ovejuna* 'sheep'.

Fuerteventura Island (Isla de Fuerteventura), CANARY ISLANDS/SPAIN *Forte Aventura*
'Good Luck Island' from *fuerte* 'strong' or 'great' and *ventura* 'luck' or 'fortune'.

Fujairah, al-, UNITED ARAB EMIRATES
An emirate named after a stream called Fujairah, whose meaning is unknown, that flows through it. It became an autonomous state in 1952, having been part of Sharjah, and a constituent emirate of the UAE in 1971.

Fuji, HONSHŪ/JAPAN
Named after Mt Fuji at the southern foot of which it lies. The meaning of the name is not clear. It may be of Ainu origin and mean 'Eternal Life'. Alternatively, the name may come from the Ainu *Huchi* 'God of Fire'. In the West the mountain is known as Fujiyama, 'Mt Fuji', as a result of some confusion with the Chinese character which can be pronounced either 'yama' or 'san'; in Japan the mountain is known as Fujisan.

Fujian, CHINA
A province which, when it was established in 760-2, had five prefectures. The names of two of them, Fuzhou and Jianzhou, were combined to give the present name.

Linguistically, the name can mean 'Happy Establishment' from *fú* 'happiness' and *jiàn* 'to build' or 'to establish'.

Fujinomiya, HONSHŪ/JAPAN
Built up around the main shrine to Mt Fuji, the name means 'Shrine of Fuji' from *Fuji*, *no* 'of', and *miya* 'shrine'.

Fukui, HONSHŪ/JAPAN
A prefecture and city meaning 'Well of Happiness' from *fuku* and *i* 'well'.

Fukuoka, KYŪSHŪ/JAPAN
A prefecture and city-port meaning 'Hill of Happiness' from *fuku* and *oka* 'hill'.

Fukushima, HONSHŪ/JAPAN
A prefecture and city meaning 'Island of Happiness' from *fuku* and *shima* 'island'.

Fukuyama, HONSHŪ/JAPAN
A city called 'Mountain of Happiness' from *fuku* and *yama* 'mountain'.

Fulmer, ENGLAND/UK *Fugelmere*
'Lake frequented by Birds' from the Old English *fugol* 'bird' and *mere* 'lake' or 'pool'.

Fulton, USA *Volney*
Missouri: laid out in 1825, it was soon renamed after Robert Fulton (1765-1815), who developed the steamboat and brought it into operational use.

Funabashi, HONSHŪ/JAPAN
'Floating Bridge' from *fune* 'boat' or 'vessel' and *hashi* 'bridge'. According to legend, the 2nd-century Emperor Keikô passed through a flooded area by making a bridge built of boats.

Funchal, PORTUGAL
Derived from *funcho* 'fennel', the herb growing here in abundance. Capital of the island of Madeira, it was founded in 1421 and named by the Portuguese explorer, João Gonçalves Zarco.

Furmanov, IVANOVO/RUSSIA *Sreda*
The original name is taken from *Sreda* 'Wednesday', that is, market day. The city was renamed in 1941 after Dmitry Furmanov (1891-1926), a Civil War hero and novelist, who was born here. The town formerly called Furmanovo in Kazakhstan, named after the same man, has been renamed Zhalpaqtal.

Furneaux Group, AUSTRALIA
A group of islands off the north-east coast of Tasmania, it is named after Tobias Furneaux (1735-81), a naval officer who discovered the islands in 1773.

Fürstenwalde, BRANDENBURG/GERMANY
Founded *c*.1255 by the Margrave of Brandenburg, it means, literally, 'Prince's

Forest' from *Fürst* 'prince' and *Wald* 'wood' or 'forest'; this may be where he went hunting and had a hunting lodge.

Fürstenzell, BAVARIA/GERMANY
Possibly 'Prince's Cell' from *Fürst* and *Zelle*. *Zelle* can mean a monk's cell (or a prison cell), but here it may indicate rather more: a small chapel for the prince.

Fürth, BAVARIA/GERMANY
Located at the confluence of the Pegnitz and Rednitz Rivers, it means 'Ford' from *Furt*. *Th* spellings were common at one time, but have been dropped in modern German except in names.

Fushun, CHINA
1. Liaoning: established as a city in 1937 with a meaning reminiscent of a Ming dynasty (1368–1644) policy towards the remnants of the Mongol Yuan dynasty (1279–1368) which was to console, comfort, or appease the people living within China's borders and subdue the barbarians living beyond the border. Thus the two characters have a meaning of 'submissiveness' from *fu* 'to console' and *shùn(cóng)* 'submissive', 'docile', or 'obedient'.

2. There is also a city with this name in Sichuan but it has different characters to the one in Liaoning.

Fuzhou, FUJIAN/CHINA *Dongye, Houguan, Minzhou*
'City of Happiness' from *fú* 'happiness', 'luck', or 'fortune' and *zhōu* which, in this case, means 'city'. In 581 it was renamed Minzhou, the 'Region of the Min', a reference to the seven ancient Min tribes whose home this was during the Chou dynasty (1111–255 BC). It received its present name in 725.

Füzuli, AZERBAIJAN *Karyagino*
Founded in 1827 and renamed in 1959 after the famous Turkish poet of Kurdish origin, Muhammad (Mehmed) bin Suleiman Füzuli (1494–1556), who wrote in the Azeri dialect. It is also spelt Fizuli.

Fyfield, ENGLAND/UK
'Five Hides of Land' from the Old English *fīf* and *hīd* 'hide of land'. A 'hide', used in Anglo-Saxon and early Norman times, denoted the area of land needed to support one free family; it varied between 60 and 120 acres depending on the nature of the terrain.

Gabon The Gabonese Republic (République Gabonaise) since 1960 when independence was achieved. Previously an autonomous republic within the French Community (1958); one of the four colonies of French Equatorial Africa (1910); part of French Congo (1886), the French having established a presence in 1839. The Portuguese came upon the Gabon Estuary in 1472 and named it Gabão 'hooded cloak' because of its shape. The country adopted the name.

Gaborone, BOTSWANA *Gaberones*
Founded in 1890 by Cecil Rhodes's[†] British South Africa Company to provide protection for the railway and telegraph lines. It was named after a long-serving chief of the Batlokwa tribe. It became the capital of Bechuanaland in 1965 and a year later of independent Botswana. In 1969 the spelling of the name was slightly changed.

Gabrovo, BULGARIA
'(The Place of) Hornbeam' from *grab*, a reference to the abundance of this type of tree.

Gadsden, USA
1. Alabama: founded in 1846 as Double Springs, it was renamed after James Gadsden (1788–1858), American minister to Mexico, who negotiated a treaty in 1853 with Mexico, known as the Gadsden Purchase, whereby land was acquired to allow the construction of a railway.
2. Arizona: some of the territory acquired by James Gadsden is now part of southern Arizona.

Gaeta, LAZIO/ITALY *Caieta*
Evolved from the Roman name which comes from the Greek *kaiatas*, itself from *kaiadas* 'cavern' or 'cavity' in the sense of an inlet or small bay. This describes the Gulf of Gaeta from which the town takes its name. It was a maritime republic in the 8th century and an independent duchy in the 10th.

Gaffney, SOUTH CAROLINA/USA
Named after Michael Gaffney, an Irish settler in the early 19th century.

Gafsa (Qafṣah), TUNISIA *Kafaz, Capsa, Justiniana*
During the Carthaginian era the town was a Berber stronghold called Kafaz, possibly meaning 'The Walled (Town)'. It was destroyed by the Romans in 106 BC and called Capsa from

which the present name has evolved. Capsa in Latin means 'chest' or 'repository', suggesting an enclosed, thus walled, town. Having been rebuilt, it fell under the control of the Byzantines who fortified it and renamed it in 540 after Justinian I[†].

Gafurov, TAJIKISTAN *Leninabad, Sovetabad, Khodzhent*
Originally called 'Lenin's[†] Town', it was renamed 'Soviet Town' in 1953. In 1962 this gave way to Khodzhent (which had been renamed Leninabad in 1936), but two years later Sovetabad was readopted. Finally, in 1978, it was given its present name after Bobodzhan Gafurov (1908–77), a senior member of the Communist Party in Tajikistan and a historian who was born near here.

Gagarin, KALUGA/RUSSIA *Gzhatsk*
Founded in 1776 and originally named after the River Gzhat. It was renamed in 1968 after the death of Yuri Gagarin (1934–68), the first man to orbit the earth in a spacecraft in April 1961; his birthplace was near here.

Gagauzia (Găgăuzia), MOLDOVA
An autonomous region in the south named after the Gagauz, Turkic-speaking Orthodox Christians whose ancestors fled Ottoman rule in Bulgaria. Encouraged by the government's declaration that they were a separate 'nation', the minority Gagauz declared an independent Republic of Gagauzia (Gagauz-Yeri 'Gagauz Land') in 1990. This independence was not recognized and the existence of the self-styled republic was terminated in 1995 when it became an autonomous region.

Gagetown, CANADA, USA
Canada (New Brunswick): founded as Grimross and renamed after General Thomas Gage (1721–87), British military commander-in-chief in North America (1763–74).

Gainesville, USA
1. Florida: founded in 1830 as Hog Town, it was renamed in 1854 after General Edmund P. Gaines (1777–1845), a military commander during the War of 1812.
2. Georgia: settled in 1818 and also named after General Gaines.

Galana, KENYA
A river whose name simply means 'River'.

Galapagos Islands (Spanish: **Islas de los Galápagos**), ECUADOR *The Enchanted (Islands)*
An Insular Region, the official name is Columbus Archipelago (Spanish: Archipiélago de Colón). The Galapagos consist of a group of islands and islets. They were discovered in 1535 by the bishop of Panama, Tomás de Berlanga, who named them Las Encantadas 'The Enchanted'. The present name comes from the Spanish *galápago* 'freshwater tortoise'.

Galashiels, SCOTLAND/UK *Galuschel*
'Huts by Gala Water' from the Middle English *schele* 'shelter' and the name of the river whose meaning is uncertain.

Galați, ROMANIA
A county and a town, possibly named after the Galatae. *See* GALATIA.

Galatia, TURKEY
An ancient region, now in central Turkey, named after the Gauls, European Celtic tribes who were called Galatae or Galatoi by contemporary writers; thus the 'Land of the Gauls' or 'Land of the Celts'. They settled in the area towards the end of the 3rd century BC, having been invited to serve as mercenaries by Nicomedes I, King of Bithynia (*c.*279–255 BC), in his fight with the Seleucid King Antiochus I (324–261 BC), who controlled most of Anatolia. Galatia became a Roman province in 25 BC.

Galesburg, ILLINOIS/USA
Named after George Washington Gale, a Presbyterian minister, who selected the site for a college community.

Galicia, POLAND-UKRAINE, SPAIN
1. Poland-Ukraine: annexed to Poland in 1349, it was attached to Austria in 1772 at the time of the first partition of Poland. In 1815 it became part of the Kingdom of Galicia. Galicia was returned to Poland at the end of the First World War. At the end of the Second World War eastern Galicia (in Russian, Galitsiya) was recognized as part of the Soviet Union (Ukraine) while western Galicia was given to Poland (in Polish, Galicja). The Austrians coined the name which may have been taken from the town of Halicz (now in Ukraine), its name possibly being connected with the salt here from the ancient Greek *alas*.
2. Spain: an autonomous community and former kingdom with a name taken from the Celtic Gallaeci who occupied the area when the Romans arrived in about 140 BC. However, it has been suggested that the name may be associated with Gaul.

Galilee, AUSTRALIA, ISRAEL
Israel: a region, in Hebrew Ha-Galil, of ancient Palestine with a name derived from the Hebrew *galil* 'district'. The Sea of Galilee, also known as Lake Tiberias or Yam Kinneret in Hebrew, is named after the region.

Gallatin, WYOMING-MONTANA/USA
A river named after Albert Gallatin (1761–1849), US secretary of the Treasury (1801–14).

Galle, SRI LANKA *Point de Galle*
Founded in the 13th century, it was under Portuguese rule in 1507–1640; it was the capital under Dutch rule until 1656. The name comes from the Sanskrit *galla* 'rock', perhaps indicating the coastal terrain on which it is situated. However, there is a legend that it was so named after the Portuguese heard a cock, *galo*, crowing.

Gallipoli, AUSTRALIA, ITALY, TURKEY
1. Italy (Apulia): has the same origin as the Gallipoli in Turkey.
2. Turkey: locally Gelibolu and originally Kallipolis. The first Ottoman Turkish conquest in Europe *c.*1356, the English and Turkish names are derived from the Greek Kallipolis 'Beautiful Town' from *kalos* 'beautiful' and *polis*.

Gallipolis, OHIO/USA
'City of the Gauls' founded in 1790 by royalists fleeing the French Revolution.

Gallitzin, PENNSYLVANIA/USA
Named after its founder, Demetrius Augustine Gallitzin (1770–1840), a Russian prince and one of the first Roman Catholic priests to serve European immigrants to the USA.

Galloway, CANADA, UK, USA
UK (Scotland): a region and now part of the unitary district of Dumfries and Galloway (*Dumfries). It has a complex early history involving Britons, Angles, Vikings (Norse and Danish), Normans and the so-called Gall Gaidhil, the 'Stranger Gaels', from whom the names of the region and its people are supposed to be derived.

Gallup, NEW MEXICO/USA
Founded as a stagecoach halt in 1880, it later became an important site for the construction of the Atlantic and Pacific Railroad. It was named after David L. Gallup, the railroad's treasurer.

Galt, CANADA, USA
Canada (Ontario): founded *c.*1816 as Shade's Mills, it was renamed in 1827 after John Galt (1779–1839), a Scottish novelist who had come to Ontario a year earlier. He founded the city of *Guelph in 1827.

Galveston, TEXAS/USA *St Louis, Gálvez*
The island on which the city is located was first
visited by the French explorer René-Robert
Cavelier, Sieur (Lord) de La Salle[†] in 1686. He
named the island after Louis XIV the Sun King
(1638–1715), King of France (1643–1715). In
1777 the Spanish governor of Louisiana,
Bernardo de Gálvez (1746–86), occupied the
island and named it after himself. This evolved
into the present name.

Galway, IRELAND, USA
Ireland: a county and a town whose Irish name
is Gaillimh. This is derived from a Gaelic word
whose modern Irish equivalent is *gall* 'stone',
the town having originated as a crossing place
over the River Corrib. Thus the name means
'Stony (River)'.

Gambia, The The Republic of the Gambia
since 1970, having achieved independence in
1965. However, in 1982–9, with French-
speaking Senegal, this English-speaking state
formed the Senegambia Confederation. In
1816 the British founded a coastal settlement
at Bathurst (now Banjul) which, by 1821, had
become a crown colony. However, in 1821–43
and 1866–89 the colony was actually
administered as a district of Sierra Leone. In
1843–66 it enjoyed the status of an
independent crown colony. In 1894 the
interior of The Gambia, as opposed to the
colony around Bathurst, became a British
protectorate. Completely surrounded by
Senegal but for a small strip of Atlantic coast,
The Gambia's borders were finally agreed in
1889 at the Paris Conference. The country is
confined to strips of land on either side of the
Gambia River and takes its name from the
river. This was so-called by the Portuguese
*c.*1455 from the local name, *Ba-Dimma* 'The
River'.

Gambier, OHIO/USA
Named after Admiral of the Fleet Sir James
Gambier (1756–1833), 1st Baron Gambier, who
was a benefactor of a college here.

Gambier Islands (French: **Îles Gambier**),
FRENCH POLYNESIA
Sighted in 1797 by Captain James Wilson and
named after Admiral of the Fleet Sir James
Gambier, 1st Baron Gambier and a British
naval commander. They are sometimes called
by their local name, the Mangareva Islands,
after the main island of Mangareva. They were
annexed by the French in 1881.

Gananoque, ONTARIO/CANADA
Founded in 1812 at the mouth of the
Gananoque River, its name is said to mean
'Rocks rising out of the Water'.

Ganda, ANGOLA *Port Mariano Machado*
'Payment'. In earlier times payments were
made to a witch doctor and the name here was
given to a large rock where the transactions
took place.

Gander, NEWFOUNDLAND/CANADA
Built up round a site chosen as an airfield by
the British Air Ministry in 1935, it is named
after the river which itself may recognize the
large numbers of wild geese in the area.

Gāndhīnagar, GUJARĀT/INDIA
Founded in 1966, it was named the 'City of
Gandhi' after 'Mahatma' Gandhi (1869–1948),
leader of the Indian nationalist movement
against British rule, who was born in Gujarāt,
with the additional *nagar*.

Ganges (Gaṅgā), BANGLADESH, INDIA
'River' from the Sanskrit *gaṅgā*. It is the holy
river of the Hindus. It is also known as Gaṅgāji,
the suffix -*ji* indicating reverence. Within
Bangladesh it is called the Padma.

Gangtok, SIKKIM/INDIA
Situated at a height of 5 600 ft (1 700m), the
name means 'Top of the Hill' from the Tibetan
gang 'hill' and *tok* 'top' or 'peak'. It was the
capital of the Kingdom of Sikkim until the
monarchy was abolished in 1975. Sikkim was
annexed by India in 1976.

Gansu, CHINA
A province whose name comes from *gān*
'gentle' and *sù* 'respected'. The name is
actually a combination of Ganzhou and
Suzhou, its two original districts.

Ganzhou, JIANGXI/CHINA *Nankang, Ganxian*
Settled as a county *c.*200 BC, it was renamed
Nankang county in 600 and Ganxiang 'Gan
county' in 608. The city lies at the confluence
of the Zhang and Gong Rivers so the place was
named Gan. The character is composed of two
parts: the left-hand side is the character for
Zhang and the right side is formed from the
character for Gong. The River Gan flows
onwards from the point at which the two
rivers meet; hence the character reflects the
terrain features here. The city is named after
the River Gan and *zhou*.

Gao, MALI *Kawkaw*
A region and a town. Founded in the 7th
century on the Niger River, the name comes
from the Fulani *kunku* 'island'. When the Arabs
took control in the 16th century they Arabized
the name to Kawkaw which in due course
became Gaogao and then, inevitably, Gao.

Gaolan Mountains, GANSU/CHINA
Take their name from *gāo* 'marsh' and *lán*
'orchid'. *Gāo* with the same pronunciation but
with a different character means 'big' or 'high'.

Garda, Lake (Lago di Garda), ITALY *Benacus*
Takes its name from the small town on its
shore. Its name means 'guard' from *guardia*. It
is also known as Benaco from the Roman name
which gave way to Garda when the town
assumed authority over the lake in the 9th
century.

Garden City, USA
There are nine cities with this name in the
USA. They were all probably given this name
because of the quality of local gardens or the
rural atmosphere.

Gardiner, CANADA, USA
USA (Maine): founded as Gardinerstown
Plantation in 1764 by, and named after,
Sylvester Gardiner, a local entrepreneur.

Garfield, USA
Kansas: named after James A. Garfield (1831–
81), President of the USA (1881); he was shot
four months after taking office and died two
and a half months later.

Garibaldi, BRAZIL, CANADA, USA
All are named, probably by immigrants from
Italy, after Giuseppe Garibaldi (1807–82), a
guerrilla leader who made a major
contribution to Italian unification and the
creation of the Kingdom of Italy in 1861.

Garies, NORTHERN CAPE/SOUTH AFRICA *Genisdal*
Named after the river here whose name comes
from a Khoikhoin word meaning 'couchgrass'.
The former name 'Genis' Valley' honoured a
Dutch schoolteacher.

Garland, USA
1. Arkansas and Texas: named after Augustus
H. Garland (1832–99), attorney general and
governor of Arkansas (1874).
2. Maine: named after Joseph Garland, the
first settler.

Garonne, FRANCE-SPAIN
A river with a name derived from a pre-Indo-
European root word *kar* 'stone' or 'rock'.

Gary, INDIANA/USA
Laid out in 1906 as an extension to the US Steel
Corporation plant, the town was named after
Elbert H. Gary (1846–1927), chairman of the
board of directors and chief executive officer
(1901–27).

Gascony (Gascogne), FRANCE *Novempopulana,
Vasconia*
A historical duchy named after the Basques
who overran it beginning in 561. The Spanish
for Basque is *Vasco*; the Basques were called the
Vascones by the Romans. Novempopulana was
the earlier Roman name when the province
was established.

Gaspé, QUEBEC/CANADA
The origin of the name is disputed. It may
come from the Christian name of the
Portuguese explorer Gaspar Corte-Real who
went down the York River at the mouth of
which the city lies *c*.1500; or it may come from
a Native American word *gespeg* 'end of the
world'. However, it lies at the mouth of the
York River, not the source.

Gastonia, NORTH CAROLINA/USA
Settled in the late 18th century, the city was
named after William Gaston (1778–1844), a
congressman and a judge.

Gatchina, LENINGRAD/RUSSIA *Khotchino, Trotsk/
Trotskoye, Krasnogvardeysk*
The original name was in use from at least
1499 until 1923. For a part of this time the
town was in Swedish possession until being
returned to Russia in 1721. It was then
renamed after Leon Trotsky (1879–1940), a
Bolshevik revolutionary leader, until 1929
when it assumed the name Krasnogvardeysk
from *Krasnaya Gvardiya* 'Red Guards' to
commemorate their role in the Bolshevik
seizure of power in Petrograd (now St
Petersburg) in November 1917. In 1944 the
original name was restored (with a slightly
different spelling) at a time of great patriotic
fervour following the lifting of the three-year
German siege of Leningrad (now St
Petersburg). *Gat* is a local word meaning a
'brushwood road' laid over marshland.

Gateshead, ENGLAND/UK *Gateshevet, Gatesheued*
'Goat's Headland' or 'Goat's Hill' from the Old
English *gāt* 'goat' and *hēafod* 'headland'.

Gatineau, QUEBEC/CANADA
It is named after the River Gatineau, near the
mouth of which it lies. The river was named
after Nicolas Gatineau, a French fur trader,
who is believed to have been drowned in the
river in about 1683.

Gaul (French: **Gaule**; Latin: **Gallia**)
An ancient region which in Roman times
comprised most of modern France (Gallia
Aquitania in the south-west, Gallia Transalpina
'Gaul beyond the Alps' or Narbonensis in the
south-east, and Gallia Celtica or Lugdunensis
in the centre), parts of Belgium and western
Germany (Gallia Belgica) and northern Italy
(Gallia Cisalpina 'Gaul this Side of the Alps'),
that was inhabited by the Gauls after whom it
was named.

Gauteng, SOUTH AFRICA *Pretoria-
Witwatersrand-Vereeniging*
A province renamed in 1995. Its present name,
'City of Gold', is derived from a Sotho-Tswana
version of *eRawutini* 'City of Gold' which is the

Xhosa name for Johannesburg, the provincial capital.

Gävle, SWEDEN *Gaeffla*
A port with a name probably derived from a stream called Gävla whose name comes from *gavel* 'gable' with the meaning of a stream that breaks through the gables, thus the place where the stream penetrates the ridge around which the town is located.

Gawler, SOUTH AUSTRALIA/AUSTRALIA
A town, river, and ranges, all named after George Gawler (1795–1869), governor of South Australia (1838–41).

Gayā, INDIA, NIGERIA
India (Bihār): named after the good demon Gaya, to whom Vishnu, one of the principal Hindu deities, gave the power to absolve sinners. It is one of the Hindus' seven sacred cities and sometimes is known as Bodhgayā.

Gaza (Arabic: **Ghazzah**; Hebrew: **'Azza**), GAZA STRIP, MOZAMBIQUE
The capital of the Gaza Strip, a small stretch of coastline some 25 miles (40 km) long and averaging 5–6 miles (8–10 km) wide. The city fell to the Ottoman Turks in the 16th century. They held it until 1917 when it was captured by the British. In 1948 it was occupied by the Egyptians, but fell to the Israelis during the Six Day War in 1967. They held it until agreeing to withdraw in 1994. Formerly known as Azza, Hazati, and Hazat, the name may come from the Hebrew *az* 'strength', in reference to an early fortress here. This was changed to Gaza after the Muslim conquest in 635 and it is usually known now as Gaza City to distinguish it from the Gaza Strip. Gaza may give its name to 'gauze', a fine wire mesh or transparent fabric. The Gaza Strip is not currently recognized as belonging to any country, although most of it is under the control of the Palestinian Authority; the rest is held by Israel, although withdrawal is planned.

Gaziantep, TURKEY *Hamtap, Ayıntab/Antep*
Falling finally to the Ottoman Turks in the 16th century, it retained its Arabic name of Ayıntab from *Ayntāb* 'Good Spring'. After a ten months' defence against a besieging French force in 1920–1 the city was awarded the title of *Gazi* 'Defender of the Faith' or 'Warriors for the Faith' by the Grand National Assembly in 1922 and its name was changed to recognize this.

Gazimammad (Qazimämmäd), AZERBAIJAN *Haji Kabul*
Named after a son of Imam Shamil (1797–1871), a Murid leader who, under the overall leadership of Ghazi Muhammad, waged a holy war against the Russians, mainly in Chechnya and Dagestan. The former name meant 'Rest Place for Pilgrims'—those en route to Mecca via Tehran.

Gazli, UZBEKISTAN
Established in 1958 on a site where there was natural gas. Thus the name simply means 'Gas (Town)'.

Gdańsk, POLAND *Gyddanyzc, Kdanzc, Danzig*
Derived from *Gutisk-anja* 'End of the Goths', to signify the limit of their territory. The Teutonic Knights captured the city in 1308 and held it until 1466 when it was retaken by the Poles. At the second partition of Poland in 1793 Prussia acquired Gdańsk. Although in 1919 its population was over 90 per cent German, it was designated a free city under the League of Nations mandate in a customs union with Poland in 1919–39; thus it was not included in the *Polish Corridor. It was seized by Nazi Germany at the outbreak of the Second World War on 1 September 1939. It was returned to Poland in 1945.

Gdynia, POLAND *Gotenhafen*
Lying only 10 miles (16 km) to the north-west, the city's name has the same origin as that of *Gdańsk. It was developed as an alternative port to Gdańsk in the Polish Corridor, which gave Poland a narrow access to the Baltic Sea after the close of the First World War in 1919. During the Second World War, while under German control, the port was known as Gotenhafen 'Goths' Harbour'.

Geelong, VICTORIA/AUSTRALIA
Founded in 1837, the origin of the name is disputed. It is said to come either from an Aboriginal word meaning a 'place in the marshes', or from another Aboriginal word, *jillong* 'place of the companion', a long-legged water bird.

Geldagana, CHECHNYA/RUSSIA *Novaya Zhizn'*
Renamed in the early 1990s, having been known as 'New Life' from *zhizn'* 'life'. This 'new life' meant 'communism'. The meaning of the present name is not known.

Gelderland, THE NETHERLANDS
A province whose name refers to a sandy stretch of terrain with a few hills in the south-east from the Germanic *gelwa* 'yellow' and *haru* 'mountain', with the additional *land*.

Gelendzhik, KRASNODAR TERRITORY/RUSSIA *Toricos, Eptala*
Popularly said to mean 'Little Bride' in Turkish from *gelin* 'bride' and a diminutive, possibly because it was once a centre of the slave trade. Eptala was the main port for the

export of local girls to the Ottoman Turkish harems.

Genadendal, WESTERN CAPE/SOUTH AFRICA
Baviaanskloof
Founded as a mission station by Protestant missionaries from Moravia (Czech Republic) and renamed 'Vale of Mercy' in 1806. The previous Afrikaans name meant 'Baboons' Ravine'.

General Belgrano, ARGENTINA
Named after Manuel Belgrano (1770–1820), commander of the army and a leader in the Argentine war for independence (1810–16).

Generalissimul Suvorov, ROMANIA
Named after the Russian prince and military commander, Alexander Suvorov (1729–1800), who won battles against the Ottoman Turks in Romania in 1789 and 1790.

General José de San Martín, ARGENTINA
Named after José de San Martín (1778–1850), a military commander and national hero who played a leading role in the revolutions against Spanish rule in Argentina (1812), Chile (1818), and Peru (1821). There is also a town named General San Martín, a suburb of Buenos Aires, in Argentina.

General Santos, MINDANAO/PHILIPPINES
Buayan
Since 1954 named after General Paulino Santos who led the first settlers into Cotabato and directed the development of the Koronadal Valley beginning in 1939. A suggestion that it should be renamed Rajah Buayan in 1967 was rejected.

General Sarmiento, ARGENTINA
Named after Domingo Faustino Sarmiento (1811–88), Argentina's first civilian president (1868–74).

Genesee, USA
A river largely contained within New York State with an Iroquois name meaning 'Beautiful Valley' or 'Shining Valley'.

Geneva, SWITZERLAND, USA
Switzerland: a lake, a canton, and a city, originally Genava, whose name may be derived from the Indo-European root word *gen* 'bend', a reference to the shape of Lake Geneva (in French, Lac Léman) at its southern end where the city lies. However, it may be of pre-Indo-European origin, namely, from *gan* 'estuary', a reference to the city's location at the point where the River Rhône debouches from the lake. Between 1864 and 1949 various treaties were signed in the city. Collectively, they are known as the Geneva Convention and they seek to establish the way soldiers

(prisoners and the wounded) and civilians are treated in war. The French name is Genève and the German Genf.

Genoa (Genova), LIGURIA/ITALY *Genua*
May be derived from the Latin *janua* 'door' or the Indo-European root word *gen* 'bend' or 'curve' since it lies on the curve of the Gulf of Genoa. A former maritime power with interests that stretched to the Crimea, it gave its name to jeans (from the French name for the city, Gènes), twilled cotton cloth trousers worn by Genoese sailors.

George, AUSTRALIA, CANADA, SOUTH AFRICA, UGANDA, USA
1. Australia (New South Wales): a lake, first discovered by a European in 1820, and named after King George IV[†].
2. Canada (Quebec): named after King George III[†] in 1811 by Moravian missionaries.
3. South Africa (Western Cape): founded in 1806 as the first British settlement in Cape Colony called George Town, it was named after King George III[†]. A shortened version of the name was adopted in 1811.
4. Uganda: a lake, originally called Beatrice Gulf in 1875 because Sir Henry Morton Stanley[†] believed it to be part of Lake Albert. He named it Beatrice after Princess Beatrice (1857–1944), the youngest child of Queen Victoria[†] and Prince Albert. It was renamed in 1908 after George, Prince of Wales, later King George V[†].
5. USA (New York): a lake called by the local Native Americans Andiatarocte 'Place where the Lake contracts'. French Jesuit missionaries saw the lake in 1642 when being escorted past it as prisoners of the Iroquois, and Father Isaac Jogues revisited it four years later on the Feast of Corpus Christi and gave it the name Lac du Saint-Sacrement 'Lake of the Holy Sacrament'. In 1755 it was renamed after King George II[†] by Major General Sir William Johnson (1715–74), superintendent of the Six Iroquois Nations (1755).

George Land (Zemlya Georga), RUSSIA *Prince George's Land*
An island of Franz Josef Land, it was named by a British explorer in 1897 after the Prince of Wales, who was to become King George V[†] in 1910.

Georgetown, ASCENSION ISLAND, AUSTRALIA, CANADA, CAYMAN ISLANDS, THE GAMBIA, GUYANA, MALAYSIA, ST VINCENT, USA
Usually spelt Georgetown but occasionally George Town and usually, but not exclusively, named after a King George of Great Britain.
1. Canada (Prince Edward Island): named in 1765 after King George II[†].

2. The Gambia: founded in 1823 as a colony for freed slaves, it was named after King George IV†.

3. Guyana: founded in 1781 and named after King George III†. It was renamed Stabroek 'Standing Pool' by the Dutch during their occupation in 1784–1812. When the British reassumed control the original name was readopted. It is the capital of Guyana.

4. Malaysia: founded in 1786 as Fort Cornwallis after Charles Cornwallis (1738–1805), 1st Marquis and 2nd Earl Cornwallis, governor-general of India (1786–93, 1805) and viceroy of Ireland (1798–1801). If not renamed after King George III†, it may have been renamed after his son, Prince George Augustus Frederick, who became King George IV† in 1820.

5. USA (Colorado): founded in 1864, it was named after a local official, George Griffith.

6. USA (Georgia and South Carolina): named after King George II†.

Georgia, AND USA

1. Georgia (Sak'art'velo) since 1998. Previously the Republic of Georgia following independence from the Soviet Union in 1991; the Georgian Soviet Socialist Republic (1936); a part of the Transcaucasian Soviet Federative Socialist Republic (with Armenia and Azerbaijan) (1922–36); independent (1918–21). Between 1801, when they abolished the Kingdom of Kartli-Kakheti (eastern Georgia), and 1864 the Russians annexed the Georgian kingdoms. The Georgian name, Sak'art'velo, means the 'Land of the Kartvelians' (also known as Karts, Kartlis, Kartlians or Kartveli), the four main branches of which are the Kartvelians, Mingrelians and Svans, all of whom live in Georgia, and the Laz, who live on Turkey's Black Sea coast. The name Sak'art'velo was not used until the 11th century when Georgia was briefly united. The Georgians claim descent from one of Noah's great-great-grandsons, Kartlos. The internationally recognized name of Georgia is derived from the Arabic and Persian words *kurj* and *gurj*, both meaning 'country' or 'land', inferring a connection with that particular territory. The patron saint of Georgia is St George, but the country's name does not come from him. Georgia was known to the Greeks as Colchis and to the Romans as Iberia.

2. USA (Georgia): a state. It was the last of the thirteen American colonies to be settled by Europeans in 1733 when it was named after King George II†. Brigadier General James Oglethorpe (1696–1785) obtained the charter for settling the colony of Georgia in 1732. Because a friend had died in a debtors' prison

in England, he became a champion of the poor. His aim was to establish a colony where poor people from England could make a fresh start. He was strongly supported by the king. It was realized, furthermore, that Georgia could provide a barrier for British colonies further north against Spanish aggression from the south. Oglethorpe was engaged in fighting off the Spanish in 1739–43. In 1753 Georgia became an English province and was the fourth state to join the Union in 1788. It seceded from the Union in 1861 and rejoined in 1870.

Georgiyevsk, STAVROPOL TERRITORY/RUSSIA
Named after a fortress built in 1777 which was itself named after St George.

Geraldton, AUSTRALIA, CANADA
Australia (Western Australia): founded in 1850 as a military outpost called Gerald Town, it was named after Governor Charles Fitzgerald.

Gerizim (Arabic: **Jabal aṭ-Ṭūr**; Hebrew: **Har Gerizim**), WEST BANK
A mountain whose Arabic name comes from the Samaritan Tura Berikha 'Mount of Blessing'. The Samaritans built a sanctuary at the top.

Germantown, PENNSYLVANIA/USA
Founded in 1683 by thirteen Quaker families from Krefeld, Germany who, suffering from religious persecution and financial hardship, emigrated to North America and established what they called the 'German Township'.

Germany (Deutschland)
The Federal Republic of Germany (Bundesrepublik Deutschland) since May 1949. At that time this referred only to West Germany, the German Democratic Republic being inaugurated in the Soviet zone of the former Germany in October 1949. The two republics united as the present Federal Republic in October 1990. Previously, at the end of the Second World War, the country was divided into American, British, French, and Soviet zones (1945–9); known by the Nazis as the Third Reich (Empire) (1933–45); the German nation, the Second Reich, was created in 1871 with the unification of its states. The name *Deutsch(land)* has its origins in the term *theudā* 'people' and its adjective *theudisca* which, in a linguistic sense, referred to various vernaculars of the German people, but as *Dutch* in the 16th century it became restricted to the Netherlanders and their language; *Deutsch* then developed into the more general term. The origin of the name 'Germany' is not clear, although the Romans called the country Germania. According to Tacitus (c.56–c.120), the Roman historian, this was the land east of the River Rhine and north of the River Danube.

It may be connected with the Celtic *gair* 'neighbour' but is traditionally derived from the Germanic *gari* 'lance' and *man* 'people'. Germany is unlike most countries in so far as its name is not universal: the French call it Allemagne and the Spanish *Alemania* after the Alemanni, a Germanic tribe of the 3rd–5th centuries; the Italians use *Germania*, but their word for German is *tedesco*; the Slavs use variations based on the root word *nem* 'mute' to mean 'not able to speak, or understand, our language' (in Russian, *Nemetchina*, in Serbo-Croat *Nemačka*, and the Romanian for German is *Neamt*); and the Finns call it *Saksa* the 'Land of the Saxons'. Following study of epidemics in Germany in the 19th century, it gave its name to German measles, otherwise known as rubella, the milder form of measles; it has also given its name to the German shepherd dog, or alsatian, bred as a working dog in Germany.

Germiston, GAUTENG/SOUTH AFRICA
Elandsfontein
Founded in 1887 and renamed in 1904 after the Scottish birthplace of John Jack, one of two gold prospectors, who helped develop the settlement.

Gettysburg, PENNSYLVANIA/USA *Gettys Town*
Named after its founder, James Gettys, when it was laid out in the 1780s. It was renamed in 1800.

Geysir, ICELAND
A place where a geyser first erupted in 1294. The Icelandic word means 'to gush' from the Old Scandinavian *geysa*. It has given the English word 'geyser' to describe a hot spring, usually in a volcanic area.

Gezira, THE SUDAN
A state derived from the Arabic *al-jazā'ir* 'the islands', a reference to the fertile land between the Blue and White Nile Rivers.

Ghana *Gold Coast*
The Republic of Ghana since 1960, the name Ghana being adopted in 1957 when the Gold Coast became independent, the first of the UK's African colonies to become so. At this time British Togoland (the western third of German Togoland, which had become separate British and French League of Nations mandates in 1919) joined the new Ghana. The Gold Coast, named Costa do Ouro by the Portuguese when they established trading posts along the coast at the end of the 15th century, became a British crown colony in 1874; *Ashanti became a crown colony in 1902 while the Northern Territories became a protectorate on the same day. The name comes from an old and extensive empire,

Ghana, to the north of modern Ghana, now Mali and Mauritania. This disintegrated in the 13th century and the clans migrated southwards. The actual word Ghana may be the title assumed by a tribal chieftain of the old empire, meaning 'king' or 'sovereign'.

Gharbīyah, al-, EGYPT
A governorate which takes its name from the Arabic *gharaba* 'to set', that is, of the sun. It means, therefore, 'The West'.

Ghardaïa, ALGERIA
'Cave of St Daïa' from the Arabic *ghār* 'cave' and the name of the female saint, Daïa, who is said to have lived in it.

Ghar el Melh, TUNISIA
'Cave of Salt' from the Arabic *ghār* 'cave' and *milh* 'salt'. This may refer to a shallow lake, although it is not known to have any connection with salt. Once an important port, it is also known as Porto Farina.

Ghāts, INDIA
Two mountain ranges, the Western Ghāts and the Eastern Ghāts, in central and southern India which take their name from the Hindi *ghāṭ* 'mountain pass'.

Ghāzīpur, UTTAR PRADESH/INDIA *Gadhīpūr*
The name was altered *c*.1330 in honour of Ghāzī Malik (Masud Malik al-Sadat), a local Muslim ruler who is said to have won a famous victory over the Hindus, with *pur* added. *Ghazi* from the Arabic *gāzī* can be used as an honorific title for a Muslim fighter against non-Muslims.

Ghazni, AFGHANISTAN *Alexandria (of the Paropanisades)*, *Ghazna*
Named originally after Alexander III the Great[†] *c*.330 BC, the present name comes from the Dari (the dialect of Persian spoken in Afghanistan) *ganj* 'treasure'. Refounded in the 9th century by Yakub, the Emir of Sistan, it was the capital of the huge Ghaznavid Empire between 977 and 1140.

Ghent (Flemish: **Gent**; French: **Gand**), BELGIUM
Probably derived from the Celtic *condate* 'confluence', a reference to its position at the junction of the Rivers Lys and Scheldt.

Gibeon, NAMIBIA
Named after Gibeon, a town north-west of Jerusalem, because the local chief wanted an appropriate name for a place where the gospel was preached.

Gibraltar, AND USA
1. An Overseas Territory of the UK. It is named after the Moorish commander, Tāriq ibn Ziyād (d. *c*.720), who captured the 'Rock' in 711, with

the additional Arabic *jabal* 'mountain'. Thus the present name is adapted from Jabal Tāriq 'Tāriq's Mountain'. The Spanish retook it from the Moors in 1462 and it was annexed to Spain in 1501. In 1704, during the War of the Spanish Succession, it was captured by British troops and formally ceded to Great Britain 'for ever' by the Treaty of Utrecht in 1713. It became a crown colony in 1830. Called in the ancient world Calpe, possibly a Phoenician name, it was one of the two Pillars of Hercules on either side of the Strait of Gibraltar. (The other is disputed: either the generally accepted Jabal Musa in Ceuta or Perejil.) It has given its name to the Strait of Gibraltar, known to the Moors as *Bāb el-Zaka* 'Gate of the Narrow Entrance (to the World)'. The Latin name was Fretum Herculeum.
2. USA (Michigan): named after the British territory.

Gibson Desert, WESTERN AUSTRALIA/
AUSTRALIA
Named in 1876 by Ernest Giles after Alfred Gibson, who was accompanying Giles as they crossed the desert but who died while searching for water.

Gigant, ROSTOV/RUSSIA
Developed from the Gigant 'Giant' State Farm established here in 1928.

Gila Bend, ARIZONA/USA
Named after the River Gila which makes a 90° turn to the west here.

Gilbert Islands, PACIFIC OCEAN
See KIRIBATI.

Gillingham, ENGLAND/UK *Gelingeham (Dorset),*
Gyllingeham, Gelingeham (Kent)
'Homestead of Gylla's People' from an Old English personal name, *-inga-*, and *hām*. The town in Dorset is pronounced with a hard *g* while the one in Kent has a soft *g*. In the Domesday Book (1086) both were called Gelingeham.

Gippsland, VICTORIA/AUSTRALIA *Caledonia*
Australis
A region originally named in 1839 by Angus McMillan, who made the first European exploration, after his native Scotland. It was renamed a year later by a Polish explorer, Paul Strzelecki, after Sir George Gipps (1791–1847), governor of New South Wales (1838–46) and a man who strongly encouraged exploration and the development of colonial resources.

Girardot, COLOMBIA *Pastor Montero*
Named after Atanasio Girardot (1791–1813), a hero of the Battle of Bárbula in 1813 during which he was killed.

Giresun, TURKEY *Choerades, Pharnacia, Kerasous*
Named after the wild cherry trees, in ancient Greek *kerasos,* which were abundant in the area, and still are. It was from here that the Roman general Lucius Lucullus (*c.*117–*c.*56 BC) introduced the cherry tree to Europe. The Greeks also called the city Pharnacia since it was founded by Pharnaces I, King of Pontus (*c.*185–*c.*157 BC). Kerasous was the Roman name.

Girga, EGYPT
Named after the monastery of St George.

Gisborne, NORTH ISLAND/NEW ZEALAND
A unitary authority and city surveyed in 1870 by, and named after, Sir William Gisborne, the British colonial secretary at the time.

Giurgiu, ROMANIA
A county and a city. The Genoese built a fortress on an island in the Danube which they called San Giorgio 'St George'. This evolved into the present name.

Giza (al-Jīzah), EGYPT
A governorate and a city also known as el-Gīza. With the city just north-east of the three great pyramids of the pharoahs, its present name is derived from *Er-ges-ḥer* 'beside the high' from *ges* 'beside' and *ḥer* 'high'.

Gjirokastër, ALBANIA *Argyrókastron, Ergeri*
Said to be named after the Greek Princess Argyro who threw herself from the tower of the citadel (in Greek, *kastron*), built by the Argyres in the 15th century, rather than surrender to a besieging Turkish army. However, it may simply have been named after the Argyres tribe as the 'Citadel of the Argyres'. Ergeri was the Ottoman Turkish name. It was occupied by the Greeks, Germans, and Italians, who called it Argirocastro, during the Second World War.

Glace Bay, NOVA SCOTIA/CANADA
So named after the ice from the French *glace* which appears each year in the Gulf of St Lawrence.

Gladstone, AUSTRALIA, CANADA, NEW
ZEALAND, USA
The nine places with this name, two in Australia (Queensland, Tasmania), one in Canada (Manitoba), one in New Zealand (North Island), and five in the USA (Michigan, Missouri, New Mexico, North Dakota, and Oregon) are all named after William Ewart Gladstone (1809–98), prime minister of the UK four times (1868–74, 1880–5, 1886, 1892–4).

Gladwin, MICHIGAN/USA
Named after Major Henry Gladwin who commanded the military outpost at Detroit at

the time of Pontiac's Conspiracy in 1763. Pontiac was an Ottawa chief who attempted, but ultimately failed, to eject the British from the Great Lakes region.

Glamorgan, Vale of (Morgannwg), WALES/UK

A former county and now a unitary district created in 1974 with a name meaning 'Morgan's Shore' from the Welsh *gwlad* or *glan* 'territory', 'land', or 'shore' and the personal name. The Welsh name means the 'Land of Morgan' with the added *wg* meaning 'territory'. Morgan is believed to have been a Welsh prince from the 7th or the 10th century.

Glarus (French: **Glaris**), SWITZERLAND

A canton, which joined the Swiss Confederation in 1352, a city, and part of the Alps. The name probably comes from the Latin *clarus* 'bright' or 'clear', either to indicate the purity of the air in the mountains or the fact that the area was not completely tree-covered.

Glasco, KANSAS/USA

Named after Glasgow, the city in Scotland, but misspelt by the first postmaster.

Glasgow, JAMAICA, UK, USA

UK (Scotland): originally Glasgu, the Gaelic name is Glaschu or Glascho 'Green Hollow' from *glas* 'green' and *cau* 'hollow'.

Glassboro, NEW JERSEY/USA

So-called because of its glass factories.

Glastonbury, UK, USA

UK (England): the previous name, Glæstingeberia, meant 'Stronghold of the People living at Glaston'. Glaston itself may mean 'Woad Place' or 'Place where Woad grew' from the Celtic *glas* 'woad' and the Old English *-inga-*, now *-ton*, to give 'Place of the Woad People'. 'Place' was strengthened by adding *burh*.

Glendale, USA

There are nine cities with this name. They are basically descriptive of the terrain in which they are situated, 'glen' and 'dale' both meaning 'valley'.

Glenelg, AUSTRALIA, UK, USA

1. Australia (Victoria): a river, originally called Nangeela, surveyed in 1836 and named after Charles Grant (1778–1866), Lord Glenelg, British secretary of state for the colonies (1835–9), and a suburb of Adelaide in South Australia.
2. UK (Scotland): Charles Grant took his title from Glenelg in Scotland. The Gaelic name is Gleann Eilge from *gleann* 'valley'; the meaning of Eilge is not known.

Glen Ellyn, ILLINOIS/USA *Babcock's Grove, DuPage Center, Stacy's Corners, Newton's Station, Danby, Prospect Park*

In 56 years (1833–89) the name changed seven times. Finally it was named after Ellyn, the wife of the then village president.

Glenrothes, SCOTLAND/UK

A New Town established in 1948 and named after the Earls of Rothes to which the word 'glen', a common element of Scottish names meaning 'valley', has been added.

Glens Falls, NEW YORK/USA *Wing's Falls*

Settled by 1770 and named after Abraham Wing, it was renamed in 1788 after Colonel Johannes Glen, also known as John Glen, who built paper mills here. The Native Americans called the Falls *Chepontuc* 'Difficult Place to get round'.

Glóssa, GREECE
'Tongue'.

Glossop, ENGLAND/UK *Glosop, Glotsop*
'Glott's Valley' from an Old English personal name and *hop* 'enclosure in a valley'.

Gloucester, AUSTRALIA, CANADA, PAPUA NEW GUINEA, UK, USA

1. UK (England): founded as Nervana in 96 by, and named briefly after, Marcus Nerva (*c.*80–98), Roman emperor (96–8). In the 2nd century it was known by the Romans as Coloniae Glevum, indicating that it was a colony for retired Roman soldiers. In the Domesday Book (1086) it is called Glowecestre '(Roman) Town called Glevum'. The present name is derived from Glevum, which itself is derived from a Celtic root word for 'bright', and *ceaster*. Thus the name can be taken to mean 'Splendid Camp'. The English county of Gloucestershire takes its name from the city with the additional *scīr*.
2. The other cities and towns with this name either recognize the English city or honour various Dukes of Gloucester.

Gloversville, NEW YORK/USA *Stump City*

Settled in the 1760s, it was renamed in 1832 as a result of the glove industry which had arisen here.

Gnadenhütten, OHIO/USA

Settled by Moravian missionaries, it was given a German name meaning 'Tabernacles of Grace' from *Gnade* 'grace' and *Hütte* 'tabernacle'.

Gniezno, POLAND *Gnesen*

According to legend, Lech, a chief of the Polanie tribe, discovered the nest (in Polish, *gniazdo*) of a white eagle while out hunting. This was taken to be a good omen. The place was given the name 'nest', although this could refer to the fact that the area was naturally defendable (as in modern parlance, a 'machine-gun nest'). Gniezno was the first capital of Poland between 966 and 1038; the eagle became the emblem of the Polish nation.

Goa, INDIA *Gowa, Govapura, Sindabur/Sandābūr*
A state with a name variously said to mean 'Fertile Land' from the local words *goe mat* or 'Cattle Country' from the Sanskrit *go* 'cow', an animal sacred to the Hindus. Under Afonso de Albuquerque, the Portuguese conquered the town in 1510 and, in due course, it became the capital of all Portuguese possessions in the Far East. In 1961 Indian troops invaded and in 1962 Goa was incorporated into India. It became a state in 1987.

Goageb, NAMIBIA
'Twin Rivers', a reference to the fact that it lies at a junction.

Gobabis, NAMIBIA
Originally a mission station, the name means 'Place of Discussion' in Khoikhoin.

Gobi Desert, CHINA-MONGOLIA
'Waterless Place' or simply 'Desert' from the Mongolian *gov*; annual rainfall is less than three inches (76 mm). The Chinese name is Shāmò 'desert' from *shā* 'sand' and *mò* 'end'.

Godalming, ENGLAND/UK *Godelmingum, Godelminge*
'Godhelm's Settlement' from an Old English personal name and *-ingas*.

Goderich, ONTARIO/CANADA
Laid out in 1828 and named after Frederick John Robinson (1782–1859), Viscount Goderich and 1st Earl of Ripon, British chancellor of the exchequer (1823–7) and prime minister from August 1827 to January 1828.

Godmanchester, ENGLAND/UK *Godmundcestre*
'(Roman) Place associated with Godmund' from an Old English personal name and *ceaster*.

Gökdepe, TURKMENISTAN *Geok Tepe*
The previous spelling was the Russian version of the Turkic name meaning 'Blue Hill' from the Turkmen *gök* 'blue' and *depe* 'hill' or 'summit'.

Golan Heights (Hebrew: **Ramat Hagolan**; Arabic: **al-Jawlān**), ISRAEL
A hilly region annexed from Syria in 1981, having been captured in 1967. It takes its name from the biblical city of Golan in Bashan mentioned in the Bible (Deuteronomy 4: 43 and Joshua 20: 8). The meaning of Golan is not known.

Golbahār, AFGHANISTAN
'Rose of Spring' from the Turkish *gül* 'rose' and *bahar* 'spring' (the season)'; *bahar* can also mean 'flowers' or 'blossom'.

Golbshtadt, ALTAY/RUSSIA *Nekrasovo*
Between 1949 and 1991 it was called Nekrasovo from *nekrasiviy* 'ugly' or 'unsightly' when Joseph Stalin[†] abolished the German National District in the Altay Republic in an act of revenge for the Nazi invasion of the Soviet Union in June 1941. The original name, probably from a personal name and the German *Stadt*, was only restored on the eve of the fiftieth anniversary of the invasion.

Gold Coast, QUEENSLAND/AUSTRALIA
A city comprising a line of beach resorts which, collectively, are named after their golden sands. *See* GHANA.

Golden, CANADA, IRELAND, USA
USA (Colorado): the origin of the name is disputed. Some sources claim that it is named after Tom Golden, a miner, it being founded as a mining town in 1857; others, that it is named after the Golden Gate, a narrow pass in the mountains in Jefferson County, Colorado.

Golden Gate, CALIFORNIA/USA
The strait between San Francisco Bay and the Pacific Ocean named by John C. Frémont (1813–90) in 1846 after the *Golden Horn. The Golden Gate Bridge spans the strait. *See* FREMONT.

Golden Horn (Haliç), TURKEY
An inlet of the Bosporus that divides the northern and southern sectors of the city of Istanbul. The curve of the inlet, some 5 miles (8 km) long, gave rise to the 'horn' while 'golden' may have been added because it turns golden in the rays of the setting sun. The Turkish *haliç* means 'inlet', 'gulf', or 'channel'.

Goldsboro, NORTH CAROLINA/USA
Settled in 1838, it was named after Matthew T. Goldsborough, who was involved with the Wilmington and Weldon Railroad which traversed the state.

Golela, SWAZILAND
'(Place where) Animals gather' in Swazi. It was probably a good area for hunting, hence the name.

Gölhisar, TURKEY
'Lake Castle' from *göl* 'lake' and *hisar*, although the nearest lake, Gölhisar Gölü, is 5 miles (8 km) away. The original town, however, was on a small hill in the lake, and was accessible by a narrow causeway.

Goliad, TEXAS/USA *Nuestra Señora del Espíritu Santo Zuñiga*
The Spanish mission 'Our Lady of the Holy Spirit of Zuniga' was established in 1749. The present name of the historical site, in use since 1829, is said to be an anagram of (H)idalgo after Miguel Hidalgo y Costilla (1753–1811), a priest revered as the father of Mexican independence. However, it is possible that the name comes from the biblical Goliath.

Goli Otok, CROATIA
'Bare Island' from the Serbo-Croat *goli* 'bare' and *otok* 'island'.

Gomera, CANARY ISLANDS/SPAIN
An island meaning 'Gum Tree' from the Spanish *gomero*.

Gómez Palacio, DURANGO/MEXICO
Founded in 1886, it was named after the governor of the state at the time, Francisco Gómez Palacio.

Gomorrah, ISRAEL
A city mentioned in the Bible (Genesis 10: 19) whose location is not known, although it may have been at the southern end of the Dead Sea. Together with Sodom, it was destroyed by 'brimstone and fire' (Genesis 19: 24) because of the wicked and immoral behaviour of its inhabitants. Located in a very fertile area, the name comes from the Hebrew *ómer* 'sheaf of corn', a reference to the crop grown here.

Gondwana, INDIA
An historic region in central India which now includes parts of the states of Madhya Pradesh, Andhra Pradesh, and Mahārāshtra. The name means the 'Land of the Gonds', a tribal group that ruled the region between the 14th and 18th centuries and still live there now. Gondwanaland is the name coined by an Australian geologist to describe a hypothetical ancient supercontinent in the southern hemisphere.

Goodenough Island, PAPUA NEW GUINEA *Morata*
One of the D'Entrecasteaux Islands, it was visited in 1873 by the British naval Captain John Moresby who named it after Commodore James Goodenough (1830–75). Morata is still used as a local name.

Good Hope, Cape of, SOUTH AFRICA
See CAPE OF GOOD HOPE.

Goodwood, WESTERN CAPE/SOUTH AFRICA
Planned as a racecourse in 1905, it was named after the famous course in Sussex, England. However, the plan was not implemented and Goodwood developed into a normal town.

Goolwa, SOUTH AUSTRALIA/AUSTRALIA
Situated close to a bend in the Murray River, the name is an Aboriginal word for 'elbow'.

Goondiwindi, QUEENSLAND/AUSTRALIA
'Resting Place for Birds' from an Aboriginal word.

Gorakhpur, UTTAR PRADESH/INDIA
Founded *c*.1400, it was named after a Hindu saint, Yogi Gorakhnāth, who is believed to have lived during the 10th and 11th centuries, with the additional *pur*. It has, however, been suggested that the name is derived from the Gurkhas, Nepalese Hindus.

Gordion, TURKEY *Gordium*
Ruins. Named after its founder, Gordius, a poor farmer who, according to legend, migrated here in a wooden cart, thus fulfilling the oracle's prophesy and becoming king. The yoke of his cart was tied to the shaft by a most complicated knot. The legend claims that it could only be undone by the future conqueror of Asia. Alexander III the Great[†], keen to be just that, was shown the cart on his arrival in the town, the key road-junction in central Anatolia, in 333 BC. Instead, apparently, of trying to untie the knot, Alexander cut through it with his sword. Thus, 'to cut the Gordian knot' is to solve a difficult problem with decisive and bold action.

Gordon's Bay, WESTERN CAPE/SOUTH AFRICA *Visch Hoek*
Originally a fishing port 'Fish Corner', it was easily confused with Fish Hoek which lay opposite it across False Bay. It was thus renamed after Colonel Robert Gordon of the Dutch East India Company who explored the coastline here in 1778.

Gore, SOUTH ISLAND/NEW ZEALAND *Longford*
Renamed after Sir Thomas Gore Browne (1807–87), governor of New Zealand (1855–62).

Göreme, TURKEY *Avcílar*
May be translated as 'Cannot be seen' or 'Not able to see' from the negative suffix *-eme* to the root *gör* 'to see'. This is probably a reference to the 'fairy chimneys', tall rocky needles, that surround the town and with which there is no comparison in terms of their beauty anywhere else. The nearby village of Avcílar means 'hunters' or 'skirmishers'.

Gorgonzola, LOMBARDY/ITALY *Argenza*
Possibly derived from Concordiola, itself from the goddess Concordia. With surplus milk on their hands, the inhabitants began to make a soft cheese which was named after the town.

Gori, GEORGIA *Tonti*
'Mountain', although this is something of a misnomer. However, the ancient and now ruined fortress, called Goristsikhe, was built on a hill overlooking the present town.

Gorizia (Slovene: **Gorica**; German: **Görz**), FRIULI-VENEZIA GIULIA/ITALY-SLOVENIA
Adapted from the Slovene *Gorica*, the diminutive of *gore* 'mountain'; thus, 'hill'. It was an Austrian possession from 1500 until 1919 when it was annexed by Italy. The northern suburbs of the town passed to Yugoslavia in 1947 and became known as Nova (New) Gorica. At that time a fence was erected to divide the city and this was only removed in 2004.

Gorkha, NEPAL
Also spelt Gurkha and named after Gorakhnāth, the patron saint of the region. The members of the local military force raised here in the 16th century came to be known as Gurkhas. Since the beginning of the 19th century significant numbers have volunteered to serve, and are still serving, in the British and Indian Armies. The name Gurkha comes from the Sanskrit *gorakṣā* 'cowherd' from *go* 'cow' and *rakṣā* 'guard' or 'protection'. To Hindus the cow is sacred.

Gorki, YAMALO-NENETS AUTONOMOUS DISTRICT/ RUSSIA *Gorki Leninskiye*
'Mountain' from *gora*. Leninskiye was added because of Lenin's[†] association with the town in 1918–24. He spent time here following an assassination attempt on him in 1918 and he died here. This town should not be confused with Gorky (now Nizhniy Novgorod).

Görlitz, SAXONY/GERMANY *Gorelić*
Until 1945 the German city lay astride the River Neisse. When the river became the border in 1945 between East Germany and Poland, the German part of the town retained its German name while the Polish part on the eastern bank took the name Zgorzelec. Both originate from a Slavonic word *goret′* 'to burn', signifying that the town was developed in a part of the forest cleared by burning.

Gorlovka, UKRAINE
Founded in 1867 as a coal-mining settlement, it is named after Pëtr (Peter) Nikolayevich Gorlov, who was instrumental in sinking the first mineshaft.

Gornji Milanovac, SERBIA/SERBIA AND MONTENEGRO *Despotovica*
First named after the river on which it lies. By a decree in 1859 of Miloš Obrenović (1780–1860), Prince of Serbia (1817–39, 1859–60), the name was changed to commemorate Miloš's son, Milan (1819–39), who died within a month of becoming Prince of Serbia in 1839; he was born here. The Serbo-Croat *gornji* means 'upper' to differentiate it from Lower *Donji* Milanovac.

Gorno-Altaysk, ALTAY TERRITORY/RUSSIA *Ulala, Oyrot-Tura*
The original Turkish name, meaning 'Great One', lasted until 1932. In 1932–48 it was renamed Oyrot-Tura 'Oyrot Town' after the Mongoloid Oyrot people. It is now named after the Altay Mountains from *altan* 'golden' and *gornyy* 'mountainous'.

Gornyak, ALTAY TERRITORY/RUSSIA
'Miner', a colloquial word and a reference to the mining that is undertaken in this area.

Gorodishche, BELARUS
'Site of an Ancient Settlement' in Russian. This probably means that there was some kind of fortified settlement here. The word can also mean 'Very Large Town', which may have been the case once but is not now.

Gorodok, BELARUS
'Small Town' or 'Site of an Ancient Settlement' from the Russian *gorod* and -*ok* denoting an ancient site.

Gort, IRELAND
'Tilled Field'.

Góry Świętokrzyskie, POLAND
'Holy Cross Mountains' from *gora*, *święty* 'holy', and *krzyz* 'cross' after an old Benedictine abbey on one of the mountains.

Gosainthan (Chinese: **Xixiabangma Feng**; Tibetan: **Shisha Pangma**), TIBET/CHINA
One of the highest mountains in the Himalayas, Gosainthan means 'Place of God' from the Sanskrit *gosāin* 'God' and *than* 'place'. The Tibetan name means 'Range above the Grassy Plain'.

Gosford, AUSTRALIA, UK
1. Australia (New South Wales): founded in 1839 and named after Archibald Acheson (1776–1849), 2nd Earl of Gosford, the Irish governor-in-chief of British North America (1835–7). His tenure was not a great success and it is not known why this town was named after him.
2. UK (England): 'Ford frequented by Geese' from the Old English *gōs* 'goose' and *ford*.

Goslar, LOWER SAXONY/GERMANY *Goslara, Geslari*
Possibly derived from the Old High German *gôse* 'flood' or 'inundation' and *lar* 'pasture' or 'site', a reference to its position on the River Gose 'the Rushing One' at the northern foot of the Harz Mountains.

Gosport, UK, USA
UK (England): originally Goseport meaning 'Market where Geese are sold' from the Old English gōs 'goose' and port.

Gotha, THURINGIA/GERMANY *Gotaha*
The original name was that used by the Frankish king, Charlemagne[†], in 775. It may have been derived from Old Saxon, *gota* 'ditch'. The British Royal Family is partially descended from the Dukes of Saxe-Coburg and Gotha, Queen Victoria[†] marrying her cousin, Albert of Saxe-Coburg and Gotha.

Gothenburg (Göteborg), SWEDEN
Founded in 1603 on the site of a Gothic settlement, it means 'Fort of the Goths' from the Swedish *Got* 'Goth' and *borg*.

Gotland, SWEDEN
A county and an island meaning 'Land of the Goths'. Originating in southern Scandinavia, they migrated to the Black Sea at the end of the 2nd century and later split into two: the Visigoths, Western Goths, and Ostrogoths, Eastern Goths.

Göttingen, LOWER SAXONY/GERMANY
Teliphordum, Gutingi
'Settlers at the Ditch' from Old Saxon *gota* 'ditch' (*see* GOTHA).

Goulburn, NEW SOUTH WALES/AUSTRALIA
Goulburn Plains
Founded in 1818 and named after Henry Goulburn (1784–1856), then British under-secretary of state for the colonies (1813–21). The name was changed in 1833 to reflect the newly won status of a town. The Goulburn Islands, off the coast of Northern Territory, and the Goulburn River in Victoria, were also named after Goulburn.

Governors Island, NEW YORK/USA *Pagganck, Nooten*
The Dutch changed the Native American name to Nooten in 1637, but in 1698 it was taken over for use by colonial governors, hence the name.

Göytäpä, AZERBAIJAN *Prishíb*
Although the area is flat, this means 'Blue Hill' from *göy* 'blue' and *täpä* 'hill'.

Gozo (Ghaudex), MALTA *Gaulos/Gaulus*
An island with the original Phoenician name of Gaulos said to mean 'Merchant Boat of Round Shape'. It was held by the Carthaginians between the 7th and 2nd centuries BC and then conquered by the Romans in 218 BC; they spelt the name Gaulus.

Graaff-Reinet, EASTERN CAPE/SOUTH AFRICA
Founded in 1786 by, and named after, Cornelius van de Graaff, a Dutch governor of

the Cape (1785–91), and his wife Cornelia, whose maiden name was Reinet.

Graciosa Island (Ilha Graciosa), AZORES/PORTUGAL
Discovered in 1451, the name means 'Elegant, or Pleasing, Island' from the Portuguese *gracioso*, possibly because of its less mountainous terrain compared with nearby islands.

Grafton, AUSTRALIA, USA
1. Australia (New South Wales): Grafton and South Grafton, both named after Augustus Henry Fitzroy (1735–1811), 3rd Duke of Grafton, British prime minister (1768–70), merged to form a single city and port in 1956.
2. USA (Massachusetts): founded in 1654 with the Native American name of Hassanisco, it was renamed after Charles Fitzroy (1683–1757), 2nd Duke of Grafton, when the first English settlers arrived in 1718.
3. USA (North Dakota): settled in 1877 and named after Grafton County in New Hampshire, the place of departure for the pioneers moving west. The county was named after the 3rd Duke of Grafton.
4. USA (West Virginia): settled in 1852 by railroad construction workers of the Baltimore and Ohio Railroad who 'grafted on' a branch line to Wheeling here.

Graham Land, ANTARCTICA *Trinity Land, Graham Coast*
The first recorded landfall on the peninsula was made in 1820 by Lieutenant Commander Edward Bransfield, of the British Royal Navy, and William Smith who called it Trinity Land. A British navigator, John Biscoe, claimed it for the UK in 1832 and named it after Sir James Graham (1792–1861), first lord of the Admiralty (1830–4, 1852–5) at the time. However, the peninsula was called the Palmer Peninsula by the Americans after Nathaniel Palmer, a sealing captain, who had also visited the area in 1820. To resolve the matter the place-name committees in the USA and UK agreed in 1964 to call the northern part of the peninsula Graham Land and the southern part Palmer Land.

Grahamstown (Afrikaans: Grahamstad; Xhosa: Rini), EASTERN CAPE/SOUTH AFRICA
Graham's Town
Founded in 1812 by, and named after, Colonel John Graham, as a military frontier post opposite Xhosa territory.

Granada, AUSTRALIA, COLOMBIA, GUATEMALA, NICARAGUA, SPAIN, USA
Spain (Andalusia): originally an Iberian settlement in the 5th century BC called

Elibyrge 'New Town' from the Old Iberian *ili* 'town' and *berri* 'new'; it became the Roman Illiberis which was Arabized to Ilbīra (to the Spanish, Elvira). A new Moorish capital, Kastīliya, was founded in 747 some 7 miles (12 km) to the north-west; this soon became known by the Spanish as (New) Elvira. This town was sacked in 1010 and the inhabitants moved back to (Old) Elvira which became the Moorish Gharnāṭah when it became the capital of the Moorish Kingdom with the same name (1238–1492). The Moorish name may mean 'Hill of Strangers'. The final Moorish stronghold in Spain, it surrendered to the armies of Ferdinand II (1452–1516), King of Aragón (1479–1516), and his wife and co-sovereign, Isabella I (1451–1504), Queen of Castile (1474–1504) in 1492. The present name is said to come from the Latin *granatum* 'pomegranate', a reference to the local abundance of this fruit. The cities and towns in the other countries are named after the Spanish city.

Granby, CANADA, USA
1. Canada (Quebec): founded in 1851 and named after the village in England whose name means 'Grani's Farmstead'.
2. USA (Connecticut and Massachusetts): named after John Manners (1721–70), given the courtesy title of Marquis of Granby, commander-in-chief of the British Army in 1766 and a hero of the Seven Years' War (1756–63).

Gran Chaco, SOUTH AMERICA
A huge lowland plain meaning 'Great Hunting Ground' from the Spanish *gran* 'great' and a Quechua word.

Grand-Bassam, CÔTE D'IVOIRE *Bassam*
The original name was the local word for a coastal village which became a French trading post towards the end of the 17th century. This was expanded in 1843 to include a military camp. When the locality became the capital of the Colony of Côte d'Ivoire in 1893 (until 1900) the French *grand* 'great' was added.

Grand Erg Occidental, ALGERIA
'Great Western Sand Sea' from the French *grand* 'great' and *occidental* 'western', and *erg*, a representative word in Arabic for 'sand sea' where the dunes are constantly on the move. The 'Great Eastern Sand Sea', *Grand Erg Oriental*, is much larger than its western counterpart.

Grand Forks, CANADA, USA
USA (North Dakota): named by French fur traders *Les Grandes Fourches* 'The Grand Forks' since their settlement was situated at the confluence of the Red River of the North and the Red Lake River.

Grand Haven, MICHIGAN/USA
So-called because it is situated on a good harbour on the east side of Lake Michigan.

Grand Island, NEBRASKA/USA
French-Canadian trappers called the island, some 25 miles (40 km) long in the Platte River, *La Grande Île* 'The Big Island', although the city actually lies some 5 miles (8 km) to the north so that it could be on the Union Pacific Railroad.

Grand Junction, USA
1. Colorado: originally founded in 1881 as Ute as a gesture after the Ute people had been ejected from the area. It was later renamed West Denver and finally after the junction of the Colorado and Gunnison Rivers.
2. Iowa: so-called because of the junction of the Keokuk and Des Moines, and the Chicago and Northwestern Railroads.

Grand-Mère, QUEBEC/CANADA
'Grandmother' in French. So-called because the local Native Americans thought that a rock in the Saint-Maurice River looked like the profile of an old woman.

Grand Rapids, CANADA, USA
USA (Michigan): founded in 1826 by a Frenchman, Louis Campau, at a point where various Native American trails met at rapids on the Grand River.

Granite City, ILLINOIS/USA
The city took its name from its principal industry: a factory devoted to graniteware (enamelled ironware) was established in 1891.

Granma, CUBA
A province since 1976 and named after the yacht that transported Fidel Castro (b. 1926/7), revolutionary leader, prime minister (1959–76), and president (1976–), and his co-revolutionaries from Mexico to Cuba in 1956 to restart the Cuban Revolution.

Granollers, CATALONIA/SPAIN *Granullaria*
Derived from its Roman name which itself came from the Latin *granum* 'grain', a reference to the agricultural importance of the city.

Gran Sasso d'Italia, ABRUZZO/ITALY
A mountain area meaning 'Great Rock of Italy' from *sasso* 'rock'.

Grantham, UK, USA
UK (England): 'Granta's Village' from an Old English personal name and *hām*, or 'Gravel Village' from a speculative Old English word *grand* 'gravel'. This would have meant a village built on gravel.

Grants, NEW MEXICO/USA *Grants Station*
Named after the Grant brothers who
established a construction camp here for the
Atchison, Topeka, and Santa Fe Railroad in
1881.

Grants Pass, OREGON/USA
Originally a caravan halt on the Sacramento–
Portland route, it became a station on the
South Pacific Railroad in 1883. It was named
after Ulysses S. Grant (1822–85), commander
of the Union armies (1864–5) during the Civil
War and President (1869–77).

Grantsville, WEST VIRGINIA/USA
Named after Ulysses S. Grant (see previous
entry).

Granville, CANADA, FRANCE, USA
Seven cities in the USA have this name, some
named after John Carteret (1690–1763), 1st
Earl of Granville, British secretary of state
(1722–4, 1742–4) and a landowner in South
Carolina, USA. The cities in Illinois and Ohio
are named after the Granville in
Massachusetts.

Grasmere, CANADA, SOUTH AFRICA, UK
UK (England): formerly Gressemere, probably
'Grass Lake' from the Old English *gres* 'grass',
and *sæ* and *mere* both 'lake'.

Grasse, PROVENCE-ALPES-CÔTE D'AZUR/FRANCE
Probably derived from a Roman personal
name, Crassus 'fat'.

Graubünden (French: **Grisons**; Italian:
Grigioni), SWITZERLAND
A canton which joined the Swiss
Confederation in 1803 with a name meaning
'Grey Leagues' from the German *grau*, the
French *gris*, and the Italian *grigio* 'grey', and the
German *Bund* 'league'. The first league, called
Grauerbund, was created in 1395 to resist the
growing power of the Habsburgs in the Upper
Rhine valley. It was so-called because its
members wore grey cloth uniforms. The
Romansh name of Grishun has the same
meaning.

Gravelines (Flemish: **Gravelinghe**), NORD-
PAS-DE-CALAIS/FRANCE *Graveninghen*
'Count's Canal' from the Flemish *gravelinghe*
after the *Graf* 'Count' of Flanders had canalized
the River Aa in the 12th century. The French
finally acquired the town at the Treaty of the
Pyrenees in 1658.

Gravesend, AUSTRALIA, UK
UK (England): previously Gravesham and
Grauessend meaning a '(Place at) the End of
the Copse' from the Old English *gráf* 'copse' or
'grove' and *ende*.

Gravina in Puglia, APULIA/ITALY
Gravina, as a southern Italian geographical
term, means 'gorge' or 'dried up river bed'.
It can also be translated more generally as the
'(place of) a twisting crevasse common in
calcareous terrain'. *Puglia* is the Italian for
Apulia, the region.

Grayling, MICHIGAN/USA
Named after the abundant grayling, once to be
found in the Au Sable River on which the city
lies.

Graz, AUSTRIA
Derived from the Slavonic *gradec* 'small fort'.
This probably refers to a castle built on the
Schlossberg 'Castle Mount', an outcrop of rock
that overlooks the city.

Great Alfold (Nagy Alföld), HUNGARY
'Great Plain' from *nagy* 'great', *ala* 'below' or
'under', and *föld* 'land' or 'ground'. It is a huge,
fertile lowland in south-eastern Hungary that
spreads into Croatia, Serbia, and Romania.

Great Barrington, MASSACHUSETTS/USA
Settled in 1726 and named by the governor of
the Massachusetts Bay Colony, probably after
his nephew, William Wildman (1717–93), 2nd
Viscount Barrington, British secretary at war
(1755–61, 1765–78). 'Great' was probably
added to distinguish it from other Barringtons
of which there are four in the USA and one in
Canada.

Great Bear Lake, NORTHWEST TERRITORIES/
CANADA
Discovered in the late 18th century by North
West Company traders, it was so named
because of the numerous bears that lived along
its shores. 'Great' was added later when the
size of the lake, some 200 miles (320 km) long
and 25–110 miles (40–175 km) wide, was
appreciated.

Great Bend, USA
1. Kansas: founded in 1871 and named after
the great bend in the Arkansas River here.
2. Pennsylvania: named after the bend in the
Susquehanna River here.

Great Britain The name adopted when
England, already incorporating Wales within
its realm, was united with Scotland on 1 May
1707. This united Kingdom of Great Britain
(1707–1800) followed the personal union of
the English and Scottish crowns, which had
already taken place in 1603 when James VI,
King of Scots, became additionally James I[†] of
England. He assumed the title of King of Great
Britain in 1604, although no such kingdom
existed. Both countries retained their own
parliaments until the full union in 1707. The

term 'Great Britain' was used earlier,
informally, to distinguish the larger Britain
from the smaller Brittany, now in France, to
which refugee Britons fled to escape Anglo-
Saxon invaders. It was also used in the title
'Commonwealth of Great Britain and Ireland'
in 1654–60, following the creation of the
Commonwealth and Free State of England,
Wales, and Ireland in 1649 after the execution
of King Charles I[†] and the abolition of the
monarchy. The term 'Great Britain', which
encompasses England, Scotland, Wales, and
most of the small offshore islands but not the
Isle of Man or the Channel Islands, is often
used, incorrectly, as a synonym for the *United
Kingdom.

Great Dividing Range, AUSTRALIA
A mountain range that runs north to south
through Queensland, New South Wales, and
Victoria and so named because it separates the
coast from the interior.

Great Falls, CANADA, USA
USA (Montana): the city lies on the Missouri
River and is named after the nearby falls, 96ft
(29m) high.

Great Lakes, CANADA-USA
Lying on the border, they are the largest group
of freshwater lakes in the world. In descending
order of size they are Lake Superior, Huron,
Michigan, Erie, and Ontario.

Great Slave Lake, NORTHWEST TERRITORIES/
CANADA
Discovered in 1771 by Samuel Hearne and
named after the Slave tribe who used to live on
its western shores. They received their name,
Awokanak locally, from the Cree who were
wont to use them as slaves.

Great Smoky Mountains, NORTH
CAROLINA-TENNESSEE/USA
So named because of the haze which often
envelops them.

Great Yarmouth, ENGLAND/UK *Gernemwa*
'(Place at) the Mouth of the River Yare' from
the Celtic river name and *mūtha*. The river
name *Gerne* may mean 'babbling stream'. The
'Great' distinguishes it from *Yarmouth on the
Isle of Wight.

Greece (Ellás), AND USA
The Hellenic Republic (Ellinikí Dhimokratía)
since 1973. Previously the Kingdom of Greece
(1830–1924, 1935–73); a military coup
established a republic in 1924–35. Although
the present republic was proclaimed in July
1973 the monarchy was not abolished until
December 1974. The Ottoman Turkish
conquest of Greece was complete by 1466 and

the country remained under Turkish rule until
the war of independence (1821–30); the new
state came into existence formally in 1832. It
was much smaller than now with some two-
thirds of the Greeks still under Turkish rule.
The desire to unite all Greeks in one
homeland, known as the *Megali Idea* 'Great
Idea', grew, but it took almost another century
to achieve it. The Greeks were called Hellenes
after Hellen, son of Deucalion and Pyrrha, and
reputed leader of the Thessalians (*see*
THESSALY). Subsequently, the name Hellenes
was applied to all Greeks. Before the monarchy
was abolished in 1974 the monarch was called
the King of the Hellenes, not the King of
Greece. The term Hellas has been used
variously for the historic region of Achaea
(modern Greek, Akhaïa) on the north coast of
the Peloponnese, and Thessaly, particularly
the area south of the River Spercheios. The
ancient name of the Hellenes living in Epirus
between the city of Thothoni (now Ioánnina)
and the Akhelóös River was Graeci who, it has
been suggested, took their name from
Graecus, a personal name. The Romans
subsequently called all Hellenes Graeci and
their land became Graecia from which
'Greece' is derived. The name may, however,
have come from Graikoi, the name used by
their Illyrian neighbours; its etymology is
unknown. The term Magna Graecia 'Great
Greece' was given to the Greek colonies in
southern Italy. Greece is the only country in
the world where the adjectives 'ancient' and
'modern' have to be applied to the country, the
people, and their language to differentiate
between the past and the present. The phrase
'It's all Greek to me' comes from
Shakespeare's play *Julius Caesar* (Act 1, Scene 2)
to mean speech that is incomprehensible to
the listener.

Greeley, USA
Colorado: founded in 1870 as Union Colony,
a cooperative agricultural enterprise. It was
renamed in recognition of the support of
Horace Greeley (1811–72), a newspaper editor
and presidential candidate in 1872.

Green Bay, ANTIGUA, USA
USA (Wisconsin): founded as a trading post in
1634 in an inlet of Lake Michigan. In 1671 the
settlement was called La Grande Baye 'The
Large Bay'. However, this gave way to Green
Bay, so-called, perhaps, by British traders
because of the woods in the area.

Greeneville, TENNESSEE/USA
Settled in 1780 and named after Major General
Nathanael Greene (1742–86), a highly able
general in the War of Independence (1775–83),

who assumed command of the revolutionary army in the south in 1778.

Greenland (Danish: **Grønland**; Greenlandic (Inuktitut): **Kalaallit Nunaat**), DENMARK
A dependency of Denmark. It was named 'Green Land' in 982 by a Norwegian, Erik the Red, who had been exiled from Iceland. He returned, however, three years later to encourage settlers from Iceland by using a little deception with the name; in this he succeeded. Greenland was annexed by Norway in 1261. After the early Norse settlements had gradually ceased to exist, the island was colonized by the Danes from 1721. It became an integral part of the Kingdom of Denmark in 1953. The Greenlandic name means 'Land of the People'.

Greenock, UK, USA
UK (Scotland): formerly Grenok 'Sunny Hillock' from the Gaelic *grianag*.

Greenodd, ENGLAND/UK *Green Odd*
'Green Point', a tongue of land from the Old Scandinavian *oddi*.

Green River, WYOMING/USA
A city named after the Green River, originally the Spanish River, but renamed probably because of its green soapstone banks.

Greensboro, NORTH CAROLINA/USA
Founded in 1808 and named after Major General Nathanael Greene, who commanded the revolutionary forces in the Battle of Guildford Courthouse near here in 1781 (*see* GREENEVILLE).

Greenville, CANADA, LIBERIA, USA
1. Liberia: settled by freed American black slaves in 1838 at the mouth of the River Sinoe after which it was originally called. Subsequently, it was given its present name after James Green, a strong American supporter of the relocation of such slaves back to Africa.
2. USA (Mississippi, North Carolina, and Ohio): named after General Nathanael Greene (*see* GREENEVILLE).
3. USA (South Carolina): settled in the 1760s as Pleasantburg, it was given its present name in 1821, possibly after an early settler, Isaac Green (1762–1831). However, it has been suggested that its name describes its appearance 'Green Town'.
4. USA (Texas): named after General Thomas J. Green, who fought in the Texas Revolution in 1836.

Greenwich, UK, USA
1. UK (England): formerly Grenewic and Grenviz meaning 'Green Port' from the Old

English *grēne* 'green' and *wīc*. It has given its name to 'Greenwich Mean Time' (GMT), the local time for the 0° line of longitude which passes through it and is the basis for time-keeping around the world.
2. USA (Connecticut): founded in 1640 and named after the village, now a borough, of Greenwich in Greater London.

Gregory, WESTERN AUSTRALIA/AUSTRALIA
A lake named after John Walter Gregory (1864–1932), an English explorer and geologist.

Greifswald, MECKLENBURG-WEST POMERANIA/GERMANY *Gripheswalde*
Although possibly from a personal name, the popular derivation is probably correct: 'Griffin Wood' from *Greif* 'griffin' and *Wald* 'wood' as the griffin is part of the coat-of-arms of the Dukes of Pomerania. The city passed to Sweden in 1648 at the Peace of Westphalia and then to Prussia in 1815 at the Congress of Vienna.

Grenada, AND USA *Camerhogne, Concepción, Granada, Grenade* (*Grenada*)
1. Grenada: independent since 1974 as a constitutional monarchy with the British monarch as chief of state. Previously an Associated State under the West Indies Act (1967), a self-governing state in association with the UK; a member of the Federation of the West Indies (1958–62); a British colony (1783–1958); and a French colony (1672–1762). Christopher Columbus[†] was the first European to see the islands in 1498 when they enjoyed the Carib Indian name of Camerhogne; Columbus renamed them 'Conception' for the Feast of the Immaculate Conception. However, passing Spanish sailors preferred Granada because the landscape reminded them of the region around Granada in Spain. The French changed this to Grenade and the British to Grenada.
2. USA (Mississippi): named after the city in Spain (with a slightly altered spelling) after it was established with the merger of Tullahoma and Pittsburg in 1836.

Grenadines, WEST INDIES
A chain of islands named after Grenada with a name representing 'Little Grenadas'. The northern islands are administered by *St Vincent and the Grenadines, while the southern element are a dependency of Grenada.

Grenoble, RHÔNE-ALPES/FRANCE *Cularo, Gratianopolis, Grelibre*
Originally a Gaulish settlement. The present name has evolved from the Roman Gratianopolis 'City of Gratian' after Gratian

(359–83), Roman emperor (375–83). Grelïbre was used in 1793 for a short time during the period of the French Revolution, begun in 1789, because *noble* was considered to show an unhealthy connection with the nobility; *libre* 'free' was thought to be more in tune with the prevailing social conditions.

Grenola, KANSAS/USA
A combination from two rival towns in the area: Greenfield and Kanola.

Gretna, CANADA, USA
USA (Louisiana): founded early in the 19th century as Mechanicsham by the owner of a plantation, it was renamed later after *Gretna Green in Scotland.

Gretna Green, SCOTLAND/UK *Gretenho, Gretenhou, Gratnay*
'Green by Gretna' with Gretna 'gravel hill' from the Old English *grēota* 'gravel' and *hōh* 'hill'. Gretna Green was a place that attracted eloping couples in the 18th–20th centuries for the ease with which they could get married. Parental approval for marriage between individuals over the age of sixteen was not required, whereas in the rest of the UK it was 21. In 1969 the legal age of consent in the whole of the UK became eighteen.

Greylock, Mt, MASSACHUSETTS/USA
Named after a Waranoke chief.

Greymouth, SOUTH ISLAND/NEW ZEALAND *Crescent City, Blaketown, Greytown*
Situated at the mouth of the River Grey which was named in 1846 after Sir George Grey (1812–98), governor of New Zealand (1845–9, 1861) and premier (1877–9).

Greytown, NEW ZEALAND, SOUTH AFRICA
Both towns, in North Island, New Zealand, and KwaZulu-Natal, South Africa, are named after Sir George Grey (see previous entry) who was also governor of Cape Colony, South Africa, in 1854–9 and 1860–1.

Grigoriopol', MOLDOVA *Chyorniy*
Founded as a settlement for Armenian refugees in 1792 and named after Prince Grigory Potëmkin (1739–91), an Army officer, governor-general of New Russia (now southern Ukraine), and favourite of Empress Catherine II the Great[†]. A 'Potëmkin village' was a term coined to describe an attractive façade hiding something dilapidated behind; when the Empress made a tour of New Russia in 1787 Potëmkin is said to have built artificial villages to deceive and impress her. During the reign of Emperor Paul I (1796–1801) it was renamed 'Black' because it is close to the Black Sea, but it reverted to its former name when Alexander I[†] became emperor.

Grimsby, CANADA, UK
1. Canada (Ontario): founded in 1783 as The Forty, possibly indicating the number of settlers, before being changed, probably because one or more of them came from Grimsby in England.
2. UK (England): formerly Grimesbi and since 1979 Great Grimsby to distinguish it from Little Grimsby. The name means 'Village of a man called Grimr' from an Old Scandinavian personal name and *bý*.

Griquatown, NORTHERN CAPE/SOUTH AFRICA *Klaarwater*
Founded in 1802 as 'Clear Water', it was renamed in 1813 after the 19th-century Griqua people who had mixed European and Khoikhoin (Hottentot) ancestry.

Grodno (Hrodna), BELARUS
'Stronghold' or 'Fortified Place' from the Slavonic *grad*. It was given the Belarusian spelling after independence in 1991. It has been under Lithuanian, Polish, and Russian rule, and most recently it was part of Poland, 1921–39.

Gronau, GERMANY
Towns in Lower Saxony and North Rhine-Westphalia have the name 'Green Meadow' from the Old High German *gron* (modern German, *grün*) 'green' or 'verdant' and *au* from *Aue* 'meadow'.

Groningen, THE NETHERLANDS, SURINAME
The Netherlands: a province and a city, originally called Villa Cruoninga, with a name derived from the Old High German *gron* 'green'. There is also a town named Gröningen in Germany.

Grootfontein, NAMIBIA *Otjivandatatjonque, Gei-/ous (/ indicates a click sound)*
Originally with a Herero name meaning 'Hill of the Leopard', it was called 'Great Spring' by the San (Bushmen). On their arrival, the Boers gave the town the Afrikaans version of this name.

Groton, USA
There are six cities with this name, all of which are named after the village of Groton in England or after the Groton in Massachusetts which itself took its name from the English village. Its name may have meant 'Gravelly Stream' from a conjectural Old English word *groten* and *ēa* 'stream'.

Grottaglie, APULIA/ITALY
Takes its name from the local grottoes, in Italian *grotta* 'cave'.

Groznyy (Chechen: **Sölz-Gala**), CHECHNYA/
RUSSIA *Groznaya*
'Awesome', 'Threatening', or 'Menacing'.
Founded as a fort in 1818 by General Aleksey
Yermolov (1777–1861), commander-in-chief of
Russian forces in the Caucasus (1816–27), as
the first one of a chain to control the Chechens
and so-called to inculcate fear into them and
indicate Russian power in the Caucasus. The
spelling was changed in 1869. In 1997 the city
was unofficially renamed by the Chechens as
Dzhokar-Gala, the 'City of Dzhokar' after
Dzhokar Dudayev, the first self-proclaimed
president of the 'independent' Republic (1991–
6); the new name has not been accepted
internationally.

Gruyères, SWITZERLAND
'Place frequented by Cranes' (tall wading bird)
from the Low Latin *gruaria*. *See* LA GRUYÈRE.

Guadalajara, MEXICO, SPAIN
1. Mexico (Jalisco): founded in 1531 by Nuño
de Guzmán and named after his home town in
Spain.
2. Spain (Castile-La Mancha): founded by the
Iberians and later taken by the Romans and
named Arriaca from an Iberian word meaning
'stony'. The present name is derived from the
Moorish name, Wādī al-Hijārah, meaning
literally 'Valley where Water flows over
Rocks', thus 'River of Stones', a reference to
the Henares River on which it lies.

Guadalcanal, SOLOMON ISLANDS
An island visited in 1568 by the Spanish
explorer, Alvaro de Mendaña de Neira, and
named by him after his home town in Spain.
Like Guadalajara (above), the name is based on
the Arabic *wādī* with the additional *el Ganar*.

Guadalquivir, SPAIN *Wādī al-Kabīr*
A river which takes its present name from its
former Arabic name 'The Great River' from
wādī and *kabīr* 'great' or 'big'.

Guadalupe, BRAZIL, COLOMBIA, COSTA RICA, EL
SALVADOR, MEXICO, SPAIN, USA
Spain (Extremadura): named after the
Guadalupe mountains on whose south-eastern
slopes the town lies. They take their name
from the Guadelupejo River from the Arabic
wādī and the Latin *lupus* 'wolf', the original
name of the river. The monastery here became
one of the most important in Spain and as a
result the name Guadalupe was adopted by a
number of cities and towns in Central and
South America.

Guadeloupe, WEST INDIES
Department of Guadeloupe (Département de
la Guadeloupe), an Overseas Department of
France since 1946. It consists of a pair of

islands, Basse-Terre 'Low Land' and Grande-
Terre 'Great Land', and several smaller ones in
the Leeward Islands. Called Karukera by the
Carib people, they were named Santa Maria de
Guadalupe de Extremadura 'Virgin Mary of
Guadalupe in Extremadura' by Christopher
Columbus[†] in 1493 after the monastery in
Spain (*see* GUADALUPE). The French arrived in
1635, colonized the islands and changed the
spelling of the name.

Guadix, ANDALUSIA/SPAIN *Acci, Wādī-Ash*
The original Roman name gave way to the
Arabic *Wādī-Ash* 'River of Life' from which the
present name has evolved.

Guam *Ladrões, Guahan*
Territory of Guam (Chamorro: Teritorion
Guam), an unincorporated territory of the USA
in Micronesia. Its subjects are US citizens. It is
said to have been discovered by the Portuguese
navigator, Ferdinand Magellan[†], in 1521; he
named the Mariana Islands, of which Guam is
the largest and southernmost, 'Thieves'
Islands' from the Portuguese *Islas dos Ladrões*
because of the conduct of the inhabitants. The
island was claimed by Spain in 1565 (Magellan
having sailed in the service of Spain). It was
ceded to the USA in 1898 under the Treaty of
Paris, following the Spanish–American War.
The name may come from that of its
indigenous people, the Chamorros.

Guanajuato, MEXICO
A state and a city, founded in 1548. The
present Castilianized name is derived from the
Tarascan Quanaxuato 'Place of Frogs'.

Guangdong, CHINA
A province, sometimes still transliterated as
Kwangtung, meaning 'Large (Area) of the
East' from *guǎng* and *dōng* 'east'. It was also
known as *Canton by the English who used
the name indiscriminately for both city and
province.

Guangxi Zhuang, CHINA *Guangnan xīlu*
An autonomous region meaning 'Large
(Area) of the West' from *guǎng* and *xī* 'west'.
The previous name, current during
the Northern Song dynasty (960–1126)
meant 'Broad South, Western Route' to
indicate the western half of the land that lay
south of the Nan Mountains. The name was
then shortened to Kwangsi and in 1958 it
became the Zhuang Autonomous Region of
Guangxi (to use the Pinyin transliteration) to
help promote the cultural aspirations of the
Zhuang people.

Guangzhou, GUANGDONG/CHINA
See CANTON.

Guarda, PORTUGAL
'Guard' from the Portuguese *guarda*. Founded in 1197 by Sancho I (1154–1211), King of Portugal (1185–1211), as a military garrison for defence against the Moors.

Guastalla, EMILIA-ROMAGNA/ITALY
Founded in 603 by Agilulf, King of the Lombards, as a military garrison with a name derived from the Lombard *wardistall* 'guard post'.

Guatemala, AND CUBA
The Republic of Guatemala (República de Guatemala) since 1839 when its present-day boundaries were finalized. Previously part of the United Provinces of Central America (1823–39) having achieved independence from Spain in 1821, although under Mexican hegemony until 1823; part of the Spanish captaincy-general of Central America (1524–1821). With its governor appointed by the Spanish king, the colony of Guatemala was sometimes referred to as the Kingdom of Guatemala from 1570. There is some dispute as to the origin of the name: some claim that it is derived from an Aztec word *Quauhtemallan* 'Land of Many Trees' or 'Land of the Eagle', while others suggest *Guhatezmalha* 'Mountain of Gushing Water', a reference to the volcano of Agua which destroyed the first capital of the captaincy-general, now called Ciudad Vieja 'Old City', 18 miles (29 km) south-west of Guatemala City.

Guayaquil, ECUADOR *Santiago de Guayaquil*
Founded in 1537 by the Spanish explorer, Francisco de Orellana, close to the original site at the mouth of the River Babahoyo which had been destroyed twice by Native Americans. He named it Santiago de Guayaquil to honour St James, on whose feast day, 25 July, it was founded, and the local Indian chief Guaya and his wife Quila.

Guelph, CANADA, USA
Canada (Ontario): founded in 1827 and named after the Guelphs, an Italian form of the baptismal name Welf, the family name of the royal house of Hanover from which the present British royal family is descended.

Guernsey *Sarnia, Greneroy, Ghernesi*
Bailiwick of Guernsey and a dependency of the British crown since 1066 (the time of the Norman invasion of England). The island, with the other Channel Islands, separated from Normandy in 1204. The name is of Scandinavian origin with *ey* added to a possible personal name to mean 'Grani's Island'. Sarnia was the Roman name. Guernsey has given its name to a breed of dairy cattle.

Guerrero, MEXICO
A state since 1849 named after Vicente Guerrero (1782–1831), a successful guerrilla leader in Mexico's wars of independence (1810–21). He became president for less than a year in 1829 before being deposed and executed, yet the name has been retained.

Guerrero Negro, BAJA CALIFORNIA SUR/ MEXICO
'Black Warrior' from the name of an American whaling ship which sank at the entrance to the nearby Laguna Ojo de Liebre in 1858.

Guildford, UK, USA
1. UK (England): previously Gyldeforda, Gyldeford, and Geldeford. The name probably means 'Ford by the Golden (sandy) Hill' from a possible Old English word *gylde* and *ford*. However, the 'golden' might refer to the golden-coloured sand on the bed of the ford.
2. USA (Connecticut): previously Menunketuk when settled by Puritans in 1639, it was renamed four years later after the town in England.
3. USA (North Carolina): named after Francis North (1637–85), 1st Earl of Guildford and lord chancellor (1682–5).

Guilin, GUANGXI ZHUANG AUTONOMOUS REGION/CHINA *Guizhou, Shian, Lingui*
Also spellt Kuei-lin. Established as a city in 1940 and standing on the Gui River, the name means 'Laurel Forest' from *guì* 'laurel' and *lín* 'forest'.

Guimarães, PORTUGAL *Vimaranes*
Possibly named after Vimara Peres who founded the town in 868. It became the first capital of Portugal *c*.1127.

Guinea, AND USA
The Republic of Guinea (République de Guinée) since 1984. Previously the People's Revolutionary Republic of Guinea (1978–84); the Republic of Guinea since independence in 1958; and French Guinea when the coastal region, then part of Senegal and known as Rivières du Sud, was detached and declared a protectorate of France in 1888, a colony in 1893 and part of the Federation of French West Africa in 1895. The name is derived from a Berber word *aguinaw* 'black man' or *akal n-iguinamen* 'land of the black men' which the Portuguese gave to a much larger part of West Africa in the middle of the 15th century. It gave its name to the former English coin, the guinea, originally made of gold from this region with the value, in decimal currency, of £1.05; also to the guinea fowl originating here and to Papua New Guinea.

Guinea-Bissau The Republic of Guinea-Bissau (República da Guiné-Bissau) since independence in 1974. Previously Portuguese Guinea: an Overseas Territory in 1951 and a colony from 1879 before which it had been a part of Cape Verde. The Portuguese first arrived in 1446. The first part of the name is as for *Guinea while the second part, to distinguish the country from Guinea, is that of the country's capital. This comes from the indigenous Bijagó people from the offshore islands.

Guisborough, ENGLAND/UK *Ghigesburg*
Probably 'Gígr's Stronghold' from an Old Scandinavian personal name and *burh*.

Guiyang, GUIZHOU/CHINA
'Sunny Side of Gui Mountain' from the nearby Gui mountain. Happily, it could also mean 'Precious Sun' from *gui* 'precious' and *yáng* 'sun' because it is so rarely seen. The region is known for its cloud cover, particularly during the summer.

Guizhou, CHINA *Juzhou*
A province meaning 'Noble Land' from *gui* 'noble' and *zhōu*, here 'land'. Also sometimes known as Kweichow. Juzhou gave way to Guizhou in 1119.

Gujarāt, INDIA
A state named after the indigenous people, the Gujars or Gurjaras, a minor tribe of the Huns, who ruled the area in the 8th and 9th centuries.

Gujrānwāla, PUNJAB/PAKISTAN
Named after the Gujars (*see* GUJARĀT).

Gujrāt, PUNJAB/PAKISTAN
Named after the Gujars (*see* GUJARĀT).

Gulfport, USA
1. Florida: a port on the Gulf of Mexico.
2. Illinois: a port on the River Mississippi.
3. Mississippi: founded in 1887 as the terminal point for the Gulf and Ship Island Railroad. The name indicates that it is a port on the Gulf of Mexico.

Gulf States Those states that have a coastline on the western and southern sides of the Persian Gulf. From the north: Kuwait, Saudi Arabia, Bahrain, Qatar, UAE, and Oman.

Gulistan, AZERBAIJAN, PAKISTAN, UZBEKISTAN
Uzbekistan: the original village took its name, Golodnaya Step 'Hungry Steppe', from the Russian *golodnyy* 'hungry' and *step'* 'steppe' in which it was located. In 1922 the name was changed to Mirzachul 'Edge of the Desert' from the Uzbek *mirza* 'edge' and *chul* 'desert'. It was renamed again in 1961, and spelt

Guliston in Uzbek, to mean 'Place of Roses' from *atirgul* 'rose' and *stan*.

Gulmarg, JAMMU AND KASHMIR/INDIA
'Meadow of Flowers' from the Hindi *gul* 'flower' and *marg* 'meadow'.

Gülşehir, TURKEY
'City of Roses' from *gül* 'rose' and *şehir*.

Gumel, JIGAWA/NIGERIA
The capital of the emirate of the same name which existed between about 1750 and 1903. It may be from the Fulani *gubelle* 'short-horned cow'.

Gümüşhane, TURKEY *Argyropolis*
'House of Silver' from *gümüs* 'silver' and *hane* 'house' or 'dwelling', in this case 'mint'. The silver mines here were worked for at least five centuries until the 19th century.

Gundagai, NEW SOUTH WALES/AUSTRALIA
Willia Ploma
Originally no more than a sheep run, the name was changed, when it was recognized as a town *c*.1840, to Gundagai, an Aboriginal word meaning 'going upstream'. It lies on the Murrumbidgee River.

Güneydoğu Anadolu, TURKEY
A geographic region 'South-East Anatolia' from *güney* 'south', *doğu* 'east', and *Anadolu*.

Gunnedah, NEW SOUTH WALES/AUSTRALIA
'White Stones' from an Aboriginal word, possibly referring to the stones in the beds of the Conadilly and Namoi Rivers.

Gunnison, COLORADO/USA
Originally a camp for silver mining, it was named in 1880 after Captain John W. Gunnison, an early explorer of the region.

Guria, GEORGIA
A region with the name of 'Heart' in Mingrelian.

Gur'yev, KAZAKHSTAN
Founded *c*.1640 by, and named after, the Guryev family, who fortified their settlement here against the Cossacks.

Gur'yevsk, KALININGRAD/RUSSIA *Neuhausen*
Renamed in 1946 after a Soviet Army officer, S. S. Guryev, who was killed here in 1945 during the advance to Königsberg (now Kaliningrad).

Gusar(i), AZERBAIJAN
'Man' from the Lezhgian *kus*.

Gusev, KALININGRAD/RUSSIA *Gumbinnen*
Renamed in 1946 after Guards Captain S. I. Gusev who was killed near here in January 1945 during the Soviet advance to Königsberg (now Kaliningrad).

Gus'-Khrustal'nyy, VLADIMIR/RUSSIA
On the River Gus, the city is famous for its glass industry which gives it its name, *Khrustal* 'cut-glass' or 'crystal'.

Gustavia, SAINT BARTHÉLEMY/WEST INDIES
Carénage
Also known as Port de Gustavia and renamed after Gustav III (1746–92), King of Sweden (1771–92). The island of St Barthélemy was ceded by France to Sweden in 1784–1878.

Guthrie, UK, USA
USA (Oklahoma): founded in 1899, it is named after Judge John Guthrie.

Guyana The Co-operative Republic of Guyana since 1970. Previously Guyana when independence was achieved in 1966; the British having acquired Guiana formally at the London Convention in 1814, the name was changed to British Guiana in 1831 when they took over the three Dutch colonies of Berbice, Demerara, and Essequibo; the Dutch had built the first permanent trading post at Essequibo in 1616. Guiana was made a British crown colony in 1928. Guiana and Guyana, an Arawak or Carib word, mean 'Land of Waters', probably because of its swampy coastline and many rivers. For the Native Americans the name actually referred to the three Guianas, Dutch Guiana (now Suriname), French Guiana, and Guyana.

Guyenne, FRANCE
Also spellt Guienne. A historic region in south-western France, which was at one time part of Aquitaine, the name Guyenne is a medieval form of the Latin Aquitania. It was part of the English realm during the 13th–15th centuries, when it was known to the English as *Gascony. It merged with Gascony during the centuries before the French Revolution in 1789.

Güzelyurt, TURKEY *Karballa, Gelvere*
'Beautiful Land' from *güzel* 'beautiful' and *yurt* 'homeland'.

Gvardeysk, KALININGRAD/RUSSIA *Tapiau*
Renamed 'Guards' in 1946, probably after 11 Guards Army which took part in the fighting in East Prussia in 1945 in the assault group of 3rd Byelorussian Front. Any Soviet Army unit could be designated 'guards' for some act of valour or particularly meritorious action. The unit would then incorporate *gvardeiskiy* in its title.

Gwalior, MADHYA PRADESH/INDIA
A former princely state, the city has expanded round an old walled fortress. According to legend, the city was founded as a result of a

hermit, Gwālipa, curing Prince Suraj Sen of leprosy in the 10th century. Thus the name is said to be derived from a small Hindu shrine dedicated to Gwālipa.

Gwandu, KEBBI/NIGERIA
Takes its name from the *gandu* 'royal farmlands' in the region at the time the Kingdom of Kebbi was founded in the 16th century.

Gwent, WALES/UK
A former county meaning 'Trading Place' from the British *venta*.

Gweru, ZIMBABWE *iKwelo, Gwelo*
Founded in 1894 on the Gweru River, the present name is derived from the original Matabele name iKwelo 'Steep Place' from *kwela* 'to climb', a reference to the high banks of the river. The name was changed to Gweru in 1982.

Gwynedd, WALES/UK
A unitary district named after a Welsh principality, 'Territory of (the) Venedoti'.

Gyandzha (Gandža, Gäncä), AZERBAIJAN
Gandja, Djanza, Yelizavetpol, Kirovabad
Lying along the Gyandzha River, it was founded in the 7th century and possibly named after the river. However, it may come from the Arabic *dzhanzar* 'treasury' or 'harvest store', or from the Gandjak tribe. It was captured by the Persians in 1606 at which time it became the capital of the Gyandzha khanate. In 1804 the city was captured by Prince Paul Tsitsianov, the Georgian-born commander-in-chief of Russian forces in Georgia (1802–6), and renamed Yelizavetpol 'City of Elizabeth' after the adopted personal name of the wife of Emperor Alexander I, the Empress Yelizaveta Alexeyevna (1779–1826) and the shortened form of *polis*; a German princess before her marriage, her name then was Louise Maria Augusta of Baden-Durlach. Nine years later, in 1813, the city was ceded to Russia. It reverted to its original name in 1918, but in 1935, a year after his assassination, it was renamed Kirovabad 'Kirov's Town' after Sergey Kirov[†], who had been first secretary of the Central Committee of the Azerbaijan Communist Party in 1921–5. Once more the city readopted its original name, this time in 1991, after Azerbaijan achieved independence from the Soviet Union. It was the capital of the Democratic Republic of Azerbaijan in 1918–20.

Gyantse (Chinese: Gyangze; Tibetan: Rgyal Rtse), TIBET/CHINA
'Victorian Peak' from the Tibetan *rtse* 'peak'.

Gympie, QUEENSLAND/AUSTRALIA *Nashville*
Originally named after James Nash who discovered gold here in 1867, it was renamed

when it became a town in 1890 from an Aboriginal word *gimpi-gimpi* 'stinging tree'.

Győr, HUNGARY *Arrabona, Janik-Kala, Raab*
The Roman name meant 'Fort on the (River) Rába' from the Celtic *bona* 'fort'. From this was derived the German name of Raab. During Ottoman Turkish rule in Hungary the town was called by the Turks Janik-Kala 'Burnt-out Town', a reference to the fact that it frequently changed hands and was often burnt and destroyed. The present name may

come from an Avar word *gyürü* 'circular fortress'.

Gyrmyzy Bazar, NAGORNO-KARABAKH/ AZERBAIJAN *Krasnyy Bazar*
'Red Market', an Azeri rendering of the former Russian name.

Gyula, HUNGARY
'Julius'. Probably named after a 10th-century Magyar chieftain.

Gyumri (Kumayri), *see* KUMAYRI

H

Haarlem, THE NETHERLANDS *Haeroleim*
Lying along the River Spaarne, the name is
derived from the previous name meaning
'Place, or Settlement, behind the Dunes'; the
present name could also mean the 'Height on
the Clayey Soil' from the Teutonic *haar*
'height' and *leem* 'clayey soil'.

Hachinohe, HONSHŪ/JAPAN
A castle town and port called 'Eight Doors'
from *hachi* 'eight', *no* 'of', and *to* 'door' in the
sense of eight families.

Hachiōji, HONSHŪ/JAPAN
'Eight Princes' from *hachi* 'eight', *ō* 'king' or
'prince', and *shi* 'child'. According to legend,
a Buddhist priest erected a temple *c*.1000 and
dedicated it to Emperor Gozu and his eight
princes.

Hacıbektaş, TURKEY
Named after Hacıbektaş Veli, a dervish who
founded the Bektaşi order of dervishes.

Hackensack, NEW JERSEY/USA *New Barbadoes*
Settled by the Dutch as New Barbadoes.
Although passing to the English in 1688, it was
not renamed until 1921, supposedly after the
Ackinchesacky tribe.

Hackettstown, NEW JERSEY/USA
Named after Samuel Hackett, owner of a
considerable amount of land in the area.

Hadera, ISRAEL
Founded in 1890 by Polish and Lithuanian Jews
on an intermittent watercourse which assisted
in the cultivation of citrus fruits. The city was
thus called 'Green' from the Arabic *khadīr*.

Haderslev, DENMARK *Hathærslefheret,
Hatherslef, Gambla hathærsløf*
All the names are derived from the Old Danish
and mean 'Hathar's Inheritance'.

Hadhramaut (Ḥaḍramawt) YEMEN
A governorate possibly meaning 'Death was
present' from the Arabic *mawt* 'death' and
ḥaḍhar 'was present'; *ḥaḍhra* can mean
'presence' but is now used as a polite form
of address. Thus the meaning of the Wādī
Hadhramaut can be taken as 'Valley where
Death is present' or 'Valley where Death
comes'. According to local mythology, the
Hadhramaut is named after a son, 'Amr,
of Qahtan, progenitor of the South Arabian

tribes. 'Amr was given the nickname
Hadhramaut because of the confrontational
times in which he lived.

Ḥadīthah, al-, IRAQ
'The New' from *jadid* in the sense of 'modern'
or 'recent', although the oasis town was
founded *c*.640 by Omar I (*c*.586–644), the
second Muslim caliph (634–44), on the site of a
Christian settlement.

Haeju, NORTH KOREA
'Region on the Sea' from *hae* 'sea' and *ju*
'region'.

Haenertsburg, NORTHERN/SOUTH AFRICA
Named in 1894 after C. F. Haenert, who
discovered gold here in 1886.

Hafnarfjörður, ICELAND
Situated on a bay, the name means 'Harbour
Fjord' from the Old Icelandic *hafner* 'harbour'
and *fjörður* 'fjord'.

Hagen, NORTH RHINE-WESTPHALIA/GERMANY
Now on the edge of a wooded mountainous
area, the name is derived from the Old High
German *hago* 'forest'.

Hagerstown, MARYLAND/USA *Elizabeth Town*
Laid out in 1762 by Jonathan Hager, a German
and one of the original landowners, as
Elizabeth Town after his wife. In 1814 the
name was changed to Hager's Town and later
to its present form.

Hague, The ('s Gravenhage, Den Haag) THE
NETHERLANDS *Haga Comitis*
'The Count's Hedge'. A settlement developed
round the original hunting lodge built in 1248
in a woodland area called Haghe 'hedge' for
Count William II. 's Gravenhage thus means
'The Counts' Private Enclosure', Den Haag
merely being a shortening of this name. It
became the principal residence of the Counts
of Holland. The 1907 Hague Convention laid
down the law governing the conduct of
international warfare. The Hague is the seat of
government and administrative capital of The
Netherlands, but not the official capital which
is Amsterdam.

Haguenau, ALSACE/FRANCE
Possibly adapted from a German personal
name, Hagino, which itself comes from the
Old High German *hago* 'forest' and *auwa*

'water'. It has been suggested, however, that it might mean 'Enclosed Meadow' from *Gehege* 'enclosure' or 'fence' and *au* from *Aue* 'meadow'. The town has been occupied by the Germans on several occasions.

Haifa (Hebrew: H̲efa), ISRAEL *Sykaminos, Caiffa/Caiphas*
Given its position on the wooded slopes of Mt Carmel, the name is probably derived from the Hebrew *kef* 'rock' or 'crag'. However, it has been suggested that it might come from the Hebrew *hof yafe* 'beautiful coast' as it overlooks the sea. In 1099, during the First Crusade, the town was captured by the Crusaders who called it Caiffa or Caiphas, possibly after Caiaphus (also spelt Caiphas), who was supposedly born in the city and became high priest of the Jews during the time of Jesus.

Haikou, HAINAN/CHINA
Situated to the west of the mouth of the Nandu River facing the mainland across the narrow Hainan Strait, the port's name means 'Mouth of the Sea' from *hǎi* and *kǒu* 'mouth'. It is known as Hoihow in Cantonese.

Haileybury, ONTARIO/CANADA
Founded by C. Farr in about 1875 and named after the school he attended in England, Haileybury College.

Hainan, CHINA *Qiongzhou, Qiongtai Island*
A province and island in the South China Sea, the name means '(In the) Southern Sea' from *hǎi* and *nán*. Its previous name only lasted between 1912 and 1921 when it was nominally independent. It became part of Guangdong province in 1950 after the Chinese take-over and only achieved separate provincial status in 1988.

Hainaut (Flemish: **Henegouwen**), BELGIUM
A province meaning 'District of the (River) Haine' which flows through it. The river's name comes from the Old High German *hago* 'forest' and *gawja* 'district' (modern German, *Gau*).

Haines, ALASKA/USA
Founded as a trading post in 1878, it became known as Haines in 1881 after Francina Haines of the Presbyterian Board of Home Missions when a mission was established.

Haiphong (Hải Phòng) VIETNAM
A seaport in the Red River Delta, the literal meaning of the name is 'Sea Room' from *hǎi* 'sea' and *phòng* 'room', a reference to the spacious harbour here; it may, however, be translated more realistically as 'Outpost by the Sea'.

Haiti *Saint Domingue*
The Republic of Haiti (Haitian Creole: Repiblik Dayti; French: République d'Haïti) when it became the first independent black republic in the world in 1804; at the same time it readopted the original Arawak name of Ayti, which became Haiti. The Arawaks called the whole island, now shared by Haiti and the Dominican Republic, Ayti 'Land of Mountains'. However, when Christopher Columbus[†] arrived in 1492, he named it La Isla Española in recognition of his Spanish sponsors; this evolved into the current name for the island, Hispaniola. Settling only in the east, the Spanish ceded the western third of the island to the French in 1697 under the Treaty of Ryswick. They called it Saint Domingue or Dominique.

Ḥajar, al-, OMAN
A mountain chain meaning 'The Stone'.

Hajdúság, HUNGARY
A region around Debrecen which takes its name from *haidus*, peasant soldiers who were granted land and various privileges by the Prince of Transylvania during the 16th century. The Ottoman Turks, whom they opposed, called these partisan fighters *Hajdúk* (modern Turkish, *haydud*), the plural of the Hungarian *hajdú* 'bandit'. Several towns in the area are prefixed *Hajdú-*.

Hakodate, HOKKAIDŌ/JAPAN *Usukishi*
'Box Castle', a reference to Goryokaku, a 15th-century fort of the Kono clan built in the shape of a five-pointed star and now a park, where the Tokugawa shogunate made its last stand in 1867. The name is derived from *hako* 'box' and *tate* 'fort'. The former name came from *usukeshi* 'edge of the bay' in Ainu.

Halden, NORWAY *Fredrikshald*
Founded in 1661 and named 'Frederick's Rock' in 1665 after Frederick III (1609–70), King of Denmark and Norway (1648–70), and *hald* 'rock'. It was given its present name in 1928.

Haleakala, HAWAII/USA
A volcanic mountain on eastern Maui island, the name means 'House of the Sun'. According to local legend, the sun was imprisoned here by the demigod Maui in order to increase the hours of daylight.

Halesowen, ENGLAND/UK *Hala, Hales Ouweyn*
'Owen's Corners of Land' from the plural of the Old English *halh* 'corner, or nook, of land' and the name of the Welsh Prince Owen, who became Lord of Hales in 1204 and occupied the manor.

Half.com, OREGON/USA *Halfway*
At the end of 1999 representatives of Half.com Inc. visited the town of Halfway, halfway between Richland and Cornucopia, to suggest that it should rename itself after their company. In exchange for a gift of computers and funds for municipal improvements, the residents agreed in 2000.

Halfway House, GAUTENG/SOUTH AFRICA
So named because it is halfway between Johannesburg and Pretoria.

Halifax, AUSTRALIA, CANADA, UK, USA
1. Canada (Nova Scotia): originally a French fishing settlement, it was developed from 1749 by the British as a stronghold and named after George Montagu Dunk (1716–71), 2nd Earl of Halifax, and at the time the president of the Board of Trade, who helped in the development of the city.
2. UK (England): formerly Halyfax, 'Nook of Land with coarse Grass' from the Old English *halh* 'nook' and *feaxe*, or something similar, 'coarse' or 'rough grass'.
3. USA (North Carolina): a historic site first settled *c*.1723, it was named in 1760 after the 2nd Earl of Halifax.
4. USA (Virginia): named after the 2nd Earl of Halifax.

Hallandale, FLORIDA/USA
Founded by Scandinavian farmers in the 1890s, it is named after one of the employees in the trading post, Luther Halland.

Halle, BELGIUM, GERMANY
Germany (Saxony-Anhalt): the full name, to distinguish it from the Halle in North Rhine-Westphalia, is Halle an der Saale 'Halle on the (River) Saale'. The name may be derived from the Middle High German *hal(le)* 'salt works' for which the city is noted.

Hallein, AUSTRIA
Close to a saltworks, the first syllable *hall* means 'salt'.

Halmahera, MOLUCCAS/INDONESIA *Batu Tjina, Moro*
An island also called Djailolo. The Portuguese and Spanish names never caught on and the local name, meaning 'Motherland', prevailed.

Ha Long, VIETNAM
Created in 1994 from the union of two towns, one of which, Hong Gai means, appropriately, 'Coal Mine'. Ha Long means 'Where the Dragon Descends to the Sea' from *long* 'dragon'. According to legend, a dragon came down from the mountains and killed a monster that had been frightening the people.

Ḥalq al-Wādī, TUNISIA *La Goulette*
Situated between Lake Tunis and the Gulf of Tunis, and linked by canal to the city of Tunis, the name literally means 'Gullet of the Dry River Bed' or 'River's Throat', a reference to the narrows here. The former French name means the same, 'The Narrows'. Also known as Halq el Oued.

Halton, ENGLAND/UK
'Farmstead in a Corner of Land' from the Old English *halh* 'corner of land' and *tūn*.

Hama (Ḥamāh) SYRIA *Hamath, Epiphaneia, Emath*
A very ancient city comprising the Kingdom of Hamath in the 11th century BC. Its name is derived from the Phoenician *khamat* 'fortress', of which nothing remains. It changed hands many times, the Seleucids calling it Epiphaneia after Antiochus IV Epiphanes (*c*.215–164 BC), Seleucid King of Hellenistic Syria (175–164 BC); in early Christian times it was known as Emath. Occupied by the Ottoman Turks in the 16th century, it passed to Syria following the end of the First World War.

Hamadan, IRAN *Hangmatana/Agbatana, Ecbatana*
An ancient city known to the Medes as Hangmatana or Agbatana and to the Greeks as Ecbatana from which the present name is derived. A personal name may be the source of the city's name. In the second half of the 12th century it was the capital of the Seljuk Turks.

Hamamatsu, HONSHŪ/JAPAN
The name reflects the fact that it is a coastal city from *hama* 'shore' or 'beach' and *matsu* 'pine tree'.

Hamburg, GERMANY, SURINAME, USA
Germany: a state and a city once known as Hammaburg. Said to have originated as a church with a moated fortress built *c*.825 between two rivers to protect it from heathens; it means 'Fortress in the Nook' from *hamma* 'nook' and *burg*. It may have given its name to the hamburger, or burger, taken by 19th-century German emigrants to the USA.

Hamden, USA
Connecticut: settled in 1664 and named after John Hampden (1594–1643), the English parliamentarian who opposed the right of King Charles I[†] to collect taxes for the Navy without the approval of Parliament.

Hämeenlinna (Swedish: **Tavastehus**), FINLAND
The old castle of Häme has given its name to the city from *hämeen* 'of Häme' and *linna* 'castle'. Formally part of the Swedish realm in

1634–1809, the city has a Swedish name meaning 'Castle of the Tavastians' from the Swedish *hus* 'castle' and the name of a local Finnish people.

Hamersley Range, WESTERN AUSTRALIA/
AUSTRALIA
A mountain range visited in 1861 by Francis Gregory, an explorer and mineral surveyor, who named it after Edward Hamersley, who backed Gregory's expedition.

Hamhŭng, NORTH KOREA
Close to the sea, the first syllable of its name means 'salty taste' from *ham* while *hung* means 'joy' or 'delight'.

Hamilton, AUSTRALIA, BERMUDA, CANADA,
NEW ZEALAND, UK, USA
1. Bermuda: founded in 1790 and named after Henry Hamilton (d. 1796), governor of the island at the time. It has been the capital since 1815.
2. Canada (Ontario): originally the site was called Burlington Bay. When it was settled in 1813 it was renamed after George Hamilton (1787–1835) who had laid out the city.
3. New Zealand (North Island): originally a military outpost erected on the site of a deserted Maori village called Kirikirioa, it was renamed after Captain John Hamilton, a British Royal Navy officer who was killed while fighting the Maori, when it became a city in 1877.
4. UK (Scotland): formerly Cadzow and renamed in 1445 after a family called Hamilton, itself probably derived from a place meaning a 'farmstead in rough country' from the Old English *hamel* 'broken' and *tūn*. The Hamiltons received it from Robert I the Bruce (1274–1329), King of Scots (1306–29), after victory over the English at the Battle of Bannockburn in 1314.
5. USA (Ohio): founded in 1794 as Fairfield adjacent to Fort Hamilton which had been named after Alexander Hamilton (1755–1804), the illegitimate son of a Scottish father, who became the first secretary of the US Treasury (1789–95). Fairfield was later renamed Hamilton.

Hamina, FINLAND *Frederikshamn*
Originally named in 1753 after Frederick I (1676–1751), King of Sweden (1720–51), when Finland was an integral part of Sweden. The Swedish *hamn* means 'harbour' from which the present name is derived.

Hammamet (al-Hammāmāt) TUNISIA
A small port with good sandy beaches, the Arabic name means 'The Bathing Places'.

Hammam Lif, TUNISIA
Derived from *Hammam en Alf* 'Bath of Noses' from the Arabic *hammān* '(hot) bath'. 'Nose' is often used euphemistically for 'penis' and the spring here has a reputation for easing syphilitic pains.

Hammerfest, NORWAY
With its harbour nestling at the foot of a cliff face on the island of Kvaløya, it takes its name from *hammer* 'steep cliff' and *feste* 'mooring place'.

Hammond, AUSTRALIA, USA
USA (Indiana): founded in 1869 as Hohman and renamed State Line since it was on the border between Illinois and Indiana. It was renamed again in 1873 after George Hammond (1836–86), one of the two founders of the meat-packing business which was set up here in 1869.

Hampden, CANADA, NEW ZEALAND, USA
USA (Massachusetts and Maine): named after John Hampden (*Hamden) who supported the establishment of Puritan communities in North America.

Hampshire, ENGLAND/UK *Hamtunscir, Hantescir, Hamptonshire/Southamptonshire*
The early English shires took their names from their principal town or estate. Thus Hampshire was originally derived from Hammtūn 'Estate on a Promontory' from *hamm*, here 'promontory'. This became Hampton, the old name for Southampton, with *scir* 'shire', an administrative division, added to indicate a county: thus, a 'District based on Southampton'. To distinguish it from the Hampton further north (now Northampton), it was given its prefix about the middle of the 10th century. The present name is therefore a shortening of Hamptonshire. The modern abbreviated form of Hants comes from an entry in the Domesday Book (1086): Hantescir.

Hampstead, CANADA, DOMINICA, UK, USA
1. Canada (Quebec): named after the district in north London, England.
2. UK (England): formerly Hemstede and Hamestede 'Homestead' from the Old English *hām* and *stede* 'place' or 'site'.
3. USA (New Hampshire): named after the Hampstead in England.

Hampton, CANADA, USA
1. USA (New Hampshire): named after Hampton Court, the Tudor palace in Richmond upon Thames, England.
2. USA (Virginia): founded on the site of a Native American village called Kecoughtan in 1609. It only became a town in 1705 when it was named after Henry Wriothesley (1573–

1624), 3rd Earl of Southampton, who was an early member of the Virginia Company (from 1609), which arrived at Jamestown in 1607. Hampton Roads, Virginia, is also named after him.

Ḥamrā', al-Ḥammādah al-, LIBYA
'The Red Plateau' from the Arabic *al-*, *ḥammādah* 'plateau', and *ḥamrā'*, the feminine of *aḥmar* 'red'. This is a reference to the colour of its rocks.

Hanalei, HAWAII/USA
Lying near a crescent-shaped bay, it simply means 'Crescent'.

Hancock, MICHIGAN/USA
Named after John Hancock (1737–93), a prominent leader in the American War of Independence (1775–83), serving nine terms as governor of Massachusetts and one of those men who signed the Declaration of Independence in 1776.

Hannibal, USA
Missouri and Ohio: named after the Carthaginian general (247–*c*.181 BC).

Hanoi (Hà Nội) VIETNAM *Dong Kinh, Dai La, Thang Long, Kecho/Cacho, Tonkin, Thanh Tich, Bac Thanh*
'(City in a Bend) in the River' from *hà* 'river' (the Song Hong 'Red River', so-called because of the huge amount of red-coloured silt it carries), and *nôi* 'inside'. The two words represent the Vietnamese pronunciation of two Chinese characters. The city was founded by the Chinese as Dong Kinh 'Capital of the East' from *kinh* 'capital' and *dong* 'east' during their occupation in the 8th century. It was later renamed Dai La. According to legend, Ly Thai To, founder of the Ly dynasty (1009–1225), saw a huge golden dragon emerge from a lake by Dai La and soar into the sky above the site. He chose it as his capital in 1010 and renamed it Thang Long 'City of the Soaring Dragon' from *thang* 'city' and *long* 'dragon'. However, Dong Kinh was restored in 1428. Kecho was used during the 17th century and meant 'Market' or 'Fair' because a market was held on the first and fifteenth day of each month. With the arrival of Europeans in the 19th century Dong Kinh became corrupted to Tonquin (*Tonkin). To its inhabitants, however, it remained Thang Long until the imperial seat was moved to Hué in 1804. Then, briefly, it was called Thanh Tich and Bac Thanh. In 1831 the city's name was changed by the Nguyen dynasty (1802–1945) to Hanoi. It was the capital of Vietnam between 1010 and 1802 and from 1976 when North and South Vietnam were united, of French Indo-China in 1902–54 and of North Vietnam in 1954–76.

Hanover, CANADA, GERMANY, SOUTH AFRICA, USA
1. Germany (Lower Saxony): German Hannover. Previously an electorate of the Holy Roman Empire (1692–1806), a kingdom (1814–66), a Prussian province (1866–1945), and a city with a name meaning 'High Bank' from *hoch* 'high' and *Ufer* 'bank'. The city lies on the River Leine and the Mittelland Canal. The House of Hanover provided five monarchs for the British crown. The first, George Louis, Elector of Hanover (1698–1727), came to the British throne as George I†; he was followed by four more kings until 1837 when the personal union between Hanover and the UK was ended with the death of William IV†. In the UK he was suceeded by Queen Victoria†, but she, as a woman, could not also succeed to the throne of Hanover because of the Salic Law that prohibited female succession. The House of Hanover was superseded by the House of Saxe-Coburg and Gotha when Victoria married her cousin, Albert of Saxe-Coburg and Gotha.
2. USA: there are twelve cities with this name and spelling, all named after the House of Hanover or the German city, or after an existing Hanover in the USA; for example, the city in New Hamsphire is named after the Hanover in Connecticut.
3. Cities in Suriname and in North Dakota, USA, are spelt in the German way.

Hanumāgarh, RĀJASTHĀN/INDIA *Bhatner*
The previous name meant 'The Fortress of the Bhattī Rājputs'. The city was renamed in 1805 when it became part of the princely state of Bikaner. The name means 'Hanumān's Fort' from Hanumān, the divine monkey chief in the Hindu mythological epic, the *Rāmāyana*, and *garh*.

Hanyang, HUBEI/CHINA
The first syllable comes from *Hàn*, the Chinese people, the Han, and the second, *yáng* 'sun'. It lies to the north, the sunny side, of the Han River. It is one of the three cities that make up the conurbation of Wuhan: Hanyang, Hankou, and Wuchang.

Haparanda, SWEDEN
On the border with Finland, the name means 'Coast where Aspens grow' from the Finnish *haapa* 'aspen' and *ranta* 'shore'.

Harare, ZIMBABWE *Fort Salisbury, Salisbury*
Founded in 1890 at the place where the British South Africa Company's Pioneer Column stopped its advance into Mashonaland. It was named after Robert Gascoyne-Cecil (1830–

1903), 3rd Marquess and Earl of Salisbury, the British Prime Minister at the time (1885–6, 1886–92, 1895–1902). The 'Fort' was dropped in 1897. The present name, adopted in 1982 two years after Zimbabwe became independent, is derived from that of Chief Neharawe whose Shona people, the Harari, occupied a hill overlooking the new settlement. It became capital of Southern Rhodesia in 1902; thereafter it was the capital of the Federation of Rhodesia and Nyasaland (1953–63), of Rhodesia during the period following the unilateral declaration of independence (1965–79), and of Zimbabwe (1980).

Harbin (Haerbin) HEILONGKIANG/CHINA
Binjiang
Developed from a small fishing village in 1905 and called Binjiang, it was renamed Binjiang County in 1913. It became a city in 1932 and was known simply as Binjiang during the existence of the Japanese puppet state of Manchukuo in 1932–45. Lying on the Sungari River, the name means 'Place where Fish are dried' or 'Place for drying Fishing Nets in the Sun' in Manchu. It has also been suggested that it is the Chinese version of a Jin dynasty (265–420) word *A-le-jin* said to mean 'honour' or 'glory'.

Harbour Grace, NEWFOUNDLAND/CANADA
Founded *c*.1550, it was probably named after Le Havre-de-Grâce (now Le Havre), France.

Harding, KWAZULU-NATAL/SOUTH AFRICA
Founded as a military post in 1877 and named after Sir Walter Harding, the first chief justice in Natal.

Hardwār, UTTAR PRADESH/INDIA *Kapila*
Also spelt Haridwar. It was originally named after the sage Gupila. The present name is derived from Haridvāra and means the 'Door, or Gate, of Hari', Hari being one of the names of Vishnu, one of the major Hindu deities. Thus, the name can be taken to mean 'Gateway to the Gods'. The town is one of the most important pilgrimage centres of Hinduism and is one of the four locations for the Kumbh Mela (*see* ALLAHĀBĀD).

Hārer, ETHIOPIA
A walled, holy, city, it was an important Muslim trading centre during the 17th and 18th centuries, hence its name which is an Amharic modification of a word for 'trading post'.

Hārim, SYRIA
Derived from the Semitic root *hrm* signifying an enclosure of sheepfolds.

Haripur, NORTH-WEST FRONTIER/PAKISTAN
'Hari's Town' after Hari Singh Nalwa, Ranjit Singh's most famous general, who was appointed governor here in the 1830s, having carried out a number of successful actions against the Hazara mountain tribes known as the Hazarawals.

Harīrūd, AFGHANISTAN-IRAN-TURKMENISTAN
A river rising in Afghanistan, the name comes from the Old Persian *harawaia* 'river rich in water' with the Persian *rūd* 'river' unnecessarily added. It forms part of the Afghan–Iranian border and of the Iranian–Turkmen border. In Turkmenistan the river is called the Tedzhen.

Harlan, USA
1. Iowa: named after Senator Harlan.
2. Kansas: named after John C. Harlan, one of the first settlers.
3. Kentucky: settled in 1819 and called Mount Pleasant. It was later renamed after Major Silas Harlan who was killed at the Battle of Blue Licks in 1782 when a band of Native Americans decisively defeated a force from Kentucky.

Harlech, WALES/UK
The name recognizes the 13th-century castle built on a rocky spur. It means 'Beautiful Rock' from words that equate to the modern Welsh *hardd* 'beautiful' and *llech* 'slab of rock'. The Yorkist siege of the castle in 1460–8 during the Wars of the Roses inspired the famous song 'Men of Harlech'.

Harlem, NEW YORK/USA
A district of New York City founded in 1658 by Peter Stuyvesant, the Dutch governor of New Netherland, who named it Nieuw Haarlem 'New Haarlem' after the Haarlem in the Netherlands.

Harlow, UK, USA
UK (England): although designated a New Town in 1947, it was mentioned in the 1086 Domesday Book as Herlaua, having been Herlawe. The name means 'A Mound, or Hill, associated with an Army' from the Old English *here* and *hlāw* 'mound' or 'hill'.

Harper, LIBERIA, USA
1. Liberia: settled *c*.1833 by a group of black American slaves who had been freed and supported by the Maryland Colonization Society. The colony was named Cape Palmas. After some turmoil with the local Grebo people in 1857, it applied to join Liberia and was renamed Harper after Robert Goodloe Harper (1766–1825), a member of the American Colonization Society.

2. USA (Kansas): named after Marion Harper, 1st sergeant of Company E, 2nd Kansas Regiment.

Harpers Ferry, WEST VIRGINIA/USA
Settled in 1734 and named after Robert Harper who organized a ferry across the River Potomac here.

Harrisburg, USA
1. Illinois: laid out in 1853 and named after James Harris, one of the first settlers.
2. Pennsylvania: first established as a trading post and ferry crossing on the Susquehanna River c.1718, it was known as Harris's Ferry after John Harris, an Englishman who traded with the Native Americans. When the settlement was developed into a town in 1785 for John Harris's son, also John Harris (1727–91), it was named Louisbourg after Louis XVI (1754–93), King of France (1774–92). However, the link with John Harris senior and his son was not forgotten and within a few years the city became known as Harrisburg, principally after the junior John Harris.

Harrismith, AUSTRALIA, SOUTH AFRICA
South Africa (Free State): laid out in 1849 as Vrededorp 'Peace Village' in Afrikaans. It was moved the next year to its present site, a village then called Gemsbokhoek 'Gemsbok Corner', because of a lack of water. Neither the names Vrededorp nor Gemsbokhoek were retained, the town being renamed after Sir Harry Smith (1787–1860), governor of Cape Colony (1847–52), in 1850.

Harrison, USA
1. Arkansas: named after General Larue Harrison who laid out the town.
2. New Jersey: named after William H. Harrison (1773–1841), President of the USA (1841) for only one month before dying of pneumonia.

Harrodsburg, KENTUCKY/USA *Harrodstown, Oldtown*
Founded in 1774 and named, and later renamed, after its founder, Colonel James Harrod, who built the first cabin.

Harrogate, AUSTRALIA, UK, USA
UK (England): formerly Harwegate. The name is of Scandinavian origin meaning the '(Place on the) Road to the Pile of Stones' from Old Scandinavian *hǫrgr* 'pile of stones' and *gata* 'road' or 'way'. In the Scandinavian sense 'road' may have meant the 'right of way for cattle to pasture'.

Hartford, LIBERIA, UK, USA
1. UK (England): the Cambridgeshire town was previously known as Hereforde 'Ford

suitable for the Crossing of an Army' from *here* and *ford*. Other towns with this name in England, however, usually mean 'Ford frequented by Harts, or Stags' from the Old English *heorot* and *ford*.
2. USA (Connecticut): originating as a Dutch fort in 1633, the settlement was named after the Hartford in England, the birthplace of Samuel Stone, one of the leaders of the First Church of Christ when it moved here in 1636 from Cambridge, Massachusetts.

Hartlepool, ENGLAND/UK *Herterpol*
'Pool, or Bay, near the Hart Peninsula' or 'Hart Island Harbour' from the Old English *heorot* 'hart' or 'stag', *ēg* 'promontory' or 'island', and *pōl* 'pool'; for coastal towns, such as Hartlepool, *pōl* can also mean 'harbour'. Presumably stags grazed on the promontory with *ēg* becoming the modern 'le'.

Har Us Nuur, MONGOLIA
'Black Water Lake' from *har* 'black', *us* 'water', and *nuur* 'lake'.

Harwell, ENGLAND/UK *Haranwylle, Harwelle*
'Spring, or Stream, by the Hill called Hāra' from the Old English *wella* 'spring' or 'stream'. Hāra meant 'the grey one' from the Old English *hār* 'grey'.

Harwich, UK, USA
1. UK (England): formerly Herwyz and Herewic 'Army Camp' from Old English *herewīc*. This may have in part supported the Danish fleet. The *z* at the end of the original name had the same sound as *ch*.
2. USA (Massachusetts): settled in 1670 and named after the Harwich in England.

Haryāna, INDIA
A state with a name meaning the 'Abode of God', in this case Vishnu, Hari being one of his names. The Sanskrit *ayana* 'home' was added since this was the birthplace of the Hindu religion. It became a state in 1966 when the Punjab was partitioned into its Punjabi- and Hindi-speaking elements.

Harz Mountains, GERMANY
A mountain range between the Elbe and Weser Rivers with a name from the Old German *hart* 'forest'.

Hasa, al- (al-Aḥsā) SAUDI ARABIA
'The Oasis', a reference to the largest oasis in the country.

Hasankale, TURKEY
'Hasan's Fortress' named after one of the citadels of Uzun Hasan, a 15th-century chief of the Akkoyunlu 'White Sheep', a Turkmen

tribe that held sway over most of eastern Anatolia.

Haslemere, ENGLAND/UK *Heselmere*
'Pool where Hazels grow' from the Old English *hæsel* and *mere*.

Hastings, AUSTRALIA, BARBADOS, CANADA, NEW ZEALAND, UK, USA
1. Canada (Ontario): named after General Francis Rawdon-Hastings (1754–1826), 1st Marquess of Hastings and 2nd Earl of Moira, who fought in the American War of Independence (1775–83) and subsequently was governor-general of Bengal and commander-in-chief of forces in India (1813–23).
2. New Zealand (North Island): settled in 1864 and named after Warren Hastings (1732–1818), the first governor-general of British India (1774–85).
3. UK (England): formerly Hæstingaceaster and Hastinges. The first name meant the '(Roman) Town of Hæsta's People' from an Old English personal name, *-ingas*, and *ceaster*; the later name meant the '(Place of) the Family, or Followers, of Hæsta'. His name probably came from the Old English *hæst* 'violent' and his tribe was known as the Hæstingas.
4. USA (Nebraska): founded in 1872 and named after Colonel Thomas D. Hastings who did much to organize a railroad through the town.

Hatay, TURKEY *Alexandretta*
A province previously known as the *sancak* '(military) district' of Alexandretta (now Iskenderun) during the Ottoman Empire. Despite being claimed by Turkey, it was awarded to Syria after the collapse of that Empire. In 1938, under a French mandate, the Alexandretta district of Syria became the autonomous republic of The Hatay, so-called by the French for reasons unknown and in reality the ancient city of *Antioch and its hinterland. As a result of the plebiscite ordered by the League of Nations, France ceded The Hatay to Turkey in 1939.

Hatfield, UK, USA
UK (England): a number of towns have this name, the two best known being in Hertfordshire and South Yorkshire. The name means 'Open Land where Heather grows' from the Old English *hæth* 'heath' or 'heather' and *feld* 'open country'. The names in the 1086 Domesday Book were Hetfelle and Hedfeld respectively. The town in Hertfordshire was designated a New Town in 1948.

Hatteras, NORTH CAROLINA/USA
A city, island, cape, and inlet named after a tribe of Native Americans.

Hattiesburg, MISSISSIPPI/USA *Twin Forks, Gordonville*
Settled in 1881 and named after his wife, Hattie, by Captain William H. Hardy, a Confederate officer and statesman.

Haugesund, NORWAY
A name that refers to Harald's Hill from *haug* 'hill', just north of the town, where Harald I Fairhair (*c*.860–*c*.940), the first king of all Norway (*c*.870–*c*.940), is thought to be buried; and the Karmsund from *sund* 'sound' or 'strait' which runs southwards between the mainland and the island of Karmøy.

Haute-Normandie, FRANCE
A region with the name 'Upper Normandy'.

Havana, CUBA, USA
Cuba: the local Spanish name is La Habana. Founded in 1515 by the Spanish conquistador Diego Velázquez de Cuéllar (*c*.1465–1524) on the south coast, this site was abandoned in 1519 due to the inequitable climate and the multitudes of mosquitoes. The name was transferred to a village, then known as Puerto Carenas, at its present location on the north coast. It was named San Cristóbal de la Habana 'St Christopher of the Habana'. The meaning of Habana is not known, but it may be that of a local tribe. Havana became the capital in 1898 when Cuba gained its independence from Spain; it is also the name of a province.

Havant, ENGLAND/UK *Hamanfuntan, Havehunte*
'Hāma's Spring' from an Old English personal name and *funta* 'spring'.

Havelock, CANADA, NEW ZEALAND, USA
New Zealand (South Island): named after Major General Sir Henry Havelock (1795–1857), who, after three unsuccessful attempts, relieved Lucknow during the Indian Mutiny in 1857. Havelock North in North Island is named after the same person.

Haverfordwest (Hwlffordd) WALES/UK
Haverfordia, Hareford, Heverford West, Herefordwest
'Western Ford used by Goats' from the Old English *hæfer* 'goat', *ford*, and *west*. The *west* was added later to distinguish this town from Hereford.

Haverhill, UK, USA
1. UK (England): formerly Hauerhella probably meaning 'Hill where Oats are grown' from the Old Scandinavian *hafri* and the Old English *hyll*.
2. USA (Massachusetts): founded in 1640 by the Revd John Ward in 1640, it is named after his birthplace in England.

Havířov, CZECH REPUBLIC
Founded as a satellite town of Ostrava in 1955,
the name is derived from *havíř* 'miner' since
most of the inhabitants were miners.

Havličkuv Brod, CZECH REPUBLIC *Deutsch Brod*
Renamed in 1945 after the Czech poet and
political journalist Karel Havliček Borovsky
(1821–56). *Brod* means 'ford' (on the River
Sazava) and is retained in memory of the
German miners who first settled here.

Havre, BELGIUM, USA
USA (Montana): named after Le Havre in
France, probably the birthplace of one of the
earliest settlers.

Hawaii, USA *Sandwich Islands*
A state consisting of a group of islands and the
name of the largest island. Captain James
Cook[†] landed on one of the islands, Kauai, in
1778 and named the group the Sandwich
Islands after John Montagu (1718–92), 4th Earl
of Sandwich, then first lord of the British
Admiralty (1748–51, 1771–82). Settled by
Polynesians, the present name may be derived
from Hawaiki, the previous name of Raiatea,
one of the French Polynesian Society Islands,
or from the Polynesian *Owhyii* 'Place of the
Gods', a reference to the two volcanoes, Mauna
Kea and Mauna Loa, on the island of Hawaii; or
it may simply mean 'Homeland'. By 1810 all
the islands of the group had been united into a
kingdom under King Kamehameha I (*c.*1758–
1819). In 1893 the monarchy was overthrown
and a republic established. In 1898 it was
annexed by the USA and in 1959 Hawaii joined
the Union as the 50th State.

Hawera, NORTH ISLAND/NEW ZEALAND
'Burned Place' from the Maori *ha* 'breath' and
wera 'burnt'. This referred to the vengeful
burning of a tribal village and the
extermination of its inhabitants by another
tribe who felt it had been slighted by them. The
correct name is Te Hawera 'The Burnt Place'.

Hawick, SCOTLAND/UK *Hawic*
'Enclosed Farm' from the Old English *haga*
'a settlement enclosed by a hedge' and *wîc*.

Hawkes Bay, CANADA, NEW ZEALAND
New Zealand (North Island): a regional council,
named by Captain James Cook[†] in 1769 after
Admiral of the Fleet Edward Hawke (1705–81),
1st Baron Hawke, who was then first lord of
the British Admiralty (1766–71). The large bay,
Hawke Bay, is similarly named after Edward
Hawke.

Hawkesbury, AUSTRALIA, CANADA
1. Australia (New South Wales): a river, named
in its upper course the Wollondilly, and then

lower down the Warragamba; after joining the
Grose, it becomes the Hawkesbury, named
after Robert Banks Jenkinson (1770–1828), 2nd
Earl of Liverpool and Baron Hawkesbury,
British secretary for war and the colonies
(1809–12) and prime minister (1812–27).
2. Canada (Ontario): founded in 1798 and
named after Charles Jenkinson (1727–1808),
1st Earl of Liverpool and Baron Hawkesbury,
secretary at war (1778–82) during the
American War of Independence (1775–83).

Hay, AUSTRALIA, USA
Australia (New South Wales): first settled in
1840 as Lang's Crossing Place, it became a
town in 1859 and was named after John
Hay, parliamentary representative of the
district.

Hayes River, MANITOBA/CANADA
Named after Sir James Hayes of the Hudson's
Bay Company.

Hayward, USA
1. California: named after William Hayward
who, having failed to find gold, opened a hotel
here instead in 1851.
2. Wisconsin: founded by, and named after,
Anthony J. Hayward.

Haywards Heath, ENGLAND/UK *Heyworth,
Hayworthe, Haywards Hoth*
'Heath by the Enclosure with a Hedge' from
the Old English *hege* 'hedge' and *worth*
'enclosure'; *hæth* was added later.

Hazārajāt, AFGHANISTAN
'Land of the Thousand' derived from the
Sanskrit *Abhisāra*. The Hazāra are Shia
'Afghans' of Mongol descent. Their ancestors
came with Genghis Khan in the 13th century
and they roamed the region in groups of a
hundred horsemen, often combined into a
force of a thousand horsemen known as a
hazār or *hazāra*. When the main Mongol force
withdrew some Hazāra stayed. During the late
18th and early 19th century they were driven
into the barren mountains of central
Afghanistan—the Hazārajāt.

Hazard, KENTUCKY/USA
Founded in 1821 and named after an American
naval officer, Commodore Oliver Hazard
Perry, who was victorious at the Battle of Lake
Erie in 1813.

Hazleton, PENNSYLVANIA/USA
So-called because of the numerous hazel
bushes in the area.

Healesville, VICTORIA/AUSTRALIA
Founded in 1860 and named after Sir Richard
Heales (1823–64), premier of Victoria at the
time.

Hebburn, ENGLAND/UK *Heabyrm*
'High Burial Place' from the Old English *hēah*
and *byrgen* 'burial place' or 'tumulus'.

Hebei, CHINA *Zhíli*
A province meaning 'North of the River', that
is, the Yellow River, from *hé* and *běi*. The
previous name, used during the Manchu
dynasty (1644–1911), meant 'Directly Ruled',
but it really only referred to the capital district
rather than to all of Hebei.

Hebrides, SCOTLAND/UK *Ebudes/Hebudes,
Suðreyjar*
A group of islands subdivided into the Inner
Hebrides and the Outer Hebrides. The origins
of the name are not known, but the present
name is said to come from a misreading of
u for ri. The Old Scandinavian name, Suðreyjar,
meant 'Southern Islands', a reference to the
fact that they were well to the south of
Orkney. They became part of the Norwegian
realm before being passed to Scotland in 1266.

Hebron (Arabic: **Khalīl ar-Rahmān**; Hebrew:
Hevron), WEST BANK *Qiryat Arba'*
A very ancient and holy city, the Arabic name
means 'Beloved, or Friend, of (God) the
Merciful' from *Khalīl* 'Friend', a reference to
Abraham who, according to tradition, is buried
here. The Hebrew name comes from *khavor* 'to
unite' or *khavoor* 'group'; it is one of the four
holy cities of Judaism. The Hebrew Qiryat
Arba' means the 'City of the Four', possibly a
reference to four united settlements in biblical
times or the fact that Hebron is built on four
hills. It was the capital of Israel for some years
during the time of King David (10th century
BC). Annexed by Jordan in 1950, it fell to Israeli
troops during the Six-Day War in June 1967. In
January 1997 it was the last of seven major
West Bank towns to be handed over to
Palestinian rule in accordance with the 1993
Oslo peace process. Although a Palestinian
city, a small part of it is under Israeli control.

Hecate Strait, CANADA
A strait between British Columbia and the
Queen Charlotte Islands named after the *Hecate*,
the ship of Captain (later Admiral Sir) George
Richards (1832–96) in which he surveyed the
coast of British Columbia in 1861–2.

Heerenveen, THE NETHERLANDS
'Peat Bog of the Lords' from the Dutch *heeren*
'lords', the plural of *heer* and *veen* 'peat bog'.

Hefei, ANHUI/CHINA *Ruyin, Lu, Luzhou*
Although renamed Hefei from the 2nd century
BC, it was given the name Lu when it became
the seat of a prefecture during the Sui (581–
618) and Tang (618–907) dynasties. As a
superior prefecture from the 15th century it

was called Luzhou. Hefei was readopted in
1912. A centre of trade routes at the
confluence of the Xia and Huai Rivers, the
name may come from *hé* 'to join' and *féi*
'fertile'.

Heidelberg, AUSTRALIA, GERMANY, SOUTH
AFRICA, USA
Germany (Baden-Württemberg): derived
from *Heidel (beere)* 'bilberry' and *Berg*. It
lies at the foot of wooded hills on the
River Neckar.

Heilbronn, BADEN-WÜRTTEMBERG/GERMANY
Heiligbronn
'Holy Spring' from *heilig* 'holy' and *Brunnen*
'well' or 'spring'. The spring refers to a stream
that appeared from under the altar of
St Kilian's Church. There is a town spelt
Heilbron, founded in 1872 and named
after the German town, in Free State,
South Africa.

Heiligenstadt, BAVARIA/GERMANY
'Place of Holy Men' (Saints) from *Heiliger* 'Saint'
and *Stadt*. It is a spa and religious city.

Hēilóngjiāng, CHINA
A province meaning 'Black Dragon River' from
hēi 'black', *lóng* 'dragon', and *jiāng*. It is named
after the River Hēilóng, the Chinese name for
the River Amur. It became a province during
the Qing dynasty (1644–1911).

Hejaz (al-Ḥijāz) SAUDI ARABIA
A region in the west separating the inland
desert from the Red Sea coast by mountains.
The terrain is recognized in the name which
derives from the Arabic *ḥajz* 'obstacle' from
ḥajāza 'to separate'. The region was occupied
by the Ottoman Turks in 1517–1916 when
Sharīf Hussein ibn Ali (*c*.1854–1931), Emir of
Mecca (1908–16), rose against them and
proclaimed himself 'King of the Arab
Countries'; the Allies recognized him only as
King of the Hejaz (1916–24).

Helena, GUYANA, USA
1. USA (Arkansas): settled in 1797 as
Monticello and renamed St Francis. In 1821
it was renamed again after the daughter of
Sylvanus Phillips.
2. USA (Montana): founded in 1864 as Last
Chance Gulch when gold was discovered. It
was quickly renamed, probably after the
community in Minnesota. However, some like
the thought that it was named after Helen of
Troy, while others believe it was named
because its location resembled that of St
Helena in California, the 'St' being dropped
later.

Helensburgh, SCOTLAND/UK
'Helen's Town'. Founded in 1776 by Sir James Colquhoun, who named it after his wife, Lady Helen Sutherland.

Helicon, Mt (Óros Elikón) GREECE
A mountain whose name describes its shape from *helix* 'spiral' or 'twisted'.

Heligoland (Helgoland) SCHLESWIG-HOLSTEIN/
GERMANY
An island with a name, 'Holy Land', which may be derived from *heilig* and *land*, to indicate some former religious centre. Coming under Danish control in 1714, it was seized by the British in 1807, and annexed to the UK in 1814. In 1890 it was given to Germany in part exchange for Zanzibar.

Heliopolis (Onu) EGYPT *On*
Ruins. A very ancient religious centre for the worship of the sun-god Re: thus 'City of the Sun' from the Greek *hēlios* 'sun' and *polis*. This area of Cairo is now known as Masr el Gedîda. The biblical name was On. The Egyptian name, Onu, means 'City of Pillars', the most famous being the pair known as Cleopatra's Needles, one now in London and the other in New York City.

Hell-Ville, MADAGASCAR
Named after Admiral Louis de Hell, the French governor of Réunion (1838–41).

Helsingborg (Hälsingborg) SWEDEN
Takes its name from the Danish port Helsingør (Elsinore) lying opposite with the added *borg*. It was ceded to Sweden by Denmark in 1658.

Helsingør, DENMARK
See ELSINORE.

Helsinki (Swedish: Helsingfors), FINLAND
The Swedish *fors* means 'waterfall', a reference to the falls at the original site of the city at the mouth of the River Vantaa, some 3 miles (5 km) north of its present location which has better access to the sea. *Helsing* comes from Helsingi, a tribal name. Helsinki is the Finnish version of the Swedish name. The city was founded in 1550 by Gustav I Vasa (*c.*1496–1560), King of Sweden (1523–60), as Helsingfors and moved in 1640. Three years after Finland was ceded to Russia in 1809, the capital of the Grand Duchy of Finland was moved to Helsinki and it has remained the capital of Finland ever since.

Hemel Hempstead, ENGLAND/UK
Hamelamestede
'Homestead in broken Country' from the Old English *hamel* 'broken' or 'undulating' terrain and *hām-stede* 'homestead'. Hemel was the old name of a district.

Hempstead, NEW YORK/USA
Settled in 1643 and named by early settlers after their home town, Hemel Hempstead in England.

Henan, CHINA
A province meaning 'South of the River', that is, the Yellow River from *hé* and *nán*, although only about one-sixth of the province is.

Henderson, NEW ZEALAND, USA
1. USA (Kentucky): laid out in 1797 by the Transylvania Land Company and named after Colonel Richard Henderson, one of its officials.
2. USA (Nevada): founded in 1942 and named after Senator Charles B. Henderson (1873–1954).
3. USA (North Carolina): settled in 1713 and laid out as a town in 1840 when it was named after Leonard Henderson (1772–1833), a former Chief Justice of the state's Supreme Court.

Henry Mountains, UTAH/USA
Named after Joseph Henry, secretary of the Smithsonian Institution, at the time when the Colorado River was being explored in 1869 and 1871.

Hengyang, HUNAN/CHINA *Hengzhou*
The present name, adopted in 1912 when Hengzhou was downgraded from prefectural status to county, means the 'Sunny Side of Heng (Mountain)' from Heng, the name of a nearby mountain, and *yáng* 'sun' or 'light'. The city was established separately from Hengyang County in 1943.

Henley-on-Thames, ENGLAND/UK *Henleiam,*
Hanleya
'High Clearing' from the Old English *hēah* and *léah*. 'Thames' indicates the river that it lies on. Henley is not on high ground and here *hēah* has the sense of 'important'.

Hennessey, OKLAHOMA/USA
Named after Pat Hennessey, well known as a fighter of Native Americans, who was killed on the site of the future town.

Henry Mountains, COLORADO/USA
A mountain range named after Joseph Henry (1797–1878), a prominent American scientist in the field of electricity.

Heraklion (Iráklion) CRETE/GREECE *Heracleum,*
El Khandaq, Chandax, Candia, Megalo Kastro
Derived from the ancient Roman port of Heracleum which was named after Hercules (Heracles) who successfully carried out the seventh of his 'labours' here: the capture of the fire-breathing mad bull that had been terrorizing Crete. It became the Saracen capital of Crete in the 9th century and was

known as El Khandaq '(Castle in) the Moat', a reference to the great ditch which surrounded it. This name was corrupted to Chandax by the Byzantines and to Candia by the Venetians to whom the island was sold in 1204; that name then came to embrace the whole island (*see* CRETE). In 1669–1897 the city was under Ottoman Turkish rule and was called Megalo Kastro 'Great Fort'. It became the capital of Crete in 1971.

Herāt, AFGHANISTAN *Herovia/Hera, Alexandria Areion*
Founded on the ancient site of Herovia, it was rebuilt and renamed 'Alexandria of the Arians' by Alexander III the Great† in 330 BC. The region was called Aria by the Greeks. The city was captured by Arabs in 660 and, after being fought over by Persians and Afghans, it became part of Afghanistan in 1863. It is now named after the river on which it lies, the Harīrūd which in Old Persian was *Harīv*.

Hérault, LANGUEDOC-ROUSSILLON/FRANCE
A department named after the Hérault River. Its name is derived from the Indo-European *ar* 'water' or 'river'.

Herbert River, QUEENSLAND/AUSTRALIA
Discovered in 1864 by George Dalrymple and named by him after Sir Robert George Herbert (1831–1905), Queensland's first premier (1860–5), after Queensland had separated from New South Wales and become an independent colony, and permanent under-secretary of state for the colonies (1871–92). The town of Herberton is also named after him.

Herculaneum, ITALY, USA
Italy (Campania): Italian Ercolano and formerly Resina. It is traditionally associated with the name Hercules (Heracles) and thus is of Greek origin. The ancient city was destroyed by the eruption of Vesuvius in 79.

Heredia, COSTA RICA *Cubujuquí, Villavieja*
Founded in the 1570s, its original name gave way to the Spanish Villavieja 'Old Town' before being renamed in 1763 after the president of the high tribunal.

Hereford, UK, USA
1. UK (England): 'Army Ford' from *here* and *ford*, possibly to indicate that the ford was wide enough for marching soldiers to cross without breaking ranks. The county of Herefordshire, from the name of the city and *scīr*, gave its name to the cattle bred here.
2. USA (Texas): named afer the breed of cattle brought here in the 1890s.

Hereroland, NAMIBIA
Named after the Herero people.

Herford, NORTH RHINE-WESTPHALIA/GERMANY
Founded as a nunnery in 789 where the River Aa flows into the River Werre. It probably has the same meaning as Hereford.

Herkimer, NEW YORK/USA *German Flats*
Settled *c*.1725 by Germans and later named after General Nicholas Herkimer (1728–77), commander of American forces at the Battle of Oriskany in 1777 who later died of his wounds received then.

Hermann, MISSOURI/USA
Settled by Germans and named after Hermann (in Latin, Arminius), who led the Germanic tribes to victory over the Romans in AD 9, thereby preventing Roman domination east of the River Rhine.

Hermanus, WESTERN CAPE/SOUTH AFRICA *Hermanuspietersfontein*
Named after Hermanus Pieters, a *trekboer* 'nomadic farmer', who settled with his flock of sheep at a *fontein* 'spring' near the coast here in 1835. The name was shortened in 1904.

Hermitage, MISSOURI/USA
Missouri: named after the home, the Hermitage near Nashville, Tennessee, of Andrew Jackson†.

Hermon, Mt (Jabal ash-Shaykh) LEBANON-SYRIA *Sirion, Senir*
A mountain ridge with a Hebrew name meaning 'consecrated'. The Israelites, under Moses and Joshua, did not progress further north and it was regarded as a sacred place even in Roman times. The Arabic name means 'Mountain of the Chief'.

Hermosa, PHILIPPINES, USA
Descriptively named 'Beautiful' in Spanish.

Hermosillo, SONORA/MEXICO *Pitic*
Founded in 1700 for the resettlement of the Pima tribe, it was renamed in 1828 after General José Maria González Hermosillo, a hero of the Mexican War of Independence (1810–21).

Herstal (French: **Héristal**), BELGIUM
'Place of the Army', meaning a permanent military garrison, from the German *Heer* 'army' and *Stelle* 'place' or 'location', itself from the Old High German *hari* and *stal*.

Herstmonceux, ENGLAND/UK *Herst, Herstmonceus*
'Wooded Hill belonging to the Monceux Family' from the Old English *hyrst* 'wooded hill' and the manorial affix. The Monceux family probably came from Normandy some time not long after the Battle of Hastings in 1066.

Hertford, UK, USA
1. UK (England): formerly Heorutford and Hertforde 'Ford (over the River Lea) frequently crossed by Harts' from the Old English *heorot* and *ford*. It gave its name to the county of Hertfordshire with the added *scīr*.
2. USA (North Carolina): named after Francis Seymour-Conway (1719–94), 1st Marquess of Hertford, who supported the development of the American colonies.

Hervey Bay, QUEENSLAND/AUSTRALIA
Named after Hervey Bay which itself was named by Captain James Cook[†] in 1770 after Admiral Augustus John Hervey (1724–79), 3rd Earl of Bristol.

Herzeg-Novi, MONTENEGRO/SERBIA AND MONTENEGRO *Sveti Stefan, Novi, Castelnuovo*
Originally founded as St Stephen from the Serbo-Croat *svetac* 'saint' in 1382 by Stephen I Tvrtko (*c*.1338–91), King of Bosnia (1353–91) and King of the Serbs and Bosnia (1376–91), as he tried to build a new port on the north side of the Bay of Kotor. However, this name did not catch on and the town was simply known as Novi 'New'. As a result of development by the Bosnian general, Duke (*Herzeg*) Stephen Vukčić Kosača, who established a factory here in 1448 and who took refuge in the port after the fall of Bosnia to the Ottoman Turks in 1463, the town came to be known as Herzeg-Novi. The Venetians renamed it Castelnuovo 'New Castle' when they held it in 1687–1797.

Herzegovina *See* BOSNIA AND HERZEGOVINA.

Herzliyya, ISRAEL
Founded in 1924 and named after Theodor Herzl (1860–1904), the founder of political Zionism, the movement to recreate a Jewish nation in Palestine.

Hesse (Hessen) GERMANY *Franconia*
A state named after the Chatti or Hassi, a Frankish tribe who lived in the area.

Hexham, ENGLAND/UK *Hagustaldes ham*
'Warrior's Homestead' from the Old English *hagustald* 'warrior' and *hām*.

Hialeah, FLORIDA/USA
Founded in 1921, its name is a Seminole word meaning 'Beautiful Prairie'.

Hiawatha, USA
Kansas and Utah: named after Hiawatha, a legendary chief of the Onondaga, who was made famous by Longfellow's poem, *Song of Hiawatha*.

Hickory, USA
Mississippi and North Carolina: named after Andrew Jackson[†] whose nickname was Old Hickory.

Hidalgo, MEXICO
A state established in its own right in 1869 and named after Miguel Hidalgo y Costilla (1753–1811), who was prominent in the struggle for Mexican independence.

Hidalgo del Parral, CHIHUAHUA/MEXICO *Parral*
Renamed to honour Miguel Hidalgo y Costilla (see previous entry).

Hierapolis, TURKEY
Ruins. Founded in the 2nd century BC, probably by Eumenes II, King of Pergamum (197–160 BC), and named the 'City of Hiera' after Hiera, the wife of Telephos, the legendary founder of Pergamum. The city was bequeathed to Rome in 133 BC.

Higashiōsaka, HONSHŪ/JAPAN
Established in 1967 with the amalgamation of Fuse, Kawachi, and Hiraoka to mean 'East of Ōsaka' from *higashi* 'east'. *See* ŌSAKA.

Highland, ILLINOIS/USA
Illinois: named after the Highlands in Scotland by Scottish settlers.

Highland Park, MICHIGAN/USA *Nabors, Whitewood*
Settled in the 1880s as Nabors. In 1889 it took its present name after a local ridge which has since been flattened.

High Point, BERMUDA, USA
USA (North Carolina): settled *c*.1750 and finally established in 1853 at the highest point of the North Carolina Railroad between Goldsboro and Charlotte.

High Wycombe, ENGLAND/UK *Wicumbe*
'(Place at) the Settlements' from *wīcum*, the dative plural of *wīc*. The 'High' relates to the greater importance of High Wycombe compared to nearby West Wycombe.

Hiiumaa, ESTONIA *Dagö, Khiuma*
An island called 'Giant's Land' from *maa* 'land' because, according to legend, a giant lived on it. The earlier Swedish (and German) name of Dagö meant 'Day Island' because it took a whole day to reach it from the mainland. Belonging to the Brothers of the Sword and the Teutonic Knights in the 13th century, it was later ruled by the Danes, Swedes, and Russians in 1721–1920; they called it Khiuma.

Hildesheim, LOWER SAXONY/GERMANY
The name was the old German personal name Hildin or Hildini from the Old High German *hiltin* 'battle' to which the suffix *-heim* has been added.

Ḥillah, al-, IRAQ *al-Jamiayn*
Founded in the 10th century on the east bank
of the River Euphrates as al-Jamiayn 'Two
Mosques'. In 1102 al-Ḥillah was founded
opposite it on the west bank. The new city was
sometimes known by its full name Hillat Bani
Mazyad after Ali bin Mazyad al-Asadī.

Hillsboro, USA
1. There are at least thirteen cities with this
name, many after a person (e.g. Kansas and
North Dakota) or a hill (e.g. Illinois and
Virginia).
2. Ohio: named after Wills Hill (1718–93), 1st
Earl of Hillsborough, British secretary of state
for the colonies (1768–72) and for the
Northern Department (1779–82).

Hillsborough, CANADA, UK, USA
1. UK (Northern Ireland): the Irish name is
Cromghlinn. Hillsborough means 'Hill's
Fortified Manor' from *burh*; 'Hill' referred to
Colonel Arthur Hill (*c.*1601–63), constable and
MP for the counties of Down, Antrim, and
Armagh. He was granted land here upon which
he built a fortress called Hillsborough Fort.
2. USA (North Carolina): laid out in 1754 on
the site of a Native American village, it was at
first called Orange and then Corbinton after a
colonial official, Francis Corbin. In 1759 it
became Childsburgh after Thomas Childs, a
provincial attorney general. Finally, in 1768, it
was renamed Hillsboro after Wills Hill (*see*
HILLSBORO). The spelling was changed in 1965.

Hilvarenbeek, THE NETHERLANDS
Possibly named after a small stream nearby,
the Hilver or Hulver, with *beek* 'stream' or
'brook'. However, in the 12th century, there
were local communities called Beke, Beeck,
and Beycke. To Beeck was added Hilvaren from
hil 'hill' and *vaart* 'low-lying area' to distinguish
it from the other similar-sounding
settlements.

Himāchal Pradesh, INDIA
A state with a name meaning 'Land of Snowy
Mountains', a reference to the Himalayas,
from the Sanskrit *hima* 'snow' and *acal*
'mountain', and *pradesh*.

Himalayas, BHUTAN-CHINA-INDIA-NEPAL
A great mountain range meaning the 'Abode
of Snow' from the Sanskrit *hima* 'snow' and
ālaya 'abode'.

Hindhead, ENGLAND/UK *Hyndehed*
'Hill frequented by Hinds' from the Old
English *hind* and *hēafod* 'headland'.

Hindu Kush, AFGHANISTAN-PAKISTAN
A huge mountain system known to Alexander
III the Great[†] as the *ᵐ*'Caucasus'. However, the

name is said to represent *Hendu Kosh* 'Hindu
Killer' or 'Killer of Indians' because, according
to the great 14th-century Arab traveller, Ibn
Battutah, so many slaves died from severe cold
while attempting to cross it.

Hindustan, INDIA
Traditionally northern India and meaning the
'Land of the Hindus'.

Hingham, UK, USA
1. UK (England): formerly Hincham and
Heingeham, probably 'Hega's Homestead'
from an Old English personal name, -*inga*- and
hām.
2. USA (Massachusetts): founded in 1633 as
Barecove Common and two years later named
after the town in England from which some
settlers had come.

Hiram, USA
Maine and Ohio: named after Hiram, the
Phoenician King of Tyre (969–936 BC). The
name means 'nobly born'.

Hirosaki, HONSHŪ/JAPAN
'Wide Cape' from *hiro* 'wide' or 'broad' and *saki*
'cape' or 'promontory', a probable reference to
the vast Tsugaru plains. It is possible, however,
that it may come from the Ainu *biro* 'cliff' and
saki.

Hiroshima, HONSHŪ/JAPAN
A prefecture and a city founded in 1593 by
Mori Terumoto when he built a castle at the
mouth of the Ōta River. The name means
'Broad Island' from *hiro* 'broad' and *shima*
'island' or 'Far-Stretching Islands', a reference
to the fact that the prefecture includes some
offshore islands.

Hisār, HARYĀNA/INDIA *Hisār Firūza, Hissār*
'Castle' as in the Turkish word or possibly
'gate' or 'barricade'. It was founded in 1356 by
Firūz Shah Tughluq, Sultan of Delhi (1351–88),
as a palace-fort and originally named 'Castle of
Firūz'.

Hispania, PORTUGAL-SPAIN
The name for the Iberian Peninsula in Roman
times. During the Second Punic War (218–201
BC), the Romans drove the Carthaginians out
of the peninsula and then divided it into
Hispania Ulterior and Hispania Citerior.
During the reign of Emperor Augustus[†] the
latter, also known as Tarraconensis, was split
into Lusitania and Baetica.

Hispaniola *Quisqueya, Española, San Domingo*
An island in the West Indies comprising the
Dominican Republic and Haiti. The local
Arawak people called the island Quisqueya
before Christopher Columbus[†] landed in 1492
and called it La Isla Española 'The Spanish

Island'. During the Spanish presence it was sometimes called San(to) Domingo. Hispaniola is the Anglicized version of the name.

Hitachi, HONSHŪ/JAPAN
'The Sun Rises' from *hi* 'sun' or 'daytime' and *tachi* 'rise'.

Hitchin, ENGLAND/UK *Hiccam, Hiz*
'(Place in the Territory of) the Hicce Tribe'. The first Hiccam is interchangeable with Hiccum, the dative of the tribal name Hicce. This may be derived from a Celtic river name meaning 'dry'.

Hòa Bình, VIETNAM
'Peace'.

Hobart, AUSTRALIA, USA
1. Australia (Tasmania): founded in 1804 as Hobart Town after Robert Hobart (1760–1816), 4th Earl of Buckinghamshire, then secretary of state for the colonies and war (1801–4).
2. USA (Indiana): laid out in 1849 by George Earle and named after his brother, Hobart.
3. USA (New York): named after Bishop Hobart.

Hoboken, BELGIUM, USA
USA (New Jersey): having bought it from the Lenni Lenape in 1630, the Dutch settlers named it Hopocan from the local *Hopocan Hackingh* 'Land of the Tobacco Pipe' from *hopocan* 'tobacco pipe'.

Ho Chi Minh City (Thanh Pho Hồ Chí Minh)
VIETNAM *Dong Nai, Phan Yen, Gia Dinh, Saigon*
Renamed in 1976 after Ho Chi Minh (1890–1969), President of the Democratic Republic of Vietnam (North Vietnam) (1946–69) and founder of the modern Vietnamese state; born as Nguyen Sing Cung, Ho Chi Minh was one of his many aliases. Within Cambodia for many centuries and built on the site of an ancient Khmer city, the Vietnamese only established a small trading settlement here, known as Gia Dinh, at the end of the 17th century. It was captured by the French in 1859 and renamed after the Sai Gon River on which it lies. Saigon, or Soai-gon or Sai Con 'kapok tree', is said to come from the Khmer *prei kor* 'forest of kapok trees' or *prei nokor* 'settlement in the forest'. The city also includes the Chinatown of Cho Lon 'Big Market', previously Ben Nghe 'Landing of the Water Buffalo', with which it became linked at the end of the 18th century. The name Ho Chi Minh has not really caught on with the public and most people still refer to the city as Saigon; the river is still called the Saigon River. It was the capital of the French Protectorate of Cochinchina in 1862–1954, of the State of Vietnam in 1949–54, and of South Vietnam in 1954–75.

Hódmezővásárhely, HUNGARY
'Place of the Fair by the Field of the Beavers' from *hód* 'beaver', *mező* 'field', *vásár* 'fair' and *hely* 'place'. Fair here probably means 'market'.

Hodonín, CZECH REPUBLIC
'Hodoňa's Place', the colloquial form of the Old Czech personal name Hodislav or Hoděmysl.

Hof, GERMANY, ICELAND
Germany (Bavaria): founded by the Dukes of Andechs-Meran, *Hof* can mean 'manor', 'court', 'palace', or simply 'household (of a noble)'.

Hofmeyr, EASTERN CAPE/SOUTH AFRICA
Maraisburg
Settled in 1873 and first named after Daniel Marais who was prominent in its establishment. To distinguish it from another town of the same name in the Transvaal, it was renamed in 1911 after Jan Hendrik Hofmeyr (1845–1909), influential and much respected leader of the (Dutch) Afrikaner Bond in the Cape Colony.

Höfn, ICELAND
'Harbour'.

Hohhot (Hu He Hao Te) INNER MONGOLIA AUTONOMOUS REGION/CHINA *Kuku-khoto, Guihua, Guisui*
Founded in the 16th century as a Mongolian city meaning 'Blue City', it was subsequently settled by the Chinese and renamed Guihua 'Civilized' or 'Naturalized' meaning 'returned to civilization'. In 1913 the city merged with a new one, Suiyüan, some 2½ miles (4 km) to the north and together they adopted the name Guisui. The present name is derived from the first one and means the same, 'Blue City', from the Mongolian *hoh* 'blue' and *hot* 'city'. The name is also spelt Huhehot.

Hôi An, VIETNAM *Dai Chien, Hai Pho/Faifo*
A name derived from *hôi* 'club', in the sense of 'to gather', and the Chinese *ăn*. It received its present name in 1954. Faifo was the 17th-century European version of Hai Pho.

Hokkaidō, JAPAN *Ezo/Yezo*
An island and region founded in 1869 as 'Province of the Northern Sea' from *hoku* 'north', *kai* 'sea', and *dō* 'province'. Only in 1868 did it become formally a part of Japan.

Holbæk, DENMARK *Holbek, Holæbæc, Holbech*
'Brook which runs through a Hollow' from *hulning* 'hollow' and *bæk* 'brook'.

Holguín, CUBA *Cubanacán, San Isidoro de Holguín*
A province and a city founded in 1523 and renamed after Captain García Holguín. He was given the region by Diego Velázquez de Cuéllar (*c.*1465–1524), who led an expedition

to conquer Cuba in 1512. The original site was a local village called 'Centre of Cuba'.

Holland, CANADA, THE NETHERLANDS, USA
1. The Netherlands: two provinces are named North Holland and South Holland. Holland may simply mean 'hollow land', a reference to the low-lying terrain, or 'scrub land' from the Germanic *hulta* 'scrub' or 'wooded' and *land*, referring to the region round Dordrecht. *See* NETHERLANDS, THE.
2. USA (Michigan): named by Dutch settlers in about 1847 after the region in Western Europe from which they emigrated.

Hollidaysburg, PENNSYLVANIA/USA
Founded in 1768 by Adam and William Holliday from Northern Ireland and named after them.

Holly Springs, USA
Mississippi: founded in 1835 and named after the spring surrounded by holly trees. The cities in Arkansas and North Carolina are named for the same reason.

Hollywood, IRELAND, USA
1. USA (California): the first serious development was begun in 1887 by Horace Wilcox and his wife, who named it after a friend's home in Chicago. This probably meant simply 'Holly Wood'.
2. USA (Florida): laid out in 1921 and named after the district in California.

Holyhead (Caergybi) WALES/UK *Halïheved, Holyhede*
'Holy Headland' from the Old English *hālig* and *hēafod* 'headland'. On Holy Island off the coast of the Isle of Anglesey, the name refers to a headland to the west. The Welsh name means 'Cybi's Fort' from *caer* and Cybi, a 6th-century saint who founded the monastery here.

Holy Island, UK
1. England: *see* LINDISFARNE.
2. Wales: in Welsh, Ynys Gybi 'Cybi's Island' (*see* HOLYHEAD). The name comes from the Old English *hālig* and *ēg-land* 'island'.

Holy Land A region generally including Israel and Palestine that is sacred to the Jews, Christians, and Muslims. It extends from the Mediterranean coast to east of the River Jordan. To Muslims it means Arabia or, at least, that part of it that was the Prophet Muhammad's homeland.

Holyoke, MASSACHUSETTS/USA
Settled in 1725 and named after either Elizur Holyoke, one of the first settlers, or the Revd Edward Holyoke, a long-time president of Harvard University (then Harvard College) (1737–69).

Holywell (Treffynnon) WALES/UK *Haliwel*
Named after the fountain (holy well) from the Old English *hālig* and *wella* which is said to have appeared on the spot where the 7th-century St Winefride (Winifred), a Welsh virgin, was beheaded after she had refused the attentions of Caradoc, the son of a local prince.

Holzkirchen, BAVARIA/GERMANY
'(Place of) Wooden Churches' from *Holz* 'wood' and *Kirche* 'church'.

Homburg (Bad Homburg) SAARLAND/GERMANY
The full name is Bad Homburg vor der Höhe which denotes a spa town at the foot of the (Taunus) mountains from *vor* 'in front of' and *Höhe* 'height'. Homburg means 'High Fortress', a reference to the 12th-century Hohenburg Fortress (now in ruins). The town has given its name to the felt hat with a lengthways furrow in the crown which was first made here.

Home Counties, ENGLAND/UK
The counties surrounding London, in particular, Essex, Kent, Surrey, and the former county of Middlesex.

Homel (Homyel') BELARUS *Gomy, Gomel'*
A province and a city overlooking the Sozh River with a name derived from the Slavonic *gom* 'hill'.

Homer, USA
1. Alaska: founded in 1895 and named after Homer Pennock, a prospector.
2. Seven states have cities with this name (and one called Homer City), most probably named after the Greek poet (9th or 8th century BC?).

Homs, SYRIA *Emesa*
A governorate, more often spelt Ḥimṣ, and a city. Captured by the Arabs in 636, they renamed it Homs, a name said to come from a Canaanite root word meaning 'shyness'. In 1516–1918 it was ruled by the Ottoman Turks.

Honda, COLORADO/USA
'Sling' or 'catapult' from the Spanish.

Honduras The Republic of Honduras (Spanish: República de Honduras) since 1838 when Honduras broke free of the United Provinces of Central America (also known as the Central American Federation); it had joined the Federation in 1823 after declaring independence from Spain in 1821. It was discovered by Christopher Columbus[†] in 1502 and colonized by Spain despite resistance from the Lenca people. Between 1570 and 1821 it was part of the Captaincy General of Guatemala. The name means 'Deep Water' from the Spanish *hondura*, a possible reference to the depth of the coastal waters.

Honey Grove, TEXAS/USA
Named by explorers who found quantities of
honey when camping in the woods.

Honfleur, CANADA, FRANCE,
France (Lower Normandy): in the River Seine
estuary and occupied by the English at various
times, the name means 'Hun's Creek' from a
Germanic personal name and the Old English
flēot 'creek' or 'estuary'.

Hong Kong (Xiānggǎng) CHINA
Hong Kong Special Administrative Region
(Xiānggǎng Tèbié Xíngzhèngqū) since 1997. It
consists principally of Hong Kong Island,
Kowloon, and the New Territories, which
include Lantau Island. With the exception of
foreign affairs and defence, a high degree of
autonomy has been granted to Hong Kong
under the concept of 'one country, two
systems'. Hong Kong was formerly a British
crown colony. The island was ceded to the UK
in perpetuity at the Treaty of Nanking (now
Nanjing) in 1842; the peninsula of Kowloon on
the mainland was ceded at the Convention of
Peking in 1860 and the New Territories, also
on the mainland, at the Second Treaty of
Peking in 1898, for 99 years. Because the island
would not be viable on its own and tacitly
accepting the Treaty of Nanking to have been
one of the 'unequal treaties', the UK agreed,
under a Joint Declaration in 1984, to return all
of Hong Kong to China on 1 July 1997 when
the lease on the New Territories expired. At
that time China agreed to establish Hong Kong
as a Special Administrative Region. The name
means 'Fragrant Harbour' from *xiāng* 'fragrant'
or 'incense' and *gǎng* 'harbour'. Several
theories exist as to how this name originated.
One is that it is due to the local abundance of
the *chénxiāng* 'deep fragrance' tree; another,
that the island was used as a base by a female
pirate known as *Xiānggū* 'Fragrant, or
beautiful, Lady'; a third that a large waterfall
near the harbour had very sweet-smelling
water from which sailors obtained fresh water.
Hong Kong is the approximate Cantonese
pronunciation of Xiānggǎng.

Honiara, SOLOMON ISLANDS
A slight abbreviation of Naghoniara meaning
'Place of the East Wind'.

Honiton, ENGLAND/UK *Honetone*
'Hūna's Farmstead' from an Old English
personal name and *tūn*. However, it is possible
that the first element of the name refers to
'honey'.

Honolulu, HAWAII/USA *Fair Haven, Brown's
Harbour*
A port sheltered by Sand Island, the name
means 'Sheltered Harbour' from the Hawaiian
hono 'port' and *lulu* 'calm' or 'quiet' and thus
sheltered. Brown's Harbour referred to
Captain William Brown who sailed into the
harbour in 1794. The Russians, British, and
French all occupied the harbour in the 19th
century. In 1850 Kamehameha III (1814–54),
King of Hawaii (1825–54), declared it to be his
capital, although it had acted as such since
1845.

Honshū, JAPAN *Hondo*
Japan's principal island, the name means
'Main District' from *hon* 'main' and *shū*
'district' or 'region'.

Hood, CANADA, USA
1. Canada (Nunavut): a river named after
Robert Hood, a member of Sir John Franklin's
expedition (1819–22) along the southern
shores of Coronation Gulf, who was murdered
by Native Americans.
2. USA (Oregon): a mountain first sighted in
1792 and named after the British Admiral
Samuel Hood (1724–1816), 1st Viscount Hood,
who fought in the American War of
Independence (1775–83) and was commander-
in-chief in the Mediterranean (1793–4). The
Hood River is also named after him.

Hood River, OREGON/USA
A city settled in 1854 and named after Admiral
Hood (see previous entry).

Hook of Holland (Hoek van Holland) THE
NETHERLANDS
Descriptively named 'Corner of Holland'.

Hooker Island (Ostrov Hooker) FRANZ JOSEF
LAND/RUSSIA
Named after Sir Joseph Dalton Hooker
(1817–1911), a widely travelled botanist and
director of the Royal Botanic Gardens at Kew
(1865–85).

Hoopstad, FREE STATE/SOUTH AFRICA *Hauptstad*
Founded in 1876 and originally named after
A. P. Haupt who surveyed the site. It was not
long before it was appreciated that this name
could be translated as 'capital' (in German,
Hauptstadt) and so it was changed to 'Hope
Town'.

Hoorn, THE NETHERLANDS
Named for its horn-shaped harbour from *hoorn*
'horn'.

Hope, CANADA, UK, USA
1. USA (Arkansas): founded in 1852 and
named after the daughter of James
Loughborough, who laid out the site.
2. USA (Indiana): named by Moravian
(Czech) settlers in accordance with their
feelings.

Hopefield, WESTERN CAPE/SOUTH AFRICA
Laid out in 1852 and named after the two officials, Hope and Field, who organized this.

Hopewell, JAMAICA, USA
USA (Virginia): named after Hopewell Farms, a holding established in 1635.

Hopkinsville, KENTUCKY/USA *Elizabethtown*
Renamed in 1797 after General Samuel Hopkins who fought in the American War of Independence (1775–83).

Hoquiam, WASHINGTON/USA
Named after the River Hoqiuam, at the mouth of which it lies. The river's name comes from the Native American *ho-qui-umpste* 'hungry for wood', a reference to the large amount of driftwood that concentrated at its mouth.

Hormuz, IRAN
An island and a strait possibly named after the Persian god Hormuzd, although this is by no means certain.

Horsham, AUSTRALIA, CANADA, UK, USA
1. Australia (Victoria): named by James Darlot, the founder in 1841, after his home town in England.
2. UK (England): 'Horse Village' meaning a 'village where horses are kept' from the Old English *hors* and *hām*.

Horta, AZORES/PORTUGAL
'Garden'.

Horton, NORTHWEST TERRITORIES/CANADA
A lake and a river discovered in 1826 and named after Wilmot Horton, British under secretary of state for the colonies at the time.

Hoshangābād, MADHYA PRADESH/INDIA
Founded in 1406 by, and named after, Sultan Hoshang Shah of Mālwa with the added *ābād*.

Hot Springs, ARKANSAS/USA
Named after the famous thermal springs much appreciated by the local Native Americans for medicinal purposes.

Hottentot Bay, NAMIBIA
Named after the Hottentot people who are now more usually known as the Khoikhoin 'Men of Men'. They were given the name Hottentot, from the expression *hotteren-totteren* 'to stammer' or 'to stutter', by Dutch settlers because of the 'clicks' in their language. It is also said that the chant used in their moon-worshipping ceremonies sounded to western ears rather like 'hottentot'.

Houghton, AUSTRALIA, UK, USA
1. UK (England): 'Farm on, or near, a Ridge' from the Old English *hōh* 'ridge' or 'spur' and *tūn*.

2. USA (Michigan): settled in 1851 and named after Douglass Houghton, formerly a state geologist.

Houma, CHINA, USA
USA (Louisiana): founded in about 1810 and named after the Houma, a minor Native American tribe.

Housatonic River, MASSACHUSETTS-CONNECTICUT/USA
Said to be from the Mahican *wussi* 'beyond' and *adene* 'mountain' to give '(Place) beyond the Mountain'. Alternatively, it has been suggested that it comes from *wassa* 'proud', *aton* 'stream', and *ick* from *azhubic* 'rocks' to give 'Proud River flowing through the Rocks'.

Houston, CANADA, GUYANA, USA
USA (Texas): founded in 1836 and named after Sam Houston (1793–1863), the first president of the independent Republic of Texas (1836–8 and 1841–4). *See* TEXAS.

Hout Bay, WESTERN CAPE/SOUTH AFRICA
'Wood Bay' from the Dutch *hout*. The slopes round the town are thickly wooded and the early settlers felled the timber here for construction purposes.

Hove, BELGIUM, UK
UK (England): formerly La Houue 'Hood-shaped Hill', thus a hill providing shelter, from the Old English *hūfe*.

Hövsgöl, MONGOLIA
A province named after Mongolia's largest freshwater lake and a town. The meaning is 'Full Lake' from *göl* 'lake'.

Howick, CANADA, NEW ZEALAND, SOUTH AFRICA, UK
1. Canada (Quebec): named after Sir Henry Grey (1802–94), Viscount Howick, British secretary of state for war and the colonies (1846–52).
2. South Africa (KwaZulu-Natal): founded in 1850 and named after Sir Henry Grey, Viscount Howick.
3. UK (England): formerly Hewic and Hawic, possibly 'High Dairy Farm' from the Old English *hēah* and possibly meaning the 'most important', and *wīc*.

Hoy Island, SCOTLAND/UK *Haey*
One of the Orkney Islands with a name meaning 'High Island'. Hoy comes from the old Scandinavian name from *há* and *ey*.

Hradec Králové, CZECH REPUBLIC *Königgrätz*
'Castle of the Queen' from *hrad* 'castle' and *králova* 'queen'. The German name only partly reflects this with *könig* 'king'. The castle is associated principally with Queen Elizabeth

(1286–1335), daughter of the King of Poland and wife of Wenceslas (Václav) II, King of Bohemia (1283–1305) and King of Poland (1300–5). The town became the seat of the widowed queens of Bohemia in the 14th century.

Hranice, CZECH REPUBLIC *Granice/Hranice, Bělokostelí/Bílý Kostel, Moravské Bělokostelí/Mährisch Weisskirchen*
The original, and present, names mean 'Border' because the town was situated on the border between Moravia and Silesia. In the 13th century it was renamed Bělokostel 'White Church', either because the town was owned by so-called 'white monks' or because the walls and towers of the church were built with white stone. As there were several towns with the same name it was renamed Moravské Bělokostelí, and also Mährisch Weisskirchen, both 'Moravian White Church'. However, in the 19th century the inhabitants began to revert to the original name.

Huambo, ANGOLA *Nova Lisboa*
Founded in 1912 by Portuguese settlers and given a Portuguese name, Huambo, of the local name Ouimbundu. In 1928 it was renamed New Lisbon as the intention was to make it the capital of Angola under Portuguese rule. When Angola achieved independence in 1975, the previous name was restored.

Huancavelica, PERU *Villa Rica de Oropesa*
An ancient Inca settlement, the modern town was founded in 1572 as the 'Rich Town of Oropesa' after the town in Spain. However, the present name was quickly adopted; it was a Spanish adaptation of the local Quechua name for the site and means 'Stone Idol'.

Huancayo, PERU
Taken from a Quechua word meaning the 'Huancas', a Native American people who lived in the Andes.

Huangshan, ANHUI/CHINA *Tunxi*
Located in a mountainous area, the name means 'Yellow Mountain' from *huáng* 'yellow' and *shān*. It was named Taiping County during the Tang dynsty (618–907), became Huangshan City in 1983, and incorporated Tunxi in 1987.

Huangshi, HUBEI/CHINA *Shidanyao*
Founded in 1950, it takes its name from either the nearby Yellow Stone Harbour or Yellow Stone Mountain from *huáng* and *shí* 'stone' or 'rock'.

Huascarán, PERU
A mountain named after Inti Cusi Huallpa Huáscar (d. 1532), an Inca chieftain, whose name means 'Sun of Joy'.

Hubei, CHINA *Jinghu*
A province meaning 'North of the Lake', a reference to Lake Dongting, the second largest freshwater lake in China, from *hú* 'lake' and *běi*. Its name was Jinghu during the Song dynasty (960–1279).

Hubli-Dhārwād, KARNĀTAKA/INDIA
Also known simply as Hubli. The present name is the result of a union of the two cities of Hubli and Dhārwād in 1961. Hubli, also known as Huballi or Pubballi, means 'Old Village'; Dhārwād, originally Daravada, means 'Gateway Town'.

Hucknall, ENGLAND/UK
'Hucca's Corner of Land' from an Old English personal name and *halh* 'corner of land'.

Huddersfield, ENGLAND/UK *Oderesfelt, Hudresfeld*
Possibly 'Open Land belonging to a man called Hudræd' from an Old English personal name and *feld*.

Hudiksvall, SWEDEN *Hoffvidvickzvaldh*
A shortened version of the original name, the first part of which was the genitive of the name of the village, Huvudvik 'Head Bay' or 'Main Bay' from the Old Scandinavian *vik* and *huvud* 'head' in the sense that it had the shape of a head or that it was the most important bay. *Vall* 'bank' or 'grazing ground' alludes to the fact that the town was built outside the village on a bank or grazing ground.

Hudson, CANADA, USA
1. Canada: a bay explored in 1610 and named after Henry Hudson (*c*.1535–1611), an English navigator, while he sought the Northwest Passage to Asia. Having failed, his crew mutinied and cast him and eight others adrift. Nothing was ever heard of any of them again. It gave its name to the renowned Hudson's Bay Company established in 1670 to find a way through to the Pacific by way of a north-west passage and to conduct trading operations with the people living in areas around the bay.
2. Canada: a strait between Baffin Island and Quebec named after Henry Hudson.
3. USA (New York): a river named after Henry Hudson who explored it in 1609 when he should have been seeking the Northeast Passage to Asia on behalf of the Dutch East India Company. Having failed in that venture, he ignored his contract and set out to discover the Northwest Passage.

Hué, VIETNAM *Phu Xuan, Thuan Hoá*
The present name evolved from the previous name, possibly just a mispronunciation: *thuan* 'allegiance' or 'submission' and *hoá*

'transformation' or 'conversion'. Phu Xuan was the name of the original citadel founded in the 17th century, now some 3 miles (5 km) north-east of the present city. It became the heart of the imperial city of the Nguyen kings. Hué lies on the Huong River, also called the Hué River or Perfume River.

Huehuetenango, GUATEMALA
Close to the city are the ruins of Zaculeu, an ancient city and this explains the present name 'Place of the Ancients'.

Huesca, ARAGÓN/SPAIN *Ileosca, Osca*
Derived from its original name given to it by its ancient Iberian founders. The Roman name probably comes from the Oscan tribe.

Huila, COLOMBIA
A department established in 1905 and named after the Nevado del Huila, a snow-capped mountain.

Huíla, ANGOLA
A province named after the Mwila who used to live on Huíla Plateau. Their name comes from *híla* 'grass', a reference to the lush grazing land here.

Hull, CANADA, UK, USA
1. Canada (Quebec): founded *c*.1800 and named after Kingston Upon Hull in England whence some of the settlers had emigrated.
2. UK (England): *see* KINGSTON UPON HULL.
3. USA (Iowa): named after a man called John Hull.
4. USA (Massachusetts): founded in 1644 and named after the English city.

Humboldt, ANTARCTICA, CANADA, USA
1. USA (Nevada): a river, a lake, a salt marsh, and a mountain range are named after Baron Alexander von Humboldt (1769–1859), a German naturalist and explorer, who spent five years in Central and South America (1799–1804).
2. Also named after him are Humboldt Bay in California, the Humboldt Current off the Peruvian coast of South America, the Humboldt Glacier in Greenland, and the Humboldt Mountains in Antarctica.

Hunan, CHINA
A province meaning '(Land) South of the Lake' from *hú* 'lake' and *nán*, referring to Lake Dongting in the north of the province. Until the 17th century Hubei and Hunan formed a single province, Huguang.

Hunedoara, ROMANIA *Eisenmarkt*
A county and a city which takes its name from the Hunaides (or Hunyadi in English), an Hungarian family, two sons from which became Kings of Hungary: János (1446–52) and

Máryás (1458–90). The suffix *-ara* represents the Hungarian *vár* to give 'Fortress of the Hunyadi'. The German name means 'Iron Market' in recognition of the iron mines which were opened during Roman times.

Hungary (Magyarország)
The Republic of Hungary (Magyar Köztársaság) from 1918 to 1949 (although for 133 days during 1919 it had been declared a Soviet republic by the communist revolutionary Béla Kun) and since 1989; previously the Hungarian People's Republic (1949–89); the Kingdom of Hungary (1000–1918), although in 1867–1918 it was part of the Dual Monarchy of Austria-Hungary. Between 1301, when the Árpád dynasty came to an end, and 1918 when the monarchy was abolished, Hungary was ruled by a succession of foreign kings with only two exceptions, one of whom was disputed. For some of this time parts of Hungary were under Ottoman Turkish suzerainty or direct rule. The Romans called the western part of modern Hungary Pannonia. The present name is derived from *On Ogur* 'Ten Arrows', the name of a group of tribes (seven Magyar and three Kavar) living along the north shore of the Black Sea before they moved to modern Hungary during the 9th century. In due course, the name of the strongest tribe, the Megyers, came to be used as a generic name for the whole group. The theory that the violence of the marauding Magyars reminded their victims of Attila and his Huns, thus attracting the name Hungarians, is not tenable. Hungary's borders have rarely been static for long. At the 1920 Treaty of Trianon Hungary was forced to cede more than two-thirds of its historic lands to the countries surrounding it. This consigned more than three million Hungarians to living outside their own country. Drawn to the side of Nazi Germany in the Second World War, Hungary shared in Germany's defeat and was forced to surrender even more territory.

Hungerford, AUSTRALIA, UK, USA
UK (England): formerly Hungreford 'Hunger Ford' from the Old English *hungor* and *ford*. This may have meant a ford which led to a barren, unfertile area or that those people who lived around the ford went hungry.

Hŭngnam, NORTH KOREA
May be 'Joy of the South' from *hung* 'joy' or 'delight' and *nam*, although the relevance of 'south' here is not apparent. The seaport on the east coast is in the central part of the country.

Hungtingburg, INDIANA/USA
Named because the surrounding area was considered to be good for hunting.

Hunter River, NEW SOUTH WALES/AUSTRALIA
Coal River
Originally called the Coal River by convicts who discovered it in 1791, it was renamed in 1797 after Vice Admiral John Hunter (1738–1821), governor of New South Wales (1795–1800).

Huntingdon, CANADA, UK, USA
1. Canada (Quebec): named after the town in England.
2. (UK) England: formerly Huntandun and Huntedun 'Huntsmen's Hill' or a 'Hill belonging to a man called Hunta' from *hunta* 'huntsman' or a personal name, *-ing-* and *dūn*. As the most important town in the area, it gave its name to the former county of Huntingdonshire with the additional *scīr*.
3. USA (Pennsylvania): originally Standing Stone, it was renamed after Selina Hastings (1707–91), Countess of Huntingdon, well known for her works of charity and generous donations to good causes, and the founder of the Countess of Huntingdon's Connexion, an association of Christian evangelicals.

Huntington, UK, USA
1. UK (England): two places have this name. That in Staffordshire, formerly Huntendon, means 'Hill of the Huntsmen' from the Old English *hunta* 'huntsman', the genitive plural being *huntena*. In Yorkshire the former name was Huntindune 'Place where Hunting takes place' from the Old English *hunting* and *dūn*.
2. USA (Indiana): previously a Native American settlement called Wepecheange 'Place of Flints', it was renamed in 1831 after Samuel Huntington, one of the 55 men who signed the Declaration of Independence in 1776.
3. USA (New York): settled in 1653 and named after the Huntingdon in England where Oliver Cromwell (1599–1658), lord protector of England, Scotland, and Ireland (1653–8), was born.
4. USA (Oregon): named after J. B. Huntington on whose ranch the town was built.
5. USA (West Virginia): named after Collis P. Huntington, president of the Chesapeake and Ohio Railway, who established a rail and river terminus here in 1870.

Huntsville, CANADA, USA
1. USA (Alabama): originally Twickenham after the home town of the English poet, Alexander Pope (1688–1744), it was renamed in 1811 after John Hunt who fought in the American War of Independence (1775–83) and first settled the area in 1805.
2. USA (Texas): founded as a trading post in 1830 and named after the founder's hometown in Alabama.

Hunyani, ZIMBABWE
A river and a town derived from *mhanyami* 'high ground'.

Hu'o'ng Hoá, VIETNAM *Khe Sanh*
Literally, a 'Mix of Perfume' from *hoá* 'mix' and *huong* 'perfume' or 'fragrance'.

Huron, CANADA, USA
1. USA (South Dakota): named after the Huron people. Huron has been said to be a corruption of the French *hure* 'head of a boar', meaning 'wild-headed'; this may have been an allusion to their hair or their headdress. The name was given to these Native Americans by Samuel de Champlain[†] in 1615.
2. USA-Canada: a lake originally named La Mer Douce 'The Freshwater Sea' by Samuel de Champlain[†], then Lac d'Orléans; this was followed by Lac des Hurons because of the French mission to the Huron.

Húsavík, ICELAND
'Bay of the Houses' from *vík* 'bay'. According to tradition, it is so named because a Swedish adventurer was blown off course and made a landfall here in 864. He ventured no further, building a dwelling here.

Huskvarna, SWEDEN *Hwsquernen*
'Mill House' from *hus* 'house', possibly a fortified stone house that used to stand here, and *kvarn* 'mill'.

Hutchinson, SOUTH AFRICA, USA
1. South Africa (Northern Cape): founded in 1885 as Victoria West Road. In 1901 it was renamed after Sir Walter Hely-Hutchinson (1849–1913), governor of Natal (1893–1901) and of Cape Colony (1901–10).
2. USA (Kansas): named after C. C. Hutchinson who founded it in 1872 at a point on the Santa Fe Railroad.

Hutt River, NORTH ISLAND/NEW ZEALAND
Named after a shareholder of the New Zealand Company, Sir William Hutt.

Hvar, CROATIA *Pharus, Lesina*
An island and a town. The town was founded by the Greeks in the 4th century as Dimos. They called the island Pharus. The Venetian name Lesina is derived from a Slavonic root word mean 'woody'. The island became part of the Kingdom of the Serbs, Croats, and Slovenes when it was created in 1918.

Hvítá, ICELAND
A river called 'White River' from *hvít* 'white' and *á* 'river'.

Hwange, ZIMBABWE *Wankie*
Founded *c.*1900 round a coal mine and named after Whanga, a local Ndebele chief. In 1982 the spelling was amended.

Hyannis, MASSACHUSETTS/USA
Named after a Native American supreme chief, Hianna. Hyannis Port, Massachusetts, is also named after him.

Hyde Park, GUYANA, USA
USA (New York): named after a local estate which itself was named after Edward Hyde (1710–52), Viscount Cornbury, governor of New York (1702–8).

Hyderābād, INDIA, PAKISTAN
1. India (Andhra Pradesh): a former princely state and a city. It has been called Bhāgnagar after a Hindu dancing girl, Bhāgmati, one of the sultan's concubines. Its principal name honours Ali ibn Abī Tālib (*c.*600–61), cousin and son-in-law of the Prophet Muhammad†. and the fourth caliph (656–61), who was given the nickname Haydar 'lion' because he was much admired for his courage in battle. Thus the name of the city, founded in 1591, means 'Lion City' from *haydar* and *ābād*. Hyderabad was coerced into joining India in 1948 after the Nizam (ruler) had initially refused to join at independence in 1947.
2. Pakistan (Sind): refounded in 1768, on the site of the ancient town of Nīrūn-Kot 'Nīrūn's Fort', and named after the fourth caliph, Ali (see 1). Nīrūn was a Hindu ruler who built a fort '*kot*' on the site. When Alexander III the Great† passed through in *c.*325 BC it was known as Patala.

Hyères, PROVENCE-ALPES-CÔTES D'AZUR/FRANCE
Occupied by Greeks and Romans, the name is derived from the Latin *area* 'vacant piece of ground'. Just off the coast opposite the town are islands called Îles d'Hyères.

Hythe, CANADA, UK
UK (England): formerly Hede 'Landing Place' or 'Harbour' from the Old English *hȳth*.

Iaşi, ROMANIA *Jassy*
A county and a city with a name possibly derived from the Cuman *jager* 'huntsman' or German *jäger* 'hunter'. The present name is the Romanian version of the German Jassy. The city was the capital of the Principality of Moldavia in 1565–1859 and of Romania in 1859–62.

Ibadan, OYO/NIGERIA
Ultimately it means 'worship' or 'adoration' from the Arabic *'ibādah* 'worship' from the verb *abada* 'to worship'; *'abd* means a 'slave' or 'servant (of God)'.

Ibaraki, HONSHŪ/JAPAN
A prefecture and a city meaning 'Thorn Tree' from *ibara* 'thorn' and *ki* 'tree'. The Chinese characters of the prefecture's name actually mean 'Thorn Castle' from *ibara* and *ki* 'castle'.

Ibarra, ECUADOR
The full name is San Antonio de Ibarra. Founded in 1606, it was named after Miguel de Ibarra, the president of the royal *audiencia* 'court' of Quito.

Iberia MISSOURI/USA
Named after the ancient name for Spain.

Iberian Peninsula The peninsula in south-west Europe comprising Spain and Portugal. It takes its name from the Bronze Age Iberian people. They took their name from the Iberus, the ancient name for the River Ebro.

Iberville, QUEBEC/CANADA *Christieville*
Renamed in 1854 after Pierre Le Moyne d'Iberville (1661–1706), a French-Canadian naval commander and explorer, who successfully attacked English trading posts in the Hudson Bay area.

Ibiza (Eivissa), BALEARIC ISLANDS/SPAIN *Ebusus*
Also spelt Iviza. The third largest of the Balearic Islands and a city-port, it was at one time inhabited by the Phoenicians. The name, therefore, may be of Phoenician origin and mean 'Island of Perfumes' from *ī* 'island' and *busim* 'perfume' or 'fragrance', a reference to the sweet-smelling vegetation on the island, or 'Island of Pines' from *brosim* 'pine'.

'Ibrī, OMAN
Named after the 'Ibriyyun tribe.

Icaria (Ikaría), GREECE
An island, traditionally said to be named after Icarus, the legendary son of Daedalus, who fell into the sea after he had flown too close to the sun and his waxen wings had melted. There is likely, however, to be a more prosaic reason for the name: possibly from the Pelasgian *īkar* 'timber', a reference to the formerly wooded terrain.

Iceland (Ísland) *Snæland*
The Republic of Iceland (Lýdhveldidh Ísland) since 1944. Originally Snæland 'Snow Land' from *c.*850 and then allegedly renamed Iceland from *ís* 'ice' by the first Norse settlers in the 9th century. Their intention was to deter visitors coming to an island which had in fact comparatively moderate annual temperatures (because of the Gulf Stream) and was much warmer than would be expected for a country so far north. Gradually settled beween 870 and 930 by Vikings from Norway, the island formally became subject to the Norwegian king in 1262. When Norway and Denmark were united in 1380, Denmark took control and this was retained until the Germans invaded Denmark in 1940 and the union was broken.

Ichihara, HONSHŪ/JAPAN
'Market in a Field' from *ichi* 'market' or 'city' and *hara* 'field' or 'uncultivated place'.

Ichikawa, HONSHŪ/JAPAN
'River Market' from *ichi* 'market' and *kawa*.

Ichinomiya, HONSHŪ/JAPAN
'Shrine of the One' from *ichi* 'one', *no* 'of', and *miya* 'shrine' or 'imperial palace'. This is a reference to Masumida Shrine, a Shintō temple around which the town began its development in the 7th century.

Ida, Mt (Kaz Daği), TURKEY
Covered in woods, the name may have come from the ancient Greek *ida* 'thick wood' or 'timber' or from the Cretan nymph Ida who went to Phrygia.

Idaho, USA
A state with a Shoshone name meaning 'Sun coming down the Mountain'. The first white men to explore the area were Meriwether Lewis (1774–1809) and William Clark (1770–1838) in 1805. Originally part of Oregon Country, it was divided between the Oregon

and Washington Territories in 1853–9 after which it became part of Washington Territory. In 1863 it became Idaho Territory and in 1890 it joined the Union as the 43rd state.

Idaho Falls, IDAHO/USA *Eagle Rock, Taylor's Bridge*
Founded in 1863 and finally renamed in 1890 after the wide but shallow waterfall on the Snake River.

Ídi, Mt, CRETE/GREECE
Also called Psiloreítis and said to have taken its name from the nymph Ida.

Idutywa, EASTERN CAPE/SOUTH AFRICA
Named after a small stream, the Dutywa. Its name is derived from the Xhosa *ukudutywa* 'one who is disturbed' and therefore 'Place of Disorder', a reference to the tribal disturbances that took place here *c*.1820. The town, laid out in 1884, was developed from a military post established in 1858.

Ife, OSUN/NIGERIA
Also called Ile-Ife. Considered by the Yoruba people to be a holy city, it may be named after Ifa, the god of divination.

Ifni, MOROCCO
A former Spanish coastal province, the name is derived from the Tuareg *isaffen*, the plural of *asif* 'water'. The fort of Santa Cruz de Mar Pequeña was taken over by the Spanish crown in 1476 but was lost to the Moors in 1524. It was regained in 1860, but the area was not occupied and developed by the Spanish until 1934. In 1969 the province was ceded to Morocco.

Ifrane, MOROCCO
Established as a hill resort for French colonial officials in 1929 with a name meaning 'Caves' from the plural of the Berber *ifri*, a reference to the limestone caves along the River Tizguit.

Iglesias, SARDINIA/ITALY
Famous for its cathedral built in 1288, the name comes from the Latin *ecclesia* 'church'.

Iguaçu, BRAZIL
Parana: a river and falls with a name derived from a Guaraní word meaning 'Great Water' or 'Much Water coming down'. There is also a town with this name near Rio de Janeiro.

Iguala, GUERRERO/MEXICO
In full, Iguala de la Independencia. Settled in 1750 and named after Agustín de Iturbide's Iguala Plan which called for an independent Mexico ruled by a monarchy. The Spanish *iguala* means 'agreement'.

Ijebu-Ode, OGUN/NIGERIA
For long the capital of the Ijebu people, a subdivision of the Yoruba, after whom the town is named.

IJsselmeer, THE NETHERLANDS
A lake, formed from the old Zuider Zee, named after the IJssel River with *meer* 'lake' added. The river's name means 'river' or 'water'.

Ilchester, ENGLAND/UK *Lindinis, Givelcestre*
'(Roman) Town on the (River) Gifl' from the Celtic river name meaning 'forked river' and *ceaster*. The Gifl was the previous name for the River Yeo.

Ilebo, DEMOCRATIC REPUBLIC OF THE CONGO *Port Francqui*
Renamed in 1972, the former name indicated its use as a port on the Kasai River and honoured Émile Francqui, a Belgian who travelled through Katanga in the 1890s.

Île-de-France, FRANCE *Francia*
A region with Paris as its capital. Originally known as Francia, the region stretched between the Rhine and Seine Rivers, but under the Carolingians (715–987) and during the 10th and 11th centuries the area was reduced in size. *Île* 'island' signifies an area between rivers. Later the Capetian dynasty (987–1328) began to spread territorially from this area, the 'Island of France', into what eventually became modern *France. The name Île-de-France did not come into use until the 14th century.

Ilford, CANADA, UK
UK (England): formerly Ilefort and Hyleford 'Ford over the (River) Hyle', a Celtic river name meaning 'trickling stream' and *ford*. The Hyle is now known as the Roding.

Ilfracombe, AUSTRALIA, UK
UK (England): formerly Alfreincome and Ilfridecumbe 'The Valley of Ælfred's People' from an Old English personal name, -*ing*-, and *cumb* 'coomb' or 'valley'.

Ilhéus, BAHIA/BRAZIL
'Islanders'. A Portuguese captaincy created in 1534 and now a port at the mouth of the River Cachoeira.

Ili, CHINA, KAZAKHSTAN
China-Kazakhstan: a river with a name said to represent the Mongolian *ili* 'glistening' to indicate clean water and a rapid flow.

Il'ich, KAZAKHSTAN
Takes its name from Vladimir Ilich Lenin's[†] patronymic.

Ilion, NEW YORK/USA *German Flats, Morgan's Landing, Remington's Corners*

Settled by Germans in 1725, it was finally named in 1852 after the Roman name for the ancient city of Troy in Turkey.

Ilkeston, ENGLAND/UK *Tilchestune, Elkesdone*
'Ēalāc's Hill' from an Old English personal name and *dūn*.

Illinois, USA
1. A state named after the Algonquian-speaking Illini people, their name simply meaning 'men'. First explored by two Frenchmen, Louis Jolliet (1645–1700) and Jacques Marquette (1637–75) in 1673, Illinois was ceded to Great Britain in 1763. In 1774 it became part of the province of Quebec, but was acquired by the USA in 1783; in 1787 it became part of the Northwest Territory. When the Northwest Territory was partitioned in 1800, Illinois became a part of Indiana Territory. In 1809, when Indiana Territory was divided, Illinois became a territory in its own right before joining the Union as the 21st state in 1818.
2. There are three rivers with this name in Illinois, Oklahoma, and Oregon.

Illiopolis, ILLINOIS/USA
'City of Illinois' from the name of the state and *polis*.

Illyria Only the Albanians claim descent from the Illyrian tribes whose territories stretched along the Adriatic coast from Slovenia in the north to Epirus in modern Greece. After defeat by the Romans in 168 BC, much of Illyria became the Roman province of Illyricum. There is no certainty as to the origin of the name. It may come from the Albanian *iliret*, the root *i lir* meaning 'free'; thus *iliret* corresponds to 'freemen' and Illyria to 'Land of the Free'.

Ilmenau, THURINGIA/GERMANY
Takes its name from the River Ilm on which it lies and a form of *Aue* 'meadow'.

Ilminster, ENGLAND/UK *Illemynister, Ileminstre*
'Large Church on the (River) Isle' from a Celtic river name and the Old English *mynster* 'minster' or 'large church'.

Iloilo, PANAY/PHILIPPINES
Adapted by the Spanish from a local word *Ilong-Ilong* 'like a nose' which is used to describe the coastal terrain, which resembles a nose, along the Jaro River, at the mouth of which it lies.

Ilulíssat, GREENLAND *Jakobshavn*
'Icebergs' in Inuktitut, a reference to the many icebergs that form in the area each year. It was originally named 'Jakob's Harbour' after Jakob Severin, a Dane, who overcame a small Dutch fleet in Disko Bay in 1739.

Imereti, GEORGIA *Colchis*
A district and in former times a West Georgian kingdom with a name meaning 'Land on the Far Side' from *imer* 'beyond' and the place-name suffix -*eti* to indicate territory beyond the Surami Range from Tbilisi, the capital of Georgia. With Mingrelia, it constituted Colchis, an ancient region which, in Greek mythology, was the destination for Jason and the Argonauts. *See* ABKHAZIA.

Immingham, ENGLAND/UK *Imungeham, Immingeham*
'Imma's Homestead' or 'The Homestead of Imma's Dependants' from an Old English personal name, -*inga*- and *hām*.

Imola, EMILIA-ROMAGNA/ITALY *Forum Cornelii*
Probably of Etruscan origin, it was known in Roman times as the 'Market of Cornelius' after Cornelius Sylla, a tyrannical Roman dictator who conquered the area in 82 BC. The present name is probably derived from the Germanic Immilo which is itself linked to the Via Aemilia (*see* EMILIA-ROMAGNA).

Imperia, LIGURIA/ITALY
Established in 1923 by the merger of Porto Maurizio, Oneglia, and a few villages, the new town's name came from a stream called Impero 'Empire' which flows close to Oneglia. The stream was renamed in the 18th century as a result of the wars between France and the Austrian Empire.

Imperial, CANADA, PERU, USA
Canada (Saskatchewan): settled by immigrants from Great Britain, the name simply conveys a connection with the British Empire.

Imphāl, MANIPUR/INDIA
'Collection of Houses', a reference to the fact that it developed as a group of villages which surrounded the royal enclosure. It was the seat of the kings of Manipur.

Inch'ŏn (Incheon), SOUTH KOREA *Chemulp'o, Jinsen*
A metropolitan city (equivalent in status to a province) lying near the mouth of the Han River with a name derived from *in* 'virtue' and *ch'ŏn* 'river'. During the Japanese occupation 1905–45 it was known as Jinsen.

Independence, USA
1. Twelve cities have this name, all celebrating, in one way or another, the independence of the USA which was declared on 4 July 1776.
2. Missouri: settled in 1827 and so-called in recognition of the enthusiasm for independence of Andrew Jackson[†].

India (Bhārat) *Hindustan*
The Republic of India since 1950 after
independence was achieved in 1947 when the
Federal Union of India (and Dominion of India)
was created. Although the English East India
Company had established its first trading post
on the west coast of India in 1608, the first step
in the creation of a British Empire in India was
only taken as a result of the victory of Robert
Clive (1725–74) at the Battle of Plassey in 1757.
At this time the Company desired no territory
other than Bengal; it was intent only on trade.
However, the collapse of the Mughal Empire
and the lack of cohesion of the Marathas
allowed the British to fill the vacuum and
more territory was gradually acquired.
Nevertheless, at the time of independence
British India comprised no more than three-
fifths of the subcontinent and 562 princely
states also existed. From 1526 the pre-eminent
power in India was the Muslim Mughal
Empire, *Mughal* being the Urdu version of
Mughul, the Persian word for Mongol, since the
rulers were partly descended from the Mongol
leaders, Genghis Khan[†] and Tamerlane[†]. The
empire began to fragment at the beginning of
the 18th century, although its emperors
retained their title with ever-diminishing
power until the Indian Mutiny in 1857–8. In
1858 the East India Company relinquished
power over India to the British crown. The
Mughal Empire incorporated the Muslim
Sultanate of Delhi which had been established
in 1206, Turkish and Afghan Muslim warlords
overpowering several major and minor Hindu
kingdoms from the 12th century. The name
India is taken from the River Indus along
which the first agricultural settlements took
root. Darius I (550–486 BC), Persian emperor
(522–486 BC), included among his territories
'Hidhu' which was probably from the Sanskrit
word *sindhu* 'the sea'. Here it referred to a great
river, the Indus, the *s* giving way to *h* in the
ancient Persian before being dropped
altogether. Somewhat ironically, the Indus
does not now flow through India, rising in
Tibet and flowing through Kashmir and
Pakistan to the Arabian Sea. The Aryans, who
had settled over the whole of northern India
by *c*.600 BC and brought with them the
language of Sanskrit, became known as
Hindus. In due course 'India', a Greek and
Latin term for 'the country of the River Indus',
spread from just being the region along the
river to the whole of the peninsula. Bhārat (or
Bhāratavarsha in full), first used officially in
1947, is taken from the most important Aryan
tribe, the Bhārata, which was probably the
name of its first king. Hindustan 'Place of the
Hindus' was the Turkish and Mughal name for

India. The expression 'Indian file' does not
come from India but from the Native
Americans whose practice it was to walk in
single file in the footsteps of the person in
front, the last man erasing the footprints to
foil trackers.

Indiana, USA
1. A state with a name meaning 'Land of
the Indians'. Various Algonquian-speaking
tribes roamed the area before the French
claimed it during the 17th century. In 1763,
at the end of the Seven Years' War (1756–63)
in Europe, which also involved French and
British rivalry in North America, the area
passed to the British under the terms of
the Treaty of Paris; twenty years later it
became part of the Northwest Territory
of the USA. In 1800 it became Indiana
Territory and joined the Union in 1816 as
the 19th state.
2. Pennsylvania: named in honour of the
collective 'Indian' tribes.

Indianapolis, INDIANA/USA
Named after the state with the added *polis*. The
motor race known as 'The Indy 500' takes its
name from the city and indicates that it is 500
miles (805 km) long and takes place near
Indianapolis.

Indianola, IOWA/USA
Founded in 1849 and named after a town with
the same name in Texas which was described
in a local newspaper.

Indio, CALIFORNIA/USA *Indian Wells*
Founded in 1876, it was later given a Spanish
name, Indio 'Indian'.

Indo-China, SOUTH-EAST ASIA *French Indo-China*
Indochina, a term which may have been
coined early in the 18th century to describe
that part of Asia which had come under the
influence of Indian and Chinese culture,
comprises Myanmar (Burma), Thailand,
Malaya, Laos, Cambodia, and Vietnam. *See*
FRENCH INDO-CHINA.

Indonesia *Dutch East Indies*
The Republic of Indonesia (Republik
Indonesia) since 1950 when a unitary
constitution was introduced. Previously the
Republic of the United States of Indonesia
(1949) with a federal constitution. The Dutch
arrived in 1595 in search of spices and
sandalwood and ejected the British who had
already ousted the Portuguese. From 1602 the
Dutch East India Company gradually
conquered the area and held sway until its
dissolution in 1798. The Dutch government
assumed control in 1816 and ruled until 1941
when the Japanese occupation began. Until

the establishment of Dutch colonial rule the region had never constituted a single political entity. In 1945 an independent republic was declared but this was not recognized by the Dutch until they transferred sovereignty in 1949. Nevertheless, 17 August 1945 is celebrated as independence day. A huge archipelago, Indonesia consists of the Greater Sunda Islands (southern Borneo (Kalimantan), Sulawesi, Java, and Sumatra), the Lesser Sunda Islands (the islands between Bali and Timor), the Moluccas (Maluku), and western New Guinea; together, they total 13 667 islands. The name is probably derived from the Greek *Indos Nesos* 'Indian Islands', its modern name being coined in 1884 by a German geographer, although it did not come into more general use until the 1920s. Some of Indonesia's islands, notably the Moluccas and Sulawesi, were famous as the 'Spice Islands'.

Indore, MADHYA PRADESH/INDIA
Founded in 1715 and later given a name derived from that of the Indreshwar Temple, built by local landowners in 1741.

Indus River, TIBET/CHINA-PAKISTAN
Derived from the Sanskrit *sindhu* 'river'. It gives its name to India and the Pakistani province of Sindh.

Ingham, AUSTRALIA, UK
1. Australia (Queensland): founded in 1864, it is named after William Ingham, who developed the sugarcane plantations here in the 1870s.
2. UK (England): possibly 'Inga's Homestead' from an Old English personal name and *hām*, although the first syllable may derive from the Germanic tribe, the Inguiones.

Inglewood, AUSTRALIA, NEW ZEALAND, USA
USA (California): laid out in 1887 by the Centinela-Inglewood Land Company which gave part of its name to the city.

Ingria, LENINGRAD/RUSSIA
A historic region also known as Ingermanland and named after its ancient Finnish inhabitants, the Ingers. The region passed from Sweden to Russia at the conclusion of the Great Northern War in 1721.

Ingushetia (Ingushetiya), RUSSIA
A republic named after the Ingush, a Muslim mountain people in the North Caucasus who call themselves Ghalghai, who became Russian subjects in 1810. Historically, they are said to be a branch of the Chechen people and take their name from the large *aul* 'mountain village' (a term used in the Caucasus) of Ingusht, or Angusht, in the Tarskaya valley. Ingushetia was united with Chechnya in 1934–

91 as a single autonomous province which became a republic in 1936. It ceased to exist in 1944–57 when Stalin[†] deported the Ingush (and Chechens) to Central Asia for 'unsocialist acts', having accused them of collaborating with the German Army. With the rehabilitation of the Chechens and Ingush in 1957 Checheno-Ingushetia was re-established with new territorial boundaries. After the Chechens had declared their independence in 1991 the separate republic of Ingushetia was established in 1992.

Inkerman, AUSTRALIA, CANADA, UKRAINE
Ukraine: probably 'New Fortress' from the Turkish *yeni* 'new' and *kerman* 'fortress'. The towns in Australia and Canada probably commemorate the Battle of Inkerman, an Anglo-French victory over Russian forces in the Crimea in 1854.

Inland Sea (Seto-Naikai), JAPAN
A sea between the islands of Honshū, Shikoku, and Kyūshū and linked to the Pacific by straits. The Japanese name has this meaning from *se* 'channel' and *to* 'door' to give 'narrow strait', and *nai* 'inside' or 'within' and *kai* 'sea'.

Inner Mongolia (Nei Monggol), CHINA
So-called after the Mongols because it is an autonomous region in northern China (as distinct from the independent state of (Outer) Mongolia further north) beyond the Great Wall. It was the southern part of traditional Mongolia, along the southern rim of the Gobi Desert. It was conquered by the Chinese in 1636, a Manchu emperor enthroning himself in Peking (now Beijing) in 1644.

Innisfail, AUSTRALIA, CANADA
Australia (Queensland): originally Geraldton but renamed after a poetic name for Ireland in 1911.

Innoshima, Honshū/Japan
Derived from *in* 'cause' or 'origin', *no* 'of' and *shima*. In the past the Chinese character for *in* meant 'house of the retired Emperor . . .'.

Innsbruck, AUSTRIA *Veldidena*
'Bridge over the (River) Inn' from the German *Brücke* 'bridge'.

Inowrocław, POLAND *Siedlce, Junior Vladislavia*
First mentioned as a trading settlement called Siedlce from the Polish word for 'settlement'. A Latinized version, Junior Vladislavia, of the Old Polish *juny Włodisław* 'young Vladislav' was then adopted in the 12th century; 'young' here indicates 'new' when compared to the older Wrocław.

Interlaken, SWITZERLAND
'Between the Lakes', a reference to its location between Lakes Brienz and Thun, from the

Latin *inter* 'between' and *lacus* 'lake'. The name is derived from Latin because the town developed around an Augustinian convent.

Inuvik, NORTHWEST TERRITORIES/CANADA
Founded in 1954 as 'Place of Man' in Inuktitut.

Invercargill, SOUTH ISLAND/NEW ZEALAND *Kelly's Point*
Settled in 1855 and named after one of the settlers, it was renamed in 1857 after Captain William Cargill (1784–1860), a Scottish colonist and Superintendent of Otago. 'Inver' from the Gaelic *inbhir* 'river mouth' denotes its position on the Waihopai River close to its junction with the New River estuary.

Inverell, NEW SOUTH WALES/AUSTRALIA
Founded in 1848, it has a Gaelic name meaning 'Meeting of the Swans', a reference to its location at the junction of the Swanbrook and Macintyre Rivers.

Invergordon, SCOTLAND/UK *Inverbreckie*
'Gordon's (Place at the) River Mouth' from *inbhir*. The local landowner was Alexander Gordon. The former name meant 'Mouth of the (River) Breckie'.

Invermere, BRITISH COLUMBIA/CANADA *Copper City*
Renamed in 1912 to 'Mouth of the Lake' from *inbhir* and *mere*. It is situated on Lake Windermere.

Inverness, CANADA, UK, USA
1. Canada (Nova Scotia): originally Broad Cove Mines, but renamed by Scottish settlers after the city in Scotland.
2. UK (Scotland): takes its name from its position at the mouth, *inbhir*, of the River Ness, whose name is ultimately associated with a word for 'moist', on the Beauly Firth.

Investigator Group, SOUTH AUSTRALIA/AUSTRALIA
A group of islands discovered in 1802 by Matthew Flinders[†] who mapped much of the Australian coast. The islands were named after his ship, the *Investigator*.

Inyanga, ZIMBABWE
A village, a district, and a national park, the name refers to the art of divining. An *inyanga* is usually a man who offers psychic and spiritual help and can act as an exorcist. The name here may come from a particularly well known or successful *inyanga*.

Inyati, ZIMBABWE
'Place of the Buffaloes'.

Ioánnina, GREECE *Thothoni, Yanina, Yanya*
Believed to have developed around a monastery dedicated to St John the Baptist from which the settlement of Agioannina took its name. Having been held by the Byzantines, it fell to the Serbs in 1349 and to the Ottoman Turks, who called it Yanya, *c.*1430. They held it until 1913 when it joined Greece.

Iona, CANADA, UK, USA
UK (Scotland): formerly Hiiensis, Ioua insula, and Hiona-Columcille. An island in the Inner Hebrides with a name meaning '(Place of) Yew Trees' from the Old Irish *eo* 'yew tree'. St Columba (*c.*521–97), known as Colum-cille, landed in 563 to undertake the conversion of Scotland. By the 8th century Iona was known in Latin as Ioua insula 'Island of Yew Trees', being renamed *c.*1100 after St Columba. It is said that Ioua was miscopied, becoming Iona.

Ionia, TURKEY
An ancient region covering part of the coastal area of western Asia Minor and named after one of the principal ancient Greek racial groups, the Ionians, who had come from central Greece *c.*1000 BC. They are said to have taken their name from Ion, grandson of Hellen (*see* GREECE). As the Ionians expanded their territory 'Ionian' became the oriental term for Greeks in general. Ionia gives its name to the Ionic order of architecture.

Ionian Islands (Iónioi Nísoi), GREECE
A geographic region of Greece often called Eftansia or Heptanesos 'Seven Islands', there being seven principal islands. They may be named after Io, virgin priestess of Hera, who, according to Greek mythology, was continually on the move to avoid the attentions of Zeus; on one of her journeys she passed up the Adriatic Sea past the islands. According to tradition, Io also gave her name to the Ionian Sea.

Iowa, USA
A state with a name meaning 'Beautiful Land' in Sioux. However, it could be said to have taken its name from the Iowa tribe who took their name from the Sioux word. First explored by the Frenchmen, Louis Jolliet (1645–1700) and Jacques Marquette (1637–75) in 1673, the area was ceded to Spain in 1762. In 1800 it returned to France which then sold it as part of the Louisiana Purchase to the USA in 1803. It became the Territory of Iowa in 1838 and joined the Union in 1846 as the 29th state.

Iowa City, IOWA/USA
Founded as the capital of the Territory of Iowa in 1839 and named after the state. The capital moved to Des Moines in 1857.

Ipoh, MALAYSIA
Takes its name from the Ipoh or Upa tree which produced a poisonous resin much

valued by Orang Asli hunters who used it on their blowpipe darts.

Ipswich, JAMAICA, UK, USA
1. UK (England): formerly Gipeswic 'Trading Place of a Man called Gip' from an Old English personal name and *wīc*.
2. USA (Massachusetts): previously Agawam when settled in 1633, but a year later renamed after the town in England which had cared for emigrants heading for Massachusetts Bay.

Iqaluit, NUNAVUT/CANADA
'Place of many Fish' in Inuktitut.

Iquique, CHILE
Founded in the 16th century, its name is derived from an Aymara word meaning 'Place of Rest'.

Iráklion, CRETE/GREECE
See HERAKLION.

Iran *Persia*
The Islamic Republic of Iran (Persian: Jomhūrī-ye Eslāmī-ye Īrān) since 1979 when the monarchy was overthrown. Previously the Kingdom of Iran from 1935 when the Persians declared that the name Iran should be used internationally instead of Persia (they had used the name Iran since Sāssānian times); a constitutional monarchy from 1906 and before that, from the 16th century, an absolute monarchy. In 1971 the 2 500th anniversary of the Persian Empire was celebrated. Iran means the '(Land of) the Aryans' from the Old Persian *aryānam*, the genitive plural of *arya* 'noble' in the sense of 'high-born'. The name Persia is a European adaptation of an ancient region called Pars which became Fars after the Arab conquest in the 7th century because there is no letter *p* in the Arabic alphabet. The name Fars, now a province, however, was never used for the whole country by the Persians, although their language is Farsi. To the Greeks the region was known as Persis. Pars took its name from the Parsi, an ancient people who settled here about the 7th century BC. Their name came from the Old Persian *parsi* 'pure'. In general terms, it may be said that 'Iranian' is used for matters concerning the state, while 'Persian' is used for cultural matters (language and literature, music, carpets, etc.).

Iraq *Mesopotamia*
The Republic of Iraq (al-Jumhūrīyah al-ʿIrāqīyah) since 1958 when the monarchy was overthrown. Until being created as the Kingdom of Iraq by the British in 1921, 'Iraq' had had no previous independent existence. Even now, though Iraq may be a state, it is not a nation: the Iraqi Kurds in the mountainous

terrain in the north and east, the Kurdish Autonomous Region, represent 15–20 per cent of the population of Iraq but maintain their separate identity and have not been fully assimilated. Faisal I (1885–1933), the first king (1921–33), was a Hashemite from the Hejaz (now in Saudi Arabia). From 1921 until 1932, when independence was achieved, Iraq remained under British administration as a League of Nations mandate. Between 1534 and 1917 it was part of the Ottoman Empire, the British completing the conquest of practically all Iraq by the end of 1918. By 1925 the three Ottoman provinces of Mosul, Baghdad, and Basra had been combined into a single political entity. The name simply represents the Arabic *al-ʿirāq* 'the (river) bank', a reference to its location astride the Euphrates and Tigris Rivers. Following the Semitic custom of calling the whole region by the name of a part of it, the entire land came to be known as Iraq in 1918. Until then it had been called Mesopotamia, a name of Greek origin meaning '(Land) between the Rivers', the Euphrates and the Tigris, from *mesos* 'middle' and *potamos* 'river'. Rather than its narrow sense, that name has come to mean an area that extended over most of modern Iraq, eastern Syria, and south-eastern Turkey. Sumer was the ancient name for southern Mesopotamia, the area between Baghdad and the Persian Gulf; it later became known as Babylonia. Northern Mesopotamia, and modern south-east Turkey constituted Assyria. Medieval Arabic sources used the term Iraq to describe what is now central and southern Iraq while that part north of Tikrīt was called al-Jazīrah 'The Island', referring to the 'island' between the Euphrates and Tigris Rivers.

Irbīl, IRAQ
See ARBĪL.

Ireland (Éire) *Ierne, Hibernia, Ériu, Scotia, Irish Free State*
Ireland comprises some four-fifths of the island of Ireland while the remainder is the province of Northern Ireland which is part of the UK. The existing boundary between the 'North' and the 'South' was agreed in 1925. The 1948 Republic of Ireland Act, inaugurated in 1949, declared Éire (in English, Ireland) to be a republic formally free of the British crown; the state's official name was confirmed as Éire while its official description became the Republic of Ireland (Poblacht na hÉireann). Earlier, under the constitution of 1937, the name Éire was adopted in place of the Irish Free State (Saorstát Éireann) (1922–37) when Southern Ireland (26 of the 32 Irish counties) became a dominion of the British Commonwealth; it had become a

part of the United Kingdom of Great Britain and Ireland when that entity was created in 1801. Gaelic Ireland lost its independence when Henry II (1133–89), King of England (1154–89) invaded in 1171 and proclaimed himself overlord of the whole island. The name is a form of Iar-en-land 'Land in the West' from the Gaelic *iar* 'west'. Poetically, it is sometimes called Eriu or Erin (Éirinn), short for Iarinnis 'West Island' from the Irish *inis* 'island'. The Latin Hibernia comes from the Old Celtic Iverna, possibly itself derived from the Greek I(w)erne. Scotia was in use up to the 10th century as a name for the island. The term 'Republic of Ireland' is sometimes used to avoid confusion with Northern Ireland, particularly where international competition is concerned.

Irian Jaya, INDONESIA
See PAPUA.

Iriga, LUZON/PHILIPPINES
Named after the nearby extinct volcano.

Irkutsk, RUSSIA
A province and a city, founded in 1652 as a Cossack fortress, lying along the Angara River at its junction with the Irkut River from which it takes its name. The river's name may mean 'Big Bend' in Ainu, the language of the Ainu people who once inhabited large areas of north Asia, but are now more or less confined to Japan and the Kuril Islands.

Ironbridge, ENGLAND/UK
Named after the iron bridge built across the River Severn in 1779.

Iron Knob, SOUTH AUSTRALIA/AUSTRALIA
Named in recognition of the rich deposits of iron ore in the area.

Iron Mountain, MICHIGAN/USA
Settled in 1879 after large deposits of iron ore had been found.

Ironwood, MICHIGAN/USA
Laid out in 1885 and named for an iron dealer, James R. Wood, who had been nicknamed 'Iron' Wood.

Iroquois, CANADA, USA
In both Ontario, Canada, and South Dakota, USA, the cities are named after the North American tribe. Iroquois is said to come from *hiro* 'I have said' and *koue* 'joy' or 'sorrow' depending on the speed with which it is spoken. Another translation is 'Real Adders'. US Army helicopters are named after Native American tribes and the name Iroquois was given to the ubiquitous HU-1 (redesignated in 1962 as the UH-1), built by Bell Helicopters and more commonly known as the 'Huey'.

Iroquois Falls, ONTARIO/CANADA
Named, according to a legend, after the falls on the River Abitibi where some Iroquois were swept to their deaths after some Huron, with whom they were at war, had untied their moored canoes one night when the Iroquois were asleep in them.

Irrawaddy (Ayeyarwady), BURMA
A river and a division whose name is believed to come from the Sanskrit *airāvati*, the name of a sun god associated with the creation of the elephant; thus 'elephant river'. It only adopts the name Irrawaddy after the confluence of the Nami Kha and Mali Kha, *kha* being the Kachin for 'river'.

Irvington, NEW JERSEY/USA *Captown*
Settled in 1666, it was renamed in 1852 after Washington Irving (1783–1859), who has been dubbed 'the first American man of letters'.

Isabela, LUZON/PHILIPPINES
A province established in 1856 and named after Isabella II (1830–1904), Queen of Spain (1833–68).

Ísafjördhur, ICELAND *Eyri*
Takes its name from the Ísa Fjord which it overlooks. The original name meant 'Sand Spit'.

Ischia, CAMPANIA/ITALY *Pithecusa, Aenaria*
An island which is probably the meaning of its name. This may have come from the Latin *insula* and then *iscla*. Its Latin name, however, was Aenaria. Pithecusa was its Greek name which may have meant 'Island of Monkeys'.

Isère, RHÔNE-ALPES/FRANCE *Isara*
A department and a river. The pre-Celtic Indo-European river name Isara meant 'water course'. There is a River Isar in Bavaria.

Isernia, MOLISE/ITALY *Aesernia*
Derived from the ancient Samnite name which is based on the root *ais* having a sense of 'to move quickly'.

Isfahan, IRAN
See ESFAHAN.

Ishikari, HOKKAIDŌ/JAPAN
A river with a name derived from the Ainu *ishikaribetsu* 'greatly meandering river', a description of its lower course. The Chinese characters literally mean 'Stone Hunting' from *ishi* 'stone' and *kari* 'hunt'.

Ishikawa, HONSHŪ/JAPAN
A prefecture and two cities with the name of 'Stone River' from *ishi* 'stone' and *kawa*.

Ishpeming, MICHIGAN/USA
Founded in 1844 and named after an Ojibwa word meaning 'heaven' or 'high up' in the sense of 'high ground'.

Iskandar, KAZAKHSTAN
Named after Alexander III the Great[†] who
campaigned in the region in 329–328 BC.

Iskenderun, TURKEY *Alexandretta*
Founded at or near the site of Alexander III the
Great's[†] victory over Darius III, King of Persia
(336–330 BC), at Alexandria ad Issum in 333 BC.
Both the previous and present names honour
Alexander, Iskender being the Turkish for
Alexander. At the end of the First World War it
became the capital of the *sancak* 'territorial
division' of Alexandretta, a French mandate
until 1939. It was then ceded to Turkey,
although Syrian maps still show the 'annexed
province' as part of Syria. *See* HATAY.

Isla de la Juventud, CUBA *Sigueanea, La
Evangelista, Isla de los Pinos*
'Island of Youth', a name adopted in 1978 in
gratitude to Cuban and foreign students who
worked on the citrus plantations and
transformed the island into a major centre for
citrus production. Previously called the 'Island
of the Pines' by the Spanish. It was also called
Parrot Island when used as a refuge for pirates.
Christopher Columbus[†] called it 'The
Evangelist' when he sighted it in 1494. The
local name was Sigueanea of unknown
meaning.

Islāmābād, PAKISTAN
'City of Islam' from the Arabic *islām*
'submission to God' and *ābād*. Following the
decision in 1959 that Karachi should no longer
be the capital of Pakistan because its location
on the coast was considered to be too distant
from other parts of the country, the site for a
new capital was chosen in 1959 and
construction began in 1961. The city became
the capital in 1967. Aurangzeb (1618–1707),
Mughal emperor (1658–1707), gave this name
to several towns in India.

Isla Mujeres, QUINTANA ROO/MEXICO
'Island of Women'. According to local legend,
a Spanish pirate fell in love with a beautiful
woman here. He built a house for her, but she
spurned him and married somebody else.
Alternatively, it is claimed that the name
comes from the discovery of female-shaped
clay idols found by the Spanish on the island.

Island Falls, CANADA, USA
USA (Maine): given the name because of a
small island in the river close to some falls.

Isle of Man (Manx: **Ellan Vannan**), and
NICOBAR ISLANDS *Mona, Monavia*
A self-governing dominion of the British
crown but not a part of the UK. The old name is
related to Môn, the Welsh name for Anglesey;
both names are obscure. The Manx (Gaelic)

ellan means 'island'. According to local legend,
however, it is named after a Celtic mythical
hero/wizard, Manannán mac Lir 'Son of the
Sea', corrupted to Vannan, who hid the Land of
Mann in cloud whenever it was threatened by
invaders. Mona was the Roman name, possibly
from the Latin *mons* 'mountain'. The island
was a dependency of Norway between *c.*800
and 1266 when it was sold to Scotland; it
came under English control in the 14th
century, but did not become a crown
possession until 1828.

Isle of Wight, UK, USA
1. UK (England): formerly the Roman Vectis
and Wit, the name in the Domesday Book
(1086). A Celtic name, it may mean something
like 'Place of the Division', indicating its
location between the two arms of the Solent.
2. USA (Virginia): although well inland,
named after the island off the south coast of
England.

Ismailia (al-Ismāʿīlīyah), EGYPT *Timsāḥ*
A governorate and city founded on the site of
the village of Timsāḥ 'Crocodile' on the lake of
the same name in 1863 by the French
engineer, Ferdinand de Lesseps (1804–95),
initially as a base camp for those working on
the construction of the Suez Canal. It was
named on the accession of Ismāʿīl Pasha (1830–
95) as Khedive of Egypt (1863–79); he was an
enthusiastic supporter of the canal project.

Israel The State of Israel (Hebrew: Medinat
Yisraʾel; Arabic: Dawlat Isrāʾīl) since 1948.
Following the destruction of the Temple in
Jerusalem by the Romans in 70 and the
expulsion of the Jews after a second rebellion
against the Romans in 135, Israel ceased to
exist as a political entity. Although without a
homeland for eighteen centuries, the Jews
retained their identity and harboured the will
to re-establish a Jewish national home in
Palestine. Between 135 and 1948 the land was
under the rule of the Romans, Byzantines,
Arabs (637–1099), Christian Crusaders (1099–
1291), Egyptian Mamlūks (1291–1516),
Ottoman Turks (1517–1918), and the British
(1918–48) who ruled under a League of Nations
mandate which began formally in 1923. The
first Zionist settlement in Palestine was
founded in 1882 and since then Jews from all
over the world have migrated to the area.
Given the presence of both Jewish and Arab
settlements in Palestine at the end of the
Second World War, the UN voted in 1947 for
its partition into Jewish and Arab states, with a
special arrangement for Jerusalem, and fixed
the borders; the Jews accepted the plan, the
Palestinians and Arabs rejected it. When the

State of Israel was proclaimed in 1948 the surrounding Arab countries declared war. Israel was victorious and acquired some of the land allocated to the Arabs so that it controlled 78 per cent of Palestine. The new borders remained the *de facto* borders until 1967. During the Six Day War of 1967 the Israelis were again victorious, capturing Sinai and the Gaza Strip from Egypt, the area west of the River Jordan (the 'West Bank') from Jordan, and the Golan Heights from Syria. The Yom Kippur War of 1973 also ended in defeat for the Arab armies. Nevertheless, since that war Israel has progressively given back captured territory to Egypt and the Palestinian Authority; however, in 1981 it annexed the Golan Heights. The present name comes from the ancient land of Israel which itself comes from Jacob, the son of Isaac and grandson of Abraham; Jacob's name was changed to Israel because he was 'one that prevailed with God' (Genesis 32: 28). Jacob-Israel fathered twelve sons, each one the progenitor of one of the twelve tribes of Israel, the 'children of Israel'. In due course, their 'Promised Land' became the Kingdom of Israel. *See* PALESTINE.

Issyk-Kul' (Ysyk-Köl), KYRGYZSTAN
A province, a town and a lake, all named after the lake. The name is said to mean 'Hot Lake' from *ysyk* 'hot' and *köl* 'lake' since it never freezes in winter. Alternatively, it could mean 'Holy Lake' from *yzykh* 'holy' or 'sacred'. The town was previously known as Rybachye 'Fishermen's (Village)'.

Issy-les-Moulineaux, ÎLE-DE-FRANCE/
FRANCE *Issiacum*
The first part of the name is derived from a Gaulish personal name, Icisius, and the place-name suffix -*acum*. The second part is the plural of a diminutive of the French *moulin* 'mill', thus 'little mills'.

Istanbul, TURKEY *Byzantium, Nea Roma, Constantinople*
Allegedly named Byzantium after Byzas who founded the Greek city-state of Byzantium in 658 BC. It was occupied by the Romans in 196. In 324 it became the capital of Constantine I the Great[†], who renamed it New Rome. When he made the city the capital of the Roman Empire in 330—because of its better strategic position—he gave it his own name, the 'City of Constantine' from the Greek Constantinoupolis. In the 10th century it was known by the Greeks as Stanbulin or Bulin and by the Arabs as Ḳusṭanṭīniyya. It remained the capital of the Byzantine Empire until captured by the Ottoman Turks in 1453. Thereafter, it was popularly known as Istanbul, a spoken Turkish corruption of the Greek *eis tin polin* 'into the city'. It was only officially renamed Istanbul in 1930, having been the capital of the Ottoman Empire between 1453 and 1923. Istanbul has been given more foreign names than any other city: for example, the Vikings called it Micklegard 'the Greatest City'; to the Bulgarians, Russians and Serbs it was Tsarigard 'City of Emperors'; to the Greeks it was simply known as Polis 'The City'; to the Arabs and Ottoman Turks, before the change to Istanbul, it was Konstantiniyye; the Ottomans also wrote of it as Der-i-Sa'adet 'the House of Good Fortune' because it was the location of the Sultan's residence; the Persians called it Asithane 'the House of State'; and to the Armenians it was Gosdantnubolis 'City of Constantine'. A Muslim name, said to have been coined by the Ottoman conqueror himself, Mehmed II (1432–81), was Islambol 'Where Islam Abounds'. The name Byzantium has given us the adjective 'byzantine' meaning 'complicated' or 'labyrinthine', like Byzantine politics. The Byzantines did not in fact call themselves Byzantines, but Romans, and they spoke Greek, not Latin.

Istiwāʾīyah, al-, THE SUDAN
'Equatoria', the southernmost state of Sudan, 5° north of the equator.

Istria (Istra), CROATIA
A county named after the Illyrian tribe, the Histri. It was seized by the Italians in 1919 from Austria in an attempt to make it a permanent part of Italy, but it was surrendered after Italy's defeat in the Second World War. The Istrian peninsula extends into Slovenia.

Italy (Italia)
The Italian Republic (Repubblica Italiana) since 1946 when the monarchy was abolished. Previously the Kingdom of Italy (1861–1946), from nine years before the complete unification of the country in 1870 when the Papal States were finally annexed. Between the fall of the Western Roman Empire in 476 and 1870 Italy largely comprised a collection of major and minor independent states. From time to time some of these were under papal or foreign rule or both. Traditionally 'Italy' is thought to come from the Vitali tribe whose name may have some connection with the Latin *vitulus* 'calf' or *witaloi* 'sons of the bull'. Another theory is that the name is derived from *diovi-telia* 'land of the day' or 'land of the light'.

Itasca, Lake, MINNESOTA/USA
In 1832 an American superintendent of Native American affairs, Henry Schoolcraft, suggested that the lake was the source of the Mississippi River and gave it the name Itasca

from the Latin *veritas* 'truth' and *caput* 'head' or 'source'. The Native American legend is that the source of the Mississippi comes from the tears of Iteska, the daughter of Hiawatha, as she goes to the underworld.

Ithaca, GREECE, USA
1. Greece: one of the Ionian islands (Itháki in Greek) with a name of unknown meaning. However, the first syllable probably comes from the Phoenician word for 'island'.
2. USA (New York): founded in 1789 and named after the Greek island in 1795. It had previously been the centre of a township called Ulysses. According to the *Odyssey*, Homer's epic poem, Ulysses (in Greek, Odysseus) was the King of Ithaca.

Itsuku-shima, HONSHŪ/JAPAN
Also called Miya-shima, it means 'Shrine Island', the entire island being consecrated as a Shintō shrine which had been built in 593. It is so-called because of this shrine which is dedicated to one, or all three, of the daughters of Susanowo, the Shintō storm god.

Ittoqqortoormiit, GREENLAND/DENMARK *Scoresbysund*
Founded in 1924 and originally named after William Scoresby (1789–1857), an English explorer, scientist, and clergyman, who charted the Scoresby Sound in 1822. It was subsequently given a local name meaning 'People with Peat'.

Iturup, KURIL ISLANDS/RUSSIA *Staten Island, Etorofu*
The largest of the Kuril Islands discovered by a Dutch navigator in 1643, it was named Staten Island. The island was occupied by the Japanese in 1800 when it was renamed Etorofu-to, possibly from the Ainu *etoropa* 'jellyfish'. It was seized by the Soviet Union at the end of the Second World War in 1945. *Urup* is the Ainu word for 'salmon'.

Ivan Gorod, LENINGRAD/RUSSIA
Developed from a fort built in 1492 and named Ivan Town after Ivan III the Great (1440–1505), Grand Prince of Moscow (1462–1505). As part of Narva, it was in Estonia between 1920 and 1945.

Ivangrad, MONTENEGRO/SERBIA AND MONTENEGRO *Berane*
Renamed in 1949 as 'Ivan's Town' from *grad* after a leading Yugoslav revolutionary, Ivan Milutinović, who was killed in 1944. It is still sometimes called Berane.

Ivanhoe, AUSTRALIA, USA
The three cities in the USA (in California, Minnesota, and Virginia) and the two in

Australia (New South Wales and Western Australia) are all thought to be named after Walter Scott's novel published in 1819. The title and the name of the hero, actually Wilfred of Ivanhoe but called Ivanhoe, are fictitious.

Ivano-Frankivs'k, UKRAINE *Stanisławów, Stanislav, Ivano-Frankovsk*
A province and city founded in 1661 as a Polish frontier town and named after a Polish prince, Stanislav (Stanisław in Polish), who owned land here. Between 1772 and 1918 it was held by Austria. It then became Polish until being annexed by the Soviet Union as a result of the Soviet–Nazi non-aggression pact in 1939. It was ceded to the Soviet Union (Ukraine) in 1945 and named Stanislav. In 1962 it was renamed Ivano-Frankovsk after Ivan Franko (1856–1910), Ukrainian poet and novelist. The spelling was slightly changed after Ukraine received its independence in 1991.

Ivanovo, RUSSIA *Ivanovo-Voznesensk*
A province and a city. The city was created in 1871 with the amalgamation of the villages of Ivanovo and Voznesensk; the latter name was dropped in 1932, probably because of Stalin's[†] crusade against religion. *Vozneseniye* means 'The Ascension' to which the original village church was dedicated. Ivanov was probably named after Ivan IV the Terrible (1530–84), first Tsar of All Russia (1547–84), although this is not certain.

Ivory Coast (Côte d'Ivoire)
The Republic of Côte d'Ivoire (République de Côte d'Ivoire) since independence in 1960. Previously an autonomous republic within the French Community (1958–60); an Overseas Territory in the French Union (1946–58); a French colony (1893–1946); and a French protectorate (1889–93). In 1946 the north broke away and became part of the new state of Upper Volta (now Burkina Faso). The conventional English name, Ivory Coast, and indeed other language versions of this, was officially changed to the present French name in 1986. In pre-colonial times the Portuguese and French confined themselves to the coast where they traded in ivory, hence the name, gold, and, to a lesser degree, slaves.

Ivrea, PIEDMONT/ITALY *Eporedia*
Derived from the original Roman name which seems to come from *epo* 'horse' and *reda* 'a Gallic vehicle with four wheels'. This may refer to the practice of the local inhabitants of defending their town by means of horse-drawn carts which could move quickly to confront the approach of any enemy.

Ivry-sur-Seine, PARIS/FRANCE *Ivriacum*
The name comes from the Medieval Latin name which itself is derived from the Gaulish *ivo* 'yew' and the Gallic-Roman place-name suffix *-acum*. The rest of the name indicates its position on the River Seine.

Iwaki, HONSHŪ/JAPAN
The northern part of the city, known as Taira, was a castle town during the Tokugawa period (1603–1867); the characters represent *iwa* 'rock' and *ki(shiro)* 'castle'.

Iwo Jima (Iō-Jima), JAPAN
An island, captured by American troops in 1945 and returned to Japan in 1968. The name means 'Sulphur Island' from *iō* 'sulphur' and *shima*.

Ixopo, KWAZULU-NATAL/SOUTH AFRICA
Stuartstown
Founded in 1878 and named after Martinhus Stuart, a local magistrate, it later reverted to its local Zulu name meaning 'marshy'.

Izalco, EL SALVADOR
A volcano named after the Izalco people.

Izhevsk, URDMURTIYA REPUBLIC/RUSSIA *Ustinov*
Founded in 1760 as an ironworks and named after the River Izh. It was renamed in 1984–90 after Marshal Dmitry Ustinov (1908–84), Soviet minister of defence (1976–84).

Izmir, TURKEY *Yazmir, Smyrna*
According to classical mythology, named after Myrrha (Smyrna or Zmyrna), daughter of a king of Cyprus. Having fled from her father when he tried to kill her, she was turned into a myrrh tree by the gods (in ancient Greek, *smurna* 'myrrh'; in modern, *myro*). These grow in the area. Izmir is derived from Smyrna and means 'To Smyrna'. Settled *c*.1000 BC and later destroyed, it was refounded by Alexander III the Great[†]. Greek during Hellenistic times

(323–31 BC), it was captured by the Ottoman Turks in 1424; during the 19th century Greek immigrants had made it largely Greek again and in 1919 Greek troops arrived to occupy it. In 1922 it was retaken by the Turks.

Izmit, TURKEY *Astacus, Olbia, Nicomedia*
Capital of the Kingdom of Bithynia as Nicomedia when rebuilt in 264 BC by, and named after, King Nicomedes I, King of Bithynia (*c*.279–255 BC). It fell to the Ottoman Turks in 1326. The present name comes from the Greek *eis Mēdian* 'to Nicomedia'.

İznik, TURKEY *Elikore, Antigonia, Nicaea*
Founded in the 4th century BC and named Antigonia after Antigonus I the One-Eyed (*c*.382–301 BC), one of Alexander III the Great's[†] generals and King of Macedonia (306–301 BC); then *c*.300 BC it was renamed Nicaea after the deceased wife of Lysimachus (*c*.360–281 BC), another of Alexander's generals and King of Thrace (306–281 BC) and also King of Macedonia. It was captured by the first sultan of the Ottoman Turks, Orhan Gazi, in 1331. He made it his capital and changed its name to İznik from the Greek *eis Nikian* 'to Nicaea'. Nicaea gave its name to a Christian statement of faith issued at the Council of Nicaea in 325; this later became known as the Nicene Creed.

Izola, SLOVENIA *Haliaetum*
Although now linked to the mainland, it takes its name from the Italian *isola* 'island'.

Iztaccíhuatl, MÉXICO-PUEBLA/MEXICO
A volcano with a Nahuatl name meaning 'White Woman' because of its snow-covered peaks which from a distance resemble parts of a woman's body.

Izumo, HONSHŪ/JAPAN
The Chinese characters represent *izu* 'jut out' and *mo* (*kumo*) 'cloud'.

Jabalpur, MADHYA PRADESH/INDIA
Surrounded by hills, it means 'Hill City' from *jabal* and *pur*.

Jablonec nad Nisou, CZECH REPUBLIC
Gablonz an der Neisse
According to legend, named after the only apple tree (in Czech, *jablon*) left standing after the area had been laid waste by the Catholic Lusatians during the Hussite Wars (1417–39). Nad Nisou means 'On the (River) Neisse'. During the first half of the 20th century it was populated largely by Germans, hence its previous German name.

Jáchymov, CZECH REPUBLIC *Joachimsthal*
The previous German name means 'Joachim's Valley', the present Czech name simply being 'Joachim'. Founded in 1516 following the discovery of rich silver deposits, the town and the valley take their names from the mine which honoured St Joachim, father of the Virgin Mary. Silver from the mines led to a silver coin, the Joachimsthaler, being minted in 1519. This was later shortened to *taler*. The word 'dollar' is derived from *taler*.

Jackpot, NEVADA/USA
Alludes to the gambling for which Nevada is famous.

Jackson, AUSTRALIA, USA
1. Seventeen states in the USA have cities with this name, most of which honour Andrew Jackson[†].
2. USA (Michigan): settled in 1829 and originally called Jacksonburgh, then Jacksonopolis and finally Jackson in 1833.
3. USA (Mississippi): settled by Louis Le Fleur, a French-Canadian merchant, in 1792, it was at first called Le Fleur's Bluff. When laid out as the state capital in 1822, it was renamed after Andrew Jackson[†], then a general.
4. USA (Tennessee): previously Alexandria, it was renamed in 1822 after Andrew Jackson[†].

Jackson Island (Ostrov Dzheksona), FRANZ
JOSEF LAND/RUSSIA
Named after the British Arctic explorer, Frederick Jackson, who spent three years in the area (1894–97).

Jacksonville, USA
1. Arkansas: named after Nicholas Jackson in 1870 after he had given land for a railroad depot.
2. Florida: settled by the French in 1564 when the area was known as Wacca Pilatka 'Cows' Crossing' because of its position on the St Johns River. During the brief English occupation in 1763–83, this became Cowford. When laid out by Americans in 1822 it was given its present name in honour of Andrew Jackson[†].
3. Illinois: laid out in 1825 and named after Andrew Jackson[†].
4. North Carolina: founded *c.*1757 as Watland's Ferry, it was renamed Courthouse and then Jacksonville after Andrew Jackson[†].
5. Oregon: originally a mining camp named after one of the prospectors.

Jacobābād, SINDH/PAKISTAN *Khānghar*
'Jacob's Town'. Developed in 1847 from the village site of Khānghar by General John Jacob (1812–58), the first deputy commissioner of the Upper Sind Frontier Region (1847–54), and named after him. A highly respected English cavalry officer who brought peace to the region, Jacob died and was buried here in 1858.

Jaén, ANDALUSIA/SPAIN *Aurinx/Auringis*
A province and a city. The name is said to be derived from the Arabic *geen* or *giyen* meaning a 'stop on a caravan route'. The name of the Moorish principality, of which Jaén was the most important town and transport hub, was Jayyán. Aurinx was the Roman name.

Jaffa (Yafo), ISRAEL *Joppa*
Now part of *Tel Aviv-Yafo. According to legend, Jaffa was built just after the Flood by Noah's son, Japhet, from whom it gets its name. In reality, it comes from the Hebrew *yafe* 'beautiful', a reference to its location on the Mediterranean coast.

Jaffna, SRI LANKA *Yalpannan*
A district, a city, and also a historic kingdom. The port-city was the capital of a Tamil kingdom until the Portuguese occupied it in 1617. They gave it a name that was a Portuguese adaptation of the Tamil for 'Port of the Lyre', a reference to the shape of its harbour.

Jahangira, NORTH-WEST FRONTIER/PAKISTAN
Named after Jahāngīr, Mughal emperor of
India (1605–27), who built a bridge composed
of boats over the Kabul River at this spot. His
name means 'Holder of the World'.

Jaipur, RĀJASTHĀN/INDIA *Jeypore*
Founded in 1727 by Maharaja Sawai Jai Singh II
(1699–1743) who wished to move his capital
(of the princely state of Jaipur) from nearby
Amber in the hills to a new site on the plains.
He named it 'Jai's Town' after himself with the
additional *pur*; he also called himself Sawai
which meant one and a quarter, meaning that
he was an additional quarter superior to all his
contemporaries.

Jaisalmer, RĀJASTHĀN/INDIA
Founded in 1156 by, and named after, the
Bhatti Rājput chieftain, Rāwal Jaisal, who
made it his capital because it had a large oasis
and was more easily defendable than his
previous capital at Lodurva.

Jajce, BOSNIA AND HERZEGOVINA
Possibly named in the 14th century by Hrvoja,
King of Bosnia and Duke of Spalato (now Split,
Croatia), after the Neapolitan Castell dell'Ovo
'Egg Castle' (in Serbo-Croat, *jaje* 'egg') to
indicate his friendship with Louis (1320–62),
King of Naples (1347–62). It was the last
Bosnian stronghold to fall to the Ottoman
Turks in 1463. The Austrians took possession
in 1878 and the town joined the new
Yugoslavia when it was created in 1918.

Jakarta, JAVA/INDONESIA *Sunda Kelapa,
Jayakarta, Batavia, Djakarta*
The original name of the small port of the last
Hindu kingdom of West Java meant 'White
Coconut'. In 1522 it was taken by the
Portuguese who built a fortress here. However,
they were driven out five years later by the
joint Islamic forces of Banten (also Bantam)
and Demak, led by Prince Fatahillah, Sultan of
Banten, who made it a vassal of the Muslim
state of Demak. He renamed the city Jayakarta
'City of Great Victory' or 'Complete Victory' in
Sundanese. In 1619 it was destroyed by the
Dutch under Jan Pieterszoon Coen who rebuilt
it as a walled town and named it Batavia in
honour of the early Germanic tribes who had
settled in Holland; Batavia was the Roman
name for that part of Europe. In due course,
the developing city took the name of the
fortress. Batavia became the capital of the
Dutch East India Company and subsequently
of the Dutch East Indies. In 1942 it was
renamed Djakarta by the Japanese when they
occupied the city as a gesture of anti-Dutch
colonialism and 'goodwill' towards the
Indonesians; Batavia, however, remained the

officially recognized name until 1949. In that
year, when Indonesia achieved full
independence, it became the capital. It is now
also a province. The *D* of Djakarta was dropped
in 1972.

Jalālābād, AFGHANISTAN *Nīkaia, Jalālkot*
'Jalāl's Town'. A very ancient site,
development of the modern town was begun
in the late 1560s by Jalāl-ud-Dīn Muhammad
Akbar[†] who named it after himself. It was
previously known as 'Jalāl's Fort' from *kot*
'fort'.

Jalal-Abad, KYRGYZSTAN
Derived from the Arabic *jalal* 'glory' or
'greatness' and *ābād* to mean 'Town of Glory'.

Jalisco, MEXICO
A state which comprises most of what was
called Nueva Galicia 'New Galicia', after the
province in Spain, until 1821. The name is
derived from Xalisco 'The Sandy Place', one of
four Chimalhuacán kingdoms in the area
before the arrival of the Spanish.

Jamaica, AND CUBA, USA
Jamaica: an independent state since 1962,
Jamaica was discovered by Christopher
Columbus[†] in 1494. He called it Santiago 'St
James', but its original Arawak name of
Xaymaca or Yamaya 'Land of Wood and Water'
has stood the test of time. The island remained
a Spanish possession until being conquered by
the British in 1655. It was officially transferred
to Britain under the Treaty of Madrid in 1670.

Jamestown, AUSTRALIA, IRELAND, ST HELENA,
SOUTH AFRICA, USA
1. St Helena: founded as a fort in 1659 and
named after Prince James (1633–1701), Duke
of York, subsequently King James II[†]. It is the
capital of the island of St Helena.
2. USA (Indiana): named after its founder,
James Mattock.
3. USA (Rhode Island): settled in 1672 and
named after King James II[†].
4. USA (New York): named after James
Prendergast who bought land here in 1811 and
built a mill.
5. USA (Virginia): founded in 1607 as the site
of the first permanent British settlement in
North America, it was named in honour of
King James I[†]. It is now a historic site.

Jammu, INDIA
According to legend, founded in the 9th
century by King Jambulochan and named after
him. Jammu is the name of a city, and Jammu
and Kashmir refers both to a state in north-
west India and to a region in the north-west of
the Indian subcontinent that has been in

dispute between India and Pakistan since partition in 1947. *See* KASHMIR.

Jamrūd, NORTH-WEST FRONTIER/PAKISTAN *Fatehgarh*
Originally named 'Victory Fort' from *garh* and the Arabic *al-Fath* 'victory' to commemorate a Sikh victory over the local tribes in 1836.

Jamshedpur, BIHĀR/INDIA *Sakchi*
Sometimes called Tatanagar. Both names honour the industrialist Jamshetji Nusserwanji Tata (1839–1904) who founded the city on the site of the village of Sakchi in 1907. Here he laid out the Iron and Steel Works because of the extensive coal and iron ore deposits in the area; the works were developed by his son Sir Dorabji Tata.

Janesville, WISCONSIN/USA
Settled in 1835 by Henry F. Janes, a pioneer who later went west and founded the Janesville in Minnesota.

Jan Mayen Island, NORWAY *Hudson's Tutches*
Possibly first sighted in 1607 by Henry Hudson who named it Hudson's Tutches (Touches), it was claimed for Holland in 1614 by, and named after, Jan May, a Dutch navigator and whaling captain. The island was incorporated into Norway in 1929.

Jansenville, EASTERN CAPE/SOUTH AFRICA
Settled in 1854 and named after Lieutenant General Jan Janssens (1762–1838), the last Dutch governor of the Cape.

Janūb Sīnāʾ, EGYPT *Sīnāʾ al-Janūbīyah*
A governorate meaning 'Southern Sinai'. *See* SINAI.

Japan (Nihon/Nippon) *Wa*
Both forms of the Japanese name are correct and derive from the different pronunciation of a Chinese character. The names come from *nichi* 'sun' and *hon* 'origin'. The English name comes from the Chinese pronunciation 'Jipen', transliterated as *ribĕn* from the Chinese characters rì (Japanese *ni*) 'sun' and *bĕn* (Japanese *pon* or *hon*) 'origin'. This is taken to mean 'Land of the Rising Sun', a reference to the fact that Japan is east of China. It is generally accepted that the original inhabitants of Japan were Ainu peoples who had come from mainland Asia. Nevertheless, the origins of the country are enmeshed in Japanese mythology which states that the empire was founded in 660 BC by Jimmu Tennō, a great-grandson of the Sun Goddess, Amaterasu. Japan was thus the land of the gods and succeeding emperors were of divine origin. Only in 1946 did the emperor become a constitutional monarch instead of a divine

ruler. A united Japan came into existence during the 4th century under the rule of the House of Yamato. After nearly 700 years of shogunate rule (although under samurai control at times), Japan's modern political era began in 1868 with the establishment of a reunified state under the rule of the Emperor Meiji (1868–1912), known as the Meiji Restoration. At the end of the Second World War in 1945 a defeated Japan was occupied by US military forces and effectively lost its sovereignty. This was regained in 1952 when the Treaty of San Francisco was ratified.

Jarash, JORDAN *Antioch-on-the Chrysorhoas, Gerasa*
Founded by soldiers of Alexander III the Great[†] *c*.332 BC, the present name is derived from the previous names, Chrysorhoas meaning the 'Golden River'.

Jarres, Plain of (Thông Haihin), LAOS
Also the Plain of Jars because of the numerous carved stone funerary jars found here by the French in the 19th century.

Jarrow, ENGLAND/UK *Gyruum, Girwe, Jaruum*
'(Settlement of) the Fen People' from an Old English tribal name *Gyrwe*, itself from the Old English *gyr* 'mud' or 'fen'; thus people who lived in or near a fen.

Jasper, CANADA, USA
1. Canada (Alberta): named after Jasper Hawes who established a fur trading post on the nearby lake, also called Jasper, *c*.1801.
2. USA (Alabama): settled in 1822 and named after Sergeant William Jasper who was prominent in the defence of Fort Moultrie in South Carolina during the American War of Independence (1775–83).

Jastrzębie-Zdrój, POLAND
'Hawks' Spring' from *jastrząb* 'hawk' and *zdrój* 'spring'. In the mid-19th century it was a popular thermal spa.

Java, INDONESIA, USA
1. Indonesia: an island, locally Jawa, whose name comes from *yavadvipa* 'island of barley', from the Sanskrit *yava* 'barley' and *dvīpa* 'island'. The fossil remains found in Java in 1891 were the first known fossils of the species *Homo erectus* and were given the name Java Man.
2. USA (South Dakota and Virginia): named after the Indonesian island.

Jayapura, WEST PAPUA/INDONESIA *Hollandia, Sukarnapura, Kota Baru*
The capital of West Papua, the name can be taken to mean 'Victorious Town' from *jaya* 'victorious', 'glorious', or 'prosperous' and *pur*.

At one time it was called Sukarnapura 'Town of Sukarno', Sukarno (1901–70) being the first President of Indonesia (1945–66).

Jazīrah, al-, IRAQ-SYRIA-TYRKEY, THE SUDAN
'The Island'. A region that extends into northern Iraq, north-east Syria, and eastern Turkey lying between the Euphrates and Tigris rivers. In The Sudan, it is an area lying south of the confluence of the Blue and White Nile Rivers.

Jedburgh, SCOTLAND/UK *Gedwearde, Geddewrde, Jeddeburgh*
'Enclosed Settlement by Jed (Water)' from the Old English *worth* 'enclosed settlement', which was replaced by the Middle English *burgh* 'town', and the name of the river on which it lies.

Jeddah (Jiddah), SAUDI ARABIA
Also spelt and pronounced Jidda. Developed from 646 as the port for Mecca and thus the place where pilgrims heading for that city and Medina made their landfall, having crossed the Red Sea. One derivation of the name is from the Arabic *jaddah* 'grandmother', a reference to Eve, whose tomb is reputed to be in Jeddah. Legend has it that she landed in Jeddah and met Adam in Mecca. It is the only city in the world named after Eve. *Jidda* itself means 'newness', modernity', or 'rebirth' and *jiddah* 'sea shore', Arabized from the Nabathaean *kadd*.

Jefferson, USA
There are at least fourteen cities with this name, another three called Jefferson City, one called Jeffersontown, and five called Jeffersonville. Many, but not all, are named after Thomas Jefferson (1743–1826), 3rd President of the USA (1801–9). There is also a Jefferson River, rising in Montana, named after the president.

Jekabpils, LATVIA *Jakobstadt*
'Jacob's (James) Castle' from the Lettish *pils* 'castle'. The German name means 'Jacob's Town' from *stadt*.

Jelenia Góra, POLAND *Hirschberg*
A province and a city with a name meaning 'Deer Mountain' from *jeleń* 'deer' and *góra* 'mountain'. The previous German name means the same from *Hirsch* 'deer' and *Berg*. The name, however, is derived from another source: Bolesław I the Brave (*c*.966–1025), later the first King of Poland (1024–5), ordered a knight, Jelnik, to build a castle as a defence against the Czechs in 1004. The settlement around the castle became known as 'Jelnik's Mountain'. The city changed hands a number of times between Bohemia, Prussia, Germany,

and Poland until that part of Silesia was transferred from Germany to Poland after the end of the Second World War.

Jelgava, LATVIA *Mitau, Mitava*
Founded as the castle of Mitau in 1226 by the Sword Brothers, a small military Order. The city passed to the Russians at the third partition of Poland in 1795 and was renamed Mitava. The *mit* in both cases is the Latvian *mit* 'to exchange' as this was a trading centre. The present name, adopted at the end of the First World War, comes from the Latvian *jalgab* 'town'.

Jemaa, KADUNA/NIGERIA
An ancient site, the modern town was founded *c*.1810 by a Muslim preacher, Malam Usman, who called it Jema'an-Darroro 'Followers of a Learned Man from Darroro'. Under his leadership Jemaa became an emirate.

Jenīn, WEST BANK *Ginae, 'Ayn Jenim*
Evolved from the original Roman name and then the Arabic. The latter may have a colloquial or legendary meaning of 'Spring of Paradise' from *'ayn* 'spring' and *junainah* 'little paradise', the plural being *janā'in*, although there is no certainty of the derivation of Jenim. A 'little paradise' is perhaps a 'garden' and thus Jenīn could be interpreted as meaning 'Gardens'.

Jerez (Jerez de la Frontera), ANDALUSIA/SPAIN
Asido Caesariana, Scheris, Xeres
It may take its name from the Roman Caesar with the added 'of the frontier', a reference to the proximity of the Christians' border with the Moors; the city was occupied by the Moors from the 8th century until recaptured in 1264. It has also been suggested, however, that the name is derived from Ceres, the Spanish name for a town in Italy which was well known for its wines. The English pronunciation of Jerez in the 16th century was 'sherry' and this is now the English word to describe this particular type of wine. The Moorish version was Scheris; Xeres is the same—the Spanish used to pronounce *x* as *sh* in the 16th century.

Jericho (Arabic: Arīḥā), WEST BANK, USA
West Bank: one of the oldest continuously inhabited cities in the world. It is said to be derived from the Hebrew equivalent of *yaréakh* 'moon' or 'month', indicating perhaps some lunar cult. To the Canaanites it was Riha 'the moon' and to the Arabs later on as Arīḥā. Biblical Jericho is known as Tel es-Sultan 'Hill of the Sultan' at the perennial spring of Ain es-Sultan 'Spring of the Sultan' or Ain Alisha 'Spring of Alisha'. The Book of Joshua 6 tells how Jericho was the first town captured by the

Israelites *c*.1250 BC after they had spent years in the wilderness; the walls fell to the sound of their priests' trumpets. The Romans called it Hierichous.

Jersey, CHANNEL ISLANDS *Caesarea, Gersoi, Jersoi, Gerseie*
An island recognized by the Old Scandinavian suffix *-ey*. The first part of the name is probably also of Scandinavian origin: perhaps a personal name, *Geirr*, to give 'Geirr's Island'. It has given its name to the pullover and to a breed of dairy cattle. *See* CHANNEL ISLANDS.

Jersey City, NEW JERSEY/USA *Paulus Hook*
Settled by Dutch trappers in 1618, it was renamed after its state in 1836.

Jerusalem (Hebrew: **Yerushalayim**; Arabic: **al-Quds**), ISRAEL *Urusalim, Zion, 'Ir David, Aelia Capitolina, Bayt al-Maqdis/Bayt al-Muqaddas*
Believed to have been founded about 1800 BC, the earliest written evidence of its existence dates from *c*.1300 BC when the city is referred to as Urusalim (or Rushalimum). It is referred to as Salem in the Old Testament (Genesis 14. 18). The exact meaning of this name is not certain, but it probably means 'Salem has founded', Salem being the Semitic Canaanite god of the evening star or twilight. Urusalim, the full name, could also mean 'Foundation of Peace from *salim* 'peace'. Having captured the fortress of Zion *c*.1000 BC, David, second King of the Israelites (*c*.1000–*c*.962 BC), made the city his capital and renamed it 'Ir David 'City of David' or 'Fortress of David'. However, this name did not really catch on and Urusalim and Zion were more commonly used. Zion comes from *ziya* 'parched desert'. With the suppression of the second Jewish rebellion against the Romans in 135 (the first having resulted in the destruction of the Temple in 70), the Jews were banished from Jerusalem and not allowed to return without risking death. A new city was built on the ruins of the old and given the name of its new founder Publius Aelius Hadrianus (76–138) (Hadrian, Roman emperor (117–38)), and a second name to honour the gods of the Capitol in Rome, thus Aelia Capitolina. This was clearly an attempt to desacralize the city and downgrade its Christian and Jewish associations. The Arabic Bayt al-Maqdis was comparatively short-lived and was derived from the Hebrew *Bayt ha-Miqdash*, the biblical name for the Temple. Jerusalem is the Holy City for Jews and Christians and ranks as the third holiest city, behind Mecca and Medina, for Muslims; thus the Arabic name, al-Quds, means 'The Holy (One)' or 'The (City of) Holiness' and comes from the Hebrew ha-Qodesh from *ha* 'the' and

kadosh 'holy'. After 400 years of Ottoman Turkish rule from 1516, Jerusalem fell to the British in 1917 and, in due course, became part of the British mandate. In 1947 the UN voted to place Jerusalem under an international trusteeship under the auspices of the UN; although accepted by the Jews, this proposal was rejected by the Arabs. In 1948–67 the city was split between Israel (West Jerusalem, the new city) and Jordan (East Jerusalem, the old city), although in 1949 it was declared to be the capital of Israel. East Jerusalem was captured by the Israelis in 1967 and the city was unified; in 1980 unified Jerusalem was confirmed as Israel's capital. *See* ISRAEL.

Jervis Bay, NEW SOUTH WALES/AUSTRALIA *Long Nose*
Discovered in 1770 and originally named by Captain James Cook[†], it was renamed in 1791 after Admiral John Jervis (1735–1823), Earl of St Vincent, a successful naval commander against the French.

Jesenice, CZECH REPUBLIC, SLOVENIA
Czech Republic: two places have this name. The village in western Bohemia takes its name from a local stream called the Jesenický Potok from *jesenický* 'water running among ash trees', itself from *jasan* 'ash tree', and *potok* 'stream' or 'brook'. The Slovene name means the same.

Jeseník, CZECH REPUBLIC *Vriwald/Freiwald, Frývaldov/Freiwaldau*
A town and mountains. The original names, Czech and German, meant 'Empty Forest', that is, nobody was living in it, from *Wald* 'forest'. In 1947 the town was renamed after the mountain range in which it lies. The German name for the mountains is Altvatergebirge 'Grandfather Mountain'.

Jessore, BANGLADESH
According to local tradition, the name is said to come from *yaśohara* 'glory depriving'. This is because the city is said to have deprived Gaur, the former capital of Bengal, of its standing.

Jewell, KANSAS/USA
Named after Lieutenant Colonel Lewis R. Jewell of the 6th Kansas Cavalry.

Jiangsu, CHINA *Wu*
A province whose name comes from its two most important prefectures, Jiangning and Suzhou, at the time it was established in 1667; the characters represent *jiāng* and *sū* 'to revive'. During the Han dynasty (206 BC–AD 220) it was known as the Wu region before becoming the independent state of Wu during the Three Kingdoms period (220–80).

Jiangxi, CHINA
A province meaning 'West of the (Yangtze) River' from *jiāng* and *xī*, although the whole province actually lies to the south of it. This is explained by several changes in provincial boundaries.

Jičín, CZECH REPUBLIC *Jitčín/Gitschin*
Until recently it was believed that the name was associated with Queen Jitka (or Guta) (1271–97), first wife of Wenceslas II, King of Bohemia (1278–1305). However, the place-name would have had to have been Jučin, the possessive case of Jitka. It is now considered that the present name is derived from a settlement called Jičina or Dičina which was situated on the Jičínský Potok 'Jičina Stream', from *jičina* 'an area full of wild boars' and *potok* 'stream (running through)'. The German name was derived from the Czech.

Jihlava, CZECH REPUBLIC *Iglau*
Founded in 799 and named after the Jihlava River on which it lies. The name may be derived from the Old Czech *igla* 'needle' (modern Czech *jehla*) because the river bed was covered with sharp needle-like stones, or from the German *Igel* 'hedgehog' because these stones resembled the spines of a hedgehog. When silver deposits were found in the nearby hills in the 1240s German miners flooded into the area, settled and gave the city the name Iglau. The Germans were expelled in 1945.

Jihočeský, CZECH REPUBLIC
'South Bohemia', a geographic region.

Jihomoravský, CZECH REPUBLIC
'South Moravia', a geographic region.

Jilin, CHINA *Yung-ki (city)*
A province created in 1907 and a city also known as Kirin. The name means 'Luck of the Forest' or 'Auspicious Forest' from *jí* 'lucky' or 'auspicious' and *lín* 'forest'. The forested areas are home to many species of wild animals, notably the Manchurian hare foxes valued for their fur, and medicinal plants,

Jilong, TAIWAN *Santissima Trinidad*
The name is believed to be derived from Ketangalan, an indigenous tribe. The city-port was occupied by the Spanish in 1626–41, when it was known as Santissima Trinidad 'Most Holy Trinity'. The name is sometimes transliterated as Keelung.

Jim Thorpe, PENNSYLVANIA/USA *Mauch Chunk*
The original name came from the Native American *machk* 'bear' and *tschunk* 'mountain'. In 1954 Mauch Chunk merged with East Mauch Chunk to form a town named after Jim Thorpe (1888–1953), one of the greatest athletes ever, an Olympic decathlon and

pentathlon champion, and a leading football and baseball player.

Jinan, SHANDONG/CHINA *Lixia, Licheng*
Also known as Tsinan, it means 'South of the (River) Ji', now the lower course of the Yellow River, from *nán*. Marco Polo called it Chingli.

Jindřichův Hradec, CZECH REPUBLIC
'Henry's Fortified Settlement' from *hradec* 'small medieval fortified settlement' and a personal name. Jindřich was the eldest son of the founder of an important noble family, the Vítkovci. The fortified settlement was located here to help protect the route from Prague into Austria.

Jingdezhen, JIANGXI/CHINA *Chang-nan-chen, Fuliang*
Took its present name 'Town of Jingde' some time between 1004 and 1007 from the title, Jingde, of the emperor reigning at the time and *zhèn* 'town'. Jingdezhen became famous during the Song dynasty (960–1297) when items made for the court were marked 'made in the Jingde period'.

Jinja, UGANDA
Founded in 1901 by the British with a name meaning 'Stones'.

Jirjā, EGYPT
Also spelt Girga. The name is derived from the old Coptic monastery of Mar Girgis dedicated to St George.

Jiujiang, JIANGXI/CHINA
A port on the Yangtze River, it means 'Nine Rivers' from *jiŭ* 'nine' and *jiāng*.

Jiulong, SICHUAN/CHINA
'Nine Dragons' from *jiŭ* 'nine' and *lóng* 'dragon', a reference to the nine hills in the vicinity.

Jiuquan, GANSU/CHINA *Suzhou*
Founded as a military outpost in 111 BC. The present name means 'Wine Spring' from *jiŭ* 'wine' or 'alcoholic drink' and *quán* 'spring' or 'stream'. According to legend, when a Han general realized that he did not have enough wine to celebrate a victory he poured what little he had into a nearby spring and invited his soldiers to drink from that.

Joachimsthal, BRANDENBURG/GERMANY
Founded in 1604 and named 'Joachim's Valley' after Joachim Frederick (1546–1608), Elector of Brandenburg (1598–1608). *See* JÁCHYMOV.

João Pessoa, PARAÍBA/BRAZIL *Filipea de Nossa Senhora das Neves, Frederikstad, Paraíba*
Founded in 1585 by the Portuguese with the name 'Filipea of our Lady of the Snows' in honour of Philip I (1527–98), King of Portugal

(1580–98), who was also Philip II, King of Spain (1556–98), and the church of Our Lady of the Snows. Between 1634 and 1654 during the Dutch occupation it was known as Frederick's Town, possibly after Frederick Henry (1584–1647), Stadholder of the United Provinces of the Netherlands (1625–47), and later as Paraíba. It was renamed in 1930 in honour of João Pessoa, former governor of the state of Paraíba and state president who was assassinated that year during the revolution associated with the national elections.

Jocotepec, JALISCO/MEXICO *Xuxutepeque, Xilotepec*
Named by the Spanish 'Hill of Guaves' (a bitter fruit) *c.*1529 from the Nahuatl *Xoco* 'acid', *tepetl* 'hill' and *k* 'place of'. The previous Xilotepec meant 'Hill of Ear of Corn'.

Jodhpur, RĀJASTHĀN/INDIA
'City of Jodha'. A former princely state founded in 1459 by, and named after, Rão Jodha, chief of a Rājput clan called the Rathores. It gave its name to 'jodhpurs', long riding breeches much favoured by the Maharaja of Jodhpur when playing polo in the 1860s.

Johannesburg, SOUTH AFRICA, USA
South Africa (Gauteng): founded in 1886 as the 'Town of Johannes'. It is not known for certain which Johannes the city is named after. However, strong claimants are Johann Rissik (1857–1925), acting surveyor general, and Christian Johannes Joubert (1834–1911), head of the mines department in the South African Republic in whose area of responsibility the goldfields were situated. The city is also known as eGoli (or iGoli) 'City of Gold' in Nguni.

John Day, OREGON/USA
Named after the John Day River, itself named after a Virginian hero of the Astor overland expedition in 1811.

John o'Groats, SCOTLAND/UK
A village named after John o'Groat (or Jan de Groot), a Dutchman who settled here with royal protection in the 15th century and established a ferry to the Orkney Islands in 1496. To travel from John o'Groats to Land's End means to cover the entire length of Great Britain, about 870 miles (1 400 km).

Johnson City, USA
1. Tennessee: settled in the 1850s and originally named Johnson's Depot after the first postmaster, Henry Johnson (1809–74). In 1859 it was renamed Haynesville after Landon C. Haynes, a senator, but two years later it reverted to Johnson with 'City' added.
2. Texas: founded in 1879 by, and named after, James P. Johnson

Johnstown, CANADA, IRELAND, USA
1. USA (New York): founded in 1762 by, and named after, Sir William Johnson, superintendent of Native American affairs.
2. USA (Pennsylvania): founded in 1800 as Conemaugh by Joseph Johns from Switzerland. It was renamed after him in 1834.

Johor, WEST MALAYSIA/MALAYSIA *Johore*
A state, and formerly a kingdom stretching into the island of Sumatra (now Indonesia), founded in 1511 after Malacca had fallen to the Portuguese. It means 'Precious Jewel' from the Arabic *jauhar*, an indication of the influence of early Arab traders.

Johor Baharu, WEST MALAYSIA/MALAYSIA *Tanjung Putri, Johore Bahru*
Founded in 1855 by, and named after, Ibrahim Temenggong, ruler of Johore (1825–62). In 1866 it was renamed Johore Bahru 'New Johore', from *baharu/baru* 'new', when it replaced Johore Lama 'Old Johore' as the state capital. *See* JOHOR.

Joinvile, SANTA CATARINA/BRAZIL *Dona Francisca*
The surrounding area was the dowry of Dona Francisca Carolina (1821–98), daughter of Pedro (Peter) I, Emperor of Brazil, when she married Francis (1818–1900), Prince of Joinville and son of Louis Philippe, King of the French. The name was changed in 1852.

Jokkmokk, SWEDEN
'Bend in the River' from the Lapp *jokk* 'bend'. It lies on the Lilla Luleälven.

Joliet, ILLINOIS/USA
Settled in 1833 and named Juliet after Juliet Campbell, the daughter of a settler. In 1845 it was renamed after Louis Jolliet (1645–1700), the French-Canadian explorer and from 1697 royal hydrographer of New France, who passed through the area in 1673. Jolliet also spelt his name Joliet and Joliette. Nearby is the town of Romeoville!

Joliette, QUEBEC/CANADA
Founded in 1841 by Barthélemi Jolliet, a descendant of Louis Jolliet (see previous entry), after whom it was named.

Jonesboro, ARKANSAS/USA
Founded in 1859 and named after William A. Jones, state senator.

Jonesborough, UK, USA
USA (Tennessee): laid out in 1799, it is named after William Jones, a prominent participant in the American War of Independence (1775–83).

Jönköping, SWEDEN
A county and a town. *Köping* means 'market settlement'; the meaning of *Jön* is not known.

Jonquière, QUEBEC/CANADA
Founded as an agricultural settlement in the 19th century, it is named after Jacques-Pierre de Taffanal, Marquis de la Jonquière, governor of New France (1749–52).

Joplin, MISSOURI/USA
Founded in 1871 by John Cox who named it after his friend, the Revd Harris Joplin, a Methodist missionary.

Jordan (al-Urdun), AND PHILIPPINES, USA
Jordan: the Hashemite Kingdom of Jordan (al-Mamlakah al-Urdunnīyah al-Hāshimīyāh) since 1949. Previously the Hashemite Kingdom of Transjordan (1946) when a monarchy was created and independence achieved, although the country was not completely free of British control until 1948 (Hashemite denotes descent from the Prophet Muhammad[†]); the Emirate of Transjordan, recognized by the UK as a national state preparing for independence under British tutelage (1923); part of the Palestinian mandate when its borders were extended eastwards (1920), but the British subdivided the mandate along the River Jordan–Gulf of Aqaba line in 1921 and created Transjordan 'Over the (River) Jordan', in the sense here of 'Beyond the Jordan', in the eastern portion. Henceforth *Palestine referred only to the territory west of the Jordan. From the beginning of the 16th century it formed part of the Ottoman Turkish *vilayet* 'province' of Damascus, having been something of a backwater for the previous 800 years. Before that it had been a part of various empires, including the Greek, Roman, and Persian, and of the Nabataean Kingdom. In 1950, following the armistice between Israel and Jordan the previous year, Jordan formally annexed the *West Bank, but this was lost to Israel as a result of the Six Day War in 1967. Between February and July 1958 Jordan and Iraq joined in a federation called the Arab Union, but this was brought to an end with the murder of the Iraqi king and the overthrow of the Iraqi monarchy. The country is named after the River Jordan whose Hebrew origin is not definitely known. It could mean the 'River of Dan', Dan being one of the sons of Jacob and thus leader of one of the twelve tribes of Israel; the cognate Hebrew name is Ha-Yarden. The Greek name was Aulon and the Arabic name is Nahr al-Urdun, although it is sometimes known as ash-SharĪah 'The Watering Place'.

Jotunheimen Mountains, NORWAY
Jotunfjell
Named in 1822 as the 'Giant's Mountains', they were renamed at the beginning of the 20th century 'Giant's Home'.

Juan Fernandez Islands (Islas Juan Fernández), CHILE
A group of three islands, the largest of which is called Robinson Crusoe Island (or Nearer Land Island), named after Juan Fernández (*c*.1536–*c*.1604), a Spanish navigator who discovered them *c*.1563.

Juárez, ARGENTINA, MEXICO
Mexico: three towns in the states of Chiapas, Chihuahua (distinct from Ciudad Juárez), and Coahuila, all named after Benito Juárez. *See* CIUDAD JUÁREZ.

Judaea (Hebrew: Yehudah), WEST BANK *Judah, Palaestina*
The southernmost of the three historical regions of ancient Palestine (the other two being Galilee in the north and Samaria in the centre) whose most important city was Jerusalem. It takes its name from Judah, one of the twelve tribes of Israel, itself named after Judah, the fourth son born to Jacob and his first wife, Leah. When the Israelites divided into two kingdoms, the southern one became the Kingdom of Judah. Becoming part of the Roman Empire in 63 BC, its name was changed to Palaestina by the Romans in about 135 in an attempt to diminish Jewish identification with the land of Israel.

Judsonia, ARKANSAS/USA
Named after the Revd Adoniram Judson, a Baptist missionary.

Jujuy, ARGENTINA
A province with a name taken from *xuxuyoc*, the title of an Inca provincial governor when the Spanish arrived in the 16th century.

Julianehåb (Qaqortoq), GREENLAND, DENMARK
'Juliana's Harbour'. Founded in 1755 by Anders Olsen, a Norwegian trader, and named after Queen Juliana Maria (1729–96) of Brunswick-Wolfenbüttel, second wife of King Frederick V of Denmark-Norway whom she married in 1752.

Jumilla, MURCIA/SPAIN *Juncellus, Jumilla/ Jumyella, Gémina Aamlet/Geminalet*
The original Roman name was an allusion to the local reeds (in Latin *juncus* 'rush' or 'reed'). This gave way to the present name or Jumyella before the Moors gave that name their own interpretation meaning 'Land of the Sons of Amlet'.

Junāgadh, GUJARĀT/INDIA *Mustafābād*
Derives its name from a very old Hindu fort from *jirna* 'old' which comprised the original settlement. It was captured by the Muslims in 1472 and renamed Mustafābād 'City of Mustafa', although to whom this refers is not known. At the time of Partition in 1947 the ruler of the small state of Junāgadh decided to join Pakistan, but his people were predominantly Hindu and he quickly found himself in exile and his wishes ignored.

Junction City, KANSAS/USA
Founded in 1858 and so-named because it lies at the confluence of the Republican and Smoky Hill Rivers.

Juneau, USA
1. Alaska: settled in 1880 and named after Joseph Juneau after he had discovered gold here.
2. Wisconsin: named after one of the founders of the city of Milwaukee in Wisconsin, another Juneau.

Junee, NEW SOUTH WALES/AUSTRALIA
Founded in 1863 with an Aboriginal name meaning 'Speak to Me'.

Jungfrau, SWITZERLAND
A mountain with a name meaning 'Maiden' or 'Virgin', possibly because of the shape of its summit and its 'virgin' snows.

Jura, FRANCE, SWITZERLAND, UK
1. France: a department in Franche-Comté taking its name from the Jura Mountains.
2. Switzerland: a French-speaking canton established in 1979 whose name means 'Forested Mountain' from the Gaulish *jor* or *juria*. The discovery of fossils in the Jura Mountains gave rise to the geologic time from *c.*215 to 145 million years ago known as the Jurassic Period.
3. UK (Scotland): formerly Doirad Eilinn 'Doirad's Island' and Dure. An island in the Inner Hebrides with its present name an abbreviation of its original name meaning 'Deer Island' from the Old Scandinavian *dýr* 'deer' and *ey*.

Jurmala, LATVIA
On the coast, the name means 'Sea Shore' from *jura* 'sea' and *mala* 'shore'.

Jutland (Jylland), DENMARK *Gotland*
North, South, and West Jutland are counties named after the Jutes, a Germanic people, some of whom left the region in the 5th century to invade southern England.

Juventud, Isla de la, CUBA
See ISLA DE LA JUVENTUD.

Jyväskylä, FINLAND
'Grain Village' from *jyvä* 'grain' and *kylä* 'village', a reference to its location in a fertile area.

K2, CHINA-PAKISTAN *Godwin-Austen*
In the Karakoram Range, K2 is the second highest mountain in the world. The *K* stands for Karakoram and the *2* signifies that it was the second peak in this range to be observed by Lieutenant Colonel Henry Godwin-Austen by theodolite from hills in Kashmir. The name 'Godwin-Austen' was proposed in 1888 by General J. T. Walker, a former surveyor-general of India, after Godwin-Austen (1834–1923), a British explorer and geologist, who first surveyed the mountain in 1856 and explored its slopes and the glaciers at its base. The government of India demurred on the grounds that it was not appropriate for Himalayan peaks to be given personal names. Thus K2 is the official name, although it has been corrupted locally to Kechu or Cheku. Nevertheless, the mountain has been known as Godwin-Austen at times.

Kabanjahe, SUMATRA/INDONESIA
'Ginger Garden' from *jahe* 'ginger'.

Kabardino-Balkaria, RUSSIA *Kabarda, Kabardin*
A republic named after the Kabardins (who are Circassians) and Balkars. Kabarda and Balkaria amalgamated in 1922 to form the Kabardino-Balkar Autonomous Province which became a republic in 1936. Accused of collaborating with the Germans by Stalin[†], the entire Balkar population was deported to Central Asia in 1944; the Balkar region was attached to the Georgian Republic, while the rest was renamed the Kabardin Autonomous Soviet Socialist Republic. When the Balkars were allowed to return in 1957, the Kabardino-Balkar Republic was restored.

Kabul (Persian: **Kābol**), AFGHANISTAN
Ortospana?
Named after the Kabul River which was called Cophes in ancient Greek and Kubha in Sanskrit. The meaning is not known, but it certainly pre-dates the advent of Islam when it was an important centre on the route between India and the Hellenic world. Capital of the Mughal Empire in 1504–26, it has been the capital of Afghanistan since 1776. Kabul may have been the city of Ortospana mentioned by Strabo[†]. The suggestion that the name is derived from the Arabic root *qbl* 'meeting' or 'receiving' is unlikely.

Kabwe, ZAMBIA *Broken Hill*
An Australian mining engineer, Thomas G. Davey, gave the site its original name from a town in New South Wales, Australia. The town developed around Broken Hill Mine opened in 1902. It was renamed Kabwe 'Small Stone' in 1965, a year after Zambian independence, in the Bantu language of the Lala people.

Kabylie, ALGERIA
A mountainous region named after the Berber Kabyle people. They call themselves Imazighen (in the singular, Amazigh) 'Free, or noble, Men', or Qbaili from the Arabic *qbaila* 'tribe'.

Kachin, BURMA
A state named after the Kachin people.

Kadoma, JAPAN, ZIMBABWE
1. Japan (Honshū): the former Chinese characters meant 'Opening Gate' from *kado* 'gate' and *ma* 'opening' or 'between'. This was a name for land which was not very fertile and thus landowners did not have to pay taxes on it. The current Chinese characters mean 'True Gate' from *kado* 'gate' and *ma* 'true'.
2. Zimbabwe: founded in 1907 and previously spelt Gatooma, it is named after a nearby hill, which was itself named after a local chief whose name in Ndebele meant '(He who) does Not Thunder, or make Noise'. The spelling was changed in 1980 after Zimbabwe achieved independence.

Kaduna, NIGERIA
'Crocodiles' in the Hausa language. A state and a city founded in 1913 by Sir Frederick (later Baron) Lugard (1858–1945), governor-general of Nigeria (1912–19). Both are named after the Kaduna River which flows through the centre of the state and on which the city lies.

Kaesŏng, NORTH KOREA *Kaegyŏng, Songak, Songdo*
Surrounded by pine-covered mountains, the previous name meant 'City of Pines' from *song* 'pine tree' and *do* 'city' and before that 'Pine Tree Peak' after Mount Songak from *ak* 'summit' or 'peak'. An old walled and fortified city, its present name means 'Open City' from *kae* 'to open' and *sŏng* 'castle' or, here, 'castle-city'. It was the capital of the Koryŏ dynasty (935–1392). The city lies just south of the 38th

parallel and therefore was within the territory
of South Korea when the country was divided
in 1945. However, it was overrun by North
Korean troops in 1950 and still held by them
when the truce talks began in 1951. When the
armistice was signed in 1953 the city was
transferred permanently to North Korea.

Kāf, al-, TUNISIA *Sicca Veneria, Colonia Julia Cirta
Nova, Shikka Banariya*
Also known as el-Kef. Situated on the slopes of
the Haut Tell at 2 559 feet (780 m), the name
comes from *kahf* and means 'The Cave' in
Arabic. Built as a Carthaginian fortress, it
became a Roman colony in the time of Caesar
Augustus† known first as Sicca Veneria, named
after a Phoenician goddess identified with
Venus, the goddess of love. The Arabic name,
Shikka Banariya, is an adaptation of the
Roman name.

Kaffeklubben Island, ARCTIC OCEAN
Discovered in 1900 by Robert E. Peary (1856–
1920), an American explorer in the US Navy
who claimed to have been the first to reach the
North Pole in 1909. Lauge Koch, a Danish
explorer, visited the island in 1921 and named
it 'Coffee Club' after the Kaffeklub at the
Mineralogical Museum in Copenhagen.

Kaffraria, SOUTH-EAST AFRICA
A coastal region colonized by the British and
Portuguese, in particular Xhosa territory. The
name comes from the Arabic *kāfir* 'infidel' or
'pagan', the Xhosa derogatorily being called
Kaffirs. The Xhosa and Zulu languages used to
be called Kaffrarian. The British part became a
crown colony in 1847 and in 1865 was
incorporated into Cape Colony.

Kafr al-Shaikh, EGYPT
A town and a governorate with the meaning of
'Village of Chief' from the Arabic *kafr*
'village' and *shaikh* 'chief'.

Kafue, ZAMBIA
Founded in 1905 and named after the Kafue
River on which it lies. Its name means
'Hippopotamus'.

Kagawa, SHIKOKU/JAPAN
A prefecture with a name meaning 'River of
Perfume' from *ka* 'perfume' and *kawa*. With
the area drained by numerous rivers, it is not
known which one has given its name to the
prefecture. However, according to legend,
perfumed water flowed from the spot where
an old birch tree stood in the upper stream of
the Kotō River.

Kagoshima, KYŪSHŪ/JAPAN
A city and prefecture, the name means 'Island
of Fawns' from *ka* 'deer', *ko* 'young' or 'child',
and *shima*.

Kahramanmaraş, TURKEY *Markasi,
Germanicia Caesarea*
Its original name was Assyrian and the second
Roman. It was conquered by the Arabs *c.*645
before falling to the Seljuk Turks in the 12th
century. In 1515 it became part of the Ottoman
Empire. Maras may be of Arabic origin and
mean 'Place of Trembling'. The Turkish
kahraman 'brave' or 'heroic' was added in
recognition of the city's stand against the
French in 1920.

Kaibab, ARIZONA/USA
A town and a plateau from a Paiute word
meaning 'Mountain lying down'.

Kaifeng, HENAN/CHINA *Daliang, Bianzhou,
Bianjing, Nanjing, Beijing*
Founded at least as early as the 4th century BC
as Daliang. At the end of the 5th century AD
the name was changed to Bianzhou when it
became a prefecture. The Northern Song
dynasty (960–1127) made it their capital. In
1127 it was captured by the Juchen (Jin) (1115–
1234), who came from Manchuria in the north;
they renamed it Bianjing and then Nanjing
'Southern Capital'. When the Ming dynasty
(1368–1644) came to power in 1368 they called
the city Beijing 'Northern Capital'. However,
in 1378 they abandoned the idea of developing
the city as an imperial capital. Its name is a
contraction of a four character phrase, *kāi* 'to
open', *tuo fēng* 'to close' or 'seal', and *jing*,
together a reference to a policy of territorial
expansion to seal off the borders to
'barbarians'.

Kai Islands (Kepulauan Kai), INDONESIA
'Thousand Islands' although there are less
than 300. *Kai* is the Portuguese for 'stone'.

Kaikoura, SOUTH ISLAND/NEW ZEALAND
A shortening of Te Ahi Kai Koura a
Tamakiterangi which means 'The Fire at
which the Crayfish were cooked for
Tamakiterangi', an early Maori explorer in the
region, from the Maori *kai* 'food' and *koura*
'crayfish'. Seafood was a staple diet of the first
people to settle here. There is also a mountain
range with this name.

Kailua, HAWAII/USA
On the island of Oahu, it means 'Two Seas'
from the Hawaiian *kai* 'seawater'.

Kairouan, TUNISIA
See QAIROUAN.

Kaiserslautern, RHINELAND-PALATINATE/
GERMANY
Derived from the Lauter, the name of a nearby
stream, and *kaiser* 'emperor' after Frederick I
Barbarossa (*c.*1123–90), German King and Holy

Roman Emperor (1152–90), who built a palace here in the 12th century.

Kaitaia, NORTH ISLAND/NEW ZEALAND
A missionary station founded in 1833, the full name being Kaitataia 'Food in Abundance' from the Maori *kai* 'food' and *tataia* 'arranged in order', thus abundant, a reference to the numerous wood pigeons, a staple diet, found in the area.

Kaitangata, SOUTH ISLAND/NEW ZEALAND
Settled in 1855, the name comes from a Maori word meaning 'Man Eater'. This refers, particularly, to Chief Mokomoko who was eaten after losing a battle. Cannabalism was not widespread and it was rare for a chief to be captured and eaten.

Kajaani, FINLAND *Kajaneborg*
Takes its name from the Swedish castle, Kajaneborg, built here in 1603–66 and from which the town developed. The Swedish name is believed to be derived from the Russian equivalent of the name for the geographical area of Kainuu in northern Finland which sounded similar to Kajane.

Kakogawa, HONSHŪ/JAPAN
A city and a river from *ka* 'add', *ko* 'old', and *kawa* 'river'.

Kalaat es Senan, TUNISIA
'Fortress of Senan' from the Arabic *qal'ah* 'fortress' and a personal name: Senan was a local bandit who resisted tax collectors.

Kalach, VORONEZH/RUSSIA
The name, from *kalachikom* indicating something 'curled up' or 'bent over', represents the town's location on a bend in a river, here the confluence of the Tolucheyevka and Podgornaya Rivers. Kalach-na-Donu 'Kalach on the (River) Don' has the same meaning.

Kalama, DEMOCRATIC REPUBLIC OF THE CONGO, USA
USA (Washington): possibly from a Native American word *okalakalama* 'goose'.

Kalamazoo, MICHIGAN/USA *Kee-Kalamazoo*
Originally a fur trading post established in the 1820s, the Algonquian name means 'Boiling Water' or 'Beautiful Water', a reference to the rapids on the Kalamazoo River. However, it has also been claimed that the name comes from the local *negikanamazo* 'otter tail'.

Kalāt, BALOCHISTAN/PAKISTAN
Sometimes called Kalāt-e Baluch to distinguish it from other towns with Kalāt in their names. The name represents the Arabic *qala* or *qal'ah* and Balochi *khilāt*, both 'citadel' or 'fortress'.

Kalgan, HEBEI/CHINA
See ZHANGJIAKOU.

Kalgoorlie, WESTERN AUSTRALIA/AUSTRALIA
Hannan's Find
Originally named after Paddy Hannan after he had discovered gold here in 1893. The town was then given a name derived from an Aboriginal word *galgurli*, a local shrub.

Kalimantan, INDONESIA
See BORNEO.

Kaliningrad, RUSSIA *Královec, Königsberg*
A province and a city. Originally founded and named by Přemysl Otaker II (1230–78), King of Bohemia (1253–78), using the Czech word for 'king' *král*. After he had led a crusade against the pagan Prussians in 1255, the name was changed to Königsberg 'King's Mountain'. However, the terrain is quite flat and the German *-berg* was probably at one time *-burg*, referring to the fortress built by the Teutonic Knights to consolidate their power in newly conquered territory. The city was captured by Soviet troops in 1945 and renamed in 1946 in memory of Mikhail Kalinin[†], the Soviet President, who died that year. It was the capital of East Prussia from the 15th century until 1945. The northern half of East Prussia was ceded to the USSR by the Potsdam Agreement in August 1945 and became a province. This met the Soviet need for ice-free ports in the Baltic Sea even though, until the German attack on the Soviet Union in 1941, the Russians had no justifiable claim to the region. It is geographically separated from the rest of Russia by 190 miles (300 km) of mainly Lithuanian territory.

Kalispell, MONTANA/USA
Named after the Kalispel tribe.

Kalisz, POLAND *Calisia*
Founded on an ancient trade route, it was known to Ptolemy in the 2nd century as Calisia. The name may be derived from a Slavonic root element *kal* 'mud' to give the meaning of a 'muddy place'. It is situated on the Prosna River.

Kalk Bay (Kalkbaai), WESTERN CAPE/SOUTH AFRICA
'Chalk Bay' from the Afrikaans *kalk* 'chalk'. In the 19th century sea shells were burnt to produce lime for whitewash.

Kalkfeld, NAMIBIA *Okovakuatjivi*
Since 1909 'Lime Field' from the German *Kalk* 'lime' and *Feld*, a reference to the limestone in the area. The original Herero name meant 'Place where People are', thus a settlement.

Kalmar, SWEDEN *Iuxta Kalmarniam*
Founded in the 12th century with a name
derived from *kalm* 'cairn' and *are* 'gravel bank'.
It gave its name to the Kalmar Union by which
Denmark, Norway, and Sweden (which
included Finland) were united in 1397–1523.

Kalmykia (Kalmykiya), RUSSIA
A republic named after the Kalmyk (or
Kalmuck), the Turkish name for a Mongoloid
people, the Oyrat, who had stayed on the
Russian steppe when the Golden Horde
dissolved in the 15th century. Their name
comes from *kalmak* 'to remain', a reference to
their putting down roots on the steppe and
also perhaps because they remained pagans
even though they had been exposed to Islam.
The republic was created in 1936 and
abolished in 1944 when Stalin[†] deported the
Kalmyks to Central Asia for their supposed
collaboration with the Germans. They were
allowed to return in 1957 and their republic
was restored.

Kaluga, RUSSIA
A province and a city founded in the 14th
century as a fortress against the Tatars. It
means 'marshland' from *luzha* 'puddle' or
'pool'.

Kalwaria Zebrzydowska, POLAND
Named after Mikolaj Zebrzydowski who
commissioned a monastery for the
Benedictine Order here in 1600 and wished to
build a town which resembled the layout of
Jerusalem. Kalwaria means 'Calvary'.

Kalyan, MAHĀRĀSHTRA/INDIA
'Beautiful' or 'Noble' from the Sanskrit *kalyana*.

Kama, BURMA, CANADA, DEMOCRATIC REPUBLIC
OF THE CONGO, NICARAGUA, RUSSIA
Russia (Sverdlovsk): originally Butysh but since
1966 named after the River Kama from the
Udmurt *kam* 'river' or 'current'.

Kamarān Island, YEMEN
An island in the Red Sea with a name that
means 'Two Moons' from the Arabic *qamr*
'moon' because a double reflection of the
moon can be seen here.

Kamchatka, RUSSIA
A province, a river, and a peninsula which take
their name from the indigenous people, the
Kamchadaly, the name used in the 18th
century for the Itel' mensy.

**Kamenets-Podol'skiy (Kam'yanets'-
Podil's'kyy),** UKRAINE
Developed from a fortress on a high spur of
rock in a loop of the Smotrich River, the first
part of the name is derived from the Russian
kamen' 'rock' or 'stone'. Podolsky has been

added to distinguish this Kamenets from
others and indicates that the city lies in the
region known as Podoliya.

Kamensk-Shakhtinskiy, ROSTOV/RUSSIA
Kamenskaya
Founded in 1686 as a Cossack settlement with
a name derived from *kamen'*. In 1927
Shakhtinsky was added when it became a
town from *shakhty* 'mines' or 'pits' because it
made mining equipment. The town of Shakhty
lies to the south.

Kamensk-Uralsky, YEKATERINBURG/RUSSIA
Named after the Kamenka River, the first part
of the name is derived from *kamen'* while the
second distinguishes it from Kamensk-
Shakhtinsky and indicates its location in the
Ural Mountains.

Kamloops, BRITISH COLUMBIA/CANADA
Cumcloups, Fort Thompson
Derived from a Native American word
meaning 'meeting of the waters'. It lies astride
the junction of the North and South
Thompson Rivers.

Kamo, ARMENIA, JAPAN, NEW ZEALAND
1. Armenia: formerly Nor-Bayazet and
renamed in 1959 after one of the
legendary figures of the Bolshevik movement.
Georgian-born, his real name was Semën
Ter-Petrosyan (1882–1922); he received his
pseudonym from Joseph Stalin[†] when Ter-
Petrosyan, with his bad Russian accent,
mispronounced the Russian *komu* 'to whom' as
kamo.
2. Japan (Honshū): three towns and two rivers
have this name. In Niigata prefecture the
Chinese characters represent *ka* 'add' and *mo*
'rampant' while in Shizuoka and Kyōto
prefectures they represent *ka(ga)* 'celebration'
and *mo* 'rampant'.

Kampala, UGANDA *Mengo, Fort Hill*
The original settlement, known as Mengo, was
scattered over seven hills and was the capital
of the Kingdom of Buganda. In 1890 Captain
(later Baron) Frederick Lugard (1858–1945) led
an expedition to the kingdom seeking British
control over the source of the River Nile. He
built Fort Hill for the Imperial British East
Africa Company on a nearby hill which was
called Kampala by the Bagandans. Eventually
the town grew to include Mengo. In 1905–62
the capital of the Ugandan Protectorate was
Entebbe, but in 1962 Uganda achieved
independence and Kampala, Lugard's
headquarters in 1890–2, became the capital. It
is said to take its name from the antelope, the
impala, locally *mpala*.

Kamphaeng Phet, THAILAND *Chakangrao, Nakhon Chum*
'Diamond Wall' from *kamphaeng* 'wall' and *phet(ch)* 'diamond', a reference to the fact that it was a walled settlement and part of the defensive line on the River Ping protecting the Kingdom of Sukhothai.

Kâmpóng Saôm, CAMBODIA
See KOMPONG SOM.

Kamyshin, VOLGOGRAD/RUSSIA *Kamyshinka, Petrovsk, Dmitriyevsk*
Originally a village on the Kamyshin River established in 1667 from *kamysh* 'reeds' or 'rushes', a fort to guard workers building the Volga–Don canal was built on the opposite bank in 1697 by Peter I the Great[†] and named after himself. In 1710 it was renamed after Dmitri 'Donskoi', victor of the Battle of Kulikovo on the River Don, close to Kamyshin, in 1380 against the Mongol Golden Horde. Due to the inhabitants' disloyalty to Catherine II the Great[†] in supporting Yemelyan Pugachov (*c.*1742–75), leader of a Cossack and peasant rebellion in 1773–5, the authorities decided in 1780 to dispense with the name Dmitriyevsk (which was now associated with treachery) and restore the name Kamyshin.

Kanab, UTAH/USA
Founded as Fort Kanab from a Ute word for 'willow'.

Kananga, DEMOCRATIC REPUBLIC OF THE CONGO *Luluabourg*
Originally Kananga, it became a German military camp in 1884 on the River Lulua, both the river and the developing city being named after the Lulua, a Central African people. The city readopted its original name, whose meaning is unknown, in 1972.

Kanash, CHUVASHIYA/RUSSIA *Shikrany*
Renamed 'Council' in 1925 from a Chuvash word, the equivalent of 'soviet'.

Kanazawa, HONSHŪ/JAPAN
From *kana* 'metal' and *zawa* 'marshland' or 'swamp'. A local traditional craft was sword-making.

Kanchanaburi, THAILAND
Founded as a defensive post against Burmese incursions in the 18th century, the name means 'City of Gold' from *kanchane* 'gold' and *buri* 'city'.

Kānchenjunga, NEPAL-SIKKIM/INDIA
A mountain with a name of Tibetan origin meaning 'Five Treasures of the Great Snow' from *kang* 'snow', *chen* 'having', *dzo* 'treasure', and *nga* 'five', a reference to its peaks.

Kānchipuram, TAMIL NĀDU/INDIA
One of India's Seven Sacred Cities, the name means 'Golden City'. It is sometimes known as Shiva Vishnu Kanchi.

Kandahār, AFGHANISTAN *Alexandria in Arachosia, Nādirābād*
Also spelt Qandahār. Originally named in 329 BC after Alexander III the Great[†], Arachosia being a part of Balochistan lying west of the Quetta Hills and a region of south-east Afghanistan in Hellenistic times. It was renamed Nādirābād after it fell to Nādir Shah (1688–1747), Shahanshah 'King of Kings' of Persia (1736–47) in 1738. The present name was coined by emigrants from Gandhāra, an historical region and ancient Indian kingdom in what is now roughly north-west Pakistan to include the Kabul and Indus Rivers. It was the first capital of a unified Afghanistan in 1747–73. It has been suggested, less plausibly, that it comes from Iskandar, the Arabic name for Alexander.

Kandalaksha, MURMANSK/RUSSIA
Located on an inlet in Kandalaksha Bay, the name is said to come from the Karelian words *kanta lakshi* 'corner inlet'.

Kandi, BENIN, INDIA
Benin: according to local tradition, founded by a hunter who came across a large group of elephants: Sinounou ba kamme 'I have come upon a great many elephants'. Kamme is said to have become Kan-ni and then Kandi. Another tradition has it that some women slipped on a river bank and broke their pitchers '*kan'di*.

Kandy (Mahnuwara), SRI LANKA *Candy*
Capital of a Sinhalese kingdom with the same name, it fell to the British in 1815. The city, perched at height of 1 600 ft (488 m), derives its name from the Sinhalese *kandha* 'mountain'. The Sinhalese name means 'Great City'.

Kaneohe, HAWAII/USA
'Bamboo Husband'. The reason for this name is not known.

Kangaroo Island, SOUTH AUSTRALIA/AUSTRALIA
Named in 1802 by Matthew Flinders[†] because of the numerous kangaroos.

KaNgwane, MPUMALANGA/SOUTH AFRICA *Swazi*
A former self-governing state created in 1971 for Swazi people living outside Swaziland. Its Swazi name means 'Land of the Ngwane', the name of a chief of the Nguni, an ethnic group from which the Swazis came, and *ka*, a place-name prefix.

k

Kanibadam, TAJIKISTAN
'Place of Almonds' for which it is famous.

Kanniyākumāri, TAMIL NĀDU/INDIA
According to legend, the goddess Kanyā
Kumāri killed a demon here and the town is
named after her.

Kano, NIGERIA
A state, city, former Hausa kingdom, and
Fulani emirate. The city is also called Kano
City. According to tradition, it was founded by
a blacksmith, called Kano, from the Gaya tribe.
He came to Dalla Hill, which overlooks the old
city, searching for iron.

Kanopolis, KANSAS/USA
Located in the centre of the state, the name is a
combination of Kansas and Centropolis
'Central City'.

Kānpur, UTTAR PRADESH/INDIA *Kanbaiyapur,
Cawnpore*
'Town of Kānh' or 'of Krishna' with the
additional *pur*.

Kansas, USA
A state and a river named after a Native
American tribe, the Kansa, who lived along the
Kansas River. This is a Sioux word meaning
'People of the South Wind'. The French
claimed the region in 1682, but sold it to the
USA in 1803 as part of the Louisiana Purchase.
It became the Territory of Kansas in 1854 and
joined the USA as the 34th state in 1861.

Kansas City, KANSAS-MISSOURI/USA
Actually two cities at the confluence of the
Kansas and Missouri Rivers separated by the
Kansas–Missouri state line.
1. Kansas: seven towns merged in 1886 and
took the name Kansas City.
2. Missouri: originally known as Westport
Landing, it became the Town of Kansas after
the river name in 1850, and Kansas City in
1889.

Kantemirovka, VORONEZH/RUSSIA
Named after Dmitry Kantemir (1673–1723),
who was born in Moldavia and became a
prince of Moldavia in 1710. In 1711 he
attempted, but failed, to conclude the merger
of Moldavia with Russia. He fled to Russia and
was awarded the title of Russian prince,
becoming Peter I the Great's[†] adviser on
eastern questions. As a further reward for his
services Peter gave him land in the area and
Kantemir founded the town.

Kantō, HONSHŪ/JAPAN
A region called 'East of the Barrier' from *kan*
'barrier' and *tō* 'east'. The barrier referred to is
the Kantō Mountain Range.

Kaoma, ZAMBIA *Mankoya*
The original name recognized the local Nkoya
people until the 1970s when the town was
renamed to mean 'Small Drum'; why is not
known.

Kapan, ARMENIA
'Locked Gate' or 'Fortified Pass'.

Karabagh, AZERBAIJAN
See NAGORNYY-KARABAKH.

Karabash, CHELYABINSK/RUSSIA
Named after the mountain here whose name
is 'Black Head', from the modern Turkish *kara*
and *baş* 'head'.

Karacadağ, TURKEY
A town on the Bulgarian border and a
mountain in the south-east both meaning
'Blackish Mountain' from *karaca* 'blackish'
from *kara* and *dağ* 'mountain'.

**Karachay-Cherkessia (Karachayevo-
Cherkesiya),** RUSSIA
A republic named after the Karachay and
Circassian peoples, but they are not related
linguistically. The Russian for Circassian is
cherkes and this is said to come from an Ossetic
word *charkas* 'eagle'. They are also known as
the Adygei (*see* ADYGEYA). The Karachay take
their name from the Karachay River 'Black
Water' from modern Turkish *kara* and *çay*
'rivulet' or 'stream'. The two came together in
1922 to form an autonomous district, but were
divided again in 1926. Accused of collaboration
with the Germans during the Second World
War, the Karachay were deported by Stalin[†] in
1943–4 to Kazakhstan and their autonomous
district was abolished. They were allowed back
in 1957 when the Karachay-Cherkessia
autonomous district was re-established. In
1991 the district became a republic.

Karachayevsk, KARACHAY-CHERKESSIA/
RUSSIA *Mikoyan-Shakhar, Klukhori*
The capital of Karachay-Cherkessia, it takes its
name from the first part of that title. In 1929–
44 it was named 'Mikoyan's Town' after
Anastas Mikoyan (1895–1978), an Armenian
who was the Soviet commissar for foreign and
domestic trade when the town was founded in
1929. The Turkic word *shakhar* is equivalent to
modern Turkish *şehir*. When Mikoyan fell out
of favour with Stalin[†] in 1944 the city was
renamed Klukhori. Only in use in 1944–7, this
was taken from the name of a pass to the south.

Karāchi, SINDH/PAKISTAN *Kulachi-jo-Kun,
Caranjee, Crochey/Krotchey, Currachee*
Said to take its name from the Kulachi, a
Balochi tribe; however, it has also been
suggested that the name comes from Kalachi, a

tribal chief or, less likely, a humble fisherman who lived in the area. In accordance with Sindh custom the *l* became an *r*. It was the first capital of Pakistan in 1947–59.

Karaganda (Qaraghandy), KAZAKHSTAN
A province and a city founded in 1926, although a settlement had appeared here in 1856. It takes its name from the Kazakh *karagan* 'caragana', a shrub native to Central Asia.

Karain, TURKEY
'Pain in the Chest'. Chest disease is quite common in the area, the people using a local 'white soil' for many purposes and this geologically complex mixture includes, among many minerals, volcanic glass fibres not unlike asbestos.

Karak, al-, JORDAN *Kir Moab, Kir Hareseth*
Also spelt Kerak and Krak. It was a walled city of the Moabites. Built on a steep-sided hill with a flat top, the first Moabite name means 'City of Potsherds' while the second Hebrew name means 'Wall of Potsherds'. The present name means 'Castle of the Raven'.

Karakalpakstan (Qoraqalpoghiston),
UZBEKISTAN
An autonomous republic named after the Karakalpak, a Turkic people, to mean 'Land of the Karakalpaks'. Their name 'Black Caps' is Turkic and is linked to modern Turkish *kara* and *kapak* 'lid' or 'cover', presumably a reference to their headgear. Having been established as an autonomous province of the Kazakh Autonomous Soviet Socialist Republic in 1925, it was detached and became part of Russia in 1930. It was incorporated into the Uzbek Soviet Socialist Republic in 1936 and into Uzbekistan when it gained independence in 1991.

Karaköl, KYRGYZSTAN *Przheval'sk*
There are two cities with almost the same name: Karaköl (in Russian, Karakol') and Kara-Köl (in Russian, Kara-Kul). The former, eastern, one, on the River Karakol, was previously known as Przheval'sk in 1889–1921 and 1939–91. It was founded in 1869 as a Russian military garrison and named after Major General Nikolay Przhevalsky (1839–88), a Russophile Pole (who Russianized his name from Przewalski) and an explorer famous for his travels throughout Central Asia on four expeditions in 1867–85. He died here, on his fifth journey, and was buried on the lakeshore. He discovered the breed of wild horse in western Mongolia in the 1870s known as Przewalski's horse. Located near Lake Issyk-

Kul, the cities' name means 'Black Lake' from *kara* 'black' and *köl* 'lake'.

Karakoram, CENTRAL ASIA
A mountain range that spreads over parts of Afghanistan, China, India, Pakistan, and Tajikistan and has a Turkic name meaning 'Black Mountain' from *kara* and *koram* 'mountain', a reference to their appearance.

Karakorum (Har Horin), MONGOLIA *Erdeni Dzu*
Ruins. Founded *c*.1220 as the ancient capital of the Mongol Empire, although it had been settled earlier than this. Despite being built in the midst of a huge grassy plain, the name means 'Black Boulder'; it has no connection with the *Karakoram Mountains which lie 1 500 miles (2 400 km) to the south-west. For a time during the 14th century the city was known as Erdeni Dzu, the Mongol name for Buddha, because Buddhism had spread during the reign of Khublai Khan (1260–94). After the collapse of the Mongol Empire at the end of the 14th century, Karakorum fell into decay and was abandoned.

Karakul', TAJIKISTAN, UZBEKISTAN
Spelt Qaraqol in Uzbek. The town in Tajikistan lies on Lake Karakul; all names have the meaning 'Black Lake'. Karakul has given its name to a sheep bred in Central Asia.

Kara-Kum (Garagum), TURKMENISTAN
A desert with a Turkic name meaning 'Black Sand' from *kara* and *kum* 'sand', a reference either to its severe climatic conditions or the fact that it is covered with quite varied vegetation.

Karaman, TURKEY *Larende*
Named after the Karamanids, a Turcoman tribe, who captured it from the Seljuk Turks in 1261 and developed it as the capital of their emirate, which was analogous to the Roman province of Karamania.

Kara Sea (Karskoye More), RUSSIA
A part of the Arctic Ocean which takes its name from the Kara River 'Black River'.

Karatau, KAZAKHSTAN
A mountain range with a Turkic name 'Black Mountain' from *kara* and *tau*, related to modern Turkish *dağ* 'mountain'. The name indicates that the range is not snow-covered throughout the year.

Karatsu, KYŪSHŪ/JAPAN
'China Port' from the Japanese word for China *Kara* and *zu* 'port'. The city was an important port for trade with China and Korea. It is said that the character for *kara* 'China' used to be *kan* 'Korea'.

k

Karbalā', IRAQ *Mashhad al-Husein*
It was given its original name 'Place where the Martyr Husayn ibn Ali died' when it became a place of pilgrimage. Husayn ibn Ali (626–80), a Shī'ite leader and the Prophet Muhammad's[†] grandson, was killed at the Battle of Karbalā' in 680 and buried here. The present name probably comes from the Aramaic Karbelā and Assyrian Karballatu, a kind of headdress.

Karelia (Russian: **Kareliya**; Finnish: **Karjala**), FINLAND-RUSSIA
The major part of the region forms a Russian republic, previously called Olonets Province after a dialect of the Karelian language, named after the Karelian people; a very small part lies in Finland. An independent Finnish state in medieval times, Eastern Karelia was acquired by Russia in 1323 and Western Karelia when Sweden relinquished it in 1721 at the end of the Great Northern War (1700–21). However, after the Bolshevik Revolution in Russia and Finland's declaration of independence in 1917, Western Karelia was awarded to Finland in 1920. In 1940 the greater part of Finnish Karelia was annexed by the Soviet Union after the Russo-Finnish War (1939–40) ended.

Karen, BURMA *Kawthulei*
A state named after the Karen people. In 1964–74 it was called by its traditional name Kawthulei 'Land of Flowers' and its inhabitants still use this name.

Kariba, ZIMBABWE
Founded in 1957 as a camp for workers building the Kariba Dam. The name may refer to the dam and mean 'Where the Waters have been trapped' or to the Kariba Gorge 'Where Animals have been trapped'. The building of the dam trapped thousands of wild animals which had to be relocated, and formed Lake Kariba.

Karl Liebknecht, KURSK/RUSSIA
Named after Karl Liebknecht (1871–1919), a German who founded the Spartacus League in 1916 which was transformed into the German Communist Party at the end of 1918.

Karl Marx Peak (Pik Karla Marksa),
TAJIKISTAN *Tsar's Peak*
A mountain renamed after Karl Marx (1818–83), a German political theorist and economist, after tsardom had been overthrown in 1917.

Karlobag, CROATIA *Vegium, Bag*
After destruction by the Turks in 1525, the town was restored in 1579 with 'Karlo', after Charles (Karl) (1540–90), Habsburg Archduke of Styria, being added to the existing name of Bag. Charles was appointed the first commander of the Military Frontier (in Serbo-Croat, *Vojna Krajina*), established in 1578 under direct Austrian control, against the Turks. Vegium was the name of the Roman settlement and in the Middle Ages this gave way to Bag.

Karlovac, CROATIA *Karlstadt*
A county and a town called 'Charles's Town'. It was founded as a fortress in 1579 to oppose the advancing Ottoman Turks and was named after the Habsburg Archduke Charles of Styria. It became one of the three generalates of the Military Frontier. *See* KARLOBAG.

Karlovo, BULGARIA *Levskigrad*
'(Town) of Karl'. This was Karl Ali-bey, a Turk who was given the town by Bayezid II, Ottoman Sultan (1481–1512). In 1953–62 the town was named Levski Town after Vasil Levski (1837–73) whose birthplace this was. His real name was Vasil Ivanov Kunchev; he was given the nickname Levski 'Lion-like' for his revolutionary activities against the Turks.

Karlovy Vary, CZECH REPUBLIC *Obora, Vary, Karlsbad*
'Charles's Spa' from the Czech *var* 'boiling' and German *Bad*. According to tradition, Charles (Karl) IV (1316–78) of Luxembourg, King of Germany (1346–78) and Holy Roman Emperor (1355–78), discovered the springs when a stag he was chasing leapt into one. His personal physician declared the springs to have healing properties and so Charles built a hunting lodge nearby from which the town developed. It was originally called Obora 'game park'. In 1396 it was named Vary, the plural of *var*, and in the 15th century Karlovy 'of Charles' was added.

Karlskrona, SWEDEN
'Charles's Crown'. Founded in 1679 by, and named after, Charles XI (1655–97), King of Sweden (1660–97).

Karlsruhe, GERMANY, USA
Germany (Baden-Württemberg): 'Charles's Retreat' from *Ruhe* 'peace' or 'rest'. Its development began when Karl III Wilhelm (d.1738), Margrave of Baden-Durlach, built a castle in 1715 close to his hunting lodge which was his retreat.

Karlstad, SWEDEN, USA
Sweden: originally Tingvalla after the *ting* (or *thing*), the local or provincial assembly of freemen, the highest decision-making authority. It was usually held in the open on raised ground: *valla* means 'mound'. In 1584 it was renamed 'Charles's Town' after Prince Charles (1550–1611), later Charles IX, King of Sweden (1604–11).

Karmi'él, ISRAEL
Founded in 1964 as 'Vineyard of God' in
Hebrew.

Karnāl, HARYĀNA/INDIA
Said to be named after its founder, Karṇa, a
warrior in the *Mahābhārata*, the epic Indian
poem.

Karnātaka, INDIA *Mysore*
A hilly state with an area of black soil in the
north-west conducive to cotton growing. The
name may mean 'High Land' in the local
Kannaḍa language and 'Land of Black Soils'
from Karnāta, itself from *kar* 'black' and *nāṭu*
'land' in Tamil. Until 1973 it was known as
Mysore.

Kärnten, AUSTRIA
See CARINTHIA.

Karoi, ZIMBABWE
'Little Witch', a reference to the local practice
of throwing witches into the nearby Angwa
River.

Karoo, NORTHERN CAPE/SOUTH AFRICA
The Great, Western, and Eastern Karoo are
vast sparsely populated regions with a name in
the Khoikhoin and San languages that means
'wasteland' or 'barren region' from *harrô* 'arid'
or 'parched'.

Karpinsk, YEKATERINBURG/RUSSIA *Bogoslovsk*
The original name was derived from the fact
that the church was dedicated to St John the
Evangelist from *bogoslov* 'theologian'. The city
was created from the settlements of Bogoslovsk
and Ugol'nye Kopi in 1941 when it took the
present name after Alexander Karpinsky (1846–
1936), a respected geologist who also had a
volcano in the Kuril Islands and a mountain in
the northern Urals named after him.

Kars, TURKEY
Named after the Kars River, although *kar*
means 'snow'; quite appropriate since winter
brings heavy snowfalls. Founded by the
Armenians, it flourished as the capital of an
Armenian principality during the 9th and 10th
centuries. It has changed hands many times,
being incorporated into the Ottoman Empire
in 1514 and being annexed by Russia in 1878;
the modern town was built largely by the
Russians. It was passed back to Turkey in 1920
when a Turkish Nationalist army captured it.

Karshi (Qarshi), UZBEKISTAN *Naksheb, Nesef,
Bek-Budi*
An ancient stop on the caravan route from
Samarkand to Afghanistan, it was renamed in
the 14th century after two fortified palaces
were built here by the Chagadai khans Kabak
and Kazanby. In Turkish *karsi* and in Uzbek

qarshi mean 'against' which can be taken here
to represent 'fort'. The name also means
'Palace' in Mongolian, a reference to the
palaces that were built here in the 14th
century for the Mongol ruler. The first name
was Sogdian and the second Arab. The
previous name was in use in 1926–37.

Kartuzy, POLAND
Named after the Carthusian monks who built
a monastery here.

Kashgar (Chinese: **Kashi**; Uighur: **Qashgar**),
SINKIANG UIGHUR AUTONOMOUS REGION/CHINA
Cascaro
Named after the River Kashgar. However, this
is a Turkic name meaning 'Hill of Jade' from
kaš 'jade' and *gar* 'rock' or 'stone'. An ancient
oasis city, it was occupied by the Turks,
Uighurs, Kara-Kitai, and the Mongols before
finally falling to the Chinese in 1755.
Kashgaria was an independent state in 1864–
77 founded by Muslims in Sinkiang who,
under the leadership of the Kokandian
adventurer Yaqub Beg (1827–77), rebelled
against the Chinese.

Kashihara, HONSHŪ/JAPAN
'Oak Field' from *kashi* or *kashiwa* 'oak (tree)' and
hara 'field'.

Kashiwa, HONSHŪ/JAPAN
'Oak (tree)'.

Kashiwara, HONSHŪ/JAPAN
'Oak (tree)' from *kashiwa* and *hara* 'field'.

Kashiwazaki, HONSHŪ/JAPAN
'Oak Cape' from *kashiwa* and *saki* 'cape'.

Kashmir, INDIA-PAKISTAN
Properly Jammu and Kashmir, both a region in
the north-west of the Indian subcontinent and
a state of India. According to legend, by means
of irrigation channels and other measures, an
ascetic named Kaśyapa reclaimed Kashmir
from a huge area of rivers, streams, and
marshes which became known as
Kaśyapamara 'Land of Kaśyapa' and, in due
course, Kashmir. Until 1346 it was ruled by
Hindus and in 1346–1819 by Muslims. It
became part of the Sikh Kingdom of Punjab in
1819 and of the Hindu Dogra princely state in
1846 until 1947. Although ruling a Muslim
majority state the Hindu maharaja, Hari Singh,
was undecided as to whether to join India or
Pakistan when faced with the choice when
British India was partitioned. While he
dithered, hoping even that Kashmir could
become an independent country, Pakistani
Pashtun tribesmen crossed into the state in
support of their fellow Muslims who had risen
in revolt. Indian troops were flown in and Hari

Singh agreed to join India. Kashmir was left divided where fighting stopped in 1948 and a UN-brokered ceasefire came into effect on 1 January 1949. In 1972 the Simla Agreement set out a 'line of control' (LOC) to separate Indian and Pakistani-administered areas of Jammu and Kashmir (*see* AZAD KASHMIR AND JAMMU). The Pakistani area, representing about a third of Jammu and Kashmir, is divided into the Northern Territories and Azad Kashmir. That part south of the LOC, roughly a half of the region, has been incorporated into the Indian state of Jammu and Kashmir. The Aksai Chin part of Kashmir, about a fifth, claimed by India, has been occupied by China since 1950. Both India and Pakistan maintain their claim on all the territory and the matter continues to defy resolution; the dispute has caused two of the three wars between India and Pakistan. Kashmir has given its name to 'cashmere', a fine, soft wool, or material made from it, from local goats. The weaving of this wool was introduced by a 15th-century ruler of Kashmir.

Kasimov, RYAZAN/RUSSIA *Gorodets/Gorodets Meschchersky*
A former khanate and city named after Kasim, son of Khan Ulugh Muhammad of Kazan. Kasim was driven out by his brother, fled to Moscow and entered the service of Vasily (Basil) II (1415–62), Grand Prince of Moscow (1425–62), who gave him the town of Gorodets which had been founded in 1152. It was given its present name in 1467 and means 'belonging to Kasim'. In 1152–1467 the name meant 'Town of the Meshcher', a local people, with *gorodets* 'little town'.

Kaspiysk, DAGESTAN/RUSSIA *Dvigatel'stroy*
Renamed 'Caspian (Town)' from *kaspiyskiy* 'Caspian'. Its original name indicated its association with engineering from *dvigatel'* 'engine' or 'motor' and *stroyka* 'building' or 'construction'.

Kassel, HESSE/GERMANY *Chassala/Casle*
A district and a city with a name derived from the Latin *castellum* 'fortress' or 'stronghold', specifically after an imperial castle built in the 9th century. It was the capital of the short-lived Kingdom of Westphalia (1807–13).

Kasserine (al-Qaṣrayn), TUNISIA *Cillium*
'The Two Palaces', a reference to the two Roman mausoleums, whose ruins can still be seen. Cillium was the Roman name; its surviving ruins may also be seen.

Kasson, MINNESOTA/USA
A Native American word meaning 'to consume'.

Kaštel, CROATIA
The collective name for a group of seven settlements, each of which developed around a *kaštel* 'castle' built in the 15th and 16th centuries in defence against the Ottoman Turks.

Kastoría, GREECE *Celetrum, Justinianopolis, Kesriye*
Captured by the Romans in 200 BC, it was renamed the 'City of Justinian', probably after Justinian I[†] in the 6th century. It was held by the Serbs in the 14th century and by the Ottoman Turks in 1385–1912 as Kesriye. Becoming part of Greece then, it was renamed in recognition of the beavers (in Greek, *kastor*) which were an important part of the local fur trade.

Kasūr, PUNJAB/PAKISTAN
According to tradition, it was founded by, and named after, Kuśa, son of Rāma, the legendary Hindu deity.

Katahdin, Mt, MAINE/USA
Taken from an Algonquian (Abnaki) word meaning 'Main Mountain'.

Katanga, DEMOCRATIC REPUBLIC OF THE CONGO *Shaba*
A province, which until 1971 was called Katanga from a Hausa word for 'ramparts', alluding to an ancient capital. This then was changed to Shaba, a Swahili word for 'copper'; appropriate, given that the province contains most of the country's copper and other minerals. The name was changed back to Katanga in 1997. Under Belgian rule from 1885, the province seceded from the newly independent Congo in 1960, but was reincorporated in 1963.

Katanning, WESTERN AUSTRALIA/AUSTRALIA
Settled in 1898, the name is said to come from the Aboriginal word *kartannin* 'meeting place'.

Katherine, NORTHERN TERRITORY/AUSTRALIA
Named after the River Katherine which itself was given its name in 1862 by John McDouall Stuart, a Scottish explorer who travelled across the continent from south to north that year, after the daughter of a friend.

Kāthmāndu, NEPAL *Manju-Patan, Kantipur*
Founded in 723 by King Gunakamadeva and later named Kantipur 'Beautiful Town' from *kānti* 'beauty' and *pur*. At the end of the 16th century a wooden temple is alleged to have been built from the wood of a single tree; this temple, called the Kasthamandap Temple, gave the town its name 'Wooden Temple' from *kāṭh* 'wood' and *mandir* 'temple' or *mandap* 'pavilion'. It may, however, have been

built some centuries earlier. Kāthmāndu has
been the capital of Nepal since 1768.

Katonah, NEW YORK/USA
Named after a local Native American chief
whose name meant 'poorly' or 'sickly'.

Katoomba, NEW SOUTH WALES/AUSTRALIA *The
Crushers*
Nearby falls, 800 ft (244m) high, give the town
its name from an Aboriginal word for
'waterfall'.

Katowice, POLAND *Kattowitz, Stalinogród*
The town became Polish in 1922 as a result of a
plebiscite in German Upper Silesia when many
communes voted to join Poland. The name is
derived from a Slavonic root word *kot* 'cat'. It
was renamed Stalinogród 'Stalin's[†] Town' two
days after his death on 5 March 1953; it
retained this name until the overthrow of the
Stalinist regime in Poland in 1956.

Katsina, NIGERIA
A former kingdom and emirate, and now a
state and a town founded *c*.1100. They are
named after Kacinna, a princess of Daura and
the wife of Janzama, a local king at the time.

Kattegat, DENMARK-SWEDEN
A strait between Denmark and Sweden with
an Old Scandinavian name from *kati* 'boat' and
gata 'strait' or 'passage'. It is, however, also
translated as 'Cat's Throat'.

Kaunas, LITHUANIA *Kowno/Kovno*
Founded as a fortress in 1030, it passed to
Russia in 1795 at the third partition of Poland,
Lithuania and Poland having amalgamated in
1569. It was the provisional capital of
Lithuania in 1920–40 while Vilnius was
occupied by the Poles. The meaning of its
name is not known for certain, but may
come from the Slavonic *kovati* 'to forge' or
from a Gothic word meaning 'humble'
or 'passive'.

Kaura Namoda, SOKOTO/NIGERIA
Named after a Fulani warlord, Namoda, who
was appointed King of Zamfara. The town was
later given the additional title of Kaura
'warlord'.

Kavála, GREECE *Neapolis, Christoupolis*
Also spelt Kaválla. 'On Horseback', a reference
to the site as a relay station for changing
horses. In Roman times it was known as 'New
Town' and by the Byzantines as 'Town of
Christ' when a bishopric was established here.
It was held by the Ottoman Turks in 1387–
1912 when it became Greek.

Kawaguchi, HONSHŪ/JAPAN
Situated at the mouth of a small tributary of
the Ara River, the name means 'River Mouth'
from *kawa* and *kuchi* 'mouth'.

Kawaihae, HAWAII/USA
'Water of Anger', a reference to an occasion
when local people came to blows over drawing
water from a pool.

Kawanishi, HONSHŪ/JAPAN
Situated on the west bank of the Ina River, the
name is an amalgamation of *kawa* and *nishi*
'west'.

Kawartha Lakes, ONTARIO/CANADA
A Huron word meaning 'Bright Waters and
Happy Lands'.

Kawasaki, HONSHŪ/JAPAN
'River Cape' from *kawa* and *saki* 'cape'. It lies on
Tokyo Bay.

Kawthoung, BURMA *Victoria Point*
Lying opposite Thailand, the present name is
derived from *thai ko sawng* 'second island'. The
former name honoured Queen Victoria[†].

Kayah, BURMA
A state named after the Kayah people who are
also known as Karenni.

Kaynardzha, BULGARIA *Küçük Kaynarca*
The present name is derived from the previous
Turkish name which meant 'Little Hot Spring'
from *küçük* 'little' and *kaynarca* 'hot spring'.

Kayseri, TURKEY *Mazarca, Eusebia, Caesarea
Cappadociae, Kaisariyah*
The original name was changed to Eusebia
after Ariarathes V Eusebes, King of Cappadocia
(163–130 BC). It was changed again by
Archelaus (d. 17), last King of Cappadocia (36
BC–AD 14) and a Roman puppet, to Caesarea (in
Cappadocia, to distinguish it from other cities
with the same name) in honour of Caesar
Augustus[†]. When the Arabs arrived they
amended the name to Kaisariyah and this
became Kayseri when the Seljuk Turks took
control *c*.1080. It was annexed to the Ottoman
Empire in 1515.

Kazakhstan *Kirgizstan*
The Republic of Kazakhstan (Qazaqstan
Respūblīkasy) since 1991 when independence
was forced upon the Soviet Central Asian
republics. Previously part of the Soviet Union
as the Kazakh Soviet Socialist Republic after it
was carved out of the Russian Soviet Federative
Socialist Republic (1936); the Kazakh
Autonomous Soviet Socialist Republic (1925–
36); the Kirgiz Autonomous Soviet Socialist
Republic in what is now northern Kazakhstan
while southern Kazakhstan became part of the

Turkestan Autonomous Soviet Socialist Republic (1920); part of Russian Turkestan after the Russians had slowly advanced southwards into the Kazakh steppe during the 18th century after the Kazakh Hordes (Great, Middle, and Little) had turned to Russia for protection from the Oyrat Mongols. By 1848 the territory of the three Hordes had been subsumed into the Russian Empire. Until 1926 the Russians called the Kazakhs Kirgiz or Kirgiz-Kazakhs to distinguish them from the Cossacks, both words being of Turkic origin and sounding very similar in Russian. The present name means the 'Land of the Kazakhs' from *stan* and the Turkic *kazak* (*qazaq* or *quzzaq*) 'Horsemen' or 'Riders of the Steppe'. However, *kazak* is more commonly translated as 'adventurer', 'outlaw', 'raider', or 'free, or independent, man'. The Kazakhs were originally Uzbeks who received their name because of their nomadic lifestyle. They wore long cloaks which came to be called cassocks in English from *kazak*, now more commonly used to describe a priest's gown. The Kazakhs have no ethnic connection with the Cossacks (*Kazaki*) although the translation of 'adventurer', etc., applies.

Kazalinsk, KAZAKHSTAN
'Place of the Goose' from *kaz* 'goose' and the possessive suffix -*ly*.

Kazan', TATARSTAN REPUBLIC/RUSSIA
Founded in the late 13th century by the Tatars, the name may possibly be taken from the Turkish *kazan* 'cauldron', a reference to the strong currents in the River Kazanka. It was at one time located some 28 miles (45 km) up the Kazanka, but was transferred to a spot where that river meets the River Volga at the end of the 14th century. Having been the capital of the Tatar Kazan khanate, which was formed in 1436 from the Golden Horde, since 1445, it was captured and annexed by the Russians in 1552.

Kazanlŭk, BULGARIA *Seuthopolis*
The name, meaning 'cauldron', from the Turkish *kazan*, recognizes the fact that the town lies in a basin. It was ceded to Bulgaria by Russia in 1877 after it had been captured from the Ottoman Turks.

Kazbegi (Qazbegi), GEORGIA
Named after Alexander Kazbegi (1848–93), a local noble who became a famous poet and whose home town this was.

Kazbek, Mt (Mqinvartsveri) GEORGIA *Stepantsminda*
Named after Kazbegi (see previous entry). Originally it was 'St Stephen'. The Georgian name means 'Glacier Mountain' from *mqinvari* 'glacier' and *tsveri* 'mountain'.

Kazimierz Dolny, POLAND
Named after Kazimierz (Casimir) III the Great (1310–70), the last Piast King of Poland (1333–70). *Dolny* 'lower' distinguishes it from Kazimierz, now a part of Cracow.

Keady (An Céide), NORTHERN IRELAND/UK *An Chéideadh*
'Flat-topped Hill'.

Kearney, CANADA, USA
USA (Nebraska): named after Fort Kearney which itself was named after General Stephen W. Kearny (1794–1848), who won New Mexico for the USA.

Kebnekaise, SWEDEN
A mountain range with a Lapp name meaning 'Kettle Top'.

Kecskemét, HUNGARY
In a farming area, the name is derived from *kecske* 'goat'.

Keele, CANADA, UK
UK (England): formerly Kiel. 'Hill where Cows graze' from the Old English *cȳ* 'cow' and *hyll*.

Keeling Islands *See* COCOS ISLANDS.

Keelung, TAIWAN
See JILONG.

Keene, USA
New Hampshire: originally Upper Ashuelot but abandoned because of Native American raids. It was moved and resettled in 1746–50, and named after Sir Benjamin Keene (1697–1757), British consul in Madrid (1724–39) and ambassador to Portugal (from 1746).

Keetmanshoop, NAMIBIA *NuGoeis, Swartmodder*
The Afrikaans name Swartmodder 'Black Mud' from *swart* 'black', adopted in 1810, had the same meaning as the original Khoikhoin name. When a German Lutheran mission station was founded here in 1866, it was named after Johann Keetman, a German industrialist who helped to establish it. The Afrikaans *hoop* 'hope' is quite common for names of mission stations.

Keewatin, CANADA, USA
Canada (Northwest Territories): a region in the south with a Cree name meaning '(People of) the North Wind'. There is also a town with this name in Ontario and one in Minnesota, USA.

Keflavík, ICELAND
'Bay of Sticks' from *kefli* 'stick', *kefla* being the genitive plural, and *vík* 'bay', supposedly a reference to the debris found in the water.

Keighley, ENGLAND/UK *Chichelai, Kikeleia*
'Cyhha's Clearing' from an Old English personal name and *lēah* 'woodland clearing' or 'glade'.

Keimoes, NORTHERN CAPE/SOUTH AFRICA
Possibly 'Great Fountain' from the Khoikhoin *gei* 'great' and *mŭs* 'fountain'. However, it is also said to mean 'Mouse's Nest' after the discovery of colonies of tree mice in the vegetation along the Orange River.

Kelantan, MALAYSIA
A state with a name meaning 'Land of the Jujube Tree' from *koli* 'jujube' and *tanah* 'land'. Under Javanese control from the 14th century, in 1780–1909 it was a vassal state of Thailand which temporarily annexed it in 1942–5.

Kellogg, IDAHO/USA *Milo*
Originally created as a camp for prospectors in 1893, it was renamed a year later after Noah S. Kellogg, who had discovered the lead mine called Bunker Hill Mine.

Kells, IRELAND, UK
1. Ireland (Meath): locally Ceanannas 'Great Residence'.
2. Ireland (Kilkenny): locally Cealla 'Churches'.
3. UK (Northern Ireland): Irish Na Cealla 'Monastic Churches'.

Kelowna, BRITISH COLUMBIA/CANADA
'Grizzly Bear', a corruption from a local Native American word.

Kelso, NEW ZEALAND, SOUTH AFRICA, UK, USA
UK (Scotland): formerly Calkou and Calcehou 'Chalk Hill Spur' from the Old English *calc* 'chalk' and *hōh* 'hill spur'. The towns in the other countries were probably named by Scotsmen who emigrated from or near to Kelso.

Kemerovo, RUSSIA *Shcheglovsk*
A province and a city founded in the 1830s. In 1918 the village of Kemerovo united with the village of Shcheglovo to form the city of Shcheglovsk. This name remained in use until 1932 when Kemerovo was readopted. This comes from the Turkish *kemer* 'fort'.

Kempsey, AUSTRALIA, UK
1. Australia (New South Wales): settled in 1836 and named after the Valley of Kempsey on the River Severn in England, the original home of some of the settlers.
2. UK (England): formerly Kemesei and Chemesege 'Dry Ground in a marshy Area belonging to a Man called Cymi' from an Old English personal name and *ēg* 'dry ground in marsh' or 'ground surrounded by water'.

Kempten, BAVARIA/GERMANY *Cambodunum*
Evolved from its Celtic name meaning 'Fortress at the Bend (in the River)' from *cambo* 'curved' and *dunum*.

Kendal, CANADA, UK
UK (England): formerly Cherchebi, Kircabikendala, and Kendale 'Village with a Church in the) Valley of the (River) Kent'. The original name was Kirkby, meaning 'Village with a Church' from the Old Scandinavian *kirkju* 'church' and *bý* 'village'. Kendal from the *Kent* River and *dal* 'valley' was added to distinguish it from other towns called Kirkby. This part of the name was later dropped to leave just Kendal.

Kengtung, BURMA *Tungkalasi, Kyaingtong*
'Walled City of Tung'. According to legend, Tungkalasi, a hermit, founded a city-state here.

Kenilworth, UK, USA
UK (England): formerly Chinewrde and Chenildeworda 'Enclosure of a Woman called Cynehild' from an Old English personal name and *worth* 'enclosure' or 'enclosed settlement'.

Kenitra (Mina Hassan Tani), MOROCCO *Port Lyautey*
Founded by the French in 1913 on the site of a small fort called Kenitra, it was later given the name of Port Lyautey after Marshal of France Louis-Hubert-Gonzalve Lyautey (1854–1934), who established the French protectorate over Morocco in 1912, became governor, and who ordered the port-city to be built in 1913. The original and present name, which it readopted in about 1958, means 'Little Fort', a diminutive of the Arabic (*al-*) *kantara* 'bridge'.

Kennebec, MAINE/USA
A river with an Algonquian name meaning 'Long Reach' or 'Long Lake' to describe that part below Augusta.

Kennebunkport, MAINE/USA *Arundel*
Although settled in 1629, it only received the name Arundel in 1717. It was renamed in 1821 from a Native American word said to mean 'Long Water Place' or 'Long Beach'.

Kenner, LOUISIANA/USA
Named after Duncan F. Kenner, an eminent Louisiana state lawyer.

Kenora, ONTARIO/CANADA *Rat Portage*
Derived from the first two letters of its sister town, Keewatin, and of the nearby Norman, and its original name of Rat Portage; the latter was adopted because of the movement of

muskrats between the Lake of the Woods and the Winnipeg River.

Kenosha, WISCONSIN/USA *Pike Creek, Southport*
Founded in 1835 and in 1850 given its present name, a Potawatomi word for 'fish', 'pike', or 'pickerel'.

Kensington, CANADA, UK, USA
1. UK (England): formerly Chenesitun 'Manor, or Estate, belonging to Cynesige' from an Old English personal name, *-ing-* and *tūn*.
2. USA-Canada: four cities in the USA and one on Prince Edward Island, Canada, originally Barretts Cross, are named after the royal borough in Greater London.

Kent, CANADA, UK, USA
1. UK (England): a county, originally Cantium, named after the Cantii who probably took their name from the Celtic *cant* 'edge' or 'rim', to refer to land on the water's edge, thus a coastal district, or it may mean 'Land of the Hosts, or Armies'. Kent became one of the seven Anglo-Saxon kingdoms.
2. USA (Ohio): settled *c.*1805 as Riedsburg, it was subsequently renamed Franklin Mills. In 1867 it was given its present name after Marvin Kent, a leading supporter of the Atlantic and Great Western Railroad.

Kentau, KAZAKHSTAN
The result of the unification of several villages in 1955 in the Karatau Mountains, the name means 'Ore Mountains' in Kazakh.

Kentucky, AUSTRALIA, USA
USA: a state. After penetration by Daniel Boone (1734–1820), the frontiersman and adventurer, in 1769, settlement followed rapidly. In 1776 Kentucky County was created as part of Virginia, but in 1792 it joined the Union as the 15th state. The name is a Wyandotte word for 'meadowland' or 'prairie', although it has been suggested that it means 'dark and bloody ground'.

Kentville, NOVA SCOTIA/CANADA *Horton Corner*
Settled *c.*1860, it was renamed in 1826 after the Prince Edward (1767–1820), Duke of Kent, a son of King George III[†].

Kenya The Republic of Kenya (Swahili: Jamhuri ya Kenya) since 1964, although Kenya had gained its independence a year earlier in 1963. Previously British East Africa as the Colony of Kenya (1920), a British crown colony, with a coastal strip of land leased from the Sultan of Zanzibar known as the Kenya Protectorate. This strip was ceded to Kenya on independence in 1963, having been held by the Imam (later Sultan) of Oman since the 17th century. In 1895 the region became part of the British East Africa Protectorate. The name is taken from the country's highest mountain, Mt Kenya, which is a shortened version of its Kikuyu name, Kirinyaga, a corruption of the Swahili *kere nyaga* 'Mountain of Whiteness'. This is a reference to its permanent covering of snow.

Keokuk, IOWA/USA
Settled in 1836, it was named after a Sauk chief, Keokuk. His name meant 'Running Fox' or 'Watchful Fox'.

Keosauqua, IOWA/USA
'Great Bend', a Native American word describing the bend in the Des Moines River.

Keota, IOWA/USA
A Native American word meaning either 'gone to visit' or 'the fire has gone out'.

Keppel Bay, QUEENSLAND/AUSTRALIA
Discovered in 1770 by Captain James Cook[†] who named it after Rear Admiral Augustus Keppel (1725–86), 1st Viscount Keppel, 1st lord of the Admiralty (1782–3).

Kerala, INDIA *Keralaputra, Travancore-Cochin*
A state created in 1956 when Malabar was added to Travancore-Cochin, both princely states in their time. The name probably comes from the Tamil *keralam* 'mountain range', a reference to the Western Ghāts which cut the state off from the interior.

Kerang, VICTORIA/AUSTRALIA
Settled in 1857, the name comes from an Aboriginal word meaning 'cockatoo' or 'moon'.

Kerch', UKRAINE *Panticapaion (Greek)/ Panticapaeum (Latin), Korchev*
A peninsula and city-port founded by the Greeks in the 6th century BC. It was the chief city of the Kingdom of the Bosporus and was later absorbed into the Roman Empire. Ceded by the Tatars to the Genoese in 1318, it was renamed Korchev from which the present name is derived. This name may have been chosen because of the iron mines in the area, *krch* being a Slavonic root word meaning 'metal worker'. The city passed to the Turks in 1475 and to the Russians in 1771. When the Crimea was transferred by the Soviet authorities to Ukraine in 1954, Kerch became Ukrainian.

Kerguelen Islands A group of islands in the Indian Ocean, they are named after a French navigator, Yves-Joseph de Kerguélen-Trémarec, who discovered them in 1772. The largest island, Kerguelen, is also called Desolation Island, as named by Captain James Cook[†] when he saw it four years later.

Kermadec Islands, NEW ZEALAND
Some of the islands were discovered by British
sailors in 1788 and others in 1793 by the
French navigator, Joseph Bruni
d'Entrecasteaux (1737–93), who named the
whole group after his first officer, Jean de
Kermadec.

Kerman, IRAN, USA *Behdesīr (Iran)*
Iran: a province and an ancient city founded in
the 3rd century. It is named after the Karmani,
a people who lived in the region.

Kermānshāh, IRAN *Kirmīsīn, Bākhtarān*
A province and a city founded in 390 by
Bahrām IV who was governor of the province
of Kermān before he came to the Sāssānian
throne (388–99). He named it the '(City of the)
King of Kermān'. The name was changed from
Kermānshāh to Bākhtarān after the 1979
revolution because of the alleged distaste of
the Iranian people for the title 'shah'. It was
admitted a decade later, however, that the
ancient name had no connection with the
overthrown Pahlavi dynasty. Kermānshāh is
now back in favour and it remains capital
of the province of Kermānshāhān. Bākhtarān
was named after the Bakhtiari tribe, the
name itself meaning 'Bearer of Good
Fortune'.

Kerry (Ciarraí), IRELAND *Clar na Cliabh, Ciarraige*
A county whose name is derived from the
Ciarrai, the people of Ciarraige 'Kingdom of
Ciar', son of King Fergus, legendary King of
Ulster in the first millennium AD. At this time the area was
known as Clar na Cliabh 'The Plain of Swords',
but by the 6th century it had become
Ciarraige.

Keshena, WISCONSIN/USA
Named after a Native American chief whose
name meant 'Swift Flying'.

Keswick, CANADA, UK
UK (Cumbria/England): formerly Kesewic, a
Scandinavian version of Cēsewīc 'Cheese
Farm', thus a farm where cheese is made, from
the Old English *cēse* 'cheese' but with a
Scandinavian *k*, and *wīc*.

Ketchikan, ALASKA/USA
'Spread Wings of a Prostrate Eagle' from a
Tlingit name, Kach Kanna.

Kętrzyn, POLAND *Rastembork/Rastenburg*
The previous German name means 'Fort of
Repose' from *Rast* 'resting place' or 'repose'
and *Burg*. In 1946 the name was changed to
honour the Polish historian Władisław
Kętrzynski (1838–1918).

Kettering, UK, USA
1. UK (England): formerly Cytringan and
Cateringe '(Settlement of) the Followers of
Cytra' from a supposed Old English personal
name and *-ingas*.
2. USA (Ohio): settled in 1841 as Van
Buren Township after Martin Van Buren
(1782–1862), President of the USA (1837–41).
It was renamed in 1952 after Charles F.
Kettering (1876–1958), an inventive engineer.

Kewanee, ILLINOIS/USA *Berriam*
Founded in 1854, it was subsequently given a
Native American name meaning 'prairie
chicken'.

Key West, FLORIDA/USA
Said to be an English version of the Spanish
Cayo Hueso 'Bone Islet' from *cayo* 'key' or 'islet'
and *hueso* 'bone', a consequence of Spanish
explorers discovering human bones in the
area. Equally plausible, however, is that the
name comes from the Spanish *cayo oeste*
'western islet' since it is at the western end of
the Florida Keys.

Khabarovsk, RUSSIA *Khabarovka*
A territory and a city founded as a military post
in 1858 by, and named after, Yerofey Khabarov
(*c*.1610–*c*.1667), a Russian explorer who
penetrated Siberia, reaching the Amur River in
1650 and travelling down it to beyond the
mouth of the Ussuri River in 1651–3.
Designated a city in 1880, it was renamed
Khabarovsk in 1893.

Khābūr River (Arabic: **Nahr al-Khābūr**;
Turkish: **Habur Nehri**), TURKEY-SYRIA
'Source of Fertility'. It rises in south-east
Turkey and joins the Euphrates in Syria.

Khakasiya, RUSSIA *Khakassia*
A republic, formerly the province of
Khakassia, named after its indigenous
inhabitants, a Siberian Turkic people, the
Khakass, whose name means 'person' from
khas.

Khamīs Mushayṭ, SAUDI ARABIA
A trading centre, the name means 'Thursday
Mushayṭ' to indicate the Thursday markets of
the Mushayṭ people.

Khanābād, AFGHANISTAN, IRAN, UZBEKISTAN
Sovetabad (Uzbekistan)
'Khan's City' from *khan* and *ābād*.

Khankendy, AZERBAIJAN
See XANKÄNDI.

Khanty-Mansi, RUSSIA *Khantia-Mansia*
A national district established in 1930 for the
Khant and Mansi peoples which became
autonomous in 1977.

Khanty-Mansisyk, KHANTY-MANSI/RUSSIA
Ostyako-Vogulsk
Named after the Khant and Mansi peoples. The
name was changed in 1940, the previous one
using the alternative names for the Khant,
Ostyak, and for the Mansi, Vogul.

Khārijah, al-, EGYPT *Kenem, Hibis*
A town with a name derived from the group of
oases in which it lies from *al-Wāḥāt al-Khārijah*
'the outer oases' from *wāḥāt* 'oases', the plural
of *wāḥa* 'oasis' and *khārijah*, the plural of *khārij*
'outer'. The 'outer' refers to the fact that this
group of oases is to the east of the 'inner'
Dakhla Oasis, *al-Wāḥāt al-Dakhla* or *al-Wāḥāt ad-
Dākhilah*. The town is also known as el-Khārga.
See DAKHLA.

Khar'kov (Kharkiv), UKRAINE
A province and a city thought to be derived
from the name of its Cossack founder, one
Kharko, who built a military fort here in 1656.
It was the capital of Soviet Ukraine in 1917–34.

Khartoum (al-Khurṭūm), THE SUDAN *Halfaya*
The full name is Ra's al-Khurṭūm 'End of the
(Elephant's) Trunk' from the Arabic *ra's*
'headland', *al-*, and *khurṭūm* 'trunk'; the Arabic
for 'elephant' is *fil*. This is a rather inaccurate
description of the strip of land betweeen the
Blue and White Nile Rivers on which the first
Egyptian Turkish military camp was founded
in 1821. One of the areas of the camp was
known by its *khartoum*, a rocky outcrop, and
the Turks adopted this name for their town.
Khartoum was the capital of the Anglo-
Egyptian Sudan between 1898 and 1956 when
it became the capital of The Sudan when
independence was achieved. On the east bank
of the Nile lies Khartoum North, a sister city.

Khaskovo, BULGARIA *Haskoy*
Founded by the Ottoman Turks in about 1385
with a name meaning 'Sultan's Village'. In due
course the *-koy* evolved into the Slavonic *-ovo*,
indicating possession.

Kherson, UKRAINE *Chersonesos, Korsun, Korsun-
Shevchenkovsky*
A province and a city. Settled by the Greeks in
the 5th century BC, Chersonesos means
'peninsula' from *khersos* 'dry land' and *nēsos*
'island'; at that time it referred to the whole of
the Crimea. It subsequently gave its shortened
name to the port which lies some 15 miles
(24 km) from the mouth of the Lower Dnieper
River and is not in the Crimea. The modern
city was founded in 1778 as a fortress to help
defend the coast, recently acquired by Russia.
The original ruins of Chersonesos lie some 3
miles (5 km) west of Sevastopol in the Crimea.
Shevchenkovsky was added in 1944 after Taras

Shevchenko (1814–61), Ukraine's most famous
poet.

Khisarya, BULGARIA *Augusta, Toplitsa,
Diocletianopolis*
First named after Caesar Augustus[†]. It was
called the 'City of Diocletian' after
Diocletian (245–316), Roman emperor
(284–305), by the Byzantines. The present
name is derived from the Turkish word *hisar*
'fortress'.

Khiva, UZBEKISTAN *Khwārezm*
An ancient city which takes its name from that
of an ancient well, known as Khejvak or
Khivak, a name it retained until the 18th
century. It was the capital of the former
Khanate of Khiva in 1512–1920. Taken by the
Russians in 1873, the khanate was abolished in
1920 and became the Khwārezm (or Khorezm)
People's Soviet Republic; and in 1921 the
Soviet Socialist Republic of Khwārezm. It was
incorporated into the Soviet Republic of
Uzbekistan in 1924. Khwārezm may mean
'Lowlands' from the Persian *zamin* 'land' and
khwar 'low' or 'abject', or 'Land of the
Rising Sun' from *khūrshīd* 'sun'. The
khanate lay along the Amu Darya (ancient
Oxus) River in what is now Turkmenistan
and Uzbekistan.

Khmel'nyts'kyy, UKRAINE *Ploskurov/Ploskyriv,
Prokuriv/Proskurov*
A province and a city founded as a Polish fort
in the 15th century and named after the River
Ploskaya from *ploskii* 'flat'. It was renamed
Proskurov when ceded to Russia at the second
partition of Poland in 1793. The city was
renamed again after the great Cossack leader
Bohdan Khmel'nyts'kyy (*c*.1595–1657),
Hetman of Ukraine (1648–57), who had
organized an uprising against the Poles, in
1954, the tercentenary of the transfer of
Ukraine east of the Dnieper River from Polish
to Russian control under the Pereyaslav
Agreement in 1654. A Russian military order,
the Order of Bogdan Khmelnitsky, was
inaugurated for outstanding military merit in
1943. The province of Khmelnytskyy was
known as Kamenets-Podolsky (also the name
of a city, now Kam'yanets'-Podil's'kyy) until
1954.

Khodzhent, TAJIKISTAN
See KHUDZHAND.

Kholm, AFGHANISTAN, RUSSIA
1. Afghanistan: the former Afghan name of
Tashkurgān, also spell Taxkorgan, meant
'Stone Tower' or 'Stone City' from the Turkic
tash 'stone'.
2. Russia (Novgorod): 'Hill'.

Khomeynishahr, IRAN *Homāyūnshahr*
'City of Khomeyni' from *shahr* and named in
honour of the Ayatollah Khomeyni (*c.*1900–
89), who precipitated the overthrow of the
Shah in 1979 and who took his name from his
home town of Khomeyn.

Khoni, GEORGIA *Tsulukidze*
Founded as the city of Khoni in 1921, it was
renamed in 1936 after Alexander Tsulukidze
(1876–1905), a literary scholar and Bolshevik
political agitator, who was born and buried
here. It readopted its original name, whose
meaning is unknown, in 1991.

Khon Kaen, THAILAND
'Heartwood Log' from *khon* 'wood' or 'log' and
kaen 'core' or 'heart'. The city is named after
Phra That Kham Kaen, a nearby *chedi* (a
monument that houses a Buddha relic).
According to legend, such a monument was
built over a tamarind tree. It came to life after
some monks taking Buddha relics to Phra That
Phanom camped here overnight. Phra That
Phanom could take no more relics so the
monks returned here and built a *chedi* named
That Kham Kaen 'Tamarind Heartwood
Reliquary' for them. Eventually a town
developed, but it was not until 1789 that it was
named Kham Kaen after the *chedi*. This evolved
into the present name.

Khorāsān, IRAN
A province in Iran and a historical region
encompassing north-east Iran, southern
Turkmenistan, and northern Afghanistan. It
was first named by the Sāssānians in about the
3rd century BC; they divided their empire into
four quarters which they named after the four
cardinal points. Khorāsān means 'Land of the
Sun' from the Persian *khawr* 'sun' and *āsān* 'to
appear'.

Khorog, TAJIKISTAN
'Settlement' from a local word *kharag*.

Khorramābād, IRAN
Two cities have this name which means 'Place
of Joy' from *khorram* 'glad' or 'joyful' and *ābād*.
Khorram can also mean 'green' or 'fresh' and is
much used to describe particularly pleasant
places.

Khorramshahr, IRAN *Muhammerah*
A very ancient city-port, it was named after the
Prophet Muhammad[†], possibly during the 8th
century. It was renamed in 1924 to mean 'City
of Joy' from *khorram* 'glad' or 'joyful' and *shahr*.

Khost, AFGHANISTAN, PAKISTAN
Also spelt Khowst in Afghanistan. The name is
probably a Persian version of *hwastu* from the
Sanskrit *suvastu* 'good site'.

Khubar, al-, SAUDI ARABIA
The plural of the Arabic *khabrā* 'a small pond
formed by rain'. It was founded in about 1923
by settlers from Bahrain.

Khudzhand (Khujand), TAJIKISTAN *Alexandreia
Eskhata, Khudzhand/Khodzhent, Leninabad*
A very ancient city on the Silk Route, it was
founded as a forward military base by ·
Alexander III the Great[†] in 329 BC and named
after him with the Greek *eskhatos* 'furthermost'
added to signify that this city was the most
distant of all the cities in his empire, more
than 30, that were named after him. Before the
Arabs arrived in the 7th century the name had
become Khudzhand. The city was captured by
the Russians in 1866 and given the Russian
version of the name, Khodzhent. In 1936 it was
renamed Leninabad 'Lenin's Town' after
Vladimir Lenin[†]. It was transferred from
Uzbekistan to Tajikistan in 1929. Following a
local referendum, it reverted to its pre-1936
Tajik name in 1991; the former province of
Leninabad retained its name, as Leninobod, for
a while before becoming Khudzhand and now
Sughd.

Khuldabad, MAHĀRĀSHTRA/INDIA
Named after Aurangzeb (1618–1707), Mughal
emperor (1658–1707), who was buried here in
1707 and given the posthumous name
Khuldmakān 'He whose abode is eternity'.

Khūzestān, IRAN *Susiana, 'Arabestān*
A province. It was named Susiana after its
capital, Sūsa, in the 3rd century BC. It was
occupied by the Arabs from *c.*640 and renamed
the 'Land of the Arabs'. The present name
means 'Land of the Khuz' with *stan*.

Kiamichi, OKLAHOMA/USA
A river and mountains with a name possibly
from a French word for a local bird, the horned
screamer.

Kickapoo, ILLINOIS/USA
Named after the Algonquian-speaking
Kickapoo tribe.

Kidderminster, ENGLAND/UK *Stour-in-Usmere,
Chideminstre, Kedeleministre*
'Cydela's Monastery' from an Old English
personal name and *mynster*, after land was
given in 731 by Aethelbald, King of Mercia
(716–57), for the purpose of building a
monastery here.

Kiel, GERMANY, USA *Kyle*
Germany (Schleswig-Holstein): 'Fjord',
possibly derived from the Anglo-Saxon *kille*
'safe haven for ships' or from *kyle* 'spring'. A
city-port, it was part of Denmark in 1773–1866
when it passed to Prussia.

k

Kielce, POLAND
Probably derived from a personal name such as Kielec from *kiel* 'fang' or 'tusk'. It was acquired by Austria at the third partition of Poland in 1795, but within twenty years had passed to Russia, which held it until 1918; it was then returned to Poland.

Kiev (Kyyiv), UKRAINE
According to legend, the city is named after the eldest of three eastern Slav brothers, Kiy, who, together with their sister, founded a city, in the 8th century, on the heights above the Dnieper River. The name may actually come from a Slavonic word for 'hill'. In 882 it became the capital of Kievan Rus', the historical heart of Russia, of Soviet Ukraine in 1934, and of Ukraine in 1991 after Ukrainian independence. It has been part of the Grand Duchy of Lithuania, Poland, and Russia. In a roundabout way it has given its name to Chicken Kiev: when the Hotel Kiev was opened in Moscow in 1957 a new chicken dish was served.

Kigali, RWANDA
Founded by the Germans at the end of the 19th century, the city, spread over four hills, is named after nearby Mt Kigali. The name comes from the Bantu prefix *ki-* and *gali* 'wide' or 'extended' in Rwandan, probably a reference to the size of the mountain. It became the capital when Rwanda achieved independence in 1962.

Kilauea, HAWAII/USA
An active volcano with a name meaning 'Much Discharging', a reference to its activity.

Kilbride, CANADA, UK
UK (Scotland): 'Church of St Bridget' from *cill* and the name of the saint who is thought to have died *c.*525.

Kildare (Cill Dara), IRELAND, USA
Ireland: a county and a town with a name meaning 'Church of, or near, the Oak' from *cill* and *doire* 'oak grove'.

Kilgore, TEXAS/USA
Settled in 1871 by, and named after, Judge C. B. Kilgore.

Kilimanjaro, Mt, TANZANIA
'Mountain of the God of Cold' from the Swahili *kilima* 'mountain' and *njaro* 'god of cold'. Although the highest mountain in Africa, it was not at first believed by Europeans to be snow-capped since it was so close to the equator.

Kilkenny (Cill Chainnigh), IRELAND
A county and town with a name meaning 'Church of St Canice (Kenneth)', an abbot

(*c.*525–*c.*600) who founded a monastery here, and others elsewhere, in the 6th century, from *cill* and the personal name.

Killarney, AUSTRALIA, CANADA, IRELAND, SOUTH AFRICA
1. Ireland: locally Cill Airne 'Church of the Sloes' from *cill* and *airne* 'sloe'.
2. Towns in the other countries testify to the presence of Irish immigrants.

Killbuck, OHIO/USA
Named after a chief of the Delaware tribe.

Killeen, TEXAS/USA
Laid out in 1882 and named after Frank P. Killeen, an engineer with the Santa Fe Railroad.

Killybegs (Na Cealla Beaga), IRELAND
Na cCealla mBicc
'The Small Churches' from *cill* and *beag* 'small'.

Kilmarnock, UK, USA
1. UK (Scotland): formerly Kelmernoke. 'Church of my little (St) Ernan' from *cill* and a modified version of the saint's name 'mo Ernanoc' 'my little Ernan' from the Gaelic *mo-* 'my' and *-oc* 'little' indicating a diminutive. Ernan, or Ernin, was a 6th-century monk from north Wales.
2. USA (Virginia): named after the town in Scotland.

Kilosa, TANZANIA
Derived from the local word *kirosa* 'Crossing Place', a reference to the bridge over the Wami River here.

Kimball, SOUTH DAKOTA/USA
Named after F. W. Kimball, chief engineer of the Chicago, Milwaukee, and St Paul Railroad.

Kimberley, CANADA, SOUTH AFRICA
1. Canada (British Columbia): founded in 1892 as Mark Creek Crossing, the city was renamed four years later after the town in South Africa.
2. South Africa (Northern Cape): founded originally as a camp in 1871 after the local discovery of diamonds. It was named after John Wodehouse (1862–1902), 1st Earl of Kimberley, British colonial secretary (1870–4).

Kimch'aek, NORTH KOREA *Sŏngjin*
A port-city which was renamed in 1952 after the death of Kim Ch'aek (1903–51), a political and military figure who commanded a front of the North Korean Army (Korean People's Army) during the Korean War (1950–3).

Kimovsk, TULA/RUSSIA *Mikhailovka*
Established as a town in 1952, it took its name from the acronym KIM, *Kommunisticheskiy*

Internatsional Molodëzhi 'Communist Youth International', an international communist youth movement that existed between 1919 and 1943 as part of the Comintern (Communist International) which was also founded in 1919.

Kinabalu, Mt, SABAH/MALAYSIA
See KOTA KINABALU.

Kinderhook, NEW YORK/USA
The Anglicized version of the Dutch *kinder hoeck* 'children's point', a reference to the many Native American children in the area.

Kingaroy, QUEENSLAND/AUSTRALIA *Kingaroy Paddock*
Founded in 1886, it takes its name from an Aboriginal word *kingerroy* 'red ant'.

Kingdom of the Two Sicilies A state in southern Italy and Sicily created in the 12th century as the Kingdom of Sicily and Apulia. Divided in 1282 between the French Angevin (mainland Italy) and Spanish Aragonese (Sicily) dynasties, the two areas were reunited as the Kingdom of the Two Sicilies in 1443 under Alfonso V (1396–1458), King of Aragon (1416–58) and King of Naples (1442–58) as Alfonso I. It was, however, commonly known as the Kingdom of Naples until 1815 when the title Kingdom of the Two Sicilies was officially adopted. It ceased to exist in 1860 during the movement to unite Italy.

King George, VIRGINIA/USA
Settled during the reign of King George I[†], it is named in his honour.

King George Sound, WESTERN AUSTRALIA/ AUSTRALIA *King George III Sound*
Charted and named by Captain George Vancouver[†] in 1791 after the reigning British king, George III[†].

Kingisepp, LENINGRAD/RUSSIA *Yam, Yamburg*
Founded as Yam after the Yam people in 1384, becoming Yamburg 'Fort of the Yam' in 1780. In 1922 it was renamed again after Viktor Kingisepp (1888–1922), Estonian leader of the Estonian Communist Party in 1918–22 when he was sentenced to death for his revolutionary activities. *See also* KURESSAARE.

King Island, AUSTRALIA, CANADA, USA
Australia (Tasmania): first sighted in 1798 and named in 1801 after Philip G. King, third governor of New South Wales. It was not settled, however, until 1855.

King Khālid Military City, SAUDI ARABIA
Built during the 1980s, it is named after Khālid ibn 'Abd Al-'Aziz As-Sa'ūd (1913–82), King of Saudi Arabia (1975–82).

King Leopold Ranges, WESTERN AUSTRALIA/ AUSTRALIA
Discovered in 1879 by Alexander Forrest who named the mountain chain after Leopold II (1835–1909), King of the Belgians (1865–1909).

Kingman, CANADA, USA
1. USA (Arizona): established in the 1880s and named after Lewis Kingman, a railroad engineer.
2. USA (Kansas): named after Chief Justice S. A. Kingman.
3. USA (Maine): named after R. S. Kingman.

King's Lynn, ENGLAND/UK *Lynn Escopi*
Renamed in 1537 by Henry VIII (1491–1547), King of England (1509–47), to indicate that he had acquired a manor here from the Bishop of Norwich, hence the previous name Lynn Escopi 'Bishop's Lynn'. The Celtic *Lynn* or *Linn* means 'pool', a reference to the mouth of the River Ouse on which the town lies.

Kings Peak, UTAH/USA
Named after Clarence King, a 19th-century geologist.

Kingsport, CANADA, USA
USA (Tennessee): settled *c.*1750 as Island Flats; it was subsequently renamed Boat Yard, Christiansville, King's Mill Station, and King's Port; the last three names have been associated with Colonel James King who constructed a mill on Reedy Creek in 1774. Situated on the River Holston, the added *port* indicates that it undertakes commercial activities.

Kingston, AUSTRALIA, CANADA, JAMAICA, NEW ZEALAND, USA
At least 21 cities and towns around the world have this name.
1. Canada (Ontario): founded in 1673 by the French on the site of a Native American village called Cataraqui. They built Fort Frontenac, named after Louis de Buade (1622–98), Comte de Frontenac, governor of New France (1672–82, 1689–98). The trading post and fort were destroyed by the British in 1758, but rebuilt and renamed Kingston in 1783, probably in honour of King George III[†].
2. Jamaica: founded in 1692 after a large earthquake had destroyed the coastal city of Port Royal, and named in honour of King William III[†]. It has been the capital since 1872.
3. USA (New York): founded as Esopus by the Dutch in 1652, it was renamed Wiltwyck in 1661. In 1669, when under new British control, it was renamed Kingston after the English family estate of the state governor.
4. USA (Rhode Island): probably named after King Charles II[†].

k

Kingston Upon Hull, ENGLAND/UK *Wike, Kyngeston super Hul*
Named after the River Hull which itself is either an Old Scandinavian word meaning 'deep one' or a Celtic one meaning 'muddy one'. Having received the port from local monks in 1293, Edward I (1239–1307), King of England (1272–1307), renamed the town Kingston Upon Hull, Kingston meaning 'The King's Estate' from the Old English *cyning* 'king' and *tūn*. The first name came from the Old English *wīc*. Today the city is usually called Hull.

Kingston Upon Thames, ENGLAND/UK *Cyningestun, Chingestune*
An evolution of the original name which meant 'Royal Estate' or 'Royal Palace' since seven Anglo-Saxon kings *cyning* were crowned here. It lies on the River Thames.

Kingstown, ST VINCENT/WEST INDIES
St Vincent was ceded to Great Britain in 1763 during the reign of King George III[†] and the name merely signifies its allegiance to the British crown.

Kingstree, SOUTH CAROLINA/USA
A large pine tree on the bank of the Black River gave the town its name.

King William Island, CANADA
Discovered in 1830, it was named after King William IV[†].

King William's Town, EASTERN CAPE/SOUTH AFRICA
Founded as a missionary station in 1826, it became a settlement as a result of the efforts of Sir Harry Smith in 1835 when it was named after the reigning British monarch, William IV[†]. Shortly afterwards it was abandoned, but then reoccupied in 1847.

Kinki, HONSHŪ/JAPAN *Kansai*
A region whose name means 'Near to the Imperial Capital' from *kin* 'proximity' and *ki* 'imperial capital', a reference to the fact that the area is close to the former imperial capital of Kyōto. Its former name meant 'Western Province'.

Kinross, CANADA, UK, USA
UK (Scotland): formerly Kynros 'End of the Promontory' from the Gaelic *ceann* 'headland' and *ros* 'promontory'.

Kinshasa, DEMOCRATIC REPUBLIC OF THE CONGO *Kintamo, Léopoldville*
Two villages, Nshasa and Ntamo, from which the present name comes, provided the basis for the modern city; when joined they became known as Kintamo. Before the name was changed to Kinshasa in 1966, the city was called Léopoldville. In 1881 Sir Henry Morton Stanley[†] established a small trading centre in Kintamo and renamed it 'Leopold's Town' in tribute to his patron, Léopold II (1835–1909), King of the Belgians (1865–1909). By 1920 it had become the capital of the Belgian Congo and remained so when the country gained its independence in 1960.

Kinston, NORTH CAROLINA/USA *Kingstown, Atkins Bank, Caswell*
Named after King George III[†]. The g was dropped after the War of Independence (1775–83) to sever any allusion to royalty. Indeed, twice the name was changed completely to honour prominent local citizens before reverting to Kinston.

Kipling, SASKATCHEWAN/CANADA *Kipling Station*
Named after the famous English writer, Rudyard Kipling (1865–1936).

Kirchberg, AUSTRIA, GERMANY, SWITZERLAND
'Church Hill' from the German *Kirche* 'church' and *Berg*.

Kiribati *Kingsmill, Gilbert Islands*
The Republic of Kiribati (Ribaberikin Kiribati) since 1979 when independence was achieved. In both Micronesia and Polynesia and straddling the international date line, Kiribati includes the former Gilbert Islands, Banaba (previously Ocean Island), the Phoenix Islands, and the Line Islands. The main group of islands was renamed in the 1820s by the Russian hydrographer Krusenstern after a British naval captain, Thomas Gilbert, who discovered the island of Tarawa in 1788. Together with the Ellice Islands (*see* TUVALU), they became a British protectorate in 1892 and the Gilbert and Ellice Islands became a crown colony in 1916. The Ellice Islands severed the link in 1975 and the colony was renamed the Gilbert Islands. Kiribati is the native pronunciation of Gilbert and is pronounced 'Kir-a-bas'.

Kırıkkale, TURKEY
'Broken Fort' from *kırık* 'broken' and *kale*, a reference to a ruined fort.

Kirillov, VOLOGDA/RUSSIA
Named after St Kirill Belozersky (1337–1427), who founded the Belozersky Monastery here in 1397. The monastery was named after a nearby lake, Beloye Ozero 'White Lake'. *See* BELOZERSK.

Kirin, CHINA
See JILIN.

Kiritimati, KIRIBATI *Christmas Island*
In the Line Islands, it was first sighted on Christmas Eve 1777 by Captain James Cook[†]. It was annexed by the UK in 1888 and

incorporated into the Gilbert and Ellice Islands Colony in 1919. Kiritimati is a local pronunciation of 'Christmas'.

Kirkbride, ENGLAND/UK *Chirchebrid*
'Church of St Brigid' from the Old Scandinavian *kirkja* and the name of the Irish abbess of Kildare, St Brigid, who died *c*.525.

Kirkby Lonsdale, ENGLAND/UK *Chwerchebi, Kircabi Lauenesdale*
'Village with a Church in the Valley of the (River) Lune' from the Old Scandinavian *kirkju-bý* 'village with a church', *dalr* 'valley', and the name of the river.

Kirkcaldy, CANADA, UK
UK (Scotland): formerly Kircalethyn. The name embraces the word 'fort' twice. *Kirk* comes from the Celtic *caer* and *caledin*, the name of a hill from *caled* 'hard', that is, rocky, and *din* 'fort'.

Kirkcudbright, SCOTLAND/UK *Kilcudbrit, Kircuthbright*
'Church of (St) Cuthbert' from the Gaelic Cil Cudbert. The present *kirk-* derives from *kirkja* but the word order is Celtic. St Cuthbert (*c*.634–87) became a monk in Scotland and Bishop of Lindisfarne (685–7) and subsequently the most popular saint in northern England. He was buried originally in Lindisfarne, but his bones were removed so as not to fall into the hands of the Danes, being taken round south-west Scotland and northern England. It is said that they lay here while on their way to Durham for final burial in 999.

Kirkintilloch, SCOTLAND/UK *Caerpentaloch*
'Fort at the End of the Ridge' from *caer, ceann* 'end' (which has replaced Pictish *pen* 'end'), and *tulaich*, the genitive of *tulach*, 'ridge' or 'hill'. A Roman fort was built here as part of the Antonine Wall in 142.

Kırklareli, TURKEY *Sarante Eklesiai, Kırk Kılıse*
Given its present name in 1924, the previous names, the first Byzantine, literally meant 'Forty Churches'. However, it is more likely that what is meant is the 'Church of Forty Saints'.

Kirksville, MISSOURI/USA *Long Point, Hopkinsville*
Founded *c*.1841, it was eventually named after Jesse Kirk, an early settler.

Kirkwall, SCOTLAND/UK *Kirkjuvagr*
'Church Bay' from the Old Scandinavian *kirkja* and *vágr* 'bay'. The church is the 12th-century cathedral of St Magnus (*c*.1075–1116), Earl of Orkney, who was murdered by his cousin. The seaport is the capital of Orkney.

Kirov, RUSSIA *Khlynov, Vyatka*
A province and a city named after Sergey Kirov[†] who was born near here. The city was originally named after the River Khlynovitse between 1181 and 1780 and then after the River Vyatka between 1780 and 1934. This may have taken its name from the local Votyak people. Unlike many other names adopted during the Soviet era, this one has not reverted to its pre-Soviet name of Vyatka.

Kirovgrad, SVERDLOVSK/RUSSIA *Kalata*
Renamed 'Kirov's Town' in 1935 after Sergey Kirov[†].

Kirovohrad, UKRAINE *Yelizavetgrad, Zinovyevsk, Kirovo, Kirovograd*
A province and a city which was founded as a fortress in 1754. In 1765 it was named 'Elizabeth's Town' after Empress Elizabeth Petrovna (1741–62). In 1924–36 it was named after Grigoriy Zinoviev (1883–1936), Bolshevik revolutionary, chairman of the Comintern (1919–26), and one of Lenin's[†] principal colleagues, whose birthplace this was. In 1936 it was renamed Kirovo and three years later Kirovograd 'Kirov's Town' after Sergey Kirov[†], for complicity in whose murder Zinoviev was executed. The present name is the Ukrainian spelling of the Russian Kirovograd. Because there was already a city called *Kirovgrad, an extra *o* was inserted.

Kirovsk, MURMANSK/RUSSIA *Khibino-Gorsk*
Originally named after the nearby Khibiny mountains from *gora*. It was renamed in 1934 after Sergey Kirov[†]. The Kirovsk in Turkmenistan is now called Babadaykhan.

Kirovskiy, KAZAKHSTAN, RUSSIA *Nikitinskiye Promysly (Russia)*
Russia (Astrakhan): first called 'Nikitin's Fisheries' from the personal name and (*rybnyy* 'fish') *promysel* 'catching'. In 1934 it was renamed after Sergey Kirov[†].

Kırşehir, TURKEY *Justinianopolis?, Kirshehri*
'Town of the Steppes' from *şehir* and *kir* 'countryside' or here 'steppes'. It may have been called Justinianopolis after Justinian I[†].

Kiryat Shmona, ISRAEL
See QIRYAT SHEMONA.

Kiryū, HONSHŪ/JAPAN
Derived from *kiri* 'paulownia', a deciduous tree of the figwort family with blue or lilac flowers which were dedicated to Anna Pavlovna (1795–1865), third daughter of the Russian Emperor Paul and wife of William II of The Netherlands, and *u* 'birth'; the Chinese character here is actually *sei* 'life' or 'existence'.

k

Kisangani, DEMOCRATIC REPUBLIC OF THE
CONGO *Falls Station, Stanleyville*
Founded in 1883 and named after the nearby
falls, it was later named 'Stanley's Town' after
Sir Henry Morton Stanley†, who travelled
across Africa through the Congo in 1874–7. In
1966 it received its present Swahili name 'In
the Sand' or 'On the Sandbank', a reference to
the fact that it is situated on the sandy
northern shore of an island in the Congo River.

Kiseljak, BOSNIA AND HERZEGOVINA
'Mineral Spring', although *kiseljak* in Serbo-
Croat can also mean 'sorrel'. This small town
was a well-known health spa during Roman
times.

Kishangarh, RĀJASTHĀN/INDIA
A city and former princely state, it was
founded as a fort in 1611 by Kishan Singh, a
warrior ruler of Rājputāna. The name means
simply 'Kishan's Fort' from *garh*.

Kishinëv, MOLDOVA
See CHIŞINĂU.

Kishiwada, HONSHŪ/JAPAN
Founded as a castle on the coast in the 14th
century by Takaie Wada and named after the
Wada family with *kishi* 'shore', 'coast', or
'bank'.

Kiskunfélegyháza, HUNGARY
'Village of the Little Cuman District' from *kis*
'little', *kun* 'Cuman', the Kipchak people who
settled here in the 14th century, *fél* 'half',
meaning 'district', *egy* 'one', and *házi* 'house';
egyházi means 'church' and in this instance can
be taken to mean 'village'.

Kislovodsk, STAVROPOL TERRITORY/RUSSIA
Founded as a spa in 1803, it means 'Sour
Waters' from *kisliye* 'sour' and *vodi* 'spa' or
'waters', plural of *voda* 'water'.

Kissidougou, GUINEA
'Town of the Kissi' from a tribal name and the
Dyula *dugu* 'town'.

Kitakami, HONSHŪ/JAPAN
A mountain range (Kitakami-sammyaku), a
river, and a town, all called 'North Summit'
from *kita* 'north' and *kami* 'summit' or 'top'.

Kita-Kyūshū, KYŪSHŪ/JAPAN
Created in 1963 from the merger of five cities,
the name simply means 'North Kyūshū' from
kita and the name of the island on which it is
situated.

Kitami, HOKKAIDŌ/JAPAN *Nokkeushi, Kitakaigan*
Founded as an Ainu settlement known as
'Edge of a Field', it was renamed Kitakaigan
'North Coast' (although it is some 25 miles
(40 km) from the coast) from *kita* and *kaigan*
'coast'. In 1942, when it became a

municipality, it was given its present name
which means 'to go to war against' or 'to
punish'. It can also be said to come from *kita*
and *mi* 'see', an indication that Sakhalin Island
could be seen from here on a fine day.

Kit Carson, USA
California and Colorado: named after Kit
Carson (1809–68), frontiersman, soldier and
Native American agent who was prominent in
the expansion westwards of the United States.

Kitchener, AUSTRALIA, CANADA
Canada (Ontario): settled as Sand Hill by Dutch
immigrants in 1805. Two years later the
German Mennonite Bishop Benjamin Eby
founded the city which was renamed after
him. This was changed to Berlin in 1824. Anti-
German feeling during the First World War
caused the city to be renamed after Horatio
Kitchener (1850–1916), 1st Earl Kitchener,
British field marshal and secretary of state for
war (1914–16), in 1916 after he drowned when
the ship taking him to Russia struck a mine
and sank.

Kittanning, PENNSYLVANIA/USA
Close to the Allegheny River, the name comes
from the Delaware *kithane* 'greatest river'.

Kittery, MAINE/USA *Piscataqua Plantation*
Settled in 1623, it was subsequently renamed
after the estate of the Champernowne family,
Kittery Point, in Devon, England.

Kizel, PERM/RUSSIA
Founded in 1788 and named after the
Kizel River whose name is said to come
from the Tatar *kyzyl* 'red', a possible
reference to the berries of the vegetation
along its banks.

Kızıl Adalar, TURKEY *Demonesi Insulae*
'Red Islands' from *kızıl* 'red' and *adalar*, the
plural of *ada* 'island'. The colour is a reference
to the copper mines on one of the islands,
Heybeli Ada and in ancient times called
Chalcitis from the Greek *chalkos* 'copper'. One
island, Büyükada, was the ancient Pityoussas
and Burgas Adası was Panormus. In English the
islands are known as Princes Islands.

Kızılırmak, TURKEY
A river, originally the Halys, with a name
meaning 'Red River' from *kızıl* and *ırmak* 'river',
a reference to the apparent colour of its
waters. It rises in the Kızıl Mountains and a
town also has this name.

Kızıltepe, TURKEY
'Red Hill' from *kızıl* and *tepe* 'hill'.

KL, MALAYSIA
A common abbreviation for *Kuala Lumpur.

Kladno, CZECH REPUBLIC
Founded in a forest and derived from the Old
Czech *kláda* 'log (of wood)' because trees from
the forest were used in the construction of the
houses.

Klagenfurt, AUSTRIA *Chlagenvurt*
Founded in the 12th century and, according to
legend, named after a *Klagefrau* 'weeping
woman', who supervised the *Furt* 'ford' over
the River Glan.

Klaipėda, LITHUANIA *Memelburg, Memel*
Destroying the original settlement, the
Teutonic Knights built a new fortress in 1252
which they called Memelburg 'Fortress on the
(River) Memel' (in Lithuanian, the Nemunas,
and known in English as the Neman); the *-burg*
was later dropped. The city was part of East
Prussia until becoming international territory
as a result of the Treaty of Versailles (1919)
and placed under French administration by
the League of Nations. The Lithuanians
drove the French out in 1923 and annexed the
area, the city becoming Lithuanian for the first
time. It was renamed Klaipeda that year,
retaining this name until it was severed from
Lithuania by Adolf Hitler[†] in 1939 when it
became Memel again. It was ceded to the
Soviet Union and renamed Klaipeda in 1945.
It became part of Lithuania in 1991 when
independence was achieved. The meaning
of the present name is unknown, but the
second half, *pėda*, means 'foot' or 'footprint'
in Lithuanian, and thus possibly 'district'
or 'territory' here, with the first
syllable conceivably associated with a
personal name.

Klamath Falls, OREGON/USA *Linkville*
A city settled in 1867 and renamed after the
Klamath tribe in 1893. Mountains and a river
have the name Klamath.

Klawer, WESTERN CAPE/SOUTH AFRICA
'Clover' in Afrikaans.

Kleinmond, WESTERN CAPE/SOUTH AFRICA
Kleinmondstrand
'Small Mouth' in Afrikaans, a reference to its
location on a small lagoon at the mouth of the
Palmiet River. It was originally 'Small Mouth
Beach'.

Klerksdorp, NORTH WEST/SOUTH AFRICA *Oude
Dorp*
Founded in 1837 as 'Old Town' on the western
bank of the Schoonspruit River, it was
renamed in 1888 when a new town sprang up
on the eastern bank. Together they were called
'Klerk's Village' after Jacob de Clercq, the
district magistrate.

Klis, CROATIA *Clissa*
Derived from the Latin *clavis* 'key', the fortress
here controlling the approaches to Split and
the Roman Salona.

Klodzko, POLAND *Glatz*
The city is situated on both sides of the River
Nysa Kłodzka from which it takes its name.
This, in turn, may come from the Slavonic
klada, and Russian *koloda*, 'log'. The city has
been under Bohemian, Austrian, and Prussian
control, hence its earlier German name; it
became Polish in 1945.

Klondike River, YUKON/CANADA
Said to come from a Native American word,
possibly *throndík* 'river with fish'. This is by no
means certain.

Klosterneuburg, AUSTRIA *Asturis*
Originally a Roman fortress, a new
development called Neuburg 'New Citadel'
arose around a castle and an Augustinian
abbey; this was later called Klosterneuburg
from the German *Kloster* 'monastery'.

Klyuč, BOSNIA AND HERZEGOVINA
'The Key', a reference to several (ruined)
castles dominating the Sana Valley.

Knaresborough, ENGLAND/UK *Chenaresburg*
Founded as a castle in 1070, the name may
mean 'Cēnheard's Stronghold' from an Old
English personal name and *burh*.

Knebworth, ENGLAND/UK *Chenepworde*
'Cnebba's Enclosure' from an Old English
personal name and *worth* 'enclosure'.

Knjaževac, SERBIA/SERBIA AND MONTENEGRO
Gurgusovac
Originally thought to be named after Gurgur,
the eldest son of Djuradj Branković, Despot
(ruler) of Serbia (1427–56). In 1859 it was
renamed on the orders of Miloš Obrenović,
Prince of Serbia (1817–39, 1859–60) to mean
'Prince Town' from the Serbo-Croat *knez*
'prince'.

Knock, IRELAND, UK
Ireland: a holy shrine since 1879 when
there was an apparition of the Virgin
Mary here. The name means 'Hill' from the
Gaelic *cnóc*.

Knoxville, TENNESSEE/USA
Originally a frontier post, it was renamed in
1791 after General Henry Knox (1750–1806),
who distinguished himself during the War of
Independence (1775–83) and became the first
secretary of war in 1785.

Knutsford, ENGLAND/UK *Cunetesford*
'Ford belonging to a man called Knútr, or Cnút'
from an Old Scandinavian personal name and
ford.

Kōbe, HONSHŪ/JAPAN
'House of God' from *kō* 'God' and *be* 'door' with
the meaning here of 'house'.

Koblenz, RHINELAND-PALATINATE/GERMANY
See COBLENZ.

Kōchi, SHIKOKU/JAPAN
A prefecture and a city with a name from *kō*
'high' and *chi* 'knowledge'.

Kodiak Island, ALASKA/USA *Kikhtak, Kadiak*
Discovered in 1763 by a Russian fur trader, it
was called Kikhtak 'Island' by the Inuit
(Eskimo). This was changed to Kadiak in 1890
and Kodiak in 1901. The island was bought by
the USA in 1867 as part of the purchase of
Alaska.

Kofarnihon, TAJIKISTAN *Ordzhonikidzeabad*
Named after the Kafirningan River, although
with a somewhat different spelling. Previously
it was named 'Ordzhonikidze's Town' after
Grigory (Sergo) Ordzhonikidze[†] and *abad*.

Kōfu, HONSHŪ/JAPAN
Although not a prefecture, the Chinese
character *fu* means 'prefecture' and *kō* 'shell'. It
is believed that a prefectural office was located
here at one time.

Kohāt, NORTH-WEST FRONTIER/PAKISTAN
The new town lies some way from the old
town of Kohāt which is believed to have been
founded by, and named after, a 14th-century
Buddhist raja called Kohāt. Additionally, Kōhāt
in Persian means 'mountains' from the plural
of *kōh* or *kūh* 'mountain'; the town is located in
hilly rugged terrain.

Kohistan, PAKISTAN/AFGHANISTAN
A district within the North-West Frontier
Province with part lying in Afghanistan, it has
also been called Yaghistan 'Land of the
Ungovernable'. The present name means
'Land of the Mountains' from the Urdu *koh*
'mountain' and *stan*.

Kokand (Quqon), UZBEKISTAN *Khavakend, Eski-
Kurgan*
'Town of the Boar' from *khuk* 'boar' and *kand*
'town'. An ancient city, the present town was
developed from a fort built in 1732 at Eski
Kurgan 'Old Tumulus (burial mound)' and
given the name Kokand in 1740; it became the
capital of the Khanate of Kokand, based on the
Ferghana Valley, in the 18th and 19th
centuries. The khanate was occupied by the
Russians in 1876, annexed, and renamed the
province of Ferghana.

Kokchetav (Kökshetaū), KAZAKHSTAN
Founded in 1824 as an outpost as the Russians
took control of the country, the name is Turkic
and means 'Green Mountain' from *taū*
'mountain'. This is a reference to the presence
of some trees and hills in the otherwise flat
and treeless steppe.

Kokkola, FINLAND *Gamlakarleby*
The former name, which was replaced in
the 20th century, meant 'Old Karl's Village'
from the Swedish *gamla* 'old', the personal
name (although the individual is not known)
and *bý* 'village'. The meaning of the present
name is not known, although *kokko* means
'bonfire'.

Kokomo, INDIANA/USA
Laid out in 1844 and named after a Miami chief
whose name meant 'Black Walnut'.

Koksoak River, QUEBEC/CANADA
'Big River' in Inuktitut.

Kokstad, KWAZULU-NATAL/SOUTH AFRICA
Nomansland
'Kok's Town'. Founded in 1861 and named
after Adam Kok (1811–75), a Griqua leader who
had no desire to live under Boer authority. He
therefore asked the British governor of Cape
Colony for some land under British protection.
Sir George Grey (1812–98), the governor
(1854–61), gave him some land called
Nomansland.

Kola, INDONESIA, RUSSIA, TANZANIA
Russia (Murmansk): a peninsula named after
the Kola River which itself comes from a Finno-
Ugric root word *kol* or *kul* 'fish'.

Kolašin, MONTENEGRO/SERBIA AND
MONTENEGRO
An Ottoman Turkish garrison, it is named after
one Kolazi, a Turkish commandant in the 17th
century. Part of medieval Serbia, it was
incorporated into Montenegro after the
Congress of Berlin in 1878.

Kolkata, WEST BENGAL/INDIA
See CALCUTTA.

Köln, NORTH RHINE-WESTPHALIA/GERMANY
See COLOGNE.

Kołobrzeg, POLAND *Kolberg*
Founded as a Slav stronghold in the 8th
century on the Baltic coast, the name means
'By the Seashore' from *kolo* 'near' or 'by' and
brzeg 'seashore' or 'coast'. It became part of
Brandenburg in 1648 and did not return to
Poland until 1945.

Komandorskiye Islands (Komandorskiye Ostrova), KAMCHATKA/RUSSIA
'Commander Islands' named after Commander Vitus Bering† who died on the largest one in 1741.

Komárno, SLOVAKIA *Komorn, Komárom*
Derived from the Slovak *komár* 'mosquito' or 'midge', a reference to their presence here at the confluence of the Vah and Nitra Rivers with the Danube. Its Austro-Hungarian associations are recognized in its German and Hungarian names; indeed, Komárno in Slovakia and Komárom in Hungary were at one time a single town split by the River Danube; in 1918 the river became the border between Hungary and the newly created Czechoslovakia and in 1920 Komárno became part of Czechoslovakia. Between 1939 and 1945 it was Hungarian.

Komatipoort, MPUMALANGA/SOUTH AFRICA
'Gorge on the (River) Komati' from the Afrikaans *poort* 'gorge'. The river's name means 'Cow'.

Komatsu, HONSHŪ/JAPAN
'Small Pine Tree' from *ko* 'small' and *matsu* 'pine tree'.

Komi, RUSSIA
A republic named after the Komi, a Finno-Ugric people.

Komi-Permyak, RUSSIA
An autonomous district named after the Komi-Permyaks, a branch of the Komis.

Kôm Ombo, EGYPT
Also spelt Kawm Umbu. 'Hill of Umbu' from the Arabic *kom* 'hill' or 'heap' and Ombos, the name of an ancient city nearby.

Kompong Som (Kâmpóng Saôm), CAMBODIA
Sihanoukville
The present and previous names have alternated more than once. Sihanoukville 'Sihanouk's Town' was named after Norodom Sihanouk (1922–), King of Cambodia (1941–55), chief of state, prime minister, president, and king again (1993–2004). *Kâmpóng* means 'village', although in many cases these have expanded into towns.

Komsomolabad, TAJIKISTAN
'Town of the Komsomol', the Young Communist League; it was disbanded in 1991.

Komsomolets, KAZAKHSTAN, RUSSIA
Russia: an island in the Arctic Ocean with a name meaning 'Member of the Komsomol' (*see* KOMSOMOLABAD). An expedition was made to the island by some members in 1931.

Komsomol'sk-na-Amure, KHABAROVSK TERRITORY/RUSSIA *Permskoye*
Founded in 1860 as a settlement for refugees from Perm. The modern city was built in 1932 by, and named after, members of the Komsomol. It lies on the River Amur, *na-Amure*, whose inclusion in the city's name distinguishes it from other towns called Komsomol'sk in Russia (the one in Kaliningrad Province had the former German name of Löwenhagen) and Uzbekistan.

Kŏmun-do, SOUTH KOREA *Port Hamilton*
Also spelt Geomundo in the Romanization system now in use in South Korea. The sense of the name is 'Island with Great Culture' from *do* 'island'. The British gave the name Port Hamilton after Captain W. A. B. Hamilton, the then secretary of the British Admiralty, when they occupied the island in 1885–7.

Königsberg, GERMANY, RUSSIA
1. Germany (Bavaria): 'King's Mountain' from *König* 'king' and *Berg*.
2. Russia. *See* KALININGRAD.

Königssee, BAVARIA/GERMANY
A lake called 'King's Lake' from *König* 'king' and *See* 'lake'. It is also called Batholomäussee 'St Bartholomew's Lake', the church on its western shore being dedicated to the saint.

Königswinter, NORTH RHINE-WESTPHALIA/GERMANY
Probably based on Late Latin *vinitorium*, from *vinitor* 'vintner', to give 'Place of Vintners' with the additional German *König* 'king', perhaps from connections with an earlier king's estate.

Konstantinovka, UKRAINE
Founded in 1869 and probably named after Grand Duke Konstantin (1827–92), fourth child of Emperor Nicholas I†.

Konstanz (French: Constance), BADEN-WÜRTTEMBERG/GERMANY
Originally a Roman fort, it was named after Constantius I Chlorus, Roman emperor (293–306). The Swiss part of the town is called Kreuzlingen. It gives its name to Lake *Constance.

Kontagora, NIGER/NIGERIA
Founded in 1864 and possibly derived from the local words *kwanta gora* 'lay down your gourds'.

Konya, TURKEY *Kawania, Ikonyon/Ikonyum/Iconium*
According to one legend, the name is derived from a story about how Prometheus, instructed by Jupiter, made men out of mud, from the Greek *eikōn* 'icon' or 'image', to replace those drowned during the Great Flood, thus repopulating Iconium; these 'mud men'

k

came to life when the wind blew on them. The city was the first to emerge when the waters subsided. Another legend has it that Perseus killed the Gorgon that had been marauding the town. The inhabitants erected a stone pillar with an icon of Perseus carved in it. The present name is derived from the previous Greek and Latin names. It became a Roman colony and the Seljuk Turkish capital of the Sultanate of Rūm between *c*.1076 and *c*.1300. When the city became a state during the reign of Suleiman I the Magnificent (*c*.1494–1566), Sultan of the Ottoman Empire (1520–66), it was known as Karaman ili, having been the capital of the province of Karamania during Roman times.

Kootenay, CANADA–USA *Flat Bow*
Also spelt Kootenai. A river and a lake with a Native American name meaning 'Water People'.

Kópavogur, ICELAND
Situated on the coast, the town's name means 'Bay of Young Seals' from *kópa*, genitive plural of *kópur* 'young seal', and *vogur* 'bay' or 'inlet'.

Koper, SLOVENIA *Insula Caprea/Capros, Aegida, Justinopolis, Caput Histriae, Capodistria*
Formerly an island (it was joined to the mainland by a causeway in 1825) Insula Caprea 'Goat Island' or Capros was probably the name of a small Roman settlement which developed into the Roman city of Aegida. It was later named 'Justin's City' after Justin II, Byzantine emperor (565–78). It was captured by the Venetians in 1279 after which it was made the capital of Istria, hence Caput Histriae from which the Italian Capodistria 'Capital of Istria' is derived. It remained in Venetian hands until 1797 and, after a brief period under the French in 1797–1813, it became Austrian until 1918 when it was incorporated into Italy. It was part of the Free Territory of Trieste until being passed to the Slovene Republic within Yugoslavia in 1954.

Kopet-Dag, IRAN–TURKMENISTAN
A mountain range with a name of Turkic origin from *kop* 'many' and *dağ*.

Kopeysk, CHELYABINSK/RUSSIA *Ugolnye Kopi*
Founded in 1920 as 'Coal Mines' from *ugol* 'coal' and *kopi* 'mines' to aid development of the local coal mines, its name was slightly changed in 1933, the -*sk* denoting a location.

Korçë, ALBANIA *Pelium, Görridje, Koritsa*
Derived from the Slav word *gorica* 'small town'. After centuries of Ottoman Turkish rule as Görridje it was occupied by the Greeks in 1912; they changed the name to Koritsa in 1915. The town was awarded to Albania in 1920.

Korčula, CROATIA *Korkyra Melaina, Corcyra Nigra, Curzola*
An island and small town with a name meaning 'Black Korkyra', possibly because it was covered in dense pine woods. Under Greek rule from the 4th century BC, the island changed hands many times before coming under Venetian rule between 1420 and 1797.

Kordestan, IRAN
A province with the Persian name 'Land of the Kurds', a geographical region named after the Kurds. Only Iran has a province so-named. *See* KURDISTAN.

Kordofan (Kurdufān), THE SUDAN
A state, once inhabited by Nubian-speaking peoples, with a name possibly derived from the Nubian *kurta* 'men'.

Korea (Chosŏn, Taehan)
Only called Korea in the West from the 1890s, Korea being the Western name for the Koryŏ dynasty (918–1392). Korea had first been united in 668, but Koryŏ, the successor to, and new shortened name for, the Kingdom of Koguryŏ, was founded in 918 by General Wang Kŏn who established a new unified kingdom in 935 by defeating the Kingdoms of Paekche and Silla. However, the ancient Kingdom of Chosŏn was founded as far back as 2333 BC and this name was re-adopted for the country in 1392 when the Confucian Yi (also known as Chosŏn) dynasty came to power. It ruled until the Japanese annexed the country in 1910, although it had become a Japanese protectorate five years earlier; the Japanese spelling was Chosen. During the next 35 years every effort was made to extinguish the Korean identity under the slogan *Nissen Ittai* 'Japan and Korea as One'. To accept the surrender of Japanese forces in Korea in 1945, Soviet troops occupied the northern half of the country and American troops the southern half; without the Koreans being consulted, the country was partitioned along the 38th parallel (38° north), an arbitrary, but supposedly temporary, line that split the peninsula roughly in two. In 1948 two separate, and rival, states were proclaimed. Koryŏ may be translated as 'High and Beautiful'. Chosŏn, the ancient Chinese name and still used by the North Koreans, means '(Land of the) Morning Calm' from *cho* 'morning' and *sŏn* 'calm' or 'freshness'. The South Koreans use Taehan 'Great Han' from *tae* 'great' or 'big', Han being another name for Korea and the Korean people. To symbolize the country's independence from China, this name was adopted in 1897 by the decree of

Emperor Kojong (d. 1907). *See* NORTH KOREA AND SOUTH KOREA.

Korhogo, CÔTE D'IVOIRE
'Heritage', possibly a reference to the ancestral line down from the founder in the 14th century, said to be a patriarch called Nangui or Nengué.

Korolev, MOSCOW/RUSSIA *Kaliningrad*
Renamed in 1996 after Sergey Korolev (1906–66), missile, rocket, and spacecraft designer. It had been named after Mikhail Kalinin[†] since 1938.

Korsakov, SAKHALIN ISLAND/RUSSIA
Muravyovsky, Korsakovsky, Otomari
Founded as a military post in 1853, it was renamed after Voin Rimsky-Korsakov (1822–71), a hydrographer who surveyed the strait between Sakhalin Island and the Russian mainland. In 1905, after the Russo-Japanese War, it was annexed by Japan and called Otomari. When it was returned to the Soviet Union in 1946, it adopted a slightly amended form of its earlier Russian name.

Koryak, RUSSIA
An autonomous district named after the Koryak people. 'Reindeer People' from *kor* 'reindeer'.

Kosciusko, AUSTRALIA, USA
1. Australia (New South Wales): a mountain named by the Polish explorer, Paul Strzelecki, in 1840 after Tadeusz Kościuszko (1746–1817), a Polish patriot who reached the rank of brigadier general fighting on the American side during the War of Independence (1775–83). He then led an insurrection in Poland against the Russians in 1794.
2. USA (Alaska): an island named after Tadeusz Kościuszko.
3. USA (Mississippi): a city named after Tadeusz Kościuszko.

Košice, SLOVAKIA *Cassovia, Kassa, Kaschau*
Derived from Koša 'clearing in the forest' to mean a 'settlement built in a clearing in the forest'. Having been founded by the Saxons, the town has experienced considerable German influence as evidenced by its German name of Kaschau. Kassa was its Hungarian name.

Kosovo (Albanian: **Kosova**), SERBIA/SERBIA AND MONTENEGRO *Dardania, Kosovo i Metohija*
A geographic, and predominantly Albanian-populated, region under Serbian sovereignty—but, in effect, a European-run colony or protectorate under UN administration since mid-1999. Previously a Serbian province which

enjoyed autonomy in 1974–90. In 1990 it declared independence and Serbia retaliated by abolishing its autonomous status. It declared its independence again in 1998 under the name of the Kosovo Republic, but this was not recognized internationally. The western half is called Metohija by the Serbs and was included in the name in 1946–71; it is derived from the Byzantine Greek *metochia* 'land of the monasteries'. Kosovo i 'and' Metohija was sometimes shortened to Kosmet. The Albanian version of Dardania (modern Kosovo, south Serbia, and Macedonia) was Dardhë 'pear'.

Kosovo Polje (Albanian: **Fushë e Kosovë**), SERBIA/SERBIA AND MONTENEGRO
'Field of the Blackbirds' from *kos* 'blackbird', *kosovo* being the genitive plural, and *polje* 'field'.

Kosovska Mitrovica (Albanian: **Mitrovicë**), SERBIA/SERBIA AND MONTENEGRO *Dimitrovica, Mitrovica, Titova Mitrovica*
Developed round the church of the warrior saint St Demetrius after whom the town is named. In 1948 *Titova* 'Tito's' was added to the name in honour of Josip Broz Tito[†]. It was dropped in 1992 and replaced by *Kosovska* to denote its location in Kosovo and to distinguish it from *Sremska Mitrovica in the Srem region of Serbia.

Kossuth, MISSISSIPPI/USA
Named after Lajos Kossuth (1802–94), a Hungarian patriot who led Hungary's fight for independence from Austria in 1848–9.

Kostrzyn, POLAND *Küstrin*
The former German and present Polish names both come from Kostrz, a personal name, the final *-yn* indicating possession, thus the '(Settlement) of Kostrz'. The town, on the border with Germany, was transferred to Poland in 1945.

Kota, RĀJASTHĀN/INDIA
Founded as a walled city in the 14th century with a name simply meaning 'Fort', it became the capital of a princely state with the same name in 1625.

Kota Baharu, KELANTAN/MALAYSIA *Kota Bahru*
'New Fort' from *kota* and *baharu/baru* 'new'.

Kota Kinabalu, SABAH/MALAYSIA *Api Api, Jesselton*
The original name meant 'Fire-Fire'. There are several theories as to the reason for this name. One is that pirates from the Sulu Archipelago kept burning it down. Another, that frequent fires occurred during festive seasons when flying sparks from firecrackers

burned the thatched roofs of the wooden structures; and a third, that it may be derived from the *avicennia* tree which grew in abundance along the coast and was used for *kayu api* 'firewood'. The original settlement was founded on Pulau Gaya, an island, but it was burnt down in 1897. A new settlement was built on the mainland in 1899 and named after Sir Charles Jessel, the vice-chairman of the British North Borneo Company. It was renamed in 1968 as the 'Fort of Kinabalu' after *kota* 'fort' and Mt Kinabalu. This name comes from the Kadazandusun *aki nabalu* 'Revered Resting Place of the Ancestral Spirits' from *aki* 'ancestor' and *nabalu* 'mountain'.

Ko Tao, THAILAND
'Turtle Island' because of its shape rather than the presence of turtles.

Kota Tinggi, JOHOR/MALAYSIA
'High Fort' from *kota* and *tinggi* 'high' or 'tall'.

Kotka, FINLAND
'Eagle', said to be named after the white-tailed eagles (in Finnish, *merikotka*) which used to nest here.

Kotor, MONTENEGRO/SERBIA AND MONTENEGRO
Acruvium?, Catarum, Cattaro
Certainly a small fortified settlement in Roman times with a sheep-fold (in Serbo-Croat *tor*) which in due course became known as Kotor from *kod tor* 'by, or near, the sheep-fold'. It took the present Slav form of its name in the 11th century, the Slavs having arrived on the Adriatic coast in the 7th century. Between *c.*1196 and 1371 it was subject to the early Serbian state and in 1391–1420 it was an independent city-republic. It also gives its name to the Gulf of Kotor.

Kotovsk, MOLDOVA, RUSSIA, UKRAINE
1. Moldova: originally Ganchesti, it was renamed Kotovskoye in 1940 and then in 1965, when it became a town, Kotovsk. Both honour the Civil War hero, Grigory Kotovsky (1881–1925), whose military career ended with his command of the 2nd Cavalry Corps. Kotovsky was born here when the town was called Ganche. It is now also referred to by its original name.
2. Russia (Tambov): until 1940 part of the city of Tambov, it was renamed after Grigory Kotovsky.
3. Ukraine: formerly Birzula, it was renamed in 1935 after Grigory Kotovsky who is buried here.

Kotzebue, ALASKA/USA
Named after the Russian naval officer and explorer, Otto von Kotzebue (1787–1846), who charted the Alaskan coast and sought the Northwest Passage in 1815–18.

Koudougou, BURKINA FASO
'Rocky Village' from the Mande *kulu* 'rock' and Dyula *dougou* 'village'.

Koulikoro, MALI
'Near the Rock' from the Mande *kulu* 'rock' and *koro* 'near'.

Kouroussa, GUINEA
Situated at the upper limit of the navigable part of the Niger River, the name means 'The End for Canoes' from the Mande *kuru* 'canoe' and *sa* 'mourning'.

Kowloon (Jiulong), HONG KONG/CHINA
'Nine Dragons' from *jiŭ* 'nine' and *lóng* 'dragon', a reference to the nine hills in the vicinity. Kowloon is the Cantonese for Jiulong.

Koyukuk River, ALASKA/USA
Named after the Koyukon, a local Native American tribe.

Kozhikode, KERALA/INDIA *Calicut*
The name is a corruption of the Tamil *kojīkoḍe*, possibly the 'Fort of Kalliai'. However, as the place of origin of the printed Indian cotton, calico, it gave its name to Calicut which was the Anglicized version of the present and original Malayalam name.

Kragujevac, SERBIA/SERBIA AND MONTENEGRO
Karajovja
Founded in the 16th century as a small Ottoman Turkish town, its present name is derived from the Serbo-Croat *kraguj* 'vulture', large numbers of which used to nest in the woods nearby. The city was the capital of Serbia in 1819–39.

Krakatoa (Kepulauan Krakatau), INDONESIA
An active volcano on an island between Sumatra and Java with a name meaning 'to split' from a Malay prefix *ke-* and Javanese *rekatak* 'to split'.

Kraków, POLAND
See CRACOW.

Kralendijk, BONAIRE/WEST INDIES
Chief town on the island of Bonaire in the Lesser Antilles. The name is derived from a Dutch word meaning 'coral dike'.

Kraljevica, CROATIA *Porto Re*
The Austrians built a new 'royal port' here in the 18th century from which the present name is derived; in Serbo-Croat *kraljevski* 'royal'.

Kraljevo, SERBIA/SERBIA AND MONTENEGRO
Karanovac, Janok, Rankovićevo
'King's Town' from *kralj* 'king'. Out of respect the Slavs took the name of Emperor Charlemagne[†] as their word for 'king'. The city was renamed in 1882 to mark the

proclamation of Serbia as a kingdom and the coronation of Milan Obrenović (1854–1901) as King of Serbia (1882–9); he had been the ruler, as a prince, of Serbia since 1868. In 1945–66 it was renamed Rankovićevo after Alexander-Leka Ranković (d. 1983), head of the Yugoslav secret police and one of Tito's closest wartime associates. When he was dismissed and disgraced in 1966, the name Kraljevo was restored.

Kramators'k, UKRAINE
Takes its name from a village called Krematorka which may come from the Slavonic *kroma* 'edge' and the former name of the river on which it lies, the Tor and now the Kazyënny Torets to mean '(Place by the) Edge of the (River) Tor'.

Kranj, SLOVENIA *Carnium, Krainburg*
Takes its name from the Roman Carnium, itself named after the Carni people. It gives its name to the central region of *Slovenia, Carniola.

Kranskop, KWAZULU-NATAL/SOUTH AFRICA
Hopetown
Established in 1894 but, to avoid confusion with another the town of the same name in Cape Province (now Northern Cape), it was given an Afrikaans name meaning 'Cliff Top', a reference to a nearby mountain.

Krasnaya Polyana, KRASNODAR TERRITORY/
RUSSIA
'Beautiful Glade' from the obsolete meaning of *krasnyy*, feminine *krasnaya*, and *polyana* 'glade' or 'clearing'.

Krasnaya Zarya, KRASNOYARSK TERRITORY/
RUSSIA *Gryaznovo*
'Red Dawn' in the revolutionary sense from *krasnaya* and *zarya* 'dawn' or 'daybreak'.

Krasneno, CHUKOT AUTONOMOUS DISTRICT/
RUSSIA
'Made Beautiful' from *krasnyy*.

Krasnoarmeysk, KAZAKHSTAN, RUSSIA,
UKRAINE, UZBEKISTAN
1. 'Red Army' from *krasnaya* and *armiya* 'army' to honour the 'Workers' and Peasants' Red Army', the forerunner of the Soviet Army.
2. Russia (Moscow): originally a village called Voznesensky 'Ascension' from *vozneseniye* because of the dedication of its church. Shortly after the Soviet Union came into existence in 1922 it was renamed *Imeni Krasnoy Armii i Flota* 'In the Name of the Red Army and Navy', abbreviated to *Kraft*. Its present name was adopted in 1946.
3. Russia (Saratov): founded in 1766 as Golyy Karamysh from the name of the river on which

it lies and *golyy* 'bare'. It was later renamed Bal'tser by German settlers, presumably after one of their number. It received its present name in 1942.
4. Ukraine: founded in about 1884 as Grishino and renamed in 1938.

Krasnodar, RUSSIA *Yekaterinodar*
A territory and a city founded *c*.1793 as a Cossack military post and named 'Catherine's Gift' from *dar* 'gift' in honour of Empress Catherine II the Great[†]. She gave the land to the Cossacks. After capture by the Red Army in 1920 during the Civil War the name was changed to a more revolutionary 'Gift of the Reds' from *krasnyy*.

Krasnodon, UKRAINE *Sorokino*
Founded in 1912 after the Sorokin family and renamed in 1938 to mean, perhaps, 'Red (Town) near the (River) Don' from *krasnyy*, here the 'revolutionary' colour. The town is in the Don basin, but over 60 miles (100 km) from the river and the name is thus more likely to refer to the Donbas (*see* DONETSK).

Krasnogorsk, MOSCOW/RUSSIA *Banki*
Renamed in 1940 to mean 'Red Mountain' from *krasnyy* and *gora*.

Krasnogvardeysk, UZBEKISTAN
A name that honours the Red Guards, in Russian *Krasnaya Gvardiya. See* GATCHINA.

Krasnohrad, UKRAINE *Konstantinograd,*
Krasnograd
Founded in 1782 as 'Constantine's Town' after the grandson of Catherine II the Great[†], Grand Prince Konstantin (1779–1831) who was heir to the throne (although he never acceded to it). It was renamed in 1922 'Red Town' from the Russian *krasnyy*, here the 'revolutionary' colour, and *grad*, which became the Ukrainian *hrad* 'town'.

Krasnokamsk, PERM/RUSSIA
Founded in 1929 on the Kama River, the name means 'Red Kama' from *krasnyy*.

Krasnoslobodsk, VOLGOGRAD/RUSSIA
'Red Settlement' from *krasnyy* and *sloboda* 'a settlement (exempted from normal state obligations)'.

Krasnoturinsk, YEKATERINBURG/RUSSIA
Turinskiye Rudniki
Founded in 1758 on the Turya River, its original name meant Turya Mines, a reference to the copper mines, from *rudnik* 'mine' or 'pit'. In 1944 it was renamed as 'red' from *krasnyy*, both to associate it with the Red Army and refer to the copper colour.

Krasnoyarsk, RUSSIA *Krasniy Yar*
A province and a city founded in 1628 as a fort on the left bank of the River Yenisey. The name means 'Red Bank' from *krasnyy* and *yar* 'steep bank' because of the reddish soil on the river banks. Although obsolete now, *krasnyy* at one time meant 'beautiful' and this could have been the original meaning. Several towns are still called Krasniy Yar.

Krasnoye Selo, LENINGRAD/RUSSIA
'Beautiful Village'. Settled by 1730 and thus pre-Russian Revolution, *krasnoye*, the neuter form of *krasnyy*, means 'beautiful' rather than 'red', and *selo* 'village'.

Krasnoye Znamya, TURKMENISTAN
'Red Banner' from the neuter form of *krasnyy* and the Russian *znamya* 'banner'. This is almost certainly a reference to the Order of the Red Banner instituted in 1924 as the first Soviet order. However, it first appeared in 1918 as the Order of the Red Banner of the Russian Federation and was awarded for exceptional courage in combat.

Krasnoznamensk, KALININGRAD/RUSSIA
Lasdehnen, Haselberg
Founded in 1734 with a German name, it also came to be known as Haselberg 'Hazelhill' from *Hasel* and *Berg* in 1938, both names continuing in use until 1945. Then, when East Prussia was ceded to the Soviet Union, it was renamed 'Red Banner'. (See previous entry.)

Krasnyy Klyuch, BASHKORTOSTAN REPUBLIC/RUSSIA
Founded in the 1890s, it was given the name 'Red Ray' from *krasnyy* and *luch* 'ray of light' or 'beam' in 1926.

Krasnyy Luch, UKRAINE *Krindachëvka*
'Red Ray' from *krasnyy* and *luch* 'ray of light' or 'beam'. It was renamed in 1929 as a symbol of a bright future.

Krasnyy Oktyabr', KURGAN/RUSSIA
'Red October', a reference to the October (Julian calendar) Revolution in 1917.

Kremenchug (Kremenchuk), UKRAINE
Founded in 1571 as a fortress, the name may be derived from the Russian *kremen'* 'flint' or from the Turkic *kermen* 'fort'.

Krishnanagar, WEST BENGAL/INDIA
'Krishna's Town' after Krishna, the Hindu god worshipped as an incarnation of the Hindu god Vishnu, and *nagar*.

Kristiansand, NORWAY
Founded in 1641 by, and named after, King Christian IV[†]. *Sand* simply means 'sand'.

Kristianstad, SWEDEN
'Kristian's Town'. A county and a city founded as a frontier post in 1614 by, and named after, King Christian IV[†] when the county of Skåne belonged to Denmark. It was ceded to Sweden in 1658, recovered by Christian V (1646–99), King of Denmark-Norway (1670–99), in 1676, and finally taken by the Swedes in 1678.

Kristiansund, NORWAY
Named after King Christian IV[†] with *sund* 'inlet', equivalent to the English 'sound'.

Kristinehamn, SWEDEN *Bro*
'Kristina's Port'. It was renamed in 1642 after Queen Christina (1626–89) who became queen at the age of six but actually only reigned for ten years (1644–54) before abdicating. Its previous name meant 'stream' or 'spring'.

Krivoy Rog (Kryvyy Rih), UKRAINE
Founded by Cossacks in the 17th century, the name literally means 'crooked horn' from the Russian *krivoy* 'crooked' and *rog* 'horn' or 'antler'. However, because the city is located at the confluence of the Ingulets and Saksagan Rivers the name is taken to mean 'curved bend'.

Križevci, CROATIA, SLOVENIA
'Holy Cross' from the Serbo-Croat *sveti* 'holy' and *križ* 'cross'. Both are named after Churches of the Holy Cross.

Krk, CROATIA *Kurik, Kurykta, Curicum, Vecla, Veglia*
The largest island in the Adriatic Sea and its main town built on a hill overlooking the sea. The present name, whose meaning is unknown, is derived from the Roman Curicum which in its turn came from the Illyrian Kurik and Greek Kurykta. After a period of Roman rule, the island passed to the Byzantines, who renamed the town Vecla, and then to the Croats before falling to Venice which ruled in 1480–1797 and used the name Veglia. In Italian this means 'vigil' or 'watch' and may be a reference to town fortifications, including a watch tower, built by the Venetians. The Austrians then held it until 1918 when it became part of the newly created Yugoslavia and adopted the present name.

Krkonoše, CZECH REPUBLIC
A mountain range, also known in German as Riesengebirge, in English as the Giant Mountains, and in Polish as Karkonosze. The Czech name comes from *krk* or *krak* 'mountain scrub' and *noš* 'to be covered (in something)', here 'mountain covered in scrub'.

Kroměříž, CZECH REPUBLIC *Kremsier*
Derived from the personal name Kroměžir who was the owner of the land here.

Kronshtadt, LENINGRAD/RUSSIA *Kronslot*
Kotlin Island, on which the port lies, was
captured from the Swedes by Peter I the Great[†]
in 1703. He built a fortress called Kronslot
'Crown Castle' in Swedish the next year to
protect his future capital, St Petersburg. In
1723 the port was renamed 'Crown City' from
the German *Krone* 'crown' and S*tadt*.

Kropotkin, KRASNODAR TERRITORY/RUSSIA
Romanovsky Khutor
Originally 'Romanov's Village' from *khutor*
'small village' or 'farmstead', it was renamed
in 1921 after Peter Alekseyevich Kropotkin
(1842–1921), geographer, geologist,
theoretician of anarchy, and revolutionary.

Krugersdorp, GAUTENG/SOUTH AFRICA
Founded in 1887 with the discovery of gold in
the area as 'Kruger's Village' from Afrikaans
dorp, it is named after the fiercely anti-British
Paul Kruger (1825–1904), President of the
Transvaal (or South African Republic) (1883–
1900), who started the Boer War with the UK
in 1899.

Krujë, ALBANIA *Kruj*
'Spring' (water).

Krumau, AUSTRIA
'Crooked Valley' from the German *krumm*
'crooked' or 'bent' and *Au*, a form of *Aue*,
'valley' or 'meadow'.

Kruševac, SERBIA/SERBIA AND MONTENEGRO
Probably derived from *kruška* 'pear' or 'pear
tree'.

Ksar-el-Kebir, MOROCCO *Oppidum Novum,
Alcazarquiver*
'The Great Fortress' from the Arabic *al-qasr* and
al-kebīr 'great'. A *ksar*, derived from the Latin
Caesar, is a fortified stronghold often
containing a large granary, *ghorfa*. Originally
occupied by the Greeks, Carthaginians,
Romans, who called it Oppidum Novum 'New
Town', and Byzantines, the Arab town was
founded in the 8th century. It was taken by the
Spanish in 1912, their name for the town
being a version of the Arabic name.

Kuala Lumpur, KUALA LUMPUR/MALAYSIA
'Mouth of the Muddy River' or 'Muddy
Confluence' from *kuala* 'mouth' or 'the place
where a tributary joins a larger river' and
lumpur 'mud'. Following the discovery of tin
ore in Perak State, the chief of Selangor State
sent a team of Chinese prospectors to search
for tin in a huge swamp in this area. In 1857
they landed at the confluence of the small
Kelang and Gombak Rivers and built a
settlement on the muddy banks. A rich deposit
was found in the present suburb of Ampang.

The city became the capital of the Federated
Malay States in 1895, of the independent
Federation of Malaya in 1957, and of Malaysia
in 1963. *See* PUTRAJAYA.

Kuching, SARAWAK/MALAYSIA *Sarawak*
Named in 1872 by Charles Brooke (1829–
1917), the second White Rajah and nephew of
the first Sir James Brooke, a British adventurer
who helped to suppress a local rebellion and
was rewarded by being given authority over
the territory and the title of White Rajah of
Sarawak (1841–63). He had founded the town
from a group of attap huts in 1839. Possibly
because the place was infested with cats at the
time it was called Kuching from the Malay
kucing 'cat'; or because of a common tree
whose fruit, *mata kuching*, resembles cats'
eyes. Another plausible explanation is that the
name is derived from the Chinese *kochin*
'harbour', the city-port lying on the Sarawak
River. It was originally named Sarawak after
the river around which an area of some 3 000
square miles (7 770 sq km) of jungle was given
to James Brooke in 1841.

Kudus, JAVA/INDONESIA
Founded by the Muslim saint, Sunan Kudus,
after whom it is named. Kudus is derived from
the Arabic *al-Quds* 'holy'.

Kuilsrivier, WESTERN CAPE/SOUTH AFRICA *De
Cuylen*
Lying on a river of the same name, the present
name is derived from the previous Dutch one
meaning 'The Pools', a reference to the fact
that in the dry season the river is reduced to
pools.

Kuito, ANGOLA *Silva Porto, Bié*
Founded in 1890 and originally named after
the Portuguese explorer António Francisco
Ferreira da Silva Porto who died here that year.
It was given a local name in 1975 meaning
'Place of Meat' from *ko* 'place' and *osito* 'meat',
a reference to the hordes of animals in the
vicinity. It is the capital of the province of Bié.

Kukawa, BORNO/NIGERIA
Named after the baobab tree, locally *kuka*.

Kulen Vakuf, BOSNIA AND HERZEGOVINA
Džisri-Kebir
A small medieval town built between 1703 and
1730 on an artificially created island in the
River Una. Its former Turkish name meant 'Big
Bridge'. The Serbo-Croat *vakuf* comes from the
Turkish *vakif*, a word to describe the property
of a Muslim religious community used for
charitable purposes. It is believed that Kulin,
the first Bosnian *ban* 'ruler' (1180–1204), who
has achieved legendary status in Bosnian

k

history, reigned here and this may explain the first part of the name.

Kulyab, TAJIKISTAN
Lying in the valley of the Yakshu River, the name is believed to be a combination of the Turkic *kul* 'lake' and Persian *ab* 'water'.

Kumamoto, KYŪSHŪ/JAPAN
A prefecture and a city with a name meaning 'Bear's Base' from *kuma* 'bear' and *moto* 'base'.

Kumasi, GHANA
According to legend, founded in the 17th century by the first King of the Ashanti Empire, Osei Tutu, who negotiated for land while sitting under a kum tree. This gave the city its name, 'Under the Kum' from *asi* 'under'. Another legend has it that the seeds of two kum trees were planted. One produced shoots indicating where the city should be. It became the capital of the Empire *c.*1680.

Kumayri (Gyumri), ARMENIA *Alexandropol', Leninakan*
A very old city probably founded by the Greeks. The Russians built a fortress on the site in 1837 and founded the nearby town of Alexandropol' 'Alexandra's Town', from *pol(is)*, three years later. This was named after Alexandra (1798–1860), the wife of Emperor Nicholas I[†]. She was born Princess Charlotte of Prussia and took the name Alexandra when she assumed the Russian Orthodox faith. In 1924 the town was renamed 'Lenin's Town' after Vladimir Lenin[†] and the Turkic *-akan* 'town'. The present name, adopted in 1990, may be associated with the Turkish *gümrük* 'customs house' since traders' dues used to be paid here.

Kumba, CAMEROON, TANZANIA
Cameroon: derived from *ekumba*, the name given to a large tree around which a group of hunters made a settlement. The first Europeans to arrive in the area simply called it Kumba.

Kumbakonam, TAMIL NĀDU/INDIA
Takes its name, according to legend, from a *kumbh* 'pitcher' which came to rest here during a great flood. The god Shiva is said to have broken it with an arrow; the contents were spilt and formed the sacred Mahamaham Tank which became a pilgrimage site.

Kumbo, CAMEROON
Derived from Nkimbo, the people of Nkim. When the Germans arrived they changed the *i* to *u* and the place became known as Kumbo.

Kumertau, BASHKORTOSTAN REPUBLIC/RUSSIA
Founded in 1953 in a coal-mining area, the name means 'Coal Mountain' from the Tatar *kömer* 'coal' and *tau*.

Kunashir, KURIL ISLANDS/RUSSIA
'Black Island' from the Ainu *kuna* 'black' and *širi* 'island', a reference perhaps to the colour of its soil. When under Japanese rule, Chinese characters were applied to give a similar sound to the Ainu name and the meaning became 'End of the Country'.

Kunduz (Qondūz), AFGHANISTAN *Drapsaca*
A province, a river, and a town with a name that probably means 'Ancient Fortress' from the Persian *kuhan* 'ancient' and *diz* 'fortress'. Its original name may have been Walwālāz.

Kunene, ANGOLA-NAMIBIA
A river, also spelt Cunene in Angola, that rises in Angola and later becomes the border between Angola and Namibia. The name comes from *okunene* 'on the right hand side', meaning that Angola lies on its right bank.

Kunming, YUNNAN/CHINA *Julan, Yizhou, Jianning, Kunchuan/Kunzhou, Tuodong/Dongdu, Shanchan*
The present name is said to come from the Kunmi, the name of a tribe in south-west China. However, other suggestions are that it derives from a word in the language of a local group meaning 'black savages'. In 1276 it was renamed Kunming County and this became Kunming City in 1928.

Kununurra, WESTERN AUSTRALIA/AUSTRALIA *Mirriwoong, Gananoorang*
'Big Water', a reference to Lake Kununurra.

Kuopio, FINLAND
Founded in 1653, the name is a Finnish version of the Swedish *köping* 'market settlement' or here 'market town'.

Kupang, WEST TIMOR/INDONESIA
'Lord' in Timorese, meaning the ruler *kupang* of the area.

Kur, GEORGIA *Cyrus, Kura*
A river called Cyrus by the Greeks, Kura by the Russians, and Kuruçay by the Turks; the river rises in Turkey. The Georgians also call it the Mtkvari from the Kartlian *mdinarée* 'river'. Kur comes from the Abhaz *a-kuara* 'river'.

Kurashiki, HONSHŪ/JAPAN
'Village of Warehouses' from *kura* 'warehouse' and *shiki* 'lay' or here 'build'. A *kurashiki* was a place where farm implements were stored in warehouses.

Kurchatov, KAZAKHSTAN *Semipalatinsk-21*
A former 'secret' city for nuclear weapons
testing, its name was changed to Kurchatov
after Igor Kurchatov (1903–60), a nuclear
physicist who supervised development of the
Soviet atomic bomb programme and the first
explosion on 29 August 1949.

Kurdistan (Arabic: **Kurdestan**), IRAN-IRAQ-
SYRIA-TURKEY
'Land of the Kurds', a large geographical area
that extends mainly over Iran, Iraq, and
Turkey, and slightly into Syria. Despite never
having been united under a single ruler nor
acquiring the status of a nation-state, the
Kurds, numbering some twenty million, have
been able to maintain a distinct sense of
identity and culture for at least the last 2 000
years; they do not, however, share a common
language or religion. They are by far the largest
group of people in the world without their
own country. Following the collapse of the
Ottoman Empire after the First World War,
the 1920 Treaty of Sèvres raised the possibility
of an autonomous homeland for the Kurds. But
at the Treaty of Lausanne in 1923 the new state
of Turkey acquired much of what would have
been Kurdistan and so its creation never took
place. Nevertheless, an independent Kurdistan
did exist on Iranian soil between December
1945 and December 1946 as the Kurdish
Republic of Mahābād before being
extinguished by Iranian troops. The name
'Kurd' can be traced back to the 7th century
and may come from the Assyrian *kardu* 'strong'
or 'heroic'; it has also been suggested that it
originally meant 'nomad'. *See* KORDESTAN.

Kuressaare, ESTONIA *Arensburg, Kingiseppe*
Founded in the middle of the 14th century
around a castle that had been built on the site
of a 12th-century Livonian fort and named
after a knight called Arnold. This name was
subsequently superseded by Kuressaare from a
personal name, Kure, and the Estonian *saare*
'island'. In 1952–91 the town was named after
Viktor Kingisepp (1888–1922), leader of the
Estonian Communist Party (1918–22), who
was born here. It then reverted to its earlier
name.

Kurgan, RUSSIA *Tsarëvo Gorodishche, Tsarëvo
Kurgan*
A province and a city founded in 1553 as a fort
on a large ancient tumulus with a name
actually meaning 'Site of an ancient
Royal Settlement'. When the fort
developed into a town in 1782 its new
name meant 'Royal Burial Mound' from
kurgan 'burial mound' or 'tumulus' and

tsarëvo 'royal'. The 'royal' was subsequently
removed.

Kurgan-Tyube (Qurghonteppa), TAJIKISTAN
'Burial Mound on a Hill' from the Turkic *tyube*
'hill' and *kurgan. See* KURGAN.

Kuril Islands, (Kuril'skiye Ostrova), RUSSIA
Chupka, Rakkoshima, Chishima
Possibly derived from the Russian *kurit'*
'to smoke', a reference to the active volcanoes.
But more likely the name comes from the
Ainu word *kur* 'man' or 'people', the Ainu
being the first known inhabitants of the
Kurils. The Ainu Chupka means 'When the
Sun rises'. The Japanese Chishima means
'One Thousand Islands' although there are
in fact only 56 and a few uninhabited rocks,
and only five are permanently inhabited. The
1855 Treaty of Simoda placed the border
between Russia and Japan between the
islands of Iturup (Japanese: Etorofu) and
Urup, but the 1875 Treaty of St Petersburg
resulted in the Russians ceding the rest of
the Kurils chain to Japan in exchange for the
Japanese-occupied part of Sakhalin Island.
In accordance with the 1945 Yalta Agreement
the entire chain was ceded to the Soviet Union
and the Japanese inhabitants were expelled.
The 1956 Soviet–Japanese Declaration that
ended the state of war between the two
countries stated that the two southernmost
islands, Shikotan and Habomai, would be
transferred to Japan when a peace treaty was
concluded. In the mean time, Japan has
continued to press its claim to have Iturup,
Kunashir, Shikotan, and the Habomai Islets,
a group they call the Northern Territories,
returned.

Kurkat, TAJIKISTAN *Cyropolis/Cryeschata*
Originally named after the Persian Cyrus II the
Great (590/580–c.529 BC), Achaemenid
emperor (c.550–c.529 BC), who founded it c.530
BC. The present name comes from the local
Kurus katha 'City of Cyrus'.

Kurri Kurri-Weston, NEW SOUTH WALES/
AUSTRALIA
Laid out in 1902 with a name from an
Aboriginal term meaning either 'man' or 'the
first'. In 1966 it merged with Weston.

Kurseong, WEST BENGAL/INDIA
Derived from the Lepcha *kursonrip*, a reference
to the small white orchid which is abundant in
the area.

Kursk, RUSSIA
A province and a city named after the River
Kur which itself comes from *kurya* 'channel'.

Kuršumlija, SERBIA/SERBIA AND MONTENEGRO
Ad Fines, Toplica, Bela Crkva
In the 11th century the Roman name gave way
to the Slav Toplica, one of the two rivers on
which the town lies, and then to Bela Crkva
'White Church' after the appearance of the
cathedral which dominates the town. The
Ottoman Turks coined the present name from
the Serbo-Croat *kuršum* 'lead' after the lead
roofs of two churches.

Kurukshetra, HARYĀNA/INDIA
A Hindu pilgrimage centre, the city's water
reservoir, often called the Kurukshetra tank, is
said to have been built by Raja Kuru; the name
means 'Kuru's Field'.

Kuşadası, TURKEY *Scala Nuova*
'Island of Birds' from *kus* 'bird' and *adası* 'island
of' from *ada* 'island'.

Kushiro, HOKKAIDŌ/JAPAN
Named after the Kushiro River at the mouth of
which it lies. The name is said to come from
kushi 'bracelet' and *ro* 'way'. The manufacture
of bracelets was an important industry here
and *kushiru* means 'gem' in Korean. However,
the origin of the name may be the Ainu *kush-ru*
'passage'.

Kustanay (Qostanay), KAZAKHSTAN *Kostana?,
Nikolayevsk*
A province and a city founded in 1883, possibly
as Kostana, which may have come from the
name of the local people, the Tana, and *kos*
'two'. In 1893–5 it was named after Emperor
Nicholas II[†] before returning to a form of its
original name.

Kūt, al-, IRAQ
'The Fort' in Arabic.

Kutaisi (K'ut'aisi), GEORGIA *Miletus, Kyta*
Derived from *kuata* 'stony' or 'rocky', possibly
a reference to its wooded hillsides and
backdrop of snow-capped mountains. It was
the capital of successive kingdoms in Georgia:
Colchis, Iberia, Abkhazia, and Imereti.

Kutná Hora, CZECH REPUBLIC *Kuttenberg*
Founded in the early 13th century as a silver-
mining town, the name comes from *kutati* 'to
mine minerals' and *hora* 'mountain' or 'rock',
a reference to the fact that at this time
minerals were mined predominantly in
mountainous country. German miners were
brought in to work the mines, hence the
former German name which has the same
meaning. The town gave its name to
kutnohorite, calcium manganese carbonate.

Kuwait (al-Kuwayt) *Grane*
The State of Kuwait (Arabic: Dawlat al-Kuwayt)
since full independence in 1961. Previously a

sovereign state under British protection
(1914–61), the UK having had control of
Kuwait's foreign affairs since 1899 when
Mubārak ibn Sabāh the Great, founder and
ruler of modern Kuwait (1896–1915), sought
British support against Ottoman forces—
although it was under nominal Ottoman
suzerainty until 1914; an autonomous
Shaikhdom (1756), Kuwait City having been
founded in about 1716. Despite the northern
border with Iraq being settled in 1923, Iraq
claimed that Kuwait belonged to it in 1961 and
again in 1990 when Iraqi forces invaded the
country, announced its annexation and
proclaimed it to be Iraq's 19th governorate;
Kuwait City was renamed Saddam City for the
next seven months. In February 1991 an
American-led multinational force liberated
Kuwait. The name Grane, for the original
coastal village, is the diminutive of the Arabic
qarn 'high hill'. In *c.*1680 a small fortress called
Kuwait was built by Barrāk, Shaikh of the Banī
Khālid tribe (1669–82), which was dominant in
eastern Arabia at the time; this name is a
diminutive of the Arabic *kūt* 'fort'. In the
language of the area this is a house built in the
shape of a fortress that can be easily defended
and which is close to water; the term was then
applied to a settlement built on such a site. By
the end of the 18th century the town which
had developed around the fort was generally
called Kuwait instead of Grane.

Kuybyshev, ARMENIA, RUSSIA
1. Named after Valerian Kuybyshev[†]. *See*
SAMARA.
2. Russia (Novosibirsk): founded in 1722 as
Kainsk, it was renamed in 1935 after the
death of Valerian Kuybyshev[†] who was
in exile here in 1907–9, during which
time he participated in revolutionary
activities.

Kuybyshevskiy, TAJIKISTAN, UKRAINE
Named after Valerian Kuybyshev[†].

Kuzbass, KEMEROVO-NOVOSIBIRSK/RUSSIA
A coal-mining region with a name that is an
abbreviation of *Kuznetskiy Basseyn* 'Kuznetsk
Basin'. *Kuznets* means 'blacksmith' and was a
name given to the local Tatars who were
famous for their skills.

Kuznetsk, PENZA/RUSSIA *Naryshkino*
Originally named after the Naryshkin family.
The name was later changed to 'Blacksmith'
from *kuznets*, presumably in acknowledgement
of a metalworks here.

Kvemo Kartli, GEORGIA *Iberia*
A region meaning 'Lower Iberia'. Iberia, or
Hiberia, was the ancient name used by the

Greeks to describe eastern Georgia along the Kura (Cyrus), now Mktvari, River. The Georgian name was Kartli, a former kingdom, named after King Kartlos, legendary father of the Georgian people and said to be a descendant of Noah's son Japheth.

KwaNdebele, SOUTH AFRICA
'Place of the Ndebele' from *kwa*, a Zulu word signifying 'at' or 'in (the place of)'. A former homeland established in 1979 for the Transvaal Ndebele people after they had been evicted from Bophuthatswana. In 1981 it became a self-governing national state, but was reincorporated into South Africa in 1994. The Ndebele were previously known as the Matabele. *See* MATABELELAND.

Kwangju, SOUTH KOREA
'Bright Province' from *kwang* 'light' or 'brightness' and *chu* 'province'.

Kwangsi, CHINA
See GUANGXI.

Kwangtung, CHINA
See GUANGDONG.

KwaZulu-Natal, SOUTH AFRICA
A province created in 1994 from the former province of Natal and the former Zulu homeland of KwaZulu. This was a tribal homeland (known as a *bantustan*) granted internal self-government in 1977; until 1972, when the name KwaZulu was adopted, it was known as Zululand 'Land of the Zulu' named after one of the clan's founding ancestors; his name is said to mean 'sky'. *Kwa* is a Zulu word signifying 'at' or 'in (the place of)'. *See* NATAL AND ZULULAND.

Kwekwe, ZIMBABWE *Que Que*
Settled in 1902 and named after the river which itself was so-called because of the noise made by frogs, 'croak-croak'. The spelling was changed in 1980.

Kwinana, WESTERN AUSTRALIA/AUSTRALIA
The name is taken from that of a freighter which was wrecked offshore in 1922. Its name is an Aboriginal word meaning 'young woman'.

Kyabram, VICTORIA/AUSTRALIA
Derived from an Aboriginal word for 'thick forest'.

Kyaikkami, BURMA *Amherst*
Founded by the British in about 1826, it was originally named after William Pitt Amherst (1773–1857), 1st Earl Amherst, governor general of India (1823–8). The meaning of the present name, adopted after the British withdrew from Burma in 1948, is unknown.

Kyŏnggi, SOUTH KOREA
A province meaning 'Near the Capital' from *kyŏng* 'capital'; the provincial capital is also the national capital, Seoul. However, the name could mean 'Royal Capital' from *ki* 'royal domain', the *ki* becoming *gi* when following the *-ng* of *kyŏng*.

Kyŏngju, SOUTH KOREA *Sŏrabŏl, Kŭmsŏng, Tongyŏng*
The capital of the Kingdom of Silla between 57 BC and 935 AD, Sŏrabŏl means 'capital'. Although a historic city, the present name means 'Beautiful Province' from *kyŏng* 'beautiful' and *chu* 'province'.

Kyōto, HONSHŪ/JAPAN *Heian-kyō, Miyako, Saikyō*
An urban prefecture and a city founded in the 6th century. The city was the Japanese capital in 794–1868 as Heian-kyō 'Capital of Tranquillity and Peace' from *hei* 'tranquillity', *an* 'peace' and *kyō* 'capital', and as Miyako 'The Capital', the imperial residence. After the Meiji Restoration in 1868 when the Imperial Household moved to Tokyo and the city ceased to be the capital, it was renamed Saikyō 'Western Capital'. In due course it became Kyōto 'Capital City' from *kyō* 'capital' and *to* 'capital', in recognition of its previous status of which its inhabitants are very proud.

Kyrenia (Greek: **Kirínia**; Turkish: **Girne**), CYPRUS *Cerynia, Corineum*
Possibly named ultimately after Kefeus, its founder and a Trojan who escaped to Cyprus after the legendary Trojan war in the 13th or 12th century BC. It has also been suggested that it is named after a mountain in the Greek homeland of the Achaeans who arrived on the north coast of Cyprus in the 10th century BC.

Kyrgyzstan The Kyrgyz Republic (Respublika Kirgizstan) since 1993. Previously the Republic of Kyrgyzstan (1990, just before independence in 1991); Kirgiziya, the Russian name, or the Kirgiz Soviet Socialist Republic (1936–91), the Kirgiz Autonomous Soviet Socialist Republic (1926–36), the Kara-Kirgiz Autonomous Province within the Russian Soviet Federated Socialist Republic (1924) when Central Asia was split into national territories, and part of the Autonomous Soviet Socialist Republic of Turkestan (1918). The Kyrgyz lands were officially incorporated into the Russian Empire in 1863, although southern Kirgizia and the Khanate of Kokand, to which it belonged, did not join until 1876. Until the mid-1920s the Kyrgyz were known as Kara-Kirgiz to prevent confusion with the Kazakhs who were called Kirgiz or Kirgiz-Kazakhs by the Russians to distinguish them from the Cossacks (in Russian, *Kazaki*). The name simply means the 'Land of the Kyrgyz' from *stan*, although the country is not a nation-state, there being some 80 nationalities living within its borders. A nomadic, pastoral Turkic-speaking people, their name may come from the Turkic *kir* 'steppe' and *gizmek* 'to wander'. It has also been suggested that the name means 'Forty Clans', a reference to the forty mythical tribes who formed the historical Kyrgyz; the new national flag shows a blazing sun emitting forty rays. Within Kyrgyzstan are three Uzbek exclaves, Iordan (Yardan), *Shakhimardan and Sokh, and the Tajik exclave of Vorukh.

Kyūshū, JAPAN
One of Japan's four main islands, the name means '(Land of) Nine Provinces' from *kyū* 'nine' and *shū* 'province', a reference to its historical administrative divisions. It is now divided into seven prefectures.

Kyustendil, BULGARIA *Pautalia, Velbuzhd, Konstandili*
In 1018 its Roman name, from a Thracian word representing 'source' or 'spring', gave way to Velbuzhd after a local chief. After the Battle of Velbuzhd in 1330 when the Serbs defeated the Bulgarians and killed the tsar the Ottoman Turks captured the town. They renamed it Konstandili 'Konstantin's Land' after Konstantin Dragaš, the Serb leader and son of a Serb nobleman. This became corrupted to the present name.

Kyzyl, RUSSIA, KYRGYZSTAN-TAJIKISTAN
1. Russia (Tuva): in 1914–18 it was known as Belotsarsk 'White Tsar (Town)' from *belyy* and

tsar'. The second name, Khem-Beldyr 'River Confluence' from *khem* 'river', the Tuvan name for the Yenisey River, and *beldyr* 'confluence', was in use in 1918–26; the town lies at the confluence of two branches of the Yenisey. In 1926 it was given its present Turkic name 'Red'. It has also been known as *Krasnyy*.
2. Kyrgyzstan-Tajikistan: a river meaning 'Red'.

Kyzyl-Kiya (Kyzyl-Kyya), KYRGYZSTAN
'Red Rock' from *kyzyl* and *kaya* 'rock', a reference to the colour of the soil.

Kyzyl Kum (Kazakh: **Qyzylqum**; Uzbek: **Qïzïl Qum**), KAZAKHSTAN-UZBEKISTAN
A desert meaning 'Red Sand' from *kyzyl* and *kum* 'sand'.

Kyzyl-Orda (Qyzylorda or Quzylorda),
KAZAKHSTAN *Ak-Mechet, Perovsky, Fort Perovsk*
Founded in 1820 as a fort called Ak-Mechet 'White Mosque' from *aq* 'white' and *meshit* 'mosque' in modern Kazakh. In 1853–1917 it was named after General Vasily Perovsky (1795–1857), the Russian commander of the force that captured the Kokandian settlement here in 1853. Ak-Mechet was readopted in 1917–25. The present Kazakh name means 'Red Fort', literally 'Red Horde' from *kyzyl* 'red' (here, in its revolutionary sense) and Turkic *ordu* 'camp' or 'army'. It served as the Kazakh capital between 1924 and 1929 until Alma-Ata (now Almaty) took over because the Bolsheviks thought that Kyzyl-Orda was too hot. The present name was adopted in 1925. It is also the name of a province.

LA, CALIFORNIA/USA
A common abbreviation for *Los Angeles.

Labé, GUINEA
Founded in the 1720s by the Dialonke, it was named after their chief, Manga Labé.

Labinsk, KRASNODAR TERRITORY/RUSSIA
Labinskaya Stanitsa
Named after the Laba River on which it lies. Until 1947 it had been known as the 'Cossack Village of the Laba'.

Labrador, NEWFOUNDLAND AND LABRADOR/CANADA
A region, the mainland section of the province of Newfoundland and Labrador, and a city. This region may have been what Leif Eriksson, the Norse explorer, called Markland 'Land of Forests' *c*.1000. It is not clear how the present name arose, but one explanation is that Gaspar Corte-Real, the Portuguese explorer, named it Terra de Lavradores 'Land of Labourers' in 1501 after he had seen the land being cultivated; another is that one of Corte-Real's sailors, a farmer, *lavrador*, from the Azores, saw Greenland which was named Terra del Lavrador. This name evolved into Labrador and was subsequently transferred to the mainland part of Newfoundland. Labrador City takes its name from the region as does the Labrador Sea between it and Greenland. Labrador gives its name to the Labrador retriever, first bred here.

Labuan, SABAH/MALAYSIA *Pulau Maida*
Derived from *pelabuhan* 'port' or 'anchorage'. The Sultan of Brunei ceded the island to the British in 1846 and it became a crown colony two years later. In 1890 its administration was assumed by the British North Borneo Company until 1907 when it became part of the Straits Settlements. In 1942 it was occupied by the Japanese and renamed Pulau Maida 'Maida Island'. In 1946 it became part of the colony of North Borneo which was renamed Sabah in 1963. It received the status of a Federal Territory of Malaysia in 1984.

La Ceiba, HONDURAS
A port named after a very large ceiba tree (kapok: *ceiba pentandra*) which at one time stood on the coast and which was used as a meeting place.

Lachine, QUEBEC/CANADA
Founded in 1667 by the French explorer René-Robert Cavelier, Sieur de La Salle[†] while attempting to find a westward way to China, it was named La Petite Chine 'Little China' which was subsequently contracted to Lachine.

Lachlan River, NEW SOUTH WALES/AUSTRALIA
Explored in 1815 by George William Evans, an Englishman, who named it after Lachlan Macquarie (1761–1824), Scottish-born governor of New South Wales (1810–21).

Lackawanna, NEW YORK/USA *Limestone Hill*
Settled in 1850, it took its name in 1899 from the Lackawanna River which itself comes from a Delaware word meaning 'Stream that forks'.

Lacon, ILLINOIS/USA
Named after Laconia in Greece. *See* LACONIA.

Laconia (Lakonía), GREECE
A department and historic province in south-eastern Greece named after the local people, the Laconians, the meaning of whose name is unknown. Under the control of their capital, the city-state of *Sparta, they gave their name to the adjective 'laconic'; the Spartans were well known for their somewhat terse speech.

La Coruña, GALICIA/SPAIN
See CORUNNA.

La Crosse, WISCONSIN/USA *Prairie La Crosse*
Developed from a trading post in 1841, the settlement was called Prairie La Crosse by French explorers. Before it was settled the area was a favourite place for the local Native Americans to play a ball game, called by the French *la crosse*. The Native Americans, who had played it long before the arrival of Christopher Columbus[†] in 1492, called it *tewaraathon* 'baggataway', but to the French the 'cross' for catching and throwing the ball looked like a bishop's crook. The sport is now known as lacrosse.

La Cygne, KANSAS/USA
Named after the River Marais des Cygnes from the French *marais* 'marsh' or 'fen' and *cygne* 'swan'.

Ladākh, JAMMU AND KASHMIR/PAKISTAN-INDIA-CHINA *Ma-lo-pho, Kachanpa, Ripul, Ladwak*

A mountainous region of Kashmir, it means '(Land of) Passes' from the Tibetan *ladag* from *la* 'pass' and *dag* 'open'. The first Chinese name meant 'Red Land', the second 'Land of Snow', and the third 'Land of Mountains'. Ladwak, from which the present name is derived, meant the 'Land of Passes'. Ladakh was divided between India and Pakistan in 1947 but, as a result of an invasion in 1962, China annexed a part belonging to India.

Ladismith, WESTERN CAPE/SOUTH AFRICA *Lady Smith*
Laid out in 1852 and named after Lady (Juana) Smith, the Spanish wife of Sir Harry Smith (1787–1860), governor of Cape Colony (1847–52). To distinguish it from the *Ladysmith in Natal, the spelling was changed in 1879.

Ladoga, Lake (Ladozhskoye Ozero), LENINGRAD/RUSSIA
Takes its name from the old town of Ladoga which itself took its name from a tributary of the Volkhov River. The tributary took its name from its Finnish name of Alodejoki 'low-lying river' from *alode* 'low place' and *joki* 'river'.

Ladushkin, KALININGRAD/RUSSIA *Ludwigsort*
Previously in East Prussia, it had a German name 'Ludwig's Place' from the personal name and *Ort* 'place'. In 1946 it was renamed after Ivan Ladushkin, a soldier of the Red Army who was killed near here in 1945.

Ladybrand, FREE STATE/SOUTH AFRICA
Settled in 1867 and named after Lady (Catharine) Brand, wife of Sir Christoffel Brand, speaker of the Cape legislative assembly.

Lady Grey, EASTERN CAPE/SOUTH AFRICA
Founded in 1858 and named after the wife of Sir George Grey (1812–98), governor of Cape Colony (1854–9, 1860–1).

Ladysmith, CANADA, SOUTH AFRICA, USA
South Africa (KwaZulu-Natal): founded as Windsor in 1850 and named after a local merchant, George Windsor. It was later renamed after Lady (Juana) Smith, the wife of Sir Harry Smith. *See* LADISMITH.

La Esmeralda, PANAMA, PARAGUAY, VENEZUELA
'The Emerald' in Spanish.

La Esperanza, BOLIVIA, CUBA, ECUADOR, HONDURAS, PERU, PUERTO RICO
'The Hope' in Spanish.

Lafayette, USA
1. Indiana: laid out in 1825 and named after the Marquis de Lafayette (1757–1834), a French

aristocrat who was making his last visit to the USA at the time; he fought with the Americans against the British, commanding a division and later an army during the War of Independence (1775–83).
2. Louisiana: founded in 1824 as Vermilionville and situated on the Vermilion River, it was renamed after the Marquis de Lafayette in 1884.

La Fe, CUBA *Santa Fe*
Founded by Americans and named after their own city of *Santa Fe in New Mexico.

Lafiagi, KWARA/NIGERIA
Founded as a fortified town in 1810 on the Niger River with a name derived from a Nupe word meaning 'Small Hill'.

Laghouat, ALGERIA
A province and a town situated in an oasis with a name derived fom the Arabic *al-wāḥāt* 'the oases' from *wāḥa* 'oasis'.

Lagos, NIGERIA, PORTUGAL
1. Nigeria: a state and a city-port founded in the 15th century by the Awori, a subgroup of the Yoruba, on Lagos Island which they called Oko. When the Portuguese arrived in 1472 they named the place 'Lakes' from *lago* 'lake'. This was a reference to the lagoons along the coast. The city was annexed by the British in 1864 as part of the Gold Coast Colony (now Ghana) and then in 1886 it became the capital of a new protectorate. In 1906 it became the capital of Southern Nigeria when merging with that protectorate and of the Protectorate of Nigeria in 1914 when Southern and Northern Nigeria amalgamated. When Nigeria gained its independence it became the national capital, retaining this status until 1991.
2. Portugal: 'Lakes', although somewhat inappropriate. It does, however, lie on the coast at the mouth of the River Alvor. The Roman name was Lacobriga and the Moorish Zawaya.

Lagosanto, EMILIA-ROMAGNA/ITALY *Fiume Carbonara*
'Saint's Lake' from *lago* 'lake' and related to St Appiano, a Benedictine monk who died *c*.800. He was sent by his abbot in Pavia to gather salt at Comacchio. In order to do the best job possible, he settled in an area of salt marshes called Lago near Comacchio. *Santo* 'saint' was added after his death to commemorate his presence here.

La Grange, GUYANA, USA
USA (Georgia): following a visit to the area by the Marquis de Lafayette (1757–1834), a French

aristocrat, in 1825, it was named after his
estate near Paris.

La Gruyère, SWITZERLAND
A region with a name that may be derived
from *gruaria* (see GRUYÈRES) or from *gruyer*
'forestry official'. The area gives its name to
the famous cheese.

Laguna Beach, CALIFORNIA/USA *Lagonas*
Founded in 1887 and named after two lagoons
nearby (in Spanish, *laguna*); it was renamed in
1904.

La Habra, CALIFORNIA/USA
Founded in 1839 with a name said to be
derived from the Spanish *abra* 'pass', a
reference to a gap in the nearby hills.

Lahaina, HAWAII/USA
'Cruel Sun'.

Laḥij, YEMEN *Laḥej, al-Hawtah*
Named after a prominent member of the
Himyar tribe, Lahdj bin Walil. During the final
years of British rule in the Aden Protectorate in
the 1960s it was called al-Hawtah.

Lahore, PUNJAB/PAKISTAN *Lohawar*
According to Hindu legend, founded by Loh or
Lava, son of Rāma, after whom it is said to be
named. Lohawar may be a corruption of *Lohpur*
'Place of Loh'. It was under British rule in
1849–1947. It was capital of the Ghaznavid
Empire in 1152–86.

Lahti, FINLAND
Founded in 1878 on the southern end of Lake
Vesijärvi, the name simply means 'bay'.

La Junta, COLORADO/USA *Otero*
'The Junction'. Founded in 1875 and originally
named after a Spanish settler, it was
subsequently renamed 'The Junction', a
reference to its position at the junction of the
old Santa Fe and Navajo trails.

Lake Charles, LOUISIANA/USA
A city named after an early inhabitant, Charles
Sallier, who settled on Lake Calcasieu to the
south in 1781.

Lake City, FLORIDA/USA *Alligator*
Founded in 1824 when the Seminole departed.
The presence of alligators was recognized in its
first name, but because of the many lakes in
the area white settlers changed the name in
1859 when the city was incorporated.

Lake District, ENGLAND/UK
A region of lakes and mountains. It has
seventeen major lakes, although only one,
Bassenthwaite, is called a lake; the rest are
called 'waters' and 'meres' from the Old
English *mere* 'lake' or 'pool'.

Lake Forest, ILLINOIS/USA
Settled in 1836, it is named after its location on
the wooded shore of Lake Michigan.

Lake Geneva, WISCONSIN/USA
A city said to be named after Geneva in New
York because their positions at the north end
of lakes are roughly similar. *See* GENEVA.

Lake Harbour, NEWFOUNDLAND/CANADA
Named after the *Lark*, one of Captain James
Cook's[†] ships used during his surveys in the
region in the 1760s.

Lakeland, FLORIDA/USA
Founded in 1883 and named after the thirteen
lakes within the city limits.

Lake Louise, ALBERTA/CANADA *Holt City,*
Laggan
Originally a camp for construction workers on
the Canadian Pacific Railway, it was renamed
in 1914 after the lake which had been
discovered in 1882 and which itself honoured
Princess Louise (1848–1939), fourth daughter
of Queen Victoria[†] and wife of the Marquess of
Lorne, governor-general of Canada (1878–83).

Lakenheath, ENGLAND/UK *Lacingahith,*
Lakingahethe
'Landing Place of People living by Streams'
from the Old English *lacu* 'stream', *-inga-* and
hȳth 'landing place' or 'harbour'.

Lake Odessa, MICHIGAN/USA
A town named after the city in Ukraine.

Lake of the Woods, CANADA-USA
So-called because of the heavily wooded
islands in the lake.

Lake Wales, FLORIDA/USA
Surveyed in 1879 by Sidney Wailes and named
after the lake, originally Lake Watts, which
was renamed after him. In 1915 the spelling
was changed.

Lakewood, OHIO/USA *Rockport, East Rockport*
First named in 1819, the name East
Rockport was in use between 1871 and
1889 when the city was given its present
name, a reference to the wooded shores of
Lake Erie.

Lakshadweep, INDIA *Laccadive, Minicoy and*
Amīndīvi Islands
A Union Territory since 1956, having passed to
India on independence in 1947 after 148 years
of British sovereignty. The name means
'Hundred Thousand Islands' from the Sanskrit
and Malayalam *laksha* 'hundred thousand' and
dvīpa 'island', although there are in fact only
27. The former name was in use in 1956–73.
The name of the island of Minicoy, the
southernmost island and historically part of

the Maldives, is said to come from *min* 'fish' and *kayam* 'deep pool'.

Lalībela, ETHIOPIA *Roha*
Renamed *c*.1185 after Lalībela, King of Ethiopia (1185–1211), the literal meaning of whose name is 'the bees recognize his sovereignty'. According to legend, a swarm of bees hovered over his cot while he lay in it; his mother, aware of the belief that the animal world could prophesy the future of important people, cried out 'Lalībela'. Thus, the younger half-brother of King Harbay was given the name Lalībela. This was his birthplace and the capital of the ruling Zagwe dynasty.

La Libertad, ECUADOR, EL SALVADOR, GUATEMALA, HONDURAS, MEXICO, NICARAGUA, PERU, PHILIPPINES
Peru: a region formed in 1821. The name means 'liberty' or 'freedom' in Spanish, but although Peru declared its independence in 1821 it did not gain its freedom until 1824 when the Spanish were finally defeated.

La Linea, ANDALUSIA/SPAIN
'The Line', a reference to the fact that it lies on the border with Gibraltar. The full name is La Línea de la Concepción.

Lalitpur, INDIA, NEPAL
1. India (Uttar Pradesh): 'Town of Lalita' and said to be named after Lalita, the wife of an Indian raja.
2. Nepal: also known as Pātan from *pāt* 'linen'. Said to have been founded in 299, the present name means 'Pleasant Town' from *lalit* 'pleasant' or 'agreeable' and *pur*.

La Mancha, CASTILE-LA MANCHA/SPAIN
al-Manshah
A flat and barren region in central Spain derived from the Arabic *al-Manshah* 'The Wilderness'. *See* CASTILE-LA MANCHA.

Lamar, MISSOURI/USA
Founded in 1856 and named after Mirabeau Buonaparte Lamar (1798–1859), president of the Texas Republic (1838–41).

Lambert's Bay, WESTERN CAPE/SOUTH AFRICA
Founded in 1913 and named after Rear Admiral Sir Robert Lambert, commander of the British naval establishment at the Cape (1820–1).

Lambourn, ENGLAND/UK *Lambourne*
Possibly 'Stream where Lambs are washed' from the Old English *lamb* and *burna* 'stream'.

La Mesa, COLOMBIA, USA
USA (California and New Mexico): 'The Table' in Spanish.

Lampedusa (Isola di Lampedusa), PELAGIE ISLANDS/ITALY *Lopadusa*
An island with a name believed to be derived from the Greek *lopax*, a kind of mollusc, which became the Latin *lopada* and then the Italian *lampita* 'limpet'.

Lampeter (Llanbedr Pont Steffan), WALES/UK
Lanpeder, Lampeter Pount Steune
'Church of St Peter' from *llan* and *Pedr*. The Welsh name means the same with the additional 'by Stephen's Bridge' from *pont* 'bridge'.

Lanai, HAWAII/USA
An island meaning 'Conquest Day', a presumed reference to some past event.

Lanark, CANADA, UK, USA
1. UK (Scotland): formerly Lannarc, a Celtic name meaning 'glade', thus '(Place in) the Glade' from the Pictish *lannerch*. Lanarkshire was a former county.
2. Canada-USA: both are named after the Lanark in Scotland.

Lancashire, ENGLAND/UK
A county with a name that is a shortening of the 14th-century Lancastreshire, Lancaster being the county town, and *scīr*.

Lancaster, CANADA, UK, USA
1. UK (England): formerly Loncastre '(Roman) Fort on the (River) Lune' from a Celtic river name and *ceaster*. The famous British four-engined Second World War bomber was named after the town.
2. USA (California, Ohio, and South Carolina): named by settlers from Lancaster, Pennsylvania.
3. USA (Pennsylvania): originally known as Gibson's Pasture and then Hickory Town, it was renamed after the English town in 1729 when it became the seat of Lancaster County.

Landau, RHINELAND-PALATINATE/GERMANY
The full name is Landau in der Pfalz, literally 'Landau in the Palatinate' from the Latin *palatinus* 'of the palace' or 'palatinate'. *Land* simply means 'land' and *au* is a form of the Old High German *Aue* 'meadow' or 'cultivated land'. Landau lies along the Queich River. The city has given its name to the landau, a four-wheeled carriage for four passengers with a coachman in front.

Land's End, ENGLAND/UK *Londeseynde*
'End of the (Main)land' from the Old English *land* and *ende*. This is said to be a translation of the Cornish *Pen an Wlas* or *Pedn an Laaz* 'End of the Land' with *pen* 'promontory' or 'end'.

Landshut, BAVARIA/GERMANY
'Protector of the District' from *Hut* 'protection' or 'guarding' and *Land* 'district'. Founded in 1204 as a fortress on the site of a Roman camp, it provided protection for the surrounding area.

Landskrona, SWEDEN
Founded by Erik (*c*.1381–*c*.1459), King of Sweden (Erik XIII), Denmark (Erik VII), and Norway (Erik III) (1397–1439), and meaning 'Crown Land' from *land* 'district' and *krona* 'crown'.

Langeland, DENMARK
An island meaning 'Long Land' from *lang* 'long' and *land* 'land'.

Langley, CANADA, UK, USA
1. Canada (British Columbia): established as Fort Langley in 1827 and moved 2 miles (3 km) upstream from its original location in 1839, it was named after Thomas Langley, a director of the Hudson's Bay Company.
2. UK (England): 'Long Wood' from the Old English *lang* and *lēah* 'wood' or 'woodland clearing'.

Langres, CHAMPAGNE-ARDENNE/FRANCE
Andematunum
Named after the Lingones, a Gallic tribe, who built a stronghold here. The former name was Roman.

Languedoc-Roussillon, FRANCE
A region whose name is derived from *langue d'oc*, the traditional medieval language, Provençal (now usually called Occitan), of southern France. It was a French dialect derived from the language spoken by the early Roman invaders where the term *hoc ille* 'this that' was used to indicate the affirmative, there being no word for 'yes' in Latin. In the north of Gaul this was contracted to *o îl* which evolved into the modern *oui*; the language was called *langue d'oïl*. In the south *hoc ille* was shortened to *oc* and from the 13th century the region where this, the *langue d'oc*, was spoken was called Languedoc. It and Roussillon were both former provinces. Roussillon takes its name from its former capital, the Roman Ruscino.

Lansing, MICHIGAN/USA *Michigan*
Founded in 1847, it was renamed the next year after the village of Lansing in New York which itself was named after John Lansing (1754–1829), a local politician.

Lantau Island, HONG KONG/CHINA
The Chinese name is Tai Yee Shan 'Big Island Mountain'. The official name means 'Broken Head' in Cantonese. It forms part of the New Territories of Hong Kong.

Lanzarote, CANARY ISLANDS/SPAIN
An island named after Lancelloti Malocello, an Italian navigator in Portuguese service, who built a castle on the island in the 14th century.

Lanzhou, GANSU/CHINA *Jincheng*
The original settlement was called 'Gold Town' from *jīn* 'gold' and *chéng* 'town'. Gold is said to have been found when the settlement was established in 81. The present name comes from the Gaolan Mountains to the south from *lán* 'orchid' and *zhōu*.

Laoag, LUZON/PHILIPPINES
'Bright' or 'Radiant' from an Ilocano word for 'light'.

Laodicea, TURKEY
Ruins. Several cities had this name, some named after Laodice, the mother of Seleucus I Nicator[†], and others after Laodice (*c*.261–*c*.241 BC), the wife of Antiochus II Theos, King of the Seleucids (261–246 BC). The most important city with this name was near the modern Denizli, originally being called Diospolis and then Rhoas.

Laois (Laoighis), IRELAND
A county, also sometimes spelled Leix, named after the Laeighis, whose leader, Lughaidh Laeighseach, was granted land here, having ejected invaders from Munster.

Laos (Pathet Lao) *Lān Xāng*
The Lao People's Democratic Republic (Sathalanalat Paxathipatai Paxaxôn Lao) since 1975 when the monarchy was abolished. Previously a constitutional monarchy, the Kingdom of Laos, under the Luang Prabang dynasty from 1947. The Laotian name for the land-locked country is Pathet Lao 'Land of the Lao', Lao being the country's legendary founder and the Lao being a branch of the Tai ethnic group. In 1893 Laos became a French protectorate, the present borders were fixed in 1896-7 and in 1899 it received its modern name from the French who put it in the plural, *Les Laos*, because of the several Lao kingdoms. The Lao, however, only use the singular. Laos was part of French Indo-China, with Cambodia and Vietnam, in 1893–1949. France recognized Laotian independence in 1949, but the country remained within the French Union until 1953 when full independence was achieved. The original name, when the first Laotian state was established from various scattered principalities in 1353, was, in full, Lān Xāng Hom Khao '(Land of) a Million Elephants and White Parasol' from *lān* 'million' and *xāng*

'elephant' to emphasize its military power and royal status.

La Palma, CHILE, EL SALVADOR, PANAMA, SPAIN, USA

Spain (Canary Islands): an island with a name meaning 'The Palm (Tree)'. Its full name is San Miguel de la Palma 'St Michael of the Palm'.

La Pampa, ARGENTINA

A province from the Spanish *la pampa* 'the pampas' or 'prairie'.

La Paz, ARGENTINA, BOLIVIA, COLOMBIA, HONDURAS, MEXICO, PHILIPPINES, URUGUAY, USA

1. Bolivia: founded in 1548 by the Spanish conquistador, Alonso de Mendoza, as Nuestra Señora de la Paz 'Our Lady of the Peace' on the site of an Inca village. It was renamed La Paz de Ayacucho 'The Peace of Ayacucho' in 1825 to commemorate the final victory over the Spanish in December 1824 at the Battle of Ayacucho in Peru after which the Bolivians declared independence. The name was shortened subsequently. It became the administrative capital in 1898; *Sucre is the judicial capital.
2. Mexico (Baja California Sur): named in 1535 Puerto de Santa Cruz 'Port of the Holy Cross', but renamed in 1596 by a Spanish sea captain who was so well treated by the local Pericus tribe that he called the bay Bahia de la Paz 'Bay of Peace' and the coastal city took this name.

La Perouse Strait (Japanese: Sōya-Kaikyō; Russian: **Proliv Laperuza**), JAPAN-RUSSIA

A strait between the Japanese island of Hokkaidō and the Russian island of Sakhalin and named after Jean-François de Galaup (1741–c.1788), Comte de la Pérouse, a French navigator who explored the Pacific Ocean and sailed through the strait in 1787.

Lapland (Finnish: **Lapi**; Swedish: **Lappland**), FINLAND-NORWAY-SWEDEN-RUSSIA

'Land of the Lapps', who are also known as the Sami. One of Finland's provinces is called Lapland.

La Plata, ARGENTINA, COLOMBIA, USA

Argentina: founded in 1882 close to the Río de la Plata 'River Plate' estuary and named after it. It was called Eva Perón in 1946–55 after Eva Perón (1919–52), the influential wife of the Argentinian president, Juan Perón. *See* (RIVER) PLATE AND ARGENTINA.

Lappeenranta, FINLAND *Lapvesi, Villmanstrand*

The harbour area used to be known as Lapvesi 'Lap Water' and was an important trading post in the early 17th century. Count Per Brahe (1602–80), the Swedish governor-general of Finland (1637–41, 1648–54), proposed to his government that Lapvesi should be raised in status to a town and in 1649 Christina (1626–89), Queen of Sweden (1644–54) agreed. On the coat of arms she received was a somewhat primitive-looking man so the town was called Villmanstrand 'Wild Man's Shore' in Swedish. The town was ceded to Russia in 1743 before becoming Finnish in 1812. The Finnish Lappeenranta 'Lap's Shore' comes from *ranta* 'shore' and *Lappeen*, the genitive of Lap.

Laptev Sea (More Laptevykh), RUSSIA

Nordenskiöld Sea, Siberian Sea

Off the northern coast of Russia in the Arctic Ocean. In 1878 Adolf Erik (later Baron) Nordenskiöld (1832–1901), a Swedish geographer and explorer, set out from Tromsö in Norway with the aim of crossing the Arctic Ocean from west to east. In achieving this, he discovered the Laptev Sea which was named after him. It was renamed in 1935 after Khariton and Dmitry Laptev, Russian naval officers and arctic explorers, who charted its shores between 1735 and 1742. It is not clear whether they were brothers or cousins. The Laptev Strait was named after Dmitry Laptev.

Lapu-Lapu, MACTAN/PHILIPPINES *Opon*

Renamed after Chief Lapulapu who killed the Portuguese navigator, Ferdinand Magellan[†], in April 1521 on Mactan Island.

L'Aquila, ABRUZZO/ITALY *Aquila degli Abruzzi*

A province and a city founded c.1240 on the order of Frederick II[†], Holy Roman Emperor, who gave it an imperial eagle, *aquila*, for its emblem from which the town took its name. The former name meant 'Eagle of the Abruzzi (Mountains)' and was in use 1863–1939.

Larache (al-Araish), MOROCCO

Originally the site of a Phoenician trading post, the name means 'The Huts' from a Spanish corruption of the Arabic *al-'arā'ish* 'from *al-* and the plural of '*arīsh* 'hut'. It was a Spanish possession in 1610–89 and 1921–56.

Laramie, WYOMING/YSA

Founded in 1868 as a settlement for construction workers on the Union Pacific Railroad and their families, and named after a French fur trader, Jacques La Ramie, who was killed near here by Native Americans c.1819. A mountain range and peak, and a river in Wyoming also have this name.

Laredo, SPAIN, USA

USA (Texas): founded in 1755 as a ferry crossing over the Rio Grande by a Spaniard, Thomas Sánchez, and named after the Laredo in Spain.

La Rioja, ARGENTINA, CHILE, SPAIN
Spain: an autonomous community named after the *Rio Oja* 'River Oja' which flows into the River Ebro. It is famous for its Rioja red wines.

Larissa (Lárisa), GREECE *Yeni Şehir-i-Fenari*
A very ancient city under Macedonian rule between 344 and 196 BC. Having been fortified by Justinian I[†], it was given the Pelasgian name Larissa 'Citadel'. Held by the Ottoman Turks in 1423–1881 it was called 'New Town' from *yeni* 'new' and *şehir*.

Lārkāna, SIND/PAKISTAN
Takes its name from a neighbouring people, the Lāraks.

Larnaca (Greek: **Lárnax;** Turkish: **Lârnaka),** CYPRUS *Kitium/Kition, Khittim, Salina, Zeno*
Settled by the Phoenicians during the 9th century BC, the present name is derived from the Greek *lárnax* 'funerary urn' or 'sarcophagus', due to a large number of tombs in the area which were discovered as a result of the activities of grave robbers. It is believed that the name was given to the city by the Ottoman Turks soon after they conquered Cyprus in 1571. Salina was adopted in recognition of the nearby salt lake; Zeno was the name used by the Lusignans and the Venetians before the arrival of the Turks.

Larne (Latharna), NORTHERN IRELAND/UK
'(Land of) the People of Lathair', a pre-Christian king. A river also has this name.

La Rochelle, POITOU-CHARENTES/FRANCE
Rupella, Rochella
Its first Latin name came from *rupes* 'rock'. This evolved into Rochella by the 12th century from the French equivalent to *rupes, roche* 'rock'.

La Roche-sur-Yon, PAYS DE LA LOIRE/FRANCE
Roca super Eon, Napoléon-Vendée, Bourbon-Vendée
'Rock on the Yon' from the pre-Latin *rocca* 'rock' on the River Yon. Having been developed by Napoleon[†] it was renamed 'Napoleon in (the department of) Vendée'. After Napoleon's abdication in 1814 and flight to Elba it was renamed Bourbon-Vendée after the Restoration of the House of Bourbon. Following Napoleon's return to France in 1815, the name Napoléon-Vendée was restored. When he abdicated a second time after his defeat at the Battle of Waterloo a few months later, Bourbon-Vendée was readopted. Finally, after the advent of the Third Republic in 1870, the original name was revived.

La Salle, CANADA, USA
1. Canada (Quebec): settled in 1668 when René-Robert Cavelier, Sieur de La Salle[†] established a fortified town which he called Saint-Sulpice after St Sulpicius (d. 647), bishop of Bourges in France. It was subsequently renamed La Petite Chine or *Lachine. The city became known as La Salle after its founder in 1912 when some of the inhabitants moved to the present site of Lachine and took the name with them.
2. USA (Illinois): settled in 1830 and named after the Sieur de la Salle[†].

Las Animas, COLORADO/USA
A contraction of the name originally given to the river: *El rio de las animas perditas* 'the River of the Lost Souls'. According to a local story, a Spanish regiment on its way to Florida was drowned in the river.

Las Cruces, CHILE, MEXICO, PUERTO RICO, USA
USA (New Mexico): 'The Crosses' from the Spanish *cruz* 'cross'. According to a local story, it was founded in 1848 after a Spanish caravan had been ambushed and massacred by the Apache in 1830. The bodies were left to lie where the city now is. Another caravan which followed the same route came across the bodies, buried them, and placed crosses over the graves.

La Serena, CHILE
Founded *c.*1543, it was named after the Spanish birthplace of the conquistador Pedro de Valdivia (*c.*1500–53).

Lashkar Gāh, AFGHANISTAN *Bost*
Renamed 'Gathering Place of Soldiers' in 1968.

Laško, SLOVENIA
Derived from *Vlaško* indicating a settlement of Vlachs, the Slav name for the Romanized pre-Slav people.

Las Palmas, CHILE, PANAMA, PUERTO RICO, SPAIN
Spain (Canary Islands): 'The Palm Trees' in Spanish. Founded in 1478, it is so-named because of the large number of palm trees in the area. The full name is Las Palmas de Gran Canaria.

La Spezia, LIGURIA/ITALY *Spezia*
The definite article was added in 1930. The meaning or origin of the name is not known for sure, but it is possible that it derives from the Greek *aspidia*, a diminutive of *aspis* and in Italian *scudo* 'shield', meaning 'defence' or 'a defender'.

Las Piedras, BOLIVIA, NICARAGUA, PUERTO RICO, URUGUAY, VENEZUELA
'The Stones' from the Spanish *piedra* 'stone' or 'rock'.

Las Rosas, ARGENTINA, MEXICO
'The Roses' from the Spanish *rosa* 'rose'.

Lassen Peak, CALIFORNIA/USA
At the southern end of the Cascade Range, it is
named after Peter Lassen (1793–1895), a
Danish explorer who acted as a guide for
pioneer settlers.

Last Mountain Lake, SASKATCHEWAN/
CANADA
Only some 2 miles (3 km) wide but 60 miles
(96 km) long, it is also called Long Lake. It is
named after a hill some 20 miles (19 km) to the
east.

Las Tunas, CUBA
A province and a city named 'The Prickly
Pears' from the Spanish *tuna* 'prickly pear'.
The full name is La Victoria de las Tunas,
named by the Spanish in 1869 to
commemorate the victory over the Cubans
during the first war of independence (1868–
78).

Las Vegas, HONDURAS, PUERTO RICO, USA
USA (Nevada): 'The Meadows' or 'The Plains'
from the Spanish *vega* 'fertile plain' or
'meadow'. As Mormons extended the Old
Spanish Trail from the Great Salt Lake to
California in the early 19th century they found
Paiute Native Americans living in an oasis with
artesian springs, mesquite, and cottonwoods
in an otherwise dry valley. Encouraged, some
of them tried to settle here in 1855, gave up
three years later, but returned with the
railroad in 1905. The original site of the Las
Vegas in New Mexico, in the middle of a fertile
meadow, was first settled 20 years earlier, in
1835.

Latakia (Arabic: **al-Lādhiqīyah**), SYRIA *Ramitha,
Leuke Akte, Laodicea ad Mare, La Liche*
A very ancient city, the first name was
Phoenician and the second Greek. The present
name is a corruption of Laodice (*c.*261–*c.*241
BC), the mother of Seleucus II, fourth King of
the Seleucid dynasty (246–225 BC), after whom
the city was named. A port and to distinguish it
from other cities called *Laodicea, it was given
the added *ad Mare* 'on the Sea'. Taken by the
Crusaders in 1103, it was renamed by them La
Liche. It is now also the name of a governorate.

Latgallia (Latgale), LATVIA *Letgallen*
A region in the east named after the Latgallian,
or Lettigallian, people. It was also known as
Polish Livonia in 1629–1772.

Latina, LAZIO/ITALY *Littoria*
Founded in 1932, it takes its name from
Latium, the former name for the region now

known as *Lazio. The city and region were both
known as Littoria until 1947.

Latin America The term embraces all those
countries in Central and South America,
including the Caribbean Islands, whose
inhabitants speak a Romance language,
descendants of Latin: French, Portuguese, and
Spanish. The introduction of these languages
began in the late 15th century with the
voyages to the New World.

Latrobe, AUSTRALIA, USA
1. Australia (Tasmania): founded in 1850 and
named in 1861 after Charles La Trobe,
administrator of Tasmania (1846–8).
2. Australia (Victoria): a river and a mountain
also named after Charles La Trobe, first
lieutenant-governor of Victoria (1851–4).
3. USA (Pennsylvania): named after Benjamin
Latrobe (1764–1820), a distinguished British-
born engineer and architect, who emigrated to
the USA in 1795.

La Tuque, QUEBEC/CANADA
Situated on the Saint-Maurice River, it is
named after a rock on the river bank that
appeared to be the shape of a *tuque*, the
woollen headgear worn by French trappers.

Latvia (Latvija) *Livonia/Livland*
The Republic of Latvia (Latvijas Republika) in
1918–40 and since 1991. Previouly the Latvian
Soviet Socialist Republic (1940–1, 1944–91)
within the Soviet Union; it was occupied by
German forces in 1941–4 during which time it
was part of what was called Ostland 'East
Land', created by Adolf Hitler[†] and comprising
Estonia, Latvia, Lithuania, and Byelorussia. It
was incorporated into the Russian Empire
(1795–1918), although parts had been taken in
1721; partitioned between Poland and Sweden
(1561–1721); under the control of the Teutonic
Knights and German landowners and bishops
(1230–1561). With Estonia it became part of
Livonia in 1346. The name is derived from
what the Latvians call themselves, Latvis; this
means 'forest clearer'. Livland is the German
translation of the Latin Livonia. The country
embraces what was southern Livonia and
Courland. Only after the War of Liberation in
1920 did the three Baltic provinces of Estonia,
Courland, and Livonia become the two states
of Estonia and Latvia. The Latvians are also
known as Letts and their language as Lettish.

Launceston, AUSTRALIA, UK
1. Australia (Tasmania): originally named
Patersonia after the founder of a nearby
settlement, Colonel William Paterson, but
renamed in 1826 after the Cornish birthplace

of Philip Gidley King (1758–1808), the third governor of New South Wales (1800–7).
2. UK (England): formerly Lanscavetone 'Estate near the Site of the Church of St Stephen' from a possible Cornish word *lann* 'church', the saint's name, and *tūn*.

Lausanne, SWITZERLAND *Lausonium/Lausonna, Lausodunum*
The present name has evolved from the last Roman name meaning 'Fort on the (River) Laus' from *dunum*. The previous names were Celtic. The small streams that used to flow through the city no longer exist. The original site was on the shore of Lake Geneva, but the inhabitants sought refuge from invasion in the hills above and built a new settlement there in the 4th century.

Lauterbrunnen, SWITZERLAND
Situated on the Lütschine River in a valley known for its waterfalls, the name means 'Clear Fountains' from the German *lauter* 'clear' or 'pure' and *Brunnen* ' fountain' or 'spring'.

Laval, CANADA, FRANCE
Canada (Quebec): now spread over Île Jésus 'Jesus Island' in the St Lawrence River following the merger of all the island's cities and towns in 1965, having first been settled in 1681. It was named in 1699 after François de Montmorency Laval (1623–1708), the first Roman Catholic bishop of Canada when he was appointed a bishop and vicar apostolic of New France in 1658.

Lavalleja, URUGUAY
A department named after Juan Antonio Lavalleja (1784–1853), one of the leading exiles who crossed back into his homeland to free it from the Spanish in 1825.

Lawang, JAVA/INDONESIA
'Door' in Javanese. Just to the north of the bigger city of Malang, it is considered to be its 'door' or 'point of entry'.

Lawrence, NEW ZEALAND, USA
1. New Zealand (South Island): originally known by its Maori name of Tuapeka when founded in 1861, it was renamed after Sir Henry Montgomery Lawrence (1806–57), one of the prominent men of British India, and the British commissioner in Lucknow who was killed at the start of the six-month siege of the residency during the Indian Mutiny in 1857; its defence owed much to his preparations and determination to resist.
2. USA (Kansas): founded in 1854 and named after Amos A. Lawrence, a textile manufacturer.

3. USA (Massachusetts): founded in 1845 and named after Abbott Lawrence, a member of a group of Boston financiers keen to promote industry here.

Lawrenceville, CANADA, USA
USA (Georgia and Illinois): both cities are named 'Lawrence's Town' after Captain James Lawrence (1781–1813), the American commander of the frigate *Chesapeake* who was killed in battle with the British on Lake Erie in 1813.

Lawton, OKLAHOMA/USA
A settlement developed close to Fort Sill which became a city in 1901 and was named after General Henry W. Lawton (1843–99).

Lazarev, KHABAROVSK TERRITORY/RUSSIA
Situated on Cape Lazarev and named after Mikhail Lazarev (1788–1851), an admiral and commander of the Black Sea Fleet, who participated in the discovery of Antarctica and completed three round-the-world voyages.

Lazarevac, SERBIA/SERBIA AND MONTENEGRO
Šopić
Renamed in 1889 after Prince Lazar Hrebeljanović (d. 1389) who ruled a principality corresponding to modern southern Serbia and Kosovo. He formed an alliance to resist the Ottoman Turks, but was killed in battle on the 'Field of Blackbirds' (*see* KOSOVO POLJE) in 1389; he became a legendary Serbian hero.

Lazio, ITALY *Latium*
A region whose Latin name, Latium, originally referred to the flat land on the left (south) bank of the River Tiber (but it now also embraces an area to the north). Latium may have an Indo-European root *stel* or *stla* from which comes the Latin *latus* 'broad' or 'wide', thus 'a plain', to describe this flat area in west-central Italy. Its first inhabitants were called the Aborigines who, it is said, were later renamed the Latini 'the Latins' after their legendary king, Latinus. Their language, Latin, was thereafter widely adopted, becoming the language of the Roman Empire.

Lead, SOUTH DAKOTA/USA
Founded in 1876 after the discovery of gold, its name comes from the lode mines, an outcrop of ore being called a 'lead'.

Leadville, COLORADO/USA
Founded in 1878 with a name recognizing the value of the lead ores mined in the area.

Leamington Spa, ENGLAND/UK *Lamintone*
The formal name is Royal Leamington Spa. Leamington means 'Farm on the (River) Leam' from *tūn*; Leam is a Celtic river name meaning

'elm river' or 'marshy river'. Spa refers to the medicinal springs here and it was to these that Princess (later Queen) Victoria† came in 1830, granting the title of 'Royal' in 1838, the year of her coronation. The town developed from the village of Leamington Priors with the discovery of saline springs.

Leatherhead, ENGLAND/UK *Leodridan, Leret*
'Grey Ford' from the supposed Celtic words *lēd* 'grey' and *rīd* 'ford'.

Leavenworth, USA
1. Indiana: named after the most prominent residents, the Leavenworth brothers.
2. Kansas: settled in 1854 and named after Colonel Henry H. Leavenworth who had already established a fort, Fort Leavenworth, on the Missouri River in 1827 to help protect caravans moving along the Santa Fe Trail.

Lebanon (Lubnān), AND USA
1. The Lebanese Republic (al-Jumhūrīyah al-Lubnānīyah), technically since 1926 when the French declared Lebanon to be a republic; independence, however, was only declared in 1941 and it was in 1946 that the country became completely independent. Put under French administration at the end of the First World War, Lebanon was created by the French in 1920 when to the previously Ottoman Turkish autonomous territory of Mount Lebanon (a region extending some 20–30 miles (32–48 km) north and south of Beirut) were added Beirut, some other coastal towns, and various districts; the new territory was called Greater Lebanon. Previously, Lebanon had been part of the Ottoman Empire since 1516–17 and of the Mamlūk state of Egypt and Syria since the 1290s. Some time after the arrival of the Phoenicians *c*.3000 BC the area of modern Lebanon came to be known as Phoenicia by the Greeks; the Phoenicians are believed to have called themselves Canaanites (*see* CANAAN). In 2000 Israel withdrew after a 22-year occupation of a security zone in southern Lebanon. The name comes from a Semitic word *lavan* 'white' or 'whitish', a reference to the country's snow-capped mountains.
2. USA: at least thirteen cities have this name, either after the mountain of the same name in Lebanon; or because of the abundance of cedar trees, reminding the inhabitants of the biblical cedars of Lebanon, cedarwood being so coveted by its neighbours; or after another town with this name in the USA.

Lebombo Mountains, MOZAMBIQUE-SOUTH AFRICA-SWAZILAND
A mountain range with a name meaning 'Big Nose', thus 'Big Ridge' from the Zulu *ubombo*.

Lebowa, LIMPOPO/SOUTH AFRICA
A former self-governing national state for the northern Sotho people established in 1972. Its name simply means 'northern'. It was reincorporated into South Africa in 1994.

Lecco, LOMBARDY/ITALY
Derived from a Gallic word *leuko*, similar to the Latin *lucus* 'wood' or 'sacred grove'.

Leeds, UK, USA
1. UK (Kent/England): previously Esledes and Hledes, it may be named after the description of a stream possibly from a *hlȳde* 'the loud brook'.
2. UK (West Yorkshire/England): originally Lādenses and then Loidis and Ledes, it lies on the River Aire. Once a district, the original Celtic name had the meaning of 'People living along the strongly flowing River (Aire)'.
3. USA (Alabama): named after the Leeds in West Yorkshire because both were industrial towns.

Leek, IRELAND, THE NETHERLANDS, UK
1. Ireland: in Irish, Liag 'Pillar Stone'.
2. UK (England): formerly Lec '(Place at) the Brook' from the Old Scandinavian *lækr*.

Leeuwarden (Frisian: **Ljouwert**), THE NETHERLANDS
The present name has evolved from the Frisian name with the first syllable, *Ljou*, coming from a personal name, and *wert* possibly meaning 'refuge'. It has been suggested that a previous name was Lieuwarden to give 'Guarded Place near Lime Trees' from *ward* 'guarded place' or 'watch tower'.

Leeward Islands, WEST INDIES
The northern and more westerly part of the Lesser Antilles. The name indicates that the islands are more protected from the prevailing easterly winds than the Windward Islands to the south. Their French name, Îles sous le Vent, and the Spanish Islas de Sotovento mean 'Islands under the Wind'.

Lefka (Turkish: **Lefke**), CYPRUS
'Poplar' in Greek, although date palms predominate.

Lefkas (Leukás), GREECE
An island and a town with the name 'White' from the ancient Greek *leuko*, a reference to the hilly limestone terrain.

Legazpi, LUZON/PHILIPPINES
Founded *c*.1639, it was named after Miguel López de Legazpi (*c*.1510–72), first Spanish governor-general of the Philippines (1565–72).

Leghorn, ITALY
See LIVORNO.

Legnica, POLAND *Liegnitz, Wahlstatt*
Possibly named after Lugus, the Celtic god of
arts and crafts.

Le Havre, UPPER NORMANDY/FRANCE *Havre-de-Grâce*
Developed from a fishing village into a
harbour in 1517 by Francis I (1494–1547), King
of France (1515–47), and called by him 'Haven
of Grace' which linked it to the existing chapel
called Notre-Dame-de-Grâce. The name was
subsequently shortened to 'The Harbour'.

Leicester, UK, USA
1. UK (England): formerly Ligera ceaster and
Ledecestre, the '-cester', from *ceaster*, indicates
that the town was a Roman camp. The first
part of the name comes from the name of a
tributary, the Leire, flowing into the River Soar
on which the city lies. It gave its name to the
local inhabitants, the Ligore, and they gave
their name to the city. Thus the name means
the '(Roman) Camp of the Ligore' or the
'(Roman) Camp of the People living by the
Leire'. The name of the county, Leicestershire,
takes its name from the city with the
additional *scīr*.
2. USA (Massachusetts): named after Robert
Dudley (1533–88), Earl of Leicester and the
favourite of Queen Elizabeth I[†].

Leichhardt QUEENSLAND/AUSTRALIA
A district of Sydney, a river, and a mountain
range all named after Ludwig Leichhardt
(1813–48?), who led exploratory expeditions
into the outback to become a national hero in
Australia, but who disappeared during the
expedition which began in March 1848.

Leighton Buzzard, ENGLAND/UK *Lestone, Letton Busard*
'Leek Garden of the Busards', a French family
name or nickname meaning 'buzzard' with
the Old English *lēac* 'leek' and *tūn*.

Leinster (Laigin), IRELAND *Galian, Laynster*
A province meaning the 'Land of the Laigin',
one of the earliest Celtic tribes to settle in
Ireland, and *tir* 'land'. The Laigin may get their
name from *láighe* 'lance'.

Leipzig, SAXONY/GERMANY *Urbs Lĭbzi, Lipsk*
Originally a Slav settlement, the name is
derived from the Slav *lipa* 'lime tree'.

Leith, UK, USA
UK (Scotland): formerly Inverlet and Inverlethe
'Mouth of the (River) Leith' from *inbhir* and the
river name which might once have been Lekta
'dripping (water)'.

Leitrim (Liatroim), IRELAND
A county meaning 'Grey Ridge' from *liath*
'grey' and *dhroim* 'ridge'.

Leixlip, IRELAND
'Salmon Leap' from the Old Scandinavian *leax*
and *hlaup* 'leap'.

Lelystad, THE NETHERLANDS
Named 'Lely's Town' after Dr Cornelius Lely
(1854–1929), the engineer who proposed plans
in 1891 to drain the Zuider Zee; they finally led
to the Zuider Zee Reclamation Act in 1918.

Le Mans, PAYS DE LA LOIRE/FRANCE *Celmans*
Named after a Gallic tribe, the Cenomani,
whose capital this was. The first syllable of the
Celtic name was later accepted as being the
French *celui* 'the one' and this evolved into *le*
'the'.

Le Mars, IOWA/USA
Named after the initials of the first ladies who
were with the founder when he first visited
the spot.

Lemnos (Límnos), GREECE
An island in the Aegean Sea with a name of
Phoenician origin meaning 'white', possibly a
reference to its volcanic rocks.

Lenape, PENNSYLVANIA/USA
Named after the Delaware whose proper name
is Lenni Lenape meaning 'Original People' or
'First People'.

Lenin, Mt (Pik Lenina), KYRGYZSTAN-TAJIKISTAN *Mount Kaufman*
1. A mountain discovered in 1871 and named
after Major General Konstantin Kaufman
(1818–82), appointed first governor-general of
Turkestan in 1865 and the architect of the
Russian conquest of Central Asia.
Subsequently, it was renamed Mount Lenin
after Vladimir Lenin[†]. At 23 405ft (7 134m),
however, it was considerably lower than
Mount Stalin (*see* COMMUNISM PEAK).
2. Although several towns in the former
Soviet Union with names associated with
Lenin have been renamed, particularly in the
non-Russian republics, some have retained
them; for example, Leninskiy in Russia and
Kazakhstan, Leninskoye, Leningradskiy, and
Leningradskaya in Russia, Lenino in Belarus in
addition to those below.

Leningrad, RUSSIA
A province named after Vladimir Lenin[†].
Although the city of Leningrad was renamed
St Petersburg in 1991, the province's name did
not change.

Leninogorsk, TATARSTAN REPUBLIC/RUSSIA *Novaya Pismyanka*
Renamed in 1955 after Vladimir Lenin[†] with
gorsk, associated with *gornyy* 'mining', when
the settlement, associated with the coal
industry, became a town. See RIDDER.

Leninsk, RUSSIA
1. Russia (Volgograd): originally Prishib, it was renamed in 1919 after Vladimir Lenin†.
2. Other towns with this name have changed as follows: in Kazakhstan, *Baykonur; in Turkmenistan, *Akdepe.

Leninsk-Kuznetskiy, KEMEROVO/RUSSIA
Kolchugino
Renamed after Vladimir Lenin† a year after his death in 1924 and for the *kuznets* 'blacksmiths' who worked in support of the coal-mining here. The Kuznetsk Coal Basin is one of the largest coalfields in Russia. -*Kuznetskiy* also helped to distinguish this Leninsk from other cities with this name.

Lenkoran (Länkäran), AZERBAIJAN
The local name is Persian, one derived from the Russian pronunciation of what was once Langarkunan 'anchorage'. One of the outcomes of the Russo-Persian War of 1804–13 was Russian occupation of the city which lasted until 1918. Thereafter, apart from a brief interlude in 1918–20, Lenkoran was part of Soviet Azerbaijan until 1991 when the country declared independence.

Lenoir, NORTH CAROLINA/USA
Named after General William Lenoir who took part in the War of American Independence (1775–83).

Lennoxville, QUEBEC/CANADA
Named after Charles Lennox (1764–1819), 4th Duke of Richmond, governor-general of British North America (1818–19).

Lenox, MASSACHUSETTS/USA *Yokuntown*
Founded *c*.1750, it was probably renamed in 1767 after Field Marshal Charles Lennox (1735–1806), 3rd Duke of Richmond and Lennox, secretary of state for the Southern Department (1766–7) and a strong supporter of the American colonists.

Leominster, UK, USA
1. UK (England): formerly Leomynster and Leominstre 'Church in Leon', Leon being an old Celtic name meaning 'at the streams' for the district on the Rivers Arrow and Lugg, with the Old English *mynster*. A religious building was erected here in 660.
2. USA (Massachusetts): named after the English town, probably by settlers who had come from there.

Leon, FRANCE, MEXICO, NICARAGUA, SPAIN, USA
1. Spain: locally León. Formerly Legio and named after the Roman 7th Gemina Felix Legion, *Legio Septima*, whose 1st-century camp grew into a city which, in turn, gave its name to the area. It is now also the name of a

province of the autonomous community of *Castile-León which used to comprise the northern part of the medieval Kingdom of León; this kingdom was in existence between *c*.910–1230 when it united with Castile.
2. Mexico (Guanajuato): founded in 1576 simply as León after the Spanish city. *De los Aldamas* was added in 1830 in honour of Juan Aldama, one of the leaders in the struggle for Mexican independence.
3. Nicaragua: founded in 1524 but destroyed by an earthquake in 1610. It was rebuilt some 20 miles (32 km) away from its previous location on the site of the old native capital of Sutiaba. Named after the Spanish city, it was the capital until 1857.
4. USA (Kansas): named after Juan Ponce de León (1460–1521), a Spanish explorer who discovered Florida.

Leonardtown, MARYLAND/USA
Named after Leonard Calvert, first governor of Maryland colony (1634–47).

Lepanto, GREECE
See NÁFPAKTOS.

Lepel, BELARUS
Named after the lake here which takes its name from either the Russian *lipa* or the Lettish *liepa* 'lime (tree)'.

Le Petit-Quevilly, UPPER NORMANDY/FRANCE
'The Small Row of Spikes' from the Latin *quevillicum* and Old French *chevilly*, both 'row of spikes'. This is a reference to the fence that enclosed a park used for hunting by Norman dukes.

Leptis Magna, LIBYA *Lpqi*
Ruins, the site now having the modern name of Labdah, although its Roman name is better known. The largest of the three cities of Tripolis, it was called *magna* 'great' to distinguish it from Leptis Minor in Tunisia, now known as Lamta. A trading port founded by the Phoenicians and called Lpqi at least as early as the 6th century BC, its name may be Punic and mean 'harbour'.

Le Puy, AUVERGNE/FRANCE *Podium*
In Auvergne *puy* means 'peak' like the Latin *podium* 'peak' or 'elevated place'. The town is surrounded by volcanic peaks.

Leriba, LESOTHO *Hlotse Heights*
Lying on the Hlotse River whose name means 'Dead Meat', a reference to the practice of people crossing the river to throw meat to the crocodiles to divert their attention. The present name may mean 'undulating' to describe the local terrain.

Lerwick, SCOTLAND/UK
'Mud Bay' from the Old Scandinavian *leirr*
'mud' and *vík* 'bay'. Capital of Shetland, it is
situated on a natural harbour.

Lesbos (Lésvos), GREECE *Ægira, Lasia, Pelasgia,*
Macaria, Pentapolis
An island which is also sometimes called
*Mytilene or Mitilíni after its capital; Midilli in
Turkish. It was called Pelasgia after the
Pelasgians who were the first inhabitants,
Macaria after Macareus, a prominent settler,
and Pentapolis alluded to its five cities. The
present name, which is pre-Hellenic, may
mean 'wooded', although Lesbos was also said
to be the son-in-law and successor of Macareus.
The word 'lesbian' is derived from Lesbos on
account of the homosexual practices
attributed to the poetess Sappho.

Lesotho *Basutoland*
The Kingdom of Lesotho since 1966 when
independence was achieved. Previously
Basutoland, a British High Commission
Territory (1884–1966); annexed by Cape
Colony (now part of South Africa) (1871–84),
having become a British protectorate in 1868
at the request of Moshoeshoe (also
Mshweshwe) I (*c*.1786–1870), founder and first
paramount chief of the Sotho nation, and King
of the Basotho (1832–70); he feared Boer
expansionism. He had established the
land-locked Basutoland Kingdom in 1832. Both
names are derived from the indigenous
people, the baSotho 'dark-skinned'. *Le-* is a
Sesotho prefix indicating the singular, *Ba-* the
plural. The name means 'Land of the Sotho'.

Lesozavodsk, PRIMORSKIY TERRITORY/RUSSIA
'Timber Mill' from *les* 'forest' or 'wood(s)' and
zavod ' factory' or 'mill'.

Lesser Antilles, WEST INDIES *Caribbees*
A group of islands comprising the Virgin
Islands, the Leeward Islands, the Windward
Islands, the Netherlands Antilles, and some
small islands off the Venezuelan coast. The
former name comes from the Carib tribe who
inhabited many of the islands when they were
first discovered. *See* ANTILLES.

Lesser Slave Lake, ALBERTA/CANADA
Named after the Slave tribe who used to live on
the lake's shores.

Letchworth, ENGLAND/UK *Leceworde*
'Lockable Enclosure' from the Old English *lycce*
'place that can be locked' and *worth*
'enclosure'.

Lethbridge, ALBERTA/CANADA *Coalbanks*
Founded in the 1880s, it was renamed in 1885
after William Lethbridge (1824–1901),

president of the Northwest Coal and
Navigation Company.

Letterkenny (Leitir Ceanainan), IRELAND
'Cannanan's Hillside' from *leitir* '(wet) hillside'.

Levallois-Perret, PARIS/FRANCE
In 1867 four communities merged to form the
city; one was Levallois, named after its
founder, Nicolas-Eugène Levallois (1816–79),
and another was Champerret which took its
name from the Latin *campus petrosus* 'stony
ground'. This coincided happily with the name
of a previous landowner, Jacques Perret, and so
his name was added to Levallois to give the
new city its name.

Levant, The From the French *levant* 'rising'
to refer to the sun and the direction in which it
rises; thus, the east. Specifically, the Levant,
now rarely used, refers to the eastern
Mediterranean, its islands, and the countries
on its borders (Syria, Lebanon, and Israel).
To the peoples further west this region
used to represent the limits of the known
world.

Leven, SCOTLAND/UK
A town, loch, and river after which the town
and loch are named. Its name, from the Gaelic
leamhain, means 'Elm River'. These are in Fife
and Kinross. There are other Levens: for
example, the River Leven that drains Loch
Lomond.

Leverkusen, NORTH RHINE-WESTPHALIA/
GERMANY
A few small villages were merged to form the
town in 1930 and it was named after a
dispensing chemist, Karl Leverkus, who had a
dyestuff factory.

Lévis, QUEBEC/CANADA *Aubigny*
Settled in 1647, it was named after Charles
Lennox (1672–1723), 1st Duke of Richmond
and Duke of Aubigny, who had been given the
Duchy by Louis XIV the Sun King[†]. It was
renamed in 1861 after François Gaston, Duke
of Lévis, who had taken over command of
French forces in Canada during the British
capture of Quebec by General James Wolfe
(1726–59) in 1759.

Levittown, PUERTO RICO, USA
USA (New York and Pennsylvania): both were
built by, and named after, Levitt & Sons. In
1952 William and Alfred Levitt, having learnt
how to erect prefabricated buildings during
the Second World War (1939–45), decided to
extend the concept. They bought land in the
two states on which they built rows of simple
and identical new houses.

Lev Tolstoy, LIPETSK/RUSSIA
Named in 1927 after Count Lev (Leo) Tolstoy
(1828–1910), the great Russian novelist who
died near here.

Lewes, UK, USA
1. UK (England): formerly Læwe from the Old
English *læw* 'incision', here meaning a 'gap'
between hills.
2. USA (Delaware): founded in 1631 as a Dutch
settlement called Zwaanendael, it was
renamed in about 1685 after the Lewes in
Sussex (now East Sussex), England, since it was
the chief town in Sussex County.

Lewisburg, WEST VIRGINIA/USA
Originally an assembly point for the Virginia
militiamen of General Andrew Lewis, after
whom it was named, just before the onset of
the American War of Independence (1775–83).

Lewis Range, CANADA-USA
Part of the Rockies and named after
Meriwether Lewis[†].

Lewiston, USA
1. Idaho: named after Meriwether Lewis[†] who,
with William Clark (1770–1838), camped here
during their journey to the Pacific coast.
2. Maine: as Lewiston Falls, said to be named
after a drunken Irishman who drowned at this
spot. However, it has also been suggested that
it was named after families called Lewis who
founded the settlement *c*.1770.

Lewistown, PENNSYLVANIA/USA
Founded on the site of a Shawnee village called
Ohesson, it is named after William Lewis who
organized the iron foundry.

Lexington, USA
1. Kentucky: settled in 1779 and named after
the Lexington in Massachusetts.
2. Massachusetts: settled in 1640 and named
Cambridge Farms in 1691, it was renamed in
1713, when it became a township, after the
Lexington in England, now Laxton, from
where the first settlers came in 1640. Laxton
means 'Leaxa's Farm'.
3. Missouri: laid out in 1822 and named after
the Lexington in Kentucky.
4. Virginia: named after the Battle of
Lexington, Massachusetts, the site of the first
skirmish between British troops and American
irregulars in April 1775 which blossomed
into the American War of Independence
(1775–83).

Leyden (Leiden), THE NETHERLANDS *Lugdunum
Batavorum*
The former name is not Roman, although it
means 'Lyon of the Batavi', a German people
who lived in this part of northern Europe; it

was coined in a 1575 poem written after the
Spanish siege in 1574. The present name is
from the Germanic *leitha* 'canal'.

Lhasa (Chinese: **Lasa Shiqu**), TIBET
AUTONOMOUS REGION/CHINA
'City of the Gods' from the Tibetan *lha* 'god'
and *sa* 'city'. It was originally the capital of
Tibet from the 7th century. Occupied by the
Chinese since 1951, it is now the capital of the
Tibet (Xizang) Autonomous Region.

Lhotse, TIBET/CHINA-NEPAL
Also known as E[1] (Everest 1), a designation
awarded by the Survey of India in 1931 as it is
sometimes thought of as being part of the
Mount Everest massif. Its name is Tibetan for
'South Peak' from *lho* 'southern' and *tse* 'peak'
or 'summit'.

Lianyun'gang, JIANGSU/CHINA
A port originally founded in 549. Although its
three constituent words, *lián* 'to join', *yún*
'cloud', and *gǎng* 'port', appear to have no clear
collective meaning, they represent three
places: Liandao 'reaches to, or is connected to,
the island' from *lián* and *dǎo*, Yuntaishan
'Cloud Terrace Mountain' from *yún*, *tái*
'terrace' and *shān* 'mountain', and Yazhugang
'Yazhu Port' from *gǎng*.

Liaoning, CHINA *Shengjing, Fengtian*
A province named after the River Liao and *níng*
'peace' or 'pacified'. Shengjing during the
early part of the Manchu dynasty (1644–1911),
it was renamed during the reign of the
Emperor Kangxi (1661–1722) to mean
'Conferred by Heaven'. It was given its
present name when its borders were
changed in 1928.

Liaoyang, LIAONANG/CHINA
Takes its name from the River Liao and means
'Sunny Side of the Liao River', in this case the
'North Side of the Liao River' from *yáng* 'sun'.

Liaoyuan, JILIN/CHINA *Xi'an*
'Source of the Liao (River)' from *láiyuán* 'source
of a river' and the river name. The city is also
called Dongliao, this being an alternative
name for the river. Founded in 1902, it was
upgraded to county status in 1913. In 1948 it
was renamed Xi'an, but to avoid confusion
with the already existing *Xi'an in Shaanxi
province, the original name was restored in
1952.

Liard, CANADA
Canada (Yukon Territory-British Columbia): a
river named after the liards, poplar trees,
along its banks. On the river is Fort Liard and
nearby is the Liard Range, both in the
Northwest Territories.

Liberal, USA
Kansas and Missouri: named because of the attitudes of its early inhabitants.

Liberec, CZECH REPUBLIC *Reichenberg, Liberk*
Founded by German settlers in the 14th century, who at first called it Am Richen Berg '(Place) next to a Rich Hill' and then Reichenberg from *reich* 'rich' and *Berg*. This name was considered to be too long and so, at least in speech, was shortened to Riberk or Riberg, which was then used as the basis for the Czech name Liberk. In the 19th century this evolved into Liberec.

Liberia, AND COSTA RICA
The Republic of Liberia since 1847. Previously the Commonwealth of Liberia (1838) when the charitable American Colonization Society (ACS) colony of Liberia and the colony of Bassa Cove (*see* BUCHANAN) merged; the fledgling ACS colony was named Liberia 'Free Land' or 'Land of the Free' in 1824 after the Latin *liber* 'free'. The oldest republic in Africa and one of only two African countries never colonized by European powers (Ethiopia is the other), the country was founded by American abolitionists who formed the ACS in 1816 to repatriate America's freed slaves to the land of their ancestors—a colony to be established on the coast of West Africa. Land was acquired along the coast in the area of Cape Mesurado in 1821 and the first permanent settlement was established in what was to become Liberia in 1822. Twenty-five years later the Americo-Liberians declared their independence of the ACS.

Libertyville, ILLINOIS/USA *Independence Grove*
Founded in 1836, but renamed 'Town of Liberty' the following year in a fit of patriotism.

Libourne, AQUITAINE/FRANCE
Founded in 1270 and named after the English seneschal of Gascony, Roger de Leybourne, who came from Leybourne in Kent, England.

Libreville, GABON *Fort d'Aumâle*
'Free Town'. In 1843 the French established a trading post with a fort here named after Henri d'Orléans (1822–97), Duke of Aumâle and fourth son of Louis-Philippe (1773–1850), King of the French (1830–48). In 1849 they gave plots of land to 52 freed slaves and called the area, together with a few Mpongwe villages, 'Free Town'. It was the capital of French Equatorial Africa in 1888–1904 and of Gabon since 1960 when independence was achieved.

Libya The Great Socialist People's Libyan Arab Jamahiriya (al-Jamāhīrīyah al-'Arabīyah al-Lībīyah ash-Sha'bīyah al-Ishtirākīyah al-

Uẓmā) since 1977; *al-uẓmā* 'the greatest' is a hyperbole and is often omitted in the English translation. Previously the Libyan Arab Republic (1969–77); the Kingdom of Libya (1951–69) when it became independent. Once German and Italian troops had been driven out of Libya in 1943, Cyrenaica and Tripolitania were put under British, and the southern desert region of Fezzan under French, military administration. The territory was annexed by Italy in 1912, although full authority was never exercised over the interior. The same was true of the Ottoman Turks who took control in 1835; although Tripoli was captured by them in 1551, their presence in the following years was confined to enclaves along the coast. Libya may have been mentioned in the Bible as Lebu and Lubim, and Lehabim (Genesis 10: 13) may refer to the Libyans. It has also been suggested that it may have been named after Libya who, according to Greek mythology, was the daughter of Epaphus and Memphis; Libya was a Greek name given to a large part of Africa. Libya was a province of western Egypt known to the Romans. The name fell out of use by the Arabs and only reappeared as an Italian creation in the 19th century, possibly taken from the Levu, the ancient Egyptian name for a Berber tribe. It applied only to the two Turkish *sancaks* of *Cyrenaica and Tripolitania (*see* TRIPOLI), the only part of the North African coast not under European control. When the Italians formed a new colony with the union of Cyrenaica and Tripolitania on 1 January 1934 they gave it the official name of Libya. *Jamāhīrīyah* is a conceptual word signifying that the people govern themselves by means of people's congresses free of the constraints of a modern bureaucratic state; it can be translated roughly as 'ruled by the masses'.

Lichfield, ENGLAND/UK *Letocetum, Licitfelda*
'Open Field by Letocetum' from a Celtic place name meaning 'grey wood' from the possible *cęd* 'wood'. To this was added *feld*; so 'Open Land in the Grey Wood'.

Lidice, CZECH REPUBLIC *L'udice*
'L'uda's Settlement' derived from the personal name, L'uda, of a local landlord who owned the settlement. The name was changed to Lidice in the 14th century.

Lidköping, SWEDEN
'Market Town on the (River) Lid' from *köping*.

Lido di Ostia, LAZIO/ITALY *Ostia Antica*
A town with a name meaning 'Shore at the Estuary' derived from its location at the mouth of the River Tiber from *lido* 'shore' or 'beach' and the Latin *os* 'mouth of a river'.

Liechtenstein The Principality of
Liechtenstein (German: Fürstentum
Liechtenstein) since 1719. It takes its name
from the family Liechtenstein 'Light Stone',
who came from the castle of Liechtenstein
near Vienna. The present boundaries were
drawn in 1434, the territory belonging to the
Count of Vaduz. The principality was created
within the Holy Roman Empire by merging
the two independent counties of Schellenburg
and Vaduz. Liechtenstein was part of the Rhine
Confederation in 1806–15 and the German
Confederation in 1815–66. It has been
independent since 1866.

Liège (Flemish: **Luik**), BELGIUM *Leodium*
A province and a city whose name may come
from the word *leudi* 'people', referring to the
Franks who inhabited the region. This became
Leodium under the Romans and this evolved
into the present name, although the grave
accent over the first *e* superseded the acute
accent only in 1946. Annexed to France in
1795, it became part of the Kingdom of the
Netherlands in 1815 and finally part of
Belgium in 1830 when it became independent.

Liepaja, LATVIA *Libau, Libava*
Derived from the Lettish *liepa* 'limetree'. It was
called Libau by the Teutonic Knights, who
built a castle here in 1263, and Libava by the
Russians after it had passed to them at the
third partition of Poland in 1795.

Ligonha, MOZAMBIQUE
A river whose name comes from the local
igonha 'crocodile'.

Ligonier, INDIANA/USA
Named after the borough in Pennsylvania
which was named after John Ligonier (1680–
1770), 1st Earl Ligonier of Ripley, who played a
prominent part in the War of the Spanish
Succession (1701–14) and became a field
marshal in 1766.

Liguria, ITALY
A region named after the Ligures, its pre-
Roman inhabitants, who may have taken their
name from the Celtic god Lugus. Napoleon[†]
created the Ligurian Republic in 1797 around
Genoa and in 1805 it was incorporated into the
French Empire until 1815 when it became part
of the Kingdom of Piedmont-Sardinia. The
region gives its name to the Ligurian Sea.

Likasi, DEMOCRATIC REPUBLIC OF THE CONGO
Jadotville
It was founded in 1892 and until 1966 was
known as Jadot's Town after a senior Belgian
mining enginer, Jean Jadot (1862–1932). The
meaning of the present name is unknown.

Lille, NORD-PAS-DE-CALAIS/FRANCE *Lisle*
Possibly taken from the Old French *L'isle*,
modern *L'Île* 'The Island', which it was often
called since it was founded in marshland. It
became part of France in 1713 following the
Treaty of Utrecht. It gave its name to 'lisle', a
fine and smooth cotton thread invented here.

Lillebonne, UPPER NORMANDY/FRANCE
Juliobona
A modification of its Roman name which
honoured Julius Caesar[†] and *bona* 'village'.

Lillehammer, NORWAY
'Little Hammer' from *hammer* 'hammer-
shaped rock'.

Lilongwe, MALAWI *Bwalia*
Founded as a police post on the Lilongwe River
in 1904, it is named after the river, the
meaning of which may simply be 'river'.
Lilongwe became the capital of Malawi in
1975.

Lima, ARGENTINA, PARAGUAY, PERU, USA
1. Peru: the Spanish city of Lima, established
in an area already long inhabited, was
originally called Ciudad de los Reyes 'City of
the Kings', since it was founded on the Feast of
Epiphany, 6 January 1535, by Francisco Pizarro
(c.1475–1541), the Spanish explorer. The
present name is derived from the Quechua
name Rímac 'Speaker', a reference to the
temple's priests. It soon became the capital of
the Viceroyalty of Peru and of Peru when it
achieved independence in 1821.
2. USA (Ohio): named after the city in Peru in
1831.

Limassol (Greek: **Lemessós**; Turkish: **Limasol**),
CYPRUS *Nemesos*
Situated between the Goerillis and Kouris
Rivers, the valley between them became
known as Nemessós from *anémessos* 'in
between (the two rivers)'. In due course
this became Lemessós which has been
Anglicized to Limassol.

Limavady (**Léim an Mhadiadh**), NORTHERN
IRELAND/UK *Newtown Limavady*
'Leap of the Dog' from *léim* 'leap'. According to
legend, a dog, carrying a message of
approaching danger, leapt over a gorge south
of the town.

Limbe, CAMEROON, MALAWI
Cameroon: founded in 1858 by an English
missionary, Alfred Saker, it was originally
called Victoria[†] after the reigning British
Queen. It was renamed in 1982 by presidential
decree after the River Limbe whose meaning is
unknown.

Limburg (French: **Limbourg**), BELGIUM-THE
NETHERLANDS
A historic region, and a duchy, which was
divided in 1839 into two provinces, one in each
country, both called Limburg after a small
community, now in Belgium, called Limbourg.
The name was adopted in 1155 and comes from
the Germanic *Lindo* 'lime tree' and *Burg*.

Limerick, CANADA, IRELAND, USA
1. Ireland: Irish Luimneach. Capital of the
Norse kingdom of the same name in the 9th
and 10th centuries, it is now a county and a
city with a name meaning 'Bare Land' from *lom*
'bare'. It may have given its name to a form of
humorous verse from the chorus of an Irish
soldier's song 'Will You Come up to Limerick?'
2. USA (Maine and Pennsylvania): named after
the city in Ireland.

Limoges, LIMOUSIN/FRANCE *Lemovices,*
Augustoritum
Named after the Lemovices, a Gallic tribe
whose name comes from the Gaulish *lemo*
'lime tree' and the Latin *vicus* 'village'. The
former Roman name honours Caesar
Augustus[†] with the Gaulish *ritu* 'ford'.

Limousin, FRANCE
A region named after the Lemovices (*see*
LIMOGES). At the beginning of the 20th century
some residents wore a distinctive caped cloak;
some early motor cars had a special roof that
resembled these hoods and they became
known as limousines.

Limpopo, BOTSWANA-MOZAMBIQUE-SOUTH
AFRICA-ZIMBABWE
A province in South Africa, until 2002 known as
Northern Province and before that as Northern
Transvaal Province, and a river. The river rises
in South Africa where it is known as the
Crocodile River, and originally to the Boers as
the Krokodil Rivier. When joined by the Marico
River it becomes the Limpopo, possibly from
the Ndebele *ilimphopho* 'river of the waterfall',
'water running over rocks' or 'rushing water'.
The Zulu name is Ukupopoza 'to rush' and the
Mozambicans call it Mogombene Mele. When
discovered by the Portuguese in 1498 it was
named the Rio Cobre 'Copper River', a
reference to the copper found along the coast.

Lincoln, ARGENTINA, CANADA, NEW ZEALAND,
UK, USA
1. UK (England): formerly Lindon, Lindum
Colonia, and Lincolia '(Roman) Colony by the
Pool', a reference to the marshes and pools of
the River Witham from the Celtic *lindo* 'lake'
or 'pool' and the Latin *colonia* 'colony'. As a
place for retired Roman legionaries, Colonia
was added *c*.90. The present name is a

combination of the first syllable of each word.
Lincoln was built as a garrison for the Roman
9th Legion Hispana *c*.60; subsequently it was
occupied by the 2nd Adiutrix Legion. The
name of the county comes from the city's
name and the additional *scīr*.
2. USA (Illinois): founded in 1853, it was
named after Abraham Lincoln (1809–65), then
a lawyer who undertook the work associated
with its incorporation in 1857 and later
President of the United States (1861–5).
3. USA (Nebraska): laid out in 1859 as
Lancaster, it was renamed in 1867, when it was
chosen as the state capital, after Abraham
Lincoln, assassinated in 1865 while still
serving as president.
4. USA: fifteen other states have cities with
this name, some after Abraham Lincoln, some
after General Benjamin Lincoln (1733–1810), a
senior commander in the American War of
Independence (1775–83) and secretary of war
(1781–3), and some from the city or county in
England.

Lincolnville, CANADA, USA
USA (Maine): 'Lincoln's Town' named after
General Benjamin Lincoln (see previous entry).

Linda, CALIFORNIA/USA
'Pretty' or 'Fine' in Spanish.

Lindau, GERMANY
Bavaria and Saxony-Anhalt: 'Meadow of
Lime-Trees' from *Aue* 'meadow' and *Linde*
'lime-tree'.

Lindisfarne, ENGLAND/UK *Lindisfarnae*
Also known as Holy Island formerly Halieland,
from the Old English *hālig* 'holy' and *ēg-land*
'island'. Lindisfarne may come from Lindsey,
an Anglo-Saxon kingdom in what is now
Lincolnshire, with the Old English *fara*
'traveller' and *ēg* to give 'Island of the
Travellers from Lindsey'; that is pilgrims
visiting the church and monastery established
in 635 by St Aidan (d. 651), the first bishop of
Lindisfarne. Alternatively, it may mean 'Place
at (a stream called) Lindis' from the Old Irish
lind 'lake' and *ferann* 'land'.

Lindsborg, KANSAS/USA
Many of the early settlers were of
Scandinavian origin with the first syllable of
their names being 'Linds'. The Swedish *borg*
'castle' was added.

Line Islands, PACIFIC OCEAN
They take their name from the fact that they
lie astride the equator—the 'Line'.

Lingfield, ENGLAND/UK *Leangafelde*
'Open Land of those who lived in the Clearing
in the Wood' from the Old English *lēah*
'woodland clearing', *-inga-* and *feld*.

Linköping, SWEDEN
'Flax Market' from *lin* 'flax' and *köping.*

Linz, AUSTRIA *Lentia*
The Roman name in the 1st century was
Lentia. The present name is probably derived
from the German *Linde* 'lime tree'.

Lipetsk, RUSSIA *Lipovka*
A province and a city founded in 1703 with a
name derived from *lipa* 'lime tree'.

Lippstadt, NORTH RHINE-WESTPHALIA/
GERMANY
'City of (the Lords of) Lippe' who probably
founded it in 1168 with *Stadt*. It lies on the
River Lippe.

Lisbon, PORTUGAL, USA
Portugal: a region, Lisbon and the Tagus
Valley, in Portuguese Lisboa e Vale do Tejo, and
a city. Its former names include Olisipo and
similar Moorish variations: ak-Oshbuna/
Lishbuna/Ulixbone/Olissibona. It has been
suggested that the original name may come
from the Greek hero of Homer's *Odyssey,*
Ulysses (an alternative spelling of Olisipo was
Ulyssipo); more likely, however, it is derived
from the Phoenician *alis ubbo* 'attractive, or
good, harbour', or *água boa* 'good water', the
city having a wonderful natural harbour. The
Phoenicians are believed to have founded the
city as a trading port *c*.1200 BC. Occupied by
the Romans (205 BC–AD 407), Julius Caesar[†]
added the official title of Felicitas Julia to the
name. The Moors held the city between 715
and 1147 when it fell to the Portuguese. It has
been the capital since 1256.

Lisburn (Lios na gCearrbhach), NORTHERN
IRELAND/UK *Lisnagarvey, Lysnecarvagh*
'Fort of the Gamblers' from *lios* 'fort', a
reference to a place nearby where gambling
took place. The English name, Lisnargarvey,
was superseded in the 17th century, perhaps
as a result of the arrival of French Huguenots.
While the *Lis* of the present name probably
comes from Lisnagarvey, the derivation of *burn*
is not known. It was elevated to the status of a
city in 2002, the year of the Golden Jubilee of
Elizabeth II, Queen of the United Kingdom
(1952–).

Lisichansk (Lysychans'k), UKRAINE *Lisya Balka*
Developed from the Cossack village whose
name meant 'Fox Gully' from *lisa* 'fox' and
balka 'gully'. This evolved into the present
name.

Lisieux, LOWER NORMANDY/FRANCE *Noviomagus
Lexoviorum, Niseux*
The present name has evolved from the
Roman name of 'New Market of the Lexovii',

a people of Gaul conquered by one of Julius
Caesar's[†] lieutenants.

Liskeard, ENGLAND/UK *Lys Cerruyt, Liscarret*
Likely to be 'Kerwyd's Court' from the Cornish
lys 'court' or 'hall' and a personal name.

Liski, VORONEZH/RUSSIA *Novopokrovka, Svoboda,
Georgiu-Dezh*
Founded in 1870 as Liski after the Lyska River
and as Novopokrovka from *novo* and *pokrov*
'cover' or 'covering', thus the dedication of its
church to the Feast of the Protection of the
Virgin Mary. In 1928–43 it was known as
Svoboda 'Freedom' or 'Liberty' before Liski was
readopted in 1943–65. From 1965 until 1990 it
was renamed after Gheorghe Gheorgiu-Dej
(1901–65), Romanian prime minister (1952–5)
and president (1961–65), in a show of
communist solidarity.

Lismore, AUSTRALIA, IRELAND, USA
1. Australia (New South Wales): possibly
named after the small Scottish island of
Lismore.
2. Ireland: the Irish name is Lios Mór, the full
name having been Lios Mór Mo-Chuta. It
means 'Big Fort' from *lios* 'fort'; this was built
in 1185 by Prince John (1167–1216), later John,
King of England (1199–1216), who was made
Lord of Ireland in 1177 by his father, King
Henry II, and visited the island in 1185.

Lisnaskea (Lios na Scéithe), NORTHERN
IRELAND/UK *Scéith Ghabhra*
'Fort of the Shield' from *lios* and the genitive of
sciath 'shield'.

Listowel, CANADA, IRELAND
Ireland: from the Irish Lios Tuathail meaning
the '(Earthen) Fort of Tuathal' from a personal
name and *lios*.

Litchfield, UK, USA
1. UK (England): formerly Liveselle and
Lieueselva, possibly a 'Ledge of Land with a
Shelter' from the Old English *hlīf* 'protection'
or 'shelter' and *scylf* 'ledge'.
2. USA (Connecticut): named after the English
town of Lichfield (not Litchfield).
3. USA (Illinois): named after one of its
founders, E. B. Litchfield.

Lithgow, NEW SOUTH WALES/AUSTRALIA
Founded in 1824 and named after William
Lithgow, a former state auditor-general.

Lithuania (Lietuva)
The Republic of Lithuania (Lietuvos
Respublika) in 1918–40 and since 1991.
Previously the Lithuanian Soviet Socialist
Republic (1940–1 and 1944–91) within the
Soviet Union; occupied by the Germans (1941–
4) during which time it was part of what was

called Ostland 'East Land', created by Adolf Hitler[†] and comprising Estonia, Latvia, Lithuania, and Byelorussia; part of the Russian Empire (1795–1918); united politically with Poland in 1569 to form the Polish-Lithuanian Commonwealth and dynastically with Poland in 1385; by 1392 its borders stretched from the Baltic Sea to the Black Sea. The deeply divided Lithuanian tribes were united into a nation in 1231 under Grand Duke Mindaugas (d. 1263) who became king in 1253. Given the present size of Lithuania, the connection between it, the Grand Duchy of Lithuania, and the Polish-Lithuanian Commonwealth is slight. The meaning of the name is not known, although it has been suggested that it may be derived from the Latin *litus* 'shore', a reference to the Baltic coast or from the small River Letavka.

Litoměřice, CZECH REPUBLIC *L'utomirici, Leitmeritz*
'Settlement of L'utomir's People' from the personal name of the leader of a Slavic tribe, the Litoměřice, which took its name from L'utomir. From the 11th century onwards German craftsmen swarmed in and the town's name was changed to a German rendition of the original. They were ejected in 1945 and the present Czech name was adopted.

Littlehampton, ENGLAND/UK *Hantone, Lyttelhampton*
'Homestead' from *hām* and *tūn*. 'Little' was added later to distinguish it from Southampton.

Little Rock, ARKANSAS/USA
In 1722 a Frenchman, Bernard de la Harpe, noticed two distinctive rock formations on the Arkansas River; he named them *La Grande Roche* and *La Petite Roche*. In due course 'The Little Rock' became the foundation of a railway bridge. In 1812, close to the spot, a trapper, William Lewis, erected a place to live and by 1821 the site had expanded to such a degree that it became the capital of the Territory of Arkansas.

Littoral, CAMEROON
A province simply meaning 'Coastal' in French.

Liupan Shan, GANSU-NINGXIA HUI/CHINA
'Six Twists Mountain' from *liù* 'six', *pán* 'twist', and *shān*. The path up the mountain used to zigzag, doubling back on itself six times.

Liuzhou, GUANGXI ZHUANG AUTONOMOUS PROVINCE/CHINA *Maping*
'Willow Region' from *liǔ* 'willow and *zhōu*.

Liverpool, AUSTRALIA, CANADA, UK, USA
1. Australia (New South Wales): founded in 1810 and named after Robert Banks Jenkinson (1770–1828), 2nd Earl of Liverpool, who was secretary of war and the colonies (1809–12) at the time, and prime minister (1812–27).
2. Canada (Nova Scotia): originally a Native American settlement called Ogumkiqueok, it was subsequently renamed Port Rossignol, Port Senior, and Port Saviour before becoming Liverpool in 1759.
3. UK (England): formerly Liuerpul 'Pool full of Weeds' or 'Muddy Pool' from the Old English *lifer* 'thick' or 'coagulated' and *pōl* after a tidal creek, now disappeared, known as the Pool.

Livingston, CANADA, GUATEMALA, UK, USA
1. UK (Scotland): formerly Villa Leuing and Leuinestun 'Leving's Farmstead' from a Middle English personal name and *toun*.
2. USA (Montana): founded in 1882 as Clark's City, it was renamed after Crawford Livingston, a railroad engineer.

Livingstone, ZAMBIA
See MARAMBA.

Livingstonia, MALAWI
A mission established in 1875 in honour of David Livingstone (1813–73), the British explorer, and now located on its third site.

Livonia (Vidzeme), ESTONIA-LATVIA, USA
1. Estonia-Latvia: the Latin name (German, Livland) for an area north of Lithuania, incorporating Latvia and the southern part of modern Estonia, named after the Livs, a Finno-Ugric people. It may be associated with the Estonian *liiv* 'sand' or Finnish *lieju* 'mud' to give the meaning of 'People living in a Muddy Place'. The name was also used to describe the territory ruled by the Teutonic Order from the beginning of the 13th century. Livonia was erased from the map in 1561 when it was partitioned between Lithuania and Poland. Sweden took possession in 1629 and Russia in 1721. Only in 1918 were the Estonians and Latvians able to found their own separate states which included parts of historic Livonia.
2. USA (Michigan): named after the city in New York.
3. USA (New York): named after the region on the Baltic coast.

Livorno, TUSCANY/ITALY *Liburnum, Legorno*
Sometimes known as Leghorn in English. A port, it may be derived from an Etruscan personal name, Liburna, or from the Liburni, an Illyrian people who once lived in the region and who were known for their fast-sailing galleys; or it may simply come from the Latin *liburna* 'fast-sailing vessel'.

Lizard, The, ENGLAND/UK *Lisart*
A peninsula in Cornwall with a Cornish name 'Court (on a) Height' from *lys* 'court' and *ardh* 'height'.

Ljubljana, SLOVENIA *Emona, Luvigana, Laibach, Lubiana*
May be derived from the Slavonic root word *ljub* 'love' to mean a well-loved place. A settlement taken over by the Romans and known to them as Emona, it was laid waste by the Huns in 452 and rebuilt by the Slavs as Luvigana. It had the German name Laibach by the middle of the 12th century and this name was retained when it became a Habsburg possession in 1277. The present name was adopted in 1918 when Slovenia became part of the Kingdom of the Serbs, Croats, and Slovenes. It has been the Slovene capital since then.

Llandudno, SOUTH AFRICA, UK
1. South Africa (Western Cape): named after the resort in Wales.
2. UK (Wales): formerly Lantudenou, a seaside resort meaning 'St Tudno's Church' from *llan* and the obscure saint's name.

Llanelli, WALES/UK
'St Elli's Church' from *llan* and the obscure saint's name.

Llanfairpwllgwyngillgogery chwyrn-drobwllllantysiliogogogoch, WALES/UK
Llan Vair y pwyll Gwinghill
A village with a name comprising 58 letters—the longest place-name in the UK. Usually known as Llanfairpwllgwyngill 'Church of St Mary in Pwllgwyngyll', Pwllgwyngyll means 'Pool of the White Hazels'. The additional syllables were added during the 19th century, but largely fell out of use until resurrected in 1973 as a tourist attraction on the signs for the railway station. The full name means 'St Mary's Church by the Pool of the white Hazel Trees, near the rapid Whirlpool, by the red Cave of the Church of St Tysilio' from *llan* 'church', *fair* a form of *Mair* '(St) Mary', *pwll* 'pool', *gwyn* 'white', *gill* a form of *cyll*, the plural of *collen* 'hazel trees', *go* 'enough', *ger* 'near', *y* 'the', *chwyrn* 'rapid', *drobwll* a form of *trobwll* 'whirlpool', *llan* 'church', *tysiliog* 'of St Tysilio', *ogo* 'cave', and *goch* a form of *coch* 'red'.

Llantrisant, WALES/UK *Landtrissen*
'Church of the Three Saints' from *llan*, *tri* 'three', and *sant* 'saint'. They were Dyfod, Gwyno, and Illtyd.

Lobito, ANGOLA
Founded by the Portuguese in 1843 with a name derived from the local *lupito* 'passage' to indicate that passage to the port was not easy.

Locke, NEW YORK/USA
Named after John Locke (1632–1704), English philosopher.

Lock Haven, PENNSYLVANIA/USA
Founded in 1834 and named after the Pennsylvania Canal lock; there were in fact two locks and a safe harbour for lumberjacks.

Lockport, NEW YORK/USA
Founded in 1821, it developed around a series of locks between Lake Erie and the Genesee River.

Lod, ISRAEL *Lodd, Lydda, Diospolis, al-Lydd, St Jorge de Lidde*
The Hebrew name Lydda may have come from a Greek tribe called the Lydda. After Septimus Severus (146–211), Roman emperor (193–211), visited in 200–1 it became a Roman colony with the name Diospolis 'City of Zeus' from the Greek *dios* 'Zeus' and *polis*; the local Jews and Samaritans, however, continued to use the name Lodd. The name was changed to al-Lydd by the Arabs after their conquest of Palestine in the 7th century. The reputed site of the martyrdom of the legendary St George, patron saint of England, in 1099–1191 it was called St Jorge de Lidde by the crusaders. Awarded to Palestine under the UN partition plan of 1947, it was occupied by Jordanian troops when Arab forces attacked immediately after the new state of Israel was proclaimed in 1948. It was quickly captured by the Israelis and renamed Lod.

Lodi, ITALY, USA
1. Italy (Lombardy): formerly Laus Pompeia. The present name is derived from the Roman name from the Latin *laus, laudis* 'praise', 'glory', or 'fame', thus 'Glory of Pompey', a reference to Pompey the Great (106–48 BC), a great Roman statesman and general.
2. USA (California): founded as Mokelumne Station in 1869, it was renamed four years later, supposedly after a racehorse.

Łódź, POLAND
A province, called Łódzkie, and a city with a name that translates as 'boat'.

Logan, AUSTRALIA, CANADA, USA
1. Australia (Queensland): a river named after a Captain Logan who was killed here by Aborigines.
2. Canada (Yukon Territory): a mountain named after Sir William Logan (1798–1875), founder of the Geological Survey of Canada.
3. USA (Utah): named after Ephraim Logan, a trapper, or Logan Fontanelle, a friendly Native American chief.
4. USA (West Virginia): originally Lawnsville and then Aracoma, it was renamed in 1907

after Logan, a Native American chief of the Mingo tribe.

Logansport, INDIANA/USA
Named after Captain Logan, a Shawnee chief.

Logroño, LA RIOJA/SPAIN
Derived from the Germanic *gronno* 'ford'. The city lies on the River Ebro.

Lolland, DENMARK
An island meaning 'Low Land'.

Lolodorf, CAMEROON
'Lolo's Village' from the name of a local chief and the German *Dorf* 'village'. The Germans occupied Cameroon in 1884–1916.

Lomas de Zamora, ARGENTINA
'Slopes of Zamora' from the Spanish *loma* 'hillock' or 'low ridge' and a personal name. This was Juan de Zamora, one of the founders of Buenos Aires, who was given land here in the 16th century.

Lombardy, CANADA, ITALY
Italy: a region, locally Lombardia and originally Langobardus, named after the Germanic Lombards or Langobards 'Long Beards' from *lang* 'long' and *bart* 'beard'. They established a kingdom in Italy in 568–774. The Spanish (1535–1713), the Austrians (1713–96), and the French (1796–1814) all ruled Lombardy before it became part of Italy in 1859.

Lombok, INDONESIA *Bumi Gora, Selaparang*
An island meaning 'Chilli' in Javanese and appropriately so because red hot chillies thrive and are harvested by the locals. The first name meant 'Dry Farmland'.

Lomé, TOGO
'Little Market'. Founded in 1880 by local merchants who chose the site just outside the new border of the British Gold Coast (now Ghana) to avoid paying British tax on imported goods. It became the capital of German Togoland in 1897 and of French Togo in 1918; it is now the national capital.

Lomita, CALIFORNIA/USA
'Little Hill' in Spanish, the diminutive of *loma*.

Lomond, Loch, CANADA, UK
1. Canada (New Brunswick and Nova Scotia): both probably named after the Scottish Loch Lomond.
2. UK (Scotland): may take its name from the River Leven or from Ben Lomond, a mountain overlooking it to the east. Its name comes from a Celtic word for 'beacon hill'.

Lomonosov, LENINGRAD/RUSSIA *Oranienbaum*
In 1707 Peter I the Great[†] gave the land to Alexander Menshikov (1673–1729), a

successful military commander during the Great Northern War (1700–21) who rose to become a field marshal and whom Peter made a prince and his closest assistant. In 1710 construction began and in due course it became a summer retreat for the Russian royal family with a name that may have been taken from the Dutch *Oranje Boom* 'Orange Tree'. Peter had worked as a ship's carpenter with the Dutch East India Company for four months in 1697. In 1948 the town was renamed after Mikhail Lomonosov (1711–65), scientist and grammarian, although the palace and park are still known as Oranienbaum.

Lompoc, CALIFORNIA/USA
Founded in 1874 as a farming community with a Chumash name meaning 'Shell Mound'.

London, CANADA, KIRITIMATI, UK, USA
UK (England): the origin is still uncertain. In *c*.115 Tacitus (*c*.56–*c*.120), the Roman historian, referred to the place as Londinium and this name may have been adopted as early as 43 when the Romans began their conquest of Britain. It may have had pre-Celtic origins. The first physical proof of the Roman name to be discovered, in 2002, came from a stone tablet dated *c*.150. Various different spellings have been used, such as Londinion and Lundinium. To denote that it was a Roman settlement the Anglo-Saxons called it Lundenceaster from *ceaster*, and it was referred to as Lundenburg and Lundene in the Anglo-Saxon Chronicle. For a period during the 4th century the city was officially known as Augusta, but this attempt at imposing a Roman title did not catch on. Between the 7th and 9th centuries a Saxon town, really a commercial centre, outside the city walls was known as Lundenwic; this area is now Covent Garden. Until about the end of the 19th century the name London only referred to the City of London. Thereafter, the term Greater London came to describe a much larger area. London was recognized as the capital of England by the end of the 12th century.

Londonderry, ST LUCIA, UK, USA
1. UK (Northern Ireland): the Irish name is Doire. Former names have included Doire Calgaigh, Doire Cholm Cille, and Derry. The latter is derived from the Irish *doire* 'oak wood', the original name meaning 'Calgach's Oak Grove' and for a time thereafter it was 'Columcille's Oak Grove', a reference to a monastery founded by St Columba (*c*.521–97) in 546. The city was granted to the city of London in 1613 for colonization, hence its present name. The Protestant inhabitants call

the city Londonderry while the Catholics prefer Derry.
2. USA (New Hampshire): named by immigrants from the city in Northern Ireland.

Londres, ARGENTINA
Founded in 1554 when Philip II (1527–98), King of Spain (1556–98), married Mary I (1516–58), Queen of England (1553–8), in London.

Lone Tree, IOWA/USA
Named after an isolated tree standing on the prairie.

Long Beach, CANADA, USA
USA (California): publicized in 1881 as a seaside resort called Willmore City after its founder, W. E. Willmore, it was renamed in 1888 because of its 8.5 mile (13.5 km) long beach.

Long Branch, NEW JERSEY/USA
Settled in 1668 and so named because it lies on a long branch of the South Shrewsbury River.

Longford, AUSTRALIA, CANADA, IRELAND, UK, USA
Ireland: a county with the local name An Longfort or Longphort 'The Fortress' from *an* 'the' and *longfort* 'fort' or 'stronghold'. The former name was Annaly or Anale, but this was superseded in the 16th century.

Long Island, ANDAMAN ISLANDS, ANTIGUA, AUSTRALIA, BAHAMAS, CANADA, PAPUA NEW GUINEA, USA
USA (New York): a descriptive name, being the Anglicized version of the Dutch Lange Eylandt. The island is 118 miles (190 km) long and between 12 and 23 miles (19–37 km) wide.

Longmont, COLORADO/USA
Founded in 1871 as a farming community, it was named after Major Stephen H. Long (1784–1864), who discovered Longs Peak (14 255ft; 4 345 m), now in the Rocky Mountain National Park, with the French *mont* 'mountain'.

Longonot, KENYA
A mountain with a name taken from the Masai *oloonong'ot* 'mountain of many ridges'.

Longueuil, QUEBEC/CANADA
Founded in 1657 by, and named after the Frenchman, Charles Le Moyne de Longueuil (1626–85).

Longview, CANADA, USA
1. USA (Texas): named in 1870 by surveyors for the Texas and Pacific Railroad because of the distant horizons afforded by a hill.
2. USA (Washington): founded in 1922 by, and named after, R. A. Long.

Longwy, LORRAINE/FRANCE
Of Germanic origin, it is equivalent to the Old English *lang* 'long' and *wīc* to mean a 'ribbon-like village along a single road'.

Lons-le-Saunier, FRANCHE-COMTÉ/FRANCE
Salinarius
Its Roman name owes its origin to the area's salt mines; the French *saunier* means 'salt worker', thus somebody who works in the mines. Lons may be derived from the Gaulish *ledone* 'stagnant water'.

Lookout, GUYANA, USA
USA (California): named because of the good views.

Lopatin, Mt, SAKHALIN ISLAND/RUSSIA
Named after Innokenty Lopatin (1839–1909), a geologist and geographer.

Lop Buri, THAILAND *Lavo/Louvo*
Founded in about the 6th century, it is named after the Lop Buri River. Given that *buri* means 'city', the river's name may be a partial back-formation.

Lop Nur, SINKIANG UIGHUR AUTONOMOUS REGION/CHINA
A former large salt lake, and now just a lake bed, with a name that is derived from the Tibetan *dap* 'mud' and Mongolian *nuur* 'lake'.

Lorain, OHIO/USA *Black River, Charlestown*
First settled in 1807 as a trading post in 1807 called Black River, it was incorporated as the village of Charlestown in 1836. When becoming a city in 1874, it was renamed after the county of Lorain which itself had been named after the province of Lorraine in France.

Lord Howe Island, AUSTRALIA, FRENCH POLYNESIA, SOLOMON ISLANDS
1. Australia (New South Wales): discovered in 1788 and named after the British Admiral, Lord Howe (1726–99), who was created a baron and earl in 1788 and was first lord of the Admiralty (1783–8).
2. French Polynesia (Society Islands): the local name for the atoll is Maupihaa, although it is also known as Mopelia. Both now are preferred to Lord Howe's Island named after Admiral Lord Howe.
3. Solomon Islands: also known by its local name of Ontong Java Atoll. It was named in 1791 after Admiral Lord Howe.

Lorestan, IRAN
A province also spelt Luristan whose name means 'Land of the Lurs', a Shī'a Muslim people.

Loreto, BOLIVIA, BRAZIL, COLOMBIA, ECUADOR, ITALY, MEXICO, PARAGUAY, PERU
Italy (Marche): takes its name from the Latin *lauretum* 'laurel grove'. According to legend, the home of the Virgin Mary in Nazareth was brought here to a laurel grove by angels in 1295; pilgrims come to see the 'Holy House'.

Lorient, BRITTANY/FRANCE *Blavet, Port-Louis, L'Orient*
A port renamed in the early 17th century after Louis XIII (1601–43), King of France (1610–43). When his successor, Louis XIV the Sun King[†], allowed a trading company, Compagnie de l'Orient '(the French) East (India) Company', to operate from here in 1664 it was renamed L'Orient 'The East'.

Lorraine, AUSTRALIA, CANADA, FRANCE, USA
France: a region whose name has evolved from the original Lotharingia which itself came from the Latin *Lotharii regnum* 'Kingdom of Lothair'. This referred to the northern part of Francia Media which was partitioned in 855 by King Lothair I (795–855) and given to his son, Lothair II (835–69), Frankish king (855–69). Possession of the region has been repeatedly disputed between France and Germany, which calls it Lothringen. It was incorporated into France in 1766, passing to Germany in 1871 when the Germans were victorious in the Franco-German War. Together, Alsace-Lorraine became known as Reichsland. At the end of the First World War, it was returned to France, but was captured by the Germans in 1940. It was restored once more to France in 1945.

Los Alamos, MEXICO, USA
USA (New Mexico): 'The Cottonwoods' from the Spanish *alamo* 'poplar'.

Los Angeles, CHILE, PERU, PUERTO RICO, USA
USA (California): founded by the Spanish in 1781 as El Pueblo de la Reyna de los Angeles 'The Town of the Queen of the Angels'; for a time it was simply called El Pueblo. In due course, the last two words of the full title, from the Spanish *angel* 'angel', were preferred for the shortened version. The city is now often simply called LA. It became an American city in 1846.

Los Baños, LUZON/PHILIPPINES
'The Baths' from the Spanish *baño* in recognition of the thermal springs at the bottom of the nearby Mount Makiling.

Los Dos Caminos, VENEZUELA
'The Two Roads' from the Spanish *dos* 'two' and *camino* 'road'.

Los Gatos, CALIFORNIA/USA
'The Cats' from the Spanish *gato*, possibly a reference to the numerous wild cats in the area.

Los Lagos, CHILE
A region created in 1974 and meaning 'The Lakes' from the Spanish *lago*.

Los Nietos, CALIFORNIA/USA
'The Grandchildren' from the Spanish *nietos*.

Los Olivos, CALIFORNIA/USA
'The Olives' from the Spanish *olivo*.

Los Rios (Los Ríos), ECUADOR
A province meaning 'The Rivers' from the Spanish *río*, a reference to the River Guayas and its headwaters.

Los Santos, PANAMA
A province meaning 'The Saints' from the Spanish *santo*.

Los Teques, VENEZUELA
Named after a local tribe.

Lothian, SCOTLAND/UK
A region divided into East Lothian, Midlothian, West Lothian, and Edinburgh city. It is said to take its name from an unknown man called Leudonus. That it may come from King Lot, the brother-in-law of King Arthur, the legendary British king of the 6th century, is highly unlikely.

Louang Namtha, LAOS *Houakhong*
Named after the River Tha from *nam* 'river' to which *luang* 'great' has been added.

Louangphrabang, LAOS *Xua, Xiang Dong Xiang Thong, Meuang Xiang Thong, Meuang Sawa/ Muong Swa, Luang Prabang*
'(City of) the Great Holy Image' from *luang* 'great' or 'royal', *phra* or *pra* 'holy', and *bang* 'image'. So-named because Fa Ngoum (1316–74), first King of the Lao Kingdom of Lan Xang (1353–73), had received in 1353 a Sinhalese gold statue of the Buddha, known as the Pra Bang, from his Khmer father-in-law. At this time the city was called Meuang Sawa. The image of the Buddha became a symbol of the sovereignty of the Kingdom of Lan Xang 'Kingdom of a Million Elephants' and it has remained so to this day. The city received the name Luang Prabang in 1563 from Setthathirat I (1534–71), King of Lan Xang (1547–71) who, although moving his capital to Vientiane in 1560, ordered that the Pra Bang should stay where it was. Meuang Sawa/Muong Swa meant 'District of Java' after the Javanese invasion of southern Laos, from *meuang* or *muong* 'district', 'principality', or 'town'. The earlier Xiang Dong Xiang Thong meant 'Copper Tree City' and Meuang Xiang Thong 'Gold City District'. The city was the capital of Lan Xang in 1353–1520 and 1545–60. After the partition of Lan Xang in 1707, Luang Prabang became the capital of the new Kingdom of

Luang Prabang in 1707 and remained so until 1947.

Loughborough, CANADA, UK
UK (England): formerly Lucteburne and Lucteburga 'Luhhede's Fortification' from an Old English personal name and *burh*.

Loughrea (Loch Riach), IRELAND
'Grey Lake' from *loch* 'lake' and *ria* 'grey', although *ria* actually means 'striped'; however, for place-names it is often translated as 'grey'. The town is situated on Lough (lake) Rea.

Louisa, VIRGINIA/USA
Named after Princess Louisa (1724–51), third daughter of King George II[†].

Louisbourg, NOVA SCOTIA/CANADA *Louisburg*
Founded in 1713 by French settlers and named after Louis XIV the Sun King[†].

Louisiana, USA
1. A state, originally known as the Territory of the Choctaw and Caddo. In 1682 a French explorer, René-Robert Cavelier, Lord de La Salle[†], claimed the Mississippi River basin for France and named it Louisiane for Louis XIV the Sun King[†]. It became a French crown colony in 1731, but the area west of the river was ceded to Spain in 1762; a year later the area east of the river, less New Orleans, passed to Great Britain and in 1783 to the USA. Under the terms of a secret treaty in 1800 the rest of the territory was restored to France with the proviso that it should never be ceded to another country. However, just three years later, to raise funds for his military campaigns in Europe, Napoleon[†] sold Louisiana to the USA for $16 million. At this time Louisiana was not the small state that it is today, but comprised all the French lands between Canada and Mexico, and between the Mississippi and the Rockies. Included in what was known as the Louisiana Purchase were the present states of Arkansas, Iowa, Missouri, and Nebraska, and parts of Louisiana, Colorado, Kansas, Minnesota, Montana, North and South Dakota, Oklahoma, and Wyoming. Their acquisition more than doubled the existing territory of the United States. The present state of Louisiana was designated the Territory of New Orleans in 1804; it joined the Union as Louisiana, the 18th state, in 1812.
2. Missouri: a city, named after the Louisiana Territory, of which it was a part when founded.

Louis Trichardt, LIMPOPO/SOUTH AFRICA
See MAKHADO.

Louisville, KENTUCKY/USA
Settled in 1778 and, when incorporated in 1780, named 'Town of Louis' after

Louis XVI (1754–93), King of France (1774–92), in gratitude for French help during the American War of Independence (1775–83).

Louny, CZECH REPUBLIC *Lunye/Lúně*
It may mean 'Lúňa's Settlement' or it may be derived from *luna*, an Old Czech word of Celtic origin, meaning 'meadow'. Thus the name might mean the 'Settlement in an Area of Meadows'.

Lourdes, CANADA, EL SALVADOR, FRANCE
France (Provence-Alpes-Côtes d'Azur): the present name may have evolved from the original Roman Lapurda. However, it may have come from a later personal name, possibly Lurdus.

Lourenço Marques, MOZAMBIQUE
See MAPUTO.

Louvain (Flemish: Leuven), BELGIUM
Lying on the Dijle River, the name may be derived from the Low German *loo* 'bushy hill' and *veen* 'swamp'. Alternatively, it may come from a personal name *Lubianos* 'Loved One'.

Loveland, COLORADO/USA
Founded in 1877 and named after W. A. H. Loveland, president of the Colorado Central Railroad.

Lovinac, CROATIA
Named after the noble Lovinčić family.

Lovran, CROATIA
'Laurel' from *lovor*.

Low Countries *See* BENELUX.

Lowell, USA
1. Maine: named after Lowell Hayden, the first baby born within its precincts.
2. Massachusetts: known originally in 1653 as the village of East Chelmsford, it was renamed after Francis Cabot Lowell (1775–1817), a textile industrialist, when it became a town in 1826.

Lower Egypt (Miṣr Baḥrī), EGYPT
That part of Egypt which is north of Cairo and which includes the Nile delta and the Mediterranean coast.

Lower Saxony (Niedersachsen), GERMANY
A state. *See* SAXONY.

Lowestoft, ENGLAND/UK *Lothu Wistoft*
'Hlothvér's Homestead' from an Old Scandinavian personal name, probably Danish, and *toft* 'homestead'.

Loxton, AUSTRALIA, SOUTH AFRICA
Australia (South Australia): named after William Loxton, a sheep rancher.

Loyalty Islands (French: Îles Loyauté), NEW CALEDONIA/FRANCE
Discovered in 1827 by a Frenchman, Jules Sébastien César Dumont d'Urville, who gave them this name because of the goodwill of the islanders. The islands were annexed to France in 1853.

Loznica, SERBIA/SERBIA AND MONTENEGRO
Derives its name from *loza* 'grape vine'.

Lualaba, DEMOCRATIC REPUBLIC OF THE CONGO
'Big River' from *lu-* 'river'.

Luanda, ANGOLA *São Paulo de Luanda*
Founded in 1576 as 'St Paul of Luanda' by Paulo Dias de Novães who claimed it as a Portuguese dependency. From 1589 it was the capital of the Portuguese colony and became the capital of Angola on independence in 1975. The name is derived from the local word *luanda* 'tax' or 'duty' and refers to cowrie shells which were used for this purpose.

Lubango, ANGOLA *Sá (or Serra) da Bandeira*
Founded in 1885 by the Portuguese and named after Bernardo de Sá da Bandeira (1795–1876), a prime minister of Portugal. In 1975 the name was changed to Lubango from *ombango* 'passage (through the mountains)', the city being surrounded by mountains.

Lubbock, TEXAS/USA
Founded in 1890 and named after Colonel Thomas S. Lubbock, a Confederate officer and one of those who signed the Texas Declaration of Independence to create the new Republic of Texas in 1836.

Lubec, MAINE/USA
Founded in 1870 and named after Lübeck in Germany.

Lübeck, SCHLESWIG-HOLSTEIN/GERMANY *Liubice*
Originally the capital of a principality of the Slavic Liubichi, who were the descendants of a leader called Liuba, whose name was equivalent to the modern Russian *liubimiy* 'beloved' or 'favourite'.

Lubumbashi, DEMOCRATIC REPUBLIC OF THE CONGO *Elisabethville*
Founded by the Belgians in 1910 as a copper-mining settlement and named after Queen Elizabeth (1876–1965), wife of Albert I, King of the Belgians. In 1966 it was renamed after a small, local stream, the Lubumbashi, whose meaning is unknown.

Lucca, TUSCANY/ITALY *Luca*
A Ligurian, Etruscan, and Roman town, the name comes from a Celtic-Ligurian root *luk* 'marshy place'. It lies in the valley of the Serchio River.

Lucerne, CANADA, SWITZERLAND, USA
1. Switzerland: a canton, a lake (named after the city and also sometimes called the Lake of the Four Cantons), and a city with the local name of Luzern in German. The most likely explanation for its name is that it is derived from the Benedictine monastery of St Leodegar which was founded in the 8th century. It was the capital of the Helvetic Republic in 1798–1803.
2. USA (California): named after the abundant growth of lucerne (also called alfalfa) in the area.

Luch, TAMBOV/RUSSIA *Gazoprovod*
'Ray' or 'Beam'. The previous name meant 'Gas Pipeline' or 'Gas Main' from *provod* 'line' or 'conductor'.

Lucknow, AUSTRALIA, CANADA, INDIA
India (Uttar Pradesh): derived from the Hindi *lakhnaū*, a version of the Sanskrit *lakshmana* 'sign', a reference to Lakshmi, the Hindu goddess of wealth and good luck, and the embodiment of beauty, and one of the wives of Vishnu.

Lüderitz, NAMIBIA *Angra das Voltas, Golfo de São Cristovão, Angra Pequena, Lüderitzbucht*
Initially the bay here was named the 'Bay of Turns' in 1487 by the Portuguese navigator Bartholomew Dias (*c.*1450–1500), then 'St Christopher's Gulf' and later still 'Little Bay'. A German merchant from Hamburg, Franz Adolf Lüderitz (1834–86), arrived in 1883 to establish the first German settlement in South West Africa and succeeded in obtaining German government protection. He renamed the bay 'Lüderitz Bay' after himself and the settlement he founded took the same name; it was later shortened.

Ludhiana, PUNJAB/INDIA
Founded in 1480 and named after the ruling dynasty in Delhi, the Afghan Lodī, who presided over the Delhi Sultanate in 1451–1526.

Luding, SICHUAN/CHINA *Luding Qiao, Jagsamka*
A shortened version of the original name meaning 'The Bridge (over the River Dadu) that Lu built' from *qiáo* 'bridge'.

Ludington, MICHIGAN/USA *Marquette*
Settled in the 1840s and named after a Jesuit explorer, Jacques Marquette, who died here in 1685. It was renamed in 1871 after James Ludington, a local lumberjack.

Ludlow, UK, USA
1. UK (England): formerly Ludelaue 'Hill by the noisy Stream' from the Old English *hlūde* 'loud' or 'noisy' and *hlāw* 'hill'.

The stream is the River Teme on which the town lies.

2. USA (Massachusetts): settled in 1751 as Stony Hill, it was renamed in 1775 after the town in England.

Ludwigsburg, BADEN-WÜRTTEMBERG/ GERMANY
'Castle of Ludwig', the city being developed during the early 18th century around the palace of Eberhard Ludwig (Louis) (1704–33), Duke of Württemberg.

Ludwigshafen, BADEN-WÜRTTEMBERG/ GERMANY *Rheinschanze*
Originally established in 1606 as Rheinschanze 'Rhine Bulwark', a fortification on the west bank of the River Rhine, it was renamed in 1843 after Ludwig (Louis) I (1786–1868), King of Bavaria (1825–48), and means 'Ludwig's Harbour'.

Lufkin, TEXAS/USA
Founded in 1882 and named after E. P. Lufkin, the son-in-law of the general manager of the Houston, East and West Texas Railroad.

Lugano, SWITZERLAND
A town with a name derived from the Gaulish *lacvanno* 'lake dweller' to describe the people living along the shores of Lake Lugano.

Lugela, MOZAMBIQUE
Derived from a local word *ologela* 'to greet' because all visitors were expected to greet the chief on arrival.

Lugo, ITALY, SPAIN
1. Italy (Emilia-Romagna): derived from the Latin *lucus* 'wood', specifically here a 'sacred grove' as opposed to a wild wood.
2. Spain (Galicia): a province and a city having the same meaning as the Italian town, although its original Roman name was Lucus Augusti 'Sacred Grove of Augustus'.

Lugovoy, KAZAKHSTAN, RUSSIA
Take their names from the Russian *lug* 'meadow', thus situated on a meadow, or it may be a reference to its fertility in an otherwise fairly barren area.

Luhansk, UKRAINE *Yekaterinoslavsk, Voroshilovgrad, Lugansk*
A province and a city founded in 1795 and originally named after Catherine II the Great[†]. Two years later it was renamed after the River Lugan whose name might be derived from *lug* 'meadow'. In 1935 the city was named Voroshilovgrad 'City of Voroshilov' after Kliment Voroshilov[†], whose birthplace was nearby, when he was appointed to the rank of marshal of the Soviet Union. The name reverted to Lugansk in 1958–70 after

Voroshilov took part in an unsuccessful attempt to overthrow the Soviet leader, Nikita Khrushchev (1894–1971), in 1957. It became Voroshilovgrad again in 1970–90 after Voroshilov's death in 1969 and his subsequent rehabilitation. As a result of a critical assessment of the first decades of Soviet rule in the late 1980s, however, Voroshilov was again discredited and the city's name once more reverted to Lugansk. The present name is the Ukrainian spelling of the former Russian name.

Luḥayyah, al-, YEMEN *Luya*
Founded in the 15th century, the present name evolved from the Portuguese name and means 'Small Beard' from the Arabic *liḥya* 'beard'.

Luján, ARGENTINA
According to legend, founded in 1630 when a statue of the Virgin Mary being taken between two churches got stuck here. This was taken as a sign that a religious shrine should be erected on the spot. However, the city is named after a conquistador, Pedro Luján, who died here in battle in 1536.

Luleå, SWEDEN
Named after the River Lule with *å* 'river' added.

Lumberton, USA
1. Mississippi: named after its major industry.
2. North Carolina: founded in 1787, soon becoming a port for the movement of lumber down river.

Lund, CANADA, DENMARK, SWEDEN, USA
Sweden: founded *c*.1020 in what is now Malmöhus County, but which was then controlled by the Danes, by Canute II (*c*.995–1035), King of Denmark (as Knut, 1019–35) and King of England (as Canute I, 1016–35) with a Medieval Latin name of Londinum Gothorum 'Londinum of the Goths'. The present name probably comes from the Old Scandinavian *lundr* 'small wood' or 'grove'.

Lundy, ENGLAND/UK *Lundeia*
'Puffin Island' from the Old Scandinavian *lundi* 'puffin' and *ey*.

Lüneburg, LOWER SAXONY/GERMANY *Liuniburg/ Luniburc*
The meaning of the first part of the name is unknown but may relate to some kind of defensive work; the second part, *Burg*, means 'fort' or 'stronghold'.

Lunenburg, CANADA, USA
Canada (Nova Scotia): originally the site of the Native American village of Malliggeak, it was

granted by Oliver Cromwell (1599–1658), lord protector of England (1653–8), in 1656 to Charles de Saint-Étienne de La Tour, governor of Acadia. However, it was not settled until Germans from Lüneburg and some Swiss arrived in the 1750s. They named their settlement after the royal house of Brunswick-Lüneburg, of which the British king, George II[†], was also Duke.

Lūni, RĀJASTHĀN/INDIA
A river whose name comes from the Sanskrit Lāvanavāri 'Salt River' due to its high salt content.

Luoyang, HENAN/CHINA *Luoyi, Henan fu*
A very ancient city, it was the capital of nine dynasties between 771 BC and 907 AD. It was sometimes known as the 'Eastern Capital' when the court moved out of Xi'an (Chang'an), and the 'Western Capital', when it was threatened from the west. The name means 'Sunny Side of the Luo River', thus 'North Side of the Luo River' from *yáng* 'sun'.

Lurgan (Lorgain), NORTHERN IRELAND/UK
Derived from *lorga* 'shin' and thus meaning 'ridge' or 'strip of land'.

Lusaka, ZAMBIA *Lusakas Village*
The area was settled at the end of the 19th century by the Lenje. The village took its name from the Lenje chief, Lusaakas; it was shortened later. The area came under the control of Cecil Rhodes's[†] British South Africa Company shortly afterwards and serious development began in 1905. Centrally located, Lusaka became the capital of Northern Rhodesia in 1935 and of Zambia on independence in 1964.

Lusatia (Lausitz), GERMANY-POLAND
A historic region named after the Slav Lužiči people, a subgroup of the Sorbs (also known as Wends or Lusatians). Their name came from *luz* 'meadow' (in modern Russian, *lug*). Taken by the Poles at the beginning of the 11th century, Lusatia passed to the Bohemian crown in 1368 and was ceded to Saxony in 1635; in 1815 Lower (southern) Lusatia became part of Prussia. At the end of the Second World War eastern Lusatia was incorporated into Poland while the rest became part of East Germany.

Lüshun, LIAONING/CHINA *Port Arthur, Ryojun*
Named Port Arthur in 1860 after a Lieutenant Arthur, a British naval officer, who was a member of a survey team that carried out a reconnaissance of the site in 1857 to see if it was suitable for a naval base. Captured by the Japanese and leased to Japan in 1895, it was quickly returned to China. Two years later the

Russians occupied the Liaodong Peninsula and in 1898 began the construction of a naval base at Port Arthur for their Pacific Fleet and a commercial port at Dalny (*Dalian) nearby. The fact that the area was ice-free all year round was particularly appealing to the Russians. Port Arthur was seized by the Japanese in 1904 and was ceded to Japan the next year; it was renamed Ryojun. It was transferred to the Soviet Union at the end of the Second World War, although both China and the Soviet Union were to have joint use of it. In 1954 China assumed complete control. The present name comes from the Chinese *lǚ* 'traveller' and *shùn* 'along'.

Lusitania, PORTUGAL
An ancient province of Hispania now roughly equivalent to modern Portugal. When Hispania was reorganized in 27 BC, Lusitania became a Roman imperial province, named after the Iberian people, the Lusitani, living here. It gave its name to a British Transatlantic liner that was sunk by a German submarine in 1915; 128 Americans (out of 1 198 passengers and crew) died and a wave of anger swept the USA, neutral in the war at the time; German submarine activity was mentioned as one of the reasons why the USA joined the First World War in 1917.

Luton, ENGLAND/UK *Lygetun, Loitone (Bedfordshire)*
'Farmstead on the (River) Lea' from a Celtic river name and *tūn*.

Luts'k, UKRAINE *Luck*
Takes its name from the Russian *luka* 'river bend' since it lies on a bend in the Styr River.

Luxembourg, AND BELGIUM, USA
1. The Grand Duchy of Luxembourg (Groussherzogtum Lëtzebuerg (Luxemburgian), Grand-Duché de Luxembourg (French), Grossherzogtum Luxemburg (German) since 1815, although William I (1772–1843), King of the Netherlands (1815–40), was allowed to take the title of the Grand Duke of Luxembourg and it remained within the Netherlands as part of the German Confederation until 1866, although having autonomy from 1839; it became independent in 1867. Previously annexed to France (1795–1814), part of the Austrian Netherlands (1714–95), and of the Spanish Netherlands (1506–1714) apart from a period of French rule (1684–97). The county of Luxembourg became a duchy in 1354. Luxembourg, also called Letzeburg, is the name of the capital city, originally Lucilinburhuc 'Little Castle', which originated as a Roman castle and which, when acquired in 963 by the Count of Arlette,

constituted a new political entity from which the city, and the surrounding territory, grew. **2.** Belgium: a province in the region of Wallonia since 1831 when the Grand Duchy of Luxembourg was divided.

Luxor (al-Uqsur), EGYPT *Wase(t), Nowe, Thebai/ Thebes, Diospolis*
Luxor, an English version of the Arabic name, actually covers only the southern half of the ruins of Thebes, Karnak being among the northern ruins of Thebes. Luxor means '(City of) The Palaces' for its temples or 'The Encampments' from *al-quṣūr*, the plural of *qaṣr*, some remains of Roman ruins having been found. An obscure village named Wase(t) after a local goddess called Wast, in the second millennium BC, it became known as Nowe 'City (of Amon)' after its chief god. In about the 5th century BC the complex was given the Greek name Thebai, corrupted to Thebes; this came from Ta-ope or Tapet 'The Capital', the name by which the area was known to the Egyptians in the 14th century BC. This was the feminine form of Apet, the name given to the annual festival that marked the annual flooding of the River Nile. Nowe was the capital of the ancient Egyptian empire. It was also known by a Greek name Diospolis 'City of Zeus' for a time by the Romans who had a legion based here; the Greek poet Homer referred to it as the 'City of a Hundred Gates'.

Luzhou, SICHUAN/CHINA *Lu County*
A port on the River Lu from which it takes its name with the additional *zhōu*, it received its present name in 1950.

Luzon, PHILIPPINES
An island meaning 'Big Light' from the Spanish *luz* 'light'.

L'viv, UKRAINE *Lwów, Lemberg, Lvov*
Founded by Danylo (Daniel) Romanovich, Prince of Galicia-Volyn (mid-13th century), as a castle-town and named after his son, Lev (Leo) 'Lion'. The German name, Lemberg, means 'Lion's Fortress'. The city came under Polish control in 1349, was given to Austria at the first partition of Poland in 1772, seized by the Poles in 1918, captured by the Russians in 1939, occupied by the Germans in 1941–4, and annexed to the Soviet Union in 1945. It became part of independent Ukraine in 1991 with the Ukrainian spelling.

Lycia, TURKEY *Milyas, Tremile*
A historic region on the Mediterranean coast bounded by ancient Caria to the west, Pamphylia to the east, and Phrygia to the north. It was named after its inhabitants who took their name from Lycus, their leader; they

were also known as the Luka. The name of Milyas came from the Milyae, who emigrated from Crete to settle here. Together with Pamphylia, it became a Roman province in 43 and a province in its own right in the 4th century.

Lydenburg (Masising), MPUMALANGA/SOUTH AFRICA
Established in 1850 as the second Voortrekker town, it means 'Town of Suffering' in Afrikaans. This alluded to the illnesses suffered at the time by the Voortrekkers (a name given to the Boers of the Great Trek into the interior from 1835). It was incorporated into the South African Republic in 1866. The local name means 'Place of Long Grass'.

Lydia, TURKEY *Mæonia*
A historic kingdom sandwiched between ancient Mysia to the north and Caria to the south, it was named after Lydus, one of its kings. At the height of its power in *c.*650–550 BC, its capital, Sardis, was the richest city in the world. In 561–546 BC, its king was Croesus. Fabulously rich, his name became synonymous with wealth: 'as rich as Croesus'.

Lyme Regis, ENGLAND/UK *Lhonborth, Lim, Lime*
The early British name meant 'Naval Harbour'. In the 8th century it was renamed after the River Lim, itself a Celtic name meaning 'stream'. *Regis* 'of the king' was added in 1285 on the order of Edward I (1239–1307), King of England (1272–1307).

Lynchburg, VIRGINIA/USA
Settled in 1757 as a ferry point on the James River, it was renamed after John Lynch, who owned the site, built a staging post here, and operated the ferry.

Lyndhurst, AUSTRALIA, UK, USA
1. UK (England): formerly Linhest 'Wooded Hill with Lime Trees' from the Old English *lind* 'lime tree' and *hyrst* 'wooded hill'.
2. USA (New Jersey): formerly Union, it was renamed in 1917 after John Singleton Copley (1772–1863), 1st Baron Lyndhurst, lord chancellor of England (1827–30, 1834–5, 1841–5).

Lynn, MASSACHUSETTS/USA *Saugas*
Founded in 1629 and renamed in 1637 after Lynn Regis (now King's Lynn) in England.

Lyons, FRANCE, USA
1. France (Rhône-Alpes): French Lyon. Founded in 43 BC as a Roman military colony on the site of two Celtic settlements and named Lugdunum 'Fort of Lugus' after the Celtic god of arts and crafts with *dunum*.

However, it is possible that *lug* means 'marshy ground', quite appropriate, given the city's position at the confluence of the Rhône and Saône Rivers. It became the capital of Gaul. For a time in 1793 during the French Revolution, it was called Ville Affranchie 'Liberated Town'.
2. USA (Kansas): named after Truman J. Lyon, the owner of the site.
3. USA (New York): named after the city in France.

Lytham St Anne's, ENGLAND/UK *Lidun*
Lytham and St Anne's were merged in 1922. The former name means '(Place at) the Slopes' from the plural of the Old English *hliþ* 'slope'. The parish church, dedicated to St Anne, gave the second part of the name.

Lyttelton, NEW ZEALAND, SOUTH AFRICA
New Zealand (South Island): used as a harbour for whalers and sealers from the late 18th century, it was later named Port Cooper and then Port Victoria. The town itself was not laid out until 1849 when it was renamed after George Lyttelton (1817–76), 4th Baron Lyttelton, under-secretary of state for the colonies (1846) and from 1849 chairman of the Canterbury Association, a Church of England foundation to promote the Church.

Lytton, BRITISH COLUMBIA/CANADA
Named in 1858 after Edward Bulwer-Lytton (1803–73), 1st Baron Lytton, secretary of state for the colonies (1858–9), and a famous novelist. His principal achievement was the organization of the new colony of British Columbia following the discovery of gold and a substantial increase in the population.

Ma'ān, JORDAN
Said to be named after Ma'ān, a son of Lot, a biblical figure who accompanied Abraham out of Egypt.

Maastricht, THE NETHERLANDS *Trajectum ad Mosam*
'Crossing over the (River) Maas' from the Latin *trajectus* 'crossing' or 'passage', referring to the Roman ford here, and the river name which in English is *Meuse.

Mablethorpe, ENGLAND/UK *Malbertorp*
'Outlying Settlement of a Man called Malbert' from an Old German personal name and the Old Scandinavian *thorp* 'outlying settlement'.

McAlester, OKLAHOMA/USA
Established in 1870 as a trading post by, and named after, James McAlester, who went on to become lieutenant-governor of the state.

McAllen, TEXAS/USA
Founded in 1905 and named after John McAllen, a Scottish settler whose ranch developed into the town.

McArthur, AUSTRALIA, USA
1. Australia (Northern Territory): a river discovered in 1845 and named after sheep ranchers James and William McArthur.
2. USA (Ohio): named after General Duncan McArthur who fought in the Native American wars in the 19th century.

Macau, BRAZIL, CHINA
China: also spelt Macao and consisting of a peninsula and two islands, Taipa and Coloane, on the west side of the Pearl River Estuary. Derived from the Chinese *A-Ma-Ngao* 'Bay of (the Goddess) A-Ma', the 'Bay of the Mother', the so-called Queen of Heaven, the goddess of seamen and fishermen, from the Cantonese *ngao* 'bay' or 'port'. Its Chinese name of Ao-men comes from *ào* 'bay' and *mén* 'gate'. It was founded as a trading post by Portuguese merchants in 1552, the first Portuguese ship having entered the Pearl River Estuary in 1513. While China retained sovereignty, the Portuguese governed their own people and other Europeans. Following the example of the cession of Hong Kong to the UK in 1842, the Portuguese expelled all Chinese officials in 1845 and declared Macau to be Portuguese territory. Their right of 'perpetual occupation'

was recognized by a weak Manchu government in 1887. In 1951 Macau became a formal overseas territory of Portugal, but in 1987 it was agreed that it should be returned to Chinese sovereignty at the end of 1999, thus bringing all mainland China under Beijing's rule for the first time in 442 years; at the time it was the last dependent state in Asia. It forms now the Macau Special Administrative Region (Aomen Tebie Xingzhengqu) and is ruled under China's 'one country, two systems' model in the same way as Hong Kong.

MacCarthy Island, GAMBIA *Lemain Island*
Also called Jangjangbure locally. In 1823 it was ceded to Captain Alexander Grant who was acting on behalf of the British crown. It was renamed subsequently after Sir Charles MacCarthy (1770–1824), the British colonial governor of Sierra Leone (1812–24), who did much to advance the cause of Christianity in Africa, but was killed by Ashanti tribesmen.

Macclesfield, AUSTRALIA, UK
UK (England): formerly Maclesfeld 'Maccel's Open Land' from an Old English personal name and *feld*. It may refer to an open area within the great forest of Macclesfield.

McClure Strait, CANADA
Between Melville Island and Banks Island, it is named after Vice Admiral Sir Robert McClure, an Irish naval officer whose ship was trapped by ice north of Banks Island while he was searching for Sir John Franklin in 1850. He entered the Northwest Passage from the west. He and his crew were rescued on Melville Island in 1854 by a ship coming from the east; thus, for the first time, the passage had been traversed.

MacDonnell Ranges, NORTHERN TERRITORY/ AUSTRALIA
Discovered in 1860 and named after Sir Richard MacDonnell (1814–81), governor of South Australia (1855–62).

McDonough, USA
Georgia and New York: named after Commodore Thomas McDonough (1783–1825), a naval commander who distinguished himself in the war of 1812 by convincingly defeating the British at the Battle of Plattsburgh on Lake Champlain in 1814.

Macedonia (Makedonija), AND GREECE, USA
1. The Republic of Macedonia (Republika Makedonija) since June 1991, five months before independence from Yugoslavia was declared; this is the name used officially by the state of Macedonia for itself. Greece protested that the name Macedonia was only a geographical term coined by the Greek historian Herodotus during the Peloponnesian War (431–404 BC) and that, furthermore, three regions in Greece already included Macedonia in their title. The Greeks were concerned that using the name might encourage the new state to lay claim some time in the future to Greek Macedonia. They suggested that the new republic should be called the Republic of *Skopje or the Vardar Republic. However, in April 1993, Macedonia was formally admitted to the UN under the name of 'The former Yugoslav Republic of Macedonia' (FYROM). Previously it was the Socialist Republic of Macedonia (1946) within Yugoslavia when it was hived off from Serbia. This sealed the concept that the geographical term 'Macedonia' should also be an ethnic one: the Slavs of Macedonia should henceforth be called Macedonians. This newly created Macedonian nation, a Serb-communist invention according to some, could thus claim, so the theory went, possession of everything Macedonian, particularly history and culture, a clear distortion of the truth. Part of the Kingdom of the Serbs, Croats, and Slovenes when that kingdom was formed in 1918, the republic had been known as South Serbia (or Vardar Macedonia after King Vardar) since 1913. At the Treaty of Bucharest that year Serbia had been awarded the mainly Slav northern and central parts of Macedonia (38 per cent), while Greece received the southern half (Aegean Macedonia) (52 per cent), which was roughly equivalent to 'historical' Macedonia in classical times, and Bulgaria 10 per cent (Pirin Macedonia). For the previous 520 years Macedonia had been subject to Ottoman Turkish rule and of much of what was generally known as Turkey-in-Europe. Macedonia is named after the Greek-speaking tribe of Makedones, or Makednoi, whose name is said to come from Makedon, the son of Zeus, supreme ruler of the Greek gods; rather, it may be derived from the fact that the early tribes came from the rugged Pindos mountains and took their names from the physical features of the landscape: from the Greek root *mak* 'tall' or 'high'. It gives its name to *macédoine*, a French word for mixed vegetables or fruit, an allusion to the ethnic mix in Macedonia, principally Macedonians, Albanians, Turks, Gypsies, Serbs, and Croats.

During the first millennium BC, Macedonia, together with Kosovo and south Serbia, was called Dardania.
2. Greece: now one region called Macedonia; in Greek, Makedonía.
3. Macedonia: an ancient kingdom, often called Macedon, which was at its height during the reigns of Philip II (359–336 BC) and his son, Alexander III the Great[†]. In 168 BC it ceased to be an independent state when it came under Roman domination, the kingdom being split into four semi-autonomous regions. Twenty years later it became a province of the Roman Empire. When the Empire was divided in 395 Macedonia became part of the eastern half, the Byzantine Empire. In the 6th and 7th centuries various Slav peoples began to settle in Macedonia and they spoke a Slavonic language called Bulgarian, but since 1944 Macedonian; it uses the Cyrillic script. The geographical term, Macedonia, today covers the Republic of Macedonia, the north and north-east of Greece and south-west Bulgaria.

Macerata, MARCHE/ITALY
Derived from the Latin *maceria* 'enclosure' or 'wall', a reference to the ruins of the ancient Helvia Ricina on which it was built in the 10th century.

Macerata Feltria, MARCHES/ITALY
As previous entry with the additional Feltria to denote that the town belonged to the Montefeltros, the ruling family of nearby Urbino.

Macgillycuddy's Reeks (Na Cruacha Dubha), IRELAND
A personal name, Mac Giolla Chuda, with *reeks* 'crests' or 'ridges'. The Irish name means 'The Black Peaks'.

Machado, BRAZIL
Minas Gerais and Roraima: a Portuguese word meaning 'axe'.

Machadodorp, MPUMALANGA/SOUTH AFRICA
'Town of Machado' after General Joaquim José Machado (1847–1925), the Portuguese governor-general of Mozambique, who had been instrumental in bringing the railway here.

Machakos, KENYA
Founded in 1889 and named after a local chief, Masaku.

Machias, MAINE/USA
Although the site of a trading post as early as 1633, it was not incorporated until 1784 when it was named after the River Machias from an Abnaki word *machisses* 'bad small falls'.

Machu Picchu, PERU
Ruins. The ancient Inca religious centre was discovered in 1911 and has a Quechua name from *machu* 'old man' and *pikchu* 'peak'. It is situated between two peaks in the Andes Mountains.

Mackay, AUSTRALIA, USA
Australia (Queensland): founded in 1862 and named after Captain John Mackay (1838–1914) who had explored the area two years earlier.

McKeesport, PENNSYLVANIA/USA
Settled *c.*1755 by David McKee and in 1795 named by his son, John McKee after his father who operated the ferry at the confluence of the Monongahela and Youghiogheny Rivers.

Mackenzie, AUSTRALIA, CANADA
1. Australia (Queensland): a seasonal river explored in 1844 by the German Ludwig Leichhardt (1813–48), who named it after Sir Evan Mackenzie, one of the early settlers.
2. Canada (Northwest Territories): a river named after Sir Alexander Mackenzie (*c.*1755–1820), a Scottish fur trader who explored the north-west of North America in 1789–93, travelling down the river in 1789. His aim was to find a river route to the Pacific, but instead the river emerged into the Arctic Ocean (the Beaufort Sea) and so he gave it the alternative name of the River of Disappointment. The local Dene name was Dehcho 'Big River'.
3. Canada (Northwest Territories); mountains named after Sir Alexander Mackenzie.

Mackinaw City, MICHIGAN/USA
Established by the French as a trading post in 1673, by 1715 it had become a military post as Fort Michilimackinac. It spawned a village called Michilimackinac which was shortened to Mackinaw in 1894. Michilimackinac is an Ojibwa word meaning 'island of the great turtle'.

McKinley, Mount, ALASKA/USA *Densmore Peak*
Named in 1889 after Frank Densmore, a prospector, it was renamed in 1896 by William A. Dickey in honour of William McKinley (1843–1901), who was shortly to become the US President (1897–1901). Its original Aleut name was Denali 'The High One' and before the Russians sold Alaska to the USA in 1867 they called it *Bolshaya Gora* 'Great Mountain'. The McKinley River in Alaska is also named after William McKinley.

Maclear, EASTERN CAPE/SOUTH AFRICA
Founded in 1876 as a military post and named after Sir Thomas Maclear (1794–1879), who was appointed the Royal Astronomer at the Cape of Good Hope in 1834; he remained there until 1870.

McLeodganj, HIMACHAL PRADESH/INDIA
Closely linked to Dharmsāla, the location of the Tibetan government-in-exile, it is named after Sir Donald McLeod (1810–72), lieutenant-governor of the Punjab (1865–70) when this hill station was named.

McMurdo Sound, ANTARCTICA
A bay discovered in 1841 by James (later Sir James) Clark Ross (1800–62), a British naval officer who explored both the Arctic and Antarctic, who named it after the commanding officer, Archibald McMurdo, of one of his ships.

Macomb, ILLINOIS/USA *Washington*
Settled in 1829 and laid out the following year when it was renamed after General Alexander Macomb, a leading figure in the war of 1812 between the UK and the USA.

Mâcon, BURGUNDY/FRANCE *Matisco*
The Roman name is derived from a Ligurian root word *mat* 'mountain' with the suffix *-asco*; the present name has evolved from the Roman. The hilly area to the west is famous for its vineyards.

Macon, USA
Cities in Georgia, Illinois, Mississippi, Missouri, North Carolina, and Tennessee are all named after Nathaniel Macon (1758–1837), a member of the US House of Representatives (1791–1815) and a US senator (1815–28). He came from North Carolina.

McPherson, KANSAS/USA
Laid out in 1872 and named after Major General James Birdseye McPherson (1828–64), killed during the Civil War (1861–5) while commanding the Army of the Tennessee against the Confederate Army.

Macquarie, AUSTRALIA
1. Australia (New South Wales): a lake named after Lachlan Macquarie (1761–1824), a Scottish-born Army officer who, while commanding the 73rd Regiment (later the 42nd and 73rd the Black Watch) assumed the appointment of governor of New South Wales in 1809. Within four years he had been promoted to major general; he remained governor until 1821.
2. Pacific Ocean: an island belonging to Tasmania, Australia, it was first sighted in 1810 and named after Lachlan Macquarie.

Macroom (Mághcromtha), IRELAND
'Plain of the Crooked Ford' from *má* 'plain', although also translated as 'Sloping Valley'.

Madagascar (Madagasikara) *Madeigascar, São Lourenço, Malagasy Republic*
The Republic of Madagascar (Repoblikan'i Madagasikara) since 1975, although 'Democratic' has been included in the title. Previously the Malagasy Republic (1958–75) when it became an autonomous state within the French Community in 1958; full independence was achieved in 1960. From 1946 it had been an Overseas Territory of France. Madagascar became a French colony in 1896, having become a protectorate a year earlier. The island was discovered on 10 August 1500, the feast day of St Laurence, a Roman deacon and martyr, by the Portuguese sea captain, Diego Dias (brother of the better known Bartholomew Dias), who gave it the name of the saint. However, the name originated with Marco Polo in the 13th century as a result of hearsay and misunderstanding. He never visited the island and mistook the Italian version of the Arab name for Mogadishu, Mogadiscio, on the Somali coast to refer to the island which he called Madeigascar. Diego Dias was not aware of this and it was not until 1531 that it was realized that the two names referred to the same place. Marco Polo's was preferred. The Arabs used the name al-Qamr '(Islands of) The Moon' to cover both Madagascar and Comoros. It was known as Bukini by the Bantus of East Africa meaning 'Place where there are Buki', Buki being the Swahili name for the Malagasy people with *ni* 'place where there are'.

Madā'in Şāliḥ, SAUDI ARABIA *Thamud*
'Cities of (the Prophet) Sālih' from *mada'in*, the plural of *madīnah* 'city'. The city is said to be the site of the settlement inhabited by the tribe of Thamud whom the Prophet Sālih was sent to visit. They ignored his message and incurred the wrath of God in the form of an earthquake. The name was changed. Sālih is a personal name meaning 'good' or 'upright'.

Madeira Islands (Arquipélago da Madeira), PORTUGAL *Insulae Purpuriae*
A group of islands, an autonomous region of Portugal, in the Atlantic Ocean. Only two are inhabited: Madeira and Porto Santo. The group takes its name from *madeiro* 'wood' since the main island, Madeira, was once covered in a variety of tropical and subtropical trees and shrubs, a few peculiar to the island. The islands were known to the Mauritanians in about the 1st century BC as the 'Purple Islands' on account of the purple dye produced. They were rediscovered by the Portuguese in 1419 and given their present name. They have given their name to the rich dark brown wine and the cake.

Madera, MEXICO, USA
USA (California): a lumber centre, the name means 'wood' in Spanish.

Madhubani, BIHĀR/INDIA
'Honey Forest' from *madhu* 'honey' and *bani* 'forest', a reference to the large quantity of honey to be found in the local forests.

Madhya Pradesh, INDIA *Malwa, Central Provinces and Berār*
A state situated in central India. Its name 'Central State' from the Sanskrit *madhya* 'central' and *pradesh* 'state' simply describes its location. Renamed in 1950, its boundaries were finally agreed in 1956.

Madīnat 'Īsā, BAHRAIN
'Isa City' after Shaikh 'Īsā ibn Salmān Āl Khalīfah (1933–99), ruler of Bahrain (1961–99) when the town was founded in the early 1960s, and the Arabic *madīnah* 'city'.

Madīnat ash-Sha'b, YEMEN *al-Ittiḥād*
'City of the People' from the Arabic *madīnah* and *sha'b* 'of the people'. Founded in 1959 as the capital of the Federation of South Arabia (*see* YEMEN), the city's original name meant 'Unity' or 'Federation'. It was renamed in 1967 when South Yemen (Aden) declared independence.

Madīnat as-Sādāt, EGYPT
'City of Sādāt' from the Arabic *madīnah*. Sādāt refers to Anwar al-Sādāt (1918–81), President of Egypt (1970–81) who was assassinated, principally because he signed a peace treaty between Egypt and Israel.

Madīnat Zāyid, ABU DHABI/UAE
'City of Zāyid' after Shaikh Zāyid bin Sultan Al-Nahyan (1918–2004), ruler of Abu Dhabi since 1966 and president of the UAE since 1971 when it gained its independence.

Madison, CANADA, USA
There are at least 22 cities with this name in the USA and one in Saskatchewan, Canada; four other cities are called Madisonville. They are generally named after James Madison (1751–1836), 4th President of the USA (1809–17). However, Madison, South Dakota, was named after the city with this name in Wisconsin because its location by lakes was said to resemble the capital of Wisconsin.

Madras, TAMIL NĀDU/INDIA
See CHENNAI.

Madre de Dios, PERU-BOLIVIA
A river, a tributary of the Amazon, named by
the Spanish 'Mother of God' in tribute to the
Virgin Mary.

Madrid, PHILIPPINES, SPAIN, USA
Spain: an autonomous community and a city.
The origins of the present name are not
known, although it is generally agreed that it
has evolved from the Arab *Majerit* which first
appeared in 932. One of the many unlikely
derivatives is 'Big Ford' from the Celtic *mago*
'big' and *rito* 'ford' but the city does not lie on a
big river. It grew from a fortress built by
Muhammad I, fifth Umayyad ruler of Muslim
Spain (852–86), overlooking the small
Manzanares River. It was captured from the
Moors in 1083 by Alfonso VI the Brave (c.1040–
1109), King of Castile and León (1072–1109).
The court moved here from Valladolid in 1561,
although the city did not officially become the
Spanish capital until 1607.

Madura, AUSTRALIA, INDONESIA
Indonesia: an island off Java with a name
derived from the Sanskrit *madhura* 'gentle',
'calm', or 'soft', literally 'honeyed' from *madhu*
'honey'. A local explanation is that it means
'Sweet Girl' from *madu* and *dara* 'girl'.

Madurai, TAMIL NĀDU/INDIA *Madura*
See MADURA. The final *i* was added in 1949. It
has been suggested, however, that it comes
from the ancient city of Mathura in Uttar
Pradesh, modified by Tamil pronunciation.

Maebashi, HONSHŪ/JAPAN *Umayabashi*
'Before the Bridge' from *mae* 'before' and *hashi*
'bridge'. Its previous name, 'Stable Bridge',
gave way to the present name some time in
1596–1615. It probably refers to a bridge over
the Tone River along which the city lies.

Maesteg, WALES/UK *Maes tege issa*
'Fair Field' from *maes* 'fair' and *teg* 'field'.

Mafikeng, NORTH WEST/SOUTH AFRICA
Mafeking
Founded in 1885 as a British military post
with a Tswana name meaning 'Place of Stones'
from *mafika*, the plural of *lefika* 'stone' or 'rock'
and *-ng* to indicate 'place'. The spelling was
corrected in 1980.

Magallanes y La Antarctica Chilena,
CHILE
A region created in 1974 and named after
Ferdinand Magellan†.

Magas, INGUSHETIA/RUSSIA
'City of the Sun' in Old Vainakh. A city of this
name, the capital of the old Alanian state, was
destroyed by the Tatars in 1239. In 1996
construction of a new city, 6 miles (10 km)

south-east of Nazran, was begun. In June 1999
it replaced Nazran, whose infrastructure was
considered to be unsuitable, as the capital of
Ingushetia, although construction was far
from complete.

Magdalena, ARGENTINA, BOLIVIA, COLOMBIA,
MEXICO, PHILIPPINES, USA
Colombia: a department bounded on its west
side by the Magdalena River from which it is
named; the river was named after St Mary
Magdalen, having been found on her feast day,
22 July 1502.

Magdeburg, SAXONY-ANHALT/GERMANY
'Magda's Fortress' from *Burg* and possibly a
personal name, itself meaning 'maid' from
Magd, or from the Old High German *magad*
'maiden' or 'virgin'. If a person, why she
should have been so honoured is not known,
but it may be that she owned land here or was
venerated in some way.

Magellan, Strait of (Spanish: **Estrecho de
Magallanes**), CHILE
Discovered in 1520 by, and named after,
Ferdinand Magellan†.

Magenta, LOMBARDY/ITALY *Castra Maxentia*
Named originally after Marcus Maxentius, a
Roman general who had his headquarters here
and later became emperor (306–12). The
present name may have evolved from this or
be derived from the name of somebody else
named Maggente or Magentus from the Latin
Magius or Italian Maggio. The French defeated
the Austrians at the Battle of Magenta in 1859
and to mark the victory the town's name was
given to a purple-pink aniline dye that was
discovered shortly after the battle.

Maggiore (Italian: **Lago Maggiore**), ITALY-
SWITZERLAND *Lacus Verbanus*
A lake meaning 'Greater' from the Italian
maggiore. This is in comparison to the nearby
Lakes Como and Lugano. The classical name is
not Latin, but is associated with the Roman
name Virbius.

Magherafelt (Machaire Theach Fiolta),
NORTHERN IRELAND/UK *Teeoffigalta*
'Plain of the House of Fioghalta' from *machaire*
'plain' or 'flat place'.

Maghnia, ALGERIA *Marnia*
Named after a local Muslim saint, Lalla
Maghnia, whose mausoleum is located here.

Maghreb Also spelt Maghrib. It is a region of
north-west Africa which, for the Arabs who
first tried to conquer it at the end of the 7th
century, meant all lands west of Egypt. In
general terms, it now comprises the Atlas
Mountains and the coastal plain of Morocco,

together with Algeria, Tunisia, and a part of Libya (Tripolitania). It is derived from the Arabic *gharb* 'west' from *gharab* 'to set', referring to the sun.

Magnetic Island, AUSTRALIA
Off the coast of Queensland and named by Captain James Cook[†] when he first saw it in 1770 because he believed that its hills contained iron deposits which were adversely affecting his ship's compass. He was wrong.

Magnitka, CHELYABINSK/RUSSIA
Derived from *magnit* 'magnet', a reference to the iron ore extracted here.

Magnitogorsk, CHELYABINSK/RUSSIA
The city grew up in 1929–31 around the Metallurgical Combine which was constructed at the same time. It was named after the magnetic iron ore which is mined from Magnitnaya Gora 'Magnetic Mountain'.

Magnolia, ARKANSAS/USA
Founded in 1853 and named after the magnolia tree, common here.

Magog, QUEBEC/CANADA *The Outlet*
Settled *c*.1776 as The Outlet because this is where Lake Memphremagog pours into the River Magog. When incorporated as a town in 1855 it took an abbreviated version of the lake's name as its name.

Mahābalipuram, TAMIL NĀDU/INDIA
Also named Māmallapura 'Town of Māmalla', a Hindu Pallava king, after whom the town was named in the 7th century.

Mahajanga, MADAGASCAR *Majunga*
Renamed in 1977 with the possible meaning of 'Healing One', a reference to the waters of the Betsiboka River, at the mouth of which it lies.

Mahalapye, BOTSWANA
Named after an impala, an East African antelope.

Mahārāshtra, INDIA *Bombay State*
A state established in 1960 which may mean 'Great Kingdom' from the Sanskrit *mahā* 'great' or 'big' and *rāshtra* 'kingdom'; by the 18th century a large Marāthā (Mahrattā) Empire, incorporating most of central and western India as well as parts of the north and east, had been established. However, the name might mean 'Mahar Kingdom', the Mahar being the most important caste of what used to be called the 'untouchables'. It is also possible that the name may have come from *rathī* 'chariot driver' with a group forming a *mahārāthis* 'great fighting force'.

Mahavavy, MADAGASCAR
A river meaning 'womanly' from the Malagasy *màha* 'able to' and *vàvy* 'woman', implying that men who refused to go near the river because of the crocodiles were 'women'.

Mahaweli Ganga, SRI LANKA
A river, the longest in Sri Lanka, meaning 'Great Sandy River' from *maha* 'great', *weli* 'sand', and *ganga* 'river'.

Mahdia (Arabic: **al-Mahdīyah**), GUYANA, TUNISIA
Tunisia: founded in 916 as a safe retreat for the imam of the Ismā'īlīs, who had emerged from hiding and proclaimed himself caliph. He was 'Ubayd Allāh, who founded the Fātimid dynasty in 909 and gave himself the title al-Mahdī 'the correctly, or divinely, guided one' and the city takes its name from this. Subsequently the city passed between Christians and Muslims on several occasions and was quite often known as Cape Africa. The title of al-Mahdī has been claimed by a number of Muslim leaders, notably by Muhammad Ahmad (1844–85) of Dongola in Sudan who, having assumed the title in 1881, created a huge Islamic state centred on Sudan and overthrew the Egyptian regime. According to popular Muslim belief, the Mahdī will come to rule before the end of the world and restore religion and justice.

Mahe, PONDICHERRY UNION TERRITORY/INDIA *Mayalli*
Captured by the French in 1726, the name was changed in honour of Bertrand François Mahé (1699–1753), Comte de Bourdonnais and commander of the French Navy.

Mahébourg, MAURITIUS
Named after Bertrand François Mahé (see previous entry).

Mahé Island, SEYCHELLES
The largest island of the archipelago named in 1742 after Bertrand François Mahé (*see* MAHE), governor of the Île de France (now Mauritius) at the time.

Mahmudiya, IRAQ
Founded in 1608 by, and named after, Mahmud Jighazadah, Pasha of Baghdad at the time.

Mahomet, ILLINOIS/USA
Named after the Prophet Muhammad[†].

Mahón, MINORCA/BALEARIC ISLANDS *Portus Magonis*
The full name is Puerto de Mahón 'Port of Mahón'. The Roman name 'Port of Magon' honoured the brother of the Carthaginian general Hannibal. The port gave its name to

m

mayonnaise, formerly *mahonnaise*, a creamy salad dressing, in 1756 when the Duke of Richelieu's chef whipped up a concoction to assuage the Duke's hunger after he had captured the port.

Maidenhead, ENGLAND/UK *Maidenhee*
Situated on the River Thames, the name means 'Maidens' Landing Place' from the Old English *mægden* 'maiden' and *hȳth* 'landing place'. It probably meant that this was a convenient place to meet.

Maidstone, CANADA, SOUTH AFRICA, UK
UK (England): formerly Mægthan stan derived from the Saxon *Maeidesstana* 'The Maidens' Stone' from which came the 1086 Domesday Book version Meddestane from the Old English *mægden* 'maiden' and *stān* 'stone'. It probably means a place to meet.

Main, GERMANY *Moenus*
A river whose name is derived from the Old European word for water, *main*, perhaps specifically meaning 'marsh'.

Mai-Ndombe, DEMOCRATIC REPUBLIC OF THE CONGO *Lake Leopold*
A lake originally named by Sir Henry Morton Stanley[†] in 1882 after Leopold II (1835–1909), King of the Belgians (1865–1909), in whose service he was. The lake was renamed in 1973 after the Ndombe people.

Maine, FRANCE, USA
1. France: a former province now comprising the departments of Mayenne and Sarthe, although there is also a department called Maine-et-Loire in the same region of Pays de la Loire. It took its name from the River Mayenne which flows through it. The river may have taken its name from the Cenomani who lived in the area.
2. USA: a state, and a city in New York State. The name of the state may come from that of the former French province, the French establishing a colony in 1604 on the St Croix River as part of the province of Acadia; on the other hand, it has been suggested that the fishermen of the islands offshore referred to the mainland as the 'Main'. It became a part of Massachusetts in 1652, but joined the Union as the 23rd state in 1820.

Mainz (French: **Mayence**), RHINELAND-PALATINATE/GERMANY *Mogontiacum, Aurea Moguntia*
A Celtic settlement which the Romans fortified *c.*10 BC for two legions for operations against the Germanic tribes. It was named after the Celtic personal name Magontios and *-acum*. The garrison was reduced to that of a single legion in AD 89 which from 92 was the 22nd Primigenia Pia Fidelis. The city has been occupied by the French on a number of occasions and was ceded to France in 1797–1816.

Maio, CAPE VERDE
An island first seen by the Portuguese on 1 May 1460 and thus named 'May'.

Maitland, AUSTRALIA, CANADA
1. Australia (New South Wales): founded as a settlement for convicts in 1818, it was first known simply as The Camp, then Molly Morgan Plains and then Wallis Plains. In 1829 a new town was surveyed nearby and called Maitland. This became East Maitland when Wallis Plains was renamed West Maitland in 1835. When these two, together with other nearby towns, were amalgamated in 1944 the resulting city was called Maitland. The British lieutenant-governor of Nova Scotia, Canada (1828–34) and previous lieutenant-governor of Upper Canada (1818–28), General Sir Peregrine Maitland (1777–1854), may be the man honoured.
2. Canada (Nova Scotia); named after General Sir Peregrine Maitland, lieutenant-governor (1828–34).

Majorca (Mallorca), BALEARIC ISLANDS/SPAIN *Majorica*
The largest of the Balearic Islands, the name is derived from the Latin *major* 'greater'. The tin-glazed earthenware introduced into Italy from Majorca was given the name 'majolica', Maiolica being the Italian name for the island.

Makarov, SAKHALIN ISLAND/RUSSIA *Shiritoru*
Named after Vice Admiral Stepan Makarov (1848–1904), a naval officer, oceanographer, and polar explorer. He commanded the Pacific Ocean Squadron during the Russo-Japanese War (1904–5), but was killed during it. While under Japanese occupation in 1905–45 the city was known as Shiritoru.

Makarska, CROATIA *Macrum/Muccurum*
A Roman port, it became a Slav stronghold and then a trading centre under the Hungarians and Ottoman Turks. Its name may come from a Slavonic word for 'wet' similar to the present Serbo-Croat word *mokar*. The village of Makar lies just inland.

Makaryev, KOSTROMA/RUSSIA
Named after a monk, Makary (Macarius), from Nizhniy Novgorod who built a new monastery here in 1439 after his earlier one, at what is now Makaryevo, was destroyed.

Makeyevka (Makiyivka), UKRAINE *Dmitriyevsk*
Founded in 1899, Dmitriyevsk merged with the village of Makeyevka, possibly named after

a Makeyev who owned a coal mine here. Another theory holds that, in much the same way that Donetsk was at one time named after a Welsh engineer, Makeyevka may have been named after a Scottish engineer called Mackay. The city became known as Makeyevka in 1931.

Makhachkala, DAGESTAN/RUSSIA *Petrovskoye, Petrovsk Port*
In a war with Persia Peter I the Great[†] gained a foothold along the western and southern coasts of the Caspian Sea in 1722–3, although it was relinquished again in 1732. This territory was reacquired by Russia at the beginning of the 19th century. In 1844, a fortress was built in Peter's name; it was renamed Peter's Port in 1857. In 1922 it was renamed again after Makhach (whose real name was Muhammad 'Ali Dakhadayev (1882–1918)), a Dagestani revolutionary leader. The Armenian *kala* 'fortress' was added.

Makhado, LIMPOPO/SOUTH AFRICA
Zoutpansberg, Schoemansdal, Louis Trichardt
Founded in 1848 by Andries Potgieter (1792–1852), a Boer leader, as the capital of a small republic with the same name, Zoutpansberg. In 1854 it was renamed by Stephanus Schoeman, Potgieter's son-in-law, after himself. His hubris was not appreciated, nor his trade in black slaves, and the town was razed to the ground in 1867 by the Venda. It then lay abandoned until being revived by the British early in the 20th century. Subsequently it became a Boer enclave named after Louis Trichardt (1783–1838), a Voortrekker leader. In pursuit of the policy to change the names of towns named after Voortrekkers, the town was renamed in 2003 as a tribute to Makhado, a Venda chief who won land here by battle. The nearby township of Makhado was renamed Dzanani at the same time, while the previous settlement of Dzanani was renamed Mphephu after a 19th-century Venda chief of this name.

Makó, HUNGARY
Named after a soldier who was given the village by King Endre II in the 13th century.

Malabar Coast, KERALA AND KARNĀTAKA/ INDIA
A name for the southern part of the west coast of India, including most of the state of Kerala and the coastal region of Karnātaka. The name probably comes from the Dravidian/Tamil *malai* 'mountain' and the Persian *bār* 'country' or Arabic *barr* 'continent'.

Malabo, EQUATORIAL GUINEA *Clarence City/Port Clarence, Santa Isabel*
Founded in 1827 by the British Vice Admiral William Owen and named by him after William Henry, Duke of Clarence, the future King William IV[†]. When the island of Bioko, then known as Fernando Pó, on which Malabo lies, passed to the Spanish in 1843 they renamed the town Santa Isabel 'St Elizabeth' after Isabella II, Queen of Spain (1833–68). After Equatorial Guinea's independence in 1968 the town was renamed in 1973 after Malabo, a paramount chief of the Bubi, who died in 1937.

Malacca (Melaka), MELAKA/MALAYSIA
A state, a city-port founded *c*.1400, and a powerful Muslim sultanate during the 15th century. Taken by the Portuguese in 1511, by the Dutch in 1641, and by the British in 1824; two years later it became one of the original Straits Settlements. The name may be derived from the Sanskrit *āmalaka* 'emblic', a deciduous tree common here. According to a Portuguese account written in 1515, Sri Paramesvara, a Malay Hindu prince of Palembang (on the island of Sumatra, Indonesia), arrived at the site of the present city-port *c*.1403 and saw a white mouse deer kick one of his hunting dogs into the water. He considered this to be a rare sign of courage for so small an animal and he took it to be a good omen for the establishment of a permanent settlement. Because he was standing under an *āmalaka* at the time he gave the settlement this name. However, it has also been suggested that the name is derived from the Sanskrit *mahā* 'great' and *lankā* 'island'. Paramesvara converted to Islam and became the first ruler of the Sultanate of Malacca. The city has given its name to the Strait of Malacca between Sumatra and Malaysia which connects the Indian Ocean with the South China Sea.

Málaga, PHILIPPINES, SPAIN, USA
Spain (Andalusia): a province and an ancient city founded by the Phoenicians in the 12th century BC, possibly with a Phoenician name *malaka* 'queen'. Alternatively, it may be derived from the Phoenician *malac* 'to salt' on account of the trade in salt fish. As Mālaka, it was under Moorish rule in 711–1487.

Malakoff, FRANCE, USA
France (Paris): named after the Russian fortress of Malakhov, a major defensive strongpoint, which was captured by French forces in September 1855 during the Crimean War and led to the fall of Sevastopol.

Malang, JAVA/INDONESIA
'Unfortunate', although the reason for this name is not known. It is a pleasant hill resort with an agreeable climate.

Malanville, BENIN
Named after Henri Malan, the French
lieutenant-governor of Dahomey (now Benin)
in 1909 and 1911.

Malawi The Republic of Malawi (Dziko la
Malaŵi) since 1966, having become the
independent state of Malawi in 1964.
Previously Nyasaland (1907–64) and part of the
Federation of Rhodesia and Nyasaland (also
known as the Central African Federation)
(1953–63); the British Central African
Protectorate (1893–1907); and the Nyasaland
Districts Protectorate when the British crown
took control of the land along the western
shore of Lake Nyasa (now Lake Malawi) in 1891
from the British South Africa Company. The
country takes its name from the Maravi (in
Portuguese, Malawi) people, whose empire
stretched well beyond Malawi's present
borders. Their name means 'flames' which
may be taken from their habit of burning off
dead grass during the dry season to prepare
the land for cultivation. Nyasaland took its
name from the Nyasa people who lived round
Lake Nyasa, the Swahili *nyasa* itself meaning
'lake'. It was thus due to a misunderstanding
by David Livingstone (1813–73), the Scottish
explorer, in 1859 that Lake Nyasa got its name.

Malaya A former country which, until 1963,
comprised the states of the southern part of
the Malay Peninsula. The name came into
vogue towards the end of the 1920s to
describe, collectively, the British crown colony
of the Straits Settlements, the Federated Malay
States, and the Unfederated Malay States.
Malaya gained its independence in 1957. The
name may be derived from a Dravidian word
which gave the Sanskrit *malaya* 'mountain';
the Tamil *malai* means 'hill country', a
reference to the peninsula's mountainous
terrain. *See* MALAYSIA.

Malaysia A Federation (Persekutuan Tanah
Malaysia) since 1963 when it was created from
the Federation of Malaya, North Borneo (now
Sabah), Sarawak, and Singapore; Singapore left
Malaysia in 1965 to become an independent
sovereign state. Malaysia consists now of two
regions, East Malaysia (Sabah and Sarawak)
and West Malaysia (eleven states), and three
Federal Territories. West Malaysia and the
Federal Territories are sometimes referred to
as Peninsular Malaysia. West Malaysia was
previously the Federation of Malaya (1948–63)
and the Malayan Union (1946–48). This
consisted of the Federated Malay States, the
Unfederated Malay States, and the Straits
Settlements of Penang and Malacca, but not
Singapore. In 1896 Negeri Sembilan, Pahang,

Perak, and Selangor became the Federated
Malay States, a group of 'protected' sovereign
states. 'Protection' here meant the
constitutional protection of their culture,
religion, and commerce. In 1909 Siam (now
Thailand) relinquished its claims to the
northern states of Kedah, Kelantan, Perlis and
Terengganu, thus fixing the present border
between Malaysia and Thailand; their sultans
refused to join the Federation and so formed
the Unfederated Malay States together with
Johor. Already in 1826 the three territories,
and trading centres, of Penang (now Pulau
Pinang, and including Province Wellesley,
now Seberang Prai, on the mainland opposite
the island), Malacca (now Melaka), and
Singapore, located along the Strait of Malacca,
had been collectively named the Straits
Settlements under the authority of British
India; in 1867 they became a separate crown
colony under the British Colonial Office.
Labuan joined in 1907. The name was coined
for the new state with the additional -*sia*
indicating its location in Asia.

Malazgirt, TURKEY *Manazkert, Manzíkirt*
Evolved from 'Dedicated to Menuas', the
Urartu King of Van, from the Armenian *kert*, a
shortened form of *kertvats* 'dedicated to' and
the personal name.

Malbork, POLAND *Marienburg*
'Fortress of (St) Mary', an estate fortified by the
Teutonic Knights in 1236 from which the town
grew. It was their capital in 1309–1457 after
which it became part of Poland. It passed to
Prussia at the first partition of Poland in 1772,
only being returned to Poland in 1945.

Malden, MASSACHUSETTS/USA *Mystic Side*
Settled in 1640 on the Mystic River, it was at
first named after the river. Nine years later it
was renamed after Malden in England from
where the speaker of the Massachusetts House
of Deputies came.

Maldives (Dhivehi Raajjeyge)
The Republic of Maldives (Dhivehi
Jumhuriyya) since 1968, having become an
independent sultanate in 1965. Previously a
sultanate under British protection from 1796
(formally becoming a protectorate in 1887);
under the protection of the Dutch rulers of Sri
Lanka during the 17th century; and occupied
by the Portuguese in 1558–73. The chain of
over 1 000 small islands probably takes its
name from the Sanskrit *mālādvīpa* 'garland of
islands' from *mālā* 'garland' or 'necklace' and
dvīpa. The indigenous name, Dhivehi
Raajjeyge, means 'Island Realm' from *Dhivehi*,
an adjective, which has come to mean
'Maldivian' from *dvīpa*, and *raajje* 'country' or

'realm' with the suffix -ge indicating the possessive.

Maldon, ENGLAND/UK *Mældune, Malduna*
'Hill with a Cross' from the Old English *mæl* 'crucifix' or 'cross' and *dūn*.

Malheur, OREGON/USA
A river and a lake with a French name meaning 'misfortune', possibly because of the barren, unpopulated, terrain.

Mali, AND BURMA, FIJI, GUINEA
1. The Republic of Mali (République du Mali) since 1960 when Senegal withdrew from the Mali Federation which had been created in 1959; one of the aims of the Federation was to give land-locked Mali access to the sea. Previously the Sudanese Republic (1958); Soudan Français 'French Sudan' an overseas territory of the French Union (1946), having become a colony with this name in 1892 and part of French West Africa in 1895. By 1898 the whole of modern Mali had been conquered by the French. The Mali Empire which flourished between the 13th and 16th centuries comprised most of modern Mali, Senegal and The Gambia as well as southern Mauritania, eastern Guinea-Bissau, and eastern Guinea. The name may come from the Malinké people, also known as the Mandinka, who are closely related to other Mande-speaking peoples who trace their ancestry to the Mali Empire. It has also been suggested that the name comes from the Mande word for 'hippopotamus'. The official language of the country is French.
2. Guinea: a town named after the Malinke people of the Mali Empire.

Malibu, CALIFORNIA/USA
Named after Umalibo, the name for a labourers' community.

Malmédy, BELGIUM *Malmundarium*
'Cleansed from Evil Ones'. Established around a 7th-century monastery, it was an ecclesiastical principality before being awarded to Prussia after the Congress of Vienna in 1815 and to Belgium after the Treaty of Versailles in 1919.

Malmesbury, SOUTH AFRICA, UK
1. South Africa (Western Cape): settled in 1829 as Swartlandskerk 'Black Country Church', it was renamed by General Sir Galbraith Lowry Cole, governor of the Cape of Good Hope (1828–33), after his father-in-law, Sir James Harris, 1st Earl of Malmesbury, who died in 1820.
2. UK (England): originating *c*.635 as St Maeldub's hermitage which was developed into an abbey, it was given the name Maldumsberg 'Maeldub's Stronghold' from an

Old Irish personal name and *burh* some 50 years later; it appeared in the 1086 Domesday Book as Malmesberie.

Malmö, SWEDEN *Malmhaug, Elbogen*
'Mineral Island' from *malm* 'mineral' and the Danish *ö* 'island'. Originally 'Sandpile' from *haug* 'mound', it was renamed by German merchants 'Elbow' because of the curve in the coastline here. It was ceded to Sweden from Denmark in 1658.

Maloarkhangel'sk, ORËL/RUSSIA
Arkhangelskoye
Named after the church dedicated to the Archangel Michael with *malo* 'little' added to differentiate it from the much bigger Arkhangel'sk (*see* ARCHANGEL) in the province of the same name.

Malopolskie, POLAND
A province meaning 'Little Poland' from *malo* 'little' and *Polska* 'Poland'.

Malta, AND LATVIA, USA
The Republic of Malta (Repubblika ta' Malta) since 1974. Situated in the Mediterranean Sea, it consists of three inhabited islands (Malta, Gozo, and Comino) and two uninhabited. Possibly occupied by the Phoenicians with the name coming from the Semitic *malat* 'Refuge', it was certainly occupied by the Carthaginians in the 6th century BC. The Romans took it in 218 BC, making it part of the province of Sicily and calling it Melita. In 1530–1798 it belonged to the Knights of St John of Jerusalem (later known as the Knights of Malta). In 1802, after Napoleon[†] had taken possession of the islands in 1798, the Maltese people requested British protection. At the Treaty of Paris in 1814 Malta was ceded to the UK, becoming independent in 1964. Famous for its honey in former times, the name may be derived from the ancient Greek *melitta* 'bee' which produces *meli* 'honey'. The island is described as Melita in the Bible (Acts of the Apostles 28: 1).

Maltahöhe, NAMIBIA
Settled in 1900 and named after Malta von Burgsdorff, wife of the German military garrison commander at Gibeon, 50 miles (80 km) to the south-east, and *Höhe* 'height'.

Maltby, ENGLAND/UK
'Malti's Village' from an Old Scandinavian personal name and *bý*, or 'Village where Malt is made' from *malt* and *bý*.

Maluku, DEMOCRATIC REPUBLIC OF THE CONGO, INDONESIA
See MOLUCCAS.

Malvern, JAMAICA, SOUTH AFRICA, UK, USA
UK (England): named after the Malvern Hills, the name, formerly Mælfern and Malferna, means 'Bare Hill' from the Welsh *moel* 'bare' and *bryn* 'hill'. The name is collective and includes Great Malvern and Little Malvern as well as the district which is known as Malvern Link from the Old English *hlinc* 'ledge' or 'ridge'.

Malvinas, UK
See FALKLAND ISLANDS.

Mamaroneck, NEW YORK/USA
Sold in 1661 by its Native American owners, its name, that of a chief and meaning 'Where the Fresh Water meets the Salt', was retained.

Mamfe, CAMEROON
A corruption of Mansfeld, the name of the area's first German district officer.

Mamonovo, KALININGRAD/RUSSIA *Heiligenbeil*
Founded in 1301 when the territory was in the hands of the Teutonic Knights, it was renamed in 1947 after N. V. Mamonov, a Hero of the Soviet Union, who was killed here during the fighting in East Prussia in 1945.

Man, Isle of *See* ISLE OF MAN.

Manabi, ECUADOR
'Butterfly' from the Guaraní *panambi*.

Managua, CUBA, NICARAGUA
Nicaragua: named after Lake Managua, locally Xolatlán, on which it lies. Managua is said to come from the Guaraní *ama* 'rain' and *nagua* 'spirit' or 'ghost', a reference to its guardian. However, an alternative suggestion is that it means 'where there is an extension of water' in Nahuatl. It has been the national capital since 1857.

Manahawkin, NEW JERSEY/USA
A Native American name meaning 'Good Corn Land' in recognition of the great productivity of the land.

Manama (al-Manāmah), BAHRAIN *Awāl*
'The Place of Dreams' or 'The Place to Rest' from *manam* 'dream', possibly a reference to a number of prehistoric burial mounds. Under British protection between 1861 and 1971, it became the capital of Bahrain in 1971.

Manapouri, SOUTH ISLAND/NEW ZEALAND
A town and a lake with a name derived from the Maori *manawa* 'heart' and *pouri* 'throbbing' to give '(Lake of) the Throbbing Heart'. According to a local legend, its waters are the tears of dying sisters.

Manasquan, NEW JERSEY/USA
A Native American name derived from *wanasquan* 'point' or 'top'.

Manatí, CUBA, PUERTO RICO
Puerto Rico: founded in 1738 and named after the manatee, a large plant-eating aquatic mammal, sometimes known as a sea cow.

Manaus, AMAZONAS/BRAZIL *São José do Rio Negrinho, Villa da Barra, Cidade da Barra do Rio Negro, Manáos*
Founded in 1699 as a small fort called St Joseph of the River Negro, it became the 'Town of the Bar', a reference to the sandbar at the mouth of the Negro. In 1850 it was renamed after a native tribe, the Manáos, who lived along the banks of the Negro. The spelling was changed in 1939.

Manche, LOWER NORMANDY/FRANCE
A department with a coastline on the English Channel and named after the French for the Channel, *La Manche* 'The Sleeve'.

Manchester, UK, USA
1. UK (England): founded *c.*80 as a Roman fort called Mamucium or Mamucio. This probably came from the Celtic *mamm* 'breast' because of the rounded hill on which the fort was built. To an abbreviated form of this name was added '-chester' from *ceaster*. Thus the meaning is '(Roman) Town on the Breast-shaped Hill'. The name appeared in the 1086 Domesday Book as Mamecestre. The centre of the cotton industry, it was popularly known as 'Cottonopolis'.
2. USA (Connecticut): settled in 1672 as Five-Mile Tract and renamed in 1772 Orford Parish. In 1823 it was incorporated as a town and renamed again after the Manchester in England.
3. USA (New Hampshire): settled in 1722 as Old Harry's Town, it was renamed in 1735 as Tyngstown when it was awarded to Captain William Tyng by the Massachusetts Bay Colony. On incorporation as a town in 1751 it was renamed once more as Derryfield. Finally, in 1810, it was named after the English Manchester, a name proposed by Samuel Blodget, who had been impressed by the barge canals in that city and who had built the first canal around the Amoskeag Falls, along which the American town lies.
4. USA (Ohio): there are two cities with this name, one believed to have come from 'Chesterman', the original owner.

Manchuria (Dongbei), CHINA *Manzhou, Manchukuo*
A historic region which takes its name from the Manchu, a people whose name means 'pure'. Dongbei, the local name, simply means 'North-east'. It was occupied by the Mongols in the 13th and 14th centuries. Invaded by the Japanese in 1931, in 1932–45 it was a Japanese

puppet state named Manchukuo 'Country of the Manchu' from the Chinese *mǎnzhōu* and *guó* 'country' or 'land', although it was nominally independent. It consists now of the provinces of Heilonjiang, Jilin, and Liaoning.

Mandalay, BURMA *Shwemyo, Yadanabon/ Yadanapone*
Named after the nearby Mandalay Hill, an isolated conical hill on which stood a gilt pagoda. The hill took its name from the Sanskrit *maṇḍala* 'circle' or Pali *mandalar* 'centre', a symbolic representation of the universe used in sacred Hindu and Buddhist rites. The city was founded in 1857–9 to replace Amarapura as King Mindon's capital and it remained the capital until 1885. The city of Ava, capital of the Kingdom of Ava, is now a suburb of Mandalay. The first Burmese name, Shwemyo, meant 'Golden City', while the official Pali name was Yadanabon 'Cluster of Gems'.

Mandan, NORTH DAKOTA/USA
Settled in 1873, it was named after the local Native American tribe.

Mandeville, CANADA, JAMAICA, USA
1. Jamaica: named after the courtesy title, Viscount Mandeville, of William Montagu (1768–1843), 5th Duke of Manchester, governor of Jamaica (1808–27).
2. USA (Louisiana): named after Mandeville de Marigny, a descendant of a French officer.

Mandi, HIMACHAL PRADESH/INDIA
'Market' which developed here because it was a place where several routes crossed.

Mandurah, WESTERN AUSTRALIA/AUSTRALIA
Founded in 1895, the name is derived from an Aboriginal term *mandjar* 'meeting place'.

Manduria, APULIA/ITALY
Derived from the Indo-European *mando* 'horse' which is similar to the Sanskrit *mandura* 'enclosure' or 'stable for horses' and may be the meaning here.

Manfredonia, APULIA/ITALY
Founded in 1256 by, and named after, Manfred (c.1232–66), King of Sicily (1258–66).

Mangalore, KARNĀTAKA/INDIA
'Town of Good Fortune' from the Sanskrit *maṅgala* 'good fortune' or 'happiness'.

Mangghystaū, KAZAKHSTAN *Siyah-Kūh, Mangyshlak*
A province, which was created in 1973 and which adopted its present name in 1990, and a city meaning 'One Thousand Winter Quarters' or 'Place of Wintering' from the Turkish *ming* and *kishlak* 'winter quarters (for an army, nomads, or animals)'. The first name meant 'Black Mountain' in Persian.

Mangochi, MALAWI *Fort Johnston*
Founded in 1891 as a military post by, and named after, the British commissioner of Nyasaland, Sir Harry Johnston (1858–1927). It was renamed in 1964 after the chief who ruled the area when the town was founded.

Manhattan, USA
New York: an island named after a Native American tribe, the Manhattan, who sold it to Peter Minuit, the first director general of the New Netherlands province, in 1626. In 1653 it became part of New Amsterdam which was transferred to the British in 1664 and renamed New York City. It has given its name to a cocktail.

Manica, MOZAMBIQUE
A province and a town named after the Manyika people. They have also given their name to Manicaland, a province in Zimbabwe.

Manicouagan, QUEBEC/CANADA
A river with a Native American name 'Where there is Bark', a reference to the fact that it drains a large forested area. Also spelt Manikuagan.

Manila, PHILIPPINES *Maynílad, Intramuros, Isigne y Siempre Leal Ciudad*
The pre-Hispanic name comes from the Tagalog (the language of northern Luzon) *may* 'there are' and *nila* 'water lilies' which were abundant along the shores of Manila Bay. The Spanish destroyed the original Malay settlement and built a new fortress city which they called Intramuros 'Within Walls' in 1571. In 1574 it was renamed the 'Noble (or Distinguished) and Ever Loyal City'. It became the capital of the new colony and of the American administration when it took power in 1898; and of the newly independent Republic of the Philippines in 1946. However, in 1948–76 Quezon City was the national capital. Manila is also the name of the National Capital Region.

Manipur, INDIA
A state meaning the 'Land of Gems' or 'Bejewelled Land'.

Manisa, TURKEY *Magnesia ad Sipylum, Magnesiopolis, Magnesia*
Named ultimately after the Magnetes, thought to be its first inhabitants in the 12th century BC. The present name has evolved from the ancient Greek name of Magnesia, the shortened version of the Attalid Magnesiopolis 'City of Magnesia'. It was renamed Manisa by a Turkmen tribal chief who captured it in 1313.

The ruins of another Magnesia, ad Maeandrum 'on the Maeander (River)', lie 55 miles (88 km) to the south.

Manistee, MICHIGAN/USA
A Chippewa name meaning 'Spirit of the Woods'.

Manitoba, CANADA *Red River Settlement*
A province which grew from the original Red River Settlement (whose official name was Assiniboia), named after the Red River, and which joined the confederation in 1870, having been ceded to Canada by the Hudson's Bay Company the year before. It takes its name from Lake Manitoba which may be derived from an Algonquian word *manito-bau* 'The Strait of the Great Spirit' or 'Place where the Spirit Lives', a reference to some narrows. The province developed from an area called Rupert's Land in the 17th century along the western shores of Hudson Bay, its borders finally being fixed in 1912.

Manitowoc, WISCONSIN/USA
Established as a trading post in 1795, the name probably comes from an Algonquian word meaning 'Abode of the Great Spirit'.

Mankato, MINNESOTA/USA
Founded in 1852 and given a Sioux name that alluded to the blue clay that was to be found along the banks of the Blue Earth River.

Mannheim, BADEN-WÜRTTEMBERG/GERMANY
Probably derived from a personal name, Manno, and *Heim* 'home'.

Manokwari, PAPUA/INDONESIA
'Old Village' in Biak. It was the site of the first English East India Company settlement in 1793 and later of a Dutch fort.

Manomet, MASSACHUSETTS/USA
An Algonquian word meaning 'Portage'.

Mansfield, AUSTRALIA, UK, USA
1. UK (England): formerly Mamesfelde 'Open Land by the (River) Maun' from a Celtic river name, itself from the nearby Mammesheved 'Mam Hill' from the Celtic *mamm* 'breast-shaped hill', and *feld*.
2. USA (Connecticut): originally Ponde Town, it was renamed after Major Moses Mansfield, an early settler and mayor of New Haven, when it became a town in 1702.
3. USA (Louisiana and Massachusetts): named after William Murray (1705–93), 1st Earl of Mansfield and Lord Chief Justice of Great Britain (1756–88).
4. USA (Ohio): laid out in 1808, it was named after Jared Mansfield, US surveyor general.

Mansūrah, al-, EGYPT
Founded originally as a military camp in 1219 and named 'The Victory' from the Arabic *al* and *manṣūr* 'one who is aided by God to be victorious', itself from *naṣr* 'victory'. This referred to the defeat and capture of a force of crusaders, mainly French, of the Sixth Crusade, including their leader, St Louis IX (1214–70), King of France (1226–70), by Muslim forces in 1250. Also spelt el-Mansura.

Manteo, NORTH CAROLINA/USA
Named after a Native American chief of Roanoke Island.

Mantiqueira, BRAZIL
Mountains which have a name derived from a Native American word meaning 'The Place where the Clouds Lie'.

Mantua, CUBA, ITALY, USA
Italy (Lombardy): Italian Mantova. Having originated as an Etruscan settlement, the name may be derived from Mantus, the Etruscan god of the underworld; or it may be named after Manto, said to be the father of the founder, one Ocnus.

Manzanillo, CUBA, MEXICO
From the Spanish *manzanilla* 'manchineel', a West Indian tree whose sap is poisonous.

Manzanita, OREGON/USA
'Little Apple', *manzanita* being the diminutive of the Spanish *manzana* 'apple'.

Manzil Bu Ruqaybah, TUNISIA *Ferryville*
Founded in 1880 by the French and named 'Town of Ferry' after the French premier, Jules François Camille Ferry (1832–93), who strongly supported French colonial activities in Africa. When the French left in 1963 the town was renamed after Habib ibn Ali Bourguiba (1903–2000), the first President of Tunisia (1957–87). The Arabic *manzil* means 'stopping place'. The name is also spelt Menzel Bourguiba.

Manzini, SWAZILAND *KwaManzini, Bremersdorp*
'Bremer's Village', from the Afrikaans *dorp* 'village', after Albert Bremer who opened a store here in 1887. In 1960 a shortened form of the original name 'Place of Manzini' was adopted. This referred to Manzini Motsa, the local chief. It was the Boer capital of Swaziland, as a dependency of Transvaal, in 1894–9; at the conclusion of the Boer War in 1902 the British moved the capital to the higher, and cooler, Mbabane.

Maple Creek, SASKATCHEWAN/CANADA
Named after the maple trees that line Maple Creek on which the town lies.

Mapulanguene, MOZAMBIQUE
'Planks' from *mapulango*, the plural of *pulango*
'plank', a reference to the timber here.

Maputo, MOZAMBIQUE *Baía da Lagoa, Lourenço
Marques*
A province and a city first named 'Bay of the
Lagoon' (in English, Delagoa Bay), but renamed
after the Portuguese trader, Lourenço
Marques, who explored the area in 1544. It was
little more than a trading post until a fort was
built in 1787 from which the town developed.
It became the capital of Portuguese East
Africa in 1907 and of Mozambique on
independence in 1975. It was renamed in 1976
after the Maputo River, itself named after a son
of a local 18th-century chief, Muagobe.

Maquelo do Zombo, ANGOLA
A name, probably devised by the Portuguese,
to recognize Maquela, a local chief of the
Zombo people, with the Portuguese *do* 'of'.

Mar, Serra do, BRAZIL
A mountain range with a Portuguese name
meaning 'Mountain Range of the Sea'. It falls
steeply to the Atlantic coast.

Maracaibo, VENEZUELA *Nueva Zamora*
Founded in 1571 as New Zamora after the city
of Zamora in Spain, it was renamed after Lake
Maracaibo, itself named after a local chief.

Maradi, NIGER
A department and a town with a name said to
be taken from the *maradi* 'chief of the
fetishers', a former title given to the regional
governor.

Marāgheh, IRAN
'Place of Pasture'. The Mongols are believed to
have kept a large number of horses here.

Marajó Island (Isla de Marajó), BRAZIL
An island of 15 500 square miles (40 100 sq.
km) in the Amazon river delta, its name
reflects its location from the Guaraní *para*
'river' and *jho* 'to go out'.

Maramba, ZAMBIA *Livingstone*
Founded in 1905 and named after the Scottish
explorer, David Livingstone (1813–73). The
present name means 'plantain', a type of
banana tree.

Maranhão, BRAZIL
A state which took its name from an offshore
island (now called São Luis, which is also the
name of the state's capital). Maranhão has
evolved from the Guaraní *para* 'river', *na*
'parent', and *jho* 'to go out'.

Marathon AUSTRALIA, CANADA, GREECE, USA
Greece: takes its name from *marathron*
'fennel', an aromatic herb that grows here. It
gave its name to the marathon race after a
courier, according to legend, ran from
Marathon to Athens to report the victory of the
Athenians over the Persians in 490 BC. After
running about 25 miles (40 km) non-stop he
delivered his message but then fell dead. The
distance for the modern marathon is 26 miles
385 yards (42.2 km)—the distance from the
start at Windsor Castle to the finish opposite
the royal box in the stadium in London at the
1908 Olympic Games.

Marburg, HESSE/GERMANY
The full name is Marburg an der Lahn
'Marburg on the (River) Lahn'. The name
means 'Frontier Fortress' from the Old
German *mar* 'boundary' and *Burg*.

Marches, The (Marche), ITALY
A region with a name taken from the plural of
the Italian *marca* 'border' or 'march'. In the
early Middle Ages the region comprised three
border provinces which acted as a buffer for
Rome against invasion.

Mar del Plata, ARGENTINA *Nuestra Señora del
Pilar, La Peregrina*
Founded as a mission station called 'Our Lady
of the Pillar' in 1746 after the cathedral in
Saragossa, Spain, dedicated to the Virgin
(Mary) of the Pillar; she is said to have appeared
standing on a pillar. After the mission had
been abandoned in 1751, a fishing village
emerged here in 1856 and was called La
Peregrina 'The Pilgrim'. The present city was
founded in 1874 and called 'Sea of the Plata',
that is, the River Plate.

Mareeba, QUEENSLAND/AUSTRALIA *Granite
Creek*
'Place to Meet' from an Aboriginal term.

Margarita Island (Isla de Margarita),
VENEZUELA
Discovered by Christopher Columbus[†] in 1498,
it quickly became famous for its pearls, hence
its name 'Island of Pearls' from the Spanish
margarita 'pearl'.

Margate, SOUTH AFRICA, UK
UK (England): formerly Meergate 'Gate, or gap,
leading to the Sea' from *mere*, here in its rarely
used meaning of 'sea' rather than 'lake', and
geat 'gate' or 'gap'.

Margherita Peak, DEMOCRATIC REPUBLIC OF
THE CONGO-UGANDA
First climbed in 1906 by an Italian team led by
Luigi Amedeo, it was named after Margherita
(1851–1926), wife of Umberto I, King of Italy
(1878–1900).

Marghilan (Margilon), UZBEKISTAN
Marginan
According to legend, when Alexander III the
Great[†] passed through in *c.*328 BC he was given
murgh 'chicken' and *nan* 'bread'; it is said that
the name derives from this.

Maria Island, AUSTRALIA
Tasmania: a few miles off Tasmania, the island
was discovered by Abel Tasman[†] in 1642 and
named by him after the wife of the governor-
general of the Dutch East Indies, Anthony van
Dieman (1593–1645). There is another island
with the same name off the coast of the
Northern Territory.

Mariana Islands *See* NORTHERN MARIANA
ISLANDS.

Mariánské Lázně, CZECH REPUBLIC *Ušovické
Lázně, Marienbad*
With numerous mineral springs, both the
previous German name, adopted in 1808, and
the present Czech name from the plural of
lázeň 'bath' mean 'Mary's Springs'. A picture of
the Virgin Mary was suspended from a tree
near to one of the local mineral springs as an
expression of thanks for recovery from illness
by an unknown patient. Maria Theresa[†]
ordered that the local springs should be
examined as a source for table salt. They were
not suitable, but her name has been
associated, wrongly, with the place.

Marias, MONTANA/USA
A river named by Meriwether Lewis[†] in 1804
after his cousin, Maria Wood.

Mariazell, AUSTRIA
Founded in 1157 by monks, it means 'Mary's
Cell'. It is a place of pilgrimage to honour the
Virgin Mary.

Maribor, SLOVENIA *Marburg/Marchburg*
Situated on the River Drava, the town's name
is derived from the medieval castle called
Marchburg from the German *Burg* which was
probably built in the 11th century to protect
the Drava march (frontier district) from the
Hungarians. Surrounded by pine forests, the
second part of the name comes from the
Slavonic *bor* 'pine'.

Marie Byrd Land, ANTARCTICA
Discovered in 1929 by the American naval
commander and polar explorer, Richard E.
Byrd (1888–1957), who flew over the
uncharted waste and named it after his wife.

Marie-Galante, GUADELOUPE
An island dependency of Guadeloupe, it was
discovered in 1493 by Christopher Columbus[†],
who named it after his ship, the *Maria Galanda*,
in Spanish *Maria Graciosa*.

Mari El, RUSSIA *Mari*
A republic named after the Mari (in Russian,
Marytsy), a Finno-Ugric people, formerly
known as the Cheremis. It was renamed in
1991, having been the Mari Autonomous
Soviet Socialist Republic from 1936 and the
Mari Autonomous Province from 1920. In the
Mari language their name means 'person',
'human being', or 'man'.

Mariental, NAMIBIA
Founded in 1912 as a railway stop, it was
named 'Mary's Valley' in honour of the Virgin
Mary by German missionaries from the
German *Tal* 'valley'.

Marietta, USA
1. Georgia: possibly named after the wife of
Thomas J. Cobb.
2. Ohio: named after Marie-Antoinette (1755–
93), Austrian wife of Louis XVI, King of France
(1774–92). She followed her husband to the
guillotine.

Mariinsk, TOMSK/RUSSIA *Kiyskoye, Kiysk*
Named after the Kiy River with the name being
shortened in 1856 when the settlement
became a town. A year later it was renamed
after Maria Alexandrovna (1824–80),
German daughter of Louis II, Grand Duke of
Hesse, and wife of Emperor Alexander II
of Russia.

Marijampole, LITHUANIA *Starapole, Kapsukas*
First known as 'Old Field' from the Slavonic
stara 'old' and *pole* 'field' in the 18th century, it
was renamed 'Mary's Field', in modern terms,
'Town of the Blessed Virgin Mary' in
recognition of its earlier existence as a
religious centre. In 1955–90 it was renamed
again after Vincas Mickevičius-Kapsukas
(1880–1935), who headed the short-lived,
Moscow-created 'Lithuanian Soviet
Government' imposed on Lithuania as the
German Army withdrew at the end of 1918.
Marijampole was readopted in 1990.

Marinette, WISCONSIN/USA
Named after the daughter of a Menominee
chief, Marinette Jacobs. Her name was a
combination of Marie and Antoinette.

Marion, AUSTRALIA, USA
1. USA (Alabama): settled in 1817 as Muckle
Ridge, it was renamed after General Francis
Marion (*c.*1732–95), a successful guerrilla
leader in the American War of Independence
(1775–83).
2. USA (Ohio): laid out *c.*1820 as Jacob's Well
after Jacob Foos, it was renamed in 1822 after
General Francis Marion.

Mariscal Estigarribia, PARAGUAY *López de Filippis*
Established as a military outpost, the name was changed in 1945 to honour General José Félix Estigarribia (1888–1940), a successful general during the Chaco War (1932–5) against Bolivia and President of Paraguay (1939–40), from the personal name and the Spanish *mariscal* 'major general'.

Maritsa, BULGARIA *Hebrus*
A river that acts as the border between Bulgaria and Greece, and between Bulgaria and Turkey. In Greek it is known as the Évros and in Turkish as the Meriç. The name comes from the Thracian *mari* 'sea' or 'swamp'.

Mariupol', UKRAINE *Pavlovsk, Zhdanov*
Possibly named after the Tsarevich Paul (later Paul I), it was renamed in 1779 Mariupol 'Mary's City' by Greek settlers. The Mary concerned was probably Maria Fëdorovna (originally the German princess Sophia Dorothea of Württemberg), wife of the future Paul I, Emperor of Russia (1796–1801). On his death in 1948 it was named after Andrey Zhdanov (1896–1948), one of Stalin's[†] closest henchmen and heir apparent, leader of the Leningrad (now St Petersburg) Communist Party organization and of that city's resistance to the German siege in 1941–4; this was his birthplace. Mariupol was restored in 1989.

Mariveles, LUZON/PHILIPPINES *Camaya*
According to legend, named after Maria Velez, a girl keen to become a nun who succumbed to the attentions of a monk in Manila in the 17th century. They fled to Camaya, but in due course were found. Maria was sent back to a convent, but the town's name was changed in her honour.

Marj, al-, LIBYA *Barca/Barce*
'The Meadows' from the Arabic *al-* and *marj* 'meadow' or 'pasture land'. Originally the ancient Greek settlement of Barca, it was captured by the Arabs in 642, subsequently by the Ottoman Turks, and then held by the Italians, who called it Barce, between 1913 and 1941 when it was taken by the British during the Second World War. Destroyed by an earthquake in 1963, a new town was built 3 miles (5 km) away and given its present name.

Market Harborough, ENGLAND/UK *Haverbergam, Mercat Heburgh*
Almost certainly 'Hill where Oats are Grown' from a conjectural Old English word *hæfera* 'oats' and *beorg* and the Middle English *merket* 'market' to denote a particularly important market.

Markham, CANADA, PAPUA NEW GUINEA
1. Canada (Ontario): named after William Markham (1719–1807), Archbishop of York from 1777.
2. Papua New Guinea: a river named after Sir Clements Markham, a noted geographer and secretary of the Royal Geographical Society in London.

Marks, RUSSIA, USA
Russia (Saratov): founded in 1767 as Baronsk, although the alternative name of Yekaterinstadt 'Catherine's Town' after Catherine II the Great[†] soon became popular. The city was given the German name of Markstadt 'Marx's Town' in 1920 after Karl Marx (1818–83), the German political theorist, economist and author of *Das Kapital* published in 1867. The name was shortened in 1941 and is spelt Marx in some atlases.

Marlboro, MASSACHUSETTS/USA
Named after the Marlborough in England.

Marlborough, AUSTRALIA, GUYANA, NEW ZEALAND, UK, USA
1. New Zealand (South Island): a unitary authority named after John Churchill (1650–1722), 1st Duke of Marlborough and a successful military commander at the highest level.
2. UK (England): formerly Merleberge, possibly 'Mærla's Hill' from an Old English personal name and *beorg*, or from the Old English *meargealla* 'gentian', thus 'Hill where Gentian grows'.
3. USA (Connecticut): probably named after the 1st Duke of Marlborough.

Marlow, UK, USA
UK (England): formerly Merelafan and Merlaue, possibly the 'Land recovered after the Lake (or Pool) has been drained' from *mere* and *lāfe*, plural of *lāf*, 'remains'.

Marmara, Sea of (Marmara Denizi), TURKEY *Propontis*
Named after the Marmara Islands which are known for their marble. This gives the islands and sea their names from the Greek *marmaros* 'marble'.

Marne, FRANCE, GERMANY
France (Champagne-Ardenne): a department named after the River Marne which takes its name from the Gaulish *matra* 'mother' or Latin *matrona* 'good lady', thus 'protectress'.

Maroa, USA, VENEZUELA
USA (Illinois): named after a Native American tribe.

Marondera, ZIMBABWE *Marandellas*
Established as a rest station between Harare
and Mutare in 1890 some 4 miles (6 km) south
of its present position, it was named after
Marondera, chief of the Barozwi people.
However, a version of the name was used
until 1982.

Maroochydore, QUEENSLAND/AUSTRALIA
Founded in 1900 at the mouth of the Maroochy
River, both the river and town were given a
name derived from an Aboriginal word
meaning 'Water where the Black Swan
Lives'.

Maroua, CAMEROON
Named after a 19th-century Fulani chief.

Marquesas Islands (Îles Marquises),
FRENCH POLYNESIA
Named by the Spanish explorer Álvaro de
Mendaña de Neira in 1595 after his patron, the
Marquesa Antonio de Mendoza (*c.*1490–1552),
the Spanish viceroy to Peru. In 1791 an
American naval captain saw a group of islands
to the north-west and called it the Washington
Islands. The entire group was annexed by
France in 1842.

Marquette, MICHIGAN/USA
Founded in 1849 and named after Jacques
Marquette, a French Jesuit missionary.

Marrakech, MOROCCO *Morocco*
Founded in 1062 when a fortress was built to
protect an Almoravid military settlement. The
later town was given the name *Marrākuŝ*
'Fortified', a Berber word. In 1147–1269
Marrakech was the capital of the Almohads, of
the Sa'adians in 1524–1668, and sporadically
between 1668 and 1900 when under Alaouite
rule. Until 1890 the city was called Morocco by
Europeans.

Marromeu, MOZAMBIQUE
'Lowland' from *marro*. The town is situated on
the right, west, bank of the Zambesi River.

Marsabit, KENYA
'Cold Place' in recognition of the low
temperatures at night.

Marsala, SICILY/ITALY *Lilybaeon/Lilybaeum, Marsa
'Alī/Marsah el-Allah*
Founded by the Carthaginians in 397 BC as
Lilybaeon, its fine harbour was developed by
the Saracens in the 9th century. They changed
the name to the 'Port of Ali' or the 'Port of
Allah' from which the present name is
derived. It has given its name to the dark
sherry-type wine.

Marseilles (Marseille), PROVENCE-ALPES-CÔTES
D'AZUR/FRANCE, USA
France: settled by Greeks in the 7th century BC,
six centuries later the Romans named it
Massilia from which the present name is
derived. The city's inhabitants were keen
supporters of the French Revolution when it
began, but their minds were changed by
the accompanying terror and blood-letting
and opposition to it grew. As a consequence
of this attitude the city temporarily lost its
name in 1793 and was called Villa-sans-Nom
'Town without a Name'. The French national
anthem, *La Marseillaise*, was named after the
city. Composed in 1792 in Strasbourg as the
Battle Song for the Army of the Rhine, it was
quickly adopted by volunteer militia units
from Marseilles as they marched north to Paris
that year. As they entered the capital singing
the song, it was dubbed *La Marseillaise*.

Marshall, LIBERIA, USA
1. Liberia: founded in 1827 by the (American)
Colonization Society of Virginia for freed black
slaves and named after the Society's chairman,
John Marshall (1755–1835), chief justice of the
USA (1801–35).
2. USA (Texas): founded in 1841 and named
after Chief Justice John Marshall.

Marshall Islands (Majōl)
The Republic of the Marshall Islands since
1979. Named after a British naval officer,
Captain John Marshall, who explored the
islands in 1788 after the Spanish had first
discovered them in 1529. They became a
German protectorate in 1886, were seized by
the Japanese in 1914 and became a Japanese
League of Nations mandate in 1919. Captured
by US forces in 1944, they became part of the
UN Trust Territory of the Pacific Islands
administered by the USA in 1947. They
became independent in 1986 and the US
Trusteeship was terminated in 1990.

Marshalltown, IOWA/USA
Named after Chief Justice John Marshall. *See*
MARSHALL.

Martha's Vineyard, MASSACHUSETTS/USA
An island named in 1602 because of its many
vines. Who 'Martha' was is not known,
although it has been claimed that it is a
corruption of 'Martin', the name of a friend of
the man who named it, either Bartholomew
Gosnold or Gabriel Archer.

Martinez, ARGENTINA, SPAIN, USA
USA (California): named after Ignacio
Martínez, the Spanish commandant at the
presidio in San Francisco.

Martinique Department of Martinique (Départment de la Martinique), an overseas department of France, since 1946. Previously a French colony since 1635, having been discovered by Christopher Columbus[†] in 1493 or 1502. The origin of the name is similarly not clear. It may be derived from a Carib name *Madinina* or be derived from St Martin.

Martins Ferry, OHIO/USA *Jefferson, Martinsville*
Laid out in 1795 by Absalom Martin on the Ohio River, it was later abandoned and then redeveloped in 1835 as Martinsville 'Martin's Town' by his son. This was again changed to Martins Ferry to commemorate the ferry service founded by Absalom Martin.

Martlesham, ENGLAND/UK *Merlesham*
'Homestead in a Clearing where Martens gather' from the Old English *mearth* 'marten', *lēah* 'woodland clearing', and *hām*. It is, however, possible that the first element is a personal name, Mertel.

Marx, SARATOV/RUSSIA
See MARKS.

Mary, TURKMENISTAN *Alexandria Margiana, Antiochia Margiana, Mouru, Merv*
Nineteen miles (30 km) west of the ruined ancient oasis city of Merv, which was founded by, and originally named after, Alexander III the Great[†]. Alexander appointed Antiochus, a general who served both his father, Philip II of Macedonia, and himself, to rule the city. Antiochus rebuilt it and called it Antiochia Margiana. The present and former names, including the Persian Mouru, all evolved from the original Margiana. In the 11th and 12th centuries it was the Seljuk Turk capital when it was regarded as the second greatest city, after Baghdad, in the Islamic world; it was known as Marvishahjahan 'Merv, Queen of the World'. The modern city was founded in 1884 when the ancient city was annexed by the Russians. However, they did not want to live close to the Turkmen so they built a new township, although they adopted the name Merv for it until 1937. The Turkmen settlement of Merv was renamed Bayram Ali (or *Baýramaly) in 1884. The surrounding area now constitutes the province of Mary.

Maryborough, AUSTRALIA
1. Queensland: founded in 1843 and named after the Mary River which itself was named after the wife of Sir Charles Fitz Roy, governor of New South Wales (1846–53).
2. Victoria: established as a sheep run called Simson's Plains and Charlotte's Plains, it was renamed when it became a town in 1854 after

the Irish birthplace (now Port Laoise) of the police commissioner.

Maryland, LIBERIA, USA
1. Liberia: a county which took its name from the colony founded by the Maryland Colonization Society in 1834 for freed black American slaves.
2. USA: a state. The land was given to Cecilius Calvert (1605–75), 2nd Baron Baltimore, by the English king, Charles I[†], in 1632 and settled two years later. The territory was named after the king's French wife, Queen Henrietta Maria (1609–69). It joined the Union as the 7th state in 1788.

Marysville, CANADA, USA
USA (California): originally a trading post, it was bought by Charles Covillaud & Co. and named after Covillaud's wife; Covillaud was one of the town's founders.

Maryville, USA
1. Missouri: founded in 1845 and named after the first girl to be born there, Mary Graham.
2. Tennessee: named after the wife of William Blount, governor of the Territory South of the River Ohio.

Mascara, ALGERIA
Founded in 949 as a military encampment and developed as an Ottoman Turkish garrison in 1701, the name means 'Mother of Soldiers' from the Arabic *umm* 'mother' and *'asker* 'soldier' or 'army'. Since 1981 it has also been spelt Mouaskar.

Mascarene Islands A collective name for the islands of Mauritius, Réunion, and Rodrigues that lie east of Madagascar in the Indian Ocean. The name is derived from that of a 16th-century Portuguese explorer, Pedro de Mascarenhas, who discovered Réunion *c*.1513. Rodrigues is a dependency of Mauritius while Réunion is a separate state.

Mascoutah, ILLINOIS/USA
A Native American word meaning 'Grassy Plain' or 'Prairie'.

Maseru, LESOTHO
Founded in 1869, after the British declared Basutoland a protectorate, from a group of Basuto settlements as a British administrative post on the top of Griffith Hill just to the west of Thaba Bosiu 'Mountain of the Night' from the Sesotho *thaba* 'mountain', the mountain capital of Moshoeshoe I (*c*.1786–1870), the first paramount chief of the Sotho nation. Maseru is a Sesotho word, the plural of *leseru* 'red sandstone', a reference to the hill. It was the capital of Basutoland in 1884–1966 and of independent Lesotho from 1966.

Mashhad, IRAN *Sanābād*
'Place where one has borne Witness', that is, 'Burial Place of a Martyr' from the Persian *ma* indicating a 'place' and *shahādat* 'martyrdom'; this, and the Arabic *shahīd*, literally mean 'witness' or 'be present at' and are equivalent to 'martyr' from the Greek *martys* 'witness'. The word can also mean the tomb of a saint which is the focus of popular veneration—a sepulchral shrine, usually of a martyr belonging to the family of the Prophet Muhammad[†]. Here, the city takes its name from the tomb of the eighth Shi'ite imam, 'Alī ibn Mūsā al-Riḍā (or Ali Reza) (*c.*765–818) who was believed by the Shias to have been poisoned by the Sunnis after he had been proclaimed the caliph-in-waiting. His shrine became a place of pilgrimage and a town grew up around it. Also buried here is Hārūn ar-Rashīd (*c.*763–809), fifth caliph (786–809) of the 'Abbāsid dynasty. This tomb ranks as the third most important shrine, after Kerbala and Najaf in Iraq, in Twelve Imam Shi'ism (which began with Ali, the fourth caliph). Also spelt Meshed. The full name is Mashhad-é Maghaddas 'Mashhad the Holy'.

Mashonaland, ZIMBABWE
A region, and former province of Southern Rhodesia, named in the mid-19th century after the indigenous Shona people, it is now divided into three provinces: Mashonaland Central, Mashonaland East, and Mashonaland West.

Mashrafah, al-, LEBANON, SYRIA
'The Elevated, or Commanding, Place'. Both towns are located in mountainous terrain.

Mason City, USA
1. Illinois: named after the county of Mason, from Mason County in Kentucky, which was named after George Mason, a good friend of George Washington[†].
2. Iowa: originally settled by Freemasons in 1853 as Shibboleth and then Masonic Grove before being simplified to Mason City.

Massachusetts, USA
A state, officially called the Commonwealth of Massachusetts. The name comes from the Massachuset, Algonquian-speaking Native Americans whose name is derived from *massadchseuck* '(People who live) near the Great Hills'. During the 17th century the modern state was composed of Plymouth Colony, founded in 1620, and Massachusetts Bay Colony, founded in 1630 by Puritan colonists. It joined the Union as the 6th state in 1788.

Massawa, ERITREA
An island and port whose name, according to popular etymology, comes from the Ethiopic *mēsūwā* 'loud call' or 'shout'. There are two competing legends: in the first, a fisherman is said to have claimed that a man shouting loudly, could make himself heard from one end of the island to the other (it is about 1 000 yards (1 km) long); in the other, traders on the mainland had to shout loudly for boats from the island to come and fetch them.

Massena, NEW YORK/USA
Named in 1792 after André Massena (1758–1817), a marshal of France during the Napoleonic Wars.

Massillon, OHIO/USA
Founded in 1811 and named in 1826 after Bishop Jean-Baptiste Massillon, a much admired preacher at the court of King Louis XIV[†] in Paris.

Masterton, NORTH ISLAND/NEW ZEALAND
Founded in 1854 and named after Joseph Masters, founder of the Wairarapa Small Farms Association.

Masuria (Mazury), POLAND
An area, now part of the province of Warmínsko-Mazurskie, named after the Mazurs. They invented the *mazurka*, a Polish folk dance in the 16th century.

Masvingo, ZIMBABWE *Fort Victoria, Nyanda*
A province and a town founded as a military post in 1890 and named after Queen Victoria[†]. On Zimbabwean independence in 1980 the name was changed to Nyanda and then in 1982 to its present name meaning 'Caves'.

Matabeleland, ZIMBABWE
A region that takes its name from the Matebele, a rarely used Tswana version of Ndebele, a Bantu-speaking people. 'Ndebele' comes from a Zulu word *amandebele* 'those who disappear'. The founder of the Ndebele was Mzilikazi who, under almost constant Zulu attack and having clashed with Shaka (*c.*1787–1828), the Zulu chief (1816–28), was forced to lead his people out of the area in 1823 and some fifteen years later settle around present-day Bulawayo, Zimbabwe, in what came to be called Matabeleland. Two provinces are now called Matabeleland North and Matabeleland South.

Matadi, DEMOCRATIC REPUBLIC OF THE CONGO
Derives its name from the Kikongo word for 'stone'. This may be traced back to Sir Henry Morton Stanley[†] who ordered local workers to break up rocks so as to build a trading post here in 1879.

Matagorda, TEXAS/USA
'Thick Shrub' from the Spanish *mata* 'shrub' or 'bush' and *gorda*, the feminine of *gordo* 'fat'. There is also an island with this name.

Matala, ANGOLA, GREECE
Angola: the original name, Capelongo, came from the local word *ulongo* which was a forked stick used for carrying loads on one's back. The second name, Artur de Paiva, was that of a junior Portuguese army officer. When Angola gained its independence in 1975 the name was changed to a word that means a 'shelf used for drying vegetables in the sun'.

Matamoros, MEXICO, USA
1. Mexico (Tamaulipas): founded in 1824 as San Juan de los Esteros Hermosos and renamed in 1826 in honour of a hero of Mexican independence, Mariano Matamoros. Its full name is Heroica Matamoros.
2. USA (Pennsylvania): 'Moor Killer' from the Spanish *matar* 'to kill' and *moro* 'Moor'.

Matapédia, QUEBEC/CANADA
A town and a river which joins the Restigouche River and has a Micmac name meaning 'Joining of Two Rivers' or 'Branching River'.

Matara, SRI LANKA
Situated at an old crossing over the River Nilwala, the name means 'Great Ford'.

Mataura, SOUTH ISLAND/NEW ZEALAND
A river whose name comes from the Maori *mata* 'red' and *ura* 'eddying (water)', a reference to the colour of the water after swamp water, reddened by iron oxide, flows into it.

Matera, BASILICATA/ITALY
May be derived from the Latin *materia* 'materials' or 'timber for building'; or from a pre-Roman root *mat-* associated with 'height'. The town overlooks a deep ravine.

Matheran, MAHĀRĀSHTRA/INDIA
Situated on a tree-clad hilltop, the name means 'Jungle Topped Head'.

Matlock, ENGLAND/UK *Meslach, Matlac*
'Oak Tree where Meetings are held' from the Old English *mæthel* 'speech' and *āc* 'oak tree'.

Matoaca, VIRGINIA/USA
Named after the Powhatan princess Matoaka (*c*.1595–1617), better known as Pocahontas. She did much to facilitate good relations between the local Native Americans and English settlers, one of whom she married.

Mato Grosso, BRAZIL
A state meaning 'Great Forest' from the Portuguese *mato* 'forest' or 'brushwood' and *grosso* 'dense' or, here, 'great'. Another state is

called Mato Grosso do Sul 'Great Forest of the South'.

Matopo Hills, ZIMBABWE
A large area of hills whose name, according to local tradition, comes from *amatobos* 'bald heads' or 'the bald-headed ones'. Their dome-shaped tops are said to resemble the bald heads of the elders of the Ndebele people in the mid-19th century.

Matrah, OMAN
Literally a place where something is put down. Since Matrah is a port this has the meaning of an 'anchorage' or 'harbour'—where ships put down their anchors. It is also spelt Mutrah.

Matsue, HONSHŪ/JAPAN
'Bay of Pines' from *matsu* 'pine' and *e* 'bay'.

Matsuyama, SHIKOKU/JAPAN
'Pine Mountain' from *matsu* 'pine' and *yama* 'mountain'.

Mattawamkeag, MAINE/USA
A river, a town, and a lake with a Native American name meaning 'Down a Stream which empties into the Main River'.

Matterhorn (French: **Mont Cervin**; Italian: **Monte Cervino**), ITALY-SWITZERLAND, USA
Italy-Switzerland: a mountain straddling the border between the two countries, the name is derived from the German *Matte* 'meadow' and *Horn* 'horn', the first word referring to the meadows at its base and the second to its curved peak. The Italian *cervino* 'deer-like' conjures up a deer's antlers.

Mattituck, NEW YORK/USA
A Native American word meaning 'Land without Woods'.

Mattoon, ILLINOIS/USA
Founded in 1854 at a railroad junction and named after William B. Mattoon, a railroad official and local landowner.

Maubeuge, NORD-PAS-DE-CALAIS/FRANCE
Malbodium
Probably evolved from the Latin name with the sense that this was a 'bad place' from *male* 'bad' or 'ill-found'. Alternatively, it may have come from a Germanic personal name of some sort. Part of the Spanish Netherlands, it was ceded to France in 1678.

Mauna Kea, HAWAII/USA
A volcano meaning 'White Mountain' from the Hawaiian *mauna* 'mountain' and *kea* 'white' because it is often snow-capped.

Mauna Loa, HAWAII/USA
A volcano meaning 'Long Mountain'.

Mauretania *Maurusia*
Now part of western Algeria and north-eastern
Morocco, Mauretania became two Roman
provinces—Mauretania Tingitana and
Mauretania Caesariensis—during the reign of
Claudius (10 BC–AD 54), Roman emperor (41–
54). The Vandals brought its existence to an
end in 429. The name is derived from the Latin
Mauri, used by the Romans to describe its
inhabitants, from the Greek *mauros* 'dark', a
reference to their dark skins. It gave its name
to a British liner, the *Mauretania*, which sailed
across the Atlantic in 1907–34. Her sister ship
was the *Lusitania*.

Mauritania The Islamic Republic of
Mauritania (al-Jumhūrīyah al-Islāmīyah al-
Mūrītānīyah) since 1958, two years before
independence was gained from France.
Previously an autonomous republic within the
French Community (1958); a colony (1920) in
French West Africa and a French protectorate
(1903). France had actually acquired territorial
rights to Mauritania in 1814 at the Treaty of
Paris, but did little to develop them until 1899
when Xavier Coppolani, a Corsican colonial
administrator, was sent to Mauritania to pacify
the Moors. The name comes from the
country's biggest ethnic group, the Mauri (in
French, *Maure*) or Moors, who are of mixed
Arab and Berber stock, and *-ania* 'land of'.

Mauritius *Dina Mozare, Ilha do Cirne, Île de France*
The Republic of Mauritius since 1992, having
gained independence in 1968. Having been
captured by the British in 1810 to assure access
to vital sea routes, it was ceded to the UK in
1814 at the Treaty of Paris when the previous
Dutch name, Mauritius, was restored.
Abandoned by the Dutch in 1710, it was
occupied five years later by the French, who
claimed it for Louis XV (1710–74), King of
France (1715–74), and called it the 'Island of
France' between 1715 and 1814. Although the
Portuguese had been the first Europeans to
discover the island some time in 1507–12, the
Dutch were the first to claim possession in
1598, although they did not attempt to settle
until 1638. They named the island Mauritius
after Maurice (1567–1625) of Nassau,
stadhouder (governor) of the Netherlands
(1585–1625). The island appeared on a map of
1153 as Dina Mozare, but was soon changed by
the geographer, Al Sharif El-Edressi, to Ilha do
Cirne 'Island of the Swan'.

Mayfield, NEW ZEALAND, UK, USA
1. UK (England/Staffordshire): formerly
Medevelde and Matherfield 'Open Land where
Madder Grows' from the Old English *mæddre*
'madder' and *feld*.

2. UK (England/Sussex): formerly Magavelde
'Open Land where Mayweed Grows' from the
Old English *mægthe* 'mayweed' and *feld*.
3. USA (Kentucky): named after a local creek
where, according to tradition, a George
Mayfield was killed by crooks.

Maykop, ADYGEYA REPUBLIC/RUSSIA
Founded as a fortress in 1857 with a name
possibly derived from the Adygey *myequape*
'river mouth of the valley of apple trees' from
miye 'apple tree', *ko* 'valley', and *pe* 'river mouth'.

Mayo, CANADA, IRELAND, TRINIDAD, USA
Ireland: locally Maigh Eo. A county and a town
meaning 'Plain of the Yew Trees' from *maigh* or
magh 'plain' and *eo* 'yew tree'.

Maysville, KENTUCKY/USA
Founded as Limestone in 1787 and
subsequently named after John May who
helped to lay it out.

Māzandarān, IRAN
A province whose economy depends on
agriculture; hence its name the 'Garden of
Iran'.

Mazār-e Sharīf, AFGHANISTAN *Khayr, Khōdja, Khayran*
'Shrine of the Prophet's Descendant' from
mazār 'a place of pilgrimage', 'shrine', or
'sanctuary' from the Persian *ma* indicating a
place and *zār* 'to visit'. *Sharīf*, besides denoting
a descendant of the Prophet Muhammad[†]
through his daughter Fatima, means 'noble',
'honourable', or 'exalted'. In this case the
descendant is Ali (ibn Abī Tālib) (*c*.600–61), the
Prophet's son-in-law, and the fourth caliph
(656–61). The site is particularly important to
Shi'ites as the shrine here is believed by many
to be Ali's tomb. After his assassination in 661,
Ali's followers, instead of burying him at the
place of his death in Kūfah, Iraq, placed his
corpse on a camel, in accordance with Ali's
wishes; he was to be buried wherever it fell
exhausted. According to local legend, this was
at the site of what is now Mazār-e Sharīf
(conventionally, Najaf in Iraq is revered as his
burial place and where, according to some, his
body was exhumed and placed on the camel).
When the mullahs of nearby Balkh heard the
story early in the 12th century they did not
believe it; however, they changed their minds
after Ali had appeared to one of them in a
dream, confirmed that it was true, and pointed
where his uncorrupted body lay hidden. The
local ruler then erected a shrine over it.

Mazatlán, SINALOA/MEXICO *Pueblo de los Mulatos, San Juan Bautista de Mazatlá*
Named by the Spanish 'Place of the Deer' in
Nahuatl. The first name meant 'Nation of the

Mulattos', that is, people of mixed (black and white) parentage from the Spanish *pueblo* 'nation' or 'people'.

Mazovia (Mazowsze), POLAND
A historic region named after the Mazowie tribe, or Mazurs. An independent principality between the middle of the 12th–15th centuries, it joined Poland in 1526. It became part of Prussia when Poland was partitioned for the second time in 1793, part of the Duchy of Warsaw in 1807, and absorbed by the Russian Empire in 1815. It became part of Poland again in 1918 when that country regained its identity. The present province has the name Mazowieckie. *See* MASURIA.

Mazowe, ZIMBABWE
Named after the river which means 'Place of Elephants'.

Mbabane, SWAZILAND
Founded in 1902 when the British took control of Swaziland and named after Chief Mbabane Kunene whose clan occupied the area. The precise meaning of his name is not known, but is said to convey 'something sharp and bitter', perhaps his attitude. It has been the national capital since 1903 and was raised to city status in 1992.

Mbala, ZAMBIA *Abercorn*
Founded in 1893 and named after James Hamilton (1838–1913), 2nd Duke of Abercorn, first chairman of the British South Africa Company. It was given a new Lala name meaning 'bullet' in 1968.

Mbandaka, DEMOCRATIC REPUBLIC OF THE CONGO *Coquilhatville*
Developed as a colonial centre in 1886 and named 'Coquilhat's Town' after Camille-Aimé Coquilhat (1853–92), the Belgian governor of the Congo Free State (now the Democratic Republic of the Congo) (1891–2). It was renamed in 1966, possibly after a local chief who held sway before the Belgians arrived.

M'Banza Congo, ANGOLA *Ambassa Congo, Bonza Congo, São Salvador do Congo*
The indigenous names after the Kongo people gave way to the Portuguese name of São Salvador do Congo 'Holy Saviour of the Congo' after they had built a cathedral here in 1534. It was given its present name 'Court, or City, of the Congo' in 1980. It was the capital of the Kingdom of Kongo between the 16th and 18th centuries.

Mbanza-Ngungu, DEMOCRATIC REPUBLIC OF THE CONGO *Thysville*
'Town of the Congo' since 1966. The former name honoured Albert Thys, a Belgian who

founded the *Compagnie du Congo* 'Congo Company' in 1886 to exploit the commercial potential of the Middle Congo.

Mbour, SENEGAL
'Royal Residence' from *bur* 'king'.

Mbuji-Mayi, DEMOCRATIC REPUBLIC OF THE CONGO *Bakwanga*
Why the town is called 'Water Goat' from the Swahili is not known, but it is probably associated with some local legend. It grew into a mining town after diamonds were discovered in 1909. Until 1966 it was called Bakwanga, a name derived from the Kwango River.

Mchinji, MALAWI *Fort Manning*
Founded as a fort in 1897 to keep the peace in the area and named after Captain (later Brigadier) Sir William Manning (1863–1932), deputy commissioner and consul for British Central Africa at the time. Its present name means 'Group of Hills'.

Mdina, MALTA *Malet, Notabile*
The original name loosely means 'shelter' or 'protected place', a reference to the Knights of Malta, one of whose duties was to care for sick and wounded Christian pilgrims. The Knights moved to Malta in 1530. The present name is derived from the Arabic *madīnah* 'town' or 'city'. It was the capital of Malta during the 15th and 16th centuries.

Mead, ARIZONA-NEVADA/USA
A man-made lake named after Elwood Mead, reclamation commissioner (1924–36).

Meath (An Mhí), IRELAND *Midhe*
A county with a name meaning 'The Middle (Kingdom)', a reference to its east-central location in the island. It was one of the five ancient kingdoms of Ireland at which time it included the modern county of Westmeath.

Meaux, ÎLE-DE-FRANCE/FRANCE *Latinum, Meldi*
First called Latinum by the Romans, it was later renamed after the Gaulish tribe, the Meldi, from whom the present name is derived.

Mecca, SAUDI ARABIA, USA
Saudi Arabia: locally Makkah. The name is said to be derived from the Arabic *mahram* 'sanctuary', meaning a place that is sacred or inviolable, or *miḥrāb* 'holy of holies', possibly a reference to the Ka'bah which, according to Islamic tradition, was built by Abraham and one of his sons, Ishmael, as the House of God. The Prophet Muhammad[†] was born here *c*.570 but, concerned for the safety of his followers, left in 622 for the agricultural oasis of Yathrib (now Medina). He returned to capture the city in 630 and then began the process whereby Mecca became the holiest city of Islam.

If possible, every adult Muslim must make the *hajj* 'pilgrimage' to Mecca once in his or her lifetime. The city was under the authority of the Egyptian Mamlūks from 1269 and of the Ottoman Turks from 1517 before becoming part of Saudi Arabia in 1925. In ancient times it was known as Bakkah and to Ptolemy[†] as Macoraba. The name is also used in the sense of a 'place that is pre-eminent for a particular activity', such as Hollywood for the film industry.

Mechanicsburg, USA
Three states (Ohio, Pennsylvania, and Virginia) have cities with this name, all probably because of the significant percentage of mechanics amongst the population.

Mechanicsville, USA
Three states (Iowa, Maryland, and Virginia) have cities with this name, probably named because of the significant percentage of mechanics amongst the population. New York has a town called Mechanicville.

Mechelen (French: **Malines**), BELGIUM
Machlina
Derived from the Old High German *mahal* 'place of judgement', a reference to the fact that Charles the Bold (1433–77), Duke of Burgundy, sited the Grand Council, the supreme court of the Low Countries, here in 1473.

Mecklenburg-West Pomerania
(**Mecklenburg-Vorpommern**), GERMANY
A state. Mecklenburg was the name of a dynasty founded by Přibislav, son of the Slav Obodrite ruler, who was made a prince (of the Holy Roman Empire) by Frederick I Barbarossa (*c*.1123–90), Holy Roman Emperor (1152–90), in 1170. In 1180, Přibislav's son, Henry Burwin I, became Prince of Mecklenburg; the principality took its name from the family castle, Mikilinborg, from the Old High German *mihil* 'big' and *Burg*. Mecklenburg experienced partition and reunification on several occasions. In 1701, however, it was divided into Mecklenburg-Strelitz and Mecklenburg-Schwerin. In 1934 they amalgamated to form the state of Mecklenburg, but in 1952 this was split into districts in what was then the German Democratic Republic (East Germany). The modern state was established after the Berlin Wall was demolished in 1989 and just before the unification of East and West Germany in 1990. *Pomerania comes from the Polish *pomorze* 'coastland'.

Medan, SUMATRA/INDONESIA *Medan Putri*
'Field of Battle', a shortened version of the Malay *medan perang* from *medan* 'field' and

perang 'battle' or 'war'. The area was the site of a long struggle between the Kingdoms of Aceh and Deli in the 17th century. The town was founded in 1682.

Medford, MASSACHUSETTS/USA
Founded in 1630 on the Mystic River with a name meaning 'Middle Ford'.

Medicine Hat, ALBERTA/CANADA
A community grew up round a Mounted Police post in 1882 which, according to a local legend, was named as a result of a Cree medicine man losing his hat here as he fled from Blackfoot warriors. The 'medicine', however, may actually come from *wakan* 'holy', 'mysterious', or 'unusual'.

Medicine Lodge, KANSAS/USA
The Plains people lived in a 'lodge' here on the banks of the Medicine Lodge River which they believed had medicinal powers.

Medina, BRAZIL, COLOMBIA, DOMINICAN REPUBLIC, PHILIPPINES, SAUDI ARABIA, USA
Saudi Arabia: adapted from the local Arabic name of al-Madīnah 'The City'. After the Prophet Muhammad[†] and his followers fled here from Mecca in 622, Yathrib, as it was then known, or Iathrippa, became the centre of Muslim faith. In due course it came to be known simply as 'The City'. Muhammad also called it Madīnat Rasūl Allah 'The City of the Messenger of God', in other words, of Muhammad himself, or al-Madīnah al-Munawwarah 'The Enlightened City' from *nūr* 'light'. Ibn Battutah, the famous 14th-century Arab traveller, amongst others, called it 'Taibah, the city of the Apostle of God', *taibah* being associated with the Arabic root for 'good'. Medina is second only to Mecca as an Islamic holy city; Muhammad is buried here. Like Mecca, Medina was under Ottoman Turkish authority from 1517 and joined Saudi Arabia in 1925. The name of the administrative region of which the city is the capital is al-Madīnah al-Munawwarah.

Medinaceli, CASTILE AND LEÓN/SPAIN *Madīnat Sālim*
Derived from the Arabic name meaning 'Town of Sālim' after a Berber from Masmūda with this name.

Mediterranean Sea *Mare Internum/Mare Nostrum*
Derived from the Latin *Mediterraneum Mare* 'Sea in the Middle of the Land' from *mediterraneus* 'midland' or 'inland', a description of its location between Europe, Africa, and Asia. The Roman names meant 'Inner Sea' or 'Our Sea'. It includes the Adriatic, Aegean, Ionian, and Tyrrhenian Seas.

Medjugorje, BOSNIA AND HERZEGOVINA
'Between the Mountains' from the Serbo-Croat *medju* 'between' and *gora* 'mountain', a simple description of its location.

Mednogorsk, ORENBURG/RUSSIA
Founded in 1939 when a copper mine was opened here. It was therefore called 'Copper Mountain' from *med'* 'copper' and *gora.*

Medvezh'yegorsk, KARELIYA REPUBLIC/RUSSIA *Medvezh'ya Gora*
'Bear Mountain' from *medved'* 'bear' and *gora* until 1938 when the name was slightly altered although keeping the same meaning. However, *medvezhiy (ugol)* means 'God-forsaken (spot)'.

Medway, UK, USA
UK (England): formerly Medeuuæge and Medwæg. A river from the Celtic *medu* 'mead', possibly a reference to the colour or sweetness of its water, and the river name *wæg/wey/wye.*

Megalópolis, GREECE
Founded *c.*370 BC after the Battle of Leuctra as a 'Great City', from *megalos* 'great' and *polis*, in Arcadia, populated by the transfer of the inhabitants of 40 surrounding villages, to oppose Sparta. It is now little more than a village itself.

Mégara, GREECE
A very ancient town named after Megareus, King of Onchestus.

Meghālaya, INDIA
A state created in 1972 and meaning 'Abode of the Clouds' from the Sanskrit *ālaya* 'abode' and *megha* 'cloud', a reference to the fact that it has some of the wettest regions on earth.

Megiddo, ISRAEL
The modern name is Tel Megiddo. Settled since *c.*3500 BC and repeatedly destroyed, Megiddo has come to represent the place of the final battle between good and evil in the Bible (Revelation 16: 16). Here the name is given as Armageddon from the Hebrew *har* 'hill' or 'mountain' and Megiddo, thus 'Hill of Megiddo'.

Megiste, GREECE *Castelrosso, Kastellórizon*
One of the eastern group of islands belonging to the Dodecanese Islands, officially called Megiste, but commonly known as Kastellórizon. This and the previous Italian Castelrosso are versions of Château-Roux 'Red Castle', a name adopted by the Knights of Rhodes who were impressed by the island's red rocks. It was occupied by the Ottoman Turks in 1512–1915, but then captured by the French. It passed to Italy in 1923 before becoming a Greek possession in 1947.

Meiningen, THURINGIA/GERMANY
'People of Magano' from a personal name related to Old High German *magan* or *megin* 'power' and *-ingen* 'people of'.

Meknès, MOROCCO *Meknessa ez-Zeitoun*
Originating as a hill-top *kasbah*, by the 10th century it had developed into an important market town of a tribe of the Meknessa Berbers. They named it after themselves, Meknessa ez-Zeitoun 'Meknès of the Olives'. Their name comes from the Arabic *miknās* from *kanasa* 'to sweep'. Moulay Ismaïl (*c.*1645–1727) made Meknès the capital of Morocco in 1673, a year after he had succeeded to the throne. After his death in 1727 the city declined and, although the French rejuvenated it when they occupied it in 1911, the capital was transferred to Rabat.

Mekong, CHINA-LAOS-CAMBODIA-VIETNAM
A river which, besides flowing through four countries, also acts as the border between Laos and Burma (Myanmar), and Laos and Thailand. Its names are Lancang Jiang 'Turbulent Flood' in Chinese, Za Qu 'Water on the Rocks' in Tibetan, Mènam Khong in Laotian, Mékôngk in Khmer, Sông Tiên Giang in Vietnamese, and Mae Nam Khong in Thai. It is the Thai name from which Mekong is derived from *menam* 'river' and *khong* 'water'.

Melaka, MELAKA/MALAYSIA
See MALACCA.

Melanesia, PACIFIC OCEAN
A major grouping of Pacific Islands to the south of Micronesia and west of Polynesia. The name is derived from the Greek *melas* 'black' and *nēsoi* 'islands'. The 'black' refers to the colour of the inhabitants' skins. Melanin is a dark brown to black pigment in the skin and hair, a characteristic shared by the Melanesians.

Melbourne, AUSTRALIA, CANADA, USA
1. Australia (Victoria): first settled in 1835, the city was named in 1837 after William Lamb (1779–1848), 2nd Viscount Melbourne, British prime minister (1834 and 1835–41) at the time. It was the Australian capital in 1901–27.
2. USA (Florida): founded in 1878 and probably named by its first postmaster, C. J. Hector, after his home town of Melbourne, Australia.

Melfi, BASILICATA/ITALY
Named after the Melpes River in ancient Lucania, now roughly equivalent to the modern region of Basilicata. Melpes may come from the stem *melf* indicating a bend in the river.

Melilla (Mlilya), SPAIN *Rusaddir*
An autonomous community and a Spanish
exclave on the Moroccan coast founded by the
Phoenicians, overrun by a succession of
invaders and finally captured by Spain in 1497.
It has been besieged and attacked several times
since then. Its border with Morocco was fixed
at the maximum range of a cannonball fired
from the fortress in 1781, but the exclave's
borders have since been extended. The
original name meant 'Cape of the Cliff' from
russ adir. The present name is derived from the
Berber root *mell* 'white', but in the Berber
dialect the name is Tamlit.

Melitopol', UKRAINE *Novo-Aleksandrovka*
Settled in the 18th century, it became a
city in 1841 and was renamed 'Honey City'
from the Greek *meli* 'honey' and *polis*. It
lies on the Molochnaya 'Milky' River, thus
inspiring the description of a 'land of milk
and honey'.

Melo, ARGENTINA, URUGUAY
Uruguay: founded in 1795 as a Spanish
military post to deter smuggling, it was named
after Pedro de Melo (1733–98), viceroy of the
Río de la Plata territory (1795–7).

Melton Mowbray, ENGLAND/UK *Medeltone,*
Melton Moubray
'Middle Farmstead of the de Moubray Family'
from the Old English *middel* 'middle' and *tūn*
with the French family name. Moubray comes
from Montbray in Normandy, France. A
member, or members, of the family probably
came to England with William I the Conqueror
in 1066 or shortly afterwards.

Melun, ÎLE-DE-FRANCE/FRANCE *Melodunum*
The present name is merely an abbreviated
form of the Roman name, which was derived
from the Gaulish *mello* 'height' and *dunu* 'fort'.

Melville Island, AUSTRALIA, CANADA
1. Australia (in the Timor Sea): the first
European to sight the island was Abel Tasman[†]
in 1644. However, it was not named until 1818
when Captain Philip Parker King named it
after Robert Saunders Dundas (1771–1851),
2nd Viscount Melville, first lord of the British
Admiralty (1812–27).
2. Canada (Northwest Territories, in the Arctic
Ocean): discovered in 1819, it was named after
the 2nd Viscount Melville.

Memphis, EGYPT, USA
1. Egypt: ruins now known as Mît Rahîna
some 10 miles (16 km) south of Cairo. The
former city is believed to have been the capital
of the Old Kingdom of Egypt *c*.2575–2130 BC.
The name is derived from Men-nefer, the
name given to the pyramid city of the Pharoah

Pepi I, who ruled some time between *c*.2300 BC
and 2150 BC. It is said that the name comes
from the good looks of Pepi from *men* 'his' and
nefer 'beauty'.
2. USA (Tennessee): founded in 1819 around a
military fort on the Mississippi River, it took its
name from the Egyptian city because of its
geographical similarity with that city located
on the River Nile.

Memphremagog, CANADA-USA
A lake stretching across the international
border, the name is an Algonquian word
meaning 'Lake of Abundance' or 'A Place
where there is much Water'.

Menasha, WISCONSIN/USA
Settled in 1843, its name comes from a
Winnebago word for 'island'. It lies opposite
an island in the Fox River.

Mendeleyevsk, TATARSTAN REPUBLIC/RUSSIA
Bondyuzhskiy
Developed from a chemical factory founded in
the mid-19th century. It was renamed in 1967
after Professor Dmitry Mendeleyev (1834–
1907), an eminent chemist who had been
employed in the factory here, and a prolific
author on scientific matters.

Menderes (Büyük Menderes Nehri), TURKEY
Maeander
A river called the Big Menderes River from
büyük 'big' and *nehri* 'river'. The Turkish
menderes 'meander' describes its twisting lower
course, the English word 'meander' coming
from its classical name. Another river, the
Küçük Menderes 'Small Menderes', was called
the Scamander and in ancient times the
Xanthus 'Golden' or 'Red-Yellow (River)' from
the Greek *xanthos*.

Mendip Hills, ENGLAND/UK *Menedepe*
The first syllable may come from the Welsh
mynydd 'hill', or a Celtic word, possibly *mönith*,
closely related to this, and possibly the Old
English *hop* 'valley'. This contradiction may
simply describe the hills and valleys of the
range. However, the second syllable may come
from the Old English *yppe* 'plateau' to describe
the Western Mendip which forms a plateau.

Mendocino, CALIFORNIA/USA
Named after Antonio de Mendoza (*c*.1490–
1552), the first viceroy of New Spain (Mexico)
(1535–50).

Mendoza, ARGENTINA, CUBA, DOMINICAN
REPUBLIC, PERU
Argentina: a province and a city founded in
1561 and named either after Antonio de
Mendoza (see previous entry) or García
Hurtado de Mendoza, governor of Chile at that
time. The province and city were transferred

from Chile to the Viceroyalty of the Río de la Plata in 1776.

Menlo Park, CALIFORNIA/USA
Takes its name from Menlough, Ireland (see next entry).

Menlough, IRELAND
Two places, both in Galway, have this name. One, locally Mionloch, means 'Small Lake'; the other, Mionlach, 'Small Place'.

Menoken, NORTH DAKOTA/USA
A Native American word meaning 'Good Growing Place'.

Menominee, MICHIGAN/USA
Founded as a fur trading post in 1796, it is named after the Algonquian-speaking Menominee who inhabited this area round the north-western shores of Lake Michigan. Their name means 'wild rice' which grew in abundance here.

Menongue, ANGOLA *Serpa Pinto*
Named after a local chief, it was renamed in the 1930s after Alexandre Alberto da Rocha Serpa Pinto (1846–1900), a Portuguese colonial administrator who became governor of Mozambique in 1889. Its original name was restored in 1980.

Menton, PROVENCE-ALPES-CÔTES D'AZUR/
FRANCE *Mentone*
Situated below a rocky amphitheatre, the name is said to come from a pre-Celtic root *men* 'rock'. The French *menton* actually means 'chin'. Held by the Genoese and then by the Grimaldis of Monaco, the town was bought by the French in 1860.

Mentor, OHIO/USA
Settled in 1815 and probably named after Hiram Mentor, one of the first inhabitants. However, it is also claimed that it is named after Mentor, the guide and adviser of Telemachus, Odysseus' son (who gave the word 'mentor').

Menzel Bourguiba, TUNISIA
See MANZIL BU RUQAYBAH.

Mequon, WISCONSIN/USA
A Native American name meaning 'ladle' and given to the River Mequon because it has a bend resembling a ladle. The town took its name from the river.

Merced, CALIFORNIA/USA
Founded in 1872 and named after a river called Nuestra Señora de la Merced 'Our Lady of Mercy' from the Spanish *merced* 'mercy' or 'favour'.

Mercedes, ARGENTINA, HONDURAS, URUGUAY, USA
Argentina (San Luis): founded in 1856 as Fuerte Constitucional 'Fort Constitution', but renamed five years later Villa Mercedes after its patroness, the 'Virgin of Mercy', from the Spanish *Virgen de Merced*.

Mercer, USA
Five states have cities with this name, most in honour of General Hugh Mercer, a Scottish-born soldier, who was killed in 1777 during the American War of Independence (1775–83).

Mercia, ENGLAND/UK
One of the seven kingdoms in Anglo-Saxon England, predominant during the 8th century. Bordering the Welsh lands in the west, the name means '(People of) the Marches' from the Old English *merce* or *mearc* 'boundary'. At its height Mercia stretched from the Welsh border to the border with East Anglia between the Humber and Thames Rivers. It lost its separate identity when Athelstan (d. 939) became king of all England in 925.

Meredith, NEW HAMPSHIRE/USA
Named after Sir William Meredith (d. 1790) , 3rd Baronet of Henbury, a lord of the British Admiralty (1765–6) and a Member of Parliament (1754–80), who supported the colonists' demands that they should not be taxed without having their own parliament.

Meredosia, ILLINOIS/USA
Adapted from a French name, *marais d'osier* 'willow marsh' from *marais* 'marsh' and *osier* 'water-willow'.

Mérida, MEXICO, PHILIPPINES, SPAIN, VENEZUELA
1. Mexico (Yucatán): founded in 1542 on the site of an ancient Mayan city, possibly known as Ichcansiho or Tihó, it is named after the Spanish city because the Mayan buildings reminded the Spaniards of the Roman ruins in Mérida.
2. Spain (Extremadura): founded in 25 BC as Augusta Emerita and the ancient capital of Lusitania for Roman veterans, *emereti*; it was dedicated to Augustus[†], a consul at the time who had taken the title Augustus in 27 BC. The present name is derived from the Roman name.
3. The state in Venezuela is named after its capital, the city of Mérida, which in its turn is named after the Spanish city, as is the city in the Philippines.

Meriden, CONNECTICUT/USA
Settled in 1661 by an Englishman, Jonathan Gilbert, who named it after his birthplace, Meriden Farm, in Dorking, Surrey. Meriden

might mean 'Valley where Merry-making takes place' from the Old English *myrge* 'merry-making' and *denu* 'valley'.

Meridian, MISSISSIPPI/USA
Settled in 1854 at the point where the Vicksburg-Montgomery and the Mobile and Ohio railway lines met. The city received its name from a settler who believed that 'meridian' meant 'junction'.

Merlo, ARGENTINA *Villa de San Antonio del Camino*
A county in the province of Buenos Aires; a small borough was established here in 1730 by Francisco de Merlo and subsequently renamed after him.

Merrimack, NEW HAMPSHIRE/USA
A town named after the River Merrimack which is said to be a Native American word meaning 'sturgeon' or 'swift water'.

Merseburg, SAXONY-ANHALT/GERMANY
Situated on the left bank of the Saale River, the name comes from the Old High German *mari* 'lake' and *Burg*. It was founded *c*.800 as a defensive post on the border with the Slavs.

Mers el-Kebir, ALGERIA
A corruption of the Arabic *al-marsā al-kabīr* 'The Great Port' from *al-*, *marsā* 'harbour' and *kabīr* 'great' or 'big'.

Mersey, AUSTRALIA, UK
1. Australia (Tasmania): named after the river in England.
2. UK (England): a river, formerly called Mǣrse 'Boundary River' from the Old English *mǣre* 'boundary' and *ēa* 'river'. The river at one time formed the boundary between the Anglo-Saxon kingdoms of Mercia and Northumbria, and between the counties of Cheshire and Lancashire.

Merseyside, ENGLAND/UK
A metropolitan county, created in 1974, lying on both sides of the River Mersey and named after it.

Mersin, TURKEY
Derived from the Greek *myrsini* 'myrtle', a tree which grows in the area.

Merthyr Tydfil, WALES/UK *Merthir, Merthyr Tutuil*
'(Grave of) the Martyr Tudful' from *merthyr* 'martyr'. Tydfil (or Tudful) was a Welsh Christian princess and saint who was killed by Saxon pagans and buried here in 480.

Meru, KENYA, MALAYSIA, TANZANIA
1. Kenya: named after a loose grouping of peoples who inhabit the eastern slopes of Mt Kenya.
2. Tanzania: a mountain, probably also named after the Meru.

Mesa, INDONESIA, USA
USA (Arizona): founded in 1878 by Mormons, the name means 'table' in Spanish, a description of the flat-topped tableland on which the settlement developed.

Mesabi Range, MINNESOTA/USA
A range of iron-ore hills with an Ojibwa name meaning 'Giant'.

Meshed, IRAN
See MASHHAD.

Mesopotamia, COLOMBIA, GREECE, ST VINCENT, SOUTH-WEST ASIA
See IRAQ.

Mesquite, BRAZIL, USA
USA (Texas): founded in 1873 and named after the mesquite shrubs that grew abundantly here at that time.

Messene (Messini), GREECE
Ruins. Probably founded *c*.370 BC, it takes its name from the region, Messenia, of which it became the capital after the Messenians were able to return to the area following more than three centuries of banishment. The name is probably derived from *mesos* 'middle' describing its location. It should not be confused with the modern town of Messíni further south.

Messina, ITALY
Italy (Sicily): a haunt of pirates from Cumae, it was founded as a colony *c*.725 BC. It was originally called Zankle by the Greeks to mean 'sickle', a description of the shape of the harbour. In the 5th century BC it was renamed Messene by Anaxilas, the tyrant of Rhegium (now Reggio di Calabria) on the other side of the Strait of Messina, after his birthplace, Messenia, a region in the south-west Peloponnese, Greece. It was also known as Messana, the Doric form of the name. It gives its name to the strait between Sicily and Italy.

Metéora, GREECE
From *meteoros* 'suspended in the air', a reference to the pillars of rock in the area, some of which are crowned with monasteries and hermitages. It was also known locally as Stous Ayious 'At the Saints' Place' and this became Stagoi.

Methuen, MASSACHUSETTS/USA
Settled in 1642, it was named after Sir Paul
Methuen (1672–1757), a lord of the British
Admiralty (1709–10) and Member of
Parliament (1715–47), by the state governor
who was a friend, when it became a town in
1725.

Metropolis, ILLINOIS/USA
Named by its founders in the hope of a grand
future for the city.

Metz, FRANCE, USA
France: the former Roman name,
Mediomatricum, recognized the
Mediomatrici, a Gallic tribe whose capital this
was. Their name comes from the Gaulish *medio*
'middle' and Matrici, the name of another
tribe in this same area. The Medieval Latin
name was Mettis from which the present
name is derived.

Meudon, ÎLE-DE-FRANCE/FRANCE *Meclodunum*
Situated on a hill, the name comes from the
Roman Meclodunum, itself from the Gaulish
metlo 'height' and *dunu* 'fort'.

Meuse, FRANCE-BELGIUM (Flemish: **Maes**)-THE
NETHERLANDS (Dutch: **Maas**) *Mosa*
A river which may derive its name from the
Germanic *mos* 'marsh'. It was known to the
Romans as the Mosa.

Mexicali, BAJA CALIFORNIA NORTE/MEXICO
It lies on the border with California opposite
Calexico. Like that name its own is a
combination of the first syllables of Mexico
and California, the result of a friendly
agreement.

Mexico (Spanish: **México**), and COSTA RICA, USA
1. The United Mexican States (Estados Unidos
Mexicanos) since 1824 when a republic was
proclaimed. Previously it had been known as
the Empire of Mexico (1821–3), independence
finally being gained from Spain in 1821.
Nevertheless, the official year of independence
is 1810 when the Mexican Revolution against
Spanish rule began. On independence Mexico
was much bigger than it is today. By 1848 it
had lost to the USA Texas, New Mexico, and
parts of Arizona, California, Colorado, and
Utah. From the time the Spanish completed
their conquest in the first half of the 16th
century until independence, the region was a
part of the Viceroyalty of New Spain. México is
the simplified Spanish version of a Nahuatl
name for the Aztec capital, Metztlixihtlico (*see*
MEXICO CITY), said to mean 'In the Navel of the
Moon'. It was akin to Mexica, by which the
Aztecs were once known, and became the
name for the country. México is also the name
of a state.

2. USA (Missouri): founded in 1836 and named
after a sign which pointed to 'Mexico that-a-
way'.

Mexico City (Ciudad de México), FEDERAL
DISTRICT/MEXICO *Tenochtitlán/Metztlixihtlico*
Early in the 14th century the nomadic Mexicas
(called by the Spanish the Aztecs) were waiting
for a sign from their sun god Huitzilopochtli to
indicate where they should found their new
nation. That place would be where they saw an
eagle—the protector of the sun—perching on
a cactus growing out of a rock and clutching a
snake—the emblem of the night—in its beak.
According to legend, they eventually found
this spot on an island in a lake called Texcoco
in 1324. The Aztecs named the place
Tenochtitlán 'Place of the High Priest
Tenoch' from the Nahuatl *tetl* 'rock'. Tenoch
was the name of a legendary high priest
who took his name from *nuchtli* 'cactus' and
gave it, as Tenochca, to the Aztecs as another
of their names. About two years after they
arrived in 1519 the Spanish dispensed with
Tenochtitlán and adapted the tribal name
Mexica, adding 'city' to distinguish it from the
country.

Meymaneh, AFGHANISTAN
'In the Middle' in Dari, although it is actually
in the north-west. It is also spelt Maimaneh.

Mezhdurechensk, KEMEROVO/RUSSIA *Posëlok*,
Olzheras
Located at the confluence of the Usa and Tom
Rivers, its first name meant simply
'Settlement'. It was later given the name
Olzheras and in 1955 was renamed again when
it became a town to recognize its location
'Between the Rivers' from *mezhdu* 'between'
and a derivative of *reka* 'river' to make a place-
name.

Mezzogiorno, ITALY
A region roughly equivalent to the former
Kingdom of Naples, that is, southern Italy
including Sicily. Today, the lack of a clear
northern limit is the subject of discussion, if
not dispute. Southern Italy is called
Mezzogiorno 'midday' because of the heat of the
sun at midday.

Mhangura, ZIMBABWE
'Copper' from a Shona word, a reference to the
copper mine here.

Mhlambanyatsi, SWAZILAND
'Buffalo Crossing'.

Miami, CANADA, USA
1. USA (Florida): originally Mayaimi, probably
the name of a local Native American tribe.
They may have taken their name from a local

word signifying that they were 'people who lived on a peninsula'. Miami is also the name of an Algonquian-speaking tribe which used to live in Wisconsin, but later moved to Indiana and Oklahoma.
2. USA (Oklahoma): originally Jimtown, but renamed after the Miami in 1890.

Miami Beach, FLORIDA/USA
A seafront city, close to Miami, it is named after that city.

Micanopy, FLORIDA/USA
Named after the chief of the Seminole; his name meant 'Chief of Chiefs'.

Michalovce, SLOVAKIA
'The Settlement of Michael's People', from the genitive of the personal name.

Michigan, USA
A state which borders four of the five Great Lakes. The Ojibwa (Chippewa) named the area *Michi Gama* 'Great Lake' or 'Great Water' and it is after Lake Michigan, the third largest, that the state is named. Part of Canada until ceded to the USA in 1783, it became the Michigan Territory when separated from Indiana in 1805. It joined the Union in 1837 as the 26th state.

Michigan City, INDIANA/USA
Laid out in 1830 as the end of the Michigan Road from the Ohio River.

Michurinsk, TAMBOV/RUSSIA *Kozlov*
Founded as a fortress in 1636, it was renamed in 1932 after Ivan Michurin (1855–1935), a horticulturist who founded an institute here and died here.

Micronesia The Federated States of Micronesia since 1979 when they were created from the Caroline Islands less the Palau group. The name means 'Small Islands' from the Greek *mikro* 'small' and *nēsos* 'island' (plural, *nēsoi*) because the islands are generally smaller than those of Melanesia, many being atoll formations. Consisting of over 600 islands in the Caroline Islands archipelago, the grouping comprises, from west to east, the four states of Yap, Chuuk (renamed from Truk in 1990 and before that Hogoleu), Pohnpei (renamed in 1984 from Ponape), and Kosrae. Parts of the Caroline and Mariana Islands were under Spanish sovereignty until 1899 when they were sold to Germany. German Micronesia was occupied by the Japanese in 1914 and they acquired a League of Nations mandate in 1920. After driving out the Japanese during the Second World War, the USA administered it on behalf of the UN as the Trust Territory of the Pacific Islands. In 1986 Micronesia entered

a free association with the USA at which time it ceased to be subject to US trusteeship and administration.

Middelburg, THE NETHERLANDS, SOUTH AFRICA
1. The Netherlands: 'Middle Town', named because of its central location on the former Walcheren Island.
2. South Africa (Mpumalanga): founded in 1866 with the biblical name of Nazareth, it was renamed in 1874 after the Dutch town.

Middlebury, USA
Vermont: it was the centre of three towns surveyed at the same time *c.*1770, midway between Salisbury and New Haven.

Middle East, The An undefined area centred on the eastern Mediterranean which is sometimes said to include lands as far west as Morocco and as far east as Pakistan. The eastern portion of these lands is sometimes known as South-West Asia. The term is generally accepted, however, as comprising Iraq, Iran, Israel, Jordan, Lebanon, Syria, and the Arabian Peninsula. The area is characterized by having a predominantly Muslim population. In the past this region was sometimes known as the Near East in comparison with the Far East.

Middlesboro, KENTUCKY/USA
Settled in 1889 and officially Middlesborough, it is named after the city with that name in England (which is spelt Middlesbrough).

Middlesbrough, ENGLAND/UK *Midelesburc*
'Middlemost Stronghold' from the Old English *midlest* 'middlemost' and *burh*, although it is not clear what it was in the middle of.

Middlesex, BELIZE, UK, USA
UK (England): formerly Middelseaxon and Midelsexe. A former county meaning '(Land of the) Middle Saxons' from *middel* and *Seaxe*. The area lay between the East Saxons (Essex) and West Saxons (Wessex) and extended beyond the boundaries of the county which ceased to exist in 1965. The Middle Saxons' territory later became a province of the Kingdom of the East Saxons.

Middletown, USA
Eleven states have cities with this name, normally because they are located midway between other cities or rivers.

Middle West, The USA
Also known as the Midwest, it is so-called because it is an area lying midway between the Appalachian and Rocky Mountains roughly in the north-central part of the USA and

comprising the states of Ohio, Indiana, Illinois, Michigan, and Wisconsin.

Midhurst, ENGLAND/UK *Middeherst*
'(Place) among Wooded Hills' from the Old English *midd* 'middle' and *hyrst* 'wooded hill'.

Midi, FRANCE
A French term for southern France meaning 'midday' because of the heat of the sun at midday.

Midland, AUSTRALIA, CANADA, USA
1. USA (Michigan): takes its name after the county of Midland, which lies roughly in the middle of the state.
2. USA (Texas): founded in 1884 and named because it is halfway between El Paso and Fort Worth.

Midlands, The, ENGLAND/UK
A term to describe the central counties of England.

Midlothian, SCOTLAND/UK *Loonia, Lodoneó, Louthian*
A unitary district. *See* LOTHIAN.

Midway Islands, USA *Middlebrooks, Brooks*
An unincorporated territory of the USA comprising two islands in the Pacific Ocean. Discovered by Captain N. C. Brooks in 1859 and named after him. When they were annexed by the USA in 1867 the name was changed to Midway, an indication of their location halfway between America and Asia.

Mie, HONSHŪ/JAPAN *Moy-i*
A prefecture meaning 'Triple' from *mi* 'three' and *-e* '-fold', a reference to its three administrative divisions. The present name is derived from the previous Ainu name.

Miguel Hidalgo, FEDERAL DISTRICT/MEXICO
Named after Miguel Hidalgo i Costilla (1753–1811), a priest and so-called father of Mexican independence who was the first leader of the revolution against Spanish rule in 1810.

Mikindani, TANZANIA
'(Place by) the Dances'. It was a place well known for the dancing of women.

Mikkeli, FINLAND *Sankt Michel*
A province and a city. The name is a shortened version of the Swedish Sankt Michel in honour of St Michael to whom the main church is dedicated. For nearly five centuries (1323–1809), Finland was subject to Swedish rule.

Milan, CANADA, ITALY, USA
Italy (Lombardy): formerly Mediolanum 'Middle of the Plain' from the Gaulish *medio* 'middle' and *lanu* 'plain'. It was founded *c.*600

BC by the Gauls on the banks of the River Po in the centre of a plain which was an economically and strategically important region. Napoleon[†] made it the capital of the Cisalpine Republic in 1797 and of the new Kingdom of Italy, with himself as king, in 1805; this only lasted until 1814. The present name, in Italian Milano, is simply an abbreviated version of the original name.

Mildenhall, ENGLAND/UK
Suffolk: formerly Mildenhale, Mitdenehalle and Middelhala, likely to be either 'Middle Corner of Land' from *middel* and *halh* 'corner of land' or 'Corner of Land belonging to a Man called (possibly) Milda'.

Mildura, VICTORIA/AUSTRALIA
'Red Earth' from an Aboriginal term.

Miles City, MONTANA/USA
Founded in 1877 and named after General Nelson A. Miles.

Miletín, CZECH REPUBLIC
Named after an unknown person called Mileta.

Milford, IRELAND, UK, USA
1. USA (Connecticut): settled in 1639 and possibly named after Milford Haven, Wales.
2. USA (Delaware): named for the several mills built here on the Mispillion River.

Milford Haven (Aberdaugleddau), WALES/UK *De Milverdico portu, Mellferth, Aber Dav Gleddyf*
'Harbour at Milford'. The modern town was founded only in 1793 by a deep, and already much used, natural harbour—'haven'—on a tidal estuary. Milford 'Sandy Inlet' comes from the Old Scandinavian *melr* 'sand' and *fjorthr* 'inlet' or 'fjord'. The Welsh name means 'Mouth of the two Rivers Cleddau', the name meaning 'sword'. The 'two' rivers referred to the Eastern and Western branches.

Milk, USA-CANADA
A river rising in Montana, USA, and flowing into Alberta, Canada, which was named by Meriwether Lewis[†] in 1805 because of the milky appearance of its waters.

Millau, MIDI-PYRÉNÉES/FRANCE *Condatomag, Aemilianum, Amigliauvo*
Its first Celtic name gave way to the Roman one which was from a personal name, Aemilius, from which the present name comes through Amigliauvo.

Millburn, NEW JERSEY/USA *Elizabethtown, Springfield*
Founded in 1664 and named after an unknown Elizabeth, it was divided in 1793, one part becoming Springfield. In 1857 the northern part of Springfield became the separate

township of Millburn, named after a 'mill on
the burn'.

Milledgeville, GEORGIA/USA
Founded in 1803 and named after John
Milledge, governor of Georgia at the time.

Millville, CANADA, USA
USA (New Jersey): the first settlement was
constructed by woodcutters along the banks of
the Maurice River in the 1700s and called
Shingle Landing. It was later renamed Maurice
River Bridge and then The Bridge. It was finally
renamed 'Mill Town' in recognition of the
mills in the area.

Milnerton, WESTERN CAPE/SOUTH AFRICA
Founded in 1902 and named after Sir Alfred
Milner (1854–1925), governor of Cape Colony
(1897–1901) and of Transvaal and Orange River
colonies (1902–5), who was created a viscount
in 1902 for his services in connection with the
Boer War (1899–1902).

Mílos, GREECE
An island, also spelt Melos, and ruins on it with
the name 'Apple' from *mîlo*.

Milton, CANADA, NEW ZEALAND, UK, USA
1. New Zealand (South Island): originally
Milltown as a result of its mills, but this
spelling was changed, when streets were
renamed after famous poets, to honour John
Milton (1608–74), a happy coincidence.
2. UK (England): a common name generally
meaning 'Middle Farmstead' from *middel* and
tūn.
3. USA (Massachusetts): originally a Native
American settlement called Uncataquisset
'Head of Tidewater', it was renamed because of
the number of mills operating on the
Neponset River at this point.
4. USA: fourteen other states have cities with
this name, some named after the poet, John
Milton, others after mills, and yet others after
people called Milton or with Milton in their
title.

Milton Keynes, ENGLAND/UK *Middeltone
Kaynes*
A 'New Town' since 1967, it was developed
from a village 'Middle Farmstead' from *middel*
and *tūn*. In the 13th century Kaynes was added
to indicate the Norman lord of the manor,
Lucas de Kaynes, from the de Cahaignes
family, who held the manor in 1221.

Milwaukee, WISCONSIN/USA
Settled in 1800 with a name said to have
evolved from the Native American name
Mahn-a-waukee which may have meant
'Gathering Place by the River', also called the
Milwaukee; alternatively, it has been

suggested that it comes from the native word
milioke 'good earth' or 'good country',
a reference to the fertility here.

Mīnāb, IRAN *Hormuz*
Close to the Strait of Hormuz, it means 'Blue
Water'.

Minas, CUBA, URUGUAY
Uruguay: founded in 1783 and named after the
local mines, in Spanish *mina* 'mine'.

Minas Gerais, BRAZIL
A state with a Portuguese name meaning
'General Mines', large deposits of gold being
discovered here in 1692. The *capitania* of Minas
Gerais was established in 1720 to regulate the
competition over mining sites.

Mindanao, PHILIPPINES
The second largest island in the the
Philippines, the name is a Spanish shortening
of Magindanau which may mean 'Place on the
Side of a Lake' from the Malay *danau* 'lake'.

Mineral'nyye Vody, STAVROPOL TERRITORY/
RUSSIA
'Mineral Waters' from *mineral'nyy* 'mineral'
and *voda* 'water'. It is a spa.

Mingrelia, GEORGIA
Annexed by Russia in 1803, it has a name of
Turkic origin meaning '(Place of) a Thousand
Springs', the first syllable coming from the
modern Turkish *bin* 'thousand'.

Minneapolis, MINNEAPOLIS/USA
Incorporated in 1856 with the first part of the
name coming from the Minnesota Territory
and the second from *polis*.

Minnesota, USA
A state and a river with a name meaning 'Sky-
Coloured Water' or 'Waters that reflect the
Sky' from the Dakota (Sioux) *minne* 'water' and
sota which probably did not represent 'blue',
but 'cloudy'. With that part of Minnesota east
of the Mississippi River in US hands by 1787,
the part west of the river was acquired by
means of the Louisiana Purchase in 1803.
Minnesota, including parts of modern North
and South Dakota, became a territory in 1849
and joined the Union as the 32nd state in 1858
with its present borders.

Minorca (Menorca), BALEARIC ISLANDS/SPAIN
Minorica
The smaller of the two main islands, the name
comes from the Latin *minor* 'lesser'.

Minot, NORTH DAKOTA/USA
Originating as a tented settlement in 1886, it
was named the following year after Henry D.
Minot who invested heavily in the Eastern
Railroad.

Minsk (Mansk), BELARUS *Mensk, Menesk*
'Exchange', in other words, 'market place'
from the Russian *menyat'* 'to exchange' or 'to
barter'. At first Russian, it passed to Lithuania
in the 14th century and then Poland before
being regained by Russia at the second
partition of Poland in 1793. It has been the
capital of the Byelorussian Soviet Socialist
Republic and of Belarus since 1919. It became
the capital of the Commonwealth of
Independent States, a partial successor to the
Soviet Union, in 1991.

Minyā, al-, EGYPT
A governorate and city which takes its name
from the very ancient town of Menat Khufu,
whose ruins are nearby.

Miraflores, ARGENTINA, CHILE, COLOMBIA,
MEXICO, PERU
Peru: although still an Inca village, it came to
be called Miraflores 'Look at the Flowers' from
the Spanish *mirar* 'look at' and *flor* 'flower' in
the 16th century because of its abundance of
bougainvillea.

Miramar, ARGENTINA, PUERTO RICO, USA
'Look at the Sea' from the Spanish *mirar* 'look
at' and *mar* 'sea'.

Miranda de Ebro, CASTILE-LEÓN/SPAIN
'Wonderful (Place) on the (River) Ebro' from
the Latin *mirandus* 'wonderful' or 'admirable'.

Mirande, MIDI-PYRÉNÉES/FRANCE
'Place of Observation', ultimately from the
Medieval Latin *mirare* 'to look' or 'watch'.

Mirandola, EMILIA-ROMAGNA/ITALY
Sometimes called La Mirandola, it has the
same meaning and derivation as *Mirande.

Mirbāṭ, OMAN
'Breastwork' or 'Sangar', a fortified post
usually built of stones above the desert floor.

Mirnyy, SAKHA REPUBLIC/RUSSIA
Founded in 1955 with a name meaning
'Peaceful'.

Mirpur Khas, SINDH/PAKISTAN
Founded in 1806 as the 'Town of the Mirs' by
Mīr 'Alī Murād Tālpur.

Mirror, ALBERTA/CANADA
Named in 1911 after the British daily
newspaper, the *Daily Mirror*.

Mirzāpur, UTTAR PRADESH/INDIA
'Prince Town' from the Hindui *mirzā* 'prince'
and *pur*.

Mishawaka, INDIANA/USA
Laid out in 1833, it may come from a
Potawatomi word meaning 'Country of Dead
Trees' or after a Potawatomi chief called

Mishiniwaka whose name could mean either
'Swift Water' or 'Red Earth'. It lies along the St
Joseph River.

Misiones, ARGENTINA
A province which takes its name from the
Spanish Jesuit missions which were set up in
the area during the 17th and 18th centuries for
the Gutrainí people.

Mission, CANADA, USA
USA (Texas): settled in 1908 and named after a
Franciscan mission established nearby in 1824.

Mississauga, ONTARIO/CANADA
At the western end of Lake Ontario, it is named
after the Mississauga tribe whose name means
'People of the Wide-Mouthed River'; in other
words, a river with many channels at its
mouth from *missi* 'many' and *saki* 'channel'.

Mississippi, USA
A state named after the largest river in the
USA. The name is a Choctaw word meaning
'Father of Waters' or simply 'Great Waters' or
'Big River'. Ceded by France to Great Britain in
1763, the area was named the Mississippi
Territory in 1798. Enlarged in 1804 and again
in 1812, the western part joined the Union in
1817 as the 20th state while the eastern part
became Alabama. Mississippi seceded from the
Union in 1861, but rejoined in 1869.

Missouri, USA
A state and a river, both named after the
Missouri people by the French. The previous
Native American name for the river was
Pekitanoui which the French took to mean 'Big
Muddy (Waters)'. It has also been suggested
that the name means 'Canoe Haver' in
Algonquian. Claimed for France in 1682, the
area was ceded to Spain in 1762 and back to
France in 1802. The following year it was
bought from France as part of the Louisiana
Purchase. It became the Missouri Territory in
1812, joining the Union as the 24th state in
1821.

Mistassini, QUEBEC/CANADA
A lake with a Cree name meaning 'Great
Stone', a reference to rocky ridges in the lake
which almost divide it in two.

Mitaka, HONSHŪ/JAPAN
'Three Hawks' from *mi* 'three' and *taka* 'hawk',
a reference to the fact that the area was once
used as an area for hawking; indeed, a place
much favoured by successive shoguns for their
falconry.

Mitchell, AUSTRALIA, CANADA, USA
1. Australia (Queensland): a town and a river
named in 1845 after Sir Thomas Mitchell
(1792–1855), surveyor general for New South

Wales from 1828 who conducted four expeditions into the interior of Australia in 1831–47.
2. USA (North Carolina): a mountain previously called Black Dome, it was renamed after Professor Elisha Mitchell, who surveyed it, died on it, and is buried at the summit.
3. USA (South Dakota): founded in 1879 and named after Alexander Mitchell, president of the Chicago, Milwaukee, and St Paul Railroad.

Mito, HONSHŪ/JAPAN
Situated on the Naka River, it was an important port. It means 'Water Gate' from *mizu* 'water' and *to* 'gate', although *to* is sometimes rendered as 'door'. Alternatively, it is possible that the name comes from the Ainu *moy-to* 'quiet marsh'.

Miyazaki, KYŪSHŪ/JAPAN
A prefecture and a city with a name derived from *miya* 'shrine' and *saki* 'cape'. The city has a shrine dedicated to the first emperor of Japan, Jimmu, who is said to have acceded to the throne in 660 BC.

Mizoram, INDIA *Lushai Hills District, Mizo Hills District*
A state created in 1987 and meaning 'Land of the Mizos'. Their name is a local word for 'highlander' with *ram* 'land', thus 'Land of the Hill People'. *Zo* is also said to mean 'wild' or 'independent'.

Mladá Boleslav, CZECH REPUBLIC *Jungbunzlau*
Founded in 995 and named after Boleslav II the Pious (d. 999), Prince of Bohemia (979–99) and son of Boleslav I; thus 'Young Boleslav' from *mladá* 'young'. The German name has the same meaning.

Mmabatho, NORTH WEST/SOUTH AFRICA
Founded in 1977 as the capital of the formerly independent homeland of Bophuthatswana, its name meaning 'Mother of the People'. In 1994 it amalgamated with Mafikeng to become capital of the newly created North-West Province.

Mnichovo Hradiště, CZECH REPUBLIC *Gradišče/Hradiště, Mnichové Hradiště, Mnichovo Hradiště, Munchengratz*
The original name simply meant 'Fortified Settlement', a place where local people could seek protection when danger threatened. In the 12th century Cistercians built a monastery here and the settlement was renamed 'Monks' Fortified Settlement'. In 1869–72, the name was slightly changed to 'Fortified Settlement for a Monk', thus a protected monastery from *mnich* 'monk' with the genitive singular *-ovo* and *hradiště*, itself from *hrad* 'castle' (the fortified residence of a nobleman).

Moab, UTAH/USA
Named after the ancient kingdom in Jordan, itself named after the Moabites who took their name from their leader, Moab, a son of Lot. Their history is not recorded after 582 BC when they were conquered by the Babylonians. The name Moab is said to mean 'Of the Father' from the Hebrew *me* from *min* 'of' and *ab* 'father'.

Mobaye, CENTRAL AFRICAN REPUBLIC
'Place on the River'. It is situated on the Oubangui River.

Mobayi-Mbongo, DEMOCRATIC REPUBLIC OF THE CONGO *Banzyville*
Lying across the river from Mobaye (see previous entry) and to distinguish the two, this town has the added Mbongo derived from the Bongo people who reside in the region. Between 1889, when it was founded, and 1972 the town was known as the 'Town of the Banzys', also people who live in the region.

Mobeetie, TEXAS/USA
'Walnut' from a Comanche word.

Mobile, ALABAMA/USA
Founded in 1702 when a French fort was moved here from further up the Mobile River. The present name is probably a French version of the name of a local Native American tribe, the Mauvillas, which meant 'canoe peddler'; however, it may come from Maubila, the name of an old native town lying on the river and also named after the tribe.

Mobridge, SOUTH DAKOTA/USA
Founded in 1906 on the River Missouri, the name is a combination of 'Mo', an abbreviation for Missouri, and 'bridge'.

Moca, DOMINICAN REPUBLIC
Founded in 1780 with a Native American name for 'partridgewood', the hard-wooded cabbage palm tree, common here.

Moçambique, MOZAMBIQUE
An alternative Portuguese form of *Mozambique, the Portuguese having settled on a hitherto Arab site here in 1507. Until 1897 it was the capital of Portuguese East Africa. The province, previously with this name, is now known as Nampula.

Moccasin, USA
Arizona, California, and Montana have cities with this name, probably from the Algonquian word *mockasin* to describe their footwear, a soft leather shoe, also worn by trappers.

Mocha (al-Mukhā), YEMEN
A seaport whose Arabic name means 'The Place (where the water) is divided (by a dam)'.

According to legend, it was founded in 1418 by Shaikh al-Shādhilī who offered an Indian sea captain some coffee as medicine. It was effective and news of its qualities quickly spread. The port, surrounded by hills on which the coffee beans were grown, became the main centre for Arabia's coffee exports and gave its name to Mocha, a well-known blend of coffee.

Mochudi, BOTSWANA
Founded by the Tswana in 1871 and named after one Motshodi, a prominent figure. His name in Setswana meant 'a person who dishes out food from a pot', a reference to the hospitality customarily shown to visitors.

Modena, ITALY, USA
Italy (Emilia-Romagna): formerly Mutina and Modana. An ancient place said to have a name of Etruscan origin, possibly *mutna* or *mutana* 'tomb' from a pre-Roman root *mut* or *mot* 'hill' or 'raised earth'; thus, a tumulus. It was called this by the Celtic Boii and by the Romans who made it a colony in 183 BC.

Modesto, CALIFORNIA/USA
Founded in 1870 by members of the Central Pacific Railroad and given its name from the Spanish *modesto* 'modest' when one of the directors from San Francisco, W. C. Ralston, modestly refused to have the settlement named after him.

Modigliana, EMILIA-ROMAGNA/ITALY
Probably derived from the Latin (*Castrum*) *Mutilium* 'Broken (Camp)'.

Modimolle, LIMPOPO/SOUTH AFRICA *Nylstroom*
Founded in 1866 and named after the river which was given the Afrikaans name 'Nile Stream' because the first Europeans to see it, a group of Voortrekkers who had fled the Cape, mistook it for the headwaters of the River Nile. A nearby hill shaped like a pyramid was a holy mountain for the indigenous people who called it Modimolle 'Place of Spirits'. This name was adopted for the town in 2002. It is said to come from the Setswana *modimo o lle* 'the forefather's spirit has eaten', a reference to the belief that those lost when climbing the mountain had been killed (eaten) by an ancestral spirit.

Modoc, KANSAS/USA
Named after the Modoc tribe, originally from California and Oregon. Their name can be interpreted as 'Southerners' in relation to their Klamath neighbours who lived to the north.

Moe, VICTORIA/AUSTRALIA
Settled in 1856 with an Aboriginal name for a 'muddy swamp'.

Moffat, CANADA, UK, USA
USA (Colorado): named after David H. Moffat (1839–1911), president of the Denver and Rio Grande Railroad. The Moffat Tunnel was also named after him.

Mogadishu (Muqdisho), SOMALIA
Hammawein, Xamar Weyne, Mogadiscio
Founded by Arabs and Persians in the 10th century, it came under control, first, of the Sultan of Oman by the end of the 17th century and then of the Sultan of Zanzibar in 1871. He leased the port-city to the Italians in 1892 for 25 years, but sold it to them in 1905, hence the Italian name Mogadiscio. From 1892 to 1960 it was the capital of Italian Somaliland and in 1960 it became the capital of independent Somalia. The name comes from the Arabic root *qds* 'holy'.

Mogilëv (Mahilyow), BELARUS
A province and a city with a name from the Russian *mogila* 'grave' and *lev* 'lion'. According to legend, a young peasant was deeply in love with a beautiful girl, but the *pan* 'local squire' refused permission for them to marry. The peasant died but his grave became known as the 'Tomb of the Lion'. It was around this burial mound that a fortress was built in 1267 from which the city developed in the 16th century when the area was part of Lithuania. This became part of Poland and in 1772 of the Russian Empire at the first partition of Poland. Only in 1991 did the city emerge from Russian or Soviet control when Belarus gained independence.

Mogok, BURMA
'Land of Rubies', the area being well known for its deposits of rubies and sapphires.

Mogollon, NEW MEXICO/USA
Named after Don Juan Mogollon, Spanish governor of New Mexico province (1712–15). The Mogollon Mountains in the state are also named after him. His name, unfortunately, means 'sponger' or 'hanger-on' in Spanish.

Mohaka River, NORTH ISLAND/NEW ZEALAND
The name is taken from a Maori term meaning 'Place for Dancing'.

Mohales Hoek, LESOTHO
Named after the half brother of a chief of the Basuto in the 1820s with the Afrikaans *hoek* 'corner', indicating that this corner of territory belonged to Mohale.

Mohammedia, ALGERIA, MOROCCO
1. Algeria: also spelt Mohammadia, its former colonial name being Perrégaux.

2. Morocco: originally Fedala, but renamed in 1959 in honour of Muhammad V (1909–61), Sultan (1927–57) and King (1957–61) of Morocco.

Mohawk, USA
Three cities in Indiana, Michigan, and New York and two rivers in New Hampshire and New York are named after the Mohawk tribe. Their name is said to mean 'eater of raw meat', referring here to bear.

Mojave Desert, SOUTH-WEST USA
Named after the Mojave tribe. Their name is also spelt Mohave.

Mokopane, LIMPOPO/SOUTH AFRICA *Makapan's Poort, Vredenburg, Piet-Potgietersrust, Potgietersrus*
Originally named after the 1850s chief of the Tlou tribe, Makapan, it was renamed Vredenburg 'Town of Peace' following the resolution of disagreements between the Voortrekker leaders, Andries Potgieter and Andries Pretorius. The settlement was named again after Andries Potgieter's son, Piet, who had been killed while fighting Makapan, who had attacked the Boers in 1854. The town thereafter fell into decline until 1870 when it underwent redevelopment and was renamed. The suffix *-rus* from the Afrikaans *rust* 'rest' indicates that this was the place where Piet Potgieter was buried. The final *-t* was dropped in 1939. The name Makapan with a different spelling was adopted in 2002. The name is said to mean 'Togetherness'.

Mokp'o, SOUTH KOREA
A port-city with a name meaning 'Forest Harbour' from *mok* 'forest' and *p'o* 'harbour'.

Mold (Yr Wyddgrug), WALES/UK *De Monte alto, Montem Altum, Moald, Flintshire*
The Welsh name means 'The Burial Mound'. The town developed from a Norman castle and derives its present name from the Old French *mont-hault* 'high hill', Bailey Hill, on which the castle was built.

Moldavia (Moldova), ROMANIA
A historic region that was once part of the Roman province of Dacia. It was subsequently ruled by a succession of invaders before falling under Ottoman Turkish rule in 1504. In 1775 its north-western territory, Bukovina, was ceded to Austria and the Russians took Bessarabia in 1812. In 1859 what remained of Moldavia, the part west of the River Prut, joined with Wallachia to form Romania. That part between the Prut and Dniester Rivers (Bessarabia) was ceded to the Soviet Union in 1940. The present Moldavia is a region in north-east Romania, called Moldova in Romanian. Indeed, the Moldovans and Romanians have always spoken of Moldova while until 1991 the rest of the world used the Latin and Russian name Moldavia. *See* MOLDOVA.

Moldova *Bogdania/Bogdan-îli, Bessarabia, Moldavia*
The Republic of Moldova (Republica Moldova) since 1991. Historically, it is part of the much larger Moldavia, a vassal state of the Ottoman Empire between the early 16th and 19th centuries. Previously the Moldavian Soviet Socialist Republic within the Soviet Union when the republic was formed in 1940 from Bessarabia and the Moldavian Autonomous Soviet Socialist Republic. This latter republic had been created in 1924 on the left (east) bank of the River Dniester within Soviet Ukraine—*Transdniestria—by the Soviet Union which refused to recognize Romania's right to Bessarabia which, as the Bessarabian Democratic Moldovan Republic from 1918, had joined Romania. Bessarabia, approximately half of the historic Romanian principality of Moldavia, was ceded to Russia by the Ottoman Turks in 1812; that part west of the River Prut remained subject to Ottoman rule (and joined Wallachia in 1859 to form Romania). According to legend, the present name is ultimately derived from the favourite hunting hound, Molda, of Bogdan Dragos, a Transylvanian (Vlach) prince. While out hunting with her master, Molda was drowned and Bogdan named the river Molda in 1359. In time this became the River Moldovo, the people living by it Moldavians and the principality Moldavia. However, it has been suggested that the name may come from the Romanian *molid* 'spruce fir'. Originally, when this region between the Carpathian Mountains and the River Dniester was founded as an independent principality in 1359, it was given the Turkish name Bogdan-ili 'Land of Bogdan' after Prince Bogdan. To justify the creation of a Moldavian Republic Joseph Stalin[†] had to create a 'Moldavian' nation which was quite distinct from both Ukraine and Romania; he adopted the name 'Moldavian' to describe the language, whose Latin alphabet he replaced with Cyrillic, and the nationality of the ethnic Romanians in Bessarabia, which he claimed were different from those of the ethnic Romanians in Romania. In fact, there is no significant difference in language, religion, culture, and traditions between the peoples of Moldova and Romania.

Molenbeek-Saint-Jean, BELGIUM
Now a suburb of Brussels, it originated as a village overlooking a stream; thus the name 'Mill Stream' from the Flemish *molenbeek*. The

additional Saint-Jean signifies that its church is dedicated to St John.

Môle Saint-Nicolas, HAITI
Named by Christopher Columbus[†] because he landed here in 1492 on the feast day, 6 December, of St Nicholas.

Moline, USA
Cities in Illinois, Kansas, and Ohio have this name from the Spanish *molino* 'mill'.

Molise, ITALY
A region whose name may come from the Latin *mola* 'mill stone' with the suffix *ensis*. However, it may be derived from the family name of a Norman count whose name is associated with Moulins-la-Marche in Lower Normandy, France.

Molochnaya, UKRAINE
A river whose name means 'milky' from the Russian *molochnaya*, a reference to the somewhat chalky appearance of its water.

Molodogvardeyskoye, KAZAKHSTAN
'(Town) of the Young Guards' from the Russian *molodaya* 'young' and *gvardiya* 'guard'; it was a branch of the Komsomol 'Young Communist League'. There is a town called Mologvardeysk with the same meaning in Ukraine honouring the Young Guard of the Krasnodon area.

Molteno, EASTERN CAPE/SOUTH AFRICA
Founded in 1873 and named after Sir John Molteno (1814–86), first prime minister of Cape Colony (1872–8).

Moluccas (Maluku), INDONESIA *Jazīrat-al-Muluk, Maluco*
An island province. The present name is a modification of the original name meaning 'Land of Many Kings' from *Jazīratul jabal maluk*, a reference to the fact that many early accounts mention that each island had its own king. Since earliest times the islands were known as the Spice Islands because of their nutmeg, cloves, and mace. The trade in spices was highly competitive (because Europeans did not believe they could be grown anywhere else) and so did much to encourage exploration of the Far East. The Portuguese were the first to arrive in 1511 and they were followed by the Dutch in 1599; they took control in 1610 and their sovereignty was recognized in 1667. Incorporated into the Muslim Republic of Indonesia in 1949, the predominantly Christian Moluccans proclaimed an independent Republic of South Moluccas (Republik Maluku Selatan) in 1950. This was quickly suppressed, but dreams of an independent 'South Moluccas' have never died.

Mombasa, KENYA *Toníka, Mvita*
Founded by Arabs in the 11th century on an island, its name comes from a town in Oman from the Arabic *mumbaşa*, whose meaning is unknown. Its old Swahili name, Mvita, may come from *fita* 'hidden', either because the island is hidden deep in an inlet almost completely surrounded by land or because the islanders were particularly good at hiding themselves when being raided. It was capital of the British East Africa Protectorate in 1895–1907.

Mon, BURMA
A state, river, and a town named after the Mon people. They established a kingdom which flourished in the 9th–11th, 13th–16th, and 18th centuries.

Monaco The Principality of Monaco (Principauté de Monaco), a sovereign hereditary state within French territory. The name may be derived from a Phoenician word signifying a place to rest. However, it may come from the Ligurian *monegu* 'rock'; a person from Monaco is called a Monegasque. Held by the Genoese in 1191–1297 and ruled by the Grimaldi family since 1297, it was annexed to France between 1793 and 1814 and was a Sardinian protectorate in 1815–61. Its present borders were drawn in 1848 when Menton and Roquebrune were lost to France, thus reducing the principality's size to 0.73 sq. mile (1.9 sq. km). A Franco-Monegasque treaty in 1861 confirmed the loss, but restored Monaco's independence.

Monaghan (Muineachán), IRELAND
A county which belonged to the historic province of Ulster. The name means 'Place of Thickets' from *muine* 'thicket'.

Monashee Mountains, BRITISH COLUMBIA/CANADA *Gold Range*
Originally named as a result of the gold found in the region, the name was later changed to Monashee 'Mountain of Peace' from the Gaelic *monadh* 'mountain' and *sith* 'peace' by a Scottish prospector, David McIntyre.

Monastir (al-Munastīr), TUNISIA *Rous, Ruspina*
Founded by the Phoenicians as Rous, it was renamed Ruspina by the Romans in 146 BC. A *ribat* 'fortified monastery' was built in the 8th century and it may be this, from the Latin *monasterium*, which is the origin of the present name.

Moncalieri, PIEDMONT/ITALY
A combination of a Roman personal name, Calerius, and *monte* 'mountain'. The town sits atop a hill.

Monchegorsk, MURMANSK/RUSSIA *Moncha-Guba*
Named after the Monchetundra mountains and *guba* 'inlet', but now with the familiar *gorsk*. The town lies on Lake Imandra.

Mönchengladbach, NORTH RHINE-WESTPHALIA/GERMANY *Münchengladbach*
Developed around a 10th-century Benedictine monastery, the name means 'Monks' Tranquil Stream' from *Mönch* 'monk', *Bach* 'stream', and the Old German equivalent of *glatt* 'smooth' and here meaning 'tranquil'. The spelling was changed in 1950.

Moncton, NEW BRUNSWICK/CANADA *The Bend, Monckton*
Located on a bend of the Petitcodiac River, it acquired its original name some time in the 18th century. In 1855 it was renamed after Lieutenant Colonel (later General Sir) Robert Monckton (1726–82), the British commander who captured the nearby Fort Beauséjour from the French in 1755. The *k* in the name was removed in 1860.

Mondamin, IOWA/USA
A Native American word for 'corn'.

Mondovì, ITALY, USA
Italy (Piedmont): originally Castrum Vici, although officially Mons Reglis. Founded in 1198 by settlers from Vicoforte. The first component of the official name, *Mons*, was later combined with *Vicus* to give Mons de Vicis; this evolved into Montem de Vico, Monte de Vi, Mundui, and finally Mondovi. The name thus means 'Mountain of the Vici'.

Monee, ILLINOIS/USA
Named after the wife of a Native American trader, Joseph Bailes, Monee being a native corruption of Mary.

Monemvasía, GREECE *Minoa*
The name comes from the fact that the town is situated at the foot of a rock that is joined to the mainland by a causeway: thus, 'Town with only one Entrance' from *moni embasis*. Known to the English as Malmsey, it has given its name to a strong, sweet wine originally from this part of the Peloponnese.

Monfalcone, FRIULI-VENEZIA-GIULIA/ITALY
'Mount Falcon' from *monte* 'mountain' and *falcone* 'falcon'.

Mongolia *Outer Mongolia*
Mongolia (Mongol Uls) since 1992. Previously the Mongolian People's Republic (1924–92); Outer Mongolia from the 17th century. During the 17th century the Chinese divided Mongolia into northern Outer Mongolia, (also known as Khalkha) and southern Inner Mongolia; and in 1691 Outer Mongolia accepted Manchu rule. It was no more than a frontier province of the Manchu Empire, guarding the border with Russia. The fall of the Manchu (Qing) dynasty in China in 1911 enabled Outer Mongolia to declare itself an independent monarchy with the throne being offered to the Living Buddha. The next year it became a Russian protectorate, but in 1915 an autonomous Mongolia was placed under Chinese suzerainty. In 1919 its autonomy was revoked and Mongolia was incorporated into the Republic of China. A successful revolt against the Chinese led to independence being proclaimed in 1921 (although not recognized by China until 1946) and the formation of a People's Republic in 1924 when the Living Buddha died. The country is named after the Mongols who took their name from *mong* 'brave' or 'undefeated'. In the 13th century Genghis Khan and his successors created a great empire (known officially as Yeke Mongol Uls 'The Great Mongol State') which extended over much of China, Central Asia, and Russia. Although now accepted as being offensive, the word 'mongol' used to be applied to people suffering from Down's syndrome.

Monmouth, UK, USA
1. UK (Wales): formerly Munwi Mutha and Monemude. In Welsh the name is Trefynwy 'Homestead on the Mynwy'. The name comes from the Monnow (Mynwy) River to mean 'Mouth of the Monnow'; the river's name may mean 'swift flowing'.
2. USA (Illinois): founded in 1831 and named after the battle fought at Monmouth in New Jersey in 1778. The Monmouth in New Jersey was named after the former county of Monmouthshire in Wales.

Monongahela, PENNSYLVANIA/USA
A city named after the Monongahela River, which is formed by the merging of the Tygart and West Fork Rivers in West Virginia, and which flows northward into Pennsylvania. The name comes from the Delaware *menaungehilla* 'river with banks that slide (into the water)'.

Monreale, SICILY/ITALY
'Royal Mountain' from *monte* and *regale* 'royal'. It was founded in the 12th century by William II the Good (1154–89), King of Sicily (1171–89), on the slopes of Mount Caputo.

Monroe, USA
1. Sixteen cities have this name, most to honour James Monroe (1758–1831), fifth President of the USA (1817–25). Two more are called Monroe City.

2. Louisiana: founded in 1785 as Fort Miro, it was renamed in 1819 after the first steamboat, the *James Monroe*, to progress along the Ouachita River.
3. Michigan: founded by the French as Frenchtown in the 1780s, it was renamed in 1817 after President James Monroe.

Monroeville, PENNSYLVANIA/USA *Patton Township*
Renamed in 1951 after Joel Monroe, who had become its first postmaster in 1851.

Monrovia, LIBERIA, USA
Liberia: founded in 1822 by the American Colonization Society (ACS), a charity which helped slaves freed in North America to return to Africa (*see* LIBERIA). Laid out on land bought from a local chief by a young Methodist clergyman, Jehudi Ashmun, he called it Christopolis 'City of Christ', but in 1824 the ACS recommended that it should be renamed Monrovia in honour of James Monroe (1758–1831), President of the USA (1817–25). It is the capital of Liberia.

Mons (Flemish: **Bergen**), BELGIUM *Castri Locus*
'Mountain' from the Latin *mons*. The Flemish Bergen means the same. Founded as a Roman camp on a mound between two rivers, the name is somewhat inappropriate.

Monson, MASSACHUSETTS/USA
Named in the 18th century after Sir John Monson (1693–1748), president of the Board of Trade and a friend of the then governor of Massachusetts.

Montagu, WESTERN CAPE/SOUTH AFRICA
Founded in 1851 and named after John Montagu (1797–1853), colonial secretary of Cape Province (1843–53).

Montana, BULGARIA, USA
1. Bulgaria: originally a Roman settlement called Montanensia from which the present name comes, it subsequently became Golyama Kutlovitsa 'Great Hollow' from the feminine form of *golyam* 'great' and *kutlovitsa* 'hollow' or 'cavity'. Between 1891 and 1945 it was called Ferdinand after Tsar Ferdinand I (1861–1948), a German prince who was chosen as Prince of Bulgaria in 1887 and the first king of modern Bulgaria (1908–18). He was forced to abdicate in 1918 following Bulgaria's defeat in the First World War. With Soviet troops in the country at the end of the Second World War and growing Communist influence, this name was superseded by Mikhaylovgrad in honour of Khristo Mikhaylov (1893–1944), the leader of a failed uprising in 1923 against the right-wing regime; he became a senior communist official.

2. USA: a state, and a city in Alaska. The state's name comes from the Spanish *montaña*, ultimately from *mons*, a reference to the Rocky Mountains in the western part of the state. The eastern part of Montana was acquired by the USA as a result of the Louisiana Purchase in 1803. After the discovery of gold Montana Territory was established in 1864 and in 1889 it joined the Union as the 41st state.

Montargis, CENTRE/FRANCE
'Hill of Argio' from *mons* and a Gaulish personal name, Argio.

Montauban, MIDI-PYRÉNÉES/FRANCE *Mons Albanus*
Derived from the Latin name meaning 'White Hill' from *mons* and *albus* 'white'.

Mont Blanc, FRANCE-ITALY-SWITZERLAND
'White Mountain' from the French *mont* and *blanc* 'white', a reference to its glacier coverage.

Montclair, NEW JERSEY/USA
Settled in 1666 as part of Newark, it became a township in its own right in 1868 and was given a name meaning 'Clear Mountain (View)'.

Montebello, CANADA, COLOMBIA, USA
USA (California): 'Beautiful Mountain' from the Spanish *monte* and *bello*.

Monte Carlo, ARGENTINA, MONACO
Monaco: 'Charles's Mountain' founded in 1866 by, and named after, Charles III (1818–89), Prince of Monaco (1856–89). The resort town is located on an escarpment at the foot of the Maritime Alps.

Montecatini Terme, TUSCANY/ITALY
Known for its *terme* 'hot springs', *catini* may come from a personal Latin name, Catinius, or, more probably, from the Italian *catino* 'basin' in the sense of a low hollow. *Monte* is quite inappropriate since the town lies at less than 100ft (30m) above sea level.

Montecristi, DOMINICAN REPUBLIC
A province and a city whose full name is San Fernando de Montecristi. Founded in 1506 and deliberately destroyed in 1606 because of its illegal trade with pirates, it was rebuilt in 1756 and called 'Christ's Mountain' from the Spanish *Cristo* 'Christ'.

Montego Bay, JAMAICA *Bahía de Manteca*
Derived from the former Spanish name which meant 'Butter Bay'; it was a lard—'hog's butter'—centre.

Montélimar, RHÔNES-ALPES/FRANCE *Acunum, Mons Adhemaris/Monteil d'Adhémar*
'Adhémar's Mount', named in medieval times after the local Adhémar family.

Montenegro, BRAZIL, CHILE, SERBIA AND MONTENEGRO
Serbia and Montenegro: in Serbo-Croat Crna Gora. A constituent republic of Serbia and Montenegro and until early 2003 of Yugoslavia. Part of the Roman province of Illyria, it was settled by Serbs in the 7th century. In the early Middle Ages it was known as Dukjla from the Roman city of Dioclea near Podgorica; it stretched from the Gulf of Kotor to Lake Scutari (now in Albania). In due course it became the independent province of Zeta. It was absorbed into the Serbian Empire in the 12th century, but when this disintegrated in 1355 the separate entity to be known as Montenegro emerged as an independent principality. Despite five centuries of conflict with the Ottoman Turks it never succumbed to them as did the Serbs after 1389. The principality's size was doubled at the Congress of Berlin in 1878 when its independence was reaffirmed. Proclaimed a kingdom in 1910, it was once again absorbed into Serbia in the new Kingdom of the Serbs, Croats, and Slovenes—with no mention of the Montenegrins—in 1918. However, Montenegro became a separate, nominally autonomous, republic of Yugoslavia on a par with Serbia in 1946. The name came into general use early in the 15th century and means 'Black Mountain', as does the local name from the Serbo-Croat *crn* 'black' and *gora*. This is said to be a reference to the dark appearance of Mt Lovćen at various times of the year and the surrounding heavily wooded areas. Montenegro is the Venetian form of the Italian *Monte Nero*. The Montenegrins are Serbs, although efforts to establish a separate national identity are being made.

Monterey, CALIFORNIA/USA
Named after the bay which was first explored by Sebastián Vizcaíno in 1602. He named the bay in honour of the Viceroy of New Spain (Mexico), Don Gaspar de Zúñiga y Acevedo (1540–1606), Conde de Monte Rey. The city was founded in 1770 and was taken by the USA in 1846.

Montería, COLOMBIA *San Jerónimo de Buenavista, San Jerónimo de Montería*
Taken from the Zenué people by the Spanish, who renamed it in 1744. A place where hunters gathered, it soon came to be known by the Spanish word for 'hunting' *montería*.

Monte Rosa, ITALY-SWITZERLAND
A mountain range. A local Italian word *roëse* 'glacier' has become *rosa* 'rose'; thus, now, 'Mount Rose'.

Monterrey, NEW LEÓN/MEXICO *Ciudad Metropolitana de Nuestra Señora de Monterrey*
Founded in 1577 but only settled succesfully in 1596. It was named after Don Gaspar de Zúñiga y Acevedo (*see* MONTEREY).

Monte Sant'Angelo, APULIA/ITALY
The city was built round the Sanctuary of St Michael which was established *c.*490 over a cave in which the Archangel Michael is said to have appeared to the Archbishop of Sipontum.

Montevideo, URUGUAY, USA
1. Uruguay: although the Portuguese fortified a hill on the site of the present city in 1717, they were driven out by the Spanish in 1724. The Spanish city was founded two years later as San Felipe de Montevideo by Bruno Mauricio de Zabala, Spanish governor of Buenos Aires, Argentina, to deter the Portuguese from advancing southwards from Brazil. The precise explanation for the name is not known, although there are plenty of theories all including *monte*, the Spanish for 'mountain' or 'hill'. This presumably refers to the Cerro de Montevideo 'Hill of Montevideo' on the west side of the bay. No theory is particularly convincing. *Video* has been suggested as meaning 'I see' from the Latin, or *vidi eo* 'It was I who saw' ascribed to the Portuguese explorer Ferdinand Magellan[†] who entered the estuary of the Río de la Plata at the end of 1519, or *vi eu* 'I saw (a hill)' uttered by a Spanish sailor as the ship approached the coast, or *VI de O*, an annotation on a Portuguese chart meaning 'sixth mountain from the west'. A department and city-port, it became the country's capital in 1828.
2. USA (Minnesota): settled in 1867 and named by Cornelius J. Nelson in 1870 'From the Mountain I see'; also said to mean 'I see the Mountain'.

Montezuma, NEW MEXICO/USA
Named after Montezuma II (1466–c.1520), ninth Aztec Emperor of Mexico (1502–c.1520), who was taken prisoner by Hernán Cortés[†].

Montgomery, UK, USA
1. UK (Wales): the Welsh name is Trefaldwyn 'Homestead of Baldwin', a Norman knight who recaptured the castle from the Welsh, from *tref* 'homestead'. The English name honours a Norman, Roger de Montgomery (d. 1093?), who fought against the English at the Battle of Hastings in 1066 and was rewarded with the title of Earl of Chichester and Arundel in 1067; in 1071 he was given the more important earldom of Shrewsbury close to the Welsh border. He built a castle here in the 11th century by which a village developed. The

present town dates from *c*.1223 when Henry III
(1207–72), King of England (1216–72), built a,
now-ruined, castle about a mile (1.5 km) from
the site of the Norman castle. In 1974 the
former county of Montgomeryshire was
subsumed into the new county of Powys.
2. USA (Alabama): founded in 1819 and named
after the Irish-born General Richard
Montgomery (1738–75), a commander during
the American War of Independence (1775–83)
who was killed in 1775 leading an
unsuccessful American assault on Quebec.
Twelve other states have cities with this name,
many in tribute to him.

Montluçon, AUVERGNE/FRANCE
Derived from the Latin *mons* and the Roman
personal name Luccius.

Montpelier, JAMAICA, USA
USA (Vermont): named after the Montpellier in
France.

Montpellier, LANGUEDOC-ROUSSILLON/FRANCE
Clapas, Mons Pislerius
Evolved from its Medieval Latin name from
mons and *pestellus* from *pastellus* 'woad' used for
dyeing. The reference to 'mount' or
'mountain' in the name is quite inappropriate.
The original name meant 'Little Pile of Stones'.

Montreal, CANADA, FRANCE, USA
Canada (Quebec): takes its name from a
mountain which was named *Mont Réal* 'Royal
Mount' in honour of Francis I (1494–1547),
King of France (1515–47), by Jacques Cartier[†]
when he visited the Huron on their island
(now Île de Montréal 'Montreal Island') in the
St Lawrence River here in 1535. By the end of
the century Hochelaga, the Huron name for
the place, had been abandoned and replaced
by a new settlement which was named Place
Royale by Samuel de Champlain[†]. The modern
city was founded in 1642 as a religious colony
by the French, who called the site Ville-Marie
de Montréal 'Mary's Town of Royal Mount' in
honour of the Virgin Mary; this was shortened
to Montreal in 1724. In 1760 the city
surrendered to the British and became part of
British North America in 1763.

Montreuil, FRANCE
Île-de-France: to differentiate it from other
towns with this name, the full name is
Montreuil-sous-Bois 'Montreuil-by-the-Wood'.
Montreuil itself comes from the Latin
monasteriolum 'little monastery'.

Montreux, SWITZERLAND
The town developed opposite an island
monastery in the 9th century and takes its
name from the Latin *monasterium* 'monastery'.

Montrose, CANADA, UK, USA
1. UK (Scotland): formerly Munros 'Moor of
the Promontory' from the Gaelic *moine* 'moor'
and *ros* 'promontory'.
2. USA (Colorado): named in 1881 after Sir
Walter Scott's novel *The Legend of Montrose*
published in 1819.

Montrouge, PARIS/FRANCE *Mons Rubicus, Le
Grand-Montrouge*
'Red Mountain' after the colour of the local
soil.

Montserrado, LIBERIA
A county that takes its name from Cape
Mesurado, itself a corruption of Montserado
'Jagged Mountain'.

Montserrat, SPAIN, WEST INDIES
1. Spain (Catalonia): a mountain called by the
Romans Mons Serratus 'Saw-tooth Mountain'
from the Latin *mons* and *serratus* 'serrated', a
reference to its jagged peaks. By the Catalans it
is known as Montsagrat 'Sacred Mountain'.
2. West Indies: an island, an Overseas
Territory of the UK since 1956, having been
part of the British federal colony of the
Leeward Islands in 1871–1956. Inhabited by
the Carib who called it Alliouagana 'Land of
the Prickly Bush', it was discovered by
Christopher Columbus[†] in 1493 and colonized
in 1632 by Irish Catholic settlers fleeing
religious persecution in Virginia, USA. It was
renamed Santa María de Montserrate by
Columbus because the terrain seemed to him
to resemble that around the Benedictine
monastery of that name near Barcelona, Spain;
the monastery was named after the mountain
on which it is situated (see 1).

Monza, LOMBARDY/ITALY *Modicia*
The former Latin name was probably a
personal one which slowly evolved through
Modicia to Mocia to Monza.

Moodus, CONNECTICUT/USA
'Place of Noises' from a contraction of a Native
American word *machemoodus*.

Moorhead, MINNESOTA/USA
Founded in 1871 as Burbank, it was renamed
after William G. Moorhead, a director of the
northern Pacific Railway.

Moorreesburg, WESTERN CAPE/SOUTH AFRICA
Founded in 1879 and named after J. C. le Febre
Moorrees, minister of the Swartland
congregation (1833–81).

Moose Jaw, SASKATCHEWAN/CANADA
The city is named after the Moose Jaw River
and was founded in 1882. The name probably
comes from *moosgaw*, a word for the warm
breezes here; when pronounced in English the

word sounded like Moose Jaw. It is unlikely that the name has anything to do with the shape of the jawbone of a moose.

Mopti, MALI
Lying on three islands at the confluence of the Niger and Bani Rivers, the name means 'Little Contact' from the Mande *mi* 'contact' and *piti* 'little' or 'unimportant'. Originally a small fishing village, it was usually no more than a brief halt for those travelling along the rivers.

Morādābād, UTTAR PRADESH/INDIA
Founded in 1625 by the Mughal general, Rustam Khan. He named it after Prince Murad Baksh.

Morava, CZECH REPUBLIC, SERBIA AND MONTENEGRO
Two rivers deriving their name from the Germanic *mar* 'marsh' and *ahwa* 'water' or, alternatively, from the German *mark* 'march'.

Moravia (Morava), CZECH REPUBLIC
A region which takes its name from the *Morava River. It was the centre of what was the medieval Kingdom of Greater Moravia and was incorporated into the Kingdom of Bohemia in 1029. It became an Austrian crownland in 1848 and a province of Czechoslovakia in 1918. It was annexed, together with Bohemia, by Nazi Germany in 1939–45 to form the Protectorate of Bohemia and Moravia.

Moray, SCOTLAND/UK *Moreb, Morauia, Murewe*
A unitary district and former county called Elginshire. A larger area called Moray was one of the seven ancient provinces of Scotland; it ceased to exist in the 12th century. The name means 'Sea Settlement' from Old Celtic words associated with modern Welsh *môr* 'sea' and *tref* 'town'. It gives its name to the Moray Firth, an inlet of the North Sea.

Morbihan, BRITTANY/FRANCE
'Little Sea' from the Breton *mor* 'sea' and *bihan* 'little'. A department, it takes its name from Morbihan Gulf.

Mordovia (Mordoviya), RUSSIA
A republic, also known as Mordvinia, and named after the Mordvin, a Finno-Ugric people.

Morecambe, ENGLAND/UK
Morikambe was first noted in a work by Ptolemy[†] *c.*150 probably from the Celtic *mori* 'sea' and *cambi* 'curved', thus 'Curved Inlet'. It did not survive. However, in the 18th century a local historian believed the name referred to the Lune estuary and suggested that the bay be called Morecambe Bay. The bay gave its name to the town which was developed as a holiday resort in the 19th century. Thus Morecambe is a modern rendering of the old Celtic name.

Moree, NEW SOUTH WALES/AUSTRALIA
Established as a livestock station in 1848, it subsequently grew into a town. Its name comes from an Aboriginal word which could mean either 'Rising Sun', 'Long Spring', or 'Water Hole'.

Morehead City, NORTH CAROLINA/USA
Shepherd's Point
Renamed in 1853 after John M. Morehead, governor of North Carolina (1841–5), who had bought land here because he believed it could be developed into a thriving Atlantic port.

Morelia, MICHOACÁN/MEXICO *Valladolid*
Founded in 1541 on the site of a Tarascan settlement and renamed in 1828 after a revolutionary priest, José María Morelos y Pavón (1765–1815). He assumed the leadership of the Mexican movement to overthrow Spanish rule after Miguel Hidalgo y Costilla, the first leader, had been captured and executed in 1811. Morelos was born here in 1765; he was captured and executed in 1815. It was previously Valladolid, named after the birthplace in Spain of Antonio de Mendoza (*c.*1490–1552), New Spain's (Mexico) first viceroy (1535–50).

Morelos, MEXICO
A state and four cities, all named after José María Morelos y Pavón (*see* MORELIA).

Moreno, ARGENTINA
Founded in 1860 and named after Mariano Moreno (1778–1811), a leader of the movement to win independence from Spain, although he died four years before it was achieved.

Moresby Island, BRITISH COLUMBIA/CANADA
Named after the British Rear Admiral (later Admiral of the Fleet) Sir Fairfax Moresby (1786–1877), who was commander-in-chief of the Pacific Station (1850–3).

Morgan City, LOUISIANA/USA *Brashear City*
Founded in 1850 and named Brashear City ten years later, it was renamed in 1876 after Charles Morgan, president of the New Orleans, Opelousas, and Great Western Railroad.

Morganton, NORTH CAROLINA/USA
Named after General Daniel Morgan, an officer who fought in the American War of Independence (1775–83).

Morgantown, WEST VIRGINIA/USA
The first community was destroyed by Native Americans in 1758, but in 1766 General

Zackquill Morgan founded a new settlement which was named after him.

Morocco, AND INDIANA/USA
The Kingdom of Morocco (al-Mamlakah al-Maghribīyah 'Kingdom of the West') since 1957 when Muhammad V (1909–61), Sultan (1927–57) and King of Morooco (1957–61), adopted the title of king because he thought it more modern. Independence from France and Spain was gained in 1956. Previously the country was a sultanate and known historically as the Sharifian Empire from the Arabic *sharif* 'noble' when the Sa'dī Sultan Ahmad I al-Manşūr (1549–1603) 'Ahmad I the Victorious' founded the Sharifian dynasty in 1578 and unified Morocco as a political entity. In 1912–56 the country was divided into a French protectorate, a Spanish protectorate (in the northern coastal zone and the Rif and Tarfaya in the south), and the international zone of Tangier. The Sultan continued to reign, but he did not rule. In 1958 Tarfaya, the northern strip of Spanish Sahara, was ceded to Morocco and in 1969 it regained the former Spanish province of Ifni lost in 1860. Within Morocco are the Spanish exclaves of Ceuta and Melilla. The English name is derived from *marrūkus*, the old Arabic version of *Marrakech, the former capital. The Arabic name of the country comes from *maghrib* 'place of the sunset' or 'west', it being on the west coast of Africa. To Muslims the country was long known as al-Maghrib al-Aqsā 'Land of the Furthest West' because it was believed to be on the edge of the world. During Roman times northern Morocco was part of a Berber kingdom called Mauretania Tingitana. The country gives its name to the flexible leather, originally made here, often used in bookbinding and shoemaking.

Morombé, MADAGASCAR
'Big Shore'.

Morón, ARGENTINA, CUBA, VENEZUELA
Argentina: takes its name from the Spanish city of *Morón de la Frontera. In 1930–43 it was called Seis de Septiembre 'Sixth of September' in memory of a military uprising that took place in 1930.

Mörön, MONGOLIA
'River'; it is located just north of the Delger River.

Morondava, MADAGASCAR
'(Place which has a) Long Sandbank'.

Morón de la Frontera, ANDALUSIA/SPAIN
Arunci
Sited by the Phoenicians and settled by the Romans who called it Arunci. With the arrival

of the Moors it was renamed from the Hebrew *moram* 'elevated site', a reference to its position near the foothills of the Penibético Mountain Range and the Spanish *frontera* 'frontier', a location on the edge of the Muslim Kingdom of Granada.

Morpeth, CANADA, UK
UK (England): formerly Morthpath 'Path where a Murder took place' from the Old English *pæth* 'path' and *morth* 'murder'.

Morphou (Turkish: **Güzelyurt**), CYPRUS
Named after Aphrodite, who was also known as Theamorfo 'looking like a goddess'. The Turkish name means 'Beautiful Home' from *güzel* 'beautiful' or 'pretty' and *yurt* 'home' or 'homeland'.

Morristown, USA
1. New Jersey: founded in 1710 as West Hanover, it was renamed in 1740 after Lewis Morris, governor of the colony.
2. Tennessee: settled in 1787 and named after Gideon Morris who was a prominent local citizen.

Moscow, RUSSIA, USA
Russia: Russian Moskva. A province and federal city mentioned for the first time as a small settlement in a chronicle dating from 1147. A few years later Muscovy was fortified by its founder, Grand Prince Yury Dolgoruky (1090–1157). The city is probably named after the Moscow River whose name is thought to come from a Finno-Ugrian word *moskva* from *mosk* or *mask* 'damp' or 'marshy'. There are several other theories, but all are related to 'water' in one way or another. It became the chief city of the Principality of *Muscovy in the 13th century, capital of Russia *c*.1478–1712 and from 1991, and of the Soviet Union 1918–91; the capital was moved from St Petersburg in 1918 because Moscow was less vulnerable to the White Russian armies opposing the Bolshevik regime. In 1937 a proposal, said to have been made by Nikolay Yezhov (1895–1940), head of the NKVD (1936–8), to curry favour with Joseph Stalin[†], to rename the city Stalinodar 'Stalin's Gift' as a 'gesture of gratitude from the people' was rejected by Stalin, who was well aware of Moscow's unique role in the history of the Russian state. Lazar Kaganovich (1893–1991), Stalin's deputy in the early 1930s and a member of the Politburo, made the same suggestion following victory in the Second World War in 1945, but again Stalin refused.

Moselle, FRANCE, GERMANY
1. France (Lorraine): a department named
after the Moselle River which flows through
it. The river's name means 'Little Meuse'
from the Latin Mosella, a diminutive of
Mosa, the Roman name for the River *Meuse.
2. Germany: the River Moselle, when
flowing through Germany, is known as
the Mosel.

Mosonmagyaróvár, HUNGARY *Wieselburg*
'Magyar Fortress on the (River) Moson' from
vár.

Mosquito Coast (Costa de Mosquitos),
HONDURAS-NICARAGUA
Also spelt Miskito. A region along the
Caribbean coast and probably named after the
Miskito people; the spelling was then
corrupted by European visitors to that of the
insect prevalent here. It is less likely that
Europeans named the coast and the
indigenous people living along it after the
insect.

Mossel Bay (Mosselbaai), WESTERN CAPE/
SOUTH AFRICA *Aliwal South*
Takes its name from the bay here which was
given its name in 1601 because of its abundant
mussel shells. The bay had formerly been
known as Angra dos Vaqueiros 'Bay of
Cowherds' because of the cattle seen by
Bartholomew Dias (*c*.1450–1500), the
Portuguese navigator, when he landed here in
1488; when Vasco da Gama (*c*.1460–1524),
another Portuguese navigator, arrived in 1497
he renamed it 'St Bras's Bay'. The town itself
was founded in 1848 and named Aliwal South
to commemorate the victory of Lieutenant
General Sir Harry Smith (1787–1860), governor
of Cape Colony (1847–52), at Aliwal in India.
This name did not find favour with the
inhabitants for long and the town was
renamed after the bay. *See* ALIWAL NORTH.

Most, BULGARIA, CZECH REPUBLIC
Czech Republic: both the former German
name, Brüx, and the present Czech one mean
'Bridge', a reference to an old bridge crossing a
marsh nearby. The Bulgarian name also means
'Bridge'.

Mostar, BOSNIA AND HERZEGOVINA *Narona,
Andetrium, Mosdar, Köprülü Hisār*
The Serbo-Croat *Stari Most* means 'Old Bridge'
and the town was at times simply called Most
'(Place of) the Bridge'. However, Mostar is
probably derived from *mostari* 'keepers of the
bridge'. The earliest mention of the name is in
1468, although the stone bridge itself was only
built in 1566 by the Ottoman Turks in honour
of Suleiman the Magnificent (*c*.1495–1566), the

Ottoman Sultan (1520–66), to replace a
wooden suspension bridge over the Neretva
River. The stone bridge was destroyed by
Croatian shelling in 1993, but rebuilt and
reopened in 2004. The town is the capital of
Herzegovina.

Mosul (al-Mawṣil), IRAQ
Lying on the Tigris River, the name comes
from the Arabic *waṣala* 'to join' or 'to connect',
a reference perhaps to the fact that it provided
a link between Persia and Syria and Anatolia.
The capital of an Ottoman province, it was
subject to Ottoman rule in 1534–1918, after
which it was occupied by the British. Its fate
was not settled until the League of Nations
awarded it to Iraq in 1925. It gives its name to
muslin, a fine cotton fabric.

Mother Lode, CALIFORNIA/USA
Originating during the gold rush from 1848,
the name comes from the idea of a main vein
of metal ore with secondary veins.

Motherwell, SCOTLAND/UK *Matervelle,
Moydirwal*
The name probably carries the meaning of a
well dedicated to the Mother of God from the
Middle English *moder* 'mother' and *wella*.

Moulay Idriss, MOROCCO
'My Lord Idris'. *Moulay* was an honorific title
meaning 'My Lord' borne by the Moroccan
sultans from certain dynasties. In English it is
usually rendered as 'mullah' from the Arabic
mawlā 'master', a title given to a Muslim well
versed in Islamic theology. The village here is a
national pilgrimage site, built round the tomb
of Moulay Idriss I the Great, the holy founder
of the first native Islamic Kingdom of Morocco
and a descendant of the Prophet Muhammad[†].
Idriss had fled Arabia to Morocco in 786,
arriving at Walīla (now known as the Roman
ruins of Volubilis) in 788. He reigned for only
two years (789–91); he was assassinated in 791
on the orders of the ʿAbbāsid caliph.

Moulins, AUVERGNE/FRANCE
'Mill' from the Medieval Latin *molina* 'mill', a
reference to a mill on the Allier River.

Moultrie, GEORGIA/USA
Named after General William Moultrie (1730–
1805), governor of South Carolina (1785–7,
1792–4) and an officer who fought valiantly
against the British during the American War of
Independence (1775–83). There is a Lake
Moultrie named after him in South Carolina.

Moundsville, WEST VIRGINIA/USA *Grave Creek,
Elizabethtown*
Settled in 1771, it was renamed Elizabethtown
in 1798. Because of what is considered to be

353

353   **Mozambique**

the highest prehistoric Native American burial mound in North America, hence its first name, a new Mound City was established nearby in 1831. This city and Elizabethtown merged in 1865 to form Moundsville.

Mount Abu, RĀJASTHĀN/INDIA
The town is named after Mt Abu on whose slopes it lies. The mountain was originally called Arbuda 'wisdom'.

Mount Athos (Áyion Óros), GREECE
'Holy Mountain' from *áyion* 'holy' or 'sacred' and *óros* 'mountain'. It has the status of a theocratic republic of Greek Orthodox monks.

Mount Ayr, IOWA/USA
Named after the Scottish town of Ayr with 'mount' signifying its elevation.

Mount Barker, WESTERN AUSTRALIA/AUSTRALIA
Named after Mt Barker which was named after Captain Collett Barker, the last military commander at Albany.

Mount Carmel, CANADA, ISRAEL, USA
Israel: a mountain derived from the Hebrew *karmel* 'garden'. The Hebrew name is Har Ha-Karmel.

Mount Clemens, MICHIGAN/USA
Settled in 1795 and named after Christian Clemens who laid out the town in 1818.

Mount Gambier, SOUTH AUSTRALIA/AUSTRALIA
Named after Mt Gambier, an extinct volcano, sighted by a British Royal Navy officer in 1800 and named by him after Admiral of the Fleet James (later Lord) Gambier (1756–1833).

Mount Holly, NEW JERSEY/USA *Northampton, Bridgetown*
Established in 1677, it was subsequently named after the holly-covered hill on which it stands.

Mount Isa, QUEENSLAND/AUSTRALIA
Said to have been named by John Campbell Miles in 1923 after he had discovered deposits of silver-lead ore here. The city's name comes from one of his leases which he called Isa after his sister Isabelle.

Mount Morgan, QUEENSLAND/AUSTRALIA
Named after Edwin and Thomas Morgan who struck gold here in 1882.

Mount of Olives (Hebrew: **Har Ha-Zetim**; Arabic: **Jabal aṭ-Ṭūr**), ISRAELI ADMINISTRATION
A limestone ridge to the east of the Old City of Jerusalem which takes its name from the olive trees here. It is mentioned in the Old and New Testaments of the Bible. It came under Israeli rule following the Six-Day War in 1967.

Mount Pleasant, AUSTRALIA, CANADA, GRAND CAYMAN, USA
Thirteen cities and towns are generally so named because of their pleasing atmosphere and surroundings.

Mount Pulaski, ILLINOIS/USA
Named after Kasimierz (Casimir) Pułaski (1747–79), a Polish patriot who took part in the uprising against the Russians in 1768 before moving to America and taking part in the American War of Independence (1775–83) against the British. He commanded the Pułaski Legion, but died of his wounds in 1779.

Mount Rainier, MARYLAND/USA
A city named after the mountain in Washington State. The mountain was named in 1792 by Captain George Vancouver[†] after his friend, the British admiral, Peter Rainier (c.1741–1808). There is a city called Rainier in Oregon.

Mount Vernon, AUSTRALIA, USA
USA: sixteen cities have this name, some after the home of George Washington[†]. His estate in Virginia was originally called Little Hunting Creek Plantation. It was renamed in 1743 by Lawrence Washington, elder half brother of George, after the British Admiral Edward Vernon (1723–94) under whom he had served in the Caribbean. George Washington inherited it in 1751.

Moura, ANGOLA, AUSTRALIA, BRAZIL, CHAD, PORTUGAL
Portugal: formerly Nova Civitas Arrucitana and al-Maniyah. According to legend, the present name comes from a Moorish girl who inadvertently helped the Christians to recapture the town in 1166.

Mourne Mountains (Beanna Boirche), NORTHERN IRELAND/UK
Named after the Mughdorna people who lived here and took their name from their leader, Mughdorn.

Moxico, ANGOLA
A province with a name from a local word for a basket with a large handle.

Moyobamba, PERU *Santiago de los Valles de Moyobamba*
Derived from the Quechua *mayupampa* 'circular plain'. The present name is merely an abbreviation of the original 'St James of the Moyobambo Valleys'.

Mozambique (Moçambique)
The Republic of Mozambique (Portuguese: República de Moçambique) since 1990. Previously the People's Republic of Mozambique from 1975 when independence

was achieved; an Overseas Province of Portugal (1951), and often referred to as Portuguese East Africa, and a colony (1752); the Portuguese navigator Vasco da Gama (c.1460–1524) made the first landfall on Mozambique Island in 1498 and it was settled nine years later. The island's name, eventually applied to the whole territory for which it became the administrative seat, is said to have come from a ruling Arab Shaikh, Musa al Biq and the town which developed here was known to medieval Arab geographers as Musanbīh and in Swahili as Musambiki. Earlier, the place was known as Bilād al-Sufāla 'Low-lying Land' from *bilād* 'land' and *sufāla* 'low-land'. It has also been suggested that the present name might come from Musa Malik from the personal name and *malik* 'king'. It gives its name to the Mozambique Channel between Mozambique and Madagascar.

Mozdok, NORTH OSSETIA/RUSSIA
Founded in 1763 in a forest and meaning 'Thick Woods' in the local language.

Mozyr', BELARUS
Derived from the Mazovian (Masurian) people.

Mpumalanga, SOUTH AFRICA *Eastern Transvaal*
A province with a name meaning roughly '(Place where) the Sun comes out' from the Zulu verb *phuma* 'to come out' or 'to appear' and *ilanga* 'sun'. The name was changed in 1995. *See* TRANSVAAL.

Mrauk U, BURMA *Myohaung*
'Old City'. Founded in 1433, the present name is the original Arakanese name; Myohaung is the Burmese name from *myo* 'city'. Myohaung is sometimes written Mrohaung, the Arakanese *r* being changed to the Burmese *y*.

Mstislaw, BELARUS *Mstislavl'*
Named 'Mstislav's (Town)' after its founder, Mstislav Vladimirovich (1076–1132), Grand Prince of Kiev (1125–32), whose name comes from the Russian *mstit'* 'to avenge' and *slava* 'glory', thus 'Avenging Glory'. He was the eldest son of Grand Prince Vladimir Monomakh and Gytha, the eldest daughter of Harold II, King of England (1066).

Mtito Andei, KENYA
Takes its name from the forest meaning 'Forest of Vultures'.

Mtskheta, GEORGIA *Armosica, Mtskheta-Armazis*
Named after Mtskhetos, son of Kartlos, the legendary father of the Georgian people and said to be a descendant of Noah's son Japheth. Mtskheta-Armazis was also sometimes called Armazistsikhe 'Castle of Armazi' from *tsikhe* 'castle', Armazi being the local name for the

Zoroastrian fire god Ahura-Mazda. The town was the capital of Kartli between the 3rd century BC and the 5th century AD. It is still regarded by some as the spiritual capital of Georgia.

Mufulira, ZAMBIA
A major copper-mining centre, the name means 'Place of Abundance'.

Muharraq, al-, BAHRAIN
The meaning is not certain but it is possible that the name could mean 'Burnt' from the Arabic *haraqa* 'to burn' to indicate a place that is exposed to intense heat.

Mühlhausen, THURINGIA/GERMANY
Its full name is Mühlhausen in Thüringen 'Thuringia' to distinguish it from Mulhouse in France. The name, 'Mill Houses', comes from *Mühle* 'mill' and *Haus* 'house', a reference to the mills on the Unstrut River.

Mülheim, NORTH RHINE-WESTPHALIA/GERMANY
The full name is Mülheim an der Ruhr 'in the Ruhr' to distinguish it from cities with this name in Hesse and Baden-Württemberg. The name comes from *Mühle* 'mill' and *Heim* to indicate a community established round a mill.

Mulhouse, ALSACE/FRANCE *Mülhausen*
Close to the German border, it has the French version of a German name from *Mühle* 'mill' and *Haus* 'house', indicating a settlement by a mill. The actual German name was used when the town was part of Germany in 1871–1918.

Mukacheve, UKRAINE *Munkács*
Founded as a fortress to guard the Carpathian mountains and named after a certain Mukach with the possessive suffix *-evo* added. Its former Hungarian name reflects its Hungarian possession in 1018–1920; it was ceded to Czechoslovakia in 1920, to the Soviet Union in 1945 and became part of Ukraine when it gained its independence in 1991.

Mukalla, al- (al-Mukallā), YEMEN
A coastal city whose name may be derived from the Arabic *qalāa* 'to guard', thus a secure anchorage or 'harbour'. Literally, it means a 'roadstead to a place that provides vessels with shelter from the winds'.

Multān, PUNJAB/PAKISTAN *Kashtpur, Hanspur Bāgpur, Sanb/Sanābpur, Mulasthān*
Derives its present name from that of the idol of the pre-Muslim sun god shrine.

Mumbai, MAHĀRĀSHTRA/INDIA *Bombaim, Buan Bahia, Bombay*
Mumbai, officially adopted in 1996, is the Marathi name for Bombay which is itself the

English version of the Portuguese Bombaim; it was also called Buan Bahia 'Good, or Beautiful, Bay' by the Portuguese. Mumbai takes its name from the local Hindu goddess Mumbadevi. Bombay Island (actually seven islands) was ceded to the Portuguese in 1534 by Gujarāt to which it belonged. In 1661 it was transferred to the British as part of the dowry of Catherine of Braganza (1638–1705), the sister of the King of Portugal, when she married the British King Charles II[†]. The city was leased by the King to the English East India Company in 1668 for an annual rent of £10. It was one of the three Presidencies of the Company, the others being Calcutta and Madras. A small fish, the bummelo, when dried, is called Bombay Duck.

Muncie, INDIANA/USA *Munseetown*
Founded in 1827 and named after the Munsee clan of the Delaware tribe who sold the land to the government in 1820.

Munich (München), BAVARIA/GERMANY *Zu den Munichen*
The capital of Bavaria was originally a tiny 8th-century settlement of friars with a church. In 1157 Henry XII the Lion (c.1130–95), Duke of Bavaria (1156–80), decided to put his plans to levy a toll over the River Isar into action. He destroyed the only bridge nearby, built a new one at the settlement, and allowed the monks to develop a market by the toll station. The original name meant 'To the Monks' from the Old High German *Muniche* 'monks' and the present name means 'Home of the Monks' from a word equivalent to the modern German *Mönch* 'monk'.

Munster (Muma), IRELAND
A province meaning 'Land of the Mumu' from *tír* 'land' and a local tribe who took their name from a pre-Christian goddess called Muma. It was one of the 'fifths', the five ancient kingdoms of Ireland, each of which comprised a group of *tuatha* 'petty kingdoms'.

Münster, NORTH RHINE-WESTPHALIA/GERMANY *Mimigernaford*
Situated on the River Aa, the original name meant 'Ford over the Aa'. It was renamed in 1068 after the Latin *monasterium* 'monastery', a bishopric having been founded here in 804.

Murchison, ANTARCTICA, AUSTRALIA, CANADA, NEW ZEALAND, UGANDA
A number of mountains and rivers in these countries, as well as the Murchison Falls (now the Kabarega Falls) in Uganda, are named after Sir Roderick Murchison (1792–1871), a geologist who was president of the British Royal Geographical Society for fifteen years, twice director of the Geological Society and

director-general of the Geological Survey from 1855. The Falls were discovered and named after Murchison by Samuel (later Sir Samuel) Baker, and his wife Florence, in 1864.

Murcia, PHILIPPINES, SPAIN
Spain: an autonomous community, city, and former Moorish kingdom, known as Mursīyah, between the 11th and 13th centuries. The present city may have been the Roman Vergilia. The present name comes from the Arabic *mursakh* 'fortified'.

Murfreesboro, TENNESSEE/USA
Founded in 1811 and named after Colonel Hardy Murfree (1752–1809), a friend of Colonel William Lytle who donated the land.

Murmansk, RUSSIA *Romanov-na-Murmane*
A province and a city-port with a name that may be derived from the Saami word *murman* 'edge of the earth' from *mur* 'sea' and *ma* 'land'. Murman was the Russian name for the coast here It was founded in 1915 as a port in the Arctic and in 1915–17 was named after the Romanov dynasty. With its fall at the time of the Bolshevik Revolution in 1917, the city was renamed.

Muro, FRANCE, SPAIN
'Wall' in Spanish.

Murom, VLADIMIR/RUSSIA
Named after a local people, the Muroma.

Muroran, HOKKAIDŌ/JAPAN
Derived from the Ainu *murueran* 'gentle road down', probably to Uchiura Bay.

Murray, AUSTRALIA, USA
1. Australia: a river in south-east Australia, it was at first named Hume after either Hamilton Hume, one of its discoverers in 1824, or his father, Andrew Hume. It was renamed in 1830 after Lieutenant General (later General) Sir George Murray (1772–1846), secretary of state for the colonies (1828–30) in the Duke of Wellington's administration.
2. USA (Kentucky): named afer the Honourable John L. Murray, a member of Congress.

Murree, PUNJAB/PAKISTAN
A former British hill station, the name is derived from *marhi* 'high place'.

Murrumbidgee, AUSTRALIA
A river flowing into the Murray River, its Aboriginal name means 'Big Water' or 'Overflowing'.

Murshidābād, WEST BENGAL/INDIA *Makhsudābād/Muxadābād*
Believed to have been founded by the Mughal Emperor Akbar[†] in the 16th century, it became

the capital of Bengal in 1704 when this was transferred from Dhākā (now Dacca) by Murshid Kulī Khan, *nawab* 'governor' of Bengal. He renamed it the 'Place of Murshid' after himself. As Muhammad Hadi, he had been given the title *murshid* 'one who gives the correct guidance' in Arabic in 1702.

Murska Sobota, SLOVENIA *Muraszombat*
'Mura Saturday', that is, the day of the market, with both the Slovene *sobota* and Hungarian *szombat* meaning 'Saturday'; the town lies close to the Mura River.

Murwillumbah, NEW SOUTH WALES/
AUSTRALIA
An Aboriginal name meaning either 'Good Campsite' or 'Place of Many Possums'.

Muş, TURKEY *Tarun*
Probably named after the Armenian King Mushel I Mamikonian who is believed to have founded the town in the 6th century. It was called Tarun by the Arabs before reverting to its original name.

Muscat (Masqaṭ), OMAN
The Arabic Masqaṭ means 'Place of Birth', the literal meaning being 'place of falling'. It gave its name to the country, Muscat and Oman, now simply Oman, and has been the capital since the late 18th century.

Muscatine, IOWA/USA *Bloomington*
Founded in 1833 as a trading post, it was renamed in 1850 after the Mascoutin people whose name means 'Burning Island', or 'Fiery Nation', or 'Dweller in the Prairie'.

Muscotah, KANSAS/USA
A Native American word meaning 'Beautiful Prairie'.

Muscovy (Moskoviya), MOSCOW/RUSSIA
A historic principality founded in the 13th century by Prince Daniel, the youngest son of St Alexander Nevsky (*c.*1200–63). It was named after Moscow, then a fortified settlement at its centre at the confluence of the Moscow and Neglinka Rivers. The Muscovite princes gradually extended their authority territorially, but it was not until the 17th century that the name Russia was adopted.

Musgrave Ranges, SOUTH AUSTRALIA/
AUSTRALIA
A group of hills first seen by the English explorer William Gosse in 1873 and named after Sir Anthony Musgrave (1828–88), colonial administrator and governor of South Australia (1873–6).

Musgravetown, NEWFOUNDLAND/CANADA
Goose Bay
Named after Sir Anthony Musgrave (1828–88), governor of Newfoundland (1864–9) and of British Columbia (1869–72). *See* MUSGRAVE RANGES.

Musina, LIMPOPO/SOUTH AFRICA *Messina*
Founded in 1904 with a Venda name meaning 'Spoiler'. This referred to the copper that contaminated the iron mined in the neighbourhood.

Muskegon, MICHIGAN/USA
Laid out in 1849 and named after a river with a name meaning 'swamp' from an Ojibwa word.

Muskogee, OKLAHOMA/USA
Founded in 1872 and named after the Muskogee tribe of the Creek Confederacy. Their name may mean 'swamp' or 'open marshy land'.

Mustvee, ESTONIA
'Black Water' from *must* 'black' and an earlier form of *vesi* 'water'. The town, on Lake Peipus, takes its name from the Chërnaya River (in Russian, 'Black River').

Mutare, ZIMBABWE *Umtali*
Founded as Fort Umtali in 1890 with a name taken from *mutare* 'piece of metal'. The river on which it lay was the Umtara 'River of Ore' and in 1982 the town was renamed after this.

Muthannā, al-, IRAQ
A governorate named after Muthannā ibn Harithā, the chief of a Bedu tribe, who played a leading role in the conquest of western Iraq.

Mutsu, HONSHŪ/JAPAN *Michinoku*
The same Chinese characters hold for both names from *michi* and *mu* 'land' and *oku* and *tsu* 'depth' or 'inner part'.

Muzaffarābād, NORTH-WEST FRONTIER/
PAKISTAN
Named 'Town of Muzaffar' after a Muzaffar Khan, who completed construction of the Red Fort in 1646, and *ābād*.

Muzaffarnagar, UTTAR PRADESH/INDIA
Founded in about 1633 by Khan-e Jahān and named 'Town of Muzaffar' after his father, Muzaffar Khan, and *nagar*.

Muzaffarpur, BIHĀR/INDIA
Founded in the 18th century by, and named after, a Muzaffar Khan, with the additional *pur* to give 'Town of Muzaffar'. Muzaffar Khan was the Emperor Akbar's[†] head of finance and later governor of Bengal and Bihār in the late 16th century.

Muztagata, SINKIANG/CHINA
A mountain called 'Ice Mountain Father' from
the Kyrgyz and Uighur *muz* 'ice', the Uighur
tagh 'mountain' and the Kyrgyz *ata* 'father'.

Mvuma, ZIMBABWE *Umvuma*
'Place of Magic Singing'.

Mwami, ZIMBABWE
'Warthog'.

Mweru, DEMOCRATIC REPUBLIC OF THE CONGO-
ZAMBIA
A lake with a Bantu name meaning 'white'.

Myanaung, BURMA *Lunhse*
'Rapid Victory'. The name was changed in
1755 by Alaungpaya (1714–60), King of Burma
(1752–60), who organized and led an army
against the Mons in southern Burma and
achieved a quick victory here.

Myanmar *See* BURMA.

Mycenae, GREECE
A prehistoric city, now in ruins, said to have
been named by its legendary founder, Perseus,
after Mycene, a nymph of Laconia.

Myitkyinā, BURMA
'Close to the Big River', a reference to the fact
that it lies on the Irrawaddy, from *myit* 'river'.

Mykolayiv, UKRAINE *Nikolayev*
A province and a city founded on 6 December
1788, the feast day of St Nicholas, the patron
saint of sailors (and Russia), as a naval base and
named after him.

Mysia, TURKEY
An ancient region in the north-west named
after the Mysians, the meaning of whose name
is not known.

Mỹ So'n, VIETNAM
Ruins situated below the My Son mountain
and named after it 'Beautiful Mountain' from
my 'beautiful' and *son* 'mountain'.

Mysore (Maisur), KARNĀTAKA/INDIA
*Mahishmati, Purigere, Mahishapura/Mahishura
Nagara*
A former state (now Karnātaka) and a city with
a name, according to popular tradition,
meaning 'Buffalo Town' from the Sanskrit
mahiṣa 'buffalo' in the sense of 'powerful'. This
stems from the legend of the slaughter of the
buffalo-demon king Mahīshasura by the Hindu
goddess Cāmundā or Durga. Less likely is the
theory that the name comes from *Maisi-ūr*,
Maisi being the name of a local goddess from
the Sanskrit Mahisha and *ūru* 'town'.

Mystic, CONNECTICUT/USA
Named after the river in Massachusetts, itself
from the Native American *missi* 'great' and *tuk*
'tidal river', thus 'the great river'.

Mỹ Tho, VIETNAM *Misar*
Founded by refugees from Taiwan in 1680 and
named after the River My Tho, the name
means 'Beautiful Perfume' from *my* 'beautiful'
and *tho* 'perfume'. It was annexed from the
Cambodians in the 17th century.

Mytilene (Mitilíni), LESBOS/GREECE
A pre-Greek name said to have come from
Mytilene, a daughter of King Macareus.

Mývatn, ICELAND
'Mosquito Lake' from *mý* 'mosquito' and *vatn*
'lake'.

Na'ama, EGYPT
On the south-eastern coast of the Sinai Peninsula, the town has a Hebrew name meaning 'Pleasant'.

Naas (An Nás), IRELAND
'The Assembly' from *an* 'the' and *nás* 'assembly'. This was the seat of the kings of Leinster.

Naberezhnyye Chelny, TATARSTAN REPUBLIC/RUSSIA *Chelny, Brezhnev*
A village called Chelny 'boats' from the plural of *chĕln* 'canoe' or an obsolete word for 'boat'. In 1930, when it became a town, Naberezhnyye was added; this came from *naberezhnaya* 'embankment' or 'quay' indicating its location on the left bank of the River Kama. On his death in 1982 it was named after Leonid Brezhnev (1906–82), Soviet leader and president (1977–82). After Mikhail Gorbachev took power in 1985 Brezhnev's reputation faded, and the city readopted its previous name in 1988.

Nabeul, TUNISIA *Neapolis*
The modern town, founded in the 12th century, lies just to the north-east of Neapolis 'New Town' which prospered between the 5th century BC and the 7th century AD. The present name is derived from Neapolis and is also spelt Nābul.

Nablus (Nābalus), WEST BANK *Shechem, Flavia Neapolis, Julia Neapolis, Naples*
A very ancient city, Shechem is mentioned (as Sichem) in the Bible (Genesis 12: 6) when Abraham came here and was promised the Land of Israel. Destroyed by the Romans in 70, the present town was refounded just to the west of the ancient town in 72 on the orders of Vespasian (9–79), Roman emperor (69–79), and called Flavia Neapolis 'New City of Flavius' after him (Titus Flavius Vespasianus) and later Julia Neapolis. The present Arabic name is a corruption of the Greek Neapolis, the Crusaders calling it Naples between 1099 and 1187.

Nacimiento, CHILE, MEXICO, USA
'Birth' or 'Nativity' in Spanish.

Nacogdoches, TEXAS/USA
Named after a subtribe of the Caddo people.

Náfpaktos, GREECE *Epakhtos, Lepanto*
A coastal town, the name is derived from *naus* 'ship' and *pegnumi* 'I make fast', thus denoting a harbour. Lepanto was the Italianized version of the original Greek name. The town's name is also spelt Návpaktos.

Náfplion, GREECE *Nauplia, Napoli di Romania*
'Naval Station' from *naus* 'ship' and *pleō* 'I sail' because it was the main port for Argos, the dominant city-state in the Peloponnese during the 7th century BC. In Greek mythology, Nauplius 'Seafarer', son of the sea god Poseidon, is said to have founded the port. Having captured it in 1388, the Venetians renamed it Napoli di Romania. It became Greek in 1822, after which it adopted its present name. It was the first capital of independent Greece in 1829–34. It is also spelt Návplion.

Nafūd, an-, SAUDI ARABIA
'The Sand Desert' in Arabic, as opposed to a stone or gravel desert.

Nāgāland, INDIA
A state established in 1963 and named after its indigenous people, the Nāga. There is no agreement as to the etymology of their name. It may come from the Sanskrit *nāga* 'snake', here a mythical creature with the body of a man and the tail of a snake; or from the Hindi *nangā* 'naked'; or from *nāga* 'hill', in recognition of the mountainous terrain; or from *nok* 'people'.

Nagano, HONSHŪ/JAPAN *Zenkōji*
A prefecture and a city with a name meaning 'Long Field' from *naga* 'long' and *no* 'field'. The original name came from the Zenkō Temple founded in the 7th century.

Nagasaki, KYŪSHŪ/JAPAN *Langasaque/ Nangasaque*
A prefecture and a city-port with a name meaning 'Long Headland' from *naga* 'long' and *saki* 'headland'. The name may, however, have come from an individual, a 13th-century feudal lord called Kotaro Nagasaki.

Nāgaur, RĀJASTHĀN/INDIA
It is believed to take its name from the Nāga Rājputs, the warrior rulers of Rājputāna, who are thought to have been the founders of the town. The name is also spelt Nagor.

Nāgercoil, TAMIL NĀDU/INDIA
'Snake Temple', a reference to the importance
of the Śaiva temple here.

Nagornyy-Karabakh (Armenian: **Lernayin
Gharabagh**; Azeri: **Dağliq, or Yuxari, Qarabağ**),
AZERBAIJAN *Arts'akh, Khachēn*
Previously an autonomous province, and a
self-proclaimed independent republic
(unrecognized internationally) since the
autumn of 1991, sometimes referred to as the
'Upper Karabakh Republic', and administered
by Karabakh separatists. With its westernmost
part lying only 5 miles (8 km) from Armenia, it
includes the five regions of the Soviet era
comprising the Nagornyy-Karabakh
Autonomous Province, together with the
Shaumyan (Shaymyanovskiy) District which
was outside the province. However, the Azeri
government considers it no more than a
geographic region within Azerbaijan. The
name means 'Black Garden in the Mountains'
from the Russian *nagornyy* 'situated in
mountains' or 'mountainous' from *na* 'on' and
gora, and the compound word *karabakh* from
the Turkish *kara* 'black' and the Persian *bakh*
'garden'. The 'black garden' is either a
reference to the thick forests or the rich soil
here. The *nagornyy* distinguishes the hilly part
of the former Turkish and Persian ruled (and
Armenian populated) khanate of Karabakh
from the lowland part between the Lesser
Caucasus Mountains and the River Kur (with an
Azeri majority). Geographically, Nagornyy-
Karabakh, a part of Karabakh, is linked to
Azerbaijan, being separated from Armenia by
mountains. Nevertheless, the influx of
Armenians gathered pace during the middle of
the 19th century and the region was occupied
by Armenian forces at the end of the First
World War in 1918. They were soon forced to
withdraw and Nagornyy-Karabakh came under
Azeri rule. In 1921 it was assigned to Armenia,
but again this decision was overturned.
Although aware that the population consisted
largely of Armenian Christians, the
government in Moscow felt the need to mollify
the Muslim population of the Soviet Union as
well as the newly created Republic of Turkey;
furthermore the Azeris claimed it. So the
region was awarded to predominantly Muslim
Azerbaijan. Two years later it became the
Nagornyy-Karabakh Autonomous Province
within the Transcaucasian Republic
(Azerbaijan)—an Armenian-populated enclave.
This decision was in line with Joseph Stalin's[†]
divide-and-rule policy for nationalities and
meant that these Armenian 'hostages' inside
Azerbaijan ensured Armenia's good behaviour,
at the same time as providing a fifth column

inside Azerbaijan which could respond to any
Azeri misbehaviour. (The same situation
applied in *Nakhichevan*.) It was at this time
that the northern tip, the Armenian populated
Shaumyan District, was excluded from the
province and placed under direct Azeri rule; it
only rejoined the self-proclaimed republic in
1992. In 1988 the Karabakhtsi voted a transfer
to Armenia, believing that the Soviet
authorities would uphold their democratic
choice and agree to reverse the territorial
injustice inflicted upon them in 1923. Moscow
demurred and imposed direct control. Fighting
broke out which resulted in Nagornyy-
Karabakh and other Azeri territory falling to
Armenian forces before a ceasefire was
engineered in 1994. The ancient name Arts'akh
is used by the Armenians.

Nagoya, HONSHŪ/JAPAN
The name refers to the great castle built here
in 1610 around which the town developed. It
may be derived from *na* 'name', *ko* 'old', and *ya*
'house', the 'old house' being the castle.
However, it could also come from the Sanskrit
nagara 'city'.

Nāgpur, MAHĀRĀSHTRA/INDIA
Founded in the early 18th century on the River
Nāg from which it gets its name. The Nāg takes
its name from the Nāga people (*see* NĀGĀLAND)
to give 'Town of the Nāgas' from the tribal
name and *pur*.

Nags Head, NORTH CAROLINA/USA
According to legend, this small town received
its name from the practice of local villains of
tying lanterns around the necks of ponies,
'nags', and then forcing them to walk along the
dunes to give the impression of boats at anchor.
This encouraged ships' skippers to bring their
boats inshore where they ran aground on the
shoals. Their cargo was then seized. There is a
town called Nag's Head on St Kitts.

Nahant, MASSACHUSETTS/USA
A town and a bay from a Native American
word meaning 'At the Point' or 'Two Things
United', a reference to two virtual islands
connected by a strip of sand.

Nahariyya, ISRAEL
Once a Phoenician harbour, the city was
refounded in 1934 as a German Jewish
agricultural settlement with a name that is
derived from the Hebrew *nahar* 'river', a
reference to the Ga'aton River which flows
through it.

Nahma, MICHIGAN/USA
Lying on the Sturgeon River, the name is
simply a local Native American word for
'sturgeon'.

Nahuel Huapí, ARGENTINA
A lake discovered in 1670 and given the
Araucanian name 'Island of the Jaguars',
presumably because of the presence of jaguars
in the wooded foothills of the Andes here;
'island' refers to the fact that within the lake
there are many islands.

Naini Tāl, UTTAR PRADESH/INDIA
Founded in 1841 as a hill resort called 'Naini
Lake' after Naini Devi, an important Hindu
goddess, and *tāl* 'lake'. According to legend,
the lake is said to be one of the emerald green
eyes of Shiva's wife, Sati.

Nairn, UK, USA
UK (Scotland): formerly Inuernaren and Narne
'Mouth of the (River) Nairn' with the river's
pre-Celtic Indo-European name possibly
meaning 'Penetrating One'. The initial part of
the original settlement name came from *inbhir*
'river mouth'.

Nairobi, KENYA
Founded by the British in 1899 at the 317th
mile point on the railway between the Indian
Ocean port of Mombasa and Lake Victoria in
Uganda. It was named after a nearby Masai
watering hole called 'Cold Water' from the
Masai *Enkare Nairobi*. It grew into a small town
and in 1905 became the capital of the British
East Africa Protectorate; it became the
national capital when Kenya gained
independence in 1963.

Naivasha, KENYA
Named after the lake here whose name means
'Heaving Waters' from the Masai *e-na-iposha*.

Najaf (an-Najaf), IRAQ
A governorate and a holy city thought to have
been founded on a ridge just west of the
Euphrates River *c.*790 with a name meaning
'Raised Land'.

Najibabad, UTTAR PRADESH/INDIA
'Najib's Town' after Najib al-Dawla, an Afghan
commander in the service of the Mughal
emperor, who built a fort one mile (1.5 km) to
the east in 1755.

Nakhichevan (Naxçivan), AZERBAIJAN
Naxuna, Nagshijahan, Nakhuntevan, Arran
An autonomous republic since 1990,
geographically separated from the rest of
Azerbaijan, and a city; at its narrowest point
only 15 miles (25 km) of Armenian territory
separate the republic from Azerbaijan proper.
It is thus a predominantly Azeri-populated
enclave within Armenia. The name is said to
be derived from Nukkhtchikhan 'Colony of
Noah'. Noah's ark is supposed to have
grounded on Mount Ararat (now just over the

border in Turkey). It might, however, be
derived from the Armenian *nakh* 'first' and
idzhevan 'landing', also a reference to the ark.
A less appealing explanation is that the name
derives from a personal name with the
Armenian suffix *-avan* 'settlement' or 'place'.
Former names were Persian and Turkish.
Arran was the name of the *vilayet* 'province' in
the Arab caliphate. The subject of dispute
between Armenia and Azerbaijan in 1918–20,
Nakhichevan was invaded by the Red Army in
1920. The following year it was confirmed by
the Treaty of Moscow as being part of
Azerbaijan. In 1924 it became an Autonomous
Soviet Republic within Azerbaijan.

Nakhodka, PRIMORSKIY/RUSSIA *Amerikanka*
'Find' in the sense of 'Discovery' or 'Godsend'
referring to a sheltered bay discovered
by chance in 1859 in the Sea of Japan. The
city-port takes its name from the Bay of
Nakhodka.

Nakhon Pathom, THAILAND
'First City' from *nakhon* 'city' and *pathom* 'first'
from the Pali *Nagara Pathama*. It is regarded as
Thailand's oldest city and is said to have been
founded over 2 000 years ago.

Nakhon Phanom, THAILAND
'City of Hills' from *nakhon* and the Khmer
phnŏm 'hill'.

Nakhon Ratchasima, THAILAND
'Border Town of the King' from *nakhon*, *racha*
'king', and *sima* 'border'. It is also known as
Khorat.

Nakhon Sawan, THAILAND
'Heavenly City' from *nakhon* and *sawankh*
'heaven' or 'paradise'. It is also known as
Paknam Pho 'River Mouth' since it lies at the
confluence of the Rivers Nan, Ping, Wang, and
Yom.

Nakhon Si Thammarat, THAILAND *Ligor,*
Tamralinga, Nagara Si Dhammaraja
The present name is the Thai rendering of the
previous Sanskrit name which meant 'City of
the Sacred Dhamma King' from *nakhon*, *si*
'good' or 'sacred', *thamm* 'Dhamma' or 'justice'
and *rat* 'royal'; or 'City of the Good and Just
King'. Ligor was a Portuguese name given to
the already exisiting city-state.

Nal'chik, KABARDINO-BALKARIYA/RUSSIA
Founded as a Russian fortress in 1818 on the
Nal'chik River, the name may possibly be
derived from a local word for 'Little
Horseshoe'.

Namangan, UZBEKISTAN
A province and a city which take their name
from the local salt mines, *Namak Kan*.

Namaqualand, NORTHERN CAPE/SOUTH AFRICA
'Land of the Nama Men', the Nama being of the Khoikhoin (Hottentot) tribe that originally inhabited this semi-desert region. The suffix -*qua* means 'men'.

Nambucca Heads, NEW SOUTH WALES/ AUSTRALIA
Founded in 1842 and named after the Nambucca River, at the mouth of which it lies. The river's Aboriginal name means 'Entrance to the Waters'.

Namibe, ANGOLA *Moçâmedes/Mossamedes*
A province and a town founded by Brazilians *c.*1849 and named after the Baron of Mossamedes, governor of Portuguese West Africa (1784–90). The present name, adopted in 1982, comes from the Namib Desert which is said to mean 'Land where nothing grows'.

Namibia *South West Africa*
The Republic of Namibia since 1990 when independence was achieved. Although there was some desultory European interest in south-west Africa before 1800 and missionaries increased their activities thereafter, it was not until 1884 that the territory became a German protectorate, officially named South West Africa. This lasted until 1915 when it was occupied by South African forces at the request of the Allies; and in 1920 it became a South African League of Nations mandate. At the end of the Second World War South Africa refused to place the territory under a United Nations Trusteeship, but it was not until 1966 that the UN terminated the mandate. Nevertheless, South Africa continued to administer the territory, in many ways as a part of South Africa, in defiance of UN resolutions. In 1968 the territory came under the nominal control of the UN (although South Africa continued to govern) which changed the name to Namibia, from the Nama word *namíb* 'shield' coined by a nationalist leader some years before. However, it is also said to take its name from the Namib Desert (*see* NAMIBE).

Namp'o, NORTH KOREA
A 'special city' whose name means 'Southern Harbour' from *nam* 'southern' and *p'o* 'harbour'.

Nampula, MOZAMBIQUE
A province and a town founded as a military post in 1907 and named after a local chief, Mpula, whose name meant 'rain'.

Nan, CHINA, THAILAND
1. China (Sichuan): because this river was difficult to ford it was given the name 'Difficult

River' from *nán* 'difficult'; however, it was also called the 'Southern River' from the homonym *nán* 'southern' because the river lay south of Ba mountain. The name 'Southern River' was formally adopted during the Ming dynasty (1368–1644).
2. Thailand: a river and a town. It was an independent kingdom as Meuang Nan. In the 14th century it became a principality in the Kingdom of Lan na and renamed Chiang Klang 'Middle City' because it is approximately half-way between Chiang Mai and Chiang Thong (Louangphrabang in Laos). It is now named after the Nan River.

Nanaimo, BRITISH COLUMBIA/CANADA
Colvilletown, Sne-ny-mo
A Hudson's Bay Company trading post was first established here. After local Native Americans had discovered gold in the vicinity a settlement grew up around it which was named after Andrew Colville, governor of the Hudson's Bay Company (1852–6). In 1860 the locals changed the name to Sne-ny-mo 'Big, Strong Tribe', a reference to the confederation of tribes here, from which the present name has evolved.

Nanchang, JIANGXI/CHINA *Yuzhang/Guanying, Hongzhou, Longxing, Hongdu*
'Flourishing South' from *nán* and *chāng* 'flourishing'. The 'south' here refers to the area south of the lower reaches of the Yangtze River. Yuzhang, also known as Guanying, was founded in 202 BC. In due course a new town, Hongzhou from *hóng* 'flood' or 'vast' was built on the north-western edge of Yuzhang and the whole town came to be known by this name during the Sui dynasty (581–617); and during the Southern Song dynasty (1127–1279) by the name of Longxing from *lóng* and *xīng*, both 'prosperous'. In 1284 the *lóng* changed to a different character with the same pronunciation meaning 'dragon'. The city was renamed Hongdu in 1362 and during the early Ming dynasty (1368–1644) it became the Nanchang Prefecture; it was retitled Nanchang City in 1927.

Nanchong, SICHUAN/CHINA
'Southern Chong'. During the Han dynasty (206 BC–AD 220) it was called Chongguo 'Prosperous Kingdom County' from *chōng* 'full', a reference to the fertile and productive agricultural plain here, and *guó* 'county'. Because it was in the southern part of the county the Sui dynasty (581–618) changed the name to Nanchong County; the city was established in 1950.

n

Nancy, LORRAINE/FRANCE *Nantiacum*
'Place of Nantio' from the place-name suffix
-acum and the name of an unknown individual.
In 1735–66 it belonged to Stanisław I (1677–
1766), King of Poland (1704–9, 1733) after he
had lost his crown and been given the Duchy
of Lorraine by his son-in-law, Louis XV (1710–
74), King of France (1715–74).

Nanda Devi, UTTAR PRADESH/INDIA
A mountain peak in the Himalayas meaning
'Goddess of Happiness' from the Hindi *nandā*
'happiness' and *devī* 'goddess'.

Nānded, MAHĀRĀSHTRA/INDIA
Derived from *Nānda Tat* 'Nanda Border', a
reference to the border of the 3rd century BC
Magadha kingdom which was ruled by the
Nanda.

Nanga Parbat, PAKISTAN-CONTROLLED SECTOR
OF KASHMIR
One of the highest mountain peaks in the
Himalayas with a Kashmiri name meaning
'Bare Mountain' from the Hindi *nanga* 'bare'
or 'naked' and *parvata* 'mountain'. The local
name is Diamir 'King of Mountains'.

Nanjing, JIANGSU/CHINA *Chien-yeh, Chien-kang,
Ching-chou, Jin-ling-fu, Tian-jing, Ying-t'ien-fu, Chiang-
ning, Nanking*
'Southern Capital' from *nán* and *jīng* 'capital
city'. Having been the capital of various
kingdoms, it became the capital of a united
China in 1368 as Ying-t'ien-fu 'Responding
to Heaven'. When the capital was moved
to Peking (now Beijing) in 1421 the city
became no more than a regional capital
and was renamed Nanjing. During the
Manchu dynasty (1644–1911), the city was
known as Chiang-ning. Other names have
been Jin-ling-fu 'Golden Hill' from *jīn* 'golden'
and *lǐng* 'hill', and Tian-jing 'Heavenly Capital'
from *tiān* 'heaven' and *jīng* when it was the
capital of the Taiping Heavenly Kingdom of
Great Peace in 1853–64, having been captured
by the rebellious Taipings in 1853. It was
also the capital of China in 1928–37, of
Japan's Chinese puppet government in
1940–5, and of the Nationalist government in
1946–9. In October 1949, when the People's
Republic of China came into existence, the
national capital once more became Beijing.
The present name is simply the Pinyin form
of Nanking.

Nan Mountains (Nan Shan), CHINA
Several mountain ranges in China are called
the 'Southern Mountains' from *nán* and *shān*,
presumably in relation to others further north.
Two, in particular, are notable. One, in the
north-west, bestrides Gansu and Shaanxi

provinces and is also called the Qinling
Mountain Range. The other, crossing four
southern provinces, is also called Nan Ling
'Southern Ranges' or simply Ling.

Nanning, GUANGXI ZHUANG AUTONOMOUS
REGION/CHINA *Yongzhou*
'Southern Peace' from *nán* and *níng* 'peaceful'.
It was in 1324, under Mongol rule, that the city
received its present name. During the
Republican period, in 1914–46, the city was
named Yongning County after the Yong River
on which it lies. The earlier name was
readopted in 1946.

Nanping, FUJIAN/CHINA *Yen-an, Yen-ping Chen,
Chien-chou, Nan-chien-chou, Yenping*
A town founded as Nanping County in 196
with a succession of names thereafter. Only in
1913 did it adopt its present name 'Southern
Peace' from *nán* and *píng* 'peaceful'.

Nanterre, PARIS/FRANCE *Nemetodor/
Nemetodurum*
The name has evolved from the Roman name
which came from the Gaulish *nemeton* 'sacred
grove' or 'sacred sanctuary' and *duru* 'door',
'house' or 'village'.

Nantes, PAYS DE LA LOIRE/FRANCE *Condevincum,
Namnetas, Civitas Namnetum*
Named after the Namnetes, a Gallic tribe
whose capital this was.

Nanticoke, CANADA, USA
Named after the Nanticoke 'Tidewater People',
a confederacy of Algonquian-speaking Native
Americans who lived in Maryland and
Delaware.

Nantong, JIANGSU/CHINA *Jinghai zhen, Tongzhou*
'Southern Communication' from *nán* and
gōutōng 'communication', a reference to its
importance as the hub of a commercial
transport system. Founded during the Five
Dynasties period (907–60) as Jinghai zhen,
it was renamed in the 960s. Subsequently,
the local people began to refer to the city
as Nantong to distinguish it from the
Tongzhou near Beijing. It was not until 1724,
however, that the need to differentiate
between the two Tongzhou was formally
acknowledged and Nan- was added and -zhou
removed.

Nantucket, MASSACHUSETTS/USA *Natocko*
An island and a town. The meaning of the
name is not clear. On the one hand, it has been
suggested that it has been derived from a
Native American word meaning 'Far Away
(Land)'; on the other, that it comes from a local
word *nantuck* 'sandy, sterile soil that tempted
no one'.

Nantwich, ENGLAND/UK *Wich, Nametwihc*
Known since Roman times for its salt deposits, hence its name 'Famous Saltworks'. The second part of the name comes from the Old English *wīc* which in the West Midlands took on a special meaning of 'salt-production centre'. *Nant* came from the Middle English *named* 'renowned' or 'famous'.

Nanyang, HENAN/CHINA *Wan-i*
The former name meant 'Wan City'. The name was first recorded as Nanyang Commandery in 272 BC. The name is said to come from the fact that the city lay in the southern part of the Central Kingdom and was situated on sunny ground, hence its name from *nán* and *yáng* 'sun'. However, it has also been claimed that the name comes from the fact that Nanyang lies on the south side of the Southern Mountains and on the north side of the Han River. Thus the name can be taken to mean something like 'Sunny Exposure to the South'.

Nanyuki, KENYA
Named after the river on which it lies, called by the Masai the 'Red River' from *Ngare Nanyuki*.

Naperville, ILLINOIS/USA
Laid out in 1832 by Captain Joseph Naper and named after him.

Napier, ANTARCTICA, AUSTRALIA, NEW ZEALAND
New Zealand (North Island): laid out in 1856 and named after General Sir Charles Napier (1782–1853), a British general who conquered Sindh (now in Pakistan) and was its governor (1843–7).

Naples, ITALY, USA
Italy (Campania): in Italian, Napoli. According to legend, the first Greek settlement was named Partenope after the dead siren Partenope 'Maiden Face', who threw herself into the sea and whose body was washed ashore after her song had been heard by Odysseus. In *c.*600 BC the Greek Neapolis 'New City' from *neos* 'new' and *polis* was founded and the conventional English name comes from this. The city gives its name to the bay here, Golfo di Napoli. It was the capital of the Kingdom of Naples (also known at various times as the Kingdom of the Two Sicilies when united with Sicily) in 1266–1860 when the city was incorporated into the Kingdom of Italy; the short-lived Parthenopean Republic (1798–9) was declared after pro-French republicans ejected Ferdinand IV (1751–1825), King of Naples (1759–98, 1799–1806).

Napoleon, USA
North Dakota and Ohio: named after Napoleon[†].

Nappanee, INDIANA/USA
Founded in 1874 with an Algonquian name said to mean 'Flour'.

Nara, HONSHŪ/JAPAN *Heijō-kyō*
'Flat'. A prefecture and a city which was the capital of Japan between 710 and 785. Its former name meant 'Citadel of Peace'.

Naracoorte, SOUTH AUSTRALIA/AUSTRALIA *Kincraig*
Founded in 1845 and renamed in 1869 as 'Large Waterhole' from a local Aboriginal word.

Naranjo, COAST RICA
'Orange Tree' in Spanish.

Narbonne, LANGUEDOC-ROUSSILLON/FRANCE *Narbo/Narbona*
Originally the capital of a tribal kingdom, it takes its name from the first Roman colony, Narbo Martius, established in Gaul in 118 BC; another was formed by Julius Caesar[†] in 45 BC for veterans of the 10th Legion. It became the capital of the Roman province, Provincia, which was renamed Gallia Narbonensis during the reign of Augustus[†]. At that time Narbonne was on the coast and the name may come from a root word *nar* 'river'.

Narimanov, ASTRAKHAN/RUSSIA *Nizhnevolzhsk*
Originally 'Lower Volga' from *nizhne* 'lower' because it is situated near the Volga delta. It was renamed in 1984 when it became a town after Nariman Nadzhaf ogly Narimanov (1870–1925), a Georgian-born government and party figure, and writer and publicist, who was exiled to Astrakhan in 1909.

Narmada, INDIA
A river in central India also called the Narbada. Second only to the River Ganges in holiness, the name means 'Giving Pleasure' from the Sanskrit *narma* 'pleasure' and *da* 'to give'. Hindus believe that the river emanated from the body of the god Shiva.

Narni, UMBRIA/ITALY *Nequinum, Narnia*
After the Roman conquest the original Umbrian name gave way to the Roman Narnia. This Latin name came from the River Nera, itself from the root word *nar* 'river'.

Narodnaya (Gora Narodnaya), KOMI REPUBLIC/RUSSIA
A mountain discovered in 1927 and named 'People's Mountain' from *narodniy* 'national', the adjective of *narod* 'people' to mark the forthcoming celebrations of the tenth anniversary of the Russian Revolution.

Narrabri, NEW SOUTH WALES/AUSTRALIA
Founded *c*.1860, its name comes from an
Aboriginal word meaning 'Big Creek' and
'Forked Stick'.

Narragansett Pier, RHODE ISLAND/USA
A summer resort named after the Algonquian-
speaking Narraganset Indian tribe. Their name
means 'People of the Point'. Narrangansett is
also the name of the bay.

Narrandera, NEW SOUTH WALES/AUSTRALIA
Founded in 1863 as a livestock post, its
Aboriginal name means 'Place of Lizards'.

Narrogin, WESTERN AUSTRALIA/AUSTRALIA
Founded in the 1880s with a name derived
from the Aboriginal *gnargajin* 'water hole'.

Narsimhapur, MADHYA PRADESH/INDIA
Chhoṭa Gadarwara
Also spelt Narsinghpur. Renamed some time
after 1800 after the Narasimha 'Man Lion'
temple from the Hindi *nar* 'male' and *siṅh*
'lion', an incarnation of the god Vishnu, and
pur.

Naruto, SHIKOKU/JAPAN
Opposite the Naruto Strait which links the
Inland Sea with the Pacific Ocean, the port's
name means 'Roaring Gateway' from *naru*
'roar' and *to* 'gate'.

Narvik, NORWAY *Victoriahavn*
'Narrow Bay' from the Old German *narwa*
'narrow' and Old Scandinavian *vik* 'bay'. It lies
at the end of a peninsula between two fjords.
The original 'Victoria's Port', which was only
valid in 1887–98, honoured the Swedish
Crown Princess Victoria (1885–1970).

Nar'yan-Mar, NENETS AUTONOMOUS DISTRICT/
RUSSIA *Beloshchelye, Dzerzhinskiy*
Originally a small community founded in 1929
and called 'White Slope' from *belyy* and *sklon*
'slope'. The name was changed in 1933 to
honour Felix Dzerzhinskiy (1877–1926), the
Polish head of the Soviet secret police, the
Cheka. In 1935, when it became a town, the
name changed again, this time to Nar'yan-Mar
'Red Town' from Nenets *nar'yan* 'red' and *mar*
'town'. This was to signify its loyalty to Soviet
power and was in complete contrast to its
earlier 'white' which denoted 'anti-
communist'.

Narym, TOMSK/RUSSIA
Named after the low-lying region surrounding
it from the Khanty *narym* 'swamp'.

Naseby, NEW ZEALAND, UK
1. New Zealand (South Island): founded in the
1860s and named after the village in England

to demonstrate its allegiance to that country
after the Indian Mutiny in 1857.
2. UK (England): formerly Navesberie. A
village and the site of a Civil War battle in 1645
when Oliver Cromwell (1599–1658), lord
protector (1653–58), decisively defeated the
royalist forces of King Charles I[†] and Prince
Rupert (1619–82), commander-in-chief of the
royalist forces (1644–5). The name means
'Fortified Place of a man called Hnæf' from the
Old English personal name and *byrig*, the
dative singular of *burh*.

Nashotah, WISCONSIN/USA
An Algonquian word meaning 'The Twins'. In
the language of the Dakota it means 'Kicks up
Smoke'.

Nashua, NEW HAMPSHIRE/USA
Settled *c*.1656 along the banks of the Nashua
River and named Dunstable in 1673. On the
other side of the river a settlement called
Indian Head was renamed Nashua in 1803 and
the two settlements amalgamated in 1837
under the name Nashua. Various theories have
been put forward as to its meaning: a Native
American word for 'the land between' or
'beautiful river with a stony bottom'.

Nashville, TENNESSEE/USA
The official name since 1963 has been
Nashville-Davidson when the city of Nashville
and the county of Davidson were joined. In
1780 Fort Nashborough was built on a site
called French Lick; the fort was named after
General Francis Nash (1742–77), who was
killed during the American War of
Independence (1775–83). The Davidson
element of the name honours General William
L. Davidson (1746–81), also killed during that
war.

Nāsik, MAHĀRĀSHTRA/INDIA *Gulshanabad*
Lying on the holy Godavari River in an area of
nine hillocks called *Nav Shikhas* from *shikhas*
'hill-top' from which the town allegedly gets
its name. However, it has been suggested that
it comes from the Sanskrit *nasika* 'nose'. The
town is also said to have been called Padma-
Aasana (after Brahmadeva had meditated
here), Tri-Kantak (after Lord Vishnu had
defeated three demons), and Padmapur. It was
called Gulshanabad 'City of Gardens' during
the Mughal period because of its beauty. The
name Nāsik, however, was restored in 1751.

Nāsirīyah, an-, IRAQ
Founded by, and named after, Nāṣir Pasha
Sadun, paramount chief of the Muntafiḳ
confederation, who became governor of the
city in 1872.

Nassau, AUSTRALIA, THE BAHAMAS, COOK
ISLANDS, GERMANY
The Bahamas (New Providence): although not
laid out until 1729, the site was given the name
in the 1690s in honour of King William III[†]
who was a member of the Dutch royal house of
Orange-Nassau (from the German duchy of
Nassau). The name means 'Wet Land' from the
German *nass* 'wet' or 'moist'. It is the capital of
The Bahamas.

Nasser, EGYPT
A lake created as a result of the construction of
the Aswān High Dam in the 1960s and named
after Gamal Abdel Nasser (1918–70), President
of Egypt (1956–70). The southern third of the
lake in the Sudan is called Lake Nubia.

Natal, BRAZIL, INDONESIA, SOUTH AFRICA
1. Brazil (Rio Grande do Norte): founded by
the Portuguese in 1597 and given the name
'Christmas' in 1611 when it became a town.
2. South Africa (KwaZulu-Natal): having
become British territory in 1843, Natal became
a separate colony in 1858 and a province in
1910. It was named by the Portuguese explorer
Vasco da Gama (*c*.1460–1524) when he sailed
into a bay on Christmas Day 1497 which he
took to be the estuary of a great river; he called
it Rio do Natal 'Christmas River'. The Bay of
Natal was given to two English naval officers
by the Zulu chief Shaka in 1824 and a trading
post called Port Natal (renamed Durban in
1843) was established. The surrounding area
became known as Natal. It joined with
KwaZulu to form a province in 1994. *See*
KWAZULU-NATAL.

Natchez, MISSISSIPPI/USA *Fort Rosalie, Fort
Panmure*
Founded in 1716 as Fort Rosalie by the French.
In 1763 the English acquired it and a year later
it was renamed. It passed to the Spanish in
1779 and to the USA in 1798. It was then
renamed after the Natchez people in memory
of their near annihilation by the French in
1729, that had been in retaliation for the
massacre of nearly 300 settlers by the Natchez.

Natchitoches, LOUISIANA/USA *Fort St Jean
Baptiste*
Founded by the French in 1714 as a trading
post on the Red River to foster trade with the
Native Americans and to prevent occupation
by the Spanish. However, in about 1825 the
river began to shift its course and it now flows
some 5 miles (8 km) to the east. The city was
later renamed after the Natchitoches tribe.

Natick, MASSACHUSETTS/USA
Founded in 1650 with a Native American name
meaning 'Place of Hills'.

Natron, TANZANIA
A lake with a name that recognizes its deposits
of natron, a form of sodium carbonate.

Natrona, WYOMING/USA
Derived from the Spanish *natron* 'native
carbonate of soda' because of the deposits
here.

Naugatuck, CONNECTICUT/USA *Judd's
Meadows, South Farms, Salem Parish/Salem Bridge*
Settled in about 1704, it took the name Salem
Parish or Salem Bridge when it became a town.
The present name is of Algonquian origin and
is thought to mean 'One Tree', presumably
because of a prominent tree. The river on
which it lies also has this name and it has been
suggested that the name might mean 'Fork of
the River'.

Nauru (Naoero) *Pleasant Island*
The Republic of Nauru since 1968 on
independence. The first European to visit was
the English navigator, Captain John Fearn, in
1798. He called it the Pleasant Island because
of the friendliness of the inhabitants. It was
incorporated into the German Marshall Islands
Protectorate in 1888 and use of the island's
native name, whose meaning is unknown,
gradually became more common. It was
occupied by Australian forces in 1914 and
continued to be administered by Australia,
New Zealand, and the UK under a joint League
of Nations mandate in 1920. After occupation
by the Japanese in 1942–5, it was placed under
a UN Trusteeship in 1947 with Australia the
administering power.

Navahrudak, BELARUS
Although one of the oldest towns in Belarus,
the name means 'New Little Town', ultimately
from the Russian *novy* and *gorodok* 'little town'.

Navajo, USA
Arizona and New Mexico: named in honour of
the Native American tribe, the Navajo (also
spelt Navaho) whose name for themselves is
Diné 'The People'. It has been suggested that
the Navajo were named by the Spanish from
navaja 'clasp knife'; however, it may come
from a Spanish word meaning 'People with Big
Fields'.

Navan, CANADA, IRELAND, UK
1. Ireland: the Irish name of the town in
Meath is An Uaimh which means 'The Cave'.
2. UK (Northern Ireland): the Irish name is An
Eamhain, but its meaning is unknown.

Navarre (Navarra), SPAIN
An autonomous community and former
Franco-Spanish kingdom founded by Basques
in the 9th century. The Spanish part joined

Castile in 1515 while the French part
continued as a separate kingdom until 1589
when it joined France. The name is taken from
the Basque 'Nafarroa', the name for two
groups of Vascones living around Pamplona.

Navidad, CHILE, USA
A town in Chile and a river in Texas, USA, with
a name meaning 'Christmas' in Spanish.

Navoi (Nawoiy), UZBEKISTAN *Kermine*
A province and a town renamed in 1958 after
Nizamaddin Mir Alisher Navoi (1441–1501), a
famous Uzbek poet, who became a provincial
governor and received the title of emir.

Návpaktos, GREECE
See NÁFPAKTOS.

Návplion, GREECE
See NÁFPLION.

Náxos, GREECE *Strongyle, Dionysus, Callipolis*
An island in the Cyclades named after Naxus,
the chief of a Carian colony on the island. As a
centre for the worship of the god Dionysus, it
was named after him for a time.

Nazaré, PORTUGAL
Named after Nazareth, the childhood home of
Jesus Christ.

Nazran, INGUSHETIA/RUSSIA
Probably 'Christian' from the Arabic *nasrani*
'Nazarene' and thus 'Christian', a name given
to the settlement at a time when the Ingush
were flirting with Christianity. The Ingush are
now predominantly Sunni Muslim.

Nazrēt, ETHIOPIA
Named after Nazareth, the childhood home of
Jesus Christ.

Ncheu, MALAWI
On the border with Mozambique, the
Chichewa name means 'Border'.

N'Djamena, CHAD *Fort Lamy*
Founded as a French military post in 1900 and
named after a French officer, François Lamy
(1858–1900), who was killed here fighting a
Sudanese adventurer who exercised a certain
authority over the area to the east of Lake
Chad. It was renamed only in 1973, despite
Chadian independence in 1960, from a local
word said to mean 'Place of Rest'.

Ndola, ZAMBIA
'Clear Spring' in Lala.

Neagh, Lough (Loch nEathach), NORTHERN
IRELAND/UK
'Eochaid's Lake' after a legendary King of
Munster, who is said to have drowned in the
lake.

Near East, The A region consisting of those
countries lying adjacent to the eastern shores
of the Mediterranean Sea including Egypt.

Neath (Castell-Nedd), WALES/UK *Neth, Neeth*
Named after the River Neath (Nedd), possibly
'Shining One' on which it lies. The Romans
built a fort here called Nidum in 75 at a
crossing place over the river, hence the Welsh
name 'Castle on the (River) Nedd'.

Nebit-Dag, TURKMENISTAN
See BALKANABAT.

Nebo, AUSTRALIA, JORDAN, USA
Jordan: a mountain whose local name is Jabal
Nabā. It takes its name from Nabu, an Assyrian-
Babylonian advocate of writing and god of
vegetation whose name means 'speaking'.

Nebraska, USA
A state which took its name from that of its
principal river, called Nibthaska by the
Omahas and Nibrathka by the Otoes, both
meaning 'Flat River' or 'Shallow River'. The
name of the river was later changed to the
*Platte, a French name meaning 'Flat' and
this well described the terrain which at the
time of the arrival of the first pioneers was
also treeless. The USA acquired Nebraska as
part of the Louisiana Purchase in 1803 and it
became the Nebraska Territory in 1854. It
joined the Union as the 37th state in 1867.

Necedah, WISCONSIN/USA
A corruption of the Ojibwa word *nissida* 'let
there be three of us'.

Needham, MASSACHUSETTS/USA
Named after Needham in England. Its name
means 'Needy (or Poor) Homestead' from the
Old English *nēd* 'needy', a reference to the
unfertile land, and *hām*.

Neenah, WISCONSIN/USA *Winnebago Rapids*
Founded in 1835 on Lake Winnebago and
renamed in 1856 with a Winnebago word for
'water'.

Nefteabad, TAJIKISTAN
'Oil Town' from the Russian *neft'* 'oil' or
'petroleum' and *abad*.

Neftegorsk, RUSSIA
1. Krasnodar Territory: 'Oil Mountain' from
neft' and *gorsk*.
2. Sakhalin: originally known as Vostok 'East',
it was renamed in 1970 'Oil Town' with *gorsk*
here probably associated with *gorod* rather
than *gora*.

Neftekumsk, STAVROPOL' TERRITORY/RUSSIA
The name explains its association with the oil
and gas industry from *neft'* and its location
close to the Kuma River.

Negaunee, MICHIGAN/USA
A Native American translation of the English word 'pioneer'; thus 'he goes ahead' or 'he goes first'.

Negeri Sembilan, MALAYSIA
A state whose name means 'Nine States' from *negeri* 'state' and *sembilan* 'nine'. With the defeat of the Bugis in the mid-1780s nine small states, owing allegiance to the Sultan of Johor and including parts of present-day Johor, Malacca, Pahang, and Selangor, merged into a loose coalition. It became one of the Federated Malay States in 1896.

Negev (Hebrew: **Ha-Negev**), ISRAEL
A semi-desert with a name derived from the Hebrew root *n-g-b* 'to dry'. Thus the name means 'Dry (Land)' or sometimes 'South (Land)'.

Negro River, SOUTH AMERICA
Three rivers have this name: one in Argentina, another that rises in Brazil and flows into Uruguay, and the third which is one of the major rivers of South America. It rises in Colombia as the Guianía and takes the name Negro when it enters Brazil, later joining the Amazon. The forests around the river periodically flood and as the flood waters recede organic matter washes into the river and gives the water its dark colour; hence the name 'Black River' from the Portuguese *negro* 'black'.

Negros, PHILIPPINES
An island in the Visayan group meaning 'Black', a reference to the colour of its inhabitants.

Neijiang, SICHUAN/CHINA
Lying on the Tuo River and meaning 'Inside the River' from *nèi* 'inside' and *jiāng*.

Neiva, COLOMBIA
Founded in 1612 when the Spanish laid claim to it and named it after the Neiva River in Haiti.

Nekrasovskoye, YAROSLAVL'/RUSSIA *Bol'shiye Soli*
First named 'Big Salts' from *sol* 'salt', it was renamed in 1938 after Nikolai Nekrasov (1821–77), a poet and literary figure.

Nelson, ANTARCTICA, AUSTRALIA, CANADA, NEW ZEALAND, UK, USA
1. Antarctica: an island named after Admiral Lord Horatio Nelson (1758–1805), the British naval commander who won the Battle of Trafalgar in 1805 although he was killed towards the end of it.
2. Australia (Victoria): a cape, probably named after Admiral Lord Nelson.

3. Canada (British Columbia): founded in 1887 and named Stanley or Salisbury, it was renamed in 1888 after Hugh Nelson (1830–93), the Irish-born lieutenant-governor of British Columbia. The river in Manitoba, discovered in 1612 by Sir Thomas Button (d. 1634), was named by him after the pilot of his ship, the *Resolution*, who died while exploring it.
4. New Zealand (South Island): settled in 1842 and named after Admiral Lord Nelson.
5. UK (England): named after a pub, the Lord Nelson Inn.

Nelspruit, MPUMALANGA/SOUTH AFRICA
Founded in 1889 and named after three brothers, Gert, Andries, and Louis Nel, who owned the farm on which the settlement was established. *Spruit* is the Afrikaans for 'stream'.

Neman, LITHUANIA, RUSSIA
1. Lithuania: a river, called Nemunas by the Lithuanians, from *nemunas* 'river'. When the area was under the control of the Teutonic Knights the German name was Memel. Part of its course forms the border between Kaliningrad Province, Russia, and Lithuania.
2. Russia (Kaliningrad): a town named after the River Neman.

Nemi (Lago di Nemi), LAZIO/ITALY *Lacus Nemorensis*
A lake also known to the Romans as Speculum Dianae 'Mirror of Diana' in recognition of the temple and *nemus* from *nemorensis* 'pertaining to a grove', particularly to one that was sacred to Diana.

Nemours, ÎLE DE FRANCE/FRANCE *Nemoracum*
Derived from the Latin *nemorosus* 'woody'; woods surrounded the town.

Nenets, RUSSIA *Nenetsia*
An autonomous district, Nenetskiy Avtonomnyy Okrug, previously the province of Nenetsia, named after the Nentsy, the plural of Nenets 'man' or 'real person'. *See* YAMALO-NENETS.

Neodesha, KANSAS/USA
Lying at the confluence of the Fall and Verdigris Rivers, its Native American name means 'Meeting of the Waters'.

Neoga, ILLINOIS/USA
A Native American name meaning 'Place of the Deity'.

Neosho, USA
A city in Missouri founded in 1839 with an Osage name meaning 'Clear and Abundant Water'. There is also a river with this name that flows through Kansas and Oklahoma and another city, Neosha Falls, in Kansas.

Nepal The Kingdom of Nepal (Nepāl
Adhirājya) since 1769 when some small
kingdoms and principalities were united by a
Gurkha warlord, Prithvi Narayan Shah (1720–
75), who took the title of king (1769–75). The
name Nepal is said to have first appeared in
879 at the end of the Licchavi dynasty and to
refer to the Kathmandu Valley only; it was
said to mean 'Beginning of a New Era', which
unfortunately turned out to be the 'dark ages'
for the Nepalese. However, several other
theories as to its etymology have been put
forward. These include it being named after a
king or kings called Nepa or an ancient tribe
living in Kathmandu Valley called the
Newar; 'Home of Wool' from the Tibetan *ne*
'home' and *pal* 'wool' since sheep were reared
in Kathmandu Valley and produced much
wool; 'Country in the Centre' from the
Newari *ne* 'centre' and *pa* 'country', a reference
to the fact that Nepal is situated between
two great countries, China and India; 'Holy
Place' in the language of the Lepchas from *ne*
'holy' and *pal* 'cave' to indicate that it was a
place of pilgrimage for Hindus and
Buddhists; or from the Sanskrit *nepāla*,
possibly from *nipat* 'to fly down' and *ālaya*
'house', meaning the settlements at the foot of
the mountains.

Neponset, USA
A town in Illinois and a river in Massachusetts
with a Native American name meaning 'He
walks in his Sleep'.

Nerchinsk, CHITA/RUSSIA
Founded as a fort in 1654 which developed
into a trading centre. It is named after the
Nercha River which may take its name from
the root element *ner* 'river'.

Nesebŭr, BULGARIA *Mesemvria*
The present name, adopted in 1934, is an
adaptation of the town's previous descriptive
name. This was of Thracian origin from *messa*
'promontory' and *vria* 'town'. It is on what
amounts to an island joined by a narrow strip
of land to the mainland.

Neskaupstaður, ICELAND *Nordfjördur*
The former name meant 'Northern Fjord'.
The present name has the meaning of
'Market Town on the Promontory' from *nes*
'nose' and *kaupstaður* 'market town', itself
from *kaup* 'to buy' and *staður* 'homestead' or
'abode'.

Nesowadnehunk, MAINE/USA
A small lake with a Native American name
meaning 'Stream among the Mountains'.

Nesterov, KALININGRAD/RUSSIA *Stallupönen,
Ebenrode*
The German Stallupönen gave way to
Ebenrode 'Level Clearing in a Wood' in 1938,
although both names continued to be used
until 1945. When East Prussia was ceded to the
Soviet Union the name was changed in 1946 to
honour S. K. Nesterov, an officer in the Red
Army who was killed here in 1944.

Netanya, ISRAEL
Founded in 1928 and named after the
American-Jewish businessman and
philanthropist, Nathan Strauss (1848–1931).
The name is also spelt Natanya.

Netherlands, The (Die Nederlanden)
The Kingdom of the Netherlands (Koninkrijk
der Nederlanden) since 1814. Previously the
Kingdom of Holland (1806–10); the Batavian
Republic (1795–1806) from the Germanic
Batavi tribe which was brought under Roman
control; the United Provinces of the
Netherlands or the Dutch Republic (1579–
1795). The Low Countries (*see* BENELUX) passed
to the Spanish crown in 1504. What came to be
known as the Revolt of the Netherlands began
in 1568 and in 1579 the United Provinces of
the Netherlands claimed independence; this,
however, was not recognized by Spain until
the Peace of Westphalia in 1648. The name
*Holland is quite often used by English
speakers to describe what the Dutch call the
Netherlands, despite the fact that North and
South Holland comprise only two of twelve
provinces. (However, it is 'Holland' which
participates in the Football and Cricket World
Cups!) Netherlands or 'Low Lands' is the literal
English translation of *Nederlanden*, itself a
translation from the Latin *inferior terra*. This
area, however, is more commonly known as
the Low Countries. The term 'Netherlands'
came to refer only to the United Provinces
during the Twelve Years' Truce (1609–21). The
adjective 'Dutch', previously applied by
English speakers to all German speakers
(*Deutsch*), was used to distinguish the people of
the United Provinces of the Netherlands from
the people of the Southern (Spanish/Austrian)
Netherlands (modern Belgium and
Luxembourg) and thus now to the inhabitants
of the modern Netherlands. 'Dutch' comes
from the Middle Dutch *duuts* and ultimately
from the old Germanic *theudā* 'people'. A
number of English terms, usually derogatory,
using the name 'Dutch' originate from Anglo-
Dutch rivalry during the 17th and 18th
centuries. They include 'Dutch courage', false
courage derived from alcohol, possibly
because the Dutch were considered heavy
drinkers or because Dutch gin encouraged the

British; to speak 'double Dutch' is to speak incomprehensibly where 'Dutch' means 'foreign' and the 'double' indicates excessively, thus reflecting a disagreeable English disdain for those not speaking English. A 'Dutch treat', when everybody pays for themselves, is clearly not a treat; and 'to go Dutch', when everybody agrees to share expenses equally, is another form of 'Dutch treat'.

Netherlands Antilles Netherlands Antilles (Nederlandse Antillen), an autonomous region of The Netherlands since 1954. They comprise two well separated island groups in the Lesser Antilles in the Caribbean Sea. In the north are the southern half of St Maarten, St Eustatius, and Saba, while off the coast of Venezuela lie Bonaire and Curaçao. First visited by the Spanish in 1499, the northern group islands were captured by the Dutch West India Company in 1630, 1635, and 1640 respectively, while Curaçao was taken in 1634 and Bonaire in 1636. Rule by the Company ended in 1828 and the Dutch crown assumed responsibility. In 1845 the Netherlands Antilles were created from the six islands, which then included Aruba (until 1986). The Netherlands Antilles are also sometimes called the Antilles of the Five. *See* ANTILLES.

Nettuno, LAZIO/ITALY
May allude to the Roman god of the sea, Neptune, to whom some temple here may have been dedicated.

Neubrandenburg, MECKLENBURG-WEST POMERANIA/GERMANY
Founded in 1248 as a military outpost by the Margraves of Brandenburg, it was given the simple name 'New Brandenburg'. *See* BRANDENBURG.

Neuchâtel (German: **Neuenburg**), SWITZERLAND *Novum Castellum*
A canton from 1815, a lake, and a town meaning 'New Castle' in the earlier Latin and from the French *neuf* 'new' and *châtel*, an earlier form of *château* 'castle'. It was a personal principality of the King of Prussia in 1707–1857. There are towns called Neufchâteau in Belgium and Lorraine, France, and Neufchâtel in Picardy, France, and Quebec, Canada.

Neumünster, SCHLESWIG-HOLSTEIN/GERMANY
'New Minster' which was built by Bishop Vicelin in 1127 in a small community then called Wippendorf.

Neustadt, GERMANY
1. Rhineland-Palatinate: the town's full name is Neustadt an der Weinstrasse 'New Town on the Wine Route' indicating its location at the centre of the wine industry. Its former name was Neustadt an der Haardt, a reference to its position on the slopes of the Haardt Mountains. **2.** A number of towns in Germany, particularly in Bavaria where there are four, have the name 'New Town'.

Neustria, FRANCE
A historic region between the 6th and 8th centuries west of the River Meuse and north of the River Loire forming the western Frankish kingdom. Its name, from the German *neu*, indicated that it was 'new land' settled by the Franks after their arrival in northern Gaul.

Neva, LENINGRAD/RUSSIA *Nevajoki*
A river, originally with a Finnish name from *neva* 'swamp' or 'marsh' and *joki* 'river'.

Nevada, USA
A state and three towns. It is a Spanish name 'Snow-clad', a reference to the Sierra Nevada mountains. The state was part of Spanish America until 1821 when it joined the newly independent state of Mexico. In 1848 Nevada joined the USA as part of California and two years later it was transferred to Utah. In 1861 it became Nevada Territory and in 1864 it joined the Union as the 36th state.

Nevel'sk, SAKHALIN ISLAND/RUSSIA *Honto*
The previous Japanese name was superseded in 1946 and the present one honours Admiral Gennady Nevelskoy (1813–76), an admiral who explored this region. A strait between Sakhalin Island and the Russian mainland is named Nevelskoy after the same officer who discovered it in 1849; thus he demonstrated that Sakhalin was an island rather than a peninsula.

Nevers, BURGUNDY/FRANCE *Noviodunum Aeduorum, Nevirnum*
The Roman names meant 'New Fort' from *novio* 'new' and *dunum*, Nevirnum being a contraction. The present name is derived from the Nièvre River on which the city lies at its confluence with the Loire. This name is probably connected with the root element *nev* 'water'.

Neves, BRAZIL, SÃO TOMÉ AND PRÍNCIPE
Brazil (Rio de Janeiro): originally a Guarulhos village, it became a Spanish religious centre with a chapel. It means 'Snows' from the Spanish *nieve*.

Nevis *See* ST KITTS AND NEVIS.

New Albany, INDIANA/USA
Founded in 1813 by three Scribner brothers who named it after their hometown, Albany, New York.

New Amsterdam, GUYANA *Fort Sint Andries*
Founded in the 1740s by the Dutch. When it
became the seat of the Dutch colonial
government in 1790 it was renamed after the
Dutch city of Amsterdam.

Newark, UK, USA
1. UK (England/Nottinghamshire): formerly
Niweweorce and Neuuerche 'New Work', that
is, a fort from the Old English *nīwe* and *weorc*
'fortification' or 'building'. The full name of
the town in Nottinghamshire is Newark-on-
Trent, a reference to the river on which it lies.
2. USA (New Jersey): founded in 1666 as
Pesayak Towne and later renamed New
Milford after Milford, Connecticut. It was
renamed again by the Revd Abraham Pierson,
possibly after his hometown in England,
Newark-on-Trent. An alternative suggestion is
that it has a biblical connection: New Ark.
3. USA (Ohio): laid out in 1802 and named
after the hometown of the first settlers,
Newark, New Jersey.

New Bedford, MASSACHUSETTS/USA *Bedford*
Founded in 1652 as part of Dartmouth. As
Bedford, it became a town in 1787. 'New' was
added later to distinguish it from Bedford in
Middlesex county. The site was owned by a
man called Russell, the family name of the
Duke of Bedford.

New Bern, NORTH CAROLINA/USA
Named in 1710 after the Bern in Switzerland,
the hometown of the first settler, Christopher
von Graffenried.

New Braunfels, TEXAS/USA
Founded in 1845 by a group of German
immigrants led by Prince Karl of Solms-
Braunfels and named after Braunfels 'Brown
Rock', then in Prussia.

New Britain, PAPUA NEW GUINEA, USA
Papua New Guinea: an island first sighted by a
European in 1616. It was given its present
name in 1699 by William Dampier (1651–
1715), a British buccaneer and explorer. When
the island became part of a German
protectorate in 1884 it was renamed Neu
Pommern 'New Pomerania'. At the end of the
First World War Australia assumed a League of
Nations mandate and the original name was
restored. It became part of Papua New Guinea
in 1975 when independence was achieved.

New Brunswick, CANADA, USA
1. Canada: a province. Part of the French
colony of Acadia, the territory passed to the
British in 1713 and in 1763 it was incorporated
into Nova Scotia. In 1784 it became a province
in its own right and was named by United

Empire Loyalists after King George III[†], one of
whose titles was Duke of Brunswick-Lüneburg.
2. USA (New Jersey): settled in 1681 as
Prigmore's Swamp and then renamed Inian's
Ferry in 1713 after John Inian, the first settler
who began a ferry service across the Raritan
River here. Subsequently, it was renamed after
King George I[†], the Duke of Brunswick-
Lüneburg.

Newbury, UK, USA
UK (England); formerly Neuberi 'New Market
Town' from the Old English *nīwe* and *burh*
which, here, means 'town' rather than 'fort'.

Newburyport, MASSACHUSETTS/USA
Settled in 1635 at the mouth of the Merrimack
River and named after the Newbury in England.

New Caledonia Territory of New Caledonia
(French: Territoire de la Nouvelle-Calédonie et
Dépendances) in Melanesia was first visited in
1774 by Captain James Cook[†]. He named it
New Caledonia because it reminded him of the
Scottish coastline, Caledonia being the Latin
name for Scotland. Annexed by France in 1853
as a dependency of Tahiti, it became an
Overseas Territory of France in 1946. It is
considered an integral part of the French
Republic. It includes the Loyalty Islands, the
Isle of Pines, and other minor islands. The
French name for the main island of New
Caledonia, La Grande Terre, means 'Mainland'.

Newcastle, AUSTRALIA, CANADA, IRELAND,
NEVIS, SOUTH AFRICA, UK, USA
1. Australia (New South Wales): established as
the Coal Harbour Penal Settlement in 1801, it
was renamed after the nearby Newcastle
coalfield, itself named after the Newcastle in
England whose principal export from the 16th
century was coal.
2. Canada (New Brunswick): founded in 1785
and almost certainly named after Thomas
Pelham-Holles (1693–1768), 1st Duke of
Newcastle-upon-Tyne and British prime
minister (1754–6 and 1757–62).
3. South Africa (KwaZulu-Natal): founded in
1864 and named after Henry Clinton (1811–
64), 5th Duke of Newcastle, British secretary of
state for the colonies (1852–4, 1859–64).
4. UK (England): although the Romans built a
fort at Newcastle-upon-Tyne, the name 'New
Castle' from the Old English *nīwe* and *castel*
dates to a Norman castle built here in 1080.
The expression 'to carry coals to Newcastle'
means to do something unnecessary, given the
city's then coal-mining industry. Newcastle
under Lyme denotes the name of a forest
which may be derived from a Celtic name
meaning 'region of elm trees'.

5. UK (Northern Ireland): in Irish, An Caisleán Nua 'The New Castle'. The castle after which the town is named belonged to the Magennis and was built in 1588.
6. USA (Wyoming): founded in 1889 as a coal-mining town, it took the name of Newcastle in England.

New Castle, JAMAICA, USA
1. USA (Delaware): founded in 1651 by the Dutch as Santhoeck and renamed in 1655 Nieuw Amstel. It was captured by the British in 1664 and given its present name, probably in honour of William Cavendish (1592–1676), 1st Duke of Newcastle, who was a Royalist commander during the English Civil War (1642–51).
2. USA (Indiana): founded in 1819 and named by Ezekiel Leavell after his hometown in Kentucky.
3. USA (Pennsylvania): founded in 1798 to incorporate an iron furnace and named after Newcastle-upon-Tyne in England.

New Delhi, INDIA
At a magnificent *durbar* 'assembly' held in Delhi in 1911 the King Emperor, George V[†], announced that the capital of British India would be transferred from Calcutta to a new site outside Delhi. This happened the following year, although construction of the site was not completed until 1931. The new city was given the name New Delhi and it remains the capital of the Republic of India. *See* DELHI.

New England, USA
A region that includes the states of Connecticut, Maine, Massachusetts, New Hampshire, Rhode Island, and Vermont. It was named by Captain John Smith in 1614 as a tribute to his home country. The first Puritans from England settled in Massachusetts in 1620 when the name was confirmed by James I[†].

Newfoundland, NEWFOUNDLAND AND LABRADOR/CANADA *The New Isle*
An island probably discovered by the Italian-born John Cabot (*c*.1450–*c*.1499) in 1497 while sailing under the English flag. He took possession of the territory in the name of Henry VII (1457–1509), King of England (1485–1509). By 1502 it had become 'The New Found Land' to make the English claim legitimate. A world map of 1507 shows it as Terra Nova—Insula Baccalauras 'New (Found) Land—Island of Codfish' as discovered by the Portuguese explorer Gaspar Corte-Real in 1501 and so named because of the abundance of fish in its waters. He had called it Terra Verde 'Green Land' although, in fact, it was not Greenland. British sovereignty was recognized by the Treaty of Utrecht in 1713. The island gave its name to the Newfoundland, a breed of working dog developed here (see next entry).

Newfoundland and Labrador, CANADA
A province consisting of the island of Newfoundland and the mainland known as *Labrador. British sovereignty was recognized in 1713 and self-government was achieved in 1855. Although Labrador became part of Newfoundland in 1927 it was not until 1949 that Newfoundland finally joined the Canadian Union as its tenth province. At the end of 2001, the name was changed to Newfoundland and Labrador.

New France (Nouvelle-France)
The name for the French possessions in North America in 1534–1763. At its zenith at the beginning of the 18th century, it stretched from the Gulf of St Lawrence to the west of Lake Superior to include most of the area of the Great Lakes, Newfoundland, Acadia (Nova Scotia), and the Mississippi valley down to the Gulf of Mexico.

New Glarus, WISCONSIN/USA
Founded in 1845 by immigrants who had been forced to flee from Glarus in Switzerland.

New Glasgow, NOVA SCOTIA/CANADA
Founded in 1809 some ten years after coal deposits were discovered and named by William Fraser, a Scot, who visualized a new Glasgow on a new River Clyde (the East River).

New Granada (Nueva Granada)
The name for the former Spanish viceroyalty between 1717 and 1810. It comprised modern Colombia, Ecuador, Panama, and Venezuela. It was named after the famous Spanish city in Andalusia.

New Guinea, INDONESIA-PAPUA NEW GUINEA
An island which comprises the Indonesian province of Papua in the west and the state of *Papua New Guinea in the east. The island was first visited by the Portuguese in 1527 and given its name in 1546 by a Spanish explorer, Ynigo Ortiz de Retes, who considered that the black-skinned people here resembled those found along the coast of Guinea in West Africa. The western half of the island became part of the Dutch East Indies in 1828; in 1884 the British assumed control of the south-eastern quadrant while the Germans took the north-east. In 1906 British New Guinea was passed to Australia which assumed a League of Nations mandate over German New Guinea in 1921.

New Hampshire, USA
A state. The land here was granted by King Charles I[†] to Captain John Mason in the 1620s

and in 1629 he named it after his home county in England. It became a colony in its own right in 1679 and a state in 1776. It was the ninth to ratify the constitution in 1788.

New Hanover, PAPUA NEW GUINEA, SOUTH AFRICA
1. Papua New Guinea: an island in the Bismarck Archipelago named after the German city by the British navigator, Philip Carteret (d. 1796) in 1767. The King of Great Britain at this time was George III† and he was also King of Hanover. Between 1884 and 1914 when the archipelago was under German control the island was renamed Neu-Hannover.
2. South Africa (KwaZulu-Natal): founded in 1850 by German settlers and named after the Hanover in Germany.

New Harmony, INDIANA/USA *Harmonie*
Settled in 1814 by George Rapp, a German preacher. The settlement was sold in 1825 to a British reformer, Robert Owen, who renamed the place New Harmony after the ill-feeling between the Harmonists and their neighbours subsided.

Newhaven, ENGLAND/UK *Mechingas, Mecinges, Newehaven*
'New Harbour' from the Old English *nīwe* and *hæfen* 'harbour'. It became 'new' in 1570 after the lower course of the River Ouse was changed. Its earlier name meant 'Mēce's Family Settlement' from an Old English personal name and -*ingas*.

New Haven, CONNECTICUT/USA *Quinnipiac*
Settled in 1638, it was renamed in 1640, probably after the Newhaven in England. It is a port at the mouth of the Quinnipiac River.

New Hebrides *See* VANUATU.

New Iberia, LOUISIANA/USA
Founded in 1835 by Spanish and French settlers and named after the Iberian Peninsula. It lies on Bayou Teche, a bayou being a small marshy river; *teche* is a local Native American word for 'snake'.

New Ireland, PAPUA NEW GUINEA *Nova Hibernia, New Mecklenburg*
First discovererd by Jakob le Maire, a Dutch navigator, who thought that it was a part of a single large island that included New Britain and New Guinea. In 1767 Philip Carteret (d.1796), a British navigator, discovered that New Britain was an island in its own right and so named the smaller island lying to the north-east Nova Hibernia 'New Ireland'. It was annexed by Germany in 1884 and renamed New Mecklenburg. The previous name was

restored when Australia assumed a League of Nations mandate after the First World War. After the Second World War it was part of the UN Trust Territory of New Guinea before joining Papua New Guinea when it achieved independence in 1975.

New Jersey, USA
A state. Although the coastline was explored in 1524 by Giovanni da Verrazzano (1485–1528), the Italian navigator, it was not permanently settled until 1660. In 1664 it came under British control and was split into western and eastern halves. King Charles II† granted the eastern half to his brother, later King James II†, who in turn granted it to Sir George Carteret (*c.*1610–80), a Royalist politician, and the western half to Quaker settlers. Carteret named it after his birthplace, the island of Jersey in the Channel Islands. In 1702 the province was reunited as a crown colony but ruled from New York; it became a separate colony in 1738. It joined the Union as the third state in 1787.

New Liskeard, ONTARIO/CANADA *Thornloe*
Settled in 1822, it was subsequently renamed after *Liskeard in Cornwall, England, the birthplace of its founder, John Armstrong.

New London, CONNECTICUT/USA *Pequot*
Founded in 1646, it was renamed after the British capital in 1658.

New Madrid, MISSOURI/USA
Developed from a Native American trading post in 1789 by General George Morgan who had been given land here by the Spanish government. He therefore named the town after the Spanish capital.

Newmarket, CANADA, IRELAND, JAMAICA, NEW ZEALAND, UK, USA
UK (England): formerly Novum Forum 'New Market (Place)', a direct translation of the Latin name. In the 16th century the villagers of nearby Exning decided to build a 'new market place'.

New Market, VIRGINIA/USA *Crossroads*
Laid out in 1784, it was renamed after the English Newmarket in 1796.

New Mexico, USA *Nuevo México*
A state which was first visited by Europeans, the Spanish, coming from Mexico in search of treasure in 1540. It received its Spanish name after the city of Mexico in New Spain in 1562, but the first settlement was not made until 1598 after missionaries had entered the area. When Mexico achieved full independence in 1821, New Mexico became a part of that new country. At the close of the Mexican War in

1848 New Mexico was ceded to the USA. It became the Territory of New Mexico in 1850 and joined the Union in 1912 as the 47th state.

New Orleans, LOUISIANA/USA *Nouvelle-Orléans*
The city was founded in 1718 as a result of a decision taken the year before in Paris to build a transshipment point here. It was named after the French Regent, Philippe (1674–1723), Duc d'Orléans. In 1763 the city was ceded to Spain, but secretly returned to France in 1800. However, as part of the Louisiana Purchase, it was bought by the USA in 1803. The French name is feminine because the feminine *ville* 'town' is understood.

Newport, AUSTRALIA, CANADA, IRELAND, JAMAICA, UK, USA
1. At least 29 cities and towns around the world have this name. In most cases, the name is appropriate for a place on the coast or on a river. However, the Old English *port* can also mean a 'market town' and thus some towns with this name can be found inland. The 'new' was usually in comparison with an older town or castle.
2. USA (Kentucky): named after Captain Christopher Newport, the captain of the first ship to visit Jamestown, Virginia, in 1607.
3. USA (Rhode Island): founded in 1639 and called a 'new port' by Puritan settlers from Massachusetts. They had come from Portsmouth at the northern end of the island and before that from Portsmouth, England.

Newport Beach, CALIFORNIA/USA *Newport Landing, McFaddens Landing, Port Orange*
Developed as a result of the need for 'new port' facilities in the bay here. In 1892 it was renamed Newport with 'Beach' being added later.

Newport News, VIRGINIA/USA
Established *c*.1621 by colonists from Ireland and named after Captain Christopher Newport, who commanded several expeditions to Jamestown, Virginia, between 1607 and 1612, and Sir William Newce, who arrived from Ireland in 1621.

Newport Pagnell, ENGLAND/UK *Neuport, Neuport Paynelle*
'New Market Town' from the Old English *nīwe* and *port* 'market town'. The affix indicated its possession by the Paynel family from 1151.

New Providence Island, THE BAHAMAS
According to tradition, the name is derived from a 16th-century governor who gave thanks to 'Divine Providence' for his survival after a shipwreck. The 'New' was added later to

distinguish it from a small island off British Honduras (now Belize) used by pirates.

Newquay, ENGLAND/UK *Newe Kaye*
Named after the new quay that was built here in the 15th century.

New Rochelle, NEW YORK/USA
Founded in 1688 by Huguenot refugees and named after La Rochelle in France.

Newry, AUSTRALIA, UK, USA
UK (Northern Ireland): the Irish name is An tIúr. Formerly Iobhar Chind Trachta 'The Yew Tree' from *iubhar* 'yew'. The original yew tree is alleged to have been planted by St Patrick at the head of Carlingford Lough. It was designated a city in 2002, the year of Queen Elizabeth II's Golden Jubilee.

New Siberian Islands (Novosibirskiye Ostrova), SAKHA REPUBLIC/RUSSIA
The archipelago takes its name from one of its islands, Ostrov Novaya Sibir' 'New Siberia Island'. When discovered by the Russian polar explorer M. Gedenshtrem in 1920, he thought it was part of the mainland of Siberia and thus called it simply 'New Siberia'.

New Smyrna Beach, FLORIDA/USA *Caparaco, Atocuimi*
Originally a Native American village, the Spanish mission of Atocuimi was established here in 1696. In 1767 an unusual group of Greek and Italian immigrants, led by Andrew Turnbull, a Scottish doctor, arrived and renamed the place after the birthplace, Smyrna (now Izmir), of Turnbull's wife. Only in 1937, in recognition of the sandy beach here, was 'Beach' added to the name.

New South Wales, AUSTRALIA
A state. Captain James Cook[†] so named the coastal area of eastern Australia in 1770 because he is said to have thought that the coastline was much like that of southern Wales. It came to refer to practically the entire eastern half of Australia—the territory east of 135° East. Subsequently, however, the territory named New South Wales became smaller and smaller as new colonies were established until it reached its present size in 1915.

New Spain (Nueve España)
The name for the former Spanish viceroyalty in Central America between 1521 and 1821. It included the territory north of the Isthmus of Panama, modern California, the south-western states of the USA, and Florida.

Newton, CANADA, UK, USA
At least fourteen cities and towns have this name, usually meaning 'New Town'. However, the city in Iowa, USA, is named after a hero of

the American War of Independence (1775–83), Sergeant John Newton. Another eight are spelt Newtown or New Town. At least two counties are named after Sir Isaac Newton (1642–1727), the famous mathematician.

Newton Abbot, ENGLAND/UK *Nyweton Abbatis* 'New Farmstead' or 'New Village of the Abbot' from the Old English *nīwe*, *tūn*, and the Latin affix indicating that it belonged to the abbot of Torre Abbey.

Newtownabbey (Baile na Mainistreach), NORTHERN IRELAND/UK
Formed in 1958 as the result of the merger of seven villages, thus 'Newtown'. 'Abbey' comes from Whiteabbey, one of the villages.

Newtownards (Baile Nua na hAirde), NORTHERN IRELAND/UK *New Town of Blathewyc* 'New Town on the Promontory' from *aird* 'point' or 'promontory' (and not from *ard* 'height' or 'high' although *aird* is often Anglicized to *ard*). Founded in 1608 on the site of a ruined Dominican friary, 'New Town' has the meaning of a settlement around a plantation. The former name came from *Uí Bhlathmhaic* 'descendants of Blathmhac'.

Newtownbutler, NORTHERN IRELAND/UK *Neetowne*
Renamed in 1715 when Theophilus Butler became a baron and took the title Baron of Newtownbutler.

New Waterford, NOVA SCOTIA/CANADA
Founded in 1608 and named after the home town of a settler, *Waterford, Ireland.

New Westminster, BRITISH COLUMBIA/CANADA *Queensborough*
Founded in 1859 as a tribute to Queen Victoria[†], but subsequently renamed following her mild disapproval; it was she who suggested the present name.

New World A term coined, possibly in 1502, by Amerigo Vespucci (1454–1512), the Spanish navigator and explorer, after his voyage to South America in 1501–2. Sailing down the South American coast, he had become convinced that this newly discovered land could not be Asia but a 'New World'. This opinion was published in his booklet *Mundus Novus* 'New World' in 1505. In 1507 Martin Waldseemüller (*c*.1470–*c*.1520), the German cartographer, published a new world map showing the 'Old World' of Ptolemy and the 'New World' of Vespucci. The new continent, he suggested, should be called Amerige or America after its discoverer.

New York, USA *New Amsterdam, New Orange*
A state and a city, New York City. The Dutch first sailed into the harbour and up the Hudson River in 1609 in search of a route to India. The first settlement in the state was made at present-day Albany in 1624 and Nieuw Amsterdam 'New Amsterdam' after the Dutch capital was established on Manhattan Island (now part of New York City) the following year. In 1626 the Dutch province of New Netherland (which included what is now New York City and parts of Connecticut and New Jersey) bought Manhattan from the Native Americans. In 1664 the British seized the city and renamed it New York after James (1633–1701), Duke of York and Albany, later King James II[†]. The Dutch territories surrounding it were given to the Duke of York and Albany by his brother, King Charles II[†]; those to the west of the Hudson River were temporarily named Albania while those to the east were called Yorkshire. The Duke passed the western lands on to Lord John Berkeley and Sir George Carteret who called them New Jersey; Yorkshire became the state of New York (and this subsequently grew to its present size). In 1673 the Dutch retook the city and renamed it New Orange in honour of the Prince of Orange, stadholder (governor) of the Netherlands at that time, who later became King William III[†]. A year later, however, British rule was restored and so was the name New York. New York joined the Union in 1788 as the eleventh state and New York City became the first capital of the USA in 1789; it remained so only until 1790.

New Zealand (Maori: **Aotearoa**)
Occupied from *c*.1400 by the Maori people who called it Aotearoa '(Land of) the Long White Cloud' from *ao* 'cloud', *tea* 'white' and *roa* 'long'. The first European to discover New Zealand was Abel Tasman[†]. At the end of 1642 he came across South Island but did not realize that it was separate from North Island. He named it Staten Landt 'Land of the States' in honour of the States General (*see* THE NETHERLANDS). In 1643 the name was changed to Nieuw Zeeland 'New Sea Land' after the Dutch province of Zeeland. In 1769–70 Captain James Cook[†] charted the two separate islands. By 1840 the British had annexed both islands as part of New South Wales, Australia, but the following year New Zealand became a separate crown colony. It became a self-governing colony in 1856 and a dominion in 1907, although it did not gain full independence until 1947. It is a constitutional monarchy with the British monarch being the formal head of state.

Neyshābūr, IRAN
Named 'Fair Shāpūr' after the man said to have founded it, Shāpūr I (d. 272), Persian king of the Sāssānian dynasty who styled himself 'King of Kings of Iran and non-Iran', and the Persian *niv* 'fair' or 'good' (modern Persian *nîk*). Some say, however, that the city was founded by Shāpūr II the Great (309–79). The name is also spelt Nīshāpūr.

Nezperce, IDAHO/USA
Named after a local Native American tribe whose French name, Nez Percé, meant 'Pierced Nose'.

Nha Trang, VIETNAM *Kauthara*
Originally one of the states of Champa, named from a region in India when it became Indianized. Re-established on the king's orders in 1924, the name is said to derive from a Cham word *yakram* or *yatran* 'bamboo river'.

Niagara Falls, CANADA, USA
1. Two cities by the famous Falls on either side of the Niagara River in Canada and the USA. Niagara may be an Iroquois word meaning 'Across the Neck', 'At the Neck', or 'Land cut in Two'. A popular meaning, however, is 'Thundering of Waters'. The Falls are in two parts, separated by Goat Island.
2. Canada (Ontario): named Elgin in 1853, Clifton in 1856, and Niagara Falls in 1881.
3. USA (New York): a British Fort Schlosser was built here in 1761 and a settlement called Manchester was established in 1805. Although both were destroyed in 1812 development continued and the city was renamed as now after the Falls.

Niagara-on-the-Lake, ONTARIO/CANADA
Newark
Founded in 1792 at the point where the Niagara River flows into Lake Ontario. The present, more appropriate, name was adopted some time after 1796.

Niamey, NIGER
Its origins are disputed. Some believe that it was a Songhai fishing village named after the local niami tree. On the other hand, according to local tradition, it was founded by a local Djerba chief, Kouri Mali, who told some captured slaves 'oua niammané' 'settle here'. This evolved into the present name. It became the capital of the French colony of Niger in 1926 and the national capital when Niger achieved independence in 1960.

Niantic, CONNECTICUT/USA
Probably named after an Algonquian-speaking tribe called the Niantic. Their name means

'(People who live) at the Point of Land on a Tidal River'.

Niassa, MOZAMBIQUE
A province meaning 'Water' or 'Lake'.

Nicaea, TURKEY
See İZNIK.

Nicaragua The Republic of Nicaragua (República de Nicaragua) since 1838. In 1826–38 it was part of the short-lived United Provinces of Central America and of the Mexican Empire (1821–3), having achieved independence from Spain in 1821. The hope of finding gold and silver brought the Spanish to Nicaragua in 1522, the first expedition being led by the conquistador Gil González Dávila. It is he who is said to have named the country after a local chief, one Nicarao. Alternatively, it has been suggested that some Spaniards heard the name Nicaragua, perhaps meaning 'Here, near the Lake'. The Mosquito Coast, on the Caribbean, was claimed as a British protectorate between 1740 and 1786. A large disputed area north of the Coco River was awarded to Honduras by the International Court of Justice in 1960. The country also gives its name to Lake Nicaragua which was called Cocibolca 'Sweet Sea' by the locals, translated as Mar Dulce by the Spanish.

Nice, PROVENCE-ALPES-CÔTE-D'AZUR/FRANCE
Nike, Nikaia
Founded by a group of Greek sailors from Massilia (now Marseilles) *c*.350 BC, who are thought to have dedicated it to Nike, the Greek goddess of victory (in Greek, *nikē* 'victory'), after the defeat of local opponents. The city-port was ceded to France in 1860.

Nicholson, AUSTRALIA, CANADA, USA
Australia (Queensland): a river rising in the Northern Territory, it is named after William Nicholson, a friend and supporter of Ludwig Leichhardt. Nicholson, however, did not accompany Leichhardt on his expeditions in Queensland.

Nicobar Islands, INDIA
See ANDAMAN AND NICOBAR ISLANDS.

Nicopolis, GREECE
Ruins also known as Nicopolis Actia or Nikópolis. A city founded by Augustus[†] to commemorate his victory (when he was known as Octavian) at Actium in 31 BC over Mark Antony (*c*.82–30 BC), a supporter of Julius Caesar[†] and triumvir. The name means 'City of Victory' from the Greek *nikē* 'victory' and *polis*.

Nicosia, CYPRUS, ITALY
1. Cyprus: in Greek Lefkosia and in Turkish Lefkoşa. Until the 4th century the city was

known as Ledra or Ledrae, possibly named
c.280 BC after Lefcon or Levcos, the elder son of
Ptolemy I Soter (c.364–c.282 BC), founder of the
Ptolemaic dynasty, who rebuilt the city.
Alternative theories are that the city was
named after the tall cypress tree, *lefki*, or as
Leukousia after the Greek *levkos* 'white' or
'brilliant'; or that *lefkon* meant 'poplar grove'
because these lined the banks of the Pedieos
River on which the city lay. The present name,
Nicosia, adopted during the 13th century, is a
modification of the Byzantine Lefkosia since
the Lusignans found Lefkosia too difficult to
pronounce. It has been the capital since the
10th century. Under the rule of the Byzantines
(330–1191), Lusignans (1192–1489), Venetians
(1489–1571), Ottoman Turks (1571–1878), and
the British (1878–1960), the city was divided in
1964 by the so-called Green Line to separate
the Greek sector in the south from the Turkish
sector.
2. Italy (Sicily); rebuilt by the Normans on the
site of an old city called Erleita di Tolomeo
'Meadows of Ptolemy' which had been
destroyed by the Arabs in the 9th century.

Nidwalden, SWITZERLAND
A demi-canton since 1291, before which it was
part of the canton of Unterwalden, one of the
three original Swiss cantons. The name means
'Below the Forest (of Kerns)' from the German
nid 'below' or 'under' and *Wald* 'forest'.

Niederösterreich, AUSTRIA
A state in the north-east called 'Lower Austria'.

Niedersachsen, GERMANY
A state with a name meaning 'Lower Saxony'
from *nieder* 'lower' and *Sachsen* 'Saxony'. It was
named after the Saxons who themselves are
possibly named after the Old High German
sahsa 'dagger', which was said to be their
favourite weapon. Two other states are called
Sachsen (Saxony) and Sachsen-Anhalt (Saxony-
Anhalt).

Nieuwkoop, THE NETHERLANDS
'New Parcel (of Land)' from the Dutch *nieuw*
'new' and *koop*, derived from *coep* and *cope*
'measurement', although the town was
founded in the 13th century.

Nieuwpoort, BELGIUM, CURAÇAO, THE
NETHERLANDS
'New Port'.

Niger, AND NIGERIA
1. The Republic of Niger (République du
Niger) since independence from France in
1960. Previously it was an autonomous
republic within the French Community (1958–
60) and a French colony (1922–58), having
become part of French West Africa in 1904.

The land-locked country takes its name from
the Niger River that flows through Guinea,
Mali, Niger and Nigeria.
2. A river which was called al-Nil 'The Nile
(River)' because contemporary Muslim
geographers believed that it was linked to the
(Egyptian) Nile. They also called it *Nahr al-
Anhur*, a misinterpretation of the Tuareg
egereou n-igereouen, both meaning 'River of
Rivers'. The present name was first seen in
1526 and it has been suggested as having come
from the Latin *niger* 'black' to mean the '(River
of) the Blacks'. However, it is more likely that
the name comes from the second and third
parts of the Tuareg name or the similar Berber
gher-n-igheren 'river of rivers'.
3. Nigeria: a state named after the Niger River
which forms its southern boundary.

Nigeria The Federal Republic of Nigeria since
1963 after independence from the UK in 1960
when it was named the Federation of Nigeria.
The northern half of the UN Trust Territory of
British Cameroons (also known as the Northern
Cameroons), formerly part of the German
protectorate of Kamerun, was incorporated
into Nigeria's Northern Region as the province
of Sardauna in 1961. Lagos was annexed by the
British in 1861. It became a colony in 1886 while
its hinterland became a protectorate; the Niger
delta had also become a protectorate, known as
the Oil Rivers Protectorate, the year before. In
1893 this protectorate was renamed the Niger
Coast Protectorate and seven years later it
merged with the territory of the Royal Niger
Company to form the Protectorate of Southern
Nigeria. Lagos Colony and Protectorate joined it
in 1906 and it was then renamed the Colony and
Protectorate of Southern Nigeria.
Simultaneously, the remainder of modern
Nigeria became the Protectorate of Northern
Nigeria. In 1914 the two parts merged to form
the Colony and Protectorate of Nigeria. The
country takes its name from the Niger River
which flows through it. The name Nigeria dates
from 1900 when the Southern Nigeria
Protectorate was created. Earlier the territory
had been known informally as Negroland or
Nigritia.

Niigata, HONSHŪ/JAPAN
A prefecture and a city on the Sea of Japan
meaning 'New Tidal Flats' from *nii* 'new' and
kata 'tidal flats'.

Niihama, SHIKOKU/JAPAN
Originally a small fishing village, the name
means 'New Beach' from *nii* 'new' and *hama*
'beach'.

Nijmegen, THE NETHERLANDS *Noviomagus (Batavorum)*
An adaptation of the Roman name 'New Market (of the Batavi)' from *novio* 'new' and *mago* 'place', 'field', or 'market'.

Nikel', MURMANSK/RUSSIA
'Nickel' from *nikel'*, a reference to its mining here.

Nikkō, HONSHŪ/JAPAN
'Sunlight', an allusion to the magnificence of its shrines, and particularly the mausoleum of Tokugawa Ieyasu (1543–1616), shogun (1603–5), and their ornate decoration. The mausoleum is so splendid that it has spawned a proverb: 'Never use the word *kekko* "magnificent" until you have seen Nikkō'.

Nikolayev (Mykolayiv), UKRAINE *Olbia*
A province and a city-port developed in 1788 from a fort built four years earlier near the ancient Greek city of Olbia with a name which, according to tradition, celebrates the Russian victory at Ochakov over the Ottoman Turks that year; this was achieved on the feast day of St Nicholas, 6 December.

Nikolayevsk-na-Amure, KHABAROVSK TERRITORY/RUSSIA
Named after Emperor Nicholas I[†] when it was established as a trading post in 1850. Na-Amure 'On the Amur (River)' was added in 1926 to distinguish this town from others with similar names.

Nikopol', BULGARIA, UKRAINE
1. Bulgaria: founded in 629 by Heraclius as Nikopolis, although to what victory it refers is not known. It is now spelt Nikopol. It has been referred to as Nikopolis Major to distinguish it from Nikopolis Minor, or the archaeological site of Nikopolis ad Istum, founded by Trajan[†] in 102 further south on the Rositsa River, to commemorate his victory over the Dacians. It has also been called Nīkbūlī.
2. Ukraine: founded as Slavyansk 'Slav Town' on a bend on the River Dnieper. It was developed and in the first half of the 17th century renamed Nikitino or Nikitin Rog 'Nikita's Horn' from the Russian *rog* 'horn', a reference to the promontory here, and the personal name Nikita, itself from the Greek *aníketos* 'unconquered' from *níkē* 'victory'. By the latter half of the 18th century names of Greek origin were in favour and so in 1782 the town was renamed Nikopol', the Slav version of Nikopolis 'Town of Victory' from the Greek *níkē* and *polis*.

Niksar, TURKEY *Cabeira, Neocaesarea*
The present name is derived from the previous Roman 'New Caesarea' which replaced the Pontic name.

Nikšić, MONTENEGRO/SERBIA AND MONTENEGRO *Anagastum, Onogošt*
Originally named after the Gothic leader, Angasta, in the 5th century. When the Slavs arrived at the end of the 6th century they built a new settlement on the site with the modified name of Onogošt. In the middle of the 14th century, the name was changed as a tribute to Nikša, the founder of the Nikšić clan, which moved here from the Gulf of Kotor.

Nile (Baḥr al-Nîl), EAST AFRICA
There are two rivers, the White Nile and the Blue Nile, which join at Khartoum in the Sudan to form the Nile. The name comes from the Semitic root word *nahal* 'river'. Sections of the river have different names such as the Victoria Nile (between Lake Victoria and Lake Albert); it becomes the Albert Nile when it leaves the northern end of that lake; then the Baḥr al-Jabal 'Mountain River (Nile)' when it enters the Sudan. It is joined by the Baḥr al-Ghazāl 'River of the Antelopes', a left-bank tributary, and becomes the White Nile (in Arabic, *al-Baḥr al-abyad* from *al, baḥr* and *abyad* 'white') after its junction with the Sobat River above Malakāl. Largely silt-free, viewed at certain times the river appears a little white. The upper reaches of the Blue Nile (in Arabic, *al-Baḥr al-azraq* from *azraq* 'blue') are known as the Abay or Abbai. At times the water reflects the sky, hence the name 'Blue Nile'.

Niles, USA
1. Michigan: settled in 1828 and named after Hezekiah Niles, the Baltimore publisher of the *Niles' Weekly Register*.
2. Ohio: settled in 1806 as the township of Heaton's Furnace, it was renamed Nilestown in 1834 after Hezekiah Niles. The name was shortened in 1843.

Nīlgiri Hills, TAMIL NĀDU/INDIA *Malai-nādu*
The original name meant 'Hill Country' from *malai* 'hill' and *nātu* 'land' or 'country'. The present name comes from the Sanskrit *Nīlagiri* 'Blue Mountain'.

Nîmes, LANGUEDOC-ROUSSILLON/FRANCE *Nemausus*
Originally the capital of a local Celtic tribe, it was Romanized, becoming a colony in 27 BC. It was given a name that comes from that of the 'spirit' of a local spring or fountain, which may be connected with the Gaulish *nemo* or Celtic *nemeton* 'grove' or 'sanctuary'. The town gave

its name to denim, a hard-wearing cotton-twill fabric, *de Nîmes* 'of Nîmes'.

Nimrūd, IRAQ *Calah, Larisa*
Ruins of one of the four great cities of Assyria and the Assyrian military headquarters founded in the 13th century BC. The Arabs named it after Nimrod, the mighty hunter of the Bible (Genesis 10: 8–12). It is also sometimes known by its original name.

Ninety-Six, SOUTH CAROLINA/USA
So named because it was 96 miles (155 km) from the Cherokee town of Keowee.

Nineveh, IRAQ
Ruins from the once great capital of the Assyrian Empire. Possibly founded during the 7th millennium BC and named after Ninus, King of Assyria and the supposed founder of the city. However, in the Bible (Genesis 10: 11), it is claimed that the city was founded by Nimrod. It was destroyed in 612 BC.

Ningbo, ZHEJIANG/CHINA *Huiji, Yinxian*
Lying on the Yung River and the seat of an independent prefecture, Mingzhou, since 738, it was renamed Ningbo 'Calm Waves' from *níng* and *bō* 'wave' in 1381 by the first emperor of the Ming dynasty to avoid using the dynastic name in the town's name. In 1914 the prefecture was abolished and became a district called Huiji. In 1927 Ningbo was re-established with city status and in 1931 it became part of Yin County and adopted the additional name of Yinxian 'Yin County' from *xiàn* 'county'. In 1949 it recovered its city status.

Ningdu, JIANGXI/CHINA
'Capital of Peace' or 'Peaceful City' from *níng* and *dū* 'capital' or 'city'.

Ninglu, SHANXI/CHINA *Ningxi Hulu, Ninglu Hulu*
'Pacify the Hu'. The Hu, or Hulu, were nomadic warriors from Central Asia and it was partly to provide a defence against them that parts of the Great Wall of China were built. Ninglu, a contraction of Ningxi and Hulu, is by the wall and it is surrounded by villages whose names mention the Hu: Weilu 'Subdue the Hu'; Pohubu 'Destroy the Hu'; Shahukou 'Kill the Hu'. The modern Chinese characters are *níng* and *lǔ* 'stupid' or 'vulgar'; this *lǔ* is a different character from the original *lǔ* which referred directly to the Hu. The Chinese character for *Hu* was changed by the Manchu so that it meant 'tiger'.

Ningxia Hui, CHINA
An autonomous region (Níngxià Huízú Zìzhìqū) given the name Ningxia 'Peaceful Xia', after its conquest by Genghis Khan[†] early in the 13th century, from *níng* and the Xi Xia

people who inhabited this area, known then as the Tangut Kingdom in the west of China, from *xī* 'west'. In the 11th century it had been called the Kingdom of Da Xia 'Great Xia' from *dà* 'great' and *xià* 'summer'. Hui is the name of another Muslim group.

Niobrara, NEBRASKA/USA
A river and a town with a Native American name meaning 'Broad Water' or 'Running Water'.

Niort, POITOU-CHARENTES/FRANCE *Noiordo, Nyrax*
The original name, and ultimately the present one, comes from Novioritu, itself from the Gaulish *novio* 'new' and *ritu* 'ford'. The town lies on the Sèvres Niortaise River.

Nipigon, ONTARIO/CANADA
A lake, river, town, bay, and strait with a local Native American name meaning 'Deep, clear Water'. The lake and river were first seen by a European in 1666.

Nipissing, ONTARIO/CANADA
A lake, discovered in 1610, and a town with a local Native American name meaning 'Little Water'.

Niš, SERBIA/SERBIA AND MONTENEGRO *Naissus, Niz, Nissa*
Derived from the River Nišava on which it lies. The previous Roman name was taken from the Celts who founded a settlement here in the 3rd century BC. The river's name may come from the Serbo-Croat *niz* 'along the course of' to mean a town built along the river.

Nishinomiya, HONSHŪ/JAPAN
'Temple of the West' from *nishi* 'west', *no* indicating the genitive 'of', and *miya* 'shrine'.

Niskayuna, NEWYORK/USA
'Extensive Corn Flats' from a Native American word.

Niterói, RIO DE JANEIRO/BRAZIL *Villa Real da Praia Grande*
Founded in 1671, it became a village with the Portuguese name Villa Real da Praia Grande 'Royal Town of the Big Beach' in 1819. It was upgraded to city status in 1836 and was given its present name from a Tupí-Guaraní word meaning 'Hidden Waters'.

Nitra, SLOVAKIA *Nitrahwa, Nitrau, Nitria*
A river and a town. There are two possibilities as to the meaning of the name. It may be from the former name of the river, Neid, which means 'to flow' or 'to run' and the Indo-European *ahwa* 'water' or 'river'; thus a '(place) where the river flows'. Alternatively, it may be derived from the Old Slavonic verb *neit* 'to

clear a forest by cutting or burning the trees' and -*a* used with the names of rivers. Thus the name could mean either a 'Settlement on the River' or a 'Settlement in a Clearing in the Forest'.

Niue, NEW ZEALAND *Nuku-tu-taha, Motusefua, Savage Island*
A self-governing state in free association with New Zealand since 1974. Its full name is Niue-fekai; *fekai* is said to mean 'food-possessing' in Old Nieuan or 'fierce' in Tongan and Samoan. Nuku-tu-taha indicates that it is an island on its own, between the Tonga Islands and Cook Islands, from *nuku* 'island', *tu* 'to stand', and *taha* 'one'. Polynesian settlers then called it Motusefua 'Island without Fruit or Offspring', but Captain James Cook[†] called it Savage Island after his landing in 1774 was opposed by the hostile inhabitants. It became a British protectorate in 1900 and was annexed the following year to New Zealand. The meaning of its native name is not known. The original name was that given to the island by early immigrants from Tonga, Samoa, and Fiji.

Nizhnekamsk, TATARSTAN REPUBLIC/RUSSIA
Lying along the left bank of the Kama River, the name means 'Lower Kama' from *nizhne* 'lower'.

Nizhniy Novgorod, RUSSIA *Novgorod, Gorky*
A province and a city founded in 1221 as 'New Town' from *novi* and *gorod*, originally a word for 'fortification'. *Nizhniy* 'lower' was added in the 14th century because it was considered inferior to *Novgorod the Great; 'lower' here could also be taken to mean 'south' (of Novgorod the Great). To celebrate his 40 years as a writer and to bind him to the Communist Party, Joseph Stalin[†] ordered the city to be renamed after Maxim Gorky (1868–1936) in 1932; this was his birthplace. Gorky's real name was Aleksey Maksimovich Peshkov; he took the name Gorky from *gor'kiy* 'bitter', a statement on the vicissitudes of his early life as an orphaned street urchin. The city's previous name was readopted in 1990.

Nizhniy Tagil, YEKATERINBURG/RUSSIA
'Lower Tagil' from *nizhniy* 'lower' and Tagil, the river on which it lies. It is 'lower' because it is further down river than Verkhniy Tagil 'Upper Tagil'. Tagil is said to mean 'river' or 'stream'.

Nizwa, OMAN
May be derived from the Arabic root *nzw* 'to flare up', thus possibly indicating a place bursting with fertility.

Nobeoka, KYŪSHŪ/JAPAN *Agata*
The name from *nobe* 'all' and *oka* 'hill' reflects the fact that it is on Kyūshū Island which is

characterized by its volcanic ranges. Agata 'Prefecture' referred to the name of the castle and this was renamed Nobeoka in 1656. As the town grew it took the name Nobeoka.

Nogales, MEXICO, USA
USA (Arizona): originally Issaac-Town named after Jacob Issaacson who built an inn here. It was renamed for the many walnut trees that once flourished here from the Spanish *nogal* 'walnut'. The Mexican town lies just across the border.

Noginsk, MOSCOW/RUSSIA *Rogozha, Bogorodsk*
Renamed in 1781 when it became a town after its church that was dedicated to the Virgin Mary (in Russian, *Bogoroditsa* 'The Virgin'). It was renamed again in 1930 after Viktor Nogin (1878–1924), a prominent Communist Party official, who began work in the Glukhovsky Factory here in 1893.

Noisy, PARIS/FRANCE
Derived from the Latin *nux* 'walnut'; it was famous for its nut trees at one time.

Nokomis, CANADA, USA
Both are named after Nokomis, daughter of the moon, in Longfellow's poem *Hiawatha*. She raises Hiawatha and helps him to acquire the wisdom and strength appropriate for a Native American leader. Nokomis is an Ojibwa word meaning 'grandmother'. There is also a Lake Nokomis in Saskatchewan, Canada.

Nola, ITALY, CENTRAL AFRICAN REPUBLIC
Italy (Campania): evolved from the Oscan Novla or Nuvla meaning 'New (Town)'. It is, in fact, ancient, having passed to the Romans in 313 BC.

Nome, CANADA, USA
USA (Alaska): following the discovery of gold in 1898 the miners' settlement was named Anvil City. It was later renamed Nome after Cape Nome. This is said to have acquired its name after a British Admiralty official had misread a naval chart of 1849 which had '?Name' for the place.

Nordhausen, THURINGIA/GERMANY
Takes its name from a Frankish settlement called Northusen from the Old High German *nord* 'north' and *husen* 'houses', thus 'settlement'.

Nord-Pas-de-Calais, FRANCE
A region meaning 'North Strait of Calais' from *nord* 'north' and *pas* 'strait', although internationally the strait is known as the 'Strait of Dover'. Nord and Pas-de-Calais are departments within the region.

Norfolk, UK, USA
1. UK (England): formerly Nordfolc, a county named after the 'Northern Folk', the northern East Anglian tribes.
2. USA (Nebraska): settled in 1866 as Norfork from North Fork and subsequently changed by the post office to Norfolk, possibly after the English county.
3. USA (Virginia): laid out in 1682 and named after the English county, the home of the early settlers.

Norfolk Island, AUSTRALIA
An external territory of Australia named in 1774 by Captain James Cook[†] after Edward Howard (1686–1777), 9th Duke of Norfolk. Formerly part of New South Wales and then of Van Dieman's Land (now Tasmania), it became a territory of Australia in 1913.

Normal, ILLINOIS/USA *North Bloomington*
Renamed in 1857 after the founding of the Illinois State Normal University. It took its name from the *normal* school, a teacher-training college, around which it developed.

Norman, AUSTRALIA, USA
USA (Oklahoma): founded in 1889 as a tent city and named after Abner Norman, an engineer on the Santa Fe Railway.

Normanby, AUSTRALIA, PAPUA NEW GUINEA, UK
1. Australia (Queensland): a river named after Sir George Phipps (1819–90), 2nd Marquess of Normanby; he was governor of Queensland (1871–4) and of Victoria, Australia (1879–84).
2. Papua New Guinea: an island in the D'Entrecasteaux group visited by Captain John Moresby, a British naval captain, in 1873. He named it after the 2nd Marquess of Normanby.
3. UK (England): several small places have this name meaning 'Village, or Homestead, of the Northmen', that is, the Norwegian Vikings.

Normandy (Normandie), FRANCE *Gallia Lugdunensis Secunda, Normandia*
A historic region and former province named after its inhabitants, the Normans. They were Vikings or Norsemen 'North Men', who date their hold on the land from 911. They became known as Normans and the region as Normandy. Normandy and England were united in the person of William I, King of England (1066–87) and Duke of Normandy. Succeeding English kings ruled, lost and regained the region until 1450 when it finally fell to the French. It is now divided into two regions called Haute-Normandie 'Upper Normandy' and Basse-Normandie 'Lower Normandy'.

Norrbotten, SWEDEN *Nurra Butn*
A county with a name meaning 'North End' from the Old Swedish *nurra* 'north' and *butn* 'end'.

Norristown, PENNSYLVANIA/USA
Established as a township in 1730 by, and named after, Isaac Norris who bought the land in 1704, having come from London in 1693.

Norrköping, SWEDEN
'Northern Market Town' from *norr* 'north' and *köping*. It is north in comparison to Söderköping 'Southern Market Town'.

Northallerton, ENGLAND/UK *Aluretune, North Alverton*
'Ælfhere's Farmstead' from an Old English personal name and *tūn*; 'north' was added in the 13th century.

Northam, AUSTRALIA, SOUTH AFRICA, UK
1. Australia (Western Australia): founded in 1833 and named after the Northam in England.
2. UK (England): 'Northern Enclosure' from the Old English *north* and *hamm*.

North America The northern half of the American landmass, that is, north of the isthmus of Panama. The first known name, Markland 'Land of Forests', was coined by Leif Eriksson, a Norse leader, *c*.1000 and probably referred to the coast of what is now southern Labrador. Certainly, the remains of a Norse settlement have been found at L'Anse aux Meadows on the northern tip of the island of Newfoundland. Also mentioned was Vinland 'Land of Wine', but because grapes cannnot possibly grow this far north, the name may have referred to Nova Scotia, Maine, or Massachusetts. Perhaps the 'grapes' the Vikings saw were not grapes at all, but berries of some kind.

Northampton, AUSTRALIA, UK, USA
1. UK (England): originally Hamtun and then Hampton 'Home Farm' from the Old English *hām* and *tūn*. 'North' was added later to give Northantone to distinguish it from Southampton. The county of Northamptonshire, abbreviated to Northants, takes its name from what was the most important city in the area with the additional *scīr*.
2. USA (Massachusetts): originally a Native American settlement called Nonotuck 'Middle of the River'. It was renamed after the English city in 1654.

North Bay, CANADA
Ontario: founded in 1882 and named after its position on the north-eastern corner of Lake Nipissing.

North Carolina, USA
See CAROLINA.

North Dakota, USA
See DAKOTA.

Northern Ireland, UK
See ULSTER.

Northern Mariana Islands *Islas das Veles, Islas dos Ladrões*
Commonwealth of the Northern Mariana Islands since 1986. Discovered in 1521 by Ferdinand Magellan[†], who named them, first, the 'Island of Sails' and then, with disgust, 'Thieves' Islands' from the Portuguese *ladrão* 'thief'. Only settled in 1668, to mark the impending conversion of the inhabitants that year, Spanish Jesuits renamed them the Islas Marianas after their patroness, Mariana (Maria Anna) of Austria, then regent of Spain after the death of her husband, Philip IV (1621–65). They were sold to Germany by Spain in 1899, occupied by Japan in 1914 and became a Japanese League of Nations mandate in 1920. They were captured by US forces in 1944 and administered by the USA as a UN Trust Territory of the Pacific Islands in 1946–86. The Trusteeship ended in 1986 when the islands became a US Commonwealth Territory in the Pacific.

Northern Territory, AUSTRALIA
A territory. It was included in the colony of New South Wales in 1825, but in 1863 it was annexed by South Australia. In 1911 it became part of the new Commonwealth of Australia, but it did not gain equal status with the other states until 1978. Attempts have been made to give the territory a more interesting or engaging name, but all have been rejected.

North Hero, VERMONT/USA
An island and a town on it. To the south are South Hero Island and South Hero. They are so named because only brave men who supported the American Revolution were intended to own them.

North Korea The Democratic People's Republic of Korea (Chosŏn Minjujuŭi In'min Konghwaguk) since September 1948 when the country was created formally three weeks after the creation of the Republic of Korea in the south; however, 'North Korea' had come into existence in 1945 as a result of

confrontation between the Soviet Union and the United States. *See* KOREA.

North Little Rock, ARKANSAS/USA *De Cantillon, Huntersville, Argenta*
Settled in 1812, it was renamed Huntersville in 1853 and then Argenta after the Hotel Argenta built a few years later. It was annexed by *Little Rock in 1891 but, lying opposite that city on the north bank of the Arkansas River, it became a separate town in 1901 and was renamed North Little Rock.

North Ossetia (Severnaya Osetiya), RUSSIA
See OSSETIA.

North Rhine-Westphalia (Nordrhein-Westfalen), GERMANY
A state created in 1946 by the amalgamation of the former Prussian province of *Westphalia and the northern part of the Prussian province of Rhine.

North Sea *Oceanus Germanicus*
A shallow arm of the Atlantic Ocean, it was known by the Romans as the 'German Sea'. It was renamed by the Dutch the Noordzee from which the English name is taken.

Northumberland, AUSTRALIA, UK, USA
1. Australia (Queensland): islands discovered in 1770 by Captain James Cook[†] who named them after Sir Hugh Percy (1715–86), 1st Duke of Northumberland and Lord Lieutenant of Ireland (1763–5).
2. UK (England): a county which was initially called Norohymbraland 'Territory of the Northhymbre (or Norohymbre)', that is, of the people living north of the River Humber, from the Old English tribal name and *land*. As the Latinized Northumbria it was one of the seven Anglo-Saxon kingdoms with the name meaning the same. At that time it extended as far north as the Firth of Forth in Scotland. After the land north of the River Tweed was ceded to Scotland in 1018 the name referred to land only in England.

North Vernon, INDIANA/USA
Named after the town of the same name in Upper Normandy, France.

Northwest Passage The sea route between the Atlantic and Pacific Oceans along the north coast of North America. The first complete journey along its sea route was only achieved in 1903–6 by Roald Amundsen (1872–1928), the Norwegian explorer.

Northwest Territories, CANADA
A territory in the north-west (although Yukon Territory lies further to the north-west). Before 1 April 1999 it was a huge area comprising the whole of northern Canada. In that year the

new territory of *Nunavut, the eastern half of the Northwest Territories, was created.

Northwich, ENGLAND/UK *Wich, Norwich*
'North Salt Works' from the Old English *north* and *wīc*, here in the sense of a salt production centre.

Norton, CANADA, UK, USA, ZIMBABWE
1. UK (England): 'North Farmstead, or Village', that is one north of another, from the Old English *north* and *tūn*. There is also a small town with this name in Wales.
2. USA (Kansas): named after Captain Orloff Norton, an officer in the 15th Kansas Cavalry.
3. USA (Massachusetts): settled in 1669 and named after the town in England.
4. Zimbabwe: named after a farm-owning family which was murdered during the Shona uprising in 1896.

Norvalspont, NORTHERN CAPE/SOUTH AFRICA
'Norval's Ferry', a reference to a Scotsman who established a ferry crossing here over the Orange River in 1848.

Norwalk, USA
1. California: founded in 1868 as Corvallis and later renamed after Norwalk in Connecticut.
2. Connecticut: named after the Norwaake tribe in 1640.
3. Ohio: part of Sufferers' Lands which had been earmarked for people from Connecticut who had lost their homes during the American War of Independence (1775–83). It was founded in 1817 and named after Norwalk in Connecticut.

Norway (Norge), AND USA
The Kingdom of Norway (Kongeriket Norge) since the 9th century and a constitutional monarchy since 1905. Previously in union with Sweden (1814–1905); ruled by Denmark (1442–1814) becoming a Danish province in 1536, the Norwegian national identity being eroded further until 1661 when the Twin Kingdoms of Denmark-Norway came into being; and united with Denmark and Sweden by the Union of Kalmar in 1397. The connection with Sweden actually began in 1319 when Haakon V (1270–1319), King of Norway (1299–1319), was succeeded by his grandson, Magnus VII Eriksson (1316–74), the 3-year-old son of a Swedish duke, who also became King of Sweden (1319–63) as Magnus II that same year. The name means 'The Way North' or 'The Northern Way' from the Old Norse *Norrevegr*, a reference to one of the routes taken by the Vikings.

Norwich, CANADA, UK, USA
UK (England): formerly Northwic and Noruic 'Northern Port' from the Old English *north* and

wīc, a reference to a port on the River Wensum and 'north' in comparison to the port of Ipswich.

Nosy-Be, MADAGASCAR
An island simply meaning 'Big Island' from *nòsy* 'island' and *be* 'big'. It is also spelt Nossi-Bé. It was ceded to France in 1840 and became part of Madagascar in 1896.

Notsé, TOGO
'Eight Town', a reference to its eight districts from *awodzoe*.

Nottingham, UK, USA
UK (England): formerly Snotengaham and Snotingeham 'Homestead of Snot's People' from an Old English personal name, -*inga*- and *hām*. The *S*, in front of a following consonant, was probably dropped due to Anglo-Norman influence in the 12th century. The county of Nottinghamshire takes its name from the most important city within it and the additional *scīr*.

Nottoway, VIRGINIA/USA
A river and a city named after a Native American tribe, their name meaning 'Snake', that is, an enemy.

Nouadhibou, MAURITANIA *Port-Étienne*
Founded by the French in 1905 and named after one of their colonial officials, Eugène Étienne (1844–1921). After Mauritania gained its independence in 1960 the name reverted to its original local name which means 'Well of Jackals'.

Nouakchott, MAURITANIA
The meaning is disputed. Originally a small fishing village, it has been suggested that the name means 'Place of the Winds', appropriate for its location near the coast its onshore winds and the surrounding shifting sand dunes; however, 'Place of Floating Seashells' from the Berber *a-n-wākshūt*, to mean a place where seashells are found at water level, has also been put forward. This is plausible even though the city is located some 3 miles (5 km) inland from the Atlantic coast. As Mauritanian independence approached the matter arose of where the capital should be, the colonial territory having been ruled by the French from Saint-Louis in Senegal. Nouakchott was chosen because it was roughly midway between Nouadhibou in the north and Saint-Louis in the south; it became the capital in 1959.

Noupoort, NORTHERN CAPE/SOUTH AFRICA
'Narrow Pass' in Afrikaans, a reference to the pass through the Carlton Hills to the north-west.

Nova Friburgo, RIO DE JANEIRO/BRAZIL
'New Fribourg'. Settled in 1818 by destitute
Swiss families who had come from Fribourg in
Switzerland.

Nova Gorica, SLOVENIA
When Italy was allowed to keep Gorizia at the
end of the Second World War, Nova Gorica
'New Hill' from *nova* and the diminutive of *gora*
was built in 1947 on the Slovenian side of the
border.

Nova Mambone, MOZAMBIQUE
'New (Place) where the Chief Lives' from
mambo 'chief' and the Portuguese *nova* 'new'
which recognized the new town which grew
up in the 1920s to replace the original
settlement of Mambone.

Nova Scotia, CANADA *Acadie/Acadia*
A province sighted in 1497 by John Cabot
(*c*.1450–*c*.1499), the Italian-born explorer, who
claimed it for England. It was the French who
were the first to settle in the area in 1605 and
they adopted the local Micmac name Acadie
'Acadia'. Also claimed by England, in 1621
King James I[†] awarded Acadia to Sir William
Alexander (*c*.1567–1640), Earl of Stirling, tutor
to the king's son, Prince Henry (1594–1612), to
found the colony of 'Nova Scotia or New
Scotland'. In 1611 Sir William had established
an order of baronets to promote 'plantation' in
the north of Ireland. This had been so
successful that he proposed doing the same in
North America; the king agreed, hence the
grant. The area changed hands on a number of
occasions until it was awarded to Great Britain
under the terms of the Treaty of Utrecht in
1713 and renamed officially Nova Scotia, the
Latin for 'New Scotland'. Prince Edward Island
and New Brunswick were detached from Nova
Scotia in 1769 and 1784 respectively; and in
1867 Nova Scotia, Ontario, Quebec, and New
Brunswick merged to form the new Dominion
of Canada.

Nova Sofala, MOZAMBIQUE
The original settlement of Sofala was founded
by the Portuguese in 1761 but it takes its name
from the Arabic *sufalah* 'lowland'. The
Portuguese *nova* 'new' was added in 1894 as
the new town was developed. Sofala is the
name of a low-lying coastal province.

Nova Varoš, SERBIA/SERBIA AND MONTENEGRO
Skenderpašina Palanka, Jeni Kasaba
'New Town' or 'Suburb' from *varoš* 'town'. The
former Turkish name, Jeni Kasaba, meant the
same. The first, 16th-century, name may have
been associated with the name of a dervish
lodge with *palanka* 'provincial town'.

Novaya Zemlya, RUSSIA
An island group called 'New Land' from *novaya*
'new' and *zemlya* 'land', presumably in contrast
to the 'old land', that is, the mainland.

Nové Zámky, SLOVAKIA *Vyuar, Olah Vyuar,
Ersekujvar*
'New Castles' from *zámok* 'castle'. A castle built
to provide protection against the Ottoman
Turks, the previous names have more or less
the same meaning. Olah was a local
archbishop with Ersekujvar meaning
'Archbishop's New Castle'. The present name
was adopted in the 18th century.

Novgorod, NOVGOROD/RUSSIA *Holmgard*
A province and a city. The former Varangian
name meant 'Island Town', although nothing
is known of it. The name may signify that the
ancient settlement arose on a hill by the source
of the River Volkhov about a mile (1.5 km) from
the present site. One of Russia's oldest cities,
first mentioned in the 9th century, it became
known as Novgorod Velikiy 'New Town the
Great' and retained this title until the 18th
century. It obtained independence from Kievan
Rus' in 1136 and styled itself 'Sovereign Great
Novgorod'. For long a rival to Moscow, it was
finally forced to recognize Moscow's
supremacy in 1478 after a military defeat. It
was retitled Novgorod the Great on 1 January
2000. *See* NIZHNIY NOVGOROD.

Novigrad, CROATIA *Castrum*
'New Town'. This port lies some 20 miles
(32 km) north-east of Zadar. Another port with
this name lies on the west coast of Istria.

Novi Pazar, SERBIA/SERBIA AND MONTENEGRO
Yeni Pazar, Novibazar
'New Bazaar' in both Serbo-Croat and the
former Turkish. It lies in the *sandžak*, originally
the name for a Turkish military district, of
Novi Pazar.

Novi Sad, SERBIA/SERBIA AND MONTENEGRO
*Petrovaradinski Šanac, Neoplanta, Neusatz/Neue
Stadt, Újvidék*
The original name, referring to a massive
Austrian fortress built in 1694, means
'Petrovaradin's Entrenchment' from *šanac*
'trench' or 'ditch'. In 1748 it was renamed
as 'New Plantation' or 'Orchard' from *plantaža*
'plantation', or, more realistically, 'New
Settlement' as the two most recent former
names, the last one Hungarian, indicate. The
present name is merely a Serbian rendering
of the previous names, literally 'New
Plantation' from *novi* 'new' and *sad*
'plantation'. Petrovaradin, on the south bank
of the Danube, was called Cusum in Roman
times.

Novocherkassk, ROSTOV/RUSSIA
'New Place of the Cherkess (Circassians)'.
Because of flooding, the original town,
Cherkassk, was moved in 1805 to its
present location. When the building of New
Cherkassk was complete, Cherkassk was
renamed Starocherkassk 'Old Place of the
Cherkess'.

Novo Hamburgo, RIO GRANDE DO SUL/BRAZIL
Founded in 1927 by German settlers and
named by them 'New Hamburg' in
Portuguese.

Novokuznetsk, KEMEROVO/RUSSIA *Kuznetsky
Ostrog, Kuznetsk, Stalinsk, Kuznetsk-Sibirsky*
Founded in 1617 as 'Iron Workers' Village'
from *kuznets* 'blacksmith' and *ostrog* 'stockade'.
When it became a town the name was
shortened. In 1932–61 it was named after
Joseph Stalin[†]. The development of a new town
on the opposite bank of the River Tom brought
about the name of Kuznetsk-in-Siberia in 1957
and New Kuznetsk in 1961 which also served
to differentiate it from the Kuznetsk in
Ulyanovsk (Simbirsk) Province.

Novo Mesto, SLOVENIA *Gradac, Rudolfswert,
Neustadt*
'New Place' from *novo* and *mesto* 'place',
although the site was first occupied *c.*1000 BC.
It was refounded in the 13th century as the
trading centre of Gradac and renamed
Rudolfswert in 1365 after the Habsburg
Rudolf IV (1339–65), Archduke of Austria
(1363–5), with *wert* 'worthy', thus
deserving of the honour. From the 15th
century it was known as Neustadt, German
for 'New Town'.

Novomoskovsk, TULA/RUSSIA *Bobriki,
Stalinogorsk*
Founded in 1930 as Bobriki from the Bobrik
River whose name is derived from *bobr*
'beaver'. In 1934, as the cult of Joseph Stalin's[†]
personality grew, it was named 'Stalin's City'
after him. After his posthumous fall from
grace it was given its present name 'New
Moscow' in 1961.

Novorossiysk, KRASNODAR TERRITORY/RUSSIA
'New Russia', a title given to the surrounding
area when it was formally annexed from the
Ottoman Turks in 1829. The city, founded as a
citadel in 1838 on the ruins of a previous
Turkish fort, took this name.

Novoshakhtinsk, ROSTOV/RUSSIA
'New Pits' from *shakhta* 'pit' or 'mine', a
reference to the new coal-mining town that
was established here in 1939 not far from
*Shakhty.

Novosibirsk, RUSSIA *Novaya Derevna, Gusevka,
Aleksandrovsky, Novonikolayevsky*
A province and a city developed from Novaya
Derevna 'New Village' (also known as
Krivoshchekovo) when this location was
selected in 1893 as a crossing point over the
River Ob for the Tran-Siberian railway. In 1894
it was named Aleksandrovsky after the death
of Alexander III (1845–94), Emperor (1881–94),
and then between 1895 and 1925 'New
Nicholas Town' in honour of the accession of
Emperor Nicholas II[†]. It was renamed 'New
Siberia' in 1925 during the process of
exorcizing the Tsarist past.

Novoural'sk, SVERDLOVSK/RUSSIA *Sverdlovsk-
44, Verkh-Neyvinsk*
Known only by its post code to start with, the
present name means 'New Urals'.

Nový Bor, CZECH REPUBLIC *Haida*
'New (Pinewood) Forest' from *nový* and *bor*
'forest'.

Novyy Bor, KOMI REPUBLIC/RUSSIA
'New Forest' from *novyy* and *bor* 'forest'.

Nowa Huta, POLAND
'New Iron Works' from *nowa* 'new' and *huta*
'iron works', a town built in 1949 to house the
workers at the nearby steel mills.

Nowa Sól, POLAND *Neusalz*
'New Salt (Town)' both in the former German
and present Polish names from *nowa* 'new' and
sól 'salt'.

Nowy Sącz, POLAND *Neusandez*
The meaning is not clear although *nowy* is
'new'. Sącz may be derived from *sączyć* 'to leak'
or 'to trickle', a reference to the Dunajec River
on which the town lies; thus, perhaps, a 'New
(Town) on a (River) which trickles'.

Noyon, PICARDY/FRANCE *Noviomagus*
The present name has evolved from the
original Roman name 'New Place'.

Nubia, EGYPT-THE SUDAN
An ancient region straddling the border and
stretching from the River Nile to the Red Sea.
The name is now used for Lake Nubia and the
Nubian Desert (as-Ṣaḥrā an-Nūbīya). The
meaning of the name is disputed. It has
generally been taken to come from the Nubian
nob 'gold', this precious metal being greatly
valued by the Nubians. However, in modern
Nubian *nub* 'black' might indicate that the
name means 'Black (Land)' or '(Land of) the
Blacks'. Furthermore, the southern part of the
region was called Kush (or Cush) during
ancient Egyptian times and Kush is believed to
have meant 'Land of Dark Silt' or 'Black Land'.

In modern Nubian *kiji* means the same and *kiji* is fairly close to Kish or Kush.

Nuesces, TEXAS/USA
A river with a name meaning 'Nut' from the Spanish *nuez*.

Nueva San Salvador, EL SALVADOR *Nueva Ciudad de San Salvador*
Founded in 1854 as the 'New City of the Holy Saviour', it became the country's capital when nearby San Salvador was severely damaged by an earthquake. The capital returned to San Salvador in 1859 after it had been rebuilt.

Nuevo Casas Grandes, CHIHUAHUA/MEXICO
Founded in 1886 4 miles (7 km) from some ancient multi-storeyed ruins called by the Spanish Casas Grandes 'Big Houses'; hence the name 'New Big Houses'.

Nuevo Laredo, NUEVO LEÓN/MEXICO *Villa de San Augustin de Laredo*
Founded in 1755 by Don Tomás Sánchez who named the settlement here Laredo after the birthplace in Cantabria, Spain, of his sponsor.

Nuevo León, MEXICO
A state established in 1824 and called New León after the former Spanish kingdom of León.

Nuku'alofa, TONGA
'Land, or Abode, of Love'. It is the capital of Tonga.

Nullarbor Plain, SOUTH AUSTRALIA/AUSTRALIA
A huge treeless plain with a name to match from the Latin *nulla* 'no' and *arbor* 'tree'.

Numazu, HONSHŪ/JAPAN
Lying at the mouth of the Kano River, it takes its name from *numa* 'marsh' and *tsu* 'port'.

Numidia An ancient kingdom and then a Roman province which now corresponds to Algeria. The name comes from the Numidians, first called Nomades or Numidae, from the Greek *nemein* 'to pasture' which gave the word 'nomad'.

Nunavut, CANADA
A territory officially created out of the Northwest Territories in 1999, although the Nunavut Act was signed in 1993. The name means 'Our Land' in the Inuktitut language of the Inuit 'The People (who are alive now)', a name to be preferred to the derogatory Cree name of Eskimo 'Raw Flesh Eater'.

Nuneaton, ENGLAND/UK *Etone, Nonne Eton*
'Farmstead by a River' from the Old English *ēa* 'river' and the prefix acknowledges the Benedictine nunnery founded here during the reign of Stephen (1097–1154), King of England (1135–54).

Nūristan, AFGHANISTAN *Kāfiristan*
A historic region and province in the north-east known to Muslims as the 'Land of the Kāfirs', i.e. infidels or unbelievers from the Arabic *kafara* 'conceal' or 'be ungrateful' with *kufr* 'unbelief'. In 1896 a *jihād* 'holy war' was launched to conquer this mountainous region inhabited by non-Muslims. Once the population had been forcibly converted to Islam and most of the region incorporated into Afghanistan, the name was changed to mean the 'Land of Light', that is, 'of the enlightened' from the Dari *nur* 'light' and *stan*.

Nusa Tenggara, INDONESIA *Lesser Sunda Islands*
Two provinces, East Nusa Tenggara (Flores, Sumba, West Timor, and scattered islands) and West Nusa Tenggara (Lombok and Sumbawa), together meaning the 'South-East Islands' from *nusa* 'island' and *tenggara* 'south-east'. The Lesser Sunda Islands are in contrast to the Greater Sunda Islands (Java, Kalimantan, and Sumatra).

Nuuk, GREENLAND/DENMARK *Godthåb*
Founded near a 10th-century Norse settlement in 1721 by Hans Egede, a Norwegian missionary, who called it 'Good Hope' from the Danish *godt* 'good' and *håb* 'hope', possibly because he had high hopes of converting the local population. It was renamed in 1979 and given an Inuktitut name meaning 'Summit' or 'Promontory'. It is Greenland's capital and thus 'summit' could refer to its status.

Nuwara Eliya, SRI LANKA
A hill resort and health spa, the name means 'City of Light' from *nuwara* 'city' and *eliya* 'light'.

Nyabira, ZIMBABWE
'Place where there is a Ford'.

Nyack, NEW YORK/USA
Settled in 1684 and named after an Algonquian-speaking tribe whose name means 'corner' or 'point'.

Nyanza, KENYA
A province with a Bantu name meaning 'Lake'; it lies on the eastern side of Lake Victoria.

Nyasa, Lake, MALAWI
See MALAWI.

Nyaungshwe, BURMA *Yaungwhe*
'Golden Banana Tree' from *shwe* 'golden'.

Nyborg, DENMARK *Nyburg(h)*
'New Castle' from *ny* 'new' and *borg*, built in 1170 to protect the Store Strait.

Nyíregyháza, HUNGARY
'Church, or village, (among) the Birch Trees'
from *nyír* 'birch' and *egyház* 'church' or
'village', itself from *egy* 'one' and *ház* 'house'.

Nykarleby, FINLAND
The Swedish name is still in use and means
'New Karl's Village' from *ny* 'new', the
personal name, and *by* 'village'. The Finnish
name, which means the same, is
Uusikaarlepyy from *uusi* 'new' and Kaarlepyy,
the Finnish transliteration of the Swedish
Karleby. Who Karl was is not known.

Nykøbing, DENMARK
Three towns, in Jutland and on the islands of
Falster and Sjælland, have this name meaning
'New Market Town'

Nyköping, SWEDEN
Lying at the mouth of the Nyköping River, the
name means 'New Market Town' from *ny*
'new' and *köping*, although it was founded in
the 13th century.

Nylstroom, LIMPOPO/SOUTH AFRICA
See MODIMOLLE.

Nyýazow, TURKMENISTAN *Tezebazar*
Originally 'New Market' from *täze* 'new' and
bazar, it was renamed after Saparmurad
Niyazov (1940–), President of Turkmenistan
(1991–). *See* TÜRKMENBASHI AND SAPARMURAD
TÜRKMENBASHI.

Oakham, ENGLAND/UK *Ocham, Ocheham*
'Occa's Homestead' from an Old English
personal name and *hām* or *hamm*.

Oakland, CALIFORNIA/USA
Founded in 1852 and named after the oak trees
along the coast.

Oamaru, SOUTH ISLAND/NEW ZEALAND
Founded in 1853. The derivation is not certain.
It could be the 'Place of Maru' from the Maori *o*
'place', *a* 'of' and the personal name or it could
mean 'Sheltered Place' from *maru* 'sheltered'.

Oaxaca, MEXICO
A state and a city founded in 1529 on the site of
an Aztec military camp established in 1486.
The name may be taken from the Nahuatl
huaxaca 'at the place of the acacia'.

Ob, SIBERIA/RUSSIA
A river whose name probably comes from the
Persian *ob* 'water'.

Oban, AUSTRALIA, CANADA, NEW ZEALAND, UK
UK (Scotland): '(Place by) the Little Bay' in
Gaelic.

Oberammergau, BAVARIA/GERMANY
'District over the (River) Ammer' from *ober*
'over', the river name, and *Gau* 'district'. The
river's name comes from the Old High German
am 'to flow'.

Oberland, LIECHTENSTEIN
One of the two regions in the principality
meaning 'Upper Land'. As its name suggests, it
is an upland region in contrast to the other
region, Unterland 'Low Land'.

Oberlin, OHIO/USA
Founded in 1833 to train priests and
missionaries for work in the West. It was
named after Johann Friedrich Oberlin (1740–
1826), a German Lutheran pastor and
philanthropist who worked for the poor living
in villages in the Vosges in France; he became
internationally known.

Oberösterreich, AUSTRIA
A state meaning 'Upper Austria' from the
German *ober* 'upper' and *Österreich* 'Austria'.
In 1938–45, when Austria was incorporated
into Germany, a larger area including Upper
Austria was called Reichsgau Oberdonau
'Reich's District of Upper Danube' from the
German *Gau* 'district' and *Donau* 'Danube'.

Obihiro, HOKKAIDŌ/JAPAN
The name may come from the Ainu *opere perep-
nai* 'stream with several mouths', i.e. a delta.
The Chinese characters represent 'Wide Belt'
from *obi* 'belt' and *hiro* 'wide'.

Obilić (Albanian: **Gllaboder**), KOSOVO/SERBIA
AND MONTENEGRO
Named after Miloš Kobilić, a Serb hero of the
Battle of Kosovo against the Ottoman Turks in
1389. He pretended to defect to the Turkish
camp and assassinated Murad I (*c.*1326–89),
Ottoman sultan (1360–89), during the battle.

Obninsk, KALUGA/RUSSIA
Developed from an estate owned by the
Obninsky family in the 19th century.

Obrovac, CROATIA
'Town of the Obri'. It was associated with the
Avars, the Slav name for whom was the Obri.

Obwalden, SWITZERLAND
A demi-canton meaning 'Above the Forest (of
Kerns)' from the German *ob* 'above' and *Wald*
'forest'. It was established in 1291 and, like
Nidwalden, it was part of the former canton of
Unterwalden.

Ocala, FLORIDA/USA
Developed from Fort King in 1827, the
meaning is disputed. It may come from a
Timucuan word for 'green (land)', thus 'fertile
(land)'; or the word may signify this part of
Florida.

Ocaña, COLOMBIA, SPAIN
Colombia: founded *c.*1570 as Nueva Madrid
'New Madrid', it was renamed later after the
city with this name in Castile-La Mancha,
Spain.

Occupied Territories, The Not an
independent state, these territories comprise
the *West Bank, including East Jerusalem, and
the *Gaza Strip, and are occupied by Israel.

Oceania A collective name for more than
10 000 islands in the Pacific Ocean.
Traditionally, it is divided into Australasia
(Australia and New Zealand), Melanesia,
Micronesia, and Polynesia. It is generally
accepted that Indonesia, Japan, the
Philippines, Taiwan, and the islands north of
Japan (the Kurils and Aleutians) are excluded.
The name was proposed in 1812 by Conrad

Malte-Brun, a Danish geographer, possibly after Oceanus, a Titan and son of Uranus (Heaven) and Gaia (Earth), who ruled the Ocean, the wide mythical stream which was believed to flow round the earth.

Oceanside, USA
The city in California indicates its location on the Pacific coast; however, the Oceanside on Long Island, New York, actually lies some miles inland.

Ocean Springs, MISSISSIPPI/USA *Fort Maurepas, Lynchburg*
The fort was built by Pierre Le Moyne d'Iberville (*see* IBERVILLE) *c.*1700 at Old Biloxi after he had rediscovered the mouth of the Mississippi River in 1699. The name was changed in 1853 and again the following year after the numerous mineral springs in the area.

Ochakiv, UKRAINE *Alektor, Kara-Kermen, Achi-Kale, Ochakov*
Originally an ancient Greek colony, a fortress was built here in 1492 and called Kara-Kermen 'Black Fort' from the Turkic *kara* and *kermen* 'fort'. This was captured by the Ottoman Turks who renamed it 'Angled Fort' from the Turkish *açi* 'angle' and *kale*. In due course this became Ochakov after the city-port passed to Russia in 1791 and to the present spelling when Ukraine achieved independence in 1991.

Ochiltree, SCOTLAND/UK *Ouchiltre*
'High Homestead' from the British *uxello* 'high' and the Welsh *tref* 'homestead' or 'village'.

Ochlockonee, USA
A river in Georgia and Florida with a Creek name meaning 'Yellow Water'.

Ochsenfurt, BAVARIA/GERMANY
'Oxen Ford' from *Ochsen*, the plural of *Ochs* 'ox' and *Furt* 'ford'. The town lies on the River Main.

Oconomowoc, WISCONSIN/USA
A Native American word meaning 'Home of the Beaver'.

Oconto, WISCONSIN/USA
A mission was established here at the mouth of the Oconto River in 1669 close to a Native American village. Its name was said to mean 'Red Ground', but after the arrival of the missionaries it was given a Menominee name, 'Place of the Pike Fish'.

October Revolution Island (Oktyabr'skoy Revolyutsii Ostrov), RUSSIA
The largest island in the North Land group, it was named in 1931 after the Bolshevik

October Revolution in 1917. This took place on 24–5 October at a time when Russia was using the Julian calendar. In 1918 the Gregorian calendar was adopted in Russia and this had the effect of advancing the date of the Revolution to 7 November.

Odawara, HONSHŪ/JAPAN
Derived from *o* 'small', *ta* 'rice field' and *hara* 'field'.

Odendaalsrus, FREE STATE/SOUTH AFRICA
Named 'Odendaal's Home' after J. J. Odendaal, who owned the farm on which the town was built in 1878. The final *rus* comes from the Afrikaans *rust* 'rest'.

Odense, DENMARK *Othenesuuigensem, Odansue, Othense, Othæsheret*
'Shrine, or Sanctuary, of Odin', the Norse god of war. The Old English form of Odin is Woden as in Woden's Day, Wednesday.

Oder (Czech/Polish: **Odra**), CZECH REPUBLIC-POLAND *Viadua*
Said to be from the Slavonic *voda* 'water', but more likely to be an 'old European' name. The river also forms part of the border between Poland and Germany.

Odessa, CANADA, UKRAINE, USA
1. Ukraine: locally Odesa. A province and a city. It originated as a Turkish fort called Khadzhibey, from the Turkish *hacı* (*hadji*) 'pilgrim (to Mecca)' and *bey* 'lord', which was captured in 1789. A new fortress and port were built around it. On the orders of Empress Catherine II the Great[†], after a proposal by the Academy of Sciences, the name was changed to Odessos after a nearby ancient Greek fishing village. Having founded the port and being a woman, Catherine decreed in 1795 that the city should have a feminine name and so it was changed to Odessa.
2. USA (Texas): the settlement for Russian workers building a railway was named by them in 1881 because the local terrain reminded them of their homeland around Odessa; the city was not actually founded until 1886.

Offaly (Uibh Fhailaí), IRELAND
A county, and an ancient kingdom, with a name meaning '(Place of) the Descendants of Failghe'. He was the son of Catháir Már, King of Ireland (120–3). The English name is merely the Anglicized version of the Irish name.

Ogaden, ETHIOPIA
A desert region named after the Ogaden people. Largely populated by Somali nomads, it has long beeen claimed by Somalia, whose government calls it Western Somalia.

Ogden, UTAH/USA *Brownsville*
Founded in 1850 around Fort Buenaventura
which had been built some six years earlier.
The city was subsequently renamed after Peter
Skene Ogden (1794–1854), a Canadian fur
trader and a prominent explorer of the
American West. Mount Ogden and the Ogden
River, both in Utah, are also named after him.

Oglethorpe, GEORGIA/USA
Named after Brigadier General James
Oglethorpe (1695–1785), an English officer and
philanthropist, who obtained the charter for
settling the colony of Georgia in 1732. *See*
GEORGIA, USA.

Oğuz, AZERBAIJAN *Vartashen*
Named after the Oğuz, a Turkic people who
came from Central Asia during the 11th
century and overthrew the Arabs. The Oğuz
were the forefathers of the Osmanlí, better
known as the Ottoman Turks.

O'Higgins, CHILE
A lake, a cape on Easter Island, a point on
Robinson Crusoe Island and a region called, in
full, Libertador General Bernardo O'Higgins.
All are named after Bernardo O'Higgins
(c.1778–1824), who was instrumental in
defeating the Spanish in 1817 and paving the
way for Chilean independence the next year.
He became the first Chilean head of state
(1817–23). His father was a Spanish officer of
Irish descent.

Ohio, USA
A state, the first to be carved from the
Northwest Territory when it joined the Union
as the 17th state in 1803. It is named after the
Ohio River, Ohio being an Iroquois word for
'great water', 'beautiful water', or 'good river'.
First explored by René-Robert Cavelier, Sieur
de la Salle[†] in 1669, it was acquired from the
French by the British in 1763. It fell to the
Americans as a result of the American War of
Independence in 1783 and became part of the
Northwest Territory.

Ohrid, MACEDONIA *Lychnidos, Okhrï*
Originally a Greek colony called Lychnidos, it
had fallen to the Romans by 217 BC. It is named
after the cliff (in Serbo-Croat, *hrid*), on which
the town was first built. The present Slav name
was first mentioned in 879. It was the capital of
the Slav Macedonian state from 971 to 1018 and
was incorporated into the medieval Serbian
state in about 1334. It fell to the Ottoman Turks
in 1395 and was held by them as a *sancak*
'territorial subdivision of a military district'
called Okhrï until 1912. The border between
the former Yugoslav Republic of Macedonia
and Albania runs through Lake Ohrid.

Oise, BELGIUM-FRANCE *Isara*
A river and a department in France named
after the river. The name has evolved from the
Roman name which itself comes from the pre-
Celtic root element *is* 'holy' and *ar* 'water' or
'river'.

Ojai, CALIFORNIA/USA *Nordhoff*
Laid out in 1874 and named after Charles
Nordhoff, an author who promoted the
benefits of living in California. It was renamed
in 1916 after the valley in which it lies. This
had a Native American name meaning 'rest'.

Okahandja, NAMIBIA
'The Small Wide One', an Herero name
referring to the Okahandja River which,
although only a tributary, is wider than the
Swakop River.

Okavango, SOUTH AFRICA
A river which rises in Angola, where it is called
the Kubango, and flows into Botswana, and a
region in Namibia. Both take their name from
the Kavango people, an ethnic group that lives
in southern Angola, northern Botswana, and
north-eastern Namibia.

Okawville, ILLINOIS/USA
'Porcupine Town' from the Native American
word *kaug* 'porcupine' and the French *ville*.

Okayama, HONSHŪ/JAPAN
A prefecture and a city meaning 'Hill' from *oka*
'hill' and *yama* 'mountain'. The prefecture is
mountainous.

Okazaki, HONSHŪ/JAPAN
Derived from *oka* 'hill' and *saki* 'promontory'.

Okeechobee, FLORIDA/USA
A lake and a city with the Seminole name 'Big
Water'. It is the third largest freshwater lake in
the country.

Okehampton, ENGLAND/UK *Ocmundtun,
Ochenemitona*
'Farmstead on the (River) Okement' from the
Celtic river name and the Old English *tūn*.

Okhotsk, Sea of (Okhotskoye More), RUSSIA
Tungus, Lama, Kamchatka
Takes its name from the port of Okhotsk, in
Khabarovsk Territory, which itself is named
after the Okhota River; its name may be an
Evenki word for 'river'. Previously it has been
called the Tungus (*see* TUNGUSKA), an old name
for the Evenk, Lama 'sea' in Evenki, and
Kamchatka after the peninsula.

Okinawa, JAPAN *Ryukyu*
An island, a prefecture, and a city, previously
called Koza, with a name meaning 'Chain (of
islands) in the Open Sea' from *oki* 'open sea' or
'offshore' and *nawa* 'rope' or 'chain'. Okinawa

is the largest island in the Ryukyu Islands archipelago and was the Kingdom of Ryukyu from the 15th century to 1879. Annexed as a vassal state by Japan in 1854, the island was captured by American troops towards the end of the Second World War in 1945. It was returned to Japan in 1972.

Oklahoma, USA
A state with a name meaning 'Red People' from a combination of the two Choctaw words *okla* 'people' and *humma* 'red'. Neither the French nor the Spanish were able to gain full control until the French did so in 1800. Three years later the USA acquired the area as part of the Louisiana Purchase and it became known as the District of Louisiana and later Louisiana Territory. In 1828 the US Congress ruled that the area should be reserved for Native Americans (those that had been driven off their lands elsewhere by white settlement) and it became known as Indian Territory. The 'Five Civilized Tribes'—Cherokee, Chickasaw, Choctaw, Creek, and Seminole—established five independent nations under US protection, although more than 60 tribes moved into the Territory. This arrangement ended in 1889 when some land in the west was opened up to non-Native Americans and was given the name Oklahoma Territory in 1890. In 1907 Oklahoma Territory and what remained of Indian Territory merged and joined the Union as the 46th state. Oklahoma City was founded on the day, 22 April 1889, when the first settlers made their 'run' (as it was called) into land previously reserved for Native Americans to stake out claims.

Okmulgee, OKLAHOMA/USA
'Boiling Water' in Creek. It was the capital of the Creek nation between 1868 and 1907.

Oktyabr'skiy, KAZAKHSTAN, RUSSIA
'October', the adjectival form of *Oktyabr'sk*, named to commemorate the Bolshevik October Revolution in 1917. *See* OCTOBER REVOLUTION ISLAND. There is also a town called Oktyabr' in Kazakhstan and three called Oktyabr'skoye in Russia.

Öland, SWEDEN
An island, which is the meaning of the name from *ö* 'island' and *land* 'land'.

Olathe, KANSAS/USA
Founded in 1857 with a Shawnee name meaning 'Beautiful'.

Olbia, ITALY, UKRAINE
1. Italy (Sardinia): said to have been founded as the Greek colony of Olbia, it was renamed Terranova in 1198 by Pisan colonists. Pausania was added in 1862 to give Terranova Pausania.

The name Olbia was only restored in 1939. It is not certain that the name is of Greek origin, although it is probably pre-Roman. It may come from a local root *olb* which was then compared with the Greek to give the auspicious meaning of 'happy' or 'fortunate', or even 'wealthy'.
2. Ukraine: ruins. Founded in the early 6th century BC as a Greek city on the north coast of the Black Sea. The export of wheat made it rich, hence its name 'Rich City' from the Greek *olbos* 'respectable wealth'.

Oldenburg, GERMANY, USA
Germany (Lower Saxony): a city and once a duchy, a grand duchy, and a state until 1946. The name means 'Old Fortress' from *Burg*.

Oldham, UK, USA
UK (England): formerly Aldholm. While the *-ham* comes from the Old Scandinavian *holmr* 'island', 'promontory', or 'raised ground in a marsh', the meaning of *ald* is not absolutely clear. It could simply be the Old English *ald* 'old' or a feature called Alt, which could refer to the spur on which the town is built.

Old World Europe and those parts of Asia and Africa that were known to exist (to Europeans) before the discovery of the Americas—the New World.

Ol'gopol' (Ol'hopil'), UKRAINE *Roguzka-Chechel'nitskaya*
Established in 1812 and renamed as 'Olga's Town', probably after Princess Olga Pavlovna, one of Emperor Paul I's six daughters. In 1795–1812 it had actually been located some 6 miles (10 km) away. In 1795 it had received the name Ol'gopol' when it had become the district capital. After the move in 1812 the previous site of Ol'gopol' reverted to its original name of Chechel'nik.

Olifants, NAMIBIA, SOUTH AFRICA
Several rivers simply meaning 'Elephant'.

Olifantshoek, NORTHERN CAPE/SOUTH AFRICA
'Elephants' Corner' from the Afrikaans *hoek* 'corner'. South Africa also has an Olifantsbosch 'Elephants' Forest' and Olifantsfontein 'Elephants' Fountain'.

Ol'khovatka, KALININGRAD/RUSSIA
Derives its name from *ol'kha* 'alder'.

Olomouc, CZECH REPUBLIC *Mons Julii, Olmütz*
Possibly a Roman fort to start with, a Slav fortress was later built on the site. The name means 'Bare Rock' from the Old Czech *holy* 'bare' or 'bald' and *mauc* 'rock'. German craftsmen and merchants were invited to settle, hence the former German name. It was the capital of Moravia in 1187–1641.

Olsztyn, POLAND *Allenstein*
The city's name is the Polish version of the former German name 'Castle on the (River) Alle', now the Łyna in Polish. The Teutonic Knights built a castle here in 1334. Becoming part of Poland in 1466, the town was annexed by Prussia at the first partition of Poland in 1772 and was not returned to Poland until 1945.

Olympia, GREECE, USA
1. Greece: a valley and ruins of purely religious buildings and those associated with athletics. It was the site in the Peloponnese of the chief sanctuary of Zeus, the principal Greek god (known to the Romans as Jupiter), who ruled heaven; according to Homer, this was located on the summit of Mt Olympus. Every four years a festival of competitive games was held in honour of Zeus. These Olympic Games, which, according to tradition, were first held here in 776 BC, gave their name to the place.
2. USA (Washington): laid out as Smithfield in 1851, it was renamed after the nearby Olympic Mountains.

Olympic Mountains, WASHINGTON/USA
First sighted by the Spanish in 1774, they were named by John Meares, an English traveller, in 1788. He called the highest summit Mt Olympus because he considered it a place fit for the gods after the Greek Mt Olympus.

Olympus, Mount, CYPRUS, GREECE, TURKEY, USA
The origin is not definitively known. It may be derived from an Indo-European root word *ulu* 'to turn', a reference to its smoothly curved summit. A volcano on Mars is called Olympus Mons. The most famous Mt Olympus is the one situated in Greece and known as Óros Ólimbos. Traditionally, it was the home of the Greek gods and was known, poetically, as heaven.

Omagh (An Ómaigh), NORTHERN IRELAND/UK
Na hOghmaighe
'The Virgin Plain' from *magh* 'plain'.

Omaha, NEBRASKA/USA
Founded in 1854 and named after the Omaha people whose own name means 'upstream (people)', a reference to the Missouri River on which the city lies.

Oman ('Umān)
The Sultanate of Oman (Salṭanat 'Umān) since 1970. Previously the Sultanate of Muscat and Oman, a title that recognized the division of the country: the sultan ruled Muscat and the coastal towns, and the imam ruled the tribal interior. In 1650 the Portuguese, who controlled the Omani coast to dominate trade

since 1507, were driven out. Since then Oman has never been occupied by a foreign power, apart from the period in 1737–47 when the Persians intervened in the civil war which raged between 1719 and 1744. The warring tribes agreed then to the appointment of Ahmad ibn Saʿīd as imam. By 1749 he had become the imam of Oman and Zanzibar (which included part of what is now Tanzania). His successors became known as sayyids and then as sultans; and they established Oman as a regional power with possessions on both sides of the Persian Gulf and in East Africa, Zanzibar becoming the second capital. In 1861 Oman and Zanzibar were divided between two of the sons of a former sultan and the two sultanates went their own way. By this time British influence was beginning to make itself felt and in due course Muscat and Oman became what amounted to an unofficial British protectorate. Within Oman the tribes continued to support their Ibādhī imam against the sultan and it was not until 1959, with British help, that the imam's dreams of a separate principality independent of the sultan, were finally ended. A number of theories exist as to the origin of the name Oman. Sumerian tablets mention a country called Magan, possibly a reference to Oman's copper-mining industry, although Magan is also said to relate to a 'seafaring people' or 'shipbuilders' in Sumerian; a *magan* is a type of ship's hull. This latter meaning, however, may refer to Mazoun, another early name, and associated with water; perhaps an abundance of water inland allowing the establishment of farming communities. The name Oman is also said to come from Uman in Yemen, from where some tribes migrated. The city of Omana is mentioned by Ptolemy[†].

Omdurman (Umm Durmān), THE SUDAN
The name honours the Muslim saint Um-Mariyam (1646–1730) who is buried here.

Ōmiya, HONSHŪ/JAPAN
The site of the ancient Hikawa shrine, the name means 'Big Shrine' from ō 'big' and *miya* 'shrine'.

Ömnögovĭ, MONGOLIA
A province meaning 'Southern Steppe' from *gov'* 'steppe' or 'desert'. There are three other provinces with *govĭ* in their title: Dornogovĭ 'East Steppe', Dundgovĭ 'Central Steppe', and Govĭ-Altay 'Steppe in the Altay Mountains'.

Omsk, RUSSIA *Omsky Ostrog*
A province and a city founded as a fortified settlement in 1716 from *ostrog* 'stockade' at the confluence of the Irtysh and Om Rivers. The name comes from the latter river and is

thought to be derived from a Tatar word for 'tranquil' to describe its flow.

Onawa, IOWA/USA
A Native American word meaning 'wide awake'.

Oneida, NEW YORK/USA
Founded in 1834 and named after the Oneida tribe. Their name represents the Iroquois *oneyote* 'granite people' or 'people of the stone'.

Oneonta, NEW YORK/USA *McDonald's Mills, Bridge, Milfordville*
Founded in about 1775 with a Native American name meaning either 'place of rest' or 'stony place'.

Oneşti, ROMANIA *Gheorghe Gheorghiu-Dej*
Built as a new town in 1953 and named after Gheorghe Gheorghiu-Dej (1901–65), the Romanian Communist leader and president (1961–5). He added *Dej* to his name after spending eleven years in prison in the town of Dej. Gheorghe Gheorghiu-Dej was renamed in 1992. The meaning of the first syllable of the present name is not known, but the suffix *-eşti* has the meaning of belonging to a community with the same ancestors.

Ongtüstik Qazaqstan, KAZAKHSTAN
Shymkent
A province 'South Kazakhstan' from *ongtüstik* 'south'.

Ontario, CANADA, USA
Canada: a province and a lake divided between Canada and the USA and first seen by French explorers in 1615. The name is said to be an Iroquois word for 'Beautiful Lake' or 'Land of Shining Waters', or it may be associated with rocks to give 'rocks near the water', a reference to the Niagara Escarpment on the lake's southern shore. Ontario was ceded by France to Great Britain in 1763. The province was known as Upper Canada in the early 19th century and then Canada West in 1841; in 1867 Canada West became the province of Ontario when the Canadian confederation was created.

Opatija, CROATIA *Abbazia*
Takes its name from the Benedictine Abbey of San Giacomo al Palo 'St James' here. *Opatija* is simply the Serbo-Croat word for the Italian *abbazia* 'abbey'.

Opatów, POLAND
Two towns have this name which comes from the Latin *abbatis* 'abbot' and the Slavonic possessive *-ow*.

Opava, CZECH REPUBLIC *Oppavia, Troppau*
Takes its name from the River Opava on which it lies. The previous German name meant

'Meadow on the (River) Oppa' from *Au*, a form of *Aue* 'meadow' and the German name of the river. The original name of the river was Opa derived from the Indo-European root word *apa* or *opa* 'water' or 'river' and under German influence this became *ahwa*. Thus the name developed from Apa to Ahwa to Apaha to Opava. As Troppau it was a duchy and the capital of Austrian Silesia.

Opelika, ALABAMA/USA
A Creek word meaning 'Great Swamp', although there is no such thing here.

Opobo, AKWA IBOM/NIGERIA *Egwanga, Ikot Abasi*
Renamed in 1870 by a ruler of the Anna Pepple house of Bonny who came here and founded the Kingdom of Opobo in honour of Opobo the Great, King of the Pepple people (1792–1830).

Opole, POLAND *Oppeln*
Derived from *pole* 'field'. Oppeln is the German form of the name.

Oporto (Porto), PORTUGAL *Cale, Portus Cale, Castrum Novum*
'The Harbour' from *o* 'the' and *porto*. It was a Roman fortified camp called Cale until the Latin *portus* 'haven' was subsequently added, referring to the settlement on the south bank of the River Douro. Castrum Novum 'New Camp' was the name given to the later Alani settlement developed on the north bank of the river and it is on this bank that most of the modern city lies. Only in the 14th century did the city become a major port with its present name and the capital of the county of Portucale, an evolution from the earlier Portus Cale. Portucale, in due course, gave its name to the country of Portugal and Porto to the rich sweet dessert wine, port.

Opuzen, CROATIA
Named after Fort Opus built by the Venetians here in 1716.

Oradea, ROMANIA *Grosswardein, Nagyvárad, Oradea Mare*
The present name is a Romanian variation of the Hungarian 'Big Town' from *nagy* 'big' and *vár* 'town'; the earlier German name meant the same. Occupied by the Ottoman Turks in 1660–92, it then fell to the Hungarians before being ceded to Romania in 1919. In 1940 at the Second Vienna Award Hungary again acquired the city, but was forced to return it to Romania in 1945. Thereafter, for a time, it was known as Oradea Mare 'Big Oradea' from the Romanian *mare* 'big'.

Oral, KAZAKHSTAN
See URAL'SK.

Oran, ALGERIA *Portus Divinus, Wahrān, Ouahran*
Founded in 903 by Muslims as a port for trade
with the hinterland on the site of a Roman
settlement called 'Divine Port'. The present
name is derived from Wahrān, the name of a
medieval Berber chief. After rule by the
Spanish and Ottoman Turks it passed to the
French in 1831 who held it until Algerian
independence in 1962.

Orange, AUSTRALIA, FRANCE, LESOTHO-
NAMIBIA-SOUTH AFRICA, USA
1. Australia (New South Wales): named in
1828 by Sir Thomas Mitchell in memory of his
commander during the Peninsular War (1808–
14), William I (1772–1843), King of the
Netherlands (1815–40) who, during the war,
was the Prince of Orange.
2. France (Provence-Alpes-Côtes d'Azur):
developed by the Romans by whom it was
known as Arausio after a Gaulish god whose
name may have come from a pre-Indo-
European root element *ar* 'mountain' with the
suffix *-aus*. In due course this evolved into the
present name. The Dutch House of Orange
took its name from the medieval principality
which originally developed from this town
which had become an independent county in
the 11th century. It was ceded to France at the
Treaty of Utrecht in 1713.
3. Lesotho-Namibia-South Africa: a river that
rises in Lesotho as the Sinqu River. It becomes
the Orange River as it enters South Africa. It
was so named after the Dutch royal House of
Orange in the person of William V (1748–
1806), Prince of Orange, by Colonel R. J.
Gordon, commander of the Dutch garrison at
Cape Town, who led an expedition to the river
in 1777.
4. USA (California): founded as Richland in
1868, it was renamed in 1875 in recognition of
its orange groves.
5. USA (New Jersey): originally called
Mountain Plantations when it was founded in
1678, it was later renamed Orange after the
Prince of Orange who became King William
III[†].
6. USA (Texas): founded in 1836 as Green's
Bluff, it was renamed Madison in 1852 and
then given its present name in 1856 after the
wild orange groves by the Sabine River.

Orange Free State, SOUTH AFRICA
See FREE STATE.

Orangeburg, SOUTH CAROLINA/USA
Founded in 1735 by German, Swiss, and Dutch
settlers who named it 'Orange Town' after
William IV (1711–51), Prince of Orange and
Nassau.

Oranienburg, BRANDENBURG/GERMANY
'Fortress of the Orange Family', a princely
dynasty which took its name from the
Principality of Orange.

Oranjemund, NAMIBIA
'Mouth of the Orange (River)', although the
town actually lies about 5 miles (8 km) to the
north of it.

Oranjestad, ARUBA, NETHERLANDS ANTILLES
1. Aruba: 'Orange Town' in Dutch, the islands
having long been occupied by the Dutch.
2. Netherlands Antilles (St Eustatius):
formerly Fort Oranje after the Dutch had built
a port here in 1636.

Ord, AUSTRALIA, USA
1. Australia (Western Australia); a mountain
and a river discovered in 1879 by Alexander
Forrest and named in 1885 after Sir Harry Ord
(1819–85), governor of Western Australia
(1877–80), shortly after his death.
2. USA (Nebraska): named after General E. O. C.
Ord.

Ordu, TURKEY *Cotyoron/Cotyora*
'Army'. It was founded as a Greek port in the
5th century BC.

Ordubad, NAKHICHEVAN/AZERBAIJAN
'Army Town' from the Turko-Persian *ordu*
'military camp' or 'army', itself from the
Mongolian *orda* 'royal encampment', and *abad*.

Ordzhonikidze, KAZAKHSTAN, RUSSIA,
UKRAINE
All towns are named after Grigory (Sergo)
Ordzhonikidze[†]. One town in Russia formerly
with this name has been renamed Denisovka
and one in Tajikistan is now Kofarnihon.
Perhaps the most famous Russian city
temporarily bearing this name is now
*Vladikavkaz.

Orebić, CROATIA *Trstenica*
Named after the Orebić family who settled
here during the 16th century and fortified the
place against the Ottoman Turks and pirates.

Örebro, SWEDEN
A county and a town with a name meaning
'Gravel Bridge' from the Old Scandinavian
aurinn, the adjective of *aurr* 'gravel' or 'mud'
and *bro* 'bridge', a reference to the medieval
gravel ford across the royal route from Oslo to
Stockholm.

Oregon, USA
A state, the name of a city in four other states,
and another called Oregon City in the north-
west of the state. Several theories have been
put forward as to the meaning of the name. It
is thought to be of Native American origin,

although one suggestion is that it is derived from origanum, a reference to the wild sage found along the coast. Alternatively, it may be an Algonquian word meaning 'Beautiful Water' or come from the Shoshonean word *ogwa* 'water' and *pe-on* 'west', the former native name for the Columbia River which forms its northern border with Washington State. The British and the Americans agreed to the joint occupation of the area in 1818, but in 1846 the Oregon Country was added to the USA. It consisted of what is now the states of Oregon, Washington, Idaho, and part of Montana. Two years later it was redesignated Oregon Territory and in 1859 the present state of Oregon was carved out of the territory and joined the Union as the 33rd state. It gives its name to the famous Oregon Trail, the longest overland route, 2 000 miles (3 220 km) long, from Independence, Missouri, to Oregon during the westward expansion of the USA. It was one of the most favoured routes and was used by settlers and those seeking gold.

Orël, RUSSIA
A province and a city located at the confluence of the Orlik and Oka Rivers, it was founded as a fortress in 1654. It takes its name from the Orlik which may come from the Turkic *ayyr* 'fork', a reference to the junction of the rivers. In Russian, *orël* means 'eagle', but there is no reason to suppose that this explains the city's name.

Orenburg, RUSSIA *Chkalov*
'Fort on the (River) Or'. A province and a city founded as a fortress in 1735 where Orsk now is. In 1743 it was moved 150 miles (240 km) down river, although it retained the same name. In 1938–57 it bore the name Chkalov after Valery Chkalov (1904–38), commander of the non-stop 63-hour flight in an ANT-25 from Moscow to Portland, Oregon, USA, via the North Pole in 1937. Chkalov, whose home town this was, was killed in an aviation accident in 1938.

Orense, ARGENTINA, SPAIN
Spain (Galicia): a province and a town whose name is thought to have evolved from the original Roman name of Aquae Originis 'Waters of the Source', a reference to its unusually hot springs. Other former names include Urentae and Aurium. It is unlikely that it comes, as has been suggested, from *oro*, the legendary 'gold' of the River Miño.

Öresund (Danish: Øresund), DENMARK-SWEDEN
'The Sound' from *sund* 'sound', the narrow channel between Sweden and the Danish island of Sjælland 'Zealand'.

Orient, The
The countries east of the Mediterranean Sea which, to the Romans, were 'the East' from the Latin *oriens* 'the quarter where the sun rises' or 'the east'. The term is now generally taken to mean 'East Asia'.

Orillia, ONTARIO/CANADA
Surveyed in 1839 and named by General Sir Peregrine Maitland (1777–1854), lieutenant-governor of Upper Canada (1818–28) and of Nova Scotia (1828–34). He had served in Spain and the name probably comes from the Spanish *orilla* 'shore' or 'bank', a reference to its location between Lakes Couchiching and Simcoe.

Orinoco, VENEZUELA
A river with the Guaraní name Ori-noko 'Place of paddling (a canoe)'.

Orissa, INDIA *Utkala, Kaliṅga, Oḍra Deśa*
A state. The former names are all associated with local peoples and then their territories. Oḍra Deśa, or the Sanskrit Odrāshtra, meant the 'Land of the Oḍras' from *deśa* 'land' or 'country'. This is said to be the Prakrit version of *uttara* 'north', a reference to the northern part of Kaliṅga. The name slowly evolved through Uḍḍiṣa to Oḍisā which was Anglicized to Orissa.

Orizaba, VERACRUZ/MEXICO
Founded by the Spanish in the 16th century on the site of an Aztec military garrison located here to guard the Veracruz–Mexico City road. It was called Ahuaializapan 'Pleasant Waters', a reference to the fertile valley in which it lies. The present name is the Spanish version of this. Nearby is Pico de Orizaba 'Mt Orizaba', also known as Citlaltépetl 'Star Mountain'.

Orkney, CANADA, SOUTH AFRICA, UK
UK (Scotland): formerly Orkas, Orcades, and Orkaneya or Orkneyjar. An island group with a Celtic name from *orc* 'boar', which was probably a tribal name. This was reinterpreted by the Norsemen as Orcades, a Romanized form, 'Islands of Seals' from the Old Scandinavian *orkn* 'seal' and *ey*. Ruled by Norway and Denmark from the 9th century, the islands passed to Scotland in 1472 as security for the unpaid dowry of Margaret (1456–86), daughter of Christian I (1425–81), King of Denmark-Norway, and of Sweden, after her marriage in 1469 to James III (1452–88), King of Scots (1460–88).

Orlando, FLORIDA/USA *Jernigan*
Settled around Fort Gatlin *c.*1844, it was renamed in 1857 after Orlando Reeves, an army sentry killed in 1835 during the Seminole Wars.

Orléans, CANADA, FRANCE, USA
1. France (Centre): its first Roman name,
Genabum, came from the combination of *gen*
'bend (in a river)' and the pre-Indo-European
apa 'water'. The city stands on the River Loire.
The present name has evolved from the city's
second name of Aurelianum, a tribute to
Aurelian (*c*.215–75), the Roman emperor
(270–5).
2. The cities in Ontario, Canada, and in five
states in the USA are spelt Orleans and are
either named after the city in France or after a
Duke of Orléans. The city in Massachusetts,
USA, was named in 1797 after Louis-Philippe-
Joseph (1747–93), Duc d'Orléans, who
renounced his title and became known as
Philippe Égalité for his strong support for
democratic principles.

Orlov, RUSSIA, SLOVAKIA *Khalturin*
Russia (Kirov): an old town founded in the 11th
century as Orlov, possibly connected with *orël*
'eagle', and renamed in 1923 after Stepan
Khalturin (1856–82), a political agitator who
was born near here. He assumed the name
Stepan Batyshkov when he obtained a job as a
carpenter in the Winter Palace in St Petersburg
with the intention of assassinating Emperor
Alexander II[†]. He failed in his attempt in 1880,
but was arrested and hanged, under the name
of Stepanov, for the murder of a military
procurator in 1882. The city readopted its
original name in 1992.

Ormond Beach, FLORIDA/USA *New Britain*
Settled in 1874 by a group from Connecticut, it
was renamed in 1880 after Captain James
Ormond.

Ormskirk, ENGLAND/UK *Ormeshirche*
'Church belonging to a Man called Orm',
either the founder or early owner, from an Old
Scandinavian personal name, Ormr, and *kirkja*.

Orontes (Nahr el-'Āṣī), LEBANON-SYRIA-TURKEY
A river whose Arabic name means the
'Rebellious River' from *nahr* 'river' and *'āṣī*
'rebel'. It may be rebellious because it is largely
unnavigable or because it flows northwards
away from Mecca.

Orsk, ORENBURG/RUSSIA
Founded in 1735 as a military post called
*Orenburg at the confluence of the Or and Ural
Rivers, taking its name from the former in
1743.

Orūmīyeh, IRAN *Urmia, Reza'iyeh*
A city just to the west of Lake Urmia (in
Persian, Daryācheh-ye Orūmīyeh) which is also
the ancient name of the city from which the
present name comes; its meaning is unknown.
In 1926–80 the city was named after Reza Shah

Pahlavi (1878–1944), Shah of Iran (1925–41),
the founder of the dynasty that was
overthrown in 1979.

Oruro, BOLIVIA *Real Villa de San Felipe de Austria*
Founded by the Spanish in 1606 as the 'Royal
Town of St Philip of Austria'. The present
Native American name means 'Black and
White' and this refers to both a department
and a city.

Orvieto, UMBRIA/ITALY *Urbs Vetus*
Founded as an Etruscan town, the present
name is derived from the former Roman name
'Old Town' from the Latin *urbs* 'walled town' or
'city'.

Osage, CANADA, USA
USA: four states have cities with this name and
the Osage River flows through Missouri. All are
named after the Osage tribe.

Ōsaka, HONSHŪ/JAPAN *Naniwa*
An urban prefecture and a city with a name
meaning 'Big Hill' from *ō* 'big' and *saka* 'hill'.
The prefecture is surrounded by mountains.
The characters do not assist in a translation
of the former name which could have
meant either 'Rapid Waves' from *nani* 'wave'
and *wa* 'rapid' or 'Difficult Waves' from *nani*
'difficult' and *wa* 'wave'. According to legend,
Jimmu, Japan's first emperor (660–585 BC),
landed here at the mouth of the Yodo
River after his passage through the Inland
Sea *c*.607 BC.

Osawatomie, KANSAS/USA
Settled in 1854, the city's name is a
combination of the names of two Native
American tribes, the Osage and Potawatomi.

Osceola, USA
Six states have cities with this name, all linked
directly or indirectly to Osceola (*c*.1804–38), a
Seminole leader during the Second Seminole
War (1835–42).

Oshawa, ONTARIO/CANADA *Skea's Corners*
Founded in 1795, it was renamed in 1842 from
a Native American word meaning 'across the
river', thus a 'river crossing'.

Oshkosh, WISCONSIN/USA *Athens*
Settled in 1836, it was renamed in 1840 after a
Menominee chief. His name is said to mean
'nail' or 'claw'.

Osijek, CROATIA *Colonia Aelia Mursa, Esseg, Eszék*
A town and a Roman colony from 133, the
later German, Hungarian, and Croat names are
all based on the Slavonic *seč* (and in Serbo-
Croat, *seći*) 'to cut', indicating that the woods
here were cut down to facilitate the building of
Roman border fortifications.

Oskaloosa, IOWA/USA
Settled in 1843 and named after one of the
wives of the Seminole leader Osceola. Her
name meant the 'Last of the Beautiful'.

Öskemen, KAZAKHSTAN
See UST′-KAMENOGORSK.

Oslo, NORWAY, USA *Ansloga, Christiania, Kristiania*
(*Norway*)
Norway: founded *c*.1050 as Ansloga which may
have had an association with the Scandinavian
god Ås. The city was burnt down in 1624 and
rebuilt further to the west. At this time it was
renamed Christiania after Christian IV (1577–
1648), King of Denmark and Norway (1588–
1648). The spelling was modified in 1877. The
city adopted its present name, a modern
version of its medieval name, in 1925. It lies at
the head of a fjord and this may be represented
by *os* 'mouth' with *lo* 'field'. It has been the
capital in *c*.1300–97 and since 1814.

Osmancık, TURKEY *'Othmāndjik*
The origin of the name is not clear. However, it
may be the Arabized form of a Turkish name
that sounded like Atman. It is said that
Othman I, better known as Osman I (*c*.1258–
1324), a Turkmen prince in north-western
Anatolia, took his name from the place which
had been given to him as a fief, but this is by no
means certain. The Osmanlí, or Ottoman
Turks, derived their name from him, the
Arabic form being 'Ûthmān; he also called
himself 'Othmāndjik 'Little Osman' to
distinguish himself from the third caliph,
'Uthmān, who was killed in 656.

Osnabrück, LOWER SAXONY/GERMANY
Possibly 'Bridge on the (River) Hase' from the
Old High German *asa* 'current', from which
the river got its name, and *brugge* 'bridge'.

Ossa, AUSTRALIA, GREECE
1. Australia (Tasmania): Mt Ossa has the same
mythological origin as the mountain range in
Greece.
2. Greece: a mountain range named after the
mountain in Greek mythology. Otus and
Ephialtes, the sons of Poseidon, attempted to
reach heaven by piling up mountains, one
upon another. They placed Ossa on Olympus
and then Pelion on Ossa.

Ossetia (Russian: **Osetiya**; Georgian:
Samachablo), GEORGIA-RUSSIA
Divided by the main Caucasus Mountain
chain, North Ossetia is a republic in Russia,
while South Ossetia is an autonomous region
in Georgia. Annexed by Russia in 1801–6,
Ossetia became part of the newly created
Gornaya Avtonomnaya Respublika 'Mountain
Autonomous Republic' in 1921. The next year,

in pursuit of a policy of divide and rule, the
Soviet authorities split Ossetia in two by
arbitrarily redrawing administrative borders;
South Ossetia was created as an autonomous
province in the Georgian Soviet Republic. In
1924 the Mountain Republic was dissolved and
North Ossetia received its autonomy,
becoming an Autonomous Soviet Socialist
Republic in 1936. Both take their names from
the Ossetians, Ossetes, or Osets whose name
may have a Persian origin from the root *os*
'rapid'. However, why they should be called
'rapid' is not known. North Ossetia is called in
Russian *Severnaya Osetiya-Alaniya*, a reference to
the fact that the Ossetians are descendants of
the Alans. *Alaniya* was added in 1994 when the
Ingush announced the name of their new
capital, Magas, the capital of the old state of
Alaniya; both the Ossetians and the Ingush
have long claimed succession to Alaniya.
Samachablo was adopted as a Georgian name
for South Ossetia following the South
Ossetians' declaration of an (unrecognized)
independent republic in 1991; it means
'Fiefdom of the Machabelis'. They also refer to
it as Shida Kartli 'Inner Kartli', although the
borders of South Ossetia and Shida Kartli do
not correspond exactly, and Samkhret' Oset'i.

Ossining, NEW YORK/USA *Philipsburg Manor, Sing
Sing*
Established in 1680, two rural communities,
Sparta and Hunters Landing, grew up and in
1813 they were combined to form a village
called Sing Sing after the Sin Sinck tribe whose
name was said to mean 'stone upon stone'. In
1901 the village was renamed Ossining
through fear that it might be associated with
Sing Sing State Prison, although this had been
in use since 1824.

Ostend (**Oostende**), BELGIUM *Oostende-ter-
Streepe*
The present name is an abbreviation of the
original name meaning 'East End of the
Strip'—the seaside resort—from the Flemish
oosten 'east' and *einde* 'end'.

Ostia Antica, LATIUM/ITALY *Ostia*
Originally at the mouth of the River Tiber, the
name comes from the Latin *ostium* 'estuary'. It
is now about 4 miles (6 km) upstream and has
been renamed 'Ancient Ostia'. The modern
seaside resort, some 3 miles (5 km) to the
south-west, is called Lido di Ostia 'Ostia Beach'.

Ostrava, CZECH REPUBLIC
Founded in 1267 as a fortified town to guard
against incursion into Moravia from the north,
the name is taken from the River Ostravice
above whose confluence with the River Oder
the town lies. The lower part of the river was

originally called Ostrava, but now all of it is called the Ostravice. *Ostra* is the feminine form of *ostry* which has several meanings including 'sharp'; in relation to the river it means 'swiftly flowing' with *-ice* indicating a small river. The Ostravice forms the border between Moravia and Silesia and that part of Ostrava situated on Moravian territory, on the left bank of the river, was originally called Německá Ostrava 'German Ostrava'; in the 17th century it was renamed Moravská Ostrava 'Moravian Ostrava'. The part of the town on Silesian territory, on the right bank of the river, was originally called Vendická Ostrava 'Slav Ostrava'; in the 15th century it was renamed Polská Ostrava 'Polish Ostrava' and in 1919 Slezská Ostrava 'Silesian Ostrava'. In 1941 the two towns were merged and simply called Ostrava.

Ostrog (Ostroh), UKRAINE
'Stockade', thus 'Fortified Place'.

Ostrołęka, POLAND
A province established in 1975 and a city on the Narew River. The name means 'Sharp Bend', a reference to the sharp change of course of the river here, from *ostry* 'sharp and *łęk* 'bow'.

Ostrov, CZECH REPUBLIC, ROMANIA, RUSSIA
1. Russia (Pskov): 'Island', here an indication that it lies between two rivers.
2. Czech Republic: formerly Schlackenwerth and now meaning 'Island'.

Ostrów Wielkopolski, POLAND
'Island in Great Poland' from *ostrów* 'island', here raised ground in the low-lying central Polish plain, *wielko* 'great', and *Polski* 'Polish'.

Ostrowiec Świętokrzyski, POLAND
'Little Island (near) the Holy Cross (Mountains)' from *ostrowiec* 'little island', indicating slightly raised ground here, and the adjectival *święty* 'holy' and *krzyz* 'cross'.

Oswego, NEW YORK/USA
It takes its name from the Oswego River at the mouth of which it lies. Its name comes from the Iroquois *osh-we-geh* 'flowing out place'. Founded as a British fur trading post in 1722, a fort was built here in 1727 and called Fort Oswego.

Oswestry, ENGLAND/UK *Oswaldestroe*
'Oswald's Tree' from an Old English personal name and *trēow* 'tree'.

Otaru, HOKKAIDŌ/JAPAN
A coastal city and port, the characters indicate 'Keg' from *o* 'small' and *taru* 'barrel' or 'cask'. Otaru used to be the name for a river from *ota* 'sand' and *nai* 'river'; this was misread as

Otarunai which was shortened to Otaru. Otarunai/Otaru can also mean 'Sandy Beach' from *ota* and *ru* 'path' since there were several routes along the beach.

Otavalo, ECUADOR
Named after the Otavalo people.

Otis, MASSACHUSETTS/USA
Named after Harrison Gray Otis (1765–1848), a prominent Massachusetts politician who served in the US House of Representatives (1797–1801), in the US Senate (1817–22), and as mayor of Boston (1829–32).

Otjiwarongo, NAMIBIA
'The Place of the Fat Cattle', named by the Herero people when they moved into the area in the early 19th century to graze their cattle.

Otorohanga, NORTH ISLAND/NEW ZEALAND
'Food for a Journey'. The literal translation comes from the Maori *o* 'place' and *torohanga* 'to extend over a distance'. This is a reference to a chief who, on his travels, ran short of food; he resorted to incantations so that his food supply would last the journey. Although the town was referred to as Harrodsville by some businessmen for a short period in 1986 as a publicity stunt, the name was never formally adopted. The practice was stopped following complaints by lawyers acting on behalf of Harrods, the emporium in Knightsbridge, London.

Otranto, APULIA/ITALY *Hydrus, Hydruntum*
A port, a cape and a strait between Italy and Albania. The original Greek name comes from *hudōr* 'water' to give 'Water (Town)'. This became the Latin Hydruntum from which the present name has evolved through Idrunta and Idronto.

Ōtsu, JAPAN
'Big Port' from *ō* 'big' and *tsu* 'port'. The town on Honshū lies on Lake Biwa, while the one on Hokkaidō is on the coast.

Ottawa, CANADA, SOUTH AFRICA, USA
1. Canada (Ontario): founded in 1827 as Bytown and named after Colonel John By (1779–1836) of the British Corps of Royal Engineers, who built the Rideau Canal here. In 1855 it was renamed after the Ottawa River on which it stands; the river is named after the Algonquian-speaking Ottawa people who lived along it and in the surrounding area. Their name may come from the Algonquian *adawe* 'trader' since they were well known in this respect. Queen Victoria[†] chose Ottawa as the capital of the United Province of Canada in 1857 and it became the capital of the Dominion of Canada in 1867.

2. USA (Illinois): originally Carbonia because of the nearby coal deposits when it was laid out in 1830, it was subsequently renamed after the Ottawa tribe.
3. USA (Kansas): founded in 1864 on Ottawa-owned land. The Ottawas relinquished the land when they moved to Oklahoma in 1867 and the city was named after them.

Ottumwa, IOWA/USA *Louisville*
Settled in 1843 on the Des Moines River, it was renamed in 1845 with a Native American word meaning 'tumbling water' or possibly 'rapids'.

Ouachita, ARKANSAS/USA
A lake, a river, and mountains that extend into Oklahoma, all named after a Native American tribe, the meaning of whose name is uncertain.

Ouagoudougou, BURKINA FASO
Founded by the Mossi people in the early 14th century. According to Mossi oral history, the original name was Woge Zabra Soba Koumbemb' tenga 'Honoured Chei Zabra Soba's Village'. In time Mande traders shortened this, using *Ouaga* for *Woge* and *dougou* 'village'. By the 16th century it had become the capital of the Mossi kingdom. Their offer of protectorate status having been refused, the French took the town in 1896. In 1919 Ouagoudougou became the capital of the colony of Upper Volta (now Burkina Faso). Upper Volta was dissolved in 1932. Nevertheless, it was reinstated as a colony in 1947 at which time Ouagoudougou became its capital once more. It retained this status when Upper Volta achieved independence in 1960. The name is also spelt Wagadugu.

Oualâta, MAURITANIA
'Place of improvised Shelter' from a Berber form of the Mande *wa* 'improvised shelter' and *la* 'place'.

Oubangui River, CENTRAL AFRICAN REPUBLIC-CONGO
See CENTRAL AFRICAN REPUBLIC.

Oudenaarde, BELGIUM
'Old Earth' or 'Old Land' from the Dutch *oude* 'old' and *aarde* 'earth'.

Oudtshoorn, WESTERN CAPE/SOUTH AFRICA
Settled in 1847 and named in 1863 after Baron Pieter van Rheede van Oudtshoorn, who had been appointed governor of the Cape in 1772 but who had died en route to take up his appointment the following year.

Oued, el-, ALGERIA
The name is a form of the more common *al-Wādi* 'The River'. A river did once flow here.

Ouessant Island, BRITTANY/FRANCE
See USHANT.

Ouezzane, MOROCCO *Dechra Jabal er-Rihan*
Founded in 1727 as a religious centre (in Arabic, *zāwiyah*) on the site of the village called 'Village on the Mount of Myrtles'. The name is derived from the Arabic *wa'z* 'preaching'. The name is also spelt Wazzan.

Oulu, FINLAND *Uleåborg*
A province and a city lying at the mouth of the Oulu River. The city's name is taken from the river whose name means 'river' or 'water'. The previous Swedish name means the same with the added *borg*.

Oum er Rbia, MOROCCO
A river with an Arabic name meaning 'Mother of Spring' from *umm* 'mother' and *rabī'* 'spring (the season)'. 'Mother' here means 'provider'.

Ouro Preto, MINAS GERAIS/BRAZIL *Vila Rica de Albuquerque, A Cidade Imperial de Ouro Preto*
A river and a city founded as a gold and silver mining settlement in 1698. It was given the name 'Rich Town' when it became a city in 1711. In 1823 it was renamed the 'Imperial City of Black Gold' after the declaration in 1822 of Brazilian independence by Peter I (Dom Pedro) (1798–1834), who became Emperor of Brazil that same year and, as Peter IV, King of Portugal (1826–34). The shortened name means 'Black Gold' from the Portuguese *ouro* 'gold' and *preto* 'black' because the gold here was discoloured by a black layer of iron oxide.

Ouse, AUSTRALIA, UK
UK (England): four rivers have this name, although the Little Ouse is a tributary of the Great Ouse. The name simply means 'water' from a Celtic or pre-Celtic root element.

Outardes River (Rivière aux Outardes), QUEBEC/CANADA
'River of Bustards' for which the river is famous.

Outeniqua Mountains, WESTERN CAPE/SOUTH AFRICA
Named after the people of a Khoi tribe whose name means 'Men Bearing Honey', the area being known for its bees.

Outer Mongolia *See* MONGOLIA.

Outremont, QUEBEC/CANADA *Côte-Sainte-Catherine*
Founded as St Catherine's Coast, it was renamed in 1857 to indicate its location with respect to Montreal; that is, on the far side of Mont-Royal from the French *outre* 'beyond' and *mont*.

Ovamboland, NAMIBIA
A region named after the Bantu-speaking
Ovambo (or Owambo) people, who are
organized into eight matrilineal clans.

Overijssel, THE NETHERLANDS
A province whose name means 'Over, or
Beyond, the IJssel (River)', that is north of the
river.

Ovid, USA
Four states have cities with this name, either
classical town names, as in New York, after
Ovid (43 BC–AD 17), the Roman poet whose full
name was Publius Ovidius Naso, or after
another city with this name. For example, the
Ovid in Michigan is named after the city in
New York State.

Ovidiopol', UKRAINE
'Ovid's Town' after Ovid (see previous entry).

Ovidiu, ROMANIA
Just north-west of Constanta, the town is
named after Ovid, who was exiled to
Constanta (then Tomis), for an unknown
reason, in AD 8 and died there. *See* OVID.

Owatonna, MINNESOTA/USA
A river and a city named after it. The Native
American name means 'Straight River'.

Owensboro, KENTUCKY/USA *Rossborough*
Founded *c.*1800 when it was popularly known
as Yellow Banks from the colour of the clay on
the Ohio River's banks. Laid out in 1816, it was
called Rossborough, but it was subsequently
renamed after Colonel Abraham Owen who
fought in the Kentucky wars and was killed at
Tippecanoe.

Owosso, MICHIGAN/USA
Named after Wasso, an Ojibwa chief, whose
name meant 'Bright Light' or 'Light falling on a
Distant Object'.

Oxford, CANADA, NEW ZEALAND, UK, USA
UK (England): formerly Oxnaforda and
Oxeneford 'Ford for Oxen' from the Old
English *oxa*, with the genitive plural *oxna*, and
ford. The county, Oxfordshire, takes its name
from the city with the additional *scīr*. OXFAM,
the Oxford Committee for Famine Relief, was
founded in the city in 1942.

Oxshott, ENGLAND/UK *Okesseta*
'Ocga's Corner of Land' from an Old English
personal name and *scēat* 'corner, or angle, of
land'.

Oxted, ENGLAND/UK *Acstede*
'Place where Oak Trees grow' from the Old
English *āc* 'oak tree' and *stede* 'place'.

Oxus River, TURKMENISTAN-UZBEKISTAN
See AMU DARYA.

Ozark, USA
A mountain range in Arkansas and Missouri
and a small town in Alabama. The name may
come from the French *aux arcs*, the name of a
French trading post established in the early
18th century. It may have taken its name from
the bends in the White River from *arc* 'bow'
and applied to the mountains through which
the river flows.

Ozersk, KALININGRAD/RUSSIA *Darkehmen*
Renamed in 1946 after East Prussia had passed
to the Soviet Union, the name comes from
ozero 'lake', a reference to the fact that it is
close to a region of lakes. There is also a town
called Ozërsk which was formerly known as
Chelyabinsk-65.

Ozurget'i, GEORGIA *Makharadze*
Based on *zurgi* 'back' or 'ridge', a reference to
the mountains to the east. In 1934 it was
renamed after Filipp Makharadze (1868–1941),
a prominent Georgian communist who was
born near here.

Paamiut, GREENLAND/DENMARK *Frederikshåb*
Originally named after Frederik V (1723–66), King of Denmark and Norway (1746–66), and meaning 'Frederik's Hope'. The present name means 'Those at the Mouth (of the Kvanefjord)'.

Paarl, WESTERN CAPE/SOUTH AFRICA
'Pearl' after the dome-shaped rocks on the mountain ridge which dominates the town. These were discovered in 1657 by Abraham Gabbema while hunting game in the Berg River Valley. Huguenot settlers moved into the area in the late 1680s, but it was not until 1720 that the Dutch founded the town.

Pacific Ocean *Sea of the South*
The largest of the world's oceans, it was named by Ferdinand Magellan[†]. Having endured a rough and stormy passage through the Strait of Magellan, he appreciated the ocean's calm and quiet waters as he crossed it in 1520–1 in search of a new westward route to the Spice Islands (the Moluccas).

Padang, SUMATRA/INDONESIA
On the coastal plain between the sea and the Padang Highlands inland and close to the mouth of the Padang River, the Malay name means 'Field'.

Paderborn, NORTH RHINE-WESTPHALIA/GERMANY
Takes its name from the Pader River on which it lies and the Old German *brunn* 'spring'. About 200 springs contribute to the emergence of the river here.

Padma, BANGLADESH
A river with a Sanskrit name meaning 'Lotus'. It is the name by which the main channel of the Ganges River, after its junction with the Brahmaputra, is known in Bangladesh.

Padstow, ENGLAND/UK *Sancte Petroces stow*
'Holy Place of St Petroc' named after Cornwall's most celebrated saint (who lived in the 6th century) and *stōw*.

Padua (Padova), VENETO/ITALY *Patavium*
A very ancient town allegedly founded by the Trojans, the meaning of its name is disputed. The former Roman name may be derived from *Pataves* 'The Paduans' who might have taken their name from an Indo-European root *pat*- leading to the Latin *pateo* 'to be open, or passable'; thus, an 'open, or flat, place' (modern Italian *aperto* 'open') in contrast to the rolling Euganean Hills. However, it has also been suggested that the name may come from the Gaulish *padi* 'pine', a reference to the local pine forests.

Paducah, KENTUCKY/USA *Pekin*
The area was passed to William Clark (1770–1838), a co-leader of the Clark and Lewis Expedition to the Pacific Northwest in 1804–6, after the death of his brother, the Revolutionary general, George Clark, who had earlier been given the site. William Cark laid out the town in 1827 and named it after Paduke, a celebrated Chickasaw chief, who had once lived in the area and was buried on the banks of the Tennessee River in a spot now within the city limits.

Pag, CROATIA *Cissa*
An island and a town settled by the Romans and known to them as Cissa. Its present name is simply 'village' from the Latin *pagus*.

Pahang, MALAYSIA
A state named after the Pahang River. It became one of the Federated Malay States in 1895.

Paide, ESTONIA *Paelinn, Weissenstein*
Many buildings are built of limestone, hence the name '(Town of) Limestone' from *paekivi* 'limestone'. The original name meant 'Fort of Limestone' from *linn* 'fort', while the German name, Weissenstein, meant 'White Stone'.

Paignton, ENGLAND/UK *Peintone*
'Village, or estate, associated with a Man called Pæga' from an Old English personal name, *-ing*- and *tūn*.

Painesville, OHIO/USA *Champion, The Opening, Oak Openings*
Laid out in 1805 and named after the original owner, Henry Champion, it received its present name in 1816 to honour General Edward Paine, who was one of the first to settle here.

Painted Desert, ARIZONA/USA
A name coined by Lieutenant Joseph C. Ives in 1858 to describe the magnificent colours of the desert floor which look as though they have been painted on.

Paisley SCOTLAND/UK *Passeleth, Passelek*
The city's means 'Church' from the Middle
Irish *baslec*, itself from the Latin *basílica*. It
developed from a village based on a Cluniac
abbey founded here in 1163. It gave its name to
the patterned shawls made here.

Pakbèng, LAOS
Lying at the point where the Bèng River flows
into the Mekong River, the name means
'Mouth of the (River) Bèng' from *paak* 'mouth'.

Pakistan The Islamic Republic of Pakistan
(Islam-i Jamhuriya-e Pakistan) since 1956.
Previously the State of Pakistan when it was
founded in 1947 from the partition of India. In
1930 Sir Muhammad Iqbal (1876–1938), a
leading Muslim philosopher, demanded the
creation of a confederated India that would
include a Muslim state comprising the four
Muslim-dominated north-west provinces of
India; a resolution to this effect was formally
adopted by the All India Muslim League in
1940. In 1933 Rahmat Ali, a Muslim Indian
student at Cambridge University, and some
fellow students proposed that the new state
should take the name Pakistan. This was
derived principally from the initial letters of
their homelands: Punjab, Afghana (North-West
Frontier), Kashmir, Iran, Sindh, Tukharistan,
Afghanistan, and Baluchistan. Thus it means
'Land of the Paks' or, alternatively, 'Land of the
(Spiritually) Pure'. Happily, *Pak* is a Persian-
derived Urdu word meaning 'ritually pure'.
Thus the name Pakistan can also be said to
classify the country by its Islamic religion and
this is also reflected in the name of its capital,
Islāmābād. Pakistan was divided into two
wings, separated by nearly 1 000 miles
(1 600 km) of Indian territory, at the time of its
creation in 1947: West Pakistan (now Pakistan)
and East Pakistan, which became *Bangladesh
in 1971. The 1933 name did not include Bengal
which was to become East Pakistan.

Pakpattan, PUNJAB/PAKISTAN
Situated on an old crossing place on the Sutlej
River, the name means 'Ferry Crossing of the
Pure' from the Urdu *pak* 'pure'.

Pakxan, LAOS
Lying at the point where the Xan River flows
into the Mekong River, the name means
'Mouth of the (River) Xan' from *paak* 'mouth'.

Pakxé, LAOS
Lying at the point where the Dôn River flows
into the Mekong River, the name means
'Mouth of the River (Dôn)' from *paak* 'mouth'
and the southern Lao word *xé* 'river'.

Palankaraya, BORNEO/INDONESIA *Pahandut*
'Great and Holy Place'.

Palau, AND ITALY, MEXICO
The Republic of Palau (Belu'u er a Belau) since
1981, although independence was only
achieved in 1994; geographically part of the
Caroline Islands. Previously part of the UN
Trust Territory of the Pacific Islands under US
administration (1947); a League of Nations
mandate administered by the Japanese (1920–
44) having been captured by the Japanese in
1914; German territory (1899–1914), having
been sold to Germany by Spain following its
defeat in the Spanish–American War; annexed
to become a part of the Spanish Empire (1886).
It was the last mandate awarded after the First
World War to run out. The meaning of the
name is unknown.

Palawan, PHILIPPINES
A large island in the south-west which acts as a
bulwark against the South China Sea; hence its
name, 'Gate of Combat'.

Paldiski, ESTONIA *Rogervik, Baltiyskiy Port*
Founded in 1718 and named in 1723, it was
renamed 'Baltic Port' in 1783. The present
name is merely an Estonian version of this,
adopted in 1917.

Palembang, SUMATRA/INDONESIA *Svarna Dvīpa*
The original Srivajayan name meant 'Golden
Island' from *svarna* 'gold' and *dvīpa* while the
present one means 'Place to pan for Gold' from
pa 'place' and *limbang* 'pan for gold'. Lying
astride the Musi River, an alternative theory is
that the name comes from *pa* 'place' and
lembang 'lowland'. It was the capital of the
Buddhist Srivajayan Empire, a great maritime
empire which spread well beyond Sumatra
between the 7th and 14th centuries; in the
15th century it became an Islamic sultanate
until this was abolished by the Dutch in 1825.

Palenque, MEXICO, PANAMA
Mexico (Chiapas): a town and ruined Mayan
site whose ancient name is not known. The
present name means 'Stockade' or 'Palisade' in
Spanish.

Palermo, SICILY/ITALY *Ziz, Panormos/Panormus,
Balarma*
'Safe Haven for all Boats' from the Greek *pan*
'all' and *ormos* 'chain (of boats)', thus an
anchorage. Despite its Greek name it was
never a Greek city. It was founded by the
Phoenicians as Ziz in the 7th or 8th century BC,
later falling to the Carthaginians, and then to
the Romans in 254 BC. After a succession of
foreign rulers, it joined Italy in 1861. It has
been the capital of Sicily since 1072.

Palestine, AND USA *Canaan*
Palestine has never been the name of a nation
or a state, and has never existed as an

autonomous entity. It is an area between the
Mediterranean coast and the River Jordan
which was mandated to the UK in 1922–48; it
is bounded in the north by the Israel–Lebanese
border and in the south includes the Negev
reaching down to the Gulf of Aqaba. Thus,
geographically, it includes modern Israel, the
West Bank, and the Gaza Strip (and this is the
definition claimed by Palestinians today). In
biblical times, during the reign of Rehoboam
c.930 BC, a part of the Kingdom of Israel was
hived off to become the southern Kingdom of
Judah (the fourth son of Jacob-Israel who gave
his name to the Jews who are said to be
descended from him). For the Jews, Palestine,
called by them **Eretz Yisra'el*, is the 'Promised
Land'. The Palestinian Arabs claim it as their
homeland since they have occupied the
territory since the Arab conquest in 637. The
name is derived from the Greek *Palaistina*,
which itself comes from the Hebrew *Peleshet*
'invaders' or 'penetrators', a reference to the
Philistine invasion in the 12th century BC.
They came from the Greek islands and settled
on a small strip of land along the coast
between what is now Tel Aviv-Yafo and Gaza
which they called Philistia 'Land of the
Philistines', a confederacy of five city-states.
Later, in the 2nd century BC, the Romans used
the name for the southern third of their
province of Syria, Syria Palaestina. With the
arrival of the Arabs in the 7th century the
name fell out of use until resurrected for the
British mandate. It is called *Falastin* by the
Arabs, their pronunciation of 'Palestine'.
While Canaan can be used to describe
ancient Palestine, its geographical
boundaries have not been defined. Over the
centuries the area has been subject to rule by
Egyptians, Israelites, Assyrians, Babylonians,
Persians, Alexander III the Great[†] and his
successors, the Ptolemies and Seleucids,
Romans, Byzantines, Arabs, Crusaders (who
called it the Holy Land), Mamlūks, Ottoman
Turks (1516–1917), the British, and Israelis.
In 1922 the League of Nations recognized
'the historical connection of the Jewish
people with Palestine' and 'the grounds
for reconstituting their national home in
that country' ('country' in the sense of
'territory'). In 1947 the UN issued a plan for the
partition of Palestine with just over half the
land earmarked for a Jewish state and
the rest for the Palestinians. The Jews accepted
the plan; the Palestinians did not. The
Philistines have given their name to the word
'philistine' to mean 'unenlightened', 'hostile
to culture', or 'lacking in intellectual
curiosity'. *See* ISRAEL, GAZA, JORDAN, AND WEST
BANK.

Palk Strait, INDIA-SRI LANKA
Named after Sir Robert Palk (1717–98),
governor of Madras, India (1763–7).

Palma, BALEARIC ISLANDS/SPAIN
'Palm Tree'.

Palm Beach, ARUBA, AUSTRALIA, USA
USA (Florida): named Palm City in 1880 after
the coconut palms that had been planted here
earlier. It was renamed in 1887 at the
beginning of its development as a resort.

Palmdale, USA
The cities in California and Florida are so
named because of their abundant palms.

Palmer Land, ANTARCTICA
Named after Nathaniel Palmer (1799–1877), an
American explorer who led an expedition here
in 1820. *See* GRAHAM LAND.

Palmerston North, NORTH ISLAND/NEW
ZEALAND
Founded in 1866 and named after Henry
John Temple (1784–1865), 3rd Viscount
Palmerston, British prime minister (1855–8,
1859–65). The 'North' was added to
distinguish it from the smaller Palmerston
in South Island.

Palmerville, QUEENSLAND/AUSTRALIA
Named after Sir Arthur Palmer (1819–98),
premier of Queensland (1870–4).

Palm Springs, USA
California: originally Agua Caliente 'Hot
Springs' in Spanish, it was renamed in 1884
after its palms and springs.

Palmyra, LINE ISLANDS, SYRIA, USA
1. Line Islands: a Pacific Ocean atoll
discovered in 1802 by sailors aboard the
American ship *Palmyra*.
2. Syria: Palmyra is the Greek and Latin form
of Tadmor or Tadmur, the pre-Semitic name
for the site which is still sometimes used
today. There is much conjecture about the
name. It has been suggested that Tadmor is
associated with *damâr* 'destruction' while local
tradition has it that it comes from *tatmor* 'to
cover' or 'to bury', a reference to the
numerous tombs in the area; another idea is
that it is derived from a Semitic root *dh-m-r* 'to
protect', i.e., a defensive post. Once an oasis of
palms in the desert, Palmyra may be linked
with the Semitic *tamr* 'date palm' to mean
'City of Palms' or it may come from a Greek
personal name.

Palo Alto, CALIFORNIA/USA
Founded in 1891 and named 'Tall Tree', a
reference to a tall redwood tree here, from the
Spanish *palo* 'tree' and *alto* 'tall'.

Palo Cedro, CALIFORNIA/USA
'Cedar Tree' from the Spanish *palo* 'tree' and *cedro* 'cedar', a reference to the many cedars here.

Palomar, BOLIVIA, CANADA, USA
USA (California): a mountain formerly called Smith Mountain and renamed in 1901 with its original Mexican name meaning '(Place of) Pigeons' from the Spanish *paloma* 'pigeon'.

Pamiers, MIDI-PYRÉNÉES/FRANCE
Derived from the 12th-century archbishopric and the castle of Apamea (now in ruins) in Syria granted to members of the Order of the Hospital of St John of Jerusalem (known as the Hospitallers). One of these Crusaders took the name for his own castle here. Apamea was founded in the 4th century BC and named after the wife, Apama, of Seleucus I Nicator[†].

Pamirs, TAJIKISTAN
Mountains, mainly in Tajikistan, but also extending into Afghanistan, China, Kyrgyzstan, and Pakistan. The name may be derived from the ancient Persian *paimir* 'Foot of Mithra', god of the sun, and used to describe the high grasslands to be found in the eastern parts of the range.

Pampa, TEXAS/USA
'Prairie' in Spanish. The word comes from a Quechua word meaning 'flat surface' and is the origin of the Pampas, a huge plain in Argentina, and the province of La Pampa.

Pamphylia, TURKEY
An ancient district with a Greek name '(Colony of) all Races' from *pan* 'all' and *pheeli* 'race', that indicated that different tribes lived here.

Pamplona, COLOMBIA, PHILIPPINES, SPAIN
Spain (Navarre): according to tradition, founded in 75 BC by the Roman statesman and general Pompey the Great (106–48 BC) who gave the city his own name. First called Pompaelo, it was also known as Pompeiopolis 'City of Pompey' by the Romans and by the Moors as Pampilona or Banbalūnah. It was the capital of the Kingdom of Navarre between the 11th century and 1841.

Pamukkale, TURKEY *Hierapolis*
Ruins. The city was founded *c.*190 BC by Eumenes II, King of Pergamum (197–159 BC), and later called Hierapolis 'Holy City', allegedly because of the number of temples built here. It was abandoned after an earthquake in 1334. The present name means 'Cotton Castle' from *pamuk* 'cotton' and *kale*. The name comes from the chalk-white stalactites that have formed on the cliff face.

Panama, AND SRI LANKA, USA
The Republic of Panama (República de Panamá) since 1903. Previously a part of the United States of Colombia (1843–1903) and part of the Federation of Gran Colombia (1821–43), having gained independence from Spain in 1821. By 1520 it had become a Spanish colony and in 1538 an *audiencia* 'court'. From 1567 Panama was attached to the Viceroyalty of Peru until 1739 when it became part of the Viceroyalty of New Granada (which encompassed modern Colombia, Venezuela, Ecuador, and Panama). The country takes its name from its capital (*see* PANAMA CITY), as does the gulf and the isthmus. The Panama Canal Zone, 5 miles (8 km) either side of the canal, was under the control of the USA between 1904 and 1979 when it was abolished; actual operation of the canal, which opened in 1914, came under full Panamanian control in 2000 and Panama became a fully sovereign state.

Panama City, PANAMA, USA
1. Panama: founded as Panamá near a village of that name in 1519. It was destroyed in 1671 but rebuilt three years later on a site a few miles west of the old town. Traditionally, the name is said to mean '(Place with) an Abundance of Fish'. However, some believe it comes from a Cuna phrase *panna mai* 'far away'; the story goes that Spanish soldiers asked a Cuna where they might be able to find gold and received the reply *panna mai* in the hope that they too would go far away. It has been the capital of Panama since 1903. It is sometimes called simply Panama.
2. USA (Florida): an English settlement dating from about 1765 and called Old Town; it was later renamed St Andrew. This fishing village merged in 1909 with another village called Panama City, named after the city in the Canal Zone in Panama, and took its name.

Panevėžys, LITHUANIA *Poneviej*
Takes its name from the Nevėžys River with the prefix *Pa-* 'On' or 'Along'.

Pangasinan, LUZON/PHILIPPINES
'Place where Salt is produced' from the Pangasinan *asin* 'salt'. A province and also the name of a cultural-linguistic group.

Pangbourne, ENGLAND/UK *Pegingaburnan, Pangeborn*
'Stream of the Family, or followers, of Pǣga' from an Old English personal name, *-inga-*, and *burna* 'stream'.

Panshīr Valley, AFGHANISTAN
Named after a former city called Banj Hir 'Five Mountains' from *banj* 'five' and *hir* 'mountain'.

p

The valley's name was later changed to Panjshīr 'Five Lions' from *shīr* 'lion'.

Paola, ITALY, MALTA, USA
1. Italy (Calabria): 'Meadow' or 'Pasture' from the Latin *pabula*.
2. Malta: founded in 1626 by, and named after, Antoine de Paule, Grand Master of the Hospitallers (Knights of St John of Jerusalem).
3. USA (Kansas): named after Baptiste Peoria, Paola being the Native American pronunciation.

Papal States (Stati Pontifici)
That part of central Italy over which the Pope had sovereignty between 756 and 1870. Although the area varied in size, it corresponded to the modern regions of Emilia-Romagna, Lazio, Marche, and Umbria.

Papeete, TAHITI/FRENCH POLYNESIA
A city-port annexed by the French in 1880, the name is derived from the Tahitian *pape* 'water' and *ete* 'basket' to mean something like '(Place where People come with) Baskets to collect Water'.

Paphos (Páfos), CYPRUS *Erythrae, Sebaste Nea Paphos, Augusta Claudia Flavia Paphos, Baffo, Basso, Ktima*
A combination of two cities, Nea 'New' (later Kato 'Lower') Paphos, founded towards the end of the 4th century BC and Ktima, and named Paphos in 1971. Old Paphos (Palaepaphos, now Kouklia, and given this name when New Paphos was founded) was located 10 miles (16 km) to the east. According to a legend whose details are somewhat confusing, the city was named by Kinyras, the husband or son of Paphos. Paphos was the daughter of King Pygmalion, who fell in love with an ivory statue he had made of his ideal woman. The goddess Venus (Aphrodite) took pity on him and brought the statue to life; Pygmalion married her. In 15 BC Nea Paphos was restored after an earthquake by Octavian (later Augustus[†]) and given the name Sebaste Nea Paphos 'Honourable New Paphos'. After the Flavians had rebuilt the city after another earthquake in 76 or 77 it was given the name Augustus Claudia Flavia Paphos to reflect the favours conferred upon the city by these Roman emperors. During the Lusignan period of control in 1192–1489 the city was called Ktima. Paphos was the pre-Roman and Roman capital of Cyprus, but when it came under Byzantine control in the 4th century it lost this status.

Papillion, NEBRASKA/USA
'Butterfly' from the French *papillon* because many butterflies were seen on the banks of the small river here.

Papua, INDONESIA *Ilhas dos Papuas, Dutch New Guinea, Irian Barat, Irian Jaya, West Papua*
A province which gives its name to the western half of the island of New Guinea (the eastern half is *Papua New Guinea). This was claimed in 1828 by the Dutch as part of the Dutch East Indies. When Indonesia declared independence in 1945 the Dutch declined to accept the demand that all former territory belonging to the Dutch East Indies should be included in the new republic. In 1949–63 the territory was known as Dutch New Guinea. Only in 1963 was it transferred to Indonesia, which renamed it Irian Barat, on condition that the population would be allowed a free vote within six years on whether it wanted to become a part of Indonesia. A plebiscite was held in 1969 and Irian Barat was annexed, becoming a province; it was renamed Irian Jaya in 1972. The Biak *Irian*, the Indonesian name for the whole island, appears to have a number of meanings, including 'Hot Land', 'beautiful' or 'light', or 'cloud-covered'. *Jaya* means 'glorious' or 'victorious', and *barat* 'west'. Irian Jaya may be said to have the meaning 'Victorious Hot Land'. At New Year 2000 Jakarta changed the name to West Papua, and later simply to Papua, in response to local demand as a symbolic concession to the largely Melanesian local identity. In 1526 Jorge de Meneses, the first governor of the 'Spice Islands' (*Indonesia), sought shelter in a cove and named the area 'Islands of the Papuans' from the Malay *papuah* 'frizzy-haired men'.

Papua New Guinea Independent State of Papua New Guinea since 1975. In 1884 the south-eastern quadrant of the island of New Guinea became a British protectorate and two years later it was annexed and called British New Guinea. Also in 1884 the Germans took over the administration of the north-eastern quadrant, calling it Schutzgebiet Kaiser-Wilhelmsland 'Protectorate of Kaiser Wilhem (Emperor William) Land'; in 1899 it became an imperial colony known as German New Guinea. In 1906 Australia assumed responsibility for British New Guinea and it became known as the Territory of Papua. In 1914–21 German New Guinea was also administered by Australia which was then given a League of Nations mandate to govern it. At the end of the Second World War this became a UN Trust Territory. In 1949 the UN Trust Territory and the Territory of Papua were merged to form the Territory of Papua and New Guinea or Papua New Guinea, a title it retained until 1975. The name comes from the Malay *papuah* 'frizzy-haired men'. The state includes the Admiralty Islands, Bougainville, New Britain, and New Ireland.

Pará, BRAZIL, INDONESIA, SURINAME
1. Brazil: a state through which the lower Amazon flows and whose Guaraní name simply means 'River'. It is also the name of a river.
2. The river in Suriname and island in Indonesia are spelt Para.

Paraguay Republic of Paraguay (República del Paraguay; Guaraní: Tetã Paraguáype) since achieving independence in 1811. Previously the land-locked region had been a part of the Spanish Viceroyalty of Río de la Plata (1776–1811); and a Spanish colony as part of the Viceroyalty of Peru (1537–1776). The country takes its name from the Paraguay River whose name comes from *para* 'river' or 'water' and *guay* 'born'. This name may well be connected with the Payaguá tribe, perhaps meaning '(People) born (along) the River'.

Paraíba, BRAZIL
A state and the name of two rivers. The name is derived from *para* and *hiba* 'arm' or 'branch of a river'.

Paralimni, CYPRUS
'Beside the Lake' from the Greek *para* 'beside' and *limni* 'lake'. It lies to the east of Paralimni Lake.

Paramaribo, SURINAME
Founded as a village on the Suriname River, its name is derived from the Guaraní *para* 'water' and *maribo* 'inhabitants'. It is the national capital.

Paramushir, KURIL ISLANDS/RUSSIA
An island with an Ainu name meaning 'Wide Island' from *para* 'wide' and *mushir* 'island'.

Paraná, ARGENTINA, BRAZIL
1. Argentina: founded in 1730 near the Paraná River after which it is also named.
2. Brazil: a state named after the river which takes its name 'Father of the Rivers' from the Guaraní *para* 'water' and *aná* 'parent' or 'union', a reference to the fact that it originates at the confluence of the Grande and Paranaíba Rivers.

Paranaíba, BRAZIL
A river with a Guaraní name meaning 'Bad Water', possibly because parts of its course were difficult to navigate.

Parati, SÃO PAULO/BRAZIL
Derived from a local word for a small fish, abundant in the waters here, the paratii.

Pardubice, CZECH REPUBLIC *Pordobice, Pardubitz*
Founded in 1295, its name is derived from the Polish personal name Porydeby or Pordoby. A

man with this name was probably the chief of the new settlement.

Paris, CANADA, FRANCE, KIRITIMATI, USA
1. France (Île-de-France): called Lutetia Parisorium from the Latin *lutum* 'mud', 'clay', or 'marsh' by Julius Caesar[†] in 53 BC. The Roman town was built on the site of an earlier settlement. The Parisii, a comparatively insignificant tribe, built their chief town on the Île de la Cité, an island in the River Seine and thus the full title meant the 'Marsh (Town) of the Parisii' or 'Midwater Dwelling of the Parisii'. It is clearly from them that the present name comes. Capital of the Capetian dynasty (987–1328) from 987, it was not recognized as the capital of France until *c*.1190. The city gives its name to 'plaster of Paris' from the gypsum quarries in Montmartre, a northern ward of Paris.
2. USA (Kentucky): founded in 1789 as Hopewell, it was briefly called Bourbontown before being renamed again in 1790 as Paris in gratitude for French help during the American War of Independence (1775–83).

Parkersburg, USA
West Virginia: settled as Neal's Station *c*.1785 and later renamed after the owner of the land, Alexander Parker.

Parkes, NEW SOUTH WALES/AUSTRALIA
Bushman's
Founded in 1862 and renamed in 1883 after Sir Henry Parkes (1815–96), who served five terms as premier of New South Wales (1872–91).

Parma, ITALY, USA
1. Italy (Emilia-Romagna): said to be named after the River Parma which may have received its name from an Etruscan people who founded the town in 183 BC. Alternatively, the name may come from the Celtic *parma* 'round shield', which might have described the shape of the original settlement. The city has given its name to the ham and violets.
2. USA (Ohio): settled as Greenbriar in 1816, it was renamed in 1826 after the Italian city.

Pärnu, ESTONIA *Pyarnu, Pernov*
Lying at the mouth of the Pärnu River, the present name, adopted in 1918, is derived from *pärn* 'lime tree'.

Parramatta, NEW SOUTH WALES/AUSTRALIA
Rose Hill
Founded in 1788 and given an Aboriginal name meaning 'Head of the River (Parramatta)' and 'Plenty of Eels' in 1791, the year after it became a town.

Parrsboro, NOVA SCOTIA/CANADA
Named after John Parr (1725–91), governor of
Nova Scotia (1782–91).

Parry Islands, NORTHWEST TERRITORIES/
CANADA
Named after Rear Admiral Sir William Parry
(1790–1855), the British Arctic explorer who
came here in 1819.

Parry Sound, ONTARIO/CANADA
Founded in the middle of the 19th century, the
town is named after Sir William Parry (see
previous entry). Nearby is Parry Island.

Parthia, IRAN
An ancient territory roughly corresponding to
the modern province of Khorāsān. Considered
by some authorities to be of Scythian origin,
the Parthians' name, possibly meaning
'banished', may have resulted from their flight
westwards from Central Asia during the 3rd
century BC.

Partizansk, PRIMORSKIY TERRITORY/RUSSIA
Suchan
Originally called after the Suchan River on
which it lies, it was renamed Partizansk in
1972 in recognition of the exploits of Partisan
fighters during the Great Patriotic War
(1941–5).

Parys, FREE STATE/SOUTH AFRICA
Founded in 1873 and possibly named by a
German surveyor called Shilbach after the
Paris in France because he had been involved
in the siege of that city in 1870 during the
Franco-Prussian War (1870–1).

Pasadena, CANADA, USA
1. USA (California): founded in 1874 by
Thomas B. Elliott who wanted a name
associated with Native Americans; he called it
Indiana Colony. The Post Office rejected the
name and Elliott asked for suggestions for a
new name. In 1875 a missionary working with
the Chippewa people proposed four names:
Gish kadenapasadena 'Peak of the Valley',
Weoquanpasadena 'Crown of the Valley',
Doegunpasadena 'Key of the Valley', and
Pequadenpasadena 'Hill of the Valley'. All were
thought to be too awkward, but all had a
common ending, Pasadena 'of the Valley', and
this was chosen.
2. USA (Texas): founded in 1895 and named
after the city in California in the mistaken
belief that the name was the Spanish for 'Land
of Flowers' to describe the fields full of flowers
along Vince's Bayou.

Pascagoula, MISSISSIPPI/USA
Located at the mouth of the Pascagoula River
after which it is named. The river's name is
said to come from the Pascagoula tribe, and
their name means 'Bread People'.

Pas-de-Calais, NORD-PAS-DE-CALAIS/FRANCE
A department meaning the 'Strait of Calais',
otherwise known as the 'Strait of Dover', from
pas 'strait' or 'pass'.

Paso Robles, CALIFORNIA/USA
'Pass of the Oak Trees' from the Spanish *paso*
and *roble* 'oak tree'.

Passaic, NEW JERSEY/USA *Acquackanonk*
Founded by the Dutch in 1678 as a fur trading
post, it was renamed after the Passaic River in
1854. The name comes from the Algonquian
passaic or *passajeek* 'peace' or 'valley' so perhaps
the name could have the meaning of 'Peaceful
Valley'.

Passau, BAVARIA/GERMANY *Bojodurum, Castra
Batava*
Originally a Celtic settlement called
Bojodurum, it subsequently became a Roman
camp. At the confluence of the Danube, Inn,
and Ilz Rivers, the name may allude to its
location from *Pass* 'pass', 'defile', or 'passage'
and *au* from *Aue* 'meadow'.

Pass Christian, MISSISSIPPI/USA
Named after the channel, called Christian's
Pass, linking Lake Pontchartrain with the Gulf
of Mexico. The pass is allegedly named after
Christian L'Adnier, a member of a French
expedition which resulted in the first
permanent settlement in the Mississippi
Valley in 1699.

Patagonia, ARGENTINA
A large region with a name said to be derived
from Patagones, the name given to the
Tehuelche people by the Spanish in the 16th
century. The name may come from the
Spanish *pata* 'paw' or 'foot', possibly an
obscure reference to their footwear. However,
it has also been suggested that Ferdinand
Magellan[†] invented the name because the
Tehuelche, dressed in animal hides, reminded
him of Patagon, a savage in a 16th-century
Spanish novel.

Pategi, KWARA/NIGERIA
'Small Hill'.

Paterson, NEW JERSEY/USA
Founded in 1791 and named after William
Paterson (1745–1806), a senator (1789–90) and
governor of the state (1790–3).

Pathein, BURMA *Kosama, Bassein*
May be derived from *pathi*, the Burmese word
for 'Muslim', given that many Muslims used to
trade here. It was probably modified by the
British.

Patna, INDIA, UK
India (Bihār): founded in the 5th century BC as Pāṭaliputra, and capital of the ancient Kingdom of Magadha, its present name is probably simply a shortened version of the original from *pāṭala* 'pale red' and *putra* 'son'. It might come, however, from the Hindi *paṭṭana* 'city'. It was abandoned in the 7th century, but refounded in 1541 as Patna by Afghans. The name Azimabad, adopted for a period from 1704, was a tribute to 'Azīm al-Shain, who made his court here; he was a grandson of Aurangzeb, Mughal Emperor of India (1658–1707).

Pátrai, GREECE *Aroe*
Also called Patras. It is said to take its name from Patreus, an Achaean leader.

Pattaya, THAILAND
A coastal town in the Gulf of Thailand, it means 'South-west Wind'.

Pau, AQUITAINE/FRANCE
May be derived from the Latin *pagus* 'village'.

Pavia, LOMBARDY/ITALY *Ticinum, Papia*
Ticinum was the Roman name while Papia was noted for the first time in the 7th century. It may be associated with the name of a Roman noble woman, possibly Papilia, corrupted to Papeia, then Paveia, and finally Pavia. *See* TICINO.

Pavlodar, KAZAKHSTAN *Koryakovsky Forpost*
A province and a city founded as a military post on the Irtysh Line in 1720, it was renamed 'Paul's Gift' in 1861 from *Pavel* 'Paul' and *dar* 'gift'. The Paul in question is probably Emperor Paul I[†] and the name was given to match his mother's town, Yekaterinodar 'Catherine's Gift' (now Krasnodar).

Pavlograd (Pavlohrad), UKRAINE *Luganskoye*
Founded in 1779. The following year a fort was built and in 1784 named in honour of the Russian heir apparent who became Emperor Paul I[†]. As soon as it became a town in 1797 *grad* was added and this became *hrad* in the Ukrainian spelling.

Pavlovsk, RUSSIA
1. St Petersburg: founded as Pavlovskoye in 1779 after Catherine II the Great[†] had given the land along the River Slavyanka to her son, later Emperor Paul I[†], for a summer residence two years earlier. When it gained the status of a town in 1796 it was renamed as now.
2. Voronezh: takes its name from the Fort of St Paul to the south which was destroyed during the Russo-Turkish Wars. On this site a new fortress was built in 1709 and manned by the men of St Paul; the name was transferred with them.

Pawhuska, OKLAHOMA/USA
Founded in 1872 and named after an Osage chief, Paw-Hiu-Skah 'White Hair'.

Pawtucket, RHODE ISLAND/USA
Settled in 1671 and given an Algonquian name 'At the Little Falls', a reference to the falls here on the River Blackstone which is also known here as the Pawtucket.

Payakumbuh, SUMATRA/INDONESIA
'Grassy Swamp' from *paya* 'marsh' or 'swamp' and *kumbuh* 'sedge grass', a type of marshy grass from which baskets and mats are made.

Paysandú, URUGUAY
Founded in 1772 by, and named after, Policarpo Sandú. He was a priest and the Native Americans who had been converted to Christianity translated the Spanish *padre* 'father' into the Guaraní *pay* to give the full name.

Pazardzhik, BULGARIA *Tatar Pazarcik*
Founded by Russian Tatars in 1485 as the 'Tatar Market' from *bazar* 'market'; the 'Tatar' was eliminated in 1934. There is a town with this name, but spelt Pazarcik, in Turkey and three towns called Pazar.

Peabody, USA
Massachusetts: originally South Danvers, it was renamed in 1868 as a tribute to George Peabody (1795–1869), a merchant banker and generous philanthropist. A city in Kansas also has this name, but it is not connected with George Peabody.

Peace River, CANADA, USA
Canada (Alberta-British Columbia): named after Peace Point, Alberta, where the Cree and Beaver tribes settled their dispute about land along the river banks.

Pearl Harbor, HAWAII/USA *Wai Momi*
The present name is merely a translation of the earlier Hawaiian name meaning 'Pearl Waters', a reference to the pearl oysters that grew here.

Pearl River, CHINA, USA
1. China (Guangdong): also known as the Zhū River from *zhū* 'pearl'.
2. USA: besides cities in Louisiana and New York, the Pearl River flows through Louisiana and Mississippi. The Native American name was Tallahatchie which the French translated as 'River of Pearls' in recognition of the abundant, but worthless, pearls found on the river's banks.

Peary Land, GREENLAND/DENMARK
Explored at the end of the 19th century by, and named after, Robert E. Peary (1856–1920), an

American Arctic explorer, who claimed to have led the first expedition to have reached the North Pole in 1909. There is still some doubt as to whether he did actually reach the Pole.

Peć (Albanian: *Pejë*), SERBIA/SERBIA AND MONTENEGRO *Siperant, Pescium, Peć, Ipek*
Derived from *pećina* 'cave' or 'grotto', a reference to the caves nearby. In 1455 the town fell to the Ottoman Turks and was renamed Ipek. When the Turks were driven out in 1912, the name reverted to Peć. Its population is largely Albanian.

Pechenga, MURMANSK/RUSSIA *Petsamo*
Petsamo was used in 1920–44 when the town was in Finnish hands and for four years afterwards. Both this name and the Russian are probably derived from a version of the Finnish *petäjä* 'pine tree'.

Pechory, PSKOV/RUSSIA *Petseri*
Possibly derived from *peshchera* 'cave'. According to legend, a hunter suddenly heard singing from somewhere underground. On searching, he found a group of holy men chanting in a cave. In 1920–40, when it was part of Estonia, it was known as Petseri.

Pecos, USA
A river and two cities lying on it in New Mexico and Texas. All are named after the Pecos people whose name means 'shepherd' from the Latin *pecus* 'flock'. They had been taught animal husbandry by the Spanish.

Pécs, HUNGARY *Sopianae, Pečůy, Fünfkirchen*
The previous name meant 'Five Churches' from the German *fünf* 'five' and *Kirche* 'church'. The present name, following from the Turkish Pečůy, means 'Cave' from the Latin *specus* 'cave' or 'cavern'.

Pedhoulas, CYPRUS
Famous for its tannery, the name is said to come from the Greek *pédila* 'sandal'.

Peebles, CANADA, UK, USA
UK (Scotland): formerly Pebles and derived from the Welsh *pabell*, plural *pebyll* 'tents' to give '(Place of) Shelter'. In the English a final *s* has been added.

Peekskill, NEW YORK/USA
Named after Jan Peek, a Dutch mariner who established a trading post in 1654 at the point where a stream (in Dutch, *kil*) joined the Hudson River.

Peel, CANADA, ISLE OF MAN
1. Canada: a river flowing through Yukon and the Northwest Territories and named after Sir Robert Peel (1788–1850), British prime minister (1834–5, 1841–6).

2. Isle of Man: originally Pelam 'The Palisade' from the Middle English *pel* 'enclosure protected by a palisade', a reference to the ruined castle. The previous name, Holmetown, meant 'Island Village' from the Old Scandinavian *holmr* 'island' and the Middle English *toun*. The Manx name is Port-na-Hinsey 'Port of the Island'.

Peenemünde, MECKLENBURG-WEST POMERANIA/GERMANY
'Mouth of the Peene (River)'. The meaning of the river's name is not known.

Peipus, Lake (Estonian: **Peipsi Järv;** Russian: **Chudskoye Ozero**), ESTONIA-RUSSIA
A lake forming part of the border between Estonia and Russia. The Estonian name is said to come from the Finnish *peipposen* 'finches', thus '(Lake of) Finches'. The Russian name comes from an Old Russian tribal name, Chud, probably associated with *chuzhoy* 'strange', 'alien', or 'foreign' to give 'strangers'.

Pekin, ILLINOIS/USA
Founded in 1824 and so named because it was thought that it was directly opposite Peking (Beijing), China, on the other side of the globe.

Peking, CHINA
See BEIJING.

Pelabuhanratu, JAVA/INDONESIA
'Harbour of the Queen'. According to legend, this was Nyai Loro Kidul, Queen of the South Seas, a vicious goddess who ensnared fishermen and swimmers (particularly those, it is said, who wore green).

Pelée, Mt (Montagne Pelée), MARTINIQUE
'Bald', athough this is only true in parts.

Pelham, AUSTRALIA, USA
USA (Massachusetts-New Hampshire): both are named after Henry Pelham (1696–1754), British prime minister (1743–54) or after his elder brother, Thomas Pelham-Holles (1693–1768), 1st Duke of Newcastle-upon-Tyne, who took over from his brother as prime minister (1754–6, 1757–62).

Pelhřimov, CZECH REPUBLIC *Pelhřzymov*
Founded in the 13th century by Peregrinus (in Czech, Pelhřim), the bishop of Prague. He took his name from the Latin *peregrinus* 'stranger', thus a 'pilgrim'.

Peloponnese (Pelopónnisos), GREECE *Morea*
A large peninsula with a name meaning 'Pelops' Island' from Pelopos, the genitive of Pelops, son of the Lydian King Tantalus and grandson of Zeus in Greek mythology, and Nisos from *nêsos* 'island'. Pelops became a powerful king himself with extensive lands so

that the whole of southern Greece was called Pelops' Island. By the 14th century Morea was in use; it came from the Latin *morus* 'mulberry tree' which grew here in great abundance.

Pemba, MOZAMBIQUE, TANZANIA, ZAMBIA
1. Mozambique: named Porto Amélia in 1899 after Amélia (1865–1951), wife of Carlos I (1863–1908), King of Portugal (1889–1908). It was renamed in 1976 after Mt Pemba 'to take action', possibly a reference to some event or action that happened here.
2. Tanzania: an island whose Arabic name is *al-Jazīrat al-khaḍrāh* 'The Green Island' to indicate that it is greener and therefore more fertile than the nearby island of Zanzibar. The meaning of Pemba is unknown.

Pembroke, CANADA, TOBAGO, UK, USA
1. Canada (Ontario): founded in 1828 and named after the Honourable Sidney Herbert (1810–61), second son of the 11th Earl of Pembroke and later 1st Baron Herbert of Lea; he was secretary for war (1852–4, 1859–60).
2. UK (Wales): formerly Pennbro and Pembroch 'Land at the End' from the Welsh *pen* 'end' and *bro* 'land'. The Welsh name is Penfro.
3. USA (New Hampshire): named after Henry Herbert (1693–1751), 9th Earl of Pembroke, a Lord Justice while King George II[†] was out of the country in 1740, 1743, and 1748; he was related by marriage to the governor of New Hampshire, Benning Wentworth.

Penang (Pulau Pinang), MALAYSIA *Prince of Wales Island*
An island state, 'Island of the Betel Nut' because its shape resembles a betelnut, the fruit of the areca tree (in Malay, *pinang*), with *pulau* 'island'. Until 1867 it was named after the Prince of Wales, who later became King George IV[†], by Captain Francis Light of the English East India Company. He founded a colony on the island in 1786 on the day of the Prince's birthday; it was ceded to Great Britain in 1791. A strip of land on the mainland opposite, Province Wellesley (named after Baron Wellesley (1760–1842), governor-general of Bengal (1797–1805), but now called Seberang Prai), was added in 1800. Penang, Malacca, and Singapore joined to create the Straits Settlements colony in 1826. Penang joined the Federation of Malaya in 1948.

Pendleton, OREGON/USA
Founded in 1869 and named after George Pendleton (1825–89), a senator and lawyer.

Pend Oreille, IDAHO/USA
A lake and a river that also flows through Washington State. Both take their name from

the French *Pend d'Oreille* for the Kalispel people. They wore ear pendants (in French, *pendant d'oreille*) and thus were given the name 'Hanging Ear'.

Pennines, The, ENGLAND/UK
A range of hills with a name not noted before the 18th century; its origin is unknown. It may be derived from the Celtic *penn* 'hill' or simply have copied the name of the Italian mountain chain, the *Apennines.

Pennsylvania, USA
A state officially called the Commonwealth of Pennsylvania. The British seized control of the territory from the Dutch in 1664 and in 1681 King Charles II[†] granted it to William Penn (1644–1718), a Quaker leader. He established a Quaker colony the following year. The region was not named after him but after his dead father, Admiral Sir William Penn (1621–70), at the insistence of the king who had owed the admiral £16 000. The admiral had been irked by his son's admiration for the Quakers and his squabbles with the establishment, and so the king was glad to be able to pay off the debt to the family by granting land to the son in a far-away country. The younger Penn wanted to call the region New Wales, but when this was denied suggested Sylvania from the Latin *silva* 'forest' or 'woodlands'. This was accepted, but 'Penn' added to it. Thus the name means 'Penn's Woodlands'. One of the original thirteen colonies, Pennsylvania was the second state to join the Union in 1787.

Penobscot, MAINE/USA
A river, a bay, and a lake with a name derived from the Native American word *penobskeag* 'rocky place' or 'river of rocks'. Living in the region, a tribe took the name Penobscot.

Penrith, AUSTRALIA, UK
1. Australia (New South Wales): founded in 1815 as Evan and then renamed Castlereagh. In 1818 it was renamed again after the English town.
2. UK (England): could mean 'Hill Ford', 'Chief Ford', or 'End of the Ford' from the Welsh *pen* 'hill', 'chief', or 'end' and the Old Welsh *rit* 'ford'.

Pensacola, ANTARCTICA, USA
USA (Florida): founded by the Spanish in 1559 with a name said to be derived from a Native American word *pan-sha-okla* 'hair people'. It was captured by the Americans in 1818 and became part of the USA in 1821.

Pentland Firth, SCOTLAND/UK *Pettaland fjorthr*
'Strait at the north end of the Land of the Picts' from the Old Scandinavian *Pett* 'Pict', *land*, and *fjorthr* 'strait' or 'inlet'.

Penzance, CANADA, UK
UK (England): formerly Pensans 'Holy
Headland' from the Cornish *penn* 'hill' or
'head' and *sans* 'holy'.

Peoria, ILLINOIS/USA
Named after one of the five Native American
tribes in the Illinois Confederacy. Their name
means 'carriers' or 'packers'.

Peotone, ILLINOIS/USA
Derived from a Native American word *petone*
'bring here'.

Pepinster, BELGIUM
Named after the Pepin family, some of whom
became the mayors of the palace in Austrasia
(the eastern part of northern France, Belgium,
Luxembourg, and western Germany) during
the Merovingian dynasty (476–750).

Pepperell, MASSACHUSETTS/USA
Named after Sir William Pepperell (1696–
1759), a lieutenant-general in the British army
and acting governor of Massachusetts (1756–7).

Perak, MALAYSIA
A state whose name means 'Silver' because of
its deposits of silver and tin. It became an
independent state after the fall of Malacca to
the Portuguese in 1511. A coastal strip,
Dindings, became part of the Straits
Settlements in 1826 and remained so until it
returned to Perak in 1935. Perak became one
of the Federated Malay States in 1896.

Perast, MONTENEGRO/SERBIA AND MONTENEGRO
Named after the Illyrian tribe, the Pirusti.

Pereira, COLOMBIA *Cartago*
Founded in 1863 on the site of Cartago and
named after Francisco Pereira Gamba who
provided the land on which the city was built.

Perejil (Isla del Perejil), SPAIN
Lying some 200 yards (180m) off the Moroccan
coast, it is also called Leila by the Moroccans.
The name means 'Parsley Island' after the
parsley which grows on this very small island.
It was ceded to Spain in 1688, but not included
in the 1912 treaty with France which
established the boundaries of the Spanish
protectorate in Morocco; thus, its possession is
now disputed between Spain and Morocco. It
may also be one of the two Pillars of Hercules
on the 'African' side opposite Gibraltar,
although the generally accepted one is *Ceuta
some 3 miles (5 km) distant.

Perekop, UKRAINE
Derived from the Russian *perekopat'* 'to dig
across', a reference to the trench that was dug
across the Perekop isthmus that links the
Crimea to the rest of Ukraine.

Père Marquette, MICHIGAN/USA
A river 'Father Marquette' named after Jacques
Marquette (1637–75), a French Jesuit
missionary, who accompanied Louis Jollet, a
fur trader, on an exploration of the Mississippi
River as the expedition's chaplain.

Pereslavl'-Zalesskiy, YAROSLAVL'/RUSSIA
Kleshchin, Pereyaslavl'
Named in the 15th century after the Pereslavl'
near Kiev. This name is derived from two old
Russian words *pereyat* (now *perenyat'*) 'to
achieve' or 'to imitate' and *slava* 'glory'; thus
the '(Town) that achieved Glory'. The suffix
-Zalesskiy was added later to describe its
location far distant from Kiev from *za lessami*,
beyond the virtually impenetrable forests to
which the local Slavs had been driven by
hostile nomads, from *za* 'beyond' or 'on the
other side of' and *les* 'forest'. The *ya* in
Pereyaslavl' was deleted at the end of the 15th
century.

Pereyaslav-Khmel'nyts'kyy, UKRAINE
Pereyaslav-Russky, Pereyaslav
See Pereslavl'-Zalesskiy above. The suffix
-Khmel'nyts'kyy, which was added in 1943,
acknowledges the leadership of Bohdan
Khmel'nyts'kyy (*c.*1595–1657), Hetman of
Ukraine (1648–57), in the uprising against the
Poles and his success in transferring Ukraine to
Russian rule in 1654.

Pergamino, ARGENTINA
Some Spaniards are said to have lost some
pergaminos 'parchment documents' here in
1626 and the spot was given this name. Only
well over a century later, however, was the
place settled.

Périgueux, AQUITAINE/FRANCE *Vesuna*
Named after a Gaulish people, the Pterocorii
'Four Armies' from the Gaulish *petro* 'four' and
corio 'army'. The Romans named it after a local
spring, the Vésone.

Perm', RUSSIA *Bryukhanovo, Yegoshikha,
Peryamaa, Molotov*
A province and a city founded as the small
settlement of Brykhanovo in 1568 at the
confluence of the Yegoshikha and Kama
Rivers. In 1723 it took the name Yegoshikha
when a copper-smelting works was built here.
It was renamed in 1780 from the Finnish *perya*
'rear' and *maa* 'land', a reference to the fact
that this was remote and distant to the Veps
who had originally come from north-west
Russia. In 1940–57 it was renamed after
Vyacheslav Molotov†.

Pernik, BULGARIA *Perunik, Dimitrovo*
Possibly first named after Perun, the god of
thunder of the pagan Slavs. In 1949–62 the

town was named after Georgi Dimitrov (1882–1949), communist prime minister (1945–9).

Perpignan, LANGUEDOC-ROUSSILLON/FRANCE
Probably developed from the Roman Villa Perpiniarum from the Gaulish name Perpennio and founded *c*.900. It changed hands several times between Spain and France before becoming part of France in 1642. In 1276–1344 it was the capital of the Aragonese Kingdom of Majorca.

Perry, CANADA, USA
USA: twelve cities have this name, a substantial number in tribute to Captain Oliver Hazard Perry (1785–1819), an American naval officer who gained almost legendary status after defeating a British squadron at the Battle of Lake Erie in the 1812 war. Perrysburg in New York and Perryville in Missouri are also named after him.

Persepolis, IRAN *Parsa*
Ruins now called Takht-e Jamshīd 'Throne of Jamshīd', but capital of the Persian Empire from the reign of Darius I the Great, King of Persia (522–486 BC) until it was partially destroyed by Alexander III the Great† in 330 BC. The name means 'Persian Town' from the Greek *Persēs* 'Persian' and *polis*.

Persia *See* IRAN. It has given its name to the Persian Gulf, now often simply called the Gulf and by some the Arabian Gulf. The fruit, peach, gets its name from the French *pêche* which is derived from the Latin *persicum* (*malum*) 'Persian (apple)'.

Perth, AUSTRALIA, CANADA, UK, USA
1. Australia (Western Australia): founded in 1829 as the Swan River Settlement some 10 miles (16 km) from the mouth of the Swan River after the Dutch navigator Willem de Vlamingh had given the river that name in 1697 after the numerous flocks of black swans in the area. It was subsequently renamed after the Scottish county of Perthshire, the home and parliamentary constituency (1823–32) of General Sir George Murray (1772–1846), the British colonial secretary (1828–30).
2. Canada (Ontario): founded in 1816 by Scottish immigrants, it was named after the city in Scotland.
3. UK (Scotland): formerly Pert '(Place by a) Copse' from the Pictish *perta* 'copse' or 'thicket'. With the first church dedicated to St John the Baptist, the city was also known as St John's Town, or St Johnstoun, alongside Perth, until the 17th century. It was the Scottish capital until *c*.1452.

Perth Amboy, NEW JERSEY/USA *Amboy*
Founded in the late 17th century as Amboy, from an earlier Native American name Ompage which may have meant 'level ground'. 'Perth' was added later in tribute to an early owner, James Drummond (1648–1716), 4th Earl, and 1st Duke, of Perth who was instrumental in attracting impoverished Scots to the area.

Peru, AND USA
The Republic of Peru (República del Perú) since 1824, having declared its independence in 1821; it did not gain its freedom until the end of the war with Spain in 1824. Previously part of the immense Viceroyalty of Peru (1543–1824), the first Spanish explorers, led by Francisco Pizarro (*c*.1475–1541), having arrived in what is now Peru in 1527; by 1533 the main body of the Incas had been defeated, although sporadic resistance continued until 1572. In 1836–9, Peru was part of the Peru–Bolivia Confederation. The name comes from the River Birú or Perú, itself from the Guaraní *biru* or *piru* 'water' or 'river'.

Perugia, UMBRIA/ITALY *Perusia*
There is no certainty as to the origins of the Roman Perusia from which the present name comes. It has been suggested that it might be associated with the Latin *parra* 'bird of ill omen', in turn connected with the Italian *sparviero* 'hawk' or *passero* 'sparrow' to give the '(City of) the Hawk, or Sparrow'.

Pervomaysk, RUSSIA, UKRAINE
1. 'First of May' from the Russian *pervyy* 'first' and *may* 'May'.
2. Russia (Nizhniy Novgorod): originally named Tashino after the wife, Tasha (the shortened form of Natasha), of the owner of the iron works here. It was renamed in 1941 to commemorate May Day. There are several other towns with similar names, such as Pervomayskiy and Pervomayskoye in Russia.
3. Ukraine (Luhansk): originally called Petro-Mar'yevka 'Peter-Mary', although which Peter and Mary are not known. Renamed as above in 1920.
4. Ukraine (Mikolayiv): spelt Pervomay'sk. Founded as a fortified post and called Orel in 1744. It was renamed Ol'viopol' in 1773 when it became a town from the Greek *olbios* 'blessed' or 'rich' and *polis*. It was renamed in 1919 in honour of the international, originally communist (workers'), holiday.

Pervoural'sk, YEKATERINBURG/RUSSIA
Shaytanka
Founded in 1732 as an iron works with a name taken from the local river. In 1933 it was renamed 'First (in the) Urals' from *pervyy*

p

'first', a reference to the fact that these ironworks were the first to be built in the Ural Mountains.

Pesaro, MARCHE/ITALY *Pisaurum*
At the mouth of the River Foglia, the ancient name for which was the Isaurus or Pisaurus, the name means 'Close to the Isaurus (River)'.

Pescadores (Penghu Qundao), TAIWAN *Penghu Liedao*
An archipelago named by the Portuguese '(Islands of) Fishermen' from *pescador* 'fisherman' in the 16th century. The islands were ceded to Japan in 1895–1945 and became part of Taiwan in 1949. The Chinese name means 'Peng Lake Archipelago' with Peng possibly coming from *pēng* 'splash' or 'the roaring of colliding waves', *hú* 'lake', *liè* 'chain', and *dǎo* 'islands'; thus Liedao means 'archipelago' as does Qundao from *qún* 'group'.

Pescara, ABRUZZO/ITALY *Aternum, Piscaria*
Lying at the mouth of the Pescara River, the name comes from the Latin *piscis* (in Italian, *pesce*) 'fish' to mean '(Place full of) Fish'.

Peshāwar, NORTH-WEST FRONTIER/PAKISTAN *Paraşawara, Puruşapura, Begrām, Parshawar*
'Town on the Frontier' from *pēsh* and *āwar*, a name given to it by Akbar[†] from the previous Persian name Parshawar. Before that it had been called the 'Town of Puruşa'. It lies close to the border with Afghanistan.

Peshtigo, WISCONSIN/USA
A city named after the River Peshtigo, a Native American word for 'Wild Goose (River)'.

Petakh Tiqva, ISRAEL
Founded in 1878 as the first modern Jewish settlement in Palestine. It acquired the Hebrew sobriquet *Em ha-Moshavot* 'Mother of Villages'. Its name means 'Gleam, or Door, of Hope' from the Hebrew *petakh* 'door' and *tiqva* 'hope; the name comes from the Bible (Hosea 2: 15).

Petaluma, CALIFORNIA/USA
Founded in 1852 and takes its name from the rancho here. Its name comes from the Miwok *pe'ta* 'flat' and *lu'ma* 'back'.

Peterborough, AUSTRALIA, CANADA, UK, USA
1. Canada (Ontario): founded as Scott's Plain, a sawmill, in 1821 by, and named after, Adam Scott. However, four years later, with the influx of Irish immigrants, the place was renamed after their leader, Colonel Peter Robinson (1785–1838).
2. UK (England): originally Medeshamstede. After the destruction of the 7th-century monastery 'Mede's Homestead' from an Old English personal name and *hām-stede*, the settlement was redeveloped and simply called Burg 'Town'. The cathedral, whose construction was started in 1118, was dedicated to St Peter and his name was added to Burg to give the name of the town, Petreburgh. In due course this became Peterborough.
3. USA (New Hampshire): settled in 1749 and named after Admiral, and General, Charles Mordaunt (1658–1735), 3rd Earl of Peterborough, first lord of the British Treasury (1689–90), who was also an active diplomatist as well as military commander.

Peterhead, SCOTLAND/UK *Inverugie, Petyrheid*
Founded in 1593 as a fishing port called 'Mouth of the (River) Ugie' from *inbhir* and the river's name, it was later renamed 'St Peter's Headland' from the saint's name and the Old English *hēafod* 'headland'. The town was named after the headland and the headland was named after the church that stood on it.

Peter Pond, SASKATCHEWAN/CANADA
A lake named after the first white man to visit and map it in 1774–6.

Petersburg, VIRGINIA/USA *Peter's Point, Peter's Town*
The present city stands on the site of Fort Henry built in 1645. A Major Peter Jones assumed command of the fort in 1675 and the name of the town is thought to honour him.

Pétionville, HAITI
Named after Alexandre Sabès Pétion (1770–1818), who helped to liberate Haiti from France in 1806 and became president of southern Haiti from 1807 until his death.

Petra, JORDAN *Reqem, Sela*
Ruins. All the names mean 'Rock' or 'Stone', the current name being the Greek. The Arabic name is Baṭrā. It was the capital of the Nabataean Kingdom between the 4th century BC and AD 106 when it was annexed by the Romans. After the Crusades the ancient city appears to have been abandoned and forgotten until it was rediscovered in 1812.

Petrodvorets, LENINGRAD/RUSSIA *Pieterhof, Peterhof*
'Peter's Palace' from the genitive of Pëtr 'Peter' and *dvorets* 'palace'. Founded in 1710 as a royal estate by Emperor Peter I the Great[†] and developed into a summer palace to rival Versailles in France later, it was given the Dutch name Pieterhof; Peter had spent four months in Holland in 1697 as a ship's carpenter. A settlement grew up round the palace and in 1840 the German spelling was adopted. Despite anti-German feeling generated by the outbreak of the First World War in 1914 the name was not changed.

However, the German siege of nearby Leningrad (now St Petersburg) in 1941–4 was too much and a Russianized version of the original name was adopted in 1944.

Petropavlovsk (Petropavl), KAZAKHSTAN
Founded in 1752 as a military outpost to protect the Siberian frontier with a name taken from its church dedicated to St Peter, Pëtr, and St Paul, Pavel. This was amended slightly when it became a town. The town formerly called Petropavlovka has been renamed Qarghaly.

Petropavlovsk-Kamchatskiy,
KAMCHATKA/RUSSIA *Petropavlovskaya Gavan'*, *Petropavlovskiy Port*
Founded in 1740 as Petropavlovsk Harbour from *gavan'* 'harbour' and the two ships of Vitus Bering[†], the *St Peter* and the *St Paul*, which had called in here during the Danish explorer's second expedition to the region. The name was changed slightly in 1822 and again in 1924 with the addition of Kamchatskiy to prevent confusion with other towns of this name or similar to it. However, these are now all outside Russia and so Kamchatskiy has officially been dropped although it is still commonly included in the name.

Petrópolis, RIO DE JANEIRO/BRAZIL
Founded in 1845 by German settlers with the encouragement of Dom Pedro II (1825–91), Emperor of Brazil (1831–89), after whom it was named 'Peter's Town' from his name and *polis*.

Petrovsk, SARATOV/RUSSIA
Named after Peter I the Great[†].

Petrovsk-Zabaykal'skiy, CHITA/RUSSIA
Petrovskiy Zavod
Founded in 1789 as an iron works and called 'Peter's Factory' from *zavod* 'factory', probably after the owner. Zabaykal'skiy 'beyond (Lake) Baykal' from *za* and the name of the lake was added in 1926 to differentiate this Petrovsk from others.

Petrozavodsk, KARELIYA/RUSSIA *Petrovskiy Zavod, Petrozavodskaya Sloboda*
Founded in 1703 by Peter I the Great[†] when he began building St Petersburg. The name means 'Peter's Factory' from *zavod* 'factory' because as an ironworks it manufactured weapons. The name was changed to 'Peter's Factory Settlement' with the additional *sloboda* 'settlement' as the workers built up their community. The shortened form was adopted in 1777 when it achieved the status of a town.

Pfaffenhofen, FRANCE, GERMANY
Germany (Bavaria): 'Farms, or Manors, owned by the Clergy' or, less likely, 'occupied by the Clergy' from *Pfaffe* 'priest' and *Hof* 'farm' or 'manor'.

Pfarrkirchen, BAVARIA/GERMANY
'Parish Churches' from *Pfarr* 'parish' and *Kirche* 'church'.

Pforzheim, BADEN-WÜRTTEMBERG/GERMANY
Porta Hercyniae
The name probably goes back to that of the Roman settlement from the Latin *porta* 'city gate'. In German a gate house or guardroom was a *Pförtnerhaus*; *Heim* originally meant 'place' or 'residence'. Thus the meaning might have been an '(Enclosed) Place with a Gate'. Its location at the confluence of the Enz, Nagold, and Würm Rivers indicates that it was an important trading place.

Phattalung, THAILAND
'Town of the Hollow Hill', a reference to the caves in the nearby limestone hills.

Philadelphia, USA
1. Pennsylvania: laid out on the order of William Penn (1644–1718) by his cousin, William Markham in 1681. Penn, an English Quaker with a classical education and keen to associate the name with a principle of the Quakers, named it the '(City of) Brotherly Love' from the ancient Greek *philéo* 'I love' and *adelphos* 'brother'.
2. Both Alaşehir in Turkey and Amman in Jordan used to have this name.

Philippi, AUSTRALIA, GREECE, USA
1. Greece: the modern town is called Fílippoi in Greek. It was founded in 356 BC by, and named after, Philip II (382–336 BC), King of Macedonia (359–336 BC), who took the site from the Thracians to protect the gold mines.
2. USA (West Virginia): settled as Anglin's Ford in 1780. It became Booths Ferry and was then renamed again Philippi in 1844 after Philip P. Barbour, a member of the US Supreme Court (1836–41).

Philippines *Islas Filipinas*
The Republic of the Philippines (Republika ng Pilipinas) since 1946. Previously the Commonwealth of the Philippines (1935–46), partially under US control; during the Japanese occupation in 1942–5, however, it was called the independent Philippine Republic (1943–5), a Japanese puppet. The Filipino uprising against the Spanish began in 1896 and two years later the USA declared war on Spain and destroyed the Spanish fleet in Manila Bay. Filipino nationalists quickly declared their independence from Spain and proclaimed a republic, subsequently known as the Malolos Republic, after the name of the market town

where the new republic was inaugurated in January 1899. This was effectively ignored by the Americans. At the end of 1898 Spain ceded the Philippines to the USA and the previous Spanish name, Islas Filipinas, was Anglicized to 'Philippine Islands'. The Filipinos felt betrayed and hostilities between them and American troops broke out at the beginning of 1899; it was not until 1901 that the back of the resistance was broken and US colonial rule established. Discovered in 1521 by Ferdinand Magellan[†], the first Spanish settlement (on Cebu) was not made until 1565. The islands were then named after Philip II (1527–98), King of Spain (1556–98).

Philippolis, FREE STATE/SOUTH AFRICA
Founded in 1823 by, and named after, Dr John Philip (1775–1851) of the London Missionary Society, to give 'Philip's Town' with *polis*.

Philipstown, NORTHERN CAPE/SOUTH AFRICA
Settled in 1863 and named after Sir Philip Wodehouse (1811–87), governor of the Cape Colony and High Commissioner in South Africa (1861–70).

Phitsanulok, THAILAND
Sometimes known as Sawng Khwae 'Two Tributaries' since it lies along the Nan River near the junction with the River Khwae Noi. It was the Thai capital between 1463 and 1488.

Phnom Penh (Phnum Pénh), CAMBODIA
Caturmukha/Chatomuk
'Hill of Abundance' from *phnõm* 'hill' and *penh* 'abundant' or 'full'. However, according to legend, it is called 'Hill of Penh'. Penh, a rich old lady, found four wooden (or one bronze) statues of Buddha washed up on the bank of the Mekong River. She hauled them/it up onto the nearest hill and constructed a shrine. The original name meant 'City of Four Faces', a reference to the fact that it lies at the junction of the Mekong River and the Tonle Sap 'Great Lake'. Founded in 1434 to be the capital of the Khmer people in place of Angkor Thom, it has been the capital of Cambodia intermittently since 1444 and from 1866.

Phnom Udong, CAMBODIA
'Hill of the Victorious' from *phnõm* 'hill'. It was the capital between 1618 and 1866.

Phocaea, TURKEY
See FOÇA.

Phoenicia, MIDDLE EAST AND NEW YORK/USA
Canaan (Middle East)
Modern Lebanon and parts of Syria and Israel. According to Greek mythology, Phoenicia is said to take its name from Phoenix, son of Agenor and the nymph Telephassa. However,

it has also been suggested that it comes from the Greek *phoinix* 'palm tree', since they were abundant here, to mean 'Land of Palms', or from the Greek *phoiníkes* 'red people', an allusion to the reddish purple cloth that they exported. The Phoenicians, indistinguishable from the Canaanites, probably arrived in the region *c*.3000 BC.

Phoenix, ARIZONA/USA
Founded in 1867 on a site that showed signs of once having been occupied. Confident that a new city would arise on the spot, it was named Phoenix after the legendary bird which burnt itself to ashes and then rose from those ashes to live another life.

Phrygia, TURKEY
An ancient region of west central Anatolia named after the Phryges or Bryges who dominated it between the 12th and 7th centuries BC. The region was incorporated into the Kingdom of Lydia in the 6th century BC.

Phuket, THAILAND *Jonkcelaon (Junk Ceylon), Ko Thalang, Tongka, Jonsalam*
An island, Ko Phuket, and a city with a name derived from the Malay *bukit* 'hill'.

Piacenza, EMILIA-ROMAGNA/ITALY *Placentia*
As the Carthaginian general Hannibal (247–*c*.183 BC) advanced southwards, the Roman general Publius Cornelius Scipio (d. 211 BC) prepared to defend a newly founded colony a little way beyond the confluence of the Rivers Po and Trebbia. The armies met on the Trebbia in December 218 BC, Hannibal emerging as the victor. The survivors of Scipio's army wintered in the colony where they found the conditions 'pleasing'. The colony was thus named Placentia from which the present name is derived.

Piatra-Neamţ, ROMANIA *Piatra lui Crăciun, Camena*
'Fort of the Germans' from *piatra* 'stone' or 'rock' and *neamţ* 'German'. It was developed on the site of a fort built by the Teutonic Knights.

Picardy (Picardie), FRANCE
A region whose name is derived from the Old French *pic* (modern French, *pique*) 'pike', a weapon that was used to great effect by the men of this area.

Pickering, CANADA, UK
UK (England): formerly Picheringa. The meaning is not clear, but it may be '(Settlement of) the Family or Followers of a Man called Pīcer' from an Old English personal name and *-ingas*.

Pico, ITALY, PORTUGAL
Portugal (Azores): an island meaning 'Peak', a reference to the volcano on the island.

Picton, CANADA, CHILE, NEW ZEALAND
1. Canada (Ontario): founded as Hallowell in 1786 and subsequently renamed after Sir Thomas Picton (1758–1815), a British major general who commanded a division at the Battle of Waterloo in 1815 and was killed leading a charge.
2. New Zealand (South Island): founded as Newton on the site of a Maori village in 1848 and renamed in 1859 after Sir Thomas Picton.

Pictou, NOVA SCOTIA/CANADA
An island and a mainland coastal town settled in 1767 with a name probably derived from the Micmac word *piktook* 'bubbling water'. On the other side of the bay is Pictou Landing.

Piedmont, ITALY, USA
Italy: a region whose local name, Piemonte, is derived from the Old Italian *pie di monte* 'foot of the mountain', a reference to its position at the foot of the Alps. It was part of the Kingdom of Sardinia in 1720–1861 and was instrumental in uniting Italy in 1861 under Victor Emmanuel II (1820–78), King of Sardinia (1849–78) and King of Italy (1861–78).

Piedras Negras, COAHUILA/MEXICO *Ciudad Porfirio Díaz*
Founded in 1849 with its present Spanish name meaning 'Black Rocks'. In 1888 it was renamed the 'City of Porfirio Díaz' (1830–1915) after the long-serving Mexican president (1877–80, 1884–1911). Díaz resigned in 1911 and went into exile. Shortly afterwards the city readopted its original name.

Pierce, NEBRASKA/USA
Named after Franklin Pierce (1804–69), President of the United States (1853–7).

Pierre, SOUTH DAKOTA/USA *Mahto*
Founded in mid-1880 with a Sioux name meaning 'Bear', it was renamed six months later after Pierre Chouteau (1789–1865), a French fur trader.

Piešt'any, SLOVAKIA *Pescan, Peskjane, Bad Pistyan, Pöstyén*
Lying on the Váh River, the name is derived from *piesak* 'sand' to mean the '(Settlement on) the Sand'. The German and Hungarian names mirrored the Slovak name.

Pietermaritzburg, KWAZULU-NATAL/SOUTH AFRICA *uMgungundlovu, Pietermauritzburg*
The Zulu paramount chief Dingane built a new capital *c*.1828 which he called uMgungundlovu 'Secret Place of the Elephant'. The modern city was founded by Boer Voortrekkers 'Pioneers' in 1838 after victory over the Zulus at Blood (now Ncome) River. It originated as a small stone church, a thanksgiving for the victory. A town developed around the church and this was called Pietermauritzburg after the Boers' leader, Pieter Mauritz Retief (1780–1838), who was killed on Dingane's orders while accepting his hospitality. In time the *u* was dropped and, at the time of the city's centenary in 1938, it was decided also to honour Gerrit Maritz (1798–1838), the leader of the second Boer trek into Natal. It remained the Boer capital only until 1843, the British having annexed the Republic of Natal the previous year. The city is generally known as Maritzburg.

Pietrasanta, TUSCANY/ITALY
Named after Guiscardo Pietrasanta, the mayor of nearby Lucca, who was instrumental in rebuilding the village after it had been razed by fire in 1242.

Piet Retief, MPUMALANGA/SOUTH AFRICA
Founded in 1882 and named after Pieter Retief (1780–1838), a leader of the Great Trek in 1837 when a group of Boers, the Voortrekkers as they became known, left British rule in Cape Colony and moved north into the unknown. A group, led by Retief, broke away and crossed the Drakensberg Mountains into Natal. While negotiating a land grant in 1838, Retief and his party were slaughtered on the orders of the Zulu chief Dingane.

Pikes Peak, COLORADO/USA
Discovered in 1806 by, and named after, Lieutenant (later Brigadier General) Zebulon Pike (1779–1813), an Army officer who led various exploratory expeditions to the west and south-west.

Piketberg, WESTERN CAPE/SOUTH AFRICA
A military post or picket (in Dutch, *piket*) was established here in the mountains in the 1670s to warn of, and guard against, any Khoikhoin movement southwards towards Cape Town. The name at first referred to the mountain here, but was adopted for the town, lying at the foot of the mountains, when it was founded in 1835.

Piła, POLAND *Schneidemühl*
'Saw'. The former German name 'Saw-mill' from *schneiden* 'to cut' and *Mühle* 'mill' reflects its possession by Prussia between 1772 and 1945.

Pilcomayo, BOLIVIA-PARAGUAY
A river with a Guaraní name meaning 'River of the Birds'.

Pilsen (Plzeň), CZECH REPUBLIC
The original town was built some 6 miles (10 km) from the present town and it is now called Starý Plzenec 'Old Little Pilsen'. The site was inappropriate for development so Václav (Wenceslas) II (1271–1305), King of Bohemia (1278–1305), founded the present town in 1295 and called it Nová Plzeň 'New Pilsen'; 'New' was subsequently dropped. Plzeň is derived from the Old Slavonic *plz* 'damp' to give '(Settlement in a) Damp (Place)', a reference to the fact that it is located at the confluence of four rivers. It is famous for its Pilsner beer.

Pima, ARIZONA/USA
Named after a Native American tribe who called themselves the 'River People' and who lived, and still live, along the nearby Gila River.

Pinar del Río, CUBA *Nueva Filipina*
A province and a city founded in 1775 and called Nueva Filipina 'New Philippines' in 1800. It was subsequently renamed after the tall pine trees found on river banks in the province from the Spanish *pinar* 'pine grove', *del* 'of the', and *río* 'river'.

Pine Bluff, ARKANSAS/USA *Mount Marie*
Settled in 1819 on bluffs overlooking the Arkansas River and renamed in 1832 because of the presence of huge pine trees in the area. There is a city called Pine Bluffs in Wyoming.

Pinetown, KWAZULU-NATAL/SOUTH AFRICA
Laid out in 1847 and named two years later after Sir Benjamin Pine (1809–91), lieutenant-governor of Natal (1849–56) and governor (1873–5).

Pingxiang, CHINA *Pingxiangzhou*
Jiangxi: founded as a military post, the name comes from *ping* 'duckweed', a reference to the abundant duckweed, and *xiāng* 'countryside' or 'hometown'. At the time of its founding during the Song dynasties (960–1279), *xiāng* referred to a district of 12 500 families or not more than 50 000 inhabitants.

Pionerskiy, KALININGRAD/RUSSIA *Neukuhren*
Named after the Pioneers, the youth branch of the Komsomol.

Piotrków Trybunalski, POLAND
Named after the Polish Tribunal whose seat this became in 1578.

Piqua, OHIO/USA *Washington*
Named after one of the four divisions of the Shawnee whose name signifies 'Ashes'. On the site of the original village, the town of Washington was laid out in 1807, but its Shawnee name was readopted in 1816.

Piraeus (Piraiés), GREECE
Founded in the 5th century BC as a new port for the Athenian fleet, its name comes from *peran* 'beyond', a reference to the fact that a marshy area separated it from the mainland.

Pirmasens, RHINELAND-PALATINATE/GERMANY
Named after St Pirmin, abbot of Reichenau, who died in 753. He is thought to have spread the Gospel here in the 8th century.

Pisa, TUSCANY/ITALY *Pisae*
Derived from the Latin name whose origin is obscure. It has been suggested that it might signify 'estuary' or an 'irrigated place', both of which would be appropriate, given its location some 6 miles (10 km) from the mouth of the River Arno.

Pisco, PERU
A river and a city founded in 1640 by the Spanish with a Quechua name 'Bird'.

Písek, CZECH REPUBLIC, USA
Czech Republic: 'Sand', a reference to the gold-producing sand of the Otava River.

Pistoia, TUSCANY/ITALY *Pistoria*
Several theories have been put forward to explain the origin of this name. None is convincing, although the one most often mentioned is associated with the Latin *pistor* 'miller' or 'baker', allegedly because the fertility of the soil attracted a group of bakers.

Pitcairn Island, UK
An Overseas Territory of the UK consisting of the islands of Pitcairn (the only inhabited one), Ducie, Henderson, and Oeno. Pitcairn was discovered in 1767 and named after Midshipman Robert Pitcairn, who was the first sailor to see it from his crow's nest on HMS *Swallow* under the command of Captain (later Rear Admiral) Philip Carteret (d. 1796), one of the greatest explorers of his time. It was first settled by British mutineers from HMS *Bounty* in 1790.

Pitești, ROMANIA *Pirum*
Derives its name from an old Roman fortification called Pirum whose meaning is unknown. The suffix *ești* has the meaning of belonging to a community with the same ancestors.

Pitkyaranta, KARELIYA/RUSSIA
On the shores of Lake Ladoga, the name means 'Long Shore' from the Finnish *pitkä* 'long' and *ranta* 'shore' or 'beach'.

Pittsburgh, PENNSYLVANIA/USA *Fort Duquesne, Fort Pitt*
Built as a French fort in 1754 and named after Michel-Ange Duquesne (1702–78), governor of

New France. The British captured it, expelling
the French and renaming it after William Pitt
the Elder (1708–78), 1st Earl of Chatham and
prime minister in all but name (1756–61,
1766–8). The city was laid out in 1764 around
the fort with the new name of Pittsburgh.

Pittsfield, MASSACHUSETTS/USA *Pontoosuc
Plantation*
Settled in the 1740s and when it became a
town in 1761 it was renamed after William Pitt
the Elder (*see* PITTSBURGH).

Pittston, PENNSYLVANIA/USA
Settled in 1762 and named after William Pitt
the Elder (*see* PITTSBURGH).

Placentia, CANADA, USA
Canada (Newfoundland): originally *Plasencia,
probably after the place with that name in
Spain given by Basque fishermen who arrived
here in the 16th century. In 1662 the French
altered the spelling to Plaisance, but this was
changed to Placentia by the British when they
took control in 1713.

Placerville, USA
California: founded in 1849 during the Gold
Rush and called Hangtown because of the
regular public hangings. It was later decided to
dispense with this rather forbidding name and
replace it with Placerville 'Pleasure Town'
from the Spanish *placer* 'pleasure' or
'enjoyment'.

Plainfield, NEW JERSEY/USA *Milltown*
So named because it was built on a scenic
plain.

Plainview, TEXAS/USA
So named in 1887 because the all-round view
to the horizon was not interrupted.

Plaistow, UK, USA
UK (England): formerly La Pleyestowe 'Play
Ground' or 'Pitch for Playing' from the Old
English *pleg-stōw* from *plega* 'play' or 'sport' and
stōw.

Plasencia, EXTRAMADURA/SPAIN *Ambroz*
A Moorish town, it was recaptured and
renamed in the 12th century by Alfonso VIII
(1155–1214), King of Castile (1158–1214), *ut
Deo placeat et hominibus* 'That it may please God
and Man'.

Plast, CHELYABINSK/RUSSIA
'Layer' or 'Stratum', a reference to the fact that
the town was founded in a goldfield where the
gold was found to be in layers.

Plate, River (Río de la Plata), ARGENTINA-
URUGUAY *Mar Dolce, Río de Solís*
The estuary of the Paraná and Uruguay Rivers
discovered in 1516 by Juan Díaz de Solís, a

Spanish navigator, who called it Mar Dolce
'Sweet Sea' before it was briefly named after
him following his murder by a local tribe. In
1526 Sebastian Cabot (*c*.1476–1557), an
explorer and navigator, sailing on behalf of
Spain on this occasion, diverted a voyage to the
Orient, having heard reports of great wealth in
the Río de la Plata area. He explored the
estuary and the contributory rivers. When he
saw the Guaraní wearing silver ornaments he
believed the reports to be true and named the
estuary the 'River of Silver' from the Spanish
plata in the hope that it might become just
that; unfortunately, the reports were not true,
the silver having been imported. *See*
ARGENTINA AND LA PLATA.

Platte, USA
Rivers in Nebraska and Missouri. The bigger
Platte flows through Nebraska and into the
Missouri River. It is formed by the junction of
the North Platte rising in Wyoming and the
South Platte rising in Colorado. It is very
shallow, hence its name from the French *plat*
'shallow'. The name comes from a French
translation of the Omaha *fit* 'river' and *thbaska*
'flat', thus 'shallow river'. Near the junction is
a city called North Platte.

Plattsburgh, NEW YORK/USA
Founded in 1784 by, and named after, Judge
Zephaniah Platt.

Plattsmouth, NEBRASKA/USA
A city founded in 1854 at the place where the
River Platte flows into the Missouri River.

Plettenberg Bay (Plettenbergbaai),
WESTERN CAPE/SOUTH AFRICA
A town named after Joachim van Plettenberg
(1739–93), governor of the Cape (1774–85).
Following their rescue some shipwrecked
Portuguese sailors called the bay Bahia
Formosa 'Beautiful Bay'.

Pleven, BULGARIA *Storgosia, Plewna, Kajluka*
Originally with a Thracian name, it was then
given a Slav name before adopting its present
one in 1270. The Pleva River, on which it lies, is
the source of the name. This comes from a
Slavonic root word for 'to swim' or 'to float'.

Ploieşti, ROMANIA
According to legend, named after Father
Ploaie, its founder, who had fled from
Transylvania. His name means 'rain'.

Plovdiv, BULGARIA *Pulpudeva, Puldin,
Philippopolis, Trimontium, Filibé/Philibe*
An ancient Thracian site, rebuilt and renamed
in 341 BC 'Philip's City' from *Pulp* 'Philip' and
deva 'city' after Philip II (382–336 BC), King of
Macedonia (359–336 BC). The Bulgarian version

of the name was Puldin, while the Greeks called it Philippopolis. Taken by the Romans in 46, it was renamed by them Trimontium 'Three Hills', a name it retained until 1364. The city fell to the Ottoman Turks that year and was renamed by them Filibé. After the Turks had been removed, the present name, a modern version of the original one, was adopted in 1919.

Plymouth, MONTSERRAT, TOBAGO, UK, USA
1. UK (England): formerly Sudtone, Sutton, and Plymmue '(Place at the) Mouth of the (River) Plym' from *mūtha* 'mouth' and the river name which is itself a back-formation from Plympton 'Farmstead of the Plum Tree' from the Old English *plȳme* and *tūn*. The first two names meant 'Southern Farm'. The Plymouth Brethren, a Christian group founded *c*.1828, take their name from the city where their first centre was established.
2. USA (Massachusetts): founded in 1620 as the first permanent European settlement in North America, the Colony of New Plymouth, and named after the port from which the settlers had sailed, Plymouth in England. At least seventeen states have cities with this name, many after the Massachusetts town.

Plzeň, CZECH REPUBLIC
See PILSEN.

Po, ITALY *Padus*
Italy's most important river has a name that is of uncertain origin. The Ligurian name was Bodincus from a possible Indo-European root *bhedh* from which comes the Latin *fundus* 'bottom'; the overall meaning therefore was 'bottomless'. Padus was probably a Celtic name meaning 'pines', a reference to the forests surrounding the delta.

Pobeda, BULGARIA
'Victory'.

Pobeda Peak (Russian: **Pobedy Pik**), CHINA-KYRGYZSTAN
'Victory Peak'. This was first climbed by Russians in 1938 and named by them 'Komsomol 20th Anniversary Peak'. It was renamed in 1943, possibly as a result of the great victory over the Germans at Stalingrad (now Volgograd) in February 1943.

Pocahontas, CANADA, USA
Named after the Powhatan princess, Pocahontas (*c*.1595–1617). This was a nickname for her and said to mean 'Playful One'. According to Captain John Smith's, probably fictitious, account, Pocahontas, aged 11, persuaded her father not to kill Smith after his capture in 1607. Subsequently, and certainly, she was of great help to English

colonists and married one, becoming Mrs John Rolfe and being received at the court of King James I[†] in London in 1616. *See* MATOACA

Pocatello, IDAHO/USA
Settled in 1882 and named after a Bannock chief who allowed the use of his land for the railroad construction here.

Poděbrady, CZECH REPUBLIC
'(Settlement) below the Fords' from *pode* 'below' meaning 'downstream' and *brady* (modern Czech, *brody*), the plural of *brod* 'ford'.

Podgorica, MONTENEGRO/SERBIA AND MONTENEGRO *Alata, Ribnica, Titograd*
A Roman staging post at the confluence of the Ribnica and Morača Rivers known as Alata, it had been renamed after the Ribnica River by the 11th century. Certainly from 1326 it was known as Podgorica 'Under the Mountain' from *pod* 'under' and *gora*, although this name was interchangeable with Ribnica until use of the latter declined in the 15th century. Between 1474 and 1879 it was held by the Ottoman Turks. In 1946 it became the Montenegrin capital and was renamed 'Tito's Town' after Marshal Josip Broz Tito[†]. Podgorica was readopted in 1992.

Podlasie, POLAND
An area in eastern Mazovia meaning '(Land) near the Forest' from *pod* 'by' or 'near' and *las* 'forest'.

Podoliya, UKRAINE
A region between the Dniester and Southern Bug Rivers that takes its name from the Russian *podol* 'lower part' from *po* 'along' and *dol* 'dale' or 'low-lying land', related to the modern Russian *dolina* 'valley'. Under foreign rule, particularly Polish, for centuries, it became part of the Soviet Union at the end of the Second World War and of Ukraine when it achieved independence in 1991.

Podol'sk, MOSCOW/RUSSIA *Podol'*
A town with a name meaning 'Lower Land' (see previous entry).

Podravska, SLOVENIA
A statistical region with a name meaning 'By the (River) Drava' which flows through it.

Pofadder, NORTHERN CAPE/SOUTH AFRICA
Theronsville
Originally a mission station established in 1875 and named after the Korana chief, Klaas Pofadder, the Afrikaans for 'puff adder', a slow-moving and venomous snake. By 1889 the residents, increasing in number, had come to dislike the name and it was changed to 'Theron's Town', T. P. Theron being a local

politician. The original name was readopted in 1936.

Poggibonsi, TUSCANY/ITALY *Poggio Bonizzi*
'Bonizo's Hill-top' from *poggio* 'hill', 'hill-top', or 'hillock' and the German personal name.

Pogradec, ALBANIA *Encheleana*
'At the Foot of the Castle' from the Slavonic *pod* 'at the foot of' or 'under' and *grad*, a reference to the ruins of an Illyrian castle on a nearby hill.

Pogranichnyy, PRIMORSKIY TERRITORY/RUSSIA *Grodekovo*
Close to the Chinese border, the name was changed in 1958 to the adjective for 'frontier' or 'boundary', thus 'Frontier (Town)'.

Pohnpei, MICRONESIA *Ponape*
An island in the eastern Caroline Islands and a state (with some coral atolls) in Micronesia. Derived from *poh* 'on', *n* 'of', and *pei* 'rock', the name can be said to mean 'Rocky (Island)'.

Pointe a la Hache, LOUISIANA/USA
'Hatchet Point' in French.

Poitiers, POITOU-CHARENTES/FRANCE *Limonum*
The previous Roman name came from the Gaulish *lemo* 'elm'. The town is now named after the Pictones or Pictavi, a Gallic tribe.

Poitou, FRANCE
A former province and historic region named after the Pictones or Pictavi, a Gallic tribe. It is now part of the region of Poitou-Charentes.

Pojoaque, NEW MEXICO/USA
'Drink-water Place' in Tewa.

Poland (Polska), AND KIRITMATI, USA
The Republic of Poland (Rzeczpospolita Polska) since 1989. Previously the People's Republic of Poland (1947–89); Second Polish Republic (1918–39, although it is argued that the presence of a Polish government-in-exile in the UK in 1940–5 continued its existence); Congress Kingdom of Poland (known as Congress Poland or Russian Poland) (1815–64) within the Russian Empire; the Russian sector of Poland was thereafter called the Western Region of the Russian Empire; Kingdom of Poland (1024–1795), although from 1596 it was called a Royal Republic. Poland was first partitioned in 1772 by Austria, Prussia, and Russia and again by Prussia and Russia in 1793; in 1795 Poland was erased from the map at the third partition when the three countries divided what remained between them. Poland did not exist as an independent state for the next 123 years, until the Second Polish Republic was created in 1918; the Poles, nevertheless, retained their strong feelings of national identity. In 1939 Poland was partitioned for the fourth time between Nazi Germany and the Soviet Union, although the status quo only lasted until June 1941 when the Germans unexpectedly attacked the Soviet Union and pushed the Russians out of eastern Poland. The Poland that reappeared in 1945 was smaller and had been shifted some 200 miles (320 km) to the west. The country is named after the Polanie 'People of the Fields, or Plain' from *pole* 'field', who settled on the banks of the Warta River in the open plain between the Oder and Vistula Rivers. Their tribal chief and progenitor of a line of princes, the legendary Piast, in *c*.870 united the scattered groups into one unit which he called Polska. The Poles used to call themselves Polaks and Polish immigrants to the USA are sometimes called Polacks. *See* LITHUANIA.

Pol-e Khomri, AFGHANISTAN
Possibly 'Brick Bridge' from *pol* 'bridge' and *khomreh* 'earthenware jug'.

Polessk, KALININGRAD/RUSSIA *Labiau*
Renamed 'Woodland' in 1946 after the Soviet Union had annexed East Prussia. The name shows that it was in a wooded area from *poles'ye* 'woodland', itself from *po* 'along' and *les* 'wood'.

Polesskoye, UKRAINE *Kabany, Kaganovich*
See POLESSK. In 1934–57 it was named after Lazar Kaganovich (1893–1991), a Bolshevik leader and devoted henchman of Stalin[†], who supervised the policy of collectivization during the 1930s and who was born here. The change of name was inevitable after an 'anti-Party' group, of which Kaganovich was a member, had tried and failed to remove Nikita Khrushchev from the position of Soviet leader in 1957.

Pólis, CYPRUS *Mario, Arsinoe*
'City' in Greek. The previous name honoured Arsinoë II, the sister of Ptolemy II Philadelphus[†].

Polish Corridor, POLAND
A comparatively narrow corridor of land, settled by Germans at the partitions of Poland although historically Polish, granted to Poland in 1919. It separated East Prussia from the rest of Germany and extended to the Baltic coast to ensure that Poland had an outlet to the sea. It was annexed by Germany in 1939, but returned to Poland, with additional territory so that it was no longer a 'corridor', at the end of the Second World War.

Polokwane, LIMPOPO/SOUTH AFRICA *Pietersburg*
Founded in 1886 and named after General Pieter Joubert (1834–1900), the commander of

Boer forces in the First Boer War (1880–1). In 2002, to get away from the colonial past, the city was renamed Polokwane 'Place of Safety' or 'Place where People care for each other'; alternative sources suggest 'Little Storage Space'.

Polotsk, BELARUS
May take its name from the Polota River from the Russian *boloto* 'marsh' since it lies at the confluence of this river and the Western Dvina; or it may come from the Polochane tribe.

Poltava, UKRAINE *Oltava/Ltava*
A province and a city which take their name from the former name, Ltava, of the Vorskla River along which the city lies. The name therefore means 'Along the Ltava' from the Russian *po* 'along'.

Polunochnoye, YEKATERINBURG/RUSSIA
Named after the Polunochnaya River when the town was founded in 1942. The river's name means 'midnight' from *polnoch*, itself from *pol* 'half' and *noch* 'night'.

Polyana, RUSSIA, UKRAINE
1. 'Glade' or 'Clearing'.
2. Russia (Sverdlovsk): the previous Russian name was Avtomat 'Automatic', possibly a reference to a machine of some kind or to a weapon.

Polyarnyy, RUSSIA
The towns in the Chukot Autonomous District and Murmansk Province both mean 'Polar', a reference to the fact that they are inside the Arctic Circle.

Polynesia 'Many Islands' from the Greek *polus* 'many' and *nēsos* 'island' (plural, *poly* and *nēsoi*). It is the largest of the Pacific Ocean's cultural regions with the distances between the island groups being greater than those of Melanesia and Micronesia. French Polynesia and the Hawaiian Islands, among others, are part of Polynesia.

Pombal, BRAZIL, PORTUGAL
Portugal: named after the *pombos* 'pigeons' that flew around the castle.

Pomerania (German: **Pommern**; Polish: **Pomorze**), GERMANY-POLAND
A historic region lying along the Baltic coast with a name meaning '(Land) by the Sea' or 'Coastland' from the Slavonic *po* 'along' and *morze* 'sea'. Sweden received Western Pomerania at the Peace of Westphalia in 1648. Eastern Pomerania was annexed by Prussia in 1772 and became known as West Prussia; by 1815 Prussia had western and central Pomerania which then went by the name

of Pommern. West Prussia and Central Pomerania were transferred to Poland in 1945 while Western Pomerania became part of the German Democratic Republic (now eastern Germany). The region has given its name to a breed of very small dog.

Pomeroy, SOUTH AFRICA, UK, USA
1. South Africa (KwaZulu-Natal): named after Major General Sir George Pomeroy Colley (1835–81), governor of Natal (1880–1), who was killed fighting the Boers at the Battle of Majuba.
2. UK (Northern Ireland): possibly 'Apple Orchard' from the French *pommeraie*.
3. USA (Ohio): named after its original owner, Samuel W. Pomeroy.

Pomfret, CONNECTICUT/USA
Named after *Pontefract in England which in past times was pronounced 'Pomfret'.

Pomme de Terre, MISSOURI/USA
A lake and a river with the French name of 'Potato'.

Pomona, BELIZE, USA
USA (California): a fruit and vegetable canning centre, it is named after Pomona, the Roman goddess of fruit from the Latin *pomum* 'fruit'.

Pomorie, BULGARIA *Anchialus/Ankhialo*
A town on the Black Sea, it was renamed in 1934 'By the Sea' from *po* 'by' or 'along' and *more* 'sea'. The previous name was derived from the Thracian *akhelo* 'water'.

Pompano Beach, FLORIDA/USA
Settled by local fishermen *c*.1900, it was named for the pompano, a type of fish found in shallow, warm waters; here, off the coast of Florida, the *Trachinotus carolinus*.

Pompeii, CAMPANIA/ITALY
Originally an Etruscan town, it fell to the Samnites in the 5th century BC and then to the Romans. It was destroyed by an eruption of Mt Vesuvius in 79. The name probably comes from the Oscan *pompe* 'five', itself from the Indo-European *penke*, a reference to the fact that it was formed from five settlements.

Pomurska, SLOVENIA *Primorska*
A statistical region meaning 'Littoral', although Slovenia's coastline is only 29 miles (47 km) long. The previous Serbo-Croat name has now been given the equivalent Slovenian spelling.

Ponca City, OKLAHOMA/USA
Named in 1893 after the Ponca tribe.

Ponce, PUERTO RICO *Nuestra Señora de Guadelupe de Ponce*
Founded in either 1670 or 1680 and named after Juan Ponce de León (1460–1521), a

Spanish explorer who established the first settlement on Puerto Rico and served briefly as its governor (1509).

Pondicherry, INDIA *Putuccĕri, Pondichéry*
A Union Territory formed in 1962 from four former French colonies and a city which was founded by the French East India Company as a trading centre in 1674 on the site of an ancient settlement. It was the chief French settlement in India between 1674 and 1954. The name means 'New Town' from the Tamil *putu* 'new' and *cĕri* 'town' or 'village'.

Ponta Delgada, AZORES/PORTUGAL
'Fine Point', a reference to the narrow headland here.

Pontchartrain, LOUISIANA/USA
A lake discovered by Pierre Le Moyne in 1699 and named by him after Louis, Comte de Pontchartrain (1643–1727), who was an early explorer of the Mississippi valley.

Ponte do Lima, PORTUGAL
'Bridge on the (River) Lima'. Roman soldiers identified this river with the River Lethe, the 'River of Oblivion' in Greek mythology, fearing that they would never return home if they crossed it.

Pontefract, ENGLAND/UK *Pontefracto, Pontfreit*
'Broken Bridge' from the Latin *pons* 'bridge' and *fractus* 'broken'. It is unusual for a name to be derived directly from the Latin. The local Anglo-Norman pronunciation, however, was Pomfret or Pumfrit. The town gives its name to liquorice Pomfret cakes.

Pontevedra, ARGENTINA, PHILIPPINES, SPAIN
Spain (Galicia): a province and a city on the Lérez River with the original name Pons Vetus 'Old Bridge' from the Latin *pons* 'bridge' and *vetus* 'long-standing', a reference to the Roman bridge which forms the basis of the modern bridge.

Pontiac, USA
1. Illinois: settled c.1830 and named after the Ottawa chief Pontiac (c.1720–69) who led a group of tribes in a campaign against the British known as Pontiac's War (1763–4).
2. Michigan: also named after the Ottawa chief.

Pontianak, BORNEO/INDONESIA
Founded in 1770 by an Arab trader who feared the *pontianak* 'spirits' in the area. According to legend, hunters became frightened of the noises they heard in the jungle at night which they likened to the screams of the ghost of a woman dying in childbirth—which is what the name translates as.

Pontivy, BRITTANY/FRANCE *Napoléonville*
Takes its name from *pont* 'bridge' and the name of a 7th-century Northumbrian saint called Iwi, or Ywi, who wished to follow the ideal of 'exile for Christ'. Without knowing their destination, he joined some sailors and ended up in Brittany where he became a hermit. Napoleon[†] built a new town just to the south and in 1805–14 the two towns were jointly named after him; and between 1852 and 1871 after his nephew Napoleon III (1808–73), Emperor of the French (1852–70).

Pontoise, PARIS/FRANCE
'Bridge on the (River) Oise' from *pont* 'bridge'.

Pontypool, CANADA, UK
UK (Wales): formerly Pont y poole 'Bridge by the Pool' from the Welsh *pont* 'bridge', *y* 'the', and English *pool*.

Pontypridd, WALES /UK *Pont y Tŷ Pridd*
'Bridge by the Earthen House' from the Welsh *pont* 'bridge', *y* 'the', *tŷ* 'house', and *pridd* 'earth'. The *Tŷ* was eliminated later because, following the *t* of *pont* and *y*, it was considered unnecessary.

Popa, Mount, BURMA
An extinct volcano with the name 'Flower' in Sanskrit.

Poperinge, BELGIUM *Pupurninga Villa, Pupurningahem*
The present name is a shortening of the previous one, first mentioned in 877, which meant 'Pupurn's Settlement' from *gem* or *hem* 'settlement' which was established in the 5th century. Pupurn is thought to be an ancient Celtic name. It is believed to have given its name to poplin.

Popocatépetl, MÉXICO-PUEBLA/MEXICO
A volcano with a name meaning 'Smoking Mountain' from the Nahuatl *popokani* 'to smoke' and *tepetl* 'mountain'.

Pordenone, FRIULI-VENEZIA GIULIA/ITALY *Portus Naonis*
A province and a river-port derived from the Latin *portus* 'harbour' or 'port' and the ancient name of the river that flows through the city, the Naone.

Porirua, NORTH ISLAND/NEW ZEALAND
'Two Tribes' from the Maori *pori* 'tribe' or 'people' and *rua* 'two'.

Poronaysk, SAKHALIN ISLAND/RUSSIA *Shikuta*
In 1946 the former Japanese name gave way to the present one which comes from the Poronay River, at the mouth of which the city lies. The river's name means 'Big River' from the Ainu *poro* 'big' and *nay* 'river'.

Póros, GREECE
A town and an island separated from the mainland by a 500 yard (450m) strait, hence its name 'The Ford'.

Portadown (Port an Dúnáin), NORTHERN IRELAND/UK
'Landing Place of the Little Fort' from *port* 'landing place', *an* 'the', and the diminutive of *dún*.

Portage, CANADA, USA
USA: seven states have cities, four have lakes, and Ohio a river, with this name. It is a French word meaning 'porterage', often a reference to the carriage of boats between one river and another.

Portage la Prairie, MANITOBA/CANADA
French fur traders coined this name to describe the carriage of their goods across the prairie between the Assiniboine River and Lake Manitoba.

Portalegre, PORTUGAL *Amoea/Ammaia*
Lying on the slopes of the Serra de São Mamede near the Spanish border, the name means 'Happy Gate' from *alegre* 'happy' or 'joyful'.

Portales, NEW MEXICO/USA
Founded in 1898 and named after the Portales Springs, themselves so named because they emerge from cave entrances which resemble an arcade (in Spanish, *portales*).

Port Alfred, EASTERN CAPE/SOUTH AFRICA *Port Frances*
Founded in 1825 and named after the wife of Colonel Henry Somerset, son of Lord Charles Somerset, governor of Cape Colony (1814–26). The name was changed as a result of the visit in 1860 by Prince Albert (1844–1900), Queen Victoria's[†] second son.

Port Arthur, AUSTRALIA, CHINA, USA
1. Australia (Tasmania): settled in 1830 by, and named after, Colonel (later lieutenant general Sir) George Arthur (1784–1854), lieutenant-governor of Tasmania (1824–37).
2. China: *see* LÜSHUN.
3. USA (Texas): named after Arthur E. Stilwell, who in 1895 developed the town into a port and railway terminus.

Port Augusta, SOUTH AUSTRALIA/AUSTRALIA *Kurdnatta*
Founded in 1852 and given the additional name of Port Augusta after the wife of Sir Henry Fox Young (1808–70), governor of South Australia (1848–54) and of Tasmania (1855–61). Its Aboriginal name means ''Place of Drifting Sand'.

Port-au-Prince, HAITI *L'Hôpital*
Founded by the French in 1749 as 'The Hospital' and later renamed after the bay 'Le Port de Prince', the 'Prince' possibly being the name of a French ship which had sought shelter in the bay. Capital of the French colony of Saint-Domingue between 1770 and 1804, it became the capital of independent Haiti in 1804.

Port Beaufort, WESTERN CAPE/SOUTH AFRICA
Founded in 1816 and named by Lord Charles Somerset, governor of Cape Colony (1814–26), after his father, Henry Somerset, 5th Duke of Beaufort.

Port Bell, UGANDA
Founded in 1908 and named after Sir Hesketh Bell (1864–1952), the first governor of Uganda (1907–10).

Port Blair, SOUTH ANDAMAN ISLAND/INDIA
Named after a naval lieutenant called Blair, who surveyed the Andaman and Nicobar Islands in 1789.

Port Bouët, CÔTE D'IVOIRE *Petit-Bassam*
Named in 1904 after the French admiral and explorer, Count Louis Bouët-Willaumez (1808–71), governor of Senegal (1843).

Port Chester, NEW YORK/USA *Saw Pits*
Founded in the 1660s with a name that alluded to its timber industry. In 1837 it was renamed, possibly after the city of Chester or the county of Cheshire in England. On the coast, 'Port' was added to distinguish it from other cities simply called Chester, of which there is one in New York State and others in nearby states.

Port Colborne, ONTARIO/CANADA *Gravelly Bay*
Settled in 1832 and renamed in tribute to Sir John Colborne (1778–1863), lieutenant-governor of Upper Canada (1828–38) and governor (1838–9), and later 1st Baron Seaton; he was appointed field marshal on retirement in 1860.

Port Elizabeth (Xhosa: **Bhayi**), EASTERN CAPE/SOUTH AFRICA *Fort Frederick*
The original fort was built in 1799 and named after Frederick Augustus (1763–1827), Duke of York and second son of King George III[†]. In 1820 it was renamed by Sir Rufane Donkin, acting governor of Cape Colony, after his wife, aged 28, who had succumbed to a fever in India two years earlier. The metropolitan area is named, locally, after Nelson Mandela (1918–), President of South Africa (1994–9).

Port Fairy, VICTORIA/AUSTRALIA *Belfast*
Settled in 1835 and subsequently renamed after a ship, the *Fairy*, that had sought shelter in the harbour in 1810.

Port Fouad (Būr Fu'ād), EGYPT
Founded in 1925 opposite Port Said at the entrance to the Suez Canal, it is named after Fu'ād I (1868–1936), Sultan of Egypt (1917–22) and first Khedive 'King' (1922–36) when Egypt achieved independence from the UK. He was the son of Ismā'īl Pasha (1830–95), Viceroy of Egypt under Ottoman suzerainty (1863–79), who was a strong supporter of the construction of the canal which took place between 1859 and 1869.

Port-Gentil, GABON
Developed from a commercial settlement and named after the French colonial administrator, Émile Gentil (1866–1914), governor of the French Congo (1904–8).

Port Harcourt, RIVERS/NIGERIA
Founded in 1912 and named after Lewis Harcourt (1863–1922), 1st Viscount Harcourt, British secretary of state for the colonies (1910–15).

Port Hawkesbury, NOVA SCOTIA/CANADA *Ship Harbour*
Renamed in 1860 after Charles Jenkinson (1727–1808), 1st Earl of Liverpool and Baron Hawkesbury, British secretary at war (1778–86).

Port Hedland, WESTERN AUSTRALIA/AUSTRALIA
Founded in 1863 and named after Captain Peter Hedland, the first European to visit the place in 1857.

Port Hood, NOVA SCOTIA/CANADA
Named after Admiral Samuel Hood (1724–1816), 1st Viscount Hood, a British naval commander on the North American station and commander-in-chief of the Mediterranean Fleet (1793–4). Port Hood Island lies just off the coast.

Port Hope, CANADA, USA
Canada (Ontario): established as a trading post in 1778 and named Smith's Creek after its owner. Having been renamed Toronto, it was then renamed again in 1817 after Colonel Henry Hope, lieutenant-governor of Quebec (1785–9).

Port Hueneme, CALIFORNIA/USA
Founded in 1874 with a Chumash name meaning 'Resting Place' from *wene me* because it was halfway between two villages.

Portici, CAMPANIA/ITALY
Possibly refers to a portico or ancient colonnade; traditionally, however, it refers to a portico in the forum of the destroyed Herculaneum.

Port Il'ič, AZERBAIJAN
A port on the Caspian Sea named after Vladimir Ilich Lenin[†].

Portland, AUSTRALIA, CANADA, UK, USA
1. Australia (Victoria): takes its name from Portland Bay, itself named after William Bentinck (1738–1809), 3rd Duke of Portland, British prime minister (1783, 1807–9). It was also given the French name of Tourville.
2. UK (England): formerly Port, Portlande, and Porland 'Estate by the Harbour' from the Old English *port* and *land*.
3. USA (Maine): settled in 1632, it was first called Machigonne and then in fairly quick succession Indigreat, Elbow, The Neck, Casco, and Falmouth after the English port because it was said that their harbours looked similar. Destroyed by the British in 1775, it was rebuilt in 1786 and named after the Isle of Portland in England.
4. USA (Oregon): settled in 1829 and named after the Portland in Maine after two settlers, one from Portland, Maine, and the other from Boston, Massachusetts, tossed a coin to choose the name.

Port Laoise, IRELAND
'Fort of the Descendants of Laois'.

Port Lincoln, SOUTH AUSTRALIA/AUSTRALIA
Developed around a good natural harbour after it had been visited in 1802 and named by Matthew Flinders[†] after his home county in England.

Port Louis, MAURITIUS
Founded *c*.1736 by the French as a revictualling halt for their ships travelling round the Cape of Good Hope. They named it after Louis XV (1710–74), King of France (1715–74).

Port Macquarie, NEW SOUTH WALES/AUSTRALIA
Named after Lachlan Macquarie (1761–1824), Scottish-born governor of New South Wales (1809–21), and known as the 'Father of Australia'.

Port Moresby, PAPUA NEW GUINEA
The bay was explored in 1873 by Captain (later Admiral) John Moresby (1830–1922), a British naval commander and explorer who named the natural harbour after his father, Admiral Sir Fairfax Moresby (1786–1877). It was annexed by the UK in 1883 and became the capital of the Australian-administered UN Trust Territory of New Guinea in 1945. It became the capital of Papua New Guinea on independence in 1975.

Port Nolloth, NORTHERN CAPE/SOUTH AFRICA
Robbe Bay
Originally named after the bay 'Seal Bay' from
the Dutch *rob* 'seal' before it became a port in
1855 for shipping the copper from
Namaqualand mines. It was named after
M. S. Nolloth, commander of HMS *Frolic*, who
had surveyed the coast of Namaqualand in
1854.

Porto, PORTUGAL
See OPORTO.

Pôrto Alegre, BRAZIL
Rio Grande do Sul: founded in 1742 by
Portuguese colonists from the Azores, the
name means 'Happy Port' from *porto* 'port' and
alegre 'happy' or 'joyful'. The original name,
Pôrto dos Casais 'Port of the Couples', signified
that the colonists were married. There is a
Porto Alegre in São Tomé and Príncipe.

Portobelo, PANAMA
Named after the bay which had been called
'Beautiful Harbour' in Spanish by Christopher
Columbus[†] in 1502. The original settlement
was founded in 1597.

Port-of-Spain, TRINIDAD AND TOBAGO *Puerto
de España*
The present name is a direct translation of the
name given by the Spanish in 1595. It is the
capital.

Porto-Novo, BENIN *Ajase*
Founded in the 17th century, it was conquered
by the Yoruba Kingdom of Oyo in 1730 and
became its chief port for the slave trade. As
Portuguese influence strengthened, they
renamed it 'New Port' in Portuguese because it
was developed from two older villages. It
became a French protectorate in the 19th
century and the capital of Dahomey (now
Benin) in 1900.

Pôrto Seguro, BAHIA/BRAZIL
Founded in 1500 as 'Safe Port' in Portuguese
because it offered a sheltered harbour.

Porto Turres, SARDINIA/ITALY *Turris Libisonis*
Originally a Phoenician port, the present name
has evolved from the name of the Roman
colony founded in 46. Torres comes from the
Latin *turris* 'tower'.

Porto Santo, MADEIRA ISLANDS/PORTUGAL
An island settled by the Portuguese in the 16th
century which takes its name from a bay called
'Blessed Harbour' on the southern coast.

Port Pirie, SOUTH AUSTRALIA/AUSTRALIA
Founded in 1848 and named after a ship called
the *John Pirie*, itself named after the Lord Mayor
of London, which had transported settlers here
in 1845.

Port Said (Būr Sa'īd**),** EGYPT
Founded in 1859 as the construction of the
Suez Canal began, it is named after
Muhammad Sa'īd Pasha (1822–63), Khedive of
Egypt (1854–63), who chose the site of the
town.

Port Saunders, NEWFOUNDLAND/CANADA
Named after Admiral Sir Charles Saunders
(*c.*1713–75), British commander-in-chief of the
Newfoundland station (1752) and of the St
Lawrence River fleet (1759).

Port Shepstone, KWAZULU-NATAL/SOUTH
AFRICA
Founded as a small port in 1867 and named in
1893 after Sir Theophilus Shepstone (1817–
93), secretary for native affairs in the late
1850s, who acquired the Transvaal as British
territory in 1877 and was its administrator
(1877–9).

Portsmouth, DOMINICA, UK, USA
1. UK (England): formerly Portesmuthan
'(Place at the) Mouth of the Harbour' from the
Old English *port* 'harbour' and *mūtha*.
2. USA (New Hampshire): the state's only
seaport, it was established on the Piscataqua
River, after which it was first named, in 1623.
Having been renamed Strawbery Banke, it was
renamed again in 1653 after the English city-
port because, like it, it was a port at a river
mouth.
3. USA (Ohio): founded in 1803 and named by
Major Henry Massie after his hometown,
Portsmouth in Virginia.
4. USA (Rhode Island): founded in 1638 as
Pocasset, an Algonquian name referring to
the width of the Sakonnet River along which
it lies. Becoming a town in 1640, it was
probably renamed after the English
Portsmouth.
5. USA (Virginia): a port at the mouth of the
Elizabeth River, it was founded in 1752 and
named after the English city-port.

Port Stanley, FALKLAND ISLANDS/UK
See STANLEY.

Port Sudan (Būr Sūdān**),** THE SUDAN
Built in 1905–9 as a replacement for the
port of Suakin, which had become choked
with coral, it takes its name from that of
the country.

Port Talbot, CANADA, UK
UK (Wales): founded in 1836 and named after
the Talbot family who owned the land.

Port Tewfik (Būr Tawfīq**),** EGYPT
At the southern end of the Suez Canal, it is
named after Tawfīq Pasha (1852–92), Khedive
of Egypt (1879–92).

Port Townsend, WASHINGTON/USA
Settled in 1851 and named after George
Townshend (1778–1855), 3rd Marquess
Townshend, the *h* being dropped later. It is
hard to know why the 3rd Marquess was
honoured, since he was disinherited by his
father and did not appear to contribute much
to public life.

Portugal *Lusitania*
The Portuguese Republic (República
Portuguesa) since 1910. Previously the
Kingdom of Portugal (1139–1910), although
between 1580 and 1640 the country was under
Spanish rule with the Spanish king Philip II
being proclaimed Philip I of Portugal (1580–
98); apart from the north, under Moorish rule
(711–1139); and a Roman province from 27 BC
named after a branch of the Celtiberians, the
Lusitani. Portugal is derived from the Latin
portus cale 'warm harbour'. This referred to a
Roman settlement, now Oporto, at the mouth
of the River Douro and the fact that the port
was never ice-bound. In due course, the name
came to represent the 'Land of Portucale'
between the Rivers Minho and Douro and
eventually the whole country.

Portugalete, BASQUE COUNTRY/SPAIN
Founded in 1322 by Maria Diaz de Haro, the
second wife of Don Juan, Prince of Castile, and
given a name which described its purpose as a
'Galley Slave Port' from the Latin *portus
galorum*.

Posad, NOVGOROD/RUSSIA *Pervomayskoye*
Historically 'Trading Quarter (situated outside
the city walls)' or 'Suburb'. *See* PERVOMAYSK.

Posadas, ARGENTINA, SPAIN
Argentina: established as a Paraguayan port
and trading post on the left bank of the Paraná
River (now in Argentina) known as Trinchera
de los Paraguayos 'Trench of the Paraguayans'
from the Spanish *trinchera* 'trench'. It was
renamed Trinchera de San José 'St Joseph's
Trench' in 1869 and then ten years later after
the Argentinian national hero, Gervasio
Antonio Posada (1757–1833).

Postmasburg, NORTHERN CAPE/SOUTH AFRICA
Sibiling, Blinkklip
Originally a mission station, when it became a
village it was given the Afrikaans name
Blinkklip 'Shining Rock'. It was renamed
'Postma's Town' in 1890 after a priest, Dirk
Postma.

Pos'yet, PRIMORSKIY TERRITORY/RUSSIA
Named after Admiral Konstantin Pos'yet
(1819–89), a navigator and naval commander
who explored the coast here.

Potchefstroom, NORTH WEST/SOUTH AFRICA
Founded in 1838 as the first capital of the
Transvaal by Andries Potgieter (1792–1852), a
Voortrekker leader. The name is derived from
the first syllable of his name with *chef* 'leader'
referring to him and *stroom* 'stream', referring
to the Mooi River on which the town lies.

Potenza, BASILICATA/ITALY *Potentia*
Founded in the 2nd century BC, the Roman
name, from which the present one is derived,
means 'Power' or 'Might'.

Poti (P'ot'i), GEORGIA *Phasis, Kale Fas*
The present name is ultimately derived from
the ancient Greek settlement of Phasis, or
Phasi, which took its name from the River
Phasis (now the Rioni) which had its source in
the Phasis Mountains. The second, Turkish,
name also comes from this source with the
additional *kale* 'fortress' which was built by the
Ottoman Turks in 1578 on the site. Phasis is
said to have given its name to the 'pheasant', a
bird stolen by Jason and the Argonauts when
searching for the Golden Fleece and
introduced into Europe.

Potomac, USA
1. A river rising in West Virginia and flowing
through Maryland and Virginia. The name
appears to come from Patawomeck, the name
registered by Captain John Smith (1580–1631),
founder of the first permanent English
settlement in North America, as a local tribal
name, incorrectly as it turned out. The
Algonquian name is said to mean a '(place)
where something is bought', thus a trading
post on the river bank.
2. Maryland: formerly Offutt's Crossroads
named after the original landowner who
opened a store here.

Potosí, BOLIVIA, MEXICO, NICARAGUA
Bolivia: a department and a city named after
Potosí Mountain, whose name is said to come
from the Quechua *potojchi* 'to explode', a
reference to the reverberations from within
the mountain. Cities and a mountain in the
USA, and a city in Guyana, are spelt Potosi.

Potsdam, GERMANY, USA
1. Germany (Brandenburg): formerly
Poztupimi 'Under the Oaks' from the Slavonic
pod 'under' and *domb* 'oak',·*dombimi* being the
instrumental case in the plural.
2. USA (New York): settled in 1803 and
named after the city in Germany because
their sandstone deposits resembled each other.

Poughkeepsie, NEW YORK/USA
Settled by the Dutch in 1683 on the Hudson
River with a Native American name meaning
'Waterfall'. It has been suggested, however,

p

that it comes from the Delaware word
apokeepsingk 'safe harbour'.

Poultney, VERMONT/USA
Named after William Poultney (1684–1764),
Earl of Bath.

Poverty Bay, NORTH ISLAND/NEW ZEALAND
So named, because there was little here
besides firewood, by Captain James Cook[†]
when he stopped in the bay in 1769.

Powder River, WYOMING/USA
A city named after the Powder River. Its name
comes from the black sand along its banks
which resembles gunpowder.

Powell, USA
Utah: a lake named after Major John Wesley
Powell, a one-armed Civil War veteran, who
led two expeditions down the Colorado River
and through the Grand Canyon in 1869 and
1871, mapping it and southern Utah.

Powhatan, USA
Three states (Arkansas, Louisiana, and
Virginia) have cities with this name, all after
the Powhatan Confederacy of over 30
Algonquian-speaking Native American tribes;
or after Powhatan himself, a famous chief who
died in Virginia in 1618. His name is said to
mean 'At the Falls'.

Powys, WALES/UK
A county formed in 1974 and named after a
historic principality with a name meaning
'Provincial' from the Low Latin *pagensis*, the
adjectival form of *pagus* 'country district'. The
sense here was country people living in open
uplands compared to those who lived in more
sheltered areas to the north and south where
there were hills and valleys.

Požarevac, SERBIA/SERBIA AND MONTENEGRO
Margus, Viminacium, Passarowitz
'Town of Fire' from *požar* 'fire', probably
meaning that the area, once wooded, had been
cleared by burning.

Poznań, POLAND *Poznani civitas, Posen*
Founded as a fort in the 9th century, its name
is probably derived from that of an early
landowner together with the title *pan* 'lord'. It
was given the German name Posen when the
Prussians occupied and annexed the city
in 1793 at the second partition of Poland.

Pozo, PARAGUAY
'Well' (excavation) in Spanish. Several
Spanish-speaking countries have places with
names that begin with Pozo.

Pozzuoli, CAMPANIA/ITALY *Dicaearchia, Puteoli*
Founded *c.*529 BC by the Greeks who called it
Dicaearchia 'City of Justice'. It was renamed by

the Romans in the 4th century BC with a name
that comes from the Latin *putere* 'to stink'
which could refer to the smell of the
sulphurous fumes from nearby Solfatara
'sulphur place'.

Prague (Praha), CZECH REPUBLIC
According to legend, some time in the 7th
or 8th centuries, Prince Krok led his people
to a rocky hill above the Vltava River where
he built a new castle; the hill is now known
as Vyšehrad 'High Castle'. His youngest
daughter, Princess Libuše, became head of
the tribe on her father's death but, because
some men did not greet this with much
enthusiasm, she decided to marry a humble
farmer, Přemysl, whom she had met earlier.
The tribal elders then chose her husband as
head of the tribe. He was called Přemysl Oráč
'ploughman' because he was busy ploughing
a field when the tribal elders arrived to tell
him of his appointment. This was the start
of the Přemysl dynasty (*c.*800–1306). Princess
Libuše was said to have special powers
allowing her to see into the future. One day
she was standing with her husband and
others on a rock near Vyšehrad overlooking
the forest above a bend in the river and saw
in a vision a glorious city which would be
situated here. She decreed that the city
should be built at a place in the forest where a
man would be found constructing the
threshold (in Czech, *prah*) of his house and that
it should be called Praha (Prague). The man
was discovered on what is now Hradčany Hill.
An attractive legend, but that is all it is. The
name is much more likely to have come from
práh 'shoal' or 'ford' because the Vltava is not
deep here and at that time could probably be
forded quite easily. Capital of Bohemia, Prague
became the capital of the newly created
Czechoslovakia in 1918 and of the Czech
Republic in 1993.

Praia, CAPE VERDE
'Beach' or 'Shore' in Portuguese. It is the
capital of Cape Verde.

Prairie du Chien, WISCONSIN/USA
'Meadow of the Dog' and named after a Native
American chief Alim 'Dog' which became
Chien in French with *prairie*.

Prairie du Sac, WISCONSIN/USA
'Grass-lands of the Sauks' in French, originally
territory belonging to the Sauk tribe.

Praslin Island, SEYCHELLES
Named after the Frenchman, Gabriel de
Choiseul-Chevigny, Duke of Praslin.

Prato, TUSCANY/ITALY *Prato in Toscana*
In 1863–1931 the town was known as Prato in Tuscany to differentiate it from two other towns called Prato. Having gained independence from vassal status, the population settled in a large meadow-land (in Italian, *prato*).

Pravda, RUSSIA, TURKMENISTAN
1. Named after the Soviet Communist Party newspaper whose name means 'Truth'. It was founded by Vladimir Lenin[†] in 1912.
2. Russia (Sakhalin Island): Hirochi was the name used by the Japanese during their occupation of Sakhalin Island until 1945.

Pravdinsk, RUSSIA
1. Kaliningrad: originally the German Friedland 'Land of Peace' from *Friede* 'peace'. It was renamed in 1946, following East Prussia's annexation by the Soviet Union, after the Soviet Communist Party daily newspaper, *Pravda* 'Truth'.
2. Nizhny Novgorod: developed around a paper mill which manufactured newsprint for *Pravda* and so named in 1932.

Prekmurje, SLOVENIA
A district meaning 'Beyond the Mura (River)'.

Prescott, CANADA, USA
1. Canada (Ontario): founded as Johnston in 1810 and renamed after General Robert Prescott (1725–1815), governor of Canada (1796–9).
2. USA (Arizona): settled in 1863 and named the following year after William H. Prescott (1796–1859), a historian and writer.
3. USA (Massachusetts): named after Colonel William Prescott who commanded the American colonist forces at the Battle of Bunker Hill in 1775.

Prešov, SLOVAKIA *Fragopolis, Epuryes, Pressow/ Prassow, Preschau*
The second, Hungarian, name, Epuryes, was derived from *eperjes* 'strawberry' meaning a '(Settlement in an Area Rich in) Strawberries'. The first Slovak name was derived from the personal name Preš or Praš with the possessive *-ov* to mean the '(Settlement) owned by Preš/ Praš'. The later German Preschau came from the earlier Slovak Pressow.

Presque Isle, MAINE/USA *Fairbanks*
Settled in 1828 and renamed in 1859 'Peninsula' from the French *presqu'île*.

Prestatyn, WALES/UK *Prestetone*
'Village, or Manor, of the Priests' from the Old English *prēost* 'priest' and *tūn*, a Welsh form of Preston.

Preston, AUSTRALIA, CANADA, UK, USA
UK (England): a very common name, the city in Lancashire formerly had the spelling Prestetune and Prestune. The name means 'Village, or Manor, of the Priests' from the Old English *prēost* 'priest' and *tūn*. The city in Lancashire received city status in 2002, the year of Queen Elizabeth II's Golden Jubilee.

Prestwick, SCOTLAND/UK *Prestwic*
'Farm of the Priests', similar to *Preston with *wīc*.

Pretoria, GAUTENG/SOUTH AFRICA *Tshwane*
Founded in 1855 by Marthinus Pretorius (1819–1901), first president of the South African Republic (1864–71), and named after his father, Andries Pretorius (1798–1853), the Boer statesman and Voortrekker leader who defeated the Zulus at Blood River (now the Ncome River) in 1837. It became the capital of the Transvaal (the South African Republic) in 1860 and the administrative capital of the Union of South Africa in 1910, a status it retained on the inauguration of the Republic of South Africa in 1961. In 2000 the metropolitan area, Greater Pretoria, was named, locally, after a chief, Tshwana, who ruled here before the arrival of white settlers. His name meant 'Black Cow' in Tshwana, not 'Likeness' or 'We are the Same' as is often suggested. The place-name appears in the locative form and therefore ends in an *e*.

Préveza, GREECE *Berenicia*
Founded *c.*290 BC, the town's present name may be an adaptation of the former name. If this is the case then it would almost certainly have been a tribute to one of the many queens or princesses in the Ptolemean family in Egypt. However, it has also been suggested that it is associated with the Italian *provvisione* 'provisioning' or the Slavonic *perevoz* 'transportation'.

Priargunsk, CHITA/RUSSIA *Tsurukhaytuy*
'Near the Argun (River)' after the river's name and *pri* 'near' or 'by'.

Pribilof Islands, ALASKA/USA
Discovered in 1788 by Gavril Pribylov (d. 1796), a Russian navigator who commanded a ship belonging to the Russian American Company. He sailed into the Bering Sea and discovered St George and St Paul Islands in the group, which was named after him in 1789. They were transferred to the USA on the purchase of Alaska in 1867.

Price, CANADA, USA
USA (Utah): settled in 1877 and named after the river discovered by, and named after,

William Price, a bishop of the Mormon Church, in 1865.

Prieska, NORTHERN CAPE/SOUTH AFRICA *Priskab, Briesschap*
Derived from the Korana *beris* 'goat' and *ga* 'lost' to give '(Place of) the Lost Goat', presumably a reference to an incident involving goats.

Prilep, MACEDONIA *Perlepe*
Possibly derived from a local word associated with the Russian *prilepit'* 'to stick to', here in the sense of the town being close to a natural object; in this case, an imposing rocky hill.

Priluki, UKRAINE
'By the (River) Bend', an approriate name given that it lies on a bend of the Uday River, from *pri* 'by' and the Russian *luka* 'bend'.

Primorsk, RUSSIA
Two towns in Kaliningrad and Leningrad Provinces have this name meaning 'By the Sea' from *primor'ye* 'seaside'. The one in Kaliningrad was previously known by its German name of Fischhausen, the one in Leningrad by its Finnish name of Koivisto.

Primorskiy Kray, RUSSIA
'Maritime Territory' from *kray* 'territory' or, literally, 'edge'. Also known as Primor'ye Kray (see previous entry).

Prince Albert, ANTARCTICA, CANADA, SOUTH AFRICA
1. Antarctica: mountains discovered between 1839 and 1843 and named after Prince Albert (1819–61), consort of Queen Victoria[†].
2. Canada (Saskatchewan): founded in 1866 as a Presbyterian mission station and named after the same Prince Albert.
3. South Africa (Western Cape): founded in 1843 and named after the same Prince Albert.

Prince Edward Island, CANADA, SOUTH AFRICA
1. Canada: a province called by the Micmacs Abegweit 'Cradled on the Waves'. The first Europeans to visit the island in 1534 are believed to have been the French and they called it Île Saint-Jean 'St John Island'. They took possession of it in 1603 and colonized it in 1720. At the end of the Seven Years' War (1756–63) it was annexed by the British, becoming a separate colony in 1769. In 1799 they renamed it after Prince Edward (1767–1820), Duke of Kent, who was then the commander of British forces in North America. It joined the Confederation in 1873.
2. South Africa: an island in the Indian Ocean and the smaller of a pair called the Prince Edward Islands. Discovered by the French in

1772 they were called the Îles des Froids 'Islands of Cold'. Captain James Cook[†] sighted them in 1776 and, unaware of the French discovery, named them after Prince Edward (1767–1820). When he learnt that Marion du Fresne had already come upon them, he named the larger island 'Marion Island'. Both islands were annexed by South Africa, Marion in 1947 and Prince Edward Island in 1948.

Prince Frederick, MARYLAND/USA
Named after Prince Frederick Louis (1707–51), eldest son of King George II[†].

Prince George, CANADA, USA
1. Canada (British Columbia): founded in 1807 as a fur trading post called Fort George after King George III[†]. The name was changed in 1915 in honour of Prince Albert Frederick Arthur George (1895–1952), later George VI, King of the United Kingdom and Northern Ireland (1936–52).
2. USA (Virginia): named after George (1653–1708), Prince of Denmark and husband of Queen Anne of Great Britain.

Prince of Wales Island, AUSTRALIA, CANADA, USA
1. Australia (Queensland): discovered by Captain James Cook[†] in 1770 and named after the future King George IV[†], then 8 years old.
2. Canada (Nunavut): discovered in 1851 and named after the future Edward VII (1841–1910), King of the United Kingdom and Ireland (1901–10), then 10 years old.
3. USA (Alaska): discovered in 1825 and named after the former Prince of Wales, who had become King George IV[†] in 1820.

Prince Patrick Island, NORTHWEST TERRITORIES/CANADA
Discovered in 1853 by Sir Francis McClintock (1819–1907), an Irish polar explorer, while on an expedition to find John Franklin; Franklin had commanded an expedition to find the Northwest Passage in 1845, but perished with his crew in the attempt. McClintock named the island after Prince Arthur William Patrick (1850–1942), third son of Queen Victoria[†]; he was governor-general of Canada (1911–16).

Prince Rupert, BRITISH COLUMBIA/CANADA
Named in 1906 after Prince Rupert (1619–82) of the Palatinate, a nephew of King Charles I[†], and the first governor of the Hudson's Bay Company. The land given to the Company was known as Rupert's Land.

Princess Anne, USA
Maryland and Virginia: named after Princess Anne (1665–1714), later Queen of Great Britain (1702–14).

Princeton, CANADA, USA
1. USA: eighteen states have cities and towns with this name, some after particular princes, some after the city in New Jersey and some after particular individuals.
2. New Jersey: settled in 1681 and originally named Stony Brook after the home of one of the settlers. It was renamed in 1724 after Prince George, the future King George II[†].

Princetown, ENGLAND/UK
Named after the Prince Regent who became King George IV[†].

Princeville, CANADA, USA
USA (Hawaii): founded on the island of Kauai in the mid-18th century as a coffee plantation. As a result of a visit in 1860 by Kamehameha IV (1834–63), King of Hawaii (1855–62) and his wife, Queen Emma, it was given the name Princeville 'Prince Town' in honour of the royal couple's son, Prince Albert (1858–62).

Príncipe, SÃO TOMÉ AND PRÍNCIPE
One of two islands comprising the island nation of São Tomé and Príncipe, Príncipe was settled by the Portuguese in the 15th century. They called it Ilha do Príncipe 'Island of the Prince' after Prince Afonso, later Afonso V (1432–81), King of Portugal (1438–81).

Priozersk, KARELIYA/RUSSIA
'By the Lake' from *pri* 'by' and *ozero* 'lake'. It lies on Lake Ladoga.

Pripet Marshes (Poles'ye), BELARUS-UKRAINE
'Woodland Marshes' from the Russian *po* 'along' and *les* 'wood', thus *poles'ye*. The English name comes from the Pripyat' River which flows through the area.

Pristan'-Przheval'sk, KYRGYZSTAN
'Przhevalsky's Jetty' from the Russian *pristan'* 'jetty' or 'pier'; the personal name referred to Nikolay Przhevalsky (1839–88), a Russophile Polish explorer (who Russianized his name from Przewalski) who travelled throughout Central Asia. He died near here and was buried on the shores of Lake Issyk-Kul. He gave his name to a wild horse, Przewalski's horse, which he discovered in Mongolia in the late 1870s.

Priština (Albanian: **Prishtinë**), SERBIA/SERBIA AND MONTENEGRO
Prišt in Serbo-Croat means 'boil' and this may be a reference to the seething waters of the nearby River Gračanka. The city came under the control of the medieval Serbian state in the late 12th century and later was its capital until the Ottoman Turkish victory at the Battle of Kosovo Polje in 1389. It is the capital of Kosovo and is largely Albanian populated.

Privol'nyy, TATARSTAN REPUBLIC/RUSSIA *Lugovoy*
'Free', but since this is a place-name its meaning is 'broad' or 'widely spread'. The former name comes from *lug* 'meadow', thus 'situated on a meadow'. There is a town called Privol'noye in Kamchatka Province with the same meaning; in this instance the adjective is in the neuter form and the missing neuter noun *selo* 'village' is understood.

Privolzhsk, IVANOVO/RUSSIA *Yakovlevskoye*
Originally named after an unknown person called Yakovlev, it was renamed in 1941 'Near the (River) Volga' from the river's name and *pri* 'near' or 'by'. The town actually lies on a tributary of the Volga.

Progreso, YUCATÁN/MEXICO
'Progress' in Spanish.

Progress, RUSSIA, USA
Russia (Amur): a name glorifying the 'progress' of communism.

Prokuplje, SERBIA/SERBIA AND MONTENEGRO *Hammeum, Komplos*
Since the 14th century it has been named after St Procopius, martyred in 303.

Proletarsk, ROSTOV/RUSSIA *Velikoknyazheskaya, Proletarskaya*
First known as the village of 'Grand Duke' from *Velikiy Knyaz'*, the desire to rid the country of reminders of tsarism following the Bolshevik Revolution in 1917 produced the name Proletariat as a tribute to the working classes of Russia; the spelling took its present form in 1970. There is also a town called Proletarskiy in Belgorod Province.

Promyshlennyy, KOMI REPUBLIC/RUSSIA
A coal-mining town, the name means 'Industrial'.

Prostějov, CZECH REPUBLIC *Prostějovice, Prossnitz*
Founded in 1213 as the 'Village of Prostěj's People' from a personal name and *ice*, a suffix often used to indicate a place associated with a personal name. In 1391, when the village became a town, the name was changed to Prostějov. It was known by the German Prossnitz for a time.

Protem, WESTERN CAPE/SOUTH AFRICA
A shortening of the Latin phrase *pro tempore* 'for the time being'. The place acquired this name because a temporary railway junction was planned here.

Provence-Alpes-Côtes d'Azur, FRANCE
A region and roughly coextensive with the historical region of Provence. Provence simply means 'Province' because in the 2nd century BC it formed part of the first Roman *provincia* 'province' to be established beyond the Alps. That was called Gallia Transalpina 'Transalpine Gaul' by the Romans. At first it stretched across the whole of southern France from the Alps to the Pyrenees, but has been much reduced in size since. It became part of the region of Provence-Alpes-Côtes d'Azur in the 1960s.

Providence, GRENADA, GUYANA, USA
USA (Rhode Island): founded in 1636 by Roger Williams, who had been ejected from Plymouth Colony for his unacceptable religious beliefs. With other like-minded colleagues he moved away and bought land from the Narraganset people. He named it for 'God's merciful providence to me in my distress'.

Provideniya, CHUKOT AUTONOMOUS DISTRICT/
RUSSIA
Takes its name from the bay of the same name, 'Providence'. It was given this name by a British sailor, Thomas Moore, who sheltered here during the winter of 1848 and called it a 'happy providence'.

Provins, ÎLE-DE-FRANCE/FRANCE
Said to take its name from a personal name, Probus, which in Latin means 'excellent', 'honourable', or 'virtuous'.

Provo, SERBIA/SERBIA AND MONTENEGRO, USA
USA (Utah): a river and a city settled in 1849 as Fort Utah and renamed the next year as a tribute to Étienne Provost, a French-Canadian trapper.

Prozor, BOSNIA AND HERZEGOVINA
'The Window', a reference to the fact that it stands at the point where the River Rama gorge opens up.

Prussia (Preussen)
A historic state with territory now in Russia, Poland, and Germany. An area on the south-eastern coast of the Baltic Sea was occupied by the Teutonic Knights in the 13th century and they called their new territory Prussia after the inhabitants, the Borussi. In 1618 the Elector of Brandenburg inherited the Duchy of Prussia (East Prussia) and in 1701 Brandenburg-Prussia became the Kingdom of Prussia; subsequently more territory further west, stretching to the Belgian frontier, was acquired, particularly as a result of the three partitions of Poland in 1772, 1793, and 1795. The kingdom was abolished in 1918 at the end of the First World War and Prussia became a state within Germany. With Germany's borders redrawn after the Second World War, Prussia ceased to exist in 1947.

Prut, MOLDOVA-ROMANIA
A river with a name whose meaning has not been satisfactorily explained. However, it may be connected with the Slavonic *brod* 'ford'. Also spelt Pruth and Prutul in Romanian.

Pskov, RUSSIA *Pleskov*
A province and a city that is spread across the Velikaya 'Great' River and its tributary, the Pskov. The present name is derived from the former Pleskov which may be derived from *plës* 'stretch of river'.

Puebla, MEXICO, SPAIN
Mexico: the first local name, Cuetlaxcoapan, meant the 'Place where Snakes change their Skin' from the Nahuatl *coatl* 'snake'. The Spanish founded a city here in 1532 and originally called it Puebla de los Angeles 'City of the Angels' because religious fervour suggested that angels had helped in its construction. The full version of its present name is Puebla de Zaragoza, adopted in 1862, as a tribute to General Ignacio Zaragoza (1829–62) who fought off the French here that year. Puebla is also a state.

Pueblo, PUERTO RICO, USA
'Town' in Spanish.

Puerto Cabello, VENEZUELA
'Port Hair' from the Spanish *puerto* and *cabello* 'hair'. According to a pleasant tradition, the name is said to be derived from the fact that the harbour's waters were so calm that a single hair was sufficient to moor a ship to the dock.

Puerto Cortés, HONDURAS *Puerto Natividad*
Renamed from the Spanish 'Nativity Port' to honour Hernán Cortés[†].

Puerto Montt, CHILE
Founded in 1853 and named after Manuel Montt (1809–80), President of Chile (1851–61).

Puerto Peñasco, SONORA/MEXICO
'Rock Port' from the Spanish *peña* 'rock'.

Puerto Real, PUERTO RICO, SPAIN
Spain (Andalusia): originally called Portus Gaditanus 'Port of Cadiz' by the Romans, it was renamed 'Royal Port' in 1488 when it was rebuilt by Isabella I (1451–1504) and Ferdinand II (1452–1516), joint Spanish monarchs (respectively 1474–1504 and 1479–1516).

Puerto Rico *Boriquén, San Juan, Porto Rico*
Commonwealth of Puerto Rico (Spanish: Estado Libre Asociado de Puerto Rico) since 1952; a commonwealth that is, in effect,

a semi-colony of the USA since its 1952 constitution. Ceded to the USA in 1898, it was previously a Spanish dependency. It was discovered in 1493 by Christopher Columbus[†] who called the bay on the north side of the island Porto Rico 'Rich Harbour' and the island itself San Juan 'St John', possibly after Don Juan (1478–97), the Spanish heir apparent. Spanish colonization began in 1508. The bay's name was later adopted for the whole island, while San Juan became the name of the capital. In 1932 the name was changed to Puerto Rico.

Puerto Vallarta, JALISCO/MEXICO *Las Peñas*
A port founded in 1851 as 'The Rocks' from the Spanish *peña* 'rock' and renamed in 1886 after Don Ignacio Vallarta, the third governor of Jalisco.

Pugachov, SARATOV/RUSSIA *Mechetnaya, Nikolayevsk*
The original name comes from *mechet'* 'mosque' and was used between 1760 and 1835. When the village became a town in 1835 it was renamed after Emperor Nicholas I[†]. With the fall of the Romanov dynasty it was renamed in 1918 after Yemelyan Pugachov (*c.*1742–75), a Don Cossack who, claiming to be Peter III (who ruled for six months in 1762 before being deposed by his wife, Catherine II the Great[†], and assassinated), led a peasant rebellion to end serfdom in the south in 1773–4 before being captured and executed.

Puget Sound, WASHINGTON/USA
Called Whulge by the Native Americans, it was explored by Peter Puget, a lieutenant serving under Captain George Vancouver[†] who led a British two-boat expedition to trace the coastline in 1792. Vancouver named the sound after Puget.

Puglia, ITALY
See APULIA.

Pukaki, SOUTH ISLAND/NEW ZEALAND
A lake with a Maori name meaning 'Head of a Stream'. It is sometimes given as 'Bunched-up Neck' and this refers to a myth whereby a god is supposed to have dug up the lake and the water took on this shape.

Pula, CROATIA *Polai, Pietas Julia, Polensium*
According to legend, the name is derived from the Greek *polai* 'the pursued', a reference to the Greek refugees from Colchis on the Black Sea. It was renamed in 40 after Julius Caesar[†] with the Latin *pietas* probably meaning 'gratitude to' here; its full name was Colonia Julia Pola Pollenta Herculanea.

Pulaski, USA
Five states have cities with this name, directly or indirectly named after Kasimierz Pułaski (1747–79), a Polish hero of the uprising against the Russians in 1768 who joined the US colonial army, became a general, and participated in the American War of Independence (1775–83) during which he died of wounds inflicted in battle.

Pullman, WASHINGTON/USA *Three Forks*
Settled in 1875, it was laid out at the junction of three creeks and named in 1882. Later it was renamed after George Pullman (1831–97), who invented the railway sleeping car named after him.

Punjab, INDIA, PAKISTAN
A state in India and a province in Pakistan. The name means '(Land of the) Five Rivers' from the Hindi *panch* 'five' (originally Persian *panj*) and *āb* 'water'. The rivers, tributaries of the Indus, are the Beas, Chenab, Jhelum, Ravi, and the Sutlej. Only the Beas and the Sutlej now lie within India's Punjab. On occasion the Sutlej has been excluded for the Indus. A powerful Sikh kingdom from 1800, the Punjab came under British rule between 1849 and 1947. It was split between India and Pakistan in 1947 with the Indian state being further split in 1966 into Punjab and Haryana, and the union territory of Chandigarh.

Punta Arenas, CHILE
Founded in 1849 with a name meaning 'Sandy Point' from the Spanish *arena* 'sand'. There is a city in Costa Rica called Puntarenas.

Punta del Este, URUGUAY
'East Point' from the Spanish *este* 'east'.

Punta Gorda, BELIZE
'Important Point' from the Spanish *punta* 'point' or 'end' and *gorda* 'important' or 'big'. A coastal town and one of the few places in Belize with an airport.

Pusan (Busan), SOUTH KOREA *Pusanp'o*
'Cauldron Mountain' from *pu* 'cauldron' and *san* 'mountain', a reference to the ring of peaks behind the city that resemble the rim of a cauldron. During the Koryo dynasty (918–1392) the name included the suffix *p'o* 'harbour', the city-port being South Korea's most important port, lying in a splendid sheltered bay. It was the temporary capital of South Korea during the Korean War (1950–3).

Pushkin, LENINGRAD/RUSSIA *Saari, Sarskoye Selo, Tsarskoye Selo, Detskoye Selo*
The settlement was captured from the Finns in 1708 when its original Finnish name meant 'Island', here to mean raised ground within an

area of lower lying terrain. It was renamed 'Island Village', an adaptation from the Finnish *saari* and the Russian *selo* 'village'. As a result of its development as a royal palace after Peter I the Great[†] had given it to his wife Catherine, it became known locally as the 'Tsar's Village', thus Tsarskoye Selo from *c.*1728. Following the merger of Tsarskoye and Sofiya in 1808 the village's name was officially recognized as Tsarskoye Selo 'Tsar's Village'. To the Bolsheviks it represented a despised symbol of Tsarist autocracy and so a month after their revolution in October 1917 and the removal of the imperial family, the palace was taken over as a holiday camp for children and workers' families; the name was changed to Detskoye Selo 'Children's Village'. In 1937 it was changed again to mark the centenary of the death of Alexander Pushkin (1799–1837), Russia's greatest poet, who was a student at the Lyceum here. There are towns called Pushkino in Moscow and Saratov Provinces, and one called Pushkinskiye Gory 'Pushkin Hills', where Pushkin is buried, in Pskov Province.

Putrajaya, MALAYSIA
A federal territory and the new federal administrative capital of Malaysia, 16 miles (25 km) south of Kuala Lumpur, which is still under construction. The first phase was completed in 1999, but the entire project may not be finished until 2010 or later. Some government offices have moved, although not all will have done so before 2012. Both the territory and the city are named after Tunku Abdul Rahman Putra Al-Haj (1903–90), the first post-independence prime minister of Malaya (1957–63) and of Malaysia (1963–70), with *jaya* 'victory'.

Puu Kukui, HAWAII/USA
A volcanic peak whose Hawaiian name means 'Candlenut Hill'.

Pyandzh, TAJIKISTAN *Saray Komar, Baumanabad, Kirovabad*
The original name may have meant 'Komar's Mansion', a rather grand description for what was probably a caravanserai or inn, from the Turkic *saray* 'mansion' or 'palace'. In 1931 the town was renamed 'Bauman's Town' after Karl Bauman (1892–1937), a Latvian Communist official, who was not noted for his activities in either Latvia or Tajikistan. Following the murder of Sergey Kirov[†] in 1934, the town was renamed in his honour in 1936. The present name, adopted in 1963, comes from the Pyandzh River which may take its name from the Persian *panj* 'five', although why this should be so is not clear.

Pyatigorsk, STAVROPOL TERRITORY/RUSSIA *Beş Dağ*
Founded in 1830 as 'Five Peaks' from *pyat* 'five' and *gora*, as was the previous Turkish name from *beş* 'five' and *dağ*, a reference to the hills surrounding the spa town.

P'yatykhaty, UKRAINE
'Five Houses' from *pyat* 'five' and *khata* 'peasant house', a word used in Ukraine, Belarus, and southern Russia. The original settlement probably consisted of only five houses.

Pyay, BURMA Śrī *Ksetra, Prome*
Also spelt Pyè. The original name meant 'City of Splendour' or literally 'Favoured Field'. It is sometimes known as the ancient site of Tjhayekhittaya, some 5 miles (8 km) south-east of modern Pyay, and now called Hmawza. Prome was the Anglicized version of Pyay which means 'The Capital', a reference to Śrī Ksetra which was one of the capitals of the Pyus in the 5th–9th centuries.

Pyin-U-Lwin, BURMA *Maymyo*
During the period of British rule (1826–1948) it was called 'May's Town' after Colonel, later Major General, James May, who was stationed here with the 5th Bengal Infantry in 1886, and *myo* 'town'. The meaning of the present name is not clear, although it too may be named after an individual.

P'yŏngsŏng, NORTH KOREA *Sainjang*
'Flat City' from *p'yŏng* 'flat' and *sŏng* 'city'. Recently built close to *P'yŏngyang, the name alludes to the surrounding terrain.

P'yŏngyang, NORTH KOREA *A-Sa-Dal, Sogyŏng*
'Flat Land' from *p'yŏng* 'flat' and *yang* 'land', a reference to the surrounding terrain; it lies on the Taedong River. According to legend, it was founded in 1122 BC and was the capital of the Kingdom of Koguryŏ in 427–668. It has been the capital of North Korea since 1948.

Pyrenees (French: **Pyrénées**; Spanish: **Pirineos**), FRANCE-SPAIN
A mountain range named after the mythological nymph Pyrène, who is said to have been buried in the mountains by Hercules, having been killed by wild beasts.

Pyrgos (Pirgos), GREECE
Several places have this name meaning simply 'Castle'.

Pythagóreio, GREECE *Samos, Tigáni*
The ancient name gave way to Tigáni 'Frying Pan', a reference to the shape of its harbour. However, Pythagoras (*c.*580–*c.*500 BC), the Greek philosopher and mathematician, was born here and in 1955 the town was renamed after him.

Q

Qādisiyah, al-, IRAQ
A governorate named to commemorate the Muslim victory over the Sāssānians in 637. The name is derived from the Arabic root *qds* representing 'holy' or 'holiness'.

Qairouan (al-Qayrawān), TUNISIA *Kamouinia*
'The Caravan' from the Persian *karwan* founded as a military base and holy city by the Arab commander, Uqba ibn Nafi, in 670 on the site of the Byzantine fort of Kamouinia during the third Arab incursion into Tunisia. In 800 it became the capital of the Aghlabid dynasty of the Maghrib. It is also spelt Kairouan.

Qaraghandy, KAZAKHSTAN *Karaganda*
A province with a name derived from the caragana bush, *karakan*, a yellow acacia that grows in the area. The present name is the Kazakh spelling of the previous Russian name.

Qarshi, UZBEKISTAN
See KARSHI.

Qasigiannguit, GREENLAND/DENMARK
Christianhåb
'Small spotted Seals'. The previous name meant 'Christian's Hope' after Christian IV (1577–1648), King of Denmark-Norway (1588–1648).

Qatar The State of Qatar (Dawlat Qatar) since 1971 when independence from the UK was achieved. Previously it had been a British protectorate (1916–71), although ruled as an absolute monarchy by the al-Thani family; a part of the Ottoman Empire (1872–1913), although the Turks did not withdraw until 1915. Prior to their arrival, Qatar had been dominated by the al-Khālifa family in Bahrain (and still its rulers) and considered a dependency of Bahrain by the British. There is no certainty as to the origin of the name. *Qatara* means 'to fall', 'drip', or 'trickle', or 'to line up camels in single file and connect them with halters'. *Qutr* means 'region' and *qutra* 'drop'. Thus the name could have been inspired by the presence of well-water or a camel park.

Qazimämmäd, AZERBAIJAN *Haji Kabul*
Now named after the son of Imam Shāmil (1797–1871), a Murīd leader who, under the overall leadership of Ghāzi Muhammad, waged a holy war against the Russians, mainly in Chechnya and Dagestan. His son also led a revolt againt the Russians. The previous name meant 'Rest Place for Pilgrims'—those en route to Mecca.

Qena, EGYPT *Caene*
An adaptation of the earlier Greek name, itself from *kainē* 'new' in comparison with the nearby Koptos (now Qift) to the south. The Wādī Qena runs away to the north.

Qeqertarsuaq, GREENLAND/DENMARK *Disko Island, Godhavn*
'Big Island' with the previous Danish name meaning 'Good Harbour'.

Qeshm, IRAN *Queixome, Kishm, Jazīrat aṭ-Ṭawīla*
The largest island in the Persian Gulf and the main town on it. The Arabic name, Jazīrat aṭ-Ṭawīla, means 'Long Island'. The present name has evolved from the Portuguese who built a fort in the 17th century around which their town of Queixome developed.

Qingdao, SHANDONG/CHINA
'Green Island' from *qīng* 'green' (also 'blue' and 'black') and *dǎo* 'island', a reference to the green of the island's rocky cliffs. Also known as Tsingtao which gives its name to the beer.

Qinghai, CHINA
A province, established in 1928, and a lake, from which it takes its name, meaning 'Blue Lake' from *qīng* 'blue' and *hǎi* 'lake' or 'sea'. The lake is actually called Qinghai Hu with *hú* 'lake'. It is also known as Koko Nor, a Mongolian name, also meaning 'Blue Lake' from *hoh* 'blue' and *nuur* 'lake'. It is still also spelt Tsinghai and was commonly known as Xihai 'West Lake'.

Qiqihaer, HEILONGJIANG/CHINA *Bukui*
It was originally a garrison called Bukui 'auspicious'. It is said that during the Yuan dynasty (1279–1368) Dawoer nomadic herdsmen settled here and called it Qiqihaer 'natural pasture'; alternatively, it is said that this name is a Chinese rendering of the Dawoer *xidijiaer* 'boundary' or 'frontier'. It is still also spelt Tsitsihar, the name coming from the Mongolian *tsetse* 'flower' with the Chinese *ěr* to denote a medium-sized place. The place is also known as Longsha from *lóng* 'dragon' and *shā* 'sand'.

q

Qiryat Shemona, ISRAEL *Khalasah*
'Town of the Eight', a reference to the group of six men and two women who died at nearby Tel Hai defending their settlement against Arab guerrillas in 1920. It was founded as a transit camp for immigrants in 1950 on the site of the Arab village of Khalasah.

Qom, IRAN
Founded by Arabs, it takes its name from the pre-Islamic village of Kumandan or Kumidān, which was merged with several other villages into a walled town in 730. Kumandan may be derived from a personal name, that of one of its founders, or possibly from *kūma*, a type of hut.

Qostanay, KAZAKHSTAN
See KUSTANAY.

Quang Tri (Quảng Trị), VIETNAM
'Big Colony' from *quáng* 'big' or 'significant' and *trị* 'to colonize'.

Quanzhou, FUJIAN/CHINA *Jinjiang, Ruitong, Licheng, Wenling, Zaiton*
Founded in 700, the port-city was given its present name in 711 from the nearby Quánshān 'Spring Mountain' where there was a well-known spring from *quán* 'spring'. The Ming (1368–1644) called it Licheng from *lǐ* 'carp' and *chéng* 'town' when the city had the shape of a carp; it also enjoyed the name Wenling from *wēn* 'warm' and *líng* 'hill' because of its year-long tropical climate. Zaiton may be derived from *citóng* 'sunshine tree' or 'coral tree' which grew in abundance just outside the city walls. The English word 'satin' comes from Zaiton which was a port of great importance during the Song and Yuan dynasties (960–1368).

Qu'Appelle, SASKATCHEWAN/CANADA
A town and a river, that also flows through Manitoba, with a French name meaning 'Who calls'. This name came from the river's Cree name Kah-tep-was 'River that calls', a reference to the sounds that are said to be made by a spirit that haunts the river.

Quatre Bornes, MAURITIUS
'Four Boundaries' from the French *quatre* 'four' and *borne* 'boundary marker, or stone', a reference to the stones that marked the limits of four large sugar estates here.

Queanbeyan, NEW SOUTH WALES/AUSTRALIA
Queen Bean
A river and a town settled in 1828 with a name that was phonetically derived from an Aboriginal word meaning 'clear water'. The present spelling represents an effort to get closer to the Aboriginal pronunciation.

Quebec, CANADA *Stadacona*
A province and a city-port which was originally a Huron village called Stadacona. This was discovered by Samuel de Champlain[†] who is credited with founding the city of Quebec in 1608. The city was captured by the British in 1759 and ceded to Great Britain in 1763. At the same time the colony of New France, claimed for France by Jacques Cartier[†] in 1534, became the province of Quebec. In 1791 it was renamed Lower Canada and in 1841 Canada East. The present Province of Quebec came into existence in 1867 when the Confederation of Canada was created. The name is derived from the Algonquian *quílílbek* 'place where the waters narrow', a reference to the lessening width of the St Lawrence River here.

Queen Alexandra Range, ANTARCTICA
A mountain range in the Ross Dependency discovered in 1908 by Sir Ernest Shackleton (1874–1922), the British explorer who led an expedition to the Antarctic in 1907–9; he named the mountains after Queen Alexandra (1844–1925), wife of Edward VII, King of the United Kingdom and Ireland (1901–10).

Queen Charlotte Islands, BRITISH COLUMBIA/CANADA
First sighted by the Spanish in 1774, they were not named until 1787 when Captain George Dixon surveyed them and named them after his ship, itself named after Queen Charlotte (1744–1818), wife of King George III[†].

Queen Elizabeth Islands, CANADA
Stretching across the Northwest Territories and Nunavut, the islands include the Parry and Sverdrup island groups, Ellesmere Island, and others. They were named as a group only in 1953 to commemorate the coronation of Elizabeth II (1926–), Queen of the United Kingdom and Northern Ireland (1952–).

Queen Maud Land (Norwegian: **Dronning Maud Land**), ANTARCTICA
Discovered by the Norwegians in 1930 and declared a Norwegian dependency in 1949. It was named after Queen Maud (1869–1934), English wife of Haakon VII, King of Norway (1905–57). The Queen Maud Mountains are also named after her.

Queens, NEW YORK/USA
The largest borough of New York City and named after Queens County created in 1683. This name was a tribute to Catherine of Braganza (1638–1705), daughter of John IV, King of Portugal (1640–56), who married the

British King Charles II[†] and thus became a queen.

Queensland, AUSTRALIA, CANADA
Australia: a state. Although its coast was charted in 1770 by Captain James Cook[†] and settled from 1842, it was part of New South Wales until 1859. On receiving its own identity it was named after Queen Victoria[†].

Queenstown, AUSTRALIA, CANADA, NEW ZEALAND, SOUTH AFRICA
1. Australia (Tasmania): founded in 1897 and named after Queen Victoria[†].
2. South Africa (Eastern Cape): founded in 1853 as a fortified village and named after Queen Victoria[†].

Quelimane, MOZAMBIQUE *Río dos Bons Sinais*
Founded as a Portuguese trading station in 1544 and named after the river on which it lies. The origin of the name is not clear, but it might come from the Swahili *kilima* 'mountain'. Vasco da Gama (*c*.1460–1524), the Portuguese navigator, came across the river in 1498 during his first voyage to India and called it the 'River of Good Omens'.

Queluz, PORTUGAL
'What Light!' from *que* 'what' and *luz* 'light'.

Quemoy (Jīnmén Dǎo), TAIWAN
An island with a name meaning 'Golden Gate' from *jīn* 'golden', *mén* 'door' or 'gate', and *dǎo* 'island'. It is sometimes referred to as Da Jinmen Dao with *dà* 'big' and the others with Xiǎo Jīnmén Dǎo with *xiǎo* 'little' which lies to its west. It was occupied by the Nationalist Chinese in 1949 when they were withdrawing from the mainland after the Communist seizure of power. Quemoy is an Anglicization of Jīnmén.

Quercy, MIDI-PYRÉNÉES/FRANCE
A historic region and former district named after the Cadurci, a Celtic tribe.

Querétaro, MEXICO
A state, whose full name is Querétaro de Arteaga, and a city founded by the Otomi people. Its name means 'Site of the Ball Game' in Purépechas. The Toltec are believed to have invented this game, *tlachtli*, which involved the players striking a hard rubber ball with their hips in an attempt to make it pass through a vertical ring set into the centre of the side walls. The game had an important ritual purpose—to divine the destiny of the Sun (represented by the ball)—and players could end up being sacrificed; their blood represented rain which nourished the fields and allowed men to be fed and life to continue. Querétaro was conquered by the Spanish in 1531. *See* TAXCO.

Quesnel, BRITISH COLUMBIA/CANADA
Quesnellemouth
A river, a lake, and a town called Quesnellemouth until 1864. All are named after Jules Maurice Quesnelle who participated in the exploration of the area in 1808.

Quetta, BALOCHISTAN/PAKISTAN *Shāl/Shālkot*
Derived from the Pashto *kwatkot* or *kota* 'fort' which evolved into *kwatta* and then Quetta; or it may come from the Pashto *kwata* 'hill', given that it lies in a very mountainous region. It was ruled by the British from 1876 after they had resolved a dispute between the Khan and his tribesmen. He leased the Bolan Pass and the nearby town of Quetta to them permanently in gratitude. In the event, it became part of Pakistan when that state was created in 1947.

Quetzaltenango, GUATEMALA
A department and a city founded in 1524 by the Spanish with a Nahuatl name meaning 'Place of the Quetzal'. This is a bird of the genus *Pharomachrus*, the males being noted specially for their dazzling plumage. It was the sacred bird of the Maya and Aztecs; and the quetzal is the basic monetary unit of Guatemala.

Quezon City, LUZON/PHILIPPINES
Originally a private estate, it was chosen in 1939 as the site of a new capital by Manuel Luis Quezon y Molina (1878–1944), who became the first president of the Philippine Commonwealth in 1935; he remained president until his death, although he had to go into exile after the Japanese invaded in 1942. The city was the Filipino capital between 1948 and 1976. There are towns called simply Quezon on the islands of Palawan and Alabat.

Qufu, SHANDONG/CHINA *Xianyuan County*
'Winding Hill' from *qū* 'winding' and *fù* 'small hill' because of the zigzag nature of the hill. Between 1012 and 1129 it was known as Xianyuan County from *xiān* 'immortal' and *yuán* 'origin' because the Yellow Emperor, the mythical founder of Chinese civilization and recognized as the common ancestor of all Chinese people, was said to have been born here.

Quibala, ANGOLA
Founded in 1828 with a name meaning 'Great Bald One', a reference to the rocks here that look like bald heads.

Quiché, GUATEMALA
A department named after the Quiché people, a branch of the Maya.

q

Quimper (Breton: **Kemper**), BRITTANY/FRANCE
Montagne-sur-Odet
The name is derived from the Breton Kemper, itself from *kember* 'confluence' since the town lies at the junction of the Odet and Steir Rivers. For a short while after the French Revolution in 1793, the town was renamed 'Mountain on the (River) Odet', an allusion to mountains to the north-east.

Quincy, USA
1. Illinois: settled in 1822 as Bluffs, it was renamed three years later on the day that John Quincy Adams (1767–1848) became the sixth president of the USA (1825–9). He was born at nearby Braintree.
2. Massachusetts: settled as Mount Wollaston in 1625 and later renamed Merry Mount. When it became a town in 1792 it was renamed after Colonel John Quincy (1689–1767), a prominent local figure.

Quintana Roo, MEXICO
A state since 1974 and named after Andrés Quintana Roo (1787–1851), a writer and one of the leaders in the independence movement in 1810–21, although he had never visited the region.

Quitman, USA
Five states have cities with this name, usually in honour of General John A. Quitman, a governor of Mississippi and prominent participant in the Mexican–American War (1846–8).

Quito, ECUADOR
Takes its name, which in full is Villa de San Francisco de Quito, from the Quitus, one of several Quechua tribes living in the area. The modern city was founded by the Spanish in 1534 after Incas had razed the ancient city to the ground to prevent it falling into Spanish hands. Once the seat of the Kingdom of Quito, it became an *audiencia* in 1563 with its territory greatly exceeding that of modern Ecuador. Until 1830, when the independent Republic of Ecuador was created, Quito was the name used for the territory. The city of Quito has been the capital since 1534.

Qwaqwa, FREE STATE/SOUTH AFRICA *Witsieshoek*
Formerly known as 'Witsie's Corner' from the personal name of a local chief and the Afrikaans *hoek* 'corner'. The present name means 'Whiter than White', a reference to the white sandstone hill that commands the area. It was a former state with self-government from 1974, within Free State, for the southern Sotho people.

Qyzylorda, KAZAKHSTAN
See KYZYL-ORDA.

q

Rabat, MALTA, MOROCCO
1. Malta: in Roman times the present area of Mdina and Rabat was called Melita. When part of the city, now Mdina, was fortified by the Arabs the parts outside the walls was called *rabat* 'suburb'.
2. Morocco: locally Ribāṭ which is a fortified monastery. It was originally Phoenician and then Roman as a self-governing city. The modern city was founded by 'Abd al-Mu'min (d. 1163), the first Almohad ruler (1130–63), in 1150 as a *ribāṭ* in which to house his troops for a *jihād* 'holy war' against Spain. It was, however, Abū Yūsuf Ya'qūb al-Manṣūr (*c.*1160–99), the third Almohad sultan (1184–99), who decided to make the camp into an imperial city. He named it Ribāṭ al-Fath 'Camp of Victory', from which the present name comes, to commemorate his victory over the Spanish at Alarcos in 1195. In Europe it was known as New Salé during the 17th century since it lay across the Bou Regreg River from a pre-Roman settlement called Sala. Although a conurbation, they remain separate cities.

Rach Giá, VIETNAM
Situated between the two arms of the Cai Lon canal which joins the port with the Bassac (Hau Giang) River, *rach* means 'canal' or 'river'; *giá* means 'beansprout'. It was part of Cambodia until 1715.

Racibórz, POLAND *Ratibor*
Said to have been founded in the 9th century by, and named after, a Slav tribal chief called Racibor. It has also been suggested that it might mean the 'Forest of Razi', a Slav god, with *bor* 'forest'. In Prussian hands in 1742–1945, its German name was Ratibor.

Racine, CANADA, USA
USA (Wisconsin): founded in 1834 and named Port Gilbert after Gilbert Knapp, a ship's captain on Lake Michigan. It was renamed in 1837 with either a French name meaning 'Root', since it lies at the mouth of the Root River, or from an Algonquian word *pakwasewin* 'place where wild rice is collected'.

Radishchevo, ULYANOVSK/RUSSIA
Dvoryanskaya Tereshka, Verkhnee Abliazovo
First known as 'Nobleman's Tereshka' from *dvoryanskiy* 'of the nobility' and the River Tereshka. In 1918 it was renamed after Alexander Radishchev (1749–1802), a radical writer, philosopher, and revolutionary who spent his childhood here.

Radivilov, UKRAINE *Radzivilov, Chervonoarmeysk*
Originally named after the Polish Radziwiłł family, it was renamed in 1940 as 'Red Army' from the Russian *chervonnyy* 'red' and *armiya* 'army'. It returned to a version of its original name after Ukrainian independence in 1991.

Radlett, ENGLAND/UK *Radelett*
'Road Junction' from the Old English *rād* and *læt* 'junction (of roads)'.

Radom, POLAND
First mentioned in 1154 with a name probably taken from the personal name Radomir or the tribal name Radimoran.

Raglan, NEW ZEALAND, UK
New Zealand (North Island): founded as a mission station in 1835 and named after Field Marshal Lord Raglan (1788–1855), 1st Baron Raglan and first British commander-in-chief during the Crimean War (1853–6). He took his title from the town in Wales.

Rainier, WASHINGTON/USA
A mountain named by Captain George Vancouver† who surveyed this part of the west coast of North America in 1792, after Rear Admiral Peter Rainier (1742–1808). Rainier, later a vice admiral and Vancouver's mentor in the British Royal Navy, never saw the mountain. There is a city with this name in Oregon, also named after the admiral. The Native American name is ˈTacoma 'mountain'.

Raipur, MADHYA PRADESH/INDIA
Founded in the 14th century by, and named after, Rai Brahma Deo as 'Rai's Town'.

Rājasthān, INDIA *Rājpūtanā*
A state, formerly comprising eighteen princely states and other small pockets of territory, with a name meaning 'Land of the Kings' from the Sanskrit *rāja* 'king' and *sthana*, itself from *stan*. Its previous name meant 'Country of the Rājpūts', 'sons of *rājas*' from *putra* 'son'. The Rājpūts are descended from the Hindu Kshattriya warrior caste.

Rājkot, GUJARĀT/INDIA
'Fort of the King' from *kot* 'fort' and *rāja* 'king'.
It was once the capital of the former princely
state of Saurāshtra.

Rājshāhi, BANGLADESH *Rampur Boalia*
A division and a town meaning 'Royal
Territory' from *rāj*.

Rakaia, SOUTH ISLAND/NEW ZEALAND
A town lying on the river of the same name
which, in Maori, means 'to arrange in ranks',
possibly a reference to the best way of
crossing it.

Rakhine, BURMA
See ARAKAN.

Raleigh, CANADA, USA
USA (North Carolina): founded in 1792 and
named after Sir Walter Raleigh (*c.*1554–1618),
an English adventurer, writer, and courtier,
who tried to establish a colony in North
Carolina (without ever going there himself) in
1584–9.

Ramallah (Rām Allāh), WEST BANK
'Height of God'.

Rāmanāthapuram, TAMIL NĀDU/INDIA
'Town of the Lord Rāma' from the Hindi *nāth*
'lord', *pur* and Rāma, a major Hindu god.

Ramat Gan, ISRAEL
Founded in 1921 as 'Hill of the Garden' from
the Hebrew *rama* 'hill' and *gan* 'garden'.

Rambouillet, PARIS/FRANCE
Derived from a personal name associated with
the Germanic name Rambo with the Gaulish
ialo 'clearing'. The town, with its famous
castle, is surrounded by forest. It gives its name
to a breed of sheep.

Ramenskoye, MOSCOW/RUSSIA
'(Settlement in a) Coniferous Forest' from a
dialect word *ramen'* 'forest'.

Ramotswa, BOTSWANA
'Father of the Village' in Tswana.

Ramsey, CANADA, ISLE OF MAN, UK, USA
1. Isle of Man: 'River where wild Garlic grows'
from the Old Scandinavian *hramsa* 'wild garlic'
and *á* 'river'.
2. UK (England): the town in Cambridgeshire
was known as Hramesege 'Island where wild
Garlic grows' from *hramsa* and *ēg* 'island', in
fact a slightly raised piece of ground in a
marshy area.

Ramsgate, SOUTH AFRICA, UK
1. South Africa (KwaZulu-Natal): founded in
1922 just south of Margate and named after
the Ramsgate in England to mirror the English
pair of towns.

2. UK (England): formerly Remmesgate
'Raven's Gap', a reference to the gap in the
chalk hills which leads to the sea, from the Old
English *hræfn* 'raven' and *geat* 'gap' or 'pass'.
What the 'raven' meant is not clear and it may
have simply been a personal name.

Randolph, MASSACHUSETTS/USA *Cochato*
Founded in 1710 and named after the Cochato
tribe, it was subsequently renamed after
Peyton Randolph (1721–75), first president of
the US Continental Congress (1774–5).

Rangoon (Yangon), BURMA *Dagon*
Written with an *r* in English because the
British learnt to speak Burmese in Arakan
where the *r* sound is used in comparison with
y in standard Burmese. The English version of
the name was officially replaced by the
Burmese in 1989. In 1754 Alaungpaya (1714–
60), King of Burma (1752–60), ejected the Mons
from Upper Burma. His final victory was at
Dagon—named after the great golden shrine
here, Shwe Dagon 'Golden Dagon'. Here he
built a new city in 1756 and called it Yangon
from *yangun* 'Peaceful' or 'End of Strife' in the
hope that the fighting was over. The name was
corrupted to Rangoon when the British
captured the city in 1852 and the city has been
the capital of Burma since 1885. The name
Dagon may have come from the Pali *Tikumbha-
nagara* 'Three Hills City' and then slowly
evolved through Tikum, Takum, and Takun to
Dagon; this explanation is disputed, however,
because *kumbha* does not mean 'hill' and there
are no hills by the site of the Shwe Dagon
pagoda. The Burmese *takun* means 'treetrunk'.

Rangpur, BANGLADESH
'Abode of Bliss' from the Sanskrit *rang* 'bliss' or
'brightness' and *pur*. Rāja Bhagadatta is said to
have had a residence here.

Rann of Kutch, INDIA-PAKISTAN
A huge salt marsh most of which lies in India.
The name is derived from the Sanskrit
irina 'salt marsh' or *aranya* 'wilderness' and
kachchha 'low, flat land'. It is also spelt Rann of
Kachchh.

Ranong, THAILAND
'Rich in Tin' from *rae* 'tin' and *nong* 'rich'. The
local tin mines brought great prosperity to the
area.

Rantoul, ILLINOIS/USA
Settled in 1854 with the arrival of the railroad,
it is named after Robert Rantoul, one of the
railroad directors.

Rapid City, CANADA, USA
USA (South Dakota): settled in 1876 on Rapid
Creek from which it derives its name; this was
noted for its rapid flow.

Rappahannock, VIRGINIA/USA
A river with a Native American name meaning 'Stream with an ebb and flow' or 'Stream with quick-rising Water'.

Raritan, NEW JERSEY/USA
A river with a probable Native American name meaning 'Stream overflows'.

Ra's al 'Ayn, LEBANON, SYRIA
'Spring Head', a reference to the springs here, from *ra's* 'head' (usually 'headland', 'cape' or 'promontory') and *'ayn*. The name used to be spelt Resulayn in Syria.

Ra's al-Khaymah, UAE *Julfar*
An emirate of the UAE and a town with a name meaning literally 'Head of the Tent' from *ra's* 'head', *al-*, and *khaymah* 'tent'. This refers to a large tent that stood here as a navigational aid. The Portuguese built a fort here known as Julfar, but they were ejected by the Persians in 1622. In 1820 it came under British control, becoming a Trucial state in 1919 (*see* UAE). In 1972 the emirate joined the UAE, having initially refused to join.

Ra's al-Naṣrānī, EGYPT
'Cape of the Christian' from *ra's* 'cape' or 'headland', *al-*, and *naṣrānī* 'Christian'.

Rasht, IRAN *Rashta Bazar*
'Low Place'. Merchants from the mountains to the west and the east used to meet here in low-lying terrain (it is 80 ft (25 m) below sea level) to trade and thus called the place Rashta Bazar. Some scholars, however, believe that the name means 'Damp Place' or a 'Deep Place of Waste and Dust'.

Rās al-Ma, ALGERIA, MALI
The Arabic name means 'Head of the Water' from *rās* 'head' and *ma* 'water' indicating that the towns lie close to the source of rivers.

Rassvet, KRASNOYARSK TERRITORY/RUSSIA
'Dawn', that is, the dawn of communism.

Ratchaburi (Ratburi), THAILAND
'City of the King' from *buri* and *racha* 'king'.

Ratmanov Island (Ostrov Ratmanova), RUSSIA
Otherwise known as Big Diomede Island, it is named after Lieutenant Makar Ratmanov. *See* DIOMEDE ISLANDS.

Ratnapura, SRI LANKA
'City of Gems' from the Hindi *ratna* 'jewel' and *pur*, a reference to the fact that many types of precious and semi-precious stones are found in the surrounding valleys.

Raton, NEW MEXICO/USA
Settled in 1871 and called 'Mouse' in Spanish because a certain breed of ground squirrel or rock squirrel swarmed over a nearby mountain.

Raub, MALAYSIA, USA
Malaysia: founded as a gold-mining settlement in the 1880s with a name meaning 'Scoop with one's Hands', a reference to the fact that the ore was very easy to collect.

Ravenna, ITALY, USA
Italy (Emilia-Romagna): possibly derived from the pre-Latin *rava* 'a stony slope subject to landslides' with the Etruscan suffix *enna*; it may have been founded by the Etruscans. The city was the capital of the Western Roman Empire in 402–76, of the Ostrogothic Kingdom in 476–540, and of Byzantine Italy in 540–751.

Ravenscar, ENGLAND/UK *Rauenesere*
'Rock frequented by Ravens' from the Old Scandinavian *hrafn* 'raven' and *sker* 'rock'.

Rāwalpindi, PUNJAB/PAKISTAN *Gajipur?*
'Village of the Ravals' from the Hindi *rāvalpiṇḍī*. They were a group of yogis. It was given its present name by a local Ghakkar chief in the 15th century. It was under British rule in 1849–1947 and was the temporary national capital in 1959–67.

Rawlins, WYOMING/USA *Rawlins Springs*
Founded in 1868 and named after General John Rawlins, secretary of war under President Grant, who found a freshwater spring here.

Rawson, ARGENTINA, USA
Argentina: founded in 1865 by Welsh settlers and named after Guillermo Rawson (1821–90), minister of the interior at the time.

Rawtenstall, ENGLAND/UK *Routonstall*
'Rough Farmstead' from the Old English *rūh* 'rough' and possibly *tūn-stall* with *stall* indicating a stall for animals.

Reading, JAMAICA, UK, USA
1. UK (England): formerly Readingum and Reddinges '(Settlement of) Rēad's People' from an Old English personal name and *-ingas*.
2. USA (Pennsylvania): laid out in 1748 on land owned by the sons of William Penn who founded Pennsylvania, they named it after their family home town in England.

Rechytsa, BELARUS
Derived from the Slavonic *reka* 'river'.

Recife, PERNAMBUCO/BRAZIL *Ciudad de Recife, Pernambuco*
Founded by the Portuguese *c*.1535 with a name meaning 'Reef (Town)' from the Portuguese

recife 'reef', a reference to the reef outside the harbour here. It was the capital of Brazil in 1537–49.

Redcar, ENGLAND/UK *Redker*
'Red, or reedy, Marsh' from the Old English *rēad* 'red' or *hrēod* 'reed' and the Old Scandinavian *kjarr* 'marsh'. Here, it is more likely to be 'Reedy Marsh' since *kjarr* was often used for a marsh overgrown with brushwood.

Redcliffe, QUEENSLAND/AUSTRALIA *Humpybong*
The original Aboriginal name was derived from *umpi bong* 'dead houses'. In 1799 Matthew Flinders† changed the name of the promontory from which the city gets its name, to Redcliffe in recognition of its red cliffs.

Red Cloud, NEBRASKA/USA
Named after Red Cloud (1822–1909), last warrior-chief of the Oglala Teton-Sioux people, who did his best to protect his hunting grounds before coming to an agreement with the US government in 1868.

Red Deer, CANADA
Alberta: a city named after the river of the same name which itself was named by Scottish settlers who mistook the local elk for the red deer of Scotland.

Redding, CALIFORNIA/USA
Founded in 1872 and named after Major B. B. Redding, an early pioneer and railroad agent.

Redditch, ENGLAND/UK *La Rededich*
'Red, or reedy, Ditch' from the Old English *rēad* 'red' or *hrēod* 'reed' and *dīc* 'ditch'.

Redlands, CALIFORNIA/USA
Founded in 1881 and simply named after its local red soil.

Redondo Beach, CALIFORNIA/USA
Named after the Rancho Sausal Redondo 'Round Willow Grove' which was nearby.

Red River (Chinese: **Yuan Jiang**; Vietnamese: **Song Hong**), CANADA, CHINA-VIETNAM, USA
1. China-Vietnam: takes its name from the large quantity of silt it carries and which colours its waters.
2. USA: the same is true of the Red River rising in New Mexico which flows partly into the Mississippi River; it is also known as the Red River of the South. The Red River of the North rises in North Dakota and empties into Lake Winnipeg, Canada. Red River is also the name of a city in New Mexico.

Redruth, ENGLAND/UK *Ridruth*
'Red Ford' from the Old Cornish *rid* 'ford' and *rudh* (modern *rüth*) 'red'.

Red Sea (Arabic: **al-Baḥr al-Aḥmar**)
While most international names translate as the 'Red Sea', the Hebrew name is Yam Sūf

'Sea of Reeds'. It has therefore been suggested in some quarters that the name should really be the 'Reed Sea'. However, several theories have been put forward for the generally accepted name, of which perhaps the most plausible is that at times the algae *Trichodesmium erythraeum* appears in the water and when it fades away it gives the water a reddish brown colour.

Redvers, SASKATCHEWAN/CANADA
Named after General Sir Redvers Buller (1839–1908), commander-in-chief (1899–1900) of British forces during the second Boer War in South Africa (1899–1902).

Redwood City, CALIFORNIA/USA *Embarcadero*
Laid out in 1854 and named because of the abundance of redwood timber in the area which was strongly exploited.

Regensburg, BAVARIA/GERMANY *Radasbona, Castra Regina Regeneopurc, Ratisbon*
'Fortified Town on the (River) Regen' from the river name and *Burg*. It originated *c.*500 BC as a Celtic stronghold from *bona* 'fort' and became a Roman garrison in 179.

Reggio di Calabria, REGGIO DI CALABRIA/ITALY *Rhegion/Rhegium, Regium Julium*
Founded by Greek settlers as Rhegion *c.*720 BC to control the Strait of Messina, it passed to the Romans *c.*270 BC. In due course they renamed it the 'Royal (Town of) Julius (Caesar)' from the Latin *regius* 'royal'. Di Calabria 'of *Calabria' was added to distinguish it from the Reggio in Emilia (now Emilia-Romagna).

Reggio nell'Emilia, EMILIA-ROMAGNA/ITALY *Regium Lepidi*
'Royal (Town) in Emilia' and previously 'Royal (Town) of Lepidus' from the Latin *regius* 'royal' and the Italian *nell* 'in the'. It was founded in the 2nd century BC by Marcus Aemilius Lepidus (d. 152 BC), a Roman statesman who also gave his name to Emilia.

Regina, BRAZIL, CANADA, MEXICO, USA
Canada (Saskatchewan): originally a hunters' camp, it received its first name, Pile O'Bones, from the remains of the buffalo that had been caught, slaughtered, and cut up here. The Cree believed that live buffalo would not desert the bones of dead buffalo and so as long as there were piles of bones there would always be buffalo to hunt. The Cree name was Okana ka-asateki 'Pile of Bones'. In 1857 the place was given a name, Wascana, that was close to its Cree name. However, when the Canadian Pacific Railway reached the place in 1882 it was given the name Regina 'Queen' by the governor-general, John Campbell (1845–1914), the Marquess of Lorne, after his wife's mother,

Queen Victoria[†] whose Latin title was *Victoria Regina* 'Victoria, Queen'; his wife was Princess Louise (1848–1939).

Rehoboth, NAMIBIA, USA
1. Namibia: originally Anis 'Steam' because of the hot springs here. In 1844 it was given a biblical name by a German missionary, who built a church here as the centre of a mission station. The name means 'Large Spaces'.
2. USA (Massachusetts): although the name has the same meaning 'Large Spaces' or perhaps 'Ample Room', it is not clear to whom credit should be given or precisely why. One theory claims that it was William Blackstone who founded the town, his aim being to provide 'room outside the narrow confines of Puritan intolerance'; another, that it was the Revd Samuel Newman who built a church here and gave thanks that 'the Lord hath made room for us' (Genesis 26: 22).

Reḥovot, ISRAEL
Founded in 1890 by Jews from Warsaw, Poland, after the biblical town of Rehoboth with a Hebrew name meaning 'Large Spaces' or 'Room'.

Reichenau, GERMANY, SWITZERLAND
Germany (Baden-Württemberg): an island in Lake Constance (Bodensee) with a name meaning 'Rich Pastures' from *reich* 'rich' and *Aue* 'pasture' or 'meadow'. These pastures were cultivated by the monks from the Benedictine monastery founded on the island in 724.

Reigate, ENGLAND/UK *Reigata*
'Gate for female Roe Deer' from the Old English *ræge* 'female roe' and *geat* 'gate'.

Reims, CHAMPAGNE-ARDENNE/FRANCE *Durocorturum*
Named after a Gallic tribe, the Remi. It is sometimes spelt Rheims in English.

Reitz, FREE STATE/SOUTH AFRICA *Singer's Post, Amsterdam*
Founded in 1884 on a site used for trade and named after one of its practitioners, it was renamed after the Dutch city. In 1889 it was renamed again after Francis Reitz, president of the Orange Free State (1889–95).

Remagen, RHINELAND-PALATINATE/GERMANY *Ricomagus*
The present name has evolved from the previous Roman name 'King's Market' from the Gaulish *rix* 'king' and *mago* 'market' or 'field'.

Remiremont, FRANCHE-COMTÉ/FRANCE *Romaraci Mons*
The Latin name meant the 'Hill of Romaric'. He was St. Romaric, who founded a monastery on a hill overlooking the town in the 7th century.

Renfrew, CANADA, UK
UK (Scotland): formerly Reinfry and Renfriu 'Point of the Current' from the Old Welsh *rhyn* 'point' and *frwd* 'current'. It lies at the point where the River Gryfe flows into the Clyde.

Rennell Island, SOLOMON ISLANDS
Annexed by the UK in 1899 and named after James Rennell (1742–1830), a prominent geographer who became surveyor general of Bengal (1764–77) after leaving the British Royal Navy.

Rennes, BRITTANY/FRANCE *Condate Rhedorum*
A shortened version of the Roman name which meant 'Confluence of the Redones', a Celtic tribe whose capital this was. The city lies at the confluence of the Ille and Vilaine Rivers which give their name to the tribe from *redo* 'current'.

Reno, ITALY, USA
USA (Nevada): settled as Lake's Crossing *c.*1860 and subsequently renamed as a tribute to General Jesse Lee Reno (1823–62) who was killed in the Civil War (1861–5).

Rensselaer, USA
New York: settled in 1631 by the Dutch and named after Kilian van Rensselaer, a diamond merchant from Amsterdam. Rensselaer Falls and Rensselaerville, previously Rensselaerwyck, are also named after him. There is also a city with this name in Indiana, probably named after John van Rensselaer.

Repino, LENINGRAD/RUSSIA *Kuokkala*
Finnish between 1917 and 1940, the town was given its Russian name in 1948 to honour Ilya Repin (1844–1930), a painter who lived and died here.

Resistencia, ARGENTINA *San Fernando del Río Negro*
Founded in the mid-18th century on the site of an old Quechua village as a Jesuit mission, it was given its present name in 1878 when it was re-established as a military outpost following the Argentine–Paraguay War (1864–70). Apparently the name refers to a local way of hunting whereby the hunters encircle their prey and then advance towards it.

Reşiţa, ROMANIA
Situated on the River Brzava, the name is derived from the Slavonic *reka* 'river'.

r

Réunion *Saint Apollina, Île Mascareigne, Île Bourbon, Île de la Réunion, Île Bonaparte*
Department of Réunion (Département de la Réunion) since 1946, having previously been a French colony. One of the Mascarene Islands and an Overseas Department of France. Most accounts claim that the island was discovered by the Portuguese explorer Pedro de Mascarenhas during his voyage to India in 1512–14. He saw it on 9 February, St Apollina's Day, hence its first name. The French claimed the island in 1638, first calling it Mascarin Island and then in 1642 Bourbon Island after the French royal house; it was finally settled by the French East India Company in 1665 and passed to the French crown in 1767. In 1793, after the French Revolution, it was renamed Reunion Island to mark the 'reunion' of some 500 revolutionaries, who had marched from Marseilles, with those in Paris in 1792. In 1801–10 it was known as Bonaparte Island after Napoleon[†], but in 1810 the island was captured by the British and the name reverted to Bourbon. However, it was returned to France four years later. With the creation of the Second Republic of France in 1848 the name was changed once more to Reunion Island. It is now simply called Réunion.

Revelstoke, BRITISH COLUMBIA/CANADA *Second Crossing*
A city and a mountain named after Edward Charles Baring (1828–97), Lord Revelstoke, the head of a British bank that helped to provide funding for the Canadian Pacific Railway which passed through here.

Revere, MASSACHUSETTS/USA *Rumney Marsh, North Chelsea*
Settled in 1626, it became part of Boston in 1632; in 1739 it became part of Chelsea until it was incorporated as the town of North Chelsea in 1846. In 1871 it was renamed after Paul Revere (1735–1818), who was born and died in Boston and who is famous for his ride through the night of 18 April 1775 to warn the inhabitants of Boston that the British were coming.

Revillagigedo, MEXICO, USA
A group of islands some 300 miles (500 km) off the tip of the peninsula of Baja California, Mexico, and a single island off British Columbia, Canada, belonging to the USA, all probably named after Juan Vincente de Güemes Pacheco de Padilla, 2nd Count of Revillagigedo, Viceroy of New Spain (1789–94).

Revolution Peak (Pik Revolyutsii),
TAJIKISTAN
Named in 1954 in honour of the Bolshevik Revolution in 1917.

Rewari, HARYĀNA/INDIA
Said to have been built by Raja Rāo for his daughter Rewati and named after her.

Rey, IRAN *Rahga, Rhagae*
'Foothill'. The ruins of the ancient city, usually spelt Rayy and one of the greatest in Iran until the 12th century, lie just to the east of the modern city, itself some 5 miles (8 km) south-east of Tehrān.

Reykjavík, ICELAND *Ingolfsholdi*
Originally named after Ingólfr Arnarson, an early Norse adventurer to Iceland *c.*870 and the first permanent settler on the island. Its present name means 'Smoky Bay' from *reykja* 'to smoke' and *vík* 'bay', a reference to the steam given off as a result of volcanic activity. It has been the capital in all but name since 1786 and of the independent Republic of Iceland since 1944.

Rheims, CHAMPAGNE-ARDENNE/FRANCE
See REIMS.

Rhine (German: **Rhein**; French: **Rhin**; Dutch: **Rijn**), WESTERN EUROPE
A river whose Latin name Rhenus came from the Rheni, people who lived along its banks.

Rhinelander, WISCONSIN/USA
Named after F. W. Rhinelander, president of the Milwaukee, Lakeshore, and Western Railroad.

Rhineland-Palatinate (Rheinland-Pfalz),
GERMANY
A state formed in 1946 with a name taken from the Rhine River and the Palatinate, a former state on the Rhine and later part of Bavaria, west of the river. A palatinate was a province that belonged to a palatine, an officer of the palace. The Palatine was the principal hill of the seven hills of Rome and, according to tradition, the first to be settled. It became the favoured area of Rome for the wealthy; it thus gave its name to the word 'palace'. At various times the German Palatinate was divided into the Upper Palatinate and the Lower Palatinate; the present Rhineland-Palatinate represents a part of the Lower Palatinate.

Rhode Island, USA
A state whose official title is the State of Rhode Island and Providence Plantations. In 1524 Giovanni da Verrazzano (1485–1528), an Italian navigator, explored the eastern coast of North America. He came across *Block Island, one of the islands of the state, which he considered resembled the island of Rhodes in the Mediterranean; he called it Rhode Island. However, Adriaen Block, a Dutch explorer, visited the island in 1614 and called it Roodt

Eylandt 'Red Island' because of its red clay. This was subsequently Anglicized to 'Rhode', possibly with the Mediterranean island also in mind. In 1636 the first settlers from Massachusetts arrived at what is now Providence on the mainland and two years later the island of Aquidneck in Narrangansett Bay was bought from local Native Americans. The settlers thought, mistakenly, that this island was the one referred to by Verrazzano and therefore called it Rhode Island. The state now comprises these and other islands and the mainland. It was the thirteenth state to join the Union in 1790.

Rhodes (Ródos), GREECE
An island and its capital. The name may be derived from the Phoenician *erod* 'snake' in recognition of the fact that the island used to be infested with snakes. Alternatively, it may come from the Greek *ródon* 'rose'. It is the site of one of the Seven Wonders of the Ancient World, the Colossus of Rhodes, a bronze statue more than 100ft (30m) high dedicated to the sun god Helios to commemmorate the raising of a long siege. It was built in *c.*292–280 BC, but was destroyed by an earthquake *c.*224 BC. Occupied by many invaders, the island was ceded to Greece in 1947.

Rhodesia *See* ZAMBIA AND ZIMBABWE.
Rhodesia was named after Cecil Rhodes[†]. In 1889 he established the British South Africa Company and it came to control what is now Zambia and Zimbabwe, but in 1894 was named Rhodesia. In 1900 the Rhodesia Protectorate, as it was called, was divided into North Western Rhodesia, North Eastern Rhodesia, both lying north of the Zambezi River, and Southern Rhodesia. In 1911 the first two became Northern Rhodesia. Northern and Southern Rhodesia, together with Nyasaland (now Malawi), formed the Central African Federation of Rhodesia and Nyasaland in 1953–63. Southern Rhodesia became Rhodesia in 1964 when Northern Rhodesia was renamed Zambia on independence. Rhodesia became Zimbabwe when it gained independence in 1980.

Rhodope Mountains (Bulgarian: **Rodopi**; Greek: **Orosirá Rodhópis**), BULGARIA-GREECE
Mainly in Bulgaria, the mountain system is said, in Greek mythology, to be named after Rhodope, wife of Haemus, King of Thrace. She was changed into this mountain form because she believed herself to be more beautiful than Juno.

Rhondda, WALES/UK *Rotheni*
'(Place on the) River Rhondda' whose name means 'Noisy One' from the Welsh *rhoddni*.

Rhyl, WALES/UK *Ryhull, Yrhill, Rhyll*
'(Place by) the Hill' from the Welsh *yr* 'the' and the Middle English *hyll* 'hill'.

Ribeira Grande, CAPE VERDE, PORTUGAL
'Big River'.

Ribeirão Prêto, SÃO PAULO/BRAZIL *Entre Rios, São Sebastião do Ribeirão Prêto*
Founded in 1856 on the Prêto River, the Portuguese name means 'Black River', a reference to the Prêto, from *ribeirão* 'stream' or 'river' and *preto* 'black'. A tributary of the Pardo River, its original name meant 'Between Rivers' and it was then renamed 'St Sebastian of the Black River'.

Richards Bay (Zulu: **Cwebeni**), KWAZULU-NATAL/SOUTH AFRICA
Named after the bay, itself named after Admiral of the Fleet Sir Frederick Richards (1833–1912), commander of the British forces against the Zulus here in 1879 and later 1st lord of the admiralty (1893–9). The Zulu name means 'At the Lagoon'.

Richard Toll, SENEGAL
'Richard's Garden', a reference to a French planter who was invited to lay out an ornamental garden on the left bank of the Senegal River. The Wolof *toll* means 'garden'.

Richelieu, CANADA, FRANCE
Canada (Quebec): a town and a river named in 1642 on the death of Cardinal de Richelieu (1585–1642), chief minister (1624–42) of Louis XIII, King of France (1610–43).

Richland, WASHINGTON/USA
Named after Nelson Rich, a local landowner, in 1905.

Richmond, AUSTRALIA, CANADA, JAMAICA, NEW ZEALAND, ST VINCENT, SOUTH AFRICA, UK, USA
1. Australia (New South Wales): named in 1789 after Charles Lennox (1764–1819), 4th Duke of Richmond and Lennox, later governor-general of British North America (1818–19).
2. Canada (Ontario and Quebec): named after the 4th Duke of Richmond and Lennox.
3. New Zealand (South Island): named after the Richmond in Greater London.
4. South Africa (KwaZulu-Natal): founded in 1850 as Beaulieu, it was renamed after the 4th Duke of Richmond and Lennox.
5. South Africa (Northern Cape): founded in 1844 and named after the 4th Duke of Richmond and Lennox, father-in-law of Sir Peregrine Maitland (1777–1854), governor of Cape Colony (1844–7).
6. UK (Greater London/England): formerly called Sceon and Sheen 'Shelters', it was

r

renamed Richemount in 1502 by Henry VII (1457–1509), King of England (1485–1509), when he rebuilt a palace which had been burnt down in 1501. He chose this name because before becoming king he had been the Earl of Richmond, after the town in Yorkshire. The full name of this town is Richmond upon Thames.
7. UK (Yorkshire/England): formerly Richemund, the name means 'Strong Hill' from the Old French *riche* and *mont*.
8. USA (Indiana): settled in 1806 as Smithville and renamed in 1818, allegedly because of the rich character of the soil.
9. USA (Kentucky): settled in 1784 and named after the city in Virginia.
10. USA (Virginia): originally a trading post established in 1637, it was named by William Byrd after his home town, Richmond in Greater London, in 1733; additionally, he may have thought that the Virginian town on the James River resembled the Richmond on the River Thames.

Rickmansworth, ENGLAND/UK
Prichemareworde, Richemaresworthe
'Enclosure of a Man (possibly) called Rīcmær' from an Old English personal name and *worth* 'enclosure' or 'enclosed settlement'.

Ridder, KAZAKHSTAN *Ridder, Leninogorsk*
Until 1941 the city was named after Philip Ridder, an Englishman who discovered a mine containing gold, silver, copper, and lead in 1786. Poor relations between the Soviet Union and the UK in 1941 (before the two countries became allies after the German attack on the Soviet Union in June 1941) caused the city to be renamed after Vladimir Lenin[†], with the Russian *gorsk* related here to *gornyy* 'mining'; it is located in the south-western Altay Mountains. In 2002 the name was changed back to Ridder.

Ridings, The, ENGLAND/UK
The name used for three administrative divisions in Yorkshire until 1974 (and still used locally), the North Riding, the West Riding, and the East Riding. In the Domesday Book of 1086 their names were Nortreding, Westreding, and Estreding respectively. The name comes from the Old Scandinavian *thrithjungr* 'third part'.

Rif, MOROCCO
See ER RIF.

Riga, INDIA, LATVIA
Latvia: founded in 1201, the name may be derived from *rija* 'barn' or 'warehouse'. The Vikings constructed such buildings to store their warlike materials for further attacks inland. German merchants may then have changed the *j* to the hard *g*. Alternatively, it

may come from the Old Latvian *rĩnga* 'curve', a reference to the bend in the Daugava River on which the city lies. Another explanation is that the name comes from the Ridzeme River which was filled in over 100 years ago. It has been the Latvian capital since 1918.

Riihimäki, FINLAND
A name which comes from *riihi* 'granary' or 'loft' and *mäki* 'hill' or 'slope'.

Rijeka, CROATIA *Tarsatica, Trsat, Rika, Fiume*
The Italian Fiume and Croatian Rijeka both mean 'River', a reference to the Riječina (known as the Fiumara or Eneo in Italian). In 1920, under the terms of the Treaty of Versailles, Fiume became a free state linked to Italy by a strip of land and in 1924 Benito Mussolini (1883–1945), Italian prime minister (1922–43), annexed it to Italy. Only in 1945 did the entire city pass to the Croats as part of Yugoslavia.

Rimavská Sobota, SLOVAKIA *Gross Steffelsdorf*
Situated on the Rimava River, it was originally a town which held a market on *Sobota* 'Saturday'. It is not certain from what Rimava may be derived; perhaps from the Old Slavonic *rym* 'tree trunk' or the Latin *rumor* 'noisy'. Thus the place-name could mean '(Settlement on) the River with many Trees' or '(Settlement on) the noisy River' with the additional 'where markets are held on Saturdays'.

Rimouski, QUEBEC/CANADA
A river and a city which may be derived from a Micmac word meaning 'Land of the Moose'.

Ringkøbing, DENMARK *Rennumkøpingh*
A county and a small town with a name derived from the parish of Rindum and *købing* 'market'.

Rio Branco, ACRE/BRAZIL
Takes its name from the Rio Branco 'White River' which flows into the Acre River here.

Rio Claro, SÃO PAULO/BRAZIL *São João Batista da Beira do Ribeirão Claro, São João Batista do Morro Azul*
'Clear River' in Portuguese. It was originally known as 'St John the Baptist of the Clear River', referring to the River Jordan in which St John baptized Jesus; it was later also called 'St John the Baptist of the Blue Hill'.

Rio de Janeiro, BRAZIL *Cidade de São Sebastião do Rio de Janeiro*
A state formed in 1975 and named after the city which was founded in 1565 and called the 'City of St Sebastian of Rio de Janeiro'; Sebastian for the 3rd-century saint and also for Sebastian (1554–78), King of Portugal (1557–78), who died during an anti-Muslim crusade in Morocco. The city was named after

the bay which was called Rio de Janeiro 'River of January' by Portuguese explorers who thought that the bay they had sailed into on 1 January 1502 was actually the mouth of a river. The city became the Portuguese colonial capital in 1763, of the united kingdom of Portugal and Brazil in 1816, and of Brazil when independence was achieved in 1822; it remained so until 1960 when the capital was transferred to Brasília. The city is commonly referred to as Rio.

Río Gallegos, ARGENTINA
A city founded in 1885 and named after Blasco Gallegos, a pilot used by the Portuguese explorer, Ferdinand Magellan[†]. Gallegos is said to have discovered the river, which is also named after him, in 1520.

Rio Grande, BRAZIL, NORTH AMERICA
1. Brazil: a river and a city-port founded in 1737. Brazil has two states called Rio Grande do Norte 'Big River of the North' and Rio Grande do Sul 'Big River of the South'.
2. North America: a river which forms a large part of the border between the USA and Mexico. Its Spanish name means simply 'Big River' while in Mexico it is known as the Río Bravo 'Wild River'.

Río Muni, EQUATORIAL GUINEA
The continental part of the country which takes its name from the Spanish río 'river' and a version of a local word for 'quiet'. Thus it means 'Quiet River' and probably refers to the Mbini which flows through it.

Río Negro, ARGENTINA
A province meaning 'Black River' and named after the Negro River which flows through it.

Ripon, CANADA, UK, USA
1. UK (England): formerly Hrypis and Ripun '(Place belonging to) the tribe called the Hrype', Ripon being derived from the dative plural of the tribal name.
2. USA (Wisconsin): settled as Ceresco after Ceres, the Roman goddess of agriculture, in 1844 and later named after the English city.

Rishon Le-Ziyyon, ISRAEL
Founded by Russian Jews, the first Jewish immigrants from Europe, in 1882 with a Hebrew name meaning 'First to Zion'. This is associated with the Bible (Isaiah 41: 27).

Rivers, NIGERIA
A state since 1967 and named because of its many rivers and mangrove swamps.

Riversdale, WESTERN CAPE/SOUTH AFRICA
Founded in 1838 and named after Harry Rivers, the local commissioner and magistrate.

Riverhead, CANADA, NEW ZEALAND, USA
USA (New York): named because of its location near the head (mouth) of the Peconic River.

Riverside, CALIFORNIA/USA *Jurupa*
Laid out in 1870 on the banks of the Santa Ana River and subsequently renamed to recognize its situation.

Riverton, CANADA, NEW ZEALAND, USA
USA (Wyoming): founded in 1906 as Wadsworth and later renamed because of its location near the junction of four rivers.

Riviera, FRANCE-ITALY
The coastal region between Cannes in France and La Spezia in Italy. The name is Italian and means simply 'Coast' or 'Seashore'. The French section is known as the *Côte d'Azur; the Italian Riviera is divided into the Riviera di Ponente 'West Coast', west of Genoa, and the Riviera di Levante 'East Coast', east of Genoa. A 'riviera' has now come to mean any popular stretch of coastline.

Rivière-du-Loup, QUEBEC/CANADA *Fraserville*
Settled in 1834, it was renamed in 1919 after the Wolf River from the French *loup* 'wolf', which was given this name because of the numerous wolves which used to roam the area.

Rivne, UKRAINE *Rovno*
A province and a city founded as a Polish settlement on the Ust'ye River. In 1795 the area passed to Russia at the third partition of Poland, but was returned to Poland in 1920–39. Both the former Russian name and the present Ukrainian one mean 'Flat' or 'Level' from the Russian *rovnyy*.

Rivoli, PIEDMONT/ITALY
Possibly derived from the Latin *ripula*, the diminutive of *ripa* 'bank of a stream'.

Riyadh (ar-Riyāḍ), SAUDI ARABIA
The presence of underground water in an oasis in a fertile wadi encouraged small settlements from which the present city grew. Its name means 'The Meadows' from *riyāḍ*, the plural of *rawḍa* 'meadow'. It was chosen as the principal city of the Saʿūd dynasty in 1824 and became the capital of the Kingdom of Saudi Arabia on its creation in 1932.

Rizal, LUZON/PHILIPPINES
Two places have this name in honour of José Rizal (1861–96), a national hero who inspired the Filipino national movement and was publicly executed by the Spanish for sedition.

Rkiz, MAURITANIA
A lake with a name meaning 'End' in the sense that the local rivers end here.

Road Town, TORTOLA/BRITISH VIRGIN ISLANDS
Takes its name from the roads offshore.
Roads or roadstead are nautical terms
meaning a sheltered area where ships may
lie at anchor.

Roanne, RHÔNE-ALPES/FRANCE *Rodumna*
Situated on the Loire River, the Roman name
probably comes from the Celtic root element
rod 'water' or 'river'.

Roanoke, USA
1. An island off the coast of North Carolina, a
river rising in Virginia and flowing through
North Carolina into the Atlantic, and five cities
have this name which is said to be an
Algonquian word meaning a 'place where
shells are found' or a 'place where shells are
used for money'. Also in North Carolina is a
city called Roanoke Rapids.
2. Virginia: settled in 1740 it was given the
name Big Lick in 1874 before being renamed
Roanoke in 1882.

Robben Island (Afrikaans: **Robbeneiland**),
WESTERN CAPE/SOUTH AFRICA
'Seals Island' from the Dutch *rob* 'seal', a
reference to the numerous seals that once
used to inhabit these waters. It became a
Dutch penal colony during the second half of
the 17th century.

Robertsport, LIBERIA
Named after Joseph Jenkins Roberts (1809–76),
a born-free American who was the first black
governor of Liberia (1842–7) and first president
(1848–56, 1872–6).

Roberval, QUEBEC/CANADA
Settled in 1855 and named after Jean-François
de la Rocque (*c*.1500–60/1), Sieur de Roberval,
the first Viceroy of Canada (1542–3).

Roca, Cape (**Cabo da Roca**), PORTUGAL
Promontorium Magnum
The westernmost point of mainland Europe,
the Roman name means the 'Great
Promontory'. The present name is 'Cape Rock'
from *roca* 'rock'.

Rochdale, UK, USA
UK (England): formerly Recedham,
Rachedham, and Rachedal 'Valley of the (River)
Roch' from the river name and the Old
Scandinavian *dalr* 'valley'. The river's name,
originally Rached, is a back-formation from
Recedham 'Homestead with a Hall' from the
Old English *reced* 'hall' and *hām*. The river
valley became known as Rached-dale and then
Rachedale; and eventually Rochdale appeared
as the name of the town.

Rochefort, BELGIUM, FRANCE
France (Poitou-Charentes): the castle built here
on the banks of the Charente River as a
defence against Norman invaders gives the
place its name. This comes from the pre-Latin
rocca 'rock' and the Latin *fortis* 'powerful' or
'strong'.

Rochester, AUSTRALIA, CANADA, UK, USA
1. UK (Kent/England): the original Roman
name, Durobrivae 'Walled Town at the
Bridges', came from the Celtic *duro* 'walled
town' or 'fort' and *briva*. The fact that it was
a Roman town shows up in the *caestir*,
cestre, and *chester* of the later names of
Hrofaescaestir, Rovecestre, and now
Rochester. When the name passed to the
English the first syllable of Durobrivae was
lost, leaving *ro* as the first syllable of the new
name. An initial *H* was gained and in time the
name became Hrofi with the additional *caestir*.
Thus the name means '(Roman) Town, or Fort,
called Hrofi'.
2. UK (Northumberland/England): formerly
Rucestr and Rouschestr, possibly meaning
'Rough (Roman) Earthwork, or Fort' from the
Old English *rūh* 'rough' and *ceaster*.
3. USA (Minnesota): settled in 1854 and named
after Rochester, New York.
4. USA (New Hampshire): named in 1722 after
Lawrence Hyde (1641–1711), 1st Earl of
Rochester, who was a friend of the governor of
New Hampshire and he named the city after
the earl.
5. USA (New York): founded as Rochesterville
in 1811 and named after Colonel Nathaniel
Rochester (1752–1831), the principal
landowner. The name was shortened in 1822.

Rochford, UK, USA
UK (England): 'Ford of the Hunting Dog' from
the Old English *ræcc* 'hunting dog' and *ford*. In
Essex it was formerly known as Rochefort and
in Worcestershire as Recesford.

Rockford, ILLINOIS/USA *Midway*
Founded in 1834 with a name that
acknowledged that it was halfway between
Chicago and Galena. It was later renamed for
the ford across the Rock River.

Rockhampton, QUEENSLAND/AUSTRALIA
Gracemere Station
Laid out in 1858 on a small settlement
founded in 1855 and named after the rock
formations in the Fitzroy River and Hampton
in England.

Rockland, CANADA, USA
USA (Maine): originally part of Thomaston, it
became a town in its own right as East

Thomaston in 1848. It was renamed Rockland in 1850 because of its local quarries.

Rocky Mount, NORTH CAROLINA/USA
Founded in 1816 and named after its rocky mounds and ridges.

Rodez, MIDI-PYRÉNÉES/FRANCE *Ruthena, Segodunum*
Derived from the early Roman name which came from a local tribe, the Ruteni. They also called it Segodunum from the Gaulish *sego* 'strength' and *dunu*.

Rodniki, KAZAKHSTAN, RUSSIA
'Springs' from the Russian *rodník'*.

Rohtak, HARYĀNA/INDIA *Rohtasgarh*
Founded as 'Fort of Rohtas' by, and named after, Raja Rohtas from the personal name and *garh*.

Roi Et, THAILAND
'101', a reference to the number of gates. It was somewhat of an exaggeration, since there were only eleven.

Rokkō, HONSHŪ/JAPAN
A mountain, Rokkō-san, with the name 'Six Hills' from *roku* 'six' and *kō* 'hill'.

Roma, AUSTRALIA, LESOTHO, ZAMBIA
1. Australia (Queensland): named after Lady Diamantina Roma Bowen, wife of Queensland's first governor, Sir George Bowen.
2. Lesotho: founded in 1862 as a Roman Catholic mission station and named in 1877 after the Italian city Roma (*see* ROME).

Roman, BULGARIA, ROMANIA
Romania: founded by, and named after, Roman Musat, the ruling prince of Moldavia (1392–4).

Romania Romania (România) since 1989. Previously the Socialist Republic of Romania (1965–89), the People's Republic of Romania (1947–65), and the Kingdom of Romania (1881–1947). After the two autonomous principalities of Wallachia and Moldavia had chosen the same man, Prince Alexandru Ion Cuza (1820–73), as their prince in 1859, the new state was created in 1861, taking the name Romania the next year; independence from the Ottoman Empire was achieved in 1878. The name comes from the Romans; some members of the Roman legions settled in Dacia (which became a Roman province in 106 and now comprises northern and central Romania), after Trajan[†] had subdued the region. They intermarried with the Dacians.

Romans-sur Isère, RHÔNES-ALPES/FRANCE
Villa Romanis
Derived from the personal name Romanus 'Roman' with Isère, the river on which the town lies, added to distinguish this particular town.

Rome, ITALY, USA
1. Italy: Italian Roma. According to the famous legend, Romulus and his twin brother Remus, sons of the war god Mars and Rhea Silvia, resolved to found a new settlement on the hills above the river where their lives had been saved in 753 BC by a she-wolf. They could not agree as to who should be the governor. As Romulus was building the wall to surround the city—rather a hut village—Remus disobeyed the order not to cross it and was killed. Named after Romulus, the city was founded on the Palatine, the chief hill of Rome, and began to increase its population by offering asylum to refugees and providing wives by arranging the abduction (or rape as the legend has it) of the Sabine women. However, this is no more than a romantic story; Romulus and Remus were mythical figures. The city's name may come from an Etruscan or Greek word—possibly from the Greek *rhome* 'strong'. Alternatively the name may come from Rumo, Ruma, or Roma, one of the ancient names of the River Tiber on which the city lies. It was the capital of the Roman Republic in 509–44 BC and of the Roman Empire in 31 BC–AD 402. Commodus (161–92), Roman emperor (180–92), had it called Colonia Commodiana 'Colony of Commodus' until he was strangled. Sacked and occupied by a succession of invaders, it was under absolute papal rule between 1420 and 1870 when it joined the Kingdom of Italy and became its capital. It has given its name to the Romance group of European languages (mainly French, Italian, Portuguese, Romanian, and Spanish), all derived from Latin, as a result of the Roman occupation of Western Europe and Romania. The English word is derived from the Old French *romanz* from Latin Romanicus to mean the speech of the people, i.e. the vernacular as opposed to classical Latin. A 'romance' was originally a novel written in the vernacular before the meaning changed to indicate the type of work rather than the language.
2. USA (Georgia): built on seven hills like its counterpart in Italy; hence the name.
3. USA (New York): the Native American name was De-O-Wain-Sta 'The Carrying Place'. This referred to the fact that it was on the only practical water route south of the St Lawrence River which connected the Great Lakes and

r

the Hudson River. Although fortified by the British in 1725, it was not until 1758 that Fort Stanwix was built. In 1786 it was renamed Lynchville after Dominic Lynch who surveyed it. It assumed the name Rome in 1819, when it became a village, in recognition of its defence of the Republic. That was a reference to the Battle of Oriskany, called 'the bloodiest battle of the Revolution', when the British were stopped in their tracks a few miles away on 6 August 1777.

Romeo, MICHIGAN/USA
Named in 1838 after the suggestion of Laura Taylor that the name should be 'short, musical, classical, and uncommon'.

Rommani, MOROCCO *Camp Marchand, Marchand*
During French rule the town was named after Jean-Baptiste Marchand, a French officer and explorer who travelled from Brazzaville in the Republic of the Congo to Fashoda (now Kodok) in The Sudan in 1897. The present name comes from the Arabic *ar-rummāni* 'the pomegranate tree'.

Romsey, ENGLAND/UK *Rummæsig, Romesy*
'Raised, or dry, Ground in a Marsh belonging to a Man called Rūm' from an Old English personal name and *ēg* 'raised ground in a marsh'.

Romulus, MICHIGAN/USA
Named after the legendary founder of Rome, Italy.

Roncevalles, NAVARRE/SPAIN
'Valleys abundant with Brambles' from the French *ronce* 'bramble' and *vallée* 'valley'.

Rondônia, BRAZIL *Guaporé*
A state established as a territory in 1943 and renamed in 1956 after Marshal Cândido Mariano da Silva Rondon (1865–1958), an explorer who did much to protect the Native Americans by founding the Indian Protection Service in 1910. The territory was upgraded to a state in 1982.

Roodeport, GAUTENG/SOUTH AFRICA
'Red Gate' in Afrikaans, the name of the farm with its red soil from which the town developed in 1888.

Rooiberg, FREE STATE/SOUTH AFRICA
'Red Mountains' in Afrikaans and so named because of the russet colour of their winter grasslands.

Roosendal, THE NETHERLANDS
'Valley of Roses' from the Dutch *roos* 'rose' and *dal* 'valley'.

Rosario, ARGENTINA, BRAZIL, COSTA RICA, MEXICO, PARAGUAY, PHILIPPINES, PUERTO RICO, URUGUAY, VENEZUELA
Argentina: founded in 1689 as a villa which later became a settlement called Pago de los Arroyos 'Region of the Rivers'. In 1725 it was renamed Rosario 'Rosary'. The town in Brazil has the Portuguese spelling: Rosário.

Roscommon, IRELAND, USA
1. Ireland: a county and a town with the Irish name of Ros Comáin meaning 'Comán's Wood'. St Comán established a monastery here in the 7th century.
2. USA (Michigan): named in 1843 after the county in Ireland by Irish immigrants.

Roseau, DOMINICA, ST LUCIA, USA
Dominica: formerly Charlotte Town, it is now the capital with a French name meaning 'Reed' in the sense of coarse grass that used to grow here.

Rosebery, AUSTRALIA, CANADA
Australia (Tasmania): founded *c.*1900 following the discovery of gold in the area and named after Archibald Primrose (1847–1929), 5th Earl of Rosebery, British prime minister (1894–5), when the gold was discovered.

Roseburg, OREGON/USA *Deer Creek*
Settled in 1851 and renamed in 1854 after Aaron Rose, one of the first settlers, who laid out the town.

Rosetta (Rashīd), EGYPT
Founded *c.*800 by, and named after, Hārūn ar-Rashīd (*c.*766–809), fifth caliph of the 'Abbāsid dynasty. Rosetta is the Anglicized form of the Arabic name. The 'Rosetta Stone', which allowed ancient Egyptian hieroglyphics to be deciphered, was found by a French officer just to the north in 1799.

Rosh Pinna, ISRAEL
'Cornerstone' in Hebrew. It was founded in 1882 as the first cooperative farming settlement in Galilee.

Roskilde, DENMARK *Roschald, Roschilde*
A county and town allegedly founded by, and named after, Hroar (or Rōir) and the *kilde* 'springs' nearby, thus 'Hroar's Spring' . It was the seat of the Danish kings from *c.*1020 and the Danish capital until 1443.

Ross, ANTARCTICA, AUSTRALIA, NEW ZEALAND, UK, USA
Antarctica: the Ross Dependency, Ross Ice Shelf, Ross Island, and Ross Sea are all named after the Scottish polar explorer and naval officer, Sir James Ross (1800–62), who carried out an expedition to the Antarctic in 1839–43.

Ross and Cromarty, SCOTLAND/UK
A former county and district with Ross coming from the Gaelic *ros* 'moorland' or 'promontory' and Cromarty from the town of that name. Its name means 'Crooked (Place)', a reference to the jagged coastline.

Rosslare (Ros Láir), IRELAND
'Middle Promontory' from *ros* 'promontory'.

Rostock, MECKLENBURG-WEST POMERANIA/
GERMANY *Rostochium, Rostek, Roztoc*
Lying at the head of the Warnow River estuary, the name is said to mean either 'Great Width at the Mouth of the River' or 'Fork in the River'.

Rostov, YAROSLAVL'/RUSSIA *Rostov Velíkiy, Rostov-Yaroslavskiy*
The original name meant 'Rostov the Great', a title bestowed upon it in the 12th century because it was the capital of the principality of Rostov; it was named after Prince Rotislav. However, it lost its title in the 17th century when its power declined with the transfer of its religious authority to Yaroslavl'. It then became known as 'Rostov near Yaroslavl'.

Rostov-on-Don (Rostov-na-Donu), ROSTOV/
RUSSIA *Temerníka*
Founded in 1749 and renamed in 1761 after the fortress-church dedicated to St Dmitry, Bishop of Rostov Velikiy (*see* ROSTOV). In 1806 it was renamed Rostov-on-(the River) Don to distinguish it from the older Rostov. Rostov is the name of a province in southern Russia.

Rotherham, NEW ZEALAND, UK
UK (England): formerly Rodreham 'Homestead on the (River) Rother' from the river name meaning 'chief river' and *hām*.

Rothesay, CANADA, UK
1. Canada (New Brunswick): named after the Duke of Cornwall and Rothesay, one of the titles of the Prince of Wales who later became Edward VII, King of the United Kingdom of Great Britain and Ireland (1901–10).
2. UK (Scotland): formerly Rothersay 'Rother's Island', Rother referring to Roderick who received the grant of Bute in the 13th century; and the additional *ey*.

Rotorua, NORTH ISLAND/NEW ZEALAND
A city founded in the early 1870s and named after Lake Rotorua whose Maori name means 'Second Lake' from *roto* 'lake' and *rua* 'two' or 'second'. It is said that it was so named by a traveller as he went along the Kaituna River; the first was Lake Rotoiti 'Small Lake'. However, this may be a convenient invention to justify claims to the area by the local tribe.

Rotterdam, THE NETHERLANDS, USA
1. The Netherlands: '(Place by a) Dam on the Rotte (River)'. It originated as a fishing village in the 13th century.
2. USA (New York): founded by the Dutch in the 17th century and named after the Dutch city.

Rottnest Island, WESTERN AUSTRALIA/
AUSTRALIA
'Rat's Nest Island' from the Dutch *rottenest*. The island was seen in 1696 by Dutch explorers to be overrun with *quokka*, the local name for small wallabies. These looked like large rats, hence the name given to the island by Captain Willem de Vlamingh or by a naval clerk some time later.

Rottweil, BADEN-WÜRTTEMBERG/GERMANY *Arae Flaviae*
The Roman name may have meant the 'Altar-like Monuments of Flavia' from the Latin *ara* 'altar'. The present name may mean the 'Camp of a Company (of troops)' from *rotte* 'company' or 'file' and *weiler* 'camp' or 'settlement'. It has given its name to the Rottweiler, a working dog left here by the departing Roman legions.

Roubaix, NORD-PAS-DE-CALAIS/FRANCE
'A Stream in the Plain' from *ros* or *ross* 'swampy plain' and *bach* or *bais* 'stream'.

Rouen, UPPER NORMANDY/FRANCE *Rotomagus*
The present name is derived from its former Roman name which may have meant the 'Market of Roto' from the Gaulish *mago* 'market' or 'field' and a personal name.

Rovaniemi, FINLAND
A compound name whose meaning is not certain, although *niemi* means 'cape' or 'headland'. The name may be of Lapp origin from *roavve* 'forested ridge' or 'site of an old forest fire' in Sami. However, in some southern Lapland dialects, *rova* means a 'heap of stones' or a 'group of rocks in rapids'.

Rovereto, TRENTINO-ALTO ADIGE/ITALY
Derived from the Medieval Latin *roboretum* 'oak grove' from *robur* 'oak (of a particularly hard kind)'.

Rovigo, VENETO/ITALY *Rodigo*
Derived from the personal Germanic name Hrodico.

Royal Oak, IRELAND, USA
USA (Michigan): settled in 1819 and said to have been named after an oak tree, but which one is not clear. It may be one in England under which Charles II[†] sheltered after his defeat at the Battle of Worcester in 1651. Alternatively, it may be one in Scotland under which Charles Edward the Young Pretender

(also known as Bonnie Prince Charlie) (1720–88) hid during the Jacobite rebellion in 1745.

Rubezhnoye, RUSSIA, UKRAINE
Ukraine: locally Rubizhne. The Russian *rubezh* means a line or geographical feature that demarcates something, often an administrative border. Founded as Rus'ko-Kraska in 1915 on the site of an earlier settlement, it was renamed Chervonyy Prapor 'Red Banner' in 1923 before assuming versions of the present name in 1930 and again c.1940.

Rubicon, ITALY, USA
Italy (Emilia-Romagna): a small river, originally the Rubico and now locally the Rubicone, that was the ancient boundary between Cisalpine Gaul and Italy during the time of the Roman Republic (509–44 BC). By crossing it with his forces in 49 BC, Julius Caesar[†] emerged from the province of which he had been given command, thus breaking the law; this was tantamount to an invasion of Italy and a challenge to the Roman Senate. Civil war ensued and brought the republic to an end. The name comes from the Latin *rubicundus* 'red' or 'ruddy', a reference to the colour of the soil here. 'To cross the Rubicon' is an English expression meaning 'a point from which there is no turning back', 'an irreversible commitment'.

Ruda, POLAND
'Ore', a reference to the deposits here. A smaller place, Ruda Śląska, means 'Silesian Ore'.

Rudnichnyy, RUSSIA
Towns in Kirov and Sverdlovsk Provinces have this name that acknowledges their locations close to iron ore deposits from *ruda* 'ore'.

Rudnik, BULGARIA, POLAND, SERBIA AND MONTENEGRO
'Mine' in the three Slav languages.

Rudnyy, KAZAKHSTAN, RUSSIA
Russia (Primorskiy): founded as Lifudzin in 1957 and subsequently given a name similar to *Rudnichnyy for the same reason.

Rudolf, Lake, ETHIOPIA-KENYA
Also called Lake Turkana in Kenya after the local Turkana people. In 1888 the Hungarian Count Samuel Teleki and the Austrian Lieutenant Ludwig von Höhnel visited the lake and named it after Archduke Rudolf (1858–89), Habsburg Crown Prince of Austria, who committed suicide at Mayerling with his mistress the following year.

Rudolph Island (Ostrov Rudol'fa), FRANZ JOSEF LAND/RUSSIA
Named after the Archduke Rudolph (see previous entry). He was the only son of Franz Josef I, Emperor of Austria. *See* FRANZ JOSEF LAND.

Rueil-Malmaison, PARIS/FRANCE *Rotoialum*
The first part comes from the Latin name from the Gaulish *roto* 'ford' or 'crossing'. The second part comes directly from the castle built here in 1622 and called Malmaison 'Bad House', thus 'House of Ill-Fortune' from *maison* 'house'.

Rugby, UK, USA
UK (England): formerly Rocheberie and Rokebi 'Hrōca's Fortified Place, or Fort' from an Old English personal name and *burh* which was later replaced with *bý* by the Danes. The game of rugby football originated in 1823 at Rugby School when one of the players, William Webb Ellis (1805–72), picked up the ball and ran with it during a game of football.

Rugeley, ENGLAND/UK *Rugelei, Ruggelega*
'Woodland Clearing on, or near, a Ridge' from the Old English *hrycg* 'ridge' and *lēah* 'woodland clearing'.

Ruhr, NORTH RHINE-WESTPHALIA/GERMANY
A large industrial region which takes its name from the River Ruhr. Its name comes from the Indo-European root element *reu* 'to hollow out', a reference to its course.

Ruijin, JIANGXI/CHINA *Xianghu*
'Rich Metal' from *rui* 'auspicious' and *jīn* 'metal'. The name was first mentioned in 904 when a precious metal, possibly gold since *jīn* can also mean 'gold', was discovered here. In 953 it became Ruijin County. In 1931 the first Communist Party *soviet* 'council' and Red Army command centre in China were established here and the city was renamed Ruijing 'Auspicious Capital' from *jīng* 'capital'. Ruijin was readopted in 1994.

Rumelia, BALKANS
The territory of the Ottoman Turks in the Balkans and called by them Rūmeli 'Land of the Rūm (Romans)', that is, the Byzantines; Muslims called the Byzantines the Rūm. The territory comprised Thrace, Macedonia, and Albania.

Runcorn, AUSTRALIA, UK
UK (England): formerly Rumfocan. On the southern bank of the River Mersey, the name means 'Wide Bay' from the Old English *rūm* 'wide' or 'roomy' and *cofa* 'bay' or 'cove'.

Runnymede, ENGLAND/UK *Ronimede*
A historic site where the Magna Carta 'Great Charter' was drafted and signed by John (1167–

1216), King of England (1199–1216), in June
1215. The name means 'Council Island
Meadow' from the Old English *rūn* 'council', *ēg*,
and *mǣd* 'meadow'. The site, the island and the
meadow, was clearly a place where important
meetings took place.

Rupert, QUEBEC/CANADA
A river discovered by Henry Hudson (*c.*1565–
1611), an English explorer, in 1610 and named
after Prince Rupert (1619–82), son of the elector
of the Palatinate and first governor of the
Hudson's Bay Company from 1670. He was a
cavalry leader under his uncle, King Charles I[†],
and an admiral in the service of King Charles II[†].

Rupert's Land, CANADA
Also called Prince Rupert's Land, a historic
region in northern and western Canada,
granted to the Hudson's Bay Company in 1670
and named after Prince Rupert (see previous
entry). It was bought by Canada in 1869.

Ruse, BULGARIA *Sexantaprista, Rusçuk/Rustchuk,*
Chervena
Founded as a protected harbour by the Romans
in the 1st century BC and called Sexantaprista
'(Harbour for) Sixty Ships'. The Ottoman Turks
built a new military base and called it Rusçuk
from which the present name is derived. It
may be associated with *rus* 'fair' or 'blond'
while *cherven* means 'red', both possibly
referring to hair colour. It is also a district
which until 1993 was called Razgrad. It is
sometimes spelt Rousse.

Russell, CANADA, NEW ZEALAND, USA
New Zealand (North Island): while still known
by its Maori name, it was chosen in 1840 to be
the first capital of New Zealand and renamed
as a tribute to Lord John Russell (1792–1878),
1st Earl Russell, British secretary of state for
the colonies and war (1839–41), during which
time New Zealand became a separate crown
colony, and prime minister (1846–52, 1865–6).
The following year, however, the capital was
moved south to Auckland. The original name,
Okiato, came from the Maori *o* 'place' and *kiato*
'receptacle for sacred objects'. Okiato
extended into the area called Kororareka, the
name used by the early Europeans before
Russell was adopted; it came from *korora*
'penguin' and *reka* 'sweet', referring to the
taste.

Rüsselsheim, HESSE/GERMANY *Rusilesheim*
Founded by, and named after, Ruzilo, a
Frankish prince, as 'Ruzilo's Home' from *Heim*
'home'.

Russia (Rossiya) *Rus', Soviet Russia*
The Russian Federation (Rossiyskaya
Federatsiya) since December 1993. *Rossiyskaya*
indicates that the Russian Federation is not a
nation state (otherwise it would have been
Russkaya) but a state that includes many
nations. Previously the Russian Soviet
Federative Socialist Republic, by far the largest
of the fifteen union republics comprising the
Union of Soviet Socialist Republics, commonly
known as the *Soviet Union (1936). Due to a
change in ideological emphasis this title was
adopted in place of the Russian Socialist
Federative Soviet Republic (1918). Following
the Revolution in February 1917 a *Soviet*
'Council of Workers' and Soldiers' Deputies'
was formed in Petrograd (now St Petersburg).
The Provisional Government, also set up in
February 1917, was overthrown in October (the
October Revolution) and power seized by the
Bolsheviks in the name of the Soviets. The
country's name was changed to Soviet Russia.
The Latinate Rossiya was not formally adopted
until Peter I the Great[†] did so when he changed
the name of the Tsardom of Muscovy to the
Empire of All Russia in 1721. According to one
theory, Rus' was the name given to the non-Slav
Vikings (the Varangians) in Scandinavia, who
migrated into the Slav-populated northern
river valleys of Russia in the 9th century; *The
Primary Chronicle* suggests that they were
invited by the quarrelling Slav tribes to come
south and rule over them. The Rus' agreed and
established themselves around Novgorod in
862. The Rus' gave their name to the area in
which they settled. By the beginning of the
10th century Kiev (now in Ukraine) had become
the centre of the first Russian state. However,
The Primary Chronicle is considered to be
unreliable by many Russian scholars; they have
suggested that the Rus' were a Slav tribe from
the south-east who founded the state of Kievan
Rus'; its existence, however, was brought to an
end when it was almost completely destroyed
by the Mongols in 1240. Gradually various
principalities emerged of which the most
important were *Muscovy, Novgorod, and
Galich (Galicia). They expanded to encompass
what is now western Russia, Ukraine, and
Belarus—the Land of the Rus' from which
Russia takes its name. The meaning of the word
Rus' has evoked considerable discussion. It has
been suggested that it comes from *Ruotsi*, the
Finnish word for the Swedes, and therefore
means 'Swedish Vikings'; or that it is a Viking
word meaning 'oarsman'. Both have been
disputed. *See* SOVIET UNION.

Russkoye Ust'ye, SAKHA REPUBLIC/RUSSIA
Polyarnoye
Formerly 'Polar' from *polyarnyy*, it was
renamed 'Russian Mouth' in 1992 from *ust'ye*
'mouth (of a river)' or 'estuary'. It lies within

the Arctic Circle close to the mouth of a river flowing into the East Siberian Sea.

Rustāq, ar-, OMAN
The Arabized version of the Persian *rōstāg* 'village', 'hut encampment' or even 'rural district'. There is also a place called Rostāq in Afghanistan with the same meaning.

Rust'avi, GEORGIA
Derived from *ru* 'canal' or 'stream' and *tavi* 'beginning' or 'source', a reference to the canal which leaves the Kura River here.

Rustenburg, NORTH WEST/SOUTH AFRICA
Founded in 1850 as 'Town of Rest' from the Afrikaans *rust* 'rest' and *burg*. This may refer to the rest and recuperation available here between attacks by local tribes or it may just mean a peaceful place, *rust* having the sense of 'home'.

Ruthenia, UKRAINE
A historic region that takes its name from the Rutheni. This is a Latinized form of *Russian*, although the Ruthenians are Ukrainian; they have, however, been called Little Russians. Part of the Austro-Hungarian Empire (where the Ukrainians were called Ruthenians or Rusyns), it was partitioned between Poland, Czechoslovakia, and Romania in 1918. When Czechoslovakia ceased to exist in March 1939, Ruthenia declared itself to be independent with the name Carpatho-Ukraine. The very next day it was occupied by Hungarian forces and annexed. It was overrun by Soviet forces at the end of the Second World War and incorporated into the Ukrainian Soviet Socialist Republic where it became the Transcarpathian Province.

Rutland, CANADA, UK, USA
1. UK (England): formerly Roteland. A county until 1974 and a unitary district since 1997 with a name meaning 'Rōta's Estate' from an Old English personal name and *land*.
2. USA (Massachusetts): founded in 1714 and named either after the Rutland in England or a Duke of Rutland.
3. USA (Vermont): named after the Rutland in Massachusetts.

Ruwenzori, DEMOCRATIC REPUBLIC OF THE CONGO-UGANDA
A mountain range with a name generally accepted as meaning 'Lord of the Clouds'; its peaks are often hidden by cloud. They are believed to be the same mountains as described by Ptolemy[†].

Ružomberok, SLOVAKIA *Rosenberg*
Founded in the 14th century by German settlers and meaning 'Mountain with Roses'

from the German *Berg* and *Rose*. The present Slovak name is derived from the German and means the same.

Rwanda The Republic of Rwanda (Republika y'u Rwanda) since 1961, although independence was not gained until the next year. Until 1962 Rwanda had been the northern part of Ruanda-Urundi which had been claimed as part of German East Africa since 1890 (and in practical terms from 1899) after the Council of Berlin had designated Ruanda-Urundi a German sphere of interest in 1885. At the time they were well-established kingdoms. Occupied by Belgian forces in 1916, Ruanda-Urundi became an official Belgian League of Nations mandate in 1923 and in 1946 it became a UN Trust Territory under Belgian administration. In 1959 the majority Hutu rose against the ruling Tutsi to end the feudal system and abolish the monarchy which occurred in 1961. At the same time both Ruanda and Urundi agreed that, given ancient antagonisms and the prevailing circumstances, their political union should be brought to an end. The spelling was changed to Rwanda on independence in 1962. The country takes its name from its indigenous people, the Vanyarwanda. *See* BURUNDI.

Ryazan, RUSSIA *Pereyaslavl-Ryazanskiy*
A historic principality, a province and a city founded *c.*1095 with a name that is derived from two old Russian words *pereyat* (now *perenyat*) 'to achieve' or 'to imitate' and *slava* 'glory', with Ryazanskiy added to distinguish it from other cities and towns beginning with Pereyaslavl. It was simply renamed Ryazan in 1778 and this name may recognize the Erzian people who used to live in the region.

Rybachiy, KALININGRAD/RUSSIA *Rossitten*
'Fishing (Place)' from *rybachiy* 'fishing', itself from *ryba* 'fish'.

Rybinsk, YAROSLAVL'/RUSSIA *Ust'-Sheksna, Rybansk, Rybnaya Sloboda, Shcherbakov, Andropov*
Originally founded as a fishing village at the confluence of the Volga and Sheksna Rivers and called the '(Place at the) Mouth of the Sheksna' in 1071–1504. Its subsequent names were associated with *ryba* 'fish'. In 1777 it became the town of Rybinsk. In 1946–57 it was named after Colonel General Alexander Shcherbakov (1901–45), who became chief of the Main Political Administration of the Red Army and deputy people's commissar of defence in 1942. Following Stalin's[†] death in 1953, the city readopted Rybinsk as its name in 1957.

However, this was changed to Andropov after the death in 1984 of Yuri Andropov (1914–84), Soviet leader (1982–4) and former head of the KGB. As his reputation decayed, the city's name once more reverted to Rybinsk in 1989. There is now a Rybnaya Sloboda in the Tatarstan Republic.

Rybnik, POLAND
Founded in the 10th century as a fishing village on the Nacyna River, the name means 'Fishmonger'.

Rybnita, MOLDOVA
Takes its name from a tributary of the Dniester River which has a name based on the Russian *ryba* 'fish'.

Ryde, ENGLAND/UK *La Ride*
'The Small Stream' from the Old English *rith*.

Rye, AUSTRALIA, DENMARK, UK, USA
1. UK (England): formerly Ria '(Place) at the Island' from the Old English *ieg* 'island'; the initial R comes from the Middle English *atter* 'at the'.
2. USA (New York): settled in 1660 and named after the Rye in England.

Ryl'sk, KURSK/RUSSIA
Takes its name from the Rylo River on which it lies. Its name comes from *ryt'* 'to dig' or 'to burrow'.

Ryukyu Islands (Ryukyu-Shotō), JAPAN
'Ball of Precious Stones' from *ryū* 'precious stone' and *kyū* 'ball'. An archipelago (also called the Nansei Shotō 'South-West Islands' from *nan* 'south', *sei* 'west' and *shotō* 'island'), it consists of over 50 islands in the Okinawa and Sakishima Island groups. The archipelago was only incorporated into Japan in 1879. The USA took control in 1945 after Japan's defeat in the Second World War, the islands being returned to Japan in 1972.

Rzeszów, POLAND
Founded in the 14th century with a name taken from *rzesza* 'empire' or 'state'.

Saar (French: **Sarre**), FRANCE-GERMANY
A river rising in France, its name derives from the Indo-European root element *ser* 'to flow'.

Saarbrücken, SAARLAND/GERMANY
'Bridge over the (River) Saar' from *Brücke* 'bridge'. The name actually comes from that of a Frankish royal castle called Sarrabrucca which, in its turn, referred to a Roman bridge over the river.

Saaremaa, ESTONIA *Ösel, Sarema*
An island simply meaning 'Island Land' from *saare* 'island' and *maa* 'land'. After occupation by the Danes, Swedes, and Russians, it became Estonian in 1918. It was known to the Swedes as Ösel and to the Russians as Sarema.

Saarland, GERMANY
A state named after the River Saar. Occupied by the French on several occasions, it was administered by the League of Nations in 1920–35 before being returned to Germany. It was removed again from Germany following the Second World War, not rejoining that country until 1957 when it became a state.

Saarlouis, SAARLAND/GERMANY *Saarlautern*
Lying along the River Saar, it was founded in 1680 by, and named after, King Louis XIV the Sun King†. It was ceded to Prussia in 1815, but was administered by the League of Nations in 1920–35. It was called Saarlautern in 1936–45 after a majority of the population of the Saarland voted in 1935 to return to Germany.

Sabah, MALAYSIA *North Borneo*
A state in East Malaysia. It was occupied in 1877 by British merchants and given the name British North Borneo the following year. They founded the British North Borneo Company in 1881, having obtained the land from the Sultans of Brunei and Sulu. The territory became a British crown colony in 1946 and joined Malaysia in 1963 when it became a state with its present name which is said to come from a local word for 'downwind'.

Sabasṭiyah, WEST BANK
See SAMARIA.

Sabie, MPUMALANGA/SOUTH AFRICA
Named after the river whose name means 'Sand'. The river flows into Mozambique where a town called Sábié also lies on it.

Sabirabad, AZERBAIJAN *Andreyevka*
'Sabir's Town' named after Mirza Tairzade (1862–1911), a satirical poet who used the pseudonym Sabir.

Sackville, NEW BRUNSWICK/CANADA
Resettled on the site of three abandoned French villages in 1761, it was named after George Sackville Germain (1716–85), 1st Viscount Sackville, British secretary of state for the colonies (1779–82).

Sacramento, BRAZIL, MEXICO, USA
USA (California): the original settlement was founded in 1839 and populated largely by Swiss immigrants, hence its first name of New Helvetia. In 1848 the modern city was laid out and named after the Sacramento River; the river received this name '(Holy) Sacrament' from the Spanish in 1808.

Sadr City (**Madīnat aş Şadr**), IRAQ *Revolution City, Saddam City*
The township in north-east Baghdad was given the name Madīnat ath Thawrah 'Revolution City' after the Ba'ath party took power in 1968. It was renamed Madīnat Saddām 'Saddam City' after Saddam Hussein (1937–), president of Iraq (1979–2003), came to power in 1979. With his overthrow in 2003 it was renamed after the prominent Shi'a cleric, Ayatollah Muhammad Sadiq al-Şadr, assassinated on Saddam's orders in 1999.

Saffron Walden, ENGLAND/UK *Wealadene, Waledana, Saffornewalden*
Originally 'Valley of the Britons' from the Old English *walh* 'Briton' or 'Welshmen' and *denu* 'valley'. The Middle English *safron* 'Saffron' was added later to distinguish this particular Walden and to acknowledge the importance of the saffron crocus that was reintroduced and cultivated here from *c.*1400; the purple-flowering plants were used to make a dye for the weaving industry in the area.

Safi, MOROCCO *Asfi*
A port settled by the Canaanites and then by the Carthaginians who named it Asfi, from the Berber for 'river', from which the present name is taken.

Safranbolu, TURKEY *Theodoropolis, Saframbolis*
Derived from *safran* 'saffron' and *bol* 'abundant'.

Saga, KYŪSHŪ/JAPAN
A prefecture from *sa* 'help' or 'support' and *ga* 'celebrate'.

Sagaing, BURMA
'Branch of a Tree called Sis'.

Sāgar, INDIA
Madhya Pradesh: built around a lake, its name simply means 'Lake'. It is also spelt Saugor.

Saginaw, USA
Michigan: a river and a city founded in 1816 near Saginaw Bay. The name is an Ojibwa (Chippewa) word meaning 'Land of the Sauks', a Native American people.

Sagunto, VALENCIA/SPAIN *Saguntum, Murbiter, Murviedro*
Possibly founded by Greeks from Zakinthos from which the Roman and present names are derived. The Moorish name, Murbiter, came from *muri veteres* 'old walls' and this later became Murviedro. It received its present name in 1868.

Sahara (Arabic: **al-Ṣaḥārā**), NORTH AFRICA
A desert whose name in Arabic simply means 'desert' from *ṣaḥrā*, the feminine of *aṣḥrā* 'tawny-coloured'. It is pronounced, however, as if from the plural *ṣaḥārā*.

Sahāranpur, UTTAR PRADESH/INDIA
Founded *c.*1340 and named after Shah Haran Chishtī, a local Muslim saint, with the additional *pur*.

Sahel (Arabic: **Sāḥil**), NORTH AFRICA
A semi-arid belt of savannah between the Sahara Desert to the north and tropical Africa to the south. It stretches eastwards from Senegal and Mauritania, through Mali, Niger, and Chad to the Sudan. The word comes from the Arabic *sāḥil* 'border', 'edge' or 'shore' (of the Sahara Desert).

Saigon, VIETNAM
See HO CHI MINH CITY.

Saint-Affrique, MIDI-PYRÉNÉES/FRANCE
Named after St Africain or Africanus, bishop of Cominges, around whose tomb the town developed in the 6th century.

Saint Albans, CANADA, UK, USA
UK (England): formerly Verulamium, Sancte Albanes stow, and Villa Sancti Albani. Originally a town built in the 1st century BC on the west bank of the River Ver and the tribal capital of the Catuvellauni, it was renamed after St Alban, a Roman who had converted to Christianity and who was martyred here; various dates have been suggested for his execution, particularly 209 and 303. *Stōw* and later the Latin *villa* were added. The

town in Newfoundland, Canada, is spelt St Alban's.

Saint-Amand-les-Eaux, NORD-PAS-DE-CALAIS/FRANCE
The first part of the name honours St Amand (*c.*584–675), a monk, missionary, and bishop, who founded a Benedictine abbey in the locality in 647. The second part refers to the mineral waters here for which the town is well known.

Saint-Amand-Montrond, CENTRE/FRANCE
A town that developed around a monastery founded by St Amand (see previous entry) near to a hill called Montrond 'round hill'.

Saint Andrews, CANADA, NEW ZEALAND, UK
UK (Scotland): earlier Kilrimont 'Church of the Royal Mount'. The earliest recorded form of the name, Cind righ monaigh, is an indication that Gaelic *cinn* 'end' had been replaced by *cill* 'church'. It was renamed Sancti Andree after the patron saint of Scotland after his relics had been brought here by St Rule, possibly in the 4th century. He built a shrine for them and the church was dedicated to St Andrew in the 8th century.

Saint Augustine, FLORIDA/USA
Founded in 1565 by the Spanish Admiral Pedro Menéndéz de Avilés and named by him after St Augustine (354–430), the bishop of Hippo, because he had sighted the coast on the bishop's feast day, 28 August. Apart from the period 1763–83, when it passed to Great Britain, it remained a Spanish possession until 1821.

Saint Austell, ENGLAND/UK *Trenance*
Named after the local church which was dedicated to a hermit called St Austol.

Saint Barthélemy, LEEWARD ISLANDS/WEST INDIES
A French island discovered by Christopher Columbus[†] in 1493 and named by him after his brother Bartholomew.

Saint-Brieuc, BRITTANY/FRANCE
Named after Brioc, a Celtic saint of the 6th century. He was probably born in Wales, but died in Brittany.

Saint Catharines, ONTARIO/CANADA
Founded in 1790 and named in 1809 after Catharine Hamilton, wife of Robert Hamilton who was a member of the first legislative council of Upper Canada.

Saint Charles, CANADA, USA
USA (Missouri): founded by the French in 1769 as Les Petites Côtes 'The Little Hills', it was transferred to Spain in 1770. The following

year it was renamed San Carlos Borromeo after the church dedicated to the Italian cardinal, St Charles Borromeo (1538–84), who became archbishop of Milan. In 1806 'Borromeo' was dropped and the remainder of the name Anglicized.

Saint Clair, CANADA-USA

A river that forms part of the boundary between Canada and the USA, and a lake, also forming part of the border, into which it flows. The river is named after the American general Arthur St Clair (1736–1818); the lake is also said to be named after him, although it was originally named by Robert Cavelier, sieur de la Salle[†], after St Clare (1194–1253) because he, or the Franciscan missionary Father Louis Hennepin, discovered it on her feast day, 12 August (now 11 August) 1679.

Saint-Claude, FRANCHE-COMTÉ/FRANCE *Condate*

Named after St Claudius, a 7th-century bishop of Besançon. Its former name meant 'Confluence', a reference to its situation at the junction of two rivers.

Saint-Cloud, PARIS/FRANCE *Novigentum*

Named after Clodoald (522–60), grandson of Clovis I (c.466–511), King of the Merovingians (481–511), although Clodoald never became king; he founded a monastery here called Novigentum.

Saint Cloud, MINNESOTA/USA

Laid out in 1854 and named after the city in France.

Saint Croix, CANADA, USA, US VIRGIN ISLANDS

1. Canada-USA: a river named by Jacques Cartier[†] who saw it on Holy Cross Day (14 September) in 1535.
2. US Virgin Islands: an island named Santa Cruz 'Holy Cross' by Christopher Columbus[†] when he visited it in 1493. The French West India Company bought the island in 1665 from the Knights of Malta. It became a French colony in 1674 when it was given the present French form of its name. In 1733 the King of Denmark bought the island and Danish possession was retained until 1917 when it was sold to the USA.

Saint-Cyr, CANADA, FRANCE

1. Canada (Quebec): a lake and a river, named after the town in France.
2. France (Paris): named after St Cyricus who is thought to have been martyred in 304. Several places in Europe and the Near East are named after him.

Saint-Denis, CANADA, FRANCE, RÉUNION, USA

All named after the patron saint of France, bishop of Paris and a martyr who was beheaded near Paris c.250. One of the two towns in France with this name is now a northern suburb of Paris.

Saint-Dié, LORRAINE/FRANCE *Sanctus Deodatus*

The town developed around the 7th-century monastery of St Dieudonné 'God Given', Bishop of Nevers, from which the name is taken.

Saint-Dizier, CHAMPAGNE-ARDENNES/FRANCE *Desiderii Fanum*

The original Roman name meant 'Temple of Desiderius'. In due course this name gave way to Didier, the French version of the Latin name.

Sainte-Foy, QUEBEC/CANADA *Notre-Dame-de-Foy*

Founded in 1698 and named after a village in France, itself named after a virgin martyr, St Faith, possibly of the 3rd century, who was put to death at Agen.

Saintes, POITOU-CHARENTES/FRANCE *Mediolanum Santonum*

The Roman name meant 'Middle Plain of the Santones', a Gallic tribe. In due course, this gave way to 'Saint', probably in connection with St Eutropius, the town's first bishop, who is buried here.

Saintes-Maries-de-la-Mer, PROVENCE-ALPES-CÔTES D'AZUR/FRANCE

According to local tradition, Mary, the sister of the Virgin Mary, Mary Magdalen, and Mary, the mother of St James and St John, with their black servant Sara, landed here c.40, having fled persecution in Judaea. The town's name comes from the church dedicated to the three Marys: 'Saint Marys of the Sea'.

Sainte-Thérèse, CANADA

Quebec: founded in 1789 and named after Thérèse Blainville, daughter of the lord of the manor who had issued the first land grants c.1730.

Saint-Étienne, RHÔNE-ALPES/FRANCE

Founded in the 11th century and named after the church around which it developed. This was dedicated to St Stephen (in French, St Étienne), the first Christian martyr who died c.35.

Saint-Eustache, QUEBEC/CANADA

Founded by the French in 1768 and named after Eustache Lambert, a prominent former citizen, who was himself named after St Eustace, a Roman martyr of unknown date.

Saint George, AUSTRALIA, BERMUDA, CANADA, USA
1. Bermuda: founded in 1612 by English colonists and named after the patron saint of England. It was Bermuda's capital until 1815.
2. USA (Utah): settled in the 1860s and named after George A. Smith, an adviser to Brigham Young (1801–77), the Mormon leader.

Saint-Germain, PARIS/FRANCE.
The full name is Saint-Germain-en-Laye, the present version of the Latin Sanctus Germanus in Laya. The personal name refers to St Germanus (c.378–448), Bishop of Auxerre from 418, who was twice sent to Britain to refute heresies. The second part of the name indicates the former forest here from the Old French l'aye (now la haie) 'the hedge'.

Saint Germans, ENGLAND/UK
Named after St Germanus (see previous entry).

Saint Helena, ATLANTIC OCEAN
An island Overseas Territory (which includes Ascension Island and Tristan da Cunha) of the UK discovered by João da Nova Castella, a Portuguese navigator, on 21 May 1502, the feast day of St Helena, hence the name. St Helena (c.250–330) became a Christian when she was over 60 and was the mother of the first Christian Roman emperor, Constantine[†]. The English East India Company took possession of the island in 1659 and it was transferred to the British crown permanently in 1834 when it became a colony.

Saint Helens, AUSTRALIA, UK, USA
1. USA (Oregon): named after Mount St Helens.
2. USA (Washington): a mountain, Mount St Helens, named after Alleyne Fitzherbert (1753–1839), Baron St Helens, a successful diplomat and British ambassador to Madrid, Spain (1790–4).

Saint Helier, JERSEY/CHANNEL ISLANDS
Named after St Helier, a 6th-century hermit and martyr from what is now Belgium.

Saint-Hubert, BELGIUM, CANADA
1. Belgium: formerly Andain. Renamed after St Hubert (d. 727), Bishop of Maastricht and Liège, who is said to have been converted while out hunting and is therefore the patron saint of huntsmen; he is buried here.
2. Canada (Quebec): also named after St Hubert.

Saint-Hyacinth, QUEBEC/CANADA
Founded in 1760 and named after Hyacinth de Lorme who bought the land in 1753.

Saint Ignace, MICHIGAN/USA
Founded in 1671 when a mission was established here. It was named after St Ignatius Loyola (1491–1556), who founded the Jesuits in 1540.

Saint Ives, ENGLAND/UK
1. Cambridgeshire: formerly Slepe or Sancto Ivo de Slepe 'Saint Ives (or Ivo) of the Slippery Place' from the Old English slæp 'slippery place'. St Ives is reputed to have been a Persian bishop who came to England to live as a hermit.
2. Cornwall: formerly Sancta Ia. St Ia was said to be an Irish virgin who had sailed across the Irish Sea on a leaf. She was later martyred.

Saint-Jean-de-Luz, AQUITAINE/FRANCE
Sanctus Johannes de Luis
The original and present names mean 'St John of Luis'. The local Basque name is Donibane-Lohizun from done 'saint', Iban 'John', and lohizun 'muddy'.

Saint John, CANADA, CHANNEL ISLANDS, GUINEA-LIBERIA, USA, US VIRGIN ISLANDS
1. Canada (New Brunswick): a fort was built here after Samuel de Champlain[†] visited the area in 1604. After the British arrival the fort was refurbished as Fort Frederick. A settlement took root in 1783 which was called Parr Town after Colonel John Parr (1725–91), governor of Nova Scotia. Together with a community called Carleton, Parr Town was renamed St John in 1785 after the river of that name, at the mouth of which it lies (see 4).
2. Canada (Quebec): a lake called Lac St-Jean and originally Piekouagami 'Flat Lake', which was discovered in 1647 by Father Jean de Quen, a Jesuit missionary, and named after him.
3. Guinea-Liberia: a river rising in Guinea and named after St John the Baptist because it was discovered on his feast day, 24 June, by the Portuguese.
4. USA-Canada: a river rising in Maine, USA, which was discovered in 1604 by de Champlain on the feast day of St John the Baptist and named after him.

Saint John's, ANTIGUA, CANADA, ISLE OF MAN, MONTSERRAT
Canada (Newfoundland): according to tradition, although evidence is lacking, the Italian explorer, John Cabot (c.1450–c.1499), sailing on behalf of the English king, Henry VII, became the first European to make a landfall here on 24 June 1497, the feast day of St John the Baptist.

Saint Johnsbury, VERMONT/USA
Settled in 1786 and named after Michel-Guillaume Jean de Crèvecoeur, the

French consul in New York, who wrote under the pseudonym J. Hector St John.

Saint Joseph, CANADA, DOMINICA, MARTINIQUE, NEW CALEDONIA, RÉUNION, TRINIDAD, USA
USA (Missouri): Joseph Robidoux, a French-Canadian trapper, established a trading post here in 1826; in 1843 he laid out the town and named it after his patron saint.

Saint Just, ENGLAND/UK
Named after its church dedicated to St Just.

Saint Kilda, AUSTRALIA, NEW ZEALAND, UK
UK (Scotland): at one time believed to be named after a saint named Kilda. However, there has never been a saint with this name. Rather, the island's name is probably a modification of the Old Scandinavian *skildir* 'shields' which was given to a group of islands. It was then applied to the island of Hirta and this became St Kilda.

Saint Kitts and Nevis The Federation of St Kitts and Nevis since 1988 and a constitutional monarchy within the Commonwealth. Previously the Federation of St Christopher and Nevis when independence was gained in 1983; an associated state of the UK, with Anguilla until 1980 (1967–83); part of the West Indies Federation (1958–67) and the Leeward Islands Federation (1871–1956). The islands united in 1882, having become British possessions in 1783 and been administered as a single colony together with Anguilla and the British Virgin Islands from 1816. The French settled St Kitts in 1627 and the British Nevis the following year. It was Christopher Columbus[†], who visited the islands in 1493, who gave the name St Christopher after his patron saint; this was shortened to St Kitts by English sailors and adopted by settlers who arrived in 1623. Nevis also comes from Columbus, who thought that the island's summit, often wreathed in cloud, looked like *las nieves* 'the snows'. The original inhabitants of St Kitts, the Caribs, called the island Liamuiga 'Fertile Land' because its volcanic soil was so conducive to agriculture.

Saint-Lambert, CANADA, FRANCE
Canada (Quebec): founded by Jesuits in 1647 and named after Lambert Closse (1618–92), the garrison sergeant-major here.

Saint-Laurent, QUEBEC/CANADA
On Montreal Island in the St Lawrence River, it takes its name from the French version of Lawrence.

Saint Lawrence, AUSTRALIA, BARBADOS, CANADA, USA
Canada-USA: a river, part of which forms the border between Canada and the USA. Explored by Jacques Cartier[†] in 1534, it was named by him because he first saw the river on 10 August, the feast day of St Lawrence (d. 258), a Roman martyr. The river gives its name to the Gulf of St Lawrence and the St Lawrence Seaway.

Saint-Lô, LOWER NORMANDY/FRANCE *Briovera*
Renamed after Laudus (Lo), the rather obscure 6th-century bishop of Coutances.

Saint Louis, CANADA, FRANCE, GUADELOUPE, RÉUNION, SENEGAL, USA
1. Some towns are spelt St Louis and others Saint-Louis. There is also a river and a lake with this name in Quebec, Canada, and a river in Minnesota, USA. They are named after St Louis IX (1214–70), King of France (1226–70).
2. Senegal: the local Wolof name is Ndar. Founded in 1659, the city-port was the administrative capital of the French West African territories of Mauritania and Senegal until 1958. It was named supposedly for the reigning French monarch, Louis XIV the Sun King[†], but in actual fact after his patron saint, St Louis IX.
3. USA (Missouri): founded as a fur trading post in 1764 by a Frenchman, Pierre Laclède Liguest, and named after St Louis IX.

Saint Lucia *Iouanalao*
A constitutional monarchy within the Commonwealth and one of the Windward Islands of the Lesser Antilles. It is thought to have been discovered by Christopher Columbus[†] in 1502, possibly on 13 December, the feast day of St Lucy (d. 304), a Sicilian virgin and martyr; this may explain its name. Settled by the French, it changed hands several times between them and the British during the 17th century, but was ceded to the UK in 1814 and became one of the Windward Islands in 1871. It was a member of the Federation of the West Indies in 1958–62 and gained its independence in 1979. The original Native American name was Iouanalao 'Place where the Iguana is found'.

Saint-Malo, CANADA, FRANCE
France (Brittany): named after the Welsh missionary monk, Maclovius or Maclou, bishop of Aleth (Saint-Servan), who fled to Brittany in the 6th century.

Saint Martin, CANADA, CHANNEL ISLANDS, FRANCE, LEEWARD ISLANDS, SWITZERLAND
Leeward Islands: an island, the southern part of which belongs to the Netherlands Antilles

and is called in Dutch Sint Maarten; the northern part belongs to the French Overseas Department of Guadeloupe. The island was discovered by Christopher Columbus[†] on 11 November 1493 and named by him after St Martin of Tours (c.316–97) whose feast day this was.

Saint Martinville, LOUISIANA/USA *Poste des Attakapas*
Settled c.1760 and originally named after a local Native American tribe. When it became a town, largely populated by refugees from the French Revolution, some time after 1812, it was renamed after St Martin of Tours (c.316–97).

Saint-Maur, PARIS/FRANCE
The full name is Saint-Maur-des-Fossés. Its name comes from the abbey founded here by Benedictine monks from Saint-Maur-sur-le-Loire, who had fled from the Viking invaders in the 7th century. St Maurus was a 6th-century monk; *fossés* comes from the Latin *fossa* 'ditch', a reference to the original fortifications.

Saint-Maurice, CANADA, FRANCE, SWITZERLAND
Canada (Quebec): a river discovered by Jacques Cartier[†] in 1535 and later named after Maurice Poulin, who was given a seigniory to the north of its mouth in 1668.

Saint Moritz, SWITZERLAND
Named after St Maurice (d. c.287), a member of the Roman Theban Legion who, when ordered to execute Christians in an official ceremony, refused and was therefore himself martyred.

Saint-Nazaire, FRANCE, FRENCH GUIANA
France (Pays de la Loire): formerly Corbilo and renamed after the 5th-century St Nazarius.

Saint Neot, ENGLAND/UK *Sanctus Neotus* (*Cornwall*)
Named after St Neot to whom the church is dedicated. St Neots in Cambridgeshire was named after the same saint after his relics had been brought here from Cornwall.

Saint-Omer, NORD-PAS-DE-CALAIS/FRANCE
Named after St Omer (Audomarus) (d. c.699), bishop of Therouanne, who founded the monastery of Sithiu here in the 7th century.

Saint-Ouen, PARIS/FRANCE *Clichy-La-Garenne*
Named after St Audoenus (c.600–84), chancellor to Clovis II (635–57), King of the Merovingians (657), and Bishop of Rouen from 641.

Saint Paul, CANADA, FRANCE, GUINEA-LIBERIA, RÉUNION, USA
1. Guinea-Liberia: a river rising in Guinea which was first seen by the Portuguese on 29 June, the feast day of St Paul (d. c.65).
2. USA (Minnesota): in c.1838 a small settlement was founded by Pierre 'Pig's Eye' Parrant and called 'Pig's Eye'. In 1841 a Canadian Catholic missionary, Father Lucian Galtier, arrived and built a log chapel which he dedicated to St Paul. Pig's Eye was then renamed.

Saint Peter Port, GUERNSEY/CHANNEL ISLANDS
Named after the church dedicated to St Peter (d. c.64), leader of the apostles, with Port added to call attention to its importance as a port with a safe harbour.

Saint Petersburg (Sankt Peterburg), RUSSIA, USA
1. Russia: the first fortress built where the River Okhta flows into the River Neva in 1300 was Swedish and called Landskrona 'Land's Crown'. Soon destroyed, a Russian settlement arose around the ruins. It came to be called Neva Town. When back in Swedish hands the fortress of Nienschants (called by the Russians Kanets or Kantsy) was built in 1611 on the site of Neva Town. The settlement around the castle grew and came to be known as Nien. In 1703 the Russians successfully stormed the fortress. The fall of Nienschants marked the founding of the modern city. It was named Sankt Piter Burkh (St Petersburg) that year by Peter I the Great[†] after his patron saint, St Peter (and conveniently, himself). When Russia entered the First World War in 1914 against Germany its German-sounding name was changed to the Russian-style Petrograd 'Peter's Town'. The cradle of the Russian Revolution, in 1905 and 1917, it was renamed Leningrad in 1924 after the death of Vladimir Lenin[†]. The name reverted to St Petersburg in 1991. The city was the capital of the Russian Empire in 1712–1917 and of the Soviet state between November 1917 and March 1918 when the capital was transferred to Moscow.
2. USA (Florida): settled in 1876, one of the settlers being Peter A. Demens. The city was named after his birthplace in Russia.

Saint-Quentin, CANADA, FRANCE
France (Picardy): originally Augusta Veromanduorum and renamed after St Quentin, possibly a Roman citizen, who is believed to have been martyred here, possibly in the 3rd century.

Saint Stephen, CANADA, USA
Canada (New Brunswick): founded as Scoodic in 1783 and, after being renamed Morristown and Dover Hill, was renamed again in 1786 after St Stephen Parish which took its name from a surveyor, Stephen Pendleton. 'Saint' was added to match the practice of surrounding parishes.

Saint Thomas, CANADA, USA, US VIRGIN ISLANDS
1. Canada (Ontario): founded as Sterling in 1817, it was renamed after Colonel Thomas Talbot (1771–1853), because he made it the capital of the settlement he had founded in 1803.
2. US Virgin Islands: the main island of the group sighted by Christopher Columbus[†] in 1493 and named by him after St Thomas, the 1st-century apostle. Colonized first by the Dutch from 1657, it later became Danish and British before being bought by the USA in 1917.

Saint Tropez, PROVENCE-ALPES-CÔTES D'AZUR/FRANCE
According to legend, said to be named after St Torpes, a Roman Christian officer who was martyred and whose headless body was washed up here.

Saint Vincent and the Grenadines A constitutional monarchy within the Commonwealth which gained its independence in 1979. The island of St Vincent was discovered by Christopher Columbus[†] on 22 January 1498, the feast day of St Vincent of Saragossa, a martyr who died from torture in 304. The islands, St Vincent and the northern Grenadines, became a British possession in 1763 although the indigenous Caribs were not finally brought under control until 1796. In 1871–1956 they were part of the Windward Islands colony; in 1958 they became part of the Windward Islands Federation and then of the West Indies Federation until 1962. At the time of Columbus's visit the Caribs called St Vincent Youlou or Hairoun 'Home of the Blessed'. *See* GRENADINES.

Saipan, NORTHERN MARIANA ISLANDS
An island under Spanish control between 1565 and 1899 when it passed to the Germans who held it from 1899 to 1914. It was a Japanese mandate in 1920–44 when it was captured by American forces. The name is Micronesian and means 'Uninhabited' because the Spanish removed the original inhabitants and the island remained deserted until the 17th century.

Saitama, HONSHŪ/JAPAN
A prefecture. The name may come from the Sakitama Shrine from *saki* 'front' and *tama*

'ball'; otherwise the Chinese characters here represent *sai* 'cape' and *tama* 'ball'.

Sakai, HONSHŪ/JAPAN
Three places and a river. In Ōsaka Urban Prefecture and in Ibaraki Prefecture Sakai has different Chinese characters but both mean 'Border', both being on administrative borders. The Sakai in Fukui Prefecture has Chinese characters *saka* 'hill' and *i* 'well'. There is also a river with this name that flows between the Tōkyō Metropolis and Kanagawa Prefecture.

Sakaide, SHIKOKU/JAPAN
The characters represent *saka* 'hill' and *ide* 'jut out'.

Sakata, HONSHŪ/JAPAN
The characters represent *saka* 'sake' (the alcoholic drink) and *ta* 'rice field'.

Sakha, RUSSIA *Yakutiya*
A republic, formerly known as the Yakut Province and named after the Yakuts. Their name may be from the Evenki *yeko* with the plural *yekot* 'outsiders' or 'strangers', a reference to the fact that they were not Evenki. To the Buryats they were *Yakhuud* which became Yakut in Russian. Sakha 'people of the edge' is what the Yakuts call themselves, an acknowledgement that they lived at the edge of the world known to the Evenki.

Sakhalin, RUSSIA *Karafuto*
An island and a province with a name derived from the Manchu *Sahalin Ula* 'Black River'. This referred actually to the lower reaches of the Amur River on the mainland which flows into the Tatar Strait opposite the northern end of the island. On an early French map the name spread across the page to include, apparently, the island. Shortly afterwards, when a new map was being prepared, the name was accepted as the name for the island and was shortened to Sakhalin. In 1855–75 the Japanese and the Russians shared the island, but in 1875 it passed completely to the Russians in exchange for the *Kuril Islands. Following the Russo-Japanese War, the southern half of the island was ceded to Japan in 1905 and renamed Karafuto, a corruption of the local Ainu name, Krafto. In 1918 the northern half was also occupied by the Japanese, but they relinquished it in 1924 and it was reoccupied by Soviet troops the following year. The southern half was returned to the Soviet Union at the end of the Second World War in 1945.

Sal (Ilha do Sal), CAPE VERDE
'Salt Island' from the Portuguese *sal* because it is well known for its saltworks.

Salaberry-de-Valleyfield, QUEBEC/CANADA
First settled after a paper mill, named after the
Valleyfield Paper Mills in Edinburgh, Scotland,
had been built here in 1870. Salaberry is a
tribute to Colonel Charles de Salaberry (1778–
1829), the commander of the French Canadian
troops who fought for the British at the Battle
of Châteauguay in 1813 against the Americans.

Ṣalāḥ ad-Dīn, IRAQ
A governorate named after Ṣalāḥ ad-Dīn Yūsuf
ibn Ayyūb (c.1137–93), the Muslim hero who
captured Jerusalem from the Crusaders in
1187; he is better known to Europeans as
Saladin. Sultan of Egypt, Palestine, Syria, and
Yemen, his name meant 'Righteousness of the
Faith, Joseph, Son of Job'.

Ṣalālah, OMAN *Zafar*
'Glittering One'. It was called the city of Zafar
(which gave its name to Dhofar) when it was
visited by Ibn Battutah (1304–68), the great
Arab traveller and writer, in the 14th century
when it was at its most prosperous. The ruins
of this city are now just to the east of modern
Ṣalālah and are called al-Balid, the local
pronunciation of al-Balad 'The Town'.

Salamanca, CHILE, MEXICO, PANAMA, SPAIN,
USA
1. Spain (Castile-León): founded c.400 BC by
Celt-Iberians, it was later called Helmantika by
the Greeks; later variations were Hermandica
and Salamántica. In due course it became part
of the Roman province of Lusitania and was
referrred to as Polis Megale 'Great City'. Its
present name, however, may be a tribute to
Salmantica, a Greek historian who lived in the
city.
2. USA (New York): founded as Bucktooth in
1854 and renamed in 1862 after a Spanish
banker with this name, because he was a
major stockholder in the Atlantic and Great
Western Railroad and had visited the town a
little earlier.

Salamis, CYPRUS, GREECE
Cyprus: now ruins, said to have been founded
after the Trojan War in the 12th or 13th
century BC by the best Greek archer, Teucer,
who named it after the Greek island of Salamis
(now the island and town of Salamís); its name
may have come from the Phoenician *salam*
'peace'. Salamis became an important Greek
colony and trading port before coming under
Persian control in 525 BC. Damage caused by a
disastrous earthquake, followed by two more
in 334 and 345, left much of the city
submerged. In 350 Constantius II (317–61),
Roman emperor (337–61), ordered that it
should be rebuilt and it was renamed
Constantia after him. It was destroyed in 647

by the Arabs and never rebuilt, although
reverting to its original name.

Salavat, BASHKORTOSTAN REPUBLIC/RUSSIA
Founded in 1854 from an oil workers'
settlement, it was named after Salavat Yulayev
(1752–1800), a Bashkir hero who was recruited
to fight against Yemelyan Pugachov (c.1742–
75) during his peasants' rebellion in 1773–4.
However, Salavat changed sides and continued
fighting even after Pugachov had been
arrested. Salavat himself was arrested shortly
afterwards and sentenced to life
imprisonment.

Saldanha, WESTERN CAPE/SOUTH AFRICA
Named after Saldanha Bay which itself was
named after António de Saldanha, a 16th-
century Portuguese navigator.

Sale, AUSTRALIA, ITALY, UK
1. Australia (Victoria): founded in 1845 and
named after Major General Sir Robert Sale
(1782–1845), a British officer who led the
defence of Jalalabad in Afghanistan in 1841–2
with great resolution and died of his wounds
during the Sikh wars in 1845.
2. UK (England): '(Place at) the Sallow (or
Willow) Tree' from the Old English *salh*.

Salé (Sla), MOROCCO
Founded as a walled city in the 10th century, it
became the Republic of Bou Regreg, a base for
Barbary pirates, in 1629–66. The name is of
Berber origin and means 'Rock'.

Salekhard, YAMALO-NENETS AUTONOMOUS
DISTRICT/RUSSIA *Obdorsk*
Founded in 1595 as a military post on the Ob
River, it took its name from that river and
the Komi *dor* 'adjacent (place)'. In 1933 it
was renamed 'Headland Settlement' from
Nenets *salya* 'headland' and *khard* 'settlement',
an indication of its location on a bend in the
river.

Salem, CANADA, INDIA, MONTSERRAT, SWEDEN,
USA
1. India (Tamil Nādu): derived from the Tamil
sēla nād, itself from *cēra nād* which signified the
visit of a Cera king.
2. USA (Massachusetts): founded in 1626
taking its name from the biblical city, which
came from the Hebrew *shalōm* 'peace'.
Conveniently, it is also a shortened form of
Jerusalem.
3. USA (New Jersey): founded by an English
Quaker in 1675 and named after *shalōm*.
4. USA (Oregon): settled in 1840 on the site of
a Native American settlement called
Chemeketa 'Place of Rest'. This was equated to
the biblical city of Salem from *shalōm*.

Salerno, CAMPANIA/ITALY *Irnthi, Salernum*
The original coastal town called Irnthi may
have been Etruscan. A Roman colony was
established on the same site in 197 BC and its
name was derived from the root word *sal*
'current (of water)' referring to a river.

Salford, ENGLAND/UK
'Ford at the Sallow (or Willow) Tree' from the
Old English *salh* 'sallow' or 'willow'.

Salinas, BRAZIL, CHILE, ECUADOR, MEXICO,
PERU, PUERTO RICO, URUGUAY, USA
USA (California): settled in 1856 and named
after the Salinas River. Its Spanish name
means 'Saltworks'.

Salisbury, AUSTRALIA, CANADA, DOMINICA,
GUAM, RUSSIA, UGANDA, UK, USA, ZIMBABWE
1. Russia: an island, Ostrov Solsberi in Franz
Josef Land, probably named after Robert
Gascoyne-Cecil (1830–1903), 3rd Marquess of
Salisbury, British prime minister (1885–6,
1886–92, 1895–1902).
2. UK (England): the original city was 1½ miles
(2½ km) to the north at Old Sarum, an Iron Age
hill-fort subsequently developed by the
Romans, who called it Sorviodunum. It was
developed further by the Saxons, who called it
Searobryg, and by the Normans, who gave it
the name Sarisberie (which appeared in the
Domesday Book in 1086). The site was
abandoned in the 13th century and
construction of a cathedral was begun on the
present site. The meaning of Sorvio is not
known but *dunum* is 'fort'. This gave way to
burh, the dative of which is *byrig* with a spelling
here of *bryg*, with the same meaning. In line
with Norman custom the first *r* of the name
was changed to *l*. Sarum, which first appeared
in the 14th century, is actually the result of a
mistake. The Latin Saresburiensis appeared in
medieval documents and was sometimes
abbreviated to Sarum because in Latin
documents *-rum* was also the abbreviation
for *-resburiensis*. In contrast to the ancient site
of Old Sarum, Salisbury also has the name New
Sarum.
3. USA: named after the city in England
are the cities in Connecticut, founded
in 1738, Maryland (1732), Massachusetts
(1640), and North Carolina (1753), although
the latter was named after the city in
Maryland.
4. Zimbabwe: *see* HARARE.

Sallisaw, OKLAHOMA/USA
Settled in the 1880s and named after the
Sallisaw Creek whose name was said to be
derived from the French *salaison* 'salt
provisions', a reference to the salt deposits
here.

Salmān Pāk, IRAQ
Named after Salmān Pāk, an early Persian
convert to Islam, who led the Muslims
across the Tigris River from Seleucia to
Ctesiphon in 638.

Salonika, GREECE
See THESSALONÍKI.

Saltash, ENGLAND/UK *Esse, Saltehasche*
Originally '(Place at) the Ash-Tree'. 'Salt' was
added later to recognize the production of salt
here.

Salt Lake City, UTAH/USA *Great Salt Lake City*
Founded in 1847 by Mormons as a place of
safety from religious persecution. Located near
the south-eastern corner of the Great Salt Lake,
it was named after the lake. 'Great' was
dropped in 1868.

Saluda, USA
A river in South Carolina which joins the
Broad River to form the Congaree River. The
name is Native American and means 'Corn
River'.

Salvador, BAHIA/BRAZIL *São Salvador*
Founded in 1549 by the Portuguese with the
name 'Saviour'. It was the capital of colonial
Brazil in 1549–1763.

Salween (Burmese: **Thanlwin**; Chinese:
Nu Jiang), CHINA-BURMA
A river called 'Olive' in Burmese. It rises in
Tibet where it is called Nagqu 'Black Water'
from *nag* 'black' and *qu* 'water'. For some 80
miles (130 km) it forms the border between
Burma and Thailand.

Salzburg, AUSTRIA *Juvavum*
A state and a city, originally a Celtic settlement
and then the Roman town of Juvavum. It is
now named 'Castle of Salt' after the nearby salt
mines from the German *Salz* 'salt' and *Burg*.
Salt was 'white gold' and people were often
paid in salt, hence the word 'salary'.

Salzgitter, LOWER SAXONY/GERMANY
Watenstedt-Salzgitter
In an area known for its iron ore and salt
extraction, the old Salzgitter merged with 27
surrounding hamlets in 1942 to form
Watenstedt-Salzgitter, a name it retained until
1951. The first part of the name comes from
salz 'salt'; the derivation of the second part is
not clear. However, it may be associated with
Güter, the plural of *Gut* 'possession', to give
'Salt Estates'.

Salzkammergut, AUSTRIA
A region with a name meaning 'Salt Chamber
Possession, or Estate', from the German *Salz*
'salt', *Kammer* 'chamber (in a mine)', and *Gut*

'possession'. This is a reference to the salt deposits which have been mined in the region since the Iron Age.

Samara, RUSSIA *Kuybyshev*
A province and a city founded as a fortified settlement named Samara in 1586. It lies at the confluence of the Volga and Samara Rivers from which it takes its name. The meaning of that name is unknown, although it has been suggested that it might be of Kyrgyz origin and mean 'Hollow One'. In 1935–91 it was named after Valerian Kuybyshev[†], a Bolshevik agitator who returned from exile to the city in 1917 and then led an uprising here. The city was the seat of the Soviet government in 1941–3.

Samaria, (Hebrew: Shomron), WEST BANK
The central region of ancient Palestine and its capital, now called Sabaṣṭiyah. The town was founded *c*.880 BC by King Omri (*c*.884–872 BC), who, as related in the Bible (1 Kings 16: 24) built it on a hill-top which he had bought from one Shemer; he called it Samaria after Shemer. It was expanded by Herod the Great (73–4 BC), King of Judaea (37–4 BC) who renamed it Sebaste in honour of Emperor Augustus[†] (in Greek, Sebastos). The present Sabaṣṭiyah is the Arabic version of this. The Good Samaritan mentioned in the Bible (Luke 10: 33-5) inspired 'The Samaritans', an organization founded in London 1953 to help the severely distressed and suicidal (and since 2002 called 'Samaritans' without the 'The').

Samarkand (Samarqand), UZBEKISTAN
Marakanda
A province and a city. The first part of the name may come from Samar or Shamur, an Arab who conquered it in the 8th century, or it may be derived from the Persian *asmara* 'stone'. The Sogdian suffix *kand* means 'town'. Ruled by several different peoples, as Marakanda it became the capital of Sogdiana in the 4th century BC, of the Central Asian Turks in the 6th century AD, and of Tamerlane's[†] empire in the 14th and 15th centuries. It was captured by the Russians in 1868 and was the capital of the Uzbek Soviet Socialist Republic in 1924–30.

Sāmarrā', IRAQ
Probably the Arabic form of the pre-Islamic name Shūma'rā. Al-Mu'taṣim (794–842), caliph (833–42), transferred the 'Abbāsid capital from Baghdad to Sāmarrā' in 836 and, according to popular tradition, he called it Surra Man-Ra'ā 'Happy is He who sees it'. This, however, was a play on words. The city remained the capital until 892 when it returned to Baghdad. Al-Mu'taṣim spared no effort to build a carefully planned and spectacular city with beautifully

decorated palaces and mosques, gardens, swimming pools, and stadiums.

Samoa Islands *Navigator Islands, German Samoa, Western Samoa*
The Independent State of Samoa (Malo Sa'oloto Tuto'atasi o Samoa) since 1997 when the 'Western' was dropped from Western Samoa. A German protectorate from 1899, the islands were occupied by New Zealand troops in 1914 at which time they became known as Western Samoa. They were awarded to New Zealand under a League of Nations mandate in 1920 and became a UN Trust Territory in 1946 administered by that country. The group of nine islands achieved independence in 1962. *See* AMERICAN SAMOA.

Samoded, ARKHANGEL'SK/RUSSIA
Founded in 1925 and named after G. I. Samoded, a hero of the Civil War (1918–20).

Samokov, BULGARIA
'Ironworks', the town being known historically for its working of local deposits of iron ore.

Sámos, GREECE
An island off the Turkish coast with a name meaning 'Dune' or 'Coastal Hill', a reference to the hills which surround the port of Tigáni in the south.

Samut Prakan, THAILAND
Lying at the mouth of the Chao Phraya River, the name means 'Ocean Wall' from *samut* 'ocean'. This refers to the Phra Chula Jawm Klao Fort a few miles to the south. It is sometimes called Paknam.

Samut Sakhon, THAILAND
Lying just a few miles from the Gulf of Thailand at the mouth of the Tha Chin River, the name of this port means 'Ocean City' from *samut* 'ocean'. It is sometimes called Mahachai because it lies at the confluence of the Tha Chin and the Mahachai Canal.

Şan'ā', YEMEN *Madīnat Sam, 'Azal*
According to popular legend, the city was founded by Shem, the son of Noah as Madīnat Sam 'City of Shem'. It was renamed after 'Azal (or Uzal in the Bible, Genesis 10. 27), the sixth son of Joktan (in Arabic, Qahtan). The present name of the city, which is also spelt Sanaa, probably comes from the Sabaic root *sn* 'well fortified'; it was a Sabaen military centre in pre-Islamic times. After the Ottoman Turkish defeat in 1917, it became the national capital. In 1948–62 it lost this status, but was reinstated as the capital in 1962 on the creation of the Yemen Arab Republic. When this merged with the People's Democratic Republic of

S

Yemen in 1990, Şan'ā' became the capital of the unified state.

Sanandaj, IRAN *Sisar*
It was at one time called Sisar 'Thirty Heads' by the travellers Ibn Khurdazib and Qudameh. It was then renamed after a royal castle built in 1667 and called Seneh or Sna from which the present name comes with the additional *dej* 'castle'.

San Angelo, TEXAS/USA *Over-the-River, Santa Angela*
Founded in 1869 at the confluence of the North, South, and Middle Concho Rivers, it was subsequently renamed after the sister-in-law of one of the founders. Later, a masculine form of the name was adopted to simplify pronunciation.

San Antonio, ARGENTINA, BELIZE, BOLIVIA, CHILE, COLOMBIA, COSTA RICA, ECUADOR, EL SALVADOR, HONDURAS, ITALY, MEXICO, PARAGUAY, PERU, PHILIPPINES, SAIPAN, URUGUAY, USA, VENEZUELA
USA (Texas): founded in 1718 as a military garrison with a mission, the Mission San Antonio de Valero, also known as the Alamo 'Cottonwood Tree', on the site of a Coahuiltecan village; this was located on the San Antonio River. In 1731 a town was laid out next to the garrison and this was called San Antonio de Béjar after the river. The river was so named because it was discovered on 19 May, the feast day of St Anthony, in 1691.

San Bernadino, PARAGUAY, SWITZERLAND, USA
1. Switzerland: a village and a pass named after St Bernadino (1380–1444) of Siena, a Franciscan friar, who preached in this area.
2. USA (California): originally a mission named by Spanish missionaries after the mountains of the same name discovered on 20 May, the feast day of St Bernadino of Siena, in 1810. The site was sold to Mormons who laid out the town in 1852.

San Carlos, ARGENTINA, BOLIVIA, CHILE, COLOMBIA, COSTA RICA, MEXICO, NICARAGUA, PANAMA, PARAGUAY, PHILIPPINES, URUGUAY, USA, VENEZUELA
Philippines (Luzon): founded in 1587, it was named in 1718 after St Charles Borromeo (1538–84), archbishop of Milan, Italy.

San Clemente, SPAIN, USA
USA (California): founded in 1925 and named after the island offshore, which itself was named by the Spanish after St Clement I (d. *c*.101), pope (*c*.91–*c*.101).

San Cristóbal de Las Casas, CHIAPAS/ MEXICO *Villa Real/Ciudad Real*
Founded as 'Royal Town' *c*.1527, it was renamed five times before it received its present name. This was bestowed in tribute to Bishop Bartolomé de Las Casas (1474–1566), a Spanish historian and Dominican missionary who became Bishop of Chiapas and strongly championed the rights of the local people.

Sancti Spíritus, CUBA, SPAIN
Cuba: founded in 1514 as 'Holy Spirit' from the Latin *sanctus* 'holy' and *spiritus* 'spirit', but moved 4 miles (6 km) away in 1522 to avoid the biting ants.

Sandakan, SABAH/MALAYSIA *Elopura*
Founded in 1879 by William Clarke Cowie who moved his base, called Sandakan, here. He named it Elopura 'Beautiful City' in recognition of the beautiful natural harbour. It was subsequently renamed Sandakan 'Place that was pawned' from the Suluk *sanda* 'to pawn' and *kan*, a suffix. Who pawned it, to whom, and why, is not known.

San Diego, CHILE, EL SALVADOR, GUATEMALA, MEXICO, USA
USA (California): founded in 1542 as San Miguel and renamed San Diego de Alcalá de Henares 'St James of Alcalá of Henares' in 1602 by the Spanish after St James (d. 44), apostle and martyr, and the patron saint of Spain.

Sandwich, UK, USA
1. UK (England): formerly Sandwicæ and Sandwice 'Sandy Harbour' from the Old English *sand* and *wīc*. Once one of the Cinque Ports, silting led to its decline as a port. It lies now 2 miles (3 km) inland on the River Stour.
2. USA (Massachusetts): founded in 1637 and named after the English port. In turn, the city in Illinois was named after the Massachusetts Sandwich.

San Felipe, BELIZE, CHILE, COLOMBIA, CUBA, ECUADOR, MEXICO, PHILIPPINES, USA, VENEZUELA
Chile: founded in 1740 as San Felipe el Real 'St Philip the Royal' after Philip V (1683–1746), King of Spain (1700–46). Although a religious man, he was never canonized.

San Fernando, ARGENTINA, CHILE, MEXICO, PERU, PHILIPPINES, PUERTO RICO, SPAIN, TRINIDAD, USA
1. Spain (Andalusia): founded in 1776 as Isla de León and renamed in 1813 after Ferdinand VII (1784–1833), King of Spain (1808–33).
2. Trinidad: founded in 1786 and named after Ferdinand II (1452–1516), King of Aragon and joint sovereign of Castile as Ferdinand V (1479–1516).

San Francisco, ARGENTINA, BOLIVIA, COLOMBIA, ECUADOR, EL SALVADOR, GUATEMALA, MEXICO, NICARAGUA, PANAMA, PARAGUAY, PERU, PHILIPPINES, PUERTO RICO, USA, VENEZUELA
USA (California): originally a Native American settlement, Spanish colonists built a military post (presidio) in 1776 while Franciscan priests established a mission, the Mission San Francisco de Asis (St Francis of Assisi (1181-1226), founder of the Franciscan order). This was one of a chain of Franciscan missions. An Englishman, Captain William Richardson, was the first person to start the construction of a village in 1835 on the shore of Yerba Buena Cove, some 2 miles (3 km) east of the mission. Under Mexican rule, it was called Yerba Buena 'Good Pasture' from *hierba* 'grass' and *buena* 'good'. This was captured by American marines in 1846 and the following year the name was changed to San Francisco in recognition of the original mission.

San Francisco Gotera, EL SALVADOR *Gotera*
Renamed in 1887 in tribute to Francisco Morazán (1792-1842), the Honduran president of the United Provinces of Central America (1830-40)—a union of the modern states of Costa Rica, El Salvador, Guatemala, Honduras, and Nicaragua.

San Gabriel, COSTA RICA, ECUADOR, PHILIPPINES, URUGUAY, USA
USA (California): founded as the Mission San Gabriel Arcangel in 1771 and named after the Archangel Gabriel.

San Gimignano, TUSCANY/ITALY
Takes its name from its patron saint, Geminius, the Bishop of Modena (d. 397), who saved the town from barbarians.

San Giovanni Rotondo, APULIA/ITALY
Named for St John with Rotondo referring to an ancient circular baptistery from the Latin *rotundus* 'circular'.

San Giuliano Terme, TUSCANY/ITALY *Bagni di San Giuliano*
Although the name was changed in 1935, its meaning is much the same. Previously it was the 'Baths of St Julian' and now it is the 'Thermal Baths of St Julian'.

Sangre de Cristo Mountains, USA
Part of the southern Rocky Mountains, they were named in 1719 by Antonio Valverde y Cosio, a Spanish explorer, who is alleged to have exclaimed 'Sangre de Cristo' 'Blood of Christ' when he saw the red hue of the snowy peaks at sunrise.

San Isidro, ARGENTINA, COSTA RICA, DOMINICAN REPUBLIC, MEXICO, PANAMA, PERU, PHILIPPINES, USA
Argentina: developed round the chapel of San Isidro Labrador, after which it was named in 1816, which had been erected in 1706 and dedicated to St Isidore the Farmer (c.1080-1130), the patron saint of Madrid.

San Jacinto, COLOMBIA, PHILIPPINES, URUGUAY, USA
USA (California): a city and mountains named in Spanish after St Hyacinth (1187-1257), a Polish Dominican friar whose feast day is 15 August.

San José, ARGENTINA, BELIZE, COLOMBIA, COSTA RICA, GUATEMALA, HONDURAS, MEXICO, PANAMA, PERU, PUERTO RICO, URUGUAY, VENEZUELA
Costa Rica: settled in 1736 as Villa Nueva 'New Town'. It was probably renamed for St Joseph in 1823 when the city became the national capital.

San Jose, CANADA, PHILIPPINES, SAIPAN, USA
USA (California): founded in 1777 as a Spanish military supply depot by José Joaquin Moraga and originally named Pueblo de San José de Guadalupe 'Town of St Joseph of Guadalupe'after him.

San Juan, ARGENTINA, BOLIVIA, CANADA, COLOMBIA, COSTA RICA, DOMINICAN REPUBLIC, HONDURAS, MEXICO, PERU, PHILIPPINES, PUERTO RICO, TRINIDAD, USA
1. Argentina: a province and a city founded in 1562 by, and named after, Juan Jufré y Montesa, governor of the captaincy general of Cuyo.
2. Puerto Rico: founded in 1508 as Caparra by Juan Ponce de León (1460-1521), the Spanish explorer who was the first European to explore the island; it was located west of the modern city and renamed 'St John' after Juan Ponce de León. In 1521 the settlement was moved to the harbour entrance and renamed Puerto Rico 'Rich Port'; the island at that time was called San Juan Bautista 'St John the Baptist', having been so named by Christopher Columbus[†] in 1492. Over time, the names were reversed. It remained under Spanish control until 1898 when the island was ceded to the USA. It is the capital.

San Juan Capistrano, CALIFORNIA/USA
Founded as one of the chain of Franciscan missions in 1776 and named after St John of Capistrano (1386-1456), an Italian Franciscan preacher.

Sankt Gallen, AUSTRIA, SWITZERLAND
Switzerland: a canton and a town named after St Gall (d. c.630), an Irish monk who built a

hermitage here in 612. Having split with
St Columban, legend has it that he stumbled
into a briar patch which he took to be a sign
from God that he should settle here.

Sankt Pölten, AUSTRIA *Aelium Cetium*
The town grew up in the 8th century around
an abbey dedicated to St Hippolytus.
Germanized, this name is St Pölten.

Sankt Wolfgang, AUSTRIA
Named after St Wolfgang (*c*.924–94), Bishop of
Regensburg, who spent some time in Austria.
The town lies on Lake Wolfgang, also named
after him.

Şanlıurfa, TURKEY *Urhai/Hurri, Edessa, Antioch,
al-Ruhā/Roucha/Rochas, Urfa*
A very ancient city named after the Hurrian
people (their name meaning 'cave'), the city
being their capital during the 2nd millennium
BC. It was refounded towards the end of the 4th
century BC by Alexander III the Great's[†] army
veterans who renamed it Edessa after their
own city in Macedonia. A century later
Seleucus I Nicator[†] changed the name to
Antioch (by the Callirrhoe 'beautiful, flowing
(water)') after his son, Antiochus. Taken by the
Arabs in 637, it was recaptured by the
Byzantines in 1032; captured by Baldwin of
Boulogne in 1098, it became the first Crusader
state in 1098–1144 before falling to the Seljuk
Turks. Its present name, adopted in 1637, is
derived from the original Aramaic name,
Urhai, with the additional Turkish *şanlı*
'glorious' or 'famous'.

Sanlúcar de Barrameda, ANDALUSIA/SPAIN
The first word of the name represents *Sant
Lugar* 'Holy Place' in Old Spanish, a reference
to a pagan temple nearby. Barrameda comes
from an Arabic word which gives the sense of a
'Sandy Gateway' from *barr* 'land', a reference
to the sandbank that impeded navigation up
the Guadalquivir River, on the estuary of
which the port city lies.

San Luis Obispo, CALIFORNIA/USA
Based on the mission of San Luis Obispo de
Tolosa 'St Louis, bishop of Toulouse' (1274–97)
from the Spanish *obispo* 'bishop', one of the
chain of Franciscan missions in California and
founded in 1772.

San Luis Potosí, MEXICO *Tangamanga, Real San
Luis Minas de Potosí*
A state and a city founded as a Franciscan
mission in 1538. Named 'St Louis' after the
then Viceroy of Mexico, Luis de Velasco, it has
the additional Spanish *potosí* 'fortune', a
reference to its location in a rich silver-mining
area.

San Marcos, ARGENTINA, CHILE, COLOMBIA,
COSTA RICA, EL SALVADOR, GUATEMALA,
HONDURAS, MEXICO, NICARAGUA, USA
USA (Texas): the original Spanish settlement
was founded in 1807 and named Villa de San
Marcos de Neve after the San Marcos 'St Mark'
river. This was thought to have been
discovered by Franciscan missionaries on
St Mark's feast day, 25 April, in 1709.

San Marino, AND USA
The Republic of San Marino, also known as the
Most Serene Republic of San Marino
(Serenissima Repubblica di San Marino).
Named after a Christian stonemason and
later saint, Marinus, who is alleged to have
fled Dalmatia to escape persecution by
Diocletian (245–316), Roman emperor
(284–305), and who founded a hermitage on
Mount Titano. Although surrounded by
Italian territory, San Marino claims to be the
world's oldest republic, dating from 301.
However, the first evidence of independence
dates only from 855 (the Montefeltro
Decree) since when sovereignty has been
maintained.

San Martín, ARGENTINA, BOLIVIA, COLOMBIA,
EL SALVADOR, MEXICO, PERU, SPAIN
Peru: a department and a city named after José
de San Martín (1778–1850), an Argentinian
soldier and national hero, who was prominent
in the rebellions against Spanish rule in
Argentina, Chile, and Peru.

San Mateo, PERU, PHILIPPINES, USA,
VENEZUELA
USA (California): named after a creek
discovered by the Spanish in 1776 which itself
was named after St Matthew.

San Miguel de Allende, GUANAJUATO/
MEXICO *San Miguel, San Miguel de los Chichimecas,
San Miguel el Grande*
Founded in 1542 by a Franciscan monk, Juan
de San Miguel, and named after him. The
name San Miguel de los Chichimecas
acknowledged that the town was in
Chichimeca territory. The name of Ignacio
Allende (1779–1811), a Mexican hero of the
rebellion against Spain, who was born here,
was added later.

San Miguel de Tucumán, ARGENTINA
Tucumán
Founded in 1565 but susceptible to flooding,
it was moved after a severe flood in 1850
to a position some 60 miles (96 km) north-
east. It was renamed after St Michael with
Tucumán referring to the province in which
it lies.

San Pedro Sula, HONDURAS *San Pedro de Puerto Caballos*
Founded in 1536 by Pedro de Alvarado, it was subsequently moved to its present site, that of a Native American village called Azula. The present name is a combination of the two names.

San Rafael, ARGENTINA, BOLIVIA, COLOMBIA, COSTA RICA, EL SALVADOR, HONDURAS, MEXICO, SPAIN, USA, VENEZUELA
In most cases named after the Archangel Raphael.

San Remo, LIGURIA/ITALY *San Romulo*
Named after St Romulus, bishop of Genoa in the 4th century. The shortened version of the name, adopted in the 15th century, may be associated with the mountain hermitage (in Italian, *eremo*) to which Romulus is said to have retired.

San Roque, ARGENTINA, COLOMBIA, SPAIN
Spain (Andalusia): 'Holy Castle' from *roque* 'castle'. In 1704 the British captured Gibraltar and the Spanish population withdrew to the small settlement of San Roque. They developed it and Philip V (1683–1746), King of Spain (1700–46), granted the title of Gibraltar en su Campo 'Gibraltar in its Countryside' to the town.

San Salvador, ARGENTINA, BAHAMAS, EL SALVADOR, GALAPAGOS ISLANDS, PERU
1. 'Holy Saviour'.
2. Bahamas: an island, thought to be the first landfall made by Christopher Columbus[†] after his first crossing of the Atlantic in 1492, although there is not universal agreement on this. The promotion of Christianity was one of the principal aims of Columbus, hence the name. Until his arrival the local name was Guanahani. The island is also called Watling's Island after a notorious pirate.
3. El Salvador: a department and a city founded in 1525 on 6 August, the feast day of the Transfiguration of the Saviour, by the Spanish. It was near Suchitoto some 20 miles (32 km) north-east of its present site to which it was moved three years later. It was the capital of the United Provinces of Central America in 1834–9 and has been the capital of El Salvador ever since. The nearby volcano of San Salvador has the Nahuatl name of Quetzaltepec 'Mountain of Quetzal Birds'.
4. Galapagos Islands: an island originally named James's Island after King James II[†]. It was also known as York since he had been the Duke of York.

San Sebastián, ARGENTINA, CHILE, EL SALVADOR, HONDURAS, PUERTO RICO, SPAIN, VENEZUELA
Spain (Basque Country): the old Basque name of Donostia is sometimes included in the name as Donostia-San Sebastián. The town is named after St Sebastián, a Roman martyr who was put to death *c*.300.

Sansepolcro, TUSCANY/ITALY *Borgo San Sepolcro, San Sepolcro*
'Holy Sepulchre' from *sepolcro* 'sepulchre'. Tradition has it that the town was founded in about the 10th century after two pilgrims had returned from Palestine and built an oratory to house some relics that they had taken from the Holy Sepulchre in Jerusalem. The original name meant simply the 'Village of the Holy Sepulchre' from *borgo* 'village'.

Santa Ana, EL SALVADOR *Cíhuatehuacán*
Now named after St Anne, the mother of the Virgin Mary. The former Nahuatl name meant 'Place of Holy Women'.

Santa Barbara, BRAZIL, CHILE, COLOMBIA, COSTA RICA, HONDURAS, MEXICO, PERU, PHILIPPINES, SPAIN, USA, VENEZUELA
USA (California): named by the Spanish explorer, Sebastián Vizcaíno, in 1602 after he had arrived on 4 December, the then feast day of St Barbara. The existence of this alleged virgin-martyr is doubtful and her feast day has been removed from the Roman calendar. The Santa Barbara Islands, also known as the Channel Islands, off the Californian coast are also named after her. In California the spelling is as above, but the usual spelling in the other countries is Santa Bárbara; in Catalonia, Spain it is Santa Bàrbara.

Santa Catalina, ARGENTINA, MEXICO, PANAMA, PERU, PHILIPPINES, SOLOMON ISLANDS, USA, VENEZUELA
USA (California): one of the Santa Barbara Islands which was named in 1602 by Sebastián Vizcaíno for the probably 4th-century St Catherine (Catalina) of Alexandria when he saw it on her feast day, 25 November.

Santa Catarina, BRAZIL, MEXICO, SÃO TOMÉ AND PRÍNCIPE
Brazil: a state which had several Spanish and Portuguese names before probably being named after the 4th-century St Catherine of Alexandria by the Italian navigator Sebastian Cabot (*c*.1476–1557) while he was in the service of Spain.

Santa Clara, CHILE, COLOMBIA, CUBA, ECUADOR, MEXICO, URUGUAY, USA
USA (California): developed from the original Spanish Mission Santa Clara de Asis 'Saint

Clare of Assisi' which had been founded in 1777 as one of the chain of Franciscan missions in California. It was named after St Clare (1194–1253), a colleague of St Francis of Assisi and a nun who founded the Poor Clares.

Santa Claus, INDIANA/USA
So named in 1846 after it was discovered that the desired name of Santa Fe was the name of another town in the state. Because it was near Christmas, it received this name.

Santa Cruz, ANGOLA, ARGENTINA, ARUBA, BOLIVIA, BRAZIL, CHILE, COSTA RICA, CURAÇAO, DOMINICAN REPUBLIC, GALAPAGOS ISLANDS, GUATEMALA, JAMAICA, MEXICO, PERU, PHILIPPINES, PORTUGAL, SÃO TOMÉ AND PRÍNCIPE, USA, VENEZUELA
'Holy Cross', a name for cities, towns, a province (Argentina), a department (Bolivia), islands, rivers, and mountains. Several cities and towns have a qualifying name, such as Santa Cruz de Tenerife on the island of that name, and Santa Cruz del Quiché, a town in the department of Quiché in Guatemala.

Santa Fe, ARGENTINA, BOLIVIA, BRAZIL, CUBA, GALAPAGOS ISLANDS, HONDURAS, MEXICO, NICARAGUA, PANAMA, PHILIPPINES, SPAIN, USA
1. Argentina: a province and a city founded in 1573 as Santa Fe de Vera Cruz 'Holy Faith of the True Cross'. It was moved to its present location in 1651 and the name shortened.
2. USA (New Mexico): founded in 1610 as a provincial capital in New Spain with the name Villa Real de la Santa Fé de San Francisco de Asis 'Royal City of the Holy Faith of St Francis of Assisi'.

Santa Marta, COLOMBIA, NICARAGUA, SPAIN
Colombia: founded in 1512 and named after the 1st-century St Martha. She is associated with Mary Magdalen and Santa Marta is the capital of the Magdalena department. There is also a mountain range with this name.

Santa Monica, PHILIPPINES, USA, VENEZUELA
USA (California): laid out in 1875 with the name of Las Lágrimas de Santa Monica 'The Tears of St Monica' in Spanish, a reference to a nearby spring. St Monica (332–87) had three children. Her tears refer to her sadness concerning her son Augustine, later St Augustine of Hippo (354–430), who led a somewhat dissolute life until his conversion to Christianity in 386 or 387.

Santander, COLOMBIA, PHILIPPINES, SPAIN
1. Colombia: a department created in 1886 and named after General Francisco de Paula Santander (1792–1840), a colleague of Simón Bolívar in the struggle for South American

independence from Spain and president of New Granada (Colombia) (1833–7).
2. Spain (Cantabria): formerly Portus Victoriae Juliobrigensium. The head of the martyr San Emeterio 'St Hemiterius' is said to have been brought here from Calahorra in the 3rd century and a monastery was subsequently built. The city takes its name from the Latinized form of his name, Sancti Emetherii, passing through various versions first: Sant Emter, San Ender, and Sant Ander.

Santarém, BRAZIL, PORTUGAL
1. Brazil (Pará): founded in 1661 as a Jesuit mission to a Tapajó community, hence its first name of Tapajós. It was renamed after St Irene (Santa Iria) when it became a town in 1758.
2. Portugal: the Roman town had the original name of Scalabis before Julius Caesar[†] renamed it Praesidium Julium. Its present name honours St Irene, a nun martyred in 653, to whom the town was dedicated by a Visigoth king who had converted to Christianity. Her body was allegedly thrown into the River Tagus and was washed ashore at this point. With the arrival of the Moors, the town was renamed Shantariyah and Shantarīn, versions that also commemorate St Irene.

Santa Rosa, ARGENTINA, BOLIVIA, BRAZIL, COLOMBIA, CURAÇAO, GUAM, GUATEMALA, MEXICO, PANAMA, PERU, PHILIPPINES, PUERTO RICO, URUGUAY, USA, VENEZUELA
USA (California): founded in 1833 and probably named after St Rose (1586–1617), a Spanish virgin born in Lima, Peru. She was the first saint of America, canonized in 1671, and became the patron saint of South America and the Philippines. Several cities and towns have a qualifying name, such as Santa Rosa de Lima in El Salvador.

Santiago, ARGENTINA, BOLIVIA, BRAZIL, CHILE, COSTA RICA, DOMINICAN REPUBLIC, MEXICO, PANAMA, PERU, PHILIPPINES
Chile: founded in 1541 as Santiago del Nuevo Extremo 'Santiago of the New Frontier' by a Spanish conquistador after the apostle St James the Great (in Spanish, Santo Iago). It has been the capital of Chile since 1818.

Santiago de Compostela, GALICIA/SPAIN
Named after the apostle St James the Great (in Spanish, Santo Iago), the patron saint of Spain. According to legend, his body was brought, or miraculously transferred, to Spain after his martyrdom at the hands of Herod Agrippa I (c.10 BC–AD 44), King of Judaea (41–4) in Jerusalem in 44. It was then lost, but supernaturally rediscovered in 813 on the site of the present cathedral. The second part of the name is believed by some to be from the

Latin *campus stellae* 'field of the star', a reference to the bright star which, again according to tradition, shone above the long-forgotten tomb to reveal its position. It may, however, come from *compos stellae* 'possession of the star' to indicate that the city has the tomb.

Santiago de los Caballeros, DOMINICAN REPUBLIC
Founded either in 1494 by Christopher Columbus[†] or by his brother Bartolomeo the following year and named after the apostle St James the Great. The second part of the name was added in 1504 after 30 *caballeros* 'gentlemen' of the Order of St James had moved here from La Isabela. Several instances of the name Santiago with qualifications exist to indicate location, such as Santiago de Cuba, a province and city in Cuba, and Santiago del Estero 'Santiago of the Marsh', a province, with lakes and marshes in the south, and a city in Argentina.

Santo Domingo, COLOMBIA, COSTA RICA, DOMINICAN REPUBLIC, MEXICO, NICARAGUA NUEVA ISABELA, CIUDAD TRUJILLO
Dominican Republic: founded in 1496 on the east bank of the Ozama River by the brother of Christopher Columbus[†], Bartolomeo, as the capital of Spain's first colony in the New World. He named it New Isabela in honour of Isabela (1451–1504), Queen of Castile (1474–1504) and of Aragon (1479–1504). It was destroyed by a hurricane but rebuilt in 1502 on the west bank of the river. Its name was changed to Santo Domingo 'Holy Sunday', which at one time was the name of part of the island, because the first settlement was established on a Sunday. In 1936–61 it was called 'Trujillo City' after Rafael Trujillo (1891–1961), dictator of the Dominican Republic (1930–61) and officially president (1930–8, 1942–52). The city readopted its previous name when he was assassinated in 1961.

Santoríni (Thíra), GREECE
See THERA.

Santos, SÃO PAULO/BRAZIL
Founded in 1543 and named after the Hospital dos Santos 'Hospital of the Saints' in Lisbon.

S. A. Nyyazow Adyndaky, TURKMENISTAN
Imeni Chapayeva, Chapayew Adyndaky
Initially named after Vasily *Chapayev from *imeni* 'in the name of', it was renamed after Saparmurad Niyazov (1940–), president (1991–) and self-styled Türkmenbashi 'Head of all Turkmen' after Turkmenistan's independence in 1991. *Adyndaky* means 'named after'.

S. A. Nyyazow Etrapy, TURKMENISTAN
Dashkhovuzskiy Rayon, Dashhowuz Rayony
'S. A. Niyazov's Region' from *etrapy* 'region' (see previous entry).

São João da Boa Vista, SÃO PAULO/BRAZIL
Santo Antônio do Jaguari, São João do Jaguari
First 'St Antony (*c*.1193–1231) (of Padua) of the Jaguars', a Franciscan friar who was born in Lisbon, Portugal, and then 'St John of the Jaguars'. Renamed again, its present name means 'St John of the Beautiful View'.

São Leopoldo, RIO GRANDE DO SUL/BRAZIL
Founded as a German colony in 1824, it was named after the Austrian Archduchess Maria Leopoldine (1797–1826), the first wife of Pedro (Peter) I, the Portuguese emperor of Brazil (1822–31). The name was subsequently put into the masculine form.

São Luís, MARANHÃO/ BRAZIL *São Luiz do Maranhão*
Founded by a French naval officer in 1612, he claimed to name it after Louis XIII (1601–43), King of France (1610–43). However, it was actually named after Louis IX (1214–70), King of France (1226–70) but also a saint; thus the name was St Louis, a name which the Portuguese adopted and converted when they captured the place in 1615.

São Paulo, BRAZIL
A state and a city founded by Portuguese Jesuit priests on 25 January 1554, the feast day of the Conversion of St Paul the Apostle (d. *c*.65), hence the name 'St Paul'.

São Tiago, CAPE VERDE
An island, discovered by António da Noli, a Genoese navigator, on 1 May 1456, the feast day of St James the Less, a 1st-century apostle, and named after him. The island has a town with the same name. Also called Santiago Island.

São Tomé, SÃO TOMÉ AND PRÍNCIPE
An island with the name 'St Thomas' in Portuguese because it was discovered by the Portuguese on 21 December 1471, the feast day of St Thomas.

São Tomé and Príncipe The Democratic Republic of São Tomé and Príncipe (República Democrática de São Tomé e Príncipe) since 1975 when independence from Portugal was achieved. Previously it had been an Overseas Province of Portugal (1951–75) and a colony before that. The islands were probably uninhabited until the Portuguese began to settle in the late 15th century; they annexed them in 1522. The name means 'St Thomas

S

and Prince' (but *see* SÃO TOMÉ AND PRÍNCIPE separately). The state consists of the two main islands and several islets.

Saparmurad Türkmenbashi,
TURKMENISTAN *Oktyabr'sk*
Originally named to commemorate the Bolshevik October Revolution in 1917, it was renamed in honour of Saparmurad Niyazov (1940–) after he had become president of Turkmenistan in 1991 and took the title Türkmenbashi 'Head of the Turkmen'. *See* TÜRKMENBASHI AND NYYAZOW.

Sapele, DELTA/NIGERIA
A saw-milling centre since 1925, it takes its name from the sapele tree.

Sapporo, HOKKAIDŌ/JAPAN
Laid out in 1871. The name may come from the Ainu *satu-poro-betsu* 'a river which runs along a plain filled with reeds or 'a long dry river bed'; or from the Ainu *sachi-poro-kotan* 'large grass-covered plain'. Most place names in Hokkaidō are from Ainu, but when the Japanese arrived they replaced these with Chinese characters.

Saragossa (Zaragoza), ARAGÓN/SPAIN *Salduba, Caesarea Augusta, Saraqustah*
The Celtiberian town of Salduba was captured by the Romans in 27 BC; it was made into a colony and renamed after Caesar Augustus[†]. In *c.*714 it was taken by the Moors and renamed again with an Arabic version of the Roman name; the present name is also a version of the Roman name. It was the capital of the Kingdom of Aragón in 1118–1497, having been recaptured by Alfonso I (*c.*1073–1134), King of Aragón (1104–34), in 1118.

Sarai, ASTRAKHAN/RUSSIA
Archaeological remains near Volgograd. The name meant 'Palace' or 'Court', a Turkic word. Sarai was the capital of the Mongol Golden Horde, the Kipchak Khanate, between 1242 and the mid-15th century and at its foundation the word meant little more than 'Encampment'. This was known as Sarai Batu after Batu (d. *c.*1255), a grandson of Genghis Khan[†], who commanded the Mongol invasion of Europe in 1240. In due course, Sarai Berke, or Sarai al-Jadid 'New Sarai', further up the Volga River was founded.

Sarajevo, BOSNIA AND HERZEGOVINA *Vrhbosna, Bosna Saray*
The Slavs built a castle on a *vrh* 'summit' to the east with *bosna* the name of the river. This was captured by the Ottoman Turks in 1428 and they built the present city in 1462–89. Among the Turkish buildings was a *saray* 'palace' or 'seraglio'. Sarajevo takes its name from *saray-*

ovasi 'the fields around the palace' or 'palace forecourt'. It became the capital of Bosnia and Herzegovina in 1850.

Saraktash, ORENBURG/RUSSIA
'Sheep Rock' from the Tatar *saryk* 'sheep' and Uighur *tash* 'rock'.

Sarandë, ALBANIA *Onchesmos*
Derived from the Greek *saranta* 'forty' from Agii Saranta 'Forty Saints', the name of the Byzantine monastery which was dedicated to 40 saints.

Sārangpur, MADHYA PRADESH/INDIA
An important trading centre in the 13th century, it is named after Sarang Singh Khichi, its ruler.

Saransk, MORDOVIYA/RUSSIA
Founded as a military fort on the Insar River in 1641 and named after it. The river's name means 'large marsh'.

Saratoga Springs, NEW YORK/USA
Originally the site of a Native American village with several similar names. The best known one is Sa-ragh-to-ga 'place of swift water' or possibly 'place of water from a rock'. It was well known for its springs.

Saratov, RUSSIA *Sarytau*
A province and a city founded in 1590 as one of a line of fortresses on high ground to protect the trade route and control movement along the Volga River. The name may come from the Turkic *sary* 'yellow' and *tau* 'mountain', a reference to its elevated position overlooking the river.

Sarawak, MALAYSIA
A state in East Malaysia named after the Sarawak River, the meaning of which is unknown. The territory was given to the English Brooke family in 1841 as a personal fief and was recognized as an independent state by the UK in 1864. It became a British crown colony in 1946 and joined Malaysia in 1963.

Saray, TURKEY
'Palace', a Turkic word, although often used for a caravanserai, an inn for people travelling with caravans.

Sardinia, GREECE, ITALY, USA
Italy: an island locally called Sardegna. Its original name is said to have been Ichnusa from the Greek *ichnos* 'footprint' or 'imprint (on a trail)', the island being seen somewhat fancifully as a stepping stone in the Tyrrhenian Sea. It may have received its present name from a people called the Sards, who inhabited it at one time. It joined the

House of Savoy in 1720 as part of the Kingdom of Piedmont-Sardinia. It may have given its name to the sardine.

Sargasso Sea, NORTH ATLANTIC OCEAN
Named after the seaweed of the Sargassum genus that floats here in huge masses.

Sarnia, ONTARIO/CANADA
Settled in 1807 and named in 1835 after the Roman name for the island of Guernsey in the Channel Islands. It was given this name by Lieutenant General (later Field Marshal) Sir John Colborne (1778–1863), lieutenant-governor of Upper Canada (1828–38), who had been lieutenant-governor of Guernsey (1821–8).

Sarov, NIZHNY NOVGOROD/RUSSIA *Moscow-2, Arzamas-60, Arzamas-16, Kremlëvsk*
The Tatars built a stronghold here which they called Sarakly 'Yellow Sword'. The present town was built in 1946–54 as a 'closed city' whose existence was a state secret until openly mentioned in the 1980s by Andrei Sakharov (1921–89), a Soviet nuclear physicist. The suffix '-60' to Arzamas was its postcode, indicating that it was 60 km (37 miles) from Arzamas. This was considered later to be too obvious and so '-16' was substituted for '-60'. At various times the nuclear weapons research and development facility has also been called the Volga Office of the Chief Municipal Construction Board, Design Office 11, Facility 550, Centre 300, and Kremlëv. The town was renamed Kremlëvsk in 1994 and the following year adopted its historical name of Sarov which may be associated with Sarakly.

Saryagach, KAZAKHSTAN
'Yellow Tree' from *sary* 'yellow' and *agash* 'tree'.

Sarysu, KAZAKHSTAN
A town and a river meaning 'Yellow Water' from *sary* 'yellow' and *su* 'water'.

Sasebo, KYŪSHŪ/JAPAN
The characters represent *sa* 'to help', *se* 'generation' or 'world', and *ho* 'guarantee'.

Saskatchewan, CANADA
A province since 1905 named after the river. Its name comes from a Cree name *Kis-is-ska-tches-wan* 'Rapid (flowing) River'. Saskatchewan was part of the Northwest Territories when they were formed in 1869 and it became a district in 1882.

Saskatoon, SASKATCHEWAN/CANADA
Founded in 1883 as the projected capital of a temperance colony. Its name is derived from

the Cree *Mis-sask-guah-too-min* 'fruit of the tree with many branches', a reference to a tree that produced edible red berries.

Sassandra, CÔTE D'IVOIRE
Takes its name from the river at whose mouth it lies. The river's name is a shortening of *Santo Andrea* 'St Andrew', an apostle and martyr. Portuguese explorers landed here on 30 November 1497, St Andrew's feast day.

Sātāra, MAHĀRĀSHTRA/INDIA
Named after the seventeen walls of its fort from the Marathi *satarā* 'seventeen'.

Sātpura Range, DECCAN/INDIA
A mountain range with the descriptive name of 'Seven Folds'.

Satu Mare, ROMANIA *Szatmárnémeti*
A county and a city first mentioned in 1181 after it had been founded to facilitate the movement of salt along the Someş River. The name means 'Big Village' from *sat* 'village' and *mare* 'big'. The early German influence is clear from the previous Hungarian name, the second part, *németi*, meaning 'German'. The city was ceded to Romania in 1920.

Satun, THAILAND
Also known as Satul. The name is derived from *setul*, a Malay name for a tree common in this area. Until 1813 Satun was a district of the Malay state of Kedah.

Saudi Arabia The Kingdom of Saudi Arabia (al-Mamlakah al-ʻArabīyah as-Saʻūdīyah) since 1932. Previously the Kingdom of the Hejaz and Najd which was recognized internationally in 1927 after ʻAbd al-Azīz ibn Saʻūd (1880–1953), first King of Saudi Arabia (1932–53), had captured the mostly desert region of Najd, the traditional homeland of the Al-Saʻūd, in 1905 from the rival Ottoman Turkish-supported Al-Rashid tribe, and the Hejaz in 1924. In 1926 he was proclaimed King of the Hejaz and Sultan of Najd. Having established the House of Saʻūd as a ruling dynasty, ʻAbd al-Aziz became known as Ibn Saʻūd. The Arabian peninsula came under the somewhat tenuous control of the Ottoman Turks at the beginning of the 16th century and in due course the Hejaz became an Ottoman province. The *Saudi* in the country's name refers to the name of the dynasty whose eponym is Saʻūd ibn Muhammad ibn Muqrin; *Arabia* refers to the geographic region, principally the Arabian Peninsula.

Sauerland, NORTH RHINE-WESTPHALIA/GERMANY
A region meaning 'Bitter Land' from *sauer* 'bitter'. According to popular tradition, this is a

reference to the alleged bitter resistance of its inhabitants against Charlemagne[†] and the Franks towards the end of the 8th century. In fact, more likely, the name refers to the poor quality of the soil and the difficulty of cultivation because of the hilly terrain.

Saugas, MASSACHUSETTS/USA
Settled in 1629 and separated from Lynn in 1815. The name is an Algonquian word said to mean 'Small Outlet'; however, it has also been suggested that it means 'Extended'.

Sauk Centre, MINNESOTA/USA
Settled in 1856 and named after the Sauk (Sac). There is also a Sauk City in Wisconsin and a Sauk River in Washington State and Minnesota. Their name means 'People living at the River Mouth'.

Sault Sainte Marie, CANADA, USA
Twin cities in Ontario, Canada, and Michigan, USA, with a name meaning 'Rapids of St Mary' from the modern French *saut*. Both cities were established at the rapids on the St Mary River which was named after the Virgin Mary. Both originated as French missions, the one in Michigan in 1668 and the one in Ontario the following year.

Sava, BALKANS, ITALY
Balkans: a river whose two branches rise and join in Slovenia and which then joins the Danube at Belgrade, Serbia. It is named after St Sava (1173–1236), who became the first archbishop of the independent Serbian Orthodox Church in 1219.

Savannah, GRAND CAYMAN, USA
USA (Georgia): founded in 1733 and named after the Savannah River, at the mouth of which it lies. The river was called the Río Dulce 'Sweet River' and the Native American name for it was Isondega 'Blue Water'. The present name may come from the Spanish *sabana* 'savannah' or 'grassy plain' or it may be a Creek version of the name of the Shawnee who lived along the river at one time.

Sawatch Range, COLORADO/USA
A mountain range with the name coming from a Ute word meaning 'Blue-Earth Spring'.

Saxmundham, ENGLAND/UK *Sasmundeham*
'Seaxmund's Homestead' from an Old English personal name and *hām*.

Saxony (Sachsen), GERMANY
A state named after the Saxons. The area covered has varied over the centuries and historically it has been a duchy, an electorate, and a kingdom in 1806–1918. In 1952–90 it did not exist as a formal territory, but when East and West Germany united in 1990 it was

reconstituted as a state. Saxony-Anhalt is a separate state created in 1990 and consists of the former principality of Anhalt and part of the former Kingdom of Saxony. The state of Lower Saxony (Niedersachsen) was created in 1946.

Scandinavia *Scandia*
Generally accepted as comprising the peninsula of Norway and Sweden with Denmark and Iceland. Some claim that Finland and the Faroe Islands should also be included. The name is derived from the Roman Scandia whose meaning is unknown. *Avia* is of Germanic origin and represents 'island'. Scandinavia has given its name to the chemical element, Scandium.

Scarborough, AUSTRALIA, CANADA, SOUTH AFRICA, TOBAGO, UK, USA
1. Canada (Ontario): formerly Glasgow and renamed in 1793 following a proposal by the wife of John Simcoe, lieutenant-governor of Ontario, who thought that the cliffs here on the shores of Lake Ontario resembled those at Scarborough, England.
2. Tobago: formerly Port Louis and probably renamed after the city in England because it is located on the slopes of a hill overlooking a harbour.
3. UK (England): formerly Escardeburg 'Skarthi's Stronghold' from an Old Scandinavian personal name and *burh*. Skarthi was probably the name of the Viking who established a small fishing settlement here in the 10th century.
4. USA (Maine): named after the city in England because of its rocky site on the Atlantic coast. It is also spelt Scarboro.

Schaffhausen (French: **Schaffhouse**), SWITZERLAND *Villa Scafhusun*
A canton, which joined the Swiss Confederation in 1501, and a city first mentioned in 1045 as Villa Scafhusun. The German name means 'Sheephouse' from *Schaf* 'sheep' and *Haus* 'house', presumably a reference to an earlier covered sheep pen of some sort.

Schast'ye, UKRAINE
'Happiness'. Probably a Soviet attempt to encourage its inhabitants.

Schenectady, NEW YORK/USA *Schaunactada*
Founded as a Dutch settlement in 1661 with a name possibly derived from the nearby Mohawk village of Schaunactada 'Beyond the Pine trees'.

Schiedam, THE NETHERLANDS
Named after the dam built on the River Schie.

Schleswig, GERMANY, USA
Germany (Schleswig-Holstein): formerly
Sliesthorp and Sliaswich. Located at the head
of the Schlei, its name consists of the river
name and the Old Scandinavian *vík* 'bay, place
of commerce'. Schleswig is also the name of a
historical region; it became a Danish duchy in
the 12th century. Following dynastic problems,
the Danes were forced to relinquish it in 1864
after Prussian and Austrian troops had invaded
and in 1866, together with the Duchy of
Holstein, it was annexed by Prussia. In a
plebiscite in 1920 the northern part (north of
Flensburg) of Schleswig voted to join Denmark
to become the county of Sønderjylland 'South
Jutland' while the southern element elected to
stay within Germany.

Schleswig-Holstein, GERMANY
A state established in 1946 as a successor to the
Prussian province of that name. The former
German-speaking Duchy of Holstein has its
name from *Holt* 'wood' and *sittan* 'to be settled'.
The name started as Holtsetar and was
corrupted, inexplicably, to Holstein with *Stein*
'stone'. *See* SCHLESWIG.

Schönberg, GERMANY, LIECHTENSTEIN
'Beautiful Mountain' from *schön* 'beautiful' and
Berg.

Schoolcraft, MICHIGAN/USA
Named after Henry R. Schoolcraft (1793–1864),
who discovered the source of the Mississippi
River and was an authority on the Native
Americans, particularly the Ojibwa.

Schouten Islands, PAPUA NEW GUINEA *Misore
Islands*
Named after Willem Schouten (*c.*1580–1625), a
Dutch navigator, who was the first European
to see them.

Schuyler, NEBRASKA/USA
Named after Schuyler Colfax (1823–85), vice-
president of the USA (1869–73) under
President Ulysses S. Grant.

Schwäbisch Hall, BADEN-WÜRTTEMBERG/
GERMANY
'Swabian Salt'. The first word indicates its
location in the historic region of Swabia while
the second refers to its saline springs and trade
in salt from the Old High German *hal(le)* 'salt
works'. *See* HALLE.

Schweizer-Reneke, NORTH WEST/SOUTH
AFRICA *Mamusa*
Originally named after a Korana chief, David
Massouw, who had a fortified camp here. The
town was founded in 1888 and named after
Captain Constantin Schweizer and Field

Cornet C. N. Reneke, who were both killed
here in 1885 fighting Massouw.

Schwyz, SWITZERLAND *Suittes*
A canton which, with Uri and Unterwalden,
was a founding member of the Everlasting
League formed in 1291 from which stemmed
the present Swiss Confederation. In its local
German form, Schweiz (now the German for
Switzerland), it gave its name to the country.
The valley in which the original village of
Suittes is situated is highly forested and thus it
may take its name from the Old High German
suedan 'to burn', indicating forest clearance.
Schwyz is also the name of the canton's capital.

Sciacca, SICILY/ITALY *Thermae Selinuntinae,
as-Sāqqah*
A coastal town and health resort with hot
sulphur springs, its name is derived from the
previous medieval Arabic name which may
have meant 'fissure' or 'crevice'.

Scilla, CALABRIA/ITALY *Scyllaeum*
Named after the mythical sea monster Scylla,
who drowned sailors navigating the Strait of
Messina.

Scotland, AUSTRALIA, CANADA, UK, USA
UK: named after the Scots, Celts who came
from northern Ireland (which was then called
Scotia) in the 5th century to settle in what was
then Caledonia. This name comes from the
Caledonii, a tribe who lived in the far north and
which was the first to be met by the Romans.
The name of their area, Caledonia, then spread
northwards to the sea. The Gaelic Kingdom of
Alba came into existence in 843 when the
separate kingdoms, Picts and Scots, united
under Kenneth I MacAlpin (d. *c.*858); this was
the forerunner of modern Scotland. The British
Kingdom of Strathclyde was brought into the
fold in 1034, but attempts to expand into
northern England failed. In 1603 England and
Scotland were joined in a personal union,
although separate kingdoms were maintained,
when James VI of Scotland became James I[1] of
England. In 1707 the Act of Union between the
two kingdoms created, together with Wales,
the Kingdom of *Great Britain. The Scottish
Parliament was dissolved and was not re-
established until 1999 in an act of devolution
from the British government.

Scottburgh, KWAZULU-NATAL/SOUTH AFRICA
Founded in 1860 and named after Sir John
Scott (1814–98), lieutenant-governor of Natal
(1856–64).

Scottsdale, AUSTRALIA, USA
USA (Arizona): settled in 1895 by Winfield
Scott (1837–1910) and named after him. Now

part of Phoenix, *dale* was probably added to make the place sound more attractive although it has no dales.

Scranton, USA
Pennsylvania: developed from a small settlement begun in 1788. Several names (Unionville, Slocum Hollow, Harrison, and Scrantonia) were used before Scranton was chosen in 1851 as a tribute to two brothers, George and Selden Scranton, who had set up the Lackawanna Iron and Coal Company here in 1840.

Scunthorpe, ENGLAND/UK *Escumetorp*
'Outlying Farmstead belonging to Skúma' from an Old Scandinavian personal name and *thorp* 'outlying, or dependent, farmstead'.

Scutari, ALBANIA, TURKEY
See Shkodër (Albania) and Üsküdar (Turkey).

Searcy, ARKANSAS/USA *White Sulphur Springs*
Founded in the 19th century, but renamed after Richard Searcy, a circuit judge, when its springs ran dry.

Seattle, WASHINGTON/USA
Laid out in 1853 and named after Seathl (1786–1866), a Duwamish chief who had befriended early white settlers, given them land, and remained loyal to them during an uprising against them in 1855–8.

Sebeș, ROMANIA *Muhlbach*
Having been a Roman settlement, it was refounded in the 12th century by Germans, hence its previous German name 'Mill Stream'. Subsequently under Ottoman Turkish and Hungarian rule, it takes its present name from the River Sebeș which, in Hungarian, means 'fast(-flowing)'.

Secunderabad, ANDHRA PRADESH/INDIA *Husain Shah Pura*
A twin city with Hyderabad, Secunderabad (Sikandarabad) was founded and named by the British early in the 19th century after the Nizam of Hyderabad, Mir Akhbar 'Ali Khan Sikander Djāh.

Sedalia, CANADA, USA
USA (Missouri): renamed after the daughter of General G. R. Smith, who laid out the town. The present name is a more pleasant-sounding version of the original Sadieville.

Sedovo, RUSSIA, UKRAINE
Ukraine: originally Krivaya Kosa 'Crooked Sandspit' from *krivaya* 'crooked' and *kosa* 'spit'. It was renamed in 1941 after Georgy Sedov (1877–1914), an Arctic explorer who was born here and died in an attempt to reach the North Pole.

Ségou, MALI
A region and a town meaning 'Fortified Enclosure' from the Mande *segu*. It was the first capital of the Bambara Kingdom of Ségu which was at its most powerful during the 17th and 18th centuries. Bambara means 'unbeliever' or 'infidel', a name acquired when the people resisted forced conversion to Islam after Ségou had fallen in a Tukulor *jihād* 'holy war' in 1861.

Segovia, COLOMBIA, SPAIN
Spain (Castile-León): founded as Segóbriga, an Iberian settlement *c*.700 BC. Its name is derived from the Celtic *sego* 'strong' and *briga*, a reference to the fortified settlement which it was hoped would thwart Muslim raiders; nevertheless, it was occupied by the Moors between the 8th century and 1079.

Selby, UK, USA, ZIMBABWE
UK (England): formerly Seleby and Salebi 'Village near Willow Trees' from a possible Old English word *sele* 'willow copse' and the Old Scandinavian *bý*.

Selenge, MONGOLIA-RUSSIA
A river, also spelt Selenga, rising in Mongolia with a name derived from the Evenki *sele* 'yellow', a reference to the yellow hue of the iron ore deposits along its course. It is also the name of a province and town in Mongolia.

Sélestat, ALSACE/FRANCE *Scalistatus*
The Medieval Latin name is associated with the Old High German *sclade* 'marshland' and *state* 'place'.

Seleucia, IRAQ *Seleukeia*
Ruins. A Hellenistic city founded by Seleucus Nicator†. He made Seleucia (on the Tigris) his eastern capital and it was named after him. It was the most important Greek city in Babylonia, but was destroyed in AD 164.

Selinus, SICILY/ITALY
Ruins. Founded in the 7th century BC by Greek settlers who gave it the name 'Wild Celery' from the Greek *selinon* that grew, and still grows, in the area.

Selkirk, CANADA, UK, USA
1. Canada (Manitoba): settled in 1812 and named after Thomas Douglas (1771–1820), 5th Earl of Selkirk, who had founded the Red River Settlement in the area in 1811. He also gave his name to the Selkirk Mountains, largely in British Columbia.
2. UK (Scotland): formerly Selechirche and Seleschirche 'Church by a Hall' from the Old English *sele* 'hall' or 'house' and *cirice* 'church'; the second element was replaced by Scottish English *kirk*.

Selma, CANADA, USA
USA (Alabama): settled as Moore's Bluff or
Landing in 1815, it was renamed Selma in 1820
from the poem by Ossian, the legendary Gaelic
bard, recovered as 'The Song of Selma' by
James Macpherson (1736–96).

Semarang, JAVA/INDONESIA
'Nest', probably a reference to fish. The city is
noted for its fishing industry.

Semey, KAZAKHSTAN *Semipalatinsk*
Founded as a Russian fortress in 1718 some
10 miles (16 km) downstream from the present
town near the ruins of a Buddhist monastery
which consisted of seven buildings. The
original name, meaning 'Seven-halled' or
'Seven Palaces' from the Russian *sem'* 'seven'
and *palata* 'palace', is a reference to these
seven buildings. To escape the spring flooding
of the Irtysh River, the town was moved to its
present location in 1778. It was the capital of
the short-lived Alash-Orda independent
Kazakh state in 1917. After Kazakhstan
achieved its independence in 1991 the name
was changed to Semey 'Seven'.

Semigallia (Zemgale), LATVIA
A historic region, below sea level in parts,
named afer the Zemgal people, who inhabited
it before the German conquest in the 13th
century. Their name means '(People of the)
Lowlands'.

Seminole, USA
At least three cities have this name honouring
the Seminole people.

Semiozernoye, KAZAKHSTAN
'(Land of) Seven Lakes' from the Russian *sem'*
'seven' and the adjective *ozërnoye* from *ozero*
'lake'.

Semporna, SABAH/MALAYSIA
'Perfect'.

Senaki, GEORGIA *Senaki, Mikha Tskhakaya,
Tskhakaya*
Its first, and present, name is said to come
from the Mingrelian word for 'cells'. In 1935 it
was renamed after Mikhail Tskhakaya (1865–
1950), a prominent communist and
revolutionary, who returned to Russia with
Vladimir Lenin[†] in 1917; Mikha was his alias.
The name was shortened in 1976 and returned
to its original form in 1991.

Sendai, JAPAN
Honshū: the characters represent *sen*
'immortal mountain fairy' and *dai* 'platform'.
However, the name may come from the Ainu
sen-nai 'river mouth'. It lies between the
Nanakita and Hirose Rivers.

Seneca, USA
Several cities have this name, directly or
indirectly named after the Seneca people.

Senegal The Republic of Senegal
(République du Sénégal) since 1960 when
independence was achieved. Previously
Senegal had united with French Sudan (now
Mali) to form the Federation of Mali in 1959;
this became independent in June 1960, but
rivalry caused the Federation to break up after
only two months; an autonomous republic
within the French Community (1958); an
Overseas Territory of France (1946); part of
French West Africa (1895), the French having
established a slave-trading post at St Louis at the
mouth of the Sénégal River in 1659. Senegal
takes its name from the river that acts as its
northern border with Mauritania. Its name may
come from the Zenaga Berbers who established
an Islamic monastery on the bank of the river
c.1040; alternatively, it may be named after the
Wolof *sunu gaal* 'our canoe'. The name only
referred to the area around St Louis until the
19th century. *See* SENEGAMBIA below.

Senegambia A confederation that merged
Senegal (once an Overseas Territory of
France) and the Gambia (once a British
protectorate) in 1982. Apart from its Atlantic
coast, The Gambia is entirely surrounded by
Senegal. Gambian fears of absorption into
Senegal brought the confederation to an end
in 1989.

Senglea, MALTA
Following the construction of a fort here in
1552 by the Knights of Malta, their grand
master, Claude de la Sengle, founded a town
nearby two years later which was named after
him.

Senigallia, MARCHE/ITALY *Sena Gallica,
Sinigaglia*
Founded by the Senonian Gauls in the 6th
century BC and named after them. The
Romans took it in 289 BC, forming a colony
and calling it Sena Gallica. Sena probably
comes from the Indo-European *sen* 'old' or
'ancient' as the Latin *senex*.

Senlis, PICARDY/FRANCE *Civitas Silvanectium*
The present name comes from the former
Roman name 'City of the Silvanectes', a Gallic
people who lived in the area.

Senno, BELARUS
'Hay' from the Russian *seno*.

Sens, BURGUNDY/FRANCE *Agedincum*
Takes its name from the Senones people, a
Gallic tribe living in the area. As with

Senigallia above, their name may come from *sen* 'old'.

Seoul (Sŏul), SOUTH KOREA *Hanyang, Hansŏng, Kyŏngsŏng, Keijō*
The city became the capital of the unified Korea in 1394 when Yi T'aejo 'Great Progenitor', otherwise King Taejo, keen to make a clean break with the past, moved his capital from Namgyong 'Southern Capital' to the small city of Hanyang which was in the middle of the country. He built it anew and it became unofficially known as Seoul 'capital'; the official name, however, was Hansŏng 'City of the Han (dynasty)' from *sŏng* 'city'. During the period of Japanese rule in 1910–45 the city was renamed Kyŏngsŏng (in Korean) 'Capital City', from *kyŏng* 'capital' or 'metropolis', and Keijō (in Japanese) with the same meaning. In 1948, when the Republic of Korea (South Korea) was created, Seoul became the official name of its capital. Seoul, or rather Sŏul, is a pure Korean word, chosen with the desire to break away from previous Chinese and Japanese associations. Today the city has 'special city' status under the direct control of the national government with the title Sŏul-t'ŭkpyŏlsi 'Seoul Special City'.

Sept-Îles, QUEBEC/CANADA
Founded in 1650 as a trading post and Jesuit mission, it was named 'Seven Islands' by Jacques Cartier[†]. There are in fact only six islands in the estuary of the St Lawrence River here, the 'seventh' actually being part of the mainland.

Serafimovich, VOLGOGRAD/RUSSIA *Ust-Medveditskaya*
Originally a village named 'Mouth of the (River) Medveditskaya' from *ust'ye* 'mouth'; *medveditsa* means 'she-bear'. In 1933 it was renamed after Alexander Serafimovich (1863–1949), a writer, Civil War correspondent, and one of the founders of the Soviet Writers' Union, who lived here.

Serbia (Srbija), SERBIA AND MONTENEGRO *Raška/Rascia*
A constituent republic named after the Serbs. They arrived in the Balkan peninsula during the 7th century, some of them settling around Raš near modern Novi Pazar. Thus the area came to be known as Raška, the first true Serbian state. Stefan I Nemanja (d. 1200), the *Veliki Župan* 'grand ruler of a tribal area called a *župa*' of Raška (1169–96), set out to unite the Serbs and by 1186 he had succeeded in uniting Raška and Zeta (*see* MONTENEGRO). From this developed the medieval Serbian empire. Having defeated the Serbs at the Battle of Kosovo in 1389, the Ottoman Turks finally

subjugated the Serbs in 1459. Only in 1878 did the Serbs regain their independence. Serbia incorporated *Vojvodina and became part of the Kingdom of the Serbs, Croats, and Slovenes in 1918.

Serbia and Montenegro *Yugoslavia*
Serbia and Montenegro (Srbija i Crna Gora) since 2003. Previously the Federal Republic of Yugoslavia since 1992 after Bosnia and Herzegovina, Croatia, Macedonia and Slovenia had declared their independence from the Socialist Federal Republic of Yugoslavia between June 1991 and March 1992. *See separately* SERBIA, MONTENEGRO, AND YUGOSLAVIA.

Serebryanyy Bor, SAKHA REPUBLIC/RUSSIA *Gosplodopitomnik*
'Silver Forest' from *serebryannyy* 'silver' and *bor* 'coniferous forest'. The former name meant 'State Fruit Farm' from *gosudarstvennyy* 'state', *plod* 'fruit', and *pitomnik* 'nursery'.

Serengeti, TANZANIA
A national park, created in 1951, which is known to the local Masai as Serenget 'Great Open Space'.

Sergiyev Posad, MOSCOW/RUSSIA *Sergiyevsky Posad, Sergiyev, Zagorsk*
'Sergius's Quarter' after St Sergius of Radonezh (1314–92) and *posad* 'trading quarter' or 'suburb', as a result of the numerous pilgrims who came here to visit the Trinity-St Sergius monastery and the commercial activities that developed to support them. In 1918–30 *Posad* was dropped. The town was renamed between 1930 and 1991 after Vladimir Zagorsky (1883–1919), secretary of the Moscow Communist Party, killed by an anarchist in 1919.

Seringapatam, KARNĀTAKA/INDIA
See SRIRANGAPATNAM

Serov, YEKATERINBURG/RUSSIA *Nadezhdinsk, Kabakovsk*
Founded in 1894 and named after Nadezhda Polovtseva, the owner of the iron works here. It was renamed in 1934, for three years only, after Ivan Kabakov (1891–1937), a Communist Party official who was executed during Joseph Stalin's[†] purges. In 1937–9 it reverted to its original name and was then once more renamed, this time after Anatoly Serov (1910–39), a military test pilot who played an important role in the Spanish Civil War (1936–9) and who was born near here.

Sessa Aurunca, CAMPANIA/ITALY *Suessa*
Suessa was the principal city of the Italic tribe, the Aurunci. It was developed following the

destruction of Aurunca and Vescia by the Romans for a failure to pay tribute. The name became Sessa and in 1864 Aurunca was added as a reminder of ancient times.

Sète, LANGUEDOC-ROUSSILLON/FRANCE *Cette*
Given a new spelling in 1936, both names being derived from the pre-Indo-European root element *set* 'mountain', a reference to Mont Saint-Clair on whose lower slopes the port lies.

Seto, HONSHŪ/JAPAN *Kusueto*
The characters represent *se* 'rapids' and *to* 'door'. However, it is said that the previous name meant 'Place that produces Chinaware'; Seto is famous for its high-quality china clay.

Setúbal, PORTUGAL *Cetobriga*
Derived from the name of the Roman fort from the Celtic for 'Wooded Fortified Hill', although it is not in exactly the same location. The ruins at Tróia are thought to be on the site of Cetobriga which was destroyed by a tidal wave in 412.

Sevastopol', UKRAINE *Chersonesos, Akhtiar, Theodorichafen*
The ancient Greek colony of Chersonesos was founded in 421 BC. Subsequently, it became a Tatar port known as Akhtiar 'White Cliff'. After a steady decline it was redeveloped by the Russians after their annexation of the Crimea in 1783; a fortress and naval base were built and the next year the new city-port was named Sevastopol 'City of Glory' from the Greek *sebastos* 'noble' and *polis*. The unofficial German name Theodorichafen only lasted while the Germans occupied the city in 1942–4. The Russians claim now that when the Crimea was transferred to Ukraine in 1654 Sevastopol' was not included, having republic status within Russia. The Ukrainians dispute this, arguing that the Soviet Constitution did not mention Sevastopol''s status as a federal city.

Sevenoaks, ENGLAND/UK *Seouenaca*
'(Place by) Seven Oak-Trees' from the Old English *seofon* 'seven' and *āc* 'oak'.

Seven Seas, The The Arctic, the North and South Atlantic, the North and South Pacific, the Indian, and the Antarctic Oceans. Before the 15th century Muslim seafarers used the term to describe the regions of their explorations; thus, the Mediterranean Sea, the Red Sea, the East African and West African Seas, the Persian Gulf, the Indian Ocean, and the China Sea.

Severnaya Zemlya, RUSSIA *Zemlya imperatora Nikolaya II*
'Northern Land' from *severnaya* 'northern' and *zemlya* 'land'. An archipelago discovered in 1913 and named 'Emperor Nicholas II[†] Land' after the reigning emperor. Following the Bolshevik Revolution in 1917, it was renamed in 1926 with the four largest islands being given suitable communist names: October Revolution, Bolshevik, Komsomolets, and Pioneer.

Severnyy, RUSSIA
'Northern (Town)' or 'Northerly (Town)'.

Severnyye Uvaly, NORTH-WESTERN RUSSIA
A range of hills called 'Northern Steep Slopes' from *severnyy* and the plural of *uval* 'steep slope'.

Severodonetsk, UKRAINE
Founded in 1934 as 'Northern Donets' from *sever* 'north' and the name of the Donets River.

Severodvinsk, ARKHANGEL'SK/RUSSIA *Molotovsk*
Situated at the mouth of the Northern Dvina River, it means 'Northern Dvina' from *sever* and Dvina. In 1938–57 it was named after Vyacheslav Molotov[†].

Severomorsk, MURMANSK/RUSSIA *Vayenga*
Renamed in 1951 'Northern Sea' from *sever* and a form of *more* 'sea'. Previously it was named after the Vayenga River.

Sevilla, COLOMBIA, PANAMA
Colombia: founded in 1903 as San Luis 'St Louis' and renamed after Seville, the city in Spain, in 1914.

Seville, SPAIN, USA
Spain (Andalusia): Spanish Sevilla. Situated in the middle of a plain, its name is derived from the Phoenician *sefala* 'plain'. The city was founded in the 2nd century BC as the Roman Hispalis on an Iberian settlement. Julius Caesar[†] renamed it Colonia Julia Romula. In 711–1248 it was held by the Moors who gave it the name Isbiliya or Ixvillia, the Arabic version of the original Roman name. It gives its name to the bitter orange used to make marmalade.

Seward, USA
Alaska: founded in 1903 and named after William H. Seward (1801–72), US secretary of state (1861–9), who bought Alaska from Russia for $7.2 million in 1867; at the time the purchase was known as 'Seward's Folly'. A peninsula is also named after him.

Seychelles *Îles de Bourdonnais, Séchelles*
The Republic of Seychelles (Creole: Repiblik Sesel) since 1976 when independence was

achieved. The republic consists of a cluster of 115 islands in the Indian Ocean. They were first sighted in 1501 by Portuguese explorers who named the largest island 'Seven Sisters'. The first landing was made by the British in 1609 and in 1742 Bertrand-François Mahé (1699–1753), Comte de la Bourdonnais, then governor of what is now Mauritius, dispatched a French naval captain to explore the islands. He did so and named them after the count. In 1756 the French laid claim to the islands and named them officially after Jean Moreau de Séchelles, the French controller-general of finance. The islands surrendered to the British in 1810 and were formally ceded to the UK in 1814. They were then administered as a dependency of Mauritius until 1903 when they became a British crown colony. The erroneous English spelling has survived.

Seyðisfjörður, ICELAND
Derived from *seydis* 'barley water' and *fjördur* 'fjord', a reference to the rather cloudy water here.

Seymour, ANTARCTICA, AUSTRALIA, CANADA, GALAPAGOS ISLANDS, SOUTH AFRICA, USA
1. Australia (Victoria): founded in 1837 and named after Edward Adolphus Seymour (1804–85), 12th Duke of Somerset, first lord of the British Admiralty (1859–66).
2. South Africa (Eastern Cape): originally a British military post built in 1846 and called Eland's Post after the animal. The town was founded in 1853 and the name was changed as a tribute to Colonel Charles Seymour, military secretary to Sir George Cathcart, governor of Cape Colony (1852–4).
3. USA (Connecticut): founded in 1678 on land bought from the Pequot who called it Naugatuck. Subsequently, it enjoyed various names: Rimmon, Chusetown after a local Native American chief, and Humphreyville after General David Humphreys. In 1850 it was renamed after Thomas H. Seymour, governor of Connecticut at the time.

Sfax (Ṣafāqis), TUNISIA *Taparura*
Built on the site of the Roman Taparura, the fortified monastery had grown into a town by the 9th century. It fell to a French attack in 1881. The name is said to be derived from the Arabic for 'City of Cucumbers', although why this should be so is not known.

's Gravenhage, THE NETHERLANDS
See HAGUE, THE.

Shaanxi, CHINA
A province meaning 'West of the Pass' from *xī* and *shān*, a reference to the Shan Pass in Shan county where the River Wei flows into the Yellow River. The province's name is spelt with a double *a* to distinguish it from the neighbouring province of Shanxi, whose first character, *shān*, means 'mountain'.

Shaba, DEMOCRATIC REPUBLIC OF THE CONGO
See KATANGA.

Shache, SINKIANG UIGHUR AUTONOMOUS REGION/CHINA *Yarkand/Yarkant*
Originally this was the ancient Kingdom of the Shache, after whom it takes its name. Lying in an oasis on the Yarkand River, by the 11th century the present city had been renamed after the river from the Turkish *yār* 'precipice' or 'vertical bank of a river' and the Persian *kand* 'town'. The city comprises several walled districts, one of which is called Yarkand and another Shache and either name can be used for the whole city.

Shaftesbury, ENGLAND/UK *Sceafetesburi, Sceftesberie*
Possibly 'Sceaft's Fortified Place' from an Old English personal name and *burh* or 'Fortified Place on a Pole-shaped Hill' from the Old English *sceaft*.

Shāhjahānpur, UTTAR PRADESH/INDIA
Founded in 1647 and named 'City of Shah Jahān' after Shah Jahān (1592–1666), Mughal emperor of India (1628–58), with the additional *pur*. His name means 'King of the World' from the Persian *shāh* 'king' and *jahān* 'world'. One of Delhi's former names honoured him.

Shāhpura, RĀJASTHĀN/INDIA
Founded *c*.1629 and named after Shah Jahān (see previous entry).

Shājāpur, MADHYA PRADESH/INDIA
Founded *c*.1640 and named after Shah Jahān. The name is a shortening of *Shāhjahānpur.

Shakaskraal, KWAZULU-NATAL/SOUTH AFRICA
'Shaka's Enclosed Village' from the Afrikaans *kraal* 'protected enclosure of huts' or 'livestock pen' and the name of Shaka (*c*.1788–1828), Zulu chief (1818–28).

Shaker Heights, OHIO/USA *North Union*
Built on the site of a former 19th-century Shaker colony called North Union. It was renamed 'Shaker Heights', indicating high ground.

Shakhimardan, UZBEKISTAN *Khamzaābād*
One of the Uzbek enclaves within Kyrgyzstan. It means 'King of Men' from the Persian *Shakh-i-Mardan*. This is a reference to Ali, the son-in-law of the Prophet Muhammad[†] and the fourth caliph (656–61), who is said to be buried here (one of a number of places). After the

Bolshevik Revolution in 1917 it was renamed the 'Town of Khamza' after Khamza Niyazi (1889–1929), a secular poet and playwright who was born here. He spoke out against Islam and announced the forthcoming destruction of Ali's mausoleum. For this, according to the Soviet authorities, he was stoned to death in 1929 by Muslim extremists—and thus became a Soviet martyr.

Shakhrisabz, UZBEKISTAN *Kesh*
Settled in the 13th century, it was renamed in the 14th century by Tamerlane[†] 'Green Town' from the Tajik *shakr-i-sabz*, in recognition of its position in a lush oasis.

Shakhtërsk, RUSSIA, UKRAINE
Towns on Sakhalin Island, Russia, and in Ukraine have this name meaning 'miner' from the Russian *shaktĕr* because of their associations with the coal-mining industry. The town in Ukraine was formerly known as Katyk.

Shakhtinsk, KAZAKHSTAN
A centre of the Karaganda Coal Basin, the name recognizes its coal-mining from the Russian *shakhta* 'mine'.

Shakhty, ROSTOV/RUSSIA *Aleksandrovsk-Grushevskiy*
Until 1920 named after an unknown Alexander, possibly an emperor, and the river, the Grushevka, on which it lies. The present name means 'pits' from the plural of *shakhta* because of the coal mines in the area.

Shamil'kala, DAGESTAN/RUSSIA *Svetogorsk*
'City of Shamil' and named after Shamil (c.1797–1871), a Muslim imam who led the Dagestani and Chechen resistance to the Russian conquest of the Caucasus in 1835–59. When he was captured in 1859 he was allowed to go on a pilgrimage to Mecca where he died. The town's former name meant 'Town of Light' from *svet* 'light' and *gorsk*.

Shamokin, PENNSYLVANIA/USA *Boyd's Stone-Coal Quarry, Boydtown, New Town*
Founded in 1835 by two coal speculators, one of whom was John C. Boyd, it was renamed at his suggestion from a Delaware word *schahamoki* 'place of eels' or 'place of horns'.

Shamva, ZIMBABWE *Abercorn*
It may take its name from the *tsamvi*, a type of wild fig that grows here. Alternatively, it may be derived from a Shona word meaning 'to become friendly'. Its former name was a tribute to James Hamilton (1838–1913), 2nd Duke of Abercorn, who took over as president of the British South Africa Company when Cecil Rhodes[†] resigned following the failure of

the Jameson raid to overthrow the Boer government in 1895.

Shan, BURMA
A state named after the Shan people who are of Thai descent.

Shandong, CHINA
A province meaning 'East of the Mountain', a reference to the Mount Xiao complex to the south-west, from *shān* and *dōng* 'east'. In Wade-Giles romanization the name is Shan-tung and Shantung is the name of the famous silk.

Shangdu, INNER MONGOLIA AUTONOMOUS REGION/CHINA *Kaiping*
'City of 108 Temples' in Mongolian and 'Upper Capital' from *shàng* 'upper' and *dū* 'capital', the name given to it c.1263 by Khubilai Khan (1215–94), Mongol emperor (1260–94), who commissioned it (first as Kaiping from *kāi* 'open up' or 'reclaim' and *píng* 'peaceful'); it was his summer capital. Marco Polo called it Ciandu which was the origin of Xanadu, a place of unimaginable splendour, in Samuel Taylor Coleridge's famous poem *Kubla Khan* written in 1797.

Shanghai, CHINA *Shanghaizhen*
A municipality established in 1267, situated at the mouth of the Huangpu River in the Yangtze delta, the name means 'By the Sea' from *shàng* 'by' or 'on' and *hǎi*. The *zhèn* in the former name meant 'garrison post', although now it is usually 'town'. Opened up to foreign trade following the Treaty of Nanking in 1842, it soon attracted adventurers and criminals. The phrase 'to shanghai' originally meant to make a person insensible by trickery to get him to serve on board a ship in need of more crewmen; to send him to Shanghai, to send him on a long voyage. Now, it more often means to abduct a person by force or coerce him or her into doing something against their will.

Shangqui, HENAN/CHINA *Zhujizhen, Zhujiaji, Zhuji City*
An ancient market town, the name comes from *shāng* 'business' or 'commerce' and *qiū* 'hillock' or 'mound'. According to legend, the local people did not know how to make fire, relying instead on naturally occurring fires which they found difficult to keep burning. The king's son built a mound on which he lit a fire under a cover so that it could not be extinguished by rain or flood. The king gave the area to his son and named it Shang. When his son died he was buried on the mound and it became known as 'Shang's Mound'. In due course this name was applied to the settlement here. As the modern city began to

grow at the beginning of the 15th century, it was called Zhujizhen from *zhū* 'vermilion', *jí* 'fair' or 'market', and *zhèn* 'garrison post' or 'town'. About 1851 this was changed to Zhujiaji from *jiā* 'family'. In 1948 it was renamed Zhuji City, but three years later the present name was adopted.

Shangzhou, SHAANXI/CHINA *Shangluo, Luozhou, Shangxian, Zhilizhou*
Originally Shangluo 'On the (River) Luo' from *shàng* 'on' and the name of the river. In 487 it was renamed Luozhou from *zhōu* and in 578 this was changed to Shangzhou from *shāng* 'business' or 'commerce' in recognition of its importance as a communications and trading centre. In the late 14th century Shangxian from *xiàn* 'county' was adopted for a short time before returning to Shangzhou. Between c.1723 and 1913 the city was called Zhilizhou before returning to Shangxian. Finally, in 1988, the present name was adopted.

Shanhaiguan, HEBEI/CHINA
A strategic 'Pass between Mountains and Sea' from *shān, hǎi,* and *guān'ài* 'pass' constructed in 1381. It has also been called Yú 'Elm'.

Shannon, CANADA, GREENLAND, IRELAND, NEW ZEALAND, USA
Ireland: a river locally called Sionainn, formerly Senos and Sinand, probably meaning 'Old (Water) Goddess' from a Celtic word associated with modern Irish *sean* 'old'.

Shantiniketan, WEST BENGAL/INDIA
'Peaceful Abode' from *shanti* 'peaceful' and *niketan* 'abode'.

Shanxi, CHINA
A province meaning 'West of the Mountain', a reference to the rugged terrain lying west of Mt Xiao in Henan Province, from *shān* and *xī*.

Shaoguan, GUANGDONG/CHINA *Hengzhou, Shaozhou*
An important communications and trading centre, the city was renamed Shaozhou from *sháo* 'harmonious', referring to the type of music played at the time, and *zhōu*. *Guān* is short for *shuiguān* 'customs house', which was established here at the end of the Ming dynasty (1368–1644). The present name was adopted in 1949.

Shaoshan, HUNAN/CHINA
'Music Mountain' from *sháo* 'harmonious' and *shān*. According to legend, the sage Emperor Shun in ancient times rested on a peak here that overlooks the valley and commanded his entourage to make music.

Shaoyang, HUNAN/CHINA *Zhaoling, Shaoling, Shaozhou, Baoqing*
Lying at the confluence of the Zi and Shao Rivers, the name was changed to Shaoling after one of the rivers in the 3rd century to avoid use of the character *zhāo* which was the emperor's personal name. In 636 it was renamed Shaozhou and in 1225 the Baoqing Prefecture during the first year of Emperor Baoqing's reign (1225–8). It was renamed Shaoyang County in 1928 and in 1950 this was divided into Shaoyang County and Shaoyang City. Shao may be a personal name with *yáng* here meaning 'north bank (of the River Shao)'.

Sharjah (ash-Shāriqah), UNITED ARAB EMIRATES
A constituent emirate of the UAE and its capital city with a name meaning 'The Eastern', possibly a reference to the fact that it lies at the eastern end of the Persian Gulf.

Sharm ash-Shaikh, EGYPT
A town named after a bay called 'Inlet of the Shaikh' from the Arabic *sharm* 'channel through reefs' or 'bay'. The Hebrew name is Mifraz Shlomo 'Solomon's Bay', a reference to the fact that King Solomon's ships probably passed through the Strait of Tiran here from Ezion-geber at the head of the Gulf of Aqaba to the land of Ophir, mentioned in the Bible (1 Kings 9: 26–8). A town, Ophira, was built on the bay in 1972. Sharm ash-Shaikh was held by the Israelis between 1967 and 1982.

Sharon, USA
Several cities have this name after the Plain of Sharon in Israel (see next entry).

Sharon, Plain of (Ha-Sharon), ISRAEL
Part of the fertile coastal plain, the name is said to come from the Hebrew *yashar* 'straight' or 'flat'. It is mentioned several times in the Bible.

Sharypovo, KRASNOYARSK TERRITORY/RUSSIA *Chernenko*
Briefly named in 1985–8 after Konstantin Chernenko (1911–85), the ineffectual Soviet leader (1984–5) who was born near here. The meaning of the present name is not known.

Shaṭṭ al-'Arab, IRAQ
A river formed by the confluence of the Tigris and Euphrates Rivers with a name literally meaning 'Bank of the Arabs' from *shaṭṭ* 'shore'or 'bank'; however, here, *shaṭṭ* refers to the river itself to mean 'River of the Arabs'. From a point south-east of Basra to the Persian Gulf the eastern bank forms the border between Iraq and Iran. The Iranians refer to it as the Arvand Rūd 'Sublime River'.

Shaumyani, GEORGIA *Shulaveri*
Renamed in 1925 after Stepan Shaumyan
(1878–1918), a Georgian and one of the leaders
of the revolutionary movement in the
Caucasus. He was particularly active in Baku,
Azerbaijan, and was one of the 26 Baku
commissars executed by Social
Revolutionaries (although, as they had a small
expeditionary force in Baku at the time, the
British have ever since been held responsible).

Shaumyanovsk, AZERBAIJAN
See AŠAGHY AGDZHAKAND.

Shawinigan, QUEBEC/CANADA
Named after the nearby Shawinigan Falls on
the Saint-Maurice River. Their name is derived
from an Algonquian word for 'crest', a
reference to the portage that led over a crest by
the falls.

Shawnee, USA
Several cities have this name after the
Shawnee people who made Gum Springs their
capital in 1828. The Kansas city was formerly
called Gum Springs.

Sheboygan, WISCONSIN/USA
Established as a trading post in 1818, it takes
its name from the river at whose mouth it lies.
Its name may be an Algonquian word meaning
'wind'; this would accord with another theory
that it is derived from the word *jibaigan*
meaning a perforated tube, perhaps a pipe
stem. However, it has also been suggested that
it comes from *shawb-wa-way* with the sense of a
loud noise coming from underground which
was heard here.

Sheerness, CANADA, UK
UK (England): formerly Scerhnesse 'Bright
Headland' from the Old English *scīr* 'bright' or
'clear' and *næss* 'headland'.

Sheffield, CANADA, UK, USA
1. Canada (New Brunswick): named after John
Baker Holroyd (1735–1821), 1st Earl of
Sheffield, a leading authority on agriculture
and commerce and lord of the British Board of
Trade from 1809.
2. UK (England): formerly Scafeld 'Open Land
by the Sheaf (River)' from the river name and
feld. The river's name comes from the Old
English *scēath* 'boundary', indicating that it
formed a border between Derbyshire and the
West Riding of Yorkshire. The first element of
Sheffield Green in Sussex, however, is
associated with 'sheep' from the Old
English *scēap*; and in Sheffield Bottom in
Berkshire it means 'Open Land with a
Shelter' from the possible Old English *scēo*
'shelter'.

Shelburne, CANADA, USA
All the places called Shelburne in Canada and
the USA are directly or indirectly named after
Sir William Petty (1737–1805), 2nd Earl of
Shelburne, British secretary of state for the
southern department (1766–8) and prime
minister (1782–3). Before becoming prime
minister he was an opponent of the
government's policy towards its American
colonies, although he said he would never
accept their independence. Nevertheless, as
prime minister, he was deeply involved in
attempts to resolve the main issues of
the peace treaty between Great Britain and
the USA.

Shelekhov, IRKUTSK/RUSSIA
Founded in 1962 and named after Grigory
Shelekhov (1747–95), a navigator and
merchant, who explored the coast of
Alaska in 1783–6 during which time the
first Russian settlements were established
there. He became governor of these
settlements in Russian America. He died in
nearby Irkutsk.

Shelikov, RUSSIA, USA
The Gulf of Shelikhov (Zaliv Shelikhova), north
of the Sea of Okhotsk, Shelikof Bay on the
Alaskan Chicagof Island, and Shelikof Strait
between the Alaskan mainland and Kodiak
Island are all named after Grigory Shelekhov
(see previous entry).

Shemakha, AZERBAIJAN
Situated in the foothills of the Caucasus
Mountains, its name comes from the Arabic
shāmīkha 'high' or 'towering'.

Shenandoah, USA
Cities, a mountain, and a river with an
Algonquian name said to mean 'Sprucy
Stream'.

Shenyang, LIAONING/CHINA *Shen, Shenzhou,
Mukden, Shengjing, Fengtian*
Originally a frontier post and then an
important frontier settlement on the
northern bank of the Hun River, the city was
first known as Shen (*Shěn*, the name of the
Hun at that time). It became Shenzhou in
928 to reflect its status as an administrative
district and in 1297 the Mongols replaced the
-*zhou* with -*yang* from *yáng* 'north bank' to
give Shenyang. This was changed by the
Manchus to Mukden (Móukèdūn in Pinyin)
'Prosperous' in Manchu in 1634 after it had
been made the capital of the Latter Jin. In
Mandarin it was known as Shengjing
'Prosperous Capital' from *shèng* 'prosperous'
and *jing* 'capital'. In 1657 it became part of a
new prefecture called Fengtian from *fèng*

'revere' and *tiān* 'heaven' and in 1923 the city was renamed Fengtian. Shenyang was readopted in 1950.

Shenzhen, GUANGDONG/CHINA
Takes its name from the Shenzhen River from *shēn* 'deep' and *zhèn* 'water channel'. The river was so named because it cuts deeply through paddy fields.

Shepherdstown, WEST VIRGINIA/USA
Mecklenburg
Settled by Germans *c*.1730, hence the name Mecklenburg which it received in 1762. It was renamed in 1798 after Thomas Shepherd who had originally laid out the town.

Shepparton, VICTORIA/AUSTRALIA *Canny-Goopna, Macguire's Punt*
Known as Canny-Goopna 'River of Big Fish' by the Aborigines, it became a sheep run in 1843 under the control of Sherbourne Sheppard. When the first European settlement was established in the early 1850s it was renamed Macguire's Punt after a ferryman. It was renamed again in 1853 after Sheppard.

Sheppey, Isle of, ENGLAND/UK *Scepeig, Scape*
'Island where Sheep graze' from the Old English *scēap* 'sheep' and *ēg*.

Sherborne ENGLAND/UK *Scireburnan, Scireburne*
(*Dorset*)
'(Place on) the Clear Stream' from *scīr* 'clear' and *burna* 'stream'. Clear Stream, or Sherborne, was the name of the river.

Sherbrooke, CANADA
Quebec: originally a fur trading post named in 1818 after General Sir John Sherbrooke (1764–1830), governor-general of Canada (1816–18).

Sheridan, CANADA, USA
USA: several cities have this name, usually in honour of General Philip H. Sheridan (1831–88), a cavalry officer who did much to encompass the final defeat of the Confederate Army in 1865, the last year of the Civil War.

Sherman, USA
1. New York: named after Roger Sherman (1721–93), a politician and one of the men who signed the American Declaration of Independence in 1776.
2. Texas: founded in the 1840s and named after General Sidney Sherman (1805–73), a cavalry officer who was prominent during the Texan Revolt against the Mexicans in 1835–6.

's Hertogenbosch (Den Bosch), THE NETHERLANDS *Den Bosch, Bois-le-Duc*
'The Duke's Wood' from the Old Dutch *des* 'of the', *Hertogen*, the genitive of *hertog* 'duke', and *Bosch* 'wood'. The duke was Henry I (d. 1235), Duke of Brabant, and the city, chartered in 1185, was so named because he had a hunting lodge nearby.

Shetland Islands, SCOTLAND/UK *Hjaltland*
A unitary district and a group of about 100 islands which came under Norse rule in the 9th century and remained so until 1469 when the islands were annexed by Scotland. The name is difficult but is claimed to have come from the Old Scandinavian *hjalt* 'high' or 'hilt (of a sword)' and *land*. This might have been a description of the shape of the group. The Shetland pony originated here.

Shiga, HONSHŪ/JAPAN
A prefecture with the characters representing *shi* 'nourish' and *ga* 'celebrate'.

Shiḥr, ash-, YEMEN
'Coastland (at the Mouth of a Wadi)', a reference to the wild mountainous coast which also gives its name to the town. It was called Escier by Marco Polo.

Shijiazhuang, HEBEI/CHINA *Shimen*
Takes its name from *shí* 'stone', *jiā* 'family', and *zhuāng* 'village'. In 1925 it merged with the neighbouring Xiumen and the two names were combined to give Shimen 'Stone Gate' from *mén* 'gate'. It reverted to its present name in 1947.

Shikarpur, INDIA, PAKISTAN
Pakistan (Sindh): founded in 1677 as 'Hunters' Town' on the hunting grounds of the Mahars originally from the Persian *shikār* 'hunting' which in Hindi became *shikārī* 'hunter' or 'stalker' and the additional *pur*.

Shikoku, JAPAN
An island region meaning 'Four Provinces' from *shi* 'four' and *koku* 'province'. These refer to four ancient feudal provinces which are now four prefectures.

Shikotan, KURIL ISLANDS/RUSSIA
'Good Place' or 'Large Place' from the Ainu *shi* 'good' or 'large' and *kotan* 'place'.

Shiloh, USA, WEST BANK
USA (Ohio): 'Place of Peace' in Hebrew and named after the Canaanite city, long in ruins, in the West Bank. The Shiloh National Military Park is in Tennessee.

Shimada, HONSHŪ/JAPAN
'Rice Field Island' from *shima* and *ta* 'rice field'.

Shimane, HONSHŪ/JAPAN
A prefecture whose characters represent *shima* and *ne* 'root'.

Shimizu, JAPAN
Honshū: here the first character represents *shin* 'clean' with *mizu* 'water'.

Shimodate, HONSHŪ/JAPAN
The characters represent *shimo* 'lower' and *date* 'castle'. Three castles were built in the late 10th century and this one was the furthest south, thus 'lower'.

Shimoni, KENYA
'Caves' from the Swahili *shimo*. The town is well-known for its caves.

Shimonoseki, HONSHŪ/JAPAN *Aka-maga-seki, Bakan*
'Lower Barrier' from *shimo* 'lower', *no* indicating the genitive, and *seki* 'barrier'. The original name has characters representing *aka* 'red', *ma* 'between', *ga* 'of', and *seki*. Bakan comes from *ba* 'horse' and *kan* 'barrier'.

Shinano, HONSHŪ/JAPAN
A river with the characters representing *shin* 'faith' and *nō* 'dark'.

Shizuoka, HONSHŪ/JAPAN *Sumpu*
A prefecture originally named Sumpu with the characters representing *sun* 'fleet' and *hu* 'prefecture'. It was renamed in 1869 'Calm Hill' from *shizu* 'calm' and *oka* 'hill'.

Shkodër, ALBANIA-SERBIA AND MONTENEGRO *Ishkodra, Scutari*
The present name is the Albanian version of the Italian Scutari which comes from the Latin *scutarii* 'shield-makers'. The lake on which the town lies has various local names: Scutari, Skadarsko Jezero 'Lake Skadar' in Serbo-Croat, and Ligeni Shkodrës in Albanian. The town is also known as Scutari, Skadar, or Shkodra. Two-thirds of the lake belong to Montenegro and one-third to Albania. *See* ÜSKÜDAR.

Shlissel'burg, LENINGRAD/RUSSIA *Oreshek, Nöteburg, Schlüsselburg, Petrokrepost'*
Both the first two Russian and Swedish names mean 'nut' (in Russian, *orekh*), the original fortress being so named in 1323 after the hazelnut shape of the island, also called Oreshek, on which it was built. It was captured in 1611 by the Swedes who built the fortress of Nöteburg 'Lake Skadar' Nut Castle'. Recaptured by Peter I the Great[†] in 1702, it was renamed Schlüsselburg 'Key Fort' from the German *schlüssel* 'key' since it would protect Peter's new capital of St Petersburg. Furthermore, situated on the River Neva where it flows out of Lake Ladoga, it was the key to the river and thus to the Baltic Sea 45 miles (70 km) away. Following the German siege of Leningrad (now St Petersburg) between September 1941 and January 1944, the German language name was changed to Petrokrepost' 'Peter's Fortress' from *krepost'* 'fortress'. The name became Shlissel'burg in 1991.

Shōdo Shima, HONSHŪ/JAPAN
An island in the Inland Sea. The characters represent *shō* 'small' and *do* 'bean', the adzuki bean, and *shima*.

Shoeburyness, ENGLAND/UK *Sceobryig, Soberia, Shoberynesse*
'Fortress providing Shelter' from the Old English *scēo* 'shelter' and *byrig*, the dative of *burh*. *Nesse* 'promontory' was added later.

Shoshone, USA
Cities, falls, a lake, a river, and mountains all have this name after the Shoshone.

Show Low, ARIZONA/USA
According to tradition, two men, C. E. Cooley and Marion Clark, agreed that their nameless settlement was too small for the two of them. The result of a game of cards would decide which had to leave. Clark allegedly said: 'If you can show low, you win.' Cooley drew the two of clubs. 'Show Low it is,' he said, and that became the name of the settlement.

Shreveport, LOUISIANA/USA
Founded in 1837 by, and named after, Henry M. Shreve (1785–1851), a river captain, who two years earlier had opened up the Red River by unblocking it of the debris which prevented navigation.

Shrewsbury, UK, USA
1. UK (England): formerly Scrobbesbyrig and Sciropesberie, probably 'Fortified Place in Scrubland' from an Old English word related to *scrobb* 'scrub' and *byrig*.
2. USA (Massachusetts and Pennsylvania): both are named after the town in England from which the early settlers came.

Shropshire, ENGLAND/UK *Scrobbesbyrigscir, Sciropescire, Salop(escire)*
A county whose name is based on the Old English form of *Shrewsbury with the additional *scīr*, thus Shrewsburyshire. Salopescira was the Norman name which was shortened to Salop, a name used officially in 1974–80. The Norman Salopescira came about because of the Norman inability to pronounce the *Scr* of *Scrobbesbyrig*; Scrob(bes) became Salop, the *Sc* becoming *Sa* and the *r* being changed to *l* (as Sarisberie became Salisbury).

Shumen, BULGARIA *Shumla, Kolarovgrad*
Derived from *shuma* 'foliage', here probably 'forest'. An important fortress town founded in 927, in 1950–65 it was renamed after Vasil Kolarov (1877–1950), a revolutionary and communist ideologist who was born here.

Under Ottoman Turkish control it was called Shumla or Chumla.

Shuraabad, AZERBAIJAN
Takes its name from the Azeri *shura* 'council' and *abad*.

Shurugwi, ZIMBABWE *Selukwe, Sebanga Poort*
Founded in 1899 and given this name because of the resemblance of a bare oval granite hill close by to the shape of a Venda pigpen, *shurugwi*, earlier spelt *selukwe*.

Shusha, AZERBAIJAN *Panakhabad*
'Glass'. The name stems from a challenge laid down by the Persian Shah Muhammad Aga who, as his army approached, said to Khan Ibrahim: 'God is pouring stones on thy head. Sit ye not then in thy fortress of glass.' Shah Muhammad died and the city held out. The name was thus changed from the earlier 'City of Panakh', a khan of Karabakh. It is also spelt Shushi.

Shwebo, BURMA *Moksobomyo, Shwebomyo*
The original name meant 'Town of the Hunter Chief' from *mokso* 'hunter', *bom* 'chief', and *myo* 'town'. In *c*.1753 the longer form of the present name was adopted and it meant 'Town of the Golden Chief' from *shwe* 'golden' and *myo*. This was a reference to King Alaungpaya (1714–60), King of Burma (1752–60), whose birthplace this was and whose tomb is here. It was the capital of the Alaungpaya dynasty in 1752–63.

Shyghys Qazaqstan, KAZAKHSTAN
A province 'East Kazakhstan' from *shyghys* 'east'.

Shymkent, KAZAKHSTAN *Chimkent*
'Turf Town', thus a town built on a grassy area from *shym* 'grass' and *kent* 'town'. Founded in the 7th century as a staging post on the Silk Road and developed as a frontier fort of the Kokand Khanate; it was captured by the Russians in 1864 and remained in Russian/ Soviet hands until Kazakhstan gained its independence in 1991. At this time the Kazakh spelling was adopted.

Siālkot, PUNJAB/PAKISTAN *Sākala*
A very ancient city which, according to legend, was originally founded by Rāja Sāla and named after him. It was then refounded by Rāja Sālivāhan or Sālbān who built a fort from which the city developed. The present name means 'Fort of Sia' from *kot* 'fort' and the fact that Sālivāhan was of the Sia caste.

Siam *See* THAILAND.

Šibenik, CROATIA *Scardona-Skradin, Castrum Sebenici, Sebenico*
Named after a Slav tribe, the Sebenici. Its first name was Illyrian, but in 1066 it was recorded as Castrum Sebenici. In 1918 it was occupied by the Italians and called Sebenico. The town adopted its present name in 1921 when it became part of the Kingdom of the Serbs, Croats, and Slovenes.

Siberia (Sibir'), RUSSIA
A region, possibly meaning 'Sleeping Land' in Tatar and first applied to a Tatar khanate in the 13th century. This was overthrown by the Cossacks in 1582 and they then began the conquest of the region between the Ural Mountains and the Pacific Ocean, giving it the name Siberia. During the 18th century, the Russians called it the 'Great Tartary' to emphasize its Asianness.

Sibi, BALOCHISTAN/PAKISTAN *Sandemanabad*
According to legend, the town derives its name from Sewi, a Hindu princess of the Sewa tribe. In 1878 it was renamed after Sir Robert Sandeman (1835–92), political agent to the governor-general of Balochistan (1877–92), after its capture by the British. He did much to promote understanding between the frontier tribes and the government of British India. Its local name was readopted after Pakistan came into existence in 1947.

Sibiu, ROMANIA *Cibinium, Hermannsdorf, Hermannstadt, Nagyszében*
Originally a Roman city and named after the River Cibin along which it lies. It became 'Hermann's Village' from *Dorf* 'village' and then 'Hermann's Town' from *Stadt* after Saxon settlers had refounded it in the 12th century and renamed it after Hermann I (1156–1217), Count Palatine of Saxony. An Ottoman Turkish vassal state in the 16th century, it was taken over by the Hungarians and given the name Nagyszében 'Big Cibin'.

Sibu, SARAWAK/MALAYSIA *Maling, New Foochow*
In 1873 the third division of Sarawak was established and Maling was renamed after the local rambutan, a fruit, which was abundant here and which in the Iban language was called *buah sibau*. When Chinese migrants from Foochow (now *Fuzhou), China, arrived in 1901 to escape oppression and begin a new life in the fertile Rejang River delta they referred to the place as New Foochow or Small Foochow.

Sichuan, CHINA
A province, well-known as Szechwan in Wade-Giles romanization. It is generally

accepted as meaning 'Four Rivers' from *si* 'four' and *chuān* 'river', a reference to the four tributaries of the Yangtze that flow through the province. However, it could mean 'Four Plains' from another meaning of *chuān* 'plain' or 'lowland area'. In 1001 the area which is now Sichuan was divided into four administrative areas, known collectively as the 'four plains provinces'. During the Yuan dynasty (1279–1368) these provinces were merged into one which retained the name of 'Four Plains'.

Sicily (Sicilia), ITALY *Trinacria*
An island and region named after the Sicels/ Siculi who were present when Greek colonization began in the 8th century BC. Trinacria 'Three Capes' recognized the triangular shape of the island. Sicily became part of Italy in 1861.

Sidi Bel Abbès, ALGERIA
Founded in about 1841 as a French military post and named after Sīdī bel 'Abbās (or Sīdī Abu 'l-'Abbās), an 18th-century Muslim saint (marabout) who is buried on a hill which dominates the town. *Sīdī*, from *sayyidī* 'my lord', is an honorific term for saints and holy men. A number of towns in North Africa start with Sidi followed by the name of a marabout buried there. The town was founded in 1849.

Sidon (Şaydā/Saida), LEBANON *Saidoon*
An ancient Phoenician coastal city called Saidoon said to mean 'Fishery' or '(Place for) Fishing'. However, the Bible (Genesis 10: 15) mentions Sidon as the first-born of Canaan, a grandson of Noah, and the city may be named after him.

Siedlce, POLAND
Derived from *osiedle* 'settlement'. The city was taken by Austria at the third partition of Poland in 1795 and returned in 1918.

Siem Reap (Siemréab), CAMBODIA *Angkor, Phibunsongkhram*
A province and a city called 'Siamese Defeated'. Although there have been occasions when Siamese incursions have been beaten back, the region was ceded to Thailand in 1867–1907 and 1941–7, and at other times its rulers have been vassals of the Thai king. When the province was annexed in 1941 it was renamed after Phibunsongkhram (1897–1964), the Thai prime minister (1938–44, 1947–57).

Siena, TUSCANY/ITALY *Sena Julia*
May be named after the Senones, a Gaulish people who invaded Etruria in 391; or it may come from an Etruscan aristocratic name such

as Seina. The colours of yellowish-brown raw siena and reddish-brown burnt siena derive from the colour of the earth of Siena. This ferruginous earth is used as a pigment in paint.

Sierra Leone The Republic of Sierra Leone since 1971, having been a constitutional monarchy since 1961 when independence from the UK was achieved. Previously a British protectorate (1896) which was proclaimed over the hinterland of the coastal colony of Sierra Leone. British abolitionists had attempted to found a colony as a refuge for freed slaves in 1787, but it was not until 1808 that the area around Freetown was declared a crown colony, the rest of modern Sierra Leone remained in the hands of the indigenous people. The name means 'Lion Mountains' from the Spanish *sierra* 'saw' and used in the sense of 'mountain chain' and *león* 'lion'. However, there are no lions here, even if there once were. In 1457 a Venetian navigator, Alvise Ca' da Mosto, wrote of the claps of thunder that were common over the mountains and it may be the noise of the thunder, rather than the roar of lions, that is the origin of the name.

Sierra Madre, MEXICO, PHILIPPINES, USA
Mexico: the country's chief mountain range with a name meaning 'Mother Range' from the Spanish *sierra* 'mountain range' and *madre* 'mother'.

Sierra Nevada, SPAIN, USA
Spain: a mountain range in the south-east with a name meaning 'Snowy Mountains' from *sierra* 'mountain range' and *nevada* 'snow-covered'.

Sighetul Marmatiei, ROMANIA
The first word is derived from the Hungarian *sziget* 'island' with the Romanian *ul*, the masculine definite article 'the'; the second word indicates that the town lies in the county of Maramureş.

Sighişoara, ROMANIA *Castrum Sex, Schässburg, Segesvár*
Originally a Roman fort, it was colonized by Saxons in the 13th century, hence the name Castrum Sex. The present name may mean 'Sigismund's Fort' in honour of Sigismund (1368–1437), King of Hungary (1387–1437), German king (1411–37), King of Bohemia (1419–37), and Holy Roman Emperor (1433–7), with the Romanian form of the Hungarian *vár* 'stronghold'.

Sigmaringen, BADEN-WÜRTTEMBERG/ GERMANY
'Sigmar's Settlement' from the personal name and *ingen* 'settlement'.

Sigourney, IOWA/USA
Named after Lydia H. Sigourney (1791–1865), a prolific writer of books and articles.

Sikkim, INDIA
A state whose name may be derived from the Sanskrit *sikhin* 'summit' or from the Limbu *su him* 'new homeland' or perhaps 'happy homeland'. For long a buffer state between British India and Nepal, it became a *de facto* British protectorate in 1817, although retaining its status as an independent Himalayan Buddhist kingdom. It ceased to be a British protectorate in 1947 and became an Indian one instead in 1950. It joined the Indian Union in 1975 as a result of a referendum.

Silesia (Śląsk), POLAND *Schlesien*
A region in the south-west named after the Ślęzanie, a Slavic people. Originally Polish, it passed to Bohemia in 1335, to the Austrian Habsburgs in 1526, and to Prussia in 1742, hence its former German name of Schlesien. The south-eastern part of Upper Silesia voted to rejoin Poland in 1921, but it fell to Nazi Germany in 1939. Practically the whole of Silesia was returned to Poland in 1945.

Silhouette, SEYCHELLES
An island named after Étienne de Silhouette (1709–67), the French minister of finance, who replaced Jean Moreau de Séchelles. Keeping strict control of the public finances, Silhouette gave his name to the word 'silhouette' to describe things made cheaply, thus without much substance or 'in outline'.

Silicon Valley, CALIFORNIA/USA
A name given to an industrial area in the San Jose and Santa Clara valleys because of the presence of many electronics enterprises. Silicon is the basic material of semiconductors.

Silifke, TURKEY *Seleucia ad Calycadnus*
The ancient town was founded by Seleucus I Nicator[†] in the 3rd century BC on the Calycadnus River (now the Gök Su) and named after him. It was also known as Seleucia Tracheotis. The modern town is some 3 miles (5 km) to the north, its name being a modification of the former name.

Silistra, BULGARIA *Durostorum*
Founded by the Romans as a fortified camp called Durostorum 'Strong Fort' in the 2nd century, its present name is a Romanian-influenced version of the Roman name. Having been under Ottoman Turkish rule from the early 15th century until 1878, it was part of Romania in 1913–40.

Sillery, QUEBEC/CANADA
Named after Noël Brûlart de Sillery, a member of the Company of New France, who helped to found a Jesuit mission and a settlement for the Abnaki people in 1637.

Silver City, USA
New Mexico: founded in 1870 as San Vincente de la Ciénaga 'St Vincent of the Marsh', it was renamed in 1876 in recognition of its value as a mining centre for silver, gold, copper, and lead.

Simcoe, ONTARIO/CANADA
A city and a lake, formerly called Lac aux Claies 'Hurdle Lake' from the French *claie* 'hurdle' because of the fishing weirs at the narrows. The lake was discovered by Samuel de Champlain[†] in 1650 and renamed by Colonel (later Lieutenant General) John Graves Simcoe (1752–1806), first lieutenant-governor of Upper Canada (now Ontario) (1792–96), in honour of his father, Captain John Simcoe, who was killed at the Battle of Quebec in 1759. The city is named after the son.

Simeonovgrad, BULGARIA *Maritsa*
Named after Simeon I the Great (864–927), Khan of Bulgaria (893–927) and Tsar of the First Bulgarian Empire (925–7).

Simferopol', UKRAINE *Neapolis, Ak-Mechet, Gotenberg*
On the site of the 2nd-century BC Scythian capital of Neapolis 'New Town', the Tatars founded a new town Ak-Mechet 'White Mosque' in the 15th century. The modern town was founded in 1784 with a Greek name, fashionable at the time, from *sumferon* 'profitable' in the sense of doing something for one's own benefit and *polis*; this could be a reference to the fact that it originated as a trading town in the centre of the Crimea and was thus a focal point for other towns. It was called Gotenberg by the Germans while under their control during the Second World War.

Simla, INDIA, USA
India (Himāchal Pradesh): the name has evolved from the former Shyamala, or Shamla Devi, another name for the goddess Kālī (in Sanskrit, 'black'). It was settled as a hill station by the British in 1817 and served as the summer capital of British India between 1864 and 1939. It is now called Shimla.

Simonstown (Simonstad), WESTERN CAPE/SOUTH AFRICA
Used by the Dutch Navy from 1741, it is named after Simon van der Stel (1639–1712), first

governor of the Cape (1691–9). In 1810 it became a British naval base as Simon's Town.

Simpson Desert, AUSTRALIA
The first European to cross it, in 1929, was Cecil Madigan. He named it after Alfred Simpson (1875–1939), president of the Royal Geographical Society of Australasia which had supported the expedition.

Sinai (Sīnā'), EGYPT
A peninsula and in the south a mountain peak, also known as Mount Horeb. It was here that, according to the Bible (Exodus 20), Moses was given the Ten Commandments and the Tablets of the Law. In Arabic Mount Sinai is called Jabal Mūsā 'Mountain of Moses'. There are various theories as to the origin of its name: it may come from the Semitic sen 'tooth' to describe the shape of the mountain, or from Sin, the moon goddess worshipped by the prehistoric inhabitants of the region.

Sinaia, ROMANIA
A monastery was first built here in 1695. The founder associated it with the monastery, St Catherine's, on Mt Sinai and gave it the name Sinaia. The town which grew up around the monastery took the same name.

Sinaloa, MEXICO
A state with a Native American name meaning 'Round prickly Pear'.

Sindh, PAKISTAN *Sind*
A province which takes its name from the Indus River, known in Pakistan as the Sindhu, which divides the province in two, from the Sanskrit *sindhu* 'the sea'. The appealing story, that when General Sir Charles Napier had completed the conquest of Sind in 1843 he sent a one-word signal in Latin (*peccavi* 'I have sinned') to the British government, is regrettably apocryphal.

Singapore *Po-Luo-Chung, Tumasik/Temasek, Singapura, Shōnan*
The Republic of Singapore (Mandarin Chinese: Xinjiapo; Malay: Republik Singapura; Tamil: Singapore Kudiyarasu) since 1965; fundamentally it is a Chinese city-state. Previously one of the states of the Federation of Malaysia when that state was established in 1963; an internal self-governing state (1959–63); a British crown colony (1945–59); part of the Straits Settlements with Penang and Malacca (1826–1945); a settlement under the direct control of the governor-general in India (1823–6), the modern city having been founded by Sir Stamford Raffles (1781–1826) of the English East India Company in 1819. Prior to that the island had been under Portuguese and then Dutch control, having

been part of the Javanese Majahapit Empire in the 14th century. After capture by Japanese forces in February 1942 it was renamed Shōnan 'Brightness of the South' from *shō* 'bright' or 'clear' and *nán*. The present name is derived from the Sanskrit *Siṃhapura* 'Lion City' from *siṃha* 'lion' and *pur*. Knowledge of Singapore's early history is sketchy but, according to Malay legend, a visiting Sumatran prince (sometimes given the name Sang Nila Utama and in other versions Sri Tri Buana) landed on the island sometime during the 13th century and saw what he took to be a lion (or a tiger in some versions); this was accepted as being a good omen. However, lions have not been found on the island, although tigers have. The 3rd-century Chinese name was Po-Luo-Chung 'Island at the End of the Peninsula'. A prosperous trading centre from early times, its name was recorded as Tumasik or Temasek 'Sea Town' from the Javanese *taṣek* 'sea' from about the 7th century. The three characters of the Chinese name were chosen to approximate to the sound of 'Singapore' in Mandarin. Literally the characters represent *xīn* 'new', *jiā* 'add', and *pō* 'slope'.

Sinkiang Uighur (Xinjiang Uygur), CHINA
Xi-yü, Sinkiang, Kashgaria, Uighur, East Turkestan
An autonomous region since 1955, before which it was Sinkiang Province from 1884. It was for long called by the Chinese Xiyu 'Western Regions'. Following its occupation by the Chinese after they had defeated the Mongols in 1760, it was renamed Sinkiang 'New Frontier' or 'New Dominion' from *xīn* 'new' and *jiāng* 'frontier' or 'border'. It was renamed Kashgaria in 1877 after the Chinese had removed Yakub Beg (1820–77), a despotic Islamic fundamentalist and ruler of Kashgar, and it was formally incorporated into the Chinese Empire in 1884. The local name for Kashgaria, often known by Westerners as East, or Chinese, Turkestan was Altynshahr 'Land of the Six Cities', a reference to the six major oases ringing the Taklamakan Desert. Largely populated by Muslim Turkic-speaking Uighurs, for a time the region was called Uighur. Uighur nationalists declared East Turkestan a republic in 1945, but this was brought to an end when Chinese communist troops occupied it in 1950.

Sinop, TURKEY *Sinope, Colonia Julia Felix*
A city-port with good harbours founded, according to legend, in the middle of the 8th century BC by the Amazons and traditionally said to have been named after their queen, Sinova. Alternatively, it is also said to have received its name from the mythological

Sinope, who was loved, and brought here, by Apollo. It was destroyed and refounded by the Milesians c.630 BC.

Sioux City, IOWA/USA *Thompsonville*
Laid out in 1848 by, and named after, a William Thompson. A year later a French-Canadian fur trader arrived with his Sioux wives and their father, Chief War Eagle. In 1857, to honour the Sioux, the settlement was renamed. 'Sioux' is an abbreviation of their Ojibwa name 'Nadouessioux' 'Adders', that is, 'enemies'.

Sioux Falls, SOUTH DAKOTA/USA
Founded on the Big Sioux River in 1857 and named after the river and its falls.

Sir Edward Pellew Group, AUSTRALIA
Pellew Islands
A group of islands off the coast of the Northern Territory named after Captain Edward Pellew (1757–1833) of the British Royal Navy in 1802. To avoid confusion with another group of the same name, the islands were given their present name after Captain Pellew had become Vice Admiral Sir Edward Pellew, 1st Viscount Exmouth, commander-in-chief of the East India station (1805–9).

Sirsa, HARYĀNA/INDIA *Sarsuti*
Both the town and the original fort are said to have been built by, and named after, Rāja Saras c.250.

Sisak, CROATIA *Segestica, Siscia*
The original Illyrian settlement was known as Segestica and the nearby Celtic one as Siscia 'swamp' or 'marsh', both being sited at the junction of three rivers. Together they came under Roman rule in the 2nd century BC and were granted colonial status in the 1st century AD as Colonia Flavia Siscia from which the present name is taken.

Sisimiut, GREENLAND/DENMARK *Holsteinborg*
Originally named 'Holstein Castle' in 1756 after the Danish Count Johan Ludwig von Holstein. The present Inuit name means 'Place where Foxes have Earths'.

Sitka, ALASKA/USA *Novo Arkhangelsk*
A fort was built here in 1799 by Alexander Baranov, the first Russian governor of Alaska. This was destroyed by the Tlingit in 1802. Two years later the construction of a city, Novo Arkhangelsk 'New Archangel', was begun. In 1867 Alaska was sold to the USA and the city became known as Sitka, probably from a Tlingit word meaning 'By the Sea'.

Sittwe, BURMA *Akyab*
Founded in 1825 as 'Crowd (as a result of) War' from *tsit-htwe* following the

development of a cantonment for British troops here because the area was considered more healthy than elsewhere. The British called the place Akyab, the name of a nearby village which had a pagoda with the name Au-kyait-dau, from which Akyab may have come.

Sivas, TURKEY *Megalopolis, Sebasteia*
Founded c.65 BC when Pompey the Great (106–48 BC), the Roman statesman, merged several settlements into the Roman city of Megalopolis 'Great City' or 'City of the Great One', i.e. Pompey. In the first century AD it was given the name Sebasteia from the Greek *sebastos* 'great' or 'magnificent'. On the arrival of the Turkmens at the end of the 11th century it received their version of the name, Sivas.

Sivrihisar, TURKEY *Justinianopolis*
Founded by, and originally named after, Justinian I† as a fortified garrison guarding the western approaches to Ancyra (now Ankara). It was subsequently renamed Sivrihisar 'Sharp-pointed Castle' from *sivri* 'sharp-pointed' and *hisar*, a reference to the castle's position on a crag above the town.

Siwālik Hills, INDIA-NEPAL-PAKISTAN
'Belonging to Shiva', one of the chief Hindu deities, in Sanskrit.

Siwān, BIHĀR/INDIA
Derived from the Sanskrit *savayāna* 'bier'. According to local legend, Buddha's bier lay here for a while while en route to cremation.

Siyāzän, AZERBAIJAN
'White Women' in Persian, the original population being largely Persian.

Sjælland, DENMARK
See ZEALAND.

Skagerrak, DENMARK-NORWAY
A strait between Norway and Denmark named after the city-port of Skagen on the northern tip of the Danish island of Jutland with the Swedish *rak* 'open channel' or 'straight way' of Dutch/Low German origin. Thus the meaning is an 'Open Channel past Skagen'.

Skegness, ENGLAND/UK *Sceggenesse*
'Skeggi's Promontory' from an Old Scandinavian personal name, possibly meaning 'bearded one', and *nes* 'promontory'.

Skeleton Coast, NAMIBIA
A treacherous coast upon which many ships foundered and many lives were lost. It was named for the skeletons of men, whales, and ships.

Skelmersdale, ENGLAND/UK *Schelmeresdele*
'Skjaldmarr's Valley' from an Old
Scandinavian personal name and *dalr* 'dale'.

Skíathos, GREECE
An island and town with a name meaning 'In
the Shadow of (Mount) Athos' from *skía*
'shadow' or 'shade'. This is figurative, rather
than actual, the distance between them being
some 75 miles (120 km).

Skikda, ALGERIA *Rusicade, Philippeville*
Founded in 1838 by the French and named
after Louis-Philippe (1773–1850), King of the
French (1830–48). The modern town was built
on the Roman settlement of Rusicade and,
when Algeria gained its independence in 1962,
a version of that name, whose meaning is
unknown, was adopted.

Skokie, ILLINOIS/USA *Niles Center*
Founded in 1834 and renamed in 1940 with a
Potawatomi word for 'swamp'.

Skópelos, GREECE
An island and town possibly meaning 'Rocky
Cliff' or '(Place of) Observation' from *skópia*.

Skopje, MACEDONIA *Skupi, Prima Justiniana,
Üsküb*
An Illyrian town, it was the native town of
Justinian I[†] who rebuilt it in 535 after an
earthquake in 518. He renamed it after himself
'First (Town) of Justinian'. It was held by the
Ottoman Turks between 1392 and 1912 and
they renamed it Üsküb. It was incorporated
into Serbia in 1913 as Skoplje, the Macedonian
spelling, and occupied by the Bulgarians
during both World Wars. It became the capital
of the Macedonian Republic within the former
Yugoslavia in 1945 and remained so when that
republic achieved its independence in 1991.
The meaning is not known.

Skovorodino, AMUR/RUSSIA *Rukhlovo*
Renamed in 1938 after A. N. Skovorodin, first
chairman of the village soviet, who was shot
by Japanese invaders in 1920.

Skye, SCOTLAND/UK *Scitis, Scia, Skith*
Popularly 'Winged (Island)' from the Gaelic
sgiath 'wing', a reference to the northern and
southern peninsulas that project from the
centre like wings. It is a pre-Gaelic name of
obscure meaning. It gives its name to the Skye
terrier that originated on the island as a
hunting dog.

Slantsy, LENINGRAD/RUSSIA
'Slates' from *slanets* 'slates' or 'shale', a
reference to the fact that it developed as a
result of slate-mining.

Slaný, CZECH REPUBLIC *Na Zlanem, Schlan*
The original fortified settlement was on a hill
overlooking the present town; it was called Na
Zlanem 'On the Salty Hill' because it was near a
salt spring. In the 12th century Benedictines
built a monastery here around which a town
arose and this was given the name Slaný
'Salty'.

Slave Coast, NIGERIA-BENIN-TOGO
Stretching roughly from the Niger delta in
Nigeria in the east to the Gold Coast (now
Ghana) in the west, the coast acquired this
name for the transatlantic slave trade that
flourished during the 17th–19th centuries.

Slave River, ALBERTA-NORTHWEST
TERRITORIES/CANADA
Samuel Hearne travelled down the river in
1771–2 and named it after the Slave tribe
which lived along its banks.

Slavgorod, BELARUS, RUSSIA, UKRAINE
'Town of Glory' from the Russian *slava* 'glory'
and *gorod*. In Ukrainian it is spelt Slavhorod
and in Belarus Slawharad.

Slavkov CZECH REPUBLIC *Novosedlice/Neusedlicz,
Austerlitz*
The original name meant '(Place of the) New
Settlers'. The German version of this was
Neusedlicz and in due course this became In
Eussedlicz, Ausserlitz, and in the 17th century
Austerlitz. However, the 14th-century owner
of the castle was a nobleman called Slavek or
Slavok and his castle was thus called *Slavkov
Hrad* 'Slavek's Castle'. *Hrad* was later dropped.

Slavonia, CROATIA
A region named after its mainly Slav
population.

Slavonska Požega, CROATIA *Incerum*
A Roman settlement in Slavonia, the present
name indicates that it has been burnt and
destroyed several times from *požar* 'fire'.

Slavonski Brod, CROATIA *Marsonia*
'Slavonian Crossing Place'. The town lies on
the River Sava where there is a crossing
between Bosnia and Slavonia from *brod* 'boat'
or, here, 'crossing place'.

Slavsk, KALININGRAD/RUSSIA *Heinrichswalde*
First known by its German name of 'Heinrich's
(Henry's) Wood', it was renamed 'Glory' from
slava in 1946 to celebrate the Soviet victory
over the Germans in the Great Patriotic War
(1941–5).

Slavyansk (Slov'yans'k), UKRAINE *Tor,
Slovensk, Slavyane*
Founded in 1676 and named after the river on
which it lies. This was changed to Slovensk in

1794 from the obsolete Russian word *Slovenye* 'Slavs'. Ten years later this became Slavyane, also 'Slavs', from which the present name is taken.

Slavyansk-na-Kubani, KRASNODAR TERRITORY/RUSSIA *Slavyanskaya*
See previous entry. Na-Kubani 'On the Kuban' denotes its location on that river. It became a city in 1958 when it assumed its present name.

Slievemore (Sliabh Mór), IRELAND
'Big Mountain' from *sliabh* 'mountain'.

Sligo, IRELAND, USA
Ireland: a county and port with the local name Sligeach 'Shelly (River or Place)' from *slige* shell, a reference to the River Garavogue.

Sliven, BULGARIA *Enidzhe Kariesi*
Derived from *slivane* 'confluence', the town lying at the confluence of the Novoselska and Asenovska Rivers. The previous Turkish name meant 'New Town'.

Sloboda, BELARUS
'Settlement (exempt from normal State obligations)' in Russian, a fairly common name at one time and related to *svoboda* 'freedom'.

Slobodskoy, KIROV/RUSSIA
The same meaning as above.

Slonim, BELARUS
'Sheltered' from a word associated with the Russian *zaslon* 'screen' or 'barrier'.

Slough, ENGLAND/UK *Slo*
A descriptive name from the Old English *slōh*, a reference to the marshy ground.

Slovakia (Slovensko) *Upper Hungary*
The Slovak Republic (Slovenská Republika) since 1993 when Czechoslovakia split in two. Previously, as part of Czechoslovakia, the Slovak Federative Republic (1990–2) and the federal Slovak Socialist Republic (1960–90); a part of the People's Republic of Czechoslovakia (1948–60) and of the Republic of Czechoslovakia (1918–39, 1945–8). A new Slovak state was created in 1938 when the Germans marched into the Czech Lands and in 1939 the Slovaks felt secure enough to declare independence. Adolf Hitler[†] agreed to the existence of a separate Slovak state and Slovakia became independent for the first time in its history, although in reality it was no more than a German puppet state. Following the defeat of Nazi Germany in 1945 Slovakia and the Czech Lands were reunited. But this lasted only until 1993. Before its creation in 1918 Slovakia had been one of the lands of the Hungarian crown since the 11th century and thus of the Austro-Hungarian Empire. The

country is named after the Slovaks, a Slav tribe which probably came from Silesia in the 6th or 7th century. Their language is called *Slovenský* which should not be confused with *Slovenski*, the language of the Slovenes.

Slovenia (Slovenija) *Dravska*
The Republic of Slovenia (Republika Slovenija) since 1991. Previously the Socialist Republic of Slovenia within the former Yugoslavia (1946–91). Between 1941–5 it was partitioned between Germany, which took the northern half, and Italy, which took the southern. As the Dravska *Banovina* 'governorship' it was part of the Kingdom of Yugoslavia (1929–41); part of the Kingdom of the Serbs, Croats, and Slovenes (1918–29) when that kingdom was created in 1918 and the name Slovenia was coined. When the Dual Monarchy of Austria-Hungary was created in 1867 the Slovenes found themselves in the Austrian part, the Austrian Habsburgs having gradually taken control of Slovene-speaking territories during the 13th and 14th centuries. The country is named after its indigenous inhabitants, the Slovenes.

Slutsk, BELARUS
Takes its name from the Sluch River on which it lies. Its name may be derived from a word associated with the Russian *luka* 'bend', a reference to its twisting course.

Slyudyanka, IRKUTSK/RUSSIA
Takes its name from its main product, mica (in Russian, *slyuda*).

Småland, SWEDEN
A province with a name meaning 'Small Land', a reference to the many small provinces which were merged to form this one.

Smederevo, SERBIA/SERBIA AND MONTENEGRO
The etymology is not clear. It has been suggested that the name might come from a medieval Serbian personal name Smender; or be a corruption of Sanctius Demetrius; or be derived from *smet* 'deep snow' and Old Serbian *drevo* (now *drvo*) 'wood'. A town on the River Danube, it was the capital of Serbia between 1427 and 1459 when it was captured by the Ottoman Turks.

Smith Center, KANSAS/USA
Founded in 1871 and named after Major J. Nelson Smith, who was killed during the Civil War in 1864.

Smithfield, SOUTH AFRICA, USA
South Africa (Free State): originally Smith Town or Smith Field when founded in 1849, it was named after Sir Harry Smith (1787–1860), governor of Cape Colony (1847–52). In due course the name was changed to New

Smithfield and later still the 'New' was dropped.

Smolensk, RUSSIA
A province and a city whose name is said to be derived from *smolěnyy* 'tarred', for the tarring of the local boats. The city lies on the River Dnieper, the direct trade route between the Baltic Sea and the Byzantine Empire. It may, alternatively, refer to the dark colour of the soil from *smola* 'tar' or 'pitch'. Occupied by the Lithuanians and the Poles, it was finally taken by Russia in 1654.

Smolyan, BULGARIA *Ezerovo, Pashmakli*
Located among lakes and forests, the Slav name Ezerovo means 'Town of Lakes' from the Slavonic *ozero* 'lake'. The former Turkish name remained until 1934 when the town was renamed after the Smoleni, a Slav tribe.

Smyrna, TURKEY, USA
1. Turkey: *see* IZMIR.
2. USA (Delaware): founded as Duck Creek Cross Roads in 1768 and renamed in 1806 after the city-port on the west coast of Asia Minor (now Turkey).

Snaefell, ISLE OF MAN
'Snow Mountain' from the Old Scandinavian *snær* 'snow' and *fjall* 'mountain'.

Snake, CANADA, USA
USA (Wyoming-Idaho): a river named after the Snake people, a group within the Shoshone.

Sneeuberg, EASTERN CAPE/SOUTH AFRICA
'Snow Mountains'. They are normally covered in snow each winter.

Snowdon (Yr Wyddfa), WALES/UK *Snawdune*
A mountain called 'Snow Hill' from the Old English *snāw* 'snow' and *dūn*. The Welsh name means 'The Mound' from *yr* 'the' and *wyddfa* 'mound' or 'tumulus', a reference to its use as a burial place.

Snowy River, NEW SOUTH WALES-VICTORIA/ AUSTRALIA
So named because it is fed by melting snows from the Snowy Mountains.

Soavinandriana, MADAGASCAR
'Favourite of the Monarch' from *sòa* 'good' and *andrìana* 'monarch'.

Sochi, KRASNODAR TERRITORY/RUSSIA *Navaginskoye*
Founded on the site of an old fort in 1896 and named after the Shacha people who used to inhabit the area.

Society Islands (Îles de la Société) A group of islands in French Polynesia claimed for

Great Britain by Captain Samuel Wallis in 1767 and named two years later after a visit by Captain James Cook[†]. He named them after his expedition's sponsor, Great Britain's Royal Society. It has also been suggested that the name was appropriate because the islands were closely grouped. They became a French protectorate in 1842 and a colony in 1881.

Socotra (Arabic: **Suquṭrā**), YEMEN
An island with a name derived from the Sanskrit *dvīpa-sakharada* or *sukhātara* 'island abode of bliss' from *dvīpa* and *sukha* 'pleasant'. The island was a British protectorate between the 1880s and 1967 when it became part of independent Yemen.

Söderköping, SWEDEN
'Southern Market Town' from *söder* 'south' and *köping*. It is south in comparison with Norrköping 'Northern Market Town'.

Sofala, MOZAMBIQUE
See NOVA SOFALA.

Sofia (Sofiya), BULGARIA *Serdnopolis, Serdica, Ulpia Serdica, Sredec, Triadica*
Originally named after the Serdi, a Thracian tribe. In the 1st century AD Ulpia was added in honour of Marcus Ulpius Trajanus (Trajan[†]). The Slavonic *Sredec* 'centre', adopted in the 9th century when the Bulgarians took the city, acknowledges that the city is roughly equidistant from the Black Sea and the Adriatic, and between Belgrade, Serbia, and Istanbul, Turkey. It was renamed Triadica, the Greek form of Sredec, when Bulgaria was incorporated into the Byzantine Empire in 1018. The city was occupied by the Ottoman Turks between 1382 and 1878 and they soon named it Sofia after the church of *Sveta Sofia* 'Holy Wisdom' which they converted into a mosque. It has been the national capital since 1879.

Sofrino, MOSCOW/RUSSIA *Suponevo, Safarino*
Originally named after a local landowner, one Suponev, it was renamed after Ivan Safarin when it changed hands. In due course this grew into Sofrino.

Soissons, PICARDY/FRANCE *Noviodunum, Augusta Suessonium*
Named after the Suessiones, a Gaulish tribe who made this their capital in the 3rd century.

Sokol, RUSSIA
'Falcon'. At least three towns have this name.

Sokolov, CZECH REPUBLIC *Falknov*
Named after an unknown falconer from *sokol* 'falcon' who lived in the area. Falknov is of German origin with the same meaning.

Sokoto, NIGERIA
A state, a town, and a river (also called the
Kebbi River) with a name that derives from the
Arabic *sūq* 'market'.

Solbad Hall, AUSTRIA
Founded near some salt mines *c.*1260, hence
the name. Both *sol* and the Old High German
hall are associated with 'salt', while *Bad*
indicates that it is a spa with mineral springs.

Soledar, UKRAINE *Karlo-Libnekhtovsk*
Previously named after Karl Liebknecht (1871–
1919), one of the German founders of the
Spartacus League, an underground group in
Berlin that was the forerunner of the
German Communist Party. The present
name is possibly related to the Russian *sol'*
'salt' and *dar* 'gift'. It has a salt mine
whose salt, it is claimed, has unique natural
curing properties.

Soligorsk, BELARUS *Novo-Starobinsk*
Located close to Starobin, it was at first called
New Starobin. In 1959 it was renamed from
the Russian *sol'* 'salt' and *gorsk* because of its
huge reserve of potassium salts.

Solihull, ENGLAND/UK
'Muddy Hill' from the conjectural Old English
sylig 'muddy' or 'boggy' and *hyll*.

Solikamsk, PERM/RUSSIA
Founded in the early 15th century near a salt
mine, it takes its name from *sol'* 'salt' and the
Kama River on which it lies.

Solnechnogorsk, MOSCOW/RUSSIA
Solnechnogorskiy
'Sunny City' from *solnechno* 'sunny' and *gorsk*.
Founded in 1928, it became a town ten years
later at which time the present form of the
name was adopted.

Solomennoye, KARELIYA/RUSSIA
'Straw (Town)', the adjective from *solomennyy*.

Solomon Islands *British Solomon Islands*
Protectorate
These islands include the islands of
Bougainville and Buka geographically, but not
politically (they belong to Papua New Guinea).
The first European to discover them in 1568
was the Spaniard Alvaro de Mendaña de Neira.
Inspired by Inca stories of islands 600 leagues
to the west of Peru that had been the source of
the gold that adorned the court of King
Solomon, King of Israel (mid-10th century BC),
Mendaña named them after the king. In the
event, the Spaniards found no evidence of gold
or silver. The northern islands became a
German protectorate in 1885 after the German
New Guinea Company had taken control; and
the southern a British protectorate in 1893.

The northern islands were transferred to the
UK in 1899. Although still a protectorate, the
islands adopted their present name in 1975.
They achieved their independence in 1978.
They give their name to the Solomon Sea.

Solothurn, GERMANY, SWITZERLAND
Switzerland: a canton, which joined the Swiss
Confederation in 1803, and a city originally
called Salodurum, possibly meaning 'Salo's
Fort' from a local personal name and the Celtic
duro 'fort', from which the present name comes.

Solovets Islands (Solovetskiye Ostrova),
RUSSIA
A group of islands in the *Beloye More* 'White
Sea' with a name meaning 'Island' from the
Lapp word *suolov*.

Soltüstik Qazaqstan, KAZAKHSTAN
A province 'North Kazakhstan' from *soltüstik*
'north'.

Sol'vychegodsk, ARKHANGEL'SK/RUSSIA *Soli*
Vychegodskiye
'Vychegda Salts' from the name of the river on
which it lies and *sol'* 'salt'.

Solway Firth, ENGLAND-SCOTLAND/UK
Possibly 'Estuary of the Pillar Ford' from the
Old Scandinavian *súl* 'pillar', *vað* 'ford', and
fjǫrðr 'estuary'.

Somalia (Soomaaliya)
The Somali Democratic Republic since 1969.
Previously the Somali Republic from 1960
when independence was gained and the
British Somaliland Protectorate and Italian-
controlled Somalia amalgamated. In 1991,
however, the self-styled Republic of
Somaliland in the north-west (the former
British protectorate) seceded and declared its
independence, but it has so far failed to win
international recognition. In 1998 the north-
eastern region declared itself to be the
'autonomous region' of Puntland, but this too
has not been recognized. The central
government, however, does not have the
power to control either region. Northern
Somalia became a British protectorate in 1886
while the Italians established a colony in the
south in 1905. In 1936 Italian Somaliland,
together with Ethiopia and Eritrea, formed the
entity known as Italian East Africa. Italian
Somaliland was captured by British forces in
1941 and in 1947 Italy renounced all its rights
to it. Nevertheless, in 1950 this territory
became the UN Trust Territory of Somalia
under an Italian mandate. The country is
named after its indigenous inhabitants, the
Somalis, or Soomaali, who may have taken
their name from a legendary ancestor, Soma
or Samale; it has also been suggested that their

name may come from *so* 'go' and *mal* 'milk', a reference to their pastoral lifestyle.

Somaliland A historic region consisting of modern Somalia and Djibouti (known as French Somaliland in 1888–1967). It was part of the Land of Punt. *See* SOMALIA.

Somerset, BERMUDA, CANADA, UK, USA
UK (England): a county called Sumortūnsæte or Sumersæton 'Dwellers around Somerton', the town being the centre of the local administration. Somerton itself means 'Summer Farm' to which *sæte* 'dwellers' or 'settlers' was added and the *tūn* lost, eventually to give Sumorsæte, the forerunner of the present name.

Somerset East, EASTERN CAPE/SOUTH AFRICA
Founded in 1825 on a tobacco farm owned by Lord Charles Somerset (1767–1831), governor of Cape Colony (1814–26). 'East' was later added to differentiate it from Somerset West.

Somerset West, WESTERN CAPE/SOUTH AFRICA
Founded in 1822 and named after Lord Charles Somerset. 'West' was added when Somerset East was founded three years later.

Somerville, AUSTRALIA, CANADA, USA
USA (Massachusetts): founded as Cow Commons in 1630 and renamed in the 19th century, allegedly after Captain Richard Somers (1778–1804), a naval officer killed during the war with Tripoli (now in Libya) which lasted between 1801 and 1805.

Somme, PICARDY/FRANCE
A department named after the river. Its name is said to come from the Celtic *samara* 'tranquil' or possibly from a Gaulish root element *sum* 'to swim'.

Somnāth, GUJARĀT/INDIA
Ruins, although a rebuilt temple exists. This is the latest version of the temple, destroyed several times by Muslims and rebuilt by Hindus, of Shiva as Somanātha 'Lord of the *soma*' which was a sacred drink that quickly led to drunkenness.

Sønderborg, DENMARK *Synderburg, Sundherburg*
'Southern Castle' after a royal castle probably founded by Valdemar I the Great (1131–82), King of Denmark (1157–82).

Sondershausen, THURINGIA/GERMANY
'Southern Settlement' from the Old High German *sunder* 'southern' and *husen* 'settlement' or 'houses'. Ten miles (16 km) to the north lies Nordhausen 'Northern Settlement'.

Songhua River, CHINA
'Pine Flower' from *sōng* 'pine' and *huā* 'flower'.

Songkhla, THAILAND
Derived from Singora, a lion-shaped mountain lying opposite the harbour, from the Sanskrit *sinha* 'lion'.

Songnim, NORTH KOREA *Wiryesŏng, Kyomipo*
'Pine Tree Forest' from *song* 'pine tree' and *nim* 'forest'. The previous name was used during the Japanese occupation in 1910–45. The Japanese *kyō* means 'capital'.

Song Shan, HENAN/CHINA
A mountain called 'Pine Mountain' from *sōng* 'pine' and *shān*.

Sonora, CANADA, MEXICO, USA
Mexico: a state and a river with a name meaning 'sonorous' in Spanish, a reference to the sweet sound made when deposits of marble are struck.

Sophiatown, GAUTENG/SOUTH AFRICA
Sophiatown, Triomf
A township on the outskirts of Johannesburg founded in 1897 by Herman Tobiansky and named by him after his wife. By 1955 it had become a hotbed of opposition to apartheid and so the place was razed and rebuilt with low-cost housing for whites; it was renamed Triomf 'Triumph'. The ending of apartheid led to the original name being restored in 1996.

Sopot, BULGARIA, POLAND, SERBIA AND MONTENEGRO
1. A Slavonic word for 'source' or 'stream'.
2. Bulgaria: in 1950–91, on the centenary of his birth, it was renamed Vazovgrad after Ivan Vazov (1850–1921), a poet and novelist who glorified Bulgarian history.
3. Poland: formerly called Zoppot, the German name.

Sorel, QUEBEC/CANADA
Named after Pierre de Saurel, the French commandant of Fort-Richelieu, in 1672.

Soroki, MOLDOVA
Derived from the Romanian *sărăcie* 'poverty', a reference to its impoverished history.

Sorrento, AUSTRALIA, ITALY, USA
Italy (Campania): the original Latin name Surrentum is derived from the Greek *surréo* 'to converge', a reference to the waters flowing down the narrow valleys and signifying 'converging waters'.

Sort, CATALONIA/SPAIN
'Luck' in Catalan.

Sosnogorsk, KOMI REPUBLIC/RUSSIA
'Pine Town' from *sosna* 'pine tree' and *gorsk*,
here in the sense of town.

Sosnovyy Bor, LENINGRAD/RUSSIA
'Pine Forest' from *sosna* 'pine tree' and *bor*
'forest'.

Sosnowiec, POLAND
'Cluster of Pine Trees' from *sosna* 'pine tree'
and *wiec* 'meeting'.

Soufrière, GUADELOUPE, MONTSERRAT, ST
LUCIA, ST VINCENT
1. 'Sulfur Mine' in French.
2. Guadeloupe: a volcano.
3. Montserrat: hills.
4. St Lucia: a town near to a volcanic crater of
the same name; this comes from its sulfur
springs.
5. St Vincent: an active volcano, the
name coming from the smell from
its eruptions.

Souk el Arbaâ du Rharb, MOROCCO
'Wednesday Market of the West' from the
Arabic *sūq* 'market', *'arba* 'Wednesday (literally
'four(th) day)', French *du* 'of the', and Arabic
gharb 'west'; in the Maghreb *sūq* is represented
as *souk* and the *gh* of *gharb* sometimes as *rh*. A
number of Moroccan towns are named after
market days: Souk el Had (de Reggada) 'Sunday
Market' (literally 'one' or 'first day'), Souk el
Tnine (Imi n Tlit) 'Monday Market' ('two'),
Souk el Tleta (des Akhassas) 'Tuesday Market'
('three'), Souk el Khemis 'Thursday Market'
('five'), Souk es Sebt (des Indouzal) 'Saturday
Market' ('Sabbath'). Friday is the Muslims' holy
day.

Soûr, LEBANON
Originally an important Phoenician port, it
was built partly on a small rocky island as a
satellite to Sidon. This name was soon
changed to Tyre under which name it was
regularly mentioned in the Bible. Both
names derive from the Phoenician *tsor* 'stone'
or 'rock'. It was well-known for its
impregnability because of its fortifications and
the fact that it was surrounded by the sea on
three sides.

Souris, CANADA, USA
1. 'Mouse' or 'Mice' in French.
2. Canada (Prince Edward Island): named
after the River Souris, so named because of
the mice that used to devastate the crops here.
There is another river with this name that
rises in Manitoba, Canada, flows through
North Dakota, USA, and into Saskatchewan,
Canada.

Sousse (Sūsah), TUNISIA *Hadrumetum,
Hunericopolis, Justinianopolis*
A governorate and a city founded by the
Phoenicians perhaps as early as the 9th
century BC. Known to the Romans as
Hadrumetum from *c*.146 BC, Julius Caesar[†]
incorporated it into the Roman province of
Africa Nova. When the Vandals arrived in the
5th century AD they changed the name to 'City
of Huneric'; he was the son of Genseric/
Gaiseric, King of the Vandals (428–77), and
succeeded his father as king. After the
Byzantine invasion in the 6th century the
name was changed again to 'City of Justinian'
to honour Justinian I[†]. The city fell to Arab
invaders in the mid-7th century and it was part
of the French protectorate in 1881–1955. The
origin of the name is unknown, but it may be
associated with the Sūsah (Apollonia) in Libya.

South Africa *Union of South Africa*
The Republic of South Africa since 1961. The
Afrikaans name is Suid-Afrika. The Dutch
established a trading post at Table Bay (now
Cape Town) at the Cape of Good Hope in 1652.
The British took the Cape in 1806, establishing
a colony, and during the 1830s many Dutch (or
Boer 'farmer') settlers trekked northwards to
establish their own republics in the Orange
Free State and the Transvaal. The UK then
annexed Natal. Confrontation between the
British and the Boers led to the Boer War
(1899–1902) which resulted in British victory
and the annexation of the Boer republics. Cape
Colony, Natal, the Orange Free State, and the
Transvaal combined in 1910 to form the Union
of South Africa.

South America The southern half of the
American land mass.

Southampton, CANADA, UK, USA
UK (England): formerly Homtun,
Suthhamtunam, and Hantone 'Settlement on
the Promontory' from the Old English *hamm*
and *tūn*. By 962 *sūth* 'south' had been added to
differentiate the city from the northern
Hampton (now Northampton) which
represented *Hāmtūn* 'home farm'.

Southampton Island, NUNAVUT/CANADA
Discovered in 1613 by Thomas Button and
named after Henry Wriothesley (1573–1624),
3rd Earl of Southampton, a member of the
Virginia Company and its treasurer (1622–4),
and of the English East India Company; he was
also Shakespeare's patron.

South Australia, AUSTRALIA
A state since 1901 when it joined the newly
formed Commonwealth of Australia. It was
first settled by the British and made a province

in 1836. It became a crown colony in 1841. Between 1863 and 1911 it included the present Northern Territory.

South Bend, USA
Indiana: founded as Big St Joseph in 1820 along the St Joseph River, it was renamed in 1830 after the great bend in the river.

South Carolina USA
See CAROLINA.

South Dakota, USA
See DAKOTA.

South-East Asia Comprises the mainland states of Burma, Cambodia, Laos, Peninsular Malaysia, Singapore, Thailand, and Vietnam; the region of East Malysia and the state of Brunei on the island of Borneo; and the insular states of Indonesia and the Philippines. See ASIA.

Southend-on-Sea, ENGLAND/UK *Sowthende*
'The Southern End (of Prittlewell Parish)'; the parish, originally a Saxon settlement, is now part of Southend, just north of the town centre.

South Georgia, UK
An island and part of the Falkland Islands Overseas Territory of the UK in 1908–85, having been annexed by Captain James Cook[†] who first landed on it in 1775. He named it after King George III[†]. Together with the *South Sandwich Islands, it is now an Overseas Territory of the UK in its own right. It is geographically south, not south in comparison with a 'north' Georgia.

South Korea The Republic of Korea (Taehan Min'guk) since August 1948 when the country was created formally. See KOREA.

South Ossetia, GEORGIA
See OSSETIA.

South Sandwich Islands, UK *Snowland, Sandwich Land*
Part of the Falkland Islands Overseas Territory in 1908–85, having been sighted by Captain James Cook[†] in 1775. He named them first Snowland and then changed his mind to honour John Montagu (1718–92), 4th Earl of Sandwich, first lord of the British Admiralty (1748–51, 1771–82) at the time. To avoid confusion with Hawaii, then called the Sandwich Islands, the present name was adopted in 1820. Together with *South Georgia, it is now an Overseas Territory of the UK in its own right.

South Shields, ENGLAND/UK *Scheles, Suthshelis*
'Temporary Sheds' used by fishermen during the summer from the Middle English *schele*

'shed' with 'south' added to differentiate it from North Shields. The collection of sheds subsequently expanded into towns.

Sovetabad, UZBEKISTAN *Karabagish*
Originally 'Black Gift' from the equivalent of the modern Turkish *kara* and *bağiş* 'gift' or 'donation', a reference to the lushness of the Ferghana Valley. In 1972 it was renamed 'Soviet City'.

Sovetsk, RUSSIA
1. Kaliningrad: founded by the Teutonic Knights in 1288, it was formerly named Tilsit after the River Tilza which itself comes from the Lithuanian *tilszus* 'marshy'. In 1946 it was renamed 'Soviet' in honour of the *Soviet Union when East Prussia was annexed by the Soviet Union at the end of the Second World War.
2. Kirov: originally Kukarka, it was renamed in 1937.

Sovetskaya Gavan', KHABAROVSK TERRITORY/RUSSIA *Imperatorskaya Gavan'*
Originally 'Imperial Harbour', so named in 1853 after Nicholas I[†]. This actually referred to the bay. The name was changed in 1923 to 'Soviet Harbour' from *gavan'* 'harbour' after the murder of the imperial family in 1918.

Soviet Union (Sovetsky Soyuz)
Proclaimed on 30 December 1922, brought into effect in July 1923, and formally brought into existence with the new constitution on 1 January 1924. Founded purely on the basis of communist ideology, not nationality, the Russian, Byelorussian (now Belarus), Ukrainian, and Transcaucasian republics combined to form the Union of Soviet Socialist Republics (in Russian, Soyuz Sovetskikh Sotsialisticheskikh Respublik); the 'Soviet Union' was the shortened version of the name. *Soviet* simply means 'council' from local to national level. By 1936 the three Soviet republics of Armenia, Azerbaijan, and Georgia had formed in place of the Transcaucasian Republic and five Central Asian Soviet Republics—Kazakhstan, Kirgiziya (now Kyrgyzstan), Tajikistan, Turkmenistan, and Uzbekistan—had also joined. In 1940 the Baltic Republics—Estonia, Latvia, and Lithuania—and Moldavia (now Moldova) were incorporated into the Soviet Union. The Soviet Union was dissolved on 25 December 1991.

Soweto, GAUTENG/SOUTH AFRICA
An acronym for 'South-Western Townships', an urban complex of 39 smaller townships for blacks south-west of Johannesburg formally established in the 1950s to accommodate black workers in the mining industry who

were forbidden to live in Johannesburg, which was reserved for whites, until 1990. The name was proposed in 1961. The first shantytowns arose here in 1904 after bubonic plague had broken out in the slums of Johannesburg.

Soyo, ANGOLA *Santo António de Zaire*
A shortening of Sonyo Sohio 'Province of the Kongo (People)'. Until 1980 it had been known for St Anthony, patron saint of the Portuguese capital, Lisbon. It is located in the province of Zaire.

Sozopol, BULGARIA *Apollonia, Susopolis*
A Greek city-state named Apollonia because the cult of Apollo was followed here and the town had a large statue of Apollo until it was stolen by the Romans in 72 BC. The present name is a version of Susopolis 'City of Salvation', from the Greek *sōzein* 'to save' and *polis*, which was adopted when Christianity spread into the region in the 3rd century.

Spa, BELGIUM
The origin of the name is not known for certain, but it may come from the Latin *spargo* 'to sprinkle' or 'bespatter' in the sense of 'bubbling up'. Its mineral springs, with curative powers, were well known to the Romans, and the name has come to mean places with such springs being called 'spas' or 'health resorts'.

Spain (España) *Iberia, Spania, Hispania al-Andalus*
The Kingdom of Spain (Reino de España) between 1516 and 1931 (the First Republic lasted for eight months in 1873–4) and a monarchy since 1947 although without a king until 1975. In 1931–47 a republic and in 1939–75 effectively a dictatorship under the rule of General Francisco Franco (1892–1975), chief of state (1939–75). The two most powerful kingdoms in Spain were joined in a personal union in 1479 when Ferdinand II (1452–1516) became King of Aragón (1479–1516), having married his cousin, Isabella I (1451–1504), Queen of Castile (1474–1504) in 1469. In 1492 they succeeded in bringing 780 years of Muslim rule in Spain to an end. The name Iberia was first used by the Greeks for the country of the Iberians who lived along the Iberus (Ebro) River. The peninsula was called Hispania by the Romans; in due course the H was dropped and the short *i* became an *E* to give España. Al-Andalus, as Islamic Spain was called and which eventually became Andalusia, means 'The Isle of the Vandals'; it became an Emirate of Damascus. The etymology of Hispania is not clear. One favoured theory is that it comes from the

Punic (the language of Carthage) *span* or *tsepan* 'rabbit', which were numerous in the peninsula; or from the Punic *sphan* 'north' since it was north of Carthage; or it may come from the Basque *ezpaña* 'lip' or 'extremity', a reference to this south-western area of Europe.

Sparta, CANADA, USA
All places are probably named, directly or indirectly, after the ancient city-state in Greece. *See* SPÁRTI.

Spárti, GREECE *Sparta, Lacedaemon*
An ancient and powerful city-state founded, according to tradition, by Lacedaemon, who named it after his wife, Sparta, the daughter of Evrótas, one of the first Kings of Laconia. Spárti lies on the Evrótas River. When the Byzantines repopulated the city after its destruction by the Visigoths, they renamed it after Lacedaemon. More probably, however, the name comes from *sparti* or *sparton* 'rope made from the shrub *spartos*' which grows abundantly and is used for making rope, brooms and baskets. The inhabitants of Sparta were known for their frugality, stern discipline, and endurance; hence the word 'spartan' to describe one who can withstand hardship without complaint. Another Greek word for Spartan was *lakónikos* 'laconic' because the Spartans were known for their concise speech.

Spartanburg, SOUTH CAROLINA/USA
Founded in 1785 and named after the Spartan Rifles, a local militia regiment that fought in the American War of Independence (1775–83) and is said to have exercised iron discipline.

Spassk, TATARSTAN REPUBLIC/RUSSIA *Spassk-Tatarskiy, Kuybyshev*
Founded in 1781 and named Spassk from *Spas* 'The Saviour' until 1926 when Tatarskiy was added. On the death of Valerian Kuybyshev[†] it was renamed after him until 1992.

Spassk-Dal'niy, PRIMORSKIY TERRITORY/RUSSIA
The first part of the name comes from *Spas* 'The Saviour' and the second from *dal'niy* 'distant' or 'remote', appropriate given its location in the Far East. Other towns begin with Spassk and then have a locational second word, such as Spassk-Ryazanskiy in Ryazan Province.

Spencer, AUSTRALIA, CANADA, USA
Australia (South Australia): Spencer Gulf and Cape Spencer were both discovered by Matthew Flinders[†] in 1802. He named them after George John Spencer (1758–1834), 2nd

Earl Spencer, who was first lord of the British Admiralty (1794–1801).

Speyer, RHINELAND-PALATINATE/GERMANY
Noviomagus, Nemetes, Spira
The present name is from the Speyer River at the mouth of which the town lies. The river's name may mean 'Winding One'. In *c*.100 BC, the town fell to the Romans who called it Noviomagus 'New Market' and then Nemetes after the local people. It was part of France between 1797 and 1815.

Spice Islands The East Indies generally, but in particular the *Moluccas.

Spišská Nová Ves, SLOVAKIA *Newendort*
In the 13th century German settlers founded a new settlement on the site of an old Slav one which had no name. They called it 'New Village' which in Slovak was Nová Ves. In due course Spišská was added to indicate that the town lay in the district of Spiš.

Spitsbergen, NORWAY
The main island within the Spitsbergen group of islands, themselves part of the *Svalbard archipelago. It was named by Willem Barents†
when he came here in 1596. The name means 'Needle Mountains' from the Dutch *spits* 'points' and *bergen* 'mountains' because of their sharp ridges.

Spittal, AUSTRIA
Named after a hospital (in German, *Spital*) founded here in 1191.

Split, CROATIA *Aspalathos, Spalatum, Spalato*
Diocletian (245–313), Roman emperor (284–305), built a huge palace on the site of the 3rd century BC Illyrico-Greek settlement of Aspalathos in which to live after his retirement. This name was Latinized to Spalatum after the arrival of the Romans. When Diocletian built his palace it was said that Spalatum was derived from the Latin *palatium* 'palace'. In *c*.614 the inhabitants of nearby Salona sought shelter in the palace from marauding Avars. The palace was then developed into a city. It was held by the Venetians between 1420 and 1797, and called by them Spalato, and by Austria between 1797 and 1918 when it joined the newly created Kingdom of the Serbs, Croats, and Slovenes.

Spokane, WASHINGTON/USA *Spokane Falls*
A trading post established in 1810 on the Spokane River, the city was settled in 1881. It is named after the Spokane people whose name is said to mean 'Children of the Sun'. 'Falls' was dropped in 1900.

Spoon River, ILLINOIS/USA
Said to be so named by an early settler due to its spoon-shaped course. However, the local Native American name was Maquon 'mussel shell' which was probably used as a spoon and this may be the origin of the name.

Sporades, GREECE
A group of of widely dispersed islands in the Aegean Sea whose collective name means 'Scattered' from *sporas*.

Spratly Islands (Chinese: **Nansha**; Pilipino: **Kalayaan**; Vietnamese: **Truong Sa**)
A group of islets and coral reefs dominating the South China Sea and claimed by Brunei, China, Malaysia, the Philippines, Taiwan, and Vietnam. They were first occupied by the French in 1933 and then by the Japanese during the Second World War. They have no indigenous inhabitants. They are said to be named after Richard Spratly, captain of the British whaler, the *Cyrus*, who sailed in the area in 1843 and reported back to the *Nautical Magazine and Naval Chronicle* that year that he had discovered 'two dangers': Ladd's Reef and what he called 'Spratly's Sandy Island'. The British Admiralty agreed the name of Spratly for the island group. The Chinese used the name Nansha Qundao 'South Sand Archipelago' from *nán, shā* 'sand' and *qúndǎo* 'archipelago' from the 3rd century.

Springbok, NORTHERN CAPE/SOUTH AFRICA
Springbokfontein
Founded in 1862 as 'Springbok Spring' and named after South Africa's national animal. The *fontein* was dropped in 1911.

Springfield, AUSTRALIA, CANADA, JAMAICA, NEW ZEALAND, USA
1. USA (Illinois): a log cabin was built here in 1818 around which the city developed. Its name comes from the nearby Spring Creek.
2. USA (Massachusetts): founded in 1635 and named after the birthplace in England of its founder, William Pynchon. The armoury here gave its name to the famous Springfield rifle in use with the US Army between 1873 and 1936.
3. USA (Missouri): settled in 1829 and named after the numerous springs here.
4. USA (Ohio): settled in 1799 on the site of Old Piqua, a Shawnee village, and named by the wife of Simon Kenton, a local scout, for the springs in the cliffs.

Sravanabelagola, KARNĀTAKA/INDIA
'Monk on the Top of the Hill'. An important Jain pilgrimage centre, the town is overlooked by a large statue of Lord Bahubali on a rocky hill.

Srebrenica, BOSNIA AND HERZEGOVINA
Argentaria
Derived from the silver mining in the area
from the Serbo-Croat *srebro* 'silver'.

Sredets, BULGARIA
'Centre' from the Slavonic *sredec. See* SOFIA.

Sremska Kamenica, SERBIA/SERBIA AND
MONTENEGRO *Villa Comanch*
'Stone (Town) in the Srem' from *kamenica*
'stone' and Sremska, the adjective to indicate
that the town lies in the Srem region.

Sremska Mitrovica, SERBIA/SERBIA AND
MONTENEGRO *Sirmium, Dimitrovica*
Named after St Demetrius, martyred here in
the early 4th century. Sremska indicates that
this Mitrovica is located in the Srem region
(another is in Kosovo).

Sremski Karlovci, SERBIA/SERBIA AND
MONTENEGRO *Castrum Caron, Karloca, Karlovica,
Karlowitz*
A town in the Srem region which originally
took its name from its earliest rulers, the de
Caron family; and then, in different forms,
from another ruler, a Duke Karl who preceded
the arrival of the Ottoman Turks in the early
16th century.

Sretensk, CHITA/RUSSIA
'Feast of the Purification (of the Virgin Mary)', a
name taken from the dedication of its church,
from *sreteniye* which also means 'meeting'.

Sri Jayewardenepura Kotte, SRI LANKA
The legislative and judicial capital of Sri Lanka
which became operational in 1982 named
after Kotte, the 15th-century Sinhalese
kingdom, and Junius Richard Jayewardene
(1906–96), President of Sri Lanka (1978–89),
with the Sanskrit *shrī* 'happiness' or 'holiness'.

Sri Lanka *Sinhaladvīpa/Sihaladipa, Serendīb/
Sarandīb, Ceilāo/Cilao, Ceylan, Tambapanni, Ceylon*
The Democratic Socialist Republic of Sri Lanka
(Sinhala: Shri Lanka Prajatantrika Samajavadi
Janarajaya; Tamil: Ilangai Jananayaka Socialisa
Kudiarasu) since 1972. Previously a Dominion
of the Commonwealth (1948–72) called
Ceylon, which had gained its independence
from the British in 1948; a crown colony
(1802–1948) (the UK's first), the British having
taken control from the Dutch East India
Company in 1796. The Kingdom of Kandy was
allowed to continue under the administration
of a British Resident. The Portuguese, who
called the island Ceilāo or Cilao, had arrived in
the early 16th century but been displaced by
the Dutch, who called it Zeilan or Ceylan,
within 60 years. The island had earlier been
called Serendīb or Sarandīb by Arab traders, an
adaptation of the Sanskrit *siṃhaladvīpa* 'Abode
of Lions Island' from *siṃha* 'lion' and *dvīpa*.
Tambapanni comes from the Sanskrit *tamba
vanna* 'copper coloured'. The name Ceylon
comes from the same source, although it is not
known if there were ever any lions on the
island. It was the scene of a fairy story devised
by Horace Walpole (1717–97), 4th Earl of
Orford and a writer, called *Three Princes of
Sarendip*; they had the happy knack of making
wonderful discoveries quite by chance. Thus
was the word 'serendipity' coined. The present
name, meaning 'Blessed Island' (also
sometimes translated as 'Resplendent Island'),
may be derived from the Sanskrit *shrī*
'holiness', 'happiness', 'prosperity', or
'honoured', a fairly recent addition to Lanka,
and *lak diga* 'land mass'. The *Rāmāyaṇa*, the
ancient Indian epic, referred to the island as
Lanka. The Tamils call it Ilangai.

Srīnagar, INDIAN SECTOR OF JAMMU AND
KASHMIR
Founded *c*.250 BC becoming known as the 'City
of Shrī (or Laksmī)', the Hindu goddess of
wealth and good fortune; thus the 'City of
Good Fortune' from the Hindi *shrī* 'fortune'
or 'happiness' and *nagar*. The modern city
lies some 3 miles (5 km) from the ancient
site.

Srirangapatnam, KARNĀTAKA/INDIA
Now little more than the ruins of the capital
city of Hyder Ali (1722–82), the ruler of Mysore
(1761–82) and his son Tipu Sultan (*c*.1751–99),
it is named after a shrine to the Hindu god Shri
Raṅga, one of the names for Vishnu with the
additional Sanskrit *patnam* 'town'.

Stafford, UK, USA
UK (England); formerly Stæfford and Stadford
'Ford at a Landing Place' from the Old English
stæth 'landing place' and *ford*. Lying on the
River Sow, it was an important trading centre
and so the landing place grew into a market
town. The county's name, Staffordshire, from
Stafford and *scīr* came into use during the 11th
century.

Staines, ENGLAND/UK *Stane*
'(Place at) the Stones' from *stān*.

Stakhanov, UKRAINE *Kadiyevka, Sergo*
Founded as Kadiyevka in the 19th century as a
coal-mining centre, in 1935–43 it was named
Sergo after Grigoriy Ordzhonikidze[†]. In 1943
Kadiyevka was restored, but in 1978 it was
renamed Stakhanov after Aleksey Stakhanov
(1906–77), a coalminer who on 30 August
1935 voluntarily dug 102 tons of coal
during a single night compared to the norm
of 6.5 tons during a 5¾ hour shift. 102 tons

represented twice the amount expected from a squad of eight men. Three weeks later he dug 227 tons in a single shift. His methods to improve personal productivity led to the creation of the Stakhanovite movement.

Stalingrad, VOLGOGRAD/RUSSIA
See VOLGOGRAD.

Stamford, AUSTRALIA, UK, USA
1. UK (England): formerly Steanford 'Stony Ford' from *stān* and *ford*.
2. USA (Connecticut): founded in 1641 and named after their home town in England by some of the early settlers.

Stanger, KWAZULU-NATAL/SOUTH AFRICA
Founded in 1873 and named after Dr William Stanger (1811–54), the first surveyor general of Natal. To the Zulu it was known as KwaDukuza 'Place of the Labyrinth', a reference to the fact that Shaka (*c.*1787–1828), chief of the Zulu (1816–28), had his largest *kraal* 'protected enclosure of huts' here.

Stanley, AUSTRALIA, CANADA, CHINA (HONG KONG), FALKLAND ISLANDS, UK, USA
1. Australia (Tasmania): founded as Circular Head in 1826 and renamed in 1833 after Edward Stanley (1799–1869), 14th Earl of Derby, British colonial secretary (1833–4, 1841–4) and prime minister (1852, 1858–9, 1866–8).
2. Falkland Islands: formerly Beau Port and Port William. Major General Richard Moody, lieutenant-governor of the Falkland Islands (1841–7), made it his official residence in 1844 and renamed it Port Stanley after Edward Stanley, 14th Earl of Derby. During the two months in 1982 when Argentinian troops occupied it four times: Puerto Rivero, Puerto de la Isla Soledad, Puerto de las Malvinas, and Puerto Argentino. It has been the capital of the Falkland Islands since 1842. 'Port' is no longer in use.
3. UK (England): 'Stony Woodland Clearing' from *stān* and *lēah* 'woodland clearing'.

Stann Creek, BELIZE
A district. When Puritan settlers arrived they established trading posts along the coast from trading stands they called *stanns*. The town formerly called Stann Creek has been renamed Dangriga.

Stanovoy Range (Stanovoy Khrebet), RUSSIA
On the border between the Sakha Republic and Amur Province, it means 'Main Range' from *stanovoy* 'main' to indicate its predominance.

Staraya Russa, NOVGOROD/RUSSIA
'Old Russia' from *staryy*. It was in this region that the Kievan Rus state, from which Russia developed, was founded.

Stara Zagora, BULGARIA *Beroea, Augusta Trajana, Vereia Irenopolis, Burue Eski Zagra*
Originally a Thracian settlement called Beroea, it was renamed in the 2nd century after Trajan[†]. Irenopolis 'Irene's Town' honoured Irene Ducas (*c.*1066–1120), wife of Alexius I Comnenus, Byzantine emperor (1081–1118). It was taken by the Turks in 1370 and they named it 'Old Fertile Land'. The Turkish *eski* 'old' was replaced by the Slavonic *stara* 'old'; *zagora* is derived from *zad gora* 'across the mountain' or 'beyond the mountain'.

Starbuck, KIRIBATI, USA
Kiribati: one of the Line Islands and formerly known as Volunteer Island. It was sighted in 1823 by, and named after, Valentine Starbuck, a British whaling captain. It was annexed by the UK in 1866.

Stari Trg, SLOVENIA
'Old Square' from *stari* 'old' and *trg* 'square'.

Staritsa, BELARUS, RUSSIA
Russia (Tver'): founded in 1297 with the name Gorodok 'Little Town'. In 1365 it was moved to the Volga and became Novy Gorodok 'New Little Town'. It was renamed Staritsa in the 15th century, its new name being that used for the 'old bed of a river', here the one flowing into the Volga.

Starnberg, BAVARIA/GERMANY
'Starling Mountain' from *Star* 'starling' and *Berg*. It is in the area of Lake Starnberg that hundreds of thousands of starlings gather each year before flying south to Africa. Starnberg lies at the northern tip of the lake.

Starobel'sk, UKRAINE *Staraya Belaya*
Founded in 1686 as 'Old White (Town)' from *staryy* and *belyy*, although the reason for the colour is not known. In due course the two words were merged to form the present name.

Starodub, BRYANSK/RUSSIA
'Old Oak Tree' from *staryy* and *dub* 'oak'.

Staryy Krym, UKRAINE *Eski-Kerim*
'Old Crimea', adopted from the previous Turkish name in 1784, the Turkish *eski* 'old' giving way to the Russian *staryy* 'old'. *See* CRIMEA.

Staten Island, NEW YORK/USA
Only 31 years after the Dutch first landed in 1630 did they achieve a permanent settlement. They named it after the *Staten Generaal* 'States

General', a group of delegates fom the seven provincial states of the Dutch Republic.

States, The The *United States of America.

Staunton, UK, USA
1. UK (England): 'Farmstead on Stony Ground' from *stān* and *tūn*.
2. USA (Virginia): founded in 1736 and named after Lady Rebecca Staunton, the wife of Sir William Gooch (1681–1751), lieutenant-governor of Virginia.

Stavropol', RUSSIA *Voroshilovsk*
A territory and a city founded in 1777 as a military post with a name meaning 'Town of the Cross' from the Greek *stavros* 'cross' and *polis*. In 1935–43 it was renamed after Kliment Voroshilov[†] to mark his promotion to the rank of Marshal of the Soviet Union in 1935. It readopted its original name on the liberation of the Caucasus from the Germans in 1943. It was the former name for *Tol'yatti

Steamboat Springs, COLORADO/USA
So named because the residents thought that the bubbly springs sounded like a paddle boat.

Stellenbosch, WESTERN CAPE/SOUTH AFRICA
'Stel's Bush' from the Dutch *bosch* 'bush'. It was founded as a camp in 1679 by, and named after, Commander Simon van der Stel (1639–1712), first governor of the Cape (1691–9).

Stepanakert, AZERBAIJAN
See XANKÄNDI.

Stepanavan, ARMENIA *Dzhalal-ogly*
First named after the *oğul* 'son' of a local landowner, it was renamed 'Stepan's Settlement' in 1924 after Stepan Shaumyan (1878–1918), a Georgian Bolshevik hero who founded the Armenian communist movement in 1912 and who was killed by the British fighting for the communist cause, and *van* 'settlement'.

Sterlitamak, BASHKORTOSTAN REPUBLIC/ RUSSIA
Founded in 1766 at the confluence of the Belaya and Sterlya Rivers from which it gets its name with the Bashkir *tamak* 'mouth'.

Steubenville, OHIO/USA
Laid out on the site of Fort Steuben in 1797 and named after Baron Frederick William von Steuben (1730–94), a Prussian officer who became a major general responsible for the training of the American colonial army during the American War of Independence (1775–83).

Stevenage, ENGLAND/USA *Stithenæce, Stigenace*
'(Place at) the Strong Oak Tree' from the Old English *stīth* 'strong' or 'stiff' and *āc* 'oak'.

Stewart Island, NEW ZEALAND *Cape South*
The third largest island of New Zealand. Captain James Cook[†] claimed that it was a peninsula of South Island in 1770, but its existence as an island was proved in 1809 by Captain William Stewart, a British whaling captain, and subsequently it was named after him.

Steyr, AUSTRIA *Styraburg*
Named after the River Steyr 'stream'; it is located at the confluence of the Enns and Steyr Rivers.

Steytlerville, EASTERN CAPE/SOUTH AFRICA *Steytlerton*
Founded in 1876 by the Dutch Reformed Church and named after the Revd Abraham Steytler.

Stirling, AUSTRALIA, CANADA, SOLOMON ISLANDS, UK, USA
1. Australia (Western Australia): a mountain range discovered in 1802 by Matthew Flinders[†] and named after Admiral Sir James Stirling, first governor of Western Australia (1828–39) and the leader of the group of initial colonists.
2. UK (Scotland): formerly Strevelin and Urbs Giudi, mentioned by the Venerable Bede (*c.*673–735), may be an earlier reference to the same place. The meaning is obscure, but it might be 'Flowing Water'.

Stockholm, CANADA, SWEDEN, USA
Sweden: 'Pole Island' from *staka* or *stock* 'pole' or 'log' and *holm* 'island'. Founded *c.*1252 by Birger Jarl 'Earl', the Swedish ruler (1248–66), who built a fort on one of the small islands as a defensive post to block the entrance to Lake Mälaren from the Baltic Sea; water traffic was controlled by a form of wooden boom and the city's name is probably derived from this. A city-port grew up around the original fort and spread onto neighbouring islands and part of the mainland. According to legend, its first name, Agnefit 'Agne's Strand', comes from a Viking warrior king, Agne, who was killed here by Finnish prisoners he had captured. The county of Stockholm surrounds the city which has been the Swedish capital since 1523. It has given its name to the 'Stockholm Syndrome', a condition experienced by some hostages who come to identify themselves with their captors even to the extent of refusing to cooperate with the police when released. The term was coined after a bank robbery in 1973.

Stockport, UK, USA
UK (England): formerly Stokeport 'Market Place at an Outlying Hamlet' from *stoc* and *port*.

Stockton, USA
California: founded as Tuleburg in 1847 and
renamed in 1850 after Commodore Robert F.
Stockton (1795–1866), who had claimed
California for the USA in 1846.

Stockton on Tees, ENGLAND/UK *Stocton*
Thought to be 'Farmstead at an Outlying
Hamlet' from *stoc* and *tūn*. This town is on the
River Tees so the name differentiates it from
several other Stocktons.

Stoke on Trent, ENGLAND/UK *Stoche*
'Outlying Hamlet' from *stoc*. It lies on the River
Trent and thus Trent has been added to
distinguish it from other places called Stoke,
such as Stoke Poges, named after the family of
le Pugeis.

Ston, CROATIA *Turris Stagni, Stagnum*
Derived from the Latin *stagnum* 'marsh land'.
To the south salt pans on marshland were laid
out by the Romans.

Stonehenge, AUSTRALIA, UK
UK (England): a monument formerly called in
Latin Circea Gigantum 'The Giants' Ring' and
the Anglo-Saxon Stanenges. It is said to mean
either 'Hanging Stones' from the layout of the
stones or 'Stone Gallows' from *stān* and *hengen*
because of the apparent resemblance to
gallows.

Stornoway, CANADA, UK
UK (Scotland): formerly Stornochway 'Steering
Bay' from the Old Scandinavian *stjórn* 'steering'
and *vágr* 'bay'. The name probably indicated
that careful manœuvring was necessary when
entering or leaving the harbour.

Stoughton, CANADA, UK, USA
1. UK (England): the place in Surrey was
formerly Stoctune 'Farmstead at an Outlying
Hamlet' from *stoc* and *tūn*.
2. USA (Massachusetts): founded as part of
Dorchester in 1713 and renamed in 1726 after
William Stoughton (1631–1701), first
lieutenant-governor of the Massachusetts Bay
Colony (1692–1701) and its chief justice.

Stour, ENGLAND/UK
The name of four rivers with the meaning
'Strong'.

Stowmarket, ENGLAND/UK *Stou*
'Meeting Place with a Market' from the Old
English *stōw* 'meeting place'; *market* was added
later to indicate that it had an important
market.

Stow on the Wold, ENGLAND/UK
Eduuardesstou, Stoua
Originally 'St Edward's Holy Place' from the
Old English *stōw*, here 'holy place', which in

due course was renamed 'Holy Place in
Moorland'.

Strabane, UK, USA
UK (Northern Ireland): Irish An Srath Bán 'The
White Riverside Land', a reference to the
colour of the earth by the River Mourne on
which it lies.

Strait of Juan de Fuca, CANADA-USA
A strait between Vancouver Island and
Washington named after Juan de Fuca, the
name adopted when sailing for the Spanish by
a Greek navigator, Apostolos Valerianus. He is
said to have claimed to have found a passage
between the Pacific and Atlantic Oceans
between the latitudes of 47° and 48° north in
1592. Although George Vancouver[†] exposed
this claim as being dishonest, the strait still
bears de Fuca's name.

Straits Settlements Created in 1826 and
comprising Penang, Malacca, and Singapore,
which bordered on the Malacca Strait. In 1867
control was transferred from the English East
India Company to the British government at
which time it became a fully fledged crown
colony. In 1907 Labuan (now part of Sabah,
Malaysia) joined the Singapore Settlement and
in 1912 it became a settlement in its own right.
In 1946 the Straits Settlements ceased to exist
when Singapore became a separate crown
colony.

Strakonice, CZECH REPUBLIC
Founded in the 12th century and named after a
local leader called Strakoň; thus the name
means the 'Village of Strakoň's People', *-ice*
being used as a suffix for place-names derived
from personal names.

Stralsund, MECKLENBURG-WEST POMERANIA/
GERMANY
'Arrow-like Strait' from a Slavonic word akin
to the modern Russian *strela* 'arrow' and the
German *Sund* 'strait'. It was settled by Slavs in
1209 on the southern coast of the Strelasund
which separates the mainland from the island
of Rügen.

Strand, WESTERN CAPE/SOUTH AFRICA *Van
Ryneveld's Town, Somerset Strand, The Strand*
Founded in about 1850 and named after D. J.
Ryneveld, a landowner and magistrate.
Because Somerset West was only 2 miles
(3 km) inland, the coastal town subsequently
became popularly known as Somerset Strand.
This was shortened to The Strand in 1918 and
to Strand in 1937.

Strasbourg, CANADA, FRANCE
France (Alsace): 'Fortress on the Street' from
the Old German *straza* 'street' and *Burg*, a

S

reference to its location on the main road between Gaul and Germany. The Germans, who occupied the city in 1871–1918 and 1940–4, spell the name Strassburg. The Romans developed the original Celtic village into a garrison town called Argentoratum; when the Franks took it in the 5th century they renamed it Strateburgum from which the present name comes.

Stratford, CANADA, NEW ZEALAND, UK, USA
1. Canada (Ontario): founded as Little Thomas in 1832 and renamed in 1835 after Stratford-upon-Avon, the birthplace in England of William Shakespeare (1564–1616), poet and dramatist.
2. New Zealand (North Island): founded as Stratford-on-Patea in 1877 after Shakespeare's birthplace. The 'on-Patea', the local river name, was dropped later.
3. UK (England): 'Ford on a Roman Road' from the Old English *strǣt* 'Roman road' and *ford*. To distinguish the various Stratfords an affix has been added; for example, 'upon-Avon' where Shakespeare was born and is buried. This town lies where a Roman road crossed the River Avon.
4. USA (Connecticut): founded as Cupheag by English settlers in 1639 and renamed in 1643, perhaps after Shakespeare's birthplace.

Strathclyde, SCOTLAND/UK
A region meaning '(Broad) Valley of the River Clyde' from the Gaelic *srath* 'valley'. It was a Kingdom of the Britons between the 6th and 11th centuries before becoming a province of Scotland.

Streator, ILLINOIS/USA *Hardscrabble, Unionville*
Laid out in 1868 on the Vermillion River and originally called Hardscrabble because the ascent from the river up to the town was hard going. It was later renamed to celebrate the conclusion of the American Civil War (1861–5) and again in 1872 after Worthy S. Streator, president of the Vermillion Coal Company.

Stroitel', RUSSIA
Belgorod and Tula: 'Builder', a reference to the manufacture of building materials here.

Stromboli, ITALY *Strongyle*
An island. The previous Latin and present names come from the Greek *strongulos* 'round (shape)'.

Stroud, UK, USA
UK (England): formerly Strode 'Marshy Ground overgrown with Brushwood' from the Old English *strōd*.

Struga, MACEDONIA, POLAND
Macedonia: 'Fishing Channel', a reference to the channels through which the Crni Drim River flows out of Lake Ohrid.

Strumica, MACEDONIA *Tiveriopol/Tiberiopolis*
The former name is said to have been adopted by the Byzantines after the relics of the fifteen martyrs of Tiberiopolis 'City of Tiberius', after Tiberius (42 BC–AD 37), Roman emperor (14–37), were brought here. The present name was used in parallel and comes from the Strumica River, a tributary of the Struma River (when in Greece, the Strimon), which may be named after Struma, the daughter of Tiberius.

Strydenburg, NORTHERN CAPE/SOUTH AFRICA
Founded by the Dutch Reformed Church in 1892 with an Afrikaans name meaning 'Town of Strife' from *strijd* 'strife' or 'conflict' and *burg*.

Stryy, UKRAINE
'Stream', a reference to the River Stryy on which it lies from the Russian *struya* 'stream'.

Štúrovo, SLOVAKIA *Parkany*
Renamed after the Slovak nationalist Ludovit Štúr (1815–56), who led the 1848 revolt against Hungary and was the seminal influence in the creation of a written Slovak language as distinct from Czech. The previous name was Hungarian.

Sturt, AUSTRALIA
A suburb of Adelaide and a stony desert in South Australia, and a mountain in New South Wales, are all named after Charles Sturt (1795–1869), an Indian-born British soldier. He explored the river systems of eastern Australia and then conducted an expedition into the interior of the continent in 1844–6.

Stutterheim, EASTERN CAPE/SOUTH AFRICA *Döhne Post*
A mission station was first established here in 1837 and a fort, called Döhne's Post after the first missionary, twenty years later. The name was changed later as a tribute to Major General Carl Gustav von Stutterheim, the German commander of the troops who built the fort.

Stuttgart, GERMANY, USA
Germany (Baden-Württemberg): the city, originally Stuotgarten, was developed from a *Stutengarten* 'stud farm' or, literally, 'Mares' Garden' from the Old High German *Stute* 'mare' and *Garten*, established *c*.950.

Stuyvesant, NEW YORK/USA
Named after Peter Stuyvesant (*c*.1592–1672), Dutch director general of all Dutch possessions in North America and the Caribbean from

1645 and of New Amsterdam (now New York City) (1647–64).

Styria (Steiermark), AUSTRIA
A state named after the town of *Steyr and the Old High German *marcha* 'march' or 'frontier district'. It was such a district of the Frankish Empire before becoming a Habsburg crown land in 1282.

Subotica, SERBIA/SERBIA AND MONTENEGRO
Castrum Szabatka, Sent Maria, Maria Tereziopolis, Szabadka
Founded in the 15th century as a Hungarian fortress, its name was changed to St Mary and then in 1779 to the 'City of Maria Theresa' in honour of Maria Theresa[†]. In 1845 the name was changed to Subotica from the Serbo-Croat *subota* 'Saturday' which indicated the weekly market on this day; the Hungarian version of the name, Szabadka (which does not mean 'Saturday') was adopted at the same time, a throwback to the original name.

Suceava, ROMANIA *Soczow*
A county and a city named after the River Suceava on which the city lies. The river's name is said to be derived from *soc* 'elder' (tree). Suceava can also mean a working part of a weaving loom where it is made of elder. Alternatively, it has been suggested that it comes from *suci* 'to twist' or 'to turn', a reference to the river's course.

Sucre, BOLIVIA, COLOMBIA, VENEZUELA
1. The judicial capital of Bolivia, a department and towns in Colombia, and a state in Venezuela are all named after Antonio José de Sucre (1795–1830), a prominent leader in the wars of independence against Spain in Bolivia and Colombia, and the liberator of Ecuador; he was the President of Bolivia (1825–8).
2. Bolivia: founded in 1539 on the site of a Charcas village called Chuquisaca, probably 'headquarters of the Charcas', and renamed La Plata 'The Silver'. It became the Bolivian capital in 1839 and was renamed after Sucre the next year. The projected move of the capital to La Paz in 1898 was hotly disputed and Sucre was allowed to remain the judicial capital while the executive and legislature moved.

Sudak, UKRAINE
Thought to have been developed as a Sogdian settlement, hence its name.

Sudan The Republic of The Sudan (Jumhūrīyat as-Sūdān) since 1956. Previously Anglo-Egyptian Sudan (1899–1956), an Anglo-Egyptian Condominium although, in fact, under British colonial administration since the UK had occupied Egypt since 1882; under

Egyptian rule (1821–85); the Egyptian–Sudanese link was split when Muhammad Ahmad (1844–85), calling himself the Mahdi, *al-Mahdī* 'the guided one', called for a *jihād* 'holy war' in 1881 and by 1885 the Mahdists had succeeded in establishing a Muslim state controlling most of modern Sudan. In 1898, however, an Anglo-Egyptian force overthrew the Mahdist state. The country's name comes from *Balad as-Sūdān* 'Land of the Blacks' from *balad* 'land', *as* 'the', and *sūdān*, the plural of *aswad* 'black'. Originally it was a term, used by geographers and travellers, that referred to the swathe of land south of the Sahara Desert stretching from the Atlantic to the mountains of Ethiopia. The ancient region of Nubia corresponded with the northern part of Sudan, north of Khartoum. Sudan should not be confused with the Sudanese Republic or what was French Sudan (*see* MALI).

Sudbury, CANADA, UK, USA
UK (England): 'Southern Fortification' from the Old English *sūth* 'south' and *burh*. The towns in both Ontario, Canada, and Massachusetts, USA, are named after the Sudbury in Suffolk, England.

Sudetenland, CZECH REPUBLIC
A part of Bohemia and named after the Sudeten mountain ranges (in Czech, *Sudety*). The region's name might possibly be translated as 'Southlands' from the German *Süd* 'south'. Although largely populated by Germans, it had never been part of Germany before 1938. Formerly belonging to the Austro-Hungarian Empire, in 1919 it was incorporated into the new state of Czechoslovakia. Following agitation by Adolf Hitler[†] in 1938, the Sudetenland was transferred to Germany. It was returned to Czechoslovakia in 1945 and the German population expelled.

Suez (as-Suways), EGYPT *Clysma, Kolsum*
A governorate and a city-port at the southern end of the Suez Canal. An ancient Greek port, the name was changed to Kolsum in the 7th century when the Muslims arrived. The Ottoman Turks converted it into an important naval and trading station in the 16th century. It gives its name to the Suez Canal and the Gulf of Suez. The meaning of the present name is obscure. Grammatically it is the diminutive of *sus* 'woodworm' or 'liquorice', although this certainly does not seem to be relevant here.

Suffolk, UK, USA
1. UK (England): a county, formerly Suthfolchi and Sudfulc, named after the 'Southern Folk', from the Old English *sūth* and *folc*, of the East

Anglian tribes. It gives its name to the Suffolk Punch, the smallest breed of draft horse which originated in Suffolk, and a breed of hornless sheep.
2. USA (Virginia): settled as Constant's Warehouse in 1720 and named after John Constant who built up a tobacco business here. In 1742 it was renamed after the English county as was the city in Massachusetts.

Sühbaatar, MONGOLIA
A province and a city founded in 1940 and named after Damdiny Sühbaatar (1893–1923), a communist revolutionary war hero, who led the Mongolian People's Revolutionary Party and was one of the founders of the Mongolian People's Republic. Fighting pro-Japanese forces in 1918, he had won the title of *baatar* 'hero' to add to his surname of Süh (also spelt Sükh) 'axe'.

Sukabumi, JAVA/INDONESIA *Soekaboemi*
'Paradise', an apt name for a hilly health resort with hot springs nearby.

Sukhothai, THAILAND
'Dawn of Happiness'. It was the first capital of the first independent Thai Kingdom (of Sukhothai) which was founded in 1238. It became a vassal state of Lan Na in 1321 and thereafter went into decline. It was incorporated into the Kingdom of Ayutthaya in 1438. At one time it stretched north into modern Laos, west to the Andaman Sea, and south into modern Malaysia.

Sukhoy Log, SVERDLOVSK/RUSSIA
'Dry Gully' from *sukhoy* 'dry' and *log* 'broad gully'.

Sukhumi (Sokhumi), GEORGIA *Dioscurias, Sebastopolis, Tskhumi, Suhumkale, Sukhum*
An ancient Greek colony, the first name referred to the mythological twins of Zeus, Castor and Pollux, the Dioscuri. It became a Roman fortified town with the Greek name of Sebastopolis 'Noble City' from *sebastos* 'noble' or 'magnificent' and *polis*. Less plausibly, it has been suggested as meaning the 'City of St Sebastian', a captain in the Roman emperor Diocletian's praetorian guard, who was martyred *c.*288. The Georgian Tskhumi 'hot' followed. When the town fell under Ottoman Turkish control in the 17th century the name was changed to Suhumkale to mean 'Fortress on the Sandy River' from the Turkish *su* 'water', *kum* 'sand', and *kale*. This became Sukhum in Russian hands, but in 1939 the present spelling was adopted. This is the form used today by advocates of Georgian unity, while Abkhaz separatists use Sukhum; it is the capital of *Abkhazia.

Sulawesi, INDONESIA *Celebes*
An island with five provinces of which four are North, Central, South, and South-East Sulawesi. The Portuguese arrived *c.*1512 and gave it a name about which there are several theories. One is that it is derived from *selihe* or *selire* 'sea current'; another, that it comes from *si-lebih* 'the one with more islands'; a third, that it comes from *Os Célebres* 'The Famous Ones', referring to the hazardous coral reefs off the north-eastern coastline. The present name may be a simple adaptation of the earlier name, Celebes. However, the Indonesian *sula* means 'sharp vertical stake' perhaps used for hunting, while *besi* 'iron' may refer to the iron deposits on the island.

Sulaymānīyah, as-, IRAQ
A Kurdish Autonomous Region and a town founded in 1781 on the site of an ancient village and named after Büyük Sulayman Pasha, governor of Baghdad (1780–1802).

Sultānpur, UTTAR PRADESH/INDIA *Kusapura/ Kushbhawanpur*
Renamed 'Town of the Sultan' having passed under the control of Muslim sultans.

Šumadija, SERBIA/SERBIA AND MONTENEGRO
'The Wooded Land' from *šuma* 'forest' or 'wood'.

Sumatra, INDONESIA, USA
Indonesia: an island with nine provinces of which three are North, South, and West Sumatra. The local name is Sumatera; at one time it was called Lesser Java. However, merchant sailors bestowed the present name which is derived from the Sanskrit *samudradvīpa* 'ocean island' from *samudra* 'ocean' and *dvīpa*; it has also been suggested that the name comes from *swarnadvīpa* 'gold island'. Samudra was a port, but its expanding influence led to the whole island taking its name. It is said to have been amended to Sumatra by Marco Polo[†] at the end of the 13th century.

Sumpango, GUATEMALA
Derived from the practice of the Toltec people of placing the skulls of sacrificed prisoners in a shrine.

Sumter, SOUTH CAROLINA/USA *Sumterville*
Founded in 1785 and named after General Thomas Sumter (1734–1832), a commander in the American War of Independence (1775–83).

Sunbury, AUSTRALIA, UK, USA
1. Australia (Victoria): originally Koora Kooracup and renamed in 1851 after the town in England.

2. UK (England): formerly Sunnanbryg and Sunneberie, probably 'Sunna's Stronghold' from an Old English personal name and *burh*.
3. USA (Pennsylvania): laid out on the site of a Susquehanna village called Shamokin in 1772 and renamed after the English town.

Sunda Islands, INDONESIA
Divided into the Greater and Lesser Sunda Islands, the name comes from *Pasundan* 'West Java' and the strait between Java and Sumatra. *See* NUSA TENGGARA.

Sundarbans, BANGLADESH *Sunderbunds*
The thickly forested coastal region named after the sundari, a type of mangrove tree.

Sunderland, CANADA, UK, USA
UK (Tyne and Wear/England): 'Separate Estate' from the Old English *sundor* 'sundered', that is, 'separate' or 'apart', and *land* in the sense of 'land that is separate from the main estate'. Here it refers to a part of Monkwearmouth that was separated from the monastery by the River Wear.

Sunnyvale, USA
California: settled as Murphy's Station in 1850 and renamed Encinal 'Oak Grove' from the Spanish *encina*. In 1912 it was incorporated and renamed again to describe its pleasant setting.

Suomenlinna, FINLAND *Sveaborg*
'Finnish Fort' from *Suomi* 'Finland' and *linna* 'fort'. The fort was built on five interconnected islands by the Swedes in 1748 to protect Helsinki from seaborne attack, hence its earlier Swedish name 'Swedish Fort'.

Suoyarvi, KARELIYA/RUSSIA
'Marshy Lake'. The town takes its name from the lake from the Finnish *suo* 'marsh' and *järvi* 'lake'.

Superior, Lake, CANADA-USA *Lac Supérieur*
Translated as 'Upper Lake' from the original French name, a reference perhaps to the fact that it was the furthest north of the five Great Lakes. It was probably discovered *c*.1622 by Étienne Brûlé, a French explorer.

Suphan Buri, THAILAND *Phanchumburi/Meuang Tharawarawadi Si Suphannaphumi, Song Phan Buri, U Thong*
'City of Gold' from *suphan* 'gold', from the Sanskrit *suvarna* or *svarna*, and *buri*. Founded in 877–82 on the left bank of the Tha Chin River, another settlement arose on the right bank and was called Song Phan Buri 'City of Two Thousand (Monks)'. Later, combined, the name became U Thong, possibly meaning 'Cradle of Gold'. The name may be associated with the mythical Suphannaphumi mentioned in early Buddhist literature.

Sūq ash-Shuyūkh, IRAQ
Founded during the first half of the 18th century as a *sūq* 'market place'. *Shuyūkh* indicated the members of the clan of the chief Shaikh of the Muntafik.

Surabaya, JAVA/INDONESIA *Sura ing Baya, Soerabaja*
'Hero when confronting Danger' from the Sundanese *sura* 'hero' and *baya* 'danger'; it is sometimes referred to as the 'City of Heroes' (*see* SURAKARTA). In 1292 a local chief and his people beat off Mongol forces sent to capture East Java and the following year the city received its name when the Majapahit Empire was founded. At three other times Surabaya has been the scene of heavy fighting: in 1610–25, 1717–23, and in 1945 and each time its inhabitants suffered severe losses. It is also said locally that the name recognizes the numerous sharks offshore and crocodiles in the rivers from the local *sura* 'shark' and *buaya* 'crocodile'. The previous version of the name was Dutch.

Surakarta, JAVA/INDONESIA *Solo, Soerakarta*
'City of Heroes' from *sura* 'hero' and *karta* 'city'. In 1745 the ruler of the Javanese Empire of Mataram, King Pakubowono II, was driven out of Kartasura and chose the nearby village of Solo, on the Solo River, to build his new palace. The new city was founded in 1755 by King Pakubowono III in 1755; Solo became a principality, a status it retained until 1946. The name Solo is the popular name for the city.

Surat Thani (Ban Don), THAILAND
'City of Good People'.

Suriname *Dutch Guiana*
The Republic of Suriname (Republiek Suriname) since 1975 when it achieved independence from The Netherlands. Previously it had been an autonomous state within the Tripartite Kingdom of the Netherlands, the Netherlands Antilles, and Suriname (1954–75); Dutch Guiana (1667–1948) after the British, who had begun to settle here in 1651, had ceded the territory to the Netherlands in exchange for the colony of New Amsterdam (now New York, USA) in 1667; it became a Dutch crown colony in 1794. The Dutch remained in control for the next 181 years but for brief periods of British control (1799–1802, 1804–14). Guiana was the name given to the north-east coast of South America by the indigenous people. The name Suriname is said to come from a local tribe called the Surinas or Surinen, its earliest inhabitants, who had been driven out by other Native Americans.

Surrey, CANADA, UK, USA
UK (England): a county, formerly Suthrige and
Sudrie, meaning 'Southern District' from the
Old English *sūther* 'southern' and possibly *gē*
'district'. The Middle Saxons had settled on
both sides of the River Thames and gave their
name to the former county of Middlesex north
of the river. The 'Southern District (of the
Middle Saxons)' was the name given to the
area south of the river in which the Middle
Saxons lived.

Surtsey, ICELAND
An island which began to erupt out of the
waters of the Atlantic Ocean in 1963 in a blaze
of fire and smoke. It was named 'Surt's Island'
in 1965 after Surtur, the fire god of Icelandic
mythology, with *ey* 'island'.

Susquehanna, USA
New York-Pennsylvania-Maryland: a river (and
a city in Pennsylvania) with a Native American
name said to mean 'Mud River' from *sisku*
'mud' and *hanna* 'river' or 'water'. It is not clear
whether the Native American tribe, the
Susquehanna, or Susquehannock, gave their
name to the river or took their name from it.

Sussex, CANADA, UK, USA
UK (England): a former county called Suth
Seaxa and Sudsexe, now split into East and
West Sussex, and meaning '(Territory of) the
South Saxons'.

Sutherland, AUSTRALIA, SOUTH AFRICA, UK,
USA
UK (Scotland): formerly Suthernelande. A
former county and now a council area named
by the Vikings Sudrland 'Southern Land' from
the Old Scandinavian *suthr* 'south' and *land*. It
was 'southern' in comparison with Orkney
and Shetland further north.

Sutlej, TIBET-INDIA-PAKISTAN *Zaradros*
A river, one of the five that gives Punjab its
name, known to the Ancient Greeks as
Zaradros. Its present name is derived from the
Sanskrit *satadru* 'flowing in a hundred
channels'.

Suvorov, TULA/RUSSIA
Named after Prince Alexander Suvorov (1729–
1800), the famous Russian military
commander who distinguished himself in the
Russo-Turkish War in 1787–91.

Suvorove, MOLDOVA *Kyzyl, Biruintsă*
The first name was from the Turkic for 'Red'. It
was subsequently renamed Biruintsă from the
Romanian for 'Victory' in 1949 to acclaim the
success of communism. In 1964 it was
renamed again after Prince Alexander Suvorov
(see previous entry) who conducted joint

operations with the Austrians in Moldavia
(now Moldova) in 1789–90. There is also a town
called Suvorovo in Bulgaria.

Suwannee, USA
Georgia-Florida: a river originally called
Guasaca Esqui 'River of Reeds'. The present
name is said to be derived from the Spanish
San Juanee 'Little St John'. There is a city in
Florida, which lies at the river's mouth, with
this name.

Suzhou, CHINA *Wumen, Wuzhou, Gusu, Pingjiang*
(*Jiangsu*)
Two towns, one in Anhui Province and the
other in Jiangsu Province, have this name,
previously known with the spelling Soochow.
Although they have the same Romanization,
the characters for Su are different. The more
famous of the two, in an area of rivers and
canals, is in Jiangsu. In 560 BC King Wu
established his capital here, expanding the city
wall and moat, and building huge gates, *mén*.
The city was therefore named Wumen 'Wu
Gates'. Later it was renamed Wuzhou after the
king's name and *zhōu*. In 589, with the Sui
dynasty conquest of southern China, it was
renamed Suzhou after Mt Gusu to the west,
although it was also called Gusu with *sū*
'perilla', a type of ornamental plant. In 724–78
it was called the Wu Prefecture, but thereafter
Suzhou became the accepted name, although
Pingjiang from *píng* 'peaceful' or 'calm' and
jiāng 'river' was also used following the
establishment of Pingjiang *Jùn* 'district'. The
Suzhou in Anhui takes its name from the
ancient Kingdom of Su.

Svalbard, NORWAY *Grumant, Spitsbergen*
An archipelago of nine principal islands visited
in 1596 by Willem Barents[†] who gave it the
name *Spitsbergen. This subsequently
changed to the Norwegian Svalbard 'Cold
Coast' from *sval* 'cold' and *bård* 'coast'. One of
the islands, however, is called Barentsøye after
him. Competing claims to possession because
of rich mineral deposits were resolved by
treaty in Norway's favour in 1920.

Svanetiya, GEORGIA
'Place of the Svans'. A rugged and
mountainous region named after its
inhabitants, the Svans, with the suffix *eti*
'place'.

Svendborg, DENMARK *Swineburgh*
'Castle of the Wild Boar' from the Old
Scandinavian *svín* 'wild boar' and *borg*.

Sverdlovsk, RUSSIA
A province named after Yakov Sverdlov (1885–
1919), a major figure in the Communist Party
and a brilliant organizer who became the first

head of the Soviet State in November 1917. *See* YEKATERINBURG.

Sverdlov'sk, UKRAINE
Founded in 1938 and named after Yakov Sverdlov (see previous entry).

Sverdrup, CANADA, RUSSIA
Canada (Nunavut): a group of islands named after Otto Sverdrup, who led a Norwegian expedition to the area in 1898–1902.

Sveti Konstantin, BULGARIA *Druzhba*
Renamed 'St Constantine' after Constantine I the Great[†] with *svet* 'saint', having been 'Friendship' until 1991. Constantine is revered as a saint in the Orthodox Church.

Sveti Stefan, MONTENEGRO/SERBIA AND MONTENEGRO
'St Stephen' from *svet* 'saint'.

Svetlogorsk, BELARUS, RUSSIA
1. Belarus: formerly Shatilki, the present Belarusian spelling is Svyetlahorsk.
2. Russia (Kaliningrad): renamed from the German Rauschen in 1946 when East Prussia was annexed by the Soviet Union. The meaning is not clear since *svetlo* (here the neuter of *svetlyy*) is associated with 'light' and can be translated in several different ways: 'light-coloured', 'bright', 'radiant', 'happy', 'joyful', 'pleasant', etc. Here it might mean 'Fair Mountain' with *gorsk*. There are several other towns with this name which may have slightly different meanings.

Svetlograd, STAVROPOL TERRITORY/RUSSIA *Petrovskoye*
Renamed in 1965 'Bright Town' from *svetlo* to indicate its rosy future and *grad*.

Svetogorsk, LENINGRAD/RUSSIA *Enso*
Renamed from the Finnish Enso in 1948 to mean 'Town of Light' from *svet* 'light' and *gorsk*, which may be a reference to the hydroelectric power station here.

Svilengrad, BULGARIA
'Silk Town' from *svila* 'silk' and *grad*.

Svir', BELARUS, RUSSIA
Russia (Leningrad): a river with a name associated with the Finnish *syvyys* 'deep'. It is the name of a town in Belarus.

Svitavy, CZECH REPUBLIC *Zuitawia, Zwittau*
Derived from the name of the River Svitava which rises in the area. The name of the river comes from the Old Czech verb *svitati* 'to be clear' with the river ending of *-ava*; thus, the 'River with Clear Water'. Zwittau was the German form of the original Czech name.

Svitlovodsk, UKRAINE *Kremges, Khrushchëv*
Named first after the Kremenchug Hydroelectric Power Station (Kremges) and then after Nikita Khrushchëv (1894–1971), Soviet leader (1953–64) and first secretary of the Ukrainian Communist Parrty (1938–49). In 1961 it became 'Bright Water' from the Russian *svetlyy* and *voda* 'water'.

Svobodnyy, AMUR/RUSSIA *Alekseyevsk*
Founded in 1912 and renamed 'Free'—at liberty or unrestrained—in 1924. The name was somewhat ironic in that a Soviet forced-labour camp was established here in the early 1930s to help in the construction of the Trans-Siberian railway system.

Swabia (Schwaben), BAVARIA/GERMANY *Alemannia*
A historic region that now encompasses part of Germany, France, and Switzerland. The present German element is a much smaller administrative district within Bavaria which takes its name from the Suebi, a Germanic people, whose name came from the Old German *sweba* 'free' or 'independent'. Originally named after the Alemanni, the name was changed in the 11th century.

Swaffham, ENGLAND/UK *Suafham (Norfolk)*
'Homestead of the Swabians' from the Old English *Swæfe* and *hām*. This would seem to indicate that the Germanic Swabians were included among the early invaders of England.

Swakopmund, NAMIBIA
'Mouth of the (River) Swakop' in German, the Germans having established a military base here in 1897. The Swakop takes its name from the Khoikhoin *tsoa-xoub* from *tsoa* 'hole' and *xoub* 'waste matter', a reference to the sludge and detritus that results whenever it floods.

Swan Hill, VICTORIA/AUSTRALIA
Kept awake by the calls of swans, Thomas Mitchell, a British explorer, gave the site this name in the 1830s.

Swan River, AUSTRALIA, CANADA, USA
Australia (Western Australia): a river named after the black swans found here in 1697 by Willem de Vlamingh. In Manitoba, Canada, and Minnesota, USA, Swan River is the name for towns.

Swansea, AUSTRALIA, UK, USA
1. Australia (Tasmania): formerly Waterloo Point and renamed in 1842 after the town in Wales.
2. UK (Wales): the Welsh name is Abertawe 'Mouth of the (River) Tawe' from *aber* and the river's name which may mean 'water'. The English name, formerly Sweynesse, Sueinesea,

and Swanesey, means 'Sveinn's Island' or
'Sveinn's Place by the Sea' after a Viking
commander with *ey*, or from the Old
Scandinavian *sóer* 'sea'.
3. USA (Massachusetts): named by an early
Welsh settler in the 1660s after his home
town.

Swartberg, WESTERN CAPE/SOUTH AFRICA
'Black Mountain', a reference to the
appearance of the mountain range.

Swartland, WESTERN CAPE/SOUTH AFRICA
'Black Land', a region which may have derived
its name from its rich, dark soil; or from the
rhenoster bush which thrived on the plain and
which turned black in summer.

Swaziland The Kingdom of Swaziland
(Umboso weSwatini) since 1968 when
independence was achieved from the UK and a
constitutional monarchy declared, although,
according to Swazi oral tradition, the kingdom
was founded *c*.1750 by the Dlamini chief
Ngwane III. Previously a British protectorate
(1903–68); and a dependency of the Boer
Transvaal (1894–9). The country is named after
the Swazis. They call themselves the Swati
after Chief Mswati II (*c*.1820–68) who became
king in 1839 and ruled until 1865. The Swazis
were a Nguni clan, taking their name from
Ngwane III, who led them to this region of
southern Africa.

Sweden (Sverige), AND USA
The Kingdom of Sweden (Konungariket
Sverige) from *c*.1000 with a constitutional
monarchy since 1809. The country is named
after a powerful Germanic people, the Svear or
Suiones (the Roman name), who inhabited the
area around Lake Mälaren. The ancient name
of the country was Svithiod. *Sverige* comes
from *Svea Rike* 'Kingdom of Svea'. Under the
Kalmar Union Sweden, Denmark, and
Norway were united between 1397 and 1523
when the Union was dissolved and Sweden
became independent. In 1814 Denmark was
forced to surrender Norway to Sweden and
the Swedish king was elected King of
Norway. The integration of the two countries
was not a success and this union was dissolved
in 1905. Sweden has given its name to suede,
originally gloves made in Sweden, *gants de
Suède*.

Swellendam, WESTERN CAPE/SOUTH AFRICA
Founded in 1743 and named after Hendrik
Swellengrebel, Dutch governor of the Cape
(1739–51), and his wife Helena, née ten
Damme.

Świętokrzyskie Gorý, POLAND
'Holy Cross Mountains', a reference to a
Benedictine abbey on Łysa Mountain, from
święty 'holy', *krzyz* 'cross', and *gorý* mountains'.

Swindon, ENGLAND/UK *Svindune (Wiltshire)*
Literally 'Swine Down' or 'Hill where Pigs are
kept' from the Old English *swīn* 'swine' and
dūn.

Świnoujście, POLAND *Swinemünde*
'Mouth of the Swina' from *ujście* 'mouth' with
Świna being the name of a strait. This comes
from the Old German *svin* 'wild boar'; with
Münde 'mouth' this gives the former German
name.

Switzerland (French: **La Suisse**; German: **Die
Schweiz**; Italian: **Svizzera**; Romansh: **Svizra**)
Helvetia, Helvetic Republic
The Swiss Confederation (French:
Confédération Suisse; German: Schweizerische
Eidgenossenschaft; Italian: Confederazione
Svizzera; Romansh: Confederaziun Svizra)
since 1291 when the German-speaking forest
communities of Schwyz, Uri, and Unterwalden
signed an agreement of mutual assistance—the
Everlasting League. The country takes its name
from Schwyz whose inhabitants became
known as Schwyzers. Napoleon[†] invaded in
1798, abolished the Confederation and
established the Helvetic Republic which he
annexed to France; it lasted only until 1803
when a new Confederation was established.
The Latin name Helvetia, after the Celtic
Helvetii people, is still used on postage
stamps.

Sydney, AUSTRALIA, CANADA
1. Australia (New South Wales): Captain James
Cook[†] was the first to discover, but not
explore, the site—a wonderful harbour (now
Sydney Harbour) which he called Port Jackson
in 1770. In 1788 Captain (later Vice Admiral)
Arthur Phillip (1738–1814), a British explorer
and first governor of New South Wales (1788–
92), arrived and he renamed it Sydney Cove
after Thomas Townshend (1733–1800), 1st
Viscount Sydney, the British home secretary
(1783–9), whose department was also
associated with the colonies at the time.
Viscount Sydney promoted the establishment
of a settlement in New South Wales for
reformed convicts. The 'Cove' was later
dropped.
2. Canada (Nova Scotia): founded in 1783 as a
refuge for United Empire Loyalists and named
after the 1st Viscount Sydney.

Syktyvkar, KOMI REPUBLIC/RUSSIA *Ust'-Sysol'sk*
Lying at the *ust'ye* 'mouth' of the River Sysola,
it was founded in 1586. Syktyv is the Komi

name for the Sysola to which has been added the Komi *kar* 'town', thus 'Town on the (River) Syktyv'. The name was changed in 1930.

Syracuse, ITALY, USA
1. Italy (Sicily): locally Siracusa, a province and a city founded *c.*734 BC by the Corinthians. The name may be derived from the Phoenician *suraku* 'salt water', a reference to a nearby marsh, or from the Phoenician *serah* 'to feel ill' because of its situation by the marsh.
2. USA (New York): its location by a marsh prevented early settlement after the site was visited by Samuel de Champlain[†] in 1615, but inspired the name in recognition of the similarities with the Sicilian city in 1820; it was founded in 1805.

Syr Darya, UZBEKISTAN-TAJIKISTAN-KAZAKHSTAN *Sayhun, Jaxartes*
A river known to the Greeks as the Jaxartes with the present name meaning 'Mysterious River' from the Uzbek *sir* 'mysterious' and the Persian *darya* 'river' or Uzbek *darë* 'river'. It is perhaps mysterious in that its course meanders with several bed changes and often channels are formed which run out into the sand. The town of Syr Dar'ya is in Uzbekistan.

Syria (Sūrīyah) *Aram*
The Syrian Arab Republic (al-Jumhūrīyah al-'Arabīyah as-Sūrīyah) since 1961 when Syria seceded from the United Arab Republic, a union between Syria and Egypt, which had been established in 1958. The Syrian Republic dates from 1941 when Syrian independence was recognized, although full independence was not achieved until French troops finally evacuated the country in 1946. During that period of five years the French continued to exercise power, having been awarded the League of Nations mandate over Syria in 1922. In March 1920 Syrian nationalists had proclaimed the Kingdom of Greater Syria, but it lasted for only a month. Between 1516 and 1918 Syria was part of the Ottoman Empire. Modern Syria comprises only a small part of historical Syria. Until the 20th century when the Western powers established the contemporary states of the Middle East, Syria (or Greater Syria) included Syria, Lebanon, Jordan, Israel, and the West Bank. With different borders Syria is also known as *al-Shām* and *ash-Shām* 'The Northern' or the 'Left-Handed Region' because in ancient times the speaker in central Arabia was taken to be facing the rising sun

and therefore Syria was on his left and to the north. *Bîlâd ash-Shām* was the name for Greater Syria and also its historic administrative centre, Damascus. The name Syria was rarely used until about 1865 when it became the name of an Ottoman Turkish province; it became the name of the country when the French mandate was established. The origin of the name Syria is not known.

Syzran', SAMARA/RUSSIA
Founded in 1683 as a military post and named after the Syzran River; the meaning of its name is unknown.

Szczecin, POLAND *Stettin*
May be derived from *szczotka* 'undergrowth', a reference to the scrub that used to grow here. It was under German rule in 1720–1945, hence the German name Stettin.

Szechwan, CHINA
See SICHUAN.

Szeged, HUNGARY *Segedin*
First mentioned in 1183, the name may be derived from *szög* 'angle', a reference to its position near a sharp bend of the Tisza River. Less plausibly, it could come from *sziget* 'island', given its location by the Tisza near its junction with the Maros River. Segedin was the Ottoman Turkish name in 1543–1688.

Székesfehérvár, HUNGARY *Alba Regia, Ustolni Belghrad, Stuhlweissenburg*
'(Royal) Seat of the White Fortress' from *szék* 'chair' or 'seat', *fehér* 'white', and *vár*. It was founded on the site of a Roman settlement *c.*972 by Prince Géza. His son St Stephen (*c.*970–1038), who received the title of king from Silvester II, Pope (999–1003), and was King of Hungary (1000–38), fortified it and made it his royal seat. It did not remain so for more than a few years, however. The Latin and German names have the same meaning. The Ottoman Turks occupied the city between 1543 and 1688, when it surrendered to the Austrians who called it Ustolni Belghrad from the Serbian *stolni belgrad* 'white capital castle'.

Szentendre, HUNGARY
'St Andrew' from *szent* 'saint'.

Szombathely, HUNGARY *Savaria, Steinamanger*
'Saturday Place' from *szombat* 'Saturday' and *hely* 'place'; this was a reference to the Saturday market.

Tabasco, MEXICO
A state and a city in Zacatecas state. The name means 'Damp Earth', a reference to the state's low-lying terrain dotted with lagoons and swamps. It has given its name to the pungent pepper sauce.

Table Bay (Afrikaans: **Tafelbaai**), WESTERN CAPE/SOUTH AFRICA *Aquada de Saldanha*
The Portuguese were the first Europeans to visit the bay *c.*1500 and they named it the 'Watering Place of Saldanha' after the Portuguese navigator, Antonio de Saldanha. In 1601 the Dutch renamed the bay after the mountain, Table Mountain, which overlooks it. At that time the name Saldanha Bay was given to another bay some 60 miles (100 km) to the north.

Table Mountain (Afrikaans: **Tafelberg**), WESTERN CAPE/SOUTH AFRICA *A Meza*
Originally 'The Table' from the Portuguese *a* 'the' and *mesa* 'table' because of the almost horizontal layers of sandstone which give it its shape.

Tabor, CZECH REPUBLIC, RUSSIA, USA
Czech Republic: spelt Tábor. Because some Celtic fortifications remained, the first Czech settlement was called Hradiště 'Fortified Settlement'. It was burnt in 1277, but was re-established in the 14th century and called Hradiště Ústské 'Fortified Settlement of Sezimovo Ústí', a neighbouring village. In 1420 this village was also burnt and its Hussite inhabitants moved to Hradiště Ústské which they renamed Hradiště Hory Tábor 'Fortified Settlement of Mt Tabor'. In due course, the 'Hradiště Hory' was dropped. Tábor refers to the biblical Mt Tabor near Nazareth, Israel. It gave its name to the Taborites, a militant bunch of Hussite reformers. *Tábor* in Czech means a place where a large number of people gather.

Tabrīz, IRAN *Gazaca, Tauris*
Popularly believed to mean a place where fever is shaken off from *tab* 'fever' and *rīz* 'to flow' or 'to pour'. Tabrīz was considered unhealthy because of its climate and the name may refer to the fact that a fever causes one to sweat and sweating helps to cool the body and get rid of the fever. It is, however, possible that it means 'hot flowing', a reference to the numerous thermal springs in the vicinity or the volcanic activity.

Tacoma, WASHINGTON/USA *Commencement City*
The bay here was the starting point for a survey and thus called Commencement Bay in 1841. The settlement on the bay was named Commencement City when it was established in 1868. Very soon it was renamed Tacoma, the Native American word for 'mountain' with particular reference to Mt Rainier, some 45 miles (72 km) to the south-east.

Tacuarembó, URUGUAY *Villa de San Fructuoso*
Founded in 1831 as the 'Town of St Fructuosus', the bishop of Tarragona in Spain, who was burnt alive in 259 with two of his deacons for refusing to worship the gods. It was later renamed and given the Guaraní name for a strong and slender reed which grows in the area.

Tadcaster, ENGLAND/UK *Tatecastre*
'(Roman) Town belonging to a Man called Tāta, or possibly Tāda' from an Old English personal name and *cæster*.

Taegu (Daegu), SOUTH KOREA *Talsong, Kyŏngsang-do*
A metropolitan city called 'Great Hill' from *tae* 'great' or 'big' and *ku* 'hill'.

Taejŏn (Daejeon), SOUTH KOREA
A metropolitan city lying on the Taejŏn River with a name meaning 'Big Field' from *tae* 'great' or 'big' and *chŏn* 'field'. It was a temporary capital of the Republic of Korea (South Korea) during the Korean War (1950–3).

Taesongdong, KOREA
'Attaining Success Town'. It is actually a village located within the 2½ mile (4 km) wide Demilitarized Zone, called simply the DMZ (but actually the most heavily fortified border on earth), between North and South Korea. It is called 'Freedom Village' by US military forces.

Taganrog, ROSTOV/RUSSIA *Troitsky*
Founded in 1698 as a fortress called Troitskaya and naval base by Peter I the Great[†]. The original name of the town that developed meant 'Trinity' from *Troitsa*. The present name, adopted in 1784, means 'Trivet Horn' from *tagan* 'trivet' and *rog* 'cape' or 'horn', the latter word in the sense of a promontory. It

may mean that some warning beacon was set up here using an iron tripod or bracket.

Tahiti, SOCIETY ISLANDS/FRENCH POLYNESIA
Otaheiti, Sagittaria, King George III Island, New Cythera
The ancient, and appropriate, name of the island is said to have been Tahiti-nui-i-te-vai-uri-rau 'Great Tahiti of the Many-Coloured Waters'. Although the largest of the Society Islands, the name means 'Little Island' from the Polynesian *iti* 'little' and *nui* 'island'. It was renamed in 1606 by its Portuguese discoverer, Fernandez de Quirós, because of the arrows (in Latin, *sagitta*) carried by the inhabitants. The island was visited by Captain Samuel Wallis of the British Royal Navy in 1767 and he named it after the reigning British monarch, George III[†]. Louis-Antoine de Bougainville (1729–1811), a French navigator, claimed the island for France in 1768. The beauty, and nakedness, of the local girls made de Bougainville think that he had discovered another island of Venus and so he renamed it Nouvelle-Cythére 'New Cythera' after the Greek island (now Kithira) where a local cult to the Greek goddess of love and beauty, Aphrodite (the Roman Venus), flourished. None of these European names found favour with the inhabitants.

Tahlequah, USA
Oklahoma: settled by Cherokees and the capital of their nation in 1839–1907, the name means 'Two are enough', a reference to a meeting between two, rather than three, commissioners associated with the Cherokee 'Trail of Tears', the forced migration westwards into Oklahoma during the winter of 1838–9.

Tahoe, CANADA, USA
USA (California-Nevada): a lake, Lake Tahoe, with a Washo name meaning 'Big Water'. Tahoe City lies on its western shore.

T'ai-chung (Taizhong), TAIWAN *Tatun*
A county and a city, founded in 1721 as Tatun, and renamed in the 1890s 'Middle Taiwan' from *Tái*, short for Taiwan, and *zhōng* 'middle' or 'central'.

Taihape, NORTH ISLAND/NEW ZEALAND *Otaihape*
Founded in 1894 as a coach stop called 'Place of Taihape', the name of a local Maori, or 'Place of Tai the Hunchback' from the Maori *o* 'place of', *tai* 'angle', and *hape* 'crooked'.

T'ai-nan, TAIWAN
A city and county called 'Southern Taiwan' from *Tái*, short for Taiwan, and *nán*.

Taipei (Táiběi), TAIWAN
'Northern Taiwan' from *Tái*, short for Taiwan, and *běi* 'northern'. Founded in the early 18th

century, the city has been the capital of Taiwan since 1894. The county is T'ai-pei.

Taiping, CHINA, MALAYSIA
Malaysia: founded in the 1840s as a Chinese tin-mining settlement called Larut and then Kelian Pauh, it was given the name '(Town of) Everlasting, or Great, Peace' in 1874 from the Chinese *tài* 'peace' and *píng* 'peaceful' to commemorate the end of the Larut war and attempt to shake off its reputation for violence.

Tai Shan, SHANDONG/CHINA
A mountain called 'Peaceful Mountain' or 'Exalted Mountain' from *tài* 'peaceful' or 'exalted' and *shān*. It has long been a place of pilgrimage and has had many other names including Yue Shan, Da Shan, Dai Shan, Dai Yue, Yue Zong, and Tai Yue.

Taiwan *Ilha Formosa*
The Republic of China (Zhonghua Minguo) since 1949. It was named 'Beautiful Island' in 1590 by the Portuguese. It was briefly occupied by the Dutch in the 17th century (1624–61) before succumbing to imperial Chinese rule for the first time in 1683 and becoming part of Fujian Province; it became a separate province of China in 1886. At the close of the Sino-Japanese War in 1895 it was ceded to Japan by the Treaty of Shimonoseki and administered as a colony; at the end of the Second World War in 1945 it was returned to China, once more becoming a province. The communist victory in the Civil War in 1949 forced the Guomindang, the National People's Party, led by General Chiang Kai-shek (1887–1975), to flee the mainland and settle in Taiwan. It still claimed to be the lawful government of all China and indeed had a permanent seat on the UN Security Council until 1971 when it was replaced by the mainland People's Republic of China (PRC). While both Republics claim sovereignty over Taiwan, they both regard it as a province of China, a renegade one as far as the PRC is concerned. The island, therefore, has no legal status as an independent country. However, Taiwan's 'One China' policy was called into question in 1999 when a 'state-to-state' relationship was announced, reinforced in 2002 when the President proclaimed that one country existed on each side of the Taiwan Strait. The name means 'Terrace Bay' from *tái* 'terrace' and *wān* 'bay', a reference to its terrain which, on the west, consists of a series of terraced tablelands descending to the sea. It gives its name to the strait between the mainland of China and Taiwan; this, too, was called Formosa by the Portuguese. The Republic of China consists not only of the main island of Taiwan, but also of several

much smaller islands. It is also referred to as
Nationalist China and has used the title
'Chinese Taipei' (notably in successive
Olympic Games and in various international
organizations) and the 'Republic of China on
Taiwan'; in 1992, as an observer to the
General Agreement on Tariffs and Trade, it
went under the name of the 'Separate
Customs Territory of Taiwan, P'enghu,
Kinmen and Matsu'.

Taiyuan, SHANXI/CHINA *Jinyang, Taiyuan Fu,
Yangzhu*
'Furthest Plain' from *tài* 'remotest' or 'big' and
yuán 'plain'. Founded in 246 BC, it became
known as Jinyang from *Jin*, the name of a river,
and *yáng* signifying that it was built on the
north bank of that river. It was renamed
Taiyuan Fu, *fū* indicating that it had become a
'prefecture', in the 14th century and it
retained this status until 1912 when it was
renamed Yangzhu. In 1947 it adopted its
present name.

Tajikistan The Republic of Tajikistan
(Jumhurii Tojikistan) since 1991 when
independence was forced upon the Soviet
Central Asian republics. Previously the Tajik
Soviet Socialist Republic (1929–91) within the
Soviet Union, having been the Tajik
Autonomous Soviet Socialist Republic within
the Uzbek Soviet Socialist Republic (1925–9);
the Bukharan People's Soviet Republic (1920–
5) formed from the Emirate of Bukhara; the
northern part of modern Tajikistan was
incorporated into the Turkestan Autonomous
Soviet Socialist Republic (1918–20), the
Bukharan Emirate becoming a Russian
protectorate in 1868; southern Tajikistan did
not come under Bolshevik Russian control
until 1921. The country takes its name from its
indigenous people, the Tajiks, with the
additional *stan*. The Tajiks get their name from
an Arab tribal name, Taiy or Tayyi, a name
widely used to describe the Arabs in pre-
Islamic times. The Sogdian form of the name
was Tazik and this was used to describe Arab
invaders into Central Asia in general and by
the 14-century sedentary Islamicized Persian
speakers. The Tajiks speak a language closely
related to that spoken now in Iran and
Afghanistan; they are thus linguistically quite
distinct from the other countries of Central
Asia whose languages belong to the Turkic
family.

Takamatsu, SHIKOKU/JAPAN
A castle built in 1588 from which a town
developed. This belonged to the Tokugawa
family in 1642–1868. Its name means 'Tall
Pines' from *taka* 'tall' and *matsu* 'pine tree'.

Takaoka, HONSHŪ/JAPAN
Founded as a castle in 1609, the name means
'High Hill' from *taka* and *oka* 'hill'.

Takarazuka, HONSHŪ/JAPAN
'Treasure Mound' from characters
representing *takara* 'treasure' and *tuka*
'mound'.

Takayama, HONSHŪ/JAPAN
In the Hida Mountains, the city's name means
'High Mountain' from *taka* and *yama*
'mountain'.

Taklamakan Desert (Tăkèlāmăgān Shāmò),
CHINA
'Empty Place' from *shāmò* 'desert'. Guide
books, either seriously or as a joke, say the
Chinese translate it as 'He who goes in won't
get out' and the Uighurs as 'Homeland of the
Past', a reference to a lost civilization.

Taldy-Kurgan (Taldyqorghan), KAZAKHSTAN
Gavrilovka
Developed from the village of Gavrilovka
which was founded in the second half of the
19th century, it was renamed in 1920 to mean
'Willow Tree Hill' from *taldy* 'an area of willow
trees' and *kurgan* 'hill'.

Talladega, ALABAMA/USA
Founded in 1834 on the site of a Creek village
with a name meaning 'Town at the End' or
'Town on the Border', thus a town on the edge
of their territory, from *talla* 'town' and *dega*
'border'. It is also the name of nearby
mountains.

Tallaght (Tamhlacht), IRELAND
'Plague Cemetery', probably a reference to a
pagan burial place. In full the name is
Tamhlacht Maolruáin after Maolruáin who
founded it in 769.

Tallahassee, FLORIDA/USA
Developed by the Spanish during the 16th
century from a Creek village with a name
meaning 'Old Town' from *talla* 'town' and *hasi*
'old'.

Tallahatchie, MISSISSIPPI/USA
A river with a Choctaw name meaning 'River
of the Rock'.

Tallinn, ESTONIA *Kolyvan', Tanin Lidna, Reval/
Revel*
Originally said to be 'Strong' or 'Brave' from
the Old Estonian *kaleva*. It was later renamed
Tanin Lidna 'Danes' Fort' (in Estonian, Taani
Linn from *taani* 'Danish' and *linn* 'fort') having
been founded in 1219 by Valdemar II (1170–
1241), King of Denmark (1202–41). The city
was sold to the Teutonic Knights in 1346 who
called it Reval after the ancient coastal district

of Rävala; this name may, however, come from the Danish word *refwall* alluding to the rock circle which rises sharply from sea level or from the Old Danish *rev* 'sandbank'. Reval passed to Sweden in 1561 and was captured by the Russians in 1710 and held by them until 1917 when the name changed to Tallinn. It has been the Estonian capital since 1918.

Tamaulipas, MEXICO
A state with a Huastec name meaning 'High Mountains', a reference to the Sierra de Tamaulipas.

Tambov, RUSSIA *Tonbov*
A province established in 1937 and a city founded in 1636 as part of the fortress system to defend the southern borders of *Muscovy. Its original name, from which the present one is derived, meant 'Whirlpool' in the Moksha dialect of Mordvin.

Tam Dao (Tam Đảo), VIETNAM
'Three Islands' from *tam* 'three' and *đảo* 'island', a reference to three mountain peaks which dominate the area and appear from a distance as three islands poking above the frequent 'sea' of clouds. It was founded by the French in 1902 as a hill station.

Tamil Nādu, INDIA
One of four states formed from the Madras Presidency in 1956 to be a home for Tamil speakers. The name means 'Homeland of the Tamils' from the Tamil *nāṭu* 'land' or 'country'.

Tamlūk, WEST BENGAL/INDIA *Tāmraliptī*
Derives its name from the Sanskrit *tāmra* 'copper' and a local name, Lipti. Now well inland, it is an ancient port known for its export of silks and copper.

Tampa, DEMOCRATIC REPUBLIC OF THE CONGO, USA
USA (Florida): founded as Fort Brooke in 1824 with a name said to be derived from the Cree *itimpi* 'close to it' or 'near it', although to what this refers is not known.

Tampere, FINLAND *Tammerfors*
The town was founded in 1775 on the *Tammerkoski* 'Tammer Rapids' from *koski* 'rapids'. This is a translation of the Swedish Tammerfors from *fors* 'rapids' from which the present name comes. Finland was an integral part of Sweden between 1634 and 1809. The meaning of Tammer is not known; it may be a personal name.

Tamworth, AUSTRALIA, CANADA, UK, USA
1. Australia (New South Wales): founded in 1848 and named after the town in England which was the parliamentary constituency of

Sir Robert Peel (1788–1850), prime minister (1834–5, 1841–6).
2. UK (England): formerly Tamouuorthig and Tamuuorde 'Enclosure on the (River) Tame' from a Celtic, or possibly pre-Celtic, river name and the Old English *worthig* 'enclosure'.

Tanganyika, DEMOCRATIC REPUBLIC OF THE CONGO-TANZANIA
A lake with Burundi and Zambia also abutting onto it. The origin of the name is unclear. Sir Henry Morton Stanley[†], who saw the lake in 1871 when he found Dr Livingstone at Ujiji, claimed that the local word *nika* meant 'plain' or 'flat' and that Africans are wont to describe large bodies of water as resembling plains; thus he was satisfied that the name meant 'Plain-like Lake'. Sir Richard Burton (1821–90), with John Hanning Speke (1827–64), were the first Europeans to see the lake in 1858 and their theory was that the name came from the local words *kou tanganyika* 'to meet', perhaps a reference to the fact that the lake is fed by a number of rivers or that tribes met here. *See* TANZANIA.

Tangier (Ṭanjah), MOROCCO *Tingis*
Possibly founded as a Phoenician trading post in the 8th century BC, but certainly established as a Carthaginian trading post *c*.400 BC. In 146 BC it became a Roman settlement, and later a colony, called Tingis from which the present name comes. According to local tradition and Greek mythology, Tinga or Tingis, a local nymph, was the widow of Anteus who was killed in a struggle with Hercules. Either Anteus founded Tangier as Tingis, or Sophax, the son of a union between Hercules and Tingis, did, giving his mother's name to the city. It was the capital of the Roman province of Mauretania Tingitana until 429. Between 1471 and 1662 it was occupied by the Spanish and Portuguese and in 1662–84 it was held by the English crown as part of the dowry of Portuguese Catherine of Braganza (1638–1705) when she married King Charles II[†] in 1662. From 1923 until 1956, when it joined Morocco, Tangier was an international city governed by an international commission. It is still sometimes spelt Tangiers.

Tangshan, HEBEI/CHINA
'Tang Mountain', the first half of the name referring to the Tang dynasty (618–907) and the second coming from *shān*.

Tanzania The United Republic of Tanzania (Jamhuri ya Muungano wa Tanzania) since October 1964 after *Tanganyika and the historically separate island of *Zanzibar had merged in April 1964 as the United Republic of Tanganyika and Zanzibar.

Tanzania comes from the first syllable of each name with the additional -ia in the sense of 'land'. Tanganyika took its name from the lake. Previously Tanganyika had become a republic (1962), having achieved independence in 1961. Between 1946 and 1961 it had been a UN Trusteeship Territory and in 1920–46 a League of Nations mandate, both with a British administration; the UK, however, treated the territory as a colony. Tanganyika was declared a German protectorate in 1885 and in 1891 it took the name German East Africa. The name Tanganyika was adopted when the League of Nations mandate came into force. Tanzania has given its name to tanzanite, a blue gem variety of zoisite, only mined in Tanzania.

Taormina, SICILY/ITALY *Tauromenium, Almoezia*
Founded in 392 BC and built on the side of Mt Tauro from which Tauromenium and now the present name come. This may have a connection with the 'Mediterranean', the hill rising directly from the sea. When it fell to the Arabs in 962 they renamed it Almoezia, but Tauromenium was restored in 1078 when the Normans ejected the Arabs.

Taoyuan, TAIWAN *Huxuzhuang, Taoziyuan, Taojian*
A county and a city with a name meaning 'Garden of Peach Trees' from *táo* 'peach' and *yuán* 'garden'. Settlers arriving in 1737 planted many peach trees and further immigrants in 1745 carried on the practice. The city developed as an agricultural market centre. The original name used characters representing *hū* 'tiger', *xù*, a type of chestnut-leaved oak tree, and *zhuāng* 'village'. In 1747 the city was renamed Taoziyuan from *zǐ* 'young animals' and it was also known as Taojian from *jiàn* 'mountain stream'. The present name was adopted in 1903.

Taranaki (Taraangaki), NORTH ISLAND/NEW ZEALAND
A regional council whose name is the Maori name for the volcanic Mt Egmont. It means 'Barren Mountain' from *tara* 'peak', *a* 'of', and *ngaki* 'clear of vegetation'. Egmont is an active volcano and therefore has no vegetation on its upper slopes. It gives its name to the Taranaki Gate, a temporary gate made of wire strands tied with a wire loop to vertical posts.

Taranto, APULIA/ITALY *Taras, Tarentum*
Traditionally founded in 706 BC by the Spartans and named Taras, possibly after the river of the same name (now the Tara). Alternatively, the name may come from the Illyrian *darandos* 'oak', in recognition of the numerous trees of this kind previously in the

area. It fell to the Romans in 272 BC and was renamed Tarentum from which the present name comes. It has given its name to the tarantula, originally the wolf-spider (*Lycosa tarentula*) found in south-east Europe.

Taraz, KAZAKHSTAN *Talas/Taraz, Auliye-Ata, Mirzoyan, Dzhambul/Zhambyl*
Founded in the 6th century on the Talas River after which the city was first named. Talas was an important halt on the Silk Road until it was destroyed by the Mongols in the 13th century. It was rebuilt by the Emirs of Kokand in the 18th century as a northern frontier fort and given the name Auliye-Ata 'Holy Father' from the Uzbek *auliye* 'holy' and *ata* 'father'. It was captured by the Russians in 1864 and became part of Russia. In 1936 it was renamed after Levon Mirzoyan (1897–1939), an Azeri who was sent to Kazakhstan in 1933 and became the senior Communist Party official (first secretary of the Central Committee) there in 1937. It was renamed Dzhambul, or Zhambyl, in 1938 after the Kazakh folk poet and singer, Dzhambul Dzhabayev (1846–1945). This is the Russian spelling of his name; in Kazakh his name is spelt Zhambyl Zhabaev and Zhambyl was the accepted spelling in 1992–7. Zhambyl reverted to its original name in 1997.

Taree, NEW SOUTH WALES/AUSTRALIA
Founded in 1854, it takes its name from the Aboriginal *taree-hin* or *tarrebit*, a reference to a local wild fig.

Tarfaya, MOROCCO *Port Victoria, Villa Bens*
Founded by an itinerant British trader in the Sahara in 1878, Donald Mackenzie, who named it after Queen Victoria[†]. It was ceded to Spain in 1885, but the Spanish did not colonize it until 1916 when they renamed it Villa Bens after Francisco Bens Argandoña, leader of the Río de Oro Dependent Protectorate (later Spanish Sahara and then Western Sahara) (1903–12). The name is believed to come from the Arabic *ṭarfā* 'tamarisk', a shrub abundant here.

Tarīfa, ANDALUSIA/SPAIN
Named after Tarīfa Abū Zur'a who was ordered to carry out an armed reconnaissance, across the Strait of Gibraltar, of the most southerly part of the Iberian Peninsula roughly opposite Tangier in 709–10. This was a precursor to the Muslim invasion of Spain in 711.

Tarim (Tǎlǐmù Hé), SINKIANG UIGHUR AUTONOMOUS REGION/CHINA
A river whose name has two possible meanings: 'the bank of a river that flows into a lake', here the Lop Nor, or a 'river that is indistinguishable from the sands of a desert'. It

515 **Tashkent**

flows through the Taklamakan Desert and gives its name to the Tarim Basin which lies between the Kunlun and Tien Shan mountains and includes the Taklamakan Desert.

Tarīm, YEMEN
Believed to be named after Tarīm bin al-Sukūn or after the earliest settler, Tarīm bin Hadramawt.

Tarkio, MISSOURI/USA
A river and a city with a Native American name meaning 'difficult to ford'.

Tarnów, POLAND
Founded as a fortified town in 1330 by the Tarn family with -ów a possessive suffix; the family name later became Tarnowski.

Tarpon Springs, FLORIDA/USA
Founded in 1882 and named after the tarpon, a large fish found in great numbers offshore in the Gulf of Mexico.

Tarquinia, LAZIO/ITALY *Tárchuna, Tarquinii, Corneto*
Founded by, and named after, Tarconte, the brother or son of Tirrenus, the eponymous hero of the Etruscan people. In 181 BC it became a Roman colony known as Tarquinii. This was the home of the Tarquin kings who ruled Rome before the Roman Republic was founded in 509 BC. It was abandoned in the 8th century and the new site, at a lower level, was renamed Corneto until 1872 when it became Corneto Tarquinia and then simply Tarquinia in 1922, a reversion to the Roman name.

Tarragona, PHILIPPINES, SPAIN
Spain (Catalonia): the present name follows from the original, Tarraco, which may have been related to the Taruscans. Julius Caesar[†] contributed to its magnificence as the capital of the Roman province of Hispania Tarraconensis and renamed it Colonia Julia Victrix Triumphalis in honour of his victories.

Tarsus, TURKEY *Antioch-on-the-(River) Cydnus, Juliopolis*
By the 8th century BC there was a Greek colony flourishing here. It was renamed temporarily after Antiochis IV Epiphanes (*c*.215–164 BC), Seleucid King of the Hellenistic Syrian Kingdom (175–164 BC), after the Seleucids had won control. After a visit by Julius Caesar[†] it was renamed for a brief time in his honour. The meaning of the present name is unknown.

Tartary Not a geographical term, but at one time or another it has been used to describe a huge area of Central Asia from the Caspian Sea to the Pacific Ocean. More recently, it has been applied to the Sinkiang Uighur (Xinjiang Uygur) Autonomous Region in China (Chinese

Turkestan) and the surrounding highlands. During the expansion of the Russian Empire eastwards all the non-Christian tribes were grouped together as 'Tartars' (previously and again now Tatars), the extra r being inserted to bring to mind the Greek word *tartarus* 'hell'. A 'tartar' is now a violent or irascible person. *See* TATARSTAN.

Tartu, ESTONIA *Tarbatu, Yur'yev, Derpt, Dorpat*
Originally a settlement to provide protection from invaders, it may be named after the ancient Estonian god Tar. It was renamed in 1030 after its founder, Yaroslav I the Wise (980–1054), Grand Prince of Kiev (1019–54), whose baptismal name was Yury 'George'; he built a fortress on the site. From the 13th century until 1893 it was called Derpt and Dorpat, whose meanings are unknown. Yur'yev was adopted again between 1893 and 1918 at which time the present name came into use.

Tarţūs, SYRIA *Antaradus, Constantia, Tortosa*
Known as Antaradus 'Town facing (the Island of) Arwād' (Aradus to the Greeks and Romans), it was rebuilt by Constantine I[†] and renamed Constantia. By the time the Crusaders captured the town in 1102 it was known as Tortosa from which the present name comes, although its association with the original name is clear. The Crusaders relinquished the city to the Arabs in 1291.

Tarutino, UKRAINE
Founded in 1814 and named to commemorate the first Russian attack on the French near the village of Tarutino, some 50 miles (80 km) south-west of Moscow, after they had occupied Moscow. The day's fighting caused Napoleon[†] to bring forward his plans to withdraw from the city by 24 hours. Early the next day, 19 October 1812, the French began to move after a stay of just 35 days. Tarutino was not a great battle, but it did catch the French by surprise and annoyed Napoleon. The name may be a personal one.

Tashkent (Toshkent), UZBEKISTAN *Dzhadzh/ Shash, Chachkent, Binkent*
A settlement may have been founded here as early as the 2nd or 1st centuries BC. By the time it was captured by the Arabs in the 8th century it was an important caravan crossroads and this was developed into a trading centre. It adopted its present name 'Town of Stone' from the Turkic *tash* 'stone' and *kand* '(fortified) town' in the 11th century. Within the Khanate of Kokand, it was taken by the Russians in 1865. The city became the capital of the Turkestan Autonomous Soviet Socialist Republic in 1918, of the Uzbek Soviet Socialist

Republic in 1930, and of Uzbekistan when it achieved independence in 1991.

Tashkepri, TURKMENISTAN
'Stone Bridge' from the Turkic *tash* 'stone' and *kepri* 'bridge' (modern Turkish *köprü*).

Taşköprü, TURKEY
'Stone Bridge' (*see* TASHKEPRI).

Tasmania, AUSTRALIA *Anthony Van Diemansland, Van Dieman's Land*
A state since 1901 and an island. In 1642 it was visited by Abel Tasman[†] who named it Anthony Van Dieman's Land after Antony van Dieman (1593–1645), governor-general of the Dutch East Indies at the time, who sponsored the expedition. A dependency of New South Wales from 1803, it was separated from New South Wales in 1825 and became a separate colony. In 1855 it was renamed Tasmania after Abel Tasman as was the Tasman Sea.

Tataouine, TUNISIA
'Springs' from a Berber word. However, the full Berber name is Foum Tataouine 'Gorge of the Springs' from *foum* 'gorge' where the French built a military post in 1892.

Tatarbunary, UKRAINE
The first part of the name comes from the Tatars and the second from the Serbo-Croat *bunar* 'well'.

Tatarsk, NOVOSIBIRSK/RUSSIA
Founded in 1911 and named after the Tatars.

Tatarstan, RUSSIA *Tatariya*
Formerly a province and now a republic meaning 'Place of the Tatars'. Originally inhabited by Bulgars, the region was settled by the Mongols of the Golden Horde during the 13th century. It became a Tatar khanate before being absorbed into the Russian Empire in 1552; and in 1920 it became the (Volga) Tatar Autonomous Soviet Socialist Republic within the Soviet Union. The name 'Tatar' (for a time spelt Tartar) was applied fairly indiscriminately to any Mongol, Turkic, or other peoples who lived in what was called "Tartary.

Tatra (Tatry), CZECH REPUBLIC-POLAND *Tritri, Turtur, Tartr, Tatr*
A mountain range in the Carpathians. The origin of the meaning is not certain but it is probably associated with 'rocks' or 'mountain peaks'.

**Taumatawhakatangihangakō-
auauotamateauripūkakapikimaunga-
horonukupōkaiwhenuakitanatahu,**
NORTH ISLAND/NEW ZEALAND
A hill called 'The Summit of the Hill where Tamatea, who is known as the Land Eater, slid

down, climbed up and swallowed Mountains, and played on his nose flute to this loved One'. Taumata was a local chief who went up the hill to serenade his girlfriend but unfortunately fell down it. Because it involved a chief this accident became notorious, particularly because chiefs were not supposed to be accident-prone or women worth the effort! With the Maori words run together this is the world's longest place-name; but *see* BANGKOK.

Taungoo, BURMA *Ketumadi*
'Hill Spur'. It was founded in 1510 and was the original seat of the Toungoo dynasty (also spelt Taungu) for the next 30 years.

Taunton, UK, USA
1. UK (England): formerly Tantun and Tantone 'Village on the (River) Tone' from the Old English *tūn* and a Celtic river name meaning 'fire', here with the sense of 'sparkling'.
2. USA (Massachusetts): bought from local Native Americans in 1638 by Elizabeth Poole, a lady from Taunton in England, after which it was named when it became a town the following year.

Taupo, NORTH ISLAND/NEW ZEALAND
A town and a lake called Taupomoana in Maori. The name comes from *Taupo nui a Tia* 'Great Cloak of Tia' after Chief Tia said that a cliff on the lakeside resembled a cloak.

Taurage, LITHUANIA *Tauroggen*
The name may be derived from *tauras* 'noble'. Tauroggen was the German name.

Tauranga, NORTH ISLAND/NEW ZEALAND
A city-port with a name derived from a Maori word meaning 'Resting Place' or 'Safe Anchorage'.

Tavistock, CANADA, UK
UK (England): formerly Tauistoce and Tavestoc 'Outlying Settlement by the (River) Tavy' from *stoc* and the river name.

Tavolzhan, KAZAKHSTAN
Takes its name from Lake Tavolzhan. This means 'meadowsweet' from the Russian *tavolga*, a plant of the rose family that is abundant here.

Taxco, GUERRERO/MEXICO *Tlacho*
A Spanish version of the previous name meaning '(Place of) the Ball Game'. The Toltec, who are thought to have invented this game, called it *tlachtli*. See QUERÉTARO.

Taxila, PUNJAB/PAKISTAN
Ruins. The present name is the Greek version of the Sanskrit name Takṣaśilā 'The Rock of Takṣa'. According to the *Rāmāyaṇa*, the Indian epic, the city was founded by Bharata, the

younger brother of Rāma, and named after his son, Takṣa, who was its first ruler. The city was destroyed by the Huns in the 7th century and was never rebuilt.

Tayga, NOVOSIBIRSK/RUSSIA
'Taiga'. Taiga is a marshy coniferous forest found, in particular, between the tundra and steppes of Siberia.

Tayshet, IRKUTSK/RUSSIA
Named after the river whose name comes from the Ket *tay* 'cold' and *shet* 'river'.

Tbilisi (T'bilisi), GEORGIA *Tiflis*
A very ancient city with a large number of sulphurous hot springs on the north-eastern slopes of Mt Tabori, hence its name 'Warm' from *tbili*. According to legend, King Vakhtang Gorgasali, out on a hunt, wounded a deer (some say a pheasant) which fell into a hot spring and was miraculously cured. Deciding that this was a good omen, he moved his capital from Mtskheta to this healthy site in 458. An Arab emirate between the 8th and 12th centuries, it was annexed by the Russians in 1801. It became the capital of the Georgian Soviet Socialist Republic in 1921. The former name is the Persian pronunciation which is also used by Russians and Armenians. The present Georgian spelling was adopted in 1936.

Tecumseh, CANADA, USA
Named after Tecumseh (1768–1813), a Shawnee chief who, although he fought against white rule, joined the British in the war of 1812 and helped in the capture of Detroit.

Tees, ENGLAND/UK
A river with a Celtic or pre-Celtic name possibly meaning 'Bubbling (One)' or 'Surging (One)', a reference to its waterfalls.

Tegelen, THE NETHERLANDS
A centre for the manufacture of tiles and pottery, the name comes from the Dutch *tegel* 'tile'.

Tegucigalpa, HONDURAS
Founded in 1578 as a silver-mining centre on the side of Mount Picacho, the name means 'Silver Mountain' in the local dialect. It became the national capital in 1880.

Tehrān, IRAN
Takes its name from a village which was located just north of the ancient city of Rayy (now *Rey). This was laid waste by the Mongols in 1220 and Tehrān developed in its place, becoming the capital of Persia/Iran under the Qajar dynasty in 1788. The meaning of the name is uncertain. It may come from *tah*

'bottom' or 'depths' and therefore here 'underground', and *ran* possibly 'place' or 'town'. During the Middle Ages the inhabitants of Tehrān lived in underground dwellings and hid there whenever attacked; one source reports that during the Mongol destruction of Rayy many of its inhabitants fled and took refuge underground in Tehrān.

Tekirdağ, TURKEY *Bisanthe?, Rhaedestus, Rodosto*
It might have been founded as a Greek settlement called Bisanthe before being renamed Rhaedestus when it became the Thracian capital in the 1st century BC. In due course this evolved into Rodosto. The city was taken by the Ottoman Turks in the 14th century and later suffered Russian, Bulgarian, and Greek occupation before being returned to the Turks in 1922. The present name means 'Grey Mountain', after a nearby mountain, from *tekir* 'tabby' or 'grey' and *dağ*.

Telavi, GEORGIA *Teleda*
Derived from *tela* 'elm' because of the abundance of elm and plane trees in the vicinity. It was the Georgian capital between 1615 and 1762.

Tel Aviv-Yafo, ISRAEL *Ahuzat Bayit*
Created in 1950 from the merger of the ancient Canaanite city-port of *Jaffa (Yafo) and its suburb, Tel Aviv. The latter was founded in 1909 as a Jewish settlement called Ahuzat Bayit near the Arab city of Jaffa. Tel Aviv means 'Hill of Spring' from the Hebrew *tel* 'hill' and *aviv* 'spring(time)'. Tel Aviv is mentioned in the Bible (Ezekiel 3: 15) as Tel-abib. Tel Aviv was the capital of Israel in 1948 when independence was declared. The following year Jerusalem was declared to be the capital, but this has not yet been accepted by the international community.

Telde, CANARY ISLANDS/SPAIN
A city on the island of Gran Canaria which was given a name derived from a local fig tree, *telle*.

Telford, ENGLAND/UK *Dawley*
Designated a 'new town' in 1963, it was renamed in 1968 after Thomas Telford (1757–1834), a Scottish civil engineer who became surveyor of public works for Shropshire in 1786 and went on to achieve national fame for his engineering designs and construction.

Tell Bastah, EGYPT *Bubastis*
Ruins. A very ancient city in the Nile delta near Zagazig named after the city's cat-headed goddess, Bast or Bastet. The Arabic *tell* means 'hill' or 'mound' which, in archaeological terms, often marks the site of an ancient city.

Tell City, INDIANA/USA
Named by its Swiss colonists after William Tell, the Swiss legendary hero.

Tel Megiddo, ISRAEL
See MEGIDDO.

Temirtau, KAZAKHSTAN, *Samarkandsky*
'Iron Mountain' from *temir* 'iron' and *tau* 'mountain', a reference to the iron ore in the area. It was built on, and at the same time as, the Samarkand Reservoir in 1934, but was renamed in 1945. There is also another town called Temir.

Temora, NEW SOUTH WALES/AUSTRALIA
Founded in 1879 during the Gold Rush, it was given a Celtic literary name meaning 'a prominent place with a good view'.

Tempe, ARIZONA/USA *Hayden's Ferry*
Founded in 1872 on the Salt River by, and named after, Charles Hayden. It was renamed in 1880 after the Vale of Tempe (modern Greek, Témbi) in northern Greece, which was dedicated to the cult of Apollo.

Temple, CANADA, UK, USA
1. Canada (Alberta): a mountain named after Sir Richard Temple (1826–1902), a British colonial administrator in India (1847–80) who visited Canada on behalf of the British Association in 1884.
2. USA (Texas): founded by the Gulf, Colorado, and Santa Fe Railroad in 1880, it was named after Major B. M. Temple, an engineer.

Temryuk, KRASNODAR TERRITORY/RUSSIA
Developed from a fortress built in 1570 by, and named after, Prince Temryuk Aydarovich.

Temuka, SOUTH ISLAND/NEW ZEALAND
An abbreviation of Te Umu Kaha 'The Fierce (or Super) Oven' from the Maori *te* 'the', *umu* 'earth oven' and *kaha* 'fierce'. Maori earth ovens were found here.

Tenancingo, EL SALVADOR, MEXICO
Mexico (México): 'Place of Little Walls'.

Tenerife, COLOMBIA, SPAIN
Spain (Canary Islands): the largest of the Canary Islands which takes its name from Pico de Teide 'Teide Peak', the volcano, that is the highest point on the island and, indeed, on Spanish soil. The former Roman name, Nivaria, meant 'Snowy' and the present name may mean the same.

Tengiz Köli, KAZAKHSTAN
A lake from *tengiz* 'sea'; *köl* means 'lake'.

Tennessee, USA
A state that takes its name from the river, a tributary of the Ohio River. The river's name may come from a Cherokee village called Tanase (one version of the spelling), whose meaning is unknown, but may be 'river'. Tennessee was part of King Charles II's[1] grant that established Carolina in 1663; in 1777 it became Washington County within North Carolina and in 1785 its settlers proclaimed it to be the free state of Franklin. This was short-lived and in 1789 North Carolina ceded Tennessee to the US government and in 1796 it became the 16th state to join the Union. Most of the state seceded in 1861 but rejoined in 1866.

Tenos (Tínos), GREECE *Ophiousa*
An island in the Cyclades group, and a town whose name is derived from the Phoenician *tenok* 'snake'. Its ancient Greek name came from *ophis* 'snake'.

Ten Sleep, WYOMING/USA
A Native American night stop and given this name because it took ten days, or 'ten sleeps' to travel between Fort Laramie, Wyoming, to Stillwater, Montana, via Yellowstone Park.

Teotihuacán, MÉXICO/MEXICO
A town and, separately, the ruins of a pre-Columbian city with a Nahuatl name meaning 'City of the Gods'.

Tepic, NAYARIT/MEXICO *Tepique*
Founded in 1542, the name is a Nahuatl word for 'Hard Stone'. However, it has also been suggested that it means 'Place between the Hills'.

Tëplaya Gora, SVERDLOVSK/RUSSIA
'Warm Mountain' from *tëplaya* 'warm' and *gora*. Situated on the southern and eastern slopes of the Urals, the snow melts earlier here in comparison to the western slopes.

Teplice, CZECH REPUBLIC *Teplice-Šanov, Teplitz-Schönau*
Well known for its warm springs, this health resort gets its name from *teply* 'warm'.

Teplichnoye, UKRAINE *Chapayevka*
Previously named after Vasily Chapayev (*see* CHAPAYEV). Its present name is the adjective of *teplitsa* 'greenhouse'or 'hothouse'.

Terceira, AZORES/PORTUGAL *Ilha de Jesus Cristo*
'The Third', meaning that this was the third island of the Azores group to be discovered by the Portuguese in 1450. At that time they named it the 'Island of Jesus Christ' because it was sighted at Easter.

Teresina, PIAUÍ/BRAZIL *Therezina*
Founded in 1852 and named after Teresa Cristina (1822–89), wife of Dom Pedro II, Brazilian emperor (1831–89).

Teresópolis, RIO DE JANEIRO/BRAZIL
Therezópolis
Founded in 1890 and named after Teresa
Cristina (see previous entry).

Terezín, CZECH REPUBLIC *Theresienstadt*
Founded in 1780 by Joseph II (1741–90), Holy
Roman Emperor (1765–90), as one of three
towns fortified against the Prussians. He
named it 'Theresa's Town' in honour of his
mother, Maria Theresa[†], and the present name
comes from this.

Termini Imerese, SICILY/ITALY *Thermae
Himerenses, Trmah, Termini*
'Springs of Himera'. Known for its thermal
saline springs, it was called Thermae
Himerenses by the Carthaginians after they
had destroyed Himera, a town nearby, in 409
BC. The Arabic name was Trmah, or Tirmah,
which gave way to Termini (in Italian, *terme*
'thermal baths' or 'hot springs') and this
remained the name until 1863.

Terni, UMBRIA/ITALY *Interamna Nahars*
The present name derives from the original
Interamna with Nahars representing the River
Nera, on which the city lies, to distinguish it
from Interamna Praetutorium (now Teramo).
Interamna is said to be of Latin origin and
mean 'between the rivers'.

Ternopol' (Ternopil'), UKRAINE *Tarnopol*
A province and a city named 'Blackthorn Field'
from the Russian *tërn* 'blackthorn' and *pole*
'field'. Founded as a Polish city, it was annexed
by Austria at the first partition of Poland in
1772 and only returned to Poland in 1920. It
was then annexed by the Soviet Union in 1939
following the Nazi–Soviet non-aggression pact
signed in August that year.

Terre Haute, INDIANA/USA
Laid out in 1816 on a plateau above the
Wabash River and given the French name
'High Ground' from *terre* 'ground' or 'land' and
haute 'high'.

Tete, MOZAMBIQUE
A province and a town meaning 'Reed'. The
town lies on the Zambezi River.

Teton, USA
A city in Idaho and a river in Montana, Teton is
also the name of a mountain range in
Wyoming. The name was coined by French fur
trappers in the early 19th century who
referred to the South, Middle, and Grand peaks
as *Les Trois Tétons* 'The Three Breasts'.

Tétouan, MOROCCO *Tamuda*
Although a Roman settlement, Tamuda, the
town really dates from 1484 when Moorish
refugees from Granada, Spain, settled here.

The Spanish occupied the town in 1913–56
and the name is a Spanish adaptation of the
Berber *tittawin*, the plural of *tit* 'spring'

Teutopolis, ILLINOIS/USA
Originally settled by German colonists from
Cincinnati, the name is a blend of *Teuton*, the
name of an ancient northern European
people, and *polis*.

Tewkesbury, CANADA, UK
UK (England): formerly Teodekesberie
'Tēodec's Fortified Place' from a possible Old
English personal name and *burh*.

Texarkana, ARKANSAS-TEXAS/USA
A dual municipality, settled in 1874, that lies
astride the Texas–Arkansas state boundary and
near the border with Louisiana. The name
comes from *Texas*, *Ark*ansas and Louisi*ana*.

Texas, AUSTRALIA, USA
USA: a state. Spanish exploration began in
1528 but it was not until 1682 that they
established their first settlement near El Paso;
in 1691 the area became a Spanish province
and it was at this time that it received the
name Texas. According to tradition, a Spanish
monk was welcomed with cries of *techas*
'friends' from the Native Americans. When
Mexico gained its independence in 1821 Texas
became part of Mexico. However, in 1836 the
Texans, dissatisfied with the Mexican
government, declared their independence as
the Republic of Texas. This attempt to prosper
as an independent nation was not a success
and in 1845 Texas joined the Union as the 28th
state. When the Civil War began in 1861 it
seceded but rejoined in 1869.

Teyateyaneng, LESOTHO
Named after the Teya-Teyane River whose
name means 'Quicksands'.

Tezebazar, TURKMENISTAN
'New Market' from *täze* 'new' and *bazar*.

Thaba Bosiu, LESOTHO
See MASERU.

Thabazimbi, LIMPOPO/SOUTH AFRICA
A town named 'Mountain of Iron' from the
Sesotho *thaba* 'mountain'. An iron ore mine
was opened here in 1931.

Thailand (Prathet Thai) *Ayutthaya, Siam/Syam*
The Kingdom of Thailand (Muang Thai, or
Prathet Thai) since 1939. It is a constitutional
monarchy, the absolute monarchy having
been abolished in 1932. The country is named
after the Thais whose name means 'Free
(People)' from *fra* 'to be free'. This denoted that
the people of the central plain round
Sukhothai had won their freedom from Khmer

rule (in the 13th century). Derived from the Sanskrit *pradesha* Prathet means 'Land' or 'Country'. Thus Thailand means 'Land of the Free'. The first Thai kingdom was that of Sukhothai and it is regarded as the birthplace of the Thai nation. However, Thailand is said to have come into existence in 1351 when the Kingdom of *Ayutthaya was founded and Sukhothai was in decline. The Khmers called the Thais *syam* or *sayam*, a name possibly derived from the Sanskrit *shyama* 'swarthy' or, in this case, 'brown', to denote the darker skin colour of those aborigines who lived in scattered settlements in the jungle along the middle reaches of the Menam River. Foreigners called the Kingdom of Ayutthaya Siam from the 16th century, but it only became the official title of the Thai kingdom in 1855. The Thai dictator, Phibun Songkhram, insisted on changing the name back to Thailand in 1939 because in his view Siam only referred to the Thai-speaking people of old Siam and not the larger nation. The name Siam was restored in 1945–9 as a sop to extreme nationalism while Phibun was out of power; he reinstated the name Thailand in 1949. Other countries gave the name Siam only to the Tai who settled in the Chao Phraya River basin. Siam has given its name to a short-haired breed of cat originally from Siam and to Siamese twins. The latter term originally referred to Chang and Eng (1811–74), twins joined at the waist, who were born in Siam and who gained world-wide notoriety on their travels.

Tha Khaek, LAOS *Sri Gotabura*
'Indian Landing', a reference to its location as a landing place for Indian traders.

Thames, CANADA, NEW ZEALAND, UK, USA
1. A river in all four countries, those in Canada, New Zealand and the USA being named after the river in England.
2. Canada (Ontario): renamed in 1792 from La Tranche.
3. UK (England): the Romano-British name Tamesis or Tamesa is thought to come from a Celtic root *tam* 'dark' to give the 'Dark(-coloured) River'. It may be, however, a pre-Celtic name. In Oxfordshire it is known as the Isis, a form of regression to Tamesis.

Thandwe, BURMA *Dvaravati, Sandoway*
'Iron-fisted'. Sandoway was the Anglicized version of the name. The Sanskrit Dvaravati meant 'Gated Kingdom' or 'Place having Gates'.

Thanet, Isle of, ENGLAND/UK *Tanatus*
A peninsula whose name may originate from a Celtic root word *tan* 'fire' to suggest 'bright', a name which may have been acquired through the presence of a beacon. In earlier times Thanet was an island.

Thanjāvūr, TAMIL NĀDU/INDIA *Tanjore*
Evolved from the ancient Tanja Nagaram 'City of Refuge'.

Thanlwin, BURMA
See SALWEEN.

Thap Cham, VIETNAM
'Cham Tower', a reference to the Cham towers, originally built as Hindu temples, in the local area.

Thar Desert, INDIA-PAKISTAN
Also called the Great Indian Desert. The name comes from the Hindi *t'hul* 'ridge', a reference to its ridges of sand.

Tharrawaddy, BURMA
Named after Tharrawaddy (d. 1846), King of Burma (1837–46).

Thásos, GREECE
An island and a town named after Thasus. In Greek mythology, he was the son of Agenor, King of Phoenicia, who sent him and his brothers to find his sister Europa, who had been carried away by Zeus. Unable to find her, he settled on the island. His name may be associated with the Greek word *thasso* 'to sit idle'.

Thaton, BURMA *Sudhammavati, Suvannabhumi, Dvaravati*
Originally 'Land of Gold' because there were large reserves of gold in the area. It was the capital of the Mons until captured in 1057 by King Anawrahta, first King of all Burma (1044–77). The previous name meant 'Place of Gates'.

Thebes, GREECE, USA
Greece: the Greek name is Thívai. A very ancient city, it was probably named after the Thebes in Egypt (see LUXOR). Some classical poets referred to it as Ogygion after the mythical Attic or Boeotian King Ogyges. So obscure was the time in which he lived that he has given his name to the adjective 'ogygian' meaning 'of dark antiquity'.

The Dalles, OREGON/USA
'The Flagstones' from the French *dalle*, a reference to the rocks in the Columbia River on which the city lies.

The Hague, THE NETHERLANDS
See HAGUE, THE.

Thera (Thíra), GREECE *Calliste, Strongyle, Santorin/Santoríni*
An island in the Cyclades group with a town of the same name. The first name, Calliste,

meant 'Most Beautiful'. Strongyle meant 'Round (Island)'. Subsequently the island was renamed after the martyr St Irene (d. 340), one of three young women who were burnt alive for treason against the emperor. The present name is said to come from Theras, a Spartan tribal leader who settled it.

Thessaloníki, GREECE *Therma, Thessalonica, Saloníka*
Founded in 315 BC by Kassandros/Cassander (358–297 BC), the husband of Thessalonikë, who was the sister of Alexander III the Great[†]. Her name meant 'Victory in Thessaly' from Thessalía (*see* THESSALY) and *nikē* 'victory'. It was the capital of the Roman province of Macedonia and in 1430–1912 was ruled by the Ottoman Turks.

Thessaly (Thessalía), GREECE
A region with many former names including Hellas. It is named after Thessalus, a King of Iolkus (now Vólos) which was located in the region. Incorporated into Macedonia as a province in 148 by the Romans, it became a province in its own right *c.*300.

Thetford, ENGLAND/UK *Theodford*
'Public Ford' from the Old English *thēod* 'public' and *ford*.

Thetford Mines, QUEBEC/CANADA *Kingsville*
The city was renamed after the Thetford in England with 'Mines' added to acknowledge its importance as a centre for asbestos mining, the discovery of asbestos deposits having been made in 1876.

Thibodaux, LOUISIANA/USA
Founded *c.*1750 and named after Henry S. Thibodaux, the acting governor of Louisiana in 1824.

Thiès, SENEGAL
The name is a local pronunciation of the French *caisse* 'crate' or 'packing-case'. It is a major transportation centre and storage depot.

Thingvellir, ICELAND
Derived from *thing* 'assembly' and *vella* 'to spurt', a reference to where the *Althing* 'Parliament' met in 930–1798, and the local geysers. This was on the northern end of Lake Thingvallavatn 'Assembly Plains Lake' from *thing*, *völlur* 'plains', and *vatn* 'lake'.

Thionville, LORRAINE/FRANCE *Diedenhofen*
'Theudo's Farm' from a Germanic personal name and the Latin *villa* 'farm' or 'dwelling'. Captured by the Germans during the Franco-Prussian War (1870–1), the German name, in use until 1919 when Lorraine was returned to France, means the same from *Hof* 'farm' or 'country house'.

Thisted, DENMARK *Tystath, Thistedtt*
Derived from the Germanic peoples' god of war and justice, Tyr, and *sted* 'place'.

Thohoyandu, LIMPOPO/SOUTH AFRICA
Construction only began in 1980. The town is said to be named after a legendary 18th-century chief whose name meant 'Head of an Elephant', representing power and perhaps a long memory.

Thompson, CANADA, USA
1. Canada (British Columbia): a river named after David Thompson (1770–1857), who was believed, wrongly, to have found its upper reaches.
2. Canada (Manitoba): established in 1961 and named after John F. Thompson, chairman of the International Nickel Company of Canada.

Thorold, ONTARIO/CANADA
Founded in 1788 and named after Sir John Thorold, a British Member of Parliament, who was not in favour of attempts to suppress the American colonies' desire for independence (1775–83).

Thrissur, KERALA/INDIA *Trichur*
'Town with the Name of Lord Shiva'.

Thunder Bay, CANADA, USA
Canada (Ontario): the result of a merger of the cities of Port Arthur and Fort William in 1970. The name comes from the bay on Lake Superior which probably got its name from Native Americans who heard thunder when in the area. It is also called Lakehead.

Thuringia (Thüringen), GERMANY
A state named after the Thuringi who used to live in the area.

Thurso, CANADA, UK
UK (Scotland): derived from the river name and formerly Thorsa '(Place on) Thor's River' from the Germanic warrior deity whose name meant 'thunder' and the Old Scandinavian *o* 'stream'. This was a centre of Norse authority until the 13th century. However, it has also been suggested that the river's pre-Norse Celtic name meant 'Bull River', which was reinterpreted by the Scandinavians.

Tianjin, CHINA *Zhigu/Gu, Haijin, Tianjinwei*
A municipality meaning 'Emperor's Ford' from *tiān*, an abbreviation for *tiānzi* 'son of heaven' and *jin* 'ford' or 'ferry crossing'. Haijin, adopted in 1316, represents the fact that the ford was over the Hai River. In 1404 it was renamed Tianjinwei 'Military Base of the Heavenly Ford' from *wèi* 'military base (usually of some 5 600 men)'. The 'wei' was dropped in 1725. The pre-Pinyin romanization system spelling was Tientsin.

Tian Shan, CHINA-KAZAKHSTAN-KYRGYZSTAN
A mountain range meaning 'Heavenly, or Celestial, Mountains' from the Chinese *tiān* 'heaven' and *shān*. It is also spelt Tien Shan.

Tianshui, GANSU/CHINA *Guirong, Shanggui, Qin Zhou*
Founded in the 11th century BC, an earthquake at the beginning of the Han dynasty (206 BC) resulted in the formation of crystal-clear freshwater lakes to the south of the town. The water was said to have fallen from heaven so the town was renamed Tianshui 'Heavenly Water' from *tiān* 'heaven' and *shuǐ* 'water'. During the Tang dynasty (618–907), the town was also known as Qin Zhou after the Qin Kingdom.

Tiantai, ZHEJIANG/CHINA *Taixing*
'Heavenly Terrace' from *tiān* 'heaven' and *tái* 'terrace'. It is also the name of a mountain within the mountain chain of the same name in Zhejiang Province.

Tiaret, ALGERIA *Tahart, Tagdempt*
Since 1981 it has also been known as Tihert. The original name, from which the present one derives, meant 'The Lioness' in Arabic.

Tiber (Tevere), ITALY *Tiberis/Thybris/Thebris*
A river whose name may be traced back to a root *tib* or possibly the Celtic root word *dubr* 'water'. It is a matter of conjecture as to whether the name is Etruscan or Latin. However, the river's name is traditionally said to be associated with Tiberinus (or Thebris), King of Alba Longa, who drowned in it.

Tiberias (Hebrew: Teverya; Arabic: **Tabariyya),** ISRAEL *Rakkat*
Built in 18 by Herod Antipas (21 BC–AD 39), a son of Herod the Great, on the ruins of the biblical Rakkat. He renamed it in honour of Tiberius (42 BC–AD 37), Roman emperor (14–37). It is one of the four holy cities of Judaism.

Tibet (Chinese: Xizang Zizhiqu; Tibetan: **Bod, Gangjong),** CHINA *Wusizang*
An autonomous region whose Chinese name literally means 'Storage Place in the West' from *zàng* 'storage place' and *xī* 'west'. The *zàng* might be an abbreviation for *bǎozàng* 'hidden treasure' or 'valuable (mineral) deposits'. It is not the same as the *zàng* in the former Tibetan name Wusizang from *wūsī* 'centre' and *zàng* 'holy and pure'. During the Qing dynasty (1644–1911) the territory became known to the Chinese as Xizang, the *zàng* coming to refer to Tibet or the Tibetans. Zizhiqu means 'autonomous region' from *zì* 'self', *zhì* 'govern', and *qū* 'region', 'district', or 'area'. Bod may come from Bon, the religion practised by the

Tibetans before the arrival of Buddhism. Gangjong, sometimes used by the Tibetans, means 'Land of Snow'. The name Tibet may be derived from Thubet, a 5th-century Mongolian prince or taken from the Arab name Tubbat. The Chinese cite a treaty between the Tibetan leaders and the Tang dynasty in the 9th century as the beginning of China's union with Tibet (which they knew as Tufan) and claim that Tibet has been a part of China since the 13th century. A considerable Chinese presence, if not control, was evident between 1705 and 1911 until the fall of the Qing dynasty. To ensure that Russia would not occupy Tibet and threaten their Indian Empire, the British also established a presence in the country in 1904. Tibet was independent between 1911 and 1950 when the Chinese invaded; by 1959 they had gained full control. The present autonomous region is smaller than historic Tibet, the Tibetan provinces of Amdo and Kham having been incorporated into 'China Proper'.

Ticino (French and German: Tessin), ITALY, SWITZERLAND
A tributary of the River Po rising in Switzerland and a canton in Switzerland named after the river. Its name is pre-Latin in origin and may be linked to the old name for the Adige, Atesis, or with Tesino, a valley in Trentino. The Latin name for the river was Ticinus which gave its name to Ticinum, the original name for *Pavia.

Ticonderoga, NEW YORK/USA *Fort Carillon*
Built by the French as Fort Carillon in 1755, it was captured by the British four years later and renamed Fort Ticonderoga to respect an old Native American portage with this Iroquois name; it meant 'Between Two Waters', those of Lake Champlain and Lake George.

Tientsin, CHINA
See TIANJIN.

Tierra del Fuego, ARGENTINA-CHILE
An archipelago, whose principal island has the same name, and a province of Argentina. It was discovered by Ferdinand Magellan[†] in 1520 as he sailed through the strait named after him. He named the archipelago 'Land of Fire' because of the fires he saw burning on the coast.

Tighina, MOLDOVA *Tigin, Bendery*
The meaning of the present name is unknown. Bendery, however, is derived from the Turkic *bender*, a variation of the Persian *bandar* 'port'. On the River Dniester, it was occupied by the Turks in the 16th century and they changed the name to Bendery. It was won and lost by Russia in the late 18th century and finally

incorporated into Russia in 1818. In 1918–40, when part of Romania, it was known as Tighina and then Bendery again until 1991.

Tigray, ETHIOPIA
A regional state, also spelt Tigre, named after the Tigrinya-speaking Tigre people. Some of these also live in Eritrea where Tigré is also spoken. Tigrinya and Tigré are separate languages. To the Eritreans, Tigray or Tigre means 'Common People' or 'Serfs'.

Tigris (Turkish: **Dicle**; Arabic: **Dijlah**), TURKEY-SYRIA-IRAQ
A river whose Arabic name comes from the Old Persian name Tigra 'Arrow', an acknowledgement that it has a faster flow than its sister river, the Euphrates.

Tijuana, MEXICO, USA
Mexico (Baja California): said to be derived from Tia Juana 'Aunt Jane', a large working ranch. However, this may have come from the Yumano who called the valley Ti-Wan 'Near the Sea'. When the area became the new border between Mexico and the USA a customs post was erected and in time the settlement grew into a city. The name Tijuana was formally adopted in 1929.

Tikhoretsk, KRASNODAR TERRITORY/RUSSIA
'Quiet River', although there is no river here, from *tikhiy* 'quiet' or 'slow-moving' and *reka* 'river'.

Tikrit, IRAQ *Birtha,Virta*
Said to have been named after a Christian woman, Takrīt bint Wā'il, since it was occupied by Arab Christians in pre-Islamic times. It was captured by the Arabs in 637.

Tiksi, SAKHA REPUBLIC/RUSSIA
Named after the bay here which has a Yakut name for 'haven'.

Tilburg, THE NETHERLANDS
Til is an affectionate shortening for Theodulus. With *burg*, the name thus means 'Stronghold dedicated to St Theodulus' who was martyred in Palestine in 309.

Tilbury, CANADA, UK
1. Canada (Ontario): founded as Tilbury West Township and Tilbury East Township at the end of the 18th century. They merged into Henderson after the postmaster, David Henderson, in 1871. In 1887 this was changed to Tilbury Centre; the 'Centre' was dropped in 1895. Lying on the River Thames, the town was named after the Tilbury in England, which also lies on the River Thames.
2. UK (England): formerly Tilaburg and Tiliberia, most likely 'Tila's Stronghold' from an Old English personal name and *burh*.

Tillabéri, NIGER
'(Place of) Tila the Great' from the name of a chief and *beri* 'big'.

Tilsit, KALININGRAD/RUSSIA
See SOVETSK.

Timaru, SOUTH ISLAND/NEW ZEALAND
Founded in 1859 with a name derived from the Maori *te maru* 'The Shelter' from *te* 'the' and *maru* 'shelter'. It refers to the harbour which is the only one in a considerable length of otherwise rugged coastline.

Timbuktu, MALI
Also spelt Tombouctou. A region and a town famous for its legendary remoteness and supposed mystery and wealth. Its comparative inaccessibility until the 20th century may be the origin of its name from the Znaga root *b-k-t* 'to be distant' or 'to be hidden' with the feminine possessive particle *tin*. However, the name has also been said to come from the Tuareg *ti-m-buktu* 'woman with a big navel'—or it might have been her name. According to tradition, she was left here to guard the possessions of Tuareg shepherds in the oasis while their flocks grazed elsewhere. On the other hand, the name could be derived from the Berber *tin* 'place of' and a personal name such as Buktu; or, founded as it was by Tuareg nomads in the 11th century, it could simply be a word meaning 'old'.

Timişoara, ROMANIA *Temesiensis, Temesvár, Temeschburg*
'Fort by the (River) Timiş', the Romanian form of the Hungarian Temesvár from the river's name and *vár*. A Roman fort called Castrum Temesiensis, it was part of Hungary when taken by the Ottoman Turks in 1552; they held it until 1716 when the town was taken by the Austrians though settled by Swabian Germans, hence the German Temeschburg with the same meaning. Having belonged to the Austro-Hungarian Empire, it was occupied by the Serbs in 1919, but the following year was allocated by the Treaty of Paris to Romania.

Timmins, ONTARIO/CANADA
Founded in 1911 after the discovery of gold here in 1905. It was named after its founder, Noah Timmins (1867–1936), whose company organized the expansion of the mine and the surrounding community.

Timor, INDONESIA-EAST TIMOR
An island. From the middle of the 16th century the Dutch and Portuguese competed to control it until they agreed to split it at the Treaty of Lisbon in 1859. The Dutch received the western half, the Portuguese the eastern half. A small exclave on the north coast of West

Timor, Ocüssi-Ambeno (also Oekussi-Ambenu), was awarded to the Portuguese in 1913 as part of East Timor. The Dutch departed in 1949, at which time West Timor became part of Indonesia. The Portuguese, however, remained in *East Timor until 1975. The name is probably derived from the Malay *timur* 'east', a reference to the fact that Timor lies to the east of Java and Sumatra. It gives its name to the Timor Sea.

Timsah (Buḥairat at-Timsāḥ), EGYPT
'Crocodile Lake' from *buḥairah* 'lake' and *timsāḥ* 'crocodile'. Crocodiles used to live here.

Tipperary, AUSTRALIA, IRELAND
Ireland: locally Tiobraid Árran. A county and a town meaning '(House of) the Well of Ara', a river on which it lies.

Tirana (Tiranë), ALBANIA
Founded in 1614 and said to be named after the nearby castle of Tirkan whose name comes from an Illyrian root. The meaning is unknown. Tirana became the Albanian capital in 1920.

Tiraspol', MOLDOVA *Tyras, Akerman*
'City on the (River) Dniester'. Founded as a Greek colony known as Tyras, the ancient Greek name for the Dniester, and developed into an independent city-state, and a shortening of *polis*. When the Ottoman Turks arrived in the 16th century they built a huge fortress which they called Akerman. The modern town was founded by Prince Alexander Suvorov (1729–1800), a Russian military commander in Moldova, in 1792 on the site of the ancient Moldavian settlement of Staraya Sukleia which had been burnt by the Turks in 1787. It was given its present Greek-style name in 1795. It was the capital of the Moldovan Autonomous Soviet Socialist Republic in 1929–40 and is now the capital of Transdniestria.

Tire, TURKEY *Arcadiopolis, Teira*
Derived from the previous name meaning 'Town'.

Tîrgovişte, ROMANIA *Eski-Djumaia*
Derived from *tîrg* 'market' or 'fair'; *tîrgoveţ* means 'inhabitant of a town'. The previous Turkish name meant 'Old Market' from *eski* 'old' and *cuma* 'Friday', the normal market day.

Tîrgu Jiu, ROMANIA
'Market (Town) on the (River) Jiu' from *tîrg* 'market'.

Tîrgu Mureş, ROMANIA *Agropolis, Neumarkt, Marosvásárhely*
'Market (Town) on the (River) Mureş' from *tîrg* 'market'. The previous names were Greek,

German, and Hungarian respectively, the latter meaning the 'Place of the Market on the (River) Maros' from *hely* 'place', *vásár* 'market' and the Hungarian name for the Mureş.

Tîrgu Neamţ, ROMANIA
'German Market (Town)' from *tîrg* 'market' and *neamţ* 'German'. The town lies on the Neamţ River.

Tirol, AUSTRIA-ITALY
See TYROL.

Tiruchchirāppalli, TAMIL NĀDU/INDIA
Trichinopoly
An imposing rock-fortress dominates the town and gave it its name. It means 'Holy Rock Town' or 'Town of the Sacred Rock' from the Tamil *tiru* 'holy', *sita* 'rock', and *palli* 'town'. A 16th-century inscription gave the name Tirussilla-palli.

Tirunelveli, TAMIL NĀDU/INDIA
Also spelt Tinnevelly. The name is derived from the Tamil *tiru* 'holy', *nel* 'paddy field', and *veli* 'fence', a reference to the legend that suggests that the Hindu god Shiva protected a follower's rice crop here.

Tiruppūr, TAMIL NĀDU/INDIA
'Holy City' from the Tamil *tiru* 'holy' and *pur*. Its temple is well-known.

Tiruvannamalai, TAMIL NĀDU/INDIA
'Red Mountain', a reference to the extinct volcano, Arunachala, nearby which gives off a red hue at dawn. However, according to legend, the name means 'Great Inaccessible Mountain' from *thiru* signifying 'greatness' and *annamalai* from *Annal*, a special name for the Hindu god Shiva, who took the form of fire to become inaccessible to Vishnu, and *malai* 'mountain' or 'hill'. Annal Malai was contracted to *annamalai*. Tiruvannamalai is a town with over 100 temples and thus the *tiru* here could be the Tamil *tiru* 'holy'.

Tiszaújváros, HUNGARY *Leninváros*
Lying on the Tisza River and having been named 'Lenin's[†] Town' for a while after the Second World War, it was renamed after the Tisza family as 'Tisza New Town' from the family name, *új* 'new' and *város* 'town'. Both Kálmán Tisza (1830–1902) and his son, Count Stephen (István) Tisza (1861–1918) were premiers of Hungary, the latter in 1903–5 and again in 1913–17.

Titicaca, BOLIVIA-PERU
A lake which straddles the international border with a name whose meaning is disputed. It is suggested that it means 'Rock of the Jaguar' from its shape or 'Crag of Lead' from the Quechua *titi* 'lead' (the metal).

Titusville, USA
1. Florida: founded as Sand Point in 1867 by Colonel Harry T. Titus after whom it was renamed in 1874.
2. Pennsylvania: founded in 1796 by, and named after, Jonathan Titus, the former owner of the town site.

Tivat, MONTENEGRO/SERBIA AND MONTENEGRO *Crni Plat*
According to legend, the name may come from the Illyrian Queen Teuta (3rd century BC) who had a summer residence here; her name seems to have come from an epithet, the Illyrian *te uta* 'the good'. Alternatively, Tivat (the area was called Theodo in the 14th century) may be derived from the Greek *theos* 'god'.

Tivoli, GRENADA, ITALY, USA
Italy (Lazio): located in the Sabine Hills, the name is derived from the original Latin name Tibur, itself possibly derived from the Sabine *teba* 'hill'. Famous as a resort, it gave its name to the Tivoli Gardens in Copenhagen, Denmark.

Tizimín, YUCATÁN/MEXICO
'Place of Many Horses'.

Tizi Ouzou, ALGERIA
Located in a valley that is connected to another valley by a pass, in Berber *tizi*, in which a flowering broom *ouzou* grows.

Tlemcen, ALGERIA *Pomaria, Agadir, Tilimsane*
Also spelt Tilimsen. Founded by the Romans in the 4th century as Pomaria 'Orchards', it was renamed Agadir 'Escarpment' by the Berbers in the 8th century after the city in Morocco. In the 13th century the settlement subsequently merged with the Almoravid military camp of Tagrart 'The Camp' and became known as Tlemcen from the Berber *tilimsàn* or *tilmsane* 'springs' because of their presence here.

Tobago, TRINIDAD AND TOBAGO
An island so named by Christopher Columbus[†] when he discovered it in 1498. Columbus was impressed by the natives' practice of stuffing the leaves of the tobacco plant in pipes and setting fire to them in the belief that this had medicinal value. The name either comes from the Haitian *tambaku* 'pipe' or from the local word *tabaco*, a reference to its crops.

Tobol'sk, TYUMEN/RUSSIA *Kashlyk*
Founded in 1587 and named after the Tobol River at whose confluence with the Irtysh River it lies. The meaning of the river's name is not known.

Tobruk (Ţubruq), LIBYA *Antipyrgos*
An ancient Greek settlement meaning 'Opposite the Tower' from *anti* 'opposite' and *pyrgos* 'tower'; it later became a Roman fortress. The present Arabic name comes from the Greek name.

Todd River, NORTHERN TERRITORY/AUSTRALIA
See ALICE SPRINGS.

Togliatti, SAMARA/RUSSIA
See TOL'YATTI.

Togo, AND CANADA
The Togolese Republic (République Togolaise) since 1960. Previously French Togo, having become an autonomous republic within the French Union in 1956 and a UN Trust Territory since 1946; a subunit of French West Africa (1936–46); a French League of Nations mandate (1919); the eastern part of German Togoland (1884–1914), Anglo-French forces occupying the German colony in 1914. (The western part of German Togoland was administered by the British from 1914 until joining Ghana as its Volta Region in 1957.) In 1884 a German specialist on Africa, Gustav Nachtigal, signed a treaty with the chief of a small coastal village, Togoville, which gave the Germans a protectorate over the coastline. He named the protectorate Togoland after the village which probably took its name from Lake Togo whose name may come from *to* 'water' and *go* 'bank' or 'shore'. After the Germans had begun their conquest of the interior in 1893 Togoland became a colony.

Togoland A former German colony in West Africa now divided between *Ghana and *Togo.

Tohoku, HONSHŪ/JAPAN
A region meaning 'North-East' from *tō* 'east' and *hoku* 'north'. It is also known simply as Ōu, an allusion to its mountain range.

Tokaj, HUNGARY
Lying at the confluence of the Bodrog and Tisza Rivers, its name comes from the Slavonic *tok* 'current', a reference to the rivers. It gives its name to the sweet white wine.

Tokelau, NEW ZEALAND *Union Islands, Tokelau Islands*
An island territory of New Zealand since 1948. It consists of three small coral atolls: Atafu (given the name Duke of York Island by the British commodore John Byron), Fakaofu (Bowditch Island), and Nukunono (Duke of Clarence Island). It became a British protectorate in 1898 and, with the name Union Islands or Group, became part of the Gilbert and Ellice Islands in 1916. It was renamed Tokelau Islands in 1946 and sovereignty was transferred to New Zealand in 1948. The 'Islands' was dropped in 1976. The Polynesian name is said to mean 'North Wind'.

Tokorozawa, HONSHŪ/JAPAN
The characters represent *tokoro* 'place' and *sawa* 'mountain stream'. Earlier *toko* had represented 'field' and *ro* 'old'.

Toktogul, KYRGYZSTAN
Founded in 1970 and named after Toktogul Satylganov (1864–1933), a composer and musician.

Tokushima, SHIKOKU/JAPAN
A prefecture and city with a name meaning 'Island of Virtue' from *toku* 'virtue' or 'goodness' and *shima*.

Tokuyama, HONSHŪ/JAPAN
'Mountain of Virtue' from *toku* 'virtue' or 'goodness' and *yama* 'mountain'.

Tokyo, HONSHŪ/JAPAN *Edo*
A metropolis, Tōkyō, and the Japanese capital city, Tokyo. At the mouth of a river, it was developed from the small fishing village of Edo 'Estuary'. It was given its present name meaning 'Eastern Capital' from *tō* 'east' and *kyō* 'capital' in 1868 when the capital was transferred from Kyōto, far to the west, to Edo with the fall of the Tokugawa shogunate and the Meiji 'Enlightened Rule' Restoration. After Tokugawa Ieyasu (1543–1616), shogun (1603–5), had become shogun he declared Edo to be his seat of power and it became the effective seat of the national government (although Kyōto remained the official capital).

Toledo, BELIZE, BRAZIL, CANADA, CHILE, PHILIPPINES, SPAIN, URUGUAY, USA
1. Spain (Castile-La Mancha): a province and a city built on a rocky promontory overlooking the River Tagus on three sides, having its name from the Celtic *tol* 'elevation' or 'rise'. It was conquered by the Romans in 193 BC and named Toletum. After occupation by the Moors it was given an Arabic version of that name, Tulayṭulah.
2. USA (Ohio): two villages, Port Lawrence and Vistula, merged in 1833 to form the new town of Toledo, named after the city in Spain.

Tolmachëvo, PSKOV/RUSSIA *Preobrazhenskaya*
The original name demonstrated the dedication of its church to the Transfiguration *Preobrazheniye*. It was renamed in 1919 after Nikolay Tolmachëv (1895–1919) who, fighting for the Red Army, shot himself near here rather than be captured by counter-revolutionary troops during the Civil War (1918–20).

Toluca, MÉXICO/MEXICO
Derived from a Nahuatl expression *tollocan* 'those who bow their heads'. The full name is Toluca de Lerdo, 'de Lerdo' being added in 1861 as a tribute to Sebastián Lerdo de Tejada, the Mexican president.

Tol'yatti, SAMARA/RUSSIA *Stavropol'-na-Volge, Tol'yattigrad*
Founded as a fortress in 1738 called 'Town of the Cross on the (River) Volga' from the Greek *stavros* 'cross' and *polis*. This was appropriate since it had been built for newly converted Christians. It was renamed in 1964 on the death of Palmiro Togliatti (1893–1964), the Italian communist leader (1926–64). The spelling was changed to the present form in 1991, although the name sometimes appears as Togliatti(-on-the-Volga).

Tomakomai, HOKKAIDŌ/JAPAN
An Ainu name derived either from *tomakuomanai* 'marshland' or *to-makomanai* 'a river lying behind a marsh'.

Tomari, JAPAN, RUSSIA
Japan (Honshū) and Russia (Sakhalin Island): both have the same Ainu name meaning 'harbour'.

Tombigbee, MISSISSIPPI-ALABAMA/USA
A river with a name derived from the Choctaw *itumbi-bikpe* 'coffin makers', a reference to those who cleaned up and placed skeletons in boxes.

Tombstone, ARIZONA/USA
In 1877 Ed Shieffelin discovered silver after he had been told that he would only find his tombstone here.

Tomsk, RUSSIA
A province and city founded in 1604 on the Tom River from which it takes its name. This may come from the Ket *toom* 'river' or from the Russian *tëmnyy* 'dark', thus 'Dark River'.

Tonbridge, ENGLAND/USA *Tonebrige*
'The Village Bridge' from *tūn* and *brycg*.

Tonga *Friendly Islands*
The Kingdom of Tonga (Pule'anga Fakatu'i 'o Tonga) since 1875. The name simply means 'South' (in relation to Samoa, roughly the centre of Polynesia) from *toga*. The Dutch discovered the islands in 1616 and then sailed on. The archipelago was named the Friendly Islands by Captain James Cook[†] in 1773. In 1905 it became a self-governing British protectorate at the request of George Tupou II, King of Tonga (1893–1918). Protectorate status was ended and independence achieved in 1970.

Tongaat, KWAZULU-NATAL/SOUTH AFRICA *Victoria*
Founded in 1849 and named after Queen Victoria[†], it was renamed following the end of

the Boer War (1899–1902) after the Tongati River whose name is said to come from the *thonga*, the fruit of the trees that grow along its banks.

Tongatapu, TONGA
The most southerly group of the islands of Tonga is called Tongatapu 'Sacred Tonga' from *tabu* 'sacred'. The English word 'taboo' comes from the Tongan word.

T'ongyŏng (Tongyeong), SOUTH KOREA
Ch'ungmu
The present name is derived from T'ongjeyŏng which in Old Korean meant 'Headquarters'. This referred to its location as the Headquarters of the Korean Navy during the Yi Dynasty (1392–1910). The previous name indirectly honoured Admiral Yi Sun-sin (1545–c.1592), the heroic commander of the Korean Navy against the Japanese, who was admired for his *ch'ung* 'loyalty' and *mu* 'military courage' and given this title posthumously.

Tonkin (Bac Bo), VIETNAM
'Eastern Capital' from *dong* 'east' and *kinh* 'capital', the Chinese name for Hanoi. Also spelt Tongking, it was a name never used by the Vietnamese. It was a French corruption which from 1883 came to mean the whole area round Hanoi. Between 1883 and 1954 it was the name of the French Protectorate in northern Vietnam. It gives its name to the Gulf of Tonkin.

Tonle Sap (Khmer: Bœng Tônlé Sab), CAMBODIA
'Large Freshwater Lake' from the Khmer *tonle* 'large lake' and *sab* 'fresh (water)'. The lake is drained by the Sab River.

Toowoomba, QUEENSLAND/AUSTRALIA *The Swamps*
Founded in 1849, it was probably renamed after the *toowoom*, the Aboriginal name for a melon.

Topeka, KANSAS/USA
Founded c.1854 as a railway town and given a name, possibly from the Sioux or Omaha word for the so-called Indian potato, meaning a 'Good Place to grow Potatoes'.

Topki, NOVOSIBIRSK/RUSSIA
'Marshy (Place)' from *topkiy* 'swampy' or 'marshy'.

Topol, HUNGARY
'Poplar Tree' from the Slavonic *topol'*.

Topola, SERBIA/SERBIA AND MONTENEGRO *Kamenica*
'White Poplar' in recognition of their presence here. The former name meant 'stone'.

Tora Bora, AFGHANISTAN
'Black Valley' in Pashtun.

Torez, UKRAINE *Chistyakovo*
Renamed in 1964 after Maurice Thorez (1900–64), the French communist leader (1930–64) and a deputy premier (1946–7), having been named presumably after a person called Chistyakov.

Torgau, SAXONY/GERMANY *Torgowy*
Possibly derived from the Slavonic *torg* 'market (place)'.

Toro, NIGERIA, SPAIN
Spain (Castile-León): 'Bull'.

Toronto, CANADA, USA
Canada (Ontario): a trading post in the 17th century and a fort, called Toronto, built by the French in 1750 which was destroyed within a few years; however, the trading post survived. In 1793 the present site was chosen for the capital of Ontario by Colonel (later Lieutenant General) John Graves Simcoe (1752–1806), lieutenant-governor of Upper Canada (now Ontario) (1792–6), and he changed the name to York to honour Frederick Augustus, Duke of York (1763–1827), son of King George III[†]. The name was changed back to Toronto in 1834. It is often said to come from the Huron *deondo* 'meeting place', but an alternative theory is that it derives from a Mohawk word meaning 'Poles in the Water', a reference to old fish weirs in The Narrows between Lake Simcoe and Lake Couchiching.

Toropets, TVER'/RUSSIA
Takes its name from the Toropa River on which it lies. Its name may come from *toropit'* 'to hurry', a reference to its rapid flow.

Torquay, CANADA, UK
UK (England): formerly Torrekay 'Quay near Torre' from the Middle English *key*.

Torrance, CANADA, USA
USA (California): founded in 1911 by, and named after, Jared S. Torrance, who owned the site.

Torre Annunziata, CAMPANIA/ITALY
Now a spa within the conurbation of Naples, it takes its name from a chapel and hospital dedicated to the Virgin of the Annunciation in 1319. The name is translated as 'Tower of the Annunciation' from *torre* 'tower'.

Torrelavaga, CANTABRIA/SPAIN
Founded in the 14th century and named after the Garcilaso de la Vega family with *torre* 'tower'.

Torremolinos, ANDALUSIA/SPAIN
Derived from *torre* 'tower' and *molino*
'windmill' around which the town was
developed.

Torrens, SOUTH AUSTRALIA/AUSTRALIA
A lake, a river, and an island, all named after
Colonel Robert Torrens (1780–1864), British
economist, soldier, and politician who was
appointed chairman of the South Australian
Colonization Commissioners in 1835 to
manage land sales.

Torres Strait A strait between Queensland,
Australia, to the south and New Guinea to the
north. It was discovered in 1606 by Luis Vaez
de Torres (*c.*1560–1614), a Spanish navigator,
when he sailed along the southern coast of
New Guinea. The existence of the strait was
not widely publicized and the name Torres
was not given to it until 1769.

Torres Vedras, PORTUGAL *Turres Veteres*
Derived from the Latin name meaning 'Old
Citadel' from *turris* 'tower', 'castle', or
'citadel'.

Torrington, CANADA, USA
USA (Connecticut): settled as New Orleans
Village or Mast Swamp *c.*1735 and renamed
after Great Torrington in England from
which some of the early settlers had come. In
1818–83 it was named Wolcottville after the
Wolcott family who had established the
woollen mill here. The English Torrington
meant 'Farmstead on the (River) Torridge'
from the Celtic river name and *tūn*.

Tórshavn, FAROE ISLANDS/DENMARK
'Thor's Harbour', Thor being a Germanic
warrior deity whose name meant 'thunder'.
Thor's day became Thursday. Founded in the
13th century as a port.

Tortola, BRITISH VIRGIN ISLANDS
Derived from the Spanish *tórtola* 'turtle dove'
because of their numbers here.

Tortuga Island (French: **Île de la Tortue**),
HAITI
An island off the north coast of Haiti settled by
the Spanish in 1629 and called by them
Tortuga 'Tortoise' because of the presence of
these creatures. When France took control of
the island in 1665 the island was given the
French version of the name.

Toruń, POLAND *Thorn*
Founded in 1231 by the Teutonic Knights,
hence its previous German name. They named
it after Toron, the name given by the
Crusaders to Tibnin, previously Taphnith, now
in southern Lebanon.

Torzhok, TVER'/RUSSIA
An important trading centre on the route
between Novgorod and Suzdal in the 14th
century, the name means 'Market' from *torg*.

Totowa, NEW JERSEY/USA
The meaning of the name is not certain. It may
mean 'Where you begin' or come from a
Native American word for 'Between
Mountains and Waters'.

Toul, LORRAINE/FRANCE *Tullum*
The former Roman, and the present, names
are derived from the Celtic *tol* 'hill' or 'height'.

Toulon, FRANCE, USA
France (Provence-Alpes-Côte d'Azur): may be
derived from the Celtic *tol* 'hill' or 'height'.
During the French Revolution in 1793 it was
called Port de la Montagne 'Mountain
Harbour'. Both names refer to high ground,
the nearby Faron Mountains which overlook
the town. As a Roman naval station it was
called Tolo Martius.

Toulouse, LANGUEDOC-ROUSSILLON/FRANCE
Tolosa
Probably derived from the Celtic *tol* 'hill' or
'height', a reference to the nearby Pyrenees.

Touraine, FRANCE
A historic region and former province named
after the Turones, a Gallic tribe.

Tournai (Flemish: **Doornik**), BELGIUM *Turnacum*
Takes its name from the former Roman name,
possibly meaning the 'Place of Turnus' from
acum and the possible name of a local Roman
leader.

Tours, CENTRE/FRANCE *Caesardunum, Civitas
Turonorum*
Named after the Gallic Turones. They called it
'Caesar's[†] Fort', but in the 5th century it was
renamed 'City of the Turones'.

Töv, MONGOLIA
A province called 'Central'.

Tovuz, AZERBAIJAN *Traubenfeld*
Founded by Germans in 1912, the name is a
shortened form of *tovuz goshur* 'peacock'. The
area was at one time known for its peacocks.

Towcester, ENGLAND/UK *Tofeceaster, Tovecestre*
'(Roman) Fort on the (River) Tove' from the
river name meaning 'slow' and *ceaster*.

Townsend, USA
Massachusetts: named after Charles
Townshend (1675–1838), 2nd Viscount, twice a
British secretary of state (1714–16, 1721–30).

Townsville, AUSTRALIA, USA
Australia (Queensland): founded in 1864 and
named after Captain Robert Towns (1791–

1873), an English officer who founded it and encouraged settlement and trade here.

Toyama, HONSHŪ/JAPAN
A prefecture and a city whose name has characters representing *to* 'to thrive' and *yama* 'mountain'. The interior of the prefecture is mountainous.

Toyohashi, HONSHŪ/JAPAN *Yoshida*
The previous medieval name was that of a local governor, although the characters represent *yoshi* 'fortune' and *ta* 'rice field'. The present name of the old castle town, adopted in 1869, has characters representing *toyo* 'abundant' and *hashi* 'bridge'.

Toyokawa, HONSHŪ/JAPAN
'Abundant River' from *toyo* 'abundant' in terms of the local fertility and *kawa*.

Toyonaka, HONSHŪ/JAPAN
The characters represent *toko* 'abundant' and *naka* 'central'.

Toyota, HONSHŪ/JAPAN *Koromo*
Renamed in 1938 after the head office of the Toyota Motor Company moved here that year. The Toyota Company was founded in 1902 by Sakichi Toyota (1867–1930) and the business was continued by his son, Kiichiroo.

Trabzon, TURKEY *Trapezount/Trapezus, Trebizond*
Founded as early as the 8th century BC, the name may be derived from the Greek *trapeza* 'table', a reference to a nearby flat-topped mountain.

Tralee (Tráigh Lí), IRELAND
'Strand of the (River) Lee' from *trá* 'strand' or 'beach' and the river name.

Trang, THAILAND *Krung Thani, Trangkhapura*
Shortened from the previous name which meant 'City of Waves'. A seaport at the mouth of the River Trang during the Ayutthaya period, *c.*1860 it was moved inland by Mongkut (1804–68) (posthumously Rama IV), King of Siam (1851–68), because of frequent flooding.

Trani, APULIA/ITALY *Turenum*
According to legend, the name comes from Tirreno, the son of Diomedes. This might explain the Latin name of Turenum, but not the present name. It has been suggested that Trani might be a shortened form of Traiano, the name assigned to the place to honour Trajan[†]. Even more probable, however, is that it is associated with a term *trana* or *traina* which, according to medieval dictionaries, has the meaning of a port well suited to the fishing industry. Trani lies on the Adriatic Sea.

Transcaucasia Comprises the three republics of Armenia, Azerbaijan, and Georgia. The Latin *trans* 'beyond' indicates that the region lies beyond the *Caucasus as far as Russia is concerned. The Transcaucasus Soviet Federative Socialist Republic was created within the Soviet Union in 1922, but was split into its three constituent republics in 1936.

Transdniestria (Transnistria), MOLDOVA
A region between the River Dniester (Nistru to the Moldovans and Romanians) and Moldova's eastern border with a name meaning the '(Land) beyond the Dniester'; it constitutes some 15 per cent of Moldova's territory, although it has never been considered part of the traditional Moldovan lands. Part of the Russian Empire since its seizure from the Ottoman Turks in the late 18th century, it was incorporated into Ukraine in 1924 as the Moldovan Autonomous Soviet Socialist Republic. This was lost to Romania, an ally of Nazi Germany, in 1941, although it was regained by the Soviet Union in 1944. By the majority Slav inhabitants of Transdniestria it is known by its Russian name Pridnestrov'ye 'The Land on the Dniester' (in Russian, the Dnestr), although neither the name nor the 'nation' existed before the uprising in 1990 when, fearful that Moldovan independence might presage reunification with Romania, Transdniestria declared its secession from Moldova. It adopted the official name of Pridnestrovsakayat Moldavskaya Respublika 'Trasndniestrian Moldavian Republic'.

Transjordan An emirate in 1921–46 and a kingdom in 1946–9 before becoming the Kingdom of *Jordan. The name indicated an area of Palestine east (or beyond) the River Jordan.

Transkei, EASTERN CAPE/SOUTH AFRICA
A former independent Bantu homeland of the Xhosa people in 1976–94 when it was incorporated into Eastern Cape Province. The name comes from *trans* and the name of the Kei River (actually the Great Kei) to mean the '(Lands) beyond the Kei', that is north-east of the Kei.

Transvaal, SOUTH AFRICA *South African Republic*
A former Boer state, which in 1994 was divided into Northern Transvaal (which became Northern Province in 1995 and then in 2003 Limpopo Province), Eastern Transvaal (now Mpumalanga), and North-West and Pretoria-Witwatersrand-Vereeniging (now Gauteng). Transvaal's independence was recognized by the UK in 1852 and it became the South African Republic in 1857. Annexed to the UK as the Transvaal in 1877, its independence was

restored in 1884; however, at the end of the Boer War (1899–1902) it became a crown colony and a province of the Union of South Africa in 1910. The name means 'Across the (River) Vaal' from *trans* to indicate that territory lying beyond, or north, of the Vaal.

Transylvania (Transilvania), ROMANIA
Siebenbürgen, Erdély
A historic region with a name meaning '(Land) beyond the Forest' from *trans* and *sílva* 'forest'; Erdély comes from the Hungarian *erdo* 'forest' to mean the 'Land of the Forests'. The Romanians claim that the Dacians were the first to inhabit the region in the 1st and 2nd centuries and that they then fused with the Romans when they arrived. This conflation of Dacian and Latin cultures allowed the Transylvanians to retain their sense of Romanian identity until union with Romania in 1918. To the Hungarians, however, Transylvania is Hungarian because when the Magyars arrived *c*.896 the land was sparsely populated by Slav tribes and the Magyars became the native people. For just over the next 1 000 years the region was a part of Hungary, although an autonomous part of the Ottoman Empire in the 16th and 17th centuries. It was partly populated by Saxons who founded seven towns in the 12th century; hence its earlier German name of Siebenbürgen 'Seven Towns'. The seven were Bistrita (Bistritz), Brasov (Kronstadt), Cluj (Klausenburg), Medias (Mediasch), Sebes (Muhlbach), Sibiu (Hermannstadt), and Sighişoara (Schässburg). With the expulsion of the Turks from Hungary towards the end of the 17th century Transylvania was separated from Hungary proper and became an Austrian autonomous province under the Habsburgs; in 1867 it was reincorporated into Hungary. The region was seized by Romania in 1918 and its possession was confirmed by the Treaty of Trianon in 1920. However, the northern part was regained by Hungary under the Vienna Award of 1940. The whole of Transylvania was returned officially to Romania in 1947.

Trapani, SICILY/ITALY *Drepana/Drepanon*
Derived from the Greek *drepanon* 'sickle'.

Traralgon, VICTORIA/AUSTRALIA
Settled in the 1840s with an Aboriginal name meaning 'Crane feeding on Frogs'.

Trás-os-Montes, PORTUGAL
A former province with a name meaning 'Beyond the Mountains'.

Travancore, KERALA/INDIA
Also known as Tiruvarankodu 'Holy Rich Kingdom' from the Tamil *tiru* 'holy', *varán*

'rich' or 'flourishing', and *kodu* 'kingdom'. A former princely state, it merged with Cochin in 1949 to form the state of Travancore and Cochin; this merged with Malabar in 1956 to form the present state of Kerala.

Travelers Rest, SOUTH CAROLINA/USA
Named after an early inn.

Traverse City, MICHIGAN/USA
Settled in 1847 and named after Grand Traverse Bay. The name, meaning 'lying across', was given by early French travellers to the bay in Lake Michigan which they crossed from headland to headland.

Travnik, BOSNIA AND HERZEGOVINA
'Green City' on account of its lush vegetation. It was the Ottoman Turkish capital of Bosnia between 1699 and 1850.

Třebíč, CZECH REPUBLIC
The meaning of the name is not clear. It might be derived from the colloquial version of the personal name Třebohost or Třebobud which was Třebek or Třebec, thus 'Třebek's Property'. Alternatively, it might come from *třebíč* or *třebež* 'lumber-producing forest'.

Trece Martires, LUZON/PHILIPPINES
'Thirteen Martyrs' in Spanish, a reference to the thirteen Filipino patriots killed by the Spanish at Cavite in 1896.

Treinta y Tres, URUGUAY
'Thirty-three' in Spanish, a reference to the 33 Uruguayan patriots who invaded what was then Brazilian-occupied territory in 1825, an act that ultimately led to Uruguayan independence in 1828.

Trenčín, SLOVAKIA
Derived from a personal name, possibly Trnka or Trenka, to give a 'Settlement of Trnka's People'.

Trent, CANADA, GERMANY, UK, USA
UK (England): a town and a river whose Celtic name gives the sense of a 'river liable to strong flooding'.

Trentino-Alto Adige, ITALY *Venetia Tridentina*
A region, one of whose provinces is "Trento. The region is mountainous, thus *alto* 'high', with Adige being the name of the principal river. It passed to Italy in 1919 and was renamed in 1947.

Trento, TRENTINO-ALTO ADIGE/ITALY *Tridentum, Trient*
The original Latin Tridentum came from *tres* 'three' and *dens* 'tooth', a reference to a local mountain with three peaks. It passed to

Austria in 1814, hence its German name
Trient. It became part of Italy in 1918.

Trenton, CANADA, USA
1. Canada: settled as Trent Port in 1792 at the
mouth of the Trent River from which it gets its
name; it has also been called Trent Town.
2. USA (Michigan): founded by Major Abram
C. Truax and called Truaxton after him in
1834. It was renamed Truago in 1837 and
Trenton ten years later after the Trenton
Limestone Series.
3. USA (New Jersey): the original settlement
was founded as The Falls in 1679. In 1714 the
town was laid out by William Trent, a
merchant from Philadelphia, and named after
him in 1721.

Treviso, VENETO/ITALY *Tarvisium*
The present name comes from the Latin
Tarvisium which itself is probably of Gallic
origin. This, in turn, probably came from the
Celtic *tarvos* 'bull'.

Trialeti, GEORGIA *Molotovo*
Derived from *triali*, meaning an area in which
to roam. Previously it was the '(City of)
Molotov' in honour of Vyacheslav Molotov[†].

Trichūr, KERALA/INDIA
With a temple the target of an annual
pilgrimage, the name means 'Small Sacred
Place'.

Trier, RHINELAND-PALATINATE/GERMANY *Augusta
Treverorum, Treveris, Trèves*
An administrative district and a city which
take their name from the Treveri, a Gallic
tribe, who had settled on the site by 400 BC and
made it their capital. Caesar Augustus[†]
founded the town in 15 BC, adding his name.
As Treveris it was the seat of the local Roman
emperor responsible for Gaul and Britain. It
was ceded to France in 1801–15 and bore the
name Trèves.

Trieste, FRIULI-VENEZIA GIULIA/ITALY *Tergeste,
Triest*
May be derived from the Illyrian *terg* 'market'.
As the principal port for the Austro-Hungarian
Empire, it was called Triest. Seized by
Germany in 1943, it was liberated by the
Yugoslavs in 1945, but two years later it
became a Free Territory under Anglo-
American military administration (Zone A
which included the city and port) and Yugoslav
military administration (Zone B to the south
called, locally, Trst). Zone B and part of Zone A
became Yugoslav with the remainder of Zone
A, which included the city, going to Italy in
1954.

Triglav (Italian: **Tricorno**) SLOVENIA
A mountain with the name 'Three-Headed'
from the Slavonic *tri* 'three' and *glava* 'head'.

Trincomalee (Thirukonamalai), SRI LANKA
Gokaṇṇa
A fine natural harbour, the Anglicized name is
said to come from the Tamil *tri* 'three', *kona*
'peak', and *malai* 'hill', a reference to the
peninsula on which the town lies. However, it
has also been suggested that the first part of
the name is derived from the Tamil *tiru* 'holy'
and the name means 'Holy Hill of the Sun'. It
was occupied by the British between 1795 and
1957.

Trinidad, ARGENTINA, BELIZE, BOLIVIA, COSTA
RICA, CUBA, HONDURAS, PANAMA, TRINIDAD AND
TOBAGO, URUGUAY, USA
1. '(Holy) Trinity'.
2. Bolivia: founded as a mission by Jesuits in
1686 and named after the Feast of the Most
Holy Trinity.
3. Cuba: founded in 1514 by the first governor
of Cuba as La Villa de la Santísima Trinidad
'The Town of the Most Holy Trinity'.
4. Republic of Trinidad and Tobago: originally
called Lere 'Land of the Humming Birds' by the
Ienian Arawaks. The island was discovered by
Christopher Columbus[†] in 1498 and he gave it
the name La Trinidad for the three peaks that
surrounded the southern bay where he
landed; these represented the Holy Trinity to
him.

Trinidad and Tobago Republic of Trinidad
and Tobago since 1976, having gained
independence in 1962. Previously part of the
West Indies Federation (1958–62); and a British
crown colony (1888), Trinidad having been
captured by the British in 1797 and ceded to
the UK in 1802 with Tobago finally acquired in
1814. *See, separately,* TRINIDAD AND TOBAGO.

Tripoli, LIBYA, LEBANON, USA
1. Libya: the full name is Ṭarābulus al-Gharb
'The Western Tripoli', an Arabic rendering of
the Greek Tripolis. It was founded by the
Phoenicians as Oea and enlarged by the Greeks
and Romans to become one of the three cities
that formed Tripolis (the others were Sabratha
and Leptis Magna) from the Greek *treis* 'three'
and *polis*. The port of Oea was renamed
Triopolis in the 3rd century. Like other towns
in North Africa it fell to the Romans, Vandals,
and Byzantines before the Arabs arrived in
645. The *al-Gharb* 'of the West' was added after
the Ottoman Turkish conquest in 1551 to
distinguish the city from what was then the
Syrian city (see 2).
2. Lebanon: the full name is Ṭarābulus ash-
Shām 'Tripoli of the Northern (Region)', in

contrast to the Tripoli in Libya, and locally
Trâblous. To the famous 14th-century Arab
traveller Ibn Battutah it was known as
Atrābulus. It was founded by the Phoenicians,
later attracting the Greek name Tripolis
because it was divided into three sectors
divided by walls. It became the capital of the
federation of city-states—Sidon, Tyre (now
Soûr), and Aradus (or Arwād).

Tripolitania (Tarābulus), LIBYA
A historic region with a Roman name 'Three
Cities', alluding to the same three Libyan cities
covered by the name *Tripoli. The region was
ruled directly and indirectly by the Ottoman
Turks in 1551–1912. It was incorporated into
the Kingdom of Italy in 1939 and into the
federal Kingdom of Libya in 1951. The name
was dispensed with in 1963 when the region
was broken down into smaller administrative
regions.

Tripura, INDIA
A state since 1972 with a Hindi name meaning
'Three Towns' from *tri* 'three' and *pur*.

Tristan da Cunha, UK
A dependency of St Helena. A group of three
islands, the largest of which is called Tristan,
in the South Atlantic Ocean. It is named after
Tristão da Cunha (1460–1540), a Portuguese
admiral, who discovered the islands in 1506.
Tristan was occupied by the British to prevent
it being used as a base by American warships
during the war of 1812. It was annexed by the
UK in 1816.

Trivandrum, KERALA/INDIA *Thiru Anthapuram/
Tiruvanantapuram*
The present name is really a shortening of the
original Malayalam name which meant 'Abode
of the Sacred Anantha', the sacred snake that
was often shown curled round the body of
Lord Vishnu, from *tiru* 'holy' or 'sacred',
Anantha, and *pur*. Its original name is now in
official use.

Trnava, SLOVAKIA *Tyrnavia, Tyrnau, Nagyszombat*
Situated on the River Trnavka, originally the
Trnava, and named after it. The river's name
signifies a river running through thorn bushes
from *trní* 'thorn bush'. The Hungarian
Nagyszombat 'Big Saturday' from *nagy* 'big'
and *szombat* 'Saturday' referred to the day
when markets were held here.

Trogir, CROATIA *Tragurion, Trau*
May be derived from the Greek *tragos* 'goat'
and *oros* 'hill' to give a '(Settlement near) Goats'
Hill'.

Trois-Rivières, CANADA, GUADELOUPE
1. 'Three Rivers' in French.

2. Canada (Quebec): the city was founded in
1634 by Samuel de Champlain[†] and so named
by him because of the three channels of the
Saint-Maurice River which flow into the St
Lawrence River.

Troitsk, CHELYABINSK/RUSSIA
Founded in 1743 and named after Trinity
Sunday from *Troitsa* 'Trinity', the day on which
the construction of the military post was
begun.

Tromsø, NORWAY
The administrative centre of Troms County, it
is situated on the island of Tromsøy which
gives its name from the Danish ø 'island' (and
in Norwegian øy). The meaning of Troms is not
known.

Trondheim, NORWAY *Kaupangr, Nidaros,
Trondhjem*
Founded as the village of Kaupangr in 997 by
Olaf I Tryggvason (*c*.964–*c*.1000), Viking King of
Norway (995–*c*.1000), the city-port may take its
present name from the fjord, Throndr (now
Trondheimsfjorden), which may itself be
derived from the Old Norwegian *thorr*
'thunder', and *heimr* 'home' or 'town'; or it
could mean 'Home of the Throne', the city
being the traditional site for royal coronations.
In 1016 the city was renamed Nidaros 'Estuary
of the (River) Nid(elva)' and in the 16th century
Trondhjem. It retained this name until
Nidaros was restored in 1930. Nidaros only
lasted a year and Trondhjem was readopted,
although spelt Trondheim.

Troodos (Greek: *Tróödhos*), CYPRUS
A mountain range where three routes meet,
thus *triodos* from *odos* 'road' or 'route'.

Troon, SCOTLAND/UK *Le Trone, Le Trune*
'(Place by) the Headland' from the Welsh *trwyn*.

Trowbridge, ENGLAND/UK *Straburg, Trobrigge*
'Tree-trunk Bridge' from the Old English *trēow*
'tree' and *brycg*.

Troy, CANADA, JAMAICA, TURKEY, USA
1. Turkey: ruins, the site now being called
Hisarlík. The name is said to come from Troas,
a legendary founder. He had three sons, one of
which was Ilus from whom the city's
alternative name came: in Greek Ilios or Ilion,
and in Latin Ilium. Archaeological evidence
has revealed nine main levels of habitation,
sometimes misleadingly called cities, with
Troy IX being the Ilium Novum of Hellenistic
and Roman times.
2. USA (Alabama): a Native American hunting
ground called Deer Stand Hill, it was renamed
Troy *c*.1838 after Alexander Troy, a lawyer.

3. USA (New York): laid out as Vanderheyden's Ferry in 1786 by the Dutch Vanderheyden family on the east bank of the Hudson River, it was renamed in 1789 after the ancient city of Troy.

Troyes, CHAMPAGNE-ARDENNE/FRANCE *Civitas Tricassium*
Named after the Tricasses, a Gallic tribe, whose capital this was. The present name evolved from the Roman name. It gave its name to the troy weight, a system of weights used principally for precious metals which was used during the great medieval fairs held in the town.

Trucial Oman or Trucial States *See* UNITED ARAB EMIRATES.

Trujillo, HONDURAS, PERU, SPAIN, USA, VENEZUELA
1. Peru: founded in 1534, it was given the status of a city the next year by Francisco Pizarro (*c*.1475–1541), the Spanish conquistador, and renamed by him after his birthplace in Spain.
2. Spain (Extremadura): formerly Turgalium and Turris Julia 'Tower of Julius', a reference to Julius Caesar[†], from which the present name comes.
3. Venezuela: named by Diego Garcia Paredes, a Spaniard, after his birthplace in Spain.

Truro, CANADA, UK, USA
1. Canada (Nova Scotia): settled as Cobequid in the 1670s on the Salmon River at the head of Cobequid Bay, it had a Micmac name meaning 'End of Flowing Water' before this was changed to Truro after the English town.
2. UK: formerly Triuero. Although the first syllable hints at 'three', the meaning of the name is not known.
3. USA (Massachusetts): named after the English city.

Truth or Consequences, NEW MEXICO/USA *Hot Springs*
Originally named for its thermal springs, it was renamed in 1950. To promote the town its authorities persuaded Ralph Edwards, who presented the radio quiz 'Truth or Consequences', to transmit his programme from the town once a year.

Trzebnica, POLAND *Treibnitz*
Named after the Trzebowian tribe.

Tsetserleg, MONGOLIA
'Garden'.

Tsinghai, CHINA
See QINGHAI.

Tsingtao, SHANDONG/CHINA.
See QINGDAO.

Tsitsihar, HEILONGJIANG/CHINA
See QIQIHAR.

Tskhenis Tskali, GEORGIA
A river with a name meaning 'Horse River' from *tskhenis* 'horse' and *tskali* 'river'. According to legend, the horses of an Arab army drowned in the river in 683.

Ts'khinval, GEORGIA *Staliniri, Ts'khinvali*
Established on the site of a 6th century settlement, the town was renamed Staliniri in 1929 to mark the 50th birthday of Joseph Stalin[†], a Georgian. It reverted to its original name 'Hornbeam Tree' after his posthumous fall from grace in 1961.

Tsu, HONSHŪ/JAPAN
At the mouth of the Ano River, the name means 'Port'.

Tsuchiura, HONSHŪ/JAPAN
The characters represent *tsuchi* 'soil' and *ura* 'port'.

Tsuruoka, HONSHŪ/JAPAN *Shōnai*
Renamed in 1601, the present characters represent *tsuru* 'crane' and *oka* 'hill'.

Tsushima, JAPAN
An island group lying in the Korea Strait. The characters represent *tsui* 'pair' or 'couple' and *ma* 'horse'. The reason for 'horse' may be that the part of Korea opposite Tsushima was called Bakan in Japanese from *ba* 'horse' and *Kan* 'Korea'. Bakan came to be known as Silla, one of the Three Kingdoms, in Korean.

Tsuyama, HONSHŪ/JAPAN
The characters represent *tsu* 'port' and *yama* 'mountain'.

Tsyurupyns'k, UKRAINE *Elissa, Olesh'ye, Alëshki*
An ancient Greek colony, the name was gradually Russified. When he died in 1928 it was named after Alexander Tsyurupa (1870–1928), a Communist Party leader.

Tuapse, KRASNODAR TERRITORY/RUSSIA *Velyaminskoye Ukrepleniye*
Founded in 1838 as a small fortress named 'Velyaminov's Fortification' after A. A. Velyaminov, a local Russian general, and *ukrepleniye* 'fortification'. As it developed into a town it was renamed 'Two Rivers' or 'Two Waters' from the Circassian *tua* 'two' and *psy* 'water' or 'river'. It is so named because the Rivers Tuapse and Pauk flow into the sea here.

Tübingen, BADEN-WÜRTTEMBERG/GERMANY
Castra Alamannorum, Tuwingen
Originally the 'Camp of the Alemanni', it was
renamed from a Middle High German word
consisting of an old German personal name,
Tuwo, and *ingen* to give 'Tuwo's Followers'.

Tubinskiy, BASHKORTOSTAN REPUBLIC/RUSSIA
'Hill' from the Bashkir *tube*.

Tucson, ARIZONA/USA *Chuk Shon*
In 1700 a Jesuit mission was established in a
Native American village called Chuk Shon
'(Village at) the Black Creek'.

Tugela (Thukela), KWAZULU-NATAL/SOUTH
AFRICA
A river whose Zulu name means 'Something
that Startles', probably a reference to its series
of five waterfalls.

Tuktoyaktuk, NORTHWEST TERRITORIES/
CANADA *Port Brabant*
Renamed in 1950 with an Inuit name
'Reindeer that looks like Caribou'. The town
lies roughly halfway along the Tuktoyaktuk
Peninsula.

Tukums, LATVIA *Tuckum/Tukhum*
Derived from the Old Liv words *tukku maegi*
'Group of Hills' or 'Mountain Range'.

Tula, ITALY, KENYA, MEXICO, RUSSIA
Russia: a province and a city formerly called
Taydula. Although some way from the Baltic
Sea, the name is said to originate from a Baltic
word *tula* 'settlement'.

Tulbagh, WESTERN CAPE/SOUTH AFRICA
Roodezand
Founded as a religious settlement in 1743
called 'Red Sand'. In 1804 it was renamed
after Ryk Tulbagh, governor of the Cape
(1751–71).

Tullahoma, TENNESSEE/USA
Settled in 1850 on the site of a Cherokee
village with a name meaning 'Nearest Town'.

Tullamore, AUSTRALIA, IRELAND
Ireland: locally Tulach Mhór 'Big Hill'. It lies on
the Tullamore River.

Ṭulmaythah, LIBYA *Ptolemais*
Originally named after Ptolemy III, King of
Egypt (c.245–221 BC), who united Cyrenaica
and Egypt. The present name is a corruption of
the original name. The town is also known as
Tolmeita.

Tulsa, OKLAHOMA/USA
Established as a Creek settlement in 1836 after
they had come from Tulsa, Alabama. The
name is said to be derived from the Creek *talwa*
'town' and *hasi* 'old'.

Tumaco, COLOMBIA
Named after Tumas, a Native American chief
who founded the village in 1570.

Tumanyan, ARMENIA *Dzagidzor*
Renamed in 1951 after Ovanes Tumanyan
(1869–1923), a poet and short story writer who
became involved in Armenian affairs. He was
born near here.

Tumut, NEW SOUTH WALES/AUSTRALIA
Lying on the Tumut River, the town has an
Aboriginal name meaning 'River Campsite'.

Tunbridge Wells (Royal Tunbridge Wells),
ENGLAND/UK
Named after the nearby *Tonbridge with Wells
referring to the springs here. These were
discovered in 1606 and the borough was
founded in the 1630s. After a visit by Queen
Victoria[†] it was designated a royal borough and
received the title of 'Royal' in 1909 from King
Edward VII.

Tunguska, KRASNOYARSK TERRITORY/RUSSIA
Three tributaries of the Yenisey River have this
name which originates from the Tungus 'Far
People', another name for the Evenk who live
in an area extending eastward from the
Yenisey River to the Pacific Ocean.There are
also towns called Podkamennaya Tunguska,
also the name of one of the tributaries, and
Sukhaya Tunguska.

Tunis, CANADA, TUNISIA
Tunisia: founded in the 9th century BC as a
Phoenician settlement, it was useful only as a
protected spot for armies besieging nearby
Carthage. When the Arabs arrived in the 7th
century their leader decided to fortify his
camp and build a city-port here. The origin of
the name is not clear, but it may be of Berber
origin from the root *e-n-s* 'halt', 'bivouac', thus
'camp' from which the former Greek name,
Tunēs, came. It became the capital of the
region during the 13th century. The city
became the national capital when Tunisia
achieved independence in 1956.

Tunisia *Africa, Tunisie*
The Tunisian Republic (al-Jumhūrīyah at-
Tūnisīyah) since 1956 when independence was
achieved. Previously a French protectorate
(1883–1956); nominally part of the Ottoman
Empire (1606–1881) as an autonomous
province ruled by local governors, the
Ottoman Turks having driven the Spanish out
of Tunis in 1574. The country is named after
the city of Tunis with the suffix -*ia* adapted
from the French name for the protectorate,
Tunisie. It was known as Africa (in Arabic,
Ifriqiya) to the Romans and to the Arabs when
they arrived in the 7th century.

Turgay, KAZAKHSTAN *Orenburg*
Lying on the Turgay River, the town was
founded in 1845 as a Russian fortress called
Orenburg. In 1868 Turgay Province was
divided into districts and the fortress-town was
renamed Turgay 'Little Bird' from the Turkish
turghay.

Türgovishte, BULGARIA *Eski Djumaia*
Famous for its cattle fair, it has the same
meaning 'Market' as *"Tîrgovişte*, the name
coming from *targovets* 'merchant'. The
Russians captured it from the Ottoman Turks
in 1878 and returned it to Bulgaria. It was
renamed in 1934.

Turin, CANADA, ITALY, USA
Italy (Piedmont): Italian *Torino*. Named after
the Taurini, a Ligurian tribe which might have
taken its name from an ancient root word
tauro 'mountains'. Thus Taurini would mean
'People of the Mountains'. The city is located
just to the east of the Alps. It was originally
called Taurisia and when it became a Roman
military colony Julia Taurinorum after Julius
Caesar†; it was renamed Augusta Taurinorum
after Caesar Augustus† after he had rebuilt it. It
became the capital of the Kingdom of Sardinia
in 1720 and was capital of Italy in 1861–4.

Turkana, KENYA
See RUDOLF, LAKE

Turkestan, CENTRAL ASIA, KAZAKHSTAN
1. Central Asia: a historic region, also spelt
Turkistan. It was meant to represent that
region in which Turkic peoples lived, 'Land of
the Turks', but this is only partly true. The
region included Tajikistan, but the Tajiks are
not Turkic; nor, of course, did it include
Turkey. Turkestan was divided in 1762 into
Russian West Turkestan, which comprised
modern southern Kazakhstan, Kyrgyzstan,
Tajikistan, Turkmenistan, and Uzbekistan,
and Chinese East Turkestan, comprising the
present Sinkiang Uighur Autonomous Region.
In 1924 Joseph Stalin† carved up the Turkestan
Autonomous Soviet Socialist Republic into
four ethnic republics (for the Kazakhs, Kyrgyz,
Turkmen, and Uzbeks), the Tajiks being
included in Uzbekistan until 1929.
2. Kazakhstan: *see* TÜRKISTAN.

Turkey (Türkiye)
The Republic of Turkey (Türkiye Cumhuriyeti)
since 1923. It was given the name in the 12th
century by Europeans to describe in general
the land in Asia Minor (as it had been called
until then) conquered by the Seljuk Turks
beginning in the 11th century. They
established the Seljuk Sultanate of Rum
'Rome' (the Turkish name for the Byzantine

Empire, or Roman Asia). The Turks themselves
used the Greek name, Anatolia, and the name
Turkey only came into official use as the name
for the new republic in 1923. As Muslims,
however, the Turks also used the title *Dar ul
Islam* 'Land (literally, House) of Islam'. In the
late 13th century the Seljuk Sultanate declined
while a small emirate in north-west Anatolia,
ruled by Osman (or Othman) I (1258–1324)
between *c.*1284 and 1324, began to expand. In
1288 Osman founded the Osmanlı dynasty—
better known as the Ottoman dynasty.
Ottoman armies spread into the Balkans in the
14th century and captured Constantinople
(now Istanbul) in 1453, bringing the Byzantine
Empire to an end. The Ottoman Empire
endured until 1922. Ninety-five per cent of the
country lies in Asia with 5 per cent, Turkish
Thrace, in Europe. The name Turk was first
recorded in the 6th century by the Chinese to
describe an empire in Central Asia founded by
a steppe people called the Ti-Kiu or Tu-Küe.
This became Türk to signify 'ruling people',
that is the Turkic-speaking tribes of Central
Asia. The country has given its name to
turkey: because African guinea-fowl were
exported to England through Turkey, the bird
came to be called the turkeycock or turkeyhen
which were subsequently shortened to turkey.
Turkish Delight, a sweet, was first made in
Turkey where it is called *Rahat Lokum*.

Türkistan, KAZAKHSTAN *Khazret, Shavgar, Yassy*
A town called Yassy after a 12th-century
Muslim saint Khwäjah Ahmad Yasawī, and
since the 15th century, Türkistan 'Land of the
Turks'. It is also spelt Turkestan and should not
to be confused with the historical regions (*see*
TURKESTAN).

Türkmenabat, TURKMENISTAN *Chahar-Su,
Novy Chardzhuy, Chardzhev*
Renamed in 2003 to mean 'City of the
Turkmen' from *ābād* 'city' or 'inhabited place'.
The previous name was derived from the 15th-
century name which meant 'Four Ways' from
the Turkic *chor* 'four', the town being a central
point where caravan routes crossed. The
'Ways' were actually tributaries of the Amu
Darya (Oxus) River which facilitated travel. It
was an Uzbek town within the Bukhara
Emirate before being included in the Turkmen
Republic in 1924 when the Soviet government
reorganized Central Asia on the basis of
nationality. The site was refounded as a
Russian military post in 1886 with the name
Novy 'New' Chardzhuy. The *Novy* was dropped
in 1937. It was also spelt Chärjew in Turkmen
and Chardzhou. It may be the site of the
ancient city of Āmul (*see* AMU DARYA).

Türkmenbashi, TURKMENISTAN *Krasnovodsk*
Founded as a Russian fort in 1869 and called
Krasnovodsk 'Red Water' from the Russian
krasnyy and *voda* 'water' after the bay here
which was called 'Red Waters'. In 1997 the city
was renamed Türkmenbashi 'Head of the
Turkmen' from the Turkish *bas* 'head' in
honour of Saparmurad Niyazov (1940–),
President of Turkmenistan (1991–). As
founder and president of the Humanitarian
Association of Turkmens of the World, he
was granted the title of Türkmenbashi in
1993. The bay has also been renamed
Türkmenbashi Bay. *See* SAPARMURAD
TÜRKMENBASHI AND NYYAZOW.

Turkmenistan Turkmenistan
(Türkmenistan) since 1991 when
independence was forced upon the Soviet
Central Asian republics. Previously the
Turkmen Soviet Socialist Republic (1924),
becoming a constituent republic of the Soviet
Union in 1925 (1925–91); the Turkestan
Autonomous Soviet Socialist Republic, which
included the Tsarist province of Transcaspia
(1918–24); the Transcaspian Province (1881–
1918), the region having fallen to the Russians
in 1881. The arrival of the Oğuz Turks in the
11th century gave the region its Turkic
character which it has retained ever since. The
name simply means 'Land of the Turkmen'
(who were also known at one time as the
Turkomans) from their name and *stan*.
Their name may mean 'Turk-like' from the
Persian *Tork* and the root of *mandan* 'to
resemble' or the suffix *men* may indicate
strength.

Turks and Caicos Islands An Overseas
Territory of the UK in the West Indies
consisting of two island groups: the Turks
group and the Caicos group. The Turks take
their name from the turk's head cactus found
here while the Caicos take their name from
the plural of the Spanish *cayo* 'islet' or 'cay'.
Settled by the British in 1678, they were
annexed to Jamaica in 1874–1959 and in 1962
they became a crown colony.

Turku, FINLAND *Åbo*
'Market Place' from the Swedish *torg* 'market
place'. At the mouth of the River Aura, the
previous Swedish name meant 'Settlement
by the River' from *å* 'river' and *bo* 'to
inhabit', thus 'settlement'. Founded in
the 11th century, it was the capital of
Finland until 1812. The capital was
then transferred to Helsinki because
Turku was considered to be too close to
Sweden.

Turlock, CALIFORNIA/USA
Founded *c*.1860 with a name from the Irish
turlough 'dry lake' or 'fen'.

Turnu Măgurele, ROMANIA
Possibly 'Tower on a Hillock' from *turn* 'tower'
and *măgură* 'hillock'.

Turpan (Turfan), SINKIANG UIGHUR
AUTONOMOUS REGION/CHINA *Huozhou/Huolu,
Gaochang, Xi Zhou, He Zhou, Huo Zhou*
An oasis town on the northern silk route, the
name means 'Lowland' in Uighur. The Uighurs
pronounce the name as Turpan, the Chinese as
Tulufan, the phonetic rendering of Turpan in
Mandarin. The previous name meant 'Land of
Fire' from the Chinese *huǒ* 'fire' and *zhōu*; *lú*
means 'stove' or 'furnace': both names are a
reference to the very high temperatures in
summer. During the Han dynasty (206 BC–AD
220) it was known as Gaochang from *gāo* 'high'
and *chāng* 'prosperous' since it was sited on
high ground and many wealthy people lived
here. During the Tang dynasty (618–907) it was
called Xi Zhou 'Western District' from *xī* 'west'
and *zhōu*.

Tursunzade, TAJIKISTAN *Stantsiya Regar, Regar*
Originally 'Regar Station', this was shortened
to Regar in 1952. In 1978 it was renamed after
Mirzo Tursun-Zade (1911–77), a poet and
literary critic who was born near here.

Turtkul', UZBEKISTAN *Petro-Aleksandrovsk*
Founded in 1873 as a fort and given its present
Turkic name 'Quadrangle' (in modern
Turkish, *dörtgen*) in 1920. This is a reference to
the shape of the ruined fort here.

Tuscaloosa, ALABAMA/USA
'Black Warrior (Town)' in honour of the
Choctaw chief Tuscaloosa from the Choctaw
tusko 'warrior' and *loosa* 'black'. He fought the
Spaniards in southern Alabama in 1540. The
Creeks established the town in 1809, but four
years later it was burnt down. The Creeks were
forced to move and built a new town in 1816
further to the west which they also called
Tuscaloosa.

Tuscany (Toscana), ITALY *Tuscia*
A region that takes its name from an Etruscan
tribe, its original inhabitants. In 1801
Napoleon[†] created the Tuscan Kingdom of
Etruria but in 1808 annexed it to France which
held it only until 1814. Declared a republic in
1849, it joined Italy in 1861.

Tuscarora, USA
Maryland: named after the Tuscarora, one of
the confederated Iroquois tribes. Their name is
said to be derived from an Iroquois term for
'hemp gatherers'.

Tuscumbia, USA *Ococoposa (Alabama)*
Alabama: founded in 1817 with a Chickasaw–
Choctaw name meaning 'Cold Water', a
reference to a local creek. It was renamed
in 1822 after Tash-Ka-Ambi, a Chickasaw
chief whose village here was destroyed in
1787.

Tutayev, YAROSLAVL'/RUSSIA *Romanov-
Borisoglebsk*
Romanov, on the left bank of the River Volga,
was founded *c.*1370 and named after Prince
Roman Vasilyevich, the great-grandson of a
grand prince who was granted the area round
the village of Borisoglebsk on the right bank of
the river. That village was founded in the 15th
century and took its name from its church
dedicated to Saints Boris and Gleb (*see*
BORISOGLEBSK). The two towns, and their
names, were merged in 1822. In 1921 it was
renamed after I. P. Tutayev, a Red Guard who
had been killed during the Yaroslavl' revolt in
1918.

Tuva, RUSSIA *Tyva/Tannu-Tuva*
Formerly a province and now a republic
named after the Tuvans. It was part of the
Chinese Empire in 1757–1911 before falling to
the Russians. It was independent as the Tannu-
Tuva People's Republic in 1921–44 when it was
annexed by the Soviet Union and established
as an autonomous province; it became an
autonomous republic in 1961. The first part of
the previous name recognized the Tannu-Ola
mountain range.

Tuvalu *Ellice Islands*
A constitutional monarchy with the chief of
state being the British monarch, represented
by a Tuvaluan governor-general. The name
means 'Eight Standing Together' from the
Tuvaluan *tu* 'to stand up' and *valu* 'eight'. The
reason for the name was that, of the nine coral
islands and atolls, only eight were inhabited
when the first Europeans arrived in the 16th
century; or it may be that, of the nine islands,
one, Nui, is in habited by people speaking a
Gilbertese dialect. The former name comes
from Alexander Ellice, the British owner of the
ship, the *Rebecca*, whose captain visited
Funafuti Atoll in 1819. The Ellice Islands
joined the Gilbert Islands Protectorate in 1892
and together they became the Gilbert and
Ellice Islands Colony (*see* KIRIBATI) in 1916.
Tuvalu separated from the colony in 1975 and
gained its independence in 1978 when it
adopted its present name.

Tuxtla Gutiérrez, CHIAPAS/MEXICO
'Tuxtla' was the Spanish pronunciation of the
Nahuatl *tuchtlán* 'where rabbits abound'. In the
19th century Gutiérrez was added in honour of

Joaquin Miguel Gutiérrez, governor of
Chiapas, who was prominent in the campaign
to prevent Chiapas becoming part of
Guatemala in the 19th century.

Tuz, TURKEY
A lake with the name 'Salt'.

Tuzla, BOSNIA AND HERZEGOVINA *Soli, Salinae*
Named after the local salt mines from the
Turkish *tuz* 'salt'. Soli meant 'Salts'.

Tver', RUSSIA *Porsy, Kalinin*
A former principality (1246–1485), a province
since 1935, and a city founded in the 12th
century at the confluence of the Tvertsa and
Volga Rivers. The name may be taken from
tverdynya 'stronghold'. In 1931–6 it was called
Porsy and then until 1990 it was named, at the
inhabitants' request, after Mikhail Kalinin[†]
who was born here.

Twinsburg, OHIO/USA *Millsville*
Renamed in 1819 after two identical twin
brothers, Aaron and Moses Wilcox, donated
six acres for a town square and $20 towards a
new school on the condition that the town's
name was changed.

Tychy, POLAND
Developed from a brewery opened in 1629 and
given a name derived from *cichy* 'quiet', 'still',
or 'silent'. This name has been quite
inappropriate since at least the early 1950s
when Nowe Tychy 'New Tychy' was built to
provide housing for over 100,000 industrial
workers.

Tyler, USA
Texas: laid out in 1846 and named after John
Tyler (1790–1862), President of the USA
(1841–5).

Tyndall, CANADA, USA
USA (South Dakota): named after John Tyndall
(1820–93), a British physicist who explained
why the sky is blue.

Tyne, ENGLAND/UK
A river with a pre-Celtic name meaning 'River'
or 'Flowing One'.

Tyre, LEBANON
See SOUR.

Tyrol, AUSTRIA, ITALY
1. Austria: a state whose name was taken from
the Castle of Tirol near Merano which itself
was named after a local family.
2. Italy: the South Tyrol is a region which
was acquired by Italy after the First World
War.

Tyrone, CANADA, UK, USA
1. UK (Northern Ireland): a former county
until 1973 whose name is derived from Tír
Eoghain 'Eoghan's Land' from *tír* 'land' or
'territory'.
2. USA (Pennsylvania): named by Irish
immigrants after the Irish county.

Tyrrhenian Sea A part of the
Mediterranean Sea between Italy and Sardinia
whose name is derived from the Latin
Tyrrhenus 'Etruscan'.

Tyumen', RUSSIA *Chingi-Tura*
A province and a city founded in 1586 on the
Tura River on the site of a Tatar town called
Chingi-Tura 'Town of Chingis' (Genghis
Khan†), founded in the 14th century. Its
present name means 'Ten Thousand' from the
Tatar *tyu* 'ten' and *men* 'thousand', perhaps a
reference to the strength of Genghis's army.

Tzaneen, LIMPOPO/SOUTH AFRICA
Derived from the Sepedi *tsaneng* 'the place
where people gather'.

Ubangi River, CENTRAL AFRICAN
REPUBLIC-CONGO
See CENTRAL AFRICAN REPUBLIC.

Ubatuba, SÃO PAULO/BRAZIL *Iperoig, Vila Nova da
Exaltação da Santa Cruz do Salvador de Ubatuba*
'Place of Canoes' or 'Place of Reeds' from the
Tupí-Guaraní *ubá* 'canoe' or from *uuba* 'wild
cane from which arrows are made' or
'mangrove reed' and *tuba* 'place where there is
an abundance of (something)'.

Ubombo, KWAZULU-NATAL/SOUTH AFRICA
Takes its name from the mountains here
whose name comes from the Zulu *lubombo*
'high ridge'.

Ubud, BALI/INDONESIA
Derived from the Balinese *ubad* 'medicine'.
The town was an important source of
medicinal plants and herbs.

Ubundu, DEMOCRATIC REPUBLIC OF THE CONGO
Ponthierville
Until 1966 named 'Ponthier's Town' after
Pierre Ponthier, a Belgian army officer. It was
then renamed 'Land of the Bunda (People)'
from the Bantu *ou* or *u* 'land'.

Uch, PUNJAB/PAKISTAN *Alexandria at the
Confluence, Iskandera/Eskanderiya*
Founded in 325 BC by Alexander III the Great[†]
near the confluence of the Sutlej and Jhelum
(then the Hydaspes) Rivers. According to local
tradition, the name was changed to Iskandera
or Eskanderiya when the Muslims first arrived
in the 8th century. The present name means a
'High Place'. It is also sometimes spelt Uchchh.

Uchaly, BASHKORTOSTAN REPUBLIC/RUSSIA
Gets its name from the lakes called Big and
Little Uchaly. This name is said to come from a
Russification of the Bashkir *asyuly* 'angry' or
'turbulent', a reference to the lakes' waters.

Udachnyy, SAKHA REPUBLIC/RUSSIA
'Successful', a reference to the success of the
gold-mine, opened here in 1968.

Udaipur, RĀJASTHĀN/INDIA
Founded in 1559 by Udai Singh II, Mahārānā of
the princely state of Udaipur (1532–72), on the
advice of a sage who claimed that if a new
Mewār capital was built here it would never be
captured. In 1568 he named it the 'City of
Sunrise' from *uday* 'birth' or 'rising' and *pur*.

Udhampur, JAMMU AND KASHMIR/INDIA
A district and a town named after Udham
Singh, the eldest son of Gulab Singh, who
founded, and was the ruler of, the state of
Jammu and Kashmir (1846–57).

Udmurtiya, RUSSIA *Votskaya*
A republic named after the Udmurt, a Finno-
Ugric people, whose name comes from *murt*, a
local word for 'person' or 'man'. Until 1932 the
Udmurt were known as the Votyaks and the
then province was called the Votskaya
Autonomous Province. It became a republic in
1990.

Uganda The Republic of Uganda (Swahili:
Jamhuri Ya Uganda) since 1963, having gained
independence from the UK in 1962.
Landlocked, it had been a British
protectorate (1894–1962), the principal
province of Buganda being acknowledged
as a native kingdom. The name Uganda
is the Swahili term for Buganda and was
adopted by the British in 1894; it means
'Land of the Ganda (People)' from the Swahili
u 'land' and *ganda*, the root word and
adjective for Buganda. The people of
Buganda are known, in the plural, as the
Baganda or baGanda.

Uglegorsk, SAKHALIN ISLAND/RUSSIA *Esutoru*
Its original Japanese name was superseded in
1946. The present name means 'Coal Town'
from *ugol'* 'coal' and *gorsk*.

Uherské Hradiště, CZECH REPUBLIC *Novum
Velehrad, Město, Hradiště*
Founded in 1275 by Otakar II (1230–78),
King of Bohemia (1253–78), to protect trade
routes to Hungary and named 'New Big
Castle' since there was another place in
the vicinity called Velehrad 'Big Castle'.
This was later changed to Město 'Place' and
then to Hradiště 'Fortified Settlement' (*see*
MNICHOVO HRADIŠTĚ). The name 'Hungarian
Fortified Settlement' from *uhry* (denoting
modern Hungary and those parts of
neighbouring countries that belonged to
the Kingdom of Hungary) indicates that
it was here on the border with what was
Upper Hungary (and now is Slovakia) that
groups of Protestant refugees from Hungary
settled.

Ûijŏngbu, SOUTH KOREA
'The Cabinet' because it was one of the sites of the cabinet office during the Yi dynasty (1392–1910).

Uinta, UTAH-WYOMING/USA
A mountain range named after a branch of the Ute tribe. The name is said to mean 'Pine Land'.

Uitenhage, EASTERN CAPE/SOUTH AFRICA
Founded in 1804 by, and named after, J. A. Uitenhage de Mist (1749–1823), a Dutch government official sent out to the colony.

Ujiji, TANZANIA
'Land of the Jiji (People)' from the Swahili *u* 'land'.

Ujjain, MADHYA PRADESH/INDIA *Avantika, Ujjayinī, Ozene*
One of the seven sacred Hindu cities, it was the capital of the ancient Aryan Avanti kingdom, hence its first name. According to legend, this was then changed to Ujjayinī 'He who Conquers with Pride'. Ptolemy[†] called it Ozene.

Ujungpandang, SULAWESI/INDONESIA
Makasar, Fort Rotterdam
Originally named after the Makasserese, the present name was adopted in 1971 to draw attention to Fort Ujung Pandang, which had been built in 1545 and in which the Javan independence hero, Prince Diponegoro, had been imprisoned for 27 years. He died here in exile in 1855. It became Fort Rotterdam in 1667 after it had been captured by the Dutch. On the south-west coast of Sulawei's south-western peninsula, the name comes from *ujung* 'at the extremity of'. An oil that was applied to people's hair came from Makassar and to prevent it soiling the backs of chairs a cover—an antimacassar—was placed over them.

Ukraine (Ukrayina) *(Kievan) Rus', Malorossiya*
Gaining independence from the Soviet Union in 1991, Ukraine was previously known as the Ukrainian Soviet Socialist Republic (1922–91), a founder member of the USSR. This followed the proclamation of the Ukrainian SSR in eastern Ukraine in 1920; in 1918 an independent Ukrainian National Republic and a Western Ukrainian National Republic were established, uniting in 1919. The name was formerly that of a region, the Ukraine (and now as a state the 'the' is omitted), and is derived from the Russian *okraina* '(land) on the edge', thus 'borderland' from *u* 'beside' and *kray* 'edge' to denote the territory between the open steppes of Russia and Asia to the east and the populated lands of the Polish-Lithuanian

Commonwealth to the west. The present name was not in wide use until the 19th century; until then the Ukrainians were often called Ruthenians and the country was known as Malorossiya 'Little Russia'. The early history of modern Russia and Ukraine is shared and can be traced back to Kievan Rus' (*see* RUSSIA). Although Ukrainian nationalism endured despite repression, for most of its history Ukraine has lacked independent statehood, its institutions imposed largely by Russia and Poland.

Ulan Bator (Ulaanbaatar), MONGOLIA *Urga, Yihe Huree (or Ikh Khureheh), Niyslel Huree (or Niislel Khureheh), Urga*
The original name came from *orgoo* 'palace', having been founded in 1639 as the residence of the Jebtsundamba Khutuktu, the Living Buddha. It was renamed in 1706 'Great Monastery' and in 1911 'Capital Monastery' from *niyslel* 'capital' and *huree* 'monastery' after Outer Mongolia declared itself independent. At this time it became the capital of Mongolia, but in the West it was still called Urga. In 1924 it was renamed '(Town of) the Red Hero' from *ulaan* 'red' and *baatar* 'hero' in honour of Damdiny Sühbaatar (*see* SÜHBAATAR) whose revolutionary troops occupied it in 1921 and who died here in 1923.

Ulanhot, INNER MONGOLIA AUTONOMOUS REGION/CHINA
'Red City' from *ulaan* 'red' and *hot* 'city' in Mongolian.

Ulan Ude, BURYATIYA REPUBLIC/RUSSIA
Udinskoye, Verkhne-Udinskaya, Verkhne-Udinsk
Founded as a Cossack settlement in 1666 and named after the River Uda. The settlement was developed as a military post and in 1689 became 'Upper Uda' from *verkhne* 'upper'. 'Upper' was added to distinguish it from a completely different town, Nizhne-Udinsk 'Lower Uda' on a different river. When Upper Uda became a town in 1783 the name was changed slightly. This remained in use until 1934. Then the name was changed again with the Buryat word *ulan* 'red', in the ideological sense, and Ude, the Buryat form of Uda.

Ulcinj, MONTENEGRO/SERBIA AND MONTENEGRO
Colchinium, Helcynio, Ulcinium, Elkinion, Dulcigno
Said to have been founded by seafarers from Colchis on the Black Sea who called it Colchinium. The name then gradually evolved into the present one. Occupied by the Ottoman Turks in 1571–1878, the town joined the Principality of Montenegro in 1879.

Ulladulla, NEW SOUTH WALES/AUSTRALIA
A port, the name is derived from an Aboriginal word for 'Safe Harbour'.

Ulster, UK *Ouolountoi, Ulaid*
A province with the Irish name 'Land of the Ulaidh', the people who inhabited the area. The origin of their name is obscure but the present name comes from Ulaidh, the Old Scandinavian genitive -s and the Irish *tír* 'district'. Ulster was a former kingdom, which reached its zenith in the 5th century, and subsequently the northernmost of the four traditional provinces of Ireland. Because the Ulster Unionists refused to accept Home Rule for Ireland, the British government was forced to pass the Government of Ireland Act in 1920 whereby Ireland was partitioned into two self-governing areas, the northern part consisting of six of the nine counties of Ulster (Antrim, Armagh, Down, Fermanagh, Londonderry, and Tyrone; the other three, Cavan, Donegal, and Monaghan, joined the Irish Free State). This new political entity became known as Northern Ireland. In 1921 the Northern Ireland Parliament was inaugurated. Early the following year an Anglo-Irish treaty was ratified, confirming the establishment of the Irish Free State (*see* IRELAND) and Northern Ireland as part of the United Kingdom of Great Britain and Northern Ireland. Northern Ireland is now often referred to as Ulster.

Ulu Dağ, TURKEY
'Big Mountain' from *ulu* 'big' and *dağ*. It is also called Mount Olympus.

Ulundi, KWAZULU-NATAL/SOUTH AFRICA
Once he had become King (1872–9) of the Zulus, Cetshwayo (c.1826–84) chose this location for his new capital which he called *UluNdi* 'The High Place'.

Uluru, NORTHERN TERRITORY/AUSTRALIA
See AYERS ROCK.

Ulverstone, TASMANIA/AUSTRALIA
Surveyed in 1855 and named after Ulverston in England. This means 'Farmstead of a Man called Wulfhere, or Ulfarr', from either an Old English or Old Scandinavian personal name and *tūn*.

Ul'yanovka, LENINGRAD/RUSSIA *Sablino*
Renamed in 1922 after Vladimir Lenin† whose original surname was Ulyanov.

Ul'yanovo, KALININGRAD/RUSSIA *Obruchevo*
Renamed in 1974 after Vladimir Lenin†.

Ul'yanovsk, UL'YANOVSK/RUSSIA *Sinbirsk, Simbirsk*
A region and a city founded in 1648 as a fortress and renamed Simbirsk 'Mountain of Winds' in 1780–1924, a reference to the frequent strong winds coming off the River Volga. Vladimir Lenin†, whose real name was Vladimir Ilich Ulyanov, was born here and on his death in 1924 the city was renamed in his honour. Unusually, the name has not reverted to its pre-Soviet name of Simbirsk.

Ulysses, USA
Three states (Kansas, Nebraska, and Pennsylvania) have places with this name, all after General Ulysses S. Grant (1822–85), President of the USA (1869–77) and commander of the Union forces (1864–5) during the Civil War (1861–5).

Umarkot, SINDH/PAKISTAN
'Fort of Umar' from *kot* 'fort'. It was founded in the 11th century by, and named after, Umar, first king of the Summa dynasty (1050–1350).

Umbria, ITALY
A region named after the pre-Etruscan tribe, the Umbri, who inhabited north-central Italy; they took their name from the River Umbro which may have taken its name from the Greek *ombros* 'heavy rain' or simply 'water'.

Umeå, SWEDEN
Derived from *uma* 'roar', a reference to the sound of the rapids on the Umeå River, and *å* 'river'.

Umm al Qaywayn, UNITED ARAB EMIRATES
A constituent emirate and its capital with a name popularly said to mean 'Mother of the Powers' from the Arabic *umm* 'mother'. However, the rest of the name is a dual suffix with an unknown meaning. It was an important dhow-building centre and these dhows did make Umm al Qaywayn a local sea power.

Umtata, EASTERN CAPE/SOUTH AFRICA
Founded as a European settlement in 1869, its name comes from the name of the river on which it lies; its name is said to mean 'The Taker' because of the considerable damage caused when it floods.

Umzimkulu, KWAZULU-NATAL/SOUTH AFRICA
A town and a river whose Zulu name means 'Great Place' from *umzi* 'place' and *kulu* 'great'. This denoted that a chief lived here.

Umzimvubu, EASTERN CAPE/SOUTH AFRICA
A town and a river whose Zulu name means 'Place of the Hippopotamus' from *umzi* 'place' and (*im*)*vubu* 'hippopotamus'.

Ungheni, MOLDOVA
Derived from the Romanian *ungher* 'corner' or 'nook', a reference to its location in a bend of

the River Prut. The suffix *eni* indicates inhabitants so the name means '(Place of) the People in the Corner'.

Union City, USA
Indiana-Ohio: so named because it lies on the border between the two states.

Union of Soviet Socialist Republics *See* SOVIET UNION.

United Arab Emirates
The United Arab Emirates (al-Imārāt al-'Arabīyah al-Muttaḥidah) since 1971 when a federation of six emirates (Abu Dhabi, 'Ajmān, Dubai, al-Fujairah, Sharjah (ash-Shāriqah), and Umm al Qaywayn) was created; Ra's al-Khaymah joined in 1972. Previously these emirates had been known collectively as the Trucial Coast, and sometimes as the Trucial States or Trucial Oman (because it had been under the nominal control of the Sultan of Oman), after the Treaty of Maritime Peace in Perpetuity had been signed with the UK in 1853. The UK's need to protect its sea routes to India provoked this interest in the Gulf. The name Trucial States comes from the maritime truce agreed in 1835 to renounce piracy during the pearl-diving season and this was later expanded into the Treaty of 1853. British protection and control of the shaikhs' foreign relations were formalized in 1892.

United Kingdom
The United Kingdom of Great Britain and Northern Ireland since 1922 when 'Southern Ireland' achieved independence as the Irish Free State. Previously the United Kingdom of Great Britain and Ireland when the two realms united on 1 January 1801. In 1707 a united Kingdom of Great Britain was established when the Scottish Parliament agreed to dissolve itself so that the Kingdom of the Scots could join the Kingdom of England and Wales. This formal union followed the personal union in 1603 when James VI, King of Scots, had also become James I†, King of England and Wales. The Channel Islands and the Isle of Man are not part of the UK although they belong to the British crown. *See* GREAT BRITAIN.

United States of America
A federal republic consisting of 50 states, 48 contiguous together with Alaska and the island state of Hawaii, and the District of Columbia. The USA was established in 1776 with the declaration of independence by the thirteen original English colonies; this was recognized by the British in 1783. Hawaii was the last state to join the Union in 1959, the same year as Alaska. The names of the states in some cases reflect their history: the influence of England and English royalty in the original thirteen, although of these Connecticut and Massachusetts reveal their association with Native Americans; the early influence of France and Spain is apparent in Vermont, and in the south and west.

Unterwalden, SWITZERLAND
A former canton which, in 1291, was one of the three original Swiss cantons. In 1340 it was split into Nidwalden and Obwalden which became demi-cantons in 1803. The name means 'Below the Forests' from the German *unter* 'below' or 'under' and the plural of *Wald* 'forest', a reference to its location at the foot of the forest slopes of the Bernese Oberland.

Upington, NORTH WEST/SOUTH AFRICA
Olijvenhoutsdrift
Founded as a mission station in 1871 with a name meaning 'Olive Wood Ford', it was renamed in 1884 after Sir Thomas Upington (1845–98), prime minister of Cape Colony (1884–6).

Upper Hutt, NORTH ISLAND/NEW ZEALAND
Founded in 1848 in the Hutt River valley and named after Sir William Hutt (1801–82), one of the original shareholders in the New Zealand Company, who was instrumental in annexing New Zealand to the UK. Lower Hutt lies to the south-west.

Uppsala, SWEDEN *Östra Aros*
'Upper Sala', that is, 'Above Sala', previously a village, from *upp* 'above'. Known until the 13th century as Östra Aros, it was founded as a trading post at the point just east of where the River Fyris becomes navigable; Aros means 'river mouth' from *ar* 'river' and *os* 'mouth'.

Ur, IRAQ
The modern name is Tell al-Muqayyar 'Hill covered in Tar' from the Arabic *tell* 'hill' and *muqayyar* 'tar' or 'pitch', although why this should be so is not clear. Ur was a Sumerian city founded during the 4th millenium BC. The Sumerian characters give the Hebrew word for 'fire', although this is not necessarily the meaning of the ancient name.

Ural, RUSSIA
A river and a mountain range (in Russian, Uralskiy Khrebet) that traditionally marks the boundary between Europe and Asia. The name probably comes from one of the highest peaks, Uraltau 'Ural Mountain'. Ural itself probably comes from a local word for 'mountain'.

Ural'sk (Oral), KAZAKHSTAN *Yaitsky Gorodok*
Founded as a Cossack fortress on the Ural River in 1613 with a name meaning 'Yaik Little Town' because the Ural was then known as the Yaik, which itself may have come from the

Turkic word *yayik* 'river'. When the river was
renamed in 1775 as now after the mountains
in which it rises, so was the town. The river is
also known as the Zhayyq; the great 14th-
century Arab traveller, Ibn Battutah, referred
to it as the Ulusu 'The Great Stream'.

Urawa, HONSHŪ/JAPAN
The characters represent *ura* 'port' and *wa*
'peace'.

Urbana, USA
1. Illinois: settled in 1822 and named after the
city with this name in Ohio.
2. Ohio: laid out in 1805 and called Urbana
after 'urban', thus 'pertaining to a city' and
'urbane' to describe the civility of its
inhabitants.

Urechcha, BELARUS *Urech'ye*
'Beside the Little River' from the Russian *u*
'beside' and *rechka* 'little river' or 'rivulet'.

Urfa, TURKEY
See ŞANLIURFA.

Uri, SWITZERLAND
One of the three German-speaking forest
communities that were founder members of
the Everlasting League in 1291; the others
were Schwyz and Unterwalden. It is now a
canton with a name probably derived from the
Latin *urus* 'aurochs', a wild ox now extinct.

Uroševac (Albanian: Ferizaj), SERBIA/SERBIA
AND MONTENEGRO *Ferizović*
In Kosovo, and therefore also with an Albanian
name. It was renamed after Stephen Uroš II,
King of Serbia (1282–1321), having formerly
beeen named after the 14th-century Turkish
governor.

Uruapan, MICHOACÁN/MEXICO
Founded in 1533 in an area of lush vegetation
with a Tarascan name meaning '(Place) where
the Flowers bloom'.

Uruguay The Oriental Republic of Uruguay
(República Oriental del Uruguay) since 1830
when the new constitution officially founding
the new republic was ratified. The 'oriental'
signified its position on the eastern bank of the
Uruguay River. Previously the territory had
become known as the Banda Oriental del
Uruguay 'East bank of the Uruguay (River)'
(1776–1828), a province of the Spanish
Viceroyalty of Río de la Plata whose capital was
Buenos Aires. In 1814 a struggle with the
Argentinians for independence began and this
led to Banda Oriental being occupied by Brazil
in 1820 and annexed to Brazil the following
year. This was resisted by the Uruguayans who
proclaimed their independence in 1825.
However, this was not recognized until a treaty

was signed between Argentina and Brazil
in 1828 when Uruguay was established as a
buffer state between those two countries.
Called Iperoig by the local Tupinambá tribe,
it took its new name from the Uruguay River.
This name may have come from *uruguá*, the
Guaraní for a species of mussel, thus 'River
of Shellfish', or from *uru*, a type of bird
that lived near the river, *gua* 'to proceed
from', and *y* 'water'. The river forms the
border between Argentina and Uruguay and
a large section of the border between
Argentina and Brazil.

Urumchi (Ürümqi), SINKIANG UIGHUR
AUTONOMOUS REGION/CHINA *Tihwa*
'Beautiful Pastureland' or 'Beautiful
Grasslands' in Mongolian, having been
renamed in 1954 from the Chinese Tihwa,
named in 1763.

Urup, KURIL ISLANDS/RUSSIA
An island with an Ainu name meaning
'Salmon'.

Ushakov Island (Ostrov Ushakova), RUSSIA
Discovered in the Kara Sea in 1935 by, and
named after, Georgy Ushakov (1901–63), an
Arctic polar explorer.

Ushant (Île d'Ouessant), FRANCE *Uxantis/
Uxisama*
The Roman names were derived from the
English *ux* 'high' and a superlative suffix *-isamo*
to give a meaning of 'very high'. Although the
island is rocky it does not have any particularly
high ground. The English name is a version of
the French which is associated with *ouest*
'west'.

Ushkovo, LENINGRAD/RUSSIA
Named after Dmitry Ushkov (1922–44), killed
while fighting near here in 1944.

Ushtobe, KAZAKHSTAN
'Three Hills' from *úsh* 'three' and *töbe* 'hill'.

Üsküdar, TURKEY *Chrysopolis, Skoutarion/Scutari*
The original name meant 'City of Gold'. The
present name may be a Turkish adaptation of
the former name which came from the Latin
scutarii 'shield-makers'; the town made shields
for the imperial army. Alternatively, it has
been suggested that it may be derived from
Eski Dar 'Old House', or simply mean 'Courier'
since it was a message station on the Asian side
of the Bosporus opposite Constantinople (now
Istanbul). See SHKODËR.

Usol'ye, PERM/RUSSIA
Founded in 1606 as a centre for salt production
with a name 'By the Salt' from *u* 'by' and *sol'*
'salt'.

Usol'ye Sibirskoye, IRKUTSK/RUSSIA
As previous entry, connected with the salt
industry with the additional Sibirskoye to
indicate its location in Siberia.

Ussuriysk, PRIMORSKIY TERRITORY/RUSSIA
Nikolskoye, Nikolsk-Ussuriyskiy, Voroshilov
Named after the Ussuri River, although it does
not lie on it. Nikolskoye was founded in 1866
and named after Emperor Nicholas I[†]. It
merged with Ketritsevo in 1898, the name
being changed with the addition of the river's
name. In 1935 it was renamed after Kliment
Voroshilov[†] on the occasion of his promotion
to marshal of the Soviet Union. It was given its
present name in 1957.

Ústí nad Labem, CZECH REPUBLIC *Aussig*
'Mouth on the (River) Labe' from *ústí* 'mouth', a
reference to the place where the Bílina River
flows into the Labe, better known as the
Elbe, and *nad* 'on'. The previous name was
German.

Ust'-Kamenogorsk (Öskemen),
KAZAKHSTAN *Ust'-Kamennaya*
Founded by the Russians as a fortress in 1720
and named after the fact that it was located at
the mouth (in Russian, *ust'ye*) of the
Kamennaya River—its junction with the Irtysh
River. The Kamennaya's name comes from the
Russian *kamen'* 'stone' or 'rock' while the *gorsk*
is associated with *gorod*.

Ust'-Kut, IRKUTSK/RUSSIA
Situated at the junction of the Kut and Lena
Rivers, the name means 'Mouth of the (River)
Kut', its name coming from the Evenki *kuta*
'swamp'.

Ust'ye, KRASNOYARSK TERRITORY/RUSSIA
'Mouth' of a river; it actually lies at the
confluence of the Chuna and Isolka Rivers.

Usulután, EL SALVADOR
A local name said to mean 'City of Ocelots'.

Utah, USA
A Rocky Mountain state with a Navajo name
meaning 'Upper (Land)'. Part of Mexico from
1821, it was ceded to the USA in 1848, a year
after the arrival of the Mormons. They
established their state of Deseret 'Honeybee'
from the Book of Mormon. They applied for
statehood with this name in 1849 but, instead,
it became a Territory with the name Utah after
the Ute tribe. Five more times statehood was
requested, but rejected each time while the
Mormons continued to practise polygamy.
Only in 1896, after polygamy had been
renounced, did Utah join the Union as the 45th
state.

Uthagamandalam, TAMIL NĀDU/INDIA
Ootacamund
Founded by the British in 1821, the previous
name came from the Badaga *Hottaga-mand*, the
name of the site of the 'Stone House', the first
European house erected in this hill station in
the Nilgiri Hills. The station was commonly
known as 'Ooty'. The present name is derived
from the Toda *udhagamandalam* 'village of
huts'.

Utica, TUNISIA, USA
USA (New York): named after the very
ancient Phoenician city in Tunisia, now in
ruins and called Utique, which, after the
destruction of Carthage in 146 BC, became the
new capital of the Roman province of Africa.
The New York name was allegedly drawn from
a hat.

Utrecht, THE NETHERLANDS, SOUTH AFRICA,
SURINAME
1. The Netherlands: a province and a city
founded in 47 by the Romans to protect an
important crossing over the Rhine. Their
name, Trajectum ad Rhenum 'Ford on the
(River) Rhine' came from the Latin *trajectus*
'river crossing'. The name Ultrajectum
which evolved into Ouda Trecht 'Old Ford' and
then into the present name.
2. The towns in South Africa and Suriname
take their names from the Dutch city.

Utsunomiya, HONSHŪ/JAPAN
A town with several old temples, the name is
derived from the characters representing *u*
'roof' or 'house', *tsu* 'capital', *no*, the
possessive, and *miya* 'Shinto temple'. The city
developed around a temple to become a
prefectural administrative capital.

Uttar Pradesh, INDIA *United Provinces of Āgra
and Oudh*
Established as a state in 1950 and renamed
'Northern State' from *uttar* 'northern' and
pradesh.

Uusikaupunki, FINLAND *Nystad*
Both names mean 'New Town'. The Swedish
Nystad was founded by Gustav Adolf II (1594–
1632), King of Sweden (1611–32) with the
present Finnish name being a translation from
uusi 'new' and *kaupunki* 'town'.

Uusimaa, FINLAND *Nylands*
A province until 1998 with both Swedish and
Finnish names meaning 'New Land' from the
Finnish *uusi* 'new' and *maa* 'land'.

Uvalde, TEXAS/USA *Encina*
Settled in 1852 and renamed in 1856 after the
county, whose seat it was. The county was
named after Guan de Ugalde, governor of

Coahuila, the Mexican state adjacent to Texas on the other side of the Rio Grande.

Uxbridge, CANADA, UK, USA
1. Canada (Ontario): named after the town in England.
2. UK (England): formerly Wixebrug 'Bridge of the Wixan Tribe' from the Old English tribal name and *brycg*.

Uxmal, YUCATÁN/MEXICO
Mayan ruins. Occupied between *c*.600 and 900, the name means 'Thrice Built', although it was in fact rebuilt four times, or 'Thrice Occupied'. However, it has also been suggested that it may mean 'Place of Abundant Harvests'.

Uyar, KRASNOYARSK TERRITORY/RUSSIA *Olginsk*
Previously named after the Grand Duchess Olga Nikolayevna (1895–1918), the eldest daughter of Emperor Nicholas II†, who was murdered with the rest of her family in 1918.

Uyedineniya Island (Ostrov Uyedineniya), RUSSIA
An island discovered in the Kara Sea in 1878 with a name meaning 'isolated' from *uyedinënnyy* 'solitary', 'secluded', or 'lonely'—which it is.

Uzbekistan The Republic of Uzbekistan (Üzbekiston Respublikasi) since 1991 when independence was forced upon the Soviet Central Asian republics. Previously the Uzbek Soviet Socialist Republic when created by the Soviet Union in 1924 from part of the Turkestan Autonomous Soviet Socialist Republic (until 1929 it included what is now Tajikistan); the Uzbek Emirate of Bukhara and the Khanates of Khiva and Kokand (18th century) until conquered by the Russians in 1868–76 when the first two became protectorates and Kokand was abolished and its territory absorbed into the Russian Empire. The country is named after the Uzbeks, a general name for the Turkic-speaking peoples of the region. Descendants of the nomadic tribes of the Golden Horde who settled here in the 15th and 16th centuries, they are said to have taken their name from Sultan Muhammad Uzbek or Öz Beg, a 14th-century Mongol khan of the Golden Horde who ruled between 1313 and 1340. It was known as Transoxiana to Ptolemy† and to the Arab conquerors of the Sāssānians as Mā Warā' an-Nahr 'Land beyond the River', both a reference to the Oxus (now Amu Darya). The area around the Zeravshan Valley in ancient times was known as Sogdiana. There are three Uzbek exclaves in *Kyrgyzstan.

Uzhgorod (Uzhhorod), UKRAINE *Ungvár*
'Town on the (River) Uzh' from *gorod*, although the previous Hungarian name meant 'Fortress on the (River) Ung', that being the Hungarian version of the river's name with *vár*. It was part of Austria-Hungary until it passed to Czechoslovakia in 1919 after the creation of that country. It passed to Hungary in 1938 and back to Czechoslovakia again temporarily in 1945 before being taken by the Soviet Union that same year.

Uzlovaya, TULA/RUSSIA
Taken from *uzel* 'junction' or 'centre', a reference to the fact that it is a railway junction.

u

Vaal, SOUTH AFRICA
A river with an Afrikaans name meaning 'grey', a reference to the muddy colour of its water when it floods during the winter.

Vaasa, FINLAND *Korsholm, Vasa, Nikolainkaupunki*
Refounded in 1606 by Charles IX (1550–1611), King of Sweden (1604–11), and given the name of the reigning dynasty, Vasa. In 1917 the name was changed to Nikolainkaupunki 'Nicholas's Town' after Emperor Nicholas II† from the personal name and *kaupunki* 'town'. Finland at that time was part of the Russian Empire. Later the same year Finland declared independence and the Finnish form of Vasa was adopted.

Vacaville, CALIFORNIA/USA
'Cow Town', a reference to the large number of cattle in the area from the Spanish *vaca* 'cow'.

Vadodara, GUJARĀT/INDIA *Vadapadraka, Chandanavati, Varāvati, Vatpatraka, Baroda*
All the names are derived from the Sanskrit *vaṭodar*, itself from *vaṭa* 'banyan tree', except for Chandanavati when the city was named after Raja Chandan. It assumed its present name in 1971.

Vaduz, LIECHTENSTEIN
Evolved from Valdutsch from the Latin *vallis* 'valley' and the Old German *Dutsch* 'German'. It is situated in the Rhine valley and is the capital of Liechtenstein.

Vakrushev, SAKHALIN ISLAND/RUSSIA
Named after Vasily Vakrushev (1902–47), people's commissar of the coal industry from 1939. The town in Ukraine, Vakrushevo, is named after the same man.

Valais (German: **Wallis**; Italian: **Vallese**), SWITZERLAND *Vallis Poenina*
A canton from 1815 deriving its name from the Latin *vallis* 'valley', the original name meaning 'Upper Rhône Valley'.

Valdemarpils, LATVIA
Named after Valdemar II (1170–1241), King of Denmark (1202–41), to mean 'Valdemar's Palace' from *pils* 'palace'.

Valdivia, CHILE, COLOMBIA, SPAIN
Chile: founded in 1552 by, and named after, Pedro de Valdivia (c.1498–1554), a Spanish conquistador who was governor of Chile at the time.

Val-d'Or, QUEBEC/CANADA
Founded in 1934 as 'Valley of Gold' in French. Although gold is mined here there is no valley.

Valdosta, GEORGIA/USA
Named after the Georgian governor's plantation, Valle d'Aosta, itself the name of a region in Italy.

Valencia, HONDURAS, SPAIN, TRINIDAD, USA, VENEZUELA
1. Spain (Valencia): an autonomous community (in Spanish, Comunidad Valenciana), a city and a former kingdom. Founded as Valentia in 138 BC for Lusitanian military veterans, the Roman name, Valentia Edetanorum 'Fortified Town of the Edetani', came from the tribal name and the Latin *valens* 'strong' or 'powerful'. The Arabic name was Medina bu-Tarab 'City of Joy'.
2. Venezuela: founded in 1555 as Nueva Valencia del Rey 'New Valencia of the King' by Alonso Diaz Moreno who came from the Spanish city of Valencia.

Valenciennes, NORD-PAS-DE-CALAIS/FRANCE
Believed to be named after Valentinian I (321–75), Roman emperor (364–75); based in Paris and Amiens, he directed operations against the Alemanni invading Gaul. It has also been suggested, however, that the name comes from *val des cygnes* 'valley of the swans' because swans appear on the city's coat-of-arms.

Valladolid, MEXICO, SPAIN
1. Mexico (Yucatán): formerly Zací and renamed after the Spanish city.
2. Spain (Castile-León): formerly the Moorish Valad-Olid and Balad-Ulid 'Town of Olid', who may have been the city's Moorish governor.

Valle d'Aosta, ITALY
A region. *See* AOSTA.

Vallejo, CALIFORNIA/USA
The area was offered by General Mariano G. Vallejo, a Mexican officer, in 1850 as the site of a new state capital for California. Named after him, it only acted as such for brief periods in 1852 and 1853.

Valletta, MALTA
Named after Jean Parisot de la Valette (1494–1568), French Grand Master of the Order of the Knights of St John, who built the town after the Ottoman Turkish siege of 1565. It became Malta's capital in 1570.

Valmiera, LATVIA *Wolmar*
Renamed from the German after Valdemar II (1170–1241), King of Denmark (1202–41).

Valparaiso, BRAZIL, CHILE, COLOMBIA, MEXICO, USA
1. Chile: a region and a city founded in 1536 by the Spanish conquistador, Juan de Saavedra, who named it after his birthplace in Spain. The name means 'Valley of Paradise' from the Spanish *valle* 'valley' and *paraíso* 'paradise', a reference to its attractive location.
2. USA (Indiana): founded in 1836 as Portersville, but subsequently renamed after the city in Chile.

Van, TURKEY, USA
Turkey: a lake, Van Gölü, named after the city of the same name on its eastern shore. The original name was Tushpa or Turushpa, the city being the capital of Urartu (*see* ARMENIA). It was renamed Bouana from the Persian *hane* 'settlement' from which the present name has evolved.

Vanadzor, ARMENIA *Karaklis, Kirovakan*
The name comes from Vankadzor, itself from *vank* 'church' and *dzor* 'gorge'; there were many churches in the gorge in which Vanadzor lies. The first name was a version of Karakilise 'Black Church' from the Turkish *kara* and *kilise* 'church'. The town was renamed Kirovakan in 1935–92 after Sergey Kirov[†] and *akan* 'mine' or 'ditch'.

Van Buren, USA
Five states have places with this name, all after Martin Van Buren (1782–1862), President of the USA (1837–41) and one of the founders of the Democratic Party.

Vancouver, CANADA, USA
1. Canada (British Columbia): settled as Granville in 1867, it was renamed in 1886 after Vancouver Island, first discovered by Captain James Cook[†] in 1778 but surveyed by, and named after, Captain George Vancouver[†] who had surveyed this part of the Pacific coast of North America in 1792 and visited the present site of the city.
2. USA (Washington): founded in 1824 as Fort Vancouver, a Hudson's Bay Company trading post named after Captain George Vancouver[†].

Vanderbijlpark, GAUTENG/SOUTH AFRICA
Founded in 1942 as a steel-producing centre, it is named after Dr Hendrik Johannes van der

Bijl (1887–1948), who helped to lay it out. The suffix *park* was added to bring attention to its 'garden' layout.

Vannes, BRITTANY/FRANCE
Named after the Veneti, a Gaulish tribe whose centre this was.

Vanua Levu, FIJI *Sandalwood Island*
Sighted by Abel Tasman[†] in 1643, it is Fiji's second largest island with a name meaning 'Great Land' from the Polynesian *vanua* 'land' and *levu* 'great'.

Vanuatu *New Hebrides*
The Republic of Vanuatu (Bislama: Ripablik blong Vanuatu) since 1980. The first European to discover the islands in 1606 was a Portuguese navigator, Pedro Fernández de Quirós, who named the largest island Espiritu Santo 'Holy Spirit'. They were rediscovered by the French in 1768 and charted by Captain James Cook[†] in 1774; he named them after the Scottish New Hebrides because of their fancied resemblance. Anglo-French rivalry resulted in the establishment of an Anglo-French Condominium in 1906. Independence was gained in 1980 at which time the name was changed to Vanuatu 'Our Land Forever' from the Polynesian/Fijian *vanua* 'land'.

Vapnyarka, UKRAINE
'(Place where) Limestone (is extracted)' from *vapno* 'lime'. There is no word *yarka* in Ukrainian, but it gives the sense here of a place associated with limestone.

Vārānasi, UTTAR PRADESH/INDIA *Kāshī, Banaras/ Benares, Muhammadābād*
The original name meant 'Luminous' or 'Resplendent', thus '(City of) Light' from the Sanskrit *kas*. Kāshī was also a kingdom and may have been the name of an ancient Aboriginal tribe. The present name means 'City between Two Rivers', the Varuana and the Asi. The Pali version of its ancient Hindu name was Bārānasi which gave Banaras which was corrupted by the British to Benares. Vārānasi was officially adopted in 1956. While subject to Muslim Mughal rule between the 13th and 16th centuries it was called Muhammadābād 'City of Muhammad'. An independent kingdom during the 18th century, the British made it a state in 1910.

Vardzia, GEORGIA
A famous cave-city with a name that may be derived from 'Ak var, dzia' 'Here I am, uncle'. According to legend, this was the call made by Tamar, daughter of King George III (12th century), when she was lost in the cave complex here.

Varna, BULGARIA, RUSSIA
1. Bulgaria: may be derived from the Slavonic root word *vran* 'the black one' from the fact that it is located on the Black Sea. Founded as the Greek city-state of Odessos in 585 BC, it came under Thracian, Macedonian, and Roman rule before becoming part of the First Bulgarian Empire and adopting its present name in 681. In 1391–1878 it was under Ottoman Turkish rule. It was renamed Stalin after Joseph Stalin[†] in 1949–56.
2. Russia (Chelyabinsk); named after the Varna in Bulgaria where the Russians won a famous victory over the Turks in 1828.

Varnavino, NIZHNIY NOVGOROD/RUSSIA
Named after a 15th-century monk, Varnava 'Barnabas', who with the help of others built a monastery here.

Varnek, NENETS AUTONOMOUS DISTRICT/RUSSIA
Takes its name from the bay which was discovered by, and named after, Alexander Varnek (1858–1930), an explorer.

Vasil'sursk, NIZHNIY NOVGOROD/RUSSIA *Vasilgorod*
Founded in 1523 during the reign of Vasily III (1479–1533), Grand Prince of Muscovy (1505–33), it was originally named 'Vasily's Town'. This was changed later to indicate that it lay on the Sura River.

Västerås, SWEDEN *Aros, Västra Aros*
'Western River Mouth' from *väster* 'western', *å* 'river', and *os* 'mouth'. The original site was to the west of the mouth of the River Svart where it flows into Lake Mälar.

Vatican City The Vatican City (Italian: Città del Vaticano) since 1929 when the Italian government recognized the Vatican City's independence and papal sovereignty in the Lateran Treaty and established the Vatican City State. It is the smallest state in the world and is an enclave within the city of Rome. The treaty also delineated the territorial extent of the temporal power of the Holy See. This is the seat of the Pope and is the term used to describe the government of the Roman Catholic Church by the Pope and his associates. The Vatican stands on Vatican Hill (not one of the 'seven hills' of Rome) whose Latin name was *Mons Vaticanus* from *vaticinator* 'prophet' or 'soothsayer'. The soothsayers were located here in Roman times and the hill took its name from them.

Vatnajökull, ICELAND
A huge ice cap called 'Lake Glacier' from *vatn* 'lake' and *jökull* 'glacier'.

Vatomandry, MADAGASCAR
'Rock that sleeps', in all probability because of some rock formation that resembles the prone body of a person.

Vättern, SWEDEN
A lake, Lake Vätter, with a name simply meaning 'Water' from *vatten*.

Vatutin, UKRAINE *Vatutino*
Founded in 1949 and named after Nikolay Vatutin (1901–44), commander of the 1st Ukrainian Front who received severe wounds, from which he later died, during an ambush by Ukrainian nationalist partisans in February 1944.

Vaud (German: **Waadt**), SWITZERLAND
A canton since 1803 whose name may be derived from what the inhabitants were called by their neighbours, *walho* 'strangers'.

Växjö, SWEDEN
Named for its location where *väg* '(trading) routes' met on a *sjö* 'lake', Lake Växjö.

Vejle, DENMARK *Wæthlæ*
Derived from *vadested* 'wading place' or 'ford'.

Veles, MACEDONIA *Bilazor/Bylazora, Veles, Kuprili, Titov Veles*
'God of Horned Animals'. The ancient Bilazor was seized by Philip V (238–179 BC), King of Macedonia (221–179 BC) in 217 BC, subsequently falling to the Romans and then the Slavs who renamed it Veles. When the Ottoman Turks took the town in 1395 they changed the name to Kuprili 'bridge' because by that time the town had spread to both sides of the River Vardar and a bridge spanned it. With the departure of the Turks in 1912 Veles was readopted, but in 1947–92 'Titov' was added to the town's name in honour of Marshal Tito[†].

Velikaya, RUSSIA
Two towns and two rivers have this name from the feminine of *velikiy* 'big'.

Velikiye Luki, PSKOV/RUSSIA
Founded in 1166 as 'Big Bends' from *velikiy* 'big' and *luka* 'bend in a river', a reference to the town's position on a bend in the Lovat River; it should therefore really be called 'Big Bend' in the singular.

Velikiy Ustyug, VOLOGDA/RUSSIA
At the mouth of the Yug River where it flows into the Sukhona, the second part of the name means 'Mouth of the (River) Yug'. *Velikiy* 'big' presumably contrasts with some other place which is smaller while *yug* means 'south'.

Veliko Tŭrnovo, BULGARIA *Tŭrnovo*
Veliko 'great' was added in 1965 to give 'Great Place of Thorns' from *trn* 'thorn'. It was the

capital of the Second Bulgarian Empire (1185–1396).

Velingrad, BULGARIA
Founded in 1948 with the amalgamation of three villages and named after Vela Peeva (1922–44), a Resistance heroine who was betrayed and executed; she was born here.

Venda, LIMPOPO/SOUTH AFRICA
A former independent homeland between 1979 and 1994 for the Venda people after whom it is named.

Veneto, ITALY
A region named after the pre-Roman Veneti people.

Venezuela, AND BONAIRE
The Bolivarian Republic of Venezuela (República Bolivariana de Venezuela) since 1830. It did not become a separate nation until 1830 although it declared independence in 1811. Previously the territory was a part of the Republic of Gran Colombia (1821–30) and the Viceroyalty of New Granada (1717–1821), becoming the Captaincy General of Venezuela in 1777 and the Audiencia of Venezuela in 1786. Christopher Columbus[†] was the first European to step ashore in 1498, naming the Península de Paria the Isla de García. The following year a Spanish expedition, led by Alonso de Ojeda and Amerigo Vespucci (1454–1512), discovered Lake Maracaibo. They named the area 'Little Venice' because on the lakeside, built out over the water, was a Native American village comprising thatched huts on stilts. This brought to mind the Italian city of Venice, hence the name.

Venice, ITALY, USA
Italy (Veneto): Italian Venezia. Named after Veneti tribes who withdrew into the lagoon under the onslaught of barbarian invasions in the 5th century. In 697 it became a republic which lasted until 1797 when it came under Austrian domination. It joined Italy in 1866.

Venlo, THE NETHERLANDS
Lying along the River Meuse, the name means 'Place in the Marsh' from *veen* 'marsh' or 'peat bog'.

Ventersdorp, NORTH WEST/SOUTH AFRICA
Founded in 1866 on a farm belonging to Joannes Venter and named after him with the Afrikaans *dorp* 'village'.

Ventimiglia, LIGURIA/ITALY *Albium Intemelium/ Albinitmulium*
Literally, it appears to mean 'Twenty Miles', but in fact this is a corruption of its original Roman name, that of a Ligurian tribe.

Ventspils, LATVIA *Windau, Vindava*
Founded in 1242 and named after the Venta River to give 'Castle on the Venta' from *pils* 'castle'. The previous Russian name, used in 1721–1918, was derived from the earlier German name, itself connected to that of the river, whose meaning is not known.

Ventura, CALIFORNIA/USA
'Good Fortune' in Spanish.

Veracruz, MEXICO, NICARAGUA, PANAMA
1. 'True Cross' in Spanish.
2. Mexico: founded in 1519 during Holy Week by Hernán Cortés[†] who originally named it La Villa Rica de la Vera Cruz 'The Rich Town of the True Cross', a reference to the cross of the Crucifixion. Veracruz-Llave is a state named in honour of General Ignacio de la Llave, governor of the state (1857–60).

Verdun, CANADA, FRANCE, URUGUAY
1. Canada (Quebec): given in 1672 to its French military governor, Zacharie Dupuis, who named it after Saverdun, his birthplace in France.
2. France (Lorraine): a shortening of the Roman name Virodunum 'Vero's Fort' from a Gaulish personal name and *dunu* 'fort'.

Vereeniging, GAUTENG/SOUTH AFRICA
Founded in 1882 after coal had been discovered here in 1878. Its name, which means 'Association' or 'Union', was the last word in the title of the Dutch company created to mine the coal.

Vereshchagino, RUSSIA *Ocherskaya, Voznesenskaya*
Perm: founded in 1898 and renamed Voznesenskaya from *Voznesenie* 'Ascension' after the dedication of its church. It was renamed again in 1915 after Vasily Vereshchagin (1842–1904), a war artist who participated in the conquest of Central Asia, in the Russo-Turkish War (1877–8) and the Russo-Japanese War (1904–5) and was well-known for his painting of battle scenes.

Verkhnedneprovsk, UKRAINE
Founded in 1780 as 'Upper Dnieper' from *verkhne* 'upper' and the River Dnepr. Although actually 'lower' Dnieper because the town is closer to the mouth of the river than its source, it was given this name because it was above some rapids. A number of other towns start with *Verkhne-, Verkhnaya,* or *Verkhniy,* many being located on rivers, e.g.Verkhnedvinsk, Verkhnaya Tura, and Verkhniy Ufaley.

V

Verkhneural'sk, CHELYABINSK/RUSSIA
Verkhneyaitsk
'Upper Ural' since it was founded as a military
post on the upper reaches of the Ural River in
1734 from *verkhne* 'upper'. It was renamed in
1775 when the river's name was changed from
the Yaik River.

Vermillion, USA
South Dakota: a city which takes its name
from the river. It gets its name from the
vermilion-coloured clay along its banks. There
are cities spelt Vermilion in both Canada and
the USA.

Vermont, USA
A state called 'Green Mountain' from the
French *vert* 'green' and *mont*; part of the
Appalachians are called the Green Mountains
because the trees are coniferous. The French
were the first Europeans to settle in 1666, but
the area passed to the British in 1763 at the
end of the Seven Years' War (1756–63). The
year after the American Revolution began in
1776 the people of Vermont declared their
territory to be the independent Republic of
New Connecticut. Later adopting the name
Vermont, this independence was retained
until the republic joined the Union as the 14th
state in 1791.

Vernon, CANADA, FRANCE, USA
Canada (British Columbia): because of the
presence of a missionary station it attracted
the name Priest's Valley and then Forge Valley
in recognition of its blacksmiths. In 1885 it
was renamed Centreville, the name of the
original site, and in 1887 Vernon after Forbes
G. Vernon, the contemporary provincial
commissioner of land and works.

Verona, CANADA, ITALY, USA
Italy (Veneto): formerly Vernomago 'Field of
Elder Trees' from the Celtic *verno* 'elder tree'
and *mago* 'field'.

Verulam, KWAZULU-NATAL/SOUTH AFRICA
Founded in 1850 and named after Lord
Robert Grimston (1816–84), 1st Earl of
Verulam, who sponsored some Methodist
settlers to come here from St Albans in
England. The Roman name of St Albans was
Verulamium.

Vesoul, FRANCHE-COMTÉ/FRANCE *Vesulium*
Derived from the Celtic *ves* 'mountain'. This
refers to the single conical hill, La Motte 'The
Height', nearby.

Vestmannaeyjar, ICELAND
An island group and their capital town,
meaning 'Islands of the Western Men' from

vestan 'western', *mann* 'man', and *eyjar*
'islands', the plural of *ey*.

Vesuvius (Vesuvio), CAMPANIA/ITALY
A volcano with a name said to come from an
Indo-European root *aues* 'to illuminate' or *eus*
'to burn' or 'to set on fire', a reference to its
volcanic activity.

Veszprém, HUNGARY
A county and a town named after Bezbriem or
Bezprím, a Polish prince.

Viareggio, TUSCANY/ITALY
Derived from the Latin *via* 'way' or 'road' and
regia 'straight' or 'direct' to describe the route
along the coastline in the vicinity.

Viborg, DENMARK, USA
Denmark: formerly Wibergum and Vvibiærgh
'Sacred Hill' from *wii* 'sacred' and *bjerg*, thus
borg 'hill', a reference to the fact that it was
once a centre of pagan worship and sacrifice,
and later of Christianity.

Vicente López, ARGENTINA
Now a part of Buenos Aires, the name is a
tribute to Vicente López (1815–1903) who
wrote the country's national anthem.

Vicenza, VENETO/ITALY *Vicetia/Vicentia*
A province and a city whose present name has
evolved from the Latin Vicetia or Vicentia
which may be derived from the Latin *vicus*
'settlement' and *et* referring to the Veneti
people.

Vichy, AUVERGNE/FRANCE *Vicus Calidus*
Derived from its Latin name meaning 'Warm
Settlement', a reference to its alkaline springs,
from *vicus* 'settlement'. It was capital of Vichy
France, also known as the French State,
between July 1940 to September 1944. This
was under nominal French sovereignty
(although its leaders collaborated with Nazi
Germany) while the rest of France was
occupied by the Germans. The inhabitants of
the town are known as *Vichyssois* while the
supporters of the wartime regime were
called *Vichystes*. Bottled Vichy water is
known internationally as is *Crème Vichyssoise*,
a thick soup created by the French chef of a
New York hotel in 1910 and usually served
cold.

Vicksburg, USA
Mississippi: after a short stay by the French a
Spanish military post called Nogales was
constructed here in 1790; it was renamed
Walnut Hills later. Around this a town grew
which was named after Newitt Vick, a
Methodist minister.

Victoria, AFRICA, ANTARCTICA, ARGENTINA, AUSTRALIA, BURMA, CANADA, CHILE, CHINA (HONG KONG), GRENADA, GUINEA, HONDURAS, MALAYSIA, NORWAY, PAPUA NEW GUINEA, PHILIPPINES, ROMANIA, RUSSIA, SEYCHELLES, USA
1. A land in Antarctica, a state in Australia, cities, towns, islands, lakes, mountains, rivers, and waterfalls have this name. Many are named after Queen Victoria[†].
2. Australia: a state. Part of the colony of New South Wales, it was hived off in 1851 to become a colony in its own right named after the queen. It became a state when the Commonwealth of Australia was established in 1901.
3. Canada (British Columbia): founded as a Hudson's Bay Company fur trading post in 1843 called Fort Camosun, it was subsequently renamed Fort Victoria in honour of the queen.
4. East Africa: a large lake called by the locals Ukerewe (which is now the name of an island within the lake) before it was given the name Victoria in honour of the queen by John Hanning Speke (1827–64), a British explorer who was the first European to see the lake in 1858 and the first to realize that it was the source of the White Nile. It is also called Victoria Nyanza from the Bantu *nyanza* 'lake'.
5. Seychelles: founded in 1841 as Port Victoria after the queen, the 'Port' later being dropped.
6. USA (Texas): founded in 1824 by the Spanish and so named as a tribute to Guadalupe Victoria (1786–1843), the first Mexican president (1824–9). He changed his name from Manuel Félix Fernández to honour Our Lady of Guadalupe, the patron saint of Mexico.
7. Zambia-Zimbabwe: waterfalls on the Zambezi River locally called Mosi-oa-Tunya 'The Smoke that thunders'. The first European to discover them, in 1855, was David Livingstone (1813–73), the Scottish explorer; he named them in honour of Queen Victoria.

Victoriaville, QUEBEC/CANADA *Demersville*
Originally named after a French bishop, the town was renamed in 1861 after Queen Victoria[†] while retaining the French *ville*.

Vidnoye, MOSCOW/RUSSIA
'Visible', 'Conspicuous', or 'Prominent' from *vidnyy*.

Viedma, ARGENTINA
Named in 1878 after Francisco de Viedma, a Spanish explorer who built a fort here in 1779 called Mercedes de Patagones 'Mercies of the Patagonians'.

Vienna, AUSTRIA, CANADA, USA
Austria: Wien in German and Bécs in Hungarian. Fortified early in the 1st century

AD and home at first to the 13th Legion, the Roman name Vindobona was probably derived from the Celtic Vindomina 'White Fort' from *vindo* 'white', referring to the splendour of the city and its location. Subsequently it was called Wenia and Wienis before assuming its present German name of Wien. It was the capital of the Holy Roman Empire (1558–1806), of the Austrian Empire (1806–67), of the Austro-Hungarian Empire (1867–1918), and of the Republic of Austria since 1918. It is also a state. It has given its name to the Vienna Convention on Diplomatic Relations signed in 1961.

Vientiane (Viangchan), LAOS
'Sandalwood City'. Vientiane is the French transliteration of the local name from *viang* 'city' or 'town' and *chan* 'sandalwood'. It was the capital in 1520–45 and then from 1560 to the present day, being moved from Louangphrabang because of the threat from the Burmese.

Vietnam (Việt Nam) *Van Lang, Au Lac, Nam Viet, Giao Chi, Giao Chau, Annam, Dai Viet, Dai Co Viet*
The Socialist Republic of Vietnam (Cộng Hòa Xã Hội Chủ Nghĩa Việt Nam) since 1976. Some 5 000 years ago the legendary name was Van Lang. In the 3rd century BC Au Lac was established when Van Lang united with the neighbouring Kingdom of Thuc. This was a kingdom of the Viet who took their name from a former principality in southern China. *Viet* is the Vietnamese pronunciation of a Chinese character meaning 'beyond' or 'far' and referred to the peoples living in the southern reaches of the Chinese Empire and the Red River delta. In 208 BC Au Lac came under the control of a renegade Chinese military commander who established the independent kingdom of Nam Viet 'Southern Viet' and known to the Chinese as Nan Yue with the same meaning; this covered part of present-day southern China and northern Vietnam. In 111 BC Chinese armies swept south to conquer the kingdom and capture the Red River delta. Nam Viet became a Chinese province called Giao Chi and later Giao Chau. In 679 the Chinese renamed it the General Protectorate of °Annam. Vietnam gained its independence after a millennium of Chinese rule in 939 and Emperor Dinh Bo Linh (d. 979) renamed it Dai Viet. In 968, by which time Dinh Bo Linh had taken control of all Dai Viet, he renamed it Dai Co Viet 'Great Viet' but Dai Viet was restored in 1054. When Nguyen Anh (1762–1820), emperor as Gia Long (1802–20), founded the last Vietnamese dynasty (1802–1945) in 1802 the name Nam Viet was adopted again, but it was inverted the following year and for the first time the country was called

V

Vietnam. In 1858–73 the French conquered Vietnam and divided it into three regions: the protectorates of Tonkin (northern Vietnam) and Annam (central), and the colony of Cochinchina (southern), which the Vietnamese called Bac Bo, Trung Bo, and Nam Bo respectively. Vietnam as a state ceased to exist. In 1945 the Vietnamese declared their independence and the establishment of the Democratic Republic of Vietnam (DRV). French forces, however, returned and the following year the Republic was recognized as a Free State within the French Union; in 1949 it was entitled the Associated State of Vietnam while the Communist world continued to call it the DRV. In 1954 France relinquished control and Vietnam was split along the 17th parallel into North Vietnam (Democratic Republic of Vietnam) and South Vietnam (State of Vietnam). South Vietnam was declared a republic in 1955 when the powerless Bao Dai (1913–97), emperor (1926–45, 1949–55), was deposed. The two countries were reunited in 1976.

Vigevano, LOMBARDY/ITALY
'Gebwin's Settlement' from the Latin *vicus* 'settlement' and a possibly Germanic personal name such as Gebwin.

Vigo, GALICIA/SPAIN *Vicus Spacorum*
A city-port with a name derived from *vicus*.

Vijayanagar, KARNĀTAKA/INDIA
Ruins. 'City of Victory' from the Sanskrit *vijaya* and *nagar*. The Hindu Kingdom of Vijayanagar came into existence in 1336 as a bulwark against Muslim invaders from the north. When Prince Harihara defeated the Hoysalas in 1343 he founded the city as his capital. In 1565, however, Muslim forces destroyed the city. The village of Hampi now incorporates part of the ruins.

Vila do Conde, PORTUGAL
'Town of the Count' from *vila* 'town' and *conde* 'count'.

Vila Machado, MOZAMBIQUE *Nova Fontesvila/ Bamboo Creek*
Founded in 1898 and named after Fontes Pereira de Melo, a Portuguese marquis; at the same time it enjoyed the English name of Bamboo Creek. It was subsequently renamed after General Joaquim Machado (1847–1925), Portuguese governor of Mozambique (1914– 15).

Vila Real, PORTUGAL *Panois*
Founded in the 13th century and later renamed 'Royal Town' from *vila* 'town' and *real* 'royal' after it was bestowed upon the Portuguese Queen Isabella (*c*.1428–96), wife of

King John II of Castile, and granted royal privileges by Afonso III (1210–79), King of Portugal (1248–79).

Vila Vasco da Gama, MOZAMBIQUE
Founded in 1924 and named after Vasco da Gama (1460–1524), the famous Portuguese navigator, who on his first two voyages to India made landfalls on the Mozambican coast.

Vila Velha, ESPÍRITO SANTO/BRAZIL
'Old Town' from the Portuguese *vila* 'town' and *velha* 'old'. It was settled in 1535.

Villahermosa, TABASCO/MEXICO *Villa Felipe II, San Juan de Villa Hermosa, Villahermosa de San Juan Bautista*
Founded by the Spanish in 1596 and originally named 'Philip II Town' after Philip II (1527– 98), King of Spain (1556–98). It became the 'Beautiful City of St John the Baptist' and received its present name 'Beautiful City' from *hermosa* 'beautiful' in 1915.

Villavicencio, COLUMBIA
Founded in 1840 and named after Antonio Villavicencio (1775–1816) who was a keen activist in the movement for independence from Spain.

Villaviciosa, ASTURIAS/SPAIN *Tierra de Maliayo*
A fishing port, it was originally called 'Bad Land' since it was not well suited to building works. This took on a new meaning and the port was renamed Villaviciosa 'Town of Vices' from *viciosa* 'depraved'.

Villedieu-les-Poêles, LOWER NORMANDY/ FRANCE
Literally 'City of God—the Frying Pans' from *poêle* 'frying pan'. For nearly a thousand years it has been noted for its metal working, including cooking utensils.

Villefranche, FRANCE
Several towns have this name 'Free Town' from *ville* and *franche* 'free' or 'open', some with a qualifying addition to indicate their location, e.g. Villefranche-sur-Saône. The title denoted a town with special tax exemptions.

Vilnius, LITHUANIA *Vilna, Wilno*
Located at the point where the Vilnya River from *vilnis* 'wave', from which it is named, flows into the Viliya River (called by the Lithuanians the Neris). According to legend, while hunting in the area, the Lithuanian ruler Gediminas (*c*.1275–1341) had a dream about an iron wolf which howled loudly and continuously. The next morning Gediminas asked a mystic in his entourage the meaning of his dream. It was that Gediminas should build an impregnable city here. He did so and the city became the capital of the Grand Duchy of

Lithuania in 1323. However, there is little doubt that the site had been occupied at least 400 years earlier. The city came under Russian rule with the name Vilna in 1655–60 and 1795–1918, under Polish rule as Wilno in 1920–39, and under German rule in 1941–4; it was subject to Soviet rule in 1944–91. It was restored as the capital of Lithuania in 1940.

Vinh, VIETNAM
Situated on the coast, the name means 'bay'.

Vinnitsa (Vinnytsya), UKRAINE
A province and a city founded in 1363 as a fortress by the Lithuanians. The province is mainly agricultural and the name probably derives from *vino* 'wine'.

Virgin Islands, UK, USA *Santa Ursula y las Once Mil Virgines*
1. The island group is divided between the UK and the USA as the British Virgin Islands and the Virgin Islands of the United States respectively. Christopher Columbus[†] landed on St Croix on 21 October 1493, the feast day of the possibly 4th-century St Ursula (but no longer in the universal calendar). She was martyred with her companions in Cologne, Germany. Columbus called the group 'St Ursula and the 11 000 (Martyred) Virgins'. The island, believed to be the largest, was named St Ursula, but it has never appeared on any map. The figure of 11 000 does not suggest the number of islands in the group but the number of virgins mentioned in the legend. It is almost certainly incorrect, the Latin *XI MV* being taken to mean *undecim millia virgines* '11 000 virgins' rather than *undecim martyres virgines* 'eleven virgin martyrs'. A European struggle for domination began in the 17th century but it was not until the 18th that the islands could be said to have fallen into two political groups: Danish and English.
2. UK: an Overseas Territory, having been a colony and in 1872–1956 part of the Colony of the Leeward Islands; the (British) islands were annexed to the Leeward Islands in 1672.
3. USA: an organized unincorporated territory previously known as the Danish West Indies. Settled by the Dutch, English, and French who sold the (American) islands to the Danes in 1733. They sold them to the USA in 1917.

Virginia, AUSTRALIA, IRELAND, SOUTH AFRICA, USA
1. South Africa (Free State): named by American surveyors in 1890, probably after their home state, for what was to become a railway halt in this gold-mining area.
2. USA: a state and Britain's first American colony founded in 1607 and named after Queen Elizabeth I[†], the so-called virgin queen

of England. In 1624 the Virginia Company's colony passed to the British crown. It was the tenth state to join the Union in 1788. It seceded in 1861 (although the western part refused to; *see* WEST VIRGINIA) but rejoined in 1870. After the first English settlements were established the name was applied to the whole coast of North America.

Virovitica, CROATIA *Wereuche*
'Place close to the Whirlpool' from *vir* 'whirlpool' or 'spring', *ovit*, an adjectival suffix indicating something nearby, and another suffix *ica* usually associated with river names. The town lies in the Drava Valley on the Odžin Potok 'Stream'.

Virpazar, MONTENEGRO/SERBIA AND MONTENEGRO
'Whirlpool Bazaar' from the Serbo-Croat *vir* 'whirlpool' and *pazar* 'bazaar'. It is an important market town.

Virunga, DEMOCRATIC REPUBLIC OF THE CONGO-UGANDA
Mountains with a Swahili name meaning 'Volcanoes'. The name is also spelt Birunga. In Uganda the name M'fumbiro 'That which cooks' is used.

Vis, CROATIA *Issa, Lissa*
An island and town founded by the Greeks in 390 BC. According to legend, it is named after Issa, a girl from Lesbos loved by Apollo.

Visalia, CALIFORNIA/USA
Founded in 1852 by, and named after, Nathaniel Vise, a local hunter.

Visayas, PHILIPPINES
An island group also known as the Bisayas and named after the indigenous inhabitants.

Visby, SWEDEN
A Stone Age settlement, it means 'Settlement at the Sacred (pagan) Site' from *wii* 'sacred (site)' and *by* 'settlement'; the *s* was added later.

Višegrad, BOSNIA AND HERZEGOVINA, HUNGARY
'Higher Castle' from the Serbo-Croat *više* 'higher' and *grad*. The Hungarian town is spelled Visegrád.

Vistula (Wisła), POLAND *Weichsel*
A river named after the Wiślanie tribe who probably took their name from an Indo-European root associated with 'water'. The former name was German.

Vitebsk (Vitsyebsk), BELARUS
A province and a city developed from a fortress first mentioned in 1021 and named after the Vitba River, whose name is said to be derived from the local *vit'* 'swamp' or 'wet place'.

Viterbo, LAZIO/ITALY
Possibly derived from the Latin *vetus urbs* 'old city'. It is of Etruscan origin and was conquered by the Romans in 310 BC.

Viti Levu, FIJI
Fiji's largest island, it means 'Great Fiji' from *Viti* 'Fiji'.

Vitoria, BRAZIL, SPAIN
1. Brazil (Espírito Santo): commemorates the victory over the Native Americans in 1551.
2. Spain (Basque Country): its Basque name is Gasteiz. Founded and named Victoriacum 'Place of Victory', with the suffix *acum*, by the Visigothic King Leogivild to commemorate his victory over the Basques in 581.

Vitry-sur-Seine, PARIS/FRANCE *Vitriacum*
'Place of Victorius' from a Roman personal name and the place-name suffix *acum*. 'on-Seine' differentiates this town from others called Vitry.

Vittoria, SICILY/ITALY
Founded in 1607 by, and named after, Vittoria Colonna, daughter of Marcantonio Colonna, viceroy of Sicily, and wife of Luigi III Enriquez of Cabrera, count of Modica.

Vittorio Veneto, VENETO/ITALY *Vittorio*
Founded as a consequence of the merger of Serravalle and Ceneda in 1866, it was named after Victor Emmanuel II (1820–78), King of Sardinia-Piedmont from 1849 and the first King of Italy (1861–78). Veneto, to indicate its location, was added in 1923.

Vittoriosa, MALTA *Birgu*
Renamed 'Victorious' to commemorate the victory of the Knights of St John of Jerusalem over the Ottoman Turks in the Great Siege of Malta in 1565.

Vizianagaram, ANDHRA PRADESH/INDIA
Founded in 1712 with a name derived from the Vijayanagar Empire, the Hindu kingdom that defied Muslim expansion in southern India during the 14th and 15th centuries. *See* VIJAYANAGAR.

Vladikavkaz, NORTH OSSETIA/RUSSIA *Zalukh, Ordzhonikidze, Dzaudzhikau*
On the site of Zalukh a fortress was built in 1783 by Count Paul Potëmkin (a cousin of the more famous Grigory) at a place where the Terek River exits from the Caucasus Mountains, the starting point of what came to be known as the Georgian Military Highway linking Vladikavkaz and Tiflis (now Tbilisi). It was to be the launch pad for the Russian conquest of the Caucasus. Potëmkin called it *Vladet′ Kavkazom* 'To have command of the Caucasus' from *vladet′* 'to control' or 'to possess' and *Kavkaz* 'Caucasus'; it is usually accepted as 'Ruler of the Caucasus'. In 1931–44 and 1954–90 it was renamed after Sergo Ordzhonikidze[†], and in 1944–54 Dzaudzhikau, the name of the village nearby and its Ossetian name which is still legally valid. This is based on a personal name and *kau* 'village'.

Vladimir, RUSSIA
A province and a city founded in 1108 and named by Vladimir II Monomakh (1053–1125), Grand Prince of Kiev (1113–25), after St Vladimir I the Great (*c*.956–1015), Grand Prince of Kiev. It was the capital of Kievan Rus′ between 1157 and *c*.1328. The name could be translated as 'Ruler of the World' or alternatively 'Possessor of Peace', *mir* meaning both 'world' and 'peace'. *See* VLADIKAVKAZ.

Vladivostok, PRIMORSKIY TERRITORY/RUSSIA
Founded in 1860 as a military post with the name 'Ruler (or Possessor) of the East' from *vladet′* 'to control' or 'to possess' and *vostok* 'east'.

Vlad Țepeș, ROMANIA
Named after Vlad Țepeș (*c*.1431–76), otherwise known as Vlad the Impaler from *țepeș* 'impaler', or Dracula. Vlad's father, Vlad II, Prince of Wallachia (1436–47), was invested with the Order of the Dragon (in Romanian, *Drac* 'dragon' with the definite article suffix *ul*) by Sigismund (1368–1437), Holy Roman Emperor (1433–37) and King of Hungary (1387–1437), and thereafter called himself Vlad Dracul. His son inherited the title. The name Dracula comes from *Dracul* which actually means 'the Devil' rather than 'the dragon'.

Vlasenica, BOSNIA AND HERZEGOVINA
May be named after the Vlachs, a people who settled in northern Albania and southern Serbia and who today are to be found in Albania, Bulgaria, northern Greece, Macedonia, and Serbia.

Vlissingen, THE NETHERLANDS
See FLUSHING.

Vlorë, ALBANIA *Aulôn, Avlona, Valona*
Also called Vlora. Founded as a Greek colony called Aulôn 'Valley', it is situated in a bay with a name meaning 'Hollow between the Hills'. When occupied by the Italians in 1915–20 and during the Second World War it was called Valona.

Vltava, CZECH REPUBLIC *Moldau*
A river with a Germanic name meaning 'Wild Water' from the Celtic *vlt* 'wild' and *va* 'water'. The name is a reference to its strong flow and

rapids. The German Moldau is a corruption of an earlier form of the river's name, Voltava.

Vodnyy, KOMI REPUBLIC/RUSSIA *Vodstroy*
Lying on the Izhma River, the name means 'Watery'.

Voghera, LOMBARDY/ITALY
Derived from the Latin *vicus* 'settlement', the *i* becoming *o*, and Iria, the ancient name of the River Staffora which flows through the town; thus 'Settlement on the (River) Iria'.

Vogtland, SAXONY/GERMANY
A region named after the title of its ruler, *Vogt* from the Latin *vocatus* 'summoned', thus 'elected'.

Vojvodina, SERBIA/SERBIA AND MONTENEGRO *Bácsko*
An autonomous province, the name meaning 'Duchy' and named after the title of the ruler (in Serbo-Croat, *vojvoda* 'duke'). This came from the Slavonic root *vojn* and in medieval Serbia indicated a high-ranking military commander or governor of a military district. Vojvodina was used for the first time in 1849 to encapsulate the districts of Bačka, Banat, and a small part of Baranja which was incorporated into Croatia-Slavonia. The region became part of Hungary in 1867 until it was included in the newly created Kingdom of the Serbs, Croats, and Slovenes in 1918.

Volchansk, RUSSIA, UKRAINE
1. Russia (Yekaterinburg): originally Lesnaya Volchanka 'Volchanka of the Woods' from *les* 'forest' and the River Volchanka from which the present name comes.
2. Ukraine: named after the Volchya River on which it lies. The river's name comes ultimately from *volk* 'wolf'. The original name, Volchi Vody, meant 'Wolf Waters' from *voda* 'water'.

Volga, RUSSIA *Ra, Itil*
A river, the meaning of whose name is not known. It may be related to the modern Russian *vlaga* 'moisture' or liquid'. The river was known by the ancient Greeks as the Ra which may have meant simply 'river'. The lower and middle sections were known as Itil a thousand years ago and this name may come from the Tatar *idel* 'big river'.

Volgodonsk, ROSTOV/RUSSIA
Takes its name from the Volga–Don Canal, it being founded when the canal was being built in 1948–52.

Volgograd, RUSSIA *Tsaritsyn, Stalingrad*
A province and a city with a name meaning 'Town on the (River) Volga'. It was originally a fortress built in 1589, its Tatar name meaning

'Town on the (River) Tsaritsa' from the Turkic *sary su* 'Yellow River' which was so-called because of the golden sands at this point on the banks of this tributary of the Volga. Although the name had nothing to do with *tsar* and the tsarist past, it was renamed in 1925 'Stalin's Town' after Joseph Stalin[†], chairman of the local military committee which had organized the defence of the city in 1919 against White Russian armies. After his fall from grace the city was given its present name in 1961, a return to Tsaritsyn being ruled out.

Volksrust, MPUMALANGA/SOUTH AFRICA
'People's Rest' from the Afrikaans *volk* 'people' and *rust* 'rest', possibly because Boers rested here after battle.

Volochayevka Vtoraya, YEVREYSKAYA AUTONOMOUS REGION/RUSSIA
Believed to be named after M. S. Volochayev, a Kuban Cossack who settled here in 1908. A second settlement appeared on the site in 1936 which became known as 'Second Volochayevka' from *vtoroy* 'second'.

Volodymyr-Volynskyy, UKRAINE *Vladimir-Volynskiy*
Founded in the 10th century by, and named after, Volodymyr I the Great (St Vladimir I the Great) (*c*.956–1015), Grand Prince of Kiev and the first Christian ruler of Kievan Rus'. Volynskyy (Volyn province) was added to differentiate between it and the Vladimir in Russia. Coming under Polish control in 1347, it returned to Russia at the third partition of Poland in 1795. It returned to Polish hands in 1919 and remained Polish until 1939 when it was seized by the Soviet Union and annexed in 1945. It became a Ukrainian city on that country's independence in 1991.

Vologda, RUSSIA
A province and a city which takes its name from the Vologda River on which it lies. Its name is of Finno-Ugric origin and means 'white'.

Vol'sk, SARATOV/RUSSIA *Malykovka*
Takes its name from the River Volga on which it lies. In 1780 it was reclassified as a town and took the name Volgsk, the g being removed later for the sake of simpler pronunciation.

Volta, BURKINA FASO-GHANA, USA
Burkina Faso-Ghana: a river, comprising the Black Volta (in Burkina Faso, the Mouhoun), the White Volta (in Burkina Faso, the Nakambe), and the Red Volta, a tributary of the White Volta. It is also the name of a lake in Ghana. The name Volta 'Turn' was given by the Portuguese in the 15th century, probably

to describe the many twists and turns in the lower course of the river.

Volta Redonda, RIO DE JANEIRO/BRAZIL
Founded in 1941 and given the name 'Complete Curve' in Portuguese to describe its location on a bend in the Paraíba do Sul River.

Volterra, TUSCANY/ITALY *Velathri, Volaterrae*
Volaterrae is the Latin version of the original Etruscan name and the name from which the present one comes. The meaning is 'High Ground' from *vel* 'high' and *terra* 'ground'.

Volturno, CAMPANIA/ITALY *Volturnus*
A river with a name from the Latin *voltur* 'vulture'.

Volzhsk, CHUVASHIYA REPUBLIC/RUSSIA *Lopatino*
Renamed in 1940 after the River Volga on which it lies.

Volzhskiy, VOLGOGRAD/RUSSIA *Derevyannyy Gorodok, Kamennyy Gorodok*
First known as 'Wooden Settlement' from *derevyannyy* 'wooden' and *gorodok* 'little town', this was subsequently changed to 'Stone Settlement' from *kamen'* 'stone'. Its present name, indicating its location on the River Volga, was adopted in 1954.

Vorarlberg, AUSTRIA *Raetia*
A state meaning 'In front of the Arlberg' from the German *vor* 'in front of' and the name of the mountainous region in western Austria. The people of Vorarlberg voted in 1919 to join Switzerland but the Peace Conference in Paris would not allow the union and nor were the Swiss keen on the idea.

Vorkuta, KOMI REPUBLIC/RUSSIA *Rudnik No. 1*
Founded as a small camp in 1931 to support a coal mine which was constructed the following year. Its original name came from *rudnik* 'mine' or 'pit'. It was to become one of the largest forced-labour camps in the Gulag system. It was later renamed after the Vorkuta River on which it lies. The river's name is said to come from the Nenets *varkuta* 'numerous bears' from *vark* 'bear'.

Voronezh, RUSSIA
A province and a city founded as a fortress in 1586 and named after the Voronezh River. This may be derived from the modern Russian *voron* 'crow' (stress on the second syllable; with stress on the first, *voron* means 'raven') to mean the 'black' waters of the river or it may be taken from a personal name.

Voskresensk, MOSCOW/RUSSIA
Founded in 1862 and took its name from the dedication of its church to the Resurrection, *Voskreseniye*.

Vostochnyy, SAKHALIN ISLAND/RUSSIA *Aleksey Orlovsky*
'Eastern'. Previously named after Prince Aleksey Orlov (1786–1861), statesman and authoritative adviser to Emperors Nicholas I[†] and Alexander II[†].

Votkinsk, URDMURTIYA/RUSSIA
Founded in 1759 and named after the Votka River on which it lies.

Vrancea, ROMANIA
A county with a name meaning 'Richly Wooded Mountain'.

Vratsa, BULGARIA *Vratitsa*
A shortened version of the original name meaning 'Small Door' or 'Small Gate'. This was probably a reference to the fact that the town is situated where the River Leva emerges from the Vratsata Gorge. Nearby a fortress had guarded a route through the mountains until it was destroyed by the Ottoman Turks in the 15th century.

Vrchlabí, CZECH REPUBLIC *Vrch Labe, Hohenelbe*
'Uplands of the (River) Elbe' in both the former German name and Czech, *Labe* being the Czech name for the Elbe. The town is situated on the upper reaches of the river.

Vrede, FREE STATE/SOUTH AFRICA
Founded in 1863 with the Afrikaans name 'Peace'.

Vredenburg, WESTERN CAPE/SOUTH AFRICA *Procesfontein*
Founded in 1883 with a name meaning 'Lawsuit Spring', a reference to a dispute about the possession of a spring. Once the church here had been dedicated, the name was changed to 'Town of Peace' from *vrede* 'peace' and *burg*.

Vreeswijk, THE NETHERLANDS
'Land of the Frisians'.

Vršac, SERBIA/SERBIA AND MONTENEGRO *Podvršac*
Situated below a hill with a fortified tower on it, the original name meant 'Below the Top' from *pod* 'below' and *vršak* 'top'. In due course the *pod* was dropped and the *k* became a *c*.

Vryburg, NORTH WEST/SOUTH AFRICA
The area around the town, called Stellaland, enjoyed the status of a republic for less than a year in 1882. Nevertheless, the citizens called themselves 'free burghers' and the town came to be known as Vryburg 'Free Town'.

Vryheid, KWAZULU-NATAL/SOUTH AFRICA
Capital of the Boer Republic of Vryheid in 1884–9, the name simply means 'Freedom'.

Vukovar, CROATIA *Vukovo*
Named after the River Vuka which flows into
the Danube here. *Vuk* 'wolf' may be associated
with a personal name. In the late 17th century
the medieval Croatian name gave way to the
present Hungarian one with *var*, Hungarian
vár 'castle' or 'stronghold'. A fortified castle
had been the core of the town since the 13th
century.

Vulcaneşti, MOLDOVA
'Owned by Vulkan' from a Moldovan family
name and *eşti* 'owned by' or 'belonging to'.

Vũng Tàu, VIETNAM *Cap St Jacques*
'Bay of Boats' from *vũng* 'bay' and *tàu* 'boat'.
The previous name, given by Portuguese
seamen in honour of their patron saint, was
superseded when the French left Vietnam in
1954.

Vyatka, RUSSIA
See KIROV.

Vyazniki, VLADIMIR/RUSSIA
Possibly '(Place) Surrounded by Elms' from
vyaz 'elm tree'.

Vyborg, LENINGRAD/RUSSIA *Viipuri*
Originally built as a fortress and held by the
Swedes in 1293–1710 and called 'Holy Fort'

from the Swedish *vi* 'holy' and *borg*. During the
Great Northern War (1700–21) in 1710 it
passed to the Russians who held it until 1918.
It then became Finnish when the name was
changed to Viipuri, a Finnish version of the
Swedish name. It was ceded back to the Soviet
Union in 1941 after the Soviet–Finnish Winter
War (1939–40) had ended.

Vyshhorod, UKRAINE
'High Town' from *vyshe* 'higher' and the
Ukrainian spelling of the Russian *gorod*. This
probably denotes a town of importance rather
than one on high ground.

Vyshniy Volochëk, TVER/RUSSIA
'Upper Portage' from *vysshiy* 'upper' and *volok*
'portage'—a place where cargo is carried
overland between two rivers.

Vyškov, CZECH REPUBLIC *Wischau*
'Height' or 'Elevation'.

Vysotsk, RUSSIA, UKRAINE
Russia (Leningrad): renamed from the Finnish
Uuras in 1948 after K. D. Vysotsky who was
killed here fighting the Finns in 1940 during
the Winter War (1939–40).

Vzmor'ye, SAKHALIN ISLAND/RUSSIA
'Sea Shore' or 'Seaside'.

V

Wabash, OHIO-INDIANA/USA
A tributary of the Ohio River with the Miami name *wuabache* 'White Water' or 'Water over White Stones'. The French called it Oubache.

Wabē Shebelē, ETHIOPIA-SOMALIA
A river, rising in Ethiopia, and called the Webi Shabeelle in Somalia. It may be named after the Shebelē people, who themselves may have been named as the people who live by the 'River (of the Land) of Leopards' from the Somali *webi* 'river' and *shabeel* 'leopard'.

Waco, CANADA, USA
USA (Texas): founded in 1849 on the site of a Waco (Huaco) village and named after the Native American tribe.

Wādī al-Jadīd, al-, EGYPT *Aṣ-Ṣahrā' al-Janūbīyah*
A governorate renamed 'The New Valley' from *wādī* and *jadīd* 'new' in 1958. Previously it was known as 'Southern Desert'.

Wad Madani, THE SUDAN
Named after Mohammad bin Madanī, who was known as Wad Madanī from *walad* 'child', a prominent 17th-century religious scholar who is buried here.

Wagga Wagga, NEW SOUTH WALES/AUSTRALIA
Settled in the 1830s with an Aboriginal name '(Place of) Many Crows', the duplication of the word indicating the plural.

Wahiawa, HAWAII/USA
'Place of Noise', a reference to its location between two arms of the Kaukonahua Stream.

Waialeale, HAWAII/USA
A mountain called 'Rippling Water'; it is one of the wettest places on earth.

Waiheke Island, NORTH ISLAND/NEW ZEALAND
'Cascading Waters' from *wai* and *heke* 'dripping'. It refers to a single place, but Europeans applied the name to the whole island.

Waikaremoana, Lake, NORTH ISLAND/NEW ZEALAND
'Sea of Rippling Waters' from *wai*, *kare* 'rippling', and *moana* 'sea'. According to legend, a Maori chief turned his daughter, Hau Mapuhia, into a *taniwha*, a sacred monster. In her struggles to get free she gouged out the lake which filled with water and her violent movements disturbed the water.

Waikato, NORTH ISLAND/NEW ZEALAND
A regional council and a river meaning 'Flowing Water' from *wai*, although the Maori were impressed by the strength of its flow and it could be taken to mean 'torrent'.

Waikiki Beach, HAWAII/USA
'Gushing Water' in Hawaiian.

Waikiwi, SOUTH ISLAND/NEW ZEALAND
A name said to have been coined by Europeans to sound 'native' from *wai*, probably a reference to the springs here, with *kiwi* being the bird.

Wailuku, HAWAII/USA
'Water of Destruction', a reference to the Battle of Kepaniwai in 1790 when the Iao Stream was filled with bodies.

Wakatipu, SOUTH ISLAND/NEW ZEALAND
A shortened version of Wakatipuawaimaori from the Maori *waka* 'trough', *tipua* 'enchanted being', in this case a giant, *wai* 'water', and *maori* 'fresh'. According to legend, a giant died and sank into the ground, leaving his outline which filled with fresh water and became a lake. The shape of the lake could be said to resemble a body.

Wakayama, HONSHŪ/JAPAN *Okayama*
A prefecture and a city founded in 1585 with the characters representing *wa* 'harmony' or 'peace', *ka* 'song', and *yama* 'mountain'. The previous name comes from *oka* 'hill' and *yama*.

Wakefield, CANADA, JAMAICA, NEW ZEALAND, UK, USA
1. New Zealand (South Island): named after Arthur Wakefield (1799–1843), brother of Edward Gibbon Wakefield (1796–1862) who did much to colonize New Zealand and who was instrumental in founding the New Zealand Association in 1837. Arthur was killed here by Maori.
2. UK (England): formerly Wachefeld 'Open Land where Festivities occur' from the Old English *wacu* 'festivity' or 'wake' and *feld*.

Wake Island, USA *Halcyon Island/Helsion Island*
An unincorporated territory of the USA and named after the British sailor William Wake

who visited it in 1796. It was formally claimed by the USA in 1899.

Wakkerstroom, MPUMALANGA/SOUTH AFRICA
Marthinus Wesselstroom
Founded in 1859 and named after Marthinus Wessel Pretorius (1819–1901), first President of the South African Republic (1857–71), with *stroom* 'stream'. The name was inevitably shortened to Wesselstroom and then changed to the present name, literally 'Awake Stream'.

Wales, GUYANA, UK, USA
UK: a principality called '(Land of the) Foreigners' from the Old English *walh* 'foreigner' (plural, *walas*) which the Anglo-Saxons called the Celts here after defeating them. They became, therefore, 'foreigners' in their own country. The Welsh name for the principality is Cymru and the Celts called themselves *Cymry* 'Compatriots'. The Roman conquest was completed by 78 and the eastern border of the territory demarcated in the 8th century. The Medieval Latin name was Cambria. Conquered in 1301 by Edward I (1239–1307), King of England (1272–1307), Wales was incorporated into the English realm under the Acts of 1536 and 1543.

Wallaceburg, ONTARIO/CANADA *The Forks*
At the confluence of two branches of the Sydenham River, it was at first called The Forks. It was later renamed after Sir William Wallace (c.1272–1305), a Scottish national hero who led the resistance against the English in 1297.

Wallachia (Țara Românească), ROMANIA
Muntenia, Eflak
A historic principality. Muntenia means '(Land of the) Mountains' from *munte* 'mountain'. The present name, '(Land of) the Vlachs', was coined by the Slavs with *vlach* meaning 'speakers of a strange language', thus 'foreigner' or 'stranger'. The Romanian name simply means 'Romanian Land' from *țara* 'land' or 'country'.

Wallasey, ENGLAND/UK *Walea, Waleyesegh*
'Britons' Island' or 'Island of the Welsh' from the Old English *walh* 'foreigner', 'Briton' or 'Welshman', with *wala* being the genitive plural, and *ēg* 'island'. Later a second *ēg* was added.

Walla Walla, WASHINGTON/USA *Fort Walla Walla, Steptoeville*
The fort was erected on the Walla Walla River 'Small Rapid River' in 1856 and quite quickly a community established itself in the vicinity. This first settlement was called Steptoeville, but in 1862 it adopted the name of the river.

Wallingford, UK, USA
1. UK (England): formerly Welingaforda and Walingeford 'Ford of Walh's People' from an Old English personal name, *-inga-* and *ford*.
2. USA (Connecticut): bought from the Native Americans in 1638, it was originally called East River, but was renamed in 1670 after the Wallingford in England.

Wallis and Futuna (Territoire de Wallis et Futuna), FRANCE
An Overseas Territory of the French Republic since 1961 also known as the Wallis Islands. The Wallis group was named in 1767 after Captain Samuel Wallis (1728–95), a British Royal Navy officer. Futuna and Alofi were named in 1616 the Hoorn Islands by a Dutch expedition. The Wallis group became a French protectorate in 1887 and Futuna followed suit in 1888. The local name for Wallis Island is Uvéa.

Wallonia, BELGIUM
A region and the French-speaking part of the country named after the Walloons. This name derives from the Germanic *walhon* 'foreigner' because they spoke French rather than the Dutch (Flemish) spoken in the north and north-east of Belgium.

Wallsend, ENGLAND/UK *Wallesende*
'End of the Wall', a reference to its location at the eastern end of Hadrian's Wall.

Walnut Creek, USA
California: founded as The Corners during the Gold Rush in 1849 and renamed in 1860 in recognition of the numerous walnut trees here.

Walpole, USA
Massachusetts-New Hampshire: both places are named after Sir Robert Walpole (1676–1745), generally regarded as Great Britain's first prime minister (1721–42).

Walsall, ENGLAND/UK *Waleshale*
'Nook of Land belonging to a Man called Walh' from an Old English personal name and *halh* 'nook of land'.

Walvis Bay (Walvisbaai), NAMIBIA
'Whale Bay' in Afrikaans. It was annexed by the UK in 1878 and included in Cape Colony in 1884. It became part of South Africa in 1910 but was administered as part of South West Africa in 1922–77. From then until 1992 it was governed by South Africa, despite Namibian independence in 1990; it was thereafter jointly governed by Namibia and South Africa until it was transferred in its entirety to Namibia in 1994.

Wanaka Lake, SOUTH ISLAND/NEW ZEALAND
Derived from the Maori *O Anaka* 'Place of Anaka', a Maori chief, with *o* 'place'.

Wanganui, NORTH ISLAND/NEW ZEALAND *Petre*
A river, properly Whanganui, and a town
founded in 1841 as Petre after William Petre
(1793–1850), 11th Baron Petre, a director of
the New Zealand Company. The town was
given a Maori name in 1844 meaning 'Big
Harbour' from *nui* 'big' and *wanga* 'harbour',
a reference to the mouth of the River
Whanganui 'Big River Mouth' on which
it lies.

Warabi, HONSHŪ/JAPAN
'Bracken'.

Warmbad, NAMIBIA *Blijde Uitkomst*
Founded as a mission station in 1805 with the
name 'Happy Deliverance'. This was later
changed to 'Warm Bath', a reference to the hot
spring here.

Warminster, UK, USA
UK (England): formerly Worgemynster and
Guerminstre 'Church on the (River) Were'
from the Old English river name meaning
'winding' and *mynster* 'church'.

Warner Robins, GEORGIA/USA *Wellston*
Robins Air Force Base was established close to
the village of Wellston from which the city
developed. It was named after Brigadier
General Augustine Warner Robins (1882–
1940), one of the pioneers of the US Army Air
Corps.

Warragul, VICTORIA/AUSTRALIA
Derived from an Aboriginal word for the
dingo.

Warren, AUSTRALIA, CANADA, UK, USA
1. USA (Michigan): established as Hickory
Township in 1837, it was renamed Aba the
following year and Warren in 1839 after
General Joseph Warren (1741–75), who was
prominent in the first months of the American
War of Independence before being killed at
the Battle of Bunker Hill in 1775.
2. USA (Ohio): settled in 1799 and named after
Moses Warren, a surveyor and early settler.
3. USA (Rhode Island): named after Admiral
Sir Peter Warren (1703–52) of the British Royal
Navy.

Warrington, UK, USA
UK (Cheshire/England): formerly Walintune
and Werrington 'Village by the Weir' from the
possible Old English *wer*(*ing*) 'weir' and *tūn*.

Warrnambool, VICTORIA/AUSTRALIA
Warnimble
Settled in 1847 as a village called Warnimble,
an Aboriginal name meaning 'Plenty of Water'
or 'Running Swamps' from which the present
name is derived.

Warsaw (Warszawa), POLAND
May be derived from a personal name such as
Warsz; he probably owned land here. The city
has been the capital of Poland since 1609
although the country was erased from the map
in 1795–1918; in 1807–15 the area was known
as the Duchy of Warsaw.

Warwick, AUSTRALIA, CANADA, UK, USA
1. UK (England): formerly Wærincwicum and
Warwic 'Settlement by the Weir' on the River
Avon from the possible Old English *wer* 'weir'
and *wic*. It gave its name to the county of
Warwickshire with *scīr*.
2. USA (Rhode Island): founded as Shawomet
in 1642 and subsequently renamed after
Robert Rich (1587–1658), 2nd Earl of Warwick,
Lord High Admiral, supporter of Cromwell
against King Charles I[†], and a Puritan who
headed a colonial government commission in
1643 which led to the establishment of Rhode
Island.

Wash, The, ENGLAND/UK *The Wasshes*
Derived from the Old English *wæsc* 'sandbank
washed by the sea'.

Washington, BONAIRE, UK, USA
1. UK (Northumberland/England): formerly
Wassyngtona 'Wassa's Village' from an Old
English personal name, -*ing*- and *tūn*.
2. USA (District of Columbia): the site for the
city, planned from the outset as the national
capital, was chosen by, and named after,
George Washington[†] in 1791. Washington
originally wanted the city to be called the
'District of Columbia' in honour of
Christopher Columbus[†]. The city began to
function as the capital in 1800.
3. USA: a state named after George
Washington[†]. Oregon County, as it was then
known, joined the USA in 1848 at which time
it was renamed the Territory of Oregon. In
1853 what is now the state of Washington was
detached from Oregon and renamed
Washington Territory. It joined the Union in
1889 as the 42nd state.

Washoe City, NEVADA/USA
Named after a Native American tribe. There is
also a New Washoe City and Lake Washoe.

Wasit, IRAQ
Ruins. Founded *c*.703 by Hajjāj ibn Yūsuf
(661–714), the Umayyad governor of Iraq from
694, who built Wasit as a military camp and as
his capital. Its meaning was the '(City) in the
Middle'—midway between Kūfah and Basra.

Waterbury, CANADA, USA
USA (Connecticut): founded as Mattatuck
Plantation in 1674 and renamed in 1686 when

it became a town. The name alludes to the good drainage here.

Waterford, CANADA, IRELAND, USA
1. Ireland: a county borough and city-port whose Gaelic name is Port Láirge 'Bank on the Haunch', a reference to the round shape of the bank of the River Suir. Waterford, originally Vadrefiord, is said to mean 'Wether Inlet' from the Old Scandinavian *vethr* 'wether' and *fjorthr* 'inlet'. Wethers, usually castrated rams, are supposed to have been exported from here, but this is difficult to prove. The city gives its name to Waterford glass.
2. USA (Connecticut): founded *c.*1653, the name derives from the shallows which could be forded here. Other cities and towns with this name in the USA are generally named after the Irish city.

Waterloo, AUSTRALIA, BELGIUM, CANADA, SIERRA LEONE, SURINAME, TRINIDAD AND TOBAGO, USA
1. Belgium: derived from the Flemish *water* 'water' and *loo* 'sacred wood'.
2. USA (Iowa): founded as Prairie Rapids in 1845, it was renamed to commemorate the Battle of Waterloo in 1815. This is true of several other places with this name in the USA and Canada.

Watford, CANADA, UK
UK (England): 'Hunters' Ford' from the Old English *wāth* 'hunting' and *ford*.

Watts, USA
California: renamed from Mud Town in 1900 after C. H. Watts, a realtor (estate agent) who established a ranch here.

Waukegan, ILLINOIS/USA *Little Fort*
In 1849 the settlement, established on the site of a former 17th-century French military post, was given the Potawatomi version of 'Little Fort'.

Waukesha, WISCONSIN/USA *Prairieville*
Settled in 1834 and later renamed 'By the Little Fox' from the Potawatomi *wauk-tsha* 'fox', a reference to its location on the Fox River.

Wausau, USA
Wisconsin: settled as Big Bull Falls in 1839 and renamed in 1872 'Faraway (Place)' from the Chippewa *wassa* 'faraway'.

Wayne, CANADA, USA
USA (New Jersey): settled in 1695 and thereafter part of different townships. In 1847 it was renamed after Major General Anthony Wayne (1745–96), prominent during the American War of Independence (1775–83) and appointed commander-in-chief of the US Army in 1792. Several other cities and towns,

variously called Waynesboro, Waynesburg, Waynesfield, and Waynesville, are named after the same man.

Wazīrābād, PUNJAB/PAKISTAN
Founded in the 17th century by, and named after, Wazir Khan, prime minister of Shah Jahan, Mughal Emperor (1628–58), with *ābād* to give the 'Town of Wazir'.

Wazīristan, PAKISTAN
A region in the North-West Frontier province, the name means 'Land of the Wazirs', a Pashtun tribe which claims to be one of the lost tribes of Israel.

Weddell Sea, ANTARCTICA *George IV Sea*
A sea that is usually ice-bound, it was penetrated in 1823 by James Weddell (1787–1834), a British explorer and sealer. He named it after King George IV[†]. It was renamed after its discoverer in 1900.

Weenen, KWAZULU-NATAL/SOUTH AFRICA
'(Place of) Weeping' in Afrikaans. It was here in 1838 that perhaps as many as 500 Boer women and children were massacred on the orders of Dingane (d.1843), ruler of the Zulu Empire (1828–40).

Weifang, SHANDONG/CHINA *Wei Zhou*
Originally in 596 it was named after the Wei River as Wei District. In 1376 it became Wei County. Lying close to Fangzi, named after its many *fāng* 'workshops', Wei County and Fangzi were merged in 1948 and given the present name.

Weihai, SHANDONG/CHINA *Weihaiwei, Port Edward*
As a *wèi* 'military base' from which it took the name Weihaiwei in 1398, the additional *wèi* at the end meant 'guard'. In 1898–1930 the city-port was leased to the British under the name Port Edward. The present name means 'Might on the Sea' from *wēi* 'might' or 'power' and *hǎi*.

Weimar, GERMANY, USA
Germany (Thuringia): originally Wimare, an early spelling of Weimar. The name was derived from the Old German *wisa* 'meadow' and *mari* 'lake' or 'spring'. After the First World War the new National Assembly met here in 1919 to draw up a constitution for the new German Republic, henceforth known as the Weimar Republic (1919–33).

Weligama, SRI LANKA
'Sandy Village'; it is situated on the coast.

Welkom, FREE STATE/SOUTH AFRICA
Founded *c.*1846 as 'Welcome' in Afrikaans.

W

Welland, CANADA, UK

Canada (Ontario): a river, a ship canal, and a
city formerly called The Aqueduct. It was
renamed in 1842 after William Merritt, one of
the canal's builders. In 1856 it was renamed
again after the Welland River in England; its
meaning is unknown.

Wellesley Islands, QUEENSLAND/AUSTRALIA

First seen by Abel Tasman[†] in 1644, they were
named by Matthew Flinders[†] in 1802 in
honour of Richard Colley Wellesley (1760–
1842), Marquess Wellesley, governor-general
of India (1797–1805). He was also the 2nd Earl
of Mornington, the name given to the largest
island of the group and the name of its main
town.

Wellingborough, ENGLAND/UK *Wellingeberie,*
Wendlingburch

'Stronghold of Wændel's Followers' from an
Old English personal name, *-inga-* and *burh.*

Wellington, AUSTRALIA, CANADA, NEW
ZEALAND, SOUTH AFRICA, UK, USA

1. Besides the UK, cities and towns with this
name all honour Arthur Wellesley, 1st Duke of
Wellington (1769–1852), commander-in-chief
of the British Army during the Napoleonic
Wars and prime minister (1828–30).
2. New Zealand (North Island): named in 1840
after the 1st Duke of Wellington. He was
honoured because of the aid he gave to the
New Zealand Company whose members had
arrived in North Island the previous year to
found a settlement. The city has been the
capital since 1865.
3. South Africa (Western Cape): founded in
1688 as Limiet Vallei 'Furthest Valley' in the
sense that this was a remote outpost and the
furthest that civilization had reached. It was
later renamed Val du Charron 'Cartwright's
Valley'. In 1840, when the settlement had
become a town, it was renamed after the 1st
Duke of Wellington.
4. UK (England): at least three towns have this
name meaning 'Wēola's Estate' from an Old
English personal name, *-ing-* and *tūn.* The Duke
of Wellington took his title from the town in
Somerset.

Wells, AUSTRALIA, CANADA, UK, USA

UK (England): formerly Willan and Welle 'The
Springs', a reference to the many springs
rising close to the cathedral.

Welwyn Garden City, ENGLAND/UK

Founded in 1920 and designated a New Town
in 1948. It takes its name from the nearby
Welwyn '(Place at) the Willow Trees' from the
dative plural *weligum* from the Old English
welig 'willow tree'.

Wembley, CANADA, UK

UK (England): formerly Wembalea 'Wembla's
Woodland Clearing' from an Old English
personal name and *lēah* 'clearing'.

Wenzhou, ZHEJIANG/CHINA *Dou*

Founded in 323 in a position sheltered by
mountains, the name means 'Warm
Region' from *wēn* 'warm' or 'mild' and *zhōu.*
The city-port was given the name Wenzhou
in 675.

Wessex, ENGLAND/UK *West Seaxe*

One of the seven Anglo-Saxon kingdoms,
centred on Winchester, founded in the 6th
century and named after the West Saxons. By
conquest it expanded to cover much of
southern England. In the 10th century the
kings of Wessex became the kings of England.
The name fell into disuse after the Norman
conquest in the 11th century, but has been
revived for some administrative purposes; and
Queen Elizabeth II's youngest son has the title
Earl of Wessex.

West Bank (Arabic: Aḍ-Ḍaffah al-Gharbīyah;
Hebrew: **Ha-Gadah Ha-Ma'aravit**)

An area of some 2 270 square miles (5 900 sq.
km) west of the River Jordan in the former
British mandate of Palestine which was
allocated to the Arabs (Palestinians) in the UN
partition plan of 1947; it includes East
Jerusalem. The area was occupied by Jordanian
forces during the war of 1948 and annexed by
Jordan in 1950; it was named the 'West Bank'.
During the Six Day War in 1967, however, it
was captured by the Israelis and the Jordan
River became the new Israeli border. Jordan
gave up its claim in 1988. Following the Oslo
Accords in 1993, the Israelis began to withdraw
from substantial pockets of territory in 1994
and transferred control to the Palestine
Authority (PA). There were to be three forms of
rule: Area A, exclusive PA civil and military
control; Area B, PA civil control, Israeli security
control; Area C, full Israeli civil and military
control. However, in response to a spate of
terrorist attacks in Israel in 2002, Israeli forces
reoccupied some Palestinian-controlled areas.
To the Israelis the West Bank is also known as
Judaea and Samaria, names used in biblical and
British mandate times (1922–48).

West Bengal (Bānglā), INDIA

A state created from the partitioning of
*Bengal in 1947 when India obtained its
independence.

West Bromwich, ENGLAND/UK *Bromwic,*
Westbromwich

'Western Farm where Broom grows' from the
Old English *brōm* and *wīc.*

Western, ZAMBIA *Barotseland*
A province established in 1964 and, until 1969, named after its inhabitants who founded an empire here in the 16th century. Previously known as the Aluyi, the tribe became known as the Barotse 'river people' in the 19th century and later still the Lozi, their present name.

Western Australia, AUSTRALIA *New Holland*
A state given this name in 1829 when it became a British colony, Captain George Vancouver[†] having taken formal possession of the territory around King George Sound for Great Britain in 1791. It became a constituent state of the Commonwealth of Australia in 1901. The earlier name was a result of Dutch exploration in the 17th century.

Western Sahara (Arabic: **Saharā' al-Gharbīyah**) *Spanish Sahara*
In 1884 Spain established a protectorate over the southern coastal area and penetration of the hinterland gradually followed; in 1904 the northern area was acquired. Full control, however, was only asserted in 1934 when the Spaniards divided their Saharan territories into two regions named after rivers: the Saguia el-Hamra in the north and the Rio de Oro in the south. After Morocco had claimed these regions in 1957 the Spanish united them in 1958 into a province they called Spanish Sahara. When the Spanish withdrew in 1976 the province was partitioned between Morocco, which took the northern two-thirds, and Mauritania, which renamed Rio de Oro Tiris el-Gharbia. Spanish Sahara became known as Western Sahara. However, to the Polisario Front, a liberation movement formed in 1973 to establish an independent state in Spanish Sahara, it became known as the Saharan (or Saharawi) Arab Democratic Republic. In 1979 Mauritania, following military reversals at the hands of the Polisario Front, renounced its share of the territory. The Moroccans immediately claimed this share, provoking further confrontation with the Polisario Front. Nevertheless, the Moroccans designated this region (and a little extra territory) their province of Oued ed-Dahab-Lagouira. This annexation has not been recognized internationally and the official status of Western Sahara has yet to be decided. Its legal status remains a 'non self-governing territory'.

West Indies *The Indies*
So named because Christopher Columbus[†] thought in 1492 that he had found a new route to the 'Indias' by sailing west instead of east. To Spain they were thus 'The Indies' until it

became evident that the islands were not those in the east; they then became known as the 'West Indies'. Politically, they comprise thirteen independent nations and several colonial dependencies, territories, and possessions.

West Java (Jawa Barat), JAVA/INDONESIA *Sunda*
A province, originally named after the Sundanese. *Sunda* is the Sanskrit for 'pure' or 'white'. *See* JAVA.

West Kilbride, SCOTLAND/UK
'Western (Place by) St Brigid's Church', the 'West' distinguishing it from East Kilbride.

Westmorland, UK, USA
UK (England): a former county with the name Westmoringaland 'District of the People living west of the Moors', thus west of the Pennines, from the Old English *west*, *mōr*, *-inga-*, and *land*.

Weston-super-Mare, ENGLAND/UK
'West Farmstead on the Sea' from the Old English *west* and *tūn*, and the Latin affix.

Westphalia, GERMANY, USA
Germany: a historic region and now part of the state of North Rhine-Westphalia. The German name is Westfalen, the second element deriving from the Old High German *falaho* 'plain dweller'.

West Virginia, USA
A state which was the western part of *Virginia until 1863 when it joined the Union as the 35th state. The reason for the split was Virginia's secession from the Union in 1861 at the start of the Civil War.

Wetaskiwin, ALBERTA/CANADA
Named 'Place of Peace' by a missionary priest following the agreement in 1867 between the Blackfoot and Cree to stop fighting.

Wexford, IRELAND, USA
Ireland: a county and seaport lying at the mouth of the River Slaney, originally the Garma 'Headland', with the Irish name of Loch Garman 'Lake of the (River) Garma'. Wexford means 'Inlet by the Sandbank' from the Old Irish *escir* 'sandbank' and Old Scandinavian *fjorthr* 'inlet'. It was named Menapia by Ptolemy[†] in his 2nd-century map. Before becoming Wexford the name was spelt Waejsford and Weysford.

W

Whakatane, NORTH ISLAND/NEW ZEALAND
'Act like a Man' in Maori. The name derives from an actual event: the town is at a river mouth and on one occasion a canoe lying on the beach began to drift out to sea. With no men around to save it a woman called Wairaka

said 'Me whakatane au i au', literally, 'I shall act like a man' to rescue the canoe. Because women were not allowed to paddle canoes this exploit captured the popular imagination and the settlement was renamed to commemorate it.

Whangarei, NORTH ISLAND/NEW ZEALAND
Said to mean 'Swampy Harbour' from the Maori *whanga* 'harbour' and *rei* 'swamp'. It has also been suggested that it means 'Rei waiting' from *whanga* 'waiting' with Rei being an abbreviation of a girl's name, Reipae; this is where she waited for a prospective husband.

Wheaton, USA
Illinois: named after Jesse and Warren Wheaton, the first settlers in 1837.

Wheeling, WEST VIRGINIA/USA
Settled in 1769 with a Delaware name *weal-ink* said to mean '(Place of the) Head' or 'Skull', a reference to the decapitation of a group of settlers or at least the display of a human head on a pole.

Whidbey, AUSTRALIA, USA
USA (Washington): an island named after Lieutenant Joseph Whidbey, one of George Vancouver's[†] officers, who played a leading role in charting parts of the Pacific coastline of North America.

Whitby, CANADA, UK
UK (N. Yorkshire/England): formerly Witeby 'White Village' or 'Hvíti's Village' from an Old Scandinavian personal name, possibly meaning the 'White One', and *bý*.

Whitchurch, UK
UK (Shropshire/England): the first Roman name, Mediolanum, meant 'Middle of the Plain' and the second name, Westune, 'West Farmstead' from *tūn*. The next two names, Album Monasterium and Whytchyrche, and the present name all mean 'White Church'.

Whitehaven, ENGLAND/UK *Qwithofhavene*
'Harbour near the White Headland' from the Old Scandinavian *hvítr* 'white', *houth* 'headland', and *hafn* 'harbour'. The 'white headland' is said to refer to a great white rock.

Whitehorse, CANADA, USA
Canada (Yukon): takes its name from the Whitehorse Rapids, now submerged, which received their name from the resemblance of the churning white water of the rapids to the manes of white horses.

White Plains, USA
New York: the former Siwanoy name, Quarropas, meant 'White Plains' because of the white balsam which grew abundantly here.

Whitney, CANADA, UK, USA
USA (California): a mountain named after Josiah D. Whitney (1819–96), a geologist who led the expedition that discovered it in 1864.

Whitstable, ENGLAND/UK *Witestaple, Witenestaple*
'White Post' from the Old English *hwīt* 'white' and *stapol* 'post'.

Whitsunday, AUSTRALIA
An island off the coast of Queensland, named by Captain James Cook[†] who saw it on Whit Sunday 1770.

Whittier, USA
California: founded in 1887 for Quakers and named after John G. Whittier (1807–92), a poet and abolitionist.

Whyalla, SOUTH AUSTRALIA/AUSTRALIA *Hummock Hill*
Founded in 1901 and renamed in 1920 after an Aboriginal term for 'Place with Deep Water'.

Wichita, USA
A city in Kansas founded in 1864, a river and a city called Wichita Falls in Texas founded in 1876, and mountains in Oklahoma, all named after the Native American Wichita tribe.

Wick, UK
1. England: 'Settlement' from *wīc*. This would be a distinctive settlement, for example, a dairy-farm or one that acted as a trading centre.
2. Scotland: formerly Vik and Weke '(Place by) the Bay' from the Old Scandinavian *vík*. It was an ancient Norse settlement which became a fishing port.

Wicklow (Cill Mhantáin), IRELAND *Wykingalo, Wykynoelo*
A county, mountains, and seaport with a name meaning 'Vikings' Meadow' from the Old Scandinavian *víkingr* 'Viking' and *ló* 'meadow'. The Irish name means 'Mantan's Church' after the obscure St Mantan who is said to have built a church here in the 5th century.

Widnes, ENGLAND/UK *Wydnes*
'Wide Promontory' from the Old English *wīd* 'wide' and *næss* 'promontory' or 'headland'.

Wielkopolskie, POLAND
A province meaning 'Great Poland', founded as a result of the unification during the 10th century of various tribes around Poznan.

Wiener Neustadt, AUSTRIA
'Viennese New Town' from the German adjective of *Wien* 'Vienna', *neu*, and *Stadt*, although it was actually founded in 1194 as a frontier fortress against the Magyars. The

'Wiener' indicates its proximity to Vienna and to distinguish it from other 'new towns'.

Wiesbaden, HESSE/GERMANY *Aquae Mattiacae/ Fontes Mattiacae, Wisibada*
A spa, known to the Romans as the 'Springs of the Mattiaci' from *aquae* and *fons* 'spring'. A Franconian palace was built here and at least by 829 the town was called Wisibada 'Meadow Spring' from the Old High German *wisa* 'meadow' and *bada* 'to bathe'.

Wigan, ENGLAND/UK
'Small Settlement' from the diminutive of the Celtic *wīg* 'settlement'.

Wight, Isle of, ENGLAND/UK
See ISLE OF WIGHT.

Wigton, ENGLAND/UK *Wiggeton*
'Wicga's Farmstead, or Village' from an Old English personal name and *tūn*.

Wigtown, SCOTLAND/UK *Wigeton*
'Dwelling Place' from the Old English *wīc* and *tūn*.

Wilberforce, AUSTRALIA, CANADA, USA
Named after William Wilberforce (1759–1833), a British politician and philanthropist well-known for his endeavours to abolish the slave trade and the slavery present in British possessions overseas.

Wilhelmshaven, LOWER SAXONY/GERMANY
Founded by Wilhelm I (1797–1888), Kaiser 'Emperor' (1871–88) and King of Prussia (1861–88), in 1853 and named after him in 1869. The second element of the name comes from *Hafen* 'port'.

Wilkes-Barre, PENNSYLVANIA/USA
Founded in 1769 and named in 1786 after John Wilkes (1725–97) and Isaac Barré (1726–82), British politicians who were outspoken in their support for the American colonies in the British Parliament.

Wilkes Land, ANTARCTICA
First sighted during the expedition of 1838–42 led by Charles Wilkes (1798–1877), a US Navy commander, and named after him.

Willemstad, CURAÇAO/NETHERLANDS ANTILLES
'William's Town' after William I the Silent (1533–84), Dutch Stadholder of the United Provinces of the Netherlands (1572–84).

Williamsburg, CANADA, USA
USA (Virginia): founded as Middle Plantation in 1633 as an outpost of Jamestown. It was the midway point of the palisade which settlers built across the peninsula. When the capital of the colony was moved from Jamestown in 1699, Williamsburg was laid out and renamed in honour of William III[†].

Willingboro, NEW JERSEY/USA *Levittown*
Settled by English Quakers in 1677 and given a name taken from the English Wellingborough in 1682. In 1959 it was renamed to recognize the work done by Levit & Sons Inc. to enhance the community. In 1963, however, the original name was readopted.

Wilmington, AUSTRALIA, USA
1. USA (Delaware): founded by Swedish settlers in 1638 and initially called Fort Christina after Christina (1626–89), Queen of Sweden (1644–54). It was captured by the Dutch in 1655 and they renamed it Altena after the German city with this name. In 1664 it was taken by the British but they did not change the name until 1739 when the owner, Thomas Penn, renamed it after Spencer Compton (1673–1743), Earl of Wilmington, a friend of his and nominal prime minister (1742–3).
2. USA (North Carolina): established with the merger of New Liverpool and New Carthage in the 1730s, it was called New Town, or Newton, at first. It was renamed in 1740 after the Earl of Wilmington.

Wilson, ANTARCTICA, AUSTRALIA, CANADA, USA
1. USA (California): a mountain named after Benjamin D. Wilson who cut out a trail to the summit in 1864.
2. USA (North Carolina): named after General Louis D. Wilson (1789–1847), who was killed during the Mexican–American War (1846–8).

Wiltshire, ENGLAND/UK *Wilton, Wiltunscir, Wiltescire*
A county 'Shire belonging to the People of Wilton', that is, the settlers on the River Wylye from the river name, *tūn* and *scīr*. The river's name is Celtic and indicates a river that is unpredictable as regards flooding.

Winchester, CANADA, UK, USA
UK (England): in about 15 the Belgae tribe established a trading centre here which subsequently came to be called Quenta. Some 200 years later the Romans began the construction of a walled city which they called Venta Belgarum. By the 8th century this had evolved into Uintancæstir. The *Venta*, which became Uin and Win, may mean 'Loved Place' while *Belgarum* is 'of the Belgae tribe'. The *chester* from *ceaster* indicates that this was a Roman town. It was the chief city of England between 871 and *c*.1145 and appeared in the 1086 Domesday Book as Wincestre.

W

Windermere, CANADA, SOUTH AFRICA, UK
UK (England): England's largest lake with a
name meaning 'Vinandr's Lake' from an Old
Scandinavian personal name and *mere*.

Windhoek, NAMIBIA *Aigams*
The original Nama name meant 'Hot Water'
from *ais* 'fire' and *gami* 'spring', a reference to
the hot springs here. It is not clear when it was
renamed or why, but a translation of the name
suggests 'Windy Corner' from the Afrikaans
hoek 'corner', although this is not appropriate.
It has been suggested that the name comes
from the birthplace or possibly a farm,
Winterhoek in Western Cape Province, of the
Nama leader, Jonker Afrikander, who founded
a community on this site in 1840. In 1892 it
became the capital of the German colony of
South West Africa. The city was occupied by
South African forces in 1915, retaining its
status as the territorial capital. When Namibia
achieved its independence in 1990 Windhoek
became the national capital.

Windsor, AUSTRALIA, CANADA, UK, USA
1. Canada (Nova Scotia): settled in 1703 by the
French with a Native American name,
Piziquid. It was renamed as Fort Edward in
1750 in recognition of its role in defending
British property and it received its present
name after the English town in 1764.
2. Canada (Ontario): settled at the beginning
of the 18th century as The Ferry, it was
renamed Richmond and then in 1836 after the
English town.
3. UK (England): formerly Windlesoran and
Windesores 'Bank with a Windlass' from
windels 'windlass' and *ōra* 'bank' or 'flat-topped
hill'. Quite what the windlass was for is not
completely certain. In 1917 Windsor gave its
name to the royal house of the UK, the town
having a royal castle.

Winnipeg, MANITOBA/CANADA *Fort Rouge, Fort
Gibraltar, Fort Garry*
A lake, a river, and a city founded in 1738 by the
French and renamed after Lake Winnipeg in
1873. The name, 'Muddy Water', comes from
the Cree *win* 'muddy' and *nipi* 'water'. The city
gave its name to 'Winnie', a female bear cub
bought by a Canadian officer from the city after
her mother had been shot by a hunter. Winnie
became the mascot of his regiment. He gave the
cub to London Zoo when his regiment came to
Europe to fight in the First World War. Winnie
became an inspiration to A. A. Milne (1882–
1956) who used the name 'Winnie the Pooh' in
his children's stories.

Winnipegosis, MANITOBA/CANADA
A lake whose name means 'Little Muddy
Water' (see previous entry).

Winnepesaukee, NEW HAMPSHIRE/USA
A lake with a Native American name said to
mean 'Good Water Outlet' or, alternatively,
'Beautiful Lake of the Highlands'. It lies by the
foothills of the White Mountains.

Winston-Salem, NORTH CAROLINA/USA
Winston was founded in 1849 and named after
Major Joseph Winston (1746–1815), an officer
who fought in the American War of
Independence (1775–83). Salem 'peace' was
laid out in 1766 by Moravian settlers. In 1913
the two towns, only a mile apart, were united
to form the present city.

Winterthur, SWITZERLAND *Vitodurum*
The present name derives from the Roman
one which probably meant something like
'Vito's Fort' from a Celtic personal name and
dur 'fort'.

Winthrop, USA
USA (Massachusetts): founded in 1635 and
named after John Winthrop (1588–1649), first
governor of the Massachusetts Bay Colony and
a prominent Puritan founder of New England.

Wisconsin, USA
A state named after the river, and a lake. The
French arrived in 1634 and retained control
until ceding the area to the British at the end of
the Seven Years' War in 1763. British control
was relinquished after the American War of
Independence (1775–83) and in 1787 the area
became part of the Northwest Territory; and of
Indiana Territory in 1800. It became part of
Wisconsin Territory, which included the
present Iowa, Minnesota, and parts of the
Dakotas, in 1836. It joined the Union in 1848 as
the 30th state. The name is Chippewa for
'Gathering (Place) of the Waters'.

Witwatersrand, GAUTENG/SOUTH AFRICA
'Ridge of White Waters' from the Afrikaans *wit*
'white', *water* 'water', and *rand* 'ridge'. It was a
part of the former province of Pretoria-
Witwatersrand-Vereeniging (now Gauteng).
Also known as the Rand, it is the watershed
between the Vaal and Limpopo Rivers. Rich in
gold deposits, this gave its name to the South
African monetary unit, the 'rand'.

Woking, CANADA, UK
UK (England): formerly Wocchingas and
Wochinges '(Territory of) Wocc's, or Wocca's,
People' from an Old English personal name
and *-ingas*. They also gave their name to
Wokingham 'Homestead of Wocc's People'
with the additional *hām*.

Wolfenbüttel, LOWER SAXONY/GERMANY
'The Dwelling Place of Ulpha' from the
personal name and *büttel* or *botl* which

sometimes indicated the property of a minor noble on which there was a settlement which had no regular market.

Wollaston, CANADA, CHILE, UK
1. Canada (Saskatchewan): a lake named by John Franklin in 1821 after Dr William Hyde Wollaston (1766–1828), an English scientist who was considered the leading chemist and mineralogist of his day.
2. UK (England): formerly Willavestune 'Wīglāf's Farmstead' from an Old English personal name and *tūn*.

Wolseley, AUSTRALIA, CANADA, SOUTH AFRICA
1. Canada (Saskatchewan): named after Field Marshal Lord Garnet Joseph Wolseley (1833–1913), who led the Red River expedition in 1870 to confront Louis Riel, who had declared a republic in Manitoba. In 1895–1901 he was commander-in-chief of the UK's Armed Forces.
2. South Africa (Western Cape): founded in 1875 as Ceres Road because it was on the road from Cape Town to Ceres. It was later renamed after General (later Field Marshal Lord) Garnet Joseph Wolseley, the British commander in South Africa who restored order in Zululand in 1879.

Wolverhampton, ENGLAND/UK *Heantune, Wolvrenehamptonia*
'Wulfrūn's High Farm', Wulfrūn being the lady to whom the manor was given in the 10th century, from an Old English personal name, *hēah* 'high' (the dative being *hēan*) and *tūn*.

Wŏnju, SOUTH KOREA
Possibly 'Principal Region' from *wŏn* 'principal' or 'first' and *chu* 'region' or 'province'.

Wŏnsan, NORTH KOREA *Genzan, Wŏnsanjin*
'Principal Mountain' from *wŏn* 'principal' or 'first' and *san* 'mountain'.

Woodstock, AUSTRALIA, CANADA, UK, USA
1. Canada (Ontario): founded by Rear Admiral Henry Vansittart (1777–1843) of the British Royal Navy, who named it after the English town.
2. UK (England): formerly Wudestoce and Wodestoch 'Settlement in Woodland' from the Old English *wudu* 'wood' and *stoc*.

Woomera, SOUTH AUSTRALIA
An Aboriginal name meaning 'Throwing Stick'.

Woonsocket, USA
Rhode Island–South Dakota: the name for both cities comes from an Algonquian word said to mean either 'At a Steep Place' or 'At the Place of Mist'.

Wooster, OHIO/USA
Laid out in 1808 and named after General David Wooster who commanded American troops besieging Quebec in 1776 during the early stages of the American War of Independence (1775–83).

Worcester, SOUTH AFRICA, UK, USA
1. South Africa (Western Cape): founded in 1818 and named after the Marquess of Worcester, the elder brother of Lord Charles Somerset, governor of the Cape at the time.
2. UK (England): formerly Weogorna civitas, Wigranceastre, and Wirecestre '(Roman) Town of the Weogora, or Wigoran, Tribe' from an Anglo-Saxon tribal name and *ceaster*. The tribal name may be that of a river near which the people lived and its pre-English name may have meant 'Winding River'. The city lies on the River Severn, although this may not have been the actual river. The county takes its name from the city with the additional *scîr*. The city gives its name to a pungent sauce first concocted here.
3. USA (Massachusetts): settled in 1673 and named after the English city when it was incorporated as a town in 1722.

Workington, ENGLAND/UK *Wirkybton*
'Estate of Weorc's People' from an Old English personal name, *-ing-*, and *tūn*.

Worksop, ENGLAND/UK *Werchesope*
'Weorc's (isolated) Valley' from an Old English personal name and *hop* '(isolated, or secluded) valley'.

Worms, RHINELAND-PALATINATE/GERMANY *Borbetomagus, Civitas Vangionum, Vormatia*
Originally 'Borbeto's Place' from a personal name and *mago* 'place' or 'field'. From this evolved Vormatia and the present name. Prior to this, by the beginning of the first millennium, its name had been changed to recognize its status as the chief town of the Vangiones.

Worthing, UK, USA
UK (England): formerly Ordinges '(Settlement) of Weorth's People' from an Old English personal name and *-ingas*.

Wrangel Island (Ostrov Vrangelya), RUSSIA
Although not formally discovered until 1867 by an American, Thomas Long, the island was named by him after Admiral Ferdinand Wrangel (1796–1870), a Russian Arctic explorer who had determined its location in 1823 from information provided by locals. In 1881 it was called New Columbia by the Americans but, after years of discussion on other proposed names, it was decided in 1926 to stick with Wrangel. Admiral Wrangel was a

W

director of the Russian American Company in 1840–9 and several geographic features are named after him, spelt Wrangell, in Alaska, USA: the Wrangell Mountains, within which is Mt Wrangell, a town, an island, and a cape.

Wrexham (Wrecsam), WALES/UK *Wristelsham, Gwregsam*
'Wryhtel's Meadow' from an Old English personal name and *hamm.*

Wrocław, POLAND *Wrotlizla, Vratislavia, Vretslav, Presslaw, Breslau, Boroszló*
A city with more than 50 names during its recorded history, Wrocław is named after Braslav, the last Slav leader of the Great Moravian Empire. *See* BRATISLAVA.

Wuhan, HUBEI/CHINA
Consists of the cities of Wuchang, Hankow, and Hanyang and takes its name from the first syllable of these when they amalgamated in 1949. Wuchang received its name in 221 because the *wǔ* 'military' made it *chāng* 'prosperous'. Hankow, or Hankou, was named because it is here that the Han River flows into the Yangtze River; this is the Han's *kǒu* 'mouth'. Hanyang was named in 606 because it lies on the *yáng* 'north bank' of the Han River. The present name, Wuhan, can be said to represent *wǔ* 'military' and *hàn*, the dynasty that ruled China (206 BC–AD 220) and gave its name to the river.

Wuhu, ANHUI/CHINA *Jiuzi*
The characters of the original name represented *jiū* 'dove' or 'pigeon' and *zǐ* 'here', a reference to the birds that flocked here. A river port, it adopted its present name 'Weedy Lake' from *wú* 'weedy' and *hú* 'lake' in 109.

Wuppertal, NORTH RHINE-WESTPHALIA/GERMANY
Lying in a narrow valley of the River Wupper, the name means 'Wupper Valley'. The city was

created in 1929 with the amalgamation of five towns, but the meaning of *Wupper* is not known.

Wutai Shan, SHANXI/CHINA
A mountain and mountain chain with a name meaning 'Five Terrace Mountain' from *wǔ* 'five', *tái* 'terrace' or 'platform', and *shān*. The mountain has five flat-topped peaks and is a place of pilgrimage for Chinese Buddhists.

Wuxi, CHINA
Three cities, in Anhui, Jiangsu, and Sichuan Provinces, have this name. It means 'No Tin' or 'Without Tin' from *wú* 'no' and *xī* 'tin'. The name is derived from the fact that during the Zhou, Qin, and Han dynasties tin was mined until none was left.

Wyandotte, USA
Michigan: settled *c.*1820 and named after the Wyandot tribe.

Wyndham, WESTERN AUSTRALIA/AUSTRALIA
Founded as a port for the Kimberley goldfield in 1885, it was named after Wyndham, the son of Sir Frederick Napier Broome (1842–96), governor of Western Australia (1883–91).

Wynyard, AUSTRALIA, CANADA
Australia (Tasmania): founded as Table Cape in 1841 and renamed in 1861, when it became a town, after Major General Edward Wynyard, commander-in-chief of British forces in Tasmania (then Van Dieman's Land) in 1850.

Wyoming, CANADA, USA
USA: a state with a Delaware name meaning 'Land of Large Plains', 'End of the Plains', or 'Large Prairie'. The population grew gradually during the 19th century, the name Wyoming Territory only being bestowed in 1868. It joined the Union as the 44th state in 1890.

Xai-Xai, MOZAMBIQUE *João Belo*
Formerly named after João Belo (1876–1928), a Portuguese naval captain who held various administrative posts in Mozambique after his arrival in 1896. Located close to the mouth of the Limpopo River, the meaning of the present name is unknown, although some say that it is a local version of the Portuguese *cheia* 'flood' said twice.

Xam Nua, LAOS
'Northern Sam', a reference to its location at the northern end of the River Sam from *nua* 'northern'.

Xankändi, AZERBAIJAN *Vararakn, Khankendy, Stepanakert*
'Town of the Khan' from *xändi* (*kendy*) 'town'. Khankendy replaced Vararakn in 1847. In 1923 the town was rebuilt as the new capital of Nagornyy-Karabakh after the destruction of Shusha and was renamed again after Stepan Shaumyan (1878–1918), a Georgian Bolshevik hero who founded the Armenian communist movement in 1912 and who was killed fighting for the communist cause. It has been suggested, wrongly, that it was renamed after Stepan Muradyan, leader of the Karabakh Dashnaks at the time of independence (1918–20) and a man inimical to the Azeris. Added to the personal name Stepan was the suffix *kert* 'dedicated to'. Captured and held by Armenian forces since 1993, it is still called Stepanakert by them, although the Azeris restored the name Khankendy in 1991. The transliterated Azeri Cyrillic form gave Xankändi and, following Azeri adoption of the roman script, this is now the official spelling.

Xenia, USA
Ohio: founded in 1803 by Joseph C. Vance who named it after the Greek word for 'hospitality'.

Xiamén, FUJIAN/CHINA
See AMOY.

Xi'an, SHAANXI/CHINA *Fengjing, Haojing, Chang'an, Siking*
Chang'an, a huge and very ancient city close to the modern city, meant 'Eternal Peace' from *cháng* 'long' and *ān* 'peace' while the present name means 'Western Peace' from *xī* and *ān*. Having been renamed Xi'an in 1369, it became Siking before returning to Xi'an in 1943. It was

the capital of China between 202 BC and AD 8 and during the Sui (581–618) and Tang (618–907) dynasties; it was one of the greatest cities of the world during the Tang dynasty. Marco Polo referred to it as Quengianfu, a variation of the Persian Kinjanfu, in the 13th-century account of his travels *Description of the World*.

Xiangfan, HUBEI/CHINA
In 1950 the two cities of Xiangyang on the south bank of the Han River and Fancheng on the north merged and the name is thus a combination of the two previous names. Xiangyang received its name from its position on the *yáng* 'north bank' of the Xiang River. Fancheng 'Fan Town' was named after the fiefdom of Fán and *chéng* 'town'.

Xiangtan, HUNAN/CHINA *Xiangnan, Hengshan*
Named after the Xiang River on which it lies at its junction with the Lian River and *tán* 'pool', a reference to some deep pools in the Xiang.

Xianyang, CHINA
Shaanxi: 'All Sunny' from *xián* 'all' or 'completely' because of the double *yáng* effect of its location south of the mountains and north of the Wei River, and thus has good exposure to the sun. Some time during the Han dynasty (206 BC–AD 220) it was renamed Wei Cheng from the Wei River and *chéng* 'town'. It reverted to its present name during the Tang dynasty (618–907).

Xī Jiāng, CHINA
'Western River', although it is only called this below Wuchow when it enters Guangdong province.

Xilitla, SAN LUIS POTOSI/MEXICO
'Place of Cozole', a type of local freshwater crab, in Nahuatl.

Xining, QINGHAI/CHINA *Huangzhongdi, Shan Zhou, Qingtang*
Its ancient name was derived from its position on the south bank of the Huang River, *zhōng* 'middle', and *dì* 'place'. The present name was adopted in 1104 when the city was taken by the Chinese from the Tibetans. It is an amalgamation of two place-names, Xidu and Changning, but the name can mean 'Peace in the West' from *xī* and *níng* 'peaceful'.

Xinjiang Uygur, CHINA
See SINKIANG UIGHUR.

Xinyang, HENAN/CHINA *Pingyang, Sanzhou*
Known as Pingyang County, it was established as Xinyang County in 976. The Xin, or *xìn*, is thought to be related to the character *shēn* 'read' from the local place-name Shen Zhou; both could have the same pronunciation and were interchangeable. Thus Xinyang might be a composite of Shen Zhou and Yiyang after the nearby Yiyang Mountains with *yáng* meaning a location south of Mt Dafu. During the Manchu dynasty (1644–1911) the city was known as Sanzhou, but it reverted to county status in 1913 and readopted its previous name. The city of Xinyang was re-established in 1949.

Xizang, CHINA
See TIBET.

Xuanhua, HEBEI/CHINA
The name is a shortened form of the expression Xuānyáng jiàohuà 'to proclaim the virtuous government of the court and to civilize the people'. Just inside the Great Wall, it was more than once a strategic frontier district and a fortified frontier post for defence against the Mongols. It has had a succession of former names as a county including Huairong, Wende, Xuande, and Guangning, and as Guihua and Shunning prefectures.

Xunantunich, BELIZE
Mayan ruins with a name meaning 'Stone Maiden'.

Yad Mordecai, ISRAEL
Founded as a kibbutz in 1943 and named after Mordecai Anielewicz (1919–43), the Polish Jewish leader of the resistance against the Germans in the Warsaw Ghetto in 1943, with *yad* 'memorial'.

Yakima, WASHINGTON/USA *North Yakima*
A river and a city founded in 1883 and named after the Yakima tribe whose name is said to mean either 'Black Bear' or 'Runaway', apparently with reference to the flow of the river. However, 'Runaway' has also been taken to mean 'those that run away'. The 'North' was dropped in 1918.

Yakutiya, RUSSIA
See SAKHA.

Yakutsk, YAKUTIYA REPUBLIC/RUSSIA *Lensky Ostrog, Yakutsky Ostrog*
Founded in 1632 on the Lena River, it was at first known as the 'Lena Stockade' from *ostrog* 'fortified town'. It was moved to its present site in 1642 and renamed 'Fortress of the Yakuts'. *See* SAKHA.

Yalta, UKRAINE *Dzhalita, Healita*
Now a popular holiday resort in the Crimea, the name is derived from the Polovtsian original, itself derived from the ancient Greek *yialos* 'sea-side' or 'shore'. According to legend, Greek sailors were blown off course one night in the Black Sea and lost their way in poor visibility. When the mist lifted the next morning the lookout saw the Crimean coast and shouted out 'yialos'. This was the name given to the place where they landed. The Polovtsians were a Turkic-speaking tribe of the Kipchak confederation living north of the Black Sea in the 11th century. Although the area came under Russian control in the late 18th century, the modern town was only developed at the beginning of the 19th century.

Yalu (Korean: *Amnok*), CHINA-NORTH KOREA
A river whose Chinese name is derived from *yā* 'duck' and *lū* 'greenish blue', said to be a comparison of the colour of its water with that of the feathers of a species of duck that lives here. The river forms a considerable part of the international border between China and North Korea.

Yalutorovsk, KURGAN/RUSSIA *Yalutorovsky*
Founded in 1639 as the military post of Yalutorovsky and named after an old Tatar fortress called Yavlu-Tura 'Warrior Town'.

Yamagata, HONSHŪ/JAPAN
A prefecture and a city with a name derived from characters representing *yama* 'mountain' and *kata* 'shape', a reference to the mountainous terrain.

Yamaguchi, HONSHŪ/JAPAN
A prefecture and a city founded in the 14th century with a name derived from characters representing *yama* and *kuchi* 'mouth', perhaps '(At the) Entrance to the Mountain'.

Yamalo-Nenets, RUSSIA *Yamalia*
An autonomous district, previously the province of Yamalia, named after the Nentsy, *Nenets* 'man' or 'real person' being the singular, a small ethnolinguistic group living in this part of northern Russia. Yamalo means 'End of the Land' from the Nenets *ya* 'end' and *ma* 'land'. *See* NENETS.

Yamanashi, HONSHŪ/JAPAN
A prefecture with characters representing *yama* and *nashi* 'pear' because of the abundance of pear trees here.

Yamoussoukro, CÔTE D'IVOIRE *Ngokro*
'Yamusa's House' or 'Yamusa's Village' from the personal name of its founder (in French, Yamoussou) and the Baule *kro* 'house' or 'village'. Because it was the birthplace of Félix Houphouët-Boigny (1905–93), the first president of the independent Côte d'Ivoire (1960–93), Yamoussoukro was designated the official capital in 1983; however, Abidjan remans the *de facto* (administrative) capital.

Yan'an, SHAANXI/CHINA *Fuzu County*
Founded as a frontier post during the Sui dynasty (581–618), it was given its present name in 1369. It gets the first part of this name from the Yan River on which it lies from *yán* 'extend' or 'prolong'. With *ān* 'peace' the name could be said to mean 'Eternal Peace'.

Yanaul, BASHKORTOSTAN REPUBLIC/RUSSIA
'New Village' from the Bashkir *yany* 'new' and *aul* 'village'.

y

Yanbuʻ al-Baḥr, SAUDI ARABIA
'Spring on-Sea' from *yanbuʻ* 'spring', 'source', or 'well' and *baḥr* 'sea'. A coastal town, also spelt Yenbo, al-Baḥr is added to differentiate it from other towns called Yanbu.

Yancheng, JIANGSU/CHINA *Yandu, Yandan*
'Salt Town' from *yán* 'salt' and *chéng* 'town' because it produced abundant quantities of sea salt. During the Han dynasty (221 BC–AD 220) it was named Yandu and Yandan County before adopting its present name in 411.

Yangibazar, KYRGYZSTAN
'New Market' from the Uzbek *yangi* 'new' and *bazar* 'market'.

Yangiyer, UZBEKISTAN *Chernyayevo*
'New Land' from *yangi* 'new' and *yer* 'land'. The previous name honoured Mikhail Chernyayev (1828–98), a Russian military commander in Central Asia during the 1860s and later governor-general of Turkestan.

Yangiyul, UZBEKISTAN *Kaunchi-Tepe*
'New Way' from *yangi* 'new' and *yoʻl* 'way' or 'road'.

Yangon, BURMA
See RANGOON.

Yangquan, SHANXI/CHINA
Situated in mountains, the name is derived from *yáng*, indicating that it is south of the mountains, and *quán* 'spring' (water). The character used to be *yàng* 'to brim over', a reference to five vigorous springs here.

Yangtze (Yangzi), CHINA
Derived from Yang, an ancient fiefdom, and *zǐ* 'son'. It rises in Qinghai Province and in its upper reaches it is called the Tongtian He and Jinsha Jiang, *hé* and *jiāng* both meaning 'river'. It becomes the Chang Jiang 'Long River' from *cháng* 'long' from Yibin in Sichuan Province onwards. Europeans have also called it the Blue River, possibly to differentiate it from the Yellow River.

Yangzhou, JIANGSU/CHINA *Han Cheng, Kuangling*
Lying a little north of the Yangtze River, the first syllable is thought to come from the phrase *yáng bō* 'the swelling of waves' from *yáng* 'swelling' and *bō* 'waves'. The city was founded as Han Town in 486 BC and it was renamed Kuangling in the 4th century BC. It received its present name in AD 588 and became the capital of the Sui dynasty (581–618) in 605.

Yanjing, YUNNAN/CHINA
'Salt Well' from *yán* 'salt' and *jìng* 'well'. The extraction of salt has continued here for some 1 000 years.

Yankton, SOUTH DAKOTA/USA
Settled in 1858 and named after the Yankton tribe, a branch of the Sioux.

Yantai, SHANDONG/CHINA *Zhifu, Chefoo*
It took its first name from that of a nearby mountain. The present name means 'Smoke Terrace' from *yān* 'smoke' and *yángtái* 'terrace' or 'patio'. Part of a coastal defence system, a bonfire system was initiated in 1398 here to warn fishing fleets of the approach of pirates, usually said to be Japanese.

Yantarnyy, KALININGRAD/RUSSIA *Palmnicken*
Noted for its amber mine and products, it means '(Town of) Amber' from *yantarʻ*. The name was changed when East Prussia was annexed by the Soviet Union in 1946.

Yao, HONSHŪ/JAPAN
The characters represent *ya* 'eight', an abbreviation of *yattsu*, and *o* 'tail'.

Yaoundé, CAMEROON
Founded as a German military garrison in 1888, the name comes from the Bantu-speaking Éwondo people, also called the *Yaounde*. In 1909 it became the capital of German Kamerun, in 1922 the capital of French Cameroun, and in 1960 the capital of independent Cameroon.

Yaqui, SONORA/MEXICO
A river and a town named after the Yaqui tribe.

Yarkand, SINKIANG UIGHUR AUTONOMOUS REGION/CHINA
See SHACHE.

Yarmouth, CANADA, UK, USA
UK (England): formerly Ermud and Ernemouth 'Gravelly Estuary' from the Old English *ēar* 'gravel' and *mūtha*. The river's name is a back-formation from the place name.

Yaroslavlʻ, RUSSIA *Medvezhy Ugol*
A province and a city founded in 1010 by Yaroslav (986–1054), then Grand Duke of Novgorod, after he had killed a bear which had attacked him. He called the fortress, which he ordered to be built here, 'Bear's Corner' from *medvedʻ* 'bear' and *ugol* 'corner'. When Yaroslav became Grand Prince of Kiev in 1019 (*see* BORISOGLEBSK) the expanding settlement was renamed 'Yaroslavl's (Town)' after him. Between 1218 and 1471 it was the capital of an independent principality.

Yarqon, ISRAEL *Nahr al-ʻAuja*
A river with a name derived from the Hebrew *yaroq* 'green' because the water appeared to reflect the vegetation along its banks. The previous Arab name meant 'The Tortuous River'.

y

Yarra, VICTORIA/AUSTRALIA *Great River, Freshwater River*
A river with an Aboriginal name meaning 'Running Water'.

Yasinovataya, UKRAINE
Named after the river, whose name comes from the Russian *yasen'* 'ash-tree'.

Yasnaya Polyana, RUSSIA
Tula: 'Bright, or Serene, Place' from *yasnaya* 'bright' or 'serene' and *polyana* literally 'glade' or 'clearing'.

Yasothon, THAILAND
Derived from the Sanskrit *yasodhara* 'Upholder of Glory' from *yasas* 'glory' and *dhara* 'supporting'.

Yatenga, BURKINA FASO
A province which takes its name from a 16th-century Mossi kingdom. It was named after its founder, one Yadega, and the region was called Yadega Tenga 'Yadega's Land'. This was then shortened to the present form.

Yatsushiro, KYŪSHŪ/JAPAN
The characters represent *yattsu* 'eight' and *shiro* 'generation'.

Yaynanyoung (Yaynanchaung), BURMA
'Stream of Petroleum'.

Yazd, IRAN *Kathah*
The original name was the Persian for a 'hollow' or 'moat' which ran round ramparts. The city is said to have acquired its present name during the reign of Yazdgerd II, King of the Sāssānians (438–57). However, it has also been suggested that the name is derived from *yazdan* 'god'. An ancient city, it has many religious buildings and is the main centre of Zoroastrianism in Iran.

Yazoo City, MISSISSIPPI/USA *Hanan's Bluff*
Founded in 1824, it was renamed after the Yazoo tribe in 1839. A tributary of the Mississippi River is called the Yazoo.

Yegor'yevsk, MOSCOW/RUSSIA *Vysokaya*
Originally called 'High' from *vysokiy* 'high'. When a church dedicated to St George was built the name became Yegor'ye Vysokoye; and when the village became a town in 1778 the present version of the name was adopted.

Yekaterinburg, RUSSIA *Sverdlovsk*
The *burg* indicates a fortified settlement which was originally named Yekaterinburg 'Catherine's Town' in 1723 after Catherine, later Empress Catherine I[†]. A Europhile, Peter I the Great[†] gave the town a German name. In 1924–91 the city was renamed after Yakov Sverdlov (1885–1919), a major figure in the Communist Party, and a professional

Bolshevik revolutionary who undertook revolutionary activities here in 1905. He became the first head of the Soviet State in November 1917.

Yélimané, MALI
A corruption of the Arabic *al-imām*, a title for the leader of prayers in a mosque.

Yelizovo, KAMCHATKA/RUSSIA *Zavoyko*
Originally named after Admiral Vasily Zavoyko (1810–98), military governor of Kamchatka from 1849, who conducted the defence of Petropavlovsk (now Petropavlovsk-Kamchatskiy) against the British and French in 1854. It was renamed in 1924 after G. Yelizov, the leader of a communist partisan group who was killed here by anti-communist White Guards in 1922.

Yellowknife, NORTHWEST TERRITORIES/CANADA
A river, a bay, and a city founded in 1935 and named after the Yellowknife tribe who got their name from their practice of making knives and other utensils from yellow copper.

Yellow River (Huáng Hé), CHINA
So-called because of the high degree of yellowish silt it carries.

Yellow Sea (Huáng Hǎi), CHINA
So-called because of the colour of its water, received from the Yellow River and others that discharge into it.

Yel'nya, SMOLENSK/RUSSIA
Derived from *yel'* 'fir tree' or 'spruce'.

Yemanzhelinsk, CHELYABINSK/RUSSIA
Developed from a fortress built in 1747 with a name derived from the Yemanzhelinka River. This comes from the Tatar *yaman* 'bad' and *yelga* 'river', probably a reference to the unpotable nature of the water.

Yemen (al-Yaman) *Saba/Sheba, Arabia Felix*
The Republic of Yemen (al-Jumhūrīyah al-Yamanīyah) since 1990 when North Yemen (Yemen Arab Republic since 1962) and South Yemen (People's Democratic Republic of Yemen since 1970) united with a 30-month period of implementation. However, in 1994 civil war broke out and the South declared itself to be the Democratic Republic of Yemen (DRY). Within a few weeks the North had prevailed and the DRY ceased to exist. Previously South Yemen had gained independence from the UK in 1967 as the People's Republic of Yemen (1967–70), having been the Federation of South Arabia (1963–7) and the Federation of Arab Emirates of the South (1959–63); the port of Aden had been captured by the British in 1839, becoming a

dependency of British India and a crown colony in 1937, while in the hinterland the British Aden Protectorate was established in 1886. North Yemen became independent in 1914 as an Imamate when Ottoman Turkish forces left, having first arrived in the 16th century; their presence was not continuous and they failed to exercise full control. When they reappeared during the middle of the 19th century it became necessary to agree a border between their and British interests and this was done in 1902–13. A *coup d'état* in 1962 brought the downfall of the Imamate and the creation of the Yemen Arab Republic. The meaning of the name Yemen is disputed. Some say that it comes from the Arabic *yamīn* 'on the right-hand side' of the Ka'bah in Mecca or to the right of the Red Sea; others that it comes from *yumn* 'good fortune' or 'prosperity' and that the Greeks translated this as *eudaemon* and the Romans as *felix*, hence Arabia Felix 'Arabia the Fortunate' (*see* ADEN AND ARABIA); yet others that it is named after Yamin bin Qahtan, a grandson of Noah and progenitor of the South Arabian tribes, or that it is simply *al-Yaman* 'the South' after the Prophet Muhammad[†] had pointed to the south and said that that was *al-Yaman*.

Yemva, KOMI REPUBLIC/RUSSIA *Obiralovka, Zheleznodorozhnaya, Zheleznodorozhnyy*
Until 1992 it was known from its connection with the railway *zheleznaya doroga* 'iron way' from *doroga* 'road', 'way', or 'route', that was built here in 1939; the spelling was amended in 1952. Why the name was changed and what it means is not known.

Yenakiyeve, UKRAINE *Rykovo, Ordzhonikidze, Yenakiyevo*
Founded as a mining settlement called Yenakiyevo in 1883 with the name probably associated with its founder or owner, one Yenakiyev. It was renamed in 1928 after Aleksey Rykov (1881–1938), who became President of the Council of People's Commissars (i.e. premier) after Lenin's[†] death in 1924. Labelled a right-winger, he was forced to stand down in 1930; he was a major defendant in the third show trial in Moscow in 1938, convicted, and executed. Three years before his execution when he was already discredited, the town was renamed after Grigory (Sergo) Ordzhonikidze[†]. Once his reputation became tarnished, the town reverted to its original name in 1943.

Yeniköy, TURKEY
There are several towns with this name which simply means 'New Village' from *yeni* 'new' and *köy* 'village'. The town on the Bosporus was

at first called Neapolis 'New City' and then in the 15th century Genikoy 'Village of the Geni', settlers who had come from Romania. The present name was adopted in the 16th century.

Yenişehir, TURKEY
'New Town' from *yeni* 'new' and *şehir*.

Yenisey, RUSSIA
A river with an Evenki-Ket name 'Big River' from the Evenki *yene* 'big river' and Ket *ses* 'river'. Yeneses then became Yenisey.

Yeovil, ENGLAND/UK *Gifle, Givele*
'(Place on) the (River) Gifl', the river's name meaning 'forked river'. It is now called the Yeo.

Yerevan, ARMENIA *Erebuni, Erivan'*
A very ancient walled citadel, the capital of Urartu, the meaning of whose name is not certain. In 1968 the inhabitants of Yerevan celebrated the 2 750th anniversary of the foundation of their city in 782 BC by King Argishti I of Urartu. The name may come from that of a local people. However, according to local legend, it was founded by Noah who, stranded in his Ark on Mt Ararat, looked out to the east and exclaimed 'Yerevats' 'I have seen it'—meaning land and thus a place in what is now the Valley of the Aras River for a new city. The present name is certainly derived from Erebuni, which is said to come from *aireri bun* 'abode of heroes' from *air* 'hero' or 'titan'. Erivan' was the official Russian spelling until 1936. It has been the capital of Armenia since 1920. Under the rule of many invaders from earliest times, it fell to the Ottoman Turks in 1582, to the Persians in 1604, and, as a Persian-protected khanate, was annexed by the Russians in 1828.

Yerofey Pavlovich, AMUR/RUSSIA
Founded in 1909 when the railway arrived and named after Yerofey Pavlovich Khabarov (*c.*1610–*c.*1667), a Russian explorer who penetrated Siberia and reached the Amur River in the middle of the 17th century.

Yeşilırmak, TURKEY *Iris*
A river, the 'Green River', from *yeşil* 'green' or 'verdant' and *ırmak* 'river'.

Yeşilköy, TURKEY *Agios Stephanios, Ayastefanos*
'Green Village' from *yeşil* 'green' and *köy* 'village'. The former names, St Stephen, were used simultaneously, the first Greek and the second Turkish. They were superseded by the present name in 1924.

Yevpatoriya, UKRAINE *Kirkinitida, Eupatoria, Gezlëv, Kozlov*
A 6th-century BC Greek colony, first called Kirkinitida and then Eupatoria, from which

the present name comes, after Mithradates VI Eupator, King of Pontus (d. 63 BC). Having been captured by the Ottoman Turks in the 14th century, the name became Gezlëv and this was Russified to Kozlov when Russia annexed the Crimea in 1783. Yevpatoriya was adopted as the sole name in the 19th century.

Yevreyskaya, RUSSIA
A Jewish autonomous province from *Yevrey* 'Jew'. However, the attempt to settle Jews here in their own autonomous province, also known as *Birobidzhan, from 1928 was a failure.

Yinchuan, NINGXIA HUI/CHINA *Fuping, Yinhan Cheng, Lu Cheng, Huaiyuan*
Originally a county in the 1st century BC, the present name means 'Silver Plain' from *yín* 'silver' and *chuān* 'plain'. The highly alkaline soil produces silvery-white streaks on the surface in winter, hence the name. It lies close to the Yellow River.

Yingkou, LIAONING/CHINA *Mogou Ying*
Near the mouth of the Liao River, the name comes from *yíng* 'camp' and *kǒu* 'mouth'. The original name was Mogou Camp in recognition of the coastal defence troops based here.

Yining, SINKIANG UIGHUR AUTONOMOUS REGION/CHINA *Ningyuan*
The first syllable comes from *yī*, a reference to the Yili Hasake region and *níng* is 'peace'. There was an ancient kingdom called Yili in this area. The city is called Gulya by the Uighurs meaning the 'Golden Roofed Temple', a reference to the temple to the north-east built at the end of the Ming dynasty (1368–1644).

Yogyakarta, JAVA/INDONESIA *Yogya*
A province and a city usually shortened to Yogya which may be derived from the Sanskrit *ayodhyā* 'invincible' or 'unconquerable (fortress)' with the Sundanese *karta* 'city'. This has been taken further to mean 'Safe City' and even 'Peaceful City'. The full name, Yogyakarta, was adopted in 1755 when the sultan moved his court here. It was the capital city of Rāma in the Hindu epic, the *Rāmāyaṇa*, and also the unofficial capital of the self-declared Republic of Indonesia between 1946 and 1949.

Yokkaichi, HONSHŪ/JAPAN
An important trading centre whose name means 'Market on the Fourth Day in the Month' from *yokka* 'fourth day in the month' and *ichi* 'market'.

Yokohama, HONSHŪ/JAPAN
Kanagawa: founded with the amalgamation of the small village of Yokohama and Kanagawa

in 1889. The name alludes to its position on the west coast of Tokyo Bay from the characters *yoko* 'beside' and *hama* 'shore'.

Yokosuka, HONSHŪ/JAPAN
Kanagawa: 'Beside the Sandy Beach' from the characters *yoko* 'beside' and *suka* 'sandy beach'.

Yola, ADAMAWA/NIGERIA
Founded in 1841 as a base for *jihad* 'holy war', the name is derived from the Fulfulde *yolde*, a word denoting a settlement on rising ground.

Yonkers, NEW YORK/USA *Nappeckamack*
Once a village belonging to the Manhattan tribe, the site was acquired by the Dutch in 1639. In 1646 Adriaen van der Donck with the title of De Konkheer, equivalent to 'squire', established a community here from which the town of Yonkers, named after his title, subsequently arose.

York, AUSTRALIA, CANADA, GREENLAND, SOUTH AFRICA, UK, USA
1. In most cases, the cities and towns with this name are taken from the English city or one of several Dukes of York.
2. Australia (Queensland): named in 1770 by Captain James Cook[†] after Edward Augustus (1739–67), Duke of York and Albany and brother of King George III[†].
3. UK (England): originally a Celtic name, Eborakon or Eboracum 'Eburos's Estate', with the personal name possibly meaning 'yew tree', but more likely 'Yew-Tree Estate'. The Romans arrived in 71 to build a walled fortress. They used the name Eboracum which later became Evorog. To the Anglo-Saxons this sounded like *eofor* 'wild boar'. They added *wīc*, thus Eoforwic, to give a possible meaning of 'Boar Farm'. The city was captured by the Danes in 867 and they took the *wīc* to be the Old Scandinavian *vik* 'bay' although York is inland. Eofor was shortened to Eor and thus the name became Eorvik. In time the 'Eor' became 'Jor' and then 'Yor' and *vik* was reduced to *k*. The former county of Yorkshire took its name from the city with the additional *scīr*. York Races include the famous Ebor Handicap.
4. USA (Maine): settled as Agamenticus in 1624 to become the first English city on North American soil. When it became a city in 1641 at the bidding of Sir Ferdinando Gorges he renamed it Gorgeana. When it reverted to a town in 1652 it was renamed York after the English city.

Yorktown, USA
Virginia: settled in 1631 and named after Charles (1600–49), Duke of York and later King Charles I[†].

Yoshkar-Ola, MARI EL REPUBLIC/RUSSIA
Tsarĕvokokshaysk, Krasnokokshaysk
Located on the River Kokshaga, the town was
originally named for tsardom, the 'Tsar's Town
on the (River) Kokshaga' in 1584–1919.
Between 1919 and 1927 it was renamed for
communism, the 'Red Town on the (River)
Kokshaga' from *krasno*. Its present name,
adopted in 1927, means much the same, 'Red
Town' from the Mari *yoshkar* 'red' and *ola*
'town'.

Youngstown, CANADA, USA
USA (Ohio): laid out originally as Young's Town
in 1797 by, and named after, John Young, a
surveyor.

Yozgat, TURKEY
'Pasture Town' fom *yoz* 'pasture' or
'uncultivated' and *gat* 'town'.

Ypacarí, PARAGUAY
A lake and a city founded in 1887 with a
Guaraní name 'Water of God'.

Ypres (Flemish: **Ieper**), BELGIUM
Derived from the Gaulish *ivo* 'yew'.

Ypsilanti, USA
Michigan: developed as Woodruff's Grove
round a trading post in the early 19th century,
it was renamed in 1833 after Demetrios
Ypsilanti (1793–1832), a Greek patriot.

Yuba City, CALIFORNIA/USA
Laid out on the Yuba River in 1849, its
name is derived from the original Spanish
name of the river Río de las Uvas 'River of
the Grapes'.

Yucatán, MEXICO *Mayapán*
A peninsula and a state. According to tradition,
while exploring the coast in 1517, the Spanish
mistook Yucatán as the name of the area when
locals they had asked replied in a local dialect
'Yucatan' 'We don't understand.' An
alternative theory, however, is that local
people told the Spanish that they grew *yuca*
'cassava' to make bread. A third theory is that
Yucatán is derived from a local word for
'slaughter' from *yuka* 'to kill' and *yetá* 'many'.
The original name acknowledges the Maya.
Many of the great cities of the Mayan
civilization, at its height *c.*600–900, were
located in the peninsula. Its conquest by the
Spanish began in 1527.

Yudu, JIANGXI/CHINA
Founded in 201 BC with a different character
for Yu: *yú* 'rain ceremony'. The name was
changed to the present *yú* 'in', 'at', 'on', 'by', or
'from'. The *dū* could mean 'city' or 'large
town'.

Yugoslavia (Jugoslavija)
The previous name for what is now the state of
Serbia and Montenegro when it was the Federal
Republic of Yugoslavia (Savezna Republika
Jugoslavija) in 1992–2003. In 1963–92 it was
called the Socialist Federal Republic of
Yugoslavia which consisted of the Republics of
Slovenia, Croatia, Serbia, Bosnia and
Herzegovina, Montenegro, and Macedonia; the
Federal People's Republic of Yugoslavia (1945–
63) and Democratic Federal Yugoslavia (1945)
with the monarchy being formally abolished in
1946; the Kingdom of Yugoslavia (1929–45);
and the Kingdom of the Serbs, Croats, and
Slovenes (Kraljevina Srba, Hrvata i Slovenaca)
(1918–29). The new country was created as a
result of the Serbs siding with the victorious
Allies in 1918, although the Croats and
Slovenes had been on the losing side in the First
World War as part of Austria-Hungary. The
kingdom also included the previously
independent Kingdom of Montenegro,
Vojvodina, Austrian Dalmatia, and Bosnia and
Herzegovina; Macedonia then was part of
Serbia. The kingdom's borders were not settled
until the Treaty of Rapallo in 1920. Yugoslavia
means 'Southern Slavs' or the '(Land of the)
South Slavs' from *jug* 'south'. In general, even in
1918, non-Serbs preferred the name Yugoslavia
because it suggested a union of equals, but as
the most powerful element, the Serbs wanted a
name that reflected their superiority.

Yukon, CANADA, USA
Canada: a territory with the full name Yukon
Territory. It is named after the Yukon River
whose name is said to come from the Native
American *yu-kun-ah* 'big river'. It was separated
from the Northwest Territories in 1898 and
became a territory in its own right.

Yuma, RUSSIA, USA
1. USA (Arizona): founded as Colorado City in
1854, renamed Arizona City in 1862 and given
the name Yuma in 1873, possibly after the
Spanish *humo* 'smoke', a reference to the
practice of the local Native Americans to make
smoke to induce rain. It is also the name of the
desert in Arizona and Sonora, Mexico.
2. USA (Colorado): named after the Yuma
people whose name is said to mean 'Sons of
the River'.

Yunnan, CHINA *Olam*
A mountainous province named by the
Mongols 'South of the Clouds'. According to
legend, Wu (157–87 BC), Emperor of China
(141–87 BC), once saw clouds of many hues and
sent some people to investigate their origins.
They ended up south of these clouds and the
county was given this name from *yún* 'cloud'

y

and *nán* 'south'. The name is also said to mean 'Cloudy South', a reference to the low cloud habitually found in the vicinity of the Yünling mountain range in Sichuan Province to the north.

Yur'yev Pol'skiy, MOSCOW/RUSSIA
'Yuri's Field'. Founded in 1152 by, and named after, Grand Prince Yuri Dolgoruky (*c*.1090–1157). Pol'skiy from *pole* 'field' was added to distinguish it from Yur'yev (now Tartu) in Estonia.

Yuryuzan', CHELYABINSK/RUSSIA
Takes its name from the Yuryuzan' River on which it lies. Its own name means 'Big River' from the Bashkir *yur* 'big' and *uzen* 'river'.

Yuzhno-Kuril'sk, KURIL ISLANDS/RUSSIA
Furukamappu

Lying at the southern end of the *Kuril Islands it was renamed 'Southern Kuril' in 1946 after Soviet acquisition of the islands from the Japanese from *yuzhno* 'south' or 'southern' and Kuril.

Yuzhno-Sakhalinsk, SAKHALIN ISLAND/
RUSSIA *Vladimirovka, Toiohara*
'South Sakhalin' from *yuzhno* 'south'. It was originally named in 1881 after a military officer and then Toiohara 'Rich Plain' from *toyo* 'rich' and *hara* 'plain' by the Japanese during their occupation in 1904–45. *See* SAKHALIN.

Yuzhnoural'sk, CHELYABINSK/RUSSIA
'Southern Urals' from *yuzhno* 'south' and Ural, the mountain range on which it lies.

Zacatecas, MEXICO *Las Minas de Nuestra Señora de los Zacatecas*
A state and a city founded in 1548 with a name meaning '(Place where) People grow Zacate Grass' from *tecatl* 'people'. The original name referred to the silver mines here.

Zadar, CROATIA *Idassa, Jader(a), Diadara, Zara*
First recorded by the Greeks as Idassa in the 4th century BC, it was later known to the Romans as Jader or Jadera. By the 10th century it had become Diadara. Between 1409 and 1797 it was in Venetian hands and Austrian between 1797 and 1920. By the Treaty of Rapallo in 1920 it was given to Italy as an enclave on the Yugoslav mainland and called Zara. In 1944 it fell to the Yugoslavs. The present name can easily be traced back to the original, but the meaning is not known.

Zadonsk, LIPETSK/RUSSIA *Teshev*
Lying at the confluence of the Don and Teshevka Rivers, it was originally named after the latter. It was renamed in 1779 'Beyond the Don' from *za* and Don.

Zagreb, CROATIA *Andautonia, Agram*
The first settlement was named after the Illyrian tribe, the Andauti. The present name may be derived from *zagrepsti* 'to dig in', indicating a settlement surrounded by earthworks; or, possibly, from *za grebom* 'behind the cliff' from *greben* 'cliff' or 'mountain range', referring to the range of wooded hills to the north. The city was developed from two rival settlements: Gradec 'fortress' and Kaptol 'bishopric'. Gradec was accorded the rights and privileges of a royal and free city by Bela IV (1206–70), King of Hungary (1235–70), after Kaptol had been sacked by the Tatars in 1242. New building in the 19th century filled the narrow gap between them which resulted in their merger in 1850. The German name Agram was in use in 1526–1918. The city has been the capital of Croatia, possibly from 1557, except in 1756–76.

Zaire, ANGOLA
A province named after the Zaire River. Its name comes from the Kikongo *nzai*, a form of *nazdi* 'river'. *See* CONGO.

Zakarpatska, UKRAINE
A province called 'Beyond the Carpathians' from *za* and *Karpaty* 'Carpathian Mountains'.

Zákynthos, GREECE *Zacinto*
An island, also known as Zante, and a town named after an ancient Arcadian chief. According to legend, he was a companion of Hercules and was bitten by a snake and died. His body was taken to an island in the Ionian Sea which was thereafter called Zákynthos or Zacynthus. The Venetians acquired the island in 1483, naming it Zacinto, and held it until 1797 when it was annexed by France. It was finally ceded to Greece in 1864.

Zaleshchiki, UKRAINE
'People who live beyond the Forest' from *za*, *les* 'forest', and *chiki* denoting a group of people.

Zambezi, SOUTH EAST AFRICA *Egwembeni*
The original Ndebele name meant 'River of Boats'. The present name may come from the root word *za* 'river' with the whole name meaning 'Grand River' or something similar.

Zambézia, MOZAMBIQUE
A province named after the Zambezi River.

Zambia The Republic of Zambia since 1964 when independence was gained from the UK. Previously named Northern Rhodesia (1911–64) after Cecil Rhodes[†]. The British South Africa Company handed over its administration to the British crown in 1924. In 1890, having been empowered by the British government, the Company concluded treaties with various local chiefs which in succeeding years led to its authority over the territory north of the Zambezi River, then part of Barotseland 'Land of the Barotse' (now known as the Lozi), and protectorate status. The country is named after the Zambezi which forms its southern border with Zimbabwe. *See* RHODESIA.

Zamboanga City, MINDANAO/PHILIPPINES
Founded by the Spanish in 1635 with a name derived from the Malay *jambangan* 'place of flowers' in recognition of the tropical flowers that flourish in the city.

Zamfara, NIGERIA
A river named after a territory which incorporated the river. It was called

Zamfarawa 'Men of Fara', Fara being the name of a local princess.

Zamość, POLAND *Himmlerstadt*
Founded in the 16th century on an estate called Zamość by Jan Zamoyski (1542–1605), chancellor and Grand Hetman of the Crown (commander-in-chief of the armed forces), who took his name from that of the estate. It might mean 'Beyond the Bridge' from the Slavonic *za* and *most* 'bridge'. It was called Himmler Town briefly during the Second World War after Heinrich Himmler (1900–45), Nazi leader and chief of the *Gestapo* (*Geheime Staatspolizei* 'Secret State Police').

Zanzibar, TANZANIA *Zanguebar*
An island, part of the autonomous region of Zanzibar and Pemba, and a city-port. The name was at one time applied to the East African coast in this region. It is derived from the Persian *Zangī-bār* 'Coastland of the Blacks' from the Zingis, a local people whose name translated as 'black', and *barr* 'coast'. The *g* was softened by the Arabs to become Zanjībār which the Portuguese transformed into Zanzibar. The capital of the Sultan of Oman from 1832, it was declared a sultanate independent of Oman in 1862. Annexed by Germany in 1885, Zanzibar became a British protectorate in 1890 when the Germans gave it and the small island of Pemba to them in exchange for two tiny, low-lying islands in the North Sea, Heligoland and Dune. It regained its status as an independent sultanate at the end of 1963, but the sultan was overthrown in early 1964 and the People's Republic of Zanzibar established. Three months later Zanzibar joined Tanganyika to form the United Republic of Tanganyika and Zanzibar, renamed a few months later as the United Republic of *Tanzania. The local name for the island is Unguja.

Zapolyarnyy, MURMANSK/RUSSIA
Founded in 1956 as 'Beyond the Polar (Circle)' from *za* and *polyarnyy* 'polar' or 'arctic'. The Arctic Circle is known to the Russians as *Severnyy Polyarnyy Krug* 'Northern Polar Circle'.

Zaporozh'ye (Zaporizhzhya), UKRAINE
Aleksandrovskaya, Aleksandrovsk
A province and a city. It was originally a fortress named after Field Marshal Alexander Golitsyn (1718–83), the commander of the First Army fighting the Ottoman Turks in the area at the time it was founded in 1770. In 1806 the town that had developed round the fortress was named Aleksandrovsk, a name it retained until 1921. The present name means 'Beyond the Rapids' from *za* and *porog* 'rapids' and is so-called because it was a place to which

peasants, tied to the land in the service of a particular landlord, fled to escape the Polish authorities. Such fugitives were known as Cossacks from the Turkic *kazak* 'outlaw' or 'adventurer'. The city lies on the River Dnieper just below its former rapids which have been submerged. On Khortytsa Island the Cossacks first formed their militaristic society in a *sich* 'fortified camp' and hence some are known as Zaporozhian Cossacks.

Zapovednyy, PRIMORSKIY TERRITORY/RUSSIA
Goszapovednik
'Prohibited'. Its former name meant 'National Park' from *gosudarstvenyy* 'state' and *zapovednik* 'reserve' or 'preserve'.

Zaragoza, ARAGON/SPAIN
See SARAGOSSA.

Zaria, KADUNA/NIGERIA
Founded *c*.1536 and named after Zaria, Queen of the Hausa state of Zazzau (16th century).

Zaslavl', BELARUS *Izyaslavl*
Named after an unknown prince called Izyaslav, thus 'Izyaslav's (Town)'.

Zastron, FREE STATE/SOUTH AFRICA
Founded in 1876 and named after Lady Johanna Brand, wife of the president of Orange Free State, whose maiden name was Zastron.

Žatec, CZECH REPUBLIC *Zateč, Saaz*
Named after a local brook with the same name. This was derived possibly from the Old Czech *zatkati* 'to block up', a reference to the clogging of the brook with sediment. It has also been suggested that it is derived from the root *žat* 'harvesting'. Žatec is the centre of the hop-growing region for the beer industry.

Zealand (Sjælland), DENMARK
An island with a name meaning 'Sea Land' from the Old Scandinavian *sjá* 'sea' and *land*.

Zeebrugge, BELGIUM
It is the port for Bruges and its name is simply 'Sea Bruges' from the Flemish *see* 'sea' and Brugge 'Bruges'.

Zeeland, THE NETHERLANDS, USA
The Netherlands: a province and a town meaning 'Sea Land', although the town is well inland.

Zeerust, NORTH WEST/SOUTH AFRICA *Coetzee-Rust*
Laid out on a farm belonging to Diederik Coetzee in 1867, it was at first known as 'Coetzee's Home' from the personal name and Afrikaans *rust* 'rest' in the sense of 'home'. The name was later shortened to the present form.

Z

Zelenodol'sk, TATARSTAN REPUBLIC, RUSSIA
Kabachishche, Zelëny Dol
Founded in 1865 with a name associated with
kabak 'tavern' before being renamed Zelëny
Dol 'Green Valley' from *zelen* 'green' and *dol*
'dale', a poetic word. In 1932 the present
version of the name was adopted. There are
quite a few towns in Russia whose names
begin with *Zelen-*, e.g. Zelenogorsk,
Zelenograd, etc.

Zelenogradsk, KALININGRAD/RUSSIA *Kranz*
'Green Town'. The name was changed in 1946
when East Prussia was annexed by the Soviet
Union at the end of the Second World War.

Zelenokumsk, STAVROPOL' TERRITORY/RUSSIA
Vorontsovo-Aleksandrovskoye, Sovetskoye
Originally with personal names, it was
renamed 'Soviet' in 1963–5. Its present name
simply means 'Green (Town)' on the Kuma
(River)'.

Železný Brod, CZECH REPUBLIC *Eisenbrod*
'Iron Ford', from *železný* 'iron' and *brod* 'ford', a
reference to the iron ore mined here since the
17th century. The former German name
meant the same from *Eisen* 'iron'.

Zeravshan, TAJIKISTAN
A mountain range and a town named after the
Zeravshan River. Its headwaters are rich in
natural resources, hence its name 'Gold
Spreader' from *zer* 'gold' and *rekhtan* 'to
spread'.

Zermatt, SWITZERLAND
'(Place) at the Meadow' from the German *zur*
'at the' and *Matte* 'meadow'.

Zernograd, ROSTOV/RUSSIA
Founded in 1933 as an experimental grain
farm, the name means 'Grain Town' from
zerno 'grain' and *grad*.

Zhaman Akkol', KAZAKHSTAN
'Bad White Lake' from *zhaman* 'bad', *ak* 'white',
and *köl* 'lake' and named because it is very salty
and appears white.

Zhambyl, KAZAKHSTAN
A province formed in 1939 and named after
the Kazakh poet, Zhambyl Zhabaev (1846–
1945). The province's capital, formerly with
this name, was renamed *Taraz in 1997.

Zhangjiakou, HEBEI/CHINA *Wanquan*
Also known as Kalgan, a Mongolian word
meaning 'gate in a barrier', a reference to the
Great Wall of China on which it lies between
two mountain peaks. Between 1911 and 1929
the city was known as Wanquan County. It has
also been known colloquially as Tung-kou
'Eastern Entry', in recognition of the fact that

it was the main point of entry for caravans
from Russia and Inner Mongolia into China.
The present formal Chinese name means
'Zhāng Family Pass', Zhāng being the name of
the commander in charge of the construction
of the fortress, built in 1429, with *jiā* 'family'
and *kŏu* 'mouth' or, here, 'mountain pass'.

Zhanjiang GUANGDONG/CHINA *Guang Zhou
Wan, Zanchuan, Fort Bayard, Tsamkong*
Occupied by the French in 1898, it was opened
as a free port the following year and renamed
after a French military hero, Seigneur de
Bayard (1473–1524). It takes its name from the
River Zhanjiang 'Clear River' from *zhàn* 'clear'
or 'transparent' and *jiāng* 'river'. It adopted its
present name in 1945.

Zharkent, KAZAKHSTAN *Dzharkent, Panfilov*
Renamed in 1942 after Major General Ivan
Panfilov (1893–1941), who was killed near
Moscow while commanding the 316th Rifle
Division against the Germans; he was a
military commissar in the Kyrgyz SSR in 1938.
The original name, possibly meaning 'Town in
a Hot Place' from *zhar* 'heat' and *kent* 'town',
was readopted after Kazakh independence in
1991. There is also a town still called Panfilovo
in Volgograd Province, Russia.

Zhdanov, AZERBAIJAN
Named after Andrey Zhdanov (1896–1948),
one of Joseph Stalin's[†] closest henchmen,
leader of the Leningrad (now St Petersburg)
Communist Party organization and of that
city's resistance to the German siege in
1941–4.

Zhejiang, CHINA
A province with a name taken from its main
river, the Zhe, from *zhé* 'curving' or 'twisty'
and *jiāng*.

Zheleznodorozhnyy, RUSSIA
Towns in Irkutsk and Kaliningrad Provinces
have this name which comes from the railway
zheleznaya doroga 'iron way' from *doroga* 'road',
'way', or 'route'. The town in Komi Republic
has been renamed Yemva. The former German
name of Gerdauen in Kaliningrad Province was
superseded in 1945 after the conquest of East
Prussia. As with *zelen* there are several Russian
towns beginning with *zhelezno-* the adjective for
'iron'.

Zheleznogorsk, KURSK/RUSSIA *Krasnoyarsk-26,
Atomgrad, Devyatka*
Founded in 1958 as a previously 'closed city',
now meaning 'City of Iron' from *zhelezno*, the
adjective for 'iron', and *gorsk*. Previous names
meant 'Atom City' and '(Group of) Nine' from
devyatka 'nine'.

Zhengzhou, HENAN/CHINA *Guan, Guan Xian, Xing Zhou, Guan Zhou, Zheng Zhou, Zheng Xian*
Named in the 6th century BC the 'City of Guan' after a locally powerful family, it was renamed when it became the seat of a prefecture. It was renamed Xing Zhou in 559, Guan Zhou in 596, and Zheng Zhou in 605, having become part of the Kingdom of Zheng which was founded in this area by a duke of that name. In 1913–52 it was called Zheng Xian from *xian* 'county' before it became Zhengzhou City.

Zhenjiang, JIANGSU/CHINA *Guyang, Dantu, Jingkou, Run Zhou*
A very ancient site, it became a military garrison in 581 on the Yangtze River; a military unit called Zhenhai was established here in 782. It got this name because the Zhen River is linked to the *hǎi* 'sea' here. It became the seat of a military governor during the Song dynasty (960–1126) and the unit changed its name to Zhenjiang in 975. The name may be derived from the abbreviation of a phrase meaning 'guarding the town defending the river'. The character *zhèn* can mean 'town', but also 'to subdue' or 'to suppress' and, in reference to the *jiāng* 'river', 'calm' or 'tranquil'.

Zhezkazgan, KAZAKHSTAN *Dzhezkazgan*
Founded in 1938 to exploit the local copper deposits, the name means 'Place where Copper is mined'. It is also spelt Zhezqazghan.

Zhidan, SHAANXI/CHINA *Bao'an*
Renamed in 1936 to honour Liu Zhidan (1903– 36) who was born here. A senior commander in the Red Army, he was killed fighting against the Guomindang. His name comes from *zhì* 'will' or 'aspiration' and *dān* 'red'. *See* BAO'AN.

Zhob, BALOCHISTAN/PAKISTAN *Apozai, Fort Sandeman*
A river and a town captured by the British in 1889 and renamed after Colonel Sir Robert Sandeman (1835–92), political agent to the governor general of Balochistan who did much to pacify the tribes on the British India north-west frontier. It was given its present name, with an unknown meaning, in the 1970s.

Zhovkva, UKRAINE *Vinniki, Zholkva, Nesterov*
Known as Vinniki from 1368, it was renamed Zholkva between 1598 and 1951. Its name was then changed to Nesterov in honour of Pëtr (Peter) Nesterov (1887–1914), a Russian pioneer military pilot who destroyed a German aircraft in the area by deliberately ramming it in September 1914, the first recorded instance of this method of attack.

Zhovten', UKRAINE
'October' in Ukrainian, a reference to the October (old style) Revolution in 1917. Another

town, north-east of Ivano-Frankivs'k, had this name until Ukrainian independence in 1991; it is now called Ezupol'.

Zhukovskiy, MOSCOW/RUSSIA *Otdykh, Stakhanovo*
Originally meaning 'rest' from *otdykh* because of its location close to the Moscow River, it was renamed in the 1930s to honour Aleksey *Stakhanov. Developed from the settlement of Stakhanov, it was renamed in 1947 to celebrate the centenary of the birth of Professor Nikolay Zhukovskiy (1847–1921), the 'father of Russian aviation' and the man who did most to establish the famous TsAGI, the Central Institute for Aerodynamics and Hydrodynamics, which was devoted to research and development in aeronautics.

Zhytomyr, UKRAINE *Zhitomir*
May be associated with the Russian *zhito* 'rye' or come from a personal name.

Ziar nad Hronom, SLOVAKIA *Kerestur, Heiligenkreuz, Svätý Kríž*
The previous German and Slovak names meant 'Holy Cross' after the dedication of the local church. In 1955, during atheistic Communist rule, the inhabitants demanded a change of name to Ziar nad Hronom 'Blazing Heat on the (River) Hron', a reference to the heat of the furnaces in the new aluminium works in the town.

Zibo, SHANDONG/CHINA
A combination of the initial characters of Zichuan and Boshan Counties. *Zī* is the name of a river which could mean 'black' and *bó* is the name of a mountain, possibly meaning 'wide' or 'extensive'.

Zielona Góra, POLAND *Grünberg*
'Green Hill' in both Polish and German. It actually lies in a hollow surrounded by hills.

Zihuatanejo, GUERRERO/MEXICO *Cihuatlan*
At one time a matriarchal society, its name means 'Place of Women'.

Žilina, CZECH REPUBLIC, SLOVAKIA
Slovakia: formerly Terra de Selinan, Sylna, Zilna, and Sylina which may be derived from the personal name Žila with the Slovak ending *ina* indicating possession, thus 'Žila's Village'. Alternatively, it might be derived from the personal name Žilin with *jane* to give 'Žilin's People'.

Zilupe, LATVIA
Takes its name from the river on which it lies. Its name means 'Blue River' from *zils* 'blue' and *upe* 'river'.

z

Zimbabwe The Republic of Zimbabwe since 1980. Previously Zimbabwe-Rhodesia (April 1979–April 1980), Rhodesia (1964–79), and Southern Rhodesia (1911–64). However, the government in Salisbury (now Harare) issued an illegal unilateral declaration of independence renouncing colonial status in 1965 and declared Rhodesia a republic in 1970. The British South Africa Company administered the region from 1890 until 1923 when Southern Rhodesia became a self-governing British colony. The present name comes from Great Zimbabwe, the ruined fortified city in the centre of the country near Masvingo (formerly Fort Victoria). It means 'Stone Enclosure' or 'Stone Dwelling' from the Bantu *zimba* 'houses', the plural of *imba* 'house' and *bahwe* 'stones'. Although Great Zimbabwe was one of many stone enclosures, it came to be an important Shona empire between 1250 and 1550. The most majestic site, it was given the title 'Great' to differentiate it from other lesser enclosures in the vicinity. *See* RHODESIA.

Zion, ST KITTS AND NEVIS, USA
USA (Illinois): named after Mount Zion, the eastern of the two hills of ancient Jerusalem and often used in the Bible instead of 'Jerusalem'. It lies just south of the old city and is now known as Mount Ophel. It comes from the Hebrew *tsiyōn* 'hill'. Zionism is the movement for a national Jewish state in Palestine.

Zlatoust, CHELYABINSK/RUSSIA
Iron and copper works were established here in 1754 and in due course the settlement was named after its church dedicated to St John Chrysostom (*c.*347–407), archbishop of Contantinople (now Istanbul) (398–403). Zlatoust 'golden-mouthed' from *zlato* 'gold' and *usta* 'mouth' is the Russian word used for Chrysostom since he became famous as a preacher.

Zlín, CZECH REPUBLIC *Slyn/Zlín, Gottwaldov*
In 1949–90 named after Klement Gottwald (1896–1953), appointed general secretary of the Czechoslovak Communist Party in 1927 and President of Czechoslovakia (1948–53). The original and present names are derived from a personal name, Zla 'Bad Man', with the possessive ending *in* to give '(Place of) the Bad Man'.

Złotoryja, POLAND
Derived from *złoto* 'gold', a reference to the gold found in the sands of the River Kaczawa on which the town lies, which was exploited for centuries.

Znamensk, KALININGRAD/RUSSIA *Wehlau*
The former German name was superseded by the present 'Banner' or 'Standard' from *znamya* after East Prussia had been overrun by the Soviet Red Army in 1945.

Znojmo, CZECH REPUBLIC *Znoim, Znaim*
The meaning is disputed. It has been suggested that the name may come from the Old Czech noun *znoj* 'Place where the Sun shines', from the Old Czech verb *znojiti* 'to be marshy' or from the Old High German *Cinahaima* 'Settlement next to a Gorge'. The former German Znaim was taken from the earlier Czech name.

Zomba, MALAWI
Founded in 1885 with a Nyanja name meaning 'Locust'. It lies on the lower slopes of Mt Zomba. It was the capital of Malawi in 1966–75.

Zrenjanin, SERBIA/SERBIA AND MONTENEGRO *Civitas Becske, Veliki Bečkerek, Petrovgrad*
Founded in the 14th century when under Hungarian rule and quickly renamed Veliki Bečkerek 'Big Bečkerek'. In 1934 it was renamed Petrovgrad 'Peter's Town' after the accession to the throne of Peter II (1923–70), King of Yugoslavia (1934–45). With the abolition of the monarchy in 1946, the city was renamed after Žarko Zrenjanin Uca (1902–42), a national hero who led the communist Partisan struggle against the Germans in Vojvodina and was killed in 1942.

Zubayr, az-, IRAQ
A town which stands on the 7th-century site of Basra, now 8 miles (13 km) to the north-east. It is named after Zubayr ibn al-'Awwām, one of the first converts to Islam, who was instrumental in raising a force to oppose Ali, the Prophet Muhammad's[†] son-in-law, in his claim to be caliph. Zubayr was killed at the Battle of the Camels in 658 and is buried here.

Zuiderzee, THE NETHERLANDS
'Southern Sea' in comparison with the North Sea. A barrier dam was built across it in 1927–32, the southern part becoming *IJsselmeer.

Zululand, KWAZULU-NATAL/SOUTH AFRICA
A historic region, the homeland of the Zulu people. In 1879 the Zulu were defeated by the British who occupied their land. This was annexed by the UK in 1887 and designated a crown colony. In 1897 its separate existence was ended when it was incorporated into Natal. *See* KWAZULU-NATAL.

Zuni, USA
New Mexico: a river and a town named after the Zuni people.

z

Zunyi, GUIZHOU/CHINA
'Follow Justice' from *zūn* 'follow' or 'abide by' and *yî* 'justice'. The name derives from a classical phrase that urges people to abide unwaveringly by the king's justice.

Zürich, SWITZERLAND *Turicum*
A canton, a city, and a lake, the name probably being derived from the Celtic *dur* 'water', a reference to the Helvetii's settlement on the edge of the lake.

Zutphen, THE NETHERLANDS *Zuidveen*
An adaptation of the previous name for the town founded in the 11th century. It meant 'Southern Peat Bog' from *zuid* 'southern' and *veen* 'peat bog' or 'marsh'.

Zvishavane, ZIMBABWE *Shabani*
Derived from the Sindebele *shavani* 'finger millet' or 'trading together'.

Zvolen, SLOVAKIA *Altsohl*, *Zólyom*
Either taken from a personal name referring to the owner of the castle and settlement to give 'Zvolen's (Settlement)' or from the Slovak *zvolit si* 'to choose' to mean the 'chosen (settlement)'.

Zweibrücken, RHINELAND-PALATINATE/ GERMANY *Bipontium*
Lying on the Schwarzenbach 'Black River', both the former Latin and present names mean 'Two Bridges' from *zwei* 'two' and *Brücke* 'bridge'.

Zwelitsha, EASTERN CAPE/SOUTH AFRICA
Founded in 1946 as a residential area for employees of a nearby textile factory with a Xhosa name 'New World'.

Żyrardów, POLAND
Named after Philippe de Girard (1775–1845), a Frenchman who opened a factory here around which the town developed. The *ów* indicates the possessive.

Z

Glossary

Note: adjectives in inflected languages are only given in the masculine singular.

Old English, previously known as Anglo-Saxon, evolved into Middle English at the beginning of the 12th century after the arrival of the Normans.

Modern English could be said to have started with William Caxton, the first English printer, in the late 15th century.

Old High German was the language of the highlands of southern and central Germany between 700 and 1100, while Old Low (Saxon) German was spoken in low-lying northern Germany.

Old Scandinavian (Icelandic, Norwegian, Danish and Swedish) covered the period from about 1050 to 1450.

Abbreviations
ML: Medieval Latin
OD: Old Dutch
OE: Old English
OF: Old French
OS: Old Scandinavian
S-C: Serbo-Croat

Å Danish, Norwegian, OS; stream, river
Āb Persian; water, river
Ābād Persian, Hindi, etc.; inhabited place, town
'Abbāsids; the family of Sunni caliphs in Baghdad and Cairo between 749 and 1517 which was descended from the Prophet Muhammad's uncle, al-'Abbas
Abd Arabic; slave, servant; widely used in names in conjunction with one of the 99 names of God, e.g. as servant of the Mighty.
Aber Pictish, Welsh; river mouth, confluence, estuary
Abu Arabic; father
-acum, -iacum ML; place of, belonging to
Adrar Berber; mountain
Aïn (pl. **aïoun**) Arabic; spring (of water), well
Ak Turkish; white
Akan Armenian; town
Akhal Georgian; new
al- Arabic; the; also **el-**; it can also appear as **an-, as-, ar-** etc. depending on the following consonant.
Āl Arabic; the family of, belonging to (designating a family or tribal name)
Albus Latin; white, light coloured
Alto Italian, Portuguese, Spanish; high, upper
Am German; on the, upon the
Amir see **Emir**
An Malagasy; denotes a place-name
Ān Chinese; peace, peaceful
Aqua (pl. **aquae**) Latin; water, spring
Áth(a) Irish/Scottish Gaelic; ford
Audiencia Spanish; a territory administered by a Spanish court with government functions in South America
'Ayn Arabic; spring

Ba Mandekan; river
Baai Afrikaans; bay
Bāb Arabic; gate, strait
Bach German; stream
Bad (pl. **Baden**) Afrikaans, German; bath, watering place, spa
Bāgh Persian; garden
Bahía Spanish; bay
Baḥr Arabic; sea, river, bay, lake
Baía Portuguese; bay
Baile Irish/Scottish Gaelic; town, townland, place, farmstead (Anglicized to Bally)
Balad Arabic; town
Ban Croat; ruler, governor
Bandar Arabic, Hindi, Malay, Persian; port, harbour, anchorage
Bani Arabic; descendants (of), hence a clan or tribe
Bánya Hungarian; mine
Barr Arabic; land (as opposed to sea)
Bas French; low, lower
Bayt Arabic; house
Béal Irish; mouth
Beau, bel French; beautiful
Běi Chinese; north, northern
Beinn Irish/Scottish Gaelic; mountain (Anglicized to Ben)
Belyy Russian (the Slavonic root is **bel-**); white
Beorg OE; hill, mound
Berg Afrikaans, Dutch, German, Norwegian, Swedish, OS; mountain, hill
Bilād Arabic; land
Bin Arabic; son of (a component of personal names); also **ibn**
Bi'r Arabic; well
Boca Portuguese, Spanish; mouth, estuary
Boer Afrikaans; farmer
Bolshevik Russian; a member of the majority faction of the Russian Social Democratic Labour Party which was renamed the Communist Party in 1918; from *bol'she* 'greater'.
Borg Danish, Swedish; fort, castle
Bourg French; small market town, fortified town
Briga Celtic; fortified hill, height
Briva Celtic; bridge
Brod S-C; boat; also used in the sense of a river-crossing
Brücke German; bridge
Brycg OE; bridge
Bryn Welsh; hill
Burg Afrikaans, German; town, stronghold, citadel
Burh OE; stronghold, fortified place
Burna OE; stream
Buri Thai; city
Bý OS; village, settlement, farmstead
Byrig OE; the dative of **burh**
Byzantine Empire; the direct heir of the Eastern Roman Empire, ruled from Constantinople (now Istanbul) until it fell to the Ottoman Turks in 1453

Cabo Portuguese, Spanish; cape, headland
Caer Welsh; fort, stronghold, fortified place

Caliph (from Arabic **khalīfah**): successor; the title of the supreme head of the Muslim community as the successor of the Prophet Muhammad

Campo Italian, Portuguese, Spanish; field, plain

Campus Latin; plain, flat space

Caravanserai Persian; an inn for travellers on caravan routes

Castra Latin; military camp, fort

Ceaster OE (from Latin **castra**); camp, walled town

Český Czech; Czech

Château French; castle

Chéng Chinese; city, town, wall of a city or town

Chiang Thai; town, city

Chërnyy Russian; black

Cill Irish/Scottish Gaelic; cell, church, churchyard (Anglicized to Kil(l))

Città Italian; city

Ciudad Spanish; city, town

Colonia Latin; colony, settlement

Conquistador Spanish; Spanish explorer-conqueror of Latin America

Costa Italian, Portuguese, Spanish; coast

Côte French; coast, slope

Crkva S-C; church

Cruz Spanish; cross

Dağ Turkish; mountain

Dal Afrikaans, Dutch, Norwegian, Swedish; valley

Dǎo Chinese; island

Dār Arabic; large house, palace, country, place

Daryā Persian; river

Deniz Azeri, Turkish; sea

-do Korean; province

Do Korean; island

Dōng Chinese; east

Dorf German; village

Dorp Afrikaans; village, town

Dūn OE; hill (suitable for a settlement)

Dùn Gaelic; fort

Dún Irish; fort

Dunum Celtic group; stronghold, town

Dvīpa Sanskrit; island

Emir various; a title of Muslim rulers with several meanings: king, prince, tribal chief, commander, governor; also **amir**

Emirate various; political entity under the rule of an emir

Ēg OE; island, dry ground in marsh

Eski Turkish; old

Ey OS; island

Fehér Hungarian; white

Feld OE, German; open land, field

Fjǫrthr OS; inlet, fjord

Fontein Afrikaans; fountain, spring

Fuku Japanese; happiness

Furt German; ford

Gǎng Chinese; harbour, port

Ganj Hindi; market

Garh Hindi; fort

Göl(ü) Turkish; lake

Gora Slavonic; mountain, hill

Gorod Russian; city, town

Gorsk Russian; a shortening of *gorskiy*, the adjective of *gorets* 'mountain-dweller'; it is also associated with *gornyy*, the adjective of **gora** 'mountainous', 'mineral', or 'mining'.

Grad Slavonic; city, town

Gród Polish; town, castle

Guǎng Chinese; large, broad, extensive, wide

Gulag Russian; *Glavnoye upravleniye lagerei* Main Camp Administration (the branch of the secret police which ran Soviet concentration camps)

Guomindang Chinese; Nationalist Party founded in 1912 and driven out of mainland China by the Communists in 1949

Gurū Sanskrit; elder, teacher (usually a Hindu spiritual teacher)

Hafen German; harbour, port

Hǎi Chinese; sea, lake

Hajj Arabic; the pilgrimage to Mecca that every adult Muslim must undertake at least once, if he or she is able

Hālig OE; holy

Hām OE; village, homestead, estate

Hamm OE; enclosure, land in a river bend, promontory, river meadow

Hamn Norwegian, Swedish; harbour

Haut French; high

Havn Danish, Norwegian; harbour

Hé Chinese; river

Hēah OE; high

Heilig German; holy

Heim German; home, dwelling place

Here OE; army

Hisar Turkish; castle, fortress

Ho Korean; lake

Hoch German; high

Holmr OS; island, promontory

Huáng Chinese; yellow

ibn Arabic; son of; also **bin**

-ice, -ovce Czech; used in place-names derived from the name of a person, river or hill

Île French; island

Ilha Portuguese; island

Imam (Arabic **imām**); leader of prayers in a mosque, title of Yemeni ruler until 1962

Inbhir Scottish-Gaelic; mouth, confluence (Anglicized to Inver)

-ing OE; place belonging to or called after

-inga- OE; genitive case of **-ingas-**

-ingas- OE; (pl.) people of, family of, followers of

In(n)is Irish/Scottish Gaelic; island (Anglicized to Ennis in Ireland, to Inch in Scotland)

Irmak Turkish; large river

Isla Spanish; island

Islam Arabic; surrender or submission to God

Isola Italian; island

Jabal Arabic; mountain, mountain range

Jazīrah (pl. **Jazā'ir**; **jazīrat** before a genitive) Arabic; island, peninsula

Jazīré Persian; island

Jiāng Chinese; river, stream

Jihād Arabic; struggle (to do what God commands to spread Islam) and often interpreted as holy war

Kalaki Georgian; town

Kale Turkish; fort, castle, citadel (**Kalesi** before a genitive)

Kamen' Russian; rock, stone

Kand Persian; town

Kar pre-Indo-European; rock, stone

Kara Turkish; black
Káto Greek; lower
Kawa Japanese; river
Kendy (Xändi) Azeri; town
KGB (Soviet) Committee of State Security
Khan Turkic; lord, prince, tribal chief, ruler of a khanate
Khedive (from Turkish **kediv**); Egyptian viceroy under Ottoman Turkish suzerainty (1867–1914)
Kirkja OS; church
Kita Japanese; north
Kızıl Turkic; red
Komsomol Russian; an abbreviation of (**Vse-Soyuznyy Leninskiy) Kommunisticheskiy Soyuz Molodëzhi** (All-Union Leninist) Young Communist League
Köping Swedish; market town
Kot Hindi; fort
Kota Malay, Indonesian; fort, city, town
Köy Turkish; village
Krasnyy Russian; red (as a colour and in the revolutionary (political) sense); beautiful (although now obsolete, for which **krasivyy** is now used)
Kray Russian; territory (territorial division)
Krishna (from Sanskrit **Krṣṇa**); a popular Indian deity, worshipped as the 8th incarnation of the Hindu god Vishnu
Ksar (pl. **ksour**) Arabic; fortified village
Kūh Persian; mountain
Kyzyl Turkic; red

Lagoa Portuguese; lagoon
Land German; state, land
Llan Welsh; church, churchyard
Lēah OE; wood, woodland clearing
Leben German; indicates a possession or inheritance
Les Czech, Russian; forest, wood
Linn, Estonian; fort
Linn, Irish/Scottish Gaelic; pool
Lios Irish; fort
Loch Irish/Scottish Gaelic; lake

Ma Arabic; water
Madīnah Arabic; city (**madīnat** before a genitive)
Magus OD; forum, market
Mahābhārata Sanskrit; 'Great Epic of the Bharata Dynasty', an epic Vedic poem
Malyy Slavonic; little
Mamlūks Arabic; owned, possessed. Usually refers to the emancipated military slaves who ruled Egypt in 1250–1517
Mare Italian; sea
Mare Romanian; big
Mark German; march (frontier district)
Mawlay Arabic; mullah (protector); generally a Muslim title equivalent to lord and given to kings, sultans or a religious leader (used especially in Morocco where it is spelt *moulay*)
Meer Afrikaans, Dutch; lake
Meer German; sea
Mere OE; lake, pool, pond
Middel OE; middle
Mīnā' Arabic; port
Monasterium ML; monastery
Mons Latin; hill, mountain
Mont French; mountain
Monte Italian, Portuguese, Spanish; mountain

More Russian, S-C; sea
Most Slavonic; bridge
Mt mount
Muslim Arabic; one who surrenders to God
Mūtha OE; river mouth, estuary
Mynster OE; monastery, minster
-myo Burmese; town

Na Bulgarian, Russian, S-C; on
Nad Czech; above, over
Nagar Hindi; city, large town
Nagara Sanskrit; city
Nagy Hungarian; big, large, great
Nahr Arabic; river
Nakhon Thai; city, town
Nam Burmese, Thai, Vietnamese; river
Nam Korean, Vietnamese; south, southern
Nán Chinese; south, southern
Nawāb Urdu; governor
Neft' Russian; oil
Negro Spanish; black
Neu German; new
Nieder German; lower
Nikē Greek; victory
Níng Chinese; peaceful, pacify, calm
Nīwe OE; new
Nizhniy Russian; lower
NKVD (Soviet) People's Commissariat for Internal Affairs; predecessor of the KGB
Nord Danish, French, German, Italian; north
Norte Portuguese, Spanish; north
Novi/y Slavonic; new
Ny Danish, Norwegian, Swedish; new

Ober German; upper
Oblast' Russian; province
Okrug Russian; district (territorial division)
Ostān Persian; province
Ostrov Russian; island
Ottoman Empire; a Turkish empire that ruled over Asia Minor, the Arab lands, the Balkans and North Africa. The dynasty took its name from Osman I (1258–1324) and lasted until 1922.

Para Guaraní river, water
Pax Latin; peace
Pervyy Russian; first
Pils Latvian; town
Píng Chinese; peaceful, calm
Pod Czech, Russian, S-C; under
Pol(is) Greek; city, town
Porto Italian, Portuguese; port, harbour
Pradesh Hindi; province, state, land
Pri Russian; near, by
Primorskiy Russian; maritime
Pueblo Spanish; town, village
Puerto Spanish; port, harbour
Pur Sanskrit, Hindi; city, town (originally village, settlement)
Pura Hindi; castle, fortified town

Qal'ah Arabic; fort, castle (**qal'at** before a genitive)
Qasr (or Kasr) Arabic; castle, fortress, palace
Qila Hindi; fort, castle

Rāj Sanskrit; rule, sovereignty, kingdom. During the period of British rule (1857–1947) British India was simply known as 'The Raj'.
Rāja Sanskrit; king

Rājput Sanskrit; son of a king
Rāma; a popular Indian deity, worshipped as the 7th incarnation of the Hindu god Vishnu
Ra's Arabic; cape, headland, promontory
Rayon Georgian, Russian; district (territorial division)
Reka Russian, S-C; river
Ribāṭ Arabic; fortified monastery, caravanserai
Rio Portuguese; river
Río Spanish; river
Rust Afrikaans; rest

Saari Finnish; island
San Italian; saint
San Japanese, Korean; mountain
Sancak Turkish; territorial subdivison of an eyalet, originally a military district
Sandžak S-C; see **sancak**
Sankt German, Swedish; saint
Santo/a Spanish; saint
Saki Japanese; cape, point
São Portuguese; saint
Saray/Sarai Persian, Turkish; palace, mansion, inn for travellers
Sāssānians; an Iranian dynasty (224–651) which took its name from Sāsān, an ancestor of Ardashir I, the founder of the dynasty.
Scīr OE; shire, district
Seaxe OE; Saxons
See German; lake
Şehir Turkish; city, town
Seljuk; ruling military family of the Oğuz Turkmen tribes taking its name from Seljuk, a chief
Selo Russian, S-C; village
Sever Slavonic; north
Shāh Persian; king (usual title of the Persian/Iranian monarch)
Shāhid Arabic; martyr (literally, witness)
Shahr Persian; city, town
Shān Chinese; mountain
Sharif Arabic; noble, high-born (a descendant of the Prophet Muhammad through his daughter Fatima)
Shaikh Arabic; tribal leader, chief, leader of a religious brotherhood
Shima Japanese; island
Shiva Sanskrit; Auspicious One; one of the chief deities of Hinduism, a member of the trinity with Brahmā and Vishnu.
Shogun Japanese; great general—hereditary military dictator
Sierra Spanish; mountain range
-sk, -ski Slavonic; often associated with a personal name or that of a river or hill/mountain in the sense of belonging to
Sloboda Russian; settlement (excused normal state obligations)
SSR Soviet Socialist Republic
Stad Afrikaans, Dutch, Norwegian, Swedish; town
Stadt German; city, town
Stān OE; stone
Stān Persian; see **ostān**
Star S-C; old
Staryy Russian; old
Stoc OE; place, outlying settlement
Stōw OE; place
Su Turkic; water

Sultān Arabic; a monarch or ruler of a Sultanate (Muslim territory)
Sund Swedish; sound, strait
Sveti S-C; holy, saint
Svetlyy Russian; light, bright, bright-coloured, radiant, joyous, pure, clear

Taka Japanese; high, tall
Tau Turkic; mountain
Tall/Tel(l) Arabic; hill, mound
Tepe Turkish; hill
Terre French; land
Thing OE, OS; assembly, meeting
Thorp OS; secondary settlement dependent on a bigger one
Timur Indonesian; east, eastern
Tīr Gaelic; land, territory
Tír Irish; land, territory
Trans Latin; across, beyond
Tūn OE; village, farmstead, enclosure, estate

Új Hungarian; new
Umm Arabic; mother, source (as used in place-names)
UAE United Arab Emirates
UK United Kingdom
Umayyads; the first Muslim dynasty (661–750). Overthrown, one member survived to found the Ummayad dynasty of Córdoba in Spain in 756; it lasted until 1031
UN United Nations
Urbs Latin; city, large town
USA United States of America
USSR Union of Soviet Socialist Republics
Usta Russian; mouth

Vár Hungarian; castle, fortress, stronghold
Város Hungarian; town
Vatn Icelandic, Norwegian; lake
Verkhniy Russian; upper
Vicus Latin; settlement
Vihara Sanskrit; (Buddhist) monastic retreat or establishment
Vijaya Sanskrit; victory
Vik Norwegian, Swedish; bay
Vila Portuguese; town
Villa Spanish; town, borough, settlement
Ville French; town
Vinh Vietnamese; bay
Vishnu (Sanskrit: **Viṣṇu**); one of the principal Hindu deities, a member of the trinity with Brahmā and Shiva
Vista Spanish; view
Voda Russian, S-C; water
Voortrekker Afrikaans; a Boer pioneer, particularly one that joined the Great Trek away from British rule in Cape Colony, South Africa, into the interior in 1836

Wādī Arabic; dry river bed which can become a water course after seasonal torrential rain, valley; it also apears as **Oued** in North Africa
Wai Maori; water
Wald German; wood
Walh OE; Briton, Welshman
Wīc OE; settlement, camp, harbour, premises
Worth OE; enclosed settlement, homestead

Xī Chinese; west, western

Yama Japanese; mountain

Yáng Chinese; sun, north bank of a river, south side of a mountain, that is, the ground that is bathed in sunshine; light, positive, active. It is the male counterpart of the female *yīn*

Yangi Uzbek; new

Yeni Turkish; new

Yīn Chinese; earth, shade; dark, passive. It is the female counterpart of the male *yáng*

Yug Russian, S-C; south

Yurt Turkish; settlement

Za Russian; beyond, on the other side of, across

Zelënyy Russian; green (adjective)

Zheleznyy Russian; iron (adjective)

Zemlya Russian; land

Zhōu Chinese; state, prefecture, region, province, county, etc.; also a term during the Zhou dynasty (1051–221 BC) for an administrative district of 2 500 families

Personalities

Akbar the Great (1542–1605), in full Abū-ul-Fatḥ Jalāl ud-Din Muhammad Akbar. The greatest Mughal emperor of India (1556–1605) who extended Mughal control over the whole of northern India.

Alexander I (1777–1825). Emperor of Russia (1801–25) at the time of Napoleon's invasion of Russia. In Russian, Alexander is Aleksandr.

Alexander II (1818–81). Emperor of Russia (1855–81). He emancipated the serfs in 1861. He was assassinated by terrorists intent on revolution.

Alexander III the Great (356–323 BC). King of Macedonia (336–323 BC). One of the greatest generals ever to have lived, he overthrew the Persian Empire and reached into India. He founded over 70 new cities, many of which were named after him in one way or another.

Atatürk, Kemal (1881–1938), born Mustafa Kemal. A Turkish Army officer who became the first president of the Republic of Turkey (1923–38). In 1924, intent on separating the spiritual from the temporal power, the disestablishment of Islam, he deposed the caliph and abolished the caliphate. In 1935, in accordance with the law, he assumed the surname Atatürk 'Father of the Turks' and dropped his Arabic name Mustafa.

Augustus, Caesar (63 BC–AD 14), born Gaius Octavius, taking the adopted name of Gaius Julius Caesar Octavianus by the will of his great-uncle Julius Caesar. Founder of the Roman empire and its first emperor (23 BC–AD 14). Called Octavian, he discarded the name in 27 BC and accepted the imperial title of Augustus 'venerable' in Latin. He gave his name to the month of August.

Barents, Willem (c.1550–97). A Dutch navigator who led three expeditions along the Arctic coast of Russia in an attempt to find the north-east passage from Europe to Asia between 1594 and 1596.

Bede, The Venerable (672/3–735). An Anglo-Saxon theologian and historian who completed his *Ecclesiastical History of the English People* c.732. It covered the period from Julius Caesar's first raids on Britain in 55 and 54 BC to the arrival of St Augustine in England in 597. Bede was canonized in 1899.

Bering, Vitus (1681–1741). A Danish navigator who joined the Russian Navy and was appointed by Peter I the Great to lead an expedition in 1728 to discover if Asia and America were joined. Subsequently he mapped much of the Siberian coast (the Great Northern Expedition) between 1733 and 1741 when he sailed towards America, but was shipwrecked on Bering Island.

Caesar, Julius (c.100–44 BC), in full Gaius Julius Caesar. A Roman general and statesman who conquered Gaul between 58 and 50 BC and briefly invaded Britain in 55 and 54 BC. He was made dictator in 47 BC and dictator for life in 45 BC, but

was assassinated the following year. Besides giving his name to various titles, the German *kaiser* and the Russian *tsar* among others, he gave his name to the Julian calendar and the month of July.

Cartier, Jacques (1491–1557). A French navigator who made three voyages of exploration between 1534 and 1542 to North America, surveying the eastern coast of Canada and the St Lawrence River.

Catherine I (1684–1727). Empress of Russia (1725–7) and the wife of Peter I the Great. Catherine was originally a Lithuanian servant girl whose name was Maria Skavronskaya. Captured by the Russians in 1702, she entered the service of Prince Menshikov, Peter's principal minister, through whom she met Peter himself; they married in 1712. In Russian, Catherine is Yekaterina.

Catherine II the Great (1729–96), born Sophie Friederike Auguste von Anhalt-Zerbst, the daughter of a minor German prince. In 1743 she was chosen as the future bride for her German cousin, Karl Ulrich, a grandson of Peter I the Great and heir to the Russian throne. Arriving in Russia in 1744, she took the title Grand Duchess Yekaterina Alekseyevna. The following year the two were married and in 1762 her husband became the emperor as Peter III. Catherine overthrew him six months after his accession and became empress the same year (1762–96). She presided over a huge acquisition of territory, stretching from Poland to Alaska and, a particular aim of hers, to the Black Sea.

Champlain, Samuel de (1567–1635). A Frenchman who explored the east coast of Canada in 1603 and thereafter proceeded inland. He was appointed lieutenant-governor of Canada in 1612. He founded Quebec and was its governor 1633–5.

Charlemagne (c.742–814). King of the Franks (768–814) and King of the Lombards (774–814). He united most of the Christian lands of western Europe. His coronation as emperor by Pope Leo III in 800 is taken as the establishment of the Holy Roman Empire.

Charles I (1600–49). King of England and Wales (Great Britain), and Ireland (1625–49). His rule provoked a civil war in England and he was executed in 1649.

Charles II (1630–85). King of England and Wales (Great Britain), and Ireland (1660–85). He was proclaimed king as Charles II by the Scots after the execution of his father in 1649, but he was prevented from ascending the throne; his invasion of England was ended with his defeat by Parliamentarian forces at the Battle of Worcester in 1651 and he went into exile in France. With the collapse of the Commonwealth in 1660, he was summoned from exile to become king.

Personalities

590

Charles II (1661–1700). King of Spain (1665–1700). Childless, he was the last monarch of the Spanish Habsburg dynasty.

Christian IV (1577–1648). King of Denmark and Norway (1588–1648).

Churchill, Sir Winston (1874–1965). British politician, statesman, and prime minister (1940–5, 1951–5). He was given honorary US citizenship by an Act of Congress in 1963.

Columbus, Christopher (1451–1506). Although born in Italy, his parents are thought to have been Spanish Jews; his Spanish name was Cristóbal Colón. He sailed in the service of King Ferdinand and Queen Isabella of Spain. Under the impression that he could reach the east by sailing west, he set off on the first of his four voyages in 1492 and returned to Spain at the end of his last one in 1504. Besides visiting several Caribbean islands, including Cuba and Hispaniola (now shared between the Dominican Republic and Haiti), he also sailed along the coast of Central America and landed briefly on the coast of Venezuela in South America. Several places in North, Central and South America are named in his honour, using both the English and Spanish forms of his name.

Constantine I the Great (c.274–337), born Flavius Valerius Constantinus. He became the Roman Emperor of the West in 312 and sole emperor in 324. He was the first Roman emperor to convert to Christianity, in either 312 or 313.

Cook, Captain James (1728–79). British navigator and explorer who sailed three times to the Pacific Ocean between 1768 and 1779 and also twice to Canada. A supremely gifted surveyor, much world mapping was corrected as a result of his discoveries. He was killed by natives in Kealakekua Bay, Hawaii.

Cortés, Hernán (1485–1547). A Spanish conquistador who overthrew the Aztec Empire between 1519 and 1521 and acquired Mexico for Spain. He was appointed captain-general of New Spain in 1522. He explored Honduras between 1524 and 1526.

Elizabeth I (1533–1603). Queen of England (1558–1603). Never married, her byname was the Virgin Queen.

Flinders, Matthew (1774–1814). An English naval officer and navigator, who twice sailed to Australia (1795 and 1801) to chart the Australian coast.

Frederick II (1194–1250). King of Sicily (1197–1250), King of Germany (1212–50), Holy Roman Emperor (1220–50). Participating in the Sixth Crusade (1228–9), he crowned himself King of Jerusalem in 1229, retaining this title until 1243 although he left the Holy Land shortly after his coronation. Much of his time was spent trying to increase imperial, and reduce papal, power in Italy.

Genghis Khan (1162/67–1227), born Temüjin. He took the title Genghis Khan 'Universal, or Mighty, Ruler' in 1206. A Mongolian conqueror and ruler, he sent his armies as far west as the Adriatic Sea and to the Pacific coast in the east; he was the founder of the Mongol Empire.

George I (1660–1727). The first German King of Great Britain (1714–27) and Elector of Hanover (1698–1727).

George II (1683–1760). King of Great Britain and Elector of Hanover (1727–60).

George III (1738–1820). King of Great Britain (1760–1800) and of the United Kingdom of Great Britain and Ireland (1801–20); Elector of Hanover (1760–1814), and King of Hanover (1814–20).

George IV (1762–1830). King of the United Kingdom of Great Britain and Ireland, and King of Hanover (1820–30).

George V (1865–1936). King of the United Kingdom of Great Britain and Ireland (1910–22) and of the United Kingdom of Great Britain and Northern Ireland (1922–36); Emperor of India (1910–36). He was a first cousin of the Russian Emperor Nicholas II.

Hitler, Adolf (1889–1945). An Austrian who became Chancellor of Germany (1933–45) and Führer 'Leader' in 1934 when the chancellorship and presidency were merged. He then established a dictatorship. His policies, including the extension of *Lebensraum* 'living space' for the Germans, precipitated the Second World War (1939–45).

Jackson, Andrew (1767–1845). A successful general during the war with the UK (1813–14) and the 7th President of the USA (1829–37). He was called Old Hickory.

James I (1566–1625). King of Scots as James VI (1567–1625) and the first Stuart King of England and Wales, as James I (1603–25). Although never crowned King of Great Britain (no such kingdom existed), he issued a decree in 1604 styling himself King of Great Britain, Ireland, and France, although for the latter country this was only titular.

James II (1633–1701). King of England, Wales and Ireland (1685–88) and King of Scots as James VII. The last Roman Catholic king, he was deposed in favour of the Protestant William of Orange who became William III.

Justinian I (483–565). Byzantine Emperor (527–65) who preserved his territory against the Persians in the east and in the west recovered North Africa, Spain, and Italy for the Empire.

Kalinin, Mikhail Ivanovich (1875–1946). The only real peasant in the Bolshevik leadership, he became head of state (president) in 1919, although his titles were Chairman of the Central Executive Committee until 1938, and then until his death Chairman of the Presidium of the Supreme Soviet.

Kirov, Sergey Mironovich (1886–1934), born Sergey Kostrikov. The communist leader of Leningrad (now St Petersburg) (1926–34) who was almost certainly assassinated on Stalin's orders. His murder started something of a cult and many towns throughout the Soviet Union were named after him in a seeming act of penance.

Kuybyshev, Valerian Vladimirovich (1888–1935). A Bolshevik leader, a Red Army commander during the Russian Civil War (1918–20), and Chairman of the Committee of (Party) Control (1934–5).

La Salle, René-Robert Cavelier, Sieur de (1643–87). A French explorer who led an expedition down the Mississippi River to the Gulf of Mexico in 1682 and claimed the region for France. His men mutinied and killed him.

Lenin, Vladimir Ilich (1870–1924), born Vladimir Ilich Ulyanov. He took the name Lenin in 1901 from the Lena River in Siberia where he was exiled (1897–1900). Founder of the Russian Communist Party, he led the Bolshevik Revolution in November 1917 and became head of the first Soviet government; he never became titular head of state of the Soviet Union. Following his death several places in the Soviet Union were renamed as a tribute to him.

Lewis, Meriwether (1774–1809). An American explorer who led the first overland expedition westwards to the Pacific Ocean in 1804–6. Following the Louisiana Purchase in 1803, the USA acquired a huge tract of unknown territory west of the Mississippi River which was ripe for exploration. From 1801 Lewis was the private secretary to Thomas Jefferson, President of the USA (1801–9), and he appointed Lewis to lead the expedition; it was called the Lewis-Clark Expedition because Lewis asked for Lieutenant William Clark to be his co-leader. Lewis was appointed governor of Louisiana Territory in 1808.

Louis XIV the Sun King (1638–1715). King of France (1643–1715). Reigning for longer than any other French king, he presided over the cultural ascendancy of France in Europe and the magnificence of his court at Versailles.

Magellan, Ferdinand (Fernão de Magalhães) (c.1480–1521). A Portuguese navigator who abandoned his allegiance to Portugal in 1517 and offered his services to Spain. In 1519–21 he sailed westwards across the Atlantic, through the Strait of Magellan, and across the Pacific Ocean. Although he was killed by natives on Mactan Island in the Philippines, one of his five ships returned to Spain, thus completing the first circumnavigation of the globe.

Maria Theresa (1717–80). Archduchess of Austria and Queen of Hungary and Bohemia (1740–80); wife of Francis I, Holy Roman Emperor (1745–65).

Molotov, Vyacheslav Mikhailovich (1890–1986), born Vyacheslav Skryabin. Soviet prime minister (1930–41) and commissar for foreign affairs (1939–49, 1953–6). He was a strong supporter of Stalin, who showed great confidence in him after his success in bringing about the Soviet-Nazi non-aggression pact signed in 1939. The alias Molotov meant 'Man of the Hammer' from *molot* 'hammer', a name he chose to further his reputation as a tough negotiator. His alias inspired the 'Molotov Cocktail', a crude home-made device consisting of a bottle filled with inflammable liquid with a rag pushed into the neck that was lit with a match.

Ironically, it was invented in 1940 by the Finns for use against Soviet tanks during the Winter War (Nov. 1939–Mar. 1940) and put into production in the Soviet Union by Molotov.

Muhammad (c.570–632). Known as the Prophet Muhammad. Originally a merchant, Muhammad received a visitation from the Archangel Gabriel in c.610; he was told that he was the messenger of God. He founded a new religion, Islam 'surrender (to the will of God)'. It dates from 622 when Muhammad and his followers fled to Medina after being persecuted in Mecca. For Muslims, the Koran is the word of God as revealed to Muhammad by Gabriel.

Napoleon I (1769–1821), in full Napoléon Bonaparte, a Corsican by birth. A French general who became First Consul (1799–1804) and Emperor of the French (1804–14/15).

Nicholas I (1796–1855). Emperor of Russia (1825–55). In Russian, Nicholas is Nikolai.

Nicholas II (1868–1918). The last Emperor of Russia (1895–1917). Forced to abdicate in 1917, he was executed sixteen months later with his family by the Bolsheviks. He became a saint of the Russian Orthodox Church in 2000. He was a first cousin of George V.

Ordzhonikidze, Grigory Konstantinovich (1886–1937). Born into the Georgian nobility, but orphaned when he was ten. A highly temperamental Bolshevik leader, known as Sergo, and close confidant of Stalin, he was responsible for the annexation of Azerbaijan and Georgia and their conversion to Bolshevism in 1920–3. He committed suicide.

Paul I (1754–1801). Emperor of Russia (1796–1801). He had two German-born wives. In 1797 he established the order of succession following the male line of the Romanov family. In Russian, Paul is Pavel.

Peter I the Great (1672–1725). Tsar of Russia who ruled jointly with his half-brother, Ivan V, between 1682 and 1696 and, after Ivan's death, alone. In 1721 he was proclaimed emperor. He fought several wars with the Ottoman Empire, Sweden, and Persia to gain access to the Black Sea, the Baltic Sea, and the western and southern coasts of the Caspian Sea. In Russian, Peter is Pëtr (pronounced Pyotr).

Polo, Marco (c.1254–1324). A Venetian merchant and traveller who set out for China in 1271 and only returned to Venice in 1295. During this period he spent seventeen years (1275–92) in the service of Kublai Khan, the Mongol emperor.

Ptolemy, Claudius (c.127–45). A Greek astronomer, mathematician, and geographer from Alexandria, Egypt. He compiled a *Guide to Geography*, a world gazetteer which listed over 8 000 places in Europe, Africa, and Asia with their geographical coordinates. His world consisted of Europe, Africa, and Asia; the lands of the Chinese ran far to the south and then to the west, completely enclosing the Indian Ocean.

Ptolemy II Philadelphus (308–246 BC). King of Egypt (285–246 BC) and a great and enlightened ruler. He extended his empire over Syria, Asia Minor, and the Aegean. His first wife was Arsinoë I, daughter of the King of Thrace. He then married his sister, Arsinoë, known as Arsinoë II.

Rhodes, Cecil (John) (1853–1902). Born in England, he became a successful entrepreneur and colonial statesman in South Africa where he did much to promote British rule by expanding British territory to incorporate Bechuanaland (now Botswana) and Rhodesia (now Zambia and Zimbabwe). Monopolizing diamond production with the creation of De Beers Consolidated Mines Ltd in 1888, Rhodes obtained exclusive mining rights from Lobengula, ruler of Matabeleland (now in Zimbabwe). In 1889 he founded the British South Africa Company and was prime minister of Cape Colony (1890–6). In his will he created scholarships for young people from the British Empire (now the Commonwealth), Germany, and the USA to study at Oxford University; they are known as Rhodes scholars.

Schouten, Willem (c.1580–1625). A Dutch navigator who served the Dutch East India Company.

Seleucus I Nicator (358/354–281 BC). One of Alexander III the Great's generals and in 312 BC the founder of the Seleucid Empire which at its height extended from Thrace to India.

Stalin, Joseph (1879–1953), born Iosif Vissarionovich Dzhugashvili, a Georgian. As a committed revolutionary, like others, he adopted various aliases, including David and Koba, and took the name Stalin 'Man of Steel' from *stal'* 'steel', probably in 1912. He was commissar for nationalities (1917–23) and became general-secretary of the Soviet Communist Party (1922–53) and premier (1941–53). He was, however, never titular head of state of the Soviet Union. He used the titles of marshal and generalissimo. In furthering his cult of personality, several cities and towns were renamed after him during his lifetime, both in the Soviet Union and in East Europe.

Stanley, Sir Henry Morton (1841–1904), born John Rowlands. Abandoned by his parents, he went as a cabin boy to New Orleans where he was adopted and took the name of his new father. He led four expeditions to Africa in 1869–89; during the first in 1871 he was ordered to find David Livingstone which he did. On his second expedition (1874–7) he crossed Africa from Zanzibar to the mouth of the Congo River on the Atlantic coast. On his third in 1879 he founded the Congo Free State. He became an American citizen in 1885, but reclaimed his British nationality in 1892.

Strabo (c.63 BC–c.AD 23). Greek geographer and historian whose *Geography* gave details of peoples and places during the reign of the Roman emperor Augustus.

Sucre, Antonio José de (1793–1830). A soldier who played a leading part in the South American wars of independence from Spain. He was the first president of Bolivia (1815–28). He resigned in 1828 but the next year, in the service of Gran Colombia, he defeated the Peruvians. He was assassinated.

Tamerlane (1336–1405). A Tatar conqueror, Timur Lenk 'Timur the Lame' with Timur meaning 'iron'. He fought across Central Asia, Persia, Syria, and northern India.

Tasman, Abel (c.1603–61). A Dutch navigator and explorer who on his first voyage to the Pacific Ocean discovered Tasmania and New Zealand in 1642, and Tonga and Fiji in 1643.

Tito, Josip Broz (1892–1980), born Josip Broz. Half Croat and half Slovene, he joined the Communist Party early in the 1920s and led the Partisans to victory over the Germans in the Second World War. He was given the title Marshal of Yugoslavia. He became prime minister in 1945 and the first Yugoslav president in 1953, a position he held until his death. To advance his cult of personality one town in each of the six Yugoslav republics and two autonomous provinces had 'Tito' added to their name, e.g. Titov Drvar and Titova Mitrovica, or were renamed, e.g. Titograd. The 'Tito' was dropped in the 1990s. Tito used many different aliases (he was always known to Stalin as Valter). According to the man himself, 'Tito' had local literary connections; the theory that it came from his habit of ordering people about, *ti to* 'you (do) that', is fanciful.

Trajan (c.53–117), born Marcus Ulpius Traianus. A Roman emperor (98–117) who extended the empire's territory to the east, acquiring Dacia as a province.

Vancouver, George (1757–98). An officer in the British Royal Navy who meticulously surveyed the Pacific coast of North America from San Francisco northwards in 1792–4.

Victoria (1819–1901), in full Alexandrina Victoria. Queen of the United Kingdom of Great Britain and Ireland (1837–1901) and Empress of India (1876–1901). She had nine children and her descendants occupied, and in some cases still occupy, ten European thrones.

Voroshilov, Kliment Yefremovich (1881–1969). An early Bolshevik, he proved to be an able military commander during the Civil War (1918–20) and was associated with Stalin during the defence of Tsaritsyn (later Stalingrad, now Volgograd) in 1919. He was the first 'red marshal', entitled Marshal of the Soviet Union, the rank only being instituted in 1935. People's commissar for defence (1934–40), he was the nominal, but largely powerless, head of the Soviet state (1953–60).

Washington, George (1732–99). American commander-in-chief of the colonial military forces that fought in the American War of Independence (1775–83). He became the first President of the USA and served two terms (1789–97).

William III (1650–1702). Stadholder of the United Provinces of the Netherlands as William III (1672–1702) and King of Great Britain (1689–1702), reigning jointly with Mary II (1662–94) until her death in 1694. As a member of the Dutch royal house of Orange-Nassau (from the German duchy of Nassau), he was known as William of Orange.

William IV (1765–1837). King of the United Kingdom of Great Britain and Ireland, and King of Hanover (1830–7). With neither of his two daughters surviving infancy, the Hanoverian crown passed to his brother, the Duke of Cumberland, while the British crown passed to his niece, Victoria. Joining the Royal Navy in 1779, he fought in the American War of Independence (1775–83) and served in the West Indies.

Select Bibliography

Abu-Hakima, Ahmad Mustafa, *The Modern History of Kuwait 1750–1965* (London: Luzac & Co., 1983).

Allworth, Edward (ed.), *Central Asia: 130 Years of Russian Dominance. A Historical Overview*, 3rd edn. (London: Duke University Press, 1994).

Appiah, Kwame Anthony, and Gates, Henry Louis Jr., *Africana: The Encyclopedia of the African and African American Experience* (New York: Basic Civitas Books, 1999).

Appleton, Richard and Barbara, *The Cambridge Dictionary of Australian Places* (Cambridge: Cambridge University Press, 1992).

Armstrong, Karen, *A History of Jerusalem: One City, Three Faiths* (London: HarperCollins, 1996).

Atlas Mira (Moscow: GUGK, 1984).

Atlas of Russia and Post-Soviet Republics (Moscow: ATKAR-PKO Kartografiya, 1993).

Barnes, Ian, and Hudson, Robert, *Historical Atlas of Asia* (Shirley, Derbys.: Arcadia Editions Ltd, 1998).

Bonavia, Judy, *The Silk Road: From Xi'an to Kashgar* (Hong Kong: Guidebook Co., 1998).

Bowker, John, *The Concise Oxford Dictionary of World Religions* (Oxford: Oxford University Press, 2000).

Cambridge Encyclopedia of China (Cambridge: Cambridge University Press, 1982).

Cameron, Kenneth, *English Place Names* (London: B. T. Batsford, 1996).

Chaliand, Gérard (ed.), *People without a Country: The Kurds and Kurdistan* (London: Zed Press, 1980).

Channon, John, *Historical Atlas of Russia* (London: Penguin Books, 1995).

Cherpillod, André, *Dictionaire Etymologique des Noms Géographiques*, 2nd edn. (Paris: Masson, 1991).

Cobban, Helena, *The Making of the Modern Lebanon* (London: Hutchinson, 1985).

Cohen, Saul. B. (ed.), *The Columbia Gazetteer of the World* (New York: Columbia University Press, 1998).

Dalby, Andrew, *Dictionary of Languages* (London: Bloomsbury, 1998).

Davies, C. Collin, *An Historical Atlas of the Indian Peninsula*, 2nd edn. (Oxford: Oxford University Press, 1959).

Davies, Norman, *Europe: A History* (Oxford: Oxford University Press, 1996).

—— *The Isles* (London: Papermac, 2000).

Ekwall, Eilert, *The Concise Oxford Dictionary of English Place-Names*, 4th edn. (Oxford: Clarendon Press, 1960).

Elliott, Jason, *An Unexpected Light: Travels in Afghanistan* (London: Picador, 1999).

Encyclopedia Britannica (London: Encyclopedia Britannica Inc., 1995).

Everett-Heath, John, *Place Names of the World: Europe* (Basingstoke: Macmillan, 2000).

Farmer, David, *The Oxford Dictionary of Saints*, 5th edn. (Oxford: Oxford University Press, 2003).

Fernández-Armesto, Felipe (ed.), *Guide to the Peoples of Europe* (London: Times Books, 1997).

Flanagan, Deirdre and Laurance, *Irish Place Names* (Dublin: Gill & Macmillan, 1994).

Gilbert, Martin, *Atlas of Russian History* (London: J. M. Dent, 1993).

Gippenreiter, Vadim, and Komech, Alexey, *Old Russian Cities* (London: Laurence King, 1991).

Great Soviet Encyclopedia (Moscow: Soviet Encyclopedia Publishing House, 1974).

Grodekov, Maj Gen N. I., *The War in Turkumania: Skobolev's Campaigns of 1880–1* (Simla: Government Central Branch Press, 1884).

Hawley, Sir Donald, *Oman and its Renaissance* (London: Stacey International, 1984).

Haywood, John, *The Historical Atlas of the Celtic World* (London: Thames & Hudson, 2001).

Herzig, Edmund, *The New Caucasus: Armenia, Azerbaijan and Georgia* (London: Royal Institute of International Affairs, 1999).

Hupchick, Dennis P., and Cox, Harold E., *A Concise Historical Atlas of Eastern Europe* (New York: St Martin's Press, 1996).

Iordan, Iorgu, *Toponimia Romaneasca* (Bucharest: Editura Academiei Republicii Populare Romane, 1963).

Lappo, G. M., *Geografiya Gorodov* (Moscow: Gumarnitarniy Izdatelskiy Tsentr, 1997).

Lempriere, J., *A Classical Dictionary* (London: George Routledge & Sons, 1902).

Lewis, Bernard, *The Middle East: 2000 Years of History from the Rise of Christianity to the Present Day* (London: Weidenfeld & Nicolson, 1995).

Louda, Jiří, and Maclagan, Michael, *Lines of Succession. Heraldry of the Royal Families of Europe* (London: Little, Brown & Co., 1999).

Lutterer, Jan, Majtán, Milan, and Šrámek, Rudolf, *Zeměpisná Jména Československa* (Prague: Mladá Fronta, 1982).

Mackintosh-Smith, Tim, *Yemen: Travels in Dictionary Land* (London: John Murray, 1997).

—— *Travels with a Tangerine: A Journey in the Footnotes of Ibn Battutah* (London: John Murray, 2001).

—— (ed.), *The Travels of Ibn Battutah* (London: Picador, 2002).

Maclean, Fitzroy, *To Caucasus: The End of all the Earth* (Boston: Little, Brown & Co., 1976).

Macleod, Calum, and Mayhew, Bradley, *Uzbekistan: The Golden Road to Samarkand* (Hong Kong: Odyssey Passport, 1997).

Macmillan, Margaret, *Peacemakers: Six Months that Changed the World* (London: John Murray 2001).

Magocsi, Paul Robert, *Historical Atlas of Central Europe* (London: Thames & Hudson, 2002).

Maier, Bernhard, *Dictionary of Celtic Religion and Culture* (Woodbridge: The Boydell Press, 1997).

Mansel, Philip, *Constantinople: City of the World's Desire, 1453–1924* (London: Penguin Books, 1997).

Marcato, Carla *et al.* (eds.), *Dizionario dei Nomi Geografici Italiani* (Turin: UTET, 1994).

Marshall, Robert, *Storm from the East: From Genghis Khan to Khubilai Khan* (London: BBC Books, 1993).

McEvedy, Colin, *The Penguin Atlas of African History*, rev. edn. (London: Penguin Books, 1995).

—— *The Penguin Historical Atlas of the Pacific* (London: Penguin Books, 1998).

Mills, A. D., *A Dictionary of English Place-Names* (Oxford: Oxford University Press, 1998).

——— *A Dictionary of British Place-Names* (Oxford: Oxford University Press, 2003).

Moorhouse, Geoffrey, *India Britannica* (London: Harvill Press, 1983).

Mostyn, Trevor (ed.), *The Cambridge Encyclopedia of the Middle East and North Africa* (Cambridge: Cambridge University Press, 1988).

Munro, David, *The Oxford Dictionary of the World* (Oxford: Oxford University Press, 1995).

Nasmyth, Peter, *Georgia: In the Mountains of Poetry* (Richmond, Surrey: Curzon Press, 1998).

National Geographic Atlas of the World, rev. 6th edn. (Washington, DC: National Geographic Society, 1996).

Nicolaisen, W. F. H. (ed.), *The Names of Towns and Cities in Britain* (London: B. T. Batsford, 1970).

Overy, Richard, *The Times History of the World* (London: HarperCollins, 1999).

Pankhurst, Richard, *The Ethiopians* (Oxford: Blackwell, 1998).

Raper, P. E., *A Dictionary of Southern African Place Names*, 2nd edn. (Johannesburg: Jonathan Ball, 1989).

Riley-Smith, Jonathan (ed.), *The Atlas of the Crusades* (London: Guild Publishing, 1991).

Room, Adrian, *Dictionary of World Place Names Derived from British Names* (London: Routledge, 1989).

—— *African Placenames* (Jefferson, NC, and London: McFarland & Co., 1994).

—— *Placenames of Russia and the Former Soviet Union* (Jefferson, NC, and London: McFarland & Co., 1996).

—— *Placenames of the World* (Jefferson, NC, and London: McFarland & Co., 1997).

Russia (Leipzig: Baedeker (Karl), 1914).

Ryan, N. J., *The Making of Modern Malaysia and Singapore: A History from Earliest Times to 1966* (Kuala Lumpur: Oxford University Press, 1969).

Saleh, Zaki, *Britain and Iraq* (London: Books and Books Ltd, 1995).

Schonfield, Victoria, *Kashmir in Conflict: India, Pakistan and the Unfinished War* (London: I. B. Tauris, 2000).

Smith, Graham (ed.), *The Nationalities Question in the Soviet Union* (London: Longman, 1992).

Speake, Graham (ed.), *Dictionary of Ancient History* (London: Penguin Books, 1995).

Talpert, Richard J. A. (ed.), *Barrington Atlas of the Greek and Roman World* (Princeton and Oxford: Princeton University Press, 2000).

The Dictionary of National Biography (London: Oxford University Press, 1996).

Tibawi, A. L., *A Modern History of Syria including Lebanon and Palestine* (London: Macmillan & Co., 1969).

The Encyclopaedia of Islam (Leiden and London: E. J. Brill, Leiden and Luzac & Co., 1960).

The Times Atlas of European History (London: Times Books, 1994).

The Times Atlas of the Bible (London: Times Books, 1996).

Treasures of Yugoslavia (Beograd: Yugoslaviapublic, 1980).

Voennyy Entsiklopedichskiy Slovar' (Moscow: Voenno Izdatelstvo, 1983).

Walker, Christopher (ed.), *Armenia and Karabakh. The Struggle for Unity* (London: Minority Rights Publications, 1991).

Ward, Philip, *Bulgaria: A Travel Guide* (Cambridge: Oleander Press, 1982).

—— *Albania: A Travel Guide* (Cambridge: Oleander Press, 1983).

Wheeler, Geoffrey, *The Modern History of Soviet Central Asia* (London: Weidenfeld & Nicolson, 1964).

Whitfield, Peter, *Mapping the World* (London: British Library, 2000).

Wild, Antony, *The East India Company. Trade and Conquest from 1600* (London: HarperCollins, 1999).

Wilford, John Noble, *The Mapmakers: The Story of the Great Pioneers in Cartography: From Antiquity to the Space Age* (London: Pimlico, 2002).

Wilson, Vincent Jr., *The Book of the States* (Washington, DC: American History Research Associates, 1972).

Wood, Michael, *In the Footsteps of Alexander the Great* (London: BBC Books, 1997).

Xenopol, A. D., *Istoria Romanilor din Dacia Traiana* (Bucharest: Editura Cartea Romaneasca, [n.d.]).

Young, Gavin, *Iraq: Land of Two Rivers* (London: Collins, 1980).

Yule, Col Henry, and Burnell, A. C., *Hobson-Jobson* (The Bengal Chamber Edition, 1990: Calcutta: Rupa & Co, 1886).

Further Reading

Berger, Dieter, *Geographische Namen in Deutschland* (Mannheim: Duden Verlag, 1993).

Coates, Richard, *The Ancient and Modern Names of the Channel Islands* (Stamford: Paul Watkins, 1991).

Dauzat, A., and Rostaing, Ch, *Dictionnaire étymologique des noms de lieux en France*, 2nd edn. (Paris: Guénégaud, 1978).

Gelling, Margaret, *Place-Names in the Landscape* (London: J. M. Dent & Sons, 1984).

—— *Signposts to the Past* (London: J. M. Dent & Sons, 1997).

Harder, Kelsie B., *Illustrated Dictionary of Place Names: United States and Canada* (New York: Van Nostrand Reinhold, 1975).

Lane, Edward, *Arabic-English Lexicon* (CD-ROM by Tradigital, USA from the publication in London 1863-93).

McKay, Patrick, *A Dictionary of Ulster Place-Names* (Belfast: Queen's University, 1999).

Nicolaisen, W. F. H., *Scottish Place-Names: Their Study and Significance*, new edn. (Edinburgh: John Donald, 2001).

Owen, Hywel Wyn, *A Pocket Guide: The Place-Names of Wales* (Cardiff: University of Wales Press, 1998).

Pamp, Bengt, *Ortnamnen i Sverige* (Lund: Studentlitteratur 1988).

Rayburn, Alan, *Dictionary of Canadian Place Names* (Toronto: Oxford University Press, 1997).

Sandnes, Jorn, and Stemshaug, Ola, *Norsk Stadnamnleksikon* (Oslo: det Norske Samlaget, 1980).

Stewart, George R., *American Place-Names* (New York: Oxford University Press, 1970).

—— *Names on the Globe* (New York: Oxford University Press, 1975).

Tanioka, Takeo, and Yamaguchi, Keü Chir (ed.), *Konsaisu Nihon Chimei Jiten*, 4th edn. (Tokyo: Sanseido, 1998).

Wahlberg, Mats (ed.), *Svenskt Ortnamnslexikon* (Uppsala: Spraak och Folkminnesinstitutet, 2003).

Watts, Victor, *The Cambridge Dictionary of English Place-Names* (Cambridge: Cambridge University Press, 2004).